Poetry Criticism

Guide to Gale Literary Criticism Series

For criticism on	Consult these Gale series
Authors now living or who died after December 31, 1959	*CONTEMPORARY LITERARY CRITICISM (CLC)*
Authors who died between 1900 and 1959	*TWENTIETH-CENTURY LITERARY CRITICISM (TCLC)*
Authors who died between 1800 and 1899	*NINETEENTH-CENTURY LITERATURE CRITICISM (NCLC)*
Authors who died between 1400 and 1799	*LITERATURE CRITICISM FROM 1400 TO 1800 (LC)* *SHAKESPEAREAN CRITICISM (SC)*
Authors who died before 1400	*CLASSICAL AND MEDIEVAL LITERATURE CRITICISM (CMLC)*
Authors of books for children and young adults	*CHILDREN'S LITERATURE REVIEW (CLR)*
Dramatists	*DRAMA CRITICISM (DC)*
Poets	*POETRY CRITICISM (PC)*
Short story writers	*SHORT STORY CRITICISM (SSC)*
Black writers of the past two hundred years	*BLACK LITERATURE CRITICISM (BLC)*
Hispanic writers of the late nineteenth and twentieth centuries	*HISPANIC LITERATURE CRITICISM (HLC)*
Native North American writers and orators of the eighteenth, nineteenth, and twentieth centuries	*NATIVE NORTH AMERICAN LITERATURE (NNAL)*
Major authors from the Renaissance to the present	*WORLD LITERATURE CRITICISM, 1500 TO THE PRESENT (WLC)*

ISSN 1052-4851

Poetry Criticism

Excerpts from Criticism of the Works of the Most Significant and Widely Studied Poets of World Literature

VOLUME 20

Carol T. Gaffke
Editor

GALE

DETROIT · NEW YORK · TORONTO · LONDON

Library of Congress Catalog Card Number 91-118494
ISBN 0-7876-1591-9
ISSN 1052-4851

Printed in the United States of America

10 9 8 7 6 5 4 3 2 1

Contents

Preface

A Comprehensive Information Source on World Poetry

Poetry Criticism (PC) provides substantial critical excerpts and biographical information on poets throughout the world who are most frequently studied in high school and undergraduate college courses. Each *PC* entry is supplemented by biographical and bibliographical material to help guide the user to a fuller understanding of the genre and its creators. Although major poets and literary movements are covered in such Gale Literary Criticism Series as *Contemporary Literary Criticism (CLC)*, *Twentieth-Century Literary Criticism (TCLC)*, *Nineteenth-Century Literature Criticism (NCLC)*, *Literature Criticism from 1400 to 1800 (LC)*, and *Classical and Medieval Literature Criticism (CMLC)*, *PC* offers more focused attention on poetry than is possible in the broader, survey-oriented entries on writers in these Gale series. Students, teachers, librarians, and researchers will find that the generous excerpts and supplementary material provided by *PC* supply them with the vital information needed to write a term paper on poetic technique, to examine a poet's most prominent themes, or to lead a poetry discussion group.

Coverage

In order to reflect the influence of tradition as well as innovation, poets of various nationalities, eras, and movements are represented in every volume of *PC*. Each author entry presents a historical survey of the critical response to that author's work; the length of an entry reflects the amount of critical attention that the author has received from critics writing in English and from foreign critics in translation. Since many poets have inspired a prodigious amount of critical explication, *PC* is necessarily selective, and the editors have chosen the most significant published criticism to aid readers and students in their research. In order to provide these important critical pieces, the editors will sometimes reprint essays that have appeared in previous volumes of Gale's Literary Criticism Series. Such duplication, however, never exceeds fifteen percent of a *PC* volume.

Organization

Each *PC* author entry consists of the following components:

- **Author Heading:** the name under which the author wrote appears at the beginning of the entry, followed by birth and death dates. If the author wrote consistently under a pseudonym, the pseudonym will be listed in the author heading and his or her legal name given in parentheses in the lines immediately preceding the Introduction. Uncertainty as to birth or death dates is indicated by question marks.

- **Introduction:** a biographical and critical essay introduces readers to the author and the critical discussions surrounding his or her work.

- **Author Portrait:** a photograph or illustration of the author is included when available.

- **Principal Works:** the author's most important works are identified in a list ordered chronologically by first publication dates. The first section comprises poetry collections and book-length poems. The second section gives information on other major works by the author. For foreign authors, original foreign-language publication information is provided, as well as the best and most complete English-language editions of their works.

- **Criticism:** critical excerpts chronologically arranged in each author entry provide perspective on changes in critical evaluation over the years. All individual titles of poems and poetry collections by the author featured in the entry are printed in boldface type to enable a reader to ascertain without difficulty the works under discussion. For purposes of easy identification, the critic's name and the publication date of the essay are given at the beginning of each piece of criticism. Unsigned criticism is preceded by the title of the journal in which it originally appeared. Publication information (such as publisher names and book prices) and parenthetical numerical references (such as footnotes or page and line references to specific editions of a work) have been deleted at the editor's discretion to enable smoother reading of the text.

- **Explanatory Notes:** introductory comments preface each critical excerpt, providing several types of useful information, including: the reputation of a critic, the importance of a work of criticism, and the specific type of criticism (biographical, psychoanalytic, historical, etc.).

- **Author Commentary:** insightful comments from the authors themselves and excerpts from author interviews are included when available.

- **Bibliographical Citations:** information preceding each piece of criticism guides the interested reader to the original essay or book.

- **Further Reading:** bibliographic references accompanied by descriptive notes at the end of each entry suggest additional materials for study of the author. Boxed material following the Further Reading provides references to other biographical and critical series published by Gale.

Other Features

- **Cumulative Author Index:** comprises all authors who have appeared in Gale's Literary Criticism Series, along with cross-references to such Gale biographical series as *Contemporary Authors* and *Dictionary of Literary Biography*. This cumulated index enables the user to locate an author within the various series.

- **Cumulative Nationality Index:** includes all authors featured in *PC,* arranged alphabetically under their respective nationalities.

- **Cumulative Title Index:** lists in alphabetical order all individual poems, book-length poems, and collection titles contained in the *PC* series. Titles of poetry collections and separately published poems are printed in italics, while titles of individual poems are printed in roman type with quotation marks. Each title is followed by the author's name and the volume and page number corresponding to the location of commentary on specific works. English-language translations of original foreign-language titles are cross-referenced to the foreign titles so that all references to discussion of a work are combined in one listing.

Citing *Poetry Criticism*

When writing papers, students who quote directly from any volume in the Literary Criticism Series may use the following general formats to footnote reprinted criticism. The first example pertains to material drawn from periodicals, the second to material reprinted from books:

[1]David Daiches, "W. H. Auden: The Search for a Public," *Poetry* LIV (June 1939), 148-56; excerpted and reprinted in *Poetry Criticism*, Vol. 1, ed. Robyn V. Young (Detroit: Gale Research, 1990), pp. 7-9.

[2]Pamela J. Annas, *A Disturbance in Mirrors: The Poetry of Sylvia Plath* (Greenwood Press, 1988); excerpted and reprinted in *Poetry Criticism*, Vol. 1, ed. Robyn V. Young (Detroit: Gale Research, 1990), pp. 410-14.

Comments Are Welcome

Readers who wish to suggest authors to appear in future volumes, or who have other suggestions, are cordially invited to contact the editors.

Acknowledgments

The editors wish to thank the copyright holders of the excerpted criticism included in this volume and the permissions managers of many book and magazine publishing companies for assisting us in securing reproduction rights. We are also grateful to the staffs of the Detroit Public Library, the Library of Congress, the University of Detroit Mercy Library, Wayne State University Purdy/Kresge Library Complex, and the University of Michigan Libraries for making their resources available to us. Following is a list of the copyright holders who have granted us permission to reproduce material in this volume of *PC*. Every effort has been made to trace copyright, but if omissions have been made, please let us know.

COPYRIGHTED EXCERPTS IN *PC*, VOLUME 17, WERE REPRODUCED FROM THE FOLLOWING PERIODICALS:

The American Book Review, v. 12, March-April, 1990. Copyright (c) 1990 by The American Book Review. Reproduced by permission.—*American Poetry*, v. 2, Fall, 1984. Reproduced by permission.—*Booklist*, v. 86, October 15, 1989. Reproduced by permission.—*Bucknell Review*, v. XVII, December, 1969. Copyright (c) Bucknell Review 1969. Reproduced by permission of Associated University Presses.—*Bulletin of Hispanic Studies*, v. XLVI, January, 1969; v. LIX, January, 1982. Both reproduced by permission of Liverpool University Press.—*The Centennial Review*, v. XXXIII, Winter, 1989 for "The Community of Love: Reading Kenneth Rexroth's Long Poems" by Lee Bartlett. Copyright (c) 1989 by The Centennial Review. Reproduced by permission of the publisher and the author.— *CLA Journal*, v. XIII, September, 1969; v. XXXIII, March, 1990. Copyright (c) 1969,1990 by The College Language Association. Both used by permission of The College Language Association.—*Contemporary Literature*, v. 10, Spring, 1969. Copyright (c) 1969 by the Regents of the University of Wisconsin. Reproduced by permission of The University of Wisconsin Press.— *The Dalhousie Review*, v. 50, Summer, 1970 for "Children in the Poetry of Yeats" by Desmond Pacey. Reproduced by permission of the publisher and the author.—*The Dublin Magazine*, v. 4, Autumn/Winter, 1965 for "From the National to the Universal" by A. G. Stock.— *English Studies*, Netherlands, v. 36, 1955. Copyright (c) 1955 by Swets & Zeitlinger B. V. Reproduced by permission.—*Esq: A Journal of the American Renaissance*, v. 22, 1976 for "'Visible' Images and the 'Still Voice': Transcendental Vision in Bryant's Thanatopsis" by E. Miller Budick. Copyright (c) 1976 Washington State University. Reproduced by permission of the publisher and the author.—*Hispania*, v. 70, March, 1987 for "Fernando Pessoa and the Cubist Perspective" by Leland Guyer. Copyright (c) 1987 The American Association of Teachers of Spanish and Portuguese, Inc. Reproduced by permission of the publisher and the author.—*The Hudson Review*, v. 42, Autumn, 1989. Copyright (c) 1989 by The Hudson Review, Inc. Reproduced by permission.—*The Listener*, v. 80 October 24, 1968 for a review of "Selectet Poems" by D. J. Enright. Copyright (c) British Broadcasting Corp. 1968. Reproduced by permission of the author.—*The Literary Review*, v. 26, Spring, 1983 for "Natural Supernaturalism: The Nature Poetry of Kenneth Rexroth" by Donald Gutierrez. Copyright (c) 1983 by Fairleigh Dickinson University. Reproduced by permission of the author.— *Luso-Brazilian Review*, v. 13, Summer, 1976. Reproduced by permission.—*The Midwest Quarterly*, v. XXV, 1983. Copyright (c) 1983 by *The Midwest Quarterly*, Pittsburg State University. Reproduced by permission.—*Modern Austrian Literature*, v. 25, 1992. Copyright (c) 1992 International Arthur Schnitzler Association. Reproduced by permission.—*The Nation*, New York, v. 206, April 22, 1968. Copyright (c) 1968 *The Nation* magazine/ The Nation Company, Inc. Reproduced by permission.—*Neophilologus*, v. LVII, October, 1973 for "Byronic Egoism and George Eliot's 'The Spanish Gypsy'" by K. M. Newton. Copyright (c) 1973 by H. D. Tjeenk Willink. Reproduced by permission of the author.—*The New Republic*, v. 197, September 7, 1987. Copyright (c) 1987 The New Republic, Inc. Reproduced by permission of *The New Republic*.—*The New York Times Book Review*, August 21, 1927; July 23, 1967; March 23, 1975; November 23, 1980. Copyright 1927, (c)1967, 1975, 1980 by The New York Times Company. All reproduced by permission.—*The Ohio Review*, v. XVII, Winter, 1976. Copyright (c) 1976 by the Editors of *The Ohio Review*. Reproduced by permission.—*Parnassus: Poetry in Review*, v. 18 & 19, 1993 for "The Threading of the Year" by David Barber. Copyright (c) 1993 Poetry in Review Foundation, NY. Reproduced by permission of the author.—*Performing Arts Journal*, v. XV, May, 1983. Copyright (c) 1983. Reproduced by permission of The Johns Hopkins University Press.—*Poetry*, v. LXV, February, 1943 for "An Uncomfortable Huamnism" by Francis C. Golffing; v. LXXVI, June, 1950 for a review of "The Art of Worldy Wisdom" by J. R. Squires; v. LXXVI, June, 1950 for a review of "The Signature of All Things" by Francis Golffing; v. XC, June, 1957 for "The Poetry of Kenneth Rexroth" by Lawrence Lipton; v. XC, June, 1957 for "Two New Books by Kenneth Rexroth" by William Carlos Williams; v. C, August, 1962 for a review of "Twenty Poems of Georg Trakl" by Theodore Holmes. Copyright 1943, renewed 1973; Copyright 1950, renewed 1978; Copyright (c) 1962, renewed 1990 by the Modern Poetry Association. All reproduced by permission of the Editor of Poetry and the respective authors./ v. XC, June, 1957 for "Two New Books by Kenneth Rexroth" by William Carlos Williams. Copyright (c) 1957, renewed 1985 by the Modern Poetry Association. Also published in *Unpublished Materials* by William Carlos Williams. Copyright (c) 1988 by New Directions Publishing Corp. Reprinted by permission of the Editor of *Poetry* and New Directions

COPYRIGHTED EXCERPTS IN PC, VOLUME 20, WERE REPRODUCED FROM THE FOLLOWING BOOKS:

PHOTOGRAPHS AND ILLUSTRATIONS APPEARING IN PC, VOLUME 20, WERE RECEIVED FROM THE FOLLOWING SOURCES:

William Cullen Bryant
1794-1878

American poet, editor, critic, travel sketch writer, translator, short story and sketch writer, satirist, and historian.

INTRODUCTION

The most accomplished and popular American poet of the first half of the nineteenth century, Bryant also was the first American poet to receive substantial international acclaim. Bryant is considered an early proponent of Romanticism in American literature, and his work is often compared thematically and stylistically to that of English Romantic poet William Wordsworth. Opposing eighteenth-century poetic conventions and using experimental iambic rhythms, Bryant's poetry usually meditates on nature and the transience of earthly things. Although its themes were few and its thought not profound, Bryant's verse possessed a simple dignity and an impeccable restrained style, most notably in "Thanatopsis" (1817) and "To a Waterfowl" (1821), the poems for which he is best remembered. Since Bryant also spent more than fifty years of his life as editor of the New York *Evening Post,* a career which ranks among the longest in American journalism, he never fully developed his poetic talents. However, Bryant's literary efforts make him an important, if somewhat overlooked, figure in American poetry.

Biographical Information

Born November 3, 1794, at Cummington, Massachusetts, Bryant began to compose verses at age nine. His first poem to gain critical attention, *The Embargo; or, Sketches of the Times,* which satirized Thomas Jefferson's laws limiting free trade, appeared in 1808. Bryant entered Williams College at age sixteen, but left without graduating and returned home, where he studied law until he was admitted to the bar in 1815. For the next ten years Bryant practiced as an attorney, a profession he came to detest. Meanwhile, he continued to write poetry and published several essays of poetry criticism. Encouraged by the highly favorable critical response to the anonymous publication of an early version of his "Thanatopsis" in the *North American Review* in 1817, Bryant established his name as a poet with his first collection, *Poems* (1821). In 1825 he moved to New York City, where he co-founded the *New York Review and Atheneum Magazine,* which eventually proved to be unsuccessful, and associated with artists Asher Durant and Thomas Cole and members of the renowned Knickerbocker school, which included writers Washington Irving, James Fenimore Cooper, Fitz-Greene Halleck, and Gulian Verplanck, each of whom later became the subjects of Bryant's biographical discourses. In 1827 Bryant was offered an editorial position at the New York *Evening Post,* and by 1829 he became

the newspaper's editor-in-chief and part owner. For nearly fifty years under his leadership the *Evening Post* espoused such liberal political causes as free trade, free speech, workers' rights, and the abolition of slavery, serving initially as an organ of the Democratic party and later the Free-Soil movement and finally the Republican party. Upon publication of his second volume of verse, *Poems* (1832), Bryant had attained national prominence as a public figure, both as poet and editor. Although Bryant published other poetry collections over the course of his life, his editorial responsibilities consumed his time and turned his attention to prose writing. Bryant also toured Europe and the United States: one visit to Illinois inspired "The Prairies," and the letters he wrote to the *Evening Post* during his trips abroad comprise three collections of travel sketches. Despite a lifetime of political, literary, and physical activity, Bryant suffered a debilitating stroke and died two weeks later on June 12, 1878.

Major Works

Distinguished by its simple dignity, didactic purpose, plain style, and a conscious concern for craftsmanship, Bryant's poetry expresses ideas derived from the Enlightenment and English Romanticism. The majority features recurrent themes of mutability, loneliness and isolation, the passing of innocence, and the somber certainty of the grave. Yet his poems are tinged by his personal interest in American politics, folklore, and history, and, above all, by his observations of the beauty and power of his native landscape, which pervades his poetic sensibilities. Bryant's poetic treatment of nature incorporates his belief that Nature is simply the visible manifestation of an omnipresent, transcendent God, who remains distinct from the natural world. For example, "To a Waterfowl" depicts the poet's vision of a lone bird on the horizon at the close of a wearisome day, which sparks his realization that all nature is directed and protected by divine providence. In "A Forest Hymn" the poet exclaims that "The groves were God's first temples," observing that even a flower possesses "an emanation of the in-dwelling Life." Many of Bryant's lyrics reveal that Nature exists to console and instruct humanity about divine purpose, which is represented by providential cycles of changes in nature and life. For instance, "Thanatopsis," whose Greek title means "view of death," gives voice to Nature, who teaches that humanity partakes of all natural processes and admonishes humanity to live well so it may not fear death. "The Death of the Flowers," written on the death of Bryant's sister, identifies the dead woman with the decay of beautiful summertime, while "To the Fringed Gentian," whose title refers to a late-blooming autumnal flower, states the poet's wish that "Hope, blossoming within my heart, / May look to heaven as I depart."

Critical Reception

Bryant's colloquial voice and celebration of nature were hailed as poetic innovations upon publication of his debut collection *Poems,* and confirmed his reputation as the most eminent American poet of the day. His status generally went unquestioned by his contemporaries until the middle of the nineteenth century, when some critics began to observe that his lyrics lacked flexibility and depth of subject and theme; that his versification failed to display poetic virtuosity and breadth of conception; and that his poetry relied too much on didactic endings and generally lacked passion. Thus, by the time the poet had achieved the heights of critical adulation, he already was being reduced to a poet of historical significance, or at least a competent wordsmith of second rank. Although most critics have agreed that Bryant's early poems represent his best work, critical assessment of his work has declined considerably in the twentieth century and is largely limited to debates about whether Bryant's poetic sensibilities are more Puritan or Romantic. A small revival of interest in Bryant's poetry has occurred since 1978, which marked the hundredth anniversary of the poet's death, but most criticism has centered on a half-dozen of individual poems, comparisons to other writers and artists, or the relation between geography and poetry. Norbert Krapf has remarked, "if we ultimately find [Bryant] to be a 'minor' poet, we must realize that it is indeed no mean accomplishment to be a minor poet."

PRINCIPAL WORKS

Poetry

The Embargo; or, Sketches of the Times 1809
*Poems 1821
Poems 1832
The Fountain and Other Poems 1846
The White-Footed Deer and Other Poems 1846
Hymns 1864
Thirty Poems 1864
Among the Trees 1874
The Poetical Works of William Cullen Bryant. 2 vols. 1883

Other Major Works

"Medfield" (short story) 1832; published in *Tales of the Glauber-Spa*
"The Skeleton's Cave" (short story) 1832; published in *Tales of the Glauber-Spa*
Letters of a Traveller; or, Notes of Things Seen in Europe and America (travel sketches) 1850
Discourse on the Life and Genius of Cooper (criticism) 1852
Letters of a Traveller, second series (travel sketches) 1859
A Discourse on the Life, Character, and Genius of Washington Irving (criticism) 1860
Letters from the East (travel sketches) 1869
Some Notices of the Life and Writings of Fitz-Greene Halleck (criticism) 1869
A Discourse on the Life, Character, and Writings of Gulian Crommelin Verplanck (criticism) 1870
The Iliad of Homer [translator] (poetry) 1870
The Odyssey of Homer [translator] (poetry) 1871
Orations and Addresses by William Cullen Bryant (speeches) 1873
The Prose Writings of William Cullen Bryant. 2 vols. (short stories, criticism, travel sketches, journalism, lectures, and speeches) 1884
The Letters of William Cullen Bryant. 3 vols. (letters) 1975

*This work includes the poems "Thanatopsis" and "To a Waterfowl."

CRITICISM

Augustus Hopkins Strong (essay date 1916)

SOURCE: "William Cullen Bryant," in *American Poets and Their Theology,* The Griffith and Rowland Press, 1916, pp. 3-48.

[*In the following excerpt, Strong discusses various aspects of Christian theology in Bryant's poetry, including the poet's expressions of divine compassion, salvation, and immortality, and also notes his limitations.*]

There are patriotic people who maintain that America is the predestined home of poetry. They point to little Greece, with her rocky cliffs and bosky vales, her purple hills and encircling isles, and ask triumphantly if Greece was not the natural habitat of liberty and beauty. When we assent, they argue *a fortiori* that our great continent was even more manifestly ordained to nourish the largest and most precious growths of the human mind. Poetry is one of those largest and most precious growths, for it is the rhythmical expression of the world's meaning, in thoughts that breathe and words that burn. Poetry therefore must be native to America.

The argument would do credit to Henry Thomas Buckle, who attributes civilization wholly to environment. But it is not convincing. Unfortunately, perhaps, poetry needs for its production something more than bigness of territory or sublimity of scenery. Switzerland has giant and snow-crowned peaks, but she has never had a great poet. Our own mountain ranges and untrodden forests, our prairie cyclones and river floods, furnish proper surroundings, but they do not furnish the needed inspiration. Our struggles with Indian ferocity and British tyranny, our combination of civil freedom with civil union, give us subjects for poetry, but not the genius to treat them. A nation of Gradgrinds would still value Niagara only for its water-power, and would be entirely content with prose.

As a matter of fact, poetry was a belated product of the American soil. We may possibly explain this by remembering that

> The Pilgrim bands, who passed the sea to keep
> Their Sabbaths in the eye of God alone,
> In his wide temple of the wilderness
> **["The Burial-place"]**

were Puritans of the most straitest sect, many of whom thought love for nature a dangerous rival to love for God. The clearing of forests and the fear of savage aggression, moreover, occupied their thoughts. The Bay Psalm Book was the nearest approach to poetical expression, and that was wholly religious. Grotesque and unmelodious as it was, it witnessed that the instinct of poetry still survived, and that men cannot long live without some such exercise of the imagination. Most wonderful it is that, after such bare and unpromising beginnings, there should have suddenly appeared the true father of American literature, the first real poet of our Western world. We wonder when we see the sun of Homer rising upon the darkness of Hellenic times; we may quite as justly wonder when we find the bizarre and tasteless lines of Trumbull and Barlow succeeded by the mature and lofty verse of William Cullen Bryant. . . .

I regard Bryant as a more truly Christian poet than even Wordsworth. Both were poets of nature. But Wordsworth came near to identifying God with nature: Bryant never confounded the two. Wordsworth would never have found delight in mountain, field, and flood, if he had not recognized in them a Spirit which through them manifested itself to mortals. That Spirit, however, never seems to utter articulate sounds, or to take personal form. But to Bryant, God was never mere impersonal spirit. "It" and "which" were not applicable to Him. God was transcendent, even more than he was immanent. The finite was never merged in the infinite. Mortal awe never became pantheistic absorption. In all this we see the abiding influence of the poet's New England training, and the happy effect of those theological sermons to which he listened in his youth.

What theology we find in Bryant's poetry must then be gathered from occasional utterances of the overflowing heart, rather than from any set effort to declare dogmatic truth. When we do find such utterances, we may be sure that they will be clear indications of his inmost thought, and not diplomatic concessions to the spirit of the times. He believed, first of all, in a personal God, and a God of love. This faith delivered him from melancholy, and made him optimistic. In this respect he was a contrast to Matthew Arnold, to whom God was only "the power, not ourselves, that makes for righteousness." One of the most astounding announcements in all literature is Matthew Arnold's assertion that this is the teaching of the Hebrew Scriptures. Without a personal God, the forward-looking spirit of Israel would be inexplicable. It is easy to see the truth of Hutton's remark that Matthew Arnold embodies in his verse "the sweetness, the gravity, the strength, the beauty, and the languor of death." Bryant's verse has sweetness and gravity, but these are the sweetness and gravity of true life, derived from the divine source of life, and sustained thereby. The solemn joy of Bryant has its analogue, not in the nocturne of Chopin, but in the largo of Handel.

Our poet saw God in the beauty and grandeur of the world. Woods, waves, and sky were vocal with praise of their great Author. Bryant was not ignorant of science, but he wished to join science to faith. Some of his noblest poetry is the expression of spontaneous emotion in presence of God's sublime manifestations in nature. **"A Forest Hymn"** illustrates this characteristic of his verse:

> The groves were God's first temples. Ere man learned
> To hew the shaft, and lay the architrave,
> And spread the roof above them—ere he framed
> The lofty vault, to gather and roll back
> The sound of anthems; in the darkling wood,
> Amidst the cool and silence, he knelt down,
> And offered to the Mightiest solemn thanks
> And supplication.

"A Hymn of the Sea" gives us, in a similar manner, the poet's recognition of God's presence in "old ocean's gray and melancholy waste":

> The sea is mighty, but a mightier sways
> His restless billows. Thou, whose hands have scooped
> His boundless gulfs and built his shore, thy breath,
> That moved in the beginning o'er his face,
> Moves o'er it evermore.

So too, there is a **"Song of the Stars,"** in which the heavenly spheres are called

> The boundless visible smile of Him
> To the veil of whose brow your lamps are dim.

Over against God's creatorship and omnipresence, Bryant recognizes the sinfulness of humanity:

> When, from the genial cradle of our race,
> Went forth the tribes of men . . .
>   . . . and there forgot
> The truth of heaven, and kneeled to gods that heard
>   them not.
>   **["The Ages"]**

> The world
> Is full of guilt and misery, . .
> Enough of all its sorrows, crimes, and cares,
> To tire thee of it.
>   **["Inscription for the Entrance to a Wood"]**

> Ha! how the murmur deepens! I perceive
> And tremble at its dreadful import. Earth
> Uplifts a general cry for guilt and wrong,
> And heaven is listening.
>   **["Earth"]**

There seems to be confession of his personal sin:

> For me, the sordid cares in which I dwell
> Shrink and consume my heart, as heat the scroll;
> And wrath has left its scar—that fire of hell
> Has left its frightful scar upon my soul.
>   **["The Future Life"]**

"The West Wind" is a symbol of human inconstancy and ingratitude:

> Ah! thou art like our wayward race;—
>   When not a shade of pain or ill
> Dims the bright smile of Nature's face,
>   Thou lov'st to sigh and murmur still.

He regrets his forgetfulness of the **"Yellow Violet"**:

> So they, who climb to wealth, forget
>   The friends in darker fortunes tried;
> I copied them—but I regret
>   That I should ape the ways of pride.

"The African Chief" depicts the cruelty of the savage:

> Chained in the market-place he stood,
>   A man of giant frame.

But his appeals for mercy are in vain:

> His heart was broken—crazed his brain:
>   At once his eye grew wild;
> He struggled fiercely with his chain,
>   Whispered, and wept, and smiled;

> Yet wore not long those fatal bands,
>   And once, at shut of day,
> They drew him forth upon the sands,
>   The foul hyena's prey.

Human sinfulness touches the divine compassion in Bryant's verse. He sees in **"The Fountain,"** that springs "from the red mould and slimy roots of earth," the symbol of God's grace:

> Thus doth God
> Bring, from the dark and foul, the pure and bright.

And in **"The Ages"** he asks:

> Has nature, in her calm, majestic march,
> Faltered with age at last? . . .

> Look on this beautiful world, and read the truth
> In her fair page.

>   . . . Eternal Love doth keep,
> In his complacent arms, the earth, the air, the deep.
>   Will then the merciful One, who stamped our race
>   With his own image, . .
> . . . leave a work so fair all blighted and accursed?

> Oh, no! a thousand cheerful omens give
> Hope of yet happier days, whose dawn in nigh.
> He who has tamed the elements, shall not live
> The slave of his own passions; he whose eye
> Unwinds the eternal dances of the sky,
> And in the abyss of brightness dares to span
> The sun's broad circle, rising yet more high,
> In God's magnificent works his will shall scan—
> And love and peace shall make their paradise with
>   man.

The poet's sympathy with nature is connected with his Puritan belief in man's fall. The external world is beautiful, because unfallen. It shares with man the effects of sin; but, whenever we retreat from the regions which man's folly has despoiled, we may find something which reminds us of our lost paradise. From the wrath and injustice of man, the Puritans fled to the untrodden wilderness, and in its solitudes they found a sanctuary. In the **"Inscription for the Entrance to a Wood,"** we read:

> The primal curse
> Fell, it is true, upon the unsinning earth,
> But not in vengeance. God hath yoked to guilt
> Her pale tormentor, misery.

And so all things work together for good, even though for the present they may seem to contradict the divine beneficence. Bryant's **"Hymn to Death"** makes even that grim messenger to be the protector of God's creatures:

> Thus, from the first of time, hast thou been found
> On virtue's side; the wicked, but for thee,
> Had been too strong for the good; the great of earth
> Had crushed the weak forever.

The **"Hymn of the Waldenses"** declares the justice of God:

> Hear, Father, hear thy faint afflicted flock
> Cry to thee, from the desert and the rock . . .
>
> Thou, Lord, dost hold the thunder; the firm land
> Tosses in billows when it feels thy hand . . .
>
> Yet, mighty God, yet shall thy frown look forth
> Unveiled, and terribly shall shake the earth.

But justice is mixed with love. He translates, from the Provençal of Bernard Rascas, the magnificent lines:

> All things that are on earth shall wholly pass away,
> Except the love of God, which shall live and last
>   for aye.
> The forms of men shall be as they had never been;
> The blasted groves shall lose their fresh and tender
>   green;
>
>   . . . . .
>
> And the great globe itself, so the holy writings tell,
> With the rolling firmament, where the starry armies
>   dwell,
> Shall melt with fervent heat—they shall all pass
>   away,
> Except the love of God, which shall live and last
>   for aye.

And from Boethius, on **"The Order of Nature"**:

> Thou who wouldst read, with an undarkened eye,
>   The laws by which the Thunderer bears sway,
> Look at the stars that keep, in yonder sky,
>   Unbroken peace from Nature's earliest day.
>
> Love binds the parts together, gladly still
>   They court the kind restraint, nor would be free;
> Unless Love held them subject to the Will
>   That gave them being, they would cease to be.

This love cares for the individual, as well as for the great whole over which it rules. The poet, in **"The Crowded Street,"** cannot think any human soul forgotten:

> Each, where his tasks or pleasures call,
>   They pass, and heed each other not.
> There is who heeds, who holds them all,
>   In his large care and boundless thought.
>
> These struggling tides of life that seem
>   In wayward, aimless course to tend,
> Are eddies of the mighty stream
>   That rolls to an appointed end.

There was a vein of humor in Bryant, which seldom came to the surface, but which his associates sometimes discovered. He invites his pastor, Doctor Dewey, to come with Mrs. Dewey and visit him at his country-seat on Long Island:

> The season wears an aspect glum and glummer,
> The icy north wind, an unwelcome comer,
> Frighting from garden walks each pretty hummer,
> Whose murmuring music lulled the noons of
>   summer,
> Roars in the woods, with grummer voice and
>   grummer,
> And thunders in the forest like a drummer.
> Dumb are the birds—they could not well be
>   dumber;
> The winter-cold, life's pitiless benumber,
> Bursts water-pipes, and makes us call the plumber.
> Now, by the fireside, toils the patient thumber
> Of ancient books, and no less patient summer
> Of long accounts, while topers fill the rummer,
> The maiden thinks what furs will best become her,
> And on the stage-boards shouts the gibing mummer.
> Shut in by storms, the dull piano-strummer
> Murders old tunes. There's nothing wearisomer!

This rhyming would have done credit to Browning or Lowell. But Bryant's humor appeared more often in his editorial work than in his poetry. A witty opponent said that his articles always began with a stale joke, and ended with a fresh lie—an accusation which only shows how greatly the journalism of the day needed reformation.

No stanza of all Bryant's writing is better known or more often quoted than that from the poem entitled **"The Battlefield"**:

> Truth, crushed to earth, shall rise again;
>   Th' eternal years of God are hers;
> But Error, wounded, writhes in pain,
>   And dies among his worshipers.

This verse has been criticized, as holding to some power of impersonal truth to conquer the world. In the light of our poet's other utterances, I must think this criticism unjust. Truth is personified only by poetic license. It has power only because it has God behind it, and because it is the very nature of God himself. And so I must interpret those noble lines in **"My Autumn Walk,"** in which Bryant exclaims:

> Oh, for that better season,
>   When the pride of the foe shall yield,
> And the hosts of God and Freedom
>   March back from the well-won field!

The hosts of truth and freedom are only the agents and instruments of God.

This persistent theism characterizes his short and fanciful, as well as his longer and more serious productions. I know of no more beautiful celebration of divine Providence than that of Bryant's address **"To a Waterfowl."** It brings down God's care into the affairs of individual life:

> Whither, midst falling dew,
> While glow the heavens with the last steps of day,
> Far, through their rosy depths, dost thou pursue
>   Thy solitary way?

Vainly the fowler's eye
Might mark thy distant flight to do thee wrong,
As, darkly seen against the crimson sky,
Thy figure floats along.

Seek'st thou the plashy brink
Of weedy lake, or marge of river wide,
Or where the rocking billows rise and sink
On the chafed ocean-side?

There is a Power whose care
Teaches thy way along that pathless coast—
The desert and illimitable air—
Lone wandering, but not lost.

All day thy wings have fanned,
At that far height, the cold, thin atmosphere,
Yet stoop not, weary, to the welcome land,
Though the dark night is near.

And soon that toil shall end;
Soon shalt thou find a summer home, and rest,
And scream among thy fellows; reeds shall bend,
Soon, o'er thy sheltered nest.

Thou'rt gone, the abyss of heaven
Hath swallowed up thy form; yet, on my heart
Deeply has sunk the lesson thou hast given,
And shall not soon depart.

He who, from zone to zone,
Guides through the boundless sky thy certain flight,
In the long way that I must tread alone,
Will lead my steps aright.

These lines were written in the poet's youth, when the world was all before him where to choose, and when competence and success were far away. They are as perfect in diction as they are in faith. Matthew Arnold agreed with Hartley Coleridge in pronouncing **"The Waterfowl"** the finest short poem in the English language. I discern the same pure and trustful spirit in his poem entitled **"Blessed are they that Mourn."** The Providence that gives us days of gladness does not forget us in our days of sorrow:

Oh, deem not they are blest alone
  Whose lives a peaceful tenor keep;
The Power who pities man, hath shown
  A blessing for the eyes that weep.

The light of smiles shall fill again
  The lids that overflow with tears;
And weary hours of woe and pain
  Are promises of happier years.

There is a day of sunny rest
  For every dark and troubled night:
And grief may bide an evening guest,
  But joy shall come with early light.

And thou, who, o'er thy friend's low bier,
  Dost shed the bitter drops like rain,

Hope that a brighter, happier sphere
  Will give him to thy arms again.

Nor let the good man's trust depart,
  Though life its common gifts deny,—
Though with a pierced and bleeding heart,
  And spurned of men, he goes to die.

For God hath marked each sorrowing day,
  And numbered every secret tear,
And heaven's long age of bliss shall pay
  For all his children suffer here.

William Cullen Bryant was a Christian. He declared his entire reliance on Christ for salvation. I do not know that his faith would have answered to the ordinary dogmatic standards, but it was certainly strong enough to lead him to confession and to baptism. He knew his own weakness and insufficiency, and he trusted in what God had done for him, and what God would do for him, in Jesus Christ. In his Phi Beta Kappa poem at Harvard, he showed

How vain,
Instead of the pure heart and innocent hands,
Are all the proud and pompous modes to gain
The smile of Heaven.

It is not generally known that he wrote hymns for public worship, for not all of these are included in most editions of his works. But Symington, in his biography, quotes for us two stanzas of a hymn founded on the saying of Mary, the mother of Jesus, at the marriage in Cana of Galilee:

Whate'er he bids observe and do;
  Such be the law that we obey,
And greater wonders men shall view
  Than that of Cana's bridal day.

The flinty heart with love shall beat,
  The chains shall fall from passion's slave,
The proud shall sit at Jesus' feet
  And learn the truths that bless and save.

His published works do, however, furnish us with another hymn which bears the title, **"Receive Thy Sight,"** and is a metrical version of the Gospel story:

When the blind suppliant in the way,
  By friendly hands to Jesus led,
Prayed to behold the light of day,
  "Receive thy sight," the Saviour said.

At once he saw the pleasant rays
  That lit the glorious firmament;
And, with firm step and words of praise,
  He followed where the Master went.

Look down in pity, Lord, we pray,
  On eyes oppressed with moral night,
And touch the darkened lids and say
  The gracious words, "Receive thy sight."

Then, in clear daylight, shall we see
   Where walked the sinless Son of God;
And, aided by new strength from Thee,
   Press onward in the path He trod.

There is a hymn to celebrate Christ's nativity:

As shadows cast by cloud and sun
   Flit o'er the summer grass,
So, in thy sight, Almighty One!
   Earth's generations pass.

And while the years, an endless host,
   Come pressing swiftly on,
The brightest names that earth can boast
   Just glisten, and are gone.

Yet doth the Star of Bethlehem shed
   A lustre pure and sweet;
And still it leads, as once it led,
   To the Messiah's feet.

O Father, may that holy Star
   Grow every year more bright,
And send its glorious beam afar
   To fill the world with light.

And a prayer for the regions of our own land that need the gospel:

Look from the sphere of endless day,
   Oh, God of mercy and of might!
In pity look on those who stray,
   Benighted, in this land of light.

In peopled vale, in lonely glen,
   In crowded mart, by stream or sea,
How many of the sons of men
   Hear not the message sent from thee.

Send forth thy heralds, Lord, to call
   The thoughtless young, the hardened old,
A wandering flock, and bring them all
   To the Good Shepherd's peaceful fold.

Send them thy mighty word to speak
   Till faith shall dawn, and doubt depart,—
To awe the bold, to stay the weak,
   And bind and heal the broken heart.

Then all these wastes, a dreary scene
   On which, with sorrowing eyes, we gaze,
Shall grow with living waters green,
   And lift to heaven the voice of praise.

There is a hymn of pity for the intemperate, and a prayer for their rescue:

When doomed to death, the Apostle lay
   At night, in Herod's dungeon-cell,
A light shone round him like the day,
   And from his limbs the fetters fell.

A messenger from God was there,
   To break his chain and bid him rise,
And lo! the Saint, as free as air,
   Walked forth beneath the open skies.

Chains yet more strong and cruel bind
   The victims of that deadly thirst
Which drowns the soul, and from the mind
   Blots the bright image stamped at first.

Oh, God of Love and Mercy, deign
   To look on those, with pitying eye,
Who struggle with that fatal chain,
   And send them succor from on high!

Send down, in its resistless might,
   Thy gracious Spirit, we implore,
And lead the captive forth to light,
   A rescued soul, a slave no more.

And even the dedication of a church draws out his prayerful sympathy and poetic feeling:

O thou whose own vast temple stands,
   Built over earth and sea,
Accept the walls that human hands
   Have raised to worship thee.

Lord, from thine inmost glory send,
   Within these walls to bide,
The peace that dwelleth without end
   Serenely by thy side.

May erring minds, that worship here,
   Be taught the better way;
And they who mourn, and they who fear,
   Be strengthened as they pray.

May faith grow firm, and love grow warm,
   And pure devotion rise,
While, round these hallowed walls, the storm
   Of earth-born passion dies.

I have yet to quote the most significant of Bryant's distinctly religious poems. It is entitled **"He hath put all things under his feet,"** and this hymn declares the worldwide supremacy of Christ:

O North, with all thy vales of green!
   O South, with all thy palms!
From peopled towns and fields between
   Uplift the voice of psalms;
Raise, ancient East! the anthem high,
And let the youthful West reply.

Lo! in the clouds of heaven appears
   God's well-belovèd Son;
He brings a train of brighter years:
   His kingdom is begun;
He comes a guilty world to bless
With mercy, truth, and righteousness.

Oh, Father! haste the promised hour,
  When, at His feet, shall lie
All rule, authority, and power
  Beneath the ample sky;
When He shall reign from pole to pole,
The Lord of every human soul;

When all shall heed the words He said
  Amid their daily cares,
And, by the loving life He led,
  Shall seek to pattern theirs;
And He, who conquered Death, shall win
The nobler conquest over Sin.

This hymn does not declare Christ's absolute deity,
nor does it indicate the poet's knowledge of that spiritual union with Christ which is the source of greatest
joy to the believer. Joy has its root in sacrifice—
Christ's sacrifice for us and our sacrifice to him. We
seldom read of the Cross, in Bryant's poetry. Yet faith
in the Cross is not wholly absent. In his poem, **"Waiting
by the Gate,"** he seems to make all final joy depend
upon Christ's death:

And some approach the threshold whose looks are
  blank with fear,
And some whose temples brighten with joy in
  drawing near,
As if they saw dear faces, and caught the gracious
  eye
Of Him, the Sinless Teacher, who came for us to
  die.

The infrequency of our poet's reference to Calvary, and
to the Christian's union with the crucified One, is the
reason why his work is so somber, so redolent of duty, so
given to external nature. If he had penetrated more deeply
into "the mystery of the gospel," which is "Christ in us,"
he would have had more of the Christian's "hope of glory."
Yet Mr. John Bigelow writes of him: "Though habitually
an attendant upon the ministrations of the Unitarian clergy
when they were accessible, no one ever recognized more
completely or more devoutly the divinity of Christ." Even
here, "divinity" may not mean the same as "deity." But
let us be thankful for what we find. His theism and his
recognition of God's providence, his faith in God's love
and revelation, have for their corollary an unwavering
belief in immortality. This appears conspicuously in his
love-songs, which were, almost without exception, addressed to his wife, with whom he spent forty-five years
of married life. Before their marriage he addressed her as
"fairest of the rural maids," and under the pseudonym of
"Genevieve" he made her the subject of one of his lightest
and sweetest poems:

Soon as the glazed and gleaming snow
  Reflects the day-dawn cold and clear,
The hunter of the West must go
  In depth of woods to seek the deer.

His rifle on his shoulder placed,
  His stores of death arranged with skill,

His moccasins and snow-shoes laced—
  Why lingers he beside the hill?

Far, in the dim and doubtful light,
  Where woody slopes a valley leave,
He sees what none but lover might,
  The dwelling of his Genevieve.

And oft he turns his truant eye,
  And pauses oft, and lingers near;
But when he marks the reddening sky,
  He bounds away to hunt the deer.

When in 1858 Mrs. Bryant had recovered from a long
and painful illness, the poet welcomed his wife in the
verses which he named **"The Life that Is,"** and of these
I quote the first and the last:

Thou, who so long hast pressed the couch of pain,
  Oh welcome, welcome back to life's free breath—
To life's free breath and day's sweet light again,
  From the chill shadows of the gate of death!

. . . . .

Now may we keep thee from the balmy air
  And radiant walks of heaven a little space,
Where He, who went before thee to prepare
  For His meek followers, shall assign thy place.

But in 1866 death finally took his wife from him. It was
an irremediable loss, for his reserved nature had found in
her his only intimate friend. His poem, **"A Lifetime,"**
begins with a treatment of grief in the third person, but it
ends most pathetically by attributing all the sorrow to
himself. It is the last poem he composed, and it summarizes his own life:

And well I know that a brightness
  From his life has passed away,
And a smile from the green earth's beauty,
  And a glory from the day.

But I behold, above him,
  In the far blue depths of air,
Dim battlements shining faintly,
  And a throng of faces there;

See over crystal barrier
  The airy figures bend,
Like those who are watching and waiting
  The coming of a friend.

And one there is among them,
  With a star upon her brow,
In her life a lovely woman,
  A sinless seraph now.

I know the sweet calm features;
  The peerless smile I know;
And I stretch my arms with transport
  From where I stand below.

And the quick tears drown my eyelids,
  But the airy figures fade,
And the shining battlements darken
  And blend with the evening shade.

I am gazing into the twilight
  Where the dim-seen meadows lie,
And the wind of night is swaying
  The trees with a heavy sigh.

He did not sorrow as those without hope, for he believed in Him who has brought life and immortality to light in his glorious gospel. He cannot think that the separation caused by death is lasting. In his poem, **"The Future Life,"** he, writes:

How shall I know thee in the sphere which keeps
  The disembodied spirits of the dead,
When all of thee that time could wither sleeps
  And perishes among the dust we tread?

For I shall feel the sting of ceaseless pain,
  If there I meet thy gentle presence not;
Nor hear the voice I love, nor read again
  In thy serenest eyes the tender thought.

    . . . . .

The love that lived through all the stormy past,
  And meekly with my harsher nature bore,
And deeper grew, and tenderer to the last,
  Shall it expire with life, and be no more?

    . . . . .

Shalt thou not teach me, in that calmer home,
  The wisdom that I learned so ill in this—
The wisdom which is love—till I become
  Thy fit companion in that land of bliss?

Indeed, he trusts that even now the separation is not complete:

May we not think that near us thou dost stand
  With loving ministrations? for we know
Thy heart was never happy when thy hand
  Was forced its tasks of mercy to forego.

May'st thou not prompt with every coming day
  The generous aim and act, and gently win
Our restless, wandering thoughts, to turn away
  From every treacherous path that ends in sin?

His poem, **"The Death of the Flowers,"** has a moving pathos, from the fact that it commemorates the loss of a beloved sister who died in her twenty-second year:

The melancholy days are come, the saddest of the
  year,
Of wailing winds, and naked woods, and meadows
  brown and sere . . .

Where are the flowers, the fair young flowers, that
  lately sprang and stood,
In brighter light and softer airs, a beauteous
  sisterhood?
Alas, they all are in their graves! The gentle race of
  flowers
Are lying in their lowly beds, with the fair and
  good of ours.

    . . . . .

And then I think of one who in her youthful beauty
  died,
The fair, meek blossom that grew up and faded by
  my side:
In the cold, moist earth we laid her, when the
  forests cast the leaf,
And we wept that one so lovely should have a life
  so brief:
Yet not unmeet it was that one, like that young
  friend of ours,
So gentle and so beautiful, should perish with the
  flowers.

He calls one of his poems **"The Past."** He sees all of earth's treasures sooner or later swallowed up by time. But, personifying the past, he writes:

  Thine for a space are they—
Yet shalt thou yield thy treasures up at last;
  Thy gates shall yet give way,
Thy bolts shall fall, inexorable Past!

  All that of good and fair
Has gone into thy womb from earliest time,
  Shall then come forth to wear
The glory and the beauty of its prime.

  They have not perished—no!
Kind words, remembered voices once so sweet,
  Smiles, radiant long ago,
And features, the great soul's apparent seat.

  All shall come back; each tie
Of pure affection shall be knit again;
  Alone shall Evil die,
And Sorrow dwell a prisoner in thy reign.

  And then shall I behold
Him, by whose kind paternal side I sprung,
  And her, who, still and cold,
Fills the next grave—the beautiful and young.

One of Bryant's noblest traits was his filial piety, the love for parents and for kindred, which many waters could not quench nor the floods drown, and which the lapse of time and the separation of death only intensified and exalted. He cannot view the glory of **"June,"** without thinking of the friends who will visit his tomb:

These to their softened hearts should bear
  The thought of what has been,

And speak of one who cannot share
  The gladness of the scene;
Whose part, in all the pomp that fills
The circuit of the summer hills,
  Is that his grave is green.

          Rest, therefore, thou
Whose early guidance trained my infant steps—
Rest, in the bosom of God, till the brief sleep
Of death is over, and a happier life
Shall dawn to waken thine insensible dust.

                    [**"Hymn to Death"**]

In **"The Indian Girl's Lament,"** the bereaved maiden comforts her soul with the thought that her lover will yet be hers:

And thou dost wait and watch to meet
  My spirit sent to join the blessed,
And, wondering what detains my feet
  From that bright land of rest,
Dost seem, in every sound, to hear
The rustling of my footsteps near.

"The Fringed Gentian" suggests to Bryant an old man's departure from this earthly life:

Thou waitest late and com'st alone,
When woods are bare and birds are flown,
And frosts and shortening days portend
The aged year is near his end.

Then doth thy sweet and quiet eye
Look through its fringes to the sky,
Blue—blue—as if that sky let fall
A flower from its cerulean wall.

I would that thus, when I shall see
The hour of death draw near to me,
Hope, blossoming within my heart,
May look to heaven as I depart.

"The Old Man's Funeral" is a poem in which Bryant might seem to be describing his own end:

Why weep ye then for him, who, having won
  The bound of man's appointed years, at last,
Life's blessings all enjoyed, life's labors done,
  Serenely to his final rest has passed;
While the soft memory of his virtues, yet,
Lingers like twilight hues, when the bright sun is
  set.

His youth was innocent; his riper age
  Marked with some act of goodness every day;
And watched by eyes that loved him, calm and
  sage,
  Faded his late declining years away.
Meekly he gave his being up, and went
To share the holy rest that waits a life well spent.

"The Journey of Life" ends with a stanza of immortal hope:

And I, with faltering footsteps, journey on,
  Watching the stars that roll the hours away,
Till the faint light that guides me now is gone,
  And, like another life, the glorious day
Shall open o'er me from the empyreal height,
With warmth, and certainty, and boundless light.

There is a **"Paradise of Tears"**:

There every heart rejoins its kindred heart;
There, in a long embrace that none may part,
Fulfilment meets desire, and that fair shore
Beholds its dwellers happy evermore.

"And I," he said, "shall sleep ere long;
  These fading gleams will soon be gone;
Shall sleep to rise refreshed and strong
  In the bright day that yet will dawn."

                    [**"The Two Travellers"**]

"The Flood of Years" will bring at length the consummation of all our hopes:

Old sorrows are forgotten now,
Or but remembered to make sweet the hour
That overpays them; wounded hearts that bled
Or broke are healed forever. In the room
Of this grief-shadowed present, there shall be
A Present in whose reign no grief shall gnaw
The heart, and never shall a tender tie
Be broken; in whose reign the eternal Change,
That waits on growth and action, shall proceed
With everlasting Concord hand in hand.

It must be acknowledged that this earliest of our American poets had his limitations. He had not the breadth of the great masters of his art. Science and philosophy did not interest him, as they interested Tennyson. The complexity of human nature is not depicted in his verse, as we find it depicted by Browning. A certain narrowness of range characterizes all his work. He is descriptive and meditative, but never lyric or dramatic. There is an ever-recurring remembrance of death and the grave. Critics have debated the question how a youth of seventeen could have chosen **"Thanatopsis"** for a subject. It is even more remarkable that the poetical writing of after years still dealt with this as its central theme. Dr. William C. Gannett, with his minute knowledge of literary history, has suggested an explanation both plausible and interesting. The first five years of Bryant's life were spent in a log house whose windows looked across the road upon the stone-walled village burying-ground. The child's earliest impressions of the world were connected with man's mortality. Puritan training traced this mortality to an original apostasy of the race from God, and to the penalty of a broken law. The thoughts of youth are long, long thoughts, and Bryant never outgrew the somberness of this early view of the universe.

Jean Paul has said that the melancholy of youth is the veil which a kind Providence throws over the faces of those who are to climb the dazzling Alpine heights of success and fame. But it surely belongs to manhood to look with unveiled face upon the realities of existence. The meagerness of Bryant's schooling prevented his emancipation. If he had gone to Yale, as he had hoped to do, association with his equals and his superiors would have drawn him out of himself, and would have made him more a man of the world. He was naturally shy and seclusive. As an editor, he disliked to meet socially those whom he might be called upon to criticize. His impartiality was sometimes like that of the reviewer whose freedom from prejudice is due to the fact that he has not read the book he criticizes. Greater variety of association would have added to the number of the themes which kindled in him the poetic fire.

But I must add to all this my belief that Bryant's mournfulness was the result of an imperfect understanding of the Christian revelation. He was a Puritan poet, and Puritanism too often lacked the recognition of a present Christ. In *The Pilgrim's Progress,* Christian expects to see his Saviour when he reaches the heavenly city, but he is destitute of his companionship on the journey thither. Though strong faith in a future life made Bryant serene, his serenity was too much like resignation—he needed more of joy in the present. Such joy would have enlarged the area of his poetic achievement, while at the same time it tempered the critical spirit of the editor.

But one thing must always be said of our poet: he was sincere and pure. There is no mawkish sentimentality in his verse, no pandering to the lower instincts of humanity, no expression of merely transient and conventional religious feeling. Lord Byron could write hymns in histrionic fashion, as a brilliant impersonator; of such hypocrisy Bryant was incapable. His limitations, therefore, are as instructive as his gifts. Like Wordsworth, he is a poet of nature. But, while Wordsworth sees in nature the immanence of God, Bryant sees in nature God's transcendence rather, and so is the greater Puritan of the two. His reverence for God's work in nature is greater than his reverence for God's work in man. But he has certainly taught us that poetry is no mere *vers de société,* but rather an embodiment of the deepest thoughts of the human soul:

> He let no empty gust
> Of passion find an utterance in his lay,
>   A blast that whirls the dust
> Along the crowded street and dies away;
> But feelings of calm power and mighty sweep,
> Like currents journeying through the windless
>   deep.
>   [**"The Poet,"** paraphrased by John Bigelow]

Marvin T. Herrick (essay date 1935)

SOURCE: "Rhetoric and Poetry in Bryant," in *American Literature,* Vol. 7, No. 2, May, 1935, pp. 188-94.

[*In the essay below, Herrick analyzes Bryant's attitude toward the relationship of poetry to rhetoric and vice versa, demonstrating its influence on the poet's theory and works.*]

Recent attempts to resurrect Bryant the editor have given students of American literature a better understanding of the man. Parrington and others have convinced us that Bryant, the liberal editor of the *Evening Post,* was quite as important a person as Bryant, the first American poet who won international fame. This new emphasis upon Bryant's journalistic achievements, while tending to push the poems into the background, has actually brought into sharper focus a fundamental problem in his poetry, a problem that the poet himself was aware of but never satisfactorily solved. I refer to the problem of the distinction between "pure" poetry and poetry that is rhetorical.

Many critics have tried to distinguish poetry from rhetoric. Milton's suggestion that poetry, as compared with rhetoric, is "less subtle and fine, but more simple, sensuous, and passionate," is profound but not altogether clear. Wordsworth, in both theory and practice, has made a clearer distinction; he has separated the materials of "pure" poetry from the rhetorical accretions of eighteenth-century verse. John Stuart Mill, perhaps because he was not himself a poet but an impartial observer, has offered the clearest explanation. "Eloquence," he says, "is *heard,* poetry is *over*heard." (Before we are through we shall have to make some distinction between *eloquence* and *rhetoric;* but, in general, the terms are synonymous.) Mill goes on to explain:

> Poetry is feeling confessiong itself to itself in moments of solitude, and embodying itself in symbols which are the nearest possible representations of the feeling in the exact shape in which it exists in the poet's mind. Eloquence is feeling pouring itself out to other minds, courting their sympathy, or endeavoring to influence their belief, or move them to passion or to action. ["Thoughts on Poetry and its Varieties," *Dissertations and Discussions* (1873)]

Professor Hoyt Hudson carries Mill's explanation further when he suggests [in "Rhetoric and Poetry," *The Quarterly Journal of Speech Education*, 1924] that the purely poetical impulse is often unexpressed, that by the time it is expressed it has often become rhetoric. If we may refine a little upon this idea, we may say that the poetical impulse, when expressed and then the expression *revised,* often becomes still more rhetorical.

This problem of the relationship of rhetoric to poetry, and of poetry to rhetoric, is admirably illustrated in Bryant's writings, in both his verse and prose. In this paper I hope to analyze Bryant's own attitude toward the problem and to demonstrate its effect upon his theory and practice of literary composition.

Bryant thought of eloquence as a common denominator of all good writing. "Eloquence is the poetry of prose; poetry is the eloquence of verse." He saw that there was some difference between eloquence and poetry: "A distinction has been attempted to be made between poetry and eloquence, and I acknowledge that there is one; but it seems to me that it consists solely in metrical arrangement." This statement closely parallels Wordsworth's discrimination between poetry and prose, but with a difference; Wordsworth's emphasis is not upon eloquence. By eloquence Bryant meant something narrower than rhetoric. "By eloquence I understand those appeals to our moral perceptions that produce emotion as soon as they are uttered." He did not think of eloquence as Aristotelian rhetoric—persuasion, logical argument—but rather as the "flowers" of rhetoric plus moral conviction. He was opposed to mere "flowers" of rhetoric, declamation; always he sought sincerity and simplicity, the "luminous style."

It appears, then, that our own logic forces us to the obvious conclusion that Bryant meant by eloquence, poetry, even "pure" poetry. True, such was his aim. His results, however, were not always "pure" poetry. Although we may make a distinction between eloquence and rhetoric, the two are closely associated, as they were in Bryant's thinking. When eloquence is the aim, rhetoric, as well as poetry, will inevitably be the result.

It would be a mistake to maintain that Bryant had a narrow view of poetry, that he always sought the eloquent. "The varieties of poetic excellence," he once said, "are as great as the varieties of beauty in flowers or in the female face." Nevertheless there is a pronounced leaning, in Bryant's criticisms, toward the eloquent, even toward the out-and-out rhetorical.

Chaucer, to Bryant's taste, was apparently not eloquent enough: "There is no majesty, no stately march of numbers, in his poetry, still less is there of fire, rapidity, or conciseness." His opinion of the English writers of the seventeenth century furnishes a more positive illustration: "The eminent divines, Barrow, Jeremy Taylor, and others, wrote nobly in prose with a genuine eloquence and a fervor scarcely less than poetic." Bryant admired Schiller for his "superhuman eloquence": "'William Tell' stirs the blood like the sound of a trumpet." Wordsworth, like Chaucer, was not eloquent enough for Bryant:

> I should say of his more stately poems in blank verse that they often lack compression—that the thought suffers by too great expansion. Wordsworth was unnecessarily afraid of being epigrammatic.

Bryant admired Fitz-Greene Halleck, his wit, his irony, his playful fancy, his fine ear. The highest praise, however, is given to Halleck's "Marco Bozzaris," particularly to the dirge over the hero's death, "a glorious outpouring of lyrical eloquence."

Bryant's own verse illustrates this leaning toward an eloquence which is often rhetorical. The most striking and familiar example is furnished by the evolution of **"Thanatopsis."** The first printed version, although it probably was written before the author had become acquainted with Wordsworth's Preface to the second edition of *Lyrical Ballads,* was simple and personal. There is more than a touch of rhetoric in this early version, but not the self-conscious rhetoric that the poet later added. Let us look at the closing lines of the poem as it appeared in *The North American Review* for September, 1817:

> Thousands more
> Will share thy destiny.—The tittering world
> Dance to the grave. The busy brood of care
> Plod on, and each one chases as before
> His favourite phantom.—Yet all these shall leave
> Their mirth and their employments, and shall come
> And make their bed with thee!

These lines were written, as Wordsworth once said of the best passages in Thomson's *The Seasons,* largely "from himself." Then came, in the revision, an addition:

> As the long train
> Of ages glide away, the sons of men,
> The youth in life's green spring, and he who goes
> In the full strength of years, matron, and maid,
> And the sweet babe, and the gray-headed man,—
> Shall one by one be gathered to thy side,
> By those, who in their turn shall follow them.

The tone has changed. The poet has written to be *heard,* not *over*-heard. Perhaps, when he first conceived the poem, it was "pure" poetry. Then he wrote it down and it became tinged with rhetoric. Then he revised the poem and it became, particularly in the closing lines, manifestly rhetorical. As Carl Van Doren has said of the revision [in "The Growth of 'Thanatopsis'," *The Nation*, 1915], "Now he was unwilling to leave in the poem so personal an air." Rhetoric had won over "pure" poetry.

There are poems wherein Bryant does seem to be writing to be *over*heard. I have in mind **"The Rivulet," "March," "Summer," "To a Fringed Gentian,"** and **"The Death of the Flowers."** But, as every student of Bryant will acknowledge, I believe, there are plenty of examples of his rhetorical verse other than **"Thanatopsis."**

William Ellery Leonard, in criticizing Bryant's prose style, compares him with Burke; both had the "poet's generalizing power." Professor Leonard selects a passage from Bryant's address on "The Electric Telegraph":

> My imagination goes down to the chambers of the middle sea, to those vast depths where repose [*sic*] the mystic wire on beds of coral, among forests of tangle, or on the bottom of the dim blue gulfs strewn with the bones of whales and sharks, skeletons of drowned men, and ribs and masts of foundered barks, laden with wedges of gold never to be coined, and pipes of the choicest vintages of earth never to be tasted. Through these watery solitudes, among the fountains of the great deep, the abode of perpetual silence, never visited by living human presence and beyond the sight of human eye, there are gliding to and fro, by night and by day, in light and in darkness, in calm and in tempest, currents of human thought borne by the electric pulse which obeys the bidding of man.

"Is not this," says Professor Leonard, "in imagination, mood, manner, even in the recurrent blank verse cadences, veritably as if an unpublished fragment of **'A Hymn of the Sea'**?"

True. I read this passage aloud to an intelligent critic, who had not looked at Bryant in years, and he could not be sure whether the selection was prose or blank verse. Then I read a passage from Bryant's **"Hymn to Death"**:

> Thou too dost purge from earth its horrible
> And old idolatries;—from the proud fanes
> Each to his grave their priests go out, till none
> Is left to teach their worship; then the fires
> Of sacrifice are chilled, and the green moss
> O'ercreeps their altars; the fallen images
> Cumber the weedy courts, and for loud hymns,
> Chanted by kneeling multitudes, the wind
> Shrieks in the solitary aisles.

Again the listener was puzzled; he could not be sure whether the selection was blank verse or prose.

Is not this last passage in imagination, mood, manner, even in its stately eloquence, like a fragment from an unpublished **"Oration on Death"**? [In a footnote the critic adds: "Bryant's poem **"A Hymn of the Sea"** offers a good comparison with the prose passage from "The Electric Telegraph," but the movement and tone of the selection from the **"Hymn to Death"** furnish a more striking parallel."] Which of the two passages quoted is the more poetic? Which is the more rhetorical? It is hard to say.

It was natural that Bryant should have delighted in rhetoric, even if he had never become the popular orator, the "old man eloquent," that he did become. Much stress has been laid upon his early upbringing and its consequent effects upon his poetry—his piety, didacticism, and his fondness for the funeral elegy. Our so-called Puritan ancestors, and many generations of their offspring, were even more taken with rhetoric than with funeral elegies. Their most important institutions were Church and Law. Sermons and orations attained a ranker growth than did elegies. In 1828 James Fenimore Cooper said of the Americans: "Their sermons and fourth of July orations are numberless." Just as nowadays few people bother to discriminate between "pure" poetry and rhetoric, so most Americans of the early nineteenth century doubtless saw no difference, beyond versification, between a splendid sermon, a stirring oration, and a fine poem. I suspect that Jefferson expressed the typical attitude of the educated American when he said of Patrick Henry's oratory, "He appeared to me to speak as Homer wrote." Bryant was a better judge of literature than Jefferson; he would never have confused Patrick Henry and Homer. But he often confused "pure" poetry and rhetoric.

I am not trying to belittle Bryant. I am not arguing that all poetry which is rhetorical is bad poetry. Such a claim would be absurd when there is so much rhetoric in some of our greatest poems. It has been demonstrated, however, that some discrimination between "pure" poetry and rhet-

oric is valuable. Bryant, I believe, was aware of such a discrimination, and tried, as did Wordsworth, to write poetry that was purer than any his countrymen had written before him. His success was only a partial success. In view of his upbringing, his surroundings, his American contemporaries, it is, perhaps, remarkable that he achieved the simplicity that he unquestionably did achieve in some of his poems. But Bryant only occasionally wrote poetry that is a "spontaneous overflow of powerful feelings . . . from emotion recollected in tranquillity." Rarely did he write poetry that is "feeling confessing itself to itself." Almost never did he write poetry that is more "sensuous and passionate" than is rhetoric. One reason for this partial failure, I must conclude, was Bryant's preoccupation with an eloquence that was essentially rhetorical.

Evans Harrington (essay date 1966)

SOURCE: "Sensuousness in the Poetry of William Cullen Bryant," in *University of Mississippi Studies in English*, Vol. 7, 1966, pp. 25-42.

[*In the following essay, Harrington investigates the "profound influence of the senses" in Bryant's poetry.*]

Even before James Russell Lowell's celebrated comparison of William Cullen Bryant to an iceberg, Bryant was accused of coldness of heart. And long after the more extreme of Lowell's remarks had been denied, similiar criticisms continued to be made. Indeed scholars of our own century have not felt inclined to exempt Bryant completely from the charge. Yet modern critics generally agree with Norman Foerster that "Bryant's genius, after all, was by no means altogether didactic and mortuary; sensuous pleasure . . . is prominent in his relation to external nature."

In a study of anything so subjective as poetry, the importance of sensuousness, pleasure in the blandishments of the senses, is undeniable. However much of the intellectual and spiritual one may acknowledge in the process of poetic composition, the profound influence of the senses is obvious. Thus, if sensuousness is a "prominent" feature of Bryant's work, a systematic investigation of it is indicated. The following observations are a result of such an investigation.

Since sensuousness is based on the five senses, it is well to note at the outset which of the senses seem most frequently and vividly registered by the poet. In the case of Bryant one may begin by dismissing altogether the sense of taste. Though Bryant sings with pleasure of the planting of apple trees and of their beautiful blooming, and though he describes vividly the making of maple sugar and apple cider, there is nowhere in his poetry any of the gustatory revelling of a Keats. The sense of taste, alone of the five, goes virtually unrepresented in Bryant's poetry.

Not surprisingly, however, Bryant's frequent evocations of walks in forests and strolls along streams decidedly involve his sense of touch. The almost omnipresent breezes of his poetry cool and soothe him. Sometimes he even effects a tactile identification with the breeze, as when in **"Green River"** a zephyr "stoops to freshen his wings." But the sun and grass are tactile pleasures, too. The poet lies languidly in a shade where the "thick turf" is "yet virgin form the kisses of the sun." Not only the sun's warmth but also its rich light seems at times to have almost a tactile appeal, as in **"June,"** where the poet visualizes his grave and muses,

> There through the long, long summer hours,
>   The golden light should lie.

or in **"Tree Burial,"** where the mother derives comfort from the image of her child not buried "Among the chilly clods where never comes / The pleasant sunshine," but bound to the bough of a tree, where the morning sun "Shall beam upon thy bed" and "the red light of the evening clouds" shall lie there "sweetly."

The color golden also seems to carry something of a tactile quality in **"The Song of the Sower."** Throughout the poem there is a warm glow, and in repeated allusions to the "golden seeds" in the "mellow mould" Bryant achieves more than a visual sensation. Here, too, occurs one of the most sensuous of all his metaphors:

> Ha! feel ye not your fingers thrill,
>   As o'er them, in the yellow grains,
> Glide the warm drops of blood that fill,
>   For mortal strife, the warrior's veins. . . .

Tactile sensation is also implicit in Bryant's pleasure in the "unmoving shade" of trees. The forest itself exudes a kind of tactile holiness in its "dim vaults" and "winding aisles," with its "cooler breath / that from the inmost darkness" comes and its "barky trunks" and "ground, / The fresh moist ground." Finally, there is another sort of tactile imagery, what might be termed the obverse of sensuousness, imbodied in phrases like "slimy roots" and "oozy banks." But this will be best discussed in another context.

Almost any of Bryant's nature poetry will testify to his keen delight in two more senses: that of hearing and that of smell. Indeed, to find this delight in lovely sounds and odors a reader need go no further than the startling product of the poet's old age, **"Among the Trees,"** in which occurs the deeply felt question:

> And when the glorious spring-time come at last,
> Have you no joy of all your bursting buds,
> And fragrant blooms, and melody of birds
> To which your young leaves shiver?

or this Keatsian luxuriance:

> the song-sparrow, warbling from her perch,
> Tells you the spring is near. The wind of May
> Is sweet with breath of Orchards, in whose boughs
> The bees and every insect of the air
> Make a perpetual murmur of delight,

> And by whose flowers the humming-bird hangs
>   poised
> In air, and draws their sweets and darts away,
> The linden, in the fervors of July,
> Hums a louder concert. When the wind
> Sweeps the broad forest in its summer prime,
> As when some master-hand exulting sweeps
> The keys of some great organ, ye give forth
> The music of the wood land depths, a hymn
> of gladness and of thanks. The hermit-thrush
> Pipes his sweet note to make your arches ring.

As Bradley has pointed out, however, it is undoubtedly the visual scene which is most outstanding in Bryant's poetry. Almost any of the poet's descriptions of natural scenes achieves a vivid pictorial effect. Witness **"Thanatopsis"** with its "hills / Rockribbed and ancient" and its gray old ocean "poured round all"; the **"Waterfowl"** darkly "painted" (as Bryant orginally expressed it) "against the crimson sky"; the towering, craggy **"Monument Mountain"**; the broad vistas of **"The Prairies"**; the haunting "ice palace" of **"Catterskill Falls"**; the **"Scene on the Banks of the Hudson"**—to choose a few almost at random. So marked is the pictorial in Bryant's work, in fact, that Bradley suggests the poet might under other circumstances have become a painter. And elsewhere Bradley observes:

> . . . while Bryant's expression is luminously transparent, it is not colorless. The very precision with which he chooses his words, especially descriptive words of form, colour, and motion, and limits them to those that best render the desired effect, while it often detracts from the musical flow of his numbers, heightens the painter-like quality which makes a constant appeal through the eye. . . . It is as if he were handling lines and colours, and not the mere symbols of these things, with the added advantage of being able to suggest that perpetual motion of wind-blown grass and moving shadows that must forever remain suspended in any vision of nature as rendered by the painter. [William Aspenwall Bradley, *William Cullen Bryant*, 1926]

The most vivid and individualistic sense impressions of Bryant's work are in his descriptive-meditative poems, like **"Thanatopsis"** and **"A Forest Hymn"**; and it is largely from this group of poems that the illustrations in the preceding paragraphs have been drawn. Bryant's work includes, however, a substantial number of poems in which the sense impressions are not at all vivid or individualistic. Yet the very triteness of these poems, together with a pattern which they reveal, seems significant for an understanding of Bryant's response to nature. The poems of this group include most of those about Indians and hunters, most of those about the few other primitives whom Bryant treated, and certain miscellaneous poems dealing with natural objects but conceived in a highly conventional fashion: for example, **"The Rivulet."**

The pattern which emerges from these poems is the marked reappearance of certain animals, natural objects, or phenomena, usually of a sort to call forth a sense impression. Thus winds under various names—zephyrs, breezes, "breaths," and airs—are almost always blowing. A stream-let, rivulet, river, or brook "prattles," "dimples," or "bick-ers." Flowers, often single violets, nod on weedy brinks. Dew glistens; deer or fawns shrink in forest glens; bees buzz and birds pipe. And always, in these poems, the elements are highly stylized; almost never is there an individualistic stroke of description. Interestingly enough, moreover, it is in poems dramatizing dreams, reveries, memories, and sentimental sorrows that this pattern is best exemplified, as though it constituted a kind of sentimen-tal ideal or escape fantasy. This Romantic stereotype would come forth most strongly when Bryant's imagination was working most feebly, of course; but the fact that the stereo-type was there, undoubtedly even behind the most vivid and individualistic strokes of description, seems signifi-cant. Readers interested in observing the pattern might read successively **"The Rivulet," "A Dream,"**"**The Hunter's Serenade,"** and **"A Maiden's Sorrow."** In **"A Dream"** nearly all the elements of the pattern are packed into two brief stanzas:

> Earth, green with spring, and fresh with dew
>   And bright with morn, before me stood;
> And airs just wakened softly blew
>   On the young blossoms of the wood.
>
> Birds sang within the sprouting shade,
>   Bees hummed amid the whispering grass,
> And children prattled as they played
>   Beside the rivulet's dimpling glass.

Before a general assessment of the quality of Bryant's sensuousness is attempted, two other aspects of it need to be noted: first, the kinds of natural objects and phenom-ena which seem to have attracted him most and elicited from him the most vivid responses; and, second, his manner of expressing the sensations in verse.

Foerster was the first to note Bryant's delight in wind. Pointing out that the poet devoted nine entire poems to that element, he says:

> "O Life! I breathe thee in the breeze," is almost as typical of [Bryant's] poetry as the view of nature as "the great tomb of man." . . . If anything in nature is endowed by Bryant with spirituality, it is the wind— "heaven's life-breathing wind," "the breath of God." [*Nature in American Literature*, 1958]

McDowell notes the almost invariably amorous nature of Bryant's winds [in *William Cullen Bryant*, 1935], and goes on to demonstrate the "even keener joy" with which Bry-ant "welcomed violent storm and tempest." He did not point out, however, that in **"The Hurricane,"** Bryant not only waited "with a thrill in every vein" for the "Silent and slow, and terribly strong" hurricane, but when it at last arrived he saw its "huge and writhing arms" as

> . . . bent
> To clasp the zone of the firmament,
> And fold at length, in their dark embrace,
> From mountain to mountain the visible space!

Perhaps because **"The Wind and the Stream"** is rather ludicrous, no one has pointed out, either, the bold dalli-ance in it of a wandering breeze with a "softly-gliding, bashful stream." When the breeze

> . . . put the o'erhanging grasses by,
> And softly stooped to kiss the stream,

the water

> Shot upward many a glancing beam,
> Dimpled and quivered more and more.

Indeed, after viewing Bryant's treatment of wind one feels that, to paraphrase Foerster, if anything in nature is en-dowed by Bryant not only with spirituality but with sen-suality (and the *if* is in either case a large one) it is the wind.

McDowell states that Bryant wooed rains, storms, and breezes "most persistently" of all things in nature, but this statement, while emphasizing real enthusiasms of Bryant, is not quite accurate. For Bryant actually devotes more poems to rivers, streams, and oceans than to any other one aspect of nature, more even than to the wind. Besides the streamlets and brooks which play through many of his poems on other subjects, nine rivers, rivulets, fountains, and streams are the exclusive subjects of poems. Two more poems are devoted to the ocean, and in two others, rivers and oceans play a major role. Nor is the importance of streams and oceans merely quantitative. Green River, in the poem of the same name, inspired some of Bryant's most sensous images and some of his happiest combina-tions of description with meter. A stream and an ocean, moreover, furnished him in **"Sella"** with one of his only two sustained fantasies: a pair of graceful and richly sen-suous poems which Bradley has called, not wholly accu-rately, "quite unlike anything else in his work."

The other fantasy in question, **"The Little Children of the Snow,"** is, in fact, an excellent example of a kind of sensuousness often overlooked in Bryant. The number of poems which he devoted exclusively to winter scenes is small. Besides this one there are only **"A Winter Scene,"** **"Catterskill Falls,"** and **"The Snow-Shower."** But the rich fancifulness in them, the unusually detailed and strik-ing images, and the noticeable quickening of the language suggest more than a coincidence in the fact that Bryant's autobiographical description of his boyhood love of na-ture contains a preponderance of references to winter scenes:

> I was always from my earliest years a delighted observer of external nature—the splendors of a winter daybreak over the wide wastes of snow seen from our windows, the glories of the autumnal woods, the gloomy approaches of the thunderstorm, and its departure amid sunshine and rainbows, the return of spring, with its flowers, and the first snowfall of winter. The poets fostered this taste in me, and though at that time I rarely heard such things spoken of, it was none the less cherished in my secret mind. Meantime the school which I attended was removed to the distance of a

mile and a quarter from our dwelling, and to it in winter we went often across the fields over the snow—when it was firm enough to bear us without breaking the glazed surface. Then the coming and going was a joyous pastime.

Reference to snow and brief treatments of it are scattered throughout Bryant's work, of course, notably in **"The Two Travellers"** and **"The Apennines."** Interestingly enough, in the former poem snow symbolizes death, as it does in **"The Little People of the Snow," "Catterskill Falls,"** and **"The Snow-Shower."** In **"The Apennines"** it is associated with purity, as it is throughout Bryant's treatments of it. In this connection it should be noted that water, too, when not polluted by proximity to "the haunts of men," is conceived by Bryant as pure and is also associated with death. The connection between ice and snow, water, purity, death, Bryant's Puritan inheritance of the Calvinistic tendency to negate natural life as depraved, and the poet's escape during the"depraved" Civil War years into fantasies of snow and water, is at least provocative.

It becomes even more provocative, in fact, when one considers that it is death, that most unnatural of all natural phenomena, which elicits the keenest and most persistent response of the senses from Bryant. This response is, of course, not properly defined as sensuous in the narrow meaning of that word; rather, as mentioned earlier, it is the obverse of sensuousness, though in such a phrase as "the oak / Shall send his roots abroad and pierce thy mould" one wonders if there is not a touch even of the sensuous. Sensuousness or revulsion, however, the impressions are vivid in the poetry. Whether Bryant is constructing an image of the earth as the tomb of man in **"Thanatopsis,"** or translating the abstract killer Time into **"The Flood of Years,"** always death, the grave, the decayed flesh of all the ages is present. Indeed if, as Foerster says, it would be absurd to list Bryant's poems about nature because the list would read like a table of contents, it would be for the same reason even more absurd to list those about death.

But if one concentrates on the evidence of Bryant's senses in his preoccupation with death, certain interesting traits appear. First, there is a physical revulsion at the mere thought of cessation of bodily and mental life. Several poems of Bryant's youth—**"Not That from Life, and All Its Woes," "A Chorus of Ghosts,"** and **"They Taught Me, and It Was a Fearful Creed,"**—from a good supplement to **"Thanatopsis"** in this connection. The young Bryant finds no consolation in talk of the release from the woes of life which death brings. He does not care to hear from "flatt'ring verse" that "this head" shall "repose in the low vale most peacefully." There is, in fact, a "sacred dread of death" which "chills" his "very soul." He shudders at "that breathless sleep, / That night of solid gloom." He envisions his "glazing eye" and "house of clay." He protests at the "fearful creed" that God abandons "to the eternity of darkness" human "thought and its organs."

It is true, of course, that even by the time of **"Thanatopsis"** Bryant had begun to achieve a kind of composure in the face of death and shortly thereafter had even begun to write his own species of "flatt'ring verse" to it. But the poignant lines at the end of **"Hymn to Death"** show that despite his new hope in "the bosom of God," Bryant's horror of death had not changed: "Oh, cut off / Untimely when thy reason in its strength, . . ." and "Shuddering I look / On what is written, . . ." Nor should one think, on the strength of the many later expressions of confidence in an after-life, that this horror greatly diminished for Bryant as he grew older. In his early forties he was writing **"Life"** and **"Earth's Children Cleave to Earth,"** both eloquent expressions of how earth's "frail / decaying children dread decay." And to skip over many similar poems, in 1876, two years before his death, he was grieving in **"The Flood of Years"** for "all the sweet lives that late were overwhelmed."

But, as indicated in some of the above quotations, it seems possible that the revulsion of Bryant's senses was even stronger against the grave—or maybe simply burial in the ground itself—than against the cessation of life. References in three of his early poems to the "eternity of darkness" and "night of solid gloom" have already been noted. In one of the same poems, **"A Chorus of Ghosts,"** Bryant speaks of the grave as a "couch of iron rest," a "dreamless bed," a "low and narrow cell." Its walls are cold and dark; and, "unfelt, the enclosing clods" keep guard above the corpse. With these impressions should be compared the "sad images" in **"Thanatopsis"** of "the stern agony, and shroud, and pall, / And breathless darkness, and the narrow house" which, according to the speaker, make one "to shudder, and grow sick at heart." It should be remembered, too, that in **"Thanatopsis"** occurs the previously cited image of the oak tree's piercing the auditor's mould.

It may be argued that these images are merely the result of the youthful Bryant's reading of Blair and Kirke White, or that at the most they express only a temporary state of religious upheaval. And it is true that as he advanced in age Bryant used fewer and fewer such direct and mordant images of the grave. It is true, also, that more and more frequently he expressed a hope for some form of happy after-life. Yet at sixty-five he was still envisioning "the clammy clay" as his resting place, and at seventy-four he was still grieving for loved ones laid "in their last rest, / their little cells," to be seen no more.

In view of his emphasis on the darkness, coldness and underground dissolution in the grave, moreover, it is interesting that some of his most successful poems, filled with some of his most sensuous images, were descriptions of graves which avoided these qualities.

> A cell within the frozen mould,
>   A coffin borne through sleet,
> And icy clods above it rolled,
>   While fierce the tempests beat—
> Away!—I will not think of these—

he tells us in **"June"** and then he proceeds to evoke that warm grave in the richly sensuous golden light described in a passage previously quoted.

But even earlier, in **"The Indian Girl's Lament,"** he had pictured that sorrowful maiden as telling her buried lover that she had pulled away shrubs which had grown too close above the head of his grave, and had broken away the boughs that had shaded the "bed," so that, ". . . shining from the sweet southwest, / The sunbeams might rejoice thy rest." And in a poem written in his sixties, **"A Sick-Bed,"** he had achieved a strikingly similar effect while dealing with a subject strikingly different.

> But bear me gently forth
>   Beneath the open sky,

a dying person pleads,

> Where, on the pleasant earth,
> Till night the sunbeams lie

And gradually the reader realizes that this "sick-bed" so pleasantly described is actually a grave.

Perhaps the most significant poem of this kind, however, is **"Tree-Burial,"** written six years before the poet's death. Here as the Indian mother talks to her dead child, whom she has suspended in animal skins and bark from the bough of a tree, the invocation of sunlight, breeze, star shine, bird song, and flower scent has a quiet, clean joy about it, a strangely tonic quality, almost hygienic, as of the dry, immensely rarified air of mountain climates. One is reminded of Bryant's Puritan heritage, and even, despite the obvious differences, of one of his striking descriptions of his native New England air on a day after a snowstorm:

> . . . The pure keen air abroad,
> Albeit it breathed no scent of herb, nor heard
> Love-call of bird nor merry hum of bee,
> Was not the air of death.

And, by contrast, by the vivid gap of its absence, one is reminded of the darkness, closeness, clamminess, coldness, and root-slimy disintegration in a subterranean grave.

Before leaving this subject, however, it is necessary to note Bryant's curiously contradictory attitude toward earth and man. For despite his apparent horror of burial in the earth, the earth itself was not evil or polluted to him, except as it was soiled by man's sins. Witness the poems **"Earth"** and **"The Apennines,"** as well as the lines in **"The River, By Night,"** where it is pointed out that the cruelties and injustices of man have stained nature. Witness, too, **"Inscription for the Entrance to a Wood":**

> Thou wilt find nothing here
> Of all that pained thee in the haunts of men,
> And made thee loathe thy life. The primal curse
> Fell, it is true, upon the unsinning earth,
> But not in vengeance.

Yet almost the entire surface of the earth has been the scene of man's wickedness and suffering. The plough is constantly striking "the scattered bones," and Bryant is constantly standing upon the "ashes" of a previous generation. In fact, only high peaks such as those of **"The Apennines"** are pure, as Bryant points out in the revealing lines:

> Yet up the radiant steps that I survey
> Death never climbed, nor life's soft breath, with
>   pain,
> Was yielded to the elements again.

Thus earth is the vast grave of **"Thanatopsis,"** and as such a constant source of somber reflections, if not outright revulsion. Yet she is also the mother of man, and in the poem **"Earth"** Bryant can lie on her "breast" and listen to her "mighty voice" complaining at the wrongs done her. He can even ask her "What then shall cleanse thy bosom, gentle Earth / From all its painful memories" of human guilt. Not all men are wicked, however; there are "all the sweet lives" mentioned in **"The Flood of Years."** The earth, therefore, as mother, grieves for them; and, in a passage which curiously mingles revulsion and sensuousness, Bryant grieves with her:

> Their graves are far away
> Upon thy mountains; yet, while I recline
> Alone, in darkness, on thy naked soil,
> The mighty nourisher and burial place
> Of man, I feel that I embrace their dust.

At this point Leonard's emphasis on the primitive nature of Bryant's imagination comes forcibly to mind [William Ellery Leonard, "Bryant and the Minor Poets," *Cambridge History of American Literature*, 1931]. Truly, there seems to be little philosophy, as such, in his attitudes toward life and death, man and nature. His pleasure in the happier aspects of nature, his fear of death and the tomb, his mingled revulsion and fondness for the enigmatic old earth-mother is indeed scarcely more complicated than "the simple thought that personifies and capitalizes." It is true also that there is a pagan emphasis in Bryant on "the phenomena of life as life, on death as death," just as Bryant's assurance of immortality scarcely touches the usual intricacies of theology and philosophy but rests "mainly on primitive man's desire to meet the loved and the lost, the father, the sister, the wife." Understanding Bryant in this way, one may also agree with Leonard that the poet's previously observed love of fairyland is

> . . . one more manifestation of the primitive in Bryant (for the fairy-tale is, as the anthopologists tell us, among the most primitive activities of man) as dreamer and poet.

The relationship between a poet's sensuousness or revulsion and his use of poetic rhythm, rhyme, vowel-and consonant-harmonies, and diction is, of course, a highly ambiguous matter. Yet no one with a feeling for poetry and nature could read lines like the following from **"Green River"**—

> Yet pure its water—its shallows are bright
> With colored pebbles and sparkles of light,

And clear the depths where its eddies play,
And dimples deepen and whirl away, . . .

or these from **"June,"** previously quoted in part—

> There through the long, long summer hours,
>   The golden light should lie,
> And thick young herbs and groups of flowers
>   Stand in their beauty by.
> The oriole should build and tell
> His love-tale close beside my cell;
>   The idle butterfly
> Should rest him there, and there be heard
> The housewife bee and humming-bird

without recognizing not only that such a relationship clearly exists but also that it plays an important part in Bryant's poetry. As a matter of fact, critics since the time of Poe—and he foremost among them—have agreed in praising Bryant's ability to make "the sound the echo of the sense." Though it is perhaps in his predominantly lyric poems and his fantasies that this "verbal sensuousness" appears most immediately, the quality is no less present in his other work. The following lines from the quietly meditative **"A Winter Piece"** probably owe much to Wordsworth, as Lowell suggested, but the tone, cadence and modulation are those in which Bryant spoke consistently throughout his poems of this sort; and the delicate observation, with the precise union of sense and sound, is, in the opinion of one reader at least, superior to Wordsworth's.

>   Nor was I slow to come
> Among them, when the clouds, from their still
>   skirts,
> Had shaken down on earth the feathery snow,
> And all was white. . . .
>
>   . . . . .
>
>   Again the wildered fancy dreams
> Of spouting fountains, frozen as they rose,
> And fixed, with all their branching jets, in air,
> And all their sluices sealed. . . .

Bradley has well described Bryant's use of meter in his didactic poetry. Pointing out that Bryant rarely failed to choose the proper meter whatever his subject, he continues:

> It is invariably for the more impressive themes. . . that he employs the blank verse which he knew how to handle with a firm grasp and with a variety of pauses that made it an instrument both of elasticity and of power. In many of these poems there is, not passion precisely, but a kind of eloquence that is his single escape from the atmosphere of tender and pervasive sentiment in which he habitually dwelt. In these moods he passes from the descriptive and reflective vein into a strain of direct invocation, as if engaged in the ritual of a sublime worship of nature.

The handling of physical details in such poems as **"Thanatopsis," "To a Waterfowl," "A Forest Hymn,"** **"Hymn to Death,"** and **"The Flood of Years"** fully illustrates Bradley's point.

It will be noticed, however, that in the preceding quotation Bradley declares the eloquence of the moral hymns to be Bryant's "single escape from the atmosphere of tender and pervasive sentiment," and thus he echoes the long-standing charge, noted at the beginning of this paper, that Bryant lacked passion, was somehow cold. It is now time to consider whether a survey of Bryant's sensuousness in any material way alters that opinion.

The answer to that question, however, depends to some extent on what is meant by the charge of coldness. If it is meant to imply that Bryant himself had little feeling, little animal pleasure in or human emotion for nature, friends, loved ones, and man in the aggregate, then a study of his sensuousness indicates an emphatic denial. On the contrary, it may be maintained that the simple, in Leonard's phrase the "primitive," emotions and instincts and sense perceptions are the very things which animate the vast majority of Bryant's poems. It even seems probable that it is precisely Bryant's abundance of feeling and poorness of intellect or imagination which limits him most as a poet. That is, if he had possessed a greater analytical power, with the accompanying strength of imagination to put the fruits of analysis into effective poetic form, he might have transcended the limitations of his age and environment, might not have reflected so clearly the sentiment of Blair, Kirke White and Cowper and the restraint of his Puritan forebears.

For if, on the other hand, it is meant by the charge of coldness simply that Bryant almost never wrote "poetry that is more 'sensuous and passionate' than is rhetoric," one is forced to agree. The precise reasons for this failure must probably forever remain uncertain, but it seems worthwhile to point out Marvin Herrick's contention that the rhetoric of Puritan sermons and the aesthetic theories of eloquence and sublimity current in Bryant's day combined to limit, in large part, the poet's ability to express naked emotion ["Rhetoric and Poetry in Bryant," *American Literature*, 1935]. Certainly, also, the Puritan strictures against uncurbed imaginations played their part in shaping the poet who could declare, in a lecture of 1825:

> There are exercises of the imagination, it must be confessed, of too gross and sordid a nature to be comprised within the confines of any divine art—revellings of the fancy amid the images of base appetites and petty and ridiculous passions. These are the hidden sins of the heart, . . .

The temperament which emerges from a study of Bryant's sensuousness is gently sensitive, moral, altruistic. It suggests a person not particularly original either in the perception or expression of his universe, so that a reader can wonder how much of his preoccupation with death or his pleasure in nature came directly from him and how much was a literary fashion, even in his most sincere moments. There is some evidence that by a native fastidiousness and fancifulness he was more naturally inclined toward dreams, pleasures of the senses, and melancholy at life's transient nature than toward an active, self-restrained career. But if such was the case, outside influences or a counterbalancing quality in his temperament—or, more likely, both—enabled him to control even the "wayward" emotions he might feel, so that he produced poetry in which the most powerful emotions were almost invariably the most moral, and the "escapes" into sensuousness and fairyland were held to a very small number and kept within proper moral bounds even when allowed.

E. Miller Budick (essay date 1976)

SOURCE: "'Visible' Images and the 'Still Voice': Transcendental Vision in Bryant's 'Thanatopsis'," in *Emerson Society Quarterly*, Vol. 22 (n.s.), No. 2, 1976, pp. 71-7.

[*Below, Budick demonstrates the relationship between images and ideas in "Thanatopsis," which represents the complexities of man's apprehension of transcendent truths in natural images.*]

In moments of discursive simplicity, William Cullen Bryant felt certain that poetry was the optic through which man's otherwise restricted vision could be made to perceive the interpenetration of nature and that which is above nature:

> Among the most remarkable of the influences of poetry is the exhibition of those analogies and correspondences which it beholds between the things of the moral and of the natural world. I refer to its adorning and illustrating each by the other—infusing a moral sentiment into natural objects, and bringing images of visible beauty and majesty to heighten the effect of moral sentiment.

Undoubtedly many of his best poems do exult, unhesitatingly and without complication, in the "analogies and correspondences" which link "things of the moral and of the natural world." Such poems as **"Inscription for the Entrance to a Wood"** and **"Green River"** enjoy the serene confidence generally associated with Romantic Idealism in the nineteenth century. Bryant's waterfowl, his fringed gentian, and the American landscape of the **"Prairies"** and **"Earth"** are nature's and poetry's carefully wrought artifacts, the primary purpose of which is to tutor man in transcendent truths and to supply him with images of the linear continuity which stretches from the mundane to the celestial.

And, yet, in one of his major works, Bryant clearly betrays a profound distrust of the naive, often facile exuberances of Idealist faith. In **"Thanatopsis"** he assumes the voice of a philosophical and religious skeptic, an agonizer over the uncertainties suggested by the twofold power of death to dissolve both natural images and the human imagination. Although Bryant might easily have availed himself of the solaces which comforted other Romantics beset by similar doubts, he chose in **"Thanatopsis"** to cut himself loose from the ego-sustaining nurture of the Romantic universe and to flounder, at least momentarily, in

an unsafe agnosticism. Albert McLean has carried Bryant's doubts to their apparently logical conclusion and argued that, according to **"Thanatopsis,"** nature may "herself project a metaphorical language, no better than the vision which changes its focus from one poem to the next. . . . Throughout the poem this emphasis upon the differences between 'forms' and some sort of transcendent reality reoccurs" [*William Cullen Bryant* (1964)]. And, yet, in the final analysis, **"Thanatopsis"** is, I believe, a compelling reaffirmation of Bryant's Romantic-Idealist faith. The poem represents the poet's valiant and successful attempt to define precisely, and without the excesses of facile Romantic rhetoric, the constituent complexities of man's apprehension of transcendent truths in natural images. This, in my view, is the poem's central achievement: its tough-minded and yet eloquent portrayal of the process whereby nature imparts to man her vision of transcendence.

The emphasis throughout the poem is on this process—on the gradual emergence of nature's loving but stern pedagogy. The rhythms and the tendency of this process are embodied in the poem's dialogic pattern of affirmation and doubt, the pattern which Bryant chose to reenforce by the addition of lines 1-17 in the 1821 edition. In the first fifteen of these lines the poem presents the world of Romantic correspondences which appears to be the immediate object of attack in line 17:

> To him who in the love of Nature holds
> Communion with her visible forms, she speaks
> A various language; for his gayer hours
> She has a voice of gladness, and a smile
> And eloquence of beauty, and she glides
> Into his darker musings, with a mild
> And healing sympathy, that steals away
> The sharpness, ere he is aware. When thoughts
> Of the last bitter hour come like a blight
> Over thy spirit, and sad images
> Of the stern agony, and shroud, and pall,
> And breathless darkness, and the narrow house,
> Make thee to shudder, and grow sick at heart;—
> Go forth, under the open sky, and list
> To Nature's teachings.

Nature, it would appear, responds to man's affection for her by speaking to him in precisely those voices he would like to hear: "a voice of gladness" to heighten his "gayer hours" and a "mild . . . healing sympathy" to mollify his "darker musings." Nature's projected images and man's emotional needs seem to harmonize perfectly; the man-nature empathy appears seamless and complete. It comes as no surprise, therefore, that the poet urges his reader, "when thoughts / Of the last bitter hour come like a blight / Over thy spirit" and "sad images / . . . Make thee to shudder," to "Go forth, under the open sky, and list / To Nature's teachings."

No sooner, of course, has the speaker uttered the conventional Romantic advice—"list / To Nature's teachings"—than he inserts a discomfiting qualification which apparently takes the poem off in another direction: "while from all around— / Earth and her waters, and the depths of air— / Comes a still voice." The dialogic pattern of the poem and the tormenting doubts which characterize its argument suggest that the "while" denotes contradiction: even as we are listening to nature's teachings, the poet tells us, a still voice, a voice from beyond nature, catches our ear and communicates a different message. "Yet a few days," the voice warns, "and thee / The all-beholding sun shall see no more." But the "while" of line 15 is not intended simply as a contradiction of the Romantic metaphors of the preceding lines. It is, in fact, meant to be an extension and an affirmation of that Romantic language as well. We must "list / To Nature's" imagistic "teachings," the speaker is arguing, while simultaneously, "from all around," a still voice comes uttering the same lessons embodied in nature's physical forms.

The dual aspect of the contradictive-continuous "while" in line 15 is central to the poem's philosophical structure. Its bifurcated meaning alerts the reader to other, related subtleties in the poem's opening lines and also signals the inauguration of a whole network of contradictive-continuous connective—simultaneously separating and joining nature and supernature—which provides the poem with its complex conditional mood. In the first fifteen lines of the poem, the speaker is not simply articulating Romantic doctrines but is struggling between his desire, on the one hand, to trust in the validity of visible forms, and his compulsion, on the other, to believe in the superiority of an unseen voice. Even as he glories in his pathetic fallacies, he hints that, to the individual who holds communion with nature's "visible" as opposed to her invisible forms, she speaks a "various," that is, inconstant, language. And, he suggests, man's dependence upon natural forms may well result in his forfeiting certain of his powers of consciousness, of perceptual focus, and of will, as nature's smiles glide secretively into his darker, more serious musings, *stealing* away their "sharpness," "ere he is aware." But the suggested opposition between voice and perceived form is not, according to Bryant, as diametrical as one might at first suppose. Nature's visible forms, we note, while ostensibly visual, do not in fact receive any pictorial illustration in the early lines of the poem. Rather they are immediately transmuted into a voice, into the "language" and "teachings" which, however "various," are still abstract and non-representational; they are a "voice of gladness"and a "healing sympathy." The still voice, on the other hand, which would appear to connote the non-visualizable dimensions of reality, is explicitly identified as a product of the physical elements of creation: "Earth and her waters, and the depths of air." Visible forms are a voice, the poet is saying; and the still voice of God or of supernature issues from the physical creation.

The still voice, for all its intimations of unmediated transcendence, is, the poet suggests, simply one more of nature's many voices, a voice which is part of the natural world. It makes its appearance in the poem, therefore, merely as the last item in the poet's catalogue of nature's teachers. This voice, the voice of stillness, speaks to man's fear of death. It is akin to the "mild / And healing sympathy" which softens man's "sad images" of the "breath-

less," still, "darkness" which awaits him. Similarly, just as the conjunction "while," which introduces the still voice, expresses both denial and continuity, so the meaning of the word "still" subtly and ironically suggests two opposite significations: the still voice speaks of death, the ultimate stilling of the natural world, but it also vocalizes nature's perpetual continuity, the still-ness implied by man's participation in ongoing natural law even after his earthly demise. Death concludes life, stills it; but death also extends life's meaning, draws it into sustained involvement with the endless cycles of the natural world. The still voice may qualify or even appear to negate the validity of the "various" forms which seduce man into a self-deceptive and naive optimism, but, in the pictorially concrete images of the next few lines, in the "ground," "ocean," "earth," and "oak," that same voice is seen to herald the reformulation of those images, albeit in a new and painfully validated perspective.

The contradictive-continuous quality of the still voice and of the conjunction "while" is echoed in the word "yet" which initiates the first of the poem's major dialogic transitions. This "yet," which was already present in the 1817 edition of the poem, begins the description of death's destructive powers and, in the context of the original version, its force was balanced and ultimately displaced by the "yet" in line 31, which ushers in the process of the poet's reconciliation with death. But with the addition of the 1821 lines, the sentiments expressed in the first lines of the 1817 poem now become the words not of the poet himself or of some unlocated source, but of the still voice, of death or of supernature itself. As such, these words seem to emerge as a direct refutation of the optimistic, Romantic perceptions described in lines 1-15 of the revised poem. Their purpose seems to be to set Romantic nature and death into an absolute and unmitigated antagonism to one another. But contained in these words is a consolation as well as a terror; and this consolation, I suggest, derives directly from the voice's careful reinstitution of naturalistic, imagistic perception. The voice speaks as follows:

> Yet a few days, and thee
> The all-beholding sun shall see no more
> In all his course; nor yet in the cold ground,
> Where thy pale form was laid, with many tears,
> Nor in the embrace of ocean, shall exist
> Thy image. Earth, that nourished thee, shall claim
> Thy growth, to be resolved to earth again,
> And, lost each human trace, surrendering up
> Thine individual being, shalt thou go
> To mix for ever with the elements.

Existence, the voice appears to be arguing, at least existence as mankind has commonly defined it, depends upon man's taking in and nature's projecting outward of images. Death, in this view, means the passing away not only of man and his image-assimilating capacity, but of nature and the validity of her imagistic projections of truth as well. When the "all-beholding sun" no longer sees man, nor man the sun, when man's "image" ceases to "exist," and when the "Earth, that nourished" man dissolves his "being," piercing his life-sustaining, identity-providing "mould," then man's faith in nature's truthfulness and the comfort which nature's imagery once supplied must also die. The implied devaluation of nature is twofold. Nature, according to the voice, first lures man into an untenable dependency on physical forms which cannot provide an accurate report of the relationship between the now and the hereafter because these forms exist only in the temporal present and perish in death; and then nature, using death as her agent, betrays man's trust in her. By simultaneously dissolving her own image and his, she robs him of the very avenues to knowledge and belief which she herself had persuaded him were authentic. Nature, as she is presented by the still voice, emerges not as a source of solace but as a force of consummate hostility, eager to plunge man into the whirlpool of his own fantastic and chaotic perceptions. Nature's "various" language of "visible" images is presented as being not only incapable of speaking to man of the grave, but as deliberately distracting him from creating the kind of non-imagistic consciousness which might be able to alleviate the terrors of death.

Nonetheless, the "yet" of line 17, which seems so clearly to signal a negation of nature's visible images, also suggests, in two ways, a temporary reprieve from death's sentence of total extinction. The conjunction "yet," as it is set in relation to lines 1-17, extends the elements of continuity—between nature and supernature—implicit in those lines and in the term "still" itself. While the skeptical, contradictive "yet" implies that, despite nature's consolations, man will die and become formless, the continuous and affirmative "yet" promises that it is "yet a few days" until man's demise. "Nor yet," the poet continues in line 19, is man buried and his image lost. There is a significant interval before man's "last bitter hour"; there is time during which he can prepare for death. Although nature's visible forms may not be able to alter the finality of death, they can forestall it, or at least remove its bitter sting. They can suggest the beauty-fostering distance between man and his destiny. The voice from earth, water, and air promises "still."

Furthermore, nature's visual images, her "ocean" and "earth" and "oak," can themselves awaken man to the meaning of death in human experience, and thereby they can help bring death itself into absolute harmony with the physical universe. The poet does not fully resolve the tension between death as a negation of nature's visual eloquence and as a continuity between visible forms and other-worldly realities until stanza two, but he begins the resolution in stanza one by imagistically depicting the elements of the creation in their proper relationship to man: as symbols of mortal demise as well as of eternal life. Out of this treatment of natural images emerges the final consolation. "Yet, not to thine eternal resting-place / Shalt thou retire alone," the second stanza begins. In death, the poet tells us, man joins the multitudes of individuals who have died before him: "patriarchs," "kings," "the wise" and "the good"—the "fair *forms*" (italics added) which represent for the poet a transcendentalized restoration of imagistic consciousness. Having apparently abandoned nature's visible images in favor of the unem-

bodied still voice of supernature, the poet in stanza two introduces a detailed catalogue of physical forms by which the reader is meant to visualize, identify with, and finally accept his destiny in death. Just when we expect the poem to assert the transcendence of idea and voice over form and vision, the poet instead begins to describe, to give form to, many of the natural events which had been inexplicably excluded from the early lines of stanza one and which had even received negative treatment in the concluding lines of that stanza. The hills, vales, woods, and rivers now all achieve beautiful pictorial prominence; and while their attributed pensiveness and complaints suggest that they are mortally imperfect, the form which is ascribed to them is majestic. Nature's visible images are "solemn decorations all / Of the great tomb of man." The sun, the planets, the stars—the whole of the physical creation—become symbolic of life and of death simultaneously.

> Visible form, [Bryant] suggests, subserves consciousness. But he emphasizes that form is still the language in which consciousness must express itself.
>
> —*E. Miller Budick*

The "yet" of stanza two negates death's powers of total dissolution by asserting the continuity of form in the realms of both nature and the hereafter. Form, the poet says, bridges the gulf which separates the living and the dead. Bryant, like at least one of his Puritan predecessors, is cautious about the use of symbols. If, Bryant suggests, man allows his definition of himself to depend solely on images taken from the natural world, he is apt to find himself dwarfed and intimidated by the physical creation. The observed phenomenon of death, by shaking man's confidence in nature's visible forms, frees the elements of man's inherent cosmic faith for a more meaningful and realistic coalescence. "The hills / Rock-ribbed and ancient as the sun," "Old ocean's . . . waste," and the "venerable woods" which decorate man's tomb are purified reincarnations of the "all-beholding sun," the "embrace of ocean," and the stolid "oak" which, only moments before, were nature's beloved visible images turned villains, the dire agents of man's uncreation in the physical universe. These demonic lords of natural sublimity, we find, are, in the larger scheme of things, merely ornaments, created forms which vivify and beautify reality and which also point to their own and man's temporality and impermanence, thereby preparing man for the greater reality yet to come.

Visible form, the poet suggests, subserves consciousness. But he emphasizes that form is still the language in which consciousness must express itself. This is the striking paradox, now fully crystallized, toward which the entire poem has been moving. Like Emerson's *Nature*, Bryant's **"Thanatopsis"** is concerned with reconciling the poet's pure, almost child-like affection for nature with his more sophisticated awareness of an Ideal reality above and beyond nature. Emerson's description of the relationship between nature and Idealist philosophy seems to me particularly relevant to Bryant's poem. Philosophical Idealism, writes Emerson, emancipates man from the "despotism of the senses, which binds us to nature as if we were a part of it." But, Emerson cautions, men must take care not to expand "too curiously the particulars of the general proposition. . . . I do not wish to fling stones at my beautiful mother, nor soil my gentle nest." In the final analysis, philosophical Idealism is not the denial of natural form but an extension of nature's meaning which originates with nature herself: "Our first institution in the Ideal philosophy," remarks Emerson, "is a hint from nature herself. Nature is made to conspire with spirit to emancipate us."

Nature's visible forms do, in the final stage of spiritual perception, convey the same truths spoken (or hinted) by the transcendental still voice. The imperative, "So live," which begins the third and last stanza of the poem, derives its meanings from the complex process of transcendental vision which the poem has been describing:

> So live, that when thy summons comes to join
> The innumerable caravan, which moves
> To that mysterious realm, where each shall take
> His chamber in the silent halls of death,
> Thou go not, like the quarry-slave at night,
> Scourged to his dungeon, but, sustained and soothed
> By an unfaltering trust, approach thy grave,
> Like one who wraps the drapery of his couch
> About him, and lies down to pleasant dreams.

In the more rigorous argument of the 1821 poem (lines 66 ff. are not part of the 1817 text), Bryant realized that it was not sufficient just to recognize, as he had done in 1817, that death is a kind of mystical participation in the movement of cosmic history. In order to reconcile himself to death, man must come to understand death *within* the context of the familiar, naturalistic universe. Therefore, Bryant's advice to his reader is that he should "live" in such a way as to enable himself to understand nature's visual language on the highest possible level; that he should, in other words, simply "live!" and enjoy it. In order to avoid becoming death's "quarry-slave" (one who is enslaved by the devastating message of nature's "insensible rock" and "sluggish clod"), man must respond to the natural world in terms of the very images and voices (the "gladness" and "beauty," for example) which seem, in moments of skepticism and mistrust, maliciously deceptive and false. While it may be true that, in death, every person must abandon his "favorite phantom," still those phantoms—the "mirth" and "employments" of humankind's days—are, in the final analysis, true, even if less refined, versions of those "pleasant dreams" out of which the substance of supernature is in fact woven. Even if death succeeds in dissolving the symbolic landscape and the symbolizing imagination, the projections and intuitions of that landscape and of that imagination have been genuine communications from the beyond.

The "lesson" of the poem's conclusion reaffirms the emergent methodology of nature's instruction; it celebrates her visible forms which the poem has been calling into question. According to Bryant, nature's paedeutics are necessarily propaedeutic, heuristic and tentative—at least in the first instance. As she is presented in the poem, nature is the intentional but affectionate baffler of human perceptions, a conjurer of many disguises who offers herself to man's imagination in a series of purposefully antithetical personae. In one attitude she supports and sustains man's faith in the virtuous simplicity of natural correspondences; in another she abruptly wrenches man from her bosom, weaning him, as it were, from his immature and ultimately debilitating dependence on the earthbound symbolism of the material world. But throughout her complex maternal relationship with man, Bryant's nature strives to one purpose: to enable man to survive, physically and spiritually, within the context of the existing universe.

In completing his revaluation of Romantic nature, the poet reasserts the centrality of visible form inhuman consciousness. The poem's summary images—the couch, chamber, and halls which nature promises man as his final resting place—are unequivocally concrete. Bryant's intention in questioning the capacity of natural and poetic symbols to convey cosmic truth has not been to deny them their legitimacy, but rather to point to the relationship which links image and idea and to suggest the complex emotional and perceptual process behind the transumption of the one into the other. **"Thanatopsis,"** the poet's contemplation of death, imitates the process of Romantic vision and transcendental revision by which man is enabled to both conserve and transcend the images of nature and the mind. The "drapery" of "dreams" which marks the poem's finale does not negate the visible "phantoms" of man's life in nature. Instead, like the revised concept of death which the poem has been suggesting, it endeavors to soften, etherealize, and distance the harsh and restrictive outlines of physical reality. Nature's visible images and her still voice do not contend with each other for the exclusive right to represent truth. Rather, they collaborate in the production of nature's perpetual pageant of sense and consciousness—her truth-revealing drama of images and ideas which inspires and comforts man during his existence in the natural world and which, like the daily replay of waking events in nightly dreams, furnishes him with images of what is familiar and pleasant as he moves onward toward death.

Edwin R. Booher (essay date 1978)

SOURCE: "The Garden Myth in 'The Prairies'," in *Western Illinois Regional Studies,* Vol. 1, No. 1, Spring, 1978, pp. 15-26.

[*In the essay below, Booher discusses Bryant's pastoral and sometimes primitive treatment of the American Midwest in "The Prairies," noting his contributions to the mythology of the American West as a literary theme.*]

One of the earliest major poems about the Midwest is William Cullen Bryant's **"The Prairies."** Written after a visit to Illinois in 1832, the poem clearly embodies significant forms of American idealism and denotes the emergence of the West as an important literary theme. For several reasons—not the least important of which is the difference between what Bryant saw on the frontier and his poetical treatment of that experience—the poem is an instructive excursion into American myth.

The lengthy journey from New York to visit two of his brothers disclosed to Bryant the realities of life in Illinois, and the letters he wrote to his wife indicate diverse and conflicting impressions. In the poem, however, the experience is transformed into a pastoral vision of the prairies, a romantic blank verse treatment on the order of his famous **"Thanatopsis"** and **"A Forest Hymn"** of the sublime aspects of Illinois scenery. First published in *Knickerbocker Magazine* in December, 1833, and subsequently included in Bryant's 1834 and later collections of poems, **"The Prairies"** has been generally praised and often anthologized. Bryant wrote other poems based on the trip to Illinois—**"The Hunter of the Prairies"** and **"The Painted Cup"**—and visited Illinois again in 1846 after his mother and brothers had moved to Princeton; but **"The Prairies"** is unquestionably his most significant poetic treatment of western material.

The route Bryant chose allowed him to see much of the American landscape. Leaving New York on May 22, 1832, he traveled by stagecoach, boat, and (briefly) train to the Ohio River. Then, by way of Cincinnati and Louisville, steamboats took him down to the Mississippi to St. Louis and up the Illinois River to a landing about twenty miles from Jacksonville. He arrived on the twelfth of June.

Interestingly enough, Bryant's western journey coincided with relevant historical circumstances that are excluded from the poem. At various river stops, he heard talk of Indian attacks in Illinois and informed his wife that he would have to return by the same route instead of crossing the prairie to Chicago as planned. A long-standing conflict between whites and Indians had resulted the previous year in the use of a volunteer army to drive Black Hawk and his Sauk and Fox people from their village at the junction of the Rock and Mississippi rivers. On April 5, 1832, Black Hawk and about a thousand persons, perhaps half of whom were warriors, recrossed the Mississippi and moved about forty miles up the Rock River, intending to exercise what they considered was their right to farm the land there and expecting to gain support from other Indian tribes as well as from the British if again confronted by the militia.

As preparations were made to send both the Illinois militia and the United States Army against him, Black Hawk came to realize that aid would not be given and that he could not remain with his people and fight. On May 14, a week before Bryant's departure from New York, Black Hawk attempted to confer under a flag of truce with an advance detachment of the militia. However, the undisciplined militiamen took his messengers prisoner, fired upon

those who had been sent to watch from a distance, and then murdered one of the captives. Following that incident and Black Hawk's retaliatory charge, the Indians were pursued through several encounters and, several weeks after Bryant's return to the East, were trapped as they attempted to cross the Mississippi. On August 2, in what is called the Bad Axe Massacre, the troops slaughtered men, women, and children who were plunging into the river in their desperate scramble for safety. By the time the poem was completed for publication the following year, Black Hawk had been imprisoned for several months and, still a prisoner, given a "celebrity's" tour of eastern cities before being freed at Rock Island. In September, 1833, most remaining tribes had been evicted by treaty from territory in Illinois.

Nor were conditions in frontier towns idyllic. John Bryant was a clerk in Jacksonville, which the poet described to his wife as "a horribly ugly village, composed of little shops and dwellings, stuck close together around a dirty square, in the middle of which stands the ugliest of possible brick courthouses, with a spire and weathercock on its top." Arthur Bryant farmed near the village, living in a two-room log cabin with kitchen and parlor separated by an open-roofed passage "large enough to drive a wagon through," as William put it. Arthur was not present to welcome his brother, however, having prudently returned to Massachusetts for a suitable wife to share his western venture.

Accompanied by John, William enthusiastically explored the prairie, with its marvelous stretches of flat lands covered by tall grasses and myriad wild flowers. Soon after his arrival, he and his brother set out on horseback toward Springfield and rode about a hundred miles over vast prairies with scattered settlements near wooded groves and rivers. Bryant found the countryside to be "the most salubrious" and fertile he had ever seen; "at the same time," he added, "I do not think it beautiful. Some of the views, however, from the highest parts of the prairie are what, I have no doubt, some would call beautiful in the highest degree. . . ." Perhaps he was thinking of these when he wrote the opening lines of **"The Painted Cup"**:

> The fresh savannas of the Sangamon
> Here rise in gentle swells, and the long grass
> Is mixed with rustling hazels.

In his letters Bryant was also candid about the people and the towns he saw. About thirty-five miles from Jacksonville, he and his brother stopped at the federal land office in Springfield to learn whether any land was available. He found the houses there "not so good" as those of Jacksonville, "and the whole town having an appearance of dirt and discomfort." After spending the night in a "filthy tavern," he and his brother rode north for several days, Bryant himself considering the purchase of a quarter section of land not far from Pekin. Once, at nightfall, the travelers found themselves on the edge of an empty stretch of prairie fifteen miles wide and sought lodging in the only habitation available, a one-room cabin. They found a man sick with fever, a half-dozen or more children, "brown with dirt," and several other travelers. The harried woman of the household gave them food about ten o'clock, and they slept on the floor—twenty men, women, and children in the same room. At another cabin Bryant asked for corn for the horses and saw "a fat dusky-looking woman, barefoot, with six children as dirty as pigs and shaggy as bears. She was cleansing one of them and cracking certain unfortunate insects between her thumbnails. I was very glad when she told me she had no corn nor oats." Shortly thereafter, however, they spotted a clean-faced youngster and, pursuing that sign of civilization, found hospitality to their liking, even though the woman had but one spoon with which to serve them and that with only half a handle.

On the return to Jacksonville, Bryant encountered one of the thirty-day companies called up in the Black Hawk campaign, which introduction him to "a hardlooking set of men" who were "unkept and unshaved, wearing shirts of dark calico, and sometimes calico capotes." The captain of the company was a lanky young man who amused Bryant with his clever talk and frontier wit. Years later, Bryant learned that the young man he had met that day was Abraham Lincoln, whom he would memorialize in 1865 as "slow to smite, and swift to spare, / Gentle and merciful and just!"

The day after Arthur returned from Massachusetts with his new wife, Bryant left for New York by the river route, concluding one of his letters with the remark that his experience must be treated in "the only form of expression in which it can be properly uttered." That form was implicit in a letter he wrote in October: "These prairies, of a soft, fertile garden soil, and a smooth undulating surface, on which you may put a horse to full speed, covered with high thinly growing grass, full of weeds and gaudy flowers, and destitute of bushes or trees, perpetually brought to my mind the idea of their having once been cultivated."

Bryant's supposition that the prairies were gardens in antiquity led him to use the agrarian myth, which informs the entire poem. As Henry Nash Smith and Leo Marx have shown, the American pastoral myth is a significant mode of belief in which the landscape, particularly the Middle West, has long been viewed as a kind of garden, an idealized middle ground of nature and art, lying midway between the primitive forest and populous city. "We are a people of cultivators . . . united by the silken bands of mild government, all respecting the laws, without dreading their power, because they are equitable," Crevecoeur wrote in the eighteenth century. And, as Marx summarizes it, *Letters from an American Farmer* is a classic illustration of the myth: "Instead of Arcadia, we have the wild yet potentially bucolic terrain of the North American continent; instead of the shepherd, the independent, democratic husbandman with his plausible 'rural scheme'; instead of the language of a decadent pastoral poetry, the exuberant idiom, verging toward the colloquial, of the farmer. . . ." The most notable political advocate of the myth was Thomas Jefferson, in whose *Notes on the State of Virginia* the familiar defense of the agrarian society is found: "Those who labor in the earth are the chosen people of God, if ever He had a chosen people, whose breast He has made His peculiar deposit for substantial and genuine virtue."

Many of the settlers who came to Illinois were deeply conscious of their roles in creating a new society on the fertile land, and the Bryants were no doubt among them. In the presence of so persistent an American belief, it is not surprising that Bryant's Illinois experience is assimilated into it. The opening lines of **"The Prairies"** establish his use of the myth:

> These are the gardens of the Desert, these
> The unshorn fields, boundless and beautiful,
> For which the speech of England has no name—
> The Prairies.

Having announced his pastoral theme, Bryant then relates how the Creator himself prepared a sublime setting for those who will cultivate the prairies:

> The hand that built the firmament hath heaved
> And smoothed these verdant swells, and sown their
>   slopes
> With herbage, planted them with island-groves,
> And hedged them round with forests.

Such natural gardens for a chosen people are "Fitting floor / For this magnificent temple of the sky," where the flowers below "rival the constellations," and the heavens bend down upon the earth in love. The hoofbeats of the horse create a "sacrilegious sound," disturbing the "dead of other days" who built great mounds overlooking the Mississippi and "in the dim forests crowded with old oaks."

Although Bryant is not explicit, the ancient inhabitants of the prairie are clearly analogous to the Arcadians of old and were "a disciplined and populous race" that built the mounds while the Greeks were yet quarrying marble to build the Parthenon. Like shepherds of the Golden Age they were rewarded for their artful affinity with nature:

> These ample fields
> Nourished their harvests, here their herds were fed,
> When haply by their stalls the bison lowed,
> And bowed his maned shoulder to the yoke.

A race so skilled in the agrarian arts that it domesticated the buffalo might well be expected to excel in the other pastoral arts of love and poetry, as indeed it did:

> . . . and lovers walked, and wooed
> In a forgotten language, and old tunes,
> From instruments of unremembered form,
> Gave the soft winds a voice.

Implicitly, the gardens of the desert are the physical and spiritual legacy bequeathed by that happy people to western settlers. *Et in Arcadia ego,* or in nineteenth-century terms, "thus change the forms of being." The civilization of Mound Builders was destroyed, Bryant relates, by the invasion of hunter-tribes, which signify the force of primitivism impinging upon the garden. With one exception, the peaceful cultivators were slaughtered as the prairie fell under the dominion of the red men.

The treatment of the Mound Builders and red men as two distinct races undergirds Bryant's use of the pastoral myth, with its counterforce of primitivism, and derives from another nineteenth-century belief generally discarded today. In a popular history which Bryant collaborated in writing in 1876, a full chapter is devoted to the Mound Builders, who are described as a shadowy people "of a singular degree of civilization" antedating the Indians found here by discoverers from the old world. It was they who built "the mighty mounds / That overlook the river," which Bryant had seen at St. Louis and which are regarded today as the relics of the Mississippian Indian culture. As for contemporary tribes, the comment in the history reflects a popular misconception that Bryant wrote or allowed to stand, at least, through editorial prerogative: "It seems irrational to assume that such a people, whose contact for two centuries and a half with the culture of another race has been unproductive of any good, can have once fallen from a semi-civilization possessed by their ancestors, but of which they have neither distinct inheritance nor even dim tradition."

The force of primitivism, epitomized by the "red man" in the poem, does not itself escape the mutability of being nor perhaps the gentle breezes of the garden landscape. According to Bryant's account, "hunter-tribes, warlike and fierce," savagely destroyed the peaceful civilization of Mound Builders. After the plain had been heaped with corpses and all but one slain, that lone survivor returned to the captured stronghold in despair, expecting nothing better than death:

> Man's better nature triumphed then. Kind words
> Welcomed and soothed him; the rude conquerors
> Seated the captive with their chiefs; he chose
> A bride among their maidens, and at length
> Seemed to forget—yet ne'er forgot. . . .

The recent conflict between whites and Indians in Illinois is completely absent from the poem. The explanation given for the Indians' departure is that the forms of being change and

> The red man, too,
> Has left the blooming wilds he ranged so long,
> And, nearer to the Rocky Mountains, sought
> A wilder hunting-ground.

Although the prairies have been the scene of earlier conflict and sorrow, they remain untainted. The poem concludes with a description of a natural garden in which men may live in perfect harmony. The birds have scarcely "learned the fear of man," and the "sliding reptiles of the ground, / [are] Startlingly beautiful." For the moment, it seems inevitable that humanity will fulfill here in this new Eden its old Utopian dream. Actual conditions that Bryant had seen are relegated to the prose; no Martin Chuzzlewit will suffer the ague in these surroundings.

Now, as the poet's horse moves over the prairie, in a bucolic and prophetic reverie, Bryant envisions an advancing multitude to build anew on the foundations of that earlier race of gardeners. Listening long to the "domestic hum" of the bee, the poet hearkens to still another sound:

> From the ground
> Comes up the laugh of children, the soft voice
> Of maidens, and the sweet and solemn hymn
> Of Sabbath worshippers. The low of herds
> Blends with the rustling of the heavy grain
> Over the dark brown furrows.

Destined to build new lives on prairies across the continent, the colonists will doubtlessly be as skilled as their predecessors in the agrarian and aeolian arts. Their virtue will be that of the child, the maiden, and the Sabbath worshipper.

The reports of travelers and of pioneers who settled the prairies—at first near the timber groves and later on the open plain—leave no doubt of the sublimity of the virgin landscape and its capacity to inspire hope. In fact, Bryant poeticizes a thought expressed more than once in accounts by early settlers of Illinois:

> I behold [the prairies] for the first,
> And my heart swells, while the dilated sight
> Takes in the encircling vastness.

In "the sound of that advancing multitude" near the end of the poem, Bryant evokes a nationalistic theme that received stronger affirmation in years following 1833 and fuller poetical expression with Whitman, whose "western youth" of "Pioneers! O Pioneers!" carry on the work of progress and regeneration when older races droop with weariness:

> All the past we leave behind,
> We debouch upon a newer mightier world, varied world,
> Fresh and strong the world we seize, world of labor and the march.
> Pioneers! O pioneers!

Eventually, as Marx points out, the American concept of progress made it imperative to introduce the machine into the garden, while the myth was assimilated into a literature of the "technologically sublime." Thus, through technology, Whitman's pioneers are enabled to transcend time and space in their spiritual passage to India and return

> To reason's early paradise,
> Back, back to wisdom's birth, to innocent intuitions,
> Again with fair creation.
>
>   ["Passage to India"]

By treating the prairies as gardens and the Mound Builders as Arcadians, Bryant, like Whitman, defines the nation's destiny in the context of a golden age and reveals the significance of the western myth to America's spiritual quest. In reality, of course, neither metropolitan corruption nor primitive anarchy were excluded from the garden. With the machine came the industrial city—big business, crowded tenements, and political dishonesty—and in the removal of the Indians beyond the Mississippi, white settlers demonstrated their own savagery; but for a poet of the nation's spirit and geography the myth of the garden was a promising and powerful theme.

R. Rio-Jelliffe (essay date 1978)

SOURCE: "'Thanatopsis' and the Development of American Literature," in *William Cullen Bryant and His America,* edited by Stanley Brodwin and Michael D'Innocenzo, AMS Press, 1983, pp. 133-46.

[In the following essay, Rio-Jelliffe considers the traditional and innovative elements of "Thanatopsis," examining its relationship to Bryant's own poetic theory and to the subsequent development of American literature.]

On reading an anonymous poem brought by Willard Phillips, his co-editor with Edward Channing of the *North American Review,* Richard Henry Dana, Jr. is said to have exclaimed: "Ah! Phillips, you have been imposed upon; no one on this side of the Atlantic is capable of writing such verses." Dana's skeptical remark identifies in the unknown author, soon discovered as the young William Cullen Bryant, the presence of a new voice, the promise of a new direction in American letters. Other critics have since concurred with Dana's estimate. H.M. Jones takes the first publication of **"Thanatopsis"** in 1817 as "the landmark . . . from which many are inclined to date the beginnings of a truly national American letters." In Bryant's first collection and Cooper's *The Spy,* both published in 1821, F.O. Matthiessen detects "the literature of the new nation, as distinct from colonial literature, [beginning] to find its voice."

"Thanatopsis" is also significant for adumbrating a concept of nature and art which generated over half a century a coherent poetic theory and practice denoting the character of the yet unborn American literature. While the historical significance of **"Thanatopsis"** is generally acknowledged, its artistic structure and the relation of that structure to the development of American literature remain undefined. This paper examines the artistic structure of **"Thanatopsis,"** a pattern of tension created by contradiction and paradox (I); and notes the relation of that structure to Bryant's theory of poetry and language, and of his theory and poetry to the development of American literature (II). Limited by space to a summary of my evidence, the paper is based on [the critic's unpublished] full-length study of Bryant's concept of nature and its relation to poetic theory and practice.

Literary historians detect in the attempts of early nineteenth century writers to assimilate and order a confusion of inherited and indigenous literary crosscurrents the be-

ginnings of an American literature. The works of Brown, Irving, Cooper, Bryant, and others record the propaedeutic struggle toward artistic independence. Bryant's precursive discovery of a subjective locus for synthesizing borrowed and native elements, of an aesthetic for giving voice to innate experience of American nature, points the way to artistic identity and integrity. His coherent system of poetics and poetry, probably the first in America, exemplifies the process of assimilation and naturalization indispensable for the advent of the great writers in the "renaissance."

At a time when American "criticism was preoccupied with the social implications of literature" and "questions of art and technique were too often neglected," Bryant discoursed on literary technique, language, and form. Contradictory assessments of Bryant's critical position and tenets require a coherent and thorough consideration of his theory and poetry. For Bryant, like Wordsworth, is a transitional writer who sets traditional material in new orientations and thus recasts them with fresh significance. Both show the influence of associational writers, the English poet primarily of the mechanist Hartley, and the American of the later intuitive-idealist Alison, whose theories anticipate romantic aesthetics. Bryant's critical and poetic works center around and are informed by an innate feeling for American nature and its implications for art. His poetic theory and practice, founded on romantic principles of emotional expression, naturalness, simplicity, spontaneity, irregularity, and freedom, set him squarely in the romantic movement which he anticipates in America by over a decade.

After the first publication of the body of the poem in 1817, generally assumed to be a fair copy of the original draft, two other versions preceded the 1821 **"Thanatopsis"** with its now famous introduction and conclusion. Two manuscripts, dated 1813-1815 and 1818-1820, contain prototypal versions of the introduction and conclusion. These variants contravene assumptions made by some readers that the 1821 introduction and conclusion were "additions . . . hastily composed" under Wordsworth's influence for the collection Dana had commissioned. The variants give evidence of an evolving view of nature which structures and informs the poem, and lies at the heart of Bryant's poetic theory and practice.

The introduction of the 1821 **"Thanatopsis"** opens with a general statement on nature's "various language" which breaks down into detailed components of gladness, beauty, sympathy, and consolation:

> To him who in the love of Nature holds
> Communion with her visible forms, she speaks
> A various language; for his gayer hours
> She has a voice of gladness, and a smile
> And eloquence of beauty, and she glides
> Into his darker musings, with a mild
> And gentle sympathy, that steals away
> Their sharpness, ere he is aware. When thoughts
> Of the last bitter hour come like a blight
> Over thy spirit, and sad images
> Of the stern agony, and shroud, and pall,

And breathless darkness, and the narrow house,
Make thee to shudder, and grow sick at heart;—
Go forth, under the open sky, and list
To Nature's teachings, while from all around—
Earth and her waters, and the depths of air—
Comes a still voice—

The next abstract reference to "thoughts of the last bitter hour" modulate from the vague "sad images" and "stern agony" to the concrete "shroud, and pall" and "narrow house." Embedded in these concrete images, and countering the impersonal generalization, are feelings of terror and grief. Material objects convert universal fact into personal experience. The movement from abstract generalities to sensuous, emotionally connotative particulars is a structural pattern reenforced by contrasting tones of detachment and involvement, and by rhythm congruent with imagery: gentle cadence among cheerful images in the first half, spasmodic rhythm among sorrowful, harsh images in the second half. These contrastive patterns recur consistently throughout the poem in various forms of expansion and development.

The body of the 1821 **"Thanatopsis"** originally published in 1817, likewise opens on an impersonal assertion of universal fact which shades into details connoting loss and grief: "cold ground," "lost each human trace," "brother to th'insensible rock." Kinetic imagery in "The oak / Shall send his roots abroad, and pierce thy mould" renders general truth into dread. No emotions are overtly named; they are inherent in particularized or concrete images. Discourse enunciates an objective cognition of ultimate doom, while poetic texture sounds undertones of feeling.

The paradoxical interplay of intellectual and emotional elements is reenforced by the contrast in landscape of eternal cosmos and transient being doomed to dissolution:

> Yet a few days, and thee
> The all-beholding sun shall see no more
> In all his course; nor yet in the cold ground,
> Where thy pale form was laid with many tears,
> Nor in the embrace of ocean shall exist
> Thy image. Earth, that nourished thee, shall claim
> Thy growth, to be resolv'd to earth again;
> And, lost each human trace, surrend'ring up
> Thine individual being, shalt thou go
> To mix forever with the elements,
> To be a brother to th'insensible rock
> And to the sluggish clod, which the rude swain
> Turns with his share, and treads upon. The oak
> Shall send his roots abroad, and pierce thy mould.

Nature the consoler in the introduction turns in this section of the body into an enemy. Imagery corroborates antithetical design in yet another way. Large natural entities of sun, ocean, earth dwindle to rock, clod, roots. The living body fades into pale form and vanishes in "mould." Contracting immensity and reducing "individual being" to mere shade underscore the sense of subsidence and deprivation.

The same contrastive patterns structure the second section which argue against grief and fear. The generalization on the magnificent sepulcher of the dead break down into component images of hills, woods, rivers, brooks, and sun, planets, stars. Yet their glory make them no less the "sad abodes of death." In the third section, the general abstraction on the infinite dead crystallizes in images of time and space whose grandeur, again paradoxically, intensifies the human being's sense of loss. The remote, impersonal background modulates to felt life in sensuous objects. In the concluding section, an abstract common destiny takes substantial form in specific details.

The conclusion of the poem repeats the pattern in preceding sections with an impersonal injunction and vague "pale realms of shade" which resolve into kinetic images celebrating nature's triumph over man's enemy:

> So live, that when thy summons comes to join
> The innumerable caravan, that moves
> To the pale realms of shade, where each shall take
> His chamber in the silent halls of death,
> Thou go not, like the quarry-slave at night,
> Scourged to his dungeon; but sustain'd and sooth'd
> By an unfaltering trust, approach thy grave,
> Like one who wraps the drapery of his couch
> About him, and lies down to pleasant dreams.

Two obverse images render the theme of the whole poem: negatively in the quarry slave, and positively in actions encapsulating nature's lessons on how to die and how to live.

The tensional interplay of intellectual abstraction and sensuous emotional objects, general and particular, detachment and involvement, eternal and transient, converts the poem from a versified disquisition on death, a commonplace at the time, to a record of dissonances in mind and heart. A structural pattern of contrast and paradox transforms intellectual discourse into a "structure of emotion" where, in Alison's terms, external objects function as "emotion-bearing" vehicles.

Consistent with the structural pattern, the dialectic, which centers on the role of nature, hinges as well on opposition and paradox. Postulated in the introduction as premise of the whole poem, nature is benefactor of human spirit, particularly in the extremity of death. Yet in the first verse paragraph of the body, the benign comforter disappears behind an indifferent cosmos threatening the individual with loss of every "human trace." The "all-beholding Sun" the transient Self "shall see no more." In the premise set by the introduction, the end of consciousness turns into the ultimate deprivation of nature herself, of access to spiritual aid. The role of nature in the first section of the poem contradicts her role premised in the introduction.

The temporary reversal in nature's role reflects the way the human being, overwhelmed with fear, views the natural universe. In contrast, nature's cosmic, timeless perspective subsumes human fear and grief in the common destiny of all things. This universal vision counters the individual's view of nature as an impersonal threat. Natural beauty, magnified in detail after concrete detail, is a metaphor of nature's all-encompassing beneficence. The sun, symbol of individual extinction in the first section now glorifies man's eternal home. Forbidding immensity and solitude on earth and sky, as in "Take the wings of morning . . ." are transformed into nature's enthralling world. Changes in descriptive mood reflect the individual's subjective alteration from fear and regret to assurance.

With this development the major paradox of the poem becomes clear. For over these natural scenes of beauty lies the shadow of grief and loss evoked in the first section. Enhancing nature's grandeur heightens the attractiveness of man's final resting place, but contrarily, intensifies rather than mitigates feelings of sorrow and loss which, from the start, imbues natural objects in the body of the poem. Working against nature's rational precepts are countersignals of feeling embedded in imagistic particulars. The rhetorical question in the final section of the body reiterates the loneliness and bitter regret of one cut off from the living. Nature's arguments address human reason, but the language of the poem betrays instinctual undertones of dismay and terror past rational argument.

The intellectual reasoning culminates in the concluding image of one who "lies down to pleasant dreams." The understructure of counter-feeling climaxes in the opposite image of a quarry slave "Scourged to his dungeon." Both, not one or the other, encapsulate the paradoxical theme of **"Thanatopsis."** This conclusion may not be what the poet had consciously intended to leave with the reader. But Bryant's own theory of language, of imagery in particular, and the preeminent role of emotion in the creative process, recognizes the power of words as accessible only to partial control. "Symbols of words," Bryant says, "suggest both the sensible object and the association." It is those associations that could undermine sense.

In style, technique, and thought, the 1821 introduction is more successfully integrated with the body than earlier variants. In the variants, a "better genius" mediates for nature whose ministry on spirit is contingent on the poet's voluntary return to the "repose of nature," a condition that holds in the later work. For the surrogate, a being with complex attributes appears in the 1821 poem, attesting to the poet's increased faith in nature as generative source of his art. This inner history is recorded in the early poems and confirmed in the centrality of nature in Bryant's critical theory.

An incremental dialectic from the introduction through the body rises to a point in the conclusion. Considered by many readers as a didactic excrescence, the conclusion brings nature's injunctions to its logical issue: in life alone man may learn how to die. To complete the lesson on death, nature must instruct man to "so live" that he dies in peace. The lesson on dying, the conclusion establishes, is primarily a lesson on living. In the context of the whole poem, from nature's ministry on spirit in the introduction to the influence of her "still voice" in the body, the conclusion clearly affirms "an unfaltering trust" in nature alone. From beginning to end, man's ultimate recourse in life or death is nature's benign government.

The introduction, body, and conclusion are integrally joined to one another with consistent structural patterns and antithetical stresses in technique and dialectic. Balanced contrast is reflected as well in diction which deviates markedly from Bryant's immediate legacies of English poetic tradition and its transplants in America. The language of **"Thanatopsis"** demonstrates the American poet's functional naturalization of poetic diction and more recent realistic modes from favorites like Cooper, Burns, and Wordsworth. In the descriptive passages, the realistic "Rock-ribb'd" operates with formulas, "ancient as the sun" and "venerable woods." Inert epithets like "th'insensible rock" obtain conceptual and affective life in the vivid actions of the "rude swain" who "turns with his share and treads upon" the "sluggish clod." In contrast to flaccid images of "cold ground" and "pale form," kinetic energy in the image of oak roots spreading out and piercing the human mould sharpens the sense of horror. Interacting with sensuous immediacy in natural or human actions, poetic diction acquires fresh viability.

Bryant prunes poetic convention to its functional essence, using formulaic simplicity to reinforce imagistic impression and consonant thought. Prosopopoeia, the preeminent figure of late eighteenth-century ornamental poetry, is transformed in Bryant's handling of personified nature into a functional device to set the premise of the poem and inform the whole structure.

Strategic placement of conventional phrases also contributes to unfolding dialectic and mood, as the infinite hosts of heaven convey as well immensity of space and eternal time; and "the continuous woods / Where rolls the Oregon" picture infinity and solitude of the dead. The two modes of language function conjointly to intensify paradoxical dissonance of universal fate and individual resistance to it in design and thought.

What might appear to modern readers as an unusual handling of nineteenth-century poetic language and form sets Bryant apart from the prevailing practice of his time. **"Thanatopsis"** diverges markedly from antecedent traditions in England. The most direct lines are the graveyard school, and the didactic strains of popular nature poetry with their sentimental, hyperbolic rhetoric, excessive analogizing of nature and human life; deliberate elevation of language with cumulative similes; periphrases, abstract personifications, extended descriptions; and loose, discursive form.

At a time when poetic diction was of universal currency, and preromantic and romantic writers like Cowper, Burns, Wordsworth, and Coleridge were generally unknown or unwelcome to American readers, Bryant fashions a multivalent language closer to the bone of American experience. Tempered language, restrained, dignified tone, and controlled structure distinguishes **"Thanatopsis"** from the prevailing poetic practice of the period. In this literary phenomenon, Bryant forges material and form, both inherited and original, in the shape of an American artist's vision of life and death.

The artistic qualities of **"Thanatopsis"** confirm the unique position accorded to it in the history of American literature. The poem is important in other ways not generally recognized. It adumbrates fundamental principles of Bryant's theory and poetic practice, a congruent system based on his concept of nature and its implications for poetic form portending the character of a national literature. The discussion below outlines basic theoretical principles of Bryant's theory of language and related techniques.

The original draft of **"Thanatopsis"** (1811) precedes by almost a decade and a half, the 1821 version by four years, Bryant's formulation of his critical theory. The four "Lectures on Poetry" (1825-1826) is a comprehensive statement of theory drawing together dispersed ideas, and in thenext five decades, consistently applied and reaffirmed in criticism and poetry. The concept of nature which unifies **"Thanatopsis"** becomes the fundamental principle of theory and practice grounded on the "premise of feeling" in associational and romantic aesthetics. Already germinal in the early poem are principles and tenets which bear on the development of American literature.

Bryant echoes an associational principle in postulating that the "great spring of poetry is emotion"; but he locates the "living and inexhaustible sources of poetic inspiration" in nature. The creative process generated by nature-inspired feelings mirrors the spontaneity of natural processes. Poetry is the product of mind quickened by nature. On these premises lies the touchstone for poetic language, style, and structure: the "natural." Bryant's organic view of mind and art prefigures the principle of organicism central to American critical theory from the renaissance to later periods.

The coadunation of mind and nature in Bryant's theory occasions a concept of poetic form now known as the doctrine of analogies or correspondences. Over a decade before the doctrine becomes central to American criticism, Bryant defines a poetic technique which exhibits "analogies and correspondences . . . between the things of the moral and of the natural worlds," and "connects all the varieties of human feelings with the works of creation," "moral associations with inanimate objects." Metaphoric analogy combines at once the main elements of Bryant's poetics: instigating and unifying emotion; nature, source, and norm of art; language and technique congruent to union of feeling and nature. It also achieves the immediate and ultimate ends of poetry, aesthetic experience and moral elevation.

The poetic structure blueprinted in the doctrine of analogies opens on a natural scene imbued with congruous feelings and thoughts, or posits an idea associated with feelings which permeate natural objects in the poem, as in **"Thanatopsis."** The fusion conjures up analogous scenes embodying inner responses. Poetic form emerges with the accretion of congruent details reenforcing the original fusion, and by accumulation grows in intensity. The "leit-

motif of romantic thought about art," the doctrine is an aesthetic formulation of the romantic vindication of mind over physical world, and outlines romantic structural forms.

In theory the doctrine of analogies combines discrete elements. In Bryant's practice, intense feeling inundates natural objects, and natural images are infused with feeling-thought. A new reality transcends the objective-subjective dualism. Irradiated with mind and feeling, imagery speaks the language of the inner world. The majestic beauty of the prairies becomes an agency of mind for projecting its own life. Under the fusion force of emotion, material and immaterial conjoin, and words function polysemously.

Anticipating in theory the metaphoric and symbolic modes of later poetry, Bryant applies the doctrine of analogies in poetic form distinguishing his nature poems from traditional descriptive-mediative types, where natural scene provides the setting for moral or intellectual reflections, or occasions a literal, often mechanical analogizing of nature. In most Bryant nature poems (except in the rare instance of a work like **"Monument Mountain"**), emotion unifies natural scene and subjective experience. From early works like **"I Cannot Forget the High Spell"** (1815) to great middle period works like **"A Forest Hymn"** (1825) and **"The Prairies"** (1832), landscape and cogitation mingle and illuminate one another.

All other components of Bryant's theory stem from the principle of emotion as unifier of mind and art. Since emotion and other mental constituents are "embodied in language" so as to affect another mind, the nature of poetic language engages Bryant over several decades. Emotion, he postulates, is the unfailing guide to poetic expression analogous to originating experience.

Bryant defines language as "the symbols of thought." Poetry selects and arranges these "arbitrary symbols" which are "as unlike as possible to the things with which it deals," and by this very limitation may render the immaterial in material "images" and "pictures." This view of poetic language as symbol advances beyond the associationists toward the romantic theory of Coleridge. It also suggests modern views on the nonrepresentational character of language.

Images or pictures are the heart of poetic language. Emotion opens up "the storehouse where the mind has laid up its images"; while imagination "shapes materials . . . into pictures of majesty and beauty." The poet's "sketches of beauty" are transformed in the reader's imagination to "noblest images" brought forward "from its own stores." Bryant, however, dissenting from writers of the time, distinguishes a poem "affluent" with "mere imagery" from the "language of passion" framed in "spontaneity or excitement." Supplanting the vogue of ornamental language and extended pictorial description, Bryant's imagism relies on a "few touches" to delineate both external reality and subjective response, and thus to activate simultaneously sense, imagination, feeling, and moral sensibility. Imagery whose materiality calls up "the idea of certain emotions" exemplifies Bryant's principle of synchronous operation in creative mind and poem.

The image, furthermore, concretizes general "lessons of wisdom" or "moral truth" in objects or particulars. Like Wordsworth, Bryant regards universal and permanent features of human and natural life as proper subjects of poetry, but requires that they be manifested in the particular or specific.

In depicting both particular and universal, outer and inner worlds, transient and permanent, imagery achieves the suggestive and effective ends of poetry. Both "picturesque and impassioned," a well-wrought image "touches the heart and kindles the imagination." The polyphonic function of imagery adumbrated in **"Thanatopsis"** appears in varying degrees of concentration in nature poems of the following decades. Bryant's view of image prefigures a line of thought from the renaissance to the present, as in Pound's definition of image as "an intellectual and emotional complex in an instant of time."

In accord with the informing principle of his thought and art, Bryant locates the source of functional imagery in nature, the "original fountain" and "standard of perfection" for poetry. He urges the poet to "go directly to nature" for original imagery true to experience, instead of the current dependence on "the common stock of the guild of poets."

Related to these tenets is Bryant's contention that only brief poems or those of moderate length may touch mind and heart. Despite the popular taste for epics of the revolutionary poets, or tales such as those he himself composed, Bryant asserts, "There is no such thing as a long poem." Presaging Poe's famous dictum by a decade, Bryant sets down a primary tenet of early nineteenth-century poetics on the lyric.

While Bryant advocates "simplicity and clearness" in language, he would admit "obscurity . . . in the phrase" and "recondite or remote allusions" to heighten poetic effect. He allows poetry to "transgress arbitrary rules" so long as it "speaks a language which reaches the heart." The end of poetry, to make the "fullest effect upon the mind," is thus attained "no matter by what system of rules." His radical prescriptions for prosody abrogate current rules and open the way for freer forms.

Even more revolutionary for his age where "artificial elevation of style" with "meretricious decorations" prevailed in poetic practice is Bryant's vehement advocacy of "simple and severe" style, or "simple and natural . . . style." he repeatedly inveighs against "strained, violent contrivances," "florid and stately" imagery and epithet popular with American poets. "Too far removed from the common idiom of our tongue," the "false sublime" subverts "pathos and feeling," and is therefore—a heinous sin in the Bryant creed—"out of nature" or "unnatural." Like Wordsworth, Bryant believes "the language of poetry is naturally figurative," but figures must be used only "to heighten the intensity of expression . . ." Unless forged in the heat of feeling they turn into "cold conceits" or "extravagance."

Bryant's obsessive demand for "simple and natural" language rests on a principle of marked historical significance: the organic correlation of verbal expression to originating emotion. From early to late critical works, he censures the "artificial and mechanical" in poetic language, and recommends "a natural and becoming dress for the conceptions of the writer," an "honest expresion of meaning." Only "natural" language gains the end Bryant extols, as did Coleridge before and Poe after him, "unity of effect." As no American writer of the time held so inflexibly, Bryant requires the language of poetry to be an organic expression of and commensurate to the originating subjective state.

Bryant locates the sources of "natural" language "in the organic expression of the people," in "the vernacular language of the poet." Consistent with his organicism, Bryant resolves the fundamental issue in the search for national literature. For all the causes adduced to account for its absence, and all the solutions to bring it about, the problem hinges primarily on locating an indigenous language to give intrinsic expression to American experience. An advanced pioneer on this question, Bryant renounces the prevailing dependence on English heritage, and locates an American language in "the copious and flexible dialect we speak." "It has grown up . . . among a simple and unlettered people," and has "accommodated itself, in the first place to things of nature, and, as civilization advanced, to the things of art. . . ." It has thus "become a language full of picturesque forms of expression. . . ." While the language of **"Thanatopsis"** is hardly the vernacular, still its chaste diction and controlled form deviates markedly from ornate expression and loose structure in similar works. Nature poems after **"Thanatopsis"** move closer to common speech in diction and rhythm. Departing from contemporary theory and poetic practice, Bryant's views on language presage the language of the emergent American literature.

> **As the demand for American literature rose in the early decades [of the 1800's], the idea of an indigenous literature became increasingly identified with romantic spirit and modes.**
>
> **—R. Rio-Jelliffe**

Bryant addresses another question in the search for national literature when he directs American writers to draw "their subjects from modern manners and the simple occurrences of common life." He anticipates the shift at about the fourth decade from elegant or sublime subjects to "real life," to "familiar and domestic life." Portending the practice of many American novelists, he claims romance puts "familiar things in a new and striking yet natural light," for its subject is not the "supernatural and the marvelous" but the "manners of our countrymen." The romancer is an "anatomist of the human heart," a title befitting such writers as Hawthorne, Melville, James, and Faulkner. Bryant grounds both language and subject matter in the life of "human beings, placed among the things of this earth."

As the demand for American literature rose in the early decades, the idea of an indigenous literature became increasingly identified with romantic spirit and modes. A complex of ideas and trends—elevation of feeling and imagination over reason; power of mind to link man and nature; with democratic socio-political ideals, the rise of the common man, and the divinity of common things; resurgence of American nature as source of poetic inspiration and expression; location of literary language rooted in American soil; subsidence of neoclassicism in literary art and taste; shifts in critical norms from absolute universal standards to historic relativism and subjective or impressionistic appeal; the moral ends of literature balanced with aesthetic pleasure; the turn from nationalism to universalism; the concept of organicism in government and art—these constituents of Bryant's thought and art identify the search for national literature with romantic confluences.

Enunciating romantic tenets in the twenties, Bryant may have promoted the shift from the rational-mechanistic to an organic view of mind and art. His poetics, grounded on emotion as the unitary creative principle, and poetry as analogue of mind quickened by nature, prefigure other major statements of organicism in America, and precede the belated reception of Alison and romantic theorists like Wordsworth and Coleridge. From the forties on, when romanticism had become "the positive movement of the time," organic unity and its allied doctrine of analogies echo in the works of Emerson, Melville, Lowell, Whitman, and others. Holding to the life principle as spirit, and to objects as symbols of inner or higher reality, Bryant prefigures transcendental organicism.

His organicism, however, falls short of the radical totality of All in Each espoused by Emerson and some contemporaries. Still relying on the human imagination to unite nature and mind, and to effect the same unity in the poem, Bryant adumbrates only in part the metaphysics to come. Similarly, his poetry in general merely foreshadows the symbolic mode after him. Still dwelling on natural beauty for its own sake as well as for its spiritual significance, the poems are essentially metaphoric in function. The nature poems nonetheless inaugurate "the organic union of art, nature, and mind of man," the salient mark of organicism in American literature.

Bryant's theory and art typifies one of two contemporaneous streams of American romanticism: an "organic emotional romanticism . . . of a slow but indigenous growth," and the imitative romanticism of Freneau, Halleck, Willis, Drake, Percival, and somewhat later, Poe, who exploited medievalism, the gothic, and other exotic trends in Europe. Two main branches of American poetry stem from Bryant and Poe, the first important poets of early nineteenth century. Poe initiates art for art's sake, the use of technique to achieve supernal beauty transcending mundane reality. Bryant inaugurates a poetic tradition founded on a total view of reality encompassing natural world and human mind. Where Poe in his poetic practice bypasses nature, Bryant takes nature for the main constituent of his art.

Bryant keeps faith in the literary potential of America when writers, misled by early associational thought, despair over a landscape empty of hoary legend and history. Virtually alone among the poets of the first three decades, he makes American landscape viable for poetry, not by drumming up external attributes of historic or mythic values, but by recreating natural scene in the crucible of impassioned imagination. For Bryant, the quest for nationality is the quest for personal artistic integrity. He discovers an inner locus for assimilating American nature and life, and for rendering it in art forms accordant to its spirit. His philosophy, aesthetics, and poetry offer a way to release American writers "from the sterile obligation to express what their own experience had not nurtured." Within the limited scope of his vision and achievement lay the seeds of the future.

Readers of his day find Bryant's poetry "complex and difficult," a testimony to the unique character of his work. For modern readers, Bryant's poems are loosely knit, lacking the tension of paradox, the oblique curve of irony, the concentration of symbol, the power of Adamic self-parturitions in Emerson, Whitman, Melville, and Dickinson. Yet for all their faults, the poems manifest a viable synthesis of tradition and innovation which prepares the ambience necessary for the great writers to come. His poetry describes and states, like poetry of the past; it also embodies, like much of the poetry to come. His "organic style," issuing from his search for language commensurate with his experience of American landscape and life, opens the way to an American literature sought after in his age, and claimed with pride in our own.

David J. Moriarty (essay date 1978)

SOURCE: "William Cullen Bryant and the Suggestive Image: Living Impact," in *William Cullen Bryant and His America,* edited by Stanley Brodwin and Michael D'Innocenzo, AMS Press, 1983, pp. 209-22.

[In the following essay, originally presented at the 1978 Centennial Conference at Hofstra University, Moriarty re-evaluates Bryant's poetic imagery from a modernist point of view, suggesting that the poet's nature images are still alive, renewable, suggestive, for the reader of today.]

One suspects that the literary critics have too often risen to defend a "denatured" Bryant, the one whose reputation as a poet has been assaulted by neglect and misunderstanding for the greater part of these one hundred years since his death. Acting as curators in a museum of dead ideas and forms, such critics do Bryant as much a disservice as the school teachers, who forced so many of us to memorize sections of William Cullen Bryant's **"Thanatopsis,"** a poem on a subject of which we had but a dim awareness and written in an unfamiliar style, all to the effect of stilling our potential for appreciating "the Dear Old Poet" before it could be developed.

The critics, by inferring that Bryant's importance rests in his distinction as one of the first Americans to capture the spirit of English Romanticism and place that spirit in a distinctly American context, only encourage a narrow view of his work, which denies the general reader access to Bryant's poetry and limits its appeal to those students of American Romanticism who would read a Bryant poem as a literary artifact. This, in turn, inevitably forces an unfair comparison of Bryant's work with that of the recognizably greater European Romantics. Leon Howard falls into just such a trap with his observation that "Bryant succeeded in naturalizing one of the great symbols of Romanticism by insisting that nature poetry make sense in terms of the American . . . experience, [but that] these symbols lost much of their power when transferred to a different cultural environment" [*Literature and the American Tradition*, 1960]. This statement is not arguable as it stands, yet is it relevant for the present-day reader's appreciation of Bryant's poetry? The misinterpretation of symbols primarily derives from a misinterpretation of context, but this very misinterpretation suggests a valid meaning and context all its own.

Another common critical opinion is that voiced by Hyatt Waggoner [in *American Poets from the Puritans to the Present* (1968)], who states that Bryant and his fellow New England poets, Longfellow, Lowell, Holmes, and Whittier, were regarded as symbolic "of America's coming of age culturally," but were not "outrageously overvalued" even in their own day. Such an evaluation leads one to conclude, with Waggoner, that these men were minor poets, too representative of the moods and manners of a simpler, more naive period of the American experience, and now "they are very hard for us to respond to sympathetically," often seeming "irrelevant or simply dull, when not ridiculous." It leaves one with the assumption that what is needed with regard to Bryant's work, as with that of any minor figure, is "an attempt to salvage something of value" from his prolific and inconsistent canon.

Albert F. McLean, Jr., sounded a somewhat different note in 1964 when he wrote in the preface to his "ritual of criticism" of Bryant's work:

> It is time to change the format, to recast our characters, to build anew the sets. For beneath the calm, sonorous surface of his verse lie traces of discord and conflict, a drama of the inner life which has been politely ignored by the critics. [*William Cullen Bryant* (1964)]

In these "traces of discord and conflict" reside Bryant's appeal to the twentieth-century reader. How is one to detect such traces, what kind of posture must the modern reader assume toward Bryant's poetry in order that it elicit a sympathetic response? These are key questions whose validity depends ultimately on Bryant's own inherent modernity.

Because he was a pioneer on the frontiers of modernism, Bryant's poetic vision is not always clear and consistent. However, that he was a modern poet most critics are willing to grant. Howard recognizes this when he observes that Bryant, together with Washington Irving, "gave the lesser symbols of their language a greater vitality than can be found in their predecessors." By his participation in this process of a breaking through the dead artificiality that afflicted much eighteenth-century verse, Bryant played a major role in initiating a tradition that finds its best expression, according to Waggoner, in the likes of Dickinson, Robinson, Frost, and Robert Lowell.

There are other hints by the critics that imply Bryant's modernity, such as McLean's notion that his poetry "relates to the search for a style on the part of the modern artist," and that nature for him "becomes, in Baudelaire's famous phrase, *un forêt de symboles*." Howard indicates a psychological depth of the poetry in that "Bryant discovered . . . that he could make serious use of external nature if he adapted his treatment of it to the stream of associations he found in his own mind and could normally anticipate in the mind of his readers."

These testimonials to the modern elements of Bryant's poetry find their justification or refutation in the poems themselves, which, of course, provide the primary source for any defense of Bryant's modernity. If Bryant's poetry foreshadows that of Robert Lowell, Frost, Dickinson, Robinson, and even that of Wallace Stevens, as McLean seems to propose at one point, then we should be able to discover these incipient indications in his poetry. If the poetry relates to the modern artist's search for a style, then elements of such should surface in the poems, and if nature is a "forest of symbols," reflecting the association of ideas in the poet's mind, then, provided these associations are still vital and valid, we should be able to discern the clues in the poems.

We are constantly on the alert for the suggestive, vital, epiphanic image in the poetry of our contemporaries, as well as those poets whom we regard as speaking to the modern situation. The image is the essential element in the modern artist's search for a style. It is the living image that proves the seedling for the modern poet's forest of symbols. If we are to read Bryant sympathetically, it seems that we should allow and take with him the same liberties that we apply in the case of a Dickinson or a Frost.

In advocating a quest for the suggestive image in Bryant's poetry, we do it no vandalism or violence. Such a practice is consistent with Bryant's own theory of poetry, expressed in his *Lectures,* where he states that "poetry, by the symbols of words, suggests both the sensible object and the association." Bryant, in fact, defines poetry as "a suggestive art" employing "arbitrary symbols," which work "like a spell upon the imagination," a faculty that is "by no means passive." The success of any poem, according to Bryant, relies on the reader's imaginative activity. The reader must take "a path which the poet only points out, and shape its visions from the scenes and allusions which he gives." It is the reader's imagination that completes the "sketches of beauty" supplied by the poet "with the noblest images its own stores can furnish." Such a theory is true to the psychology of association that informs and structures much of Bryant's poetry, making the poem "an exhibition of those analogies and correspondences which it beholds between the things of the moral and of the natural world." It is by "bringing images of visible beauty . . . to heighten the effect of moral sentiment," so that the poem "binds into one all the passages of human life and connects all the varieties of human feeling within the work of creation," that the poet accomplishes his aesthetic.

Bryant's aesthetic is quite similar to that of Whitman. It was Whitman's concept that the poem gives the clue, that the reader must involve himself or herself in a "gymnast's struggle" with an "alert creativity," thus making his own poem from the raw material of the poet's perceptions. Such a concept is at the heart of any sympathetic response to Bryant's poetry, as well as Whitman's. Any modern reader of Bryant must meet him half way, come to him on equal terms, without the conventional critical preconceptions, without the patronizing attitude accorded the period figure, willing to allow Bryant his suggestive insights.

McLean notes Whitman's recognition of indebtedness to Bryant in "My Tribute to Four Poets," from *Specimen Days*. Whitman wrote of a "Bryant pulsing the first interior verse—throbs of a mighty world—bard of the river and wood, ever conveying a taste of the open air, with scents as from hay fields, grapes, birch-borders. . . ." Whitman found "here and there through all, poems of passages of poems, touching the highest universal truths. . . ." Bryant is no symbolist poet. His idea of a poem is something that is not "merely a tissue of striking images," yet there is, even in this denial, an implicit realization that the "striking image" plays an important role in the poem's construct. Indeed, one detects in Bryant's poetry vestiges of the liberal Protestant imagination, that which informs the poetry of both Whitman and Blake, two poets attractive to the symbol seeker. It is a vision that reads the forms of images in nature as evidence of the types and symbols of the eternal verities. One finds this in Bryant's **"A Forest Hymn"** (1825), when the poet, entering the Temple of Nature, that repository of symbols, beholds there images that suggest the hand of the Master Artist. We do not need to share Bryant's idea of the Deity to appreciate the aesthetic ramifications of such a response to nature. In these moments, the poet becomes the priest-mediator observing and interpreting the forms and images in nature that correspond with the images in the mind of his reader. It is these images in the forest of nature that give evidence of the eternal, becoming analogues of the images in the forest of the mind, which are emanations of the "inner light," the God within, of liberal Protestant theology, or the shared racial consciousness of our modern Jungian psychology.

The secular metaphor is the poet as wizard, whose verse casts a spell over the receptive reader, enabling him or her to put aside the selfish concerns of the everyday life, a life that Bryant felt "begets desulatory habits of thought," and enter into the magical realm of poetic images. Bryant used this metaphor in **"The Poet"** (1864):

> What witchery hangs upon this poet's page!
> What art it his written spells to find
> That sway from mood to mood the willing mind!

We are less susceptible to this sense of self-abnegation, the ecstasy of the poet-priest and mystic, the magical mediator of the grandeur of God's creation, yet it is a theme that runs throughout Bryant's poetry and is captured especially well in an image from **"A Forest Hymn,"** where the poet confronts a form suggesting stasis and permanence in the ancient religious totem of the Druids, "This mighty oak—By whose immovable stem I stand and seem / Almost annihilated—."

It is the modern reader, who has depleted to the point of exhaustion his store of noblest images, whose imagination has been lulled into a dull passivity by the uncontrolled onslaught of myriad sensations, who has experienced first hand man's alienation from nature, and whose moral sense is so lacking as to prevent him from distinguishing the correlations between the natural and the moral spheres, that has difficulty responding to the magic spell of Bryant's poetry. The fault is in ourselves, not in the poetry. As McLean perceives, we must struggle to recognize with Bryant "that his poetic dialogue was no simple dialectic between subject-Man and object-Nature; it was . . . an involved process of creation in which physical objects and poetic images were not easily distinguishable." In such instances, the best moments Bryant's poetry has to offer us, Mclean indicates, "the fine line which generally divides imagery from metaphor becomes gently obscured as all the phenomena of Nature assume the task of suggestion.

This process of the blurring of distinctions between metaphor and image in Bryant's poetry is a counter to the charge of "imagistic incoherence" levelled at Bryant and said to parallel and/or reflect an "incoherence of vision." Granted there are times when Bryant's imagery works suggestively and metaphorically and times when the images are only elaborately stated clichés. This is an "inconsistency of vision," an "imagistic inconsistency," the very thing that makes Bryant a minor poet, but it is not an incoherence. No critic would ever charge a modern poet in such a way, no matter how unintelligible the work. Rather, the critic would apply terms like paradox, tension, irony, and the like to the poetry.

The variety of images one finds in Bryant's poetry is impressive. The imagery not only reflects the profusiveness of his source, nature, but partakes of these modern qualities of irony and paradox, these "traces of discord and conflict" that McLean detects. Nature herself in Bryant's poetry is a paradox. At times it provides "an image of that calm life," that sense of repose from the bustling, grubbing rat race of life. The final stanza of **"Green River"** (1820) is a good example. Note how Bryant uses different consonant sounds to convey the contrast in mood from the first half of the stanza, where the sounds of dissonant d's and strident s's prevail to the last half of the stanza, dominated by fluffy f's, murmuring m's, and lovely l's.

> Though forced to drudge for the dregs of men,
> And scrawl strange words with the barbarous pen,
> And mingle among the justling crowd,
> Where the sons of strife are subtle and loud—
> I often come to this quiet place,
> To breathe the airs that ruffle thy face,
> And gaze upon thee in silent dream,
> For in thy lonely and lovely stream
> An image of that calm life appears
> That won my heart in greener years.

At other times, as in **"The Prairies"** (1832), "the encircling vastness" of nature diminishes, even threatens man. Initially the vastness of the prairie suggests the sensation of stasis, permanent motionlessness, stillness, which Bryant expresses with an image of the prairie as ocean, fixed and motionless, and there is a tension established between the vastness and the claustrophobic motionlessness.

> Lo! they stretch,
> In airy undulations, far away,
> As if the ocean, in his gentlest swell,
> Stood still, with all his rounded billows fixed,
> And motionless forever.

Indeed, this sense of motionlessness proves a momentary optical illusion as the poet's eye discerns all manner of movement.

> —Motionless?—
> No—they are all unchained again. The clouds
> Sweep over with their shadows, and, beneath,
> The surface rolls and fluctuates to the eye;
> Dark hollows seem to glide along and chase
> The sunny ridges.

Here the paradox is deepened by the image, since the very sense of movement in the landscape, created by the moving shadows of the clouds crossing the stationary ridges, is as much an illusion as the stillness. Another image, following immediately, reiterates this paradox of motionless motion, "the prairie-hawk that, poised on high, / Flaps his broad wings, yet moves not." This illusion is also undercut by the poet's concession, "ye have played / Among the palms of Mexico and vines / Of Texas, and have crisped the limpid brooks / That from the fountains of Sonora glide / Into the calm Pacific."

The hawk's vast range confirms the paradox in nature; beneath the seemingly still and motionless illusions of permanence and stasis in nature, ripples an energy, power, change, and evanescence that is suggested in the image of the hawk "crisping" the placid surface of some remote "limpid" brook. Before the paradox of nature, the poet

stands in awe, "almost annihilated." Aware of his own insignificance in nature's scheme and his own limited range, the poet indulges in a reverie of images of changefulness, called up from the vast interior of his imagination: decay and death, the "sad images of the stern agony" that pervade **"Thanatopsis."** Images that formerly found their expression "In a forgotten language, and old tunes, / From instruments of unremembered form," which, like Bryant's own images, "Gave the soft winds a voice," and are subject to the change that all "the forms of being" undergo.

It must be admitted that such an awareness gives the lie to the grand illusions of Bryant's time: Progress, Manifest Destiny, and "rugged individualism." When the poet awakes from his reverie at the close of **"The Prairies,"** he finds himself "in the wilderness alone," not "almost annihilated," but, in a sense, alienated from the forces of nature over which he has no control, a realistic statement of the consequences of "rugged individualism." In the poem there is a definite progression from the poet's intial discovery of the paradox in nature, to the reflections on the enigmatic forces of nature, to the final recognition that man has no tools to challenge this enigma, except the sad images and instruments of soon to be forgotten form.

If there is much irony implicit in Bryant's recognition that "the old tunes" are not immune to the vicissitudes of change, there is also irony in his sending his artist friend, Thomas Cole, off to Europe with a sonnet that envisions Cole as bearing in his heart "a living image of our own bright land" by way of preparing him for the images of decay and death that he will witness there:

> —everywhere the trace of men,
> Paths, homes, graves, ruins, from the lowest glen
> To where life shrinks from the fierce Alpine air.
> **["To Cole, The Painter, Departing For Europe"**
> (1830)]

His exhortation to Cole to "keep that earlier, wilder image bright" amounts not only to a romantic vision of the mutual intent of their respective arts, to keep the preternaturally vivid image of the New World alive for as long as possible, but an equally romantic awareness that such preternatural images will eventually suffer decay and death as the source of civilization moves inexorably westward.

Bryant, one feels could not but appreciate the very irony inherent in the remarks of the critic who finds in his poetry "honesty, not irony in the modern manner," who proclaims that he wrote his best poetry before he was forty and who indicts him with the term "incoherent" because of his ability to celebrate Progress, while advocating the essential absurdity of human ideas of Progress in the face of an inexorable nature. The final lines of his sonnet **"Mutation"** (1842) contain Bryant's response to such critics, "Weep not that the world changes—did it keep / A stable, changeless state, 'twere cause indeed to weep." Progress, after all, presumes an openness to change, and nature surely enforces the law of change without quarter, and man's response to nature is more timeless than his response to political ideas, though more complex and thus "inconsistent."

There is no perversion and no contradiction of Bryant's vision if critics, searching for signs of life among his literary remains, often ignore an early poem like **"The Ages"** (1821), based on the idea of Progress rather than the natural imagery of change. This is because there is an element of incipient self-destruction in the political poems that Bryant wrote for his contemporaries that is not present in his nature poems, where the natural, living image has "an enduring freshness and vividness," a longer "half-life," that outlives the mechanism of the personification of the abstract idea.

It is to Bryant's lasting credit that he was honestly aware of the irony in this idea of the evanescence of the image, it is this honesty that makes his poems which treat of the natural image more expressive of the human condition and more relevant for us now than any of the overtly political poems. Waggoner, who comments on "an almost classic simplicity and fitness about the images" in **"To A Waterfowl"** (1821), seems impervious to the one image in the poem that conveys this ironic nature of Bryant's vision, that the ultimate image is inexpressible, "Thou art gone, the abyss of heaven / Hath swallowed up thy form." The image of the waterfowl, like other symbolic bird images, in its propensity to fade out, to disappear into the horizon, to be "swallowed up" in nature, is a fitting metaphor for the processes of art and the momentary epiphanic quality of the natural image.

As the individual grows old and the senses dim and are dulled and desensitized, the finely tuned ability to perceive the evanescent image fades. As Bryant noted in **"Earth,"** written in Europe in 1835, "All in vain, / Turns the tired eye in search of form." Five years later, in **"The Old Man's Counsel,"** Bryant wrote that life "Darts by so swiftly that [its] . . . images / Dwell not upon the mind, or only dwell/In dim confusion." Like Wordsworth, the British poet Bryant is most often compared with, he experienced this loss of the visionary gleam, and this failure of the vision was even more devastating to the American poet's reputation because he supposedly had access to the preternatural forms of the New World, through a proximity and an experience not available to a European Romantic. Because the "living image" seemed so accessible, so near, so real, to Bryant, in contrast to the Europeans, for whom the preternatural was more an abstract idea than a vital image, the death of the imagination, the decay of the poetic vision, the sense of loss is also more real and more tragic. For this reason, that Bryant turned, like Wordsworth, in his later years to poetry dealing with the abstract idea, becomes more forgivable, but all of this only indicates how easily one falls into this trap of reading Bryant in terms of the Romantic mythology.

What should be considered are the images themselves, those that are still alive, renewable, suggestive, for the reader of today, and it is the natural images, the ones that sparkle and furnish a momentary, evanescent vision of the human condition before they fade and are swallowed

up in the abyss of eternity, that are this. These images that have outlived their percipient are surrounded by much "dead wood" in the poetry, and they require of the reader, who wishes to perceive them anew, an almost childlike openness to the wonder and surprise and epiphanic joy that Bryant himself felt when he came upon the yellow violet in the still dead forest of April [in **"The Yellow Violet"**], or the fringed gentian [of **"The Fringed Gentian"**], its "blossom bright" in the dying Autumn wood. This is not to indicate that such images must be taken out of context. In truth, they have a life of their own, and thus provide their own context, and, as I stated previously, they must be sought with alert senses, not dimmed by the light of common day.

In **"Inscription for the Entrance to a Wood"** (1821), the following lines appear: ". . . The primal curse / Felt, it is true, upon the unsinning earth / But not in vengeance." These lines contain the essence of Bryant's double-edged and ironic vision of nature. The whole of nature is innocent and blameless. "We observe no sin in her grander operations and vicissitudes," Bryant once mused; and yet nature is cursed by the sin of man and subject to the very law of decay and death that it is called upon to enforce. However, such is not laid on "in vengeance," as it is with man, and nature has a reprieve not granted man. It is apparently renewable. The cyclical process in nature affords the natural image the chance to renew itself for readers of all time so that, as Bryant assures us, "The cool wind, / That stirs the stream in play, shall come to thee, / Like one that loves thee nor will let thee pass / Ungreeted, and shall give its light embrace." There is a delicate irony in this "light embrace" for we are all chilled by the melancholy "cool wind" of change and the cold wind of death that constitutes the primal curse.

There is this same kind of irony, the "equivocation" that McLean notices in **"Oh Fairest of the Rural Maids"** (1820). By making a particular individual, Frances Fairchild, his future wife, an expression of the natural image, a "child of nature," Bryant grants her the same exemption, in her innocence, that nature holds, "The forest depths, by foot unpressed, / Are not more sinless than thy breast." Frances has long ago been annihilated by the primal curse, but the natural image of her beauty is still vital because, "Thy sports, thy wanderings, when a child, / Were ever in the sylvan wild; / And all the beauty of the place / Is in thy heart and on thy face."

The final result of the primal curse, man's severance from nature, sets up a tension in Bryant's best poems between the processes of nature and her temporal artifice, when a tentative and ephemeral bond is reset and a glimpse of the preternatural state, when the bond was permanent and fixed, is allowed. A fine example of this is **"A Winter Piece"** (1821) where an image like ". . . the clouds from their still skirts, / Had shaken down on earth the feathery snow, / And all was white," skirts, if you will, a line of delicate balance between the static and artificial personification of nature prevalent in the eighteenth century and the more modern natural image, striking and suggestive, and evidencing this tension. Particularly fortunate is the use of "still," implying the paradox and the tension, and indicating both a temporalness and a frozen stasis. The image itself is stiff, yet intimate, the formality of nature's dress undercut by the informality of the gesture, and the "ambiguity of the word" is reinforced further by the punning on "down" and "feathery" in the next line, and by the fact that "all was white," that most suggestive and ambiguous of colors, containing the potentiality of everything, lacking the actuality of anything.

This initial image prepares the way for an even more ambiguous image, one offering a glimpse of preternatural stasis and brightness, a moment when

> . . . the wildered fancy dreams
> Of spouting fountains, frozen as they rose,
> And fixed, with all their branching jets, in air,
> And all their sluices sealed. All, all is light;
> Light without shade.

Such an image succinctly prefigures the later nineteenth century's preoccupation with form and style. It is a photographic image of nature frozen and eviscerated, in an attitude that celebrates the superiority of art over nature, while denying the reality, and it is this reality that Bryant reinforces as he shatters this precise, frozen, and pristine image, immediately, dissolving all in a confusion of melting, dissonance, and impending darkness:

> But all shall pass away
> With the next sun. From numberless vast trunks,
> Loosened, the crashing ice shall make a sound
> Like the far roar of rivers, and the eve
> Shall close o'er the brown woods as it was wont.

Near the close of this **"Winter Piece,"** Bryant gives us the physical object as metaphor, that is the essential expression of the way the suggestive image operates in his poetry.

> Lodged in sunny cleft,
> Where the cold breezes come not, blooms alone
> The little wind-flower, whose just opened eye
> Is blue as the spring heaven it gazes at—
> Startling the loiterer in the naked groves
> With unexpected beauty. . . .

There are poems of Bryant in which the sacred bond between man and nature is shown as irretrievable, the preternatural state where all is "sweetness and light" as irrecoverable. In these poems the death of man and the decay of nature intermingle in a prophetic and apocalyptic way that is especially compelling for the modern reader. The later poem, **"The Crowded Street,"** is an example. Here urban existence is depicted as cut off from nature, and Godless and dead due to this separation. In their deadened state, the city dwellers evidence a "sense of futility and indifference," to use McLean's phrase. Man is victim, nature no better than a survivor, but in **"An Indian at the Burial-Ground of His Fathers"** (1824), man and nature guarantee each other's doom. The Indian narrator of this work is not the "noble savage" of the European Romantics, but, rather, he is the poet's persona and the alter ego of us all. As a displaced alien, he is able to see clearly from his distanced perspective the disease of modern society, which is a threat to all of us.

If an ecological balance existed between the Indian and the land, it was because the Indian considered nature "sacred when the soil was ours," but now Bryant's Indian sees the land as having been defiled by the usurping, death-dealing white race, "the pale race who waste us now. . . . They waste us—ay—like April snow / In the warm noon, we shrink away." These lines have a poignant topicality for, just five years after they were written, Andrew Jackson's infamous Indian Removal Act opened up the "Trail of Tears" and forced thousands of Indians from the Southeast to migrate to the Oklahoma Territory, a march that "wasted" many.

Bryant's Indian gives substance to the vision that we of the "pale race" often feel but are too horrified to express, that there is a "fearful sign" to behold in "the white stones above the dead." The headstones in the Caucasian churchyard suggest a veritable "thanatopolis," a metaphor in miniature of the city of the dead. There is an implicit tension between the more natural image of the white April snow melting away in the noon sun, and the equally ironic, more pretentious, because it appears permanent, whiteness and artifice of the man-crafted grave stones. Our own contemporary, Allen Ginsberg, can extend and transvalue such imagery to indicate that the stone skyscrapers, built on the Indian's sacred ground and Whitman's beloved Manahatta, are also pretentious cenotaphs to the deadness of modern man. A vision of nature dying, of course, presumes the death of poetry because it is exceedingly more difficult, if not impossible, to make poetry out of the attempts of others, their art and craft, than it is to make poetry about nature. One is all coldness and style, the other has warmth and vitality. One is the image of a cold, dead thing, the other a living image of the bright land.

As the Indian interprets the signs of the white man's violation of nature, he conjures a vision of nature polluted, corrupted, dying, a vision that has supplied Rachel Carson with the controlling metaphor for her telling book on the ecological catastrophe, *The Silent Spring*. It is a time when Bryant's future horror becomes our present reality:

> . . . grateful sound are heard no more,
>   The springs are silent in the sun;
> The rivers, by the blackened shore,
>   With lessening current run;
> The realm our tribes are crushed to get
> May be a barren desert yet.

It is a vision that anyone who has been in certain parts of New Jersey can confirm as prophetic; it is the dying image of our now tarnished land.

William Cullen Bryant, in his Indian mask, stands apart from the pretentiousness that too often blocks our true appreciation of his vision and accomplishment. All that

Bryant ever sought from his dear nature, as he tells us in **"November"** (1824), was a coax "Yet one smile more . . . / Yet one rich smile, and we will try to bear / The piercing winter frost, and winds, and darkened air." Likewise, all that the suggestive image in the poetry seeks to elicit is a wry, Gioconda-like, smile of joy, surprise, discovery, what you will, when we loiterers come upon those "little wind-flowers" and are unexpectedly startled in the "naked groves" of poetry, before, that is, the cold wind of the critic blows all away.

Linden Peach (essay date 1982)

SOURCE: "Man, Nature and Wordsworth: American Versions," in *British Influence on the Birth of American Literature,* Macmillan Press Ltd., 1982, pp. 29-57.

[*In the following excerpt, Peach shows how Bryant made use of Wordsworth's poetry, highlighting the similarities and differences of British and American literary romanticism.*]

> Every sympathy is the admission of a power over us, a line in which sympathetic magic is at play.
> —Robert Duncan (*The Truth & Life of Myth*)

The possibilities of establishing an intimate relationship with nature and an awareness of its healing and cleansing power forcefully entered Western literature and thought with the writings of Hegel, Kant, Herder, Rousseau, Goethe and Wordsworth. As one scholar has shown, however, direct German influence upon American literature in the first four decades of the nineteenth century was very limited and basically confined to those scholars who studied at the University of Göttingen. Only a few American intellectuals were fluent in German. Emerson's reliance upon translations in the early 1830s suggests that he had little direct knowledge of German at that time. In 1831 he borrowed Coleridge's translation of Schiller's *Wallenstein* from the Boston Athenaeum and T. Churchill's translation of Herder's *Outlines of a Philosophy of the History of Man* (1803) and, in the following year, Coleridge's translation of Goethe's *Wilhelm Meister's Apprenticeship* (1821). Among the Transcendentalists there was no general reading of German literature or philosophy in the original, and even those who became proficient in German by the 1840s—Clarke, Dwight, Brooks, Margaret Fuller—were not well read in German literature.

The new attitudes to nature entered American literature initially through the poetry of Wordsworth. Both William Cullen Bryant and Ralph Waldo Emerson, who must take pride of place in any discussion of American attitudes towards nature in the early nineteenth century, read Wordsworth's poetry in their early years and were influenced by it.

Wordsworth did not receive sympathetic reviews in America until after 1824, and the *North American Review* especially opposed his work. In July 1821, Edward Everett,

for example, criticised Wordsworth and Coleridge for their involved mysticism and in January 1824, a reviewer repeated the criticisms of the *Edinburgh Review* that Wordsworth's subjects were too mundane:

> He is right in believing that feelings, imaginations, reasonings, occupations and habits of those in humble life are proper subjects for poetry; but he is wrong in compelling poetry to repeat their commonplace ideas, and seriously investigate their ordinary household arrangements and domestic implements; and particularly wrong in making her blow a trumpet before every shepherd's door, and to swell out into vast importance those circumstances which, if discussed at all, should have been treated with brevity and indifference suited to their station.

The *North American Review*'s slow acceptance of Wordsworth was the result of its conservatism for which William Charvat has offered two explanations. Firstly, almost all of its writers were allied to the Federalist Party, which represented the propertied classes, and were therefore suspicious of literature which condoned rebellion against the existing social and economic order. Secondly, its critical standards were those of the Scottish Common Sense School, opposed to complex mystical theories.

The American public were prepared to receive Wordsworth, however, through the poetry of James Thomson and William Cowper which had been popular in America long before 1800 and with which Wordsworth's own work had many affinities. Before the appearance of the *Lyrical Ballads* Thomas Odiorne wrote nature poetry which in a small way anticipates Wordsworth and reveals that Wordsworth's view of nature was not quite as foreign to the American mind as his poor reception by the critics might suggest. William Bryant was prepared to receive the *Lyrical Ballads* sympathetically by one work in particular: Archibald Alison, *Essays on the Nature and Principles of Taste.*

Tony Tanner, developing [Charles] Olson's thesis [in his *Call Me Ishmael* (1947)] that space is 'the central fact to man born in America', has argued that Wordsworth's 'fruitful intermingling of Nature's and Man's creative potencies . . . is absent from American Romantic writing' [*Journal of American Studies*, 1968]. Such 'intermingling' does occur in American writing, however, but is less intimate than in Wordsworth's poetry and has a different set of emphases. It is often handled less fluently and with a great sense of unease.

William Bryant's attempts to articulate a close, intimate relationship with nature are evident in poems such as **"After A Tempest," "Lines on Revisiting the Country," "A Winter Piece"** and **"A Summer Ramble"** and they confess the influence of Wordsworth's *Lyrical Ballads* which Bryant read first at the age of sixteen. Although Bryant's autobiography is left unfinished at the description of the literary influences on his life, Richard Henry Dana has recorded Bryant's enthusiasm for Wordsworth and how the *Lyrical Ballads* heightened Bryant's general awareness of nature:

I never shall forget with what feeling my friend Bryant, some years ago, described to me the effect produced upon him by his meeting for the first time with Wordsworth's ballads. He said that, upon opening the book, a thousand springs seemed to gush up at once in his heart, and the face of nature, of a sudden, to change into a strange freshness and life. He had felt the sympathetic touch from an according mind, and you see how instantly his powers and affections shot over the earth and through his kind.

Bryant's interest in the new possibilities which the *Lyrical Ballads* offered poetry is evident from his essay 'Poets and Poetry of the English Language' which draws upon Wordsworth's Preface to his poems. The recommended subject matter for poetry in Bryant's essay is that of the *Lyrical Ballads*: 'the vicissitudes of human life,' 'the emotions of the human heart' and 'the relations of man to man.' In the *Lyrical Ballads* Wordsworth was concerned with the emotions of ordinary people, of 'humble and rustic life.' Bryant believed poetry should deal with emotions near 'the common track of the human intelligence.' In this way the poet would be certain 'of the sympathy of his own generation and of those who shall come after him.' Wordsworth wrote 'of sympathies in which, without any other discipline than that of our daily life, we are fitted to take delight.' For Wordsworth the poetry was in the way in which objects and sentiments are described in 'connection with each other' so that 'the understanding of the Reader must necessarily be in some degree enlightened, and his affections strengthened and purified.' Bryant hoped to achieve 'combinations and lights which at once affect the mind with a deep sense of their truth and beauty.' These adaptations show that Bryant was one of the few to respond sympathetically to Wordsworth's Preface which generally aroused much controversy in America, as an essay in the *Southern Literary Messenger* in 1844 recalled:

The lovers of poetry were at the outset repelled by a poet whose Prelude was an argument; who presented a Theory in prose to win the judgement. It was like being detained at the door of a Cathedral by a dull Cicerone, who before granting admittance, must needs deliver a long homily on the grandeur of the interior, and explain its deficiencies.

While Wordsworth's poetry offered Bryant the possibility of exploring and articulating new areas of intimacy with nature, Bryant never successfully developed his own possibilities as a nature poet. Consequently, he often appears as a poor imitator of Wordsworth. For example, Wordsworth's 'Resolution and Independence' (1802) offered Bryant the possibility of presenting the particular kind of emotional involvement with nature which follows a prolonged and heavy storm. Thus, Bryant's **"After A Tempest"** (1824) overtly confesses the influence of the opening stanzas of Wordsworth's poem. Bryant:

The day had been a day of cloud and storm,
  The wind was laid, the rain was overpast,
And stooping from the zenith, bright and warm,
  Shone the great sun on the wide earth at last.

Wordsworth:

There was a roaring in the wind all night;
The rain came heavily and fell in floods;
But now the sun is rising calm and bright;

Wordsworth's conscientious use of vowels and stress upon the verb 'roaring' project the energy of the storm. There is a sudden transition to calm in the third line and the image of the rising sun is underscored and sharply focused by the unusual epithets 'calm and bright' which are generally applied to the moon rather than the sun. In comparison with Wordsworth's, Bryant's description is very flat and his use of language far less conscientious, as is evident, for example, in the careless repetition of 'day' in the first line. The imagery is self-conscious and together with the rhetorical diction connotes an artificial sense of grandeur. We do not feel that Bryant is as emotionally and intimately involved with the aftermath of the storm as Wordsworth. Both poems then concentrate upon the narrator, who absorbs the quiet of the scene before moving to a description of the slow awakening after the rain. In Wordsworth's poem 'the grass is bright with rain-drops' and a hare 'raises a mist; that, glittering in the sun, / Runs with her . . .' In **"After A Tempest"**:

The rain-drops glistened on the trees around,
Those shadows on the tall grass were not stirred,
Save when a shower of diamonds, to the ground,
Was shaken by the flight of a startled bird;

These lines by Bryant are better than the previous ones but are flawed by the trite comparison of falling rain-drops to a shower of diamonds. This lack of precision makes Bryant's nature poetry generally less convincing than Wordsworth's. Here he fails to convey the stealth with which nature once again begins to stir after the storm as adequately as Wordsworth and because of the failure of the previous lines we remain unconvinced by the narrator's presence at the scene.

The influence of Wordsworth's 'Lines composed a few miles above Tintern Abbey, On Revisiting the Banks of the Wye' upon Bryant's **"Lines on Revisiting the Country"** (1825) reveals Bryant's uneasiness with a Wordsworthian involvement with nature at the same time as he tried himself to achieve it. In the opening of his poem Bryant attempts the same kind of emotional context which Wordsworth establishes in his poem:

I stand upon my native hills again,
  Broad, round, and green, that in the summer sky
With garniture of waving grass and grain,
  Orchards, and beechen forests, basking lie,
While deep the sunless glens are scooped between,
Where brawl o'er shallow beds the streams unseen.

Wordsworth's 'Tintern Abbey' opens:

Five years have past; five summers, with the length
Of five long winters! and again I hear
These waters, rolling from their mountain—springs

With a soft inland murmur—Once again
Do I behold these steep and lofty cliffs,
That on a wild secluded scene impress
Thoughts of more deep seclusion; and connect
The landscape with the quiet of the sky.

Here again Wordsworth's more immediate relationship with nature is evident in the specificity of his writing. Moreover, he seems more intimately involved with his writing than Bryant, betrayed in the way in which throughout the poem rhythms and mood are closely interrelated. While Bryant attempts a similar emotional experience in his opening line—'I stand upon my native hills again'—nature is far more removed from him. He is confronted by a sense of space which undermines any real sense of interrelationship between himself and the natural landscape. Consequently his description of nature is more generalised and panoramic.

How far Bryant had been prepared to follow Wordsworth and enter for himself the kind of experience which Wordsworth describes is evident, however, from the other close parallels between the two poems. Both poets have recently come from the city; Wordsworth from 'lonely rooms' and 'the din of towns and cities' while Bryant has 'scaped the city's stifling heat, / Its horrid sounds, and its polluted air.' Both poets share their return with a female companion; in Wordsworth's poem it is his sister and in Bryant's poem it is his four-year-old girl. Like Wordsworth's sister, she reflects the beauty and freedom of life in contact with nature: 'There plays a gladness o'er her fair young brow / As breaks the varied sense upon her sight, / Up-heaved and spread in verdu and in light'. Wordsworth finds in his sister's voice 'the language of my former heart' and 'my former pleasures in the shooting lights / Of thy wild eyes.' Both teach their companions the 'ministry of nature.' Wordsworth tells his sister: 'let the misty mountain-winds be free/To blow against thee.' He looks forward to a time when 'these wild ecstasies shall be matured / Into a sober pleasure' and 'thy mind / Shall be a mansion for all lovely forms.' Bryant writes:

For I have taught her, with delighted eye,
  To gaze upon the mountains,—to behold,
With deep affection, the pure ample sky,
  And clouds along its blue abysses rolled,
To love the song of waters, and to hear
The melody of winds with charmed ear.

Here, however, Bryant once again lapses into a general, stilted description of nature which undermines the emotional sincerity.

The parallels between 'Tintern Abbey' and **"A Winter Piece"** (1821) reveal that Bryant's appreciation of the cleansing and healing power of nature was due mainly to Wordsworth's influence. But Bryant's own attempt to write about this particular aspect of nature involves a typically European romanticism of the wild solitudes of America. This, together with the way in which his lines roll carelessly off the tongue, detracts from any deep sense of liberation through contact with nature:

The time has been that these wild solitudes,
  Yet beautiful as wild, were trod by me
Oftener than now; and when the ills of life
Had chafed my spirit—when the unsteady pulse
Beat with strange flutterings—I would wander forth
And seek the woods!

Wordsworth in 'Tintern Abbey' turns to the Wye for the same reason as Bryant to the woods. But Wordsworth, through an emphasis upon 'fretful stir', 'fever of the world', 'beatings of my heart' at the end of each of three lines, more successfully connotes the languid life rhythm of one who is wearied by everyday life in the city:

In darkness and amid the many shapes
O joyless daylight; when the fretful stir
Unprofitable, and the fever of the world
Have hung upon the beatings of my heart—
How oft in spirit, have I turned to thee,
O Sylvan Wye!

Bryant's corresponding 'ills of life' and 'unsteady pulse' are more casual, introduced into the poem without the same force.

The failure to involve himself fully in an intimate relationship with nature, together with his inability to free himself from eighteenth-century poetic diction and thought patterns, is largely responsible for the weaknesses in Bryant's nature poetry. His failure is betrayed, also, by the fact that his attempts at a close communion with nature usually constitute several stanzas in a poem concerned with larger political themes and is rarely as in *Lyrical Ballads* the subject of an entire poem.

Ironically, Bryant most successfully followed Wordsworth when the latter was most light-hearted and glib! Bryant's derivation of the concept of joy in nature from Wordsworth is evident in the way in which **"A Summer Ramble"** (1826) confesses the influence of Wordsworth's 'To My Sister.' In both poems the poet decides to spend a day relaxing in the wooded countryside and calls to a female companion. Wordsworth takes his sister and a young boy, while Bryant is accompanied by his wife. Wordsworth's poem does not involve a detailed working out of an intimate, emotional involvement with nature but the projection of a sense of ease, joy and happiness in contact with nature:

My sister! (tis a wish of mine)
Now that our morning meal is done,
Make haste, your morning task resign;
Come forth and feel the sun.
Edward will come with you;—and, pray,
Put on with speed your woodland dress;
And bring no book: for this one day
We'll give to idleness.

The rhythms are colloquial and the lines significant for their gaiety rather than any profundity of thought. Their influence upon Bryant's poem is easily seen in the similar sentiments and colloquial rhythms:

Away! I will not be, to-day,
   The only slave of toil and care,
Away from desk and dust! away!
   I'l be idle as the air.

Bryant calls to his wife:

   Come, thou, in whose soft eyes I see
      The gentle meanings of thy heart,
   One day amid the woods with me,
      From men and all their cares apart.

However, when Bryant tried to develop Wordsworth's concept of joy he failed badly. Wordsworth's influence upon **"The Gladness of Nature"** (1826) is betrayed in Bryant's use of the word 'breathed' which Wordsworth uses for similar purposes in one of the *Lyrical Ballads*. In Bryant's poem 'gladness breathes from the blossoming ground', while in the *Lyrical Ballads* there is a sense of joy and 'spontaneous wisdom breathed by health, / Truth breathed by cheerfulness'. In Bryant's poem there is, also, the same kind of rebuke at not responding to the joyfulness of nature which is central to some of Wordsworth's poems, 'The Tables Turned' and the 'Matthew Poems', for example. Bryant goes much farther than Wordsworth and tries to bridge the distance between man and the non-human, physical universe by using metaphors describing nature which bring to mind an intimate, close-knit and joyful, human community. The result is slightly bizarre since the metaphors are not always appropriate to the natural objects which they describe: the swallows gossip, the wilding bee hums merrily, but the winds titter, the leaves dance, the flowers smile, the brooks laugh.

Bryant is more successful when describing less intimate involvements with nature than those with which Wordsworth generally concerned himself. **"The Prairies"** (1833), one of Bryant's most anthologised poems, is a response to the vast geography of America. Through its wide-sweeping rhythms and images such as the prairie hawk it connotes a sense of space which anticipates the fuller realisations of Ralph Waldo Emerson and Walt Whitman. While the rolling and fluctuating landscape of America is acknowledged, Bryant, however, conveys here a sense of static calm rather than the energy which Emerson and Whitman embrace in their work. But **"The Prairies"** is a more conscientious poem than those which attempt a Wordsworthian communion with nature:

   Breezes of the South!
Who toss the golden and the flame-like flowers
And pass the prairie-hawk, that, poised on high,
Flaps his broad wings, yet moves not—ye have
      played
Among the palms of Mexico and vines
Of Texas, and have inspired the limpid brooks
That from the fountains of Sonora glide
Into the calm Pacific.

Bryant also achieves a greater degree of success in poems concerned with a darker view of nature than that which Wordsworth usually contemplated. After 'Guilt and Sor-

row' Wordsworth never wrote a poem comparable to Bryant's **"The Murdered Traveller"** (1824) where nature is dark, mysterious and violent. It seems almost as if the universe itself has struck a blow against the man: 'The northern dawn was red, / The mountain-wolf and wild-cat stole / To banquet on the dead'. The ominous colour of the dawn, the death itself which is lonely and savage and the use of the word 'banquet' contribute to the poem's chilling atmosphere. A similar menace at the heart of nature occurs in **'The Prairies'** where 'the brown vultures of the wood / Flocked to the vast uncovered sepulchres, / And sat unscared and silent at their feast.'

This greater sense of space and of the dark, destructive forces within nature tended to obviate the kind of intimacy with nature which Wordsworth achieved in the *Lyrical Ballads*. Bryant was, also, more conscious than Wordsworth of a sexual impulse in his yearning for nature:

   For me, I lie
Languidly in the shade, where the thick turf,
Yet virgin from the kisses of the sun,
Retains some freshness, and I woo the wind
That still delays his coming.

Here communion with nature is a sexual embrace and in **"The West Wind"** (1821), written three years earlier, Bryant rests beneath the forest's skirt and listens to 'the thread-like foliage sigh'. The sexual exuberance of summer is suggested by the river which flows full to its banks and the June roses which meet the west wind's kiss. But beside the sexuality of nature Bryant remains unfulfilled; in **"Summer Wind"** the wind 'still delays his coming'. Because the consummation which Bryant seeks is more sexual than Wordsworth's, Bryant is left less satisfied than Wordsworth by contact with nature.

Bryant's sexual self-consciousness is so strong in poems such as **"The Yellow Violet"** that the sexuality he sees in nature is an overt, anthropomorphic projection and this again obviates any real sense of contact with nature. In **"The Yellow Violet"** the flower has the self-conscious modesty of a virgin maid. The yellow violet's 'modest bell / Peeps from the last years leaves below' and its 'faint *Perfume* / Alone is in the virgin air.' References are made to its 'glowing *lip*' and the '*gentle eye*' cast earthward to avoid the eyes of passers by. Compared with the violet's reticence there are other 'loftier flowers . . . *flaunting* nigh.' Moreover, the sexual forces in nature are as ambivalent as the rest of it. Anxiety enters **"The West Wind"** when the 'branching pines rising dark and high' reach mysterious and perhaps disturbing heights and the 'new-fledged bird / Takes wing, half happy, half afraid'. In the opening of **"Inscription for an Entrance to a Wood"** the woodland creatures celebrate their sexuality, but the winged plunderer, simultaneously the despoiler and perpetrator of nature, introduces the violence of sexuality: 'Scarce less the cleft born wild-flower seems to enjoy / Existence than the winged plunderer / That sucks its sweets'. This menacing sexual ambivalence in nature further obscures Bryant's attempt at communion with her.

Bryant assumed Wordsworth's conviction that nature was morally significant and recommended in **"Thanatopsis"** (1817):

> Go forth, under the open sky, and list
> To Nature's teaching, while from all around—
> Earth and her waters, and the depths of air—
> Comes a still voice—

Wordsworth had suggested in *Lyrical Ballads*: 'Come forth into the light of things, / Let Nature be your Teacher.' Bryant even imported into his poetry Wordsworth's indebtedness to Matthew for introducing him to the ministry of nature. The bond between Wordsworth and the aged Matthew were such that in 'The Two Mornings' Wordsworth reports that although Matthew is dead 'I see him stand, / As at that moment, with a bough, / Of wilding in his hand.' Bryant's **"The Old Man's Counsel"** (1840), like the Matthew Poems, is a conversation poem in which youth is contrasted with the sombre understanding of old age. Here the young poet is similarly indebted to the old man for his spiritual development and the strength of the bond between them is such that even after death the Old Man, like Matthew, appears beside the youth:

> Long since that white-haired ancient slept—but still,
> When the red flower-buds crowd the orchard-bough,
> And the muffled grouse is drumming far within
> The woods, his venerable form again
> Is at my side, his voice is in my ear.

But because Bryant was never able to achieve as convincing an intimacy with nature as Wordsworth, he never accepted nature, like Wordsworth, as an exclusive moral teacher. His attempts to do so, and to establish a relationship with nature, are the subjects of poems written mainly in the 1820s. Thereafter, he was more willing to describe a distance between himself and nature—**"The Prairies,"** for example, was written in 1833—and emphasises not only her vast inaccessibility but her dark, mysterious, sexual ambivalence and potential destructiveness. . . .

While both Bryant and Emerson were influenced in their early years by Wordsworth, neither can be called an 'American Wordsworth' or even a disciple of Wordsworth. However, Wordsworth was an important influence upon them because he contributed to their understanding of man's relationship with nature. Contrary to Tony Tanner's argument, there is in both their works an interrelationship between mind and nature.

Tony Tanner is ultimately correct in arguing that a greater awareness of space distinguishes the English and American nature poets. But the differences between them are manifest in the American poet's failure (or refusal) to develop as extensive and as intimate a relationship with nature as that which occurs in most of Wordsworth's poetry rather than in his total abstinence from such a relationship. . . .

Albert F. McLean (essay date 1989)

SOURCE: "The Divided Voice," in his *William Cullen Bryant,* updated edition, Twayne Publishers, 1989, pp. 106-31.

[In the excerpt below, McLean focuses on Bryant's poetic theory and poetic technique, observing a distinct division between the poet's artistic intention and his poetic achievement.]

If Bryant's vacillation between epideictic and contemplative verse in his poems of progress was, on one level, a re-enactment of the age-old dilemma of the personal poet who feels compelled to tithe his talent to the social good, on a more profound level this indecision was too symptomatic of the fundamental weakness of his poetry. Bryant was seldom able to speak with the firm, clear, original voice of his own genius. Though he sensed early and rightly that his was the way of the poet, he never truly understood the terms of his vocation. Though his voice in a few great poems rises to uniqueness, the grounds for his triumphs were never clear to him. And though at times he brought into the realm of the articulate his personal vision of the universal experience, he seemed unable to sustain his best insights and to profit by his successes.

This basic criticism of Bryant as a poet need not obscure, however, our appreciation of his many accomplishments. Bryant—given his nature and environment—faced an inevitable and nearly unsolvable dilemma. His preternaturally early development, his search for parental approval, the facile action of his mind as it worked backward and forward between experience and introspection, the unquestioned authority of British culture, the fluid state of American letters, and criticism during the years of his maturation—all of these militated against the kind of ultimate commitment required of the creative artist. Out of his dilemma he made the best that might have been anticipated. He dignified nature both as a subject and as a metaphor, he made some of his deeper thoughts available to the masses, he not only expressed himself in the discipline of traditional meters but also pioneered in the use of freer, more natural rhythms.

Yet Bryant could never make the basic decision that Emerson was to formulate as the choice between self-reliance and conformity. To have fallen back upon his own resources would have meant isolation and obscurity; to have molded himself deliberately on the pattern of an acknowledged poet—Wordsworth or Byron—would have meant the sacrifice of his independence as a Yankee and an American. Either choice would have guaranteed his work a fullness and consistency; either choice would have allowed him to mine his talent more deeply and to understand the dynamics of his creative process. But the choice was not made. His poetic gift broadened—to use Emerson's figure—in concentric circles and not according to any linear directive. As a poet he was an eclectic, as an individual, a pragmatist. Unlike the great modern poets—Yeats, Rilke, Eliot, Stevens—who would build in part upon the failures of their predecessors, Bryant faced the problems of multiplicity and divided purpose with a gift for adaptability rather than with integrity and self-awareness. Lacking within him the tight knot of conviction, he could never fulfill the promise implicit in his vocation.

This pathetic flaw influenced every aspect of his poetry, but it is most noticeable in the two areas with which this chapter will deal: poetic theory and poetic technique. In his infrequent attempts to reflect upon his art, Bryant was never able to formulate an adequate conception of the relationship between poetic ends and poetic means. If he resisted the mechanical functionalism of the classical rhetoric he had absorbed through his formal education, he also balked at the obvious alternative—a thoroughgoing aestheticism. Neither "art for morality's sake" nor "art for art's sake" provided him with a rationale for his own creativity. Thus, his critical fumblings expose only too well his policy of drifting between the neoclassical Scylla and the romantic Charybdis.

Poetic Theory

His sole effort at sustained criticism, The *Lectures on Poetry* (1825-26), manfully attempted to declare a position on this issue of ends and means. In the second of the four lectures, entitled "On the Value and Uses of Poetry," he defined the ultimate end of poetry as moral uplift and spiritual refinement. While admitting that a good deal of poetry is mere "amusement, an agreeable intellectual exercise," Bryant stressed the nobler goals: "[Poetry] has, however, a still higher value when regarded as in some sort the support of our innocence, for there is ever something pure and elevated in the creations of poetry. Its spirit is an aspiration after superhuman beauty and majesty, which, if it has no affinity with, has at least some likeness to virtue."

How are these goals to be reached? Three positive recommendations may be gleaned from the *Lectures:* first, American poetry should tap the rich resources of native speech and natural imagery; second, poetry should profit from the poetic "experiments" of the past rather than strive for novelty; third, poetry should be "suggestive" and not attempt literal representation. Independently, each of these methods could produce an aesthetic experience that might be considered ennobling and spiritual. The first—that of tapping native resources—is, indeed, the way that Whitman chose; the second is that of the traditionalist Longfellow; the third approximates the path of mysterious ambiguity by which Poe climbed toward the "supernal." But, in combination, the methods are unstable and too often ineffective. Like the man who believed in all religions in hopes of hitting upon one that was right, Bryant, in his criticism as well as in his poetry, obscured his purpose through the multiplicity of his means. While there is nothing intrinsically wrong about using traditional verse forms to praise American scenery, as Bryant did repeatedly, the total effect of the poem is as much conditioned by the imported stanzaic patterns as it is by the vastness and wildness of the landscape. And in similar fashion the total effect of the poem derives as much from the "suggestive" manner in which the scene is described as it does

upon the natural details of physical location. Thus, what Bryant conceived as various roads to the same city were actually variable determinants that could shift the locus of the destination across the surface of a map. Bryant failed to see that the poetic end was absolutely dependent upon the poetic means—that a diversity of means did not simplify but, to the contrary, complicated the creative process.

Particularly in his treatment of the idea of "suggestion" does his theorizing expose his confusion. For Bryant, the "suggestive" power of poetry arose from its capacity to encourage the imagination along "the path which the poet only points out, and shapes its visions from the scenes and allusions which he gives." As a "suggestive art" poetry stands in contrast to the "imitative" arts of painting and sculpture, which only reproduce "sensible objects." While these "imitative" arts carefully define reality in its form and substance, poetry utilizes "arbitrary symbols" (language) in order to excite the imagination "most powerfully and delightfully." To Bryant, examples of great poetry that affect the imagination are Milton's portrayals of Eve and Satan. In each case the imagination feeds upon a few hints in order to visualize the physical and moral qualities of the character. Had Bryant been satisfied to expand upon this point, his conception of poetry would have been unified and usable—perhaps even comparable to that put forward by Poe in "The Poetic Principle." But, still suspicious of the currents of unregulated "imagination," he foundered upon the shoals of common sense.

From the point at which Bryant took up in his essay the roles of *emotion* and *intellect* in poetry, the idea of "suggestion" is all but forgotten. Once the door has been opened to "the language of the passions" and to "direct lessons of wisdom," then the sources of imaginative vitality—mystery, wonder, spontaneity—retire to their private chambers. Once the "suggestive" power of poetry becomes comprehensive enough to include the familiar rhetorical devices for kindling emotions and instilling ideas, there is little left in poetry to distinguish it from prose. In fact, such is the conclusion at which Bryant, at the close of his first *Lecture,* sadly and quietly arrives. He admits that the only way in which he can distinguish between poetry and "eloquence" is by metrical arrangement. This conclusion, far removed from the brave premise upon which he had built his critical remarks, is a clear indication of his inability to maintain a consistent understanding of his creative work.

Form and Diction

In Bryant's attitude toward poetic form, as in his theories of poetry, there is a fundamental deficiency. Even a rapid perusal of the collected poetry reveals his constant experimentation with rhyme schemes, stanzaic units, and meter. Although much of his verse is in rhymed quatrains, he adapted easily to the sonnet form, the Spenserian measure, and the ballad. He was adept at both conventional rhyme schemes and improvised patterns. In **"To a Waterfowl,"** for example, he skillfully combines trimeters and pentameters within the rhymed quatrain. **"Green River"** is a marvelous use of rhymed tetrameter couplets to create a variety of effects. And in a number of poems, **"Catterskill Falls"** for one, he affixes this rhymed tetrameter couplet as a braking device at the conclusion of each conventional stanza. Perhaps Bryant can be praised, as Professor McDowell has praised him, for the estimable virtues of versatility and liberality in his use of poetic form. But for the poet such praise is, at best, a kind of honorable mention. With each successive mastery of a form Bryant reaffirms his technical competence but seldom does the novel device stimulate discoveries of fresh ideas or emotions. Too often the experiment suggests that the poet is still straining for the better vehicle, still seeking for the external order of discipline that will bring his work to life. Instead of pressing the more viable forms to the limit of their capacity, he dissipates his strength upon a variety of minor problems. That very breadth and restlessness that characterized Bryant as a student of nature and society and makes him interesting as a journalist and traveler tended to produce a body of verse with more amplitude than depth, more intelligence than conviction.

Bryant appears not to have come to grips with the problem of language. His critical observations usually revolved around two key points. The first is obviously indebted to the viewpoint of Wordsworth, expressed in the preface to *The Lyrical Ballads,* in its appeal for a less stylized and more natural diction in poetry. Thus the poet—by omitting "stiff Latinisms," "hackneyed phrases," and "the recondite or remote allusion" from his verses—can acquire a "household" or "luminous" style. Bryant praised the tendency of contemporary poets to go "directly to nature for their imagery, instead of taking it from what once had been regarded as the common stock of the guild of poets."

The second point Bryant made about language in the *Lectures* was that the tongue spoken by Americans and available to the native poet was a successfully transplanted version of a basic Anglo-Saxon. Having the flexibility to meet the new political and scientific conditions of American life, this language still retained the beauty and integrity of its early roots. Bryant summarized his position thus: "It has grown up, as every forcible and beautiful language has done, among a simple and unlettered people; it has accommodated itself, in the first place, to the things of nature, and, as civilization advanced, to the things of art; and thus it has become a language full of picturesque forms of expression, yet fitted for the purposes of science."

Both of these points were to become axiomatic for generations of American writers, not merely because they provided a rationalization for a national literature, but because their implications opened up new and exciting visitas for expression. The downright earthiness of the American vernacular, the latent ironies and humor of dialect, the possibilities of "organic" expression that united matter and idea in a single word or phrase—all of these were to announce those great experiments in language by Whitman, Thoreau, Melville, and Mark Twain. But Bryant failed to sense the implications of his theory. For him the return to nature for diction meant merely the naming of indigenous plants, birds, and animals in the simple vernacular and the brief, infrequent mention of place names in his poems. For Bryant the historical condition of the transplanted language impliednone of the high ironies that ring through the rhetoric of *Moby Dick;* to the contrary, the diction of the poet should abhor "subtleties of thought" and adhere "to the common track of human intelligence."

His confusion over the "suggestive" function of poetry spills over into this area of diction. On the one hand, he explains in the *Lectures* that language, for all its achievements, "is still limited and imperfect, and . . . falls infinitely short of the mighty and diversified world of matter and thought of which it professes to be the representative." And he conceives of the way in which descriptive passages function as "glimpses of things thrown into the mind; here and there a trace of an outline; here a gleam of light, and there a dash of shade." Yet, on the other hand, he could speak of language as "a great machine" and employ—as we have seen in his epideictic verse—all of the mechanical devices for persuasion typical of utilitarian rhetoric. Lacking any theoretical approach to language that did any more than describe the current situation, Bryant was not prepared to formulate an original position for his own work. His poetic diction avoids the more obvious pedantry and artifice of earlier American poets, which he had pointed out in some detail in an essay-review of 1818; yet he retained many vestiges of the former style. And while the notion of "suggestion" brought an imaginative vitality to his better poems, a workable concept was never to emerge from the clouded background evoked by the *Lectures*.

Bryant sought no half-way house in prosody, as he had in poetic diction. Instead, like Wordsworth and the Victorians, he stretched his talent over both the traditional, melodic verse and the less inhibited rhythms of blank verse. In both areas, as previous chapters have illustrated, he had notable successes. Yet in neither area did he develop, in theory or in practice, a prosody that could be relied upon to sustain him through his creative adventures. Unlike a formalist such as Frost, Bryant did not find endless "the possibilities for tune from the dramatic tones of meaning struck across the rigidity of a limited meter." Indeed, his "dramatic tones" have, through the collected works, a discouraging similarity. Nor in blank verse did he always find the pitch and cadence that could keep pace with his intellectual and emotional discoveries. At times during his career—in **"Thanatopsis," "The Fountain,"** and **"The Antiquity of Freedom"**—his poetic intent coincided with his choice of blank verse, and the promise of a forceful and original voice is made manifest. At other times, however, the long sequence of iambic pentameter lines (which are best read, as Northrop Frye points out [in *Anatomy of Criticism*, 1957] as a four-stress, running rhythm), performed a pedestrain service, doing little to raise prose description and meditation to a level of poetic intensity.

The Formal Voice

Several examples of his formal voice at work can be found among Bryant's experiments in the sonnet form. No established poet in America had, previous to Bryant, been equal to the rigid demands of either the English or Italian variations of the form, and thus Bryant's achievements in this particular area take on a historical and artistic importance. Two sonnets composed in 1824, **"Mutation"** and **"November,"** indicate the two directions opened up by the poet's concern for form; a third, **"To Cole, the Painter, Departing for Europe,"** illustrates the level of achievement of which Bryant was capable had he persevered in his use of the sonnet.

In **"Mutation"** Bryant ambitiously adopted an interlocking rhyme scheme in which the fifth and eighth lines of the sonnet pick up the rhyme of the preceding line: a b a *b b* c b *c c* d c d e e. Yet in spite of the continuity effected by the rhyme, the sonnet breaks into three firm quatrains and a definitive couplet. The initial quatrain argues that grief and remorse are short-lived, the second states that peace inevitably follows pain, and the third quatrain asserts the positive and remedial influence of suffering. Generalizing upon this cycle in the emotional life of man, the concluding couplet urges an acceptance of change or mutation as preferable to "a stable, changeless state." Such a paraphrase is no substitute for the poem, but it does serve to point up Bryant's sensitivity to the structure of progressive quatrains, typical of the sonnet form as it had developed in the work of Shakespeare, Milton, and Wordsworth. Also, it may be suggested that the interlocking rhyme scheme in **"Mutation,"** similar in its effect to the terza rima in English verse, serves to reinforce through the pattern of sounds the theme of gradual and unceasing "mutation." Bryant employs the iambic pentameter line skillfully to convey the tone of optimistic certitude in the first two quatrains, and in order to make his couplet sufficiently reflective, he inserts an additional stress to make an iambic hexameter of the fourteenth line.

Nevertheless, the disciplined voice falters, starting at line eight; it has overreached itself. The transition to rhythms of emergent joy is less than successful, in spite of the vigorous emphasis effected by the heavy consonance of lines 8 to 11. The verse strains for its rhymes in lines 11 and 12, and is nearly overcome by the resultant wordiness and awkwardness. In raising more formal problems than he could successfully handle, Bryant shows in **"Mutation"** (cited here in full) both his enterprising nature and his limitations as a poetic craftsman:

> They talk of short-lived pleasure—be it so—
>   Pain dies as quickly: stern, hard-featured Pain
> Expires, and lets her weary prisoner go.
>   The fiercest agonies have shortest reign;
>
> And after dreams of horror, comes again
> The welcome morning with its rays of peace.
>   Oblivion, softly wiping out the stain,
> Makes the strong secret pangs of shame to cease:
>
> Remorse is virtue's root; its fair increase
>   Are fruits of innocence and blessedness:
> Thus joy, o'erborne and bound, doth still release
>   His young limbs from the chains that round him
>   press.

> Weep not that the world changes—did it keep
>   A stable, changeless state, 'twere cause indeed to
>   weep.

Less ambitious in its structure and simpler in its progression of mood is the sonnet **"November."** Although the quatrains contrast with one another and reinforce the Janus-faced quality which the poet imputes to November, the rhymes are simpler and the rhythm is fairly uniform throughout. The elements of the sonnet form, even though they are not fully exploited here, work harmoniously together to define the lyrical response of the poet to the season:

> Yet one smile more, departing, distant sun!
>   One mellow smile through the soft vapory air,
> Ere, o'er the frozen earth, the loud winds run,
>   Or snows are sifted o'er the meadows bare.
> One smile on the brown hills and naked trees,
>   And the dark rocks whose summer wreaths are
>   cast,
> And the blue gentian-flower, that, in the breeze,
>   Nods lonely, of her beauteous race the last.
> Yet a few sunny days, in which the bee
>   Shall murmur by the hedge that skirts the way,
> The cricket chirp upon the russet lea,
>   And man delight to linger in thy ray.
> Yet one rich smile, and we will try to bear
> The piercing winter frost, and winds, and darkened
>   air.

The melodic element prevails in **"November,"** much more than it does in **"Mutation."** The soothing alliterative effects contribute to the mood and, through their distribution of stress, to the rhythm. By his skillful combination of a restricted meter and rhyme with a pervasive musicality, Bryant was able in the sonnet, in the elegy, and in numerous other regular stanzaic patterns to tap the nonrational and simply emotive sources of his creativity. At those points where he permitted the form itself, either traditional or improvised, to bear the responsibilities of order and coherence, Bryant most fully capitalized upon the virtues of his formal voice. Where euphony was permitted to prevail over meaning, his imagination was least inhibited.

Thus the sonnet **"To Cole,"** which relies principally upon its imagery to convey its meaning, sustains its forceful rhythms and its militant harmonies throughout. The structure is implicit in the poem, modestly hiding its logic in thick folds of sensory experience. The sonnet is simply a reminder, addressed directly to the painter, to view the European scenes he is about to visit through the eyes of his early piety, nationalism, and optimism. In observing the picturesque melancholy of cultures eroded by the forces of history—"paths, homes, graves, ruins"—Cole should bear in mind "A living image of our own bright land." Against the imagery of European decay and dissolution, Bryant opposes the vision that Cole had imparted through his huge canvases—of a new world with unsullied open spaces. Without an obtrusive statement to this effect, Bryant draws upon the two accepted denominators of cultivated taste in his day, the "picturesque" and the "sublime," and contrasts them neatly within the limits of the form. One quatrain of exhortation, one quatrain of strident description of the divine wilderness of Cole's canvases, one quatrain of subdued preview of European sights—a thumping heroic couplet restating the exhortation—and a wealth of poetic experience has been condensed into the fourteen lines of **"To Cole, the Painter, Departing for Europe"**:

> Thine eyes shall see the light of distant skies;
> > Yet, Cole! thy heart shall bear to Europe's strand
> > A living image of our own bright land,
> Such as upon thy glorious canvas lies;
>
> Lone lakes—savannas where the bison roves—
> > Rocks rich with summer garlands—solemn
> >   streams—
> Skies, where the desert eagle wheels and
>   screams—
> Spring bloom and autumn blaze of boundless
> > groves.
>
> Fair scenes shall greet thee where thou goest—fair,
> > But different—everywhere the trace of men,
> > Paths, homes, graves, ruins, from the lowest glen
> To where life shrinks from the fierce Alpine air—
>
> > Gaze on them, till the tears shall dim thy sight,
> > But keep that earlier, wilder image bright.

Similarly, in his use of his classical elegy Bryant relies less upon the structure of ideas than upon the unity imposed by the rhyme and rhythm of the form. In the case of the elegy, the problems are less of rhyme and more of meter, for the basic unit of the eight foot couplet is easily worked into the conventional quatrain. But the meter of the elegy, as Bryant practiced it, even though the seventh and eighth feet of each couplet asserted a basic iambic pentameter, allowed for considerable substitution in the remaining six feet. For Bryant—who had written in the *North American Review* of 1819 that poetry should avoid "tame iambics" and the "dead waste of dissyllabic feet," and cultivate, instead, "a freer use of trisyllabic feet"—the elegy had the notable advantage of combining a fundamental metrical regularity with a degree of license. Within an elegy, such as **"To the Fringed Gentian,"** Bryant availed himself of his freedom and used effectively both the anapest and spondee without disturbing the smooth movement of the lines. Only two places in **"To the Fringed Gentian"** reveal Bryant's failure to provide the discipline of the seventh and eighth feet, and both cases can be easily justified by their metrical context. The success of **"To the Fringed Gentian"** is more than technical, however, and it is the rhythm of temperate despair caught by each successive couplet that combines sound with sense. It is rhythm, more than thought, which builds the quiet tension through the poem and carefully restrains it until the moment of brief, climactic release—"Blue—blue—. . . ."

The melodies of this poem speak for themselves, yet the principle of symmetrical construction, essential to the classical elegy, deserves comment. Through a combination of alliteration and internal rhyme, Bryant shapes line after line into a delicate fabric of total harmony. The principle of balance may be obvious in a line such as "Thou waitest late and comest alone," but the equilibrium of "The hour of death draw near to me" is less clear until the repeated consonant sounds—*th, d,* and *r,*—are distinguished. And the internal rhyme in the line, "The aged *year* is *near* his end," is also easy to overlook in the anticipation of the end rhyme. When variety was needed to break the pattern of the symmetrical line, Bryant was capable of constructing an asymmetrical line of great beauty. The high point of **"To a Fringed Gentian,"** "Blue—blue—as if that sky let fall / A flower from its cerulean wall," is created by an intricate patterning of the repeated vowel sound of *oo,* and the soft consonants *l* and *f.*

One path toward greater lyrical intensity is the shortened poetic line of three or four stresses. Although the pentameter line is generally accepted as the norm for poetry in English, the shorter line has several advantages. It compresses the language, thus demanding more involvement by the reader, it lends itself to suggestive, less explicit expression, and, if used adroitly, it encourages an intensity of emotion. Recent criticism, from feminist critics in particular, has argued that the pentameter line is predominately masculine and thus its use is a "code" for male dominance. How one reconciles this with the fact that most nineteenth-century male poets adapted themselves to the shorter lines to achieve certain effects, is not certain, but it is clear that the shorter line is more muted, gives itself to more subtle expression, and generally suggests a greater degree of intimacy than the more sedate and formal pentameter.

Such is the case in Bryant's hymns, first collected and published in 1864. He wrote them largely in his early years but continued to produce them sporadically throughout his career. They were most often composed in a four-foot line, and many of them follow the basic metrics of the old New England standby, Watt's *Hymns,* organized into quatrains of iambic tetrameter, with three-foot lines interpolated into the stanzas in various patterns. Bryant's hymn **"In Memoriam"** (1856), for example, scans according to what was known as the "common meter," in which the second and fourth line of each quatrain are shortened to three feet (4 3 4 3):

> Two hundred times has June renewed
> > Her roses since the day
> Where here, amid the lonely wood,
> > Our fathers met to pray.

The rhythm established here is familiar to church-goers even today and connotes a delicate pathos and tenderness difficult to achieve with the pentameter line.

A more heavily stressed hymn, **"This Do, in Remembrance of Me,"** still gives the effect of the dying fall in the second and fourth lines:

All praise to Him of Nazareth
 The Holy One who came
For love of man, to die a death
 Of agony and shame.

Most of the hymns, however, are composed in regular quatrains of iambic tetrameter, appropriate to the worship of praise and exaltation. In 1842, Bryant wrote, evidently considering it to be a hymn, a brief lyric poem that mourns the death of William Ellery Channing, the preeminent voice of nineteenth-century Unitarianism. Consistent with Channing's message of optimism and hope, its rhythms have a calm lilt to them and anticipate the message of joy in the concluding stanza:

While yet the harvest-fields are white,
 And few the toiling reapers stand,
Called from his task before the night,
 We miss the mightiest of the band.

Oh, thou of strong and gentle mind,
 Thy thrilling voice shall plead no more
For Truth, for Freedom, and Mankind—
 The lesson of thy life is o'er.

But thou in brightness, far above
 The fairest dream of human thought,
Before the seat of Power and Love,
 Art with the Truth that thou has sought.
     ["The Death of Channing"]

Among his secular poems, a few, such as **"A Sick Bed"** (1858) and **"The Return of the Birds"** (1864), actually come close to the traditional hymn meter, but Bryant's more usual practice was simply to establish in the opening lines of his poem a foundation line of three or four feet and then to expand or compress it as the tone or subject matter seemed to require. Thus, **"My Autumn Walk"** (1865) sets the rhythmic thrust of the three stress line in the first stanza:

On woodlands ruddy with autumn
 The amber sunshine lies;
I look on the beauty round me,
 And tears come into my eyes.

This meditation on the personal tragedies attendant on the Civil War continues for a full sixteen stanzas that vary considerably in their content and rhythm. Some of them are disconsolate comments on those who have lost sons or husbands, while others present patriotic justifications for this suffering. In a stanza of mourning, for instance, Bryant attenuates the lines and the stresses are muted:

But who shall comfort the living,
 The light of whose homes is gone:
The bride that early widowed,
 Lives broken-hearted on.

But in the more militant stanzas the trimeter is forcefully asserted:

Oh, for that better season,
 When the pride of the foe shall yield
And the host of God and Freedom
 March back from the well-worn field.

Most significant in **"My Autumn Walk"** is that Bryant works against the prevailing metric, discards the iamb in favor of longer feet, closes his lines with feminine endings that are often dangling half feet, and is even willing to overload his line with heavily accented syllables, as he does, for example, in "The mock-grape's blood-red banner." For all the pious and conventional language of the poem, it is an excellent exercise in rhythmic control and illustrates the kind of invention of which Bryant was capable in his use of the shortened line. Other poems show this same craftsmanship. **"A Scene on the Banks of the Hudson"** (1828) applies a four-foot line to capture the mood of the fugitive poet seeking respite in natural beauty: "River: in this still hour thou hast / Too much of heaven on earth to last."

Not that Bryant's use of the short line was always effective. **"A Lifetime"** (1876) attempts too much in making the trimeter sustain his nostalgic musings and self-explorations over 148 lines, much too long to sustain the fragile line structure. But it has a few fine moments. The opening stanza, for instance, is nicely paced and sets the reflective mood:

I sit in the early twilight,
 And, through the gathering shade,
I look on the fields around me
 Where yet a child I played.

And as he looks to the heavens, imagining that his deceased wife appears, his restrained and simple eloquence cuts through the banality of the situation:

I know the sweet calm features;
 The peerless smile I know,
And I stretch my arms with transport
 From where I stand below.

There is no finer use of the abbreviated line, however, than that in an obscure little verse, a translation from the Spanish of a Mexican poet, José Rosas. In its compression, in its precise diction, and in its rhythmic modulations, **"The Cost of Pleasure"** invites comparison in its handling of the trimeter line with Emily Dickinson's "I Never Saw a Moor." The metaphor, with its hint of sexuality, is strictly that of the Mexican poet (and probably did not even occur to Bryant). But even more than the play upon dew drops and the rose, the rhyme and rhythm of the translation are what make **"The Cost of Pleasure"** work:

Upon the valley's lap
 The liberal morning throws
A thousand drops of dew
 To wake a single rose.

Thus often, in the course
 Of life's few fleeting years,

A single pleasure costs
  The soul a thousand tears.

Blank Verse

In spite of its value in leading him to the sensuous and suggestive core of his subject matter, the formal voice, even if perfected, could not fully realize Bryant's total response to his experience. For the demands of form and his own limitations made one thing certain: if he were to cultivate his aesthetic sensibility, he must sacrifice those intellectual qualities he considered to be essential to noble and elevated poetry. His respect for the reasoning faculties of the mind—not, as some might have it, any moral scruples about pleasure—led him into another area of poetic technique where intellect could have its say. Blank verse had the advantages of scope and permissiveness, and while Bryant was well aware of the fruits of metrical discipline, the very breadth and inclusiveness of his experience demanded a more open form.

There are several appropriate ways of considering the technique of his blank verse, but some are obvious and others are blind alleys. To say that Bryant drew from a vital tradition of poetry in the English language—a tradition that runs from Shakespeare through Milton and down to Wordsworth—contributes little to our understanding of his motivation or of the spirit in which he adopted this verse form. We know that he was stimulated by Cowper's "The Task" and that the possibilities for combining natural imagery with blank verse were further revealed to him by Thomson's *The Seasons*. But, if books from abroad provided him with certain basic idioms and perhaps with some of his rhythms, such devices tended to be the tools of his art rather than its substance. While Bryant appears to have felt secure in the shadow of precedent, his concern was for personal expression—not for the perpetuation of an art form.

Yet in this direction there is not much to guide us. Bryant offers little criticism, or even unpublished correspondence, that suggests what he felt to be the function of blank verse or its place in his own work. His remarks in the *Lectures,* upon which this discussion must draw, are addressed not to the problems of blank verse but to those of poetry as a whole. This critical silence on an important phase of his work, however, is in itself important. For in this area particularly, Bryant preferred to work intuitively. The meticulous craftsmanship of the elegies and of the sonnets reveals a conscious attention to the details of composition, but the blank verse gives every sign of being written whole and revised diffidently. Even the case McDowell makes for Bryant's careful reworking of his material hinges largely upon **"Thanatopsis"**—which he most certainly did labor over—and upon the formal lyrics. In the body of the blank verse there is little to indicate that Bryant did more than polish the more evident rough spots and attend to flaws in organization.

In practice, the voice that speaks out of the blank verse was conditioned by two dominant influences, neither of them, in any strict sense, poetic. The first of these was

Bryant's own prose style, a simplified version of the neoclassical rhetoric. At its worst, the old rhetoric was pedantic, inflated, and intemperate; at its best, it harnessed the forces of wit, logic, and fancy into a well-matched team. In political and religious tracts toward the close of the eighteenth century, this rhetoric strove for an eloquence that would combine rational persuasion with the elevated style of the grand manner. Bryant had pruned from his own prose the more glaring absurdities of the "false sublime," and his own career in journalism further encouraged him toward a more direct, honest expression of thought and feeling. Yet the temper of "eloquence" remained, and its assumed relationship between writer and reader was seldom far from Bryant's mind.

Next to this eloquence, the theory of the "association of ideas" was instrumental in molding the blank verse. From this theory, as subsequent discussion will attempt to make clear, Bryant derived both an articulated justification of what impulse led him to do anyway, and a poetic technique for themanagement of metaphor and symbol. The act of association, as Bryant adapted it to his own purposes, became a vehicle for reflective reverie. Conditioned by the experiences of the past and dependent upon the solitude and silence of nature for its operation, this voice—perhaps best called the "voice of eloquent reverie"—would give expression to Bryant's greatest poem, **"Thanatopsis,"** and to the other major works in blank verse: **"Inscription for the Entrance to a Wood," "The Prairies," "Monument Mountain," "The Antiquity of Freedom,"** and **"The Fountain"** . . . .

The Pitfalls of Blank Verse

If the blank verse drew from [Bryant's prose style and the ideas of association psychology], and was indeed the "voice of eloquent revery," its continued success depended upon a delicate coordination. This is the irony of Bryant's style. While the rhetoric of eloquence could provide him with a stable center for his creative activity, it could also leave his expression vaporous, void of content, and out of touch with his listeners. Though the association of ideas might secure for him the freedom and inwardness that brought his poetry to life, it could easily become a stylistic trick—and one without relevance either to his deeper thoughts or to the eternal truths of nature. Even in the blank verse of his middle periods—**"Earth"** (1834), for example—the rhetorical effects could take over and not only leave the language flaccid but also detract from the smooth and suggestive train of ideas. And, as a previous chapter has pointed out, the association of ideas becomes an inert principle once the sense of communion with nature is lost. Thus, while **"Among the Trees"** (1868) has many fine lines, its language gradually loses contact with any substantial reality; the poem therefore concludes lamely with a banal figure that might easily have been drawn from an eighteenth-century political tract:

  The hand of ruffian Violence, that now
  Is insolently raised to smite, shall fall
  Unnerved before the calm rebuke of Law,
  And Fraud, his sly confederate, shrink, in shame,
  Back to his covert, and forego his prey.

As a poet, Bryant is no exceptional case; for any creative artist, the pitfalls lie on all sides. If he had bad habits impressed upon him during his back-country education, he made the most of them. If his reading in British literature and philosophy opened up promising new vistas for him, these insights too quickly became mannerisms. Though he developed an extraordinary ear for the musical effects of language early in his career, these very effects militated against the full articulation of his thought. Though he claimed to speak authoritatively for the role of imagination in literature, his aptitude lay not in the creation of startling new effects and prophetic questions but rather in the restatement of old truths and in the resolution of contemporary crises of the heart and mind.

To say that Bryant spoke with a divided voice is an essential criticism, but it need not be a severe one. Along each of the trails that he tramped alone, he left a number of memorable literary landmarks. Nor was his failure absolute, depending as it does upon our assessment of his talent. If we take his best poems, however, as a true index of his ability, he falls short of his own standard of achievement. Unable to assess himself completely as a poet, unwilling to formulate the fast, guiding principles by which his genius would be directed, and uncompromising in his attachment to the two divergent paths along which he was wont to stray, Bryant failed to realize that distinctive originalitywhich is the mark of the great poets of his day and ours.

FURTHER READING

Biography

Bigelow, John. *William Cullen Bryant.* New York: Houghton Mifflin Company, 1890, 355 p.

> General biography by Bryant's close friend and colleague at the New York *Evening Post,* including numerous letters and other correspondence.

McDowell, Tremaine. "Introduction" to *William Cullen Bryant,* pp. xiii-lxviii. New York: American Book Company, 1935.

> Perceptive survey of Bryant's life and literary career, including the poet's early conservatism, political idealism, religious liberalism, views on nature, and literary romanticism.

Criticism

Berbrich, Joan D. "Part II: William Cullen Bryant," in her *Three Voices from Paumanok: The Influence of Long Island on James Fenimore Cooper, William Cullen Bryant, Walt Whitman,* pp. 61-109. Port Washington, NY: Ira J. Friedman, Inc., 1969.

> Studies the geographical, social, and historical significance of various Long Island, New York, locales in the literary works of Cooper, Bryant, and Whitman,

observing that "editorials [Bryant] wrote in Manhattan; poems he wrote on Paumanok!"

Bryant, William Cullen II. "Bryant and Poe: A Reacquaintance." In *Studies in the American Renaissance,* edited by Joel Myerson, pp. 147-52. Charlottesville: University Press of Virginia, 1993.

> Reviews Bryant's and Poe's often misinterpreted literary and personal opinions of each other.

Budick, E. Miller. "The Disappearing Image in William Cullen Bryant's 'To a Waterfowl.'" *Concerning Poetry* 11, No. 3 (Fall 1978): 13-16.

> Analyzes the symbolic value of the bird in Bryant's poem, emphasizing the meaning of its disappearance near the poem's conclusion.

Duffey, Bernard. *Poetry in America: Expression and Its Values in the Times of Bryant, Whitman, and Pound.* Durham, NC: Duke University Press, 1978, 358 p.

> Examines the relation between American poetry and culture "to each other and to the changing imaginative life of the nation," classifying Bryant's work as the "first major" expression of European romanticism in the United States.

Ferguson, Robert A. "William Cullen Bryant: The Creative Context of the Poet." *The New England Quarterly* LIII, No. 4 (December 1980): 431-63.

> Discusses professional and intellectual influences in Bryant's nature poetry written before 1840, challenging the widely-held notion that Bryant was an "American Wordsworth."

Freeman, John, and Gregory Green. "A Literary Cul-de-Sac: The Sonnet and the Schoolroom Poets." *The American Transcendental Quarterly,* No. 42 (Spring 1979): 105-22.

> Treats the various uses of the sonnet form by American poets Longfellow, Lowell, Whittier, and Bryant, contending that the latter's sonnet "To Cole" represents an indigenous formal expression of American values.

Justus, James H. "The Fireside Poets: Hearthside Values and the Language of Care." In *Nineteenth-Century American Poetry,* edited by A. Robert Lee, pp. 146-65. Totowa, NJ: Barnes & Noble, 1985.

> Offers close readings of the public, national values of American culture expressed in the poetry of Bryant, Lowell, Longfellow, Whittier, and Holmes.

Koppenhaver, Allen J. "The Dark View of Things: The Isolated Figure in the American Landscapes of Cole and Bryant." In *View of American Landscapes,* edited by Mick Gidley and Robert Lawson-Peebles, pp. 183-98. Cambridge, NY: Cambridge University Press, 1989.

> Compares the sense of isolation and loneliness expressed in Bryant's poetry and in Thomas Cole's paintings and writings.

Krapf, Norbert. *Under Open Sky: Poets on William Cullen Bryant.* New York: Fordham University Press, 1986, 107 p.

> Collection of poems and prose pieces by twenty modern

American poets responding to "the voice, vision, and legacy" of Bryant.

Olson, Steve. "A Perverted Poetics: Bryant's and Emerson's Concern for a Developing American Literature." *The American Transcendental Quarterly,* No. 61 (October 1986): 15-21.

Demonstrates Bryant's influence on American poetical theory by closely reading a passage from the poet's Fourth Lecture on Poetry, which illuminates "the complex relationship among poetry and nature and the influence of the past."

Poger, Sidney. "William Cullen Bryant: Emblem Poet." *Emerson Society Quarterly* 43, No. 3 (1966): 103-06.

Considers the relation between Bryant's poetry and the conventions of nineteenth-century visual art, demonstrating the poet's pictorial talent in "The Planting of the Apple-Tree."

Spencer, Benjamin T. "Bryant: The Melancholy Progressive." *Emerson Society Quarterly* 43, No. 3 (1966): 99-103.

Detects a dialectic relationship throughout Bryant's poetic canon between the poet's belief in humanity's progress to a better quality of life and the sadness of individual existence.

Wortham, Thomas. "William Cullen Bryant and the Fireside Poets." In *Columbia Literary History of the United States,* edited by Emory Elliott, et al., pp.278-88. New York: Columbia University Press, 1988.

Accounts for the diminished significance of the Fireside Poets in the American literary canon, but acknowledges their collective achievement.

Additional coverage of Bryant's life and career is contained in the following sources published by Gale Research: *Nineteenth-Century Literature Criticism* Vols. 6, 46; *DISCovering Authors; DISCovering Authors: Most-Studied Authors Module; DISCovering Authors: Poets Module; Concise Dictionary of American Literary Biography, 1640-1865;* and *Dictionary of Literary Biography,* Vols. 3, 43, 59.

Countee Cullen
1903-1946

(Born Countee Leroy Porter) American poet, novelist, critic, journalist, and dramatist.

INTRODUCTION

Cullen was one of the foremost figures of the Harlem Renaissance, a cultural movement of unprecedented creative achievement among black American writers, musicians, and artists centered in the Harlem section of New York City during the 1920s. While Cullen strove to establish himself as the author of romantic poetry on such universal topics as love and death, he also wrote numerous poems treating contemporary racial issues, and it is for these that he is best remembered.

Biographical Information

The details of Cullen's early years are uncertain, and Cullen himself maintained a lifelong reticence about his youth. Nonetheless, scholars have determined that he was born in Louisville, Kentucky, and then raised in New York City by his paternal grandmother. Following her death in 1918, he was adopted by the Reverend and Mrs. Frederick Cullen of the Salem Methodist Episcopal Church in Harlem. In the home of his adoptive parents, Cullen was exposed to religious concerns as well as the political issues of the day through the work and influence of his adopted father. Reverend Cullen had helped found the National Urban League and served as president of the Harlem chapter of the National Association for the Advancement of Colored People (NAACP). An excellent student, Cullen attended DeWitt Clinton High School, then New York's premier preparatory school, before enrolling at New York University in 1922. During high school and college Cullen's poems appeared in campus and national publications and won numerous literary prizes, including second place in the Witter Bynner Poetry Contest for undergraduates for *The Ballad of the Brown Girl*, a retelling of an English folk ballad. *Color*, Cullen's first volume of poetry, was published in 1925, the same year he graduated from New York University. Cullen matriculated to Harvard University and received his M.A. in 1926. Returning to New York where he was already considered a leading literary figure, Cullen began writing "From the Dark Tower," a column on literary and social issues for *Opportunity*, the journal of the National Urban League. He published several volumes of poetry, including *Copper Sun* (1927) and *The Ballad of the Brown Girl* (1927), and edited *Caroling Dusk: An Anthology of Verse by Negro Poets* (1927).

In 1928 Cullen's editorial work on *Opportunity* in addition to his reputation as a poet earned him a Guggenheim

grant to study in France for one year. Prior to his departure, he married Nina Yolande DuBois, daughter of the prominent black scholar and intellectual W.E.B. Du Bois, in an April ceremony that was the highlight of the African-American social community. The marriage rapidly deteriorated, however, so that by July of the same year, when Cullen departed for Paris, Yolande did not accompany him, remaining instead in the United States. They divorced in 1930 upon Cullen's return to New York, having lived apart for two years. During his time in Paris, Cullen wrote *The Black Christ and Other Poems* (1929) which expressed the agony and pain of lost love and betrayal. Cullen's time in France was both invigorating and liberating, as he was able to escape the effects of racism and to mingle with writers, painters, and artists; the effect was not apparent in his published work, however, as *The Black Christ and Other Poems* received little critical approbation.

To help pay the bills, Cullen turned his attention to other forms of writing, and in 1932 he published *One Way to Heaven*, a novel that was praised for its accurate portrayal of Harlem life, and also published stories and verse for children. Cullen refused several academic teaching positions at various southern universities, not wanting to leave the more racially tolerant North, and in 1934 he accepted a position as a junior high French instructor at an all black school in New York. Teaching, writing, lecturing, and community projects occupied the remainder of his life. Cullen wrote little poetry during this period, instead contributing editorials to New York newspapers and collaborating with Arna Bontemps on the play *St. Louis Woman* (1945). The one exception to this was *The Medea and Some Poems* (1935), which, although it enjoyed some favorable reviews, was not as widely circulated as his earlier volumes. In 1940 Cullen married Ida Mae Roberson, with whom he enjoyed a happy relationship until his death. In the mid-1940s Cullen began preparing a definitive collection of those poems he considered his best: *On These I Stand: An Anthology of the Best Poems of Countee Cullen* was published posthumously in 1947.

Major Works

Cullen contended that poetry consisted of "lofty thoughts beautifully expressed," and he preferred poetic forms characterized by dignity and control." Strongly influenced by Keats and other Romantic poets, Cullen wrote traditional poetry with formal structure full of religious imagery and classical allusions. Throughout his career, Cullen tried to downplay the influence of race on his poetry, preferring to be respected as a poet, not as a Negro poet. Still, race was not something he could escape, and Cullen was criticized by the African American community for his failure to write about black life and social issues. Today, his best-known poems—"Yet Do I Marvel," "Incident," and "Uncle Jim"—are those which address the issues of racial discrimination and the inequality between blacks and whites in American society. "Yet Do I Marvel" exemplifies Cullen's belief that blacks could write poetry as well as any other race or ethnic group, and that they were not limited in scope, subject, or language, which is why much of his poetry focuses on such universal themes as love, morality, faith, and doubt. "Yet Do I Marvel" challenges the perceived contradiction between his status as a member of an oppressed race and his poetic skill, asking how God could "make a poet black, and bid him sing!" Indeed, in *Color* (1925), as the title suggests, many of Cullen's poems express his anger at the unfair treatment of blacks, although his vociferations are markedly more low-key than those of Langston Hughes or Claude McKay due to Cullen's natural reserve and his traditional poetics. It is difficult to overlook his condemnation of racism in "Incident," which relates the experience of an eight-year-old child who is the object of a racial slur on a Baltimore bus, an adaptation of a personal experience.

The Ballad of the Brown Girl (1927), one of Cullen's more popular works, revises a traditional English folk ballad that tells the story of Lord Thomas, who must choose between a white maiden and a "brown girl." In Cullen's version, which earned him second prize in the prestigious Witter Bynner Poetry Contest for undergraduates, the choice the man must make reflects the tension between blacks and whites, and the brown girl seeks to avenge the insult to her blackness by the white maiden. This poem was publicly praised by Harvard University's recognized expert on ballads, Irving Babbit, increasing Cullen's reputation and standing as a poet with cross-cultural appeal. This issue of racial identity appears in other examples of Cullen's love poems, most notably "A Song of Praise," in which Cullen examines the differences between loving a black woman and loving a white one.

Religious themes also prevail in Cullen's work, reflecting his Romantic inclination to write about spirituality, love, and idealism. "The Black Christ" (1929) for example, recounts the lynching and resurrection of a Southern black man. "Heritage"—deemed by Langston Hughes to be the most beautiful poem he knew—reflects the tension Cullen felt between his identification with Christian values and traditions and his desire to claim an African heritage.

Critical Reception

While some critics have praised Cullen's skill at traditional versification, others suggest that his restrained, controlled style was not suited to the treatment of such emotionally charged matters as contemporary racial issues and that his adherence to conventional forms resulted in poems that are insincere and unconvincing. Nevertheless, "Heritage" and "The Ballad of the Brown Girl," two poems by Cullen that address racial inequality, are among his major successes. Despite the controversy surrounding his traditional poetic style and his ambivalence toward racial subject matter in art, Cullen can still be considered a representative voice of the Harlem Renaissance.

It is felt by some that Cullen never fully realized the potential displayed in his earliest works, his traditional and conservative verse forms not being suited to contemporary social issues. The critically acclaimed collections *Color* (1925) and *The Ballad of the Brown Girl and Other Poems* (1927) came early in Cullen's career and showed mature lyricism and mastery of verse forms. Subsequent collections, *Copper Sun* (1927) and *The Black Christ and Other Poems* (1929), garnered critical reaction that was mixed at best. *Copper Sun* perhaps would have fared better if it were Cullen's first collection instead of his second: after the stunning debut of *Color*, the poems contained in *Copper Sun* appeared pale and Cullen displayed little, if any, literary growth. "The Black Christ" is considered to be Cullen's least successful poem, due in part to his failed attempt to combine religious and romantic themes: Christ's crucifixion and resurrection and the romantic image of the death of spring. Attempting to recount the lynching and resurrection of a black man, the poem fails to recreate the horror of the subject or to forge any believable link between the concrete subject and the religious metaphor.

Cullen too felt his early poems were among his best, as just prior to his death, he began compiling the poems for which he wanted to be remembered and included many from *Color* and his other early works. *On These I Stand:*

An Anthology of the Best Poems of Countee Cullen (1947) was published one year after his death and contained such racially charged poems as "Heritage," "For a Lady I Know," and even the unpopular "The Black Christ." All of the poems in the collection represented his traditional lyricism and what Gwendolyn Brooks call his "careful talent." Despite the relatively small volume of his work, Cullen is the most-often anthologized black poet.

PRINCIPAL WORKS

Poetry

Color 1925
The Ballad of the Brown Girl: An Old Ballad Retold 1927
Copper Sun 1927
The Black Christ, and Other Poems 1929
The Medea, and Some Poems 1935
On These I Stand: An Anthology of the Best Poems of Countee Cullen 1947
My Soul's High Song: The Collected Writings of Countee Cullen, Voice of the Harlem Renaissance 1991

Other Major Works

Caroling Dusk: An Anthology of Verse by Negro Poets [editor] (poetry) 1927
One Way to Heaven (novel) 1932
The Lost Zoo (A Rhyme for the Young, but Not Too Young) (children's poetry) 1940
My Lives and How I Lost Them (juvenile fiction) 1942
St. Louis Woman [with Arna Bontemps] (drama) 1946
Complete Works (novels, poetry, essays, satires, letters, and rules to games) 1939

CRITICISM

Babette Deutsch (essay date 1925)

SOURCE: "Let It Be Allowed," in *The Nation and the Athenaeum,* Vol. 121, No. 3156, December 30, 1925, pp. 763-64.

[*In the following review, Deutsch asserts that* Color *represents the voice of the African-American people and declares Cullen a poet with great potential.*]

These lyrics [*Color*] by the youngest of the Negro poets—Countee Cullen is just past his majority—are likely to be considered less as the work of a gifted individual than as the utterance of a gifted, and enslaved, people. And indeed Mr. Cullen's poems are intensely race-conscious. He writes out of the pain of inflamed memories, and with a wilful harking back to the primitive heritage of his own folk. The peculiar flavor which the book gets from the fact that it was written by a colored man is to be had most

sharply in the first section, from which the volume takes its title. This tang is the essence of such pieces as **"Atlantic City Waiter," "Fruit of the Flower,"** and **"Heritage,"** with their insistence on the savage past; it is the essence, too, of the lovely **"Song of Praise,"** and of that shrewd lyric **"To My Fairer Brethren":**

> Though I score you with my best,
>   Treble circumstance
> Must confirm the verdict, lest
>   It be laid to chance.
>
> Insufficient that I match you
>   Every coin you flip;
> Your demand is that I catch you
>   Squarely on the hip.
>
> Should I wear my wreaths a bit
>   Rakishly and proud,
> I have bought my right to it;
>   Let it be allowed.

Again and again Mr. Cullen strikes the harsh note which carries the scorn of the oppressed, the arrogance of the insulted and injured. He is engaged by the somber power and terrible brilliance of Africa as a Jew might be engaged by the purple days of Solomon's glory, or as the Gael is moved by the bright bloody history of his island. The poem by which Mr. Cullen is perhaps best known, **"The Shroud of Color,"** could have been written only by a Negro. It is a piece which, in spite of its sad lack of concision and its many cliches, yet abounds in true spiritual vigor.

But though one may recognize that certain of Mr. Cullen's verses owe their being to the fact that he shares the tragedy of his people, it must be owned that the real virtue of his work lies in his personal response to an experience which, however conditioned by his race, is not so much racial as profoundly human. The color of his mind is more important than the color of his skin. The faint acridness that gives an edge to many of these lyrics is a quality which one finds in Housman, or even in the minor strains of Herrick and of Horace. There is, for example, the song **"To a Brown Girl";** and the same pungency is felt in the companion piece, **"To a Brown Boy,"** or in **"Wisdom Cometh with the Years."** The twenty-eight rhymed Epitaphs have, almost without exception, a pure Gallic salt, as witness the one **"For a Lovely Lady":**

> A creature slender as a reed,
>   And sad-eyed as a doe
> Lies here (but take my word for it,
>   And do not pry below).

And even in what might be called his African poems it is Mr. Cullen's endowment of music and imagery and emotional awareness that matters, over and above the presence of jungle shapes and shadows.

These excellences—fantasy, lyricism, and fine sensitiveness—the book undoubtedly has. It has also faults, the faults of youth. The poet does not shrink from such rub-ber-stamp phrases as "costly fee," "crimson vintage," "ensanguined mead," "coral lips." He clutches at stars and clings to dreams like any neophyte, and lives in the pleasant reassurance that after death he will return to talk to his love "in liquid words of rain." But there seems little doubt that he will shed these puerilities before his youth is over, that he will discipline and develop his unquestionable gift.

Alain Locke (essay date 1926)

SOURCE: "*Color*—A Review," in *Opportunity,* Vol. 4, No. 37, January, 1926, pp. 14-15.

[*In the following assessment of* Color, *Locke proclaims Cullen a rare talent whose verse is firmly rooted in poetic tradition and in the African-American experience.*]

Ladies and gentlemen! A genius! Posterity will laugh at us if we do not proclaim him now. *Color* transcends all the limiting qualifications that might be brought forward if it were merely a work of talent. It is a first book, but it would be treasurable if it were the last; it is a work of extreme youth and youthfulness over which the author later may care to write the apology of "juvenilia," but it has already the integration of a distinctive and matured style; it is the work of a Negro poet writing for the most part out of the intimate emotional experience of race, but the adjective is for the first time made irrelevant, so thoroughly has he poetized the substance and fused it with the universally human moods of life. Cullen's own Villonesque poetic preface to the contrary, time will not outsing these lyrics.

The authentic lyric gift is rare today for another reason than the rarity of poetic genius, and especially so in contemporary American poetry—for the substance of modern life brings a heavy sediment not easy to filter out in the poetic process. Only a few can distill a clear flowing product, Housman, de la Mare, Sara Teasdale, Edna St. Vincent Millay, one or two more perhaps. Countee Cullen's affinity with these has been instantly recognized. But he has grown in sandier soil and taken up a murkier substance; it has taken a longer tap-root to reach down to the deep tradition upon which great English poetry is nourished, and the achievement is notable. More than a personal temperament flowers, a race experience blooms; more than a reminiscent crop is gathered, a new stalk has sprouted and within the flower are, we believe, the seeds of a new stock, richly parented by two cultures. It is no disparagement to our earlier Negro poets to say this: men do not choose their time, and time is the gardener.

Why argue? Why analyze? The poet himself tells us

> Drink while my blood
> Colors the wine.

But it is that strange bouquet of the verses themselves that must be mulled to be rightly appreciated. Pour into the vat all the Tennyson, Swinburne, Housman, Patmore, Teasdale you want, and add a dash of Pope for this strange modern skill of sparkling couplets,—and all these I daresay have been intellectually culled and added to the brew, and still there is another evident ingredient, fruit of the Negro inheritance and experience, that has stored up the tropic sun and ripened under the storm and stress of the American transplanting. Out of this clash and final blend of the pagan with the Christian, the sensual with the Puritanically religious, the pariah with the prodigal, has come this strange new thing. The paradoxes of Negro life and feeling that have been sad and plaintive and whimsical in the age of Dunbar and that were rhetorical and troubled, vibrant and accusatory with the Johnsons and MacKay now glow and shine and sing in this poetry of the youngest generation.

This maturing of an ancestral heritage is a constant note in Cullen's poetry. **"Fruit of the Flower"** states it as a personal experience:

> My father is a quiet man
>   With sober, steady ways;
> For simile, a folded fan;
>   His nights are like his days.
>
> My mother's life is puritan,
>   No hint of cavalier,
> A pool so calm you're sure it can
>   Have little depth to fear.
>
> And yet my father's eyes can boast
>   How full his life has been;
> There haunts them yet the languid ghost
>   Of some still sacred sin.
>
> And though my mother chants of God,
>   And of the mystic river,
> I've seen a bit of checkered sod
>   Set all her flesh aquiver.
>
> Why should he deem it pure mischance
>   A son of his is fain
> To do a naked tribal dance
>   Each time he hears the rain?
>
> Why should she think it devil's art
>   That all my songs should be
> Of love and lovers, broken heart,
>   And wild sweet agony?
>
> Who plants a seed begets a bud,
>   Extract of that same root;
> Why marvel at the hectic blood
>   That flushes this wild fruit?

Better than syllogisms, **"Gods"** states the same thing racially:

> I fast and pray and go to church,
>   And put my penny in,
> But God's not fooled by such slight tricks,
>   And I'm not saved from sin.

I cannot hide from Him the gods
   That revel in my heart,
Nor can I find an easy word
   To tell them to depart:

God's alabaster turrets gleam
   Too high for me to win,
Unless He turns His face and lets
   Me bring my own gods in.

Here as indubitably as in Petrarch or Cellini or Stella, there is the renaissance note. What body of culture would not gladly let it in! In still more conscious conviction we have this message in the **"Shroud of Color"**:

Lord, not for what I saw in flesh or bone
Of fairer men; not raised on faith alone;
Lord, I will live persuaded by mine own.
I cannot play the recreant to these;
My spirit has come home, that sailed the
    doubtful seas.

The latter is from one of the two long poems in the volume; both it and **"Heritage"** are unusual achievements. They prove Mr. Cullen capable of an unusually sustained message. There is in them perhaps a too exuberant or at least too swiftly changing imagery, but nevertheless they have a power and promise unusual in this day of the short poem and the sketchy theme. They suggest the sources of our most classic tradition, and like so much that is most moving in English style seem bred from the Bible. Occasionally one is impressed with the fault of too great verbal facility, as though words were married on the lips rather than mated in the heart and mind, but never is there pathos or sentimentality, and the poetic idea always has taste and significance.

Classic as are the fundamentals of this verse, the overtones are most modernly enlightened:

The earth that writhes eternally with pain
Of birth, and woe of taking back her slain
Laid bare her teeming bosom to my sight,
And all was struggle, gasping breath, and fight.
A blind worm here dug tunnels to the light,
And there a seed, tacked with heroic pain,
Thrust eager tentacles to sun and rain.

Still more scientifically motivated, is:

Who shall declare
   My whereabouts;
Say if in the air
   My being shouts
Along light ways,
   Or if in the sea
Or deep earth stays
   The germ of me?

The lilt is that of youth, but the body of thought is most mature. Few lyric poets carry so sane and sober a philosophy. I would sum it up as a beautiful and not too optimistic pantheism, a rare gift to a disillusioned age. Let me quote at the end my favorite poem, one of its best expressions:

"The Wise"

Dead men are wisest, for they know
How far the roots of flowers go,
How long a seed must rot to grow.

Dead men alone bear frost and rain
On throbless heart and heatless brain,
And feel no stir of joy or pain.

Dead men alone are satiate;
They sleep and dream and have no weight,
To curb their rest, of love or hate.

Strange, men should flee their company,
Or think me strange who long to be
Wrapped in their cool immunity.

George H. Dillon (essay date 1926)

SOURCE: "Mr. Cullen's First Book," in *Poetry,* Vol. 28, No. 1, April, 1926, pp. 50-3.

[*In the following review of* Color, *Dillon notes the tendency of Cullen's verse to become "stilted and prosy" and finds the poet most successful when he is "spare and direct."*]

This first volume of musical verses [*Color*] offers promise of distinction for its author, shows him to be a young poet of uncommon earnestness and diligence. Serious purpose and careful work are apparent in all of his poems. One feels that he will cultivate his fine talent with intelligence, and reap its full harvest. He has already developed a lyric idiom which is not, perhaps, very unusual or striking in itself, but which he has learned to employ with considerable virtuosity. To be sure, the many elements which have entered that reservoir below the threshold of his consciousness have undergone as yet no thorough chemistry. But although some of his poems are flagrantly reminiscent, not only in detail but in outline, one never catches him resting idly on his fulcrums. Indeed, he accepts them with such dignity and appreciation, and often uses them to such telling advantage, that one is inclined to call attention to them only by remarking that he "has taken his own where he has found it."

Perhaps the only protest to Mr. Cullen that one cares to insist on is against his frequent use of a rhetorical style which is surely neither instinctive in origin nor agreeable in effect. "Yet do I marvel," he writes, instead of, "And yet I marvel," the natural and fitting phrase; and many of his poems are marred by similar distortions. Lofty diction in poetry, when it is unwarranted by feeling (and therefore, intermediately, by rhythm) is liable to seem only stilted and prosy. Neither can personal emotion survive conventional expression. It is because of this, I think, that I find Mr. Cullen's longest poem, **"The Shroud of Color,"** the least moving of any he has written.

Mr. Cullen is most winning when he is most spare and direct. In **"The Wise,"** which seems to me very nearly a perfect poem, he achieves great intensity with an almost colloquial style:

> Dead men are wisest, for they know
> How far the roots of flowers go,
> How long a seed must rot to grow.
>
> Dead men alone bear frost and rain
> On throbless heart and heatless brain,
> And feel no stir of joy or pain.
>
> Dead men alone are satiate;
> They sleep and dream and have no weight,
> To curb their rest, of love or hate.
>
> Strange, men should flee their company,
> Or think me strange who long to be
> Wrapped in their cool immunity.

Some of the dramatic lyrics communicate a sense of life so quickly and sheerly that they seem like heart-beats. Here is one called **"Caprice,"** to choose from a dozen others equally illustrative:

> "I'll tell him, when he comes," she said,
> "Body and baggage, to go,
> Though the night be darker than my hair,
> And the ground be hard with snow."
>
> But when he came with his gay black head
> Thrown back, and his lips apart,
> She flipped a light hair from his coat,
> And sobbed against his heart.

This is an epitaph **"For a Lovely Lady"**:

> A creature slender as a reed,
> And sad-eyed as a doe,
> Lies here (but take my word for it,
> And do not pry below).

And here is **"A Brown Girl Dead"**:

> With two white roses on her breasts,
> White candles at head and feet,
> Dark Madonna of the grave she rests.
> Lord Death has found her sweet.
>
> Her mother pawned her wedding-ring
> To lay her out in white;
> She'd be so proud, she'd dance and sing
> To see herself tonight.

Poems like these have a kind of mysterious simplicity a note which Mr. Cullen has struck untutored. Here, translated into poetry, is something of the freshness and sever-

ity of vision toward the profound commonplaces of life and death; and something of the poignant naïveté of expression that one associates with the great Russian storytellers. In reading such poems, one is aware of a tender and sensitive soul commanding language of ingenuous sweetness and accuracy.

Perhaps this distinctive quality of this poet's work is of some racial significance, but such a speculation is hardly relevant here. Much can be said about the unique interest of Mr. Cullen's book as a personal document; but this is a general rather than a special interest, and has already been widely emphasized. I have thought it more appropriate here to consider Mr. Cullen's work simply as poetry, especially since it is so highly deserving of such consideration.

Robert T. Kerlin (essay date 1926)

SOURCE: "Singers of New Songs," in *Opportunity,* Vol. 4, No. 41, May, 1926, pp. 162-64.

[*In the following excerpt, Kerlin maintains that Cullen's poems in* Color *contain particular insights and wisdom that are absent from the works of Caucasian poets.*]

In 1923 a Negro student in New York University won second place among the seven hundred undergraduates of American colleges who competed for the Witter Bynner prize in poetry. The next year he was still second, and in 1925 he was first. This was Countee Cullen, aged 23. On the publication of **"The Ballad of the Brown Girl"** I wrote, in *The Southern Workman,* that it placed Mr. Cullen by the side of the best modern masters of the ballad— Morris, Rossetti, and any others that may be named. Of course it is imitative—all modern ballads are, and are successful just in degree as they are imitative of the old folk ballads. But there is a felicity possible in imitation, and a creativeness, which are capable of producing the thrill we expect of supreme art. I still think, **"The Ballad of the Brown Girl"** worthy of the praise I gave it.

But now appears Mr. Cullen's first book [*Color*] and this ballad is nowhere in it! My first thought is, What must be the severity of self-criticism, and the audacity, of a poet of twenty-three who will exclude from his book a poem of such merit? It was a most conceited thing to do. But I have no sooner read his ballad entitled **"Judas Iscariot"** than I am able to guess the reason of the exclusion. Like the author, I am willing to rest his case upon this ballad without the assistance of **"The Brown Girl."**

I return to his apologia, as it were, **"To You Who Read My Book"**:

> Juice of the first
> Grapes of my vine,
> I proffer your thirst
> My own heart's wine.
> Here of my growing

A red rose sways,
Seed of my sowing,
And work of my days.

It is in an altogether manly strain, albeit with an undertone of melancholy—Mr. Cullen did well to entitle his book **Color**. It is impregnated with color. Something exotic to the Caucasian, call it *color,* call it *Africanism,* call it what you will, impregnates the fabric of Cullen's verse as the murex dye impregnated the cloth of the Tyrian looms, and made the purples worn by kings. A brown girl is thus brought before you:

Her walk is like the replica
Of some barbaric dance
Wherein the soul of Africa
Is winged with arrogance.

An Atlantic City waiter whose subtle poise as with his tray aloft he carves dexterous avenues, as it were through a jungle, on his way to serve choice viands to ladies who pause and gaze, is thus presented:

Sheer through his acquiescent mask
Of bland gentility,
The jungle flames like a copper cask
Set where the sun strikes free.

In such imagery we have a poet who is going on his own. We have here a Negro poet who is as sure of himself as Keats was. [I particularly esteem the two poems **"Black Magdalens"** and **"Simon the Cyrenian Speaks,"** primarily for] their merits as poems, and incidentally because they exemplify, as the **"Judas Iscariot"** already mentioned does, the Negro's easy penetration to the meanings we of the occidental and white mind so easily miss in "our" gospel narratives. . . .

These two poems, which are quite typical of Mr. Cullen's quality as a poet, suggest something in the way of spiritual discernment and wisdom which is the Negro's peculiar possession. It is the same quality which appears in Mr. Roland Hayes' singing—a quality that so gets hold of your heart. It surely omens a new element in our literature, art and life. Will the Negro be duly impressed with the idea that he has this contribution to make? And, a more important question, will the Caucasian, proud of his "supreme Caucasian mind," be humbly or otherwise receptive?

Herbert S. Gorman (essay date 1927)

SOURCE: "Countee Cullen Is a Poet First and a Negro Afterward," in *The New York Times Book Review,* August 21, 1927, pp. 5, 17.

[*In the following excerpt, Gorman states that Cullen's poetry transcends racial boundaries.*]

Countee Cullen's **Copper Sun** is his second volume and it is encouraging to observe that it reveals a profounder depth than **Color**. Any exploration of his substance of being will immediately reveal inborn negro impulses disciplined by culture and an awareness of restraint and the more delicate nuances of emotionalized intellect. A primitive naïveté underlies his work, yet, curiously enough, the surface values are sophisticated enough. There are times when he is the more obvious negro poet sentimentalizing about himself and his people, but the admirable aspect of his work is the direct evidence in **Copper Sun** that he transcends this limitation time and again and becomes sheer poet. What is meant here is that his best work does not suggest the descriptive "negro poet" any more than the work of Mark Van Doren, for instance, suggests the "white poet." He is unlike Langston Hughes, who is nearly always the "negro poet." It is surely no disparagement to assert that a writer is the poet of a race, for Walt Whitman was one and so is William Butler Yeats; but there is a cul-de-sac into which the free mind of the poet should not be driven. That cul-de-sac does not contain the universal gestures of a groping humanity, but the peculiar emanations of a specific people. The great national poets transcended it. Homer for instance, being as universal as he was Greek. Countee Cullen, because he escapes this cul-de-sac so often, speaks as much for the younger era of poets in America as he does for the negro.

E. Merrill Root (essay date 1927)

SOURCE: "Keats in Labrador," in *Opportunity,* Vol. 5, No. 9, September, 1927, pp. 270-71.

[*In the following review of* Copper Sun, *Root contends that Cullen's poetry demonstrates a vitality that sets it apart from the predominantly intellectual and lifeless verse of the day.*]

Modern American poetry has had two chief faults: a hard clear technique; a hard objective content. With brilliant exceptions, like Edna Millay (that tiger, tiger burning bright), or like the grace notes of Robert Frost (that eagle-sized lark), it has seldom been poetry that sings and that shines. If it shone—as in Amy Lowell's scissor-blades and patchwork, it did not sing; if it sang—as in the jazz records to be played on the Victrola of Vachel, it did not shine. Much of the rest of it has not been Christian enough to escape the hard intellectuality of Puritanism: like the bleak Pilgrim Fathers, it wears black: it knows little of the Lilies of the Field and the Many Mansions. It has been "just a plate of current fashion" with "not a softness anywhere about it," like the formal lady in "Patterns"; it has seldom been "Eve with her body white, supple and smooth to her slim fingertips."

Therefore I, for one, welcome poetry that sings and that shines; poetry that is no plumed hearse, but a dancing star.

I who adore exotic things
Would shape a sound
To be your name, a word that sings
Until the head goes round.

So sings Countee Cullen, unashamed. And it is no boasting: it is a literal description of his sensuous rhythms, his translation of heart's blood into words, his imagery that is not the decorative cameos of the Imagists, but the suns that roar through heaven and the scarlet flowers that grow mystically from the black and humorous earth. Here is poetry that is not written with phosphorescent brains, but with the soul's blood. Here is poetry that soars on deep-damasked wings.

Countee Cullen's title is *Copper Sun*. And in the book we are transported into a fresher world, where the sun is a blazing copper drum sounding reveille over the morning hills, and the trees are heavy with the "golden increment of bursting fruit," and the delicate reeds quiver under the feet of the wind, that angel of the unknown color.

Technically considered, the book is a delight and a triumph. Whether we stir to the rolling echoes and the dying fall of its music, as in that haunting and perfect poem, **"Threnody"**; or thrill to the subtlety of emotion incarnated in the simplicity of art—the tears, idle tears of **"Pity the Deep in Love"**; or marvel at imagery as inevitable as the green hills haloed with the copper sun of morning, we acknowledge Countee Cullen a master of living magic.

> One to her are flame and frost;
> Silence is her singing lark;
> We alone are children, lost,
> Crying in the dark.
> Varied feature now, and form,
> Change has bred upon her;
> Crush no bug nor nauseous worm
> Lest you tread upon her.
>
> Pluck no flower lest she scream;
> Bruise no slender reed,
> Lest it prove more than it seem,
> Lest she groan and bleed.
> More than ever trust your brother,
> Read him golden, pure;
> It, may be she finds no other
> House so safe and sure.
>
> . . . . .
>
> Lay upon her no white stone
> From a foreign quarry;
> Earth and sky be these alone
> Her obituary.

Such lines seem the earth's own green hieroglyphs. To paraphrase the poet: Earth and sky be these alone Poetry's commentary!

And (as always) it is only out of the fullness of the blood that the mouth chants. These are no Arrows of Scorning shot by an impotent brain, no acrobatics of a honeyless wasp, no finger-exercises by the Precocious Child trying to see how different he can be from Mr. Longfellow. These are pulses translated into poetry. Here is the revolt, fierce but forgiving, of **"From the Dark Tower"**; the

"grief wound up to a mysteriousness" of **"Threnody,"** where personal anguish merges into pantheistic mysticism; the ache and ecstasy of love, sung with a simple inevitability that equals A. E. Housman, and a breadth of range that surpasses Edna Millay; the fear of all flesh (as in **"Protest"**) for the dark halo . . . Here are magic casements opening on many seas: and Countee Cullen has himself stood at every casement and looked from each with his own eyes. His is no poetry at second brain: no tinsel of words, but a tissue of experience. He is no mirror but a face; no phonograph but a voice.

In lyricism more musical and rich, in a subtle sensuousness which shows that the years have brought him more philosophic eyes, *Copper Sun* surpasses *Color*. If I find any luck and lapse, I miss those great poems, those longer epics of philosophy, **"Heritage"** and **"Shroud of Color."** I want to see Countee Cullen again fight a campaign and not merely a battle, and with full pomp and circumstance justify man's ways to God. Yet tho he perhaps shows a relapse in scope of attack, he shows an advance in the quality of his philosophy. He is still death-shadowed; he still feels the "little room" which fifty—or fifty times fifty—Springs give to our immortal longings; but he wanders less resolutely in the Valley of the Shadow. In **"Threnody,"** in **"Epilogue,"** he shows a philosophic advance: he steps out of the dark halo that hovers over us as from an eagle's wings: he sees death as it is—an accident and not an essence—a relapse of the mortal body, but a return to the immortal energy: he may yet say, with Whitman, "To die is different from what we expect—and luckier." Also, in the **"Litany of the Dark Peoples,"** he has written one of the finest manifestoes of generosity that has been written in modern years: in serenity of vision and triumph it transcends even those great poems (which belong to our common race of Adam) **"Heritage"** and **"Shroud of Color."**

> And if we hunger now and thirst,
> Grant our witholders may,
> When heaven's constellations burst
> Upon Thy crowning day,
> Be fed by us and given to see
> Thy mercy in our eyes,
> When Bethlehem and Calvary
> Are merged in Paradise.

And Countee Cullen has developed, too, a new suggestion of fighting faith, a gay insouciance of Yea-saying, that is an advance. Thus the poet is one whose

> Ears are tuned to all sharp cries
> Of travail and complaining,
> His vision stalks a new moon's rise
> In every old moon's waning.
> And in his heart pride's red flag flies
> Too high for sorrow's gaining."

Hegelian paradox set to gay music (**"More than a Fool's Song"**), banter with the superstition called Fate (**"Ultimatum"**), the Higher Scepticism of Epilogue, show that he is, more than most of our modern American poets, a singer after sunset—and before sunrise. Whether he knows it or not, the best in him is shaking itself loose of Disillusionment and Decay and Fallen-petal Pessimism and all our resolute, dreary Apostles of the Unholy Catholic Church of Death Everlasting, from Masters to Mencken.

I am presumptuous, but if a critic has any worth, he must be conscious of the artist's unconscious: he must translate into idea the urge and ultimatum of the blood which the artist translates into image. What, then, is the *elan vital* back of Countee Cullen's blood?—An emphasis on color and on copper suns, on the subjective and the lyric, on the heart as well as the head, on poetry that shines and that sings: in short, on Romance. That is his peculiar worth: that makes him rare and radiant. And, in future, what should be his further path and destiny? It seems to me that, having done all he can do to give immortal poignance to the ache and transience of flesh, he should go beyond good and evil, above life and death, into spirit. In denial of negation and in acceptance of affirmation, in the victorious synthesis of animal and angel, in instincts made rhythmic with intellect, in spirit defeated yet superb like Spartacus . . . there, with Shelley, he will find "life, empire, and victory." My wish for him is that he leap to the forefront of the battle; that he become the first poet in modern America to accept the universe like a master-spirit. And my wish is not merely a love and a hope, but (thanks to the tocsin that already sounds in his poetry) a faith.

Countee Cullen belongs to a great race that, because of American savagery, stupidity, and jealousy, has had to walk the Valley of the Shadow. If he will rise above tragic circumstance, as we poor dwellers on Waste Lands and Main Streets are not strong enough to do, if he will (to quote Carlyle) "seek within himself for that consistency and sequence which external events will always refuse him (and us)," he can be the first American poet to become Nietzsche's child—"Innocence is the child, and forgetfulness, a new beginning, a game, a self-rolling wheel, a first movement, a Holy Yea."

Meanwhile, tho he is not yet the spiritual leader of a new day, he is one of the few poets of our generation. He sings and shines like Edna Millay, and has more wholesome life in his blood; his blood (if not always his brain) is world-accepting and life-affirming like Frost's grey elfin mysticism, and he has richer color, tho not an idiom as unique and great as Frost's tang and accent.

Countee Cullen loves Keats; therefore he will know what I mean—and how much I mean—when I say that in his sensuous richness of phrase, in his sweetness of heart, in his death-shadowed joy, he reminds me of Keats. The great tree has fallen: but from the mystic root comes up this shoot and sapling with the same rich leaves. Countee Cullen, it seems to me, is much what the young Keats would be if he wore flesh again in this minor and maddening age, this fever and fret of a fiercer Capitalism, this welter thru which war has plunged like a dinosaur trampling daffodils, this fox-fire age of cerebral realism, this Labrador of the soul which we call America.

Poetry (essay date 1928)

SOURCE: "Mr. Cullen's Second Book," in *Poetry*, Vol. 31, No. 5, February, 1928, pp. 284-86.

[*In the following review, the critic states that* Copper Sun *is of mixes quality yet the best poems of the collection are memorable.*]

Countee Cullen's second book [*Copper Sun*] has evidently suffered somewhat from the effort to pad the pages with poems written during his formative period. If the book's reputation were to stand on the quality of the more important poems about which it has been built, then it would take its place as a more mature volume than *Color*. Unfortunately readers and critics are apt to judge by the worst as well as by the best, and the average falls slightly below that of the first volume. The poems which mark the height of the author's achievement are **"Threnody for a Brown Girl,"** which won the John Reed Memorial Prize in 1925, **"From the Dark Tower," "The Spark," "The Wind Bloweth Where It Listeth,"** and a few other memorable lyrics of less length. The **"Threnody"** includes a stanza not in *Poetry*'s original version, one which mars the dignity of the elegy with the intrusion of race feeling:

> Plain to her why fevered blisters
> Made her dark hands run,
> While her favored fairer sisters
> Neither wrought nor spun.

It is difficult to be wholly fair in judging the poems of colored poets. The delight one feels in a poet is naturally intensified in inverse ratio with the advantages the poet has received, but in thecase of Mr. Cullen this ought not to apply. His intellectual background is that of a person of culture, of a Phi Beta Kappa, a Harvard student, reared in a metropolis and endowed with natural intellectual power. In his poetry the African tradition is negligible, and only the bitterness of his rebellion against biological injustice would betray his origin. Quite aside from any critical prejudice in his favor, there are poems in this volume which express great breadth of vision, and others which have a tenacious hold upon concrete and earthy beauty. For instance, the second part of **"Variations on a Theme"**:

> All through an empty place I go
> And find her not in any room;
> The candles and the lamps I light
> Go down before a wind of gloom.
>
> Thick-spraddled lies the dust about—
> A fit, sad place to write her name,
> Or draw her face the way she looked
> That legendary night she came.
>
> The old house crumbles bit by bit;
> Each day I hear the ominous thud
> That says another rent is there
> For winds to pierce and storms to flood.

My orchards groan and sag with fruit
Where Indian-wise the bees go round.
I let it rot upon the bough,
I eat what falls upon the ground.

For these, and for many other lines in **Copper Sun** no sympathy is asked or needed. They will stand very well upon their own merits.

Bertha Ten Eyck James (essay date 1930)

SOURCE: "On The Danger Line," in *Poetry,* Vol. 24, No. 5, February, 1930, pp. 286-89.

[*In the following review, James examines poetic style in* The Black Christ, and Other Poems.]

[*The Black Christ, and Other Poems*] proves again that Countee Cullen is an accomplished poet, but it shows also the danger in being an accomplished poet. He writes well, he uses the proper subjects, the strong verbs, rare adjectives and inverted order of modern verse, but the polished results seem to lack that lyric freshness that makes this type of verse worth while. To give an example, here is **"Nothing Endures"**:

> Nothing endures,
> Not even love,
> Though the warm heart purrs
> Of the length thereof.
>
> Though beauty wax,
> Yet shall it wane;
> Time lays a tax
> On the subtlest brain.
>
> Let the blood riot,
> Give it its will;
> It shall grow quiet.
> It shall grow still.
>
> Nirvana gapes
> For all things given;
> Nothing escapes,
> Love not even.

In this poem one may see charm and skill, and a complete unimportance. Too many of the lyrics here are of this type, even the more serious, such as **"The Foolish Heart"**:

> "Be still, heart, cease those measured strokes;
> Lie quiet in your hollow bed;
> This moving frame is but a hoax
> To make you think you are not dead."
>
> Thus spake I to my body's slave,
> With beats still to be answerèd;
> Poor foolish heart that needs a grave
> To prove to it that it is dead.

That is very skiful and quotable, but it shares the common lot of too much modern verse: it has nothing new to say and it says that in a fresh form, perhaps, but without a fresh feeling. The newness of a phrase does not lend life to an old idea; there must be a new point of view. When Andrew Marvell said, "Time's winged chariot hurrying near" he gave a fresh idea with his new image.

With us the time-honored emotions of love and decay are given intricate sentence-patterns, but one usually feels a lack of vitality in the resultant poem. Is it because we do not feel deeply? It may be that love and death seem less powerful, that man seems less important, but we still have trouble with us. Even though our verse suggests the Cavalier lyricists rather than the poets of a more deep-rooted emotional life, there are modern tragedies.

And the proof of this lies in the title-poem of this book, which comes last, **"The Black Christ."** It is an episode that must be associated with the deepest emotion, dedicated "hopefully" to white America. Reading it, one wishes to feel to the full the sorrow and triumph of the author, but there are barriers to that sympathy.

There are several ways of writing down such an event as the lynching of a brother for forgetting himself so far as to share love in springtime with a white girl. It could be done with violence and bitterness, or with simple realism. Countee Cullen has visualized this episode as the mirror of the death of Christ, and of the eternal Fair Young God; he makes a religious experience of it, told to further brotherhood and faith. Yet he writes it in very "poetic" language.

One has no right, perhaps, to criticize an artist's style; that is his own affair. But if it blur the force of the experience, one is inevitably disappointed.

This poem is written in an involved way, with free use of image and comparison. Such sentences as these from the speech of Jim seem to me too fanciful to be convincing:

> But when I answer I'll pay back
> The late revenge long overdue
> A thousand of my kind and hue,
> A thousand black men long since gone
> Will guide my hand, stiffen the brawn,
> And speed one life-divesting blow
> Into some granite face of snow.
> And I may swing, but not before
> I send some pale ambassador
> Hot-footing it to hell to say
> A proud black man is on his way.

The same practice of poetic law and manner that makes the briefer poems in this volume pleasant and musical and slight prevents this long poem from seeming to have a style as simple, devout and important as its theme.

Mildred Boie (essay date 1935)

SOURCE: "The Proof of the Poet," in *Opportunity,* Vol. 13, No. 12, December, 1935, pp. 381-82.

[*In the following excerpt, Boie offers a generally positive assessment of the verse in* The Medea, and Some Poems.]

"Some Poems" [in *The Medea, and Some Poems*] include a number of sonnets which are moving in the blending of emotion with thought, and almost perfect in form. The sonnet beginning "These are no wind-blown rumors," for example, contains phrases of inevitable beauty, of turns that charge remembered feelings with fresh intensity—"I know . . . That spring is faithless to the brightest bird." Its images are original and striking—

> At beauty's birth the scythe was honed, the nail
> Dipped for her hands, the cowls clipped for her
> face.

At the same time this and some of his other sonnets reveal flaws which seem to fleck most modern poets' use of this restricted and very conventional form—phrases and words not quite at ease in modern verse, phrases such as "nailed star," lists such as "My winged joy, my pride, my utmost mirth," rather worn generalizations such as "Two win from Time and Death a moment's grace," and, in other sonnets, occasional forced inversions and poetic elisions. But on the whole the sonnets are excellent.

So too are the short translations and some of the lyrics, though the later seem less successful. **"After a visit"** shows Mr. Cullen's singing and sincere appreciation of song, and rare and beautiful use of repetition—"I had known joy and sorrow I had surely known." **"Magnets"** is unified, intense yet light, and full of good lines like "The bitter mouth, its kissing done." But **"Any Human to Another,"** seems inharmonious in meter and subject, the very short lines being at once too jerky and too airy for the theme; and the nonsense rhymes are not delightful enough to justify their inclusion. The Scottsboro song reads like a forced occasional lyric that is self-conscious and not transmuted from social indignation into poetic truth.

This is a fault (if a generalization will be forgiven) which naturally but too often distracts the poets who happen to be Negroes from the objectiveness and fine playfulness which poetry of universal appeal and trueness requires.

Arna Bontemps (essay date 1947)

SOURCE: "The Harlem Renaissance," in *The Saturday Review,* Vol. XXX, No. 12, March 22, 1947, pp. 12-13, 44.

[*In the following excerpt, Bontemps contrasts Cullen with Langston Hughes, a fellow Harlem Renaissance poet, and offers a reminiscence of Cullen that subsequently became under-quoted.*]

New books of poems by Langston Hughes and Countée Cullen have appeared this year [*Fields of Wonder* and *On These I Stand,* respectively]. Some readers, no doubt, will be reminded of the shy, disarming bows made by these new writers before literary circles back in the twenties, when neither of them had yet finished college. In the case of Cullen, who died a year ago January, there will be a tendency to summarize as well as reflect. His stature as a poet will be estimated. With Hughes, of course, only a tentative and partial measurement can be attempted. But whatever evaluations may follow, whatever ranks and positions may finally fall to them in American literature, there isn't likely to be much question about their importance to the Harlem renaissance, so well remembered by many. They were its heralds and its brightest stars.

Except for their ages (there was a difference of about a year) and the fact that each was a Negro American, they were not much alike. An observer got the impression that while they were drawn together by the common experience of writing poetry, they actually had remarkably little in common. Their personal backgrounds, their reading, their moods, their attitudes, their tastes and preferences—everything one saw in their personalities was different. Even when they wrote poems on identical subjects, as in Cullen's **"Epitaph for a Poet"** and Hughes's "The Dreamkeeper," the contrast was striking. Cullen's stanza goes:

> I have wrapped my dreams in a silken cloth.
> And laid them away in a box of gold!
> Where long will cling the lips of the moth,
> I have wrapped my dreams in a silken cloth;
> I hide no hate; I am not even wroth
> Who found earth's breath so keen and cold.
> I have wrapped my dreams in a silken cloth,
> And laid them away in a box of gold.

Hughes put the same idea in these words:

> Bring me all of your dreams,
> You dreamers,
> Bring me all of your
> Heart melodies
> That I may wrap them
> In a blue cloud-cloth
> Away from the too-rough fingers
> Of the world.

Cullen's verses skip; those by Hughes glide. But in life Hughes is the merry one. Cullen was a worrier. If these traits in the two poets stood out with less emphasis in the days of cultural and artistic awakening among Negroes, twenty-odd years ago, they were nevertheless present. Equally evident, then as later, was Cullen's tendency to get his inspiration, his rhythms and patterns as wellas much of his substance from books and the world's lore of scholarship; while Hughes made a ceremony of standing on the deck of a tramp steamer and tossing into the sea, one by one, all the books he had accumulated before his twenty-first birthday. He need not have done it, of course, for he had never been chained to any tradition, and there isn't the least danger that he ever will be; yet this stern renunciation was in keeping with his old habit of using living models and taking poetic forms as well as content from folk sources.

Cullen was in many ways an old-fashioned poet. He never ventured very far from the Methodist parsonage in which he grew up in New York. A foster child, drawn into this shelter at an early age, he continued to cherish it gratefully. He paid his adopted parents a devotion, one is almost inclined to say a submission, only rarely rendered by natural sons. But it was all a part of his own choice. He did not stand in fear of his foster parents. He simply preferred pleasing them to having his own way. It is possible that he felt or imagined the cords of this relationship to be the kind that would not stand strain, but the decisions he made later do not seem to support such an idea.

By the time he was half way through DeWitt Clinton High School, Countee Cullen had written at least one of the poems on which his reputation was to be built. Those readers who now complain of Pre-Raphaelite Victorian echoes in his work, perhaps find significance in the fact that the composition was called **"I Have a Rendezvous with Life"** and that it was offered by the eager youngster "with apologies to the memory of Alan Seeger." At the time it came to notice, however, after winning a city-wide poetry prize for high school students, most responses were enthusiastic. Ministers in prominent pulpits took the poem as a text and preached sermons on it. Editorials quoted it. A cheerful shout went up.

Here, some voices cried, was a poetic voice—a Negro at that—who thought that life was good. Here was a fledgling singer, praise God, who gave you a tune you could hum. A Cullen rooting section, consisting mainly of readers who had little truck with most of the new poetry, stood by anxiously. A year or two passed. Cullen became a conspicuous high school graduate, took home medals and ribbons galore, and went to college fully dedicated to literature. He continued to be a good student—good enough, in fact, for Phi Beta Kappa—but his pride was in his poetry.

About half of his "best poems" were written while he was a student of New York University, and it was during these years that he first came up for consideration as an authentic American writer, the goal to which he aspired. Up at "The Dark Tower," a gathering place of awakened Harlem, the very name of which was taken from one of Cullen's sonnets, there was never any doubt that he would make it. At the *Opportunity* banquets, where prizes were awarded by that once-influential magazine in order to encourage the efforts of new Negro writers, it was taken for granted that Cullen was in. Before he finished college, his poems had been published in a dozen or more magazines, including *The Nation, Poetry, The American Mercury,* and *Harper's. Color,* the first collection of these lyrics, made a solid impression in 1925, the year in which Cullen cele-

brated his twenty-second birthday, and *Copper Sun* and *The Ballad of the Brown Girl,* both presenting more of his undergraduate output, followed in 1926 and 1928. Meanwhile, the young poet went abroad on a Guggenheim Fellowship, perhaps, as much as anything else, to take stock.

His stay in France was extended a year beyond his original plans, but even that wasn't long enough. His springtime leaves had fallen, and he was still waiting for a new season to bring another yield. He kept writing as a matter of habit, and the little shelf of his books increased steadily, but that wasn't the real thing; that wasn't what he was waiting for. A decade later he wrote to a friend: "My muse is either dead or taking a twenty-year sleep. . . ."

The literary and artistic movement which Cullen and Hughes highlighted was regarded sympathetically, but it was never quite certified or approved as a phase of America's cultural growth. In the twenties the Negro's gifts were still departmentalized. There were poets in the United States, and there were Negro poets. There were musicians, and there were Negro musicians. There were painters, and there were Negro painters. Cullen abhorred this attitude. Almost his only public comments about the art in which he expressed himself were pleas for an evaluation of his work strictly on its merits, without racial considerations. He was to learn, however, that this was no small matter.

Cullen did not live to see another springtime resurgence of his own creative powers comparable with the impulse that produced his first three books of poetry, the books which give his selected poems most of their lilt and brightness. He did live to see young poets like Gwendolyn Brooks and Robert E. Hayden coming up for the kind of evaluation he had hoped to receive. Before he was forty, a second generation of the renaissance, owing much to him and to Langston Hughes, was on the way.

European influences on Cullen's poetry:

[The poems in *The Medea, and Some Poems*] are the harvest of Mr. Cullen's pleasure trip to Europe. He responds to the beauty and to the social equality between races in France with gratitude and with imitation, or so it seems, of the American expatriates who have written verse since the war. His is a curious compound of the Baroque, the classic English sonnet and the flowers of Baudelaire. The verses do not fall below a high level of skill, feeling, and success. They mark a growth that will profit him, but America will not read his verses again with the avidity of the past until he comes back to his own and confronts his talent with realities.

I.F. "'Medea' to Scottsboro," in Christian Science Monitor, *Vol. XXVII, No. 236, September 4, 1985,*
p. 12.

Beulah Reimherr (essay date 1963)

SOURCE: "Race Consciousness in Countee Cullen's Poetry," in *Susquehanna University Studies,* Vol. 7, No. 2, June, 1963, pp. 65-82.

[*In the following excerpt, Reimherr argues that race is thematically central to Cullen's poetry.*]

The theme of race consciousness is one of several themes that run through the poetry of Countee Cullen. Nature, classical mythology, love, death, religion, the animals that failed to reach Noah's ark, even cats, captured his pen. Although Cullen stoutly defended his right to deal with any subject that interested him, James Weldon Johnson felt that the best of Cullen's poetry was motivated by race. . . .

In Cullen's poetry, the themes of love and religion hold a place of equal importance with the theme of race consciousness. Cullen was essentially a lyric poet; however, an awareness of color and the difference it made in America influenced his early poetry and ran as an undercurrent of frustration and depression in his later writing. There was a much greater consciousness of race in *Color* than in his subsequent books. One-third of the poems in *Color* have some reference to race, but only one-seventh of the poems in *Copper Sun* and *The Black Christ* have any racial overtones, and only two poems in *The Medea*.

There was a tension between Cullen's desire to be purely a lyric poet and his feelings of race-consciousness. Cullen stated: "Most things I write, I do for the sheer love of the music in them. Somehow or other, however, I find my poetry of itself treating of the Negro, of his joys and his sorrows—mostly of the latter, and of the heights and the depths of emotion which I feel as a Negro."

This was especially true of *Color,* which was impregnated with race consciousness. A reviewer of *Color* stated: "Every bright glancing line abounds in color," the designation used by Cullen for his racial poems [*Crisis,* March, 1926]. This critic pointed out that there are a few poems with no mention of color which any genuine poet, black or white, could have written. These are best exemplified by such poems as **"To John Keats, Poet At Spring Time,"** the numerous epitaphs, and the shorter poems on love, death, and the swift passing of life. A second group of poems have the adjectives "black," "brown" or "ebony" deliberately introduced to show that the author had color in mind. Such poems include **"To a Brown Girl," "To a Brown Boy," "Black Magadalens," "A Brown Girl Dead," "Bread and Wine," "Wisdom Cometh with the Years,"** and **"Threnody for a Brown Girl."** Others arise with full race consciousness. These include the many poems describing the prejudice of America toward the Negro and his reactions to discrimination. As stated by Owen Dodson, if one were to ask any Negro what he found in Cullen's poetry, he would say: "All my dilemmas are written here—the hurt pride, the indignation, the satirical thrusts, the agony of being black in America ["Countee Cullen," *Phylon,* First Quarter, 1946].

Cullen's first important poem to contain feelings of race consciousness is **"The Shroud of Color."** Before condemning it for its echoes of Milton and Edna St. Vincent Millay, it should be noted that the poem was written when Cullen was barely twenty. Yet Laurence Stallings considered it the most distinguished poem to appear in *American Mercury* for 1924.

Cullen introduced the poem by describing his joy in the beauty of the world and his idealism that saw in man "a high-perfected glass where loveliness could lie reflected." However, truth taught him that because of his color, man would kill his dreams. His color was "a shroud" that was strangling him, for it prevented others from seeing him as an individual.

> "Lord, being dark," I said, "I cannot bear
>   The further touch of earth, the scented air;
>   Lord, being dark, forewilled to that despair
>   My color shrouds me in, I am as dirt
>   Beneath my brother's heel. . . .

In a series of four visions God showed him that struggle, not suicide is the law of life. In the first vision, the struggle of the plant kingdom toward fulfillment was described. Some seeds thrust eager tentacles to sun and rain, climb, yet die; but others burst into triumphant bloom. The second vision revealed the struggle within the animal kingdom for life. In beautiful lines Cullen stated:

> And no thing died that did not give
> A testimony that it longed to live.
> Man, strange composite blend of brute and god,
> Pushed on, nor backward glanced where last he
>   trod.
> He seemed to mount a misty ladder flung
> Pendant from a cloud, yet never gained a rung
> But at his feet another tugged and clung.

But still, his conclusion was that, "those whose flesh is fair" can fight on. The scene shifted to heaven where even God had to struggle to preserve his mastery against the forces of Lucifer. The last scene was a vision of his own people, of their flourishing life of freedom in Africa followed by the dark days of slavery. In spite of having been enslaved, the Negro maintained faith in man. His grief now seemed "puny" in light of the suffering that his people had lived through. The poem thus ended on a note of racial pride, a salient feature of the Negro Renaissance.

> With music all their hopes and hates
> Were changed, not to be downed by all the fates.
> And somehow it was borne upon my brain
> How being dark, and living through the pain
> Of it, is courage more than angels have . . .
> The cries of all dark people near or far
> Were billowed over me, a mighty surge
> Of suffering in which my puny grief must merge
> And lose itself; I had no further claim to urge
> For death. . . .

Some of Cullen's best expressions of race consciousness appear in his sonnets. In an early sonnet, **"Yet Do I Marvel,"** he presented four paradoxes and then "gathering up an infinity of irony, pathos and tragedy in the final couplet" stated the problem that most vitally concerned him. According to James Weldon Johnson, these are "the two most poignant lines in American literature [*The Book of American Negro Poetry*, 1931]. When one is oppressed for a difference beyond his control, how can he sing?

> I doubt not God is good, well-meaning, kind,
> And did He stoop to quibble could tell why
> The little buried mole continues blind,
> Why flesh that mirrors Him must some day die,
> Make plain the reason tortured Tantalus
> Is baited by the fickle fruit, declare
> If merely brute caprice dooms Sisyphus
> To struggle up a never-ending stair.
> Inscrutable His ways are, and immune
> To catechism by a mind too strewn
> With petty cares to slightly understand
> What awful brain compels His awful hand.
> Yet do I marvel at this curious thing:
> To make a poet black, and bid him sing!"

Sorrow at the restrictions excluding Negroes from the mainstream of American life deepened in **"Hunger"** and **"The Dark Tower"** to a contemplation of suicide in **"Mood."** In **"Hunger"** Cullen expressed restlessness with the limited measure alloted him in a world that is "a pageant permeate with bliss." In **"The Dark Tower,"** Cullen cried out against the inferior position accorded Negroes. There was a place for both black and white in creation; surely then God did not intend subjection and sorrow to be the Negroes' eternal lot.

> We shall not always plant while others reap
> The golden increment of bursting fruit,
> Not always countenance, abject and mute,
> That lesser men should hold their brothers cheap;
> Not everlastingly while others sleep
> Shall we beguile their limbs with mellow flute,
> We were not made eternally to weep.
> The night whose sable breast relieves the stark,
> White stars is no less lovely being dark,
> And there are buds that cannot bloom at all
> In light, but crumple, piteous, and fall;
> So in the dark we hide the heart that bleeds,
> And wait, and tend our agonizing seeds.

In **"A Thorn Forever in The Breast,"** he continued the thought of how far short the actual world was from the ideal world, or for the Negro, the black world from the white. Should he through his writing struggle to bring the actual closer to the ideal? He implied futility when he noted that Christ, the world's greatest idealist, died on a cross.

> A hungry cancer will not let him rest
> Whose heart is loyal to the least of dreams;
> There is a thorn forever in his breast
> Who cannot take his world for what it seems;

> Aloof and lonely must he ever walk,
> Plying a strange and unaccustomed tongue,
> An alien to the daily round of talk,
> Mute when the sordid songs of earth are sung.
> This is the certain end his dream achieves:
> He sweats his blood and prayers while others sleep,
> And shoulders his own coffin up a steep
> Immortal mountain, there to meet his doom
> Between two wretched dying men, of whom
> One doubts, and one for pity's sake believes.

All was not sorrow in Cullen's racial poems for some joy and racial pride are expressed. According to Sterling Brown, the complete picture of the Negro in America is not all tragedy. In his words: "I have heard laughter, high spirited enjoyment of living and not always—or mainly, among the lucky few—but rather among the harassed many. The Negro has ability to take it, to endure, and to wring out of life something of joy" [*The Quarterly Review of Higher Education Among Negroes*, July, 1941]. **"Harlem Wine,"** according to Arthur Davis, glorified the "uncontrollable strength of black living, contrasting it by implication with the 'watery' life of the other group" [*Phylon*, Fourth Quarter, 1953].

> This is not water running here,
>   These thick rebellious streams
> That hurtle flesh and bone past fear
>   Down alleyways of dreams.

> This is a wine that must flow on
>   Not caring how not where,
> So it has ways to flow upon
>   Where song is in the air. . . .

An equal picture of joy appeared in **"She of the Dancing Feet Sings,"** in which a girl felt her singing and dancing were out of place in heaven; she would rather join the "wistful angels down in hell."

> And what would I do in heaven, pray,
>   Me with my dancing feet,
> And limbs like apple boughs that sway
>   When the gusty rain winds beat?

> And how would I thrive in a perfect place
>   Where dancing would be sin,
> With not a man to love my face
>   Nor an arm to hold me in?

Racial pride characterized the Negro Renaissance. Instead of trying to submerge their differences, Negro writers gloried in them. In **"A Song of Praise"** Cullen pictured dark girls as being lovelier and more passionate than white girls.

> You have not heard my love's dark throats,
>   Slow-fluting like a reed,
> Release the perfect golden note
>   She caged there for my need.

> Her walk is like the replica
>   Of some barbaric dance

Wherein the soul of Africa
  Is winged with arrogance . . .

My love is dark as yours is fair,
  Yet lovelier I hold her
Than listless maids with pallid hair,
  And blood that's thin and colder . . .

Africa was a source of racial pride. In the Negro's search for a heritage to which he could look with pride, Africa became his dream world. The discovery of ancient Negro sculpture revealed Africa as once the possessor of an advanced civilization. America was discovered as an alien country and Africa pictured as a land of beauty and peace in **"Brown Boy to Brown Girl."**

                 . . . in no least wise
Am I uncertain that these alien skies
Do not our whole life measure and confine.
No less, once in a land of scarlet suns
And brooding winds, before the hurricane
Bore down upon us, long before this pain,
We found a place where quiet waters run;
I felt your hand this way upon a hill,
And felt my heart forebear, my pulse grow still.

In this distant heritage there were Negroes who were kings and queens. Thus, Jim the handsome hero of **"The Black Christ"** was of "imperial breed." The heroine of **"The Ballad of The Brown Girl"** "comes of kings" and her dagger had once been used by "a dusky queen, in a dusky, dream-lit land." One of Cullen's best sonnets [**"Black Majesty"**] described the heroic rulers of Haiti who fought for their independence against Napoleon. . . .

Cullen's treatment of Africa was influenced by the twin concepts of primitivism and atavism. For the primitivists, the Negro according to Robert Bone, had an especial appeal as "he represented the unspoiled child of nature, the noble savage—carefree, spontaneous, and sexually uninhibited" [*The Negro Novel in America*]. Atavism, in this context, was the persistence in present civilization of "old remembered ways" from Africa, a concept employed by Vachel Lindsay in "The Congo." A yearning for the African jungles, a desire to dance naked under palm trees, the imagined throbbing of tomtoms, and the feeling of savages were the expressions of atavism.

Several writers exposed the falsity of associating primitivism and atavism with the Negro. Although Wallace Thurman in his novel *Infants of the Spring* suggested that Alain Locke, Carl Van Vechten, and Countee Cullen favored atavism, he showed its falseness in his satiric description of a literary meeting at which the main writers of the Negro Renaissance debated whether African origins still persist in the American Negro. In this debate (quite the best thing in the entire book) Claude McKay, a poet and novelist of Jamaican background, proved conclusively that African origins do not persist in the American Negro, but that he is a perfect product of the melting pot. Hugh Gloster, in criticizing Van Vechten's novel *Nigger Heaven*, stated that "Van Vechten knows, or

should know, that the Negro is no more primitivistic and atavistic than any other racial group that has been transplanted to America. He was merely a literary faddist capitalizing upon a current vogue and a popular demand" [*Infants of the Spring,* 1932]. Yet while the fad lasted, echoes of it appeared in Cullen's writing, especially in *Color*. In **"The Shroud of Color"** Cullen described the awakening of a chord long impotent in him.

Now suddenly a strange wild music smote
A chord long impotent in me; a note
Of jungles, primitive and subtle, throbbed
Against my echoing breast, and tom-toms sobbed
In every pulse-beat of my frame. The din
A hollow log bound with a python's skin
Can make wrought every nerve to ecstasy,
And I was wind and sky again, and sea,
And all sweet things that flourish, being free.

Here the poet looked with longing to Africa because of the imagined freedom enjoyed there. A fuller statement of atavism is given in Cullen's famous poem, **"Heritage."** He introduced the poem by asking just what Africa could mean to one three centuries removed. Although the sights and sounds of Africa were forgotten, within the Negro's blood beat the savage rhythm of his "heritage". . . .

In **"Atlantic City Waiter,"** Cullen indulged in the fantasy of a waiter being more dexterous in his footwork because of a heritage of "ten thousand years on jungle clues." The spirit of the jungle flamed through his acquiescent mask.

Sheer through his acquiescent mask
Of bland gentility,
The jungle flames like a copper cask
Set where the sun strikes free.

To conclude, Cullen knew nothing about Africa save what he had gleaned in the course of his considerable reading. In the words of Arthur Davis, "Africa in his poems is not a place but a symbol; it is an idealized land in which the Negro had once been happy, kingly, and free."

Only five of Cullen's poems of love and friendship possess race consciousness, and in these five, his treatment was stereotyped rather than factual. **"Tableau"** pictures the absence of prejudice in children, but its presence in adults who have been conditioned by society.

Locked arm in arm they cross the way,
  The black boy and the white,
The golden splendor of the day,
  The sable pride of night.

From lowered blinds the dark folk stare,
  And here the fair folk talk,
Indignant that these two should dare
  In unison to walk. . . .

A more subtle picture of interracial friendship appears in **"Uncle Jim"** from *Copper Sun*. It is a puzzling but interesting poem. Because of the disagreement between the young man and his bitter uncle about white people, one can assume that the young man's friend was white. When he was with his friend, his mind reverted to Uncle Jim. Does this suggest that he was wondering whether there was any truth in his uncle's attitude that white folks were different, not to be trusted?

> "White folks is white," says Uncle Jim;
>   "A platitude," I sneer;
> And then I tell him so is milk,
>   And the froth upon his beer.
>
> His heart walled up with bitterness,
>   He smokes his pungent pipe,
> And nods at me as if to say,
>   "Young fool, you'll soon be ripe!"
>
> I have a friend who eats his heart
>   Away with grief of mine,
> Who drinks my joy as tipplers drain
>   Deep goblets filled with wine.
>
> I wonder why here at his side,
>   Face-in-the-grass with him,
> My mind should stray the Grecian urn
>   To muse on Uncle Jim.

Cullen's attitude toward God and the church was frequently interwoven with race consciousness. In **"Simon the Cyrenian Speaks"** he assumed that the man who carried the cross of Christ was a Negro because be came from Cyrene, a country of North Africa. Cullen somewhat falsely attributed to the Cyrenian his own sensitivity about color.

> He never spoke a word to me,
>   And yet He called my name;
> He never gave a sign to me,
>   And yet I knew and came.
>
> At first I said, "I will not bear
>   His cross upon my back;
> He only seeks to place it there
>   Because my skin is black". . .
>
> It was Himself my pity brought;
>   I did for Christ alone
> What all of Rome could not have wrought
>   With bruise of lash or stone.

In **"Pagan Prayer,"** Cullen made his own acceptance of Christ contingent upon his people being fully accepted by society, especially by the church whose doors seemed barred from within. In this poem, he stated that his people are religious, but as for himself, he will not yield his heartuntil he sees more evidence that God is a God of both white and black people.

> Not for myself I make this prayer,
>   But for this race of mine
> That stretches forth from shadowed places
>   Dark hands for bread and wine.

> For me, my heart is pagan mad,
>   My feet are never still,
> But give them hearths to keep them warm
>   In homes high on a hill. . . .
>
> Our Father, God; our Brother, Christ,
>   Or are we bastard kin,
> That to our plaints your ears are closed,
>   Your doors barred from within?
>
> Our Father, God; our Brother, Christ,
>   Retrieve my race again;
> So shall you compass this black sheep,
>   This pagan heart. Amen.

He went so far in **"Heritage"** as to wish for a God who was dark, feeling then that "this flesh would know Yours had borne a kindred woe."

"The Black Christ" is Cullen's fullest synthesis of the racial with the religious theme. In this poem, as the title suggests, he came to the realization that Christ was also the God of the black people. It is both the story of a boy who was lynched and the journey from agnosticism to religious faith on the part of one who finds it hard to reconcile injustice with the rule of God. Cullen, through the description of the mother, presented the unquestioning faith of the older generation; through the speech of Jim and his brother, the doubts and agnosticism of the younger.

In the prologue, Cullen stated that the purpose of the poem was to restore the brother's faith. He also foreshadowed his conclusion that Christ is crucified afresh with every lynching and act of violence.

> How God, who needs no man's applause,
> For love of my stark soul, of flaws
> Composed, seeing it slip, did stoop
> And in the hollow of His hand
> Enact again at my command
> The world's supremest tragedy,
> Until I die my burthen be:
> How Calvary in Palestine,
> Extending down to me and mine
> Was but the first leaf in a line
> Of trees on which a Man should swing,
> World without end, in suffering
> For all men's healing, let me sing.

The parallel between lynching victims and the crucified Christ interested Cullen for he had already suggested the idea in a brief poem in *Copper Sun*.

> The play is done, the crowds depart; and see
> That twisted tortured thing hung from a tree,
> Swart victim of a newer Calvary.
>
>   **["Colors"]**

. . . . .

Could a God, who permitted lynchings to take place, actually exist?

"A man was lynched last night."
"Why?" Jim would ask, his eyes star-bright.
"A white man struck him; he showed fight.
    Maybe God thinks such things are right."
"Maybe God never thinks at all—
    Of us," and Jim would clench his small,
    Hard fingers tight into a ball.
"Likely there ain't no God at all,"

Although the mother expressed the belief that God, who made them, would guide and protect them, Jim and his brother felt God was too far away to be concerned about them. . . .

The brother's faith in God was restored as a result of a miracle. Jim was reincarnated.

The very door he once came through
To death, now framed for us anew
His vital self, his and no other's
Live body of the dead, my brother's.

He hurried in amazement to the lynching tree, but Jim's body was not there. Throughout the poem, Cullen parallels the crucifixion suggesting that Christ substituted himself for the doomed Negro. Although the handling of the miracle is ambiguous, the thought which Cullen wished to express, that God is not worlds away but present and concerned about the pains of his people, comes out clearly.

O lovely Head to dust brought low
More times than we can ever know
Whose small regard, dust-ridden eye,
Behold Your doom, yet doubt You die;
O Form immaculately born,
Betrayed a thousand times each morn,
As many times each night denied,
Surrendered, tortured, crucified!
Nor have we seen beyond degree!
That love which has no boundary;
Our eyes have looked on Calvary". . . .

In **"The Black Christ,"** the white girl and black boy forgot hue and race in their common appreciation of the beauty of spring. Cullen did not look "to a fusion of the races as the true end, but to a cooperation in which each would share with the other, its best gifts." In a speech just before his lynching, Jim expressed the common humanity uniting black and white.

This is the song that dead men sing:
One spark of spirit Godhead gave
To all alike, to sire and slave,
From earth's red core to each white pole,
This one identity of soul;

Cullen's poems possessing race consciousness steadily declined after *Color*. **"The Black Christ"** was a *tour de force* which he wrote to aid his people. Witter Bynner, a close friend of Cullen's, did not like the poem; he told Cullen not to let himself be crucified on a Guggenheim cross. There were only two poems possessing race con-

sciousness in *The Medea*: the two sonnets expressing his abiding love for France. In Europe, he found no discrimination, and as a result spent twelve summers there. In the first sonnet, he stated that life in France brought him warmth and completeness, and in the second sonnet, he stated his desire to die in France.

As he whose eyes are gouged craves light to see,
As he whose limbs are broken strength to run,
So have I sought in you that alchemy
That knits my bones and turns me to the sun;
And found across a continent of foam
What was denied my hungry heart at home.

[**"To France"**]

Cullen bid farewell to the racial theme in a poem in *The Black Christ*.

Then call me traitor if you must,
Shout treason and default!
Say I betray a sacred trust
Aching beyond this vault.
I'll bear your censure as your praise,
For never shall the clan
Confine my singing to its ways
Beyond the ways of man.

[**"To Certain Critics"**]

Thus, race consciousness has influenced Countee Cullen's poetry. It has added a mood of sorrow and protest to his poetry and influenced his choice of subject matter. Cullen's poems will live, for in the words of Arthur Davis, "They have made articulate the agony of racial oppression during a dark period in our continuing struggle for democracy."

More important, his poetry will live because of his lyrical beauty, manifested in such poems as **"Threnody for a Brown Girl"** and **"To John Keats, Poet at Spring Time."**

David F. Dorsey, Jr. (essay date 1969)

SOURCE: "Countee Cullen's Use of Greek Mythology," in *CLA Journal,* Vol. XIII, No. 1, September, 1969, pp. 68-77.

[*In the following excerpt, Dorsey argues that Cullen often invented the circumstances of Greek myths when incorporating them into his poetry in order to create irony and to achieve originality.*]

In *The Crisis* for November, 1929, Countee Cullen reviewed Claire Goll's novel, *Le Nègre Jupiter Enlève Europe*. Regarding the title, the review contains the following criticism:

The mythical allusion does not seem to me altogether well-chosen, for Europa was a young and beautiful maiden whom Jupiter, who never allowed the vast and exacting duties of godhead to interfere with his amatory holidays, bore off and seduced after having first transformed himself into a bull in order that Juno might not recognize her dallying and recreant spouse. But Jupiter was the king of all the gods, more of an autocrat than the former czars of all the Russias, and an *enlèvement* by him was a neat and finished job. On the other hand, irrespective of the inroad that black men in various capacities are making into European life, swallowed up as they are among the white population they are no more to be feared than a handful of sand added to the millions of grains that make the Sahara, no more than a cup of water thrown into the sea.

The *Clintonian 1921,* the yearbook for New York's Clinton High School, published a poem, **"Icarian Wings,"** by Cullen, who was then in the junior class:

> At dusk when drowsy zephyrs blow,
> My soul goes clad like Icarus
> To genie lands of summer snow;
> Rejuvenated impetus
> For laggard limbs is there; the lamp
> Of far Cathay, my passive slave,
> Works mighty change in court and camp,
> And none my ire have strength to brave.
>
> When silver rifts disturb the night,
> And herald light's diurnal reign,
> My airy oars my pleas requite
> With disobedience; in vain
> Cajoleries and arts; once more
> My lot to don the drab dull husk
> You know; by golden wings I store
> And wait the halcyon time of dusk.

Of course this poem lacks the technical perfection of his later works, but its employment of Greek mythology is characteristic of Cullen. The poet's soul flies only at night; in the day his wings refuse to fly. But Icarus flew in daylight; it was the sun which destroyed him. Or rather, it was the very obedience of his wings which caused his tragic fall. The young poet laments the intransigence of his wings in the sunlight. Should we not bow to the critic Cullen and deplore this distortion of the original myth? Or can we see in the poem a judicious fear of the sun and a conscious intent to avoid the fate of Icarus?

In *Color,* Cullen's first published book of poems, I have noted only two poems with classical allusions. Chimeras are found in **"The Shroud of Color."** The ancient chimera was a fire-breathing monster, usually with a lion's head a goat's body and a serpent's tail. It is above all an overwhelming threat to life, and without killing it, the hero Bellerophon could win no peace or happiness. In a sloppy poet we might ignore the ancient description and concentrate on the modern meaning of chimera: an idle fancy. But even current usage connotes a horrifying creature of one's imagination. And Cullen is never sloppy. Besides, he has told us to be careful in using classical allusions. Of his chimeras he says,

> My heart will laugh a little yet, if I
> May win of Thee this grace, Lord: on this high
> And sacrificial hill 'twixt earth and sky,

> To dream still pure all that I loved, and die.
> There is no other way to keep secure
> My wild chimeras; grave-locked against the lure
> Of truth, the small hard teeth of worms, yet less
> Envenomed than the mouth of Truth, will bless
> Them into dust and happy nothingness.
> Lord, Thou art God; and I, Lord, what am I
> But dust? With dust my place. Lord let me die.

The speaker wishes to cherish and protect his chimeras. He prays for death if that is necessary to preserve them. The ancient purveyor of death becomes the purpose for living and the only things worth dying for. Lest this conversion seem accidental, we may interrupt chronological order to examine another poem, **"That Bright Chimeric Beast."** Here the chimera, the unicorn, the phoenix and the leviathan are all sacred, inviolate, eternally resurrected, bright beasts "conceived yet never born, / Save in the poet's breast."

In Cullen's most famous poem, **"Yet Do I Marvel"** the poet 'doubts not' that God could

> Make plain the reason tortured Tantalus
> Is baited by the fickle fruit, declare
> If merely brute caprice dooms Sisyphus
> To struggle up a never-ending stair.

But this is almost blasphemous. The spectacular punishments of Tantalus and Sisyphus are intended as clear examples of the wages of sin. Everyone who knows how Tantalus suffers, knows also why. These are peculiarly inappropriate examples of the inscrutability of divine Providence. In context, of course, this problem dissolves. The poet wishes to question every aspect of God's justice, not merely those which scandalize us all. For such breadth he requires cases where the tradition feels no cause to doubt. For this, no examples could surpass those Cullen has chosen.

Before leaving *Color* I must mention the poem **"Judas Iscariot"** in order to note that Cullen's patterns of reversal are confined neither to Greek myth nor to brief passages. This whole poem is a narrative suggesting that, because Judas was Christ's most devoted disciple, Jesus assigned to him the hardest task in His divine, inscrutable design.

In **"One Day We Played a Game"** two lovers express the intensity of their love by investing each other with the names of famous lovers: Abelard and Heloise, Melisande and Pelleas, Tristan and Isolde, Ninus and Semiramis, Guinevere and Lancelot, Adam and Eve. A misguided game. Each pair named was marked by betrayal, separation, tragedy or sin. Only at the end do the players glimpse and reject the implicit omen.

In **"To Endymion"** the subtle use of myth is multi-leveled. The poem is entirely devoted to Keats, not Endymion. This conflation of the two is possible not simply because of Keats' and Endymion's embrace of spring woodlands and beauty in the nineteenth century poem, but also because Cullen's poem is addressed to the Keats supposedly sleeping in his grave. The entire poem presupposes, and finally declares, that Endymion is not asleep (as the myth would have it), but with the goddess of the woodlands, he rides as a star which can look down to see the untrue epitaph on his (that is Keats') grave.

In the dedicatory poem of *The Black Christ and Other Poems,* Cullen employs a very simplistic tone, rhyme scheme and rhythm. Allusions from Greek, Hebrew and various other mythologies abound. For example:

> That venemous head
> On a woman fair,—
> Medusa's dead
> Of the hissing hair.

and

> Pale Theseus
> Would have no need,
> Were he with us,
> Of sword or thread;
> For long has been set
> The baleful star
> Of Pasiphaë's pet
> The Minotaur.

In the first case we have Cullen's own brand of Medusa, which we shall see again: lethally attractive, but attractive. All the other extinct monsters mentioned are treated like the Minotaur. Nothing could seem more straightforward. But they are all replaced later in the poem by the modern, surviving monster, Mammon, who is repeatedly and vividly presented as a typical Cullenesque Medusa. Only then do we discover what we might have noticed before. Each moster listed is specifically stated to be attractive or desirable or loved by somebody. The point of the poem is that modern youth is, by crass materialism, rushing fervently to its own destruction *en masse*. To make the Minotaur and Medusa, dragons, griffins and basilisks all analogous to this situation required a most supple manipulation of contexts and conventional imagery. In that respect at least the poem is a *tour de force*.

In the first of two sonnets entitled **"Two Poets,"** the poet is asked to sing of ordinary, little people, or of war, instead of 'the love-mad lark' who died with last year's rose. He is then told

> . . . cease playing Orpheus; no blast
> You blow can raise Eurydice once dead.

The poet complies, but as the sonnet ends, he smiles at dawn and sheds tears "at sight of gulls departing from his skies."

The manipulation of the traditional significance of Orpheus and Eurydice is here only slight. The carping malcontents can only imagine functional song, and poetry devoted to past springs or past loves would only impress them if it resurrected what is lost. The nostalgic smile and tears of the poet suggest that his friends have missed the

point of poetry. The Greek allusion makes a strong case for them which is only refuted when we learn its irrelevance and their stupidity.

If one accepts the apparent religious sincerity of the poem, **"The Black Christ,"** one must be disturbed by certain discordant notes in the narrative. It offends at least a naive understanding of psychology and any romantic notions of heroism to imagine a rebellious, blasphemous youth could stand beside his brother while the brother is beaten to the ground, kicked senseless, dragged from their own home and lynched. In literature if not in life surely the futile defense is required here. But in this poem a devoted, passionate, admiring brother in exactly such a scene remains utterly passive, because helpless. This anomaly is expressed (but not explained) in intensely ironic allusions.

One of the most famous passages concerning ethics to be found in Lucretius' *de Rerum Natura* is the following, which begins his second book:

> What joy it is, when out at sea the storm winds are lashing the waters, to gaze from the shore at the heavy stress some other man is enduring! Not that anyone's afflictions are in themselves a source of delight; but to realize from what troubles you yourself are free is joy indeed. What joy, again, to watch opposing hosts marshalled on the field of battle when you have yourself no part in their peril! But this is the greatest joy of all: to stand alone in a quiet citadel, stoutly fortified by the teaching of the wise, and to gaze down from that elevation on others wandering aimlessly in a vain search for the way of life, pitting their wits one against another, disputing for precedence, struggling night and day with unstinted effort to scale the pinnacles of wealth and power.

Cullen's narrator describes his brother's 'arrest' as follows:

> They charged. I saw him stagger, fall
> Beneath a mill of hands, feet, staves.
> And I like one who sees huge waves
> In hunger rise above the skiff
> At sea, yet watching from a cliff
> Far off can lend no feeblest aid,
> No more than can a fragile blade
> Of grass in some far distant land,
> That has no heart to wrench, nor hand
> To stretch in vain, could only stand
> With streaming eyes and watch the play.

The passage in Lucretius continues:

> O joyless hearts of men! O minds without vision! How dark and dangerous the life in which this tiny span is lived away! Do you not see that nature is clamouring for two things only, a body free from pain, a mind released from worry and fear for the enjoyment of pleasurable sensations?

The essential demand of Epicurean ethics is that each man achieve his own individual *ataraxia,* that is, a state of philosophic calm which will render him emotionless in the face of any castastrophe whatsoever, especially if it happens to others rather than to himself. Love, whether familial or sexual, religious or reasoned, is virulently forbidden. And the most frequently cited and the most poetic expression of this doctrine to be found in Lucretius is this passage. In other words, Cullen's most passionate expression of love for a brother, of religious commitment, of frustrated pain attending someone else's suffering, borrows from language famous for preaching the exact antithesis of his views. Later, looking at the body hanging from the tree, the narrator says

> My Lycidas was dead. There swung
> In all his glory, lusty, young,
> My Jonathan, my Patrocles,
> (For with his death there perished these)
> And I had neither sword nor song . . .
> For vengeance nor for threnody.

But Lycidas died at sea, far from the poet who sang him. So Jonathan at war far from David. And Achilles avenged Patrocles though he knew it meant his own death. Each of these allusions emphasizes, by its inapplicability, the inaction of the speaker. The poet is calling attention to some inadequacy in the speaker's compromise with reality, even his perception of reality. The purpose of this discrepancy is to prepare the reader for others. Once we question the speaker's present convictions, we may note that the Black Christ's apparition after death imitates Jesus' in brevity and exceeds it in selectivity. The brother is not miraculously restored to life in a way which would warrant the paeons which conclude the poem and refute the blasphemies which precede the climax. Indeed a quite prosaic and typical hallucination could utterly explain the speaker's experience. But if God did indeed return the brother to life for a moment, He has demonstrated His power, but neither answered nor undermined any of the charges and criticisms which caused the boys' original agnosticism.

When these discordant passages of the story are assembled, the poem makes far better ammunition for the atheist than the Christian. And it can be no surprise to find another among Cullen's several statements of sometimes gravest and sometimes trivial reservations about Christian dogma and morality. But like **"The Shroud of Color,"** this blasphemous work is cloaked in a Christian disguise.

In **"After a Visit,"** the uninspired poet can neither speak nor write until a visit with other poets reminds him to await humbly the muse's favours. The description of despair begins

> Last night I lay upon my bed and would have slept;
> But all around my head was wet with tears. I wept
> As bitter dreams swarmed in like bees to sting my
>   brain,
> While others kissed like endless snakes forged in a
>   chain,
> Dull-eyed Euminedes estranging me and sleep,
> Each soft insidious caress biting me deep.
> And I wept not what I had done but what let go . . .

The Euminedes here are a long line of snakes who caressingly kiss the speaker, but of course a snake's kiss bites deep. But the Greek Euminedes have here been modified in critical ways. They are only three. Blood drips from their eyes, they wear in their hair snakes which they use as whips to flail their prey. The blows and bites are anything but insidious and soft. Finally, their purpose is to revenge the most outrageous crimes of murder and sacrilege. Sins of omission do not warrant their attention. Thus, by overtly mentioning and modifying every element in the inconography of the Euminedes save one, namely revenge, Cullen chisels out an image exactly suited to his purpose. And the major point of the allusion is stated only by allusion and gives the entire poem a level of meaning nowhere else even hinted. The poet feels that he is betraying those who love him because he has not written anything for a year. This betrayal neither warrants nor receives the flailing whips of the usual furies. Instead they kiss him lightly, as a snake would. These furies do not spew blood from their eyes because the poet has not shed blood. But as Greek furies do, they punish betrayal of kinfolk, albeit unwilling betrayal. If this interpretation is valid, it demonstrates that Cullen does not use mythological allusions for erudition or color, but as essential and very pregnant bearers of meaning.

In a sonnet Cullen imagines a poet who thinks himself immune to his former mistress' powers.

> And then he too, as I, will turn to look
> Upon his instrument of discontent
> Thinking himself a Perseus, and fit to brook
> Her columned throat and every blandishment;
> And looking know what brittle arms we wield,
> Whose pencil is our sword, whose page our shield.

The poet had supposed that he, like Perseus, had weapons and plans to survive any petrifying confrontation with Medusa. But Medusa conquers by the frightening horror of her appearance; the beloved by her beauty. Medusa repels; the mistress explicitly inveigles. A means for avoiding direct confrontation is Perseus' decisive strategem, but here the poet looks directly at the girl. Perseus' aim is murder; the poet's is love. Everything fits only when exactly reversed. The myth enhances the poem not through the similarities between Perseus and the poet, but through their differences. Ironic contrast is the essential function of the allusion to Perseus, and without him the whole sextet is meaningless, or at best insipid.

In the poem entitled **"Medusa"** the poet although forewarned has "stood to meet" an appropriately dangerous, but un-Hellenically beautiful Medusa. Now blinded and despoiled by her, with dire prophecies fulfilled, he still swears, "I know it was a lovely face I braved." Here the development and reversal of the symbolic reference is patent.

In another sonnet which begins, "Some things incredible I still believe," the unicorn, the phoenix and the leviathan are utterly accepted as real, but the worth of the beloved is questioned. Here the point depends on reversing the modern symbolic convention. Paramount examples of the impossible become proofs of the speaker's credulity.

One sonnet which is weak for several reasons ends by making an allusion to Greek myth and then declaring it gratuitous and inappropriate.

> My mother never dipped me in the Styx,
> And who would find me weak and vulnerable
> Need never aim his arrow at my heel.

I have tried to demonstrate that it is characteristic of Cullen's poetic technique to reverse the symbolic content of his allusions to Greek (and sometimes Christian) mythology, thereby doubling their semantic content, that is, their significance in his own contexts. It would be outside the scope of this paper to argue, but it is inevitable to suggest that this practice is intimately related to the severely paradoxical, aporetic and ironical content of his poetic genius. For subtle precision of form, however, his allusive technique surely "doth magnify the glory of our poet."

Eugenia W. Collier (essay date 1973)

SOURCE: "I Do Not Marvel, Countee Cullen," in *Modern Black Poets,* Prentice-Hall, Inc., 1973, pp. 69-83.

[*In the following excerpt, Collier cites Cullen's "From the Dark Tower" as a poem that expresses "the spirit of the Harlem Renaissance."*]

Literary historians and critics have a way of saying that the Negro poet faces a dilemma: Should he write as a Negro, or should he write as an American? They seem to mean, should he write poetry of social protest, or is he free to write of love and nature and God? I am convinced that this dilemma is only a straw man, created by the critics themselves.

Of course, Negro poets write of other subjects than social protest. Of the poets of the Harlem Renaissance, the fiery McKay wrote gentle lyrics of love, and tender poems of his childhood in Jamaica. Countee Cullen's delicate sonnets of love and life are among the most beautiful produced by the America of his time. Anne Spencer, writing in Lynchburg, produced lovely, feminine poetry on a wide range of subjects.

But for the Negro poet, from the slave poet Jupiter Hammon to our contemporary Julian Bond and LeRoi Jones, race is a basic and primary truth. In an article in *Phylon* in 1950, Gwendolyn Brooks said: "Every Negro poet has 'something to say.' Simply because he is a Negro, he cannot escape having important things to say. His mere body, for that matter, is an eloquence. His quiet walk down the street is a speech to the people. Is a rebuke, is a plea, is a school."

I submit that in those instances when the Negro poet effectively uses the advantages of his racial experience, combined with a high degree of artistry, he is writing the most American poetry possible. In his protest against hatred and injustice, in his pride in himself, in his quest for social and economic equality, he is expressing both the feelings and the logic which the Founding Fathers expressed in the Declaration of Independence; he is expressing the hope of the immigrant seeing the Statue of Liberty for the first time; he is, in short, voicing the American Dream. The Harlem Renaissance saw the first abundant outpouring of such poetry.

Since it is not possible for us here today to examine all, or even most of this poetry, I thought we might look in depth at three poems that represent some of the principal themes of the Negro poetry of the 1920's, and to cite incidentally other poems which deal effectively with these themes.

It seems to me that a poem which effectively expresses the spirit of Harlem Renaissance poetry is **"From the Dark Tower,"** by Countee Cullen. It is a restrained, dignified, poignant work, influenced in form by Keats and Shelley rather than by the moderns. Incidentally, The Dark Tower was actually a place on 136th Street in Harlem, where a number of the poets used to gather. Perhaps Cullen knew he was speaking for the others, too, when he wrote:

> We shall not always plant while others reap
> The golden increment of bursting fruit,
> Not always countenance, abject and mute
> That lesser men should hold their brothers cheap;
> Not everlastingly while others sleep
> Shall we beguile their limbs with mellow flute,
> Not always bend to some more subtle brute;
> We were not made eternally to weep.
>
> The night whose sable breast relieves the stark
> White stars is no less lovely being dark,
> And there are buds that cannot bloom at all
> In light, but crumple, piteous, and fall;
> So in the dark we hide the heart that bleeds,
> And wait, and tend our agonizing seeds.

Let us examine the symbolism contained in the poem. Here we have the often-used symbol of planting seeds and reaping fruit. This symbol invariably refers to the natural sequence of things—the hope eventually realized, or the "just deserts" finally obtained. The sowing-reaping symbol here effectively expresses the frustration that inevitably falls to the individual or group of people caught in an unjust system. The image of a person planting the seeds of his labor, knowing even as he plants that "others" will pluck the fruit, is a picture of the frustration which is so often the Negro's lot. The image necessarily (and perhaps unconsciously) implies certain questions: What must be the feelings of the one who plants? How long will he continue to plant without reward? Will he not eventually stop planting, or perhaps begin seizing the fruit which is rightfully his? In what light does he see himself? How does he regard the "others" who "reap the golden increment of bursting fruit"? What physical and emotional damage results to the laborer from this arrangement to which obviously he never consented?

In his basic symbol, then, Cullen expresses the crux of the protest peom which so flourished in the Harlem Renaissance. In poem after poem, articulate young Negroes answered these questions or asked them again, these questions and many more. And in the asking, and in the answering, they were speaking of the old, well-worn (though never quite realized) American ideals.

In the octave of the poem, Cullen answers some of these questions. The grim promise "not always" tolls ominously like an iron bell through the first eight lines. "We shall not always plant while others reap," he promises. By degrees he probes deeper and deeper into the actual meaning of the image. In the next two lines he points out one of many strange paradoxes of social injustice: that the "abject and mute" victim must permit himself to be considered inferior by "lesser men"—that is, men who have lost a measure of their humanity because they have degraded their brothers. This image is a statement of a loss of human values—the "abject and mute" victim of an unjust social system, bereft of spirit, silently serving another who has himself suffered a different kind of loss in robbing his fellow man of his potential—that is, the fruit of his seed. Perhaps this destruction of the human spirit is the "more subtle brute" of which the poet speaks. The last line of the octave promises eventual change in the words, "We were not made eternally to weep." Yet it implies that relief is still a long way off.

It is in the sestet that the poem itself blossoms into full-blown dark beauty. With the skill of an impressionist painter, the poet juxtaposes black and white into a canvas of brilliant contrasts. The night is pictured as being beautiful because it is dark—a welcome relief from the stark whiteness of the stars. The image suggests the pride in Negritude which became important in the Harlem Renaissance—the pride in the physical beauty of black people, the Negro folk culture which has enriched America, the strength which the Negro has earned through suffering. Cullen describes the night as being not only a lovely thing, but also a sheltering thing. The image of the buds that cannot bloom in light suggests that the Negro's experience has created a unique place for him in American culture: there are songs that he alone can sing.

The final couplet combines the beautiful and sheltering concept of darkness with the basic symbol of futile planting. The poet now splashes a shocking red onto his black and white canvas. The dark becomes not only a shelter for developing buds, but also a place to conceal gaping wounds. These two lines are quiet but extremely disturbing: "So in the dark we hide the heart that bleeds, / And wait, and tend our agonizing seeds." And the reader cannot help wondering, what sort of fruit will grow from these "agonizing seeds"?

Cullen's sonnet is one of the best produced by the Harlem Renaissance. Not every poet had Cullen's technical control over his medium, even over the exacting sonnet form. Yet with varying degrees of skill and with differing emphasis on various aspects, variations appeared on the themes that issued from the Dark Tower. Arna Bontemps

used the agrarian symbol in "A Black Man Talks of Reaping." Fenton Johnson years before had captured the utter despair of thwarted potential in "Tired." Claude McKay points out the quiet desperation of ceaseless and hopeless toil in "The Tired Worker." Langston Hughes treats with gentle humor the dignity and importance of the humble worker in "Brass Spittoons." Sterling Brown in "Old Lem" adapts a folk poem into a work of art to protest the system in which the toil of the worker is exploited.

Cullen's concept of black as being beautiful was not unique. Along with his increasing conviction of *who* he was and *what* he was, the Negro poet gained a realization that in the experience of the black masses was rich material for poetic expression. More and more, then, he turned to the music, the ballads, and the folklore that were his heritage. As he used the subject matter of the folk as a vehicle for his poetry, the Negro poet also began to utilize the language of the people.

James H. Smylie (essay date 1981)

SOURCE: "Countee Cullen's 'The Black Christ,'" in *Theology Today*, Vol. 38, No. 2, July, 1981, pp. 160-73.

[*In the following excerpt, Smylie analyzes Cullen's poem* "The Black Christ."]

Cullen was not the first to relate crucifixion and lynching, nor did he compose his song ["**The Black Christ**"] in a theological vacuum. Fundamentalists and Modernists of various grades were locked in abrasive public combat in the 1920s, and heirs of the "social gospel" were interpreting the benefitsof Christ's atoning work in terms of an oppressive economic system. The black community, including Cullen's minister father, could not help but be influenced by the doctrines blowing in the wind of the larger Christian community. But Cullen wrote primarily in the context of the black tradition.

As Eugene Genovese had reminded us, in *Roll, Jordan Roll* (1974), black religion was best expressed in experiential terms and with a fusion of the work of deliverer Moses and deliverer Jesus. Just as blacks found it natural to think analogically about the similarity between their own experience of bondage and that of the children of Israel in Egypt, so they thought of Christ's cry of dereliction and death on the cross in terms of their own dark experience with lynching. Blacks looked for identity, dignity, and for the assurance of God's presence with them.

Some whites considered lynching as the crime of crimes, and took steps to control and eliminate the scandal. There is some evidence that it illuminated the theological discussion of the atonement during these years. Conservatives sang about the cross as an "emblem of suffering and shame," on a "hill far away," not down at the end of a dusty street, and insisted that atonement be interpreted in a theological formula of a blood sacrifice made once for all to satisfy divine justice. Liberals were embarrassed with those who sang about the "power in the blood."

Among the liberal options, the young Cullen may have found the concerns of the "Social Gospel" of special interest. Worshiping, he probably sang the hymn of Methodist Frank Mason North, "Where cross the crowded ways of life / Where sound the cries of race and clan," and perhaps he heard his father speak about the prophet, Walter Rauschenbusch. In *A Theology for the Social Gospel* (1917), Rauschenbusch described the conflict between the kingdom of evil and the kingdom of God. Christ's crucifixion was described as a lynching in an analysis of the atonement, an act of mob spirit and mob action. Acquiescence of the civil and spiritual powers exposed the corruption of and cant about just society. Christ's death demonstrated God's solidarity with the human family, according to Rauschenbusch, not through sympathy expressed at a distance, but by self-sacrificing love, "the chief guarantee for the love of God and the chief incentive of self-sacrificing love in men." The cross was the motive and method of true believers.

Contemporary liberal professions about how Christ confirmed "the fatherhood of God and the brotherhood of man" may have sounded hollow to blacks confronted with lynching in which seemingly respectable Christians conspired. But perhaps Cullen's spirit resonated with something he got from North. It is worth noting that Herman Melville's *Billy Budd* was published posthumously in 1924 although we have no evidence that Cullen read it.

As a child of the manse, Cullen sang other hymns beside "On a hill far away" and "Where cross the crowded ways of life." "Go down, Moses" and "Were you there when they crucified my Lord" have been a special part of the black consciousness about God's relationship to the black. Cullen could also draw upon the work of sensitive black intelligentsia. In *Caroling Dusk*, Cullen collected the poems of a number of Negroes, as they were called in those days, who had reflected on deliverance in the black community. One was James Weldon Johnson, who published *God's Trombones* (1927) to preserve as well as pay tribute to "Black and Unknown Bards" who "sang a race from wood and stone to Christ" and who spoke of Moses and Jesus. In these verse sermons, Johnson recalled the importance of "The Crucifixion" for blacks. He sang of the "gentle Jesus," the "burdened Jesus," the "sorrowing Jesus," the "blameless Jesus," the "loving Jesus," the "lamb-like Jesus," through whom God, with tenderness over the human condition identified and dignified life's sufferers. Johnson placed the sermon on Moses after that on the crucifixion. In it he addressed the "sons of Pharaoh" and warned of the "Judgment Day" when "God's a-going to rain down fire." W. E. B. DuBois was another who wrote poignantly of black religion. He published *The Soul of Black Folks* in 1903, the year of Cullen's birth, in which he indicted lynching. In *Darkwaters* (1920), DuBois collected some of his own prose and poetry in a powerful put-down of the soul of white folk. In "A Litany of Atlanta," written after an outbreak of violence against blacks in 1906, DuBois cried out to the "blind" God, the "silent" God, the "deaf" God:

> Bewildered we are, the passion-tost, mad with the
> madness of a mobbed and mocked and murdered

people; straining at armposts of Thy Throne, we raise our shackled hands and charge Thee, God, by the bones of our stolen fathers, by the tears of our dead mothers, by the very blood of Thy crucified Christ: What meaneth this? Tell us the Plan: give us the sign!

In "The Prayers of God," DuBois directly connected crucifixion with lynching. Reflecting on the judgment scene in Matthew 25, DuBois puts into the mouth of a troubled white:

> Thou?

> Thee?

> I lynched Thee?

When did I lynch you, Lord? Inasmuch as you lynched one of the least of these "niggers," you lynched me. DuBois wanted the God of the "lamb-like Jesus" to vindicate those who suffered from the oppressive pharaohs of this world.

Writing in his preface to *Caroling Dusk,* in which he included poems of Johnson and DuBois, Cullen claimed that his problem was a conflict between his Christian-self and his pagan-self. He exposed this struggle in his first book of verse, *Color.* "What is Africa to Me?" he asked in one. In another, he offered a **"Pagan Prayer,"** using some "Social Gospel" phrases and addressing his own need:

> Our Father, God; our Brother, Christ,
>   Retrieve my race again;
> So shall you compass this black sheep,
>   This pagan heart. Amen.

In **"Heritage,"** Cullen expressed this tension even more poignantly. He confessed that he belonged to "Jesus of the twice-turned cheek," but he was uneasy about making Jesus, with "precedent of pain," black like himself:

> Lord, I fashion dark gods, too,
> Daring even to give You
> Dark despairing features where,
> Crowned with dark rebellious hair,
> Patience wavers just so much as
> Mortal grief compels, while touches
> Quick and hot, of anger, rise
> To smitten cheek and weary eyes.
> Lord forgive me if my need
> Sometimes shapes a human creed.

Cullen did not resolve his tension in these early poems. As early as 1922 he began to link Christ's crucifixion with the *via dolorosa* of the American black. He wrote of **"Christ Recrucified"**:

> The South is crucifying Christ again

> . . . . .

> Christ's awful wrong is that he's dark of hue
> The sin for which no blamelessness atones;

But lest the sameness of the cross should tire,
They kill him now with famished tongues of fire,
And while he burns, good men, and women, too,
Shout, battling for his black and brittle bones.

This early cry of the heart against this obscene violence of the lynch mob and the lynch spirit, turning from rope to faggot, reverberated in Cullen's heart throughout the 1920s. In 1927, Sacco and Vanzetti were hanged in Boston, and Cullen expressed his disagreement with the decision and with capital punishment in general. Apparently finding no comforting analogy in his pagan-self, he turned to his Christian-self for insight to help him with his excruciating problem.

Cullen transformed his problem into one of the human condition. How does "Calvary in Palestine" extend down for "all men's healing," Cullen asked in the opening lines of **"The Black Christ"**? Christ "by his loss," bought "redemption on a cross." But how? Cullen does not interpret Christ's crucifixion in terms of a sacrifice to satisfy wounded honor or a debt for human sin, but rather in terms of *theo pathes,* the God who is with us and for us in our human agony.

Cullen had explored other interpretations of the atonement. In **"The Shroud of Color"** which appeared in *Color,* he described the awesome clash between cosmic powers, between God and evil, God's archangels, angels and Christ against Lucifer, all in Miltonian terms:

And strange it was to see God with his back
Against a wall, to see Christ hew and hack
Till Lucifer, pressed by the mighty pair,
And losing inch by inch, clawed at the air
With fevered wings; then, lost beyond repair,
He tricked a mass of stars into his hair;
He filled his hands with stars, crying as he fell,
"A star's a star although it burns in hell."
So God was left to his divinity,
Omnipotent at that most costly fee.

God so triumphant and so distant did not appeal to Cullen. It did not do justice to the mystery of human suffering and sacrificial love, and God's own concern for the human condition. In the same poem, Cullen explored another dimension of atonement. While he expressed his own lack of "strength to sacrifice," he submerged his own "puny grief" in the struggle of "all dark people" in "life's abattoir," and he looked to a "mighty surge" of suffering through which blacks would overcome the world in victory. This turn away from Christ to the collective suffering of black people as redemptive was not really satisfying. In **"The Shroud of Color,"** he expresses a lingering doubt with a reference early in the poem to Abraham and Isaac:

. . . hast Thou, Lord, somewhere I cannot see
A lamb imprisoned in a bush for me?

Cullen's last and longest attempt to deal with this tension of atonement is **"The Black Christ."** He sings about a black boy, Jim, growing to manhood, proud and handsome, about his temptation to reject the faith in the face of injustice, about his crucifixion for the sake of love, and murder, and about his resurrection appearance. He sings about Jim's brother, who acknowledges Jesus as well as Jim as of the same kin. This brother is the narrator, perhaps Cullen himself, who faces his own rebellion when his brother is lynched and his own trial of faith. And Cullen sings about the mother, "Job's dark sister," who embodies Calvary's sorrow in her heart, yet is "still unconquered Lady, Faith." She is the instrument through whom God's Spirit works to keep her sons faithful. And through this black passion play, Cullen expressed his own credo about Christ's atonement.

The mother is a Black Madonna, the Christ-bearer, and her long-suffering as a handmaiden of the Lord indicates how important the black mother has been for the household of faith. She knows the South as a "cruel land" which has bled her and hers. She speaks of her own "soul's ecstasy" to her boys:

No man, . . . can batter down
The star-flung ramparts of the mind.
So much for flesh; I am resigned,
Whom God has made shall he not guide?

Her resignation is lightened by the confidence of a deliverance, and in confessing God's mighty acts, she recalls Moses and Israel to her children:

Once there had been somewhere as now
A people harried, low in the dust;
But such had been their utter trust
In heaven and its field of stars
They had broken down their bars,
And walked across a parted sea
Praising his name who set them free.

Wise with the experience of suffering, she is deeply disturbed about what the "cruel land" may do to her sons, and she attempts to fill their hearts with the power of a new affection for Christ. . . .

After temptation, then crucifixion, and a rebellious son dies as a man of sorrows. Jim, proud, handsome, and imperial, meets his mother and brother next in panic, fleeing the sickening howls of "two-limbed dogs" on their way to lynch him. The occasion for this lynch mob and lynch spirit is Jim's love for a white girl and his murder of a white man. Cullen describes the sequence of events. Jim—"Spring's gayest cavalier"—is attracted to and falls in love with a white girl. It is an innocent love "(Taught on a bloody Christless road)," without regard to "hue and race," without regard to "rank or caste," a love which from the heart of both lovers was a voice "high and clear." Jim and his lover are discovered together by a white man, violating what one southerner has called the South's "gynecolatry." This "bit of crass and filthy clay" strikes the woman for a slut. Because this man laid a "hand on spring" and insulted his love, Jim laid a hand on the defiler, striking and killing him, as Moses did the Egyptian. As Jim breathlessly tells of his plight to his mother and brother the lynchers close in for mob action. When the "Blood-sniffing crowd" breaks into the home of this cowed holy family, Cullen borrows from the passion narratives of the Gospels to describe the surrender of Jim to his tormentors. He leaves to his brother a word of reassurance and instruction so that his death may not be in vain:

> Brother . . . then prove
> Out of your charity and love
> That I was not unduly slain,
> That this my death was not in vain.
> For no life should go to the tomb
> Unless from it a new life bloom,
> A clearer faith, a clearer sight,
> A wiser groping for the light.

And to his mother, grief-stricken, though dry-eyed, he confesses his faith:

> Mother, not poorer losing one,
> Look now upon your dying son.

Beaten, as Jesus was before him, he is dragged out and hanged on a "virgin tree / Awaiting its fecundity."

This crucifixion stirs outrage in Jim's brother. He is now tempted as he had not been before with his own dark doubts until his brother appears again in resurrection and causes his own "soul's ecstasy." With no eyes to see or ears to hear, he turns his anger against his mother's child-like submission to this work of evil. He mocks her faith:

> . . . Why was he flung
> Like common dirt to death? Why, stone,
> Must he of all the earth atone
> For what? . . .
>   . . . Christ who conquered Death and Hell
> What has he done for you who spent
> A bleeding life for his content?
> Or is the white Christ, too, distraught
> By these dark sins his Father wrought?

Hearing these blasphemies, the mother holds fast. The God to whom she traveled, Cullen writes,

> Was judge of all that men might do
> To such as she who trusted him
> Faith was a tower for her, grim
> And insurmountable. . . .

Suddenly God gives to Jim and his mother the sign of the prophet Jonah when Jim shows his "vital self" in a resurrection appearance, thus providing, as do the Gospels, the eschatological ground for belief. While the lynching was an experience of abandonment, resurrection was the sign and seal of God's presence even in tragedy. Jim is able to see, with his mother, the grace and glory of the Lord in Christ's work of atonement.

Cullen transforms the existential black experience into a universal message about Christ's passion and triumph. Out of Jim's temptation, crucifixion, and resurrection, Cullen arrives at his interpretation of the atonement, expressed in a brother's words:

> If I am blind he does not see;
> If I am lame he halts with me;
> There is no hood of pain I wear
> That has not rested on his hair
> Making him first initiate
> Beneath its harsh and hairy weight.
> He grew with me within the womb;
> He will receive me at the tomb.
> He will make plain the misty path
> He makes me tread in love and wrath,
> And bending down in peace and grace
> May wear again my brother's face.

Countee Cullen left his readers problems with both form and substance. Some critics were not kind with regard to the form of "**The Black Christ**." They were disappointed, as was Granville Hicks writing for the *Nation,* because the poet was not developing properly. The critics considered the rhymed tetrameter used for the narrative and meditations in the epic arbitrary, constricting, and unconvincing. One even called it comic. Unfortunately, Cullen had not taken into consideration that T. S. Eliot published the *Wasteland* in 1922, and that poets were exploring new idioms to express a sense of alienation. He picked Milton as a model by which to explore America's racist wasteland, and his contemporaries considered him anachronistic. With rhymed tetrameter he trivialized the awesome. He failed to move the lost generation even though some recognized the maturity of his theme. Here they strained at meter and rhyme and swallowed a camel, and probably discouraged Cullen who wanted so much to be considered a poet.

Blacks, made more militant than Cullen by the Garvey movement and more troubled by the Depression, did not fully appreciate the poet's effort either. But DuBois, who had been Cullen's father-in-law for a brief period, was kind. He noted in 1929 that **"The Black Christ"** was a poem of "religious mysticism, of beauty, and finish." DuBois himself was moving further and further toward Marxism, economically, politically, and religiously, and away from his Christian roots. Langston Hughes, part of the Harlem Renaissance like Cullen, demonstrated in his poetry what he thought of attempts like Cullen's to express a viable Christian theology in the face of frustration. . . .

In developing Jim, Cullen had the same trouble Melville had with *Billy Budd.* Like Billy, Jim is tempted and rebellious, but resists temptation. Like Billy, Jim kills another man. While Billy goes to the gallows to satisfy the demands of the king's law, Jim hangs on the tree for his challenge of the racist taboo and his impulse to avenge innocent love. He also satisfied the demands of custom and law. Here the figure of Moses may fuse with that of Jesus. Jim, like Billy, becomes a judgment on the injustices of the society. But Jim is not portrayed as the savior. God through Christ is the savior, and the new Calvary leads back to the first, where God identified with our human condition and dignified our lives even when we meet with the most arbitrary human estrangement and alienation. The experience of lynching illuminates the meaning of the "old rugged cross" on a hill far away, and makes existential the question of the spiritual, "Were you there when they crucified my Lord." Cullen showed his theological acumen in other ways.

While he does not describe in this poem a bodily resurrection so important to Fundamentalists in his day, he did know the importance of resurrection. When he described the appearance of Jim's "vital self"—perhaps a Bergsonian conception—he also indicated that crucifixion without resurrection and hope would lead to despair. Moreover, Cullen also saw that faith and hope in the Christian must manifest themselves in love. That is the last invitation which Jim gives to his brother to prove that his death has not been in vain. What Redding calls "childish mysticism" in Cullen, Wagner calls a "Christ-mysticism" and desire for union with Christ which is as old as the gospel itself.

Cullen did not dissolve the brutality of crucifixion in the abstraction of a correctly phrased doctrine of the atonement. He wanted his readers to experience the first Calvary and God's sacrificial love by looking on lynching. Lynching was a sacramental reminder of God's solidarity with the human family, first demonstrated in Christ's crucifixion. Moreover, in the summons of a life of hope and love, Cullen suggested that the cross was the source of our common brotherhood in suffering and a paradigm for Christian living.

In his poetic musings, Cullen may have reminded blacks of an old time religion, described by Maysin *The Negro's God,* which preached submission to oppression and promised compensation in a cloudy cuckoo-land-of-bye-and-bye. In any case, Cullen seemed to resolve the tension between his Christian and his pagan self and was himself satisfied. In 1946, he issued a collection of verse in a volume entitled **On These I Stand** just before his premature death of that year. He republished **"The Black Christ"** and a number of the poems already mentioned as a reaffirmation of faith. He included, for example, **"The Litany of Dark People"** from *Copper Sun.* There he maintained that while the black may be crucified, still would he confess Christ:

> . . . no assault the old gods make
> Upon our agony
> Shall swerve our footsteps from the wake
> Of Thine toward Calvary.

He also included a poem written in 1929 called **"Mood"** in which he suggested some of his own restiveness and impatience with things as they were. Yes, he belonged to "Jesus of the twice-turned cheek" and remembered Jim's words about love. But he complained:

> God knows I would be kind, let live, speak fair,
> Require an honest debt with more than just,
> And love for Christ's deat sake these shapes that

> wear
> A pride that has its genesis in dust,—
> The meek are promised much in a book I know
> But one grows weary turning cheek to blow.

"The Black Christ," according to this collection of poems, was Cullen's strongest attack on "man's consistent cruelty / To man."

Martin Luther King, Jr., born the same year Cullen wrote **"The Black Christ,"** hailed in his mature years as the Black Moses, incarnated in his own person and work the central insight of Cullen in his poem about the crucifixion. Reinhold Niebuhr suggested, in *Moral Man and Immoral Society* (1932), that Gandhi might provide help to blacks in dealing with powerlessness and injustice in America. There is no question that King profited from Gandhi's freedom struggle in India, and biographers such as Leone Bennett in *What Manner of Man* (1963) emphasize over and over again the Gandhian connection. But so often attention is given to Gandhi at the expense of King's dependence on the person and work of Christ. Bennett, by the way, opens his biography by indicating Gandhi's own attraction to the Galilean. He tells of a visit in 1935 of American blacks to Gandhi who unexpectedly asked them to sing one of his favorite songs: "Were you there when they crucified my Lord."

While there is no evidence that King read Cullen's poem, King did know Cullen as a poet and referred to him. Using insights from Gandhi, from Rauschenbusch, Niebuhr, and Anders Nygren's *Agape and Eros* (1938, 1939), King developed his view of suffering love into a force to challenge the conscience, customs, and laws of America. In *Strength to Love* (1963), a collection of sermons, King notes that while the world looks upon Christ's crucifixion as weakness and foolishness, Christians see there God's power and wisdom to lift up the last, the least, and the lost. It is not simply a guarantee of God's self-sacrificing love and identification with the human condition, but also it is the incentive of sacrificial love among human beings for human beings. It is not a paradigm for cowards, but for those who are strong in faith and hope and love.

King maintained that it was only through suffering love that we could love the enemy, even modern Pharoahs, curb desire for retaliation and the humiliation of others, and bring about reconciliation and healing to all people, black and white. As King joined with his followers to sing "We shall overcome," he was considered a Black Moses in the line of Marcus Garvey. King himself wanted to be more like Jesus. He deliberately chose Easter week of 1963 to hold demonstrations in Birmingham to witness to the one in whose footsteps he was trying to walk. He paid for his witness by being lynched, not by hanging, not by fire, but by being shot and killed by an assassin's bullet. King's death, in Cullen's vision, was another leaf in "a line / Of trees" bringing "Calvary in Palestine" down to us for "all men's healing."

Cullen lost some of his lyric powers and his reputation as a poet after the publication of **"The Black Christ."** He did not die the death of a martyr in protest against human cruelty to other human beings. He lived the quieter life of a school teacher to go to an early grave in 1946 mourned by over three thousand who attended his funeral. Apparently he had spoken a word which at least some of his generation heard. Eleanor Roosevelt wrote about **"The Black Christ"** in 1945 that it ought to be read by people as soon as they are mature enough to comprehend it.

Gary Smith (essay date 1984)

SOURCE: "The Black Protest Sonnet," in *American Poetry,* Vol. 2, No. 41, Fall, 1984, pp. 2-12.

[In the following excerpt, Smith comments on Cullen's use of the sonnet as a vehicle for protest.]

To more than one commentator on the poetry of the Harlem Renaissance, the central paradox of the movement, as a literary phenomenon, is the discrepancy between theory and practice: what the poets proposed in theory and what they actually accomplished in their poetry. This paradox appears in poets like Countee Cullen and Claude McKay, who considered themselves poets first and blacks second, yet their most memorable poetry draws its strength from racial identity. In matters of literary style, this paradox surfaces in the choices of conventional forms that were often at odds with radical literary themes. The most striking instance of this paradoxical relationship between theory and practice, style and content, is found in the use of the European sonnet, an art form that attracted the interest of most of the major Renaissance poets. One naturally wonders why the New Negro poets were drawn to the European sonnet—a four-hundred-year old, genteel literary form that traces its roots to the sixteenth century Italian sonnet—as opposed to folk forms more native to the black American experience, such as the antebellum sermon, folk songs, blues, and spirituals.

The answer to this paradox lies in a number of areas. In the case of Cullen, his attraction to the European sonnet reflected his traditional academic training and romantic temperament. . . .

The early poetic training of Cullen and McKay attracted them to what was universal in literature as opposed to the topical. For both poets, race was incidental to art. And since the sonnet had been the cutting stone for most of the great poets writing in the English language, it naturally appealed to both as the most important means of sharpening their skills, while reaching a universal audience with their poetry. In McKay's *Selected Poems,* for example, no less than thirty-five sonnets appear, several of which are among his most anthologized poems: "If We Must Die," "The Harlem Dancer," and "To America." In Cullen's personal collection, ***On These I Stand,*** the poet includes the sonnets, **"Yet Do I Marvel," "From the Dark Tower,"** and **"Hunger,"** among his most memorable poems.

While the New Negro poets, like Cullen and McKay, were drawn to the sonnet because of its syllogistic form, its dis-

cipline, as well as its genteel beauty and long tradition, they were equally attracted to its discursive possibilities. Indeed, the most prevalent theme in the black protest sonnet is not unrequited love but rather the unrequited desire for socio-economic justice. While the Shakespearean sonnet almost invariably discourses upon some aspect of human life, the New Negro poets primarily wrote sonnets about social inequality. Furthermore, while the Shakespearean sonnet points to the paradoxes of life, the black protest sonnet singles out America's often hypocritical social values and constitutional law. Therefore, in one sense, the black protest sonnet takes a radical shift in theme from its genteel, quietly reasoned European counterpart; but, again, in its tendency to present a syllogistic argument, the black protest sonnet is largely indebted to the European sonnet tradition. . . .

Cullen's sonnet, **"From the Dark Tower,"** provides an even more striking turn from the conventional European sonnet. Structurally, the poem bears a strong resemblance to the Italian sonnet with its two rhyming quatrains, but it actually conforms to the English sonnet with its sestet of three rhyming couplets:

> We shall not always plant while others reap
> The golden increment of bursting fruit,
> Not always countenance, abject and mute,
> That lesser men should hold their brother cheap;
> Not everlastingly while others sleep
> Shall we beguile their limbs with mellow flute,
> Not always bend to some more subtle brute;
> We were not made eternally to weep.
>
> The night whose sable breast relieves the stark
> White stars is no less lovely being dark,
> And there are buds that cannot bloom at all
> In light, but crumble, piteous, and fall;
> So in the dark we hide the heart that bleeds,
> And wait, and tend our agonizing seeds. . . .

Cullen's theme is an unrequited appeal for socio-economic justice. Its question is how "we"—presumably the black masses—can remain indifferent, "abject and mute," to inhuman treatment and retain those characteristics that make us distinctly human. . . .

In retrospect, the black protest sonnet of the post-renaissance poets, in some ways, foreshadows the Black Arts Movement of the 1960s. Although their sonnets display the careful attention to craft that was the hallmark of the New Negro poets, there is also a sharper, more bitter assault upon racism in American society.

Alan R. Shucard (essay date 1984)

SOURCE: "Countee Cullen and the Harlem Renaissance" and "The Racial Poet," in *Countee Cullen,* Twayne Publishers, 1984, pp. 1-12, 13-24.

[In the following excerpt, Shucard argues that Cullen naturally created race dominated poetry despite his intellectual intent to place artistry above all other concerns.]

It is a peculiar sensation, this double consciousness, this sense of always looking at one's self through the eyes of others, of measuring one's soul by the tape of a world that looks on in amused contempt and pity. One ever feels his twoness,—an American, a Negro; two souls, two thoughts, two unreconciled strivings; two warring ideals in one dark body. . . .

The history of the American Negro is the history of this strife,—this longing to attain self-conscious manhood, to merge his double self into a better and truer self. In this merging, he wishes neither of the older selves to be lost. He would not Africanize America, for America has too much to teach the world and Africa. He would not bleach his Negro soul in a flood of white Americanism, for he knows that Negro blood has a message for the world. He simply wishes to make it possible for a man to be both a Negro and an American. . . .

> [W. E. B. DuBois, *The Souls of Black Folk*, 1953]

Though Cullen devoted a good measure of his life to the spiritual and artistic integration of the races, he could never, understandably, eradicate or fuse the double-consciousness of which DuBois had spoken; and, in fact, in his only novel, *One Way to Heaven,* he mocked what he took to be the superficiality of those who could. There the irrepressible Constancia Brandon is oblivious to "the free masonry existing between the races in New York" (*One Way to Heaven,* 1932) simply because she regards everyone as an extension of her own ego.

Cullen's ego was not as simple a device as Constancia's. By affinity, training, and experience, it was divided. If it was largely black, it was substantially white—or perhaps it would be more exact to say that if his consciousness was black, the white world exercised a strong claim on it. How could it be otherwise? When fifteen-year-old Countee Porter was adopted in 1918 by the Reverend Cullen and his wife, he acquired the name and entered the family of the influential pastor of the large Salem Methodist Episcopal Church. There was no avoiding black awareness in the rectory of that church, and there was no wish to avoid it. Cullen's adoptive father was at the center of Harlem's reaction to racial violence across the country. Frederick Cullen was part of the embassy of black men who went to the White House after World War I to induce Woodrow Wilson to halt at thirteen the number of black soldiers hanged for allegedly firing weapons in Houston; the President acquiesced and caused the remaining soldiers in custody to be released. Later, the Reverend Cullen was elected President of the National Association for the Advancement of Colored People for the Harlem Chapter. . . . Such activities and the bitter circumstances that evoked them did not escape Countee Cullen's notice, of course; he was an exemplar of what Henry James had in mind when he exhorted writers to be the kinds of people "upon whom nothing is lost." Vivid descriptions that he overheard in the rectory of lynchings and of the relish that some whites derived from them caused him to become physically ill. This, balanced against the energetic good humor that sent him on an insatiable quest for a good time at parties and among hordes of friends and ac-

quaintances among Harlem's genuine and striving intellectuals, represented his essential informal black education.

If his informal training was black, his formal education was mainly and, given the circumstances of time and place, inevitably white. In schools and universities he was taught white things—most significant for his writing career, the English literary tradition—by white teachers. He did well in that world because he was highly intelligent, sensitive, and motivated; his winning approbation in the white world could not help but drive him to seek more, a habit that was not readily broken. Some years later he confessed to the closest friend of his young manhood, Harold Jackman: "There is actually no excuse for enjoying the plaudits of the populace as I do. I fairly revel in public commendation. Perhaps I am the one living poet who will confess that he doesn't write *for his own amusement,* and that what others think of his work can affect him." He accumulated excellent grades at New York's DeWitt Clinton High School, a ride uptown from Harlem, that brought him honors in several academic subjects at graduation; he won contests for poetry and oratory; he was elected to the honor society and the vice-presidency of his graduating class; he became editor of the school newspaper. In his last year of secondary school, the DeWitt Clinton literary magazine, the *Magpie,* under his editorship published some of his poetic juvenilia, for example:

> Poet, poet what's your mission
> Here mid earth's grief and pain? . . .
> Poet, Poet what do you ask
> As pay for each glad song?
> Thy thanks will pay me doubly well
> And last my whole life long.

It also brought to light **"Life's Rendezvous,"** a far more mature piece that won him a first prize in the Federation of Women's Clubs' poetry contest.

Cullen was wrong about his having no excuse for his applause-seeking. He was human, with an appetite whetted by successes in both black and white cultures, and he was young. A crucial fact of Countee Cullen's artistic life—and one that is easily overlooked or forgotten—is that he streaked only briefly across the poetic heavens in his mid-twenties.

Perhaps nowhere does a more convincing reminder of his youthful vivacity reside than in his letters to Jackman in the 1920s composed during Cullen's Harvard days and summer trips abroad. Full of the harmless, catty remarks of two friends deriding their Harlem acquaintances, occasionally with references to people they call "niggers"—by which they signify Harlemites with low-class proclivities and high-class pretentions—they are characterized by a studiousness balanced by jocularity and gusto. Thus he wrote to Jackman from Harvard in April of 1926, the year after the publication of *Color* and the year preceding publication of *Copper Sun, Ballad of the Brown Girl,* and *Caroling Dusk,* capturing the flavor of his life there. He describes William Stanley Braithwaite, one of his Harvard mentors, as "a fine person and quite prodigal with his wine." Cullen had been seeing both Braithwaite's daughter Fiona and Sydonia Byrd, a friend of hers, and, flaring his feathers a bit, he boasted in the same letter: "Rumor has already engaged me to both young ladies who share my unstable affections; so that for the first time in my life I feel what it means to be a shiek [*sic*]— even if only on a small scale." With too lithe a mind to stay on any subject unduly long, even his newly acquired sheikdom, Cullen turned then to "the Liszt Symphony based on *Faust.* A gorgeous piece of characterization I call it, although that probably means nothing from one who has no musical discrimination."

In the afterglow of his exuberant and youthful celebrity, which coincided with the dying down of the Harlem Renaissance as the Depression cast its shadow across the United States, he published some more poems, a novel, a translation of the *Medea,* and a couple of children's books; he worked on theater projects, including, with Arna Bontemps, a dramatic adaptation of Bontemps's novel *God Sends Sunday,* which was produced as *St. Louis Woman* after Cullen's unexpected death from uremic poisoning in 1946. But particularly beginning in 1934, when he took a teaching post at Frederick Douglass Jr. High School, Cullen's literary light was dimmed by his concentration on teaching English and French skillfully and lovingly to primarily black children for the rest of his short life.

Since the adulation and predictions of a deathless future that Cullen's work aroused in the 1920s and '30s, it has surely declined in critical notice. Then and since, when it has been examined, there has been a tendency on the part of commentators on his work to praise it, and sometimes to attack it, on the basis of its being "Negro"—or, conversely, on the basis of its being insufficiently "Negro" or, in later years, "black." In either case, it has been evaluated largely on nonliterary grounds.

It is clearly important to clarify the nature of Cullen's work and to evaluate it, in literary terms insofar as that is possible, but it is no simple matter, for Cullen himself is ambivalent about his intent, and seems often to vacillate between playing the pure aesthete and the racial spokesman. Many of his poems and critical attitudes, of course, as well as his fiction, derive from his sense of race. Despite his own frequent denials, Cullen writes a great deal of racial poetry, though he writes, too, naturally, of religion, of death, of the nature of poetry, of love. His wider vision, his treatment of other themes, couched in extremely traditional forms consciously derivative of Keats, is usually presented through the squint of his racial views. Cullen's poetry, in short, does not permit the critic to forget his Negroness, but the final judgment of him as a poet must be made from his poetry alone.

The cry "Black is Beautiful," a shibboleth among Negroes in America seeking to evoke self-esteem within themselves and respect among whites, may serve a desirable sociological end, but it cannot, of course, be taken as a literary assumption. The poetry of Countee Cullen, a black man, is often interesting and sometimes poignant,

but may be too literarily flawed to be regarded as first-rate; indeed, if it should be shown that only the epithets "interesting" and "poignant" and few others apply, the poetry could scarcely be taken to be beautiful. It should not be taken as axiomatic that it can even be called "black," though it was composed by a black man, for Cullen himself denied that there is such a literary phenomenon as "black poetry." In a limited sense, he was correct: after all, black American poets are American; use, except for dialect poems, general American English; and heed the same urge to create as their white counterparts—are bound to the same muse, even if they might argue against white Attic origins. Cullen summarized his denial of "black poetry" in his foreword to the 1927 anthology he gathered of poems by black poets, *Caroling Dusk,* which he carefully subtitled: *An Anthology of Verse by Negro Poets.* The point is an important one, and so it is worth quoting the segment of the foreword that pertains:

> I have called this collection an anthology of verse by Negro poets rather than an anthology of Negro verse, since this latter designation would be more confusing than accurate. Negro poetry, it seems to me, in the sense that we speak of Russian, French, or Chinese poetry, must emanate from some country other than this in some language other than our own. Moreover, the attempts to corral the outbursts of the ebony muse into some definite mold to which all poetry by Negroes will conform seems altogether futile and aside from the facts. This country's Negro writers may here and there turn some singular facet toward the literary sun, but in the main, since theirs is also the heritage of the English language, their work will not present any serious aberration from the poetic tendencies of their times. The conservatives, the middlers, and the arch heretics will be found among them as among the white poets; and to say that the pulse beat of their verse shows generally such a fever, or the symptoms of such an ague, will prove on closer examination merely the moment's exaggeration of a physician anxious to establish a new literary aliment. As heretical as it may sound, there is the probability that Negro poets, dependent as they are on the English Language, may have more to gain from the rich background of English and American poetry than from any nebulous atavistic yearnings toward an African inheritance.

Cullen is partially right, yes, but he is largely wrong; there are issues here more genuine than those raised merely by his anxious physician. Of course, American Negro poetry does not exist in the linguistic sense of Russian, French, or Chinese poetry, but to mention that obvious fact is to camouflage one that should be equally obvious. Poets are human beings who organize in verse the forces of the lives they share with other humans; they belong to and write of a sociological and cultural milieu, which for the black American has been in many respects different from that of the white American. The black and the white have, theoretically, shared the same institutions, the same governments, for example, but they have seldom shared the same relationships to those institutions. Thus insofar as the experiences of the black poets and the white have coincided, their poems may be expected to be more or less indistinguishable: Cullen had an early and unfortunate marriage before a later, happier one, and there is nothing "Negro" about many of his love poems; he was profoundly preoccupied with the interplay of death and life, and in many of the poems in which he treats this theme, he sounds in attitude and technique like A. E. Housman, or Emily Dickinson, or, above all, like John Keats, his acknowledged idol. But, where the experiences of the black and the white have been fundamentally different, and often under conditions coercive for the black, the poetry might be expected to be different, and an examination of the work of black poets, of Cullen himself, shows that expectation to be valid (indeed, the impact of different conditions sometimes is felt in areas of universal human experience, in the bitterness of some of Cullen's religious or love poems, for instance). Therefore, there is every reason to anticipate that black poetry will be distinguishable by an intense concentration on the racial theme because the life from which it springs is of people who have been made excruciatingly aware of racial (often, really cultural) differences, real and imagined—and this is, in fact, the case. This is not to say that every black writer composes his every piece on the race theme. In general, "black poetry" does exist, and most of Cullen's own poetry operates under this definition: it is clearly and simply poetry arising from the tension between blacks and whites in the United States, written from the point of view of the black, whether the attitude he assumes in a given poem is one of strong protest or of placid acceptance. None but a black man like Don Lee could write the bulk of his verse, or a black woman like Gwendolyn Brooks the main body of hers, or a black poet like Countee Cullen the majority and the most significant of his work.

In this sense, there is undeniably a black poetry, and however much, in his laudable desire for integration and his belief in art without racial boundaries as a means to eradicate racial lines in society Cullen tried to deny the phenomenon, a study of his own verse and criticism demonstrates the extent to which he helped to promulgate it. In terms of bulk alone, Cullen provides his own proof that his denial of black poetry was erroneous. He was a sensitive black man who heard and heeded the need to try to be a poet in a world that made it difficult—when not impossible—for the black; this is the most central fact of Cullen's artistic life. Although he could take Langston Hughes to task for Hughes's having fallen "into that gaping pit that lies before all Negro writers, in the confines of which they become racial artists rather than artists pure and simple," all seven of Cullen's volumes of poetry (including the anthology, *Caroling Dusk*) are racially oriented wholly or in great measure. They bear the mark that definitively characterizes black poetry: the venting of feelings toward the racial problem from the black point of view.

Cullen's very first collection reveals this proclivity even in its title, *Color* (1925, a year after he had upbraided Hughes). The next book he published, *The Ballad of the Brown Girl: An Old Ballad Retold* (1927), is a single poem dealing with the comparison of a brown girl and a lily-white maid, and their association with a white nobleman; race is the forceful undertow pulling in this inter-

pretation of the love triangle. Subsequent volumes contain a great number of poems touching matters racial, gathered normally in a section called "Color." And despite his protestations during his lifetime against being known as a racial poet—not to say against the existence of a category of poetry called "Negro"—the volume *On These I Stand* (1947), which comprises all the pieces for which he wanted to be remembered (he collected the poems before his death, and the book was published posthumously), is considerably more than half devoted to poems on the racial theme. His voice was not as strident in protest as that of other black poets of his time, Langston Hughes, say, or Claude McKay crying out "If We Must Die" "To the White Fiends." They themselves are tame by standards invented decades later. Perhaps it is because he did not want to be a protesting writer of black poetry that Cullen's voice sometimes sounds effete. But disclaimers though he may issue, admonitions to other black poets though he may minister, the body of his work shows him to be a writer of black verse.

There is more evidence attesting to Cullen's particular race-consciousness than just the volume of his poetic output. He produced a number of magazine pieces from 1926 to 1929 that reflect much of his notion of the relationship between race and literature. Chiefly, these were in the form of a literary column, "The Dark Tower," that he wrote for *Opportunity,* the Urban League organ, while he was a member of the editorial staff. Taken as a whole, these articles suggest not only that Cullen was deeply concerned with racial matters, but that he was ambivalent in his attitudes toward them. His comments seem to stem not only from his conventional religious upbringing in Harlem by the Reverend Frederick A. Cullen and his wife, and from his conservative education, but also from the pressure of being oppressed for being black and wanting to fit into the white world on the one hand, while feeling a strong sense of pride in and allegiance to his race on the other. Remember the young and human Cullen admitting how he reveled in "public commendation." The impact upon him of the blanched environment in which he was educated can only be surmised. In the review of *The Weary Blues* in which he warns Langston Hughes against the menace of becoming a "racial artist," Cullen seems rather abashed by the jazz beat in Hughes's poems. He questions whether the jazz poem is not too exciting, in the manner of the revival meeting: "I wonder if the quiet way of communing is not more spiritual for the God-seeking heart," he asks—which is to say that the jazz pieces of *The Weary Blues* are not sufficiently dignified for Cullen. Yet in the "Dark Tower" column of December 1926, while apologizing for earlier boosting a young poet named Chaliss Silvay under the mistaken impression that Silvay was "of our pigmentary persuasion," Cullen claims "reason for a proper pride in us that 'one of ours' had a hand in it"—that is, in the publication by Silvay of some poems. A few months later Cullen defends the actions of the Negro heroine of a play, *Stigma,* by Dorothy Manley and Donald Duff; in the play, set in the South, the girl has been made pregnant by a white man, who offers to marry her, and Cullen is evidently annoyed that white critics cannot comprehend what motivates the Negro girl's refusal: "Mina, the colored girl in the play, does not reject the white father of her unborn because either he or she is against miscegenation. The pivot of her refusal is that she feels that she as an individual is superior to this clay-footed god." And he continues, implying much about his sense of and wishes for race relations: "Not one of the critics seems to have an adequate notion what sort of person Mina really was; they all took her at face value as 'a Negro maid of all work' not seeing that she wore a mask to protect her intelligence which would have been objectionable in the South."

There is no cause to believe that Cullen is guilty of hypocrisy; far from it. But his periodical material does indicate that he is a man pulled by allegiances not easy to reconcile. It must be remembered that the very nature of his position in journalism, that of literary writer for a black journal, forced him to focus upon the association between Negroes and the arts, both within and without the Negro community. Even if he wished to assume a "neutral," that is, "non-black" perspective, always it was incumbent upon him to interpret the world of letters exactly from the vantage point the title of his column suggests—"The Dark Tower." This is a matter of emphasis, of course, for he could and did recommend literature not written by or about blacks, E. A. Robinson's *Tristram*, for example, and Dorothy Parker's *Enough Rope*. But mainly he could not forget he was a black contributing to a black periodical, even if he did forget to be consistent in his views within the limits of his situation.

It is certainly not easy for one to reconcile Cullen's attack, in the *Weary Blues* review, on Hughes's black folk poetry with the racial pride that Cullen expresses elsewhere—for example, in speaking of the help that he, as a black critic, had been able to give the white poet Silvay toward the publication of Silvay's poems. But even harder is it to square, on racial grounds, Cullen's deprecation of Hughes's work in black rhythms with his treatment of Amy Spingarn's *Pride and Humility* in which Cullen finds the poet's "clearest notes in those poems which have a racial framework." It seems to be to Hughes's detriment that he should make "Negro poetry," but to Miss Spingarn's credit; at least, she is at her best when she is being a "racial artist." If any pattern can finally be discerned in Cullen's prose discussions, it is basically this: the conflict he suffered between his pride in the black (perhaps tainted with a trace of shame) and his drive to achieve harmony with the white (if not to simply placate the white) stimulates a tendency to urge caution, a soft blackness that will not be offensive to whites. There is no premeditated Uncle Tomism implied here, but a genuine altruistic hope to attain respect and equality between the races, and to use art as a means to that end. Militancy might be offensive to whites. So might something as Negroid as jazz poetry. To protest decorously, however, and to expose the Negro's plight in a palatable way might effect change. "Decorously" and "palatable" are the operative words, as Cullen makes clear in a "Dark Tower" exhortation of March 1928. He observes that "American life is so constituted, the wealth of power is so unequally distributed that whether they relish the situation or not, *Negroes should*

be concerned with making good impressions [italics inserted here to stress this basic tenet of Cullen's view]." There are things, Cullen insists, that must be hidden in order to make those impressions; the Negro must remove his heart from public exhibition:

> The sins committed under shibboleths of art and truth are many, but we doubt if art and truth glibly flowing from the tongue are extenuating enough alibis. There is no more childish untruth than the axiom that the truth will set you free; in many cases it will merely free one from the concealment of facts which will later bind you hand and foot in ridicule and mockery. Let art portray things as they are, no matter what the consequences, no matter who is hurt, is a blind bit of philosophy. There are some things, some truths of Negro life and thought, of Negro inhibitions, that all Negroes know, but take no pride in. To broadcast them to the world will but strengthen the bitterness of our enemies, and in some instances turn away the interest of our friends. Every phase of Negro life should not be the white man's concern.

There are, then, for Cullen, secret and shameful Negro things that should remain secret; and even those that are public should not necessarily command the attention of the black artist merely because he is black. Further, the implication of a reply Cullen wrote to an article by Frank Luther Mott called "The Harlem Poets," in *Midland* (May 1927), is that the black artist ought to write about the experiences Negroes share with whites, and not concentrate especially upon "Negro experiences." Mott had urged Negro writers not to imitate white forms and values, not to forget "the materials of Negro life." Cullen's rebuttal was to argue for a more complete freedom than Mott would allow:

> The mind of man has always ridden a capricious wandering nag, that just will not stay reined. . . . Let us not . . . be stricken into such dire lamentation when the Negro goes excursioning. Let the test be how much of a pleasant day he himself has had, and how much he has been enabled to impart to us.

A logical extension of Cullen's insistence on freedom for the Negro artist to draw upon any sort of material for his work is his belief that the artist owes fealty to art before race. In the introduction to *Four Negro Poets* Alain Locke had contended that "the present-day Negro poet regards his racial heritage as a more precious endowment than his own personal genius, and to the common legacy of his art adds the peculiar experiences and emotions of his folk." Although by the time Locke made this declaration, Cullen had written sufficient poetry of racial awareness to justify his inclusion in the generalization, Cullen went immediately to the trouble of disagreeing with Locke. He wrote:

> As one, to a slight extent, in the know of things, we have serious doubts that Negro poets feel themselves more strongly obligated to their race than to their own degree of personal talent.

He admitted that two of the poets represented in *Four Negro Poets* might subscribe to Locke's ideas (undoubtedly

McKay and Hughes), but others (he himself and Jean Toomer) "are less racially altruistic."

These portions of Cullen's prose pieces shed light into the rational construct that he evolved of the relationship between poetry and race. His obligation was to his "own degree of personal talent," and he believed himself to be "less racially altruistic" than some poets—and than some readers of his poetry, including Locke, thought him to be. The question as to which assessment of Cullen is more accurate, his own or Locke's, is to be answered hereafter, but it should first be pointed out to his credit that Cullen's intention not to be restricted by racial ties leads to a praise-worthy sense of fairness in his periodical writing—even if it leads, too, to the kind of self-contradiction that has been demonstrated.

Another excellent example of his impartiality is contained in an account he wrote of a visit he had in Paris with Madame Claire Goll, a French novelist and Negrophile, who had recently written a novel, *Le Nègre Jupiter Enlève Europe,* on the theme of miscegenation. His hostess was of the opinion that the vein of white American literature had been utterly depleted, and the only promising mine of future American letters was Negro literature. With gentle humor Cullen recounts his reaction, though perhaps in his humor there is a hint of the mixed loyalties that tugged at him:

> In vain I mention some names: Frost and Robinson and Millay; Anderson and Cather and O'Neill; timidly I venture the opinion that these are names before whom it is just to bow below the knee, and that their ore does not seem to have run out. Madame makes me feel that I am recreant, disloyal, a literary heretic, a blind man stumbling along in the light of the new day. Just archly enough not to offend me, yet accusingly, she turns to one of my poems, and indicts me for my love of Keats, for concerning myself with names like Endymion and Lancelot and Jupiter. It is on the tip of my tongue to ask why Keats himself should have concerned himself with themes like Endymion and Hyperion, but I am drinking Madame's tea. . . . Later, out in the cool Parisian air, I ponder where all this will lead us. Must we, willy-nilly, be forced into writing of the old atavistic urges, the more savage and none too beautiful aspects of our lives? May we not chant a hymn to the Sun God if we will, create a bit of phantasy in which not a spiritual or a blues appears, write a tract defending Christianity, though its practitioners aid us so little in our argument; in short do, write, create, what we will, our only concern being that we do it well and with all the power in us? Ah Madame, I have drunk your tea and read your book and thought you a charming hostess, but I have not been converted.

And so, indeed, Cullen was not converted, not then by Madame Goll, nor at any other time, as far as can be determined, by anyone else. But it was his *intellectual* conception of poetry and race that could not be changed. Even in this there was ambivalence, though he generally adhered to the proposition that art came first for any artist, well ahead of race. But the writing of poetry is not entirely an act of the intellect (except for a few—Milton,

perhaps). It is a matter of exercising intellectual control upon visceral reactions to life, and for Countee Cullen that meant imposing rational control over the visceral reactions of a black man living the black experience. It is true that he was less isolated from white life than many black men, but this was, in part, the very mixed blessing that accounts for the disparity in point of view among some of his critical pieces, and for the clear incongruity between his artistic racial theory and his poetic practice. An examination of his poetry discloses that more than just in mass but in the range and importance of themes, Cullen was a writer of black verse; that Alain Locke's categorizing of Cullen's poetry was more valid than the poet's own; that Negro poetry is a matter of theme and vantage—or disadvantage—point, and not merely of the inclusion of dialect, of spiritual and blues elements, or the jazz rhythms he deprecated in Hughes.

Michael L. Lomax (essay date 1987)

SOURCE: "Countee Cullen: A Key to the Puzzle," in *The Harlem Renaissance Re-examined,* AMS Press, 1987, pp. 213-22.

[*In the following excerpt, Lomax alleges that Cullen's attitude toward race ultimately stunted his artistic development.*]

Color and Cullen did not entirely escape negative criticism . . . and significantly it was white reviewers who pointed to Cullen's arch-traditionalism and lack of stylistic originality as major flaws in his work. Locke's review had mentioned Cullen's rhyming, but glossed over it by invoking Pope as the model for what he euphemistically termed "this strange modern skill of sparkling couplets" [*Opportunity,* January, 1926]. The white reviewers were not, however, so quick to justify Cullen's old-fashioned style. "Perhaps the only protest to Mr. Cullen that one cares to insist on is against his frequent use of rhetorical style which is surely neither instinctive in origin nor agreeable in effect," wrote *Poetry*'s reviewer. "Lofty diction in poetry when it is unwarranted by feeling . . . is liable to seem only stilted and prosy" [George H. Dillon, *Poetry,* 1926]. the general silence of black reviewers on this point seems to suggest their own agreement with Cullen. The majority black critical view was that New Negro artists should express themselves in time-honored forms and thus give stature to their racial themes. By performing well, within the confines of established literary traditions, black artists would demonstrate their capabilities in a way that could not be disputed.

White reviews of *Color* included one uniform and rather predictable response. They all stated that Cullen's real importance was not merely as a black poet writing of his people's experiences but as a poet expressing the universal human experience. "But though one may recognize that certain of Mr. Cullen's verses owe their being to the fact that he shares the tragedy of his people," wrote Babette Deutsch in *The Nation* [December 30, 1925], "it must be owned that the real virtue of his work lies in his personal response to an experience which, however conditioned by his race, is not so much racial as profoundly human. The color of his mind is more important than the color of his skin."

Ironically, though, it was this specifically racial element in his work which most forcefully appealed to black reviewers. "His race and its sufferings," wrote Walter White, "give him depth and an understanding of pain and sorrow" [*Saturday Review of Literature,* February 13, 1926]. White's emphasis was echoed in other black reviews which praised Cullen as the first real spokesman for sensitive and educated blacks who daily suffered through the pressures and hardships of the American racial experience. "The poems which arise out of the consciousness of being a 'Negro in a day like this' in America," wrote Jessie Fauset in *The Crisis,* ". . . are not only the most beautifully done but they are by far the most significant in the book. . . . Here I am convinced is Mr. Cullen's forte; he has the feelings and the gift to express colored-ness in a world of whiteness. I hope he will not be deflected from continuing to do that of which he has made such a brave and beautiful beginning" [*Crisis,* March, 1926].

Certainly the "colored-ness" which Jessie Fauset praised as an essential feature of Cullen's first volume was a quality which she sensed rather than a sentiment which she found expressed in clear and forthright statements. There were too many non-racial poems for that; and too many poems in which, as she herself pointed out, "the adjectives 'black' or 'brown' or 'ebony' are deliberately introduced to show that the type which the author had in mind was not white." At least in part, though, this inclusion of non-racial and peripherally black poems did suggest Cullen's own particular brand of "colored-ness." For within the context of *Color* as a whole, they implied the tentativeness of Cullen's assertions of a strong sense of his own black identity. These poems, appearing along side verse dealing with specifically racial themes, point to the Du Boisean "double-consciousness" as the central contradiction in Cullen's appraisal of his own racial identity. Neither black nor white, Cullen saw himself somewhere in between, an undefined individual consciousness for whom "colored" became as good a label as any. Thus, the volume as a whole and several poems in particular are haunted by the unresolved conflict in Cullen's perception of himself as simultaneously a black man and a culturally assimilated though, admittedly, socially ostracized Westerner. This central tension became the source of dramatic conflict in Cullen's and *Color*'s best known poem, **"Heritage."** In it, Cullen confronted the contradictions within his own identity and, though finally incapable of resolving them, he articulated his emotional and intellectual struggle with honesty and a rarely-achieved eloquence.

"Heritage" leans towards bonds of racial unity. So does *Color* as a whole, and so do Cullen's works of the early twenties. In light of Cullen's later sift to the opposite pole of assimilation, and his easier acceptance of a more catholic and eclectic Western identity, one wonders why his first volume bore this black stamp. The answer lies in the *milieu*

of the 1920s. *Color* is the product of personal struggle in an atmosphere which reinforced all that was racially distinctive. Sophisticated whites were Negrophiles who wanted to see blacks as essentially different from their own boringly Western selves. Cullen, in spite of strong misgivings, was willing to do as many other New Negroes did, and thus he bowed to white desires. So, much of his later writing became a retraction of the position taken during the twenties. But whatever Cullen did and said later, *Color* remains an impressive and landmark volume, one which quickly established its author as the New Negro poet *par excellence*. To many critics, it also suggested a promise and future which Cullen did not fulfill.

Countee Cullen's sudden and premature death in 1946 at the age of forty-two shocked those who remembered him as he had been at the time of *Color*'s publication, just two brief decades before, then a youthful poet with an auspicious future. At the time of his death, he was still a relatively young man and certainly, in terms of sheer talent, a gifted one as well. And in spite of what had appeared to be a too lengthy hiatus, there were those close to him who felt that his future might have been more productive. "Creative writers sometimes have long periods of silence," mused Langston Hughes, "Had he lived he might have written brilliantly and beautifully again" [*Chicago Defender,* February 2, 1946]. But Cullen's untimely death certainly put an end to such speculations. Neither his youthful promise nor his more matured talent were to be fulfilled. And when Cullen's career is viewed in a more dispassionate and, perhaps, somewhat less generous light than Hughes affords, such sanguine prognostications of what might have been had Cullen only lived hardly seem realistic. In fact, there is a real sense in which Cullen's death, rather than cutting short a still potentially productive career, instead marked a final coda to the poet's bitter period of decline. At forty-two, Cullen had not been a progressively maturing artist confidently expressing his own vision of life—in this case, his vision of black life in America. Rather, with his original gifts atrophying from disuse, Cullen remained a forced-black man who never adjusted comfortably to his racial identity.

During the bleak years which followed the Harlem Renaissance, Cullen continued to publish but without his earlier success. The Depression cut short white interest in black art, and Cullen barely survived the loss of his white audience. Without their interest he rejected entirely the racial themes of the 1920s, limiting himself to the more conventional poetic concerns of love and death. By the 1940s, he had exhausted these and, except for occasional forays into children's literature, wrote practically nothing at all.

Fittingly enough, Cullen made plans before his death to take a final bow in the role of poet. In 1945, he compiled a collection of his published poems and appropriately titled it *On These I Stand*. the volume was to be "an anthology of the best poems of Countee Cullen." He clearly intended the collection to be a final monument to his poetic career and thus, whatever else he might do in the future, it could serve as a basis for evaluating that favored part of his literary life. The volume appeared in 1947, almost exactly one year after his death, and, as he had anticipated, critics used *On These I Stand* as a scale for measuring his entire career. Unfortunately, the final evaluations were not so impressive as Cullen had apparently anticipated.

John Ciardi pointed out that the keyword for Cullen's early career had been "promise." But with his death, "this edition of his selected poems is total. And . . . the total disappoints the large claims that have been made for him" [*Atlantic Monthly,* March, 1947]. Looking through the volume, Ciardi and other critics reviewed Cullen's chronologically arranged poems and discerned a pattern of slow but unquestionable decline. His career was a "descending curve," wrote *Poetry*'s reviewer [in July, 1947], as he traced the lines of deterioration from Cullen's best serious verse of the 1920s through the mediocre and poorer products of later years. Everyone seemed to agree that at the time of his death Cullen had reached a literary low point. Still the question remained: Why? The answers were not so uniform.

Some critics answered that the problem lay in Cullen's conservative response to literary traditions:

> Cullen was singularly unaware of what was going on in the world of poetry. In the age of Pound and Eliot, he tortured syntax and used such words as "aught" and "albeit." He nowhere shows any evidence of studying the styles of any modern poets other than Millay, Wylie, and Housman, although, according to Robert Hillyer, he wrote imitations of most of the older poets in the days at Harvard that preceded the publication of *Color* Perhaps because of his failure to absorb the technical discoveries of his contemporaries, he was singularly unself-critical and could allow such monstrosities . . . to be printed. Certainly his failure to study carefully what other poets did is in part responsible for his never developing a style peculiarly his own. Even the good poems in *On These I Stand* could have been written by any other craftsman, they bear no stylistic signature. [*Poetry,* July, 1947]

Yet, while one of Cullen's deficiencies was obviously a problem of technique, such stylistic considerations do not satisfactorily resolve the issue. For Cullen could at times, through content, overcome his largely self-imposed limitations. "When the observation contained in the poem is directed and personal, dealing immediately with people seen and events that really occurred," Ciardi pointed out, "the poem emerges movingly." That, however, occurred only rarely. Generally, Cullen substituted literary sentiments for sense and feeling and real, intimate response. In later poems, he seemed to have lost whatever original ability he had had to discern between artificial feelings and personal perceptions. He lost the ability to capture essential experiences, as he had done in **"Heritage."** The result for his later poetry was a bland mixture; trite sentimentality expressed in the most outmoded style.

Most white critics thought that Cullen had lapsed into clichés because the demands of race had driven him away from the sincere, personal introspection which was his true concern. According to them, Cullen's natural impulse led toward intimate expression in such pristine forms as the sonnet and "the neat, sensitive, and immediate lyric." Yet, "Increasingly, Cullen's poetry . . . evidences a triumph of conscience over his particular gift, as if he told himself, 'don't you play now. Just do your work'" [*PM,* March 16, 1947]. To work, according to this view, was to write of racial matters—a necessary subject because he was black, an unfortunate one since he was a poet. In this view, the moral and the aesthetic responsibilities were incompatible, irreconcilable. In spite of personal inclinations to do otherwise, Cullen tragically chose race above art. "Somehow or other . . . ," Cullen had admitted, as if to substantiate this argument, "I find my poetry of itself treating of the Negro, of his joys and sorrows—mostly of the latter, and of the heights and depths of emotion which I feel as a Negro." The result of such a decision was that Cullen lost his personal roots and in the process his basis for an individual vision. Without the direction he might have achieved as an integrated individual, this argument went, Cullen's only refuge was in the expression of worn and meaningless sentiments.

Race does indeed appear to be at the root of Cullen's problem, but not for those reasons suggested by white critics. Cullen had once said that he viewed poetry ideally as "a lofty thought beautifully expressed." The issues of race in America constrained this ideal and trespassed upon Cullen's separate pristine world of poetry and art. For race meant harshness, violence and ugliness, all directly opposite to the delicate beauties which he envisioned as the true concerns of poetry. During the 1920s, when whites were enthusiastic Negrophiles, Cullen joined with other New Negroes in, to quote Langston Hughes, expressing their "individual dark-skinned selves without fear or shame" [*The Nation,* June 23, 1926]. The result for Cullen was a vital and often electric poetry, full of the tensions produced by an unresolved sense of his own racial identity in direct conflict with his desire to gain recognition from an enthusiastic white audience which demanded that blacks be different. With the waning white enthusiasm of the Depression, however, Cullen reasserted his intention to be a poet, not a black poet, and accordingly moved away from racial themes. His rejection of race as a thematic priority is nowhere more strongly expressed than in his short poem, **"To Certain Critics,"** in which Cullen defiantly asserted: "I'll bear your censure as your praise, / For never shall the clan / Confine my singing to its ways / Beyond the ways of man." With his rejection of race, Cullen concentrated on the essentially fatuous literary artificialities which were, according to him, the poet's true concern.

Cullen's refusal to accept race as a basic and valuable segment of his total identity was an evasion which prevented him from further straightforward and clear development. Race did not have to be a circumscribing point of view. Nor was Cullen compelled to do as Langston Hughes did and make it the conscious subject of all he wrote. Race was, however, an inescapable aspect of his identity which, in spite of all he said to the contrary, did affect him. . . . Cullen's racial equivocations were rooted deeply in the Harlem Renaissance itself. For the decade of the 1920s was a period of racial confusion and contradiction. Blacks were in vogue, but the values many New Negroes lived by, and the goals they sought, were white. Blacks were forced to play racial roles they did not find comfortable in order to achieve recognition from whites. Few New Negroes overcame the limitations of the period and were able to assert and maintain their own more solid racial and personal integrity. Langston Hughes was one of those few. Countee Cullen was not.

James W. Tuttleton (essay date 1989)

SOURCE: "Countee Cullen at 'The Heights,'" in *The Harlem Renaissance: Revaluations,* Garland Publishing, Inc., 1989, pp. 101-37.

[*In the following excerpt. Tuttleton attempts to demonstrate that Cullen's college experience was a source of considerable influence on his poetry*]

The present work undertakes to describe the undergraduate career of Countee Cullen at New York University between 1922 and 1925 and to present an edited text of his most significant surviving piece of undergraduate critical prose, the senior honors thesis he presented to the Department of English on May 1, 1925: "The Poetry of Edna St. Vincent Millay: An Appreciation." In both biographical and critical treatments of Cullen, these years have received scant attention, although they were immensely formative in his experience as a poet. In fact, the thesis that is presented here has never been published and is largely unknown to Cullen's readers or to students of the Harlem Renaissance.

The mind of a poet, the poetic influences to which he is exposed at an impressionable moment in his life, the critical context in which these influences are received, and the personalities of those having a decisive effect on the shaping of his perceptions and values—all of these are essential in understanding his originality, his development, and his reception. In the case of Countee Cullen, an adequate account of these influences—including the impact of Millay's love lyrics and ballad forms—would require a full-length biography, one devoted with greater rigor to the facts and their critical meaning, moreover, than is evident in Blanche E. Ferguson's *Countee Cullen and the Negro Renaissance* (1966). In the space available here, no such full account is possible. But something of a start may be made by presenting his essay on Millay and by bringing to light some of the facts—hitherto unknown or forgotten—of this remarkable poet's education at New York University.

As will be evident to anyone reading this thesis, Countee Cullen, though only twenty one years old when he wrote the work, was an accomplished and subtle student of poetry. The essay reflects a sensitive understanding of the varied generic and metrical gifts of Millay. And it is passionately responsive to her sense of the fragility and transience of beauty and love in a world where all must change and die. Students of Cullen's poetry have sometimes noted, without demonstrating at any length, the impact on him of Millay's lyric verse. (An exception is Margaret Perry's suggestive comparison, in the work cited below, of **"The Shroud of Color"** with Millay's "Renascence.") The present thesis offers, I believe, the critical ground on which a fuller influence study and a more informed comparative evaluation can be based. For here, in Cullen's "appreciation," will be found a description of the thematic and technical features of Millay's art that Cullen most admired, as well as a commentary on those defects of her performance of which he was most critical.

I am not of course the first to note the relation of Cullen's art to that of Millay. Walter White, for example, linked Cullen to a poetic tradition "of which A.E. Housman and Edna St. Vincent Millay are the bright stars" (quoted in Margaret Perry, *A Bio-Bibliography of Countee P. Cullen, 1903-1946,* 1971). Perry herself has remarked that "Countee Cullen's poetry also bears a close resemblance to both the poetry of Edward Arlington Robinson (whom Cullen considered to be America's finest poet) and of Edna St. Vincent Millay." But Perry was apparently not aware that Cullen had written this thesis—it is not listed among the "Unpublished Works" in her bibliography—so that the ground for a more extensive comparison was not available to her. . . .

[If] in 1930 Cullen gave to Robinson the laurel as the best American poet, in 1925—when he wrote his thesis and published *Color*—Millay was foremost in his mind. Further, while granting that some of the following themes may also be found in Houseman and Keats, I . . . argue that common to both Cullen and Millay are these thematic elements: 1) A profound recognition of the transience of life; 2) a sense of the world as the vale of inexplicable agony and suffering; 3) an awareness of the inadequacy of the usual Christian explanation of why God permits, if he does not authorize, human suffering; 4) the impulse, therefore, to seize the day, to indulge in and celebrate poetically the pleasures of life—especially love in its erotic character and sensuous beauty in all of its forms. I would call this a frank aesthetic and sexual paganism, typical of the disillusioned youth of the 1920s; 5) nevertheless, a recognition that love is transient and sexual pleasure is fleeting—a recognition conveyed in both poets in wry, flip, cynical, and anguished tones; 6) yet the implied wish that it might be otherwise, that the order of existence might fulfill the heart's desire, especially in relation to love and sexuality, together with an occasional affirmation, sometimes like resignation, that there *is* a providential ordering, somehow, of human affairs. All this is just perhaps another way of saying what Countee Cullen himself said in a headnote in *Caroling Dusk,* namely, that one of his chief difficulties had always been "reconciling a Christian upbringing with a pagan inclination." This aesthetic and sexual hedonism, or paganism, in Millay was one of the chief appeals of her work. To these six thematic elements that link Millay and Cullen I would add a seventh, technical parallel: both poets' preference for the conventional forms of the poetic tradition—in relation to rhythms, rhyme schemes, stanzaic structures, and genres—especially the sonnet and the ballad.

. . . . .

Cullen matriculated at University College of Arts and Pure Science [New York University] in February of 1922 and was graduated on June 10, 1925, with a B.A. degree. This college, familiarly called "The Heights," was one of two undergraduate liberal arts colleges of New York University at that time; it was located at University Heights, overlooking the Harlem River in the Bronx. There Cullen majored in English and took a First Minor in French and a Second Minor in Philosophy. Since there has been, as yet, no detailed account of Cullen's educational development, and since he was a poet, it will perhaps be of value to future students of his life and art if I discuss his coursework at The Heights. . . .

Cullen's program of studies and his manifest distinction as a student . . . indicate that he received a solid liberal arts education with a strong emphasis on languages and literature, history and philosophy. He was well-prepared for graduate study at Harvard in either English or French, both of which he later taught in New York City. But even more importantly, for our purposes, this undergraduate education—although just the foundation of his career as a poet—made him acquainted with a wide range of literary forms, styles, and techniques; it educated him about the culture of writers in several national traditions; and it helped him to understand the literary heritage in its historical and philosophical contexts. This much, of course, can be inferred from the poems alone, for his engagement with the literary heritage is implicit in all his characteristic themes and subjects, in his literary allusions, and in his strategies of versification and language use.

When one studies the transcript information against the college bulletins for the years 1922-1925, one particular facet of Cullen's program appears remarkable. Although the English Department boasted a faculty of between fifteen and twenty professors during these years—including local eminences like Dean Archibald L. Bouton, Francis Henry Stoddard, Vernon Loggins, Arthur Huntington Nason, and Homer Watt—almost all of Cullen's English coursework was taken with one man, Professor Hyder E. Rollins. . . .

I shall later return to the influence of Rollins on Countee Cullen's development. But it should be noted that Cullen's apprenticeship as a poet was not limited to the classrooms at The Heights. For he was deeply involved in the extracurricular literary life of the university—in ways that are not evident in the published biographies and bibliographies of his work.

For one thing, Cullen was published in the university literary magazines as early as 1922; and in his junior and senior years, Cullen was in fact the poetry editor of *The Arch: The Literary Magazine of New York University*. The issues of November 1924, and January, March, and May 1925 list him on the masthead. In this role, Cullen corresponded and conferred with other student writers, selected verse for publication, and oversaw the printing of this department of the magazine, which incidentally served students of every college of the university. Even more important, Cullen's own verse appeared in *The Arch*. Neither his poetry editorship nor his publications in *The Arch* have been noted in previous bibliographies of his work. This is worth stressing because critical treatments of volumes like *Color* (1925) and *Copper Sun* (1927) sometimes suggest that the poems in these volumes appeared only in national publications like *Harper's, The Nation, Poetry, Vanity Fair,* etc. However, some verses in these volumes first appeared in *The Arch*. For the sake of clarifying the record, therefore, some attention to his extracurricular work in *The Arch* and its relation to other sites of publication seems warranted.

In Volume I, Number 8 of *The Arch* (June, 1922), p. 13, there appears a "Triolet" beginning "I did not know she'd take it so"; this "Triolet" had first appeared in *The Magpie* (Christmas, 1921), the literary magazine of the De Witt Clinton High School. It was renamed **"Under the Mistletoe"** and republished in *Copper Sun*.

In Volume II (misprinted Volume I), Number 1 of *The Arch* (November, 1923), p. 8, appear two poems. The first is "To——," beginning "Whatever I have loved has wounded me"; this poem is retitled **"A Poem Once Significant, Now Happily Not,"** and is reprinted in *Copper Sun*. The second is "Triolet," beginning "I have wrapped my dreams in a silken cloth"; this poem, retitled **"For a Poet,"** was dedicated to John Gaston Edgar and was republished in *Harper's* (December, 1924) and in *Color*.

In Volume II, Number 2 of *The Arch* (January, 1924), pp. 40-42, appears one of Cullen's most well-known poems, **"The Ballad of the Brown Girl."** This was of course the Second Prize poem in the Witter Bynner Intercollegiate Poetry Contest. Bynner thought it should have won, and advised Cullen to send it for republication to *Palms,* where it appeared in the Early Summer Issue of 1924. Finally, it was republished in book form by Harper and Brothers in 1927.

In Volume II, Number 3 of *The Arch* (March, 1924), p. 88, appeared **"The Love Tree,"** which was reprinted in *Copper Sun*. And in Volume II, Number 4 (May, 1924), p. 122, appeared **"Sacrament,"** which was reprinted in *Color*.

Finally, in Volume III, Number 1 of *The Arch* (November, 1924), p. 17, appeared **"Variations on a Theme,"** which was reprinted in *Copper Sun;* and in the March 1925 issue appeared **"The Poet,"** also reprinted in *Copper Sun*. (This very early poem first appeared in *The Magpie* in November of 1920.)

This record of Cullen's student publications in *The Arch* suggests several things: first, that some of the poems appearing in national periodicals were first tried out in *The Arch;* second, that a number of his other poems in the published volumes first appeared in the NYU student literary magazine; and third, that some of the poems re-printed in *Copper Sun* as "juvenilia" were indeed the work of either his high school or undergraduate years, poems that he had not deemed worth including in *Color*. The pressure to publish his second volume led him to recycle them in order to expand *Copper Sun* to a proper book length.

. . . . .

[A course on Keats] had a permanent influence on Roll-ins's future career—as on Cullen's as well. For Rollins became enchanted with Keats and devoted to his life and work. Out of this ardor came, after Cullen's graduation, several of Rollins's major publications: *Keats' Reputation in America to 1848* (1946), the two-volume *The Keats Circle: Letters and Papers, 1816-1878* (1948), *Keats and the Bostonians* (1951), *More Letters and Poems of the Keats Circle* (1955), and the magisterial two-volume edition of *The Letters of John Keats, 1814-1821* (1958). In my judgment, the many Keatsian thematic and technical characteristics of Cullen's verse—not to speak of the encomia in **"To John Keats, Poet. At Springtime"** and **"To Endymion"**—are directly attributable to Rollins's impassioned lectures on Keats in *English Poets of the Nineteenth Century* during Cullen's junior year, 1923-1924. . . .

Setting aside Keats for the moment, Rollins's mind was also profoundly oriented toward the Renaissance, where his research involved the compilation of an immense collection of popular broadside ballads. On these ballads he worked assiduously during Cullen's undergraduate years. . . .

But if Rollins communicated enthusiasm for ballads to Countee Cullen, behind Rollins—forming a link with Cullen—was Rollins's own mentor, George Lyman Kittredge, who lectured on the ballad form at Harvard and inspired students like Rollins to carry on the work. Kittredge was a man of formidable erudition whose knowledge of the English ballad was founded on the work of *his* Harvard master, F.J. Child. The five-volume *The English and Scottish Popular Ballads*, edited by Francis James Child (to which the young Kittredge had supplied notes and annotations), was the groundwork upon which the work of Kittredge and thereafter Rollins was based. Ultimately, it was also the source of Cullen's ballad poems. Kittredge's one-volume edition of *The English and Scottish Popular Ballads* (1904) also served as the introduction to these poems for generations of Harvard students such as Rollins. But Rollins went even beyond his mentor Kittredge and rivalled Child's monumental work in preparing the original collections I have already named, as well as others published after Cullen's graduation.

Is it any wonder, then, that Cullen's first three volumes, *Color* (1925), *Copper Sun* (1927), and *The Ballad of the Brown Girl* (1927), are full of ballad settings, characters, and stylistic features? Or that he wrote his thesis on a woman poet who, in "The Ballad of the Harp Weaver," had established her claim to eminence with a Pulitzer Prize? Such lines as Cullen's "He rode across like a cavalier, / Spurs clicking hard and loud" (**"Two Who Crossed a Line"**), are unimaginable except under the influence of Rollins's *Cavalier and Puritan: Ballads and Broadsides.* . . . Cullen's portrait of his parents in **"Fruit of the Flower"** is a reflection of Rollins's influence: "My mother's life is puritan, / No hint of cavalier. . . ." Such narrative poems as **"Judas Iscariot,"** as well as Cullen's recurrent use of the *abcb* quatrain, culminate in **"The Ballad of the Brown Girl,"** published in *The Arch* in 1924. This is not the place to offer a full critique of that remarkable poem, which grew directly out of Millay's experiments and out of Rollins's lectures on the ballad tradition and his editing of four volumes of ballads during Cullen's undergraduate years. Yet some observations and clarifications of fact may perhaps be offered here. First, it is very unlikely that Cullen found the source for the ballad in *The Oxford Book of Ballads* or *The Ballad Book*, as Alan R. Shucard has suggested in *Countee Cullen*. In view of Rollins's intimate involvement with Kittredge, with whom he continually corresponded about his ballad work, and in view of Kittredge's connection to F.J. Child, it is more likely that Rollins steered Cullen to the source in Child's edition of "Lord Thomas and Fair Annet" and its variants like "The Nut-Brown Bride," "The Brown Bride and Lord Thomas," "Lord Thomas and Fair Elinor," or "Sweet Willie and Fair Annie." These Child versions of the ballad give the full dramatis personae of Cullen's poem, as the abbreviated versions in the *Oxford* and *The Ballad Book* collections do not. Further, it is beside the point to criticize Cullen for verboseness in expanding the ballad from ten (*Oxford* version) or fifteen (*Ballad Book*) stanzas to fifty. Cullen's poem is only slightly longer than the "E" version of the ballad ("Sweet Willie and Fair Annie"), which runs to forty-two stanzas. Nor is there any point in faulting Cullen, as Houston A. Baker, Jr., does in *A Many-Colored Coat of Dreams: The Poetry of Countee Cullen,* for making Lord Thomas dependent on his mother, since this aspect of Lord Thomas is found in the originals. . . .

Was [Cullen's] individualism, as a black, "eradicated" by the program of English studies he undertook with Rollins and others? Was it inhibited by his turning to the wrong models—to Keats, Millay, Housman, Robinson, the ballad, the white English literary tradition—rather than to the literature of rising black consciousness, represented by Dunbar, McKay, Hughes, and others in Harlem? Or should his models have been the literary modernists then bursting on the scene—Pound, Eliot, cummings, and Hart Crane? Whatever the case, Dean Munn improbably remarked that "If the poetry of youth be ardently sincere, its promise frequently makes its very imperfections insignificant. Let the young poet not fear the critic who, Jeffrey-like, says 'This will never do'" [Introduction to *Some Recent New York University Verse,* edited by David L. Blum, 1926].

One New York University critic who was not afraid to say what would not do was Professor Eda Lou Walton, who taught English at the Washington Square Campus. (I have found no information on whether Cullen knew the playwright and future novelist Thomas Wolfe, who also taught at the Square.) She and Cullen sometimes read or listened to other poets. In *The Critical Review* issue in which Martin Russak fondly remembered his freshman awe of Cullen, Professor Walton undertook to criticize the negative effects on individualism of the "Teasdale-Millay school" then so popular in colleges. In view of the defensive tone of Cullen's thesis on Millay, Walton's comments in "The Undergraduate Poet" deserve serious attention. Speaking of the impact of Teasdale and Millay on youthful writers, Walton remarked: "These young poets upon first falling in love begin to sing sweetly and tritely of their hearts and souls, of longing and yearning, and burning. If they confuse their hearts and souls with trees and stars, with moons and seas, so much the better. They lift and fall with the tides; they are swept by storms, they are lonely as clouds. They are safe in the uniqueness of their emotion and blind, for the most part, to its amusing commonplaceness. Then comes the first disillusionment. They begin 'burning the candle at both ends' and pretending that 'it makes a lovely light,' although often they do not believe a word of it. They turn a bit cleverly cynical and can never end a lyric without some ironical fillip. They announce stridently the uselessness and stupidity of the opposite sex. They try to pick out figs, but are more intent on thistles." For Walton, the "Teasdale-Millays" had little to say, in contrast to another camp of undergraduate poets, whom she identified as the "Cerebrals," whose masters were T.S. Eliot, Hart Crane, e.e. cummings, and Marianne Moore. In characterizing these two camps, Walton was of course implicitly highlighting—and condemning—the conventional academic romanticism of the kind of poetry Cullen was writing, although she never mentions Cullen by name. Cullen's indifference to those currents of poetic modernism, developing on the campus as well as in the international literary culture, has indeed been a constant factor in the definition of his work as "minor."

Whatever one may claim to have been the proper model for Cullen's art, there is no doubt that for Hyder Rollins the English tradition from the Middle Ages onward was the right foundation for a poet. . . .

This overview of Countee Cullen's undergraduate years at "The Heights" suggests several conclusions. First, Cullen was a highly popular and academically successful student who attained an impressive celebrity with his classmates and professors. Trained in a conventional academic program that emphasized the classic writers of the white English tradition, Cullen naturally gravitated to the work of Keats, Robinson, Millay, Masters, and the old ballad writers. Essentially shaped by Hyder E. Rollins, an international scholar with a deep affinity for Keats and the ballad forms, Cullen supplemented his studies by extra-curricular activities like publishing in the student literary periodical, *The Arch,* even editing the magazine in his last two years, and by attending and giving readings of poetry on campus and throughout the country. His achievement was thus an inspiration to other young poets. Some have suggested that Harvard, with its erudition, may have "ruined" Cullen for the task of elevating the quality of down-home, right-on black poetry in the twentieth century. But for better or for worse, Cullen's direction was set well before he got to Harvard: the route was fixed at The Heights.

There is no doubt that his work would have benefited from deeper immersion in the modernist poets then attaining fame—writers like Eliot, Pound, Stevens, and Williams. And it is highly probable that the application of modernist techniques to problems of racial identity and experience would have deepened the impact of poems like **"Heritage," "The Black Christ,"** and others that express his sense of the meaning of blackness in white America, thereby allying him more intimately with the poetic projects of Claude McKay, Langston Hughes, and other figures of the Harlem Renaissance. But Cullen was the product of the forces that shaped him and of the choices and models that he elected. Within those terms and limits, he attained exceptional distinction as a lyric poet with an impassioned romantic sensibility. If he failed to scale the highest point of Parnassus, he did reach the lesser heights.

FURTHER READING

Criticism

Canaday Jr., Nicholas. "Major Themes in the Poetry of Countee Cullen." In *The Harlem Renaissance Remembered,* edited by Arna Bontemps, pp. 103-25. New York: Dodd, Mead & Company, 1972.

> Section on Cullen examines his most significant themes as represented in selected poems.

Davis, Arthur P. *From the Dark Tower: Afro-American Writers 1900 to 1960.* Washington: Howard University Press, 1974, 306 p.

> Contains essays on African American literature in the twentieth century; chapter on Cullen.

Gibson Donald B. "Introduction." In *Modern Black Poets: A Collection of Critical Essays*, pp. 1-17. New Jersey: Prentice-Hall, Inc., 1973.

> Introduction provides excellent background on contemporary Black poetry with special emphasis on the socio-economic context.

Lindberg, John. "Thematic Black Anthologies." *North American Review* 255, No. 1 (Spring 1970): 69-73.

> Compares and contrasts ten anthologies of black poetry, including Cullen's *Caroling Dusk*, and comments upon each volume's approach.

Pinckney, Darryl. "The Sweet Singer Tuckahoe." *The New York Review of Books* 39, No. 5 (March 5, 1992): 14.

> Provides a general biographical background; occasioned by the publication of Cullen's collected writings.

Additional coverage of Cullen's life and career is contained in the following sources published by Gale Research: *Twentieth-Century Literary Criticism*, Vols. 4, 37; *Black Literature Criticism*; *DISCovering Authors*; *Black Writers*, Vol. 1; *Contemporary Authors*, Vols. 108, 124; *Concise Dictionary of American Literary Biography, 1917-1929*; *Dictionary of Literary Biography*, Vols. 4, 48, 51; *Major Twentieth-Century Writers*; and *Something About the Author*, Vol. 18.

George Eliot
1819-1880

(Pseudonym of Mary Ann, or Marian, Evans) English poet, novelist, essayist, editor, short story writer, and translator.

INTRODUCTION

While George Eliot is remembered first and foremost for her insightful novels set in rural England, she also wrote several works of poetry, some of which have been compared favorably with the poems of her contemporary, Elizabeth Barrett Browning, and even with Shakespeare's dramatic verse. Although considered inferior to her novels, Eliot's poetry shares with them the author's interest in moral and philosophical issues as well as her realistic and penetrating approach to character.

Biographical Information

Eliot was raised in Warwickshire, England, by her strict Methodist family, whose views she accepted until she befriended the skeptical philosophers Charles Bray and Charles Hennell. Eliot's association with these two men caused her to challenge and eventually to reject the rigid religious principles of her upbringing. This questioning of values also inspired her first published work, a translation of *Das Leben Jesu* (*The Life of Jesus*) by the German religious philosopher D. F. Strauss. The incident caused a rift with her father, but they later reconciled and she lived with him until his death in 1849.

After her father's death, Eliot moved to London and became acquainted with John Chapman, who hired her as an assistant editor on the *Westminster Review* and introduced her to his literary circle. This group included the philosopher Herbert Spencer, through whom Eliot met the versatile writer and intellectual, George Henry Lewes. Although Lewes was married (he refused to divorce his estranged wife), the two openly lived together until Lewes's death in 1878, defying the strict moral code of the Victorian era. Lewes's influence on Eliot's writing was great: it was he who first encouraged her to write fiction, and he acted as intermediary between the pseudonymous "George Eliot" and her first publisher, *Blackwood's Magazine*. Lewes also sheltered her from adverse criticism of her works, censoring letters and reviews from periodicals. Extremely sensitive to negative reactions to her writing, Eliot removed herself from any controversy surrounding her work.

Eliot's critical acclaim occurred early in her career, and by the end of her life she was regarded as one of the greatest English novelists of her time. Although her reputation declined shortly after her death, her works have been the focus of renewed interest and respect since the late 1940s.

Major Works

Like her novels, Eliot's poetry reflects a variety of influences: her rural English background and family life; her travels abroad (particularly to Spain); and her study of Jewish customs and religious beliefs.

Eliot's sonnet sequence, *Brother and Sister,* was based on affectionate memories of her childhood. Her first book of dramatic verse, *The Spanish Gypsy,* was influenced both by the works of the Romantic poet William Wordsworth and by Greek tragedy. Here, her aim was to find a "suitable set of historical and local conditions" with which to give this tragic poem "a clothing." The novelist Henry James praised *The Spanish Gypsy* for its "extraordinary rhetorical energy and elegance." Although the poem was ultimately considered flawed, the memorable characters of Zarca and Don Silva are often discussed in literary scholarship. "Armgart," thought to be the best poem from the collection *The Legend of Jubal and Other Poems,* has also been lauded for its understanding of the psychological aspect of human characters and their internal conflicts and desires. Like *The Spanish Gypsy,* "Armgart" is a dramatic poem. It has been described as capturing the personal and public divisions of the female artist as well as Eliot's personal concerns about the exposure of recognition. Taken as a whole, Eliot's poetry is thought to highlight her sensitivity to the sound of language and her preoccupation with the thematic concerns of religion and morality.

Critical Reception

Eliot's poetry has generally been assessed as significantly inferior to her novels. In fact, scholars have speculated that Eliot ultimately abandoned writing poetry as a result of unenthusiastic critical reception. Yet while her poetic career is most often deemed a "failure," *The Spanish Gypsy* has been praised for its authentic presentation of the struggles of the Jewish "gypsy" in Spain. This poem is thought to be fertile ground for her later novel, *Daniel Deronda*. *The Legend of Jubal and Other Poems* is similarly considered a necessary step toward Eliot's later novels and essays. Thus, study of her poems today is often undertaken to achieve a better understanding of her novels and the poetic qualities of her prose style.

PRINCIPAL WORKS

Poetry

The Spanish Gypsy: A Poem 1868
Brother and Sister 1869
"Armgart" 1871
The Legend of Jubal and Other Poems 1874

Other Major Works

The Life of Jesus [translation] (essay) 1846
Scenes of Clerical Life (short stories) 1858
Adam Bede (novel) 1859
"The Lifted Veil" (short story) 1859
The Mill on the Floss (novel) 1860
Silas Marner (novel) 1861
Romola (novel) 1863
"Brother Jacob" (short story) 1864
Felix Holt (novel) 1866
Middlemarch (novel) 1872
Daniel Deronda (novel) 1876
Impressions of Theophrastus Such (essays) 1879

CRITICISM

The Nation (review date 1868)

SOURCE: Review of *The Spanish Gypsy*, in *The Nation: A Weekly Journal*, Vol. VII, No. 157, July 2, 1868, pp. 12-14.

[*In the following excerpt, the critic considers* The Spanish Gypsy *unsuccessful as a poem.*]

[George Eliot is] one of the best of English writers; she is, incidentally to this, an excellent story-teller—a real novelist, in fact—and she is, finally, an elegant moralist. In her novels she had never struck us as possessing the poetic character. But at last, to-day, late in her career, she surprises the world with a long poem, which, if it fails materially to deepen our esteem for her remarkable talents, will certainly not diminish it. We should have read George Eliot to but little purpose if we could still suppose her capable of doing anything inconsiderable. Her mind is of that superior quality that impresses its distinction even upon works misbegotten and abortive. *The Spanish Gypsy* is certainly very far from being such a work; but to those who have read the author's novels attentively it will possess no further novelty than that of outward form. It exhibits the delightful qualities of *Romola, The Mill on the Floss,* and even *Silas Marner,* applied to a new order of objects, and in a new fashion; but it exhibits, to our perception, no new qualities. George Eliot could not possess the large and rich intellect which shines in her writings without being something of a poet. We imagine that the poetic note could be not unfrequently detected by a delicate observer who should go through her novels in quest of it; but we believe, at the same time, that it would be found to sound neither very loud nor very long. There is a passage in the *Mill on the Floss* which may illustrate our meaning. The author is speaking of the eternal difference between the patient, drearily-vigilant lives of women, and the passionate, turbulent existence of men; of the difference having existed from the days of Hecuba and Hector; of the women crowding within the gates with streaming eyes and praying hands; of the men without on the plain (we quote only from recollection) "quenching memory in the stronger light of purpose, and losing the sense of battle and even of wounds in the hurrying ardor of action." Elsewhere, in *Romola,* she speaks of the purifying influence of public confession, springing from the fact that "by it the hope in lies is for ever swept away, and *the soul recovers the noble attitude of simplicity.*" In these two sentences, if we are not mistaken, there is a certain poetic light, a poetic ring. The qualities are not intense—they gleam, tremble, and vanish; but they indicate the manner in which a brilliant mind, when reason and sense guard the helm and direct the course, may yet, without effort, touch and hover upon the verge of poetry. *The Spanish Gypsy* contains far finer things than either of these simple specimens—things, indeed, marvellously fine; but they have been gathered, inour opinion, upon this cold outer verge—they are not the glowing, scented fruit that ripens beneath the meridian.

The poem was composed, the author intimates, while Spain was yet known to her only by descriptions and recitals; it was then, after a visit to the country, rewritten and enlarged. These facts correspond somehow to an impression made upon the reader's mind. The work is primarily—like the author's other productions, we think—an eminently intellectual performance; not the result of experience, or of moral and sensuous impressions. In this circumstance reside at once its strength and its weakness; its want of heat, of a quickening central flame; and its admirable perfection of manner, its densely wrought, richly embroidered garment of thought and language. Never, assuredly, was a somewhat inefficient spirit so richly supplied with the outward organs and faculties of maturity and manhood. George Eliot has nothing in common, either in her merits or her defects, with the late Mrs. Browning. The critic is certainly not at his case with Mrs. Browning until he has admitted, once for all, that she is a born poet. But she is without tact and without taste; her faults of detail are unceasing. George Eliot is not a born poet; but, on the other hand, her intellectual tact is equally delicate and vigorous, her taste is infallible, she is never guilty of errors or excesses. In the whole length of the volume before us we have not observed a single slovenly line, a single sentence unpolished or unfinished. And of strong and beautiful lines what a number; of thoughts deep and clear, of images vivid and complete, of heavily-burdened sentences happily delivered of their meaning, what an endless variety! The whole poem is a tissue of the most elegant, most intelligent rhetoric.

Henry James (review date 1868)

SOURCE: A review of *The Spanish Gypsy*, in *A Century of George Eliot Criticism*, edited by Gordon S. Haight, Houghton Mifflin Company, 1965, pp. 55-64.

[*In the following review, which was originally published in* The North American Review *in October 1868, James comments on the inferiority of Eliot's poetry in comparison with her novels.*]

I know not whether George Eliot has any enemies, nor why she should have any; but if perchance she has, I can imagine them to have hailed the announcement of a poem from her pen as a piece of particularly good news. "Now, finally," I fancy them saying, "this sadly overrated author will exhibit all the weakness that is in her; now she will prove herself what we have all along affirmed her to be,—not a serene, self-directing genius of the first order, knowing her powers and respecting them, and content to leave well enough alone, but a mere showy rhetorician, possessed and prompted, not by the humble spirit of truth, but by an insatiable longing for applause." Suppose Mr. Tennyson were to come out with a novel, or Madame George Sand were to produce a tragedy in French alexandrines. The reader will agree with me, that these are hard suppositions; yet the world has seen stranger things, and been reconciled to them. Nevertheless, with the best possible will toward our illustrious novelist, it is easy to put ourselves in the shoes of these hypothetical detractors. No one, assuredly, but George Eliot could mar George Eliot's reputation; but there was room for the fear that she might do it. This reputation was essentially prose-built, and in the attempt to insert a figment of verse of the magnitude of *The Spanish Gypsy*, it was quite possible that she might injure its fair proportions.

In consulting her past works, for approval of their hopes and their fears, I think both her friends and her foes would have found sufficient ground for their arguments. Of all our English prose-writers of the present day I think I may say, that, as a writer simply, a mistress of style, I have been very near preferring the author of *Silas Marner* and of *Romola*,—the author, too, of *Felix Holt*. The motive of my great regard for her style I take to have been that I fancied it such perfect solid prose. Brilliant and lax as it was in tissue, it seemed to contain very few of the silken threads of poetry; it lay on the ground like a carpet, instead of floating in the air like a banner. If my impression was correct, *The Spanish Gypsy* is not a genuine poem. And yet, looking over the author's novels in memory, looking over them in the light of her unexpected assumption of the poetical function, I find it hard at times not to mistrust my impression. I like George Eliot well enough, in fact, to admit, for the time, that I might have been in the wrong. If I had liked her less, if I had rated lower the quality of her prose, I should have estimated coldly the possibilities of her verse. Of course, therefore, if, as I am told many persons do in England, who consider carpenters and weavers and millers' daughters no legitimate subject for reputable fiction, I had denied her novels any qualities at all, I should have made haste, on reading the announcement of her poem, to speak of her as the world speaks of a lady, who, having reached a comfortable middle age, with her shoulders decently covered, "for reasons deep below the reach of thought," (to quote our author,) begins to go out to dinner in a low-necked dress "of the period," and say in fine, in three words, that she was going to make a fool of herself.

But here, meanwhile, is the book before me, to arrest all this *a priori* argumentation. Time enough has elapsed since its appearance for most readers to have uttered their opinons, and for the general verdict of criticism to have been formed. In looking over several of the published reviews, I am struck with the fact that those immediately issued are full of the warmest delight and approval, and that, as the work ceases to be a novelty, objections, exceptions, and protests multiply. This is quite logical. Not only does it take a much longer time than the reviewer on a weekly journal has at his command to properly appreciate a work of the importance of *The Spanish Gypsy*, but the poem was actually much more of a poem than was to be expected. The foremost feeling of many readers must have been—it was certainly my own—that we had hitherto only half known George Eliot. Adding this dazzling new half to the old one, readers constructed for the moment a really splendid literary figure. But gradually the old half began to absorb the new, and to assimilate its virtues and failings, and critics finally remembered that the cleverest writer in the world is after all nothing and no one but himself.

The most striking quality in *The Spanish Gypsy*, on a first reading, I think, is its extraordinary rhetorical energy and elegance. The richness of the author's style in her novels gives but an inadequate idea of the splendid generosity of diction displayed in the poem. She is so much of a thinker and an observer that she draws very heavily on her powers of expression, and one may certainly say that they not only never fail her, but that verbal utterance almost always bestows upon her ideas a peculiar beauty and fulness, apart from their significance. The result produced in this manner, the reader will see, may come very near being poetry; it is assuredly eloquence. The faults in the present work are very seldom faults of weakness, except in so far as it is weak to lack an absolute mastery of one's powers: they arise rather from an excess of rhetorical energy, from a desire to attain to perfect fulness and roundness of utterance; they are faults of overstatement. . . .

I may say in general, that the author's admirers must have found in *The Spanish Gypsy* a presentment of her various special gifts stronger and fuller, on the whole, than any to be found in her novels. Those who valued her chiefly for her humor—the gentle humor which provokes a smile, but deprecates a laugh—will recognize that delightful gift in Blasco, and Lorenzo, and Roldan, and Juan,—slighter in quantity than in her prose-writings, but quite equal, I think, in quality. Those who prize most her descriptive powers will see them wondrously well embodied in these pages. As for those who have felt compelled to declare that she possesses the Shakespearian touch, they must consent, with what grace they may, to be disappointed. I have never thought our author a great dramatist, nor even a particularly dramatic writer. A real dramatist, I imagine, could never have reconciled himself to the odd mixture of the narrative and dramatic forms by which the present work is distinguished; and that George Eliot's genius should have needed to work under these conditions seems to me strong evidence of the partial and incomplete character of her dramatic instincts. An English critic lately described her, with much correctness, as a critic rather than a creator of characters. She puts her figures into action very successfully, but on the whole she thinks for them more than they think for themselves. She thinks, however, to wonderfully good purpose. In none of her works, are there two more distinctly human representations than the characters of Silva and Juan. The latter, indeed, if I am not mistaken, ranks with Tito Melema and Hetty Sorrel, as one of her very best conceptions. . . .

But now to reach the real substance of the poem, and to allow the reader to appreciate the author's treatment of human character and passion, I must speak briefly of the story. I shall hardly misrepresent it, when I say that it is a very old one, and that it illustrates that very common occurrence in human affairs,—the conflict of love and duty. Such, at least, is the general impression made by the poem as it stands. It is very possible that the author's primary intention may have had a breadth which has been curtailed in the execution of the work,—that it was her wish to present a struggle between nature and culture, between education and the instinct of race. You can detect in such a theme the stuff of a very good drama,—a somewhat stouter stuff, however, than *The Spanish Gypsy* is made of. George Eliot, true to that didactic tendency for which she has hitherto been remarkable, has preferred to make her heroine's predicament a problem in morals, and has thereby, I think, given herself hard work to reach a

satisfactory solution. She has, indeed, committed herself to a signal error, in a psychological sense,—that of making a Gypsy girl with a conscience. Either Fedalma was a perfect Zincala in temper and instinct,—in which case her adhesion to her father and her race was a blind, passionate, sensuous movement which is almost expressly contradicted,—or else she was a pure and intelligent Catholic, in which case nothing in the nature of a struggle can bepredicted. The character of Fedalma, I may say, comes very near being a failure,—a very beautiful one; but in point of fact it misses it.

It misses it, I think, thanks to that circumstance which in reading and criticising *The Spanish Gypsy* we must not cease to bear in mind, the fact that the work is emphatically a *romance*. We may contest its being a poem, but we must admit that it is a romance in the fullest sense of the word. Whether the term may be absolutely defined I know not; but we may say of it, comparing it with the novel, that it carries much farther that compromise with reality which is the basis of all imaginative writing. In the romance this principle of compromise pervades the superstructure as well as the basis. The most that we exact is that the fable be consistent with itself. Fedalma is not a real Gypsy maiden. The conviction is strong in the reader's mind that a genuine Spanish Zincala would have somehow contrived both to follow her tribe and to keep her lover. If Fedalma is not real, Zarca is even less so. He is interesting, imposing, picturesque; but he is very far, I take it, from being a genuine *Gypsy* chieftain. They are both ideal figures,—the offspring of a strong mental desire for creatures well rounded in their elevation and heroism,—creatures who should illustrate the nobleness of human nature divorced from its smallness. Don Silva has decidedly more of the common stuff of human feeling, more charming natural passion and weakness. But he, too, is largely a vision of the intellect; his constitution is adapted to the atmosphere and the climate of romance. Juan, indeed, has one foot well planted on the lower earth; but Juan is only an accessory figure. I have said enough to lead the reader to perceive that the poem should not be regarded as a rigid transcript of actual or possible fact,—that the action goes on in an artificial world, and that properly to comprehend it he must regard it with a generous mind.

Viewed in this manner, as efficient figures in an essentially ideal and romantic drama, Fedalma and Zarca seem to gain vastly, and to shine with a brilliant radiance. If we reduce Fedalma to the level of the heroines of our modern novels, in which the interest aroused by a young girl is in proportion to the similarity of her circumstances to those of the reader, and in which none but the commonest feelings are required, provided they be expressed with energy, we shall be tempted to call her a solemn and cold-blooded jilt. In a novel it would have been next to impossible for the author to make the heroine renounce her lover. In novels we not only forgive that weakness which is common and familiar and human, but we actually demand it. But in poetry, although we are compelled to adhere to the few elementary passions of our nature, we do our best to dress them in a new and exquisite garb. Men and women in a poetical drama are nothing, if not distinguished.

Our dear young love,—its breath was happiness!
But it had grown upon a larger life,
Which tore its roots asunder.

These words are uttered by Fedalma at the close of the poem, and in them she emphatically claims the distinction of having her own private interests invaded by those of a people. The manner of her kinship with the Zincali is in fact very much "larger life" than her marriage with Don Silva. We may, indeed, challenge the probability of her relationship to her tribe impressing her mind with a force equal to that of her love,—her "dear young love." We may declare that this is an unnatural and violent result. For my part, I think it is very far from violent; I think the author has employed art in reducing the apparently arbitrary quality of her preference for her tribe. I say reducing; I do not say effacing; because it seems to me, as I have intimated, that just at this point her art has been wanting, and we are not sufficiently prepared for Fedalma's movement by a sense of her Gypsy temper and instincts. Still, we are in some degree prepared for it by various passages in the opening scenes of the book,—by all the magnificent description of her dance in the Plaza. . . .

We are better prepared for it, however, than by anything else, by the whole impression we receive of the exquisite refinement and elevation of the young girl's mind,—by all that makes her so bad a Gypsy. She possesses evidently a very high-strung intellect, and her whole conduct is in a higher key, as I may say, than that of ordinary women, or even ordinary heroines. She is natural, I think, in a poetical sense. She is consistent with her own prodigiously superfine character. From a lower point of view than that of the author, she lacks several of the desirable feminine qualities,—a certain womanly warmth and petulance, a graceful irrationality. Her mind is very much too lucid, and her aspirations too lofty. Her conscience, especially, is decidedly over-active. But this is a distinction which she shares with all the author's heroines,—Dinah Morris, Maggie Tulliver, Romola, and Esther Lyon,—a distinction, moreover, for which I should be very sorry to hold George Eliot to account. There are most assuredly women and women. While Messrs. Charles Reade and Wilkie Collins, and Miss Braddon and her school, tell one half the story, it is no more than fair that the author of *The Spanish Gypsy* should, all unassisted attempt to relate the other.

Whenever a story really interests one, he is very fond of paying it the compliment of imagining it otherwise constructed, and of capping it with a different termination. In the present case, one is irresistibly tempted to fancy *The Spanish Gypsy* in prose,—a compact, regular drama: not George Eliot's prose, however: in a diction much more nervous and heated and rapid, written with short speeches as well as long. (The reader will have observed the want of brevity, retort, interruption, rapid alternation, in the dialogue of the poem. The characters all talk, as it were, standing still.) In such a play as the one indicated one imagines a truly dramatic Fedalma,—a passionate, sensuous, irrational Bohemian, as elegant as good breeding and native good taste could make her, and as pure as her

actual sister in the poem,—but rushing into her father's arms with a cry of joy, and losing the sense of her lover's sorrow in what the author has elsewhere described as "the hurrying ardor of action." Or in the way of a different termination, suppose that Fedalma should for the time value at once her own love and her lover's enough to make her prefer the latter's destiny to that represented by her father. Imagine, then, that, after marriage, the Gypsy blood and nature should begin to flow and throb in quicker pulsations,—and that the poor girl should sadly contrast the sunny freedom and lawless joy of her people's lot with the splendid rigidity and formalism of her own. You may conceive at this point that she should pass from sadness to despair, and from despair to revolt. Here the catastrophe may occur in a dozen different ways. Fedalma may die before her husband's eyes, of unsatisfied longing for the fate she has rejected; or she may make an attempt actually to recover her fate, by wandering off and seeking out her people. The cultivated mind, however, it seems to me, imperiously demands that, on finally overtaking them, she shall die of mingled weariness and shame, as neither a good Gypsy nor a good Christian, but simply a good figure for a tragedy. But there is a degree of levity which almost amounts to irreverence in fancying this admirable performance as anything other than it is.

After Fedalma comes Zarca, and here our imagination flags. Not so George Eliot's: for as simple imagination, I think that in the conception of this impressive and unreal figure it appears decidedly at its strongest. With Zarca, we stand at the very heart of the realm of romance. There is truly a grand simplicity, to my mind, in the outline of his character, and a remarkable air of majesty in his poise and attitude. He is a *père noble* in perfection. His speeches have an exquisite eloquence. In strictness, he is to the last degree unreal, illogical, and rhetorical; but a certain dramatic unity is diffused through his character by the depth and energy of the colors in which he is painted. With a little less simplicity, his figure would be decidedly modern. As it stands, it is neither modern nor mediaeval; it belongs to the world of intellectual dreams and visions. The reader will admit that it is a vision of no small beauty, the conception of a stalwart chieftain who distils the cold exaltation of his purpose from the utter loneliness and obloquy of his race. . . .

Better than Fedalma or than Zarca is the remarkably beautiful and elaborate portrait of Don Silva, in whom the author has wished to present a young nobleman as splendid in person and in soul as the dawning splendor of his native country. In the composition of his figure, the real and the romantic, brilliancy and pathos, are equally commingled. He cannot be said to stand out in vivid relief. As a piece of painting, there is nothing commanding, aggressive, brutal, as I may say, in his lineaments. But they will bear close scrutiny. Place yourself within the circumscription of the work, breathe its atmosphere, and you will see that Don Silva is portrayed with a delicacy to which English story-tellers, whether in prose or verse, have not accustomed us. There are better portraits in Browning, but there are also worse; in Tennyson there are none as good; and in the other great poets of the present century there are no attempts, that I can remember, to which we may compare it. In spite of the poem being called in honor of his mistress, Don Silva is in fact the central figure in the work. Much more than Fedalma, he is the passive object of the converging blows of Fate. The young girl, after all, did what was easiest; but he is entangled in a network of agony, without choice or compliance of his own. It is an admirable subject admirably treated. I may describe it by saying that it exhibits a perfect aristocratic nature, (born and bred at a time when democratic aspirations were quite irrelevant to happiness), dragged down by no fault of its own into the vulgar mire of error and expiation. The interest which attaches to Don Silva's character revolves about its exquisite human weakness, its manly scepticism, its antipathy to the trenchant, the absolute, and arbitrary. . . . Throughout the poem, we are conscious, during the evolution of his character, of the presence of these high mystical influences, which, combined with his personal pride, his knightly temper, his delicate culture, form a splendid background for passionate dramatic action. The finest pages in the book, to my taste, are those which describe his lonely vigil in the Gypsy camp, after he has failed in winning back Fedalma, and has pledged his faith to Zarca. Placed under guard, and left to his own stern thoughts, his soul begins to react against the hideous disorder to which he has committed it, to proclaim its kinship with "customs and bonds and laws," and its sacred need of the light of human esteem. . . . To be appreciated at their worth, these pages should be attentively read. Nowhere has the author's marvellous power of expression, the mingled dignity and pliancy of her style, obtained a greater triumph. She has reproduced the expression of a mind with the same vigorous distinctness as that with which a great painter represents the expression of a countenance.

The character which accords best with my own taste is that of the minstrel Juan, an extremely generous conception. He fills no great part in the drama; he is by nature the reverse of a man of action; and, strictly, the story could very well dispense with him. Yet, for all that, I should be sorry to lose him, and lose thereby the various excellent things which are said of him and by him. I do not include his songs among the latter. Only two of the lyrics in the work strike me as good: the song of Pablo, "The world is great: the birds all fly from me"; and, in a lower degree, the chant of the Zincali, in the fourth book. . . .

When Juan talks at his ease, he strikes the note of poetry much more surely than when he lifts his voice in song:—

> Yet if your graciousness will not disdain
> A poor plucked songster, shall he sing to you?
> *Some lay of afternoons,—some ballad strain*
> *Of those who ached once, but are sleeping now*
> *Under the sun-warmed flowers?*

Juan's link of connection with the story is, in the first place, that he is in love with Fedalma, and, in the second, as a piece of local color. . . .

In every human imbroglio, be it of a comic or a tragic nature, it is good to think of an observer standing aloof, the critic, the idle commentator of it all, taking notes, as we may say, in the interest of truth. The exercise of this function is the chief ground of our interest in Juan. Yet as a man of action, too, he once appeals most irresistibly to our sympathies: I mean in the admirable scene with Hinda, in which he wins back his stolen finery by his lute-playing. This scene, which is written in prose, has a simple, realistic power which renders it a truly remarkable composition.

Of the different parts of **The Spanish Gypsy** I have spoken with such fulness as my space allows: it remains to add a few remarks upon the work as a whole. Its great fault is simply that it is not a genuine poem. It lacks the hurrying quickness, the palpitating warmth, the bursting melody of such a creation. A genuine poem is a tree that breaks into blossom and shakes in the wind. George Eliot's elaborate composition is like a vast mural design in mosaic-work, where great slabs and delicate morsels of stone are laid together with wonderful art, where there are plenty of noble lines and generous hues, but where everything is rigid, measured, and cold,—nothing dazzling, magical, and vocal. The poem contains a number of faulty lines,—lines of twelve, of eleven, and of eight syllables,—of which it is easy to suppose that a more sacredly commissioned versifier would not have been guilty. Occasionally, in the search for poetic effect, the author decidedly misses her way:

> All her being paused
> In resolution, *as some leonine wave,* etc.

A "leonine" wave is rather too much of a lion and too little of a wave. The work possesses imagination, I think, in no small measure. The description of Silva's feelings during the sojourn in the Gypsy camp is strongly pervaded by it; or if perchance the author achieved these passages without rising on the wings of fancy, her glory is all the greater. But the poem is wanting in passion. The reader is annoyed by a perpetual sense of effort and of intellectual tension. It is a characteristic of George Eliot, I imagine, to allow her impressions to linger a long time in her mind, so that by the time they are ready for use they have lost much of their original freshness and vigor. They have acquired, of course, a number of artificial charms but they have parted with their primal natural simplicity. In this poem, we see the landscape, the people, the manners of Spain as through a glass smoked by the flame of meditative vigils, just as we saw the outward aspect of Florence in *Romola*. The brightness of coloring is there, the artful *chiaroscuro*, and all the consecrated properties of the scene; but they gleam in an artificial light. The background of the action is admirable in spots, but is cold and mechanical as a whole. The immense rhetorical ingenuity and elegance of the work, which constitute its main distinction, interfere with the faithful uncompromising reflection of the primary elements of the subject.

The great merit of the characters is that they are marvelously well *understood,*—far better understood than in the ordinary picturesque romance of action, adventure and mystery. And yet they are not understood to the bottom;

they retain an indefinably factitious air, which is not sufficiently justified by their position as ideal figures. The reader who has attentively read the closing scene of the poem will know what I mean. The scene shows remarkable talent; it is eloquent, it is beautiful; but it is arbitrary and fanciful, more than unreal,—untrue. The reader silently chafes and protests, and finally breaks forth and cries, "O for a blast from the outer world!" Silva and Fedalma have developed themselves so daintily and elaborately within the close-sealed precincts of the author's mind, that they strike us at last as acting not as simple human creatures, but as downright *amateurs* of the morally graceful and picturesque. To say that this is the ultimate impression of the poem is to say that it is not a great work. It is in fact not a great drama. It is, in the first place, an admirable study of character,—an essay, as they say, toward the solution of a given problem in conduct. In the second, it is a noble literary performance. It can be read neither without interest in the former respect, nor without profit for its signal merits of style,—and this in spite of the fact that the versification is, as the French say, as little *réussi* as was to be expected in a writer beginning at a bound with a kind of verse which is very much more difficult than even the best prose,—the author's own prose. I shall indicate most of its merits and defects, great and small, if I say it is a romance,—a romance written by one who is emphatically a thinker.

London Quarterly Review (review date 1868)

SOURCE: Review of *The Spanish Gypsy*, in *London Quarterly Review*, Vol. 31, No. LXI, 1868, pp. 160-88.

[*In the following assessment of* The Spanish Gypsy, *the reviewer argues that the poem "must be considered rather as a highly poetic work elaborated in the prose method, than as a production strictly poetical in all respects."*]

Hitherto she has kept just on the verge of verse, at the extreme pitch of poetry in prose; and this is, perhaps, one of her greatest merits in workmanship. In writing high-toned and intensely-poetic prose, a besetting difficulty is to avoid breaking into rhythm. To one with a thorough command of language, the mere transit from prose to blank verse would present no difficulty whatever, and would often be a great relief; but the great feat, when under the excitement of working prose artistically, is to keep it thoroughly true to prose principles; and, at the same time, it is absolutely essential that no effort be betrayed in keeping prose prose. Still, George Eliot has done this; and the grand outline and features of her art show nowhere any distortion of struggle or hard repression. At length, however, the rhythmic impulse has got the upper hand, and we have a work from George Eliot in verse. . . .

Without entering upon a discussion of the *minutia* of morality involved in this story, we may remark that the philosophical resources of the plot are made use of to the utmost. The amount of discussion which finds utterance in the pages of *The Spanish Gypsy,* and the valuable

series of analyses of mental phenomena which have been effected, are nothing less than startling; and there can be no question that a book of more noble intention or more lofty thought is hard to find, if it be at all discoverable. The highest poetical qualities George Eliot has not before failed of reaching—those qualities summed up under the the head of idealisation—she has here grasped with a hand strong as ever. But is the seeker after the technical beauties of poetry satisfied, when he comes to these pages, in a degree nearly approaching that in which the seeker for the technical beauties of high prose is satisfied in her former works? In this question, we but restate the problem whether *The Spanish Gypsy* is a new birth calling for congratulation, in respect of the method of its execution. To those who look critically at the external forms of poetry there is something not quite attractive, in the first place, in the composite form which the author has selected for this poem—or rather invented, for it is quite a new thing. *The Spanish Gypsy* opens with descriptive narration in blank verse, which passes into dialogue, interrupted by greater and smaller passages of description and explanation in blank verse, besides a copious supply of lyrics, and very elaborate stage directions in prose. One or two of the dramatic scenes, also, are entirely in prose. Now a first glance at the outline of this poem would lead one conversant with the author's works to the idea that the old method had been adopted—that the work had been produced on the same principles of procedure as her prose works, with the exception of the sense being conveyed rhythmically instead of unrhythmically. But it would be rash to come to such a conclusion without a thorough examination of the work page by page and line by line.

The characteristic of the modern novel method, in contradistinction to the dramatic method, is that the personages are not made to depend solely on their own utterances and reflective utterances of fellow-characters for the impression which the reader gets of them, but are constantly assisted by a running commentary analytical and explanatory. In a prose work of art, too, we get bits of landscape &c. which are left to the imagination in the drama, and the effects of this and that circumstance are constantly analysed and explained by the narrator, instead of being implied in the general action of the drama, or in subtly condensed touches of dialogue or monologue. Now, although we get all these prose characteristics in *The Spanish Gypsy,* they alone would not be sufficient to stamp the method as the prose method, unless minute examination lent its support to such an imputation. After making a minute examination of the work, we are of opinion that, taken as a whole, and notwithstanding the exquisite touches of true poetic expression scattered through it, it must be considered rather as a highly poetic work elaborated in the prose method, than as a production strictly poetical in all respects.

The Spanish Gypsy would be known anywhere for the production of George Eliot, by virtue of the ideas which go to furnish its fabric; but no distinct individual poetic manner is traceable from page to page, as is the case with Tennyson and Browning, or such poets of less perfection in manner as Mrs. Browning and Edgar Poe. In the following magnificent passage there is a wealth and breadth of thought, and a certain catholic and historic class of thought, that is but seldom to be found in the works of other artists than George Eliot; but what is there to distinguish the style as hers? Indeed, in the most exquisitely *expressed* passage, those which have been italicised might, with a shade less breadth of view, have passed for extract from some of the best works of Mrs. Browning:—

> But other futures stir the world's great heart.
> Europe is come to her majority,
> And enters on the vast inheritance
> Won from the tombs of mighty ancestors,
> The seeds, the gold, the gems, the silent harps
> That lay deep buried with the memories
> Of old renown.
> *No more, as once in sunny Avignon,*
> *The poet-scholar spreads the Homeric page,*
> *And gazes sadly, like the deaf at song;*
> *For now the old epic voices ring again*
> *And vibrate with the beat and melody*
> *Stirred by the warmth of old Ionian days.*
> The martyred sage, the Attic orator,
> Immortally incarnate, like the gods,
> In spiritual bodies, wingèd words
> Holding a universe impalpable,
> Find a new audience. For evermore,
> With grander resurrection than was feigned
> Of Attila's fierce Huns, the soul of Greece
> Conquers the bulk of Persia. *The maimed form*
> *Of calmly-joyous beauty, marble-limbed,*
> *Yet breathing with the thought that shaped its lips,*
> *Looks mild reproach from out its opened grave*
> *At creeds of terror; and the vine-wreathed god*
> *Rising, a stifled question from the silence,*
> *Fronts the pierced Image with the crown of thorns.*
> The soul of man is widening towards the past:
> No longer hanging at the breast of life
> Feeding in blindness to his parentage—
> Quenching all wonder with Omnipotence,
> Praising a name with indolent piety—
> He spells the record of his long descent,
> More largely conscious of the life that was.
> And from the height that shows where morning
>   shone
> On far-off summits pale and gloomy now,
> The horizon widens round him, and the west
> Looks vast with untracked waves whereon his gaze
> Follows the flight of the swift-vanished bird
> That like the sunken sun is mirrored still
> Upon the yearning soul within the eye.

We must not be misunderstood as insinuating that George Eliot has plagiarised in the slightest degree the expressions of Mrs. Browning, or of any other poet; but in judging whether a new poem is to be regarded as truly and unmistakably poetic in expression, it is necessary as a preliminary induction to bring together such passages as are most striking; and, having ranged them before him, the critic must decide whether they constitute a manner of expression original as well as beautiful. This method of procedure discovers in **The Spanish Gypsy** the fact that

such distinctly poetic style as the author has developed has been the result of the unconsciously assimilative faculty. This is frequently the case with writers of intense poetic feeling, whose mode of expression is other than the poetic mode. A happy thought comes, and is happily expressed; but, when analysed technically, it is found to be expressed as A or B would have expressed it, had his mind been the fortunate nursing-ground of the idea:—not that the actual possessor of the idea has borrowed a single word from A or B; but that antecedent familiarity with A's or B's work has stamped certain forms or lines of speech on a mind which, if occupied by a poetic technical equipment of its own, would not have assimilated such forms or lines. And thus it is that we meet in **The Spanish Gypsy** passages which, without perhaps the slightest resemblance to any special passage by another poet, are so distinctly in the manner which we associate with some well-known name, that, had we met them as detached quotations, we should have said, "Tennyson," "Shakespeare," "Mrs. Browning," "Shelley," as the case might be. Who, for instance, would not take these exquisite lines for the product of the Laureate's mind:—

> Through all her frame there ran the shock
> Of some sharp-wounding joy, like his who hastes
> And dreads to come too late, and comes in time
> To press a loved hand dying?

Not only does the ring of the words recall Tennyson, but there is that Tennysonian structure which gives an inevitable rhythmic flow, divide the words into lines how you will. Write the passage thus—

> Through all her frame
> There ran the shock of some sharp-wounding joy,
> Like his who hastes and dreads to come too late,
> And comes in time to press a loved hand dying

and you get scansion as distinct and pure as before, though not quite so stately. Here is a line suggestive of Shelley—

> 'Twas Pablo, like the wounded spirit of song.

And in the lines—

> The pillars tower so large
> You cross yourself to scan them lest white Death
> Should hide behind their dark

we have a remarkable expression, which has always struck us as peculiarly appropriate in Mr. Swinburne's rondel, *Kissing her Hair*. It was not in that rondel that the happy term "white Death" was first used, for it occurs in the *Prometheus Unbound* of Shelley, in whose *Alastor* we get also "black Death." The names most frequently forced on the mind in connection with matters of expression in **The Spanish Gypsy** are, however, Shakspeare and Mrs. Browning. The following lines are peculiarly suggestive of the great poetess:—

> All deities
> Thronging Olympus in fine attitudes;

O'r all hell's heroes whom the poet saw
Tremble like lions, writhe like demigods.

And when we read farther on—

One pulse of Time makes the base hollow—sends
The towering certainty we built so high
Toppling in fragments meaningless

we are forced by identity of metaphor to revert to some
lines in *Aurora Leigh,* describing Romney (in far less
elegant terms, truly) as a man who

builds his goodness up so high,
It topples down the other side, and makes
A sort of badness.

Of Shakespearian cuttings from this poem by one of the
most Shakespearian of our modern authors, it would be
easy to give a long array. Here is one:—

I thrust myself
Between you and some beckoning intent
That wears a face more smiling than my own.

This next, a lyrical one, is at least Elizabethan:—

It was in the prime
Of the sweet spring-time.
In the linnet's throat
Trembled the love-note.

And many more distinctly Shakespearian passages will
suggest themselves to readers of the work, or of a more
considerable extract which we give farther on. Even Milton is not unrepresented, as witness the line—

When with obliquely soaring bend altern.

An appraisal of the lyrics of **The Spanish Gypsy** yields a
result similar to that obtained by examining the miscellaneous pieces of expression which are pointedly beautiful—
that is to say, the lyrics do not support any claim to com-
petency in the matter of individual technical expression. A
lyric to be entirely satisfying should combine perfection of
music with perfection of sense. In the short space of a lyric
we expect to get this combination even from a poet who
does not sustain it when working on a larger scale; but,
charming as are many of the songs of this volume, hardly
any come up to the standard of lyrical excellence which we
should demand of a new poet as a diploma-condition. In
one instance George Eliot has given us a song as thoroughly exquisite in sense and sound as anything can possibly be.
It is this sad, sweet song of Pablo's:—

Warm whispering through the slender olive leaves
Came to me a gentle sound,
Whispering of a secret found
In the clear sunshine 'mid the golden sheaves:
Said it was sleeping for me in the morn,
Called it gladness, called it joy,
Drew me on—"Come hither, boy"—

To where the blue wings rested on the corn.
I thought the gentle sound had whispered true—
Thought the little heaven mine—
Leaned to clutch the thing divine,
And saw the blue wings melt within the blue.

But in another of Pablo's songs, equally exquisite in
thought, and perhaps fuller of pathos, there is a lack of
music, rising partly from the somewhat unlyrical construction of the verse, and partly from the slightly stiff
manner in which the division of sense involves a division
of the lines:—

The world is great: the birds all fly from me,
The stars are golden fruit upon a tree
All out of reach: my little sister went,
And I am lonely.

The world is great: I tried to mount the hill
Above the pines, where the light lies so still,
But it rose higher: little Lisa went,
And I am lonely.

The world is great: the wind comes rushing by,
I wonder where it comes from; sea-birds cry
And hurt my heart: my little sister went,
And I am lonely.

The world is great: the people laugh and talk,
And make loud holiday: how fast they walk!
I'm lame, they push me: little Lisa went,
And I am lonely.

Two of the songs, to which attention is invited in the
author's prefatory note, are written in trochaic assonant—
a metre eminently unsuited for the purposes of an English
lyrist. A line composed of four trochees does not in itself
furnish a good basis for lyric utterance in our language,
however well it may suit the sonorous tongue of the
Spaniard. With all their spirit and *vis*, the following verses
have no ring of music:—

At the battle of Clavijo
In the days of King Ramiro,
Help us, Allah! cried the Moslem,
Cried the Spaniard, Heaven's chosen,
God and Santiago!

Straight out-flushing like the rainbow,
See him come, celestial Baron,
Mounted knight, with red-crossed banner,
Plunging earthward to the battle,
Glorious Santiago!

As the flame before the swift wind,
See, he fires us, we burn with him!
Flash our swords, dash Pagans backward—
Victory he! pale fear is Allah!
God with Santiago!

The assonant quality is one which would not strike an
English reader at first sight. He would look upon the metre

as a blank-verse metre, unless near inspection perhaps revealed to him that in every couplet the two vowels of the final foot are identical in each line, while the consonants are independent. In the other trochaic assonant song (the final verse of which, by-the-bye, affords another sample of Elizabethan assimilation), this correspondence is in the quatrain instead of the couplet form: here is the last verse:—

> Beauty has no mortal father,
>   Holy light her form engendered
> Out of tremor, yearning, gladness,
>   Presage sweet and joy remembered—
>   Child of Light, Fedalma!

There is one more lyric which we must not omit to quote here; it is this:—

> There was a holy hermit,
>   Who counted all things loss
> For Christ his Master's glory:
>   He made an ivory cross,
> And as he knelt before it
>   And wept his murdered Lord,
> The ivory turned to iron,
>   The cross became a sword.
>
> The tears that fell upon it,
>   They turned to red, red rust;
> The tears that fell from off it
>   Made writing in the dust.
> The holy hermit, gazing,
>   Saw words upon the ground:
> 'The sword be red for ever
>   With the blood of false Mahound.'

Splendidly strong as these two verses are—great as is the historical keenness which prompted the thought—we cannot but think that even these bear out the charge of want of music; and indeed, in our opinion, the only song in the book which seriously opposes that charge is the first we quoted.

As great stress was laid, some pages back on the polarising of language as an element of poetic style, it may naturally be asked, what, in that respect, is elicited by searching the pages of *The Spanish Gypsy,* to help us to a conclusion on the style of the volume? To tell the truth, we have only discovered two instances in which any use has been made of this instrument of the poet. In one case, Don Silva is described as "too proudly special for obedience"—a happy term in which the force of the word *special* exceeds by a degree its usual value. In the other case, Prior Isidor, reproaching Don Silva, exclaims—

> "O fallen knighthood, penitent of high vows!"

Here, the word penitent is placed in such unusual company as to convey an intensified sarcasm highly artistic in its propriety under the circumstances of the dialogue, throughout which the Prior has been working himself up to a higher and higher pitch of bitter invective.

However, setting aside the question of special polarisations of language, it would be absurd to say that *The Spanish Gypsy* is entirely devoid of individualities of expression such as would help to make up a style. Indeed, there are numerous *minutiæ* of utterance, scattered throughout it, which are unmistakably born and bred in the most original recesses of this most original mind. In this passage, for instance, the italicised words are unquestionably such as would be met in no other author:—

> And in love's spring all good seems possible:
> No threats, all promise, brooklets ripple full
> And bathe the rushes, *vicious crawling things
> Are pretty eggs.*

The same may be said of the following:—

> Little shadows danced
>   Each a tiny elf
> Happy in large light
>   And the thinnest self.
>
>   . . . . .
>
> Small legs and arms
> With pleasant agitation purposeless
> Go up and down like pretty fruits in gales.
>
>   . . . . .
>
>   Twixt the rails
> The little Pepe showed his two black beads,
> His flat-ringed hair and small Semitic nose
> Complete and tiny as a new-born minnow.

And there are plenty of other instances. But, while those decorations are peculiarly individual and pointed, and would stand out as very attractive gems in the excellent setting of a page of George Eliot's high prose, it does not seem to us that they have sufficient intensity to grace the more exacting setting of verse; and, indeed, striking as the expressions are, they are a little below the dignity blank verse assumes with that inexpressible *afflatus* which we have already mentioned as the inevitable accompaniment of anything like a serious attempt at poetry strictly so called.

While on this subject, we must not fail to remark that at times the execution seems to fall more distinctly short of poetic dignity. Sometimes the incidents chosen for description are to blame for this, and at others the expressions. In the first scene on the Plaça, the tricks of the juggler seem unduly dwelt on—described at greater length than could be well afforded for such trivial matters; and the monkey's performances occupy a greater space than seems in keeping with the serious nature of the book.

We are aware that the minute observations we have been making stand a good chance of being included in the category of considerations referred to in *Macmillan's Magazine,* when the writer of the article on *The Spanish Gypsy* talks of *peddling in the lesser things of criticism;* but we must dare the consequences of our procedure, even should they take the form of an implied censure from so distinguished a pen as that of Mr. John Morley, who is obviously the "J. M." of that article.

A little more peddling, then, and we have done. The heterogeneity of method involved in brusque transitions from narration to dramatisation—from stage directions and descriptions in verse, to stage directions and descriptions in prose—the heterogeneity which, while never coming near the soul of the work, has been shown to have entered so far into its flesh and blood, as to show itself in a variety of elements of style assimilated from other authors—may be traced farther in smaller details. We find it still when we examine the grammar. *Bad* grammar is a thing the most aspiring enemy could never hope to find in any composition of George Eliot; but heterogeneous grammar has come to an abundant crop in the work before us, no doubt through unfamiliarity with this class of composition. We find change of person and tense in the dialogues and descriptions coming upon us with unanticipated rapidity, and without apparent reason. In one instance, Fedalma says to Hinda:—

"*You* would obey then? Part from him for ever?"

And after receiving Hinda's answer, she resumes:—

"No, Hinda, no!
Thou never shalt be called to part from him."

In the next dialogue, Don Silva first addresses Fedalma in the plural, then in the singular, then again in the plural, thus:—

"*You* could do nought
That was not pure and loving."

. . . . .

"True misery is not begun
Until I cease to love *thee*."

. . . . .

"There was no way else
To find *you* safely."

An instance of sudden change of tense—transition from the past to the historic present—may be found quite close to the opening of the book:—

"I said the souls *were* five,—besides the dog,
But there *was* still a sixth, with wrinkled face,
Grave and disgusted with all merriment
Not less than Roldan. It *is* Annibal,
The experienced monkey who *performs* the tricks."

These last few quotations are but specimens of what occurs frequently throughout the volume.

There is yet one symptom of minute heterogeneity that we have to name—the excessive variations in length and style to which the blank verse is subjected. The type of the metrical stock of *The Spanish Gypsy* is the blank line of five iambuses; but with so little strictness is this type adhered to that, making every deduction for legitimate and easy elision, there is an immense residue of irregular lines. Some have six distinct iambuses, some only four, some few less; and many have no distinct form at all. The lines that have caught our attention and arrested us by virtue of their obvious irregularity amount to about seventy; and this without including many that, though they may be scanned by difficult elision, are not such as have an inherent conformity to the type selected. These small irregularities may be defended; but to our thinking they are blemishes of greater importance than they would at first sight appear to be—simply because they frequently arrest attention by their eccentricity at points where there is no other reason for halting. But when all has been said about these minute faults, it must be admitted that it is not on them that the strongest attack on the execution of the work could be mainly based, but on the larger outlines of the method.

To tell a tale in verse in the prose method is fatal in one respect. Few authors are sufficiently temerarious to carry a work in verse to as great a length as a work in prose; and in reducing to the necessary limits a work in verse which is not thoroughly poetic in method—not thoroughly condensed in expression—the danger is that much will be left out which, if told out in prose, would save the characters from the great fault of shadowiness. Some such fatal error has, we venture to submit, attended the production of *The Spanish Gypsy,* in which the characters are too vague, too mere embodiments of noble thoughts and sentiments: they do not take a living and active place in our minds as do the Marners and Maggies, the Dodsons and Tullivers, and all the persons of George Eliot's other books. Juan is the only character here who is *personally* much more than a ghost—because in the treatment of him the method is more fully dramatic than elsewhere. In the other characters we feel more that we are listening to the noble oratory of the author than that we are in the presence of a group of variously-endowed human beings.

Juan, however, lives distinctly before us, and better recalls the dramatic breadth of Shakspeare than anything in the book: whatever he says is thoroughly characteristic; his various figurings before us furnish a homogeneous series of aspects which make up an evident man—and that a very noble one. His nobility, we may observe in passing, consists chiefly in a pure and disinterested devotion to Fedalma, and a genial kindliness to everyone, together with a cheerful acceptance of the position in life which places him out of all possibility of reward for his devotedness. But it is with the drawing of him, not the nobility, we are now concerned; and this we have described as more truly dramatic than that of the other personages. The work is evidently framed with a view to being as unsuitable for the stage as possible; and it is very intelligible that an artist of a high class should wish to avoid the remote contingency of being made to figure on a degenerate stage such as ours. Still, the drama and the stage are subjectively so intimate in relationship, that a fine drama is usually found to meet the exigencies of the stage. So with Juan—the scenes in which he is introduced are not only fuller of dramatic portraiture, but also more instinct with dramatic life, and that most difficult thing to treat in the drama, motion. Take, for instance, the beautiful scene in which he is among the gypsies, and in which he has been robbed of his various articles of finery by the wild girls. How full it is of motion, as well as deep thought and exquisite portraiture. . . .

Our final quotation shall be one of the finest passages in the book; it is from the last speech of the unhappy Duke Silva, as he takes farewell of Fedalma, about to start for Africa with her Zincali:—

"I will not leave my name in infamy,
I will not be perpetual rottenness
Upon the Spaniard's air. If I must sink
At last to hell, I will not take my stand
Among the coward crew who could not bear
The harm themselves had done, which others bore.
My young life still may fill a breach,
And I will take no pardon, not my own,
Not God's—no pardon idly on my knees;
But it shall come to me upon my feet
And in the thick of action, and each deed
That carried shame and wrong shall be the sting
That drives me higher up the steep of honour
In deeds of duteous service to that Spain
Who nourished me on her expectant breast,
The heir of highest gifts. I will not fling
My earthly being down for carrion
To fill the air with loathing: I will be
The living prey of some fierce noble death
That leaps upon me while I move."

To students, and those who have assimilated the code of morality implied in George Eliot's works, this last production must ever be dear for intimate companionship, as affording innumerable new renderings of the great sentiments of the author; but by the *dilettante,* the seeker after technical beauty in poetry, and the stickler for unity of form, it will not be greatly loved. Here and there the *dilettante* will get, if he tries, exquisite touches of true poetry, in the truly poetic method; but even if that method, in its essence of condensation, were closely followed throughout the poem, the fact that narration and dramatisation, verse and prose, are indiscriminately used for similar purposes, constitutes too grave a rupture of what the generality of readers require in respect of form, for the poem to be popular. It is, of course, not desired to erect popularity as the final criterion of excellence in judging of a work of art of such high feeling and subtle intellectuality as *The Spanish Gypsy;* but we may safely say that, had the subject been treated in prose, a large and intelligent class of readers now unappealed to would have come readily within the influence of the work. The subject of *The Spanish Gypsy* could never have been worked into a tale as popular (and therefore wide in influence for good) as *Adam Bede;* but it might easily have extended its influence as far as that of *Romola* has extended, and the circuit of that influence is no mean one. Had *The*

Spanish Gypsy, in fine, been perfect, which it must have been in prose, so complete is the author's mastery over that her special method, its production would have been a matter of widespread gratitude; but being, as it is, imperfect, the general public will probably forget it far sooner than it deserves to be forgotten, and while it is still treasured up in the hearts of those who thoroughly sympathise with the author. Looking at the work in this light, we cannot but call it, on the whole, a failure; yet, so high a value do we set upon it, that we should certainly restrain ourselves from using so harsh an expression, but for one consideration:—we look of course that George Eliot shall produce us many more books yet: in *The Spanish Gypsy* we see no promise of perfection in this lately-assumed method; while in the other method, perfection is at her command: every sincere critic who sees the shortcomings of the present work is therefore bound to protest against the use of the instruments which have been employed in its elaboration. For our own part, we cannot but express the opinion that the abandonment by George Eliot of her own walk of art for the continued production of works in the manner of *The Spanish Gypsy* would be a national calamity.

The Spectator   (review date 1874)

Review of *The Legend of Jubal and other Poems,* in *The Spectator,* Vol. 47, No. 2395, May 23, 1874, pp. 660-61.

[*In the excerpt below, the critic contends that the majority of poems in Eliot's collection* The Legend of Jubal, and Other Poems, *though eloquent, lack imagination.*]

[Certainly] it is an even greater transposition from one to another province of the realm of Art, which our great novelist has experienced in writing these poems. Verse supplies her with a fresh, unhackneyed material in which to shape her more delicate conceptions, and lends to it the special fascinations proper to the new mould. The volume is, of course, a study in itself, if only because it shows where the great novelist seemed to feel most the need for recourse to poetry, and the kind of poetry to which, under these circumstances, she has recourse,—and this we could hardly have learnt from a long poem like *The Spanish Gipsy,* where she was committed to the poetic form throughout the story. Nevertheless, one feels in reading the volume that remarkable as these poems would be from any unknown hand, they are not the most impressive, though they may be the most characteristic expressions of the great mind that produced them,—nay, that they are only in one sense even the most characteristic, namely, in Mr. Browning's sense, that their author here deliberately prefers, instead of blowing "thro' brass," "to breathe thro' silver,"—deliberately chooses the new medium for expressing this most individual and intense kind of thought and feeling.

What one notices specially in these minor poems, as in *The Spanish Gipsy,* is that George Eliot's marvellous dramatic power seems to fade away in great measure in the delicate medium of verse, that the ideal ends which draw her to verse absorb her while she is occupied in it, and prevent her from moulding her characters with anything like the force we expect from her. Jubal, Agatha, Armgart and her friends (Leo partly excepted), and Lisa, are all more or less the dreams of ideal reverie. George Eliot's brooding fancies and her moral enthusiasms are expressed in them, but not her living imagination. We get fine lines, exquisite passages, great imaginative expressions here and there, which she could hardly have used in prose, but only one really perfect poem, and that a study, of the idyllic kind, of the relations of a sister and brother. **"Jubal,"** the poem in praise of death, the poem which expresses the idea that death in life is the great cause of life in death, that the good which the fear of death drives into the soul is the origin of that creative power which enables individual genius to live again in the blessings it confers on the world, is a reverie full of delicate touches and of a sedate melancholy; but the oftener we read it, the more the close of it, which is of course its peroration and its moral, strikes us as unworthy, even in a merely artistic sense, of the conception of the poem. A death-vision, in which the first inventor of music sees the face of his "loved Past," and hears, from that somewhat strange impersonation, a Positivist lecture on the glory of living again in the souls of all the other men whom music is to bless, certainly makes a feeble ending to the melodious but rather monotonous poem which delineates so pathetically the origin of music and of song. All that contains what we may fairly regard as artistic autobiography is exceedingly fine and instructive. . . .

But when we pass beyond those beautiful passages in the poem which describe the secrets of the writer's own imaginative experience, to the delineation of the moral,—that death is no evil, but a good, and that an impersonal immortality is better than a personal,—we get sweet and fluent didactic verse, without either that keen psychological truth which arrests the attention as all vivid portraiture arrests it, or that bold flight of imagination which carries us with it into a purer and sublimer region. Such passages . . . have neither the ease nor the force which mark a great poem. The effort in them is visible. They are verse, not poetry, and they throw their air of tremulous endeavour over the whole poem of which they form so important an element . . . .

"Agatha" and **"Armgart"** seem to us less imperfect than the **"Legend of Jubal,"** partly because they do not aim so high, and partly because there is more of the dramatic form and less of the purely poetic form in them. **"Agatha,"** indeed, is little more than an effort to paint a 'beautiful soul' of the humbler South-German kind, in its old-fashioned piety and mystic, but not the less beneficent, saintliness; and the picture is very beautiful, though rather slight. It gains a certain idyllic grace from its poetic form; and the little village night-song with which it concludes is full of simple beauty. But it seems to us that it is a success mainly because it passes so little beyond the idyllic aims of many of the author's sketches in prose. We see a very delicate picture framed in melodious verse, but the poem hardly attempts to give expression to anything

deeper than George Eliot's always sensitive appreciation of moral simplicity and loveliness. That which chiefly drives her into poetry, the desire for a fitter medium of intense feeling than any which prose can afford, is hardly perceivable here. In **"Armgart,"** however, the moral yearning is uppermost again. On the whole, it seems to us the most successful of those of George Eliot's poems which she would not have thought of giving us in any shape if she could not have given them in verse. It contains sentences of extraordinary grandeur,—again, in all probability, sentences representing the author's own personal experience of the artistic life,—and it paints the necessary limitation and apparent selfishness of genius, and the exorbitant claim of right divine which exclusive gifts are apt to breed in the minds of those who possess them, with marvellous force. No one has ever shown so powerfully how even a genius which delights in itself merely for the joy it diffuses amongst mankind, thinks not of mankind, but of itself, as the great loser, when the gift is withdrawn; and no one has ever enforced so earnestly the lesson of disinterested sympathy with those "toiling millions of men" who are "sunk in labour and pain." What a fine expression is this of the inborn feeling of power! (Armgart, we need hardly say, by way of explanation, is a great singer):—

> For herself,
> She often wonders what her life had been
> Without that voice for channel to her soul.
> She says, it must have leaped through all her
>   limbs—
> Made her a Mænad—made her snatch a brand
> And fire some forest, that her rage might mount
> In crashing roaring flames through half a land,
> Leaving her still and patient for a while.
> 'Poor wretch!' she says, of any murderess—
> 'The world was cruel, and she could not sing:
> I carry my revenges in my throat;
> I love in singing, and am loved again.

And what, again, can be more Shakespearian than this reply to Leo's remark, that a great artist in the moment of success knows not "pain from pleasure in such joy"?—

> O, pleasure has cramped dwelling in our souls,
> And when full Being comes must call on pain
> To lend it liberal space.

And here, again, is another such terse saying, in which we hardly know whether the form or the thought is the finer:—

> True greatness ever wills—
> It lives in wholeness, if it live at all,
> And all its strength is knit with constancy.

Still even in **"Armgart,"** the nearest, we think, to a poetic whole of all the poems not purely idyllic, there is a sense of defect, of fragmentariness, and baldness at the end, which tells one that the poetic form is not the form which is the most appropriate to its author's genius. What remains in the mind of the reader as he looks back on it, is not form and thought fused perfectly together, but the thought glimmering somewhat vaguely through an imperfect form. **"Lisa"** is the least good of all the longer poems. It is eloquent verse and tender narrative, and nothing more.

The most complete and successful of the poems is the series of twelve Shakespearian sonnets called **"Brother and Sister."** This is indeed the "soul of a dead past" revisiting the world with a true imaginative beauty. But it is a poem of the idyllic order,—an exalted form of some of the pure idylls in the *Mill on the Floss,* hardly a poem written from the depth of ideal emotions which could choose no form but poetry. No picture of a sister's childish delight in common joys with her brother was ever more delicate; but what is more beautiful still is the air of dreamy wonder, partly, no doubt, a feeling reflected back from a later age, but partly remembered, in which the first recollections of natural beauty are steeped. . . .

On the whole, it seems to us that this little volume of poems is strongest where it keeps to realistic pictures steeped in emotion, and weakest where it springs into the ardour of the ideal life. The verse is too sedate, and almost too tame for the language of passion, and adequate to the thought only when it is the reflection of deeply felt experience. There is a want of ease and swiftness and motion in it, whenever it tries to soar. While the author invests her real self-knowledge or memories in a liquid cloud of soft external beauty, she is truly poetical, though in a modest region of poetry. But when she embodies an impassioned faith of her own in an imaginative form, she seems to us to show how far her visionary power lags behind her imaginative insight. In meditative melancholy, in tender recollection, she can reach a point of true poetic beauty; but she is too self-conscious, too intrinsically sober-minded, too sensible of the urgent limits upon her thought, too true to the world she knows, for those flights of genius beyond the region of experience in which only the higher kind of poets succeed. George Eliot's poems will add great interest to her novels. But her name and genius will always be identified with her delineations of life.

Rose Elizabeth Cleveland (essay date 1885)

SOURCE: "George Eliot's Poetry," in *George Eliot's Poetry and Other Studies,* Funk and Wagnalls, 1885, pp. 9-23.

[*In the following excerpt, Cleveland contends that Eliot's verses lack the lyricism and vision which, she argues, are marks of genuine poetry.*]

I come at once to the consideration of George Eliot's verse in the mention of two qualities which it seems to me to lack, and which I hold to be essentials of poetry.

The first of these two qualities has to do with form, and is a property, if not the whole, of the outside, that which affects and (if anything could do this) stops with the senses.

Yet here, as elsewhere in this department of criticism, it is diffcult to be exact. I ask myself, Is it her prosody? and am obliged to find it faultless as Pope's. There is never in her metres a syllable too much or too little. Mrs. Browning's metre is often slovenly, her rhymes are often false. Yet, explain it who will, Elizabeth Browning's verse has always poetry and music, which George Eliot's lacks.

What was work to write is work to read. Ruskin's dictum— "No great intellectual thing was ever done by great effort"—I suspect to be wholly true, and that it is pre-eminently true in the production of poetry. Poetry must be the natural manner of the poet, and can never be assumed. I do not mean by this to ignore the aids which study gives to genius; I only mean to say that no mere labor and culture can simulate poetic fire, or atone for its absence. George Eliot puts her wealth of message into the mould of poetic form by continuous effort. No secret of hydraulics could cause a dewdrop to hang upon a rose-leaf in a cube. Her torrents of thought were predestined to a cubical deliverance. Never was the Calvinistic dilemma more intrusive. Her free will cannot squeeze them spherical.

George Eliot's prose carries easily its enormous burdens of concentrated gift. It is like the incomparable trained elephants of Eastern monarchs, which bear at once every treasure—the iron of agriculture, the gem of royalty; and in its cumbrous momentum it out-distances all competitors. But poesy should betray no burdens. Its rider should sit lightly, with no hint of spur. It should sport along its course and reach its goal unwearied.

The born poet has no agony in the deliverance of his song. The uttering is to him that soothing balm which the utterance is to his reader. Burns said, "My passions when once lighted raged like so many devils till they got vent in rhyme; and then the conning over my verses, like a spell, soothed all into quiet." But where will one find a lullaby in George Eliot's verses?

Poets do, indeed, learn in suffering what they teach in song; but the singing quiets the suffering. It is the weeping, not the tear wept, that gives relief. Mrs. Browning makes no secret of the headache.

> If heads that hold a rhythmic thought must ache perforce,
> Then I, for one, choose headaches.

In a private letter she writes: "I have not shrunk from any amount of labor where labor could do anything." *Where labor could do anything!* There it is!

George Eliot has been said to possess Shakespearian qualities. Perhaps just here, in the relation of manner to matter, is seen her greatest resemblance and greatest difference. No writer, all concede, ever carried and delivered so much as Shakespeare. Never was human utterance so packed with wealthy meaning, so loaded with all things that can be thought or felt, inferred or dreamed, as his. And it all comes with gush and rush, or with gentle, murmuring flow, just as it can come, just as it must come. He takes no trouble, and he gives none. From one of his plays, replete with his incomparable wit, wisdom, and conceit, you emerge as from an ocean bath, exhilarated by the tossing of billows whose rough embrace dissolves to tenderest caress, yet carries in itself hints of central fire, of utmost horizon, of contact with things in heaven and earth undreamt of in our philosophy. You come from one of George Eliot's poems as from a Turkish bath of latest science and refinement,—appreciative of benefit, but so battered, beaten, and disjointed as to need repose before you can be conscious of refreshment.

The irony of fate spares not one shining mark. George Eliot cared most to have the name of poet. But her gait betrays her in the borrowed robe. It is as if the parish priest should insist on wearing in his desk my lady's evening costume. It is too much and not enough. He cannot achieve my lady's trick which causes the queenly train to float behind her like the smoke-plume of a gliding engine. He steps on it and stumbles. You step on it and fall. . . .

> **With the attitude and atterance of [George Eliot's] spirit confronting me, I cannot allow her verse to be poetry. She is the *raconteur*, not the *vates*; the scientist, not the seer.**
>
> —*Rose Elizabeth Cleveland*

A second quality which George Eliot's poetry lacks is internal and intrinsic, pertaining to matter rather than manner, though, as will be suggested later on, standing, perhaps, in the relation to manner of cause to effect. It is that, indeed, which all her works lack, but which prose, as prose, can get along without; call it what you will, faith or transcendentalism; I prefer to define it negatively as the *antipode of agnosticism.*

No capable student of her works but must admit the existence of this deficiency. Everywhere and in all things it is apparent. Between all her lines is written the stern, self-imposed thus far and no farther. Her noblest characters move, majestic and sad, up to a—stone-wall! There is no need that argument be brought to establish this proposition. It demands—nay, admits of, no proof, for it is self-evident.

The question which concerns us here is simply, What has this fact to do with George Eliot's poetry?

I answer, Much, every way. Herein, indeed, is matter. But my suspicions must not be disclosed in their full heterodoxy. I venture, however, to affirm that agnosticism can never exist in true poetry. Let verse have every quality which delights sense, captivates intellect, and stirs the heart, yet lack that ray which, coming from a sun beyond our system, reaches, blends with, vivifies, and assures the

intimation of and longing for immortality in man—lacking this, you have not poetry.

It is the necessity of the poet, his *raison d'être,* to meet and join the moving of men's minds toward the hereafter. For all minds tend thither. The dullest mortal spirit must at times grope restlessly and expectantly in the outer darkness for something beyond; and this something must exist, will exist, in a true poem. It need not be defined as Heaven, or Paradise, or Hades, or Nirvâna; but we must not be confronted with silence; there must be in some way recognition of and sympathy with this deepest yearning of the soul. Many a one, not knowing what, not seeing where, but trusting in somewhat and trusting in somewhere, has been a poet and an inspiration to his race. The simplest bead-telling Margaret is appeased with the creedless faith of her Faust, though it be told in "phrases slightly different" from the parish priest's. Faust, the lore-crammed, the knowledge-sated, yet feels the unseen, and longs and trusts. His proud will brings no cold, impenetrable extinguisher to place upon this leaping flame of spirit, which sends its groping ray far beyond his finite horizon, ever moving, moving in its search; because he feels assurance of the existence of the something toward which it moves.

George Eliot, confronted by Margaret's question, answers sadly, with submission born of a proud ignorance, "I do not know. My feeling that there is something somewhere is, itself, unaccountable, and proves nothing. I simply do—not—know. I will not conjecture. It is idle and impertinent to guess. There is that of which you and I both do know, because we have experience of it. Of this only will I speak. All else is but verbiage. We stop here."

And she stops here, before a great stone-wall, higher than we can see over, thicker than we can measure, so cold that we recoil at the touch. There is no getting any farther. It is the very end.

Now, this can never be poetry; for the poet must ever open and widen our horizon. He need not be on the wing, but his wings must be in sight. He need not—nay, he must not, deal with man-made creeds and dogmas. He need not deal with ethics even. Homer knows nothing of most of George Eliot's sweet humanities, and confuses shockingly all things which, since his poor day, have come to be catalogued under the heads of virtue and vice. . . .

George Eliot, with brain surcharged with richest thought and choicest, carefulest culture; with heart to hold all humanity, if that could save; with tongue of men and angels to tell the knowledge of her intellect, the charity of her heart—yet, having not faith, becomes, for all of satisfaction that she gives the soul, but sounding brass and tinkling cymbal! She will not bid me hope when she herself has no assurance of the thing hoped for. She must not speak of faith in the unknown. She cannot be cruel, but she can be dumb; and so her long procession of glorious thoughts, and sweet humanities, and noblest ethics, and stern renunciations, and gracious common lots, and lofty ideal lives, with their scalding tears, and bursting laughter, and flaming passion—all that enters into mortal life and time's story—makes its matchless march before our captured vision up to—the stone-wall. "And here," she says, "is *the end!*" We may accept her dictum and be brave, silent, undeceived, and undeceiving agnostics; but, as such, we must say to her (of *The Spanish Gypsy,* for instance), "This is not poetry! It is the richest realism, presenting indubitable phenomena from which you draw, with strictest science, best deduction and inference concerning the known or the knowable. But, by virtue of all this, it is not poetry. The flattering lies and pretty guesses are not there, and will be missed. You must put them in as do the Christians, the transcendentalists, and the fools generally. The 'poet' comes from these ranks. If you will persist in this sheer stop when you reach the confines of the known, you must not attempt to pass your work off as poetry. Even pagans will not be attracted by such verse. They want and will have predication. It is not so much that you do not know—nobody knows—as that you will not guess, or dream, or fancy, to their whim; that you will be so plainly, simply silent concerning the hereafter. Your readers will not endure that in poetry. There was John Milton, his learning as great as yours, his metres not more exact, yet nothing saves his Paradises from being theological treatises except the imagination in them, which stops not with the seen, but invades and appropriates the unseen. This blind old Titan sees and interprets the heavens by his inner vision. His sublime audacity of faith aërates the ponderous craft of his verse and keeps it from sinking into the abyss of theologic pedantry. . . .

George Eliot herself says, in a private letter lately given to the public, referring to the evolution of her Dinah from the germ sown in her mind years before by the person of an aunt, and speaking of the unlikeness of the two, as well as the likeness, "The difference was not merely physical. *No difference is.*"

No one knows better than George Eliot knew how the spiritual body gives curve, and feature, and expression to the material body. Mrs. Browning herself did not more keenly realize and everywhere acknowledge the truth that spirit makes the form.

> . . . Inward evermore
> To outward, so in life and so in art,
> Which still is life.

No one bows with profounder recognition to the dictum "it is the spirit which quickeneth" than does the author of *Adam Bede* and *The Spanish Gypsy.* It is this which she thinks it worth while to teach, without which she would have no heart to teach at all. But her teaching takes its shape from the attitude of her own soul.

To epitomize, then. George Eliot's pages are a labyrinth of wonder and beauty; crowded with ethics lofty and pure as Plato's; with human natures fine and fresh as Shakespeare's; but a labyrinth in which you lose the guiding cord! With the attitude and utterance of her spirit confronting me, I cannot allow her verse to be poetry. She is the *raconteur,* not the *vates;* the scientist, not the seer.

Miriam Allott (essay date 1961)

SOURCE: "George Eliot in the 1860's," in *Victorian Studies,* Vol. 5, No. 2, December, 1961, pp. 93-108.

[*In the following excerpt, Allott argues that Eliot's fascination with Greek tragedy is reflected in her poem* The Spanish Gypsy.]

George Eliot's imagination . . . is from the first most at home in a region where the sense of tragic entanglement is acute and her "meliorism"—her philosophy of moral betterment—faces its stiffest challenge. By the mid-1860's she was sufficiently familiar with her own methods to recognise that the tragic mode was the one which came most naturally to her. "It is my way (rather too much so perhaps) to urge the human sanctities through tragedy," she wrote during the summer of 1866, when she was brooding over her unfinished tragic drama, *The Spanish Gypsy*. It was sometime during this period that she put together her "Notes on *The Spanish Gypsy* and Tragedy in General," a short essay which provides a valuable guide to her thoughts and feelings during these years.

She explains in this document that the original inspiration for her poem came from an Annunciation seen in the Scuola di San Rocco at Venice. This was probably in June 1860, and it seems appropriate that she should open this decade by finding even in so familiar a theme—she "had seen numerous pictures of this subject before"—still further evidence of the intransigence of the individual human lot. Here was a young, hopeful girl who had suddenly to learn that she must "fulfil a great destiny, entailing a terribly different experience from that of ordinary womanhood," and who had no choice at all in the matter because everything in life "is the result of foregoing hereditary conditions." Presented with "a great dramatic motive of the same class as those used by the Greek dramatists," George Eliot hunted for "a suitable set of historical and local conditions" with which "to give the motive a clothing."

She chose her subject, then, because it was representative of "the part played in the general lot by hereditary conditions in the largest sense, and of the fact that what we call duty is entirely made up of such conditions; for even in cases of just antagonism to the narrow view of hereditary claims, the whole background of the particular struggle is made up of our inherited nature." The true nature of the tragic situation consists in "the terrible difficulty" of

> adjustment of our individual needs to the dire necessities of our lot, partly as to our natural constitution, partly as sharers of life with our fellow-beings—

> . . . the dire strife

> Of poor Humanity's afflicted will

> Struggling in vain with ruthless destiny.

Looking at individual lots, I seem to see in each the same story, wrought out with more or less of tragedy, and I determined the elements of my drama under the influence of these ideas.

The tragic subject, then, "must represent irreparable collision between the individual and the general . . . It is the individual with whom we sympathise and the general of which we recognise the irresistible power." This is true of Greek tragedy, where the collision takes place between "hereditary entailed Nemesis, and the peculiar individual lot, awaking our sympathy, of the particular man or woman whom the Nemesis is shown to grasp with terrific force." She discovers nothing "artificial" or "erroneous" in this mode of writing for it reflects the permanent truths of ordinary human experience. The Greeks "had the same essential elements of life presented to them as we have, and their art symbolized these in grand schematic terms." The Prometheus story is characteristic because it "represents the ineffectual struggle to redeem the small and miserable race of man against the stronger adverse ordinances that govern the frame of things with a triumphant power."

Because her interpretation of life is now penetrated by this preternaturally acute sense of heredity as one of the strongest of our "adverse ordinances" she experiences little difficulty in relating to the Greek conception of tragedy the "modern" or Shakespearian kind. *Othello* is "a great tragic subject" because "this story of a jealous husband is elevated into a most pathetic tragedy by the hereditary conditions of Othello's lot, which give him a subjective ground for distrust." She notes as relevant to her discussion here, "Faust, Rigoletto (Le Roi s'Amuse), Brutus."

At this point she is compelled to face the moral implications of her argument and in her final paragraphs we find her doing her utmost to see that her humanist beliefs remain firmly in control. She recognises that tragedy "has not to expound why the individual must give way to the general: it has to show that it is compelled to give way, the tragedy consisting in the struggle involved, and often in the entirely calamitous issue in spite of a grand submission." The only "moral 'solution'," in fact, is the inward impulse stimulated by "an imagination actively interested in the lot of mankind generally." This impulse is towards feelings of "love, pity, constituting sympathy, and generous joy" for the lot of our fellow-creatures, feelings which in effect "become piety—i.e. loving willing submission, and heroic Promethean effort towards high possibilities, which may result from our individual life." So "the will of God is the same thing as the will of other men," compelling us to avoid "what they have seen as harmful to social existence." Any other notion of the divine will "comes from the supposition of arbitrary revelation"—a supposition which she had, of course, long ago rejected. Finally, returning to the particularities of her own work, she explains that "the two convictions or sentiments" which, in *The Spanish Gypsy,* are the "very warp on which the whole action is woven," are "(1) The importance of individual deeds; (2) The all sufficiency of the soul's passions in determining sympathetic action.". . .

By the logic of her own arguments . . . , as well as her natural emotional bias, she is drawn towards pure tragedy— that is, an art which expresses a sense of the total arbitrariness of human destiny, akin let us say to Hardy's or to that of some twentieth-century French writers who are concerned, as Camus is for example, with the "absurd" in human experience. In George Eliot's case, however, moral scruples intervene. "The art which leaves the soul in despair is laming to the soul," she writes at the close of her "Notes on *The Spanish Gypsy* and Tragedy in General" and all the evidence shows that her sense of responsibility for the spiritual comfort of her readers increased with her sales. This aspect of her Victorianism (we find it again in Tennyson) distinguishes her sharply from her successors in the next generation, most of whom defend "that absolute loyalty towards his feelings and sensations" which, as Conrad says and as Hardy and Henry James would agree, "an author should keep hold of in his most exalted moments of creation. Not so many years after the 1860's people reading *The Return of the Native* or *Jude the Obscure* would find themselves exposed with no protection from the author— apart, that is, from the imaginative vitality fostered by his artistic truth—to a vision of "adverse ordinances that govern the frame of things with a triumphant power." But however compelling her own vision of such ordinances might be, George Eliot protected herreaders from any "laming" effects by continuing to preach her meliorism with all that survived of her indestructible Evangelicalism.

The staunchness of her moral purpose reminds us how closely she clung to Christian ethics while rejecting Christian dogma. For a temperament like hers, hyper-sensitive, easily discouraged, continually responsive to the universal plight of "struggling, erring human creatures" and always deeply conscientious, it was imperative to discover even in the darkest experiences the unmistakable working of a firm moral order. In the 1860's, then, it was more than ever her task to "convince her nerves" not, as Keats says, "of the existence of Pain and Sickness and Heartbreak"—they were already sensitive to these things—nor indeed of "the balance of good and evil"—she had always been able to see that some things in human experience could produce admiration and delight—but of the meaningfulness of the total human condition. In other words it was herself as much as her readers whom she now needed to convince of the truth of her meliorist beliefs.

The cost of this effort was high. There was an incalculable toll in health, energy, and artistic vitality as she toiled on, trying to ennoble her readers by her teachings in *Romola* and *The Spanish Gypsy* and *Felix Holt* while the "horrible scepticism about all things" paralyzed her mind and imagination. It is more than coincidence that what still emerges in her novels with occasional flashes of imaginative power is the experience of hidden personal anguish.

K. M. Newton (essay date 1973)

SOURCE: "Byronic Egoism and George Eliot's *The Spanish Gypsy,*" in *Neophilologus,* Vol. LVII, No. 4, October, 1973, pp. 388-400.

[In the following excerpt, Newton asserts that Don Silva, a rebellious character in Eliot's The Spanish Gypsy, *is a strong example of a Byronic egoist.]*

Though almost all critics of George Eliot have recognized her concern with egoism, she is not generally considered among those nineteenth-century writers who were interested in the Byronic egoist, the character who had emerged from Gothic literature and the *Sturm und Drang* and who came to the greatest prominence in the works of Byron. This figure played an important part in nineteenth-century literature and was used by numerous writers to signify revolt or egoistic aspiration. Perhaps the fundamental attribute of the Byronic egoist is that he refuses to recognize any external source of authority which can define him. He either defies all sources of authority which try to assert their superiority over the self, like Byron's Manfred, or else he thinks he can create his own values by an act of will quite independently of all generally accepted moral sanctions. A reading of the novels alone might suggest that George Eliot was not greatly interested in Byronic egoism, though there are several characters who possess some Byronic attributes, notably the Princess Halm-Eberstein in *Daniel Deronda.* But Byronic characters emerge clearly in her poetry, particularly in the character of Armgart in the poem of the same name, and in *The Spanish Gypsy,* in the figure of Don Silva, and it is arguable that this is a feature of her work which deserves some attention from critics. George Eliot was, of course, very much opposed to Byronic egoism, but it is important to try tosuggest why she was interested in the subject as late as the 1860's and 1870's, and took the trouble to attack it.

In the early Romantic period, the Byronic egoist can be seen as symbolizing the revolt against a universe which was, as Carlyle put it in *Sartor Resartus,* "all void of Life, of Purpose, of Volition, even of Hostility: it was one huge, dead, immeasurable Steam-engine, rolling on, in its dead indifference, to grind me limb from limb" (Book II, Chap. vii). Against this the egoist had asserted his "Everlasting No". The early Romantics and Carlyle were subsequently able to transcend such egoistic defiance, most closely associated with Byron's heroes, primarily by discovering the presence of God in an organic universe. But in the later nineteenth century, with developments in philosophy and science, culminating in Darwin, the concept of a mechanical, amoral, Godless universe was more powerfully present than it had ever been. Was the Byronic egoist's stance of defiance and revolt not still a valid one? Also, in the course of the nineteenth century, there were expressions of egoism which went much further than Byron or the early Romantics. George Eliot's concern with this was perhaps heightened by the fact that in Germany the work of David Strauss and especially Feuerbach, both of whom she had translated, had been used to justify the most extreme egoistic views. According to F. A. Lange [in *History of Materialism,* 1880] "intelligent opponents have often urged it against Feuerbach that his system must morally lead to pure Egoism". George Eliot, who was very familiar with German intellectual life, may have been aware of this. It is interesting that the most uncompromising expression of egoism in the nineteenth century was strongly influenced by Feuerbach's philosophy. . . .

George Eliot, who said she completely agreed with Feuerbach, would surely have been worried at this development of ideas she accepted, and which led Stirner to assert that all values stemmed from the self: "*I* decide whether it is the *right thing* in me; there is no right *outside* me. If it is right for *me,* it is right" [*The Ego and His Own,* 1912]. Similar views can be found in Nietzsche, an admirer of Byron's *Manfred:* "The distinguished type of human being feels *himself* as value-determining; . . . he knows that *he* is the something which gives honor to objects; he *creates values*" [*Beyond Good and Evil,* 1967].

George Eliot, who had rejected all belief in a transcendent reality, cannot refute the Byronic egoist's claim that in an amoral universe the individual is free to rebel or assert his own chosen values by proclaiming like Carlyle in *Sartor Resartus* that nature is the "Living Garment of God". Though she recognized the value of religion when she praised church assemblies because their very nature expressed "the recognition of a binding belief or spiritual law which is to lift us into willing obedience and save us from the slavery of unregulated passion or impulse" [*The George Eliot Letters,* 1954-56], she herself could not argue that the truth of religion supported Christian morality and refuted the egoist's claim that there is no moral order which can define the self. For her, the moral order to which the self must submit must first of all be discovered within the self as feeling. This could then lead to a larger social and moral vision. Even if the universe was amoral and Godless, the egoist could not simply dismiss all moral and religious sanctions and adhere to his own chosen value.

The above discussion helps, I think, towards an understanding of *The Spanish Gypsy,* a work George Eliot regarded highly, and perhaps explains why she was interested in a character like Don Silva. In the notes on tragedy she left regarding the poem she wrote:

> A tragedy has not to expound why the individual must give way to the general: it has to show that it is compelled to give way, the tragedy consisting in the struggle involved, and often in the entirely calamitious issue in spite of a grand submission. Silva represents the tragedy of entire rebellion: Fedalma of a grand submission, which is rendered vain by the effects of Silva's rebellion: Zarca, the struggle for a great end, rendered vain by the surrounding conditions of life. [*George Eliot's Life as Narrated in Her Letters and Journals,* n.d.]

Though no one would make great claims for the poem as a work of art, *The Spanish Gypsy* is important because it gives considerable insight into George Eliot's ideas and shows that her interests extended to areas not commonly associated with her. In the following analysis I shall concentrate mainly on Don Silva, her clearest portrait of a Byronic egoist.

II

Silva is a Spanish knight who is disillusioned with his Spanish heritage, primarily because of the nature of the war against the Moors and the activities of the Inquisition. He is contemptuous of Spanish policies. Because of this he feels that his heritage has no claim on his respect and that he is justified in rebelling against it. Yet he has no alternative plan of action in mind. He still serves the Spanish cause though he regards himself as being free to do as he likes. His rebellion only manifests itself as negative defiance. He is opposed and reproached by his uncle, the Prior, the personification of the Spanish aristocrat and an eager Inquisitor. Silva's resolve to marry the non-Spanish Fedalma is seen by the Prior as an implicit rejection of his duty to Spain. Silva replies with defiance, a key word of the Byronic rebel:

> 'Tis you, not I, will gibbet our great name
> To rot in infamy. If I am strong
> In patience now, trust me, I can be strong
> Then in defiance.

But the Prior makes the prophetic statement that if he utterly rejects the claims of the past for his own self-chosen value he will never find a stable identity:

>   you will walk
> For ever with a tortured double self,
> A self that will be hungry while you feast,
> Will blush with shame while you are glorified,
> Will feel the ache and chill of desolation,
> Even in the very bosom of your love.

Brought up in a tradition he can no longer accept, unable to feel any allegiance to a Christianity perverted into persecution, Silva has created his own personal value out of love. He literally worships Fedalma. She is his substitute for the values he has lost: in her "Silva found a heaven / Where faith and hope were drowned as stars in day". Even if this blasphemy will damn him, he will choose her and reject his former God:

>   Is there no God for me
> Save him whose cross I have forsaken?—Well,
> I am for ever exiled—but with her!

In the extremes to which Silva takes it, love is largely a projection onto Fedalma of his own inner needs. It is an attempt at a purely subjective creation of value to overcome his despair. He has come to believe that the world is meaningless and valueless, for both the world of nature and man revolts him:

> Death is the king of this world; 'tis his park
> Where he breeds life to feed him. Cries of pain
> Are music for his banquet; and the masque—
> The last grand masque for his diversion, is
> The Holy Inquisition.

Love for him is a desperate effort to choose consciously his own value in order that the self can transcend the amorality of life. A later speech makes particularly clear the despair which underlies it:

> I meant, all life is but poor mockery:
> Action, place, power, the visible wide world
> Are tattered masquerading of this self,
> This pulse of conscious mystery: all change,
> Whether to high or low, is change of rags.
> But for her love, I would not take a good
> Save to burn out in battle, in a flame
> Of madness that would feel no mangled limbs,
> And die not knowing death, but passing straight
> —Well, well, to other flames—in purgatory.

Given this vision of life, with love his only protection against despair, Silva cannot give up Fedalma when she decides to honour her Gypsy heritage. He thinks that his chosen value of love is superior to the claims of his past and all his former allegiances. It justifies the breaking of all bonds or duties, and he is prepared to commit any action, no matter how immoral in traditional terms, to retain it: "I will sin, / If sin I must, to win my life again". To lose her is to lose his own self: "that lost self my life is aching with". He declares that his love for her, his means of realizing his selfhood, "Makes highest law, must be the voice of God".

Silva's rejection of his Spanish past and his adoption of the Gypsy cause in order to marry Fedalma is an assertion that he can choose his own identity and values by an act of will. He dismisses any authority superior to the self:

> I will elect my deeds, and be the liege
> Not of my birth, but of that good alone
> I have discerned and chosen.

Anything that threatens to deprive him of her or places itself above his own will "Is what I last will bend to—most defy". This is an extreme expression of Byronic egoism. There is nothing esternal to the self that can define it, and all past claims or present obstacles must be crushed by the will. Since the mind can recognize no values beyond the self as valid, then it must create its own value. George Eliot tests this philosophy against experience in the poem.

But though Silva has rebelled against his Spanish past, he has not liberated himself from it. His identity is still basically defined by the fact that he is a Spanish Knight. The way of life and the attitudes of the latter are an inherent part of him which he does not even think of rejecting. It is an important part of George Eliot's treatment of Byronic egoism to show that social factors are among its most important causes. Byron and the Romantics in general tend to treat the egoist's defiance and creation of his own values at the level of a purely personal choice. But George Eliot, with her knowledge of sociology and psychology, places the egoist in a social situation. His attitudes and behaviour cannot be considered in isolation, but only in relation to the particular society of which he is a product. For example, Silva unquestioningly adopts the attitudes of one who has been brought up as an aristocrat. When he learns of Fedalma's flight and Gypsy birth, he regards these as "momentary crosses, hindrances / A Spanish noble might despise". He is quite confident he can regain her:

> What could a Spanish noble not command?
> He only helped the Queen, because he chose;
> Could war on Spaniards, and could spare the Moor;
> Buy justice, or defeat it—if he would:
> Was loyal, not from weakness but from strength
> Of high resolve to use his birthright well.

The will which he celebrates is the product of the aristocratic background he professes to despise. Thus his assertion of personal will to defy the demands of the tradition in which he has been brought up is only a negative expression of the social domination inherent in that tradition, as the following passage illustrates:

> Don Silva had been suckled in that creed
> (A high-taught speculative noble else),
> Held it absurd as foolish argument
> If any failed in deference, was too proud
> Not to be courteous to so poor a knave
> As one who knew not necessary truths
> Of birth and dues of rank; but cross his will,
> The miracle-working will, his rage leapt out
> As by a right divine to rage more fatal
> Than a mere mortal man's.

His claim, then, that one can create one's own value by the power of the will is fatally flawed. Instead of discovering a new basis for his identity, he is merely exploiting Spanish aristocratic values in his personal interests. The following assertion of his will-philosophy and of Byronic egoism is thus undermined by its implicit assumptions.

> I have no help
> Save reptile secrecy, and no revenge
> Save that I *will* do what he [the Prior] schemes to
>   hinder.
> Ay, secrecy, and disobedience—these
> No tyranny can master. Disobey!
> You may divide the universe with God,
> Keeping your will unbent, and hold a world
> Where He is not supreme.

George Eliot attacks this philosophy by showing that it is not a freely chosen position, the only possible response to a world without acceptable values. In Silva's case, it is rather the product of his alienation from his social background and the negative assertion of the social attitudes in which he has been brought up. He is another variation on the comment in *Felix Holt* that "there is no private life which has not been determined by a wider public life . . .". The narrator also acknowledges that underlying his outward will-assertion and defiance, he felt "Murmurs of doubt, the weakness of a self / That is not one . . .". But this insecurity only makes him rebel the more against the Prior, who possesses an absolutely stable identity:

> With all his outflung rage
> Silva half shrank before the steadfast man

> Whose life was one compacted whole, a realm
> Where the rule changed not, and the law was
>   strong.
> Then that reluctant homage stirred new hate,
> And gave rebellion an intenser will.

Even his rebellion, then, is not freely chosen but is the outcome of the psychological strain which results from his social alienation.

One of the most important debates in the poem, in which George Eliot's alternative to Silva's Byronic egoism becomes plain, is that between Silva and his Jewish servant Sephardo, clearly the representative of the author's point of view. To Silva's assertion that "Death is the king of this world", Sephardo replies that even if this were so, the good would still exist as human feeling in the hearts of men. A physician would know that mercy existed within himself even if all the angles in heaven denied it. This expresses George Eliot's own view that even if God does not exist and the world is as Silva describes it, which Sephardo makes no attempt to deny, the good would still exist as a purely human construct based on human feeling. The individual was therefore not justified in creating his own personal values by an act of will. He was inextricably a part of mankind and could never achieve complete cultural transcendence. The ego itself was in a large degree a cultural product. It was an illusion, then, to believe that the egoist could completely separate himself from his fellow-men and feel totally self-sufficient.

Silva goes on to proclaim the need for "naked manhood", for men who are unattached to any beliefs or systems and can stand alone. Sephardo replies that there is no such thing. We all owe allegiance to something larger than ourselves, in his case to his Jewish heritage. It is monstrous to consider all things without preferences; we are compelled to have certain priorities: "My father is first father and then man". But Silva is prepared to cast aside all claims in choosing to marry Fedalma:

> That I'm a Christian knight and Spanish duke!
> The consequence? Why, that I know. It lies
> In my own hands and not on raven tongues.

But the hollowness of his view that these characteristics are mere accidental features has already been made apparent. Sephardo, in contrast, refers "to the brand / Of brotherhood that limits every pledge." We need some law that is superior to the will in order to define the self:

> Our law must be without us or within.
> The Highest speaks through all our people's voice,
> Custom, tradition, and old sanctities;
> Or he reveals himself by new decrees
> Of inward certitude.

For George Eliot, the self's inner need for a sense of meaning and value is projected outwardly in customs and traditions, but if these become outdated and moribund, their essential content, which corresponds to this need within the self, must be reformulated. Silva makes no attempt to do this. The Spanish society he is a part of has become decadent since it strives to maintain itself through domination and persecution of other races and religious groups. Silva therefore finds it valueless and thinks he can reject it. Instead of trying to find a new form for the valuable content of his heritage or acting against corrupt forces within it, he constructs a self-created philosophy of the will. George Eliot tests this philosophy against experience and shows that it offers no possibility of a stable identity. One cannot choose to reject the past completely without fragmenting the self.

Silva soon discovers this. The town of Bedmár is taken by the Gypsies, and many of his former friends are killed and the Prior is executed. This crushingly brings home to him how deep-rooted is his connection with the heritage he thinks he can reject: his own acts against his former stronghold are felt as self-inflicted wounds. In this crisis, he realizes that his Spanish past is a fundamental part of his being, and his inner life becomes "cancerous":

> Silva had but rebelled—he was not free;
> And all the subtle cords that bound his soul
> Were tightened by the strain of one rash leap
> Made in defiance.

He is unable to escape from "his past-created, unchanged self". The self cannot totally deny continuity of being, and any rejection of the defining elements in his past by an act of will must inflict terrible psychological wounds. He even realizes that the Prior embodies certain values which are an integral part of his selfhood. He repudiates the role he has chosen: "I am a Catholic knight, / A Spaniard who will die a Spaniard's death!" and kills Zarca.

The consequence of rejecting his past is an intolerable sense of self-division. This leads to a severe identity crisis which makes him commit murder. The valuable content of his past life must be the basis for any unified sense of selfhood. Even in a Spain ruled by the Inquisition this is so; he cannot simply reject Christianity and the Spanish tradition and worship a God of his own. At the end of the poem he realizes this and commits himself to serving

> that Spain
> Who nourished me on her expectant breast,
> The heir of highest gifts.

III

It is the misfortune of both Silva and Fedalma that neither of them can wholeheartedly accept the tradition they belong to. Fedalma, though she adopts the opposite position to Silva, and chooses to obey her father and accept her Gypsy origin, derives no happiness from this choice. It is probably George Eliot's intention to suggest that their dissociation from their respective traditions represents the alienated response of the modern consciousness to the claims of the past. In contrast, both the Prior and Zarca, in different ways, possess utterly stable identities. The Prior believes totally in the objective truth of his religion, and Zarca has identified himself with the ideal of Gypsy

nationhood. But Silva is naturally alienated from a Spain dominated by the Inquisition, and Fedalma has been brought up outside the Gypsy tradition and can thus only make a conscious decision to accept it. She cannot respond to it with an undivided consciousness.

The Prior and Zarca, being certain of their commitments, are free from the sense of self-division created by excess of self-consciousness. Even the prospect of death cannot undermine the Prior's absolutely secure sense of identity. He possessed "The strength of resolute undivided souls / Who, owning law, obey it." For Fedalma and Silva, such certainty is impossible: their situations have necessarily made them self-conscious and self-divided. Silva is "Doom-gifted with long resonant consciousness / And perilous heightening of the sentient soul," and after his desertion suffers from the "tortured double self" the Prior had prophesied.

Fedalma's self-division is also evident though she does not suffer the same identity crisis as Silva. Her acceptance of her Gypsy role and rejection of love means she must choose sorrow, the "sublimer pain", for her choice "cut her heart with smiles beneath the knife, / Like a sweet babe foredoomed by prophecy". Though she makes a conscious decision to adopt the Gypsy way of life, she feels emotionally detached from it. She contrasts her own condition with that of her Gypsy servant, Hinda:

> She knows no struggles, sees no double path:
> Here fate is freedom, for her will is one
> With her own people's law, the only law
> She ever knew. For me—I have fire within,
> But on my will there falls the chilling snow
> Of thoughts that come as subtly as soft flakes,
> Yet press at last with hard and icy weight.

Fedalma's situation, and surely George Eliot regards it as symbolic of the modern or post-Romantic situation, has deprived her of the stability and certainty of her servant. She is cut off from such a sense of tribal consciousness. She is an example of the isolated, self-conscious ego, detached from those traditional beliefs, those "cosmic syntaxes", which could integrate the self within a single world-view that was accepted as true.

Fedalma's adoption of Gypsy life only makes her more aware of her divided consciousness. When she feels the power of Zarca's vision, she thinks she can "walk erect, hiding my life-long wound". At such times she feels strong in her resolve. But this feeling is only temporary: self-consciousness returns and the sense that "There's nought but chill grey silence, or the hum / And fitful discord of a vulgar world". Love for both Silva and Fedalma had been an attempt to heal the division they felt in themselves. It was a substitute for the lack of a heritage or a belief with which they could identify completely.

Silva's position is the more difficult since the tradition he is a part of has clearly become corrupt and decadent. Fedalma can at least assent intellectually and with part of her feelings to the Gypsy purpose. Silva's Byronic rebellion is a logical response to his situation. He employs self-conscious thought to try to create an identity for himself which will give him a sense of meaning in what he regards as a meaningless world:

> Thus he called on Thought,
> On dexterous Thought, with its swift alchemy
> To change all forms, dissolve all prejudice
> Of man's long heritage, and yield him up
> A crude fused world to fashion as he would.

But he discovers that there are deeper forces in the self that cannot be rejected by the will. He yearns for the memories and associations of the past, for human contact. The alienation and isolation involved in rejecting his roots and confronting the indifferent universe alone proves too much:

> He could not grasp Night's black blank mystery
> And wear it for a spiritual garb
> Creed-proof: he shuddered at its passionless touch.

The strain his rebellion places on his inner self is intolerable. Though among his people "he had played / In sceptic ease with saints and litanies" he now comes to realize their symbolic value. The religious and ancestral symbols connected with Spanish life are forms which express a meaning which is inextricably a part of himself; they even supported him while he scorned them:

> Sustaining him even when he idly played
> With rules, beliefs, charges, and ceremonies
> As arbitrary fooling.

For George Eliot, such symbols express an essentially human meaning which possesses a human truth. By means of self-conscious thought, Silva can consider these symbols as "arbitrary fooling", but in his moment of crisis he comes to realize how much the essential human content manifested in them means to him. The religious and social forms he has tried to reject are not mere outward symbols of an evil system: they express the fundamental human values of the way of life in which he has been brought up, and more than that, they symbolize the human truths created by feeling in its encounter with external reality. Silva's ordeal makes him accept this. The essential identity of Spain still exists even if it has been corrupted by the Inquisition, and it is this he must serve. He discovers by experience that the philosophy of the ego and the will is an intolerable violation of his inner self which cannot be borne. Any valid sense of identity must be rooted in his past experience. To try to reject this utterly leads at best to alienation and at worst to a psychological crisis in which the self seems to become infected by disease:

> Forcing each pulse to feed its anguish, turning
> All sweetest residues of healthy life
> To fibrous clutches of slow misery.

But George Eliot's intention is not simply to attack egoism. Despite his rebellion, Silva is clearly a man of heroic qualities and it is his egoism and strength of will that are central to these. She does not believe that these should be suppressed, but only that the energies generated by the ego be properly directed. This is apparent in her characterization of Zarca, in many ways as supreme an egoist as Silva. But Zarca commits all his egoistic energies to furthering the best interests of his people, in creating for them a valid nationhood.

His vision resembles that of a religious prophet. Fedalma implicitly compares him to Moses, Christ, and Mahomet. He is treated in the poem like a Carlylean hero who creates history by the force of his vision. For him it is a value-creating act. He knows that there is nothing beyond it, no providence, that guarantees its success:

> No good is certain, but the steadfast mind,
> The undivided will to seek the good:
> 'Tis that compels the elements, and wrings
> A human music from the indifferent air.
> The greatest gift the hero leaves his race
> Is to have been a hero.

The good does not exist external to man, it must be created by him. In contrast to Silva, Zarca does not regard the lack of immanent meaning and value in the world as a justification for Byronic egoism, but rather as urging man himself to create value through a social vision.

But it might appear that Zarca's vision is questionable because it seems to be characterized by the same dangerous idealism that underlies the Prior's beliefs. Both men are prepared to commit acts of evil to achieve what they regard as the good. This is a recurrent problem in George Eliot's works. The Prior's belief in the absolute truth of his religion convinces him that acts of evil cease to be evil if they favour what he regards as God's purpose: "'Tis so God governs, using wicked men—/ Nay, scheming fiends, to work his purposes". In this way he can justify the Inquisition.

This kind of reasoning is the consequence of identifying his beliefs with an objective truth beyond the human realm. If the good is seen as something external to man, whatever helps to achieve it is regarded as right. Good and evil are not defined in relation to humanity but in terms of a rigid doctrine which is more important than the human, and has become separated from it. But for Zarca, evil is always evil. It cannot be redeemed even if it furthers his concept of the good. No good that will be achieved will ever lift the burden of evil. It may serve as grounds to defend an act of evil but it can never, as the Prior believes, change its nature.

Since the Zíncali have no philosophy or religion which will allow them to come to terms with problems of this kind, Zarca must heroically elect to bear this burden for them. In this he again greatly resembles the Carlylean hero who identifies his deepest insight with the divine, and uses his possession of it to justify his authority over his people. Cruel acts are necessary if the Gypsies are to survive:

> they shall be justified
> By my high purpose, by the clear-seen good

That grew into my vision as I grew,
And makes my nature's function, the full pulse
Of inbred kingship. . . .

        The Zíncali have no god
Who speaks to them and calls them his, unless
I, Zarca, carry living in my frame
The power divine that chooses them and saves.

He knows that killing the Spaniards is evil, but there is no alternative. Yet his essential humanity is shown in his sympathy with the dead of Bedmár. This act was initiated before Silva joined the Gypsies. Even the execution of the Prior shows humanity. He decrees that he should not be burned as an act of vengeance, though the Prior is one of those "human fiends / Who carry hell for pattern in their souls". Instead he is executed with due ceremony.

But though George Eliot sympathizes with Zarca's aim, external reality remains indifferent to human aspirations. Moral good must be projected onto a valueless world, but the amoral development of events can frustrate this. With Zarca's death, the only force that could hold the Gypsies together disintegrates and results in a kind of Gypsy diaspora.

Zarca is the exemplification of Carlyle's view that the Byronic egoist must convert his rebellion and will-assertion into devotion to the best interests of his society. This was one means of socially transforming Romantic egoism. But possibly George Eliot regarded the transcendentalism underlyingZarca's certainty in his vision as a less modern position than the state of alienated self-consciousness that afflicts both Silva and Fedalma. Though both Silva and Fedalma are finally true to their respective traditions, this does not heal their self-division, and it also deprives them of love. Their commitment is a tragic one.

George Eliot's dissatisfaction with the pessimistic conclusion is perhaps shown by her return to the central ideas of *The Spanish Gypsy* in her last novel. In *Daniel Deronda*, George Eliot used certain features of the poem as the basis of her novel. There are obvious similarities between Zarca and the Gypsies and Mordecai and the Jews; Deronda's situation is very similar to Fedalma's; and the problem of Byronic egoism re-emerges in the characterization of Gwendolen and the Princess. In the novel George Eliot attempts to find a non-tragic solution to the problems the poem had raised: to suggest that the vision of a Zarca or a Mordecai can be realized and that the modern consciousness can recover from its self-division.

William Baker   (essay date 1975)

SOURCE: "'The Lifted Veil,' *Romola* and *The Spanish Gypsy*," in *George Eliot and Judaism*, Universität Salzburg, 1975, pp. 81-116.

[*In the following excerpt, Baker considers the sources of Eliot's* The Spanish Gypsy.]

Romola . . . provides evidence of the development of George Eliot's Jewish interests and knowledge of history, and her increasing readiness by comparison with "The Lifted Veil" to put them to fictional use. Her dramatic poem *The Spanish Gypsy* on which she began work in 1864, . . . a year after finishing her Italian novel, shows these developments at a further stage, and, in addition, provides further evidence of a thorough pre-occupation with values and desires which are to find their fictional fruition in *Daniel Deronda*. An examination of the sources of the poem helps in an assessment of George Eliot's Jewish knowledge after 1864, illuminates it, and provides background material for a discussion of her last novel.

The philosophical and moral basis of the poem have not gone unnoticed. G. W. Cooke in his *George Eliot: A Critical Study of her Life, Writings and Philosophy* (1883) writes that George Eliot's "faith in tradition, as giving the basis of all our best life, is perhaps nowhere so expressively set forth . . . as in *The Spanish Gypsy*." He points to the works of Comte as an important source for George Eliot's ideas and believes that in the poem George Eliot shows her awareness that "true wisdom is always social, always grows out of the experience of the race, and not out of any personal inspiration or enlightenment." In a similar way, a modern critic B. J. Paris in his account of *The Spanish Gypsy* in *Experiments in Life* (1965) stresses its moral elements. To Paris the tragedy in the poem is a result of "Don Silva's rebellion against the unalterable conditions of his lot, . . . [he] feels that love and reason are superior to hereditary bonds." Alfred Abraham Möller in his *George Eliots Beschäftigung mit dem Judentum* concentrates upon the poem as representing "den Konflikt zwischen Egoismus und Altruismus, Recht des Individuums und der Gemeinschaft," and indicates the firm psychological and sociological basis of George Eliot's presentation of her characters in *The Spanish Gypsy*.

Henry James, reviewing the poem in *The North America Review,* CVII (October 1868), praises George Eliot's humour, and considers that Juan ranks "with Tito Melema and Hetty Sorrel, as one of [George Eliot's] very best conceptions." He has, however, the sense that George Eliot's "primary intention . . . her wish to present a struggle between nature and culture, between education and the instinct of race" result in her overlooking realistic details of presentation. The poem, he believes, "is emphatically a *romance*" and its two central characters, Fedalma and Zarca, are unreal: "Fedalma is not a real Gypsy maiden" and Zarca is "very far . . . from being a genuine Gypsy chieftain." This kind of criticism has found a modern adherent in F. R. Leavis, who in *The Great Tradition* has written of *The Spanish Gypsy* that "the essential function of the quasi-historical setting is one with that of the verse form: it is to evade any serious test for reality." Discussion of some of the literary and historical sources of *The Spanish Gypsy* shows that George Eliot paid close attention to problems of historical veracity and that she placed her characters and chosen historical environment upon sound foundations.

Before turning to these sources it is worthwhile noting that there are German literary parallels in setting, structure, theme, and general intention to *The Spanish Gypsy,* which George Eliot would have known, and which point forward to *Daniel Deronda.* . . . [By] 1856 George Eliot knew Heinrich Heine's tragic play *Almansor* which is set at the time of the conflict between the Moors and the Spanish in fifteenth-century Spain. Both lovers in *Almansor* are Moors although the heroine Zuleima has been converted to Christianity. Heine's play ends tragically with Zuleima and her lover Almansor flinging themselves from a rock in defiance of their Spanish pursuers. George Eliot's summary of the preoccupations of Heine's play would serve equally well for her own poem. Of *Almansor* she wrote in her review "German Wit: Heinrich Heine": "The tragic collision lies in in the conflict between natural affection and the deadly hatred of religion and of race in the sacrifice of youthful lovers to the strife between Moor and Spaniard, Moslem and Christian," (*Westminster Review,* LXV, January, 1856, 11). It would seem that George Eliot had *Almansor* in mind during the composition of *The Spanish Gypsy.* In a letter to John Blackwood of 21 April 1868, George Eliot tells him that "The Poem will be less tragic than I threatened," and G. S. Haight notes that "At one time [George Eliot] apparently contemplated the death of both Fedalma and Silva" (*Letters,* IV, 431 and fn. 4).

Another play which prefigures the poem is Augustin Daly's adaptation of S. H. Mosenthal's *Deborah,—Leah the Forsaken,* which George Henry Lewes and George Eliot saw performed at the Adelphi Theatre on 10 February 1864. Lewes wonders in his Journal "at the badness of the piece and the success it has" [*Letters,* IV, 10 February 1864]. Daly's drama is set in an Austro-Hungarian border village in the early eighteenth-century. Like *Almansor* and *The Spanish Gypsy,* it deals with the theme of love and conflict between members of different religions and races. A Jewish maiden, Leah, is rescued from death by a Christian youth, Rudolf, who immediately falls in love with her. Their relationship and mistrust of one another, a result of their different backgrounds, forms the material for the dramatic action. Daly's intention is to impress upon his audience his sense of a common humanity. Leah treats Rudolf as a rescuer and as a saviour. She is no longer merely a persecuted animal but a human worthy of attention and love. She says to Rudolf: "Had you not stopped by the brink—not looked down in pity on my wistful eyes, but gone your way and heeded me no more—perchance you might have been happy and I content . . . You placed me in the revivifying sunlight of love . . . You have shown me the sun, and it has fired me with pride." Daly suggests that outside of Europe the Jew will be able to regain his pride. In Act II Leah and Rudolf plot to escape from a Europe of suffering. Leah pleads with her lover, "Let us leave this old Mizriam, and wander through the desert into the promised land." Rudolf and Leah "will plough the soil, and on it rear the altar of a new religion, that shall teach love and brotherhood to all men." *Leah* concludes with a description of "an emigrant Jewish tribe with all their goods on their way to America." And in the final words of the drama Leah says that she "shall wander into the far-off-the promised land!"—America.

To return to the historical sources for *The Spanish Gypsy,* George Eliot in her Journal, 14-18 November 1864, recorded that she "read Prescott again and made notes" (*Letters,* IV). W. H. Prescott in his *History of Ferdinand and Isabella* lays the blame for the initiation of, and the excesses of the Inquisition, upon Queen Isabella's confessor, the Dominican Monk, Thomas de Torquemada. Prescott wrote of Torquemada that he

> concealed more pride under his monastic weeds than might have furnished forth a convent of his order, was one of that class with whom zeal passes for religion, and who testify their zeal by a fiery persecution of those whose creed differs from their own; who compensate for their abstinence from sensual indulgence, by giving scope to those deadlier vices of the heart, pride, bigotry and intolerance, which are no less opposed to virtue, and are far more extensively mischievous to society.

In *The Spanish Gypsy,* George Eliot's Prior is not the Grand Inquisitor but a relatively minor member of the Inquisition, a state functionary enacting a prescribed task at a border town. The Host describes the "monk within our city walls," as "A holy, high born, stern Dominican." According to Juan's description which compliments Prescott's:

> . . . he seems less a man
> With struggling aims, than pure incarnate Will,
> Fit to subdue rebellious nations, nay,
> That human Flesh he breathes in, charged with passion
> Which quivers in his nostril and his lip,
> But disciplined by long-indwelling will
> To silent labour in the yoke of law.

During his lengthy soliloquies the Prior admits to temptations and that he has had human desires. However, in his function as Inquisitor enacting holy orders, he must not give way to pity. Hence mercy

> Sees that to save is greatly to destroy.
> 'Tis so the Holy Inquisition sees; its wrath
> Is fed from the strong heart of wisest love.
> For love must needs make hatred.

His hatred becomes a vehicle for repressed passions.

The background George Eliot chose for *The Spanish Gypsy* was "that moment in Spanish history when the struggle within the Moors was attaining its climax." ["Notes on *The Spanish Gypsy* and Tragedy in General," J. W. Cross, *George Eliot's Life,* 1885]. W. H. Prescott's *Ferdinand and Isabella* contains a "Review of the Political and Intellectual Condition of the Spanish Arabs Previous to the War of Granada," and in his second volume, a detailed account of Ferdinand's Granada campaign. Prescott relates how in order to defend the frontier of Eaja from Moorish attack, one Don Alonso de Cardena, an entrusted servant of Ferdinand, levies local support from "the principal chiefs on the borders; amongst others, . . . Don Pedro Henriquez, adelantado of Andalusia, Don Juan de Silva, count of Cifuentes, Don Alonso de Aguilar, and the Marquis of Cadiz." In *The Spanish Gypsy* George

Eliot retains the name of the Moorish leader El Zagal. She transforms an insignificant border potentate, Don Juan de Silva, into the tragic protagonist of her poetic drama. She uses this technique of populating her work with actual human beings to great effect. J. C. Pratt, in "A Middlemarch Miscellany," after a discussion of the impact upon George Eliot of the ideas of the German historian Wilhelm Becker, writes that

> Perhaps refusing to depend completely even on fictional antiquity, she created her novel's *Middlemarch's* people as composites of literary, historical, contemporary and mythical persons, striving always to echo the lesser known, the lower ranked, the patently unheroic. It was not the Byronic hero which appealed to her, but the Bekkerian, a figure whose insignificant actions assured his historical obscurity.

In other words she took Don Juan de Silva out of the "unvisited tombs" [*Middlemarch: A Study of Provincial Life,* edited W. J. Harvey, 1965] of Iberian history and transformed him into Byronic dimensions.

Prescott gives information on Spanish Hebrew culture in his section "a general survey of the History of the Jews in Spain, their institutions, customs, poetry, achievements, etc.," and in this section he refers to "the golden age of modern Jewish literature" in medieval Spain. However, for Jewish information George Eliot would also have made use of George Ticknor's, *History of Spanish Literature* (1863), which according to her journal she was reading on 20 November, 1866. Ticknor emphasises Jewish cultural attainments in Spain and it is these achievements which are presented in *The Spanish Gypsy*. I quote Ticknor's summary of the Jewish Spanish cultural heritage:

> The Jews . . . down to the time of their expulsion from Spain, in 1492 and even later, often appear in the history of Spanish literature. This was natural, for the Jews of Spain, from the appearance in 962 of four learned Talmudists, who were carried there by pirates, down to the fifteenth century, were more strongly marked by elegant culture than were their countrymen at the same period in any other part of Europe. Of Hebrew poetry in the Hebrew language,—which begins in Spain with the Rabbi Salomo ben Jehudah Gabirol, who died in 1064,—a history has been written entitled *Die Religiöse Poesie der Juden in Spanien,* von Dr. Michael Sachs (Berlin, 1845). But the great repository of everything relating to the culture of the Spanish Jews is the Biblioteca of Rodriquez de Castro, Tom. I. . . . It may be worth while to add that during the Moorish occupation of Spain, the Jews partook often of the Arabic culture, then so prevalent and brilliant;—a striking instance of which may be found in the case of the Castilian Jew, Juda ha-Levi, who took also the Arabic cognomen of Abu'l' Hussan, and whose poems were translated into German, and published by A. Geiger, at Breslau, in a very small neat volume, in 1851. Juda was born about 1080, and died, probably, soon after 1140.

George Eliot's knowledge of Spanish Jewish life in the poem is shown through the differing responses of Gentiles to Jews and through the reaction of Jews to their own situation and both these methods of presentation cohere in her finely drawn study of the astronomer Salomo Sephardo. Young Don Silva confides his secrets to his teacher Sephardo whom he begs not to betray him: "Kings of Spain / Like me have found their refuge in a Jew / and trusted in his counsel. You will help me?" Don Silva's appeal demonstrates George Eliot's awareness of the high position Jewish advisers had in Spanish Court Life. Prescott informs us that "we find eminent Jews residing in the courts of the Christian princes, directing their studies, attending them as physicians, or more frequently administering their finances. . . . Their astronomical science recommended them in a special manner to Alfonso the Wise." Ticknor tells us that it was not only in King Alfonso's court that Jews held high positions. He cites the example of Salomo Halevi, who "in 1330, when he was forty years old, was baptised as Pablo da Santa Maria, and rose subsequently . . . to . . . highest places in the Spanish church." It is noticeable that Salomo Sephardo ('Sephardo' literally meaning Spanish Jew) refuses to become a Christian and asserts his Judaism. His apparel reveals the practising orthodox Jew. He is dressed "In skullcap bordered close with crisp grey curls." When Don Silva appeals to him in very personal terms: "I have a double want / First a confessor—not a Catholic; / A heart without a livery—naked manhood," Sephardo's reply

> there's no such thing
> As naked manhood. . . .
> While my heart beats, it shall wear livery—
> My people's livery, whose yellow badge
> Marks them for Christian scorn

reinforces the moral of the drama. The claims of race, memory and tradition, are stronger than those of affection. Sephardo clearly states his uncompromising position, I am no Catholic / but Salomo Sephardo, a born Jew, / willing to serve Don Silva. Sephardo is, of course, fortunate in receiving the protection of an influential person—Don Silva. Others were not so fortunate. Sephardo tells Don Silva that he will not adopt the position of "the rich *marranos*" or converted Jews who take the attitude that "Man is first man" to them rather than "Jew or Gentile." But George Eliot presents her readers not with a wealthy convert but with a man who wants to survive. Her host, unlike Sephardo, has no access to the court. His motives are shown with sly humour,

> His father was a convert, chose the chrism
> As men choose physic, kept his chimney warm
> With smokiest wood upon a Saturday,
> Counted his gains and grudges on a chaplet,
> And crossed himself asleep for fear of spies;
> Trusting the Gods of Israel would see
> 'Twas Christian tyranny that made him base.

There is here a delightful set of juxtapositions: "chrism" and "physic"; the Jewish Sabbath and work; monetary concern and the use of Christian ritual objects. Underlying all is the sense of living a fugitive existence, of the continual fear of being found out, of the double life being exploded—that "fear of spies."

George Eliot's portrait of Sephardo is a complicated one. The dichotomies in Sephardo's views represent not only his own internal struggles but wider ones. Sephardo's concern is whether man is capable of controlling his own destiny? This question obsessed Jewish and Arabic medieval metaphysicians, for if man had some control over his future then God was not completely in command. The area in which this problem was most debated was that of astrology. If by reading the stars man could foresee his future, God's omnipotence was in question. Don Silva believes in a fate told by the stars. His tutor cannot be as certain as his pupil, and tells Don Silva that he believes that the stars "are not absolute, And tell no fortunes." Sephardo relies on tradition and reason rather than the results of man's discoveries: "we walk evermore / To higher paths, by brightening Reason's lamp / Still we are purblind, tottering." Sephardo explains the basis of his belief by an appeal to traditional Judaic discussion. He tells Don Silva that

> Two angels guide
> The path of man, both aged and yet young,
> As angels are, ripening through endless years.
> On one he leans: some call her Memory,
> And some, Tradition;

In order to place Sephardo's difficulties within a specific historical context George Eliot deliberately introduces the name of "the best known and most admired Jewish author in the [medieval] Christian world" [S. W. Baron, *A Social and Religious History of the Jews,* 1937-], Rabbi Abraham Aben-Ezra (c. 1092-c. 1167). Sephardo tells Don Silva,

> I hold less
> Than Aben-Ezra, of that aged lore
> Brought by long centuries from Chaldaean plains,
> The Jew-taught Florentine rejects it all.
> For still the light is measured by the eye,
> And the weak organ fails. I may see ill;
> But over all belief is faithfulness,
> Which fulfils vision with obedience.

Long before nineteenth-century Biblical scholarship and the work of Spinoza, the wandering scholar and poet Aben-Ezra in his Biblical Exegesis questioned the authenticity of the Old Testament texts, showing that many verses in the Torah had originated at a period later than the Mosaic events which they described. Aben-Ezra wrote several works of an astrological nature and argued that the influence of the stars on human destiny was unalterable.

Sephardo's affirmation of belief in memory and tradition, and his rejection of Aben-Ezra's philosophy has affinities with the response of some Victorian thinkers to their own spiritual doubts and uncertainties when confronted with Biblical criticism and the results of scientific and biological research. As George Eliot writes to John Blackwood on 21 March 1867, her poem "is not historic, but has merely historic connections" (*Letters,* IV). Similarly Matthew Arnold in *Literature and Dogma* (1873), found some relief from his overwhelming sense of isolation in the universe by arguing that science and art, the domain that constitutes "Hellenism," make up between them but one-fourth of life, the remaining three-fourths being allotted to conduct. Arnold emphasised ethical behaviour—"Hebraism"—and like Auguste Comte, Herbert Spencer, and G. H. Lewes, based his attitudes upon a belief in man's relationship with past wisdom, memory and tradition. For Arnold, as for the younger Samuel Butler and many Victorians, the past irrevocably shaped a man's present and affected his attitudes and conduct. Butler went as far as to write in his *Unconscious Memory* (1880) that all life is "the being possessed of a memory—the life of a thing at any moment is the memories which at the moment it retains."

In *The Spanish Gypsy* Sephardo continually appeals to his sense of a long Judaic tradition and affirms his belief in the traditional Judaic conception of God. His pupil Don Silva believes not only in the results of star-gazing but in the permanence of his passion for Fedalma for whom he is prepared to sacrifice home, religion and throne, and to become a fellow-gypsy. The past is too great for Fedalma, who returns to her people to seek an ancestral home, the ancient centre of Gypsy civilisation. Don Silva, at the conclusion of the poems, when he realises that his passion is no longer a reality, undertakes a pilgrimage to Rome in order to return to the centre of wisdom, memory and tradition of his Spanish European world.

In her Notes on "The Spanish Gypsy and Tragedy in general" George Eliot wrote that she "could not use the Jews . . . because the facts of their history were too conspicuously opposed to the working out of my catastrophe" [*George Eliot's Life as Related in Her Letters and Journals,* 1885]. George Eliot chose the Gypsies, a nomadic oppressed race who had rarely intermingled within the countries in which they lived. They had little in the way of sophisticated cultural traditions and highly developed institutions as cohering communal focal points. One of the main sources for George Eliot's knowledge of the Gypsies was, according to her "Commonplace Book," George Borrow's, *The Zincali; or, An Account of the Gypsies of Spain* (1841). Borrow relates how the Inquisition and the Spanish treated the Gypsy as "Gente burrat y despreciable." George Eliot noted how "*Jews and even Moorish families—could* much less have any scruples than the Spanish monarchs in laying hands on the Gypsy. The edict for their extermination was published in the year 1492. But, instead of passing the boundaries, they slunk into hiding-places, and shortly after appeared everywhere in as great numbers as before." Borrow stressed how, as a result of persecution, despite their internal differences, there was a highly developed feeling of racial affinity amongst Gypsies. He found in Spain of the 1830's "much of that fellow-feeling which springs from a consciousness of proceeding from one common origin, or, as they love to term it, 'blood'" (*The Zincali*).

Borrow's explanation of the differences between the Jews and the Gypsies, illustrates George Eliot's choice of the Gypsies for her poem. Borrow writes "Both have had an exodus, both as exiles and dispersed among the Gentiles

. . . both, though speaking the language of the Gentiles, possess a peculiar tongue . . . and both possess a peculiar cast of countenance." Fedalma looking at the captured Gypsy leader—whom she does not know to be her father—seems to see in his eyes

> the sadness of the world
> Rebuking her, the great bell's hidden thought
> Now first unveiled—the sorrows unredeemed
> Of races outcast, scorned, and wandering.

For Borrow the Gypsies have no real religion whilst the Jews have one "to which they are fanatically attached" (*The Zincali*). The Jews, unlike the Gypsies, possess a great tradition of learning and historical memory, rooted in an actual and historical homeland. The Gypsies do not really "know the name of their original country, and the only tradition which they possess, that of their Egyptian origin is a false one" (*The Zincali*). George Eliot notes in her "Commonplace Book" that "One story (said to be told by the Gypsies themselves) was that their wandering from Egypt was inflicted on them as a punishment for the sin of their ancestors in refusing an asylum to the Infant Jesus."

Zarca tells his daughter Fedalma of his dream of leading a return of his people to Africa:

> They have a promised land beyond the sea:
> There I may lead them, raise my standard, call
> The wandering Zincali to that home,
> And make a nation—bring light, order, law,
> Instead of chaos.

The concrete nouns reinforce, in order of dominance, national virtues as Zarca sees them. Pre-eminent is "light" which will replace the darkness of Gypsy diaspora life. Zarca tells his daughter that the Gypsy people have "no home in memory / No dimmest lore of giant ancestors / To make a common hearth for piety." Fedalma too has few illusions and is less idealistic. Her reaction to her father indicates a fierce internal struggle between the claims of race and duty and the influence of her Spanish upbringing. She speaks of the Gypsies as

> A race that lives on prey as foxes do
> With stealthy, petty rapine: so despised,
> It is not persecuted, only spurned,
> Crushed underfoot, warred on by chance like rats.

Such self-humiliation and lack of national pride serves as a reflection of the low state into which her people have fallen. Fedalma is seeing the Gypsies from a double vision: as an outside educated in Christian society; and as one born a Gypsy. At the conclusion of the poems she understands her renunciation of her past life and her lover in terms of duty to her father rather than as the product of a blind passionate ideal. Fedalma tells Don Silva in their final interview that she will "plant" her father's "sacred hope within the sanctuary and die its priestess." Even at the end she is not blinded with false hope.

Fedalma has blood ties which finally entrap her. In the poem, "race" as applied to a specific group of people who have a strong sense of kinship, becomes evident. The use of the idea thus differs from its usage by W. H. Riehl and later developments of *volk* ideology. G. L. Mosse explains in *The Crisis of German Ideology* (1966) that "*Volk* was limited to a particular national unit. . . . The term 'rooted' was constantly invoked by Volkish thinkers" and it implied those who had lived in the same rural environment for centuries. The Jews and the Gypsies were neither from the small town, the village or peasants, but were restless and rootless, had no home and occupied no specific territory. It is significant that George Eliot extolls no specific 'rooted' kind of life but in this poem dealing with kinship, history and tradition, she uses the Gypsies, a group of people without a definite ancestral tradition and cohering communal institutions, and the Jews who possess tradition and institutions but are dispersed and exiled. She does not choose the *volk* of contemporary and later German thought: the idyllic Medieval *volk*, or those of the remote Germanic past celebrated for instance in Wagner's opera, *Nibelungen*, which George Eliot and George Henry Lewes saw in Dresden on 18 September 1867. Lewes comments in his Journal that this opera "Interested us very much, though it is a subject ill suited to the opera, better left in the twilight of Mythology."

In her "Notes on *The Spanish Gypsy* and Tragedy in General" George Eliot wrote of the universal significance of the local conflict between the Moors, Jews, Gypsies and Christians in late medieval Spain and of the need to renounce "the expectation of marriage." The subject "might be taken as a symbol of the part which is played in the general human lot by hereditary conditions in the largest sense, and of the fact that what we call duty is entirely made up of such conditions." Individual desires, such as that of wishing to marry a person from a different ethnic background, should be resisted. It is necessary to adjust

> our individual needs to the dire necessities of our
>   lot,
> partly as to our natural constitution, partly as
>   sharers
> of life with our fellow-beings. Tragedy consists in
>   the
> terrible difficulty of this adjustment—
>   "The dire strife
>   Of poor Humanity's afflicted will,
>   Struggling in vain with ruthless destiny."
> Looking at individual lots, I seemed to see in each
>   the
> same story, wrought out with more or less of
>   tragedy.

Two months after the publication of *The Spanish Gypsy* George Eliot wrote to Clifford Allbutt that "the inspiring principle which alone gives me courage to write is, that of so presenting our human life as to help my readers in getting a clearer conception and a more active admiration of those vital elements which bind men together and give a higher worthiness to their existence." In *The Spanish Gypsy* "those vital elements" are the tremendous influences of memory and tradition amongst persecuted people and an aspiration which gives a "higher worthiness to their existence" (*Letters,* IV, August 1868) to—in Zarca's case—to return to the country where he believes his people's roots lie.

Kathleen Blake (essay date 1980)

SOURCE: "*Armgart*—George Eliot on the Woman Artist," in *Victorian Poetry,* Vol. 18, No. 1, Spring, 1980, pp. 75-80.

[*In the following excerpt, Blake argues that the poem "Armgart" centers around the conflict between love and art that exists for female artists.*]

A more indefatigable and psychologically adept husband-therapist of a woman's creative drive than George Henry Lewes cannot be imagined. George Eliot dedicated her *Legend of Jubal and Other Poems* (1871) "To my beloved Husband, George Henry Lewes, whose cherishing tenderness for twenty years has alone made my work possible to me." And yet *Jubal* contains the dramatic poem "**Armgart,**" which like *Middlemarch* and *Daniel Deronda* (1871-72, 1876) poses the incompatibility of love and art for the artist who is a woman. . . .

"**Armgart**" is . . . very divided about the female artist who is "not a loving woman." The poem is quite resolute in supporting Armgart against the threats posed by men and motherhood, but it introduces another version of the conflict of love and art for a woman, one even more foundering, and fascinating.

"**Armgart**" is a dramatic poem that Henry James thought the best of the four long poems in the *Jubal* collection but that, like the rest of Eliot's verse, is almost completely unrecognized by criticism. As James says, it is difficult not to overrate or underrate the poetry by measure of the fiction. The latter impulse has dominated. Swinburne says it would be unmanly to treat the poetry critically at all [*A Note on Charlotte Brontë,* 1877]. A recent article called "George Eliot's Great Poetry" is practically the only one to be found that promises to treat the subject, and it turns out to concern *The Mill on the Floss* [John Freeman, 1970].

If "**Armgart**" is not great, it surely has great interest in respect to the double dilemma into which it plunges its laureled prima donna. One develops from a proposal of marriage from Graf Dornberg, the other from the loss of voice in illness. Armgart rejects the Graf's addresses because he separates her art from herself as expendable. She disdains his various wooing arguments. One is that unlike men, women are what they are, not what they achieve:

> Men rise the higher as their task is high,
> The task being well achieved. A woman's rank
> Lies in the fullness of her womanhood.
> Therein alone she is royal.

Armgart receives this with irony:

> Woman, thy desire
> Shall be that all superlatives on earth
> Belong to men, save the one highest kind—
> To be a mother.

The Graf's second argument is that a woman not only suffers less but achieves more without her art, in "home delights / Which penetrate and purify the world." Armgart's rejecting irony is again bitter: should she sing in her chimney corner to inspire her husband at his newspaper?

The Graf has attempted to set her artistry off against her womanhood, as if it were unnatural. The art of singing offers a fine riposte because a soprano voice comes from nature and is not furnishable by a man. Armgart refuses to recognize a conflict, except as one made by men:

> I am an artist by my birth—
> By the same warrant that I am a woman:
>
> . . . . .
>
> . . . if a conflict comes,
> Perish, no, not the woman, but the joys
> Which men make narrow by their narrowness.

The joys that must perish are those of love. Eliot dramatizes the conflict through a convoluted and convincing route of motivation. The Graf does not overtly demand that Armgart renounce her art to marry him, but she feels the pressure anyway from a man who grudgingly tolerates instead of rejoicing in her singing. The interdiction of art by love would come from within herself, "My love would be accomplice of your will." So she will repress love and transform the pain into art.

It turns out that for Armgart to sacrifice her art is essential to her appeal to the Graf, though he doesn't say so outright. Armgart holds that his affection depends on all she has to give up for him: "my charm / Was half that I could win fame yet renounce!" He fancies "a wife with glory possible absorbed / Into her husband's actual." When she loses her voice he does not return to renew his suit. This vouches for Armgart's blame to men for setting love and art at odds for a woman. The poem seems to be with her.

I think it is with her in recognizing the intensity and ambition that the world so little credits in a woman. Some of the best passages of the poem concern Armgart's exaltation of celebrity. She revels in fame and impact on the multitude. She needs their applause and flowers and jewels to register her powerful self to herself: "splendours which flash out the glow I make." Her ambition is treated seriously as a source of artistic identity and energy. The poem gives a deeply felt case for the artist's overweening pride. In the end it does turn out to be overweening, however, and sympathy for Armgart becomes divided.

Again the issue is love versus art, but recast into new terms. When Armgart loses her voice she cannot bear to live within the mediocrity that she sees as the common fate of women. She feels suicidal rebellion against "woman's penury." Her cousin and attendant, the plain, self-effacing, hitherto almost unheeded Walpurga, now replaces Graf Dornberg in the argument over love and art. Walpurga contends that Armgart's glory as an artist had so removed her from the common lot that she despised it, so that the communication with the audience on which the singer exalted herself was at base factitious and cynical: natures like hers perform "in mere mock knowledge of their fellows' woe, / Thinking their smiles may heal it." Walpurga tasks Armgart with egotistical lack of care for others, of the same sort that made her oblivious to Walpurga's own care for her; she dismisses that unobtrusive tenderness as petty, mere "thwarted life," "woman's penury." Eliot gives vent inWalpurga to the anger of the ordinary woman at being the measure of everything escaped by the extraordinary one. Walpurga defines one of the escapes as a loss: the loss of love. Walpurga has found a meaning for her monotone life in loving Armgart. She is impatient with Armgart's despair because it pridefully rejects as worthless what Walpurga has based her life on.

Therefore the poem presents a double critique of the conflict of love and art for a woman. It expresses indignation at the unnecessary sacrifices demanded by men of women in marriage. Armgart is right not to marry the Graf. But it also deepens the conflict until vindication is harder to come by. It seems that glory saps loving-kindness. This constitutes a particular liability for a woman artist because her glory is so exceptional in a world which devalues women's achievements (as the poem shows) that it exaggerates the gap between herself and her sex. Armgart is wrong to recoil utterly from the lot to which she is reduced because it is no better than the lots of millions of women like Walpurga.

The conclusion of the poem takes careful sorting. Marriage offers no compensation for a lost voice. Singing versus marriage was a falsely imposed set of alternatives to begin with. Armgart ends up teaching music in a small town. She thereby remains true to her art. She refuses to denigrate it by becoming a poor actress; instead she will help to form other fine singers. She also shows care for Walpurga because the small town is the home that Walpurga had left in order to serve Armgart. Love and art are here in some sense reconciled. The poem appears to say that this reconciliation is necessary for true art, and that for a woman artist love and art are destructively divided, but not so importantly in the relation one first thinks of, between the sexes. There the division must be suffered, because anything else means capitulation to the unfair demands of men. Rather the poem identifies the more dangerous result of the division of art and love as the woman artist's contempt for her own sex. This becomes a species of suicidal self-hatred when she suffers the common feminine lot herself, and it provides no basis for the best in art, because communication must be communion.

Karen B. Mann (essay date 1980)

SOURCE: "George Eliot and Wordsworth: The Power of Sound and the Power of Mind," in *Studies in English Literature*, Vol. 20, No. 4, Autumn, 1980, pp. 675-94.

[*In the following excerpt, Mann examines the importance of Wordsworth's influence on George Eliot's poem "The Legend of Jubal," and shows that both writers consider sound a powerful metaphor for the human imagination.*]

George Eliot's appreciation for Wordsworth's poetry extends from her earliest evangelical years to the end of her life; and the simplified Wordsworth of nature and rural goodness has often been recognized as an influence upon her work. What is perhaps less noticed is the degree, to which Wordsworth and George Eliot share a similar conception of imagination as the crucial faculty of mind. . . . [The] Romantic conception of imagination as the central faculty of mind is not so much negated by George Eliot as re-examined in the light of a different aesthetic form, with its own, new perception of the importance of imagination. Wordsworth is the figure who is most important for George Eliot here, although sufficient evidence of the influence of Coleridge and Shelley is apparent. After a general discussion of the similarities between Wordsworth and George Eliot concerning the nature and results of "the power of mind," I will indicate how a single, dominant metaphor for that power—sound—is transferred by George Eliot from the work of the poet into her fiction. The full implications of that transference will be most apparent in George Eliot's poem **"The Legend of Jubal,"** which underlines both her kinship with and her difference from the Romantic conceptions of William Wordsworth. . . .

I

The final books of *The Prelude* detail the poet's sense of the importance of imagination as a faculty which allows man to infuse his own spirit into the alien world, thereby comprehending directly the nature of life for the non-self. But this conception of the imagination is inherent as well in the poems composed during the same period as *The Prelude,* which were published and therefore available to Mary Ann Evans before 1850. For instance, in "Tintern Abbey" Wordsworth writes of an essentially imaginative perception which transcends ordinary or natural vision and yet brings about the poet's commitment to such "natural" vision:

> Therefore am I still
> A lover of the meadows and the woods,
> And mountains; and of all that we behold
> From this green earth; of all the mighty world
> Of eye, and ear,—both what they half crate,
> And what perceive: well pleased to recognize
> In nature and the language of the sense
> The anchor of my purest thoughts, the nurse,
> The guide, the guardian of my heart, and soul
> Of all my moral being.

In the works of George Eliot, this acquisition of knowledge through a process essentially aesthetic is an inherent activity in both the narrator's loving attention to his story and the imaginative vision necessary for the full maturity of the characters. It is the imagination which, for Wordsworth and for Eliot, grasps and accepts the idea of the world as a concrete whole in which individual and milieu function as one unit. Moral and rational judgments can thus only be drawn from the sympathetic perception of a situation in its totality.

Wordsworth and George Eliot express this metaphysical insight in essentially similar ways. The "Elegiac Stanzas," a later poem which shows Wordsworth's own domestication of imagination in a more Victorian world, might stand as a sufficient guide to the central problem of George Eliot's novels. The timeless, serene image of Peele Castle which Wordsworth fashions in his youth dissolves with the intrusion of death into his life. But the changed outlook of the soul thus "humanized" by "deep distress" is no less imaginative; for the poet grasps anew the image of Peele Castle as painted by Beaumont and sympathizes with its passion and sublimity. George Eliot echoes the terms of "Elegiac Stanzas" closely in *Felix Holt the Radical*, when Esther discerns the difference between the earlier "Elysian" picture of wealthy life and her new interpretation of that vision after a closer view of the world of Transome Court. Even the word "Elysian" occurs in both works. For both Wordsworth and George Eliot the earlier vision has been replaced by the understanding of a larger relation between the image in the mind and an external world of suffering.

There is also a great deal of similarity between the conception of maturation as it is portrayed in the works of Wordsworth and George Eliot. As the "Ode: Intimations of Immortality" implies, the child's unthinking, imaginative appropriation of the outer world as food for the self is gradually dissolved by a sense of both outward menace and inward difference. Eliot echoes, in fragmentary form, this aspect of growing up, which Wordsworth narrates most completely in the first books of *The Prelude*. Little Maggie Tulliver experiences the natural world as a playground for body and mind in which she reigns supreme; and Gwendolen Harleth in girlhood is subject to those feelings of separation from and menace in nature which occasionally overtook the young poet (cf. *The Prelude*, I, 425-63). What this sense of menace indicates in both Wordsworth and, by implication, in George Eliot, is a fear of separation from the natural world, of "traumatic breaks: *Natura non facit saltus*." Wordsworth evades these breaks or moments of separateness by recommitting himself to nature in poetry; George Eliot finds her connection with the world through the acceptance of a pervasive network of physical and psychological law.

Let me move from the abstract assertion of likeness between Wordsworth and George Eliot to an examination of the specific and vital similarities in their usage of certain metaphors for the power of mind. A passage from one of George Eliot's letters written on June 4, 1848, is doubly useful since it is often quoted by critics to exemplify the "realistic" or anti-imaginative qualities of her work, whereas in actuality it offers a direct example of the degree to which George Eliot is a "Romantic" believer in the imagination:

> Alas for the fate of poor mortals which condemns them to wake up some fine morning and find all the poetry in which their world was bathed only the evening before utterly gone—the hard angular world of chairs and tables and looking-glasses staring at them in all its naked prose. It is so in all stages of life—the poetry of girlhood goes—the poetry of love and marriage—the poetry of maternity—and at last the very poetry of duty forsakes us for a season and we see ourselves and all about us as nothing more than miserable agglomerations of atoms—poor tentative efforts of the Nature Princip to mould a personality. This is the state of prostration—the self-abnegation through which the soul must go, and to which perhaps it must again and again return, that its poetry or religion, which is the same thing, may be a real ever-flowing river fresh from the windows of heaven and the fountains of the great deep—not an artificial basin with grotto work and gold fish.

The George Eliot Letters

The influence of Wordsworth's many streams and fountains is apparent here, and it is the exact nature of Wordsworth's influence which is revealing for George Eliot's fiction. In the first place, the passage implies that poetry and religion are not systems of rules but forces—rivers. It also implies that such forces have access to a realm beyond this world of tables and chairs, whether envisioned as a heaven above or a deep below everyday human experience. The unnamed link between such a realm and the everyday world is *imagination*, conceived as the "power" of mind. It is this faculty—the common term between art and morality, or, in George Eliot's words, poetry and religion—which George Eliot wishes to examine through the medium of fiction, not simply to point up its dangers, but also to establish its necessity, so that human life will indeed not become an "artificial basin with grotto work and gold fish."

George Eliot's "The Legend of Jubal" focuses upon power, order, and the transcendence through harmony of time and death.

—*Karen B. Mann*

It is important that George Eliot turned to the metaphoric heritage of the Romantic poets to express her conception of this power of mind. Metaphor itself is the paradigm of the imagination in its blending of inner and outer. And while the image of the river in the above passage takes us far in our understanding of the imagination as a power, it is not so revelatory of the nature of that power as is the equally if not more predominant metaphor of sound in the works of both Wordsworth and George Eliot. There is, of course, an interesting transition from the one metaphor to the other, in that the rivers and fountains of Wordsworth's poetry are preeminently vocal. But beyond this, sound has certain significant characteristics as a phenomenon which suits it peculiarly to the needs of both poet and novelist. Like smell, with which it is sometimes combined, hearing is an "intangible" sense, one which indicates how man can be touched by the invisible and the subtle. Further, sound's effect upon the mind is a function of time or duration rather than space, and so it becomes a means for unification both of past and present self, and of self and world, by a means less immediately mechanical than mere sight. Linked with this last, and perhaps central to the preoccupation with sound in both Wordsworth and George Eliot, is the power of sound to create a sense of spiritual life in the world surrounding man *speaking* to him.

Thus, in George Eliot's novels, metaphors of sound and music operate to characterize the qualities of mind of her characters and even of her narrator. When with these metaphors are included references to that fruitfully ambiguous term "harmony," a sense of how George Eliot values an imaginative response to the outer world emerges.

II

Wordsworth's "On the Power of Sound" (pub. 1835) and George Eliot's **"The Legend of Jubal"** (pub. 1870) help exemplify the significance each writer attaches to the nature of sound. Their common subject—the power of sound as an expression of the power of mind—is reinforced by the fact that George Eliot recorded her admiration of Wordsworth's poem in a letter to Maria Lewis on 1 October 1840 (*Letters*). That she should choose the same topic some 29 years later for one of her few efforts at poetry suggests the degree to which Wordsworth's complex metaphor had meaning for her own conception of the mind as a power. Repeatedly in her novels, her characters and her narrator reveal their imaginative powers through their unconscious susceptibilities to sounds and music and their conscious responses to such sounds as expressions of harmony and order. But before discussing this issue, I need to explain more fully what place sound has in Wordsworth's own canon.

The list of lines containing the various forms of the word "sound" in the Concordance of Wordsworth's poetry occupies three and a half columns; references to music and harmony lengthen that list. Decidedly represented are *The Prelude* and *The Excursion,* as well as the "Poems of the Imagination" in the collected *Works;* but, of course, anything so central to the concept of poetry as sound and song is present virtually everywhere in Wordsworth's poems. Briefly stated, the usage of sound suggests two important, connected processes: the power of mind to hear the living world speaking to man, and the subsequent power of mind to answer that external voice. The sounds of importance to the first of these reciprocal processes are, of course, natural ones. These sounds are for Wordsworth a "ghostly language of the ancient earth" (*The Prelude,* II, 309). Appropriately, the most predominant

earth sounds arise from streams and torrents, and quickly become identified with the parallel streams of verse overflowing from the poet's imagination:

> Was it for this
> That one, the fairest of all rivers, loved
> To blend his murmurs with my nurse's song,
> And, from his alder shades and rocky falls,
> And from his fords and shallows, sent a voice
> That flowed along my dreams?
>
> (*The Prelude*)

In *The Excursion,* this external voice has become "the mighty stream of tendency / Uttering, for elevation of our thought, / A clear sonorous voice". Sensitivity to such a voice from nature is a sign of awakening imaginative power. From the boy of Winander to Peter Bell, Wordsworth's characters exhibit the reciprocal powers of outer and inner life through the presence of and response to portentous sounds. . . . [Much] the same thing occurs with George Eliot's fictional characters. These sounds or voices help to exhibit the mind's awareness of the spirit alive in the external world to which the imagination must give answer. That answer in Wordsworth is frequently the sound of music, an expression of perceived and created harmony which becomes a hymn of praise. The full statement of this two-fold process is contained in the poem which, appropriately enough, climaxes Wordsworth's "Poems of the Imagination": "On the Power of Sound."

Wordsworth's poem begins with the conception of a spirit which inhabits the organ of the ear, to whom the sounds of the world are subservient. Yet the relationship between mind and sound is not really so simple, as the subsequent verses show. Certain sounds, particularly measured sounds or songs, appear to influence and even dominate the mind, sometimes making inroads for man's "dangerous Passions." But at the same time, such domination allows the mind in turn to conquer external circumstance:

> For the tired slave, Song lifts the languid oar,
> And bids it aptly fall, with chime
> That beautifies the fairest shore,
> And mitigates the harshest clime.

In terms sometimes used by critics of George Eliot's fiction, such an imaginative avoidance of harsh reality might be a sign of moral torpor. But for Wordsworth (and, in **"The Legend of Jubal,"** for George Eliot), this response to external power by the assertion of inner power is a hint of transcendent order, or harmony between mind and universe:

> As Conscience, to the centre
> Of being, smites with irresistible pain,
> So shall a solemn cadence, if it enter
> The mouldy vaults of the dull idiot's brain,
> Transmute him to a wretch from quiet hurled—
> Convulsed as by a jarring din;
> And then aghast, as at the world
> Of reason partially let in
> By concords winding with a sway

Terrible for sense and soul!
Or awed he weeps, struggling to quell dismay.
Point not these mysteries to an Art
Lodged above the starry pole;
Pure modulations flowing from the heart
Of divine Love, where Wisdom, Beauty, Truth
With Order dwell, in endless youth?

By implication, the movement of mind under the power of measured sound corresponds to a letting in of divine or transcendent reason, to a momentary touch with the infinite.

In the succeeding stanzas of the poem, Wordsworth seems to assert, through the myths of Orpheus, Amphion, and Pan, how the power of the mind's response to music becomes a means to conquer time, space, and death. George Eliot attempts much the same task in her myth of Jubal. But when Wordsworth—aware that such myths belong to the "rapt imagination" of earlier times—tries to express the awakening of the mind through more ordinary external sounds, his examples become peculiarly ominous. The portentous sounds he chooses from everyday life offer a striking contrast to the gaiety of the satyrs under the influence of Pan's music, for he details the echo of dirt upon the coffinlid, the bell which rings the convict's knell, and the final note of the sinking ship's distress gun.

As a countermovement to this lapse into the world of death, where sound may be "heard, and heard no more," Wordsworth again prays for an order to make the power of sound a guarantee of universal order:

Ye wandering Utterances, has earth no scheme,
No scale of moral music—to unite
Powers that survive but in the faintest dream
Of memory?—O that ye might stoop to bear
Chains, such precious chains of sight
As laboured minstrelsies through ages wear!
O for a balance fit the truth to tell
Of the Unsubstantial, pondered well!

What Wordsworth desired to accomplish as minstrel in this poem is an assertion of the reciprocal and benevolent connection between mind and world accomplished by means of sound. The power of the mind to respond to outer harmony—apparent not only in sounds themselves but also in the "music" of the heavens, the ocean, and the seasons—triggers a second power: the power to give out again an answering hymn of thanksgiving which asserts a recognition of the world's order, and the Being to whom such order is due. Significantly, the poem ends with the recollection that the outer world itself came into being through sound, through the Word; and the Word, according to Wordsworth, alone is immortal.

III

Like "On the Power of Sound," George Eliot's **"The Legend of Jubal"** focuses upon power, order, and the transcendence through harmony of time and death. What is immediately different about George Eliot's treatment—

and this is revelatory of her own imaginative bent—is her choice of a narrative for her exploration of the subject. While at first this would appear to suggest that George Eliot localizes her assertions about harmony within the particular beliefs of a person bound by time and space, the workings of the poem as a whole indicate that she perceives the legend to be a form of parable which perhaps gives the potentials of sound more necessary relevance to man's worldly condition than the less immediately time-bound meditations of Wordsworth.

The frame story of the invention of music by Jubal implies that music becomes necessary as a counterbalance to the actual existence of time and death, although time itself is ironically made known through sound as the measure of duration: "Time, vague as air before, new terrors stirred, / With measured wing now audibly arose / Throbbing through all things to some unknown close." In fact, it is the presence of time itself which calls for a means to transmute its pulsations from perpetual reminders of death into expressions of man's immortal power. In the terms of the narrative, with the recognition of death in the image of Lamech's son, the children of Cain feel the need for a means to obliterate or transmute the sense of passing time and to reach by that means immortality. Thus the greater portion of the poem, after this awakening shock of personal mortality common to all of George Eliot's fiction, is focused upon the resurgence of mental power by means of music. This pattern corresponds directly to the pattern in Wordsworth's poem, where the poet reaches after a larger harmony which will allay the fears of eternal silence. The keys to such immortality in **"The Legend of Jubal"** are action and sound:

Then while the soul its way with sound can cleave,
And while the arm is strong to strike and heave,
Let soul and arm give shape that will abide
And rule above our graves, and power divide
With that great god of day, whose rays must bend
As we shall make the moving shadows tend.

Most of George Eliot's fictional characters try to assert power through the "arm," that is, through action, through the molding of events. Tubal-Cain in this poem represents the most exemplary form of this assertion, for he is the plastic artist whose shapes, the outward results of "inspiring vision," provide useful tools for man. But such creation, linked as it is with materialthings, has "mixed ends," unlike the "invisible" creation of Jubal. Yet Jubal's first stirrings of power are an imaginative response to his brother's industry with outward things:

Jubal, too, watched the hammer, till his eyes,
No longer following its fall or rise,
Seemed glad with something that they could not
  see,
But only listened to—some melody,
Wherein dumb longings inward speech had found,
Won from the common store of struggling sound.
Then, as the metal shapes more various grew,
And, hurled upon each other, resonance drew,
Each gave new tones, the revelations dim

Of some external soul that spoke for him:
The hollow vessel's clang, the clash, the boom,
Like light that makes wide spiritual room
And skyey spaces in the spaceless thought,
To Jubal such enlarged passion brought
That love, hope, rage, and all experience,
Were fused in vaster being, fetching thence
Concords and discords, cadences and cries
That seemed from some world-shrouded soul to
    rise,
Some rapture more intense, some mightier rage,
Some living sea that burst the bounds of man's
    brief age.

What Jubal wakens to is the power of his imagination discovering a means for expressing itself in response to external stimuli, and finding eternity in the expression. The blankness of space around him is filled with "tremors" arising from the "giant soul of earth." Indeed, what had been empty space is filled by the presence of Jubal and his music, and the result is not only a filling of that vacuum with sound, but a binding of those listening to that sound into a unity of time past and to come, for the old remember their youth and the young look to their futures. The completed union in time and space occurs as all arise and begin to dance with "ringèd feet swayed by each close-linked palm."

It seems apparent from the passage describing Jubal's intentions and success that Eliot means for music to symbolize mental power of a particular sort. Music brings order or form to brute matter, where the super-abundance of artistry itself "informs the sense / With fuller union, finer difference." This balance of opposing drives toward wholeness and distinctness is echoed in the description of Jubal's first invention, the lyre:

He made it, and from out its measured frame
Drew the harmonic soul, whose answers came
With guidance sweet and lessons of delight
Teaching to ear and hand the blissful Right,
Where strictest law is gladness to the sense,
And all desire bends toward obedience.

What is crucial for Eliot, both here and in her fiction, is the union of desire and obedience: order in this case is no stern taskmaster who requires the bending of the will away from all that is joyful. Joy itself arises from the perception of an order which pleases both the outward sense and the inward soul. What Jubal has found is a "heart of music in the might of sound"—that is, a center and source of potent feeling within the raw power of outward "noise." Thus Eliot, like Wordsworth, finds in the correlation between sound and music a metaphor for the power of imaginative perception and the harnessing of that power.

Having had his imaginative insight and his outward proof of its potency in the response of his people, Jubal goes out in confidence to bless the world with harmony and bring more and more of life's disparate materials under his command. In this regard he is a kind of prototype of all of George Eliot's "imaginative" characters, from Hetty

Sorrel to Mordecai Cohen. Like them, his first expectation of ever higher personal success, exemplified in the poem in the climbing of higher and higher mountains which will eventually allow him to hear the true music of the spheres, is frustrated. Instead of one final solid peak to stand upon, Jubal finds the sea: "this main—/ Myriads of maddened horses thundering o'er the plain." Jubal's sense of the largeness of the world embodied in the roaring of the sea, and the growing weakness of his personal power to order what that sea speaks to him, brings a crippling paralysis.

When Jubal, like Wordsworth in "On the Power of Sound," feels the pull of death foreshadowed in his growing imaginative inadequacy, he chooses to return to his place of origin, to find in his past that successful creativity which now eludes him. What Jubal does meet on his return is not that past itself, but his own powers of mind made visible in the stream of singing people:

Brought like fulfilment of forgotten prayer;
As if his soul, breathed out upon the air,
Had held the invisible seeds of harmony
Quick with the various strains of life to be.

As a kind of gloss on Wordsworth's own immortal Word, the divine word which is being sung, "The common need, love, joy, that knits them in one whole," is "Jubal," the name "For glorious power untouched by that slow death / Which creeps with creeping time."

The man Jubal, a poor "remnant" of mortality, is, in comparison to this invisible power, but a feeble bell in a lake of silence, and the hope of immortality which the poem offers is certainly not a personal one. What Jubal is given as an answer to his coming physical dissolution is the same sort of transcendent consolation which Wordsworth offers at the close of "On the Power of Sound." It is the eternal presence of "power" itself, released into the world of inert matter, which connects man with the infinite. Ironically, that power first makes itself recognized as a hunger after the "senses' beauteous Right." From that hunger Jubal had created the music which then feeds his soul; and further, that music feeds the souls of others:

But thy expanding joy was still to give,
And with the generous air in song to live,
Feeding the wave of ever-widening bliss
Where fellowship means equal perfectness.

Jubal then dies amid a symphony of sound and sight corresponding to the mighty harmonies hidden in the vastness of space. Appropriately, George Eliot's last metaphor for him is "a quenched sun-wave." The "power" which is a common denominator between the two poems by Wordsworth and Eliot, then, is an essentially two-fold one: the power to be moved and the power to move. Both are an expression of the perception of harmony or order. In Wordsworth's poetry as a whole, the world calls forth song as the poet is stimulated by his milieu, and gives forth song, which the poet recognizes as an answer to his need for harmony. What George Eliot details in the career of Jubal is an essentially similar duality: Jubal's yearning is awakened by a "resonance" which confirms the difference yet likeness between inner mind and outward nature. To bring that resonance into full, conscious existence and to express it for others, he must create music, which itself is a praise of that resonance. The final resting place of poetic music for Wordsworth and for Eliot, then, is hymn.

F. B. Pinion (essay date 1981)

SOURCE: "*The Spanish Gypsy* and Other Poems," in *A George Eliot Companion,* Barnes and Noble, 1981, pp. 166-78.

[*In the following excerpt, Pinion closely examines* The Spanish Gypsy *as well as individual verses in* The Legend of Jubal and Other Poems, *observing that while much of Eliot's poetry is flawed, there are also those poems which display deep feeling and dramatic power.*]

George Eliot's notes on **The Spanish Gypsy** stress the 'irreparable collision between the individual and the general' in tragedy. For Mrs Transome the 'general' is moral tradition; for Maggie Tulliver it is a conjunction of moral tradition, hereditary nature, and loyalties; with Fedalma and Don Silva it turns on hereditary obligations. 'Silva presents the tragedy of entire rebellion: Fedalma of a grand submission, which is rendered vain by the effects of Silva's rebellion', George Eliot writes. Although she finds tragedy in Zarca's 'struggle for a great end, rendered vain by the surrounding conditions of life', it makes little dramatic impact on the reader; he is an inspiring and intractable power which Fedalma finds irresistible in his presence, but which she can hardly sustain when he is dead. Yet, in conjunction with symbolism, the struggle between the individual and the general creates the most dramatic tragic scene in the whole work. Fedalma, whose gipsy instinct makes her yearn for the open air and join in the dancing, is stirred by 'old imperious memories' when, ignorant of her origin, she is fascinated by her father's necklace. Late on the eve of her expected marriage, a bird falls dead at her feet; it carries the message that her father comes. When he reveals himself, it is clear that the gold necklace symbolizes the fate which binds her to Zarca and to her past and future. He snatches the circlet of rubies from her brow, and asks her, as he grasps her hand and shoulder, if she chooses to be forgetful. She believes she can show her loyalty to him by securing his freedom after her marriage; she has divided loyalties and memories:

> Look at these hands! You say when they were little
> They played about the gold upon your neck.
> I do believe it, for their tiny pulse
> Made record of it in the inmost coil
> Of growing memory. But see them now!
> Oh, they have made fresh record; twined themselves
> With other throbbing hands whose pulses feed
> Not memories only but a blended life—
> Life that will bleed to death if it be severed.

Zarca insists that she has a higher compulsion; hers is no ordinary lot. As his successor, queen of the gipsies, she is expected to perform royally. She consents unwillingly, 'an unslain sacrifice', removes her bridal gems, and accepts her fate, to wed her people. Her 'young joy' dies like the bird which announced Zarca's coming.

Don Silva's conflict is not externalized. It occurs in the black solitude of night after he has joined the Zincali unconditionally. In this inner drama thought is weaker and less trustworthy than feeling; he defends his action reflectively but 'the universe / Looks down inhospitable' and 'the human heart / Finds nowhere shelter but in human kind'. There are no specifically Positivist overtones here or elsewhere in the work, although Dr Congreve ascribed 'a mass of Positivism' to it, and Edmund Gosse more than half a century later described it as 'a Comtist tragedy'. Silva's 'larger soul' cannot scorn those memories from ancestral homes, that 'hereditary right' which troubles his conscience as if it were 'the voice divine of human loyalty'. The great trust he has broken turns reproach on him from those human and divine faces which had witnessed his knightly pledges as a champion of the Cross. Such is the revenge 'wrought by the long travail of mankind / On him who scorns it, and would shape his life / Without obedience'. Significantly, at the end, when Silva is intent on redeeming his honour with his 'knightly sword', the blackness he sees with Fedalma's departure is 'overhung by stars'. Taking her cue perhaps from Matthew Arnold's preface to the 1853 edition of his poems, George Eliot expressed the view that 'art which leaves the soul in despair is laming to the soul', and attributed the fostering of nobler sentiments in her tragedy to individual deeds and 'the all-sufficiency of the soul's passions in determining sympathetic action'. The critical weakness of **The Spanish Gypsy** is that, although the tragic conflict is clear in Fedalma and Silva, it rarely succeeds in lifting the passions to tragic heights.

The introduction is leisurely; like the proem of *Romola* it begins with a descriptive approach which is cinematic in technique, taking the reader by stages from an aerial view of Spain 'leaning with equal love / On the Mid Sea that moans with memories, / And on the untravelled Ocean's restless tides' (before Columbus's voyage to America) to Bedmár and a tavern courtyard. Here a group of characters provides a chorus, commenting on events which introduce the main action. The individualization of this group in description and action is justified by the sequel, for all play minor stage roles, none more importantly than the minstrel Juan and the juggler Roldan, with the lame boy Pablo (another singer). The first dramatic note is sounded by the booming bell which calls to prayer and ends the dancing in the plaza, where Fedalma's joy is quelled by the rebuking gaze of the prisoner gipsy chief. With the confrontation between the prior Isidor and Silva, and events leading to Zarca's winning of Fedalma, the remainder of the first book (which comprises almost half the work) reaches a level of dramatic tension which is rarely equalled and never long sustained in the sequel. The most imaginative of the incidents and episodes which follow occurs in the third book,and acquires its power when a brief climactic action is almost suspended with tableau effect to give symbolic concentration to the tragic dilemma at the heart of the work. Silva has found Fedalma; they embrace; she starts back with a look of terror, still holding him by the hand, and says:

> Silva, if now between us came a sword,
> Severed my arm, and left our two hands clasped,
> This poor maimed arm would feel the clasp till
>   death.
> What parts us is a sword . . .

Her speech is cut short: Zarca, after approaching from the background, has drawn his sword and thrust the naked blade between them.

George Eliot recognised the supremacy of the feelings in making great moral decisions but, unlike Emily Brontë, lacked the imaginative power to express feelings with sustained dramatic life and intensity. She shows that she can engineer dramatic situations, and indeed achieve some lively vigour in dramatic scenes; but thought and noble sentiments tend to predominate over feeling. Even so, it would be a mistake to regard the verse as a failure. The songs, however, are not inherently lyrical, and seem to have been composed to imaginary music, Juan's 'Day is dying! Float, O song' (which conveys an admirable picture) and his song to Pepita are two of the more successful. With the exception of two short lighter scenes in prose, the remainder of the work is in blank verse, which every-where bears the mark of careful composition, even in such detail as the astrologer Sephardo's mouth:

>   shut firm, with curves
> So subtly turned to meanings exquisite,
> You seem to read them as you read a word
> Full-vowelled, long-descended, pregnant—rich
> With legacies from long, laborious lives.

The monkey Annibal, left with Pablo in Sephardo's care, while his master, the juggler Roldan, seeks Fedalma for Silva,

>   keeps a neutral air
> As aiming at a metaphysic state
> 'Twixt 'is' and 'is not'; lets his chain be loosed
> By sage Sephardo's hands, sits still at first,
> Then trembles out of his neutrality,
> Looks up and leaps into Sephardo's lap,
> And chatters forth his agitated soul,
> Turning to peep at Pablo on the floor.

The style suits the action in movement, as in the description of Roldan's juggling or of Silva's hurried search for Fedalma, after hearing that she has been seen dancing in the plaza. As she dances, the admiring tension of the spectators finds relief which is exquisitely expressed in 'Sighs of delight, applausive murmurs low, / And stirrings gentle as of earéd corn / Or seed-bent grasses, when the ocean's breath / Spreads landward'. Pictorial effects are equally fine. The verse is often dramatic and clear-cut; elsewhere (deliberately with the minstrel Juan), with-

out being lavishly rich or superfluous, it is over-poetic in texture, tending to express thought in imagery. It is no wonder that Henry James found *The Spanish Gypsy* 'much more of a poem than was to be expected', though his admiration of 'its extraordinary rhetorical energy and elegance', 'its splendid generosity of diction', and 'its marvellous power of expression' is probably rather over-pitched. By comparison, however, Elizabeth Barrett Browning's *Aurora Leigh* seems improvized, prolix, and prosaic.

Unable to make progress with her first version of *The Spanish Gypsy*, George Eliot continued the writing of verse in '**My Vegetarian Friend**' (which she had sketched in prose three or four years earlier) and in '**Utopias**', both being completed in January 1865. They were combined, it seems, to form '**A Minor Prophet**' as it appeared in *The Legend of Jubal and Other Poems* (1874). The first part, the prophecy of Elias Baptist Butterworth, is satirical and witty, the opening lines resembling a parody of Wordsworthian matter-of-factness; it glances at contemporary spiritualism, and entertains the idea that rappings come from the Thought-atmosphere, to which people will have unimpeded recourse in the vegetarian era, when all will be ideal. The poet, however, prefers an imperfect world where amelioration is bought with sacrifice. In a world that moves to smiles and tears, the 'twists and cracks in our poor earthenware' (an allusion to the main image of Browning's 'Rabbi Ben Ezra', which had appeared in 1864) touch her to 'more conscious fellowship' with her coevals. She believes in progress towards the ideal, but her faith springs from the past, from noble and gentle deeds, heroic love, and even (a Browning thought) from failure and yearning. When she adds that it comes from 'every force that stirs our souls / To admiration, self-renouncing love', her Positivist sympathies are clear.

'**Two Lovers**', a lyric composed in September 1866, communicates deep feeling in excellent form, rounded to give a sense of life's wholeness. '**O May I Join the Choir Invisible**' expresses a Positivist view of immortality, the hope that the author's 'better self' will always be remembered and become a source of strength to others. For many it is the only poem by which George Eliot is remembered as a poet. It was written in Germany during the summer of 1867.

The following summer, after completing *The Spanish Gypsy*, she made a further study of English verse. It had been a principle with her, which she found supported in practice by 'all the finest writers', occasionally to use lines of irregular length, especially of twelve syllables, in blank verse. She was impressed by Milton's example ('such listening for new melodies and harmonies with *instructed* ears'); and it is significant that her August reading included *Samson Agonistes* and Guest's *English Rhythms*. Among the projects she listed for 1869 were *Middlemarch,* a long poem on Timoleon, and several shorter ones, including '**(Tubalcain) Vision of Jubal**', '**Agatha**', '**Stradivarius**', and '**Arion**'.

'**Agatha**' was finished in January. It is a sketch based on recollections of a visit George Eliot and Lewes made the previous July with the Gräfin von Baudissin (the countess) and her daughter to a peasant's cottage among the mountains of southwestern Germany. Description of the scenery is followed by the dialogue of Countess Linda and Agatha ('sweet antiphony of young and old'); and the poem concludes with a song, purportedly by Hans the tailor in honour of Agatha and her cousins Kate and Nell, whom she houses because, though younger, they are 'feeble, with small withered wits'. The influence of Agatha's piety, even on the young, makes her a link between 'faulty folk and God'. Tennyson did this sort of thing better, Swinburne wrote; he also did worse. The subject has no pretensions to profundity, but it is tactfully observed and gracefully composed. *The Atlantic Monthly* paid £300 for it, and the author probably never made money more easily.

Three weeks later she had finished **'How Lisa Loved the King'**, a greater achievement which alone would make George Eliot worthy to be remembered. It is an amplification of a Boccaccio story (*Il Decamerone*, X. vii), and its rhymed verse suggests the influence of *The Canterbury Tales,* familiarity with which is to be seen among the epigraphs of *Middlemarch*. With excellent judgment she frequently uses alexandrines to bring paragraphs to a close. It is creative work, a free translation, notable as much for the originality and delicacy of its imagery as for the technical mastery which is often displayed in variety and ease of movement within the regular insistencies of its medium.

The last of the **'Brother and Sister'** sonnets was written at the end of July, just before the original opening of *Middlemarch* was begun. Initially entitled 'Sonnets on Childhood', they suggest that incidents in *The Mill on the Floss* which are commonly regarded as autobiographical have been modified for fictional ends. The recollections have a twofold significance. Like Wordsworth's 'spots of time' they record memories which have enriching or renovating virtues:

> The firmaments of daisies since to me
> Have had those mornings in their opening eyes,
> The bunchèd cowslip's pale transparency
> Carries that sunshine of sweet memories.

George Eliot's soul, like Wordsworth's, had its 'fair seedtime'; those early hours were 'seed' to all her 'after good', and she ascribes her moral development to childhood experiences fostering love and fear, 'the primal passionate store, / Whose shaping impulses make manhood whole'. They were her 'root of piety'. The sonnets also show how brother and sister helped to enlarge each other's world, the author describing them as 'little descriptive bits on the mutual influences in their small lives'. Through him she became more aware of reality, and found less satisfaction in the world of dreams. With school their shared life came to an end. The subsequent rift between Mrs Lewes and her brother Isaac is alluded to in the 'Change' that is 'pitiless'. Another Shakespearian sonnet, written subsequently as an epigraph does not belong to this sequence; it is made to fit the fiction but it recalls the author's love of Scott's *Waverley* in her childhood, and how

she wrote out the story when the book had to be returned before she could finish it.

'The Legend of Jubal' was begun when *Middlemarch* was interrupted by Thornton Lewes's fatal illness, and finished 'about Christmas' (1869). The passage on Death was written under the shadow of great grief when he passed away, Lewes told Alexander Main. The thought that life must end imparts 'new dearness' to everything, 'finer tenderness' to love, and ambition to achieve something that will abide:

> Come, let us fashion acts that are to be,
> When we shall lie in darkness silently,
> As our young brother doth, whom yet we see
> Fallen and slain, but reigning in our will
> By that one image of him pale and still.

The poem returns to the rhymed couplet form of **'How Lisa Loved the King'** with occasional alexandrine variations. The legend is imaginary, starting from Genesis and *Paradise Lost*. After inventing the lyre and discovering the power of music over his own race, Jubal seeks inspiration in new lands. When from a mountain peak he sees the ocean, and hears 'its multitudinous roar, / Its plunge and hiss upon the pebbled shore', he can no longer respond to new voices, and turns back to rejoin his brethren, hoping that 'fresh-voiced youth' will express all that is in his soul. He travels far, losing his way and his ancient lyre. When at length he returns white-haired, 'the rune-writ story of a man', he sees 'dread Change' around. Utterly exhausted and near death, he lies watching an approaching procession and hears it chanting to many instruments in praise of Jubal. At this his joy revives, giving him strength to run and meet them. When he tells them that he is Jubal, the inventor of the lyre, he is greeted with derision, beaten, and left to find refuge among thorny thickets. 'The immortal name of Jubal filled the sky, / While Jubal lonely laid him down to die.' He feels shadowy wings enclose him, sees the loving face of his dedication in the past, and hears praise of the glorious heritage he has left melt into symphony as he is upborne. There is a Positivist inspiration in this heroic theme, but the poem, like so much of George Eliot's poetry, though it contains much that is impressive and exquisite, suggests a finished composition rather than the living voice and passion of the highest art.

'Armgart' is a rather slight dramatic sketch in five scenes which was begun 'under much depression' in August 1870; the subject had engaged George Eliot's interest a few weeks earlier at Harrogate. In one respect she was like the singer Armgart, who is asked how she can bear 'the poise of eminence' with 'dread of sliding'; in another, she was more fortunate, for Armgart is expected to renounce her art when she marries. She refuses, but a year later loses her voice, and vents her bitterness in proud anger. Her outbursts bring the verse to life, but her haughty egoism is pricked with surprising suddenness by the lame cousin who has waited on her for years:

> Now, then, you are lame—
> Maimed, as you said, and levelled with the crowd:

Call it new birth—birth from that monstrous Self
Which, smiling down upon a race oppressed,
Says, 'All is good, for I am throned at ease.'

Armgart admits that she has been blind, and that true vision comes only, it seems, with sorrow. She will make amends to her cousin, and become a teacher of music and singing (a career she has despised). She is confirmed in her resolution when she learns that her master had suffered the same disappointment.

Two shorter poems belong to 1873. **'Arion',** written in the stanza of Marvell's Horatian ode on Cromwell's return from Ireland, is a splendid composition until it falters at the very end. **'Stradivarius'** is admirable from start to finish. Mainly a duologue, it is dramatic throughout and influenced by Browning's style. The painter Naldo, a believer in the inspiration derived from 'drinking, gambling, talk turned wild' or 'moody misery and lack of food', with 'every dithyrambic fine excess', speaks slightingly of the 'painful nicety' with which Stradivari works. Stradivari contends that he will be appreciated by master violinists of the future, that the 'fullest good' one gives is God, and that 'not God Himself can make man's best / Without best men to help Him'. Naldo ends his excuses for not finishing his latest picture with 'A great idea is an eagle's egg, / Craves time for hatching'; and the poem closes with Stradivari's rejoinder:

> If thou wilt call thy pictures eggs
> I call the hatching, Work. 'Tis God gives skill,
> But not without men's hands: He could not make
> Antonio Stradivari's violins
> Without Antonio. Get thee to thy easel.

'A College Breakfast-Party' provides very different fare. Written in April 1874, it developed from talks with Trinity men during George Eliot's visit to Cambridge the previous May. A metaphysician may enjoy it, but most readers probably wish the author had persisted in her intention never to publish it. Lewes arranged for its publication in *Macmillan's Magazine* for a £250 fee, and it was added to the *Legend of Jubal* volume when Blackwood asked if she had more poems to 'swell it out to the required length' in the Cabinet Edition. To satirize without tedium the prolixity, non sequiturs, and inconclusiveness of philosophical discussion presents an artistic dilemma which was beyond George Eliot's invention. The verse copes admirably with the eloquence of academic sophistry, but such a subject needs either a structural idea which can quintessentialize it or the continual relief of witty comment and amusing incident. The device of a dialogue between selected *Hamlet* characters, with the indecisive prince left to form his own conclusions, is promising; but a long succession of argument in which 'None said, "Let Darkness be", but Darkness was' is inevitably tedious. The high debate oscillates from abstract to real, from absolute to relative, and from the scientifically explicable to the unknown of religion. After hearing that analogies in reasoning have as much significance as a crow and a bar to a crowbar, the priest, trying to supply an imperative to Hamlet's thronging doubts, discourses learnedly

and, after proving by analogy to his own satisfaction that everything said supports belief in a Presence, leaves for another appointment. Discussion on the relative leads to taste, and taste to the ideal beauty which is seen in art and poetry, and which exists independently of all human turmoil and philosophical change. Guildenstern insists that beauty and taste develop in accordance with human evolution, but Hamlet, uncertain to the last, thinks that poetry could belong to 'a transfigured realm' which is free from our grosser world.

> And then he dreamed a dream so luminous
> He woke (he says) convinced; but what it taught
> Withholds as yet. Perhaps those graver shades
> Admonished him that visions told in haste
> Part with their virtues to the squandering lips
> And leave the soul in wider emptiness.

No uncertainty on George Eliot's attitude to transcendentalism in philosophy and aesthetic theory can remain after this conclusion.

'Stradivarius' suggests that George Eliot's poetic gifts were not inconsiderable. With *Daniel Deronda* in hand she could do no more in verse than continue the practice she had begun in *Felix Holt* of supplying her own chapter epigraphs where nothing more suitable came to mind. They can be lyrical or humorous; but the gravely philosophical tend to be more impressive, as when Gwendolen Harleth, her murderous thought making her feel guilty of her husband's death, experiences 'that new terrible life lying on the other side of the deed which fulfils a criminal desire':

> Deeds are the pulse of Time, his beating life,
> And righteous or unrighteous, being done,
> Must throb in after-throbs till Time itself
> Be laid in stillness, and the universe
> Quiver and breathe upon no mirror more.

They are often dramatic, one of the most apt and poetical referring to that 'moment of naturalness' between Lydgate and Rosamond which 'shook flirtation into love':

> How will you know the pitch of that great bell
> Too large for you to stir? Let but a flute
> Play 'neath the fine-mixed metal: listen close
> Till the right note flows forth, a silvery rill:
> Then shall the huge bell tremble—then the mass
> With myriad waves concurrent shall respond
> In low soft unison.

Victor A. Neufeldt (essay date 1983)

SOURCE: "The Madonna and The Gypsy," in *Studies in the Novel,* Vol. 15, No. 1, Spring, 1983, pp. 44-54.

[*In the following excerpt, Neufeldt compares* The Spanish Gypsy *with several of Eliot's novels in order to trace the emotional and spiritual progression of Eliot's heroines.*]

It has been suggested that *Romola* marked a turning point in Eliot's development as a novelist. And indeed, Cross later recalled his wife's telling him that "the writing of *Romola* ploughed into her more than the writing of any of her other books. She told me she could put her finger on it as marking a well-defined transition in her life. In her own words, 'I began it as a young woman—I finished it an old woman'" [*George Eliot's Life as Related in Her Letters and Journals,* ed. by J. W. Cross, 1885]. I would argue, however, that in at least one respect her next work, *The Spanish Gypsy* marked an equally significant turning point for Eliot. *Romola* ends with the heroine finding fulfillment in the role of a Madonna; *Middlemarch* ends with a would-be Madonna finding fulfillment as a wife and mother. In between Eliot depicts a heroine, variously denominated as angel, goddess, and priestess, who finds only frustration and futility. The progression denotes Eliot's growing realization that the claims of public duty and responsibility must not be satisfied at the expense of personal fulfillment and happiness. . . .

In *The Spanish Gypsy* Eliot portrays a heroine who sacrifices the joys of "ordinary womanhood" to dedicate her life to her father's dream of creating a new nation, of instructing and liberating her people, only to announce at the end that the dream she has dedicated herself to at great cost is an illusion.

Eliot began her drama of renunciation in the summer of 1864, and evidence of her difficulty with it began to appear almost immediately: "Horrible scepticism about all things—paralyzing my mind. Shall I ever be good for anything again?—ever do anything again?" [Gordon S. Haight, *George Eliot: A Biography,* 1968]. By February of 1865, while struggling with the fourth act, Eliot recorded: "George has taken my drama away from me." Her complaints were of headaches, feebleness of mind and body; yet one cannot help wonder (even after acknowledging that she was working with a new form) whether these were not the physical symptoms of much more deep-seated difficulties she was having with her subject matter, for within five weeks she was at work on *Felix Holt,* having witnessed with much joy the marriage of Charles Lewes and Gertrude Hill in the interval. Only after she had finished *Felix Holt,* had seen its enthusiastic reception, had nostalgically retraced with Lewes part of the first trip they had made together the descriptions of which are filled with a sense of health, ease, relaxation, and a delight that was "immense—greatly from old recollections," and had seen a steady increase in her fame, her circle of staunch friends, and her social acceptability, could she return to *The Spanish Gypsy* in March of 1867. Yet she had never lost interest in the unfinished work. In August 1866 (not long after the completion of *Felix Holt*), she wrote to Frederic Harrison: "Now when I read it again, I find it impossible to abandon it: the conceptions move me deeply, and they have never been wrought out before. There is not a thought or a symbol that I do not long to use: but the whole thing requires recasting, and as I never recast anything before, I think of the issue very doubtfully" (*Letters,* IV). The recasting she spoke of involved the change from a drama in verse to the form in which we know the poem, but

what more, one wonders, did she have to recast? Was the writing of *Felix Holt* important to the completion of *The Spanish Gypsy*? I believe it was.

Significantly, there is no suggestion in *Felix Holt* of Esther Lyon seeking her happiness outside "the ordinary lot of womanhood." The renunciation of marriage is not one of the possibilities offered her. At the end of Chapter 44, the narrator says, "In the ages since Adam's marriage, it has been good for some men to be alone, and for some women also. But Esther was not one of these women; she was intensely of the feminine type, verging neither towards the saint nor the angel. She was 'a fair divided excellence, whose fulness of perfection' must be in marriage." In short she was no Romola, nor, like her Biblical namesake or Fedalma, could she sacrifice herself for her people. In choosing between Harold and Felix, Esther had to choose between the claims of her hereditary past and the claims of her personal history. She was saved from the tragic consequences of an involvement in the Transome history because she gave precedence to the claims of her personal past, which involved both her duty to her foster father and her emotional ties to Felix. After Esther testified at Felix's trial, the narrator comments: "In this, at least, her woman's lot was perfect: that the man she loved was her hero; that her woman's passion and her reverence for rarest goodness rushed together in an undivided current." It is precisely this fusion of public and private good that enables the narrator to say in the Epilogue that Esther never repented her decision.

The Spanish Gypsy again sets up for the heroine the conflict between hereditary claims and personal history, between duty and personal fulfillment, but for Fedalma there is no happy fusion of public and private good. At the beginning, love seems to her such an easy bliss, yet one has only to recall the statement in *Felix Holt* that "it is not true that love makes all things easy; it makes us choose what is difficult" to realize how naive she is. When Zarca places before Fedalma her duty to renounce Silva and take up "the heirship of a gypsy's child"

> To be the angel of a homeless tribe;
> To help me bless a race taught by no prophet
> And make their name, now but a badge of scorn,
> A glorious banner floating in their midst.

and to help him found the new gypsy nation, Fedalma sees no reason why she cannot have it both ways; she will marry the Duke, then declare her heritage and enlist the Duke's aid for his new father-in-law. Zarca rejects such a scheme as unheroic—"A woman's dream—who thinks by smiling well / To ripen figs in frost." When Fedalma counters that the love she has pledged "is nature too, / Issuing a fresher law than laws of birth." Zarca replies scathingly:

> Round your proud eyes to foolish kitten looks;
> Walk mincingly, and smirk, and twitch your robe;
> Unmake yourself—doff all the eagle plumes
> And be a parrot, chained to a ring that slips
> Upon a Spaniard's thumb.

Because Zarca is obsessed with his dream, he sees things in overly simple black and white terms. He can state without a moment's hesitation that Fedalma was born not to the slavery of marriage, but to reign. "You belong," he says, "Not to the petty round of circumstance / That makes a woman's lot, but to your tribe." Later, in Book Three, he tells Silva that Fedalma's destiny is to

> . . . live a goddess, sanctifying oaths,
> Enforcing right, and ruling consciences,
> By law deep-graven in exalting deeds,
> Through the long ages of her people's life.
> If she can leave that lot for silken shame,
>
> . . . . .
>
> Then let her go!

When he says to Fedalma in Book One, "Now choose your deed: to save or to destroy." Fedalma and the reader both know that things are not that simple. In fact, such over-simplification with its concomitant lack of awareness of the consequences involved is the fatal weakness of both Zarca and Silva. While Zarca understands well what the consequences of Fedalma's marriage would be for him, he has little understanding of the price she will have to pay to obey him:

> And, for your sadness—you are young—the bruise
> Will leave no mark.

It is the woman, one should note, who quickly comes to understand the full implications of the choices being offered. When Zarca calls Fedalma to "feed the high tradition of the world." he calls on her to accept the "higher" demands of civilization and society, of the collective will of which the fathers are the guardians, and to renounce the "lower" pleasures of passion, instinct, and sexual desire, of the natural world of regeneration, birth and growth associated with the mother. He calls on her, in other words, to renounce her personal history and her desire for individual love and fulfillment. Fedalma's response is that she has pledged to Silva "A woman's truth," and such a love for another person takes precedence over abstract ideals of duty and honor. Thus she is faced with the choice of betraying her father or the man she loves, and will have to pay a high price whatever choice she makes. She chooses to obey her father, but as she does so, she asks:

> O father, will the women of our tribe
> Suffer as I do, in the years to come
> When you have made them great in Africa?
> Redeemed from ignorant ills only to feel
> A conscious woe? Then—is it worth the pains?

"I will take / This yearning self of mine and strangle it," she says to Zarca, "Die, my young joy—die, all my hungry hopes." She closes Book One with the words:

> O love, you were my crown. No other crown
> Is aught but thorns on my poor woman's brow.

It is clear from the beginning, then, that public duty and personal happiness cannot be reconciled. Fedalma, by the end of Book One, has committed herself to public duty, yet the tragic outcome of that commitment is foreshadowed when she says of Zarca,

> I thought his eyes
> Spoke not of hatred—seemed to say he bore
> The pain of those who never could be saved.

The foreshadowing leads one to suspect that Eliot's recasting of this work after the completion of *Felix Holt* involved much more than just the form.

Despite her commitment, Fedalma's ambivalence continues in the books that follow. In Book Three she yearns for Silva, then reproaches herself for her infirmity—for being "clogged with self." When Zarca asks her, "Are you aught less than a true Zincala?" she replies, "No; but I am more. The Spaniards fostered me." In the middle of Book Three, after testing the primitive animal-like Hinda on what she would do if she had to choose between love and loyalty to the tribe (Hinda chooses loyalty to the tribe), Fedalma utters perhaps the most poignant description of her situation, a description one cannot help but feel the author identifies with strongly;

> For her, good, right, and law are all summed up
> In what is possible. . . .
> She knows no struggles, sees no double path:
> Her fate is freedom, for her will is one
> With her own people's law, the only law
> She ever knew. For me—I have a fire within,
> But on my will there falls the chilling snow
> Of thoughts that come as subtly as soft flakes,
> Yet press at last with hard and icy weight.
> I could be firm, could give myself the wrench
> And walk erect, hiding my life-long wound,
> If I but saw the fruit of all my pain
> With that strong vision which commands the soul,
> And makes great awe the monarch of desire.
> But now I totter, seeing no far goal.

Precisely because she can see the "double path," Fedalma knows that Silva, like Zarca, oversimplifies the situation, that he is unaware of the tragic consequences inherent in his decisions and actions. It is she who tells Silva that once one has made a decision there can be no return to what once was:

> There lies a grave
> Between this visionary present and the past.
> Our joy is dead, and only smiles on us
> A loving shade from out the place of tombs.

To her clear-eyed perceptions, Silva can only reply with sentimental, romantic platitudes:

> Fedalma, women know no perfect love:
> Loving the strong, they can forsake the strong;
> Man clings because the being whom he loves
> Is weak and needs him. I can never turn

And leave you to your difficult wandering. . . .
    I should feel nought
But your imagined pains: in my own steps
See your feet bleeding, taste your silent tears,
And feel no presence but your loneliness.
No, I will never leave you!

Like Esther, Fedalma and Silva are given a choice of renunciations. Unlike Esther, both deny their personal past. In contrast to *Felix Holt,* however, the choices here carry far more serious consequences. Renunciation carried out with clear-eyed understanding is painful indeed; but renunciation carried out blindly and naively, as in Silva's case, will have disastrous consequences. Because of his tragic blindness, Silva kills Zarca, and in so doing forces Fedalma to commit herself irrevocably to the fulfillment of her father's dream, thus assuring the separation Silva sought to avoid. As a result, Silva's soul, in Zarca's words, "is locked 'twixt two opposing crimes," and Fedalma is committed to a dream she knows she can never bring into reality:

                      For in her thought
Already she has left the fading shore,
Sails with her people, seeks an unknown land,
And bears the burning length of weary days
That parching fall upon her father's hope,
Which she must plant and see it wither only—
Wither and die. She saw the end begun.

"Father," she says, "I renounced the joy; / You must forgive the sorrow." For her, there is only the ironic realization that she must share with Silva "each deed / Our love was root of." We are left at the end with a broken man, and a woman following a dream she knows to be an illusion, both gazing into the gathering darkness. It is a bitterly ironic ending for a woman who has been hailed an angel, a goddess, and a priestess. There is about her a terrible sense of futility and sterility, which, when taken together with the ending of *Felix Holt,* denies emphatically the supposed happiness of Romola in the role of Madonna. Her future, Fedalma says to Silva in their final meeting, is to keep her father's trust:

My life shall be its temple. I will plant
His sacred hope within the sanctuary
And die its priestess—though I die alone,
A hoary woman on the altar-step,
Cold 'mid cold ashes. That is my chief good.

That might be Fedalma's good, but as *Middlemarch* makes clear, it could never be Eliot's. The complete subjugation of personal passion in the name of duty is for her an untenable ideal.

At the end of *The Mill on the Floss,* Maggie is prepared to renounce all personal happiness. . . .

But Eliot cannot condemn young Maggie to such a bleak future, to such a life of self-abnegation, so she puts her into a boat and mercifully allows her the oblivion of death. When Romola reaches a point of absolute self-despair

after the death of her godfather, she too launches out in a boat, in this case hoping for the oblivion of death. Eliot cannot oblige her, but neither can she condemn Romola to a bleak future of self-despair, so she transforms her most unconvincingly into a Madonna, a practitioner of the Religion of Humanity. Only in *The Spanish Gypsy,* does Eliot finally have her young heroine confront fully the emptiness and bleakness, the nothingness of a future based on a denial of personal happiness. Here, as Fedalma is about to board her boat to cross to North Africa, there is no moment of tragic insight, no moment of consolation in memory, no oblivion of death. One experiences only the sense of a useless sacrifice produced by her total self-abnegation.

Eliot was able to have Fedalma face what she could not require either Maggie or Romola to confront because she had by now found an antidote to such a vision of existence in her personal happiness as wife and foster mother, and in the growing sense of security her ever-increasing fame was giving her, especially from 1866 on. Her return from the Continent in that year was a homecoming, Redinger suggests, "in harmony with the adult life she had created for herself." [Rudy Redinger, *George Eliot: The Emergent Self*, 1975]. In the killing of Zarca, I believe Eliot finally purged the sense of guilt she had felt over having betrayed her father. She had demonstrated what the consequence of following his code of morality would have been, and had asserted her right to the personal happiness she had found with Lewes. After *The Spanish Gypsy,* therefore, Eliot's gaze, as the ending of *Middlemarch* shows, turned outward and forward.

Sylvia Kasey Marks (essay date 1983)

SOURCE: "A Brief Glance at George Eliot's *The Spanish Gypsy*," in *Victorian Poetry,* Vol. 21, No. 2, Summer, 1983, pp. 184-90.

[*In the following excerpt, Marks argues that Eliot's novels and her poem* The Spanish Gypsy *explore similar themes and delineate similar characters.*]

In a footnote to their discussion of George Eliot, the authors of *A Literary History of England* observe that her long dramatic poem *The Spanish Gypsy* "to which she devoted only too much labor and learning, has sunk out of sight under its own weight." Another modern critic called it "a long-winded narrative in pedestrian blank verse about the destiny of the gypsy race during the Moorish struggles in Spain, [which] now seems virtually unreadable." Yet *The Spanish Gypsy* appears less of an oddity when viewed in the context of George Eliot's total canon, particularly when we see its kinship to the themes, situations, and characters found in the novels, where most of the scholarly attention has been directed. . . .

In its time, *The Spanish Gypsy* was successful. The reviews were not unfavorable and several editions were published, including one in the United States; by 1878,

Eliot had earned £1000 from its sales. It is difficult to account for the lack of popularity of the poem today. One possible reason is that it is a hybrid work which does not successfully blend the various forms contained in it. Thus, while it is subtitled, "A Poem," Henry James declared that it was "not a genuine poem." Indeed, Eliot had originally intended to write a play, and the five parts of the poem, the authorial comments, and even stage directions in the text are possibly remnants of this idea. The marks of the epic and medieval romance are evident as well. Don Silva, for example, is described as "Born of a goddess with a mortal sire," while the poet in the poem, Juan, a character who mingles comfortably in tavern, Spanish court, and gypsy camp, is identified with the messenger Mercury. In epic simile fashion reminiscent of Milton's resonating similes Fedalma's dancing in the Plaça Santiago

> Moved as, in dance religious, Miriam,
> When on the Red Sea shore she raised her voice,
> And led the chorus of her people's joy;
> Or as the Trojan maids that reverent sang
> Watching the sorrow-crownéd Hecuba.

Fedalma, of course, will accompany her people to a new homeland in Africa, though she and the Zincali are less triumphant than Miriam and the Israelites after escaping the Egyptians. Fedalma will also sorrow after the murder of her father, much as Hecuba mourned the sacrifice of herdaughter Polyxena and the murder of her son Polydorus. In epics, too, the gods takes sides in battles, and Zarca, Fedalma's father, observes, "The Catholics, / Arabs, and Hebrews have their god apiece / To fight and conquer for them." There is even a necklace and a child's dress which identify the grown-up Fedalma as Zarca's kidnapped infant daughter, a typical convention of the romance genre. The lack of psychological character development associated with epic and medieval romance may also account for the modern reader's shying away from the poem; we do not see enough of the internal struggle of Fedalma and Don Silva as they come to terms with the conflicts confronting them. Yet, even if we regard this dramatic poem as artistically less successful than George Eliot's novels, from a thematic perspective it is certainly an important reference point from which to reflect on her earlier novels, as well as to anticipate those which follow the poem.

First of all, at a very fundamental level, there are the glimmers of the typical situations and characters found in Eliot's novels. The action occurs, as it does in *Romola* and the other novels, in a generation different from Eliot's. The opening scene at Lorenzo's inn reminds us of Silas Marner at the Rainbow, the dinner at the Poyser's in *Adam Bede,* and the cronies congregating at Nello's barbershop in *Romola.* When Fedalma's father Zarca, his true identity unknown to her, first catches her eye, "As if the meeting light between their eyes / Made permanent union," we recall Tito's first accidental meeting with his father, Baldassare, in *Romola.* Fedalma, like Esther Lyon in *Felix Holt,* finds herself at odds with her adoptive home. She is mistrusted by Father Isidor, who warns his nephew Don Silva, "That maiden's blood / Is as unchristian as the leopard's." She also joins George Eliot's other characters who are estranged from their real parents: Esther Lyon, Harold Transome in *Felix Holt,* Tito Melema, Daniel Deronda, and Eppie in *Silas Marner.* Among the secondary characters in **The Spanish Gypsy,** Blasco functions as a male counterpart to sharp-tongued, yet perceptive, female characters in the novels such as Jane Dodson Glegg in *The Mill on the Floss,* Dolly Winthrop in *Silas Marner,* Mrs. Cadwallader in *Middlemarch,* Mrs. Poyser, and Mrs. Holt. A silversmith, Blasco shrewdly recognizes that war and weddings are good for business. Finally, Seneca, that "solemn mastiff," Annibal, a very human monkey, as well as Bavieca, Don Silva's black charger that "Thrills with the zeal to bear him royally" take their places alongside George Eliot's other animals who often have human feelings ascribed to them.

Most important, however, is the dilemma of the heroes and heroines of the novels. In his discussion of the characters in George Eliot's works, D. R. Carroll traces a movement "from illusion through disenchantment to regeneration" ["An Image of Disenchantment in the Novels of George Eliot," *RES* II, 1960]; Barbara Hardy also identifies a change or metamorphosis experienced by the characters ["The Moment of Disenchantment in George Eliot's Novels, *George Eliot,* 1970]. With minor variations, the circumstances in the novels and **The Spanish Gypsy** are markedly similar. To begin with, in the novels, the reader meets one or two characters who suffer from a myopic view of their immediate world. Surveying their circumstances through rose-colored glasses, they may be selfish and harbor misplaced idealism. *Middlemarch*'s Dorothea Brooke, Maggie Tulliver in *The Mill on the Floss,* Esther Lyon, and Romola are examples of this. In the case of Fedalma and Don Silva, both unrealistically view their marriage as feasible in spite of Father Isidor's objections to Fedalma's parentage and her own independent spirit. Sympathizing with the gypsy prisoners she reveals

> Why, I with all my bliss
> Have longed sometimes to fly and be at large;
> Have felt imprisoned in my luxury
> With servants for my jailers.

Even the wedding jewels Don Silva presents to her provoke a similar reflection:

> Their prisoned souls are throbbing like my own.
> Perchance they loved once, were ambitious, proud;
> Or do they only dream of wider life,
> Ache from intenseness, yearn to burst the wall
> Compact of crystal splendor, and to flood
> Some wider space with glory? Poor, poor gems!
> We must be patient in our prison-house,
> And find our space in loving.

Don Silva, too, is committed to fight for his country's cause against the Moors. The tavern folk are amused by his decision "to wait a siege / Instead of laying one. Therefore—meantime— / He will be married straightway." Father Isidor responds angrily to Don Silva's marital intentions and scornfully rebukes him, "You, a Spanish duke, / Christ's general, would marry like a clown."

Returning to the pattern of Eliot's works, we find that the state of illusion is followed by a crisis which shatters the misperception; suddenly, in Pauline fashion, the scales fall from the eyes. The illusion is seen for what it really is, and the characters correspondingly realize that they can no longer depend on the narcotic effect of that illusion. In *Felix Holt,* for example, this occurs when Esther realizes what life would really be like at Transome Court. This phase of recognition is accompanied by the necessity of making a choice. George Eliot elaborates on the dilemma posed by this choice in her "Notes on the Spanish Gypsy and Tragedy in general," identifying the alternatives of personal happiness and the good of others as the "two irreconcilable 'oughts.'" Eliot prepares the reader for Fedalma's awakening early in the poem. Raised in sheltered circumstances, Fedalma decides to "see the town, / The people, everything" and cajoles her old nurse Iñez to accompany her to the Plaça, where she is moved to dance before the crowd. During her brief excursion the sight of the gypsy prisoners arrests her, and when she returns to the castle she confides to Don Silva, "I seemed new-waked / To life in unison with a multitude." She adds, "We were out four hours. / I feel so wise." Fedalma's crisis occurs when her marriage plans are suddenly halted by the appearance of Zarca, her father, who confronts her with her gypsy heritage. She is forced to choose between her love for the Spaniard and the role her father expects her to play as a ruler's daughter: "You, my only heir, / Are called to reign for me when I am gone." When he further argues against her plan to marry first and then use her new position as the wife of a Spanish duke to free the imprisoned Zincali, she reluctantly concedes that she must cast her lot with the gypsies. But she longs to tell Don Silva that "The chain that dragged me from him could [never] be aught / But scorching iron entering in my soul." Eliot's title for the poem further underscores Fedalma's dilemma. Nothing can erase the gypsy part of her background. Zarca firmly admonishes that her Zincala blood is "Unmixed as virgin wine-juice." Yet her Spanish upbringing desperately argues with her father, "But I am more [than a Zincala]. The Spaniards fostered me." The Spanish and the gypsy in her are truly irreconcilable—Fedalma cannot choose both.

Don Silva, interestingly, makes two choices. His crisis arises when he realizes that Fedalma remains firm in her commitment to her father and the Zincali. This prompts him to reject the Spanish cause, to join Fedalma and her father, and to swear to become a gypsy. To Zarca he insists, "She shall be my people, / And where she gives her life I will give mine." But in Eliot's terms, such a decision is an aberration. The narrator comments that "Silva had but rebelled,—He was not free." And Father Isidor, the determined Spanish inquisitor, affirms even more strongly that Don Silva's turning traitor against his people makes him "Fouler than Cain who struck his brother down / In jealous rage." The Prior's judgment is echoed by Zarca, whose devotion to the Zincali brotherhood is equally strong and whose standard for a correct choice applies to all characters: "Our poor faith / Allows not rightful choice, save of the right / Our birth has made for us." Silva returns to Bed már as a member of the gypsy

clan only to find his three best friends executed by Zarca's orders. Stirred, too, by the mute accusatory figure of Father Isidor after he is hanged by the triumphant gypsies, Don Silva mortally wounds Zarca and makes a second choice: he discards the gypsy badge for the cross of the Spanish side, resolving not to receive "pardon idly on my knees; / But it shall come to me upon my feet / And in the thick of action." He, like Fedalma, renounces his own happiness in favor of his heritage, as well as in favor of spending himself for the good of his people. What makes **The Spanish Gypsy** particularly intriguing is that all the novels up to and including *Felix Holt* portray a character who opts for the past of his experience, or his adopted past. In **The Spanish Gypsy,** and in *Daniel Deronda* which follows it, the character determines in favor of his hereditary or racial past.

Once a decision has been made, the characters are, in a sense, reborn. Putting their own interests aside, they respond to the call of duty. Maggie Tulliver and Esther are but two instances of this in the novels. Significantly, Tito Melema in *Romola* is always serving himself and never achieves the resigned kind of satisfaction that Romola and the other characters do. In **The Spanish Gypsy,** Fedalma assumes the leadership of the gypsies after her father's death. Early in the poem she had reservations about the cause:

> I could be firm, could give myself the wrench
> And walk erect, hiding my life-long wound,
> If I but saw the fruit of all my pain
>
> . . . . .
>
> But now I totter, seeing no far goal.

As her father's heir she

> bears the burning length of weary days
> That parching fall upon her father's hope,
> Which she must plant and see it wither only,—
> Wither and die. She saw the end begun.

Lacking her father's charisma, "the constant stress / Of his command" and faced in the first week with defections, she nevertheless carries on. Don Silva, living with the consequences of his second decision to return to the Spanish cause, fits this pattern, too. He loves Fedalma, sorrows because it is her father he has killed, but resolves to go to Rome "to be absolved, to have my life / Washed into fitness for an offering / To injured Spain." Both individuals now see with clarity. They have gained insight. At their final parting, Fedalma asks Don Silva to think of her "as one who sees / A light serene and strong on one sole path / Which she will tread till death." George Eliot once wrote that "the highest 'calling and election' is to *do without opium* and live through all our pain with conscious, clear-eyed endurance" (*Letters,* III). Fedalma echoes this as she says to Silva before boarding the boat to Africa, "We must walk / Apart unto the end. Our marriage rite / Is our resolve that we will each be true / To high allegiance, higher than our love."

The journey of George Eliot's characters from blindness to insight manifested in service is captured in the first lines of another Eliot poem, **"O May I join the Choir Invisible"**:

> O may I join the choir invisible
> Of those immortal dead who live again
> In minds made better by their presence: live
> In pulses stirred to generosity,
> In deeds of daring rectitude, in scorn
> For miserable aims that end with self,
> In thoughts sublime that pierce the night like stars,
> And with their mild persistence urge man's search
> To vaster issues.

Bonnie J. Lisle (essay date 1984)

SOURCE: "Art and Egoism in George Eliot's Poetry," in *Victorian Poetry,* Vol. 22, No. 3, Autumn, 1984, pp. 263-78.

[*In the following excerpt, Lisle argues that while Eliot's poems are flawed, they are nevertheless worth pursuing as avenues to understanding George Eliot and her novels.*]

One of the greatest English novelists, George Eliot remains at best a second-rate poet. That the poems are so pedestrain, in fact, may tempt us to overlook their real importance. George Eliot insisted that "every one . . . represents an idea which I care for strongly and wish to propagate as far as I can. Else I should forbid myself from adding to the mountainous heap of poetical collections" [*The George Eliot Letters,* 1954-78]. Whatever their dubious merits as verse, the poems embody "ideas" that afford us insight into the writer and her fiction.

George Eliot's poetry can help us particularly to understand her troublesome insistence on marriage as the only happy ending available to her heroines. Perhaps the most obvious alternative to the "home epic" is the one George Eliot herself chose—the life of the artist. Art offers the ardent spirit a way of connecting with others, of transcending the limitations and obscurity of domesticity, yet the novelist refuses to allow her heroines this privilege. For all their passionate sensibility, women like Dorothea Brooke and Maggie Tulliver possess no artistic skill or ambition. The denial seems particularly deliberate in *Middlemarch,* where Dorothea condemns "the simpering pictures in the drawing-room" as a falsification of social reality. This conscious rejection of art is even more striking because George Eliot seems to have been preoccupied with questions of art and artists at the time she began the novel: of five poems written after **The Spanish Gypsy** and before the publication of *Middlemarch,* the two longest—**The Legend of Jubal** (1869) and **"Armgart"** (1870)—explore the origins, nature, and responsibilities of artistry. In order to understand why George Eliot's heroines cannot follow her own example, we need to look more closely at these two poems.

The Legend of Jubal is George Eliot's original myth about the birth of music. Written "under the shadow of a great grief," the death of her stepson (*Letters,* V), the poem examines the relationship of human mortality to the eternal life of art. In this tale, George Eliot imagines art arising as a response to the consciousness of death. Cain, "driven from Jehovah's land," resolves to found a race that shall never know the meaning of death: "My happy offspring shall not know / That the red life from out a man may flow / When smitten by his brother." Generations grow and thrive in a timeless world until a youth is accidentally killed during athletic play. Cain finds that he cannot flee the knowledge of death, as the idyllic world he has created begins to change:

> a new spirit from that hour came o'er
> The race of Cain: soft idlesse was no more

> . . . . .

> Death was now lord of Life, and at his word
> Time, vague as air before, new terrors stirred.

The consciousness of mortality acts as a spur to sympathy and love: "No form, no shadow, but new dearness took / From the one thought that life must have an end." Memory becomes precious for its ability to recall the dead. But the greatest change is a new sense of urgency to work, to achieve while there is yet time, for

> "There comes a night when all too late
> The mind shall long to prompt the achieving hand,
> The eager thought behind closed portals stand,
> And the last wishes to the mute lips press
> Buried ere death in silent helplessness."

Like George Eliot's aspiring heroines, Cain's progeny hope to leave a mark, to transcend personal mortality: "Come, let us fashion acts that are to be, / When we shall lie in darkness silently." From this desire culture is born.

Three brothers, "heroes of their race," devise the major forms of human endeavor. Calm Jubal domesticates animals and initiates pastoral life. The more restless Tubal-Cain harnesses fire and creates the tools of agriculture, industry, commerce, and war. Their work prospers, assuring collective immortality through the continuity of culture:

> The home of Cain with industry was rife,
> And glimpses of a strong persistent life,
> Panting through generations as one breath,
> And filling with its soul the blank of death.

But Jubal accomplishes a greater task by creating music, humanity's "larger soul." Jubal wanders the earth for many ages, imparting the gift of music wherever he goes, but at last he resolves to return to his own tribe.

Nearing his home, Jubal encounters a musical procession—a religious celebration honoring his creation. Jubal feels "the burning need / To claim his fuller self," to enjoy this moment of personal glory, so he identifies himself to the crowd. But he is now old and frail, whereas in the people's memory he has attained mythic proportions: "Jubal was but a name in each man's faith / For glorious power untouched by that slow death / Which creeps with creeping time." Scorned as a madman and driven away by the angry worshippers, "The immortal name of Jubal filled the sky, / While Jubal lonely laid him down to die." As he expires, Jubal's incorporate past arises to comfort him. She quenches the "little pulse of self" that had demanded recognition and shows him the higher glory that lives on in his music:

"Thy limbs shall lie dark, tombless on this sod,
Because thou shinest in man's soul, a god,
Who found and gave new passion and new joy
That naught but Earth's destruction can destroy."

Jubal attains what others are denied—personal immortality; ironically, the price of this apotheosis is complete loss of individual identity. Jubal the man has been subsumed by his greater art; thus the crowd that sings his praises spurns him for being merely human. Great art is an act of purely disinterested giving. The voice of the Past concludes with these curious words:

"Thy gifts to give was thine of men alone:
'Twas but in giving that thou couldst atone
For too much wealth amid their poverty."

The artist's high privilege, George Eliot suggests, must be redeemed by suffering and self-annihilation. Relinquishing self-consciousness, winning "a moment's freedom . . . / From in and outer," Jubal dies. Perfect transcendence of self coincides with death; now purified of mortal weakness, Jubal becomes part of the very spirit of creation, "Quitting mortality, a quenched sun-wave, / The All-creating Presence for his grave."

The Legend of Jubal celebrates the artist's ideal mission and glory; however, the ideal rests upon an essential contradiction. Death is the stimulus to creation. The reward art holds out is immortality. Even Jubal dreams of undying fame when he invents the lyre: "'So shall men call me sire of harmony, / And where great Song is, there my life shall be.'" Yet the true artist must at the same time be purely selfless, willing to sacrifice his life utterly to art. Self-annihilation is at once a debt he owes humanity and, paradoxically, the only way to attain the immortality he seeks. Thus, an unresolved tension between severely pure and selfish motives, between the ideal duty and real feelings of the artist informs the poem. The same tension underlies George Eliot's attitude toward her work.

Thoughts of mortality urged her, like Jubal, to produce something lasting. When Marian Evans and George Lewes decided not to have children, authorship promised another means of self-perpetuation—of living on in future generations. As John Blackwood remarked, "Certainly she does seem to feel that in producing her books she is producing a living thing, and no doubt her books will live longer than is given to children of the flesh" (*Letters,* IX). Even as an established novelist, George Eliot felt the pressure

of time; an 1868 journal entry laments, "I am not yet engaged in any work that makes a higher life for me—a life that is young and grows, though in my other life I am getting old and decaying" (*Letters,* IV). Yet to pursue authorship for personal immortality is to fall into the conceit, if not the futility, of an Edward Casaubon, for whom "the consolations of the Christian hope in immortality seemed to lean on the immortality of the still unwritten Key to all Mythologies" (*Middlemarch,* Ch. 29). Indeed, George Eliot admitted, "I feat that the Casaubontints are not quite foreign to my own mental complexion" (*Letters,* V), and when asked who served as the vain scholar's model, she "pointed to her own heart" (*Biography*). She perpetually suspected her motives as an author, castigating herself for "strong egoism" and "a fastidious yet hungry ambition" (*Letters,* V). Such moments of candor alternate with defensive denials of self-interest; she writes to Alexander Main about the success of *Middlemarch:* "I am . . . too fearful lest the impression which it might make (I mean for the good of those who read) should turn to nought" (*Letters,* V). The hasty parenthesis betrays George Eliot's fear of revealing—especially to an admirer—the egoism of which she was so conscious.

Convinced of her own weakness, George Eliot nevertheless maintained a rigorous, almost impossible standard for her art and her responsibility as an artist. According to her relentlessly moral aesthetic, any art that fails to benefit others is mere self-indulgence. In an unpublished essay on authorship, she condemns "that troublesome disposition to authorship . . . which turns a growing rush of vanity and ambition into this current." Selfish motives produce trifling, inferior work which, because it does no social good, becomes actively pernicious—a kind of "spiritual gin" ["Authorship," *Essays of George* Eliot, 1963]. In effect, writing cannot be morally neutral. It would require supreme self-confidence to face this prospect without misgivings, and George Eliot felt keen doubts about the value of her fiction: "I have read my own books hardly at all after once giving them forth—dreading to find them other than I wish. . . . Every one who contributes to the 'too much' of literature is doing grave social injury. And that thought naturally makes one anxious" (*Letters,* V). The threat of failure was so palpable that the mere sight of artistic incompetence shook her deeply: "Great art, in any kind, inspirits me and makes me feel the worth of devoted effort, but from bad pictures, bad books, vulgar music, I come away with a paralyzing depression" (*Letters,* VI). She could justify her work only by its effect on others.

A wide, sympathetic response to her novels offered reassurance that her efforts and ambitions were more than egoistic delusions; signs that her work was misunderstood or ineffective tended to confirm her worst fears. Mere popularity she dismissed as ephemeral, demanding proof of a deeper, more lasting influence: "Even success needs its consolation. Wide effects are rarely other than superficial and would breed a miserable scepticism about one's work if it were not now and then for an earnest assurance . . . that there are lives in which the work has done something to 'strengthen the good andmitigate the evil'" (*Let-*

ters, VI). Ironically, the fear of egoism was indirectly responsible for George Eliot's susceptibility to the bald flattery of admirers like Alexander Main (whom Blackwood aptly nicknamed "the Gusher") and her dependence on the sometimes embarrassing adoration of devotees like Edith Simcox. In their uncritical ardor she could read her influence and feel that her work had the moral power she demanded of true art.

Evidence that she did genuinely affect her readers raised another kind of conflict for this self-divided artist. On the one hand, Lewes writes, "The deep feelings she creates in others react upon herself and make her prize her power" (*Letters,* VI). On the other, confirmation of her gift rendered her sense of responsibility more imperative. Like Jubal, she owed her art to humanity; she must "atone" by giving of herself. To fall short of her abilities thus induced not merely disappointment but guilt: Lewes reports that George Eliot "was horribly depressed on Saturday, feeling as she said 'quite guilty and that every one would be despising her feeble performance'" (*Letters,* VI). The words are both revealing and typical in their conjunction of selfless duty and egoism—guilt at failing to perform her work well and fear of being despised for it.

These conflicting impulses find expression in the widely different stories of Jubal and Armgart. If Jubal, rising above mortal weakness to merge with the "All-creating Presence," represents George Eliot's vision of the ideal, Armgart with her all-too-human frailties reflects the dilemma of the real artist. Jubal's apotheosis is pure fantasy, and George Eliot accordingly distances the action by setting it in the remote, mythic past, and by maintaining the dispassionate third person narration of a fable. **"Armgart"** strikes closer to home emotionally, so its presentation is more immediate, with an identifiable contemporary setting and a dramatic structure that allows the heroine to speak directly to us.

Armgart, despite her singularly unmelodious name, is a young opera singer just reaching the peak of her powers. She has the voice and the sensibility of a great artist and ambition to equal her talent: "I triumph or I fail. / I never strove for any second prize." Armgart's aspirations create conflict when she rejects the marriage proposal of a long-time suitor, Graf Dornberg. The Graf charges that "Too much ambition has unwomaned her," but Armgart insists that she cannot "divide her will" between husband and art; she asserts, moreover, that the latter claim is the more imperative:

> I am an artist by my birth—
> By the same warrant that I am a woman
> Nay, in the added rarer gift I see
> Supreme vocation.

Kathleen Blake reads this debate on womanhood and art as a sign of George Eliot's preoccupation with "an antagonism that she herself almost totally evaded." Rightly pointing to Lewes' unfailing support of his wife's artistic career, Blake argues that **"Armgart"** nevertheless "expresses indignation at the unnecessary sacrifices demanded by men of women in marriage. Armgart is right not to marry the Graf." This reading misses the essence of Armgart's—and George Eliot's—dilemma.

Armgart fears that succumbing to the Graf would "divide her will" and threaten her devotion to art; she fails to recognize that her own character poses a more serious threat to her integrity, both as an artist and as a woman, than does the Graf's proposal. While Armgart is prepared to sacrifice love for art, she cannot fully give herself to either. Her will is divided not by masculine demands but by egoism. Ambition and desire for glory inspire Armgart to strive for the highest achievement:

> I am only glad,
> Being praised for what I know is worth the praise;
> Glad of the proof that I myself have part
> In what I worship.

Yet among these mixed motives, egoism dominates the impersonal love of excellence, and she values her artistry most because it sets her apart from the common herd:

> I cannot bear to think what life would be
> With high hope shrunk to endurance,
>
> . . . . .
>
> A self sunk down to look with level eyes
> At low achievement.

She defends her ambition, emphasizing the joy her singing gives others ("For what is fame / But the benignant strength of One, transformed / To joy of Many?"), but no purely selfless love of art sustains Armgart. She nearly achieves loss of self-consciousness as she sings Gluck's music, feeling that "every linkéd note / Was his immortal pulse that stirred in mine"; however, even in this moment of near-transcendence, she indulges in an ill-judged trill that wins popular applause at the expense of artistic integrity. Her devotion to art remains inseparable from her egoistic need to taste personal triumph. This self-centeredness not only trivializes but falsifies her artistry. Armgart's pride in her own achievement distorts her view of life, and she mistakes "A strain of lyric passion for a life / Which in the spending is a chronicle / With ugly pages." Art that remains unconscious of human reality lacks the essential value of truth; Armgart's understanding of the artist's role is thus exposed as vain, morally bankrupt: she is one of those "who can live / In mere mock knowledge of their fellows' woe, / Thinking their smiles may heal it." Armgart represents the attitude to which Dorothea objects when she criticizes "simpering pictures" that take no account of "how hard the truth is for [our] neighbors."

Graf Dornberg understands Armgart's precarious position: with no source of impersonal delight in her life, she is at the mercy of "the very fate / Of human powers, which tread at every step / On possible verges." As Armgart's egoism threatens to debase her art, it also unfits her for ordinary life: the Graf tells her, "Ambition exquisite as yours which soars / Towards something quintessential you call fame, / Is not robust enough for this gross world." The Graf's premonitions are confirmed when Armgart loses her purity of voice after a serious illness. Her "human powers" having failed her vaunting ambition, she sees no reason to live: "Oh, I had meaning once / Like day and sweetest air. What am I now? / The millionth woman in superfluous herds." Indeed, when Armgart discovers that it was not the illness but the doctor's "strong remedies" that have ruined her voice, she assails him for not allowing her "To die a singer, lightning-struck, unmaimed" rather than live on as an ordinary woman.

Armgart's conflict arises less from external than from internal pressures, for egoistic ambition divides her from both her art and her humanity. The question of marriage to Graf Dornberg is not the central issue of the poem; George Eliot presents both sides of the question fully and never clearly endorses either position. The unambiguous message, the real significance of the Graf's proposal and rejection, lies in Armgart's incapacity to love anything (man or art) selflessly. Her companion, Walpurga, points out that what Armgart had thought was supreme devotion to art was in fact supreme egoism: "you claimed the universe; naught less / Than all existence working in sure tracks / Toward your supremacy." It is only her loss of voice that jolts Armgart out of self-absorption. Then she sees her own failure thrown into relief by two people who have successfully subdued egoism through love *and* art.

Before her illness, Armgart treats these people as subordinate players in her personal drama: Walpurga, her humble cousin/attendant, merely serves as an appreciative audience; old Leo, the voice master, helps her to satisfy her ambitions as a singer. Both find their happiness in her reflected glory—and both represent the kind of undistinguished life that Armgart disdainfully rejects. But suddenly bereft of her ambition, she begins to see that their common lives have a solid center of value that hers lacks. Walpurga finds fulfillment in "Love nurtured even with that strength of self / Which found no room save in another's life." Leo is sustained by an impersonal devotion to art. A composer, he too once dreamed of fame, but now he teaches and practices his art without hope of recognition: "The time was, I drank that home-brewed wine / And found it heady, while my blood was young: / Now it scarce warms me". Armgart's new perception is, as Walpurga says, "new birth—birth from that monstrous Self" which had possessed her. She resolves to teach music in the small town where Walpurga was born, thus returning her companion's devotion and serving art selflessly (for George Eliot makes it clear that teaching is a more purely generous act than performing). Armgart explains her choice to Leo: "I would take humble work and do it well—/ Teach music, singing . . . pass your gift / To others who can use it for delight." Armgart follows the example of both her friends: she embraces a life of service, the subordination of self to others.

Significantly, though, Armgart's sacrifice is not voluntary. Only the loss of creative power enables her to transcend egoism; the death of the artist allows her to become fully human. While **"Jubal"** and **"Armgart"** depict very different aspects of the creative mind, they concur on one point: to choose the life of the artist is in some sense to choose death. Jubal dies for the glory of art, and Armgart lives only because her art perishes; when the life-giving cure destroys her voice, she mourns the "little corpse" of her "dead joy." If on the one hand, the consciousness of mortality and the quest for something undying provide the impetus to create, on the other, the high demands of art prove incompatible with mortal life. There is an inherent conflict between life and art that is fully resolved only by death, either of the artist or of her creativity.

Another George Eliot poem, **"Arion,"** presents the conjunction of art and death even more dramatically than the longer tales of Jubal and Armgart. Arion, a poet-minstrel of ancient Corinth who has won wealth and fame in another land, sets sail for home as the poem begins:

> Then weighted with his glorious name
> And bags of gold, aboard he came
>   'Mid harsh seafaring men
>   To Corinth bound again.

The rough sailors set upon Arion, intending to murder him for his gold, but he persuades them to allow him one final song before he dies. The power of his music strikes awe into these "wolfish men": "They said, with mutual stare, / Some god was present there." While the sailors appear moved by the song to grant him a reprieve, Arion refuses to degrade his art by using it for a purely personal end, even to save his life. Before the sailors can respond to the song, he leaps into the sea:

> But lo! Arion leaped on high,
> Ready, his descant done, to die;
>   Not asking, "Is it well?"
>   Like a pierced eagle fell.

As in **"Jubal,"** George Eliot depicts the artist as ideal, as mythic hero; again, death proves the heroism and offers escape from a less glorious reality that threatens the artist.

Like George Eliot's verse generally, these poems reveal the writer's tensions more directly than does the carefully controlled public voice of the novels. On one level, the consistent association of art with death reflects the completeness with which she assumed her authorial role: the birth of "George Eliot" in a sense signalled the death of her former self, as Marian Evans was subsumed by the persona of the novelist. The association of art and death also points to a deep division within the artist. . . .

The public persona "George Eliot" was intended, at least in part, to compensate for the social transgressions of Marian Evans; as Alexander Welsh observes, "The adoption of the literary pseudonym . . . substituted one secret for another, but a secret that would be potentially triumphant rather than embarrassing" ["The Secrets of George Eliot," *YR* 68, 1979]. The strategy worked: the carefully cultivated image of the great novelist and wise moralist obscured the "immoral" woman who lived openly with a married man. Whereas plain Marian Evans Lewes had been pointedly ostracized, the "Madonna," as Lewes called her, was courted by polite company and quoted approvingly in sermons. (*Biography*).

The weapon proved double-edged. Fame brought wider public acceptance, but at least initially, it alienated some of George Eliot's oldest friends. Sara Hennell lamented—in verse that unconsciously proved her point—the distance her friend's triumphant authorship had put between them:

> Dear Friend, when all thy greatness suddenly
> Burst out, and thou wert other than I thought,
> At first I wept—for Marian, whom I sought,
> Now passed beyond herself, seemed lost to me.
>
> (*Biography*)

Herbert Spencer's jealousy was so ill-disguised that it hurt her deeply; she welcomed a new pug puppy as a comforting presence "to fill up the void left by false and narrow-hearted friends. I see already that he is without envy, hatred, or malice" (*Biography*). Fame failed, moreover, to placate George Eliot's puritanical and unforgiving brother Isaac. After enduring twelve years of his obdurate silence, she remarked, "I cling strongly to kith and kin, even though they reject *me*" (*Letters,* V). Continued rejection in the quarter where she most wanted acceptance impelled George Eliot to cling to and reaffirm the ideal image she had created for herself. The portraits of Jubal and Arion can be read as self-justifying fantasies of this ideal self. Both protagonists are artists who have won renown far from home; when they attempt to return, they are prevented, either by outright repudiation or by envious greed. Yet by sacrificing their lives for art, they rise above those who deny or injure them, and even become godlike. In these poems, art is the best revenge. **"Jubal"** and **"Arion"** exalt the artist and thereby shed reflected glory on their creator.

But if the ideal self redeemed, it also reproved its weaker counterpart. As George Levine observes, George Eliot's public persona "was, we know, a deliberate fiction . . . it was an hypothesis testing the possibility of the abolition of the common self" ["George Eliot's Hypothesis of Reality," *NCF* 35, 1980]. Of course, such an experiment can never completely succeed: the flawed human reality inevitably fails to live up to the grander image and rebels against its imposition. George Eliot took the role of Madonna seriously, but as Edith Simcox reports, she felt "the difficulty, after living an ideal life—thinking of things and people as they might be—to come back into the real world and exercise the virtues one had been dreaming about" (*Letters,* IX). George Eliot seems to have felt this tension particularly in her relationship to John Cross, who, like most of her later acquaintances, had initially been drawn to the famous novelist. She writes to "Nephew Johnny" that "It is a precious thought to me that you care for that part of me which will live when the 'Auntship' is gone—'Non omnis moriar' is a keen hope with me. Yet I like to be loved in this faulty, frail (yet venerable) flesh" (*Letters,* IX). The words echo the description of Jubal in his moment of weakness; like him, George Eliot found

adulation gratifying, but no substitute for personal affection:

> he as from a tomb, with lonely heart,
> Warmed by no meeting glance, no hand that
>   pressed,
> Lay chill amid the life his life had blessed.
> What though his song should spread from man's
>   small race
> Out through the myriad worlds what people space,
> And make the heavens one joy-diffusing quire?—
> Still 'mid that vast would throb the keen desire
> Of this poor aged flesh.

Also like Jubal, she had been claimed by the public and no longer belonged entirely to herself. She worried how her readers would respond to her marrying the much-younger Cross: "She had twice broken it off as impossible—had thought of all the difficulties—the effect upon her influence and all the rest" (*Letters,* IX). But unlike her idealized poet, George Eliot was not rescued by death at the crucial moment; instead of being rapt into eternity as a god, she submitted to her "frail flesh" and went ahead with the marriage.

As the letters show George Eliot was extremely self-conscious about her failures to live up to the public image she had assumed. Egoistic needs helped to fuel her artistic aspirations yet were incompatible with that selfless ideal. In **"Armgart"** she seems to play out the guilt that arises from this discrepancy. George Eliot allows her ambition to speak freely through Armgart, deliberately abandoning the wise narrative voice and giving us unmediated dialogue; she then absolves her higher responsibility by punishing the singer for egoism. Guilt over not working hard enough, fear of failing to accomplish anything significant made creation a difficult and painful process. A journal entry critically reviews her efforts:

> We found the cold here more severe than at Ryde, and the papers tell of still harder weather about Paris where our fellow-men are suffering and inflicting horrors. Am I doing anything that will add the weight of a sandgrain against the persistence of such evil?

> Here is the last day of 1870. I have written only 100 pages—good printed pages—of a story which I began about the opening of November, and at present mean to call "Miss Brooke." Poetry halts just now.

> In my private lot I am unspeakably happy, loving and beloved. But I am doing little for others. (*Letters,* V)

The sense of failure clearly dominates the accomplishment; even counting the blessings of private life calls forth a cry of unworthiness.

Personal happiness, while it made creative life possible for George Eliot, also appears to have complicated matters. One senses that both love and a successful creative life burdened her with a consciousness of excessive wealth. She did not have to face the test of supreme self-sacrifice that she imposes on her artistic protagonists. Therefore, the only "atonement" available was self-punishment, "For when one's outward lot is perfect, the sense of inward imperfection is the more pressing" (*Letters,* V). Indeed, George Eliot evidences some of Dorothea's "fanaticism of sympathy" when a simple report of domestic comfort calls up an apologetic reflection on the misery in the world: "We are in our usual train of home procedures—thinking, reading, talking much en tête-à-tête, and hoping that there are many others . . . who are as happy as we are. One is too sure of the many who are not at all happy" (*Letters,* V). The shift from first person to third signals the intrusion of the public voice, carefully editing even these private expressions to avoid appearing self-indulgent. Other references to private happiness are guarded by irony: "We are alarmingly happy"; "We are dangerously happy"; "I hope we are not the happiest people in the world, but we must be among the happiest" (*Letters,* V). Perhaps she suspected that personal contentment verged perilously on egoistic complacency.

Although her life seems to represent an instance of love and art successfully combined, George Eliot remained uneasy about the conjunction. The two were deeply interdependent—love had called forth the art and art in turn had justified the love—yet in a more subtle way they remained divided in George Eliot's mind and work. Writing to Harriet Beecher Stowe, she alludes to "the peculiar struggles of a nature which is made twofold in its demands by the yearnings of the author as well as of the woman" (*Letters,* V). The words point, like **"Armgart,"** to a purely internal division. It is not the external demands of husband versus career that disturb George Eliot, but the yearnings of the authoras distinct from the yearnings of the woman.

How do these yearnings differ? If George Eliot's novels have one dominant theme, it is that all human beings yearn for love. Love is a unifying power: it subdues egoism and joins us to the human community; it binds our present to our past; it can give us a single, unambiguous purpose in the midst of life's uncertainties. But love is not enough for the artist, who also longs for fame and applause. Thus, as George Eliot's own experience had shown her, the life of the artist was deeply divisive and indissolubly mingled with egoism. Love and art stand opposed in another way as well. Love reconciles us to living, as we see in the verse dialogue **"Self and Life."** Self challenges Life to acquit itself before death: "Ere I lose my hold of thee / Justify thyself to me." Rejecting Life's proffered gifts—the joy of childhood, the excitement of growth and discovery, the wisdom of maturity—Self complains that each good is vitiated by pain and sorrow. But when love appears, Self gratefully embraces Life:

> Self and thou, no more at strife,
>   Shall wed in hallowed state.
> Willing spousals now shall prove
> Life is justified by love.

George Eliot's disbelief in an afterlife allowed her no comforting illusion of reunion beyond the grave, so for her love necessarily clung to mortal existence. Only the

threat of separation marred her calm acceptance of death: "The idea of dying has no melancholy for me, except in the parting and leaving behind which Love makes so hard to contemplate" (*Letters,* V). But this one thought held terrors she could not suppress: "Sometimes in the midst of happiness I cry suddenly at the thought that there must come a parting" (*Letters,* V). An unpublished verse fragment [found in Bernard J. Paris, "George Eliot's Unpublished Poetry," *SP* 56, 1959] expresses the conflict between love and death most poignantly:

> Master in loving! till we met
> I lacked the pattern thy sweet love hath set:
> I hear Death's footstep—must we then forget?—
>   Stay, stay—not yet!

By contrast, art finds its perfection in death. **"Oh May I Join the Choir Invisible"** expresses a longing to die out of the imperfect self and "inherit that sweet purity / For which we struggled, failed, and agonized"; the poem imagines the "discords" of "rebellious flesh" dissolving into harmony. George Eliot must have recognized that death promised to resolve her own struggle in a very literal way. Her fame and influence now assured, she could die knowing that the books she called "that best part of me," "the seed of one's soul" (*Letters,* V), would perpetuate the ideal self she could never fully claim in her lifetime. Death meant freedom to the novelist, loss of love to the wife: in this way, too, George Eliot's yearnings as author and as woman remained divided.

A number of strong motives are therefore at work in George Eliot's refusal to allow her heroines to become artists as well as wives. On the most conscious and practical level, she did not want to encourage the production of mediocre and thus morally degrading art; the world suffered from more than enough silly lady novelists already. Artistry for her was fraught with unresolved conflicts and would hardly provide a satisfactory solution for her self-divided heroines. The artist cannot escape egoism, yet the moral purpose of her fiction demanded that the pattern of her heroines' growth must be away from self. Love, though, represented unity and selflessness; it provided the kind of morally satisfying resolution she sought in her novels and also pleased the reading public with a conventionally happy ending. Finally, love and art pull in opposite directions—love toward life, and art toward death. Since the novels address the problem of living in this world, they naturally endorse love, which reconciles us to life, rather than art, which seduces us from it.

This last point requires some clarification. In both **"Jubal"** and **"Armgart,"** George Eliot speaks of art as one of life's greatest gifts; like love, it can unify experience: in Jubal's song "love, hope, rage, and all experience, / Were fused in vaster being," and "Joy took the air, and took each breathing soul, / Embracing them in one entranced whole." Yet this joyous act of creation is an unalloyed good only for the auditors, not for Jubal himself. While art enriches the lives of others, it saps the strength of the artist and ultimately demands his life as the price of vision. Jubal, foreseeing his future as an artist, confronts

the high task,
The struggling unborn spirit that doth ask
With irresistible cry for blood and breath,
Till feeding its great life we sink in death.

Similarly, the unpublished ode **"Erinna"** depicts the poet-heroine winning artistic insight only at the expense of great suffering and early death. In the case of art, it appears more blessed (or at least less traumatic) to receive than to give.

James Krasner (essay date 1994)

SOURCE: "'Where No Man Praised': The Retreat from Fame in George Eliot's *The Spanish Gypsy*," in *Victorian Poetry*, Vol. 32, No. 1, Spring, 1994, pp. 55-74.

[*In the following essay, Krasner explores the personal costs of "exposure" as defined in George Eliot's poetry.*]

As she was completing her long dramatic poem **The Spanish Gypsy**, George Eliot responded to an inquiring publisher by drawing attention to the difference between this work and her novels:

> The book I am writing is *not* a novel, and is likely to be dead against the taste of that large public which a publisher is for the most part obliged (rather unhappily) to take into account [*The George Eliot Letters*, 1955].

While it seems rather self-defeating for an author to warn a publisher that her new work will never sell, it is typical of George Eliot's attempt, at this point in her career, to distance herself from the fame and publicity surrounding her literary success. Much of George Eliot's poetry deals with the tension between fame and artistry, and **The Spanish Gypsy** offers a particularly trenchant portrayal of her attempt to absolve herself of the guilt she associated with public exposure. In the character of Fedalma, George Eliot offers us a public heroine who deplores publicity, a celebrated artist who retreats from her celebrity, and a political spokesperson who eloquently denies the significance of her words.

Recent critical attention to George Eliot's poetry has focused on **"Armgart"** and **"The Legend of Jubal"** as demonstrations of George Eliot's personal conflicts about being a woman artist. Bonnie J. Lisle and Rosemarie Bodenheimer identify Armgart and *Daniel Deronda*'s Alcharisi as women who must choose between patriarchal standards and their own artistic ambitions [Lisle, "Art and Egoism in George Eliot's Poetry," 1984; Bodenheimer, "Ambition and its Audiences: George Eliot's Performing Figures, 1990]. Lisle considers Armgart's final abandonment of her singing for a life of service a "selfless" act; through her character George Eliot voices her own ambition and then "absolves her higher responsibility by punishing the singer for egoism." Bodenheimer's more satisfying analysis shows Armgart rejecting both her ambitions for public performance and the patriarchal mold of mar-

riage to Graf Dorn to dedicate herself selflessly to artistry. Both critics read **"The Legend of Jubal,"** in which the artist is destroyed by his followers, as suggestive of George Eliot's anxiety about living in the public eye while maintaining an unscrutinized private life.

The Spanish Gypsy offers a rather unusual angle on the plight of the ambitious woman. Fedalma has ambition thrust upon her by an external patriarchal figure; pursuing her ambition amounts to being selfless and fulfilling social expectations. Fedalma herself can vigorously reject ambition and complain against it, while at the same time being lauded as a queen and national inspiration. This suggests George Eliot's own desire to fulfill her ambition while at the same time rejecting it as vanity. While Armgart and Alcharisi offer clearer versions of the problems involved for an ambitious woman, Fedalma embodies a resolution to these problems. She cannot be blamed for her fame and manages to maintain a private identity in a public context. In *The Spanish Gypsy* George Eliot portrays artists who achieve popular success without being tained by it.

I would thus call into question the typical reading of *The Spanish Gypsy* as another demonstration of George Eliot's belief in the importance of social duty over personal desire. Sylvia Kasey Marks finds it fits the "pattern" of George Eliot's novels in which characters who are "selfish and harbor misplaced idealism" lose their illusions and putting "their own interests aside, . . . respond to the call of duty" ["A Brief Glance at George Eliot's Poetry," *VP* 22, 1984]. In Fedalma's case this means relinquishing her love for Don Silva and accepting the duty of her Gypsy heritage by joining her father, Zarca, in his military campaign against the Spanish. George Eliot herself supports this reading in "Notes on the Spanish Gypsy and Tragedy in General":

> A good tragic subject must represent . . . irreparable collision between the individual and the general. . . . Silva presents the tragedy of entire rebellion: Fedalma of a grand submission . . . Zarca, the struggle for a great end [*George Eliot's Life*, 1884]

But as Bodenheimer so effectively demonstrates in George Eliot's letters, and as becomes apparent on a close reading of *Gypsy* and "Notes," such a choice between ambition and submissionis belied by George Eliot's desire to have both. Through Fedalma, George Eliot manages to resolve this conflict by presenting a character who retains her private vision in her public life and remains unambitious in the midst of widespread fame.

George Eliot creates this grafting of common and extraordinary experience through what she describes as a uniquely feminine kind of tragedy. Intertwining the myths of Iphigenia and the Virgin Mary, she presents Fedalma as a tragic heroine who is violently compelled to humiliating and painful public sacrifice but who establishes her own identity by focusing on that very pain and humiliation. George Eliot also applies the imagery of compelled public sacrifice to artistic practice. Fedalma and the minstrel Juan remove themselves from the world of economic exchange and popular success through an artistic self-sacrifice in which they abandon their wills to the crowd and voices to a common voice.

I

George Eliot begins her "Notes on the Spanish Gypsy and Tragedy in General" with the following provocative passage:

> The subject of "The Spanish Gypsy" was originally suggested to me by a picture which hangs in the Scuola di San Rocco at Venice, over the door of the large Sala containing Tintoretto's frescoes. It is an Annunciation, said to be by Titian. . . . It occurred to me that here was a great dramatic motive of the same class as those used by the Greek dramatists, yet specifically differing from them. A young maiden, believing herself to be on the eve of the chief event of her life—marriage—about to share in the ordinary lot of womanhood, full of young hope, has suddenly announced to her that she is chosen to fulfil a great destiny, entailing a terribly different experience from that of ordinary womanhood. She is chosen, not by any momentary arbitrariness, but as a result of foregoing hereditary conditions: she obeys. "Behold the handmaid of the Lord." Here, I thought, is a subject grander than that of Iphigenia, and it has never been used (*Life*).

The relevant questions here are: Why is Mary's fate "tragic"? What does the link between Mary and Iphigenia suggest? What "subject" is George Eliot referring to when she claims that "it has never been used"?

The "annunciation" scene in **The Spanish Gypsy** comes at the end of the first act when Zarca, king of the Gypsies and Fedalma's father, announces his presence and her true identity. In Titian's *Annunciation* Mary sits in a palatial room, beyond which is seen a garden by moonlight; she is working at a desk. A partridge walks across the ground toward her, symbolizing both her fertility and, as birds often do in annunciation scenes, the Holy Spirit. The angel, arrayed in military regalia, hovers above the balustrade. In **The Spanish Gypsy** Fedalma sits in a "large chamber richly furnished opening on a terrace-garden, the trees visible through the window in faint moon-light" looking at a casket of jewels. A "little bird falls softly on the floor"; picking it up, she finds that the bird has been killed and, on a slip around its broken wing, a message has been written in its blood. Zarca, in military apparel, appears at the window.

The parallels are obvious enough, but the variations are disturbing. That Zarca's first dramatic act should be to kill a small creature that could easily have been spared makes him seem repellant; the jarring contrast between dead bird and Holy Spirit makes him seem infernal. Fedalma says that the bird "was seeking sanctuary, / And died, perhaps of fright, at the altar foot." But if her room is an altar where the human meets the divine, then the paternal god entering is, in fact, the destroyer from which the bird has fled.

Throughout the work, Zarca is portrayed as a cruel father, imposing a "terrible" destiny on his daughter. These elements of terror suggest that the individual daughter's compulsion to follow the destiny determined by her father (as embodiment of "the general") may be something more sinister than an announcement followed by meek obedience. If Mary is Iphigenia then God must be Agamemnon. Fedalma responds to her father's request in words strongly reminiscent of Iphigenia:

> Father, since I am yours,
> Since I must walk an unslain sacrifice,
> Carrying the knife within me, quivering,—
> Put cords upon me, drag me to the doom
> My birth has laid upon me. See, I kneel:
> I cannot will to go.

This is a far cry from "Behold, the handmaid of the Lord," and makes the violence implicit in George Eliot's elision of Mary and Iphigenia explicit. When Fedalma chooses her father over Silva in section III, the narrator smoothly combines imagery of Mary's annunciation and Iphigenia's sacrifice, linking divine authority to brutal torture:

> wrought upon by awe,
> Her own brief life seeming a little isle
> Remote through visions of a wider world
> With fates close-crowded; firm to slay her joy
> That cut her heart with smiles beneath the knife,
> Like a sweet babe foredoomed by prophecy.
>
> . . . . .
>
> . . . Now the father stood
> Present and silent and unchangeable
> As a celestial portent.

Diane Sadoff has described how, in the novels written after *Romola*, fathers or father-figures are portrayed as "failed and apparently illegitimate authorit[ies]" who are idealized by foolish heroines [*Monsters of Affection: Dickens, Eliot and Bronte on Fatherhood*, 1982]. The imagery of **The Spanish Gypsy** presents Zarca not only as an illegitimate authority, but as a brutal and sadistic one. Fedalma is described as bound with chains, submerged in lava, strangled, tortured, and dismembered by her father's sword; nowhere else in George Eliot's work do we see familial power dynamics enunciated in such violent imagery. Here allegiance to the father is not only foolish but terribly dangerous.

In "Notes on the Spanish Gypsy and Tragedy in General," George Eliot's choice of tragic models points towards a preoccupation with male familial brutality. She focuses on *Othello* and Euripides' *Iphigenia*, mentioning the *Oresteia* (with reference to Orestes' predicament but not Clytemnestra's), and the stories of Faust and Rigoletto. This is rather an odd selection for a discussion of "Tragedy in General"; one wonders why *Oedipus* does not make the list while *Rigoletto* does, except that *Rigoletto* involves a father killing a daughter while *Oedipus* involves a son killing a father. Fear of violent compulsion intertwines imagistically with the submission to social and hereditary duty in George Eliot's conception of Fedalma's tragedy.

Yet this portrayal of compelled ambition is consistent with what Bodenheimer describes as George Eliot's strategy for avoiding the "Victorian stigma of 'the public woman' with its automatic associations of self-display":

> This representation of ambition as a form of impotent suffering . . . had its strategic uses as well as its truth. By separating her ambition from her achievement and transforming it into suffering, George Eliot could feminize and conceal it, both to her own satisfaction and for the benefit of her audiences and admirers.

While Bodenheimer is referring to George Eliot's own psychological suffering, expressed in her letters and journals, we see the same psychological mechanism made physical and violent in Fedalma. Fedalma confronts ambition as an impotent sufferer; this sacrificial victim seems to be just the opposite of the ambitious woman courting public fame. Bodenheimer goes on to suggest that George Eliot created her public persona as a disembodied narrative voice in an attempt to avoid "the public display of the performing or performed body." Like George Eliot, Fedalma wishes to avoid the public eye, to remain invisible and bodiless, but Zarca insists that heroism and sacrifice must be public acts. His insistence that she should "save" her people by abandoning her love for Don Silva is predicated on the understanding of her identity as public. "You belong / Not to the petty round of circumstance / That makes a woman's lot, but to your tribe," he tells her. Her elevation to the public role of queen of the Gypsies occurred at birth and parallels the sacrificial violation of Iphigenia's body or the public sanctification of Mary's womb:

>   the woman who would save her tribe
> Must help its heroes,—not by wordy breath,
> By easy prayers strong in a lover's ear,
>
>   . . . . .
>
>   . . . not to such trim merit
> As soils its dainty shoes for charity
> And simpers meekly at the pious stain,
> But never trod with naked bleeding feet
> Where no man praised it, and where no Church
>   blessed:
> Not to such almsdeeds fit for holidays
> Were you, my daughter, consecrated, bound
>
>   . . . . .
>
> When you were born in the Zincalo's tent,
> And lifted up in sight of all your tribe,
> Who greeted you with shouts of loyal joy,
> Sole offspring of the chief in whom they trust.

The moment of sacrifice is the moment of exposure, when the private body becomes public. Fedalma's good wishes, or good words, are not enough; her "naked bleeding feet,"

her body itself, has been promised—"bound" in both senses of the word—as a public sacrifice. The father holding his newborn child up to his people imagistically echoes the father holding his daughter up as a sacrificial offering.

Fedalma also describes her future through images of public display, and again public display of the body is elided with public violation:

> On the close-thronged spaces of the earth
> A battle rages: Fate has carried me
> 'Mid the thick arrows: I will keep my stand,—
> Not shrink and let the shaft pass by my breast
> To pierce another.
>
> Die, my young joy,—die, all my hungry hopes,—
>
>   . . . . .
>
> The saints were cowards who stood by to see
> Christ crucified: they should have flung themselves
> Upon the Roman spears . . .
> That death shall be my bridegroom. I will wed
> The curse of the Zincali.

Fedalma's descriptions of her sacrifice betray George Eliot's fear of public exposure. Her death will be both public ritual and festival; the battle, the public execution, civic martyrdom, and wedding feast are the social events to which she compares her acceptance of her public role. Death and marriage are elided, for both involve the loss of a private body through public, patriarchal ritual.

In her poem **"Oh May I Join the Choir Invisible,"** written in the same year as the final revisions of *The Spanish Gypsy*, George Eliot describes a different kind of martyrdom, one that balances fame and anonymity, and that avoids the public exposure of the victim's body. She wishes to join "the choir invisible / Of those immortal dead who live again / In minds made better by their presence." These great souls manage to serve as examples of goodness while remaining nameless and faceless:

>   This is life to come,
> Which martyred men have made more glorious
> For us who strive to follow. May I reach
> That purest heaven . . .
>
>   . . . . .
>
> And in diffusion ever more intense.

This poem points to George Eliot's desire to retain the moral influence of fame while allowing the body to be "diffused" rather than objectified. While martyrdom serves humanity, it serves it more effectively, becomes "ever more intense" if it is not accompanied by celebrity.

In Fedalma, George Eliot offers us the example of a martyr who seeks, like the narrator of the poem, to diffuse her public fame and maintain a private identity. Despite the "close-thronged" crowd of her audience, Fedelma is able rhetorically to transform her public sacrifice and public suffering into a private, even lonely, misery and reclaim her private body by emphasizing the personal pain caused by this public violation. Several times she distinguishes between her father's ambitious vision and her awareness of her own immediate suffering:

> Father, my soul is weak, the mist of tears
> Still rises to my eyes, and hides the goal
> Which to your undimmed sight is clear and
>   changeless
>
> . . . . .
>
> If it were needed, this poor trembling hand
> Should grasp the torch,—strive not to let it fall
> Though it were burning down close to my flesh,
> No beacon lighted yet: through the damp dark
> I should still hear the cry of gasping swimmers.
>
> But on my will there falls the chilling snow
> Of thoughts that come as subtly as soft flakes,
> Yet press at last with hard and icy weight.
> I could be firm, could give myself the wrench
> And walk erect, hiding my life-long wound
> If I but saw the fruit of all my pain
> With that strong vision which commands the soul,
>
> . . . . .
>
> But now I totter, seeing no far goal;
> I tread the rocky pass, and pause and grasp,
> Guided by flashes.

Fedalma compares herself unfavorably to her father. He has a grand historical vision; she does not. He understands his pain to be necessary and redemptive; she perceives it only as pain. But in dwelling on this pain, she undercuts Zarca's grandiose rhetoric and returns the reader to an awareness of her private pain. Fedalma's singed fingers, like her bound hands, arrow-pierced breast, ice-encrusted scalp, all attest to the ultimately private nature of her suffering. She may be a public figure, but when she is pricked, or sacrificed, she bleeds.

At the end of the poem, Zarca's death leaves Fedalma queen and sole ruler, allowing her to perfect her persona as a lonely sufferer:

> For me,
> I am but as the funeral urn that bears
> The ashes of a leader.
>
> . . . . .
>
> He trusted me, and I will keep his trust:
> My life shall be its temple. I will plant
> His sacred hope within the sanctuary
> And die its priestess,—though I die alone,
> A hoary woman on the altar step,
> Cold 'mid cold ashes.

Fedalma rewrites public service as an act of private contrition; the leader becomes a priestess; the nation becomes a "sanctuary." Like the "rocky pass" or the "damp dark," this claustrophobic temple limits and encloses Zarca's grand nationalistic vision. Fedalma's portrayal of herself as a solitary priestess calls to mind Mary's solitude in Titian's *Annunciation.* The Tintoretto frescoes on the walls of the Scuola di San Rocco, which George Eliot directs her gaze away from in order to concentrate on Titian's *Annunciation,* portray the life of Christ in a series of panoramic crowd scenes. Christ, at his birth, preaching, crucifixion, is a small figure surrounded by multitudes— a public savior. This panoramic portrayal of self-sacrifice does not impress George Eliot. Rather, she is drawn to the much more intimate painting representing the moment before Mary becomes a public figure, the moment when she realizes "the irreparable collision between the individual and the general." Tintoretto's frescoes seem of a piece with Zarca's heroic rhetoric, which sets the national hero above the throngs of his followers in a fantastic, Utopian landscape:

> I your father wait
> That you may lead us forth to liberty—
>
> . . . . .
>
> And plant them as a mighty nation's seed.
>
> . . . . .
>
> They have a promised land beyond the sea:
> There I may lead them, raise my standard, call
> All wandering Zincali to that home,
> And make a nation,—bring light, order, law,
> Instead of chaos. You, my only heir,
> Are called to reign for me when I am gone.

The impulse toward public display, from which George Eliot shrinks in horror, characterizes Zarca's conception of sacrifice. Titian's *Annunciation* is far less theatrical than Tintoretto's frescoes, his version of sacrifice more private and secluded. George Eliot chooses the second as Fedalma's.

In **"A Minor Prophet"** George Eliot sets up a similar contrast between the "victorious world-hero" and "the patched and plodding citizen." Ultimately, she rejects the idea that the world is made better by heroes with panoramic vision:

> Bitterly
> I feel that every change upon this earth
> Is bought with sacrifice. My yearnings fail
> To reach that high apocalyptic mount
> Which shows in bird's-eye view a perfect world,
> Or enter warmly into other joys
> Than those of faulty, struggling human kind.

Like Fedalma, the narrator of this poem compares herself to another, more theatrical prophet, and finds her vision narrow and confined. But in this narrowness lies its human-

ity. Unlike Elias Baptist Butterworth, the fanatical vegetarian satirized in **"A Minor Prophet,"** the narrator has a
link to the common citizen who can not see "in bird's eye
view a perfect world," but "from that dazzling curtain of
bright hues / [turns] to the familiar face of fields." Such
private sacrifice serves humanity in infinite small ways,
"As patriots who seem to die in vain." Anonymous, painful,
and apparently purposeless sacrifice emerges as George
Eliot's vision of true heroism.

**Much of George Eliot's poetry deals with
the tension between fame and artistry,
and *The Spanish Gypsy* offers a
particularly trenchant portrayal of her
attempt to absolve herself of the guilt she
associated with public exposure**.

—*James Krasner*

George Eliot's choice of Titian over Tintoretto suggests
also that she considers Mary's sacrifice preferable to Christ's.
Unlike the son of God, she is an ordinary woman who must
have "a terribly different experience from that of ordinary
womanhood." In the "tragic relations of the individual and
general" the element of hereditary and historical compulsion defines Mary's experience. Unlike Christ, she does not
choose: "she is chosen"; she "is compelled to give way."
George Eliot's "tragic subject" that "has never been used"
culminates in obedience rather than death: "she obeys."
While the common woman obeys her husband in marriage,
the tragic heroine obeys hereditary compulsion, or male
society, in a more visible, although equally subservient,
condition. Mary is elevated from the handmaid of her
husband to the "handmaid of the Lord." When Zarca tells
Fedalma that she is "called to reign for me when I am
gone. . . . You, woman and Zincala, fortunate, / Above
your fellows," he clearly echoes the angel's words to Mary,
"blessed art thou among women" (Luke 1.28). In both
cases, however, the "blessing" consists of suffering, and the
subsequent position as "queen" is chosen for the woman by
an irresistible patriarch. The crucial difference between Mary
and Christ, George Eliot suggests, is that while Christ's
obedience to God's plan makes him a hero and a savior,
Mary's makes her a "handmaid." Fedalma, in becoming a
queen, becomes only a different kind of slave:

> ZARCA: I would compel you to go forth.
> FEDALMA: You tell me that?
> ZARCA: Yes, for I'd have you choose;
>   Though, being of the blood you are,—my
> blood,—
>   You have no right to choose.
> FEDALMA: I only owe
>   A daughter's debt; I was not born a slave.
> ZARCA: No, not a slave; but you were born to
> reign.
>   'T is a compulsion of a higher sort,

> Whose fetters are the net invisible
> That holds all life together.

The "terribly different" experience of being a famous
woman is, then, simply a making general, or making
public, of her experience as a common woman; she must
obey a national will rather than an individual one. The
famous woman suffers the exposure of publicity without
gaining power from it; she thus has more in common
with the common woman than would Zarca, or Christ,
with the common man. Where Christ and Zarca stand for
their people symbolically, their public power differentiates their lives from the lives of individual people. Fedalma
serves as a better representative of common experience,
and a better sacrifice, because her fame can not lift from
her a crucial connection to those she represents; she serves
both as a symbol of her people and as a demonstration of
their suffering, particularly the suffering of women.

This drawing together of public and private experience is
George Eliot's model for the female tragic hero. Titian's
Annunciation shows Mary before she becomes a public
figure, but it continues to be the image through which she
is portrayed 1900 years after her elevation into the public
eye; she will always be alone with the angel. Mary succeeds in remaining always a private figure in the midst of
universal publicity, and George Eliot finds in the bridging
of public and private a model for a heroine who can be
at once publicly sacrificed and privately self-determined.

Through Fedalma's response to Zarca George Eliot manages to rewrite personal ambition as social sacrifice. Fedalma and Juan, her minstrel and confidante, serve a similar function for George Eliot's anxieties about popular
and financial success. During the period in which *The
Spanish Gypsy* was being written, George Eliot's fame
and financial success made her anxious to justify the
originality and social value of her art. Bodenheimer describes how in order "to defend herself against the idea
that she wrote only for fame and fortune" George Eliot
had to establish that her audience "needed her ideas". In
Fedalma and Juan she presents artist figures who, rather
than foisting unwanted and egoistic works on the public,
perform by public acclamation in a way that meets a strong
social need. Far from being self-indulgent or mercenary,
these artists empty themselves of ego in order to speak
for others, receiving no reward for their self-effacing acts.

In a letter to Frederic Harrison, written in August 1866,
George Eliot announces that she is "taking up again"
The Spanish Gypsy, which she had put aside in February
of 1865, "precisely because it was in that stage of Creation
or 'Werden,' in which the idea of the characters predominates over the incarnation." Such artistry fails because it
"lapses . . . from the picture to the diagram," teaching
through a "scientific and expository" mode, rather than
an aesthetic one. Throughout the letter, George Eliot describes the difficulty of the artistic task as a mediation
between spirit and flesh:

> [I] have gone through again and again the severe effort
> of trying to make certain ideas thoroughly incarnate,

as if they had revealed themselves to me first in the flesh and not in the spirit. . . . Well, then, consider the sort of agonizing labour to an English-fed imagination to make art a sufficiently real back-ground, for the desired picture, to get breathing, individual forms, and group them in the needful relations, so that the presentation will lay hold on the emotions as human experience—will, as you say, "flash" conviction on the world by means of aroused sympathy. . . . When one has to work out the dramatic action for one's self under the inspiration of an idea, instead of having a grand myth or an Italian novel ready to one's hand, one feels anything but omnipotent.

Given George Eliot's location of Mary as inspiration for *The Spanish Gypsy,* the terms she uses to describe the artistic process here are quite provocative. The artist must "incarnate . . . in the flesh" what was "revealed" to her "in the spirit." The process is a "sort of agonizing labour" and makes her feel "anything but omnipotent." Rather than God omnipotently creating a universe, the artist must be Mary, translating idea into flesh, and experiencing great pain in doing so. The artist takes upon herself the "severe effort" of artistic incarnation in order to "teach" the truth.

As an example, she cites her process of writing *Romola* for which she "took unspeakable pains" and which brought her to the edge of a complete breakdown. Her labor of making idea into incarnate art involved exhaustive research into Florentine history because "I felt that the necessary idealization could only be attained by adopting the clothing of the past." The "agonizing labour" of aesthetic translation involves opening one's mind to another frame of reference. For *Romola* the "English-fed imagination" had to adopt "the 'Idiom' of Florence, in the largest sense one could stretch the word." Whether or not the artist is dealing in historical material, however, the artistic process involves the adoption of an "Idiom" that allows the artist to speak for human experience, a voice that can "lay hold on the emotions" and thus "'flash' conviction on the world."

In Fedalma's one moment of pure artistry in *The Spanish Gypsy,* her dance in the Placa Santiago that reveals her Gypsy blood, she literally incarnates her art, moving her body in such a way that a message is "flashed" to those who behold her:

> Sudden, with gliding motion like a flame
> That through dim vapor makes a path of glory,
> A figure lithe, all white and saffron-robed,
> Flashed right across the circle . . .
>
>   . . . . .
>
> Moved as, in dance religious, Miriam,
> When on the Red Sea shore she raised her voice,
> And led the chorus of her people's joy.
>
>   . . . . .
>
> The exquisite hour, the ardor of the crowd,
> The strains more plenteous, and the gathering might
> Of action passionate where no effort is.

> But self's poor gates open to rushing power
> That blends the inward ebb and outward vast,—
> All gathering influences culminate
> And urge Fedalma . . .
>
>   . . . . .
>
>   . . . now the crowd
> Exultant shouts, forgetting poverty
> In the rich moment of possessing her.

George Eliot wants to make her ideas "thoroughly incarnate, as if they had revealed themselves to me first in the flesh." This moment of pure, physical, sympathetic artistry seems like one such fleshly revelation; Fedalma communicates immediately to the crowd in a "flash" of emotion. The reference to Miriam emphasizes both the political and the aesthetic significance of Fedalma's artistry. In Exodus 15 Moses sings a discursive, political song, celebrating Israel's victory over Egypt. Miriam's dance, which follows, expresses the same ideas aesthetically; it bears the same relationship to Moses' song that, in George Eliot's terms, the picture bears to the diagram. Fedalma's dance serves as an "Idiom" through which she can communicate directly, and like that adopted by George Eliot in writing *Romola,* it nearly destroys her, as the "self's poor gates open to rushing power / That blends the inward ebb and outward vast."

Even in this most self-displaying moment, however, Fedalma avoids the stigma of the performing woman. By eliding the compulsion of "foregoing hereditary conditions" with the compulsion of the audience, George Eliot exonerates Fedalma of any charges of undue ambition or inappropriate display. Like the violent images described earlier, the images in the dance sequence emphasize the intense compulsion of an outward force that overcomes "the self's poor gates." Fedalma only dances after her audience cries out, not simply to be entertained, but to be instructed by an artist capable of putting ideas into breathing, individual form:

> All long in common for the expressive act
> Yet wait for it; as in the olden time.
> Men waited for the bard to tell their thought.
> "The dance! the dance!" is shouted all around.

Artistic expression emerges as a social obligation for Fedalma; the display of her body remains innocent because she is simply answering the call of the people for a translator and representative, one who can speak to them in sympathetic terms. Like Miriam, who "led the chorus of her people's joy," Fedalma becomes a representative of the crowd, translating Moses' words into terms that "flash conviction on the world by aroused sympathy." George Eliot's belief in more descriptive political and artistic representation, which Catherine Gallagher has discussed in relation to *Felix Holt,* emerges in *The Spanish Gypsy* as a way of justifying popular success ["George Eliot and *Daniel Deronda*: The Prostitute and the Jewish Question," *Sex, Politics and Science in the Nineteenth-Century Novel,* 1986]. "Men waited for the bard to tell their thought"; the bard not only speaks in a way the audience can understand, she actually voices the audience's thoughts; they "possess" her:

> And all the people felt a common joy . . .
>   . . . The joy, the life
> Around, within me, were one heaven: I longed
> To blend them visibly: I longed to dance
> Before the people . . .
>   . . . Nay, I danced;
> There was no longing: I but did the deed
> Being moved to do it.

Fedalma slips from an assertion of personal desire "I longed" to an assertion of will-less acquiescence to "a common joy," for which "there was no longing." The defined edges of the self that distinguish interior from exterior blend: "Soon I lost / All sense of separateness."

The conception of the artist as an egoless representative of others, a vessel through which others speak, recurs throughout the poem. Juan describes his art as a way of speaking through other voices:

> Juan is not a living man all by himself:
> His life is breathed in him by other men,
> And they speak out of him. He is their voice.
>
>   . . . . .
>
> We old, old poets, if we kept our hearts,
> Should hardly know them from another man's.
> They shrink to make room for the many more
> We keep within us.

Rather than inspiration from the Muse, the artist receives it from other men who literally inspire ("breath into") him. Juan's artistry involves emptying out the self and "telling" the "thought" of others. As [Catherine] Gallagher points out, George Eliot yearned to "become the medium of the collective project of culture" but was much too cynical about the operation of artistic representation to accept such a direct translation from people to artist as Juan suggests. The naiveté of Juan's aesthetic overstates, rather than expresses, George Eliot's ideas, thus putting this artist beyond blame. Like the unnecessarily violent intensity of Zarca's rhetoric of social sacrifice, Juan's intense idealism suggests how far George Eliot will go to rid her art of any appearance of egoism. The letter to Harrison, with all its talk of pain and suffering, suggests how tightly George Eliot was putting the screws to her ambition, trying to transform an omnipotent creator into a meek and willing handmaid of the truth. Clearly, George Eliot is more comfortable with omnipotence, and throughout *The Spanish Gypsy* we see a vigorous disavowal of poetic and personal power. In Fedalma's relationship with Zarca, this disavowal emerges as a violent assault on her will. In an artistic context we find a spontaneous and complete jettisoning of the ego that George Eliot herself could never achieve. "I am a thing of rhythm and redondillas," says Juan, "The momentary rainbow on the spray / Made by the thundering torrent of men's lives." The

artist must be insubstantial, ephemeral, having no "substantial self that holds a weight," having life breathed into him by others, something carried on the tide or rolled by "larger things." During the dance, Fedalma experiences "life in unison with a multitude . . . Soon I lost / All sense of separateness: Fedalma died / As a star dies, and melts into the light." Like the narrator of **"Oh May I Join the Choir Invisible,"** the artist dissolves like light or spray or the ebbing tide, into the multitude. Juan and Fedalma become utterly selfless in the artistic process, capable of speaking only for others, voluntarily sacrificing their egos.

Within George Eliot's elision of Mary / Iphigenia / Fedalma, moreover, the social worth of art is grounded on its ability to give voice to the voiceless populace, particularly women. George Eliot does seem to hold out hope for descriptive representation in the context of gender issues. In a letter to Mrs. Nassau Senior, she describes Iphigenia as a sacrificial victim who gives voice to her country-women's suffering:

> The influence of one woman's life on the lot of other women is getting greater and greater with the quickening spread of all influences. One likes to think, though, that two thousand years ago Euripides made Iphigenia count it a reason for facing her sacrifice bravely that thereby she might help to save Greek women (from a wrong like Helen's) in times to come. There is no knife at your throat, happily.

George Eliot is referring to Iphigenia's last speech, in which she states that "Because of me, never more will / Barbarians wrong and ravish Greek women, / Drag them from happiness and their homes / In Hellas." George Eliot interprets the lines with more of an eye to gender than to country, as she admits. The crucial connection between Mrs. Nassau Senior (who had just been appointed inspector of workhouses) and Iphigenia, is not that both are sacrificed (Mrs. Nassau Senior does not have a knife at her throat), but that both further the "quickening spread of all influences" whereby women's wrongs are made public; both serve as social representatives. This is also the crucial similarity between Iphigenia and Fedalma, who conceives of her sacrifice to Zarca as a way of making women's wrongs visible:

> O father, will the women of our tribe
> Suffer as I do, in the years to come
> When you have made them great in Africa?
> Redeemed from ignorant ills only to feel
> A conscious woe? Then,—is it worth the pains?
> Were it not better when we reach that shore
> To raise a funeral-pile and perish all?
> So closing up a myriad avenues
> To misery yet unwrought? My soul is faint,
> Will these sharp pangs buy any certain good?

As before, Fedalma differentiates between the "sharp pangs" of her own private, painful vision and her father's nationalistic pride, but here she explicitly takes up the cause of those who, like herself, are subjected to "ignorant ills." Like Mrs. Nassau Senior she considers herself an intercessor between her countrywomen and her leader. Like Iphigenia, she identifies herself as a representative of her countrywomen, not just her country.

While this representative aesthetic is consistent with George Eliot's description of the artist opening to a new idiom, it seems to undercut her firm belief that the artist must have something original to teach. Worse, it invokes George Eliot's other main anxiety about literary success—that she was pandering to the crowd for fame and fortune. In **"Armgart"** Leo claims that Armgart's attention to her audience grows out of her immoral, egoistic artistry: "Will you ask the house / To teach you singing? . . . lift your audience / To see your vision, not trick forth a show / To please the grossest taste of grossest numbers." Yet, in *The Spanish Gypsy* Fedalma comes very close to being the mere instrument of the crowd.

Partly this inconsistency demonstrates George Eliot's psychological bind. By escaping the egoism of "scientific and expository" thought and incarnating her art, she indulges in the egoism of populism. But there are significant differences between Armgart's crowd-pleasing and Fedalma's. The dance in the square and Juan's minstrelsy are the epitome of popular art, but they are still "expressive acts." Fedalma and Juan faithfully translate the crowd's ideas ("tell their thought") rather than just tickling their fancy. Armgart revels in the control over the crowd her art gives her. "For what is fame / But the benignant strength of One, transformed / To joy of Many?" For Fedalma, on the other hand, the strength of the many, the "common joy," transforms the one artist. Armgart, like Zarca, portrays herself elevated from the crowd; she is a "spiritual star" pouring forth "glory wide-diffused," but not diffusing herself. Fedalma's star is dying "As a star dies, and melts into the light. / I was not, but joy was."

George Eliot goes out of her way to show that Juan and Fedalma's denial of self removes their art and their sacrifices from the world of social and financial exchange. In this *The Spanish Gypsy* differs from George Eliot's novels which, as Catherine Gallagher has convincingly demonstrated, George Eliot conceived of as necessarily marketable commodities. Her descriptions of *The Spanish Gypsy* to her publisher John Blackwood and to George Smith, publisher of the *Cornhill,* continually sound these themes:

> I need not tell you that I am not hopeful—but I am quite sure the subject is fine. . . . The plot was wrought out entirely as an incorporation of my own ideas.

> The book I am writing is not a novel, and is likely to be dead against the taste of that large public which a publisher is for the most part obliged (rather unhappily) to take into account.

> As to the matter of pounds and shillings I had not, before I received your letter, formed any definite idea beyond this: that I was to be paid only for the number of copies *sold.* You appear to offer me £300 unconditionally for 2000 copies printed. This I do not wish.

The message is clear. She does not write to be popular. Her art is based on ideas beyond mere entertainment. She is not interested in money. While she justifies popular art within the text, she retreats from it outside the text, casting the poem as sublime work, well beyond the comprehension of her audience. Her description of her agonizing struggle to incarnate her ideas, and flash conviction on her audience, must be balanced against her denial of any fit audience or any audience at all. Both claims, however, remove her work from the realm of exchange. Whether she writes only for herself or annihilates herself in writing, she does not sell her art for gold or applause.

George Eliot responds to her concerns about egoism by presenting Juan and Fedalma as self-sacrificing, egoless artists, as we have seen. But she does not stop there. She makes sure that even self-sacrifice can not be interpreted as a hidden bargain for fame and wealth. Bonnie J. Lisle has pointed out how, in **"The Legend of Jubal,"** the artist strikes a bargain, whereby the loss of identity brings fame: "The artist's high privilege, George Eliot suggests, must be redeemed by suffering and self-annihilation. . . . Self-annihilation is at once a debt he owes humanity and, paradoxically, the only way to attain the immortality he seeks." In *The Spanish Gypsy,* however, self-annihilation does not bring immortality, only silence. Fedalma celebrates Juan's sacrifice because he so fully, and so permanently, erases his own identity:

> Good Juan, I could have no nobler friend.
> You'd ope your veins and let your life-blood out
> To save another's pain, yet hide the deed
> With jesting,—say, 't was merest accident,
>
> . . . . .
>
> And die content with men's slight thought of you,
> Finding your glory in another's joy.

Like Dorothea Brooke, Juan will die without fame and rest in an unvisited grave. Lisle's conception of the artist losing his identity to achieve the "reward" of immortality operates through the same logic of self-interested exchange that Fedalma praises Juan for surpassing. If the artist does not desire fame, her suffering does not serve as a "debt [s]he owes" for this fame, but is an expression of pure love for others.

Juan also explicitly removes his artistry from the realm of exchange, describing it as a form of "service" and, again, sacrifice. He explains to Fedalma that one must lose oneself wholly, without attention to how much value can be placed on one's love:

> What is lovely seen
> Priced in a tariff?—lapis lazuli,
> Such bulk, so many drachmas: amethysts
> Quoted at so much; sapphires higher still.
> The stone like solid heaven in its blueness
> Is what I care for, not its name or price.
> So, if I live or die to serve my friend
> 'Tis for my love—'tis for my friend alone,

And not for any rate that friendship bears
In heaven or on earth.

To be purged of the earthly taint of the marketplace, sacrifice must be performed freely. This poet does not bargain his identity for fame but relinquishes his identity so as to perfect his artistic obligation of speaking for others. The act of giving oneself to the crowd, of dissolving into light or ebbing into the ocean, can not be conceived of as a bargain, for once it is done no self is left to reap the reward. Just as Juan whimsically pours his life's blood out, Fedalma thoughtlessly squanders her identity; the crowd "possesses" Fedalma because she has given herself away. Her dance is imaged as an anarchic redistribution of wealth: "now the crowd / Exultant shouts, forgetting poverty / In the rich moment of possessing her." The artistic dissolution of self is elided with the scattering of coins or jewels, like Fedalma's subsequent abandonment of Silva's royal jewelry.

In her poem **"Arion"** George Eliot also enacts the jettisoning of mercantile artistry. Arion is a financially successful artist who is "weighted with his glorious name / And bags of gold." Set upon by thieves aboard ship, he tries to trade the gold for his life, but is refused. Having sold his art for gold, he now discovers the gold is valueless, and his art degraded. He then proposes to give the thieves "a song unsung before," that had never been marketed to "men who paid their gold / For what a poet sold." Pouring forth the song "for naught," he inspires the thieves to call him a god, then suddenly, leaps over the side to his death.

By choosing such an extreme surprise ending, George Eliot shows her intention not to compromise the artist in any way. Arion is clearly a true artist, but he has been "weighted" by years of fame and fortune; both drag him to earth. By moving beyond the buying and selling of poetry he achieves a kind of "liberty" and "lofty passion." But were he to accept the acclamations of the thieves and remain alive, he would simply be weighted with more fame. Moreover, if they allow him to redeem his life through song, he will once again be participating in artistic exchange, as Lisle has noted. His suicide registers both George Eliot's determination to find a selfless aesthetic and her frustration at being unable to do so.

Fedalma's expression of concern for the Gypsy women also raises the question of exchange value, with reference to Fedalma's sacrifice. The question is phrased in terms of exchange. Will the suffering be "worth the pains"? Will the sacrifice "buy" anything of value? The "redemption" of the people will be paid with the coin of Fedalma's suffering. Zarca has consistently portrayed Fedalma using the language of exchange value. "I lost you as a man may lose a diamond / Wherein he has compressed his total wealth," he tells her, and having found her, "I come to claim you." Fedalma recognizes that she is expected to participate in this historical bargain: "Even in the womb you vowed me to the fire . . . And pledged me to redeem!—I'll pay the debt."

Fedalma ultimately rejects a model of sacrifice based on financial redemption, however. In the last few lines of this passage Fedalma answers the question she poses at first—yes, the women will suffer then as she does now, regardless of how great Zarca or his armies become. Women who are "Redeemed from ignorant ills only to feel / A conscious woe" are not "redeemed" in any true sense. Fedalma chooses to describe her sacrifice as an act of pure selflessness, not as a bargain. She has no illusions that the debt can ever fully be paid, or that the process of redemption will be successful. Her sacrifice will consist of pure suffering, and through it, she will embody the suffering of others:

Yes, say that we shall fail! I will not count
On aught but being faithful. I will take
This yearning self of mine and strangle it.

. . . . .

The grandest death, to die in vain, for love
Greater than sways the forces of the world.

The "forces of the world," such as Zarca and his armies, are swayed by political motives; they are willing to sacrifice if they will get something in return; her sacrifice is "greater" because her motive is "love."

If we look again at George Eliot's letter announcing her recommitment to *The Spanish Gypsy* in comparison with "Notes on The Spanish Gypsy and Tragedy in General," some striking similarities emerge. The tragic heroine is caught in the "irreparable collision between the individual and the general . . . of which we recognize the irresistible power." The artist is caught between her own individual ideas and their incarnation in a work of art that will appeal to the general public. The submission to the general, in both cases, involves "unspeakable pains" and "severe effort." Fedalma, George Eliot tells us, represents "the tragedy of a grand submission." Both as a political figure and as an artist, Fedalma submits herself to the irresistible power of the general. In making her work accessible, in incarnating her ideas in a sympathetic idiom, the artist has done the right thing, but George Eliot still imagines it as a "tragedy." We have seen how Fedalma serves to resolve, rather than highlight, George Eliot's conflicts as a female artist; George Eliot constructs characters and circumstances that will guarantee this artist will be blameless of all the charges George Eliot leveled against herself. But ultimately, George Eliot can not accept her as her own. Even as she writes to Harrison asserting the necessity of agonizingly denying the artistic ego, she considers Fedalma's self-denial tragic.

Michael Ragussis (essay date 1995)

SOURCE: "Writing Spanish History: The Inquisition and 'the Secret Race'," in *Figures of Conversion: "The Jewish Question" and English National Identity,* Duke University Press, 1995, pp. 127-73.

[*In the following excerpt, Ragussis explores the idea of woman as the daughter, or preserver, of a race, and the historical implications of Jewish culture in Eliot's* The Spanish Gypsy.]

Fedalma in George Eliot's **The Spanish Gypsy** is a portrait of the heroism of the female heart. The entire project of **The Spanish Gypsy** was framed from the beginning by an attempt to understand in what ways the genre of tragedy could function as a category of the feminine—that is, as a representation of a specifically female action. The project began with Eliot's meditation on a painting of the Annunciation, as she records in her "Notes on the Spanish Gypsy and Tragedy in General":

> It occurred to me that here was a great dramatic motive of the same class as those used by the Greek dramatists, yet specifically differing from them. A young maiden, believing herself to be on the eve of the chief event of her life—marriage—about to share in the ordinary lot of womanhood, full of young hope, has suddenly announced to her that she is chosen to fulfil a great destiny, entailing a terribly different experience from that of ordinary womanhood. She is chosen, not by any momentary arbitrariness, but as a result of foregoing hereditary conditions: she obeys. "Behold the handmaid of the Lord." Here, I thought, is a subject grander than that of Iphigenia, and it has never been used.

Eliot's example of the Annunciation invites us to see the way in which the mortal father becomes transformed into a kind of god for whom the daughter functions as the obedient handmaid or sacrificial victim. . . . [In] **The Spanish Gypsy** the daughter is sacrificed to the father as God. Hence Fedalma "knelt, / Clinging with piety and awed resolve / Beside this altar of her father's life, where she obediently sacrifices her own life while taking the pledge of worship: "He trusted me, and I will keep his trust: / My life shall be its temple. I will plant / His sacred hope within the sanctuary / And die its priestess."

While Eliot defined the function of "hereditary conditions" in tragic plots in a variety of ways, more and more she came to mean *racial* conditions: "A story simply of a jealous husband is elevated into a most pathetic tragedy by the hereditary conditions of Othello's lot, which give him a subjective ground for distrust"; "a woman, say, finds herself on the earth with an inherited organization; she may be lame, she may inherit a disease, or what is tantamount to a disease; she may be a negress, or have other marks of race repulsive in the community where she is born" [*George Eliot's Life as Related in Her Letters and Journals*, 1885]. Even in the central paradigms of Iphigenia and Mary, Eliot represents woman's tragic hereditary function as the sacrifice of the daughter either to preserve or to found a people. In the tradition of historical romance within which **The Spanish Gypsy** is written, such a function becomes concentrated in the notion of woman as the daughter of a race—Rebecca, "the daughter of Israel," or Leila, the "daughter of the great Hebrew race." Once the nineteenth-century concept of race became the medium through which Eliot would realize the

tragic circumstances of her own version of the Annunciation, fifteenth-century Spain seemed the inevitable choice for the "set of historical and local conditions" that would embody her idea: "My reflections brought me nothing that would serve me except that moment in Spanish history when the struggle with the Moors was attaining its climax, and when there was the gypsy race present under such conditions as would enable me to get my heroine and the hereditary claim on her among the gypsies. I required the opposition of race to give the need for renouncing the expectation of marriage" [*George Eliot's Life*]

In choosing fifteenth-century Spain, Eliot selected what had become for the nineteenth century a kind of historical laboratory in which experiments on the question of race could be performed. Moreover, her growing concern over national and racial injustices climaxed in her decision to record the Gypsies' historic plight and to represent through it, at least at one level, the persecution of more than one racial minority. As early as 1856, Eliot was praising Harriet Beecher Stowe for the invention of "the Negro novel" and was comparing Stowe with Scott in the use of "that grand element—conflict of races [*Essays of George Eliot*, 1963] So, in **The Spanish Gypsy,** the chief of the Gypsies encourages the other persecuted minorities of fifteenth-century Spain, "Whether of Moorish or of Hebrew blood, / Who, being galled by the hard Spaniard's yoke," to become allies of the Gypsies. He addresses the Moors and the Jews as "Our kindred by the warmth of Eastern blood" and thereby begins a series of oppositions that pit the "white Castilian" against "the dark men." When the Gypsy chief mocks the conversion of the Gypsies by taunting, "Take holy water, cross your dark skin white," Eliot alludes to both the historic Spanish missions to the Americas and the contemporary English missions to Africa and India.

At the center of Eliot's text is the question of the heroine's identity, or how she is to be named. Fedalma is raised a *Christian*, rumored to be a *Jew*, dressed as a *Moor* at one point, and claimed by the chief of the Zincali as a *Gypsy*. While Father Isidor, cast in the conventional role of the fanatical Dominican Inquisitor, contemplates Fedalma's torture and death, Zarca, the chief of the Zincali, arrives to save her from the Inquisition. Zarca explains to Fedalma that he is her father and that she was stolen from him by a band of Spaniards when she was a young child. In requiring that she not marry Silva, her Spanish lover, the father asks his daughter to sacrifice herself in the name of the father, or the name of race, and thereby to exchange her individual identity for a corporate identity: "Fedalma dies / In leaving Silva: all that lives henceforth / Is the poor Zincala," the Spanish Gypsy of the title. This is the moment of the daughter's obedience. Zarca explains that as the sole offspring of her widowed father, she is the "Chief woman of her tribe" and that after his death she will be the tribe's leader. In prohibiting the marriage with Silva, the father offers the daughter a different kind of marriage, and Fedalma accepts: "I will wed / The curse that blights my people," and "Father, now I go / To wed my people's lot." The conventional marriage plot is reconfigured here as the means by which the daughter serves her father as the bride of his people. Intermarriage with the racial other is canceled in a figure: marriage with the entire body of one's own race.

With the death of the father, the text ends with the daughter's journey to Africa in an attempt to realize his plans to establish his people's national identity. Fedalma's journey is represented as the kind of exile we associate with Scott's Rebecca—an exile based in the sacrifice of the erotic. Moreover, Eliot makes clear the hopelessness of Fedalma's political ambitions. With the death of her father, "the tribe / That was to be the ensign of the race, . . . would still disperse / And propagate forgetfulness," in a diaspora in which Fedalma's relinquishment of marriage and childbirth turns into a bitterly ironic form of propagation, the engendering not of ancestral continuity but of forgetfulness. Fedalma's procreative function is reinvented through a tragic pun: "I am but as the funeral urn that bears the ashes of a leader." The daughter's body becomes no more than a kind of grave for the memorialization of the dead father.

But this kind of tragic irony does not finally displace the central ideology of the text, voiced in the father's scathing denunciation of intermarriage and conversion:

> Such love is common: I have seen it oft—
> Seen many women rend the sacred ties
> That bind them in high fellowship with men,
> Making them mothers of a people's virtue:
> Seen them so levelled to a handsome steed
> That yesterday was Moorish property,
> To-day is Christian—wears new-fashioned gear,
> Neighs to new feeders, and will prance alike
> Under all banners, so the banner be
> A master's who caresses. Such light change
> You call conversion; but we Zincali call
> Conversion infamy.

In recording the procedures by which women of a minority race or religion are absorbed by the men of the more powerful group, Zarca adds conversion to the crimes of rapine and murder by which the systematic genocide of a people proceeds. And Eliot, however she might sympathize with the tragic loss and suffering of her title character, upholds the paternal critique of conversion.

Eliot uses the specific example of the "hurry to convert the Jews" in fifteenth-century Spain to ground historically what often appears to be her text's exaggerated horror of apostasy. While the main characters of *The Spanish Gypsy* are Catholics (Silva and Isidor) and Gypsies (Fedalma and Zarca), it is in her depiction of a converted Jew (Lorenzo) and a practicing Jew (Sephardo) that she attempts to provide the historical basis for her study of conversion. Even the portrait of her Gypsy heroine takes as its model the more well-known example of the converted Jewish woman; while Silva points to Fedalma's baptism, Father Isidor protests: "Ay, as a thousand Jewesses, who yet / Are brides of Satan." But Eliot fails to represent the historical complexities of the issue of conversion in Spain. Instead, she is quick to make an example of the Jews to advance her argument against conversion. This results in making the converted Jew no more than the kind of opportunist Zarca warns Fedalma of becoming—the man or woman who would convert to "win / The prize of renegades":

> Thus baptism seemed to him [Lorenzo] a merry
>   game
> Not tried before, all sacraments a mode
> Of doing homage for one's property,
> And all religions a queer human whim
> Or else a vice, according to degrees.

Because Eliot focuses on the converted Jew who easily quits his Judaism to assume a new religion for self-advantage, as in the case of the "fathanded" Lorenzo, her Jewish convert never seems to be the product of the fierce religious intolerance and racism that periodically erupted in Spain, especially in the pogroms of 1391, when masses of Jews were converted on threat of death. Instead, her portrait of the converted Jew seems to function as an indictment of Jewish hypocrisy and opportunism.

This was the prevalent picture of the Jewish *conversos* in general, and the crypto-Jews in particular, throughout the nineteenth century, as Aguilar well knew: "The fact that the most Catholic kingdom of Spain was literally peopled with secret Jews brands this unhappy people with a degree of hypocrisy, in addition to the various other evil propensities with which they have been so plentifully charged. Nay, even amongst themselves in modern times this charge has gained ascendency." During the nineteenth century the growth of European nationalism and incipient Zionism had this effect on the historiography of the Spanish Jews: those who became martyrs for their religion and race were praised as heroes, while those who converted were vilified as cowardly opportunists and hypocrites. The Jewish historian Heinrich Graetz, an important spokesperson for Jewish rights and a major source of Eliot's knowledge of Jewish history [William Baker, *George Eliot and Judaism*, 1975], cast Spanish Jews in the opposing roles of martyrs versus cowards, those who "remained true to their faith" versus the "weaklings." Even in the midst of acknowledging the "violent assaults" suffered by the Jews, Graetz spoke of "the weak and lukewarm among them, the comfort-loving and worldly-minded, [who] succumbed to the temptation, and saved themselves by baptism" [Graetz, *History of the Jews,* 1891-98].

Eliot makes her most scathing critique of the converted Jew through the words of Sephardo, the Jew who takes his entire identity, including his name, from his Jewish ancestry and belief. Sephardo argues against Silva's universal humanism:

> . . . there's no such thing
> As naked manhood. . . .
> While my heart beats, it shall wear livery—
> My people's livery, whose yellow badge
> Marks them for Christian scorn. I will not say

Man is first man to me, then Jew or Gentile:
That suits the rich *marranos;* but to me
My father is first father, and then man.

. . . . .

Sephardo declares his desire to wear the garment of his race—no disguises, and no conversion, for him. But Sephardo's representation of the Marranos as opportunists who reject their fathers and their faith—"I am a Jew, and not that infamous life / That takes on bastardy, will know no father"—is historically inaccurate. In a note to Sephardo's speech, Eliot defines "Marrano" as a name for the converted Jew, but she does not designate by it the more specific meaning, the converted Jew who secretly practices Judaism—as represented, for example, in Aguilar's work, in which Marranism is shown as a way of honoring one's father—by handing down through the generations a faith that was threatened and eventually outlawed in Spain. Eliot's depiction of the converted Jew therefore is one-sided, neglecting both those *conversos* who converted out of genuine conviction, to worship devoutly and sincerely as Catholics, and those crypto-Jews who converted to Catholicism (sometimes on the threat of death) while secretly practicing Judaism.

This kind of flattening out of difference, this use of a single name to characterize a complicated and diverse population, was the means by which religious affiliation became overwritten in Spain by racial genealogy. I mean here that the creation of various *estatutos de limpieza de sangre* in the fifteenth century, prohibiting *conversos* from holding various offices and titles, in effect "reconverted" *all* New Christians to Jews, despite the fact that some were sincere Catholics and others were Marranos or crypto-Jews. All New Christians were suspected of relapsing into Judaism, and thereby all were conceived as members of a special race against which legislation was enacted. This meant that, on the basis of their Jewish ancestry, the New Christians could be prevented from assimilating into Spanish Catholic life and enjoying its privileges. In short, when those Christians who had Jewish ancestors, even as far back as several generations, began to reach the highest positions of power, in the Church, the military, and the government, the doctrine of blood was used to supersede the institution of conversion and to reinstate against *Christians*—of Jewish ancestry—the old laws against the Jews. "The Old Christians" were divided from "the New Christians," so that Christianity became based on family line and race, and a Christian's authenticity depended less on the sincerity of his religious convictions and practices than on how many Jewish ancestors, how many generations ago, "polluted" his blood. Father Isidor complains about Fedalma, "That maiden's blood / Is as unchristian as the leopard's"—despite her Christian education, and despite Silva's insistence that "Fedalma is a daughter of the Church—/ Has been baptized and nurtured in the faith."

The Spanish Gypsy does contain some version of this history, including, as part of the conventional English attack on the Catholic Inquisition, the odor of burning flesh, of "flames that, fed on heretics, still gape, / And must have heretics made to feed them still." But Eliot fails to make clear the conditions of crypto-Judaic life in the fifteenth century, including the dangers that crypto-Jews suffered to preserve their ancestral faith and heritage when the Inquisition made returning to the faith of Judaism virtually impossible. The Inquisition initially was aimed at those converted Jews who were suspected of secretly performing Judaic rituals; from 1485 until 1500, more than 99 percent of the cases that came before the Spanish Inquisition concerned converted Jews. The institution of the Inquisition crystallized the dilemma of the ideology of conversion by seeking to destroy what the missionary effort had produced. Eliot understood the historical reasons behind this system of destruction, including the economic ones, so that *The Spanish Gypsy* depicts characters callously arguing over whether a live Jew or "a well-burnt Jew" would most benefit the pocket of the Church's bishops or the nation's merchants. Indeed, she even recognizes that the term "Marrano" became a slur by which all *conversos* were stigmatized as Jews, and thereby she understands how sincere converts were libeled by the slanderous epithet "Jew": "The 'old Christians' learned to use the word [Marrano] as a term of contempt for the 'new Christians,' or converted Jews and their descendants; but not too monotonously, for they often interchanged it with the fine old crusted opprobrium of the name *Jew*." But such an apparently philo-Semitic view is part of a traditional argument that in effect did not sympathize with Jewish persecution but with sincere converts to Christianity who were stigmatized as Jews. In *The Spanish Gypsy,* then, we have a late development in the historiography of the Spanish Inquisition in England: an anti-Catholic attack that in fact includes the representation of the Jews under the Inquisition, but that understands the Jewish convert in an entirely unsympathetic light. *The Spanish Gypsy*'s horror of conversion (at least in part fueled by Eliot's knowledge of the consequences of Christian proselytism in fifteenth-century Spain) contributes to the anti-Semitic stereotype of the Jewish convert as hypocrite and opportunist, a figure reborn in the pages of Trollope's novels and in the anti-Semitic attack aimed at English converts like Disraeli.

FURTHER READING

Biography

Haight, Gordon S. *George Eliot: A Biography*. London: Clarendon Press, 1968, 616 p.
    Regarded by many as the definitive biography of Eliot.

May, J. Lewis. *George Eliot*. Indianapolis: The Bobbs-Merrill Company, 1930, 359 p.
    Early biography of Eliot which aims to revive interest in the author and her works.

Redinger, Ruby V. *George Eliot: The Emergent Self*. New York: Alfred A. Knopf, 1975, 540 p.

Approaches Eliot's life and work from a psychoanalytical point of view.

Criticism

Bloom, Harold, ed. *George Eliot*. New York: Chelsea House Publishers, 1986, 260 p.
  Collection of essays on Eliot's novels by well-known critics such as F. R. Leavis, Dorothy Van Ghent, Barbara Hardy, and J. Hillis Miller.

Ermarth, Elizabeth Deeds. *George Eliot*. Boston: Twayne Publishers, 1985, 163 p.
  Brief overview of Eliot's life, followed by analyses of the themes and aesthetics which dominate her work, particularly her novels.

Godwin, Gail. "Would We Have Heard of Marian Evans?" *Ms.* 3, No. 3 (September 1974): 72-5.
  Examines the characters in George Eliot's novels in relation to the author's own life, gender, and physical appearance.

Haight, Gordon S., ed. *The George Eliot Letters: Volume VIII: 1840-1870*. New Haven, Conn.: Yale University Press, 1978.

Includes a letter from Anthony Trollope to Eliot's companion, George Henry Lewes, critiquing Eliot's *The Spanish Gypsy*.

Holmstrom, John, and Lerner, Laurence, eds. *George Eliot and Her Readers*. New York: Barnes and Noble, 1966, 190 p.
  Anthology of contemporary reviews, mainly of Eliot's novels; meant to demonstrate the opinions of Eliot's readers during her lifetime.

Pangallo, Karen L., ed. *The Critical Response To George Eliot*. Westport, Conn.: Greenwood Press, 1994, 233 p.
  Provides a representative selection of essays on and reviews of Eliot's novels.

Speirs, John. "Poetry into Novel." In his *Poetry towards Novel*, pp. 283-333. London: Faber and Faber, 1971.
  Argues that there is a strong relationship between Eliot's novels and the works of poets such as Shakespeare.

Wade, Rosalind. "George Eliot and Her Poetry." *Contemporary Review* 204 (July 1963): 38-42.
  Briefly examines the concern with human emotions revealed in Eliot's poetry.

Additional coverage of Eliot's life and career is contained in the following sources published by Gale Research: *Nineteenth-Century Literature Criticism*, **Vols. 4, 13, 23, 41, 49;** *DISCovering Authors*; *World Literature Criticism*; *Dictionary of Literary Biography*, **Vols. 21, 35, 55; and** *Concise Dictionary of British Literary Biography*..

Fernando (António Nogueira) Pessoa
1888-1935

(Also wrote under the heteronyms of Alberto Caeiro, Ricardo Reis, Alvaro de Campos, Alexander Search, Bernardo Soares, Baron de Teive and others) Portuguese poet, essayist, and critic.

INTRODUCTION

Pessoa, considered to be the greatest Portuguese poet of the twentieth century and, indeed, the greatest since Vas de Camões in the sixteenth-century, holds a prominent position in twentieth-century literature. His works are felt to epitomize the themes and techniques of modernism, and his experimental approach to poetic composition explores the questions—psychological, philosophical and spiritual—that define the modern age. Pessoa created a set of literary alter egos called "heteronyms," which allowed him to explore many disparate aspects of human nature without the limitations of a single literary persona.

Biographical Information

Pessoa was born into an artistic, cultured family in Lisbon, Portugal on June 13, 1888. His father, a music critic, died when Pessoa was five years old. In the following year, his mother married the Portuguese consul to South Africa and moved the family to Durban, where Pessoa spent the remainder of his youth. In South Africa, Pessoa attended an English secondary school where he excelled in languages, and became proficient in English. Young Pessoa was an admirer of Shakespeare, and, by the age of fifteen, was composing sonnets in English. These sonnets were later collected and published as *35 Sonnets* (1918). Pessoa returned to Portugal in 1905 and enrolled at the University of Lisbon only to leave the school after just one year. His fluent English was a desirable skill and he soon found himself a position as a business correspondent for Portuguese commercial firms, an occupation that was to last his entire life. Although he continued to write poetry, it was not until 1912 that he began to compose poems in Portuguese. Around that time he also became associated with poets of the nationalistic *saudosismo* movement, which celebrated a romanticized Portuguese past. By 1915 Pessoa was well known in the cultural circles of Lisbon, having established himself as a poet and critic well in tune with the modernist movements that flourished in Europe during the first decades of the twentieth century. He was also one of the founders of *Orpheu* and *Presença,* the most influential journals of modern Portuguese literature. For a brief time he also edited his own journal, *Athena,* where many of his poems and essays were first published. He died in November 1935 in Lisbon, Portugal after long suffering from alcoholism. At the time of his death, his work was not widely known outside of Portu-

gal, as it was not collected or published in books until after his death. His reputation has grown posthumously through the publication of many collections of poetry and by a number of English translations which made his work available to a much wider audience than during his lifetime.

Major Works

As Pessoa was not known in literary circles outside of Portugal until after his death, there was no critical or scholarly attention given to his work prior to the posthumous publication of collections and translations. In the early part of his career, after his return to Portugal from South Africa in 1905, Pessoa wrote English sonnets, using the pseudonym Alexander Search. It was not until around 1912 that he began writing in Portuguese; he became politically active and involved with the *saudosismo* movement and, by 1915 had produced a considerable body of work in Portuguese. During his lifetime, he published several volumes of his English poems: *35 Sonnets* (1918), *Antinous* (1918), *English Poems (I, II and III)* (1921). He also published one volume of Portuguese poems, *Mensagem* (1934), which is considered his greatest work. *Mensagem* is composed of a sequence of poems on the history of Portugal, and created controversy in that it is possible to interpret it as a "nationalist" work in which Pessoa apologizes for the authoritarian regime that had come to power in 1926. Since his death, numerous volumes of his poetry have been published, and his poetry has been translated into several languages. Among these posthumous editions are *Poemas de F. P.* (1942), *Fernando Pessoa: Selected Poems* (1974), and *Poems of Fernando Pessoa* (1987). The poems themselves are not his only successful poetic creations. Among the most remarkable of Pessoa's poetic achievements are those alter-egos, or "heteronyms," that he created to be the authors of much of his poetry. Distinct from pen-names, or "pseudonyms," these do not simply disguise the author, Pessoa argued, but replace the author, allowing the author to affect a completely different persona.

Critical Reception

The history of twentieth-century literature, and modernist poetry in particular, would not be complete without Fernando Pessoa. Critics often speak of Pessoa in the same breath as such modernist legends as T. S. Eliot, Ezra Pound and Rainer Maria Rilke. Because of his invention and frequent use of "heteronyms" in his poetry however, Pessoa stands out as an idiosyncratic figure in twentieth-century letters. Critics have analyzed Pessoa's three most frequently used heteronyms and agree that each has a distinctive personality and distinguishing literary characteristics. The first heteronym, Alberto Caeiro, wrote in free verse and expressed the philosophic views of a pagan materialist. This author-persona disavowed any sense of the supernatural, and in "Guardador de Rebanhos" ("The Shepherd") maintains that the senses are the only certain sources of knowledge. Another heteronym, Ricardo Reis, acknowledges Caeiro as a mentor and expands upon the view that sensory experience is the only true knowledge. Reis writes in a fatalistic, world-weary manner and employs fixed forms. A third philosophical stance is explored by the Alvaro de Campos heteronym, which, of all of Pessoa's heteronyms, most embodies the modernist philosophy. Campos' poems display the opposing desires to have both everything and nothing, and comment on the elusive nature of identity.

Pessoa's canonical status, however, is not surprising when one considers the implications of this ostensibly bizarre poetic accomplishment. His use of heteronyms constitutes an intense examination of identity and how individuals come to develop identities, a concern not only of Pessoa's contemporaries but of modern critics, as well. The poet whose conventional English sonnets critics have hailed as expert imitations of Shakespeare went on to become a poet who sought to undermine conventional notions of authorship. By creating so many personae of authorship, Pessoa forced his contemporaries, and forces his readers today, to question the stability of identity, not only of the author, but of all individuals. Many critics have remarked on the irony of the fact that Pessoa's name means "person" in Portuguese and is derived from the Latin "persona," appropriate for a poet who had so many personae.

PRINCIPAL WORKS

Poetry

Antinous 1918
35 Sonnets 1918
English Poems. 3 vols. 1921
Mensagem 1934
Poemas de F. P. 1942
Poemas de Álvaro de Campos 1944
Poemas de Alberto Caeiro 1946
Poemas de Ricardo Reis 1946
Poemas dramáticos I 1952
Poesias inéditas: 1930-35 1955
Poesias inéditas: 1919-30 1956
F.P.: Antologia (edited by Octavio Paz) 1962
Selected Poems 1971
Sixty Portuguese Poems 1971
Fernando Pessoa: Selected Poems 1974
Poems of Fernando Pessoa (translated by Edwin Honig and Susan M. Brown) 1987

Other Major Works

Faust (unfinished drama) 1906-1935
The Mariner (drama) 1914
Obras completas de Fernando Pessoa 11 Vols. (criti-

cism, poetry and essays) [still in progress] 1942
Páginas de doutrina estética [Pages on Aesthetic Doctrine; edited by J. de Sena] (criticism and essays) 1946
Always Astonished: Selected Prose (prose) 1988

CRITICISM

Jane M. Sheets (essay date 1969)

SOURCE: "Fernando Pessoa as Anti-Poet: Alberto Caeiro," in *Bulletin of Hispanic Studies,* Vol. XLVI, No. 1, January 1969, pp. 39-47.

[*In this excerpt, Sheets discusses Pessoa's Alberto Caeiro heteronym, and relates his poetic aesthetic to Zen Buddhism, existentialism, and that of French writer Alain Robbe-Grillet.*]

If one accepts poetry in the traditional sense, as a way of looking at things, not directly, but following the poet's eye, if one thus accepts the poet as a perceptive *interpreter* of his surroundings, then the intention of Alberto Caeiro, Fernando Pessoa's first heteronym, is distinctly antipoetical. . . .

In the 1935 letter to Casais Monteiro in which he discusses the genesis of the heteronyms, Pessoa describes his conscious attempts, early in March, 1914, to create a pastoral poet; when at last he gave up, lacking inspiration, he was suddenly compelled to go to his desk, where he took out paper and began to write. Without stopping, he produced, on the 8th of March, more than thirty poems, all assigned to Alberto Caeiro. The poems were written in a kind of 'indefinable ecstasy . . .'—. . . . From the very beginning, Pessoa was certain not only that the moment itself was supreme and sublime, but also that the poems were superior to any of his own to that time and would perhaps even surpass any subsequent work. . . .

Immediately after this burst of inspiration, Pessoa took another paper and wrote six poems, **"Chuva Oblíqua"**, signed with his own name. These are 'poemas interseccionistas', characteristic in mood and content of what had been up to then a main stream in Pessoa's work: they are vague, subtle, complex, with intersecting images within a static framework. Their appearance marked a return from Fernando Pessoa Alberto Caeiro to, simply, Fernando Pessoa. . . .

The three parts of Caeiro's work vary slightly in their point of view. In the first group of poems, **"O Guardador de Rebanhos,"** Caeiro's gentle, but increasingly persistent, message about Nature is that it has no interior, that it is parts without a whole, that there is, in fact, no Nature: there are only mountains, flowers, rivers and stones, and Caeiro's self-appointed task is to bring these objects to the reader's attention, as directly and simply as possible, without the use of metaphor or other poetic devices. . . .

The six poems of **"O Pastor Amoroso"** represent a second, but very brief, phase in Caeiro's thought. The once-solitary shepherd is still in touch with Nature, but he is also in love. The sense of sight, once so essential, gives way to feelings. There is no longer a looking outward, but 'Toda a realidade olha para mim como um girassol com a cara dela no meio'. The most obvious change in attitude is the willing reversion to thought. In **"Keeper of the Flocks"** thinking was scorned, but now, very simply: 'Amar é pensar' and 'Quero só / Pensar nela'.

In the third and last section, 'Poemas Inconjuntos', the theme, once again, is *seeing,* a direct experience of objects, but there are now other concerns: disappointment in love ('Sentir é estar distraido'), the acknowledgment and acceptance of all things in the world, including injustices, an absolute focus on the present, on one's being and, as he contemplates death, a self-portrayal: 'Sou fácil de definir / Vi como um danado'. Although Caeiro's perspective shifts slightly, his original purpose remains: to confront objects *as they are,* without thought or analysis, to acknowledge *Dinge-an-sich* without attempting to generalize or to compare and, above all, to make no attempt to create or to invent reciprocal relationships between man and nature. Feelings are acknowledged, but are unexplored: 'Eu não tenho filosofia, tenho sentidos'.

Caeiro's point of view is frequently labelled 'anti': he has been called 'anti-intellectual' [Moisés Massaud, 1962], 'anti-Romantic' [Adolpho Casais Monteiro, 1958], 'Anti-subjektivist' [Bruno Linnartz, 1966], 'anti-metaphysical' [Jacinto do Prado Coelho, 1963], even an 'anti-metaphysical philosopher' [*Dizionario Letterario Bompiani,* III, 1957]. Other critics suggest that Caeiro's claim to objectivity is cancelled by the very formulation of his impressions. Still another common thread in the criticism is that the poet and his works, because of their surfeit of clarity, seem to belong to other periods in literary time: Pessoa is 'half-Greek, half-Bedouin', a 'modern classicist', his poems 'lack Atlantic softness'. Two suggestions of this kind will be taken up here: Adolpho Casais Monteiro's belief that Caeiro's technique is related to that of Robbe-Grillet, and Thomas Merton's observation on the Zen-like quality of certain of Caeiro's experiences. Both approaches reveal much more of Pessoa-Caeiro's literary precocity and, more important, his spontaneous assumption of a universal way of seeing, than do evaluations based solely on Western and often conceptual terms. By looking in detail at Caeiro's works in these seemingly disparate and remote contexts, accepting Pessoa's assertion that Caeiro is the most sincere, the master of the other heteronyms and himself ('. . . se há parte da minha obra que tenha um cunho de sinceridade essa parte é . . . a obra de Caeiro') [*Cartas a Armando Côrtes-Rodrigues,* 1945], the idea of Fernando Pessoa Alberto Caeiro as anti-poet, but as purposive anti-poet, as a strengthening opposition and a necessary part of a foundation for subsequent poems, is reinforced.

Casais Monteiro, in two short articles, compares Caeiro's attitudes to those found in Robbe-Grillet's essay, 'Nature, humanisme, tragédie', published in 1958. Both writers, he explains, believe the sense of sight is pre-eminent and they share the conviction that things have no interior, so that there is no need for the eye to explore beneath the surface of objects. They reject metaphor as false and artificial complicity and share a direct acknowledgement of the independence of Nature and its obliviousness of man.

Rejection of the interiority of things, denial of metaphysics and of an anthropocentric world—all are explicit attitudes of Caeiro. . . .

Casais Monteiro, like other critics, believes that Caeiro's poems are a reaction to the sentimentality and preciosity of the poetry of his time, but he proposes no answer to why they appear at first glance to be so closely related to an aesthetics which was elaborated half a century after his poems were written. He suggests a study of the coincidence from the point of view of phenomenology and existentialism, but offers only one collective and unsatisfactory term: Robbe-Grillet and Caeiro are materialists, or at least anti-spiritualists.

In Robbe-Grillet's other essays, in 'Une voie pour le roman futur', 'Temps et description dans le récit d'aujourd'hui', and in 'Du réalisme à la réalité' [*Pour un nouveau roman,* 1963] one finds further correlations, particularly concerning the kind of language which characterizes a literature consisting of presences, of objects; that is, words of a visceral, analogical or incantatory character, 'vertical' or 'deep' words, are replaced by visual or descriptive adjectives, words which measure, locate, limit, define. Caeiro's poems, written with simple vocabulary and syntax, consist of this kind of language, and take the same matter-of-fact approach to objects. . . .

Movement becomes crucial for both writers in this environment of objects. Yet by shifting merely from one object to another, from one isolated part of a scene to another, time itself assumes a new role: it can no longer complete anything, reveal any destinies, or lead to any conclusions. One is aware not so much of time passing as of change which occurs *within the present.* No past is created, no headway made, there is no evolution, only 'travelling'.

The fifth poem of 'Poemas Inconjuntos' illustrates the dilemma: as Caeiro begins to consider the meaning of the terms 'Truth, lie, certainty, uncertainty', flirting, one might say, with signification, a blind man appears in the street. The poet crosses his legs. He folds his hands over his upper knee. The consideration begins again. . . . The blind man stops, the poet unfolds his hands and repeats the words once more. A new awareness intervenes: some part of reality is changing, he says. . . .

Even though Caeiro makes a conscious effort to focus on words which evoke comparisons and trains of thought, on concepts, what he sees and what he does, simple actions and gestures, alone fill his consciousness. For him, existence and reality consist here of a limited scene, slight changes of the scene and an awareness of this change. If there are to be any configurations or patterns, they must be established by the reader himself, in his own mind.

He, the reader, is presented only with a description, with the *sight,* not a *vision,* of limited surroundings; any profound or transcendent signification occurs not within the work, but outside it.

When Robbe-Grillet insists on equating surfaces with the whole, he is attempting to resolve, to 'melt down', as he says, pairs of contraries—to rid his work specifically of the dualism which opposes interior to exterior. Robbe-Grillet's experiments with form have therefore a supporting philosophical context; he works within a developing framework of ideas, and he writes, moreover, on a conscious, intellectual, nearly clinical level. But how can one account for Caeiro's similar approach, developed fifty years earlier, especially recalling the way in which his poems were written, spontaneously, unconsciously and with almost frightening suddenness?

The existential awareness shared by Robbe-Grillet and Pessoa as Caeiro can be attributed in part to *Angst,* a condition associated with the world of Robbe-Grillet's era, while Pessoa's personal version is explained in his essays. And although this condition causes them to share certain qualities—both are anti-metaphysical, anti-poetic, and both focus at least initially on particular objects in their environment, naming and describing—their continuing stance in relation to the objects they confront is unlike.

From the beginning, Robbe-Grillet is reserved and aloof, and remains so, while Caeiro's glance is more receptive, his descriptions generic rather than exact. The issue is one of personal mobility, even daring, and Caeiro, who surprises and momentarily outreaches his author, who assumes a mood and posture which is awesome to Pessoa even without being identified, and from which he withdraws almost immediately, fits only briefly into Robbe-Grillet's delimited atmosphere of theory and measured clarity, and then moves on. Especially in his late poems, Caeiro still sees clearly, but also *savours* things, moves irresistibly towards them, imbibes them. Poetic tools and concepts such as beauty and Nature are still rejected, but his apprehension by means of sight deepens and intensifies.

Contemporary theory, then, relates only to part of Caeiro's production; Octavio Paz suggests in fact that Caeiro's reality goes *back* in time, to the epoch before language begins, when innocent poets were first applying names to things, before words and things were made separate: 'Caeiro es una afirmación absoluta del existir y de ahí que sus palabras nos parezcan verdades de otro tiempo, ese tiempo en el que todo era uno y lo mismo' [*Antologia,* 1962]. This general assignement of an ancientcontext is made specific by Thomas Merton, who suggests that Caeiro's 'way of seeing', his mode of apprehension, is akin to that of Zen Buddhists [Thomas Merton, introduction to "Twelve Poems," 1966]. The denial of metaphysics or any intellectual or poetic role, the insistence on resolving contraries, but especially his 'knack of full awareness', which takes Caeiro a step beyond description and movement among objects, and which finally distin-

guishes his work from Robbe-Grillet's theory—these also are Zen attitudes.

To move with Caeiro from Robbe-Grillet's essays to Zen Buddhism is not as unsettling or incongruous as it might seem, especially if one accepts Merton's definition of Zen as 'an Asian form of religious existentialism', [Thomas Merton, *Mystics and Zen Masters*, 1967] as 'philosophic monism', and if one considers the Zenists' aim: 'ultimate emancipation from duality', by means of 'direct and immediate contact with light and reality in their existential source'. The Zen insight is a direct grasp of being *in itself,* not an intuition of the nature of being.

Caeiro's gaze, 'clear as a sunflower's', is the initial step in the real, spiritual instruction in Zen: purification of the powers of vision. The viewer is required to perceive objects in all their sensuous fullness; one is immersed in the contents of perception, for Caeiro objects in Nature, until they are known by heart and can be called to mind in their maximum clarity [Eugen Herrigel, "The Method of Zen," 1964]. . . .

Then, when that is fully mastered, one aims at intensification.

And when he drops in the grass and closes his eyes, Caeiro's physical contact with Nature is complete; he experiences reality and truth. . . .

Caeiro thus apprehends with a *kind* of primal vision, with heightened awareness; he achieves 'o pasmo essencial . . . que tem uma criança . . . ao nascer' which Thomas Merton translates as 'the knack of full awareness', a stage along the Zen way of seeing.

But although Caeiro is persistent in presenting objects as they are, in striving for an unmediated relation to reality, at the point at which Zen goes beyond reason, becomes superconscious, Caeiro is still conscious in a worldly way, and insists on remaining so; he is reluctant, it seems, to yield completely to his senses and seeks distractions, drawing comparisons between artifacts and Nature, falling in love in the few poems of 'O Pastor Amoroso', and experimenting with yet another way of seeing. Almost immediately, in fact, Pessoa-Caeiro is pulled back to the immediate world of Fernando Pessoa, who shared at that time the more rational ambiance and inclinations of his literary colleagues.

This 'note of self-conscious and programmatic insistence', as Merton calls it, was dramatically displaced by a poem written in 1917, in which one senses, as in no other experience Caeiro relates, a complete identification and oneness with life. There had been, in the poems of 1914, lines in which Caeiro moved beyond description and seemed to stand on the threshold of pure realization, describing 'days of perfect and exact light, days in which objects were saturated with reality', but in the later work the theme of reality is explored in fifty-three lines, a long poem for Caeiro.

Not the reality of the world, but that of the self is questioned: 'Ser real quer dizer não estar dentro de mim'. My body and the world are more typical of reality than my soul, and 'item for item', 'coisa por coisa, o Mundo é mais certo'. . . .

However cautious one must be in interpreting extrasensory or supersensory states of mind, depending always on written description, which is again nearly always prefaced by an apology for its inadequacy, nevertheless the experience *does* coincide with descriptions of Zen enlightenment: not self-realization, not possession by the ego, but realization pure and simple; no movement from lower to higher worlds, as often occurs in Western mysticism; not, in fact, a mystical experience nor a withdrawal from the world, but a unity with it, in which the subject-object relationship is abolished and material realities become simply irrelevant; not a looking inward but a direct grasp of being in itself.

The range of this poem—the world, the universe—surpasses by far Caeiro's usual terrain, and each adjective contributes to the idea of selflessness and affirmation . . . Caeiro's apprehension of the universe is complete and 'sublime', but he is also fully alert, superconscious rather than unconscious; Caeiro 'sees' with 'perfect natural lucidity' because he is suffused with an awareness of being.

Like Robbe-Grillet, Caeiro insists on the monism of phenomena and creates literature which consists of what he *sees,* describing with exactness and great clarity; but he also participated, if only briefly, with his own being in the harmony of a universe consisting of material realities, a position which Robbe-Grillet would find untenable, unnecessary, perhaps absurd, even frightening.

Caeiro emerged out of Pessoa's semi-conscious compulsion to experiment and to escape the currents of contemporary literary movements. By creating Caeiro, a forceful, if somewhat over-insistent, representative of yet another programme, anti-interpretation, Pessoa succeeded in renewing and expanding his awarenesses far beyond his expectations; his original intention, after all, was simply to create a pastoral poet.

Pessoa had studied Rosicrucianism, theosophy and other forms of the occult, yet when authentic inspiration came, it was not due to, or like, those esoteric rites, but resembled instead the form of Buddhism which is both positive and practical. This spontaneous shedding of mystical philosophies and simultaneous release on two levels from the ego (the pseudonym eventually suppresses his own fictitious ego) revealed a new and pure plane of Pessoa's personality. . . .

By means of this artless yet affirmative anti-poet, Caeiro, a short-lived but vital member of his coterie, Pessoa acquired the base of an experienced and universal poetic vision. After Caeiro's tenets had been established, the avowedly poetic voices of Campos, Reis and Pessoa himself spoke with greater assurance.

Geoffrey R. Barrow (essay date 1976)

SOURCE: "The Personal Lyric Disguised: Fernando Pessoa's *Mensagem,*" in *Luso-Brasilian Review,* Summer, 1976, pp. 90-9.

[*In the following excerpt, Barrow examines the dramatic and lyric elements of* Mensagem, *considered to be Pessoa's most significant work.*]

The author of **Mensagem** was preoccupied with the future of Portugal and conscious of her spiritual and historical past. In a spirit of messianism he associated himself in 1912 with the movement *Renascença Portuguesa* and wrote an essay concerning "A Nova Poesia Portuguesa Sociològicamente Considerada" for *A Águia,* the principal organ of this movement. Eight years later, the assassination of Sidónio Paes, the President of Portugal, was the subject of a long ode by the poet, **"À Memória do President Rei Sidónio Paes."** In this poem the late President is identified with King Sebastian and his return is expected at some future date. It is not, however, the political present which attracts the attention of the poet. . . .

There can be no illusions about the political capacity of Pessoa: he was a poet, and it was as a poet that he expressed himself when he approached even the most concrete subjects.

More perceptive critics of Pessoa do not consider **Mensagem** to be public poetry, that is, poetry directed at the world of practical politics or poetry in which the poet consciously makes his voice that of his age . . . [Octavio Paz] implies that the individual poems are linked by a certain principle of presentation yet are not inherently related to one another, and because [he] insists that **Mensagem** treats history creatively in the manner of the poet. The first observation, however, poses the question of how we should classify **Mensagem,** for while it is true that the work is a combination of lyric and epic elements, it is no less true that certain parts of the poem are akin to drama.

As those critics who would call **Mensagem** an epic themselves point out, the subject matter of the poem forms the basis of their generic distinction. The work concerns itself with the history of Portugal, a history with an epic potentiality. Yet **Mensagem** lacks the continuous narrative usually associated with the epic, maintains a peculiarly personal view of Portuguese history and is as much concerned with what is to come as with the past. Considered in its entirety **Mensagem** is not an epic poem, although it must be admitted that in certain individual poems there is some attempt to preserve that convention of recitation which is perhaps the distinguishing feature of epic poetry.

In a note upon the poetic technique of the heteronyms, Pessoa examines the distinction between what for him are the two most important generic terms, the lyric and the dramatic. He establishes a gradual progression from the one to the other based upon the increasing distance placed between the poet and his persona. According to Pessoa, the salient feature of dramatic poetry is the objectivity afforded the poet. He fails to make his case clearly, however, because he does not emphasize adequately the distinction between dramatic poetry and drama. . . . .

In this respect the technique of **Mensagem** is somewhat similar to that of the heteronyms. Both in **Mensagem** and in the poetry of Caeiro, Reis and Campos, the poet attempts to lend his literary production a certain degree of objectivity. Admittedly, there is hardly any attempt to conceal himself in such poems as **"'Screvo meu livro à beira-mágoa . . ."** but certainly in Part I of **Mensagem,** and even in the majority of the poems in Part II, Pessoa places a good distance between himself and the persona, or speaker of the poem. If we pursue the comparison between **Mensagem** and the heteronyms a little further we discover that in certain poems of **Mensagem,** especially those in **As Quinas,** the third section of Part I, there is an effort on the part of the poet both to achieve the highest degree of distantiation between himself and his personae and at the same time to express himself with the highest degree of lyrical freedom. Here, as in the poetry of the heteronyms, the poem becomes a mask behind which Pessoa can conceal himself yet through which he can express himself freely.

While it is arguable that with regard to the heteronyms Pessoa completely disassociates himself from the persona of his lyric poems, the persona becomes increasingly identifiable with the poet himself as **Mensagem** progresses. There is, in effect, a distinctive tone in each part of the work, suggesting that the closer we are to the awaited, prophesied moment, the more intimately lyric Pessoa becomes. The poems based upon the heraldic symbols of the Portuguese shield in Part I, for example, are predominantly explanatory, signpost poems which guide the reader along the prophetic road. The poems in Part II are more descriptive and show the incomplete nature of the maritime conquests of Portugal. The lyric tone of **"Prece,"** however, does anticipate the more emphatically vatic and strongly lyric tone of the poems in Part III. In fact, if we distinguish between explanatory-historic and lyric-prophetic poems in **Mensagem** we discover that the rather depersonalized, explanatory-historic poem becomes less frequent while the more personal lyric-prophetic poem becomes more so as we approach the end of the work.

In Part I, Pessoa establishes firmly and immediately his criteria for progress. Were he not to do this it is quite possible that the reader would confuse history and poetry, not perceive exactly the message of the work, and not fully appreciate its fictional validity. The explanatory-signpost poem aids the poet although it must be stressed that he avoids sounding didactic and programmatic.

The opening poem of **Mensagem, "O dos Castelos,"** though informing us that the West is where the future lies, is for the most part descriptive, whereas the following poem **"O das Quinas"** broaches the central preoccupation of Pessoa, progress and its human cost, in a rather sententious tone. . . . .

In *Os Castelos*, the importance of myth, the need for man to be conscious of his mythic heritage and the need for intervention of an external authority if myth and reality are to be united is explained poetically. Pessoa addresses or discusses historical characters and the tone is aphoristic. . . .

There is, of course, a potential lyricism in the imprecations of several of the poems of *Os Castelos* and in the five brief autobiographical accounts of *As Quinas.* Nevertheless, the poem which explains and presents Pessoa's vision of history to his reader predominates in Part I. The poet is declaring the rudimentary assumption upon which his vision is based: progress depends upon a significant amalgam of myth and life.

In Part II Pessoa does not attempt to explain his vision of history but describes a particular set of events: Portuguese expansion in the fourteenth and fifteenth centuries. Rather than interpreting these events for his audience, Pessoa assumes they will be assimilated and interpreted according to the principal formulated in Part I. Some indication of how this is carried out emerges when **"Epitáfiode B. Dias,"** **"Fernão de Magalães"** and **"Ascensão de Vasco da Gama"** are examined. The death of an important character in the maritime expansion of Portugal is the subject of each of the three poems, but in each it is dealt with in a different manner. The first poem is a brief epitaph which opens with the traditional "Here lies," then identifies the occupant of the grave symbolically as Atlas and concisely extols his maritime achievements. **"Fernão de Magalhães"** is longer and describes the demonic dance which occurs after the mariner's death. Myth and reality fuse momentarily when he dies and the Titans celebrate the event by dancing. A visual account of a similar fusion which occurs on the death of Vasco da Gama is given in **"Ascensão de Vasco da Gama."** Here the "Deuses da tormenta e os gigantes da terra" suspend their hostility while the soul of the Argonaut ascends to heaven.

Each of the three poems gives an example of that brief moment of union between myth and reality which signifies progress. Atlas, the Titans and the "Deuses da tormenta e os gigantes da terra" represent myth, whereas Dias, Magalhães and Gama represent reality. The Poems corroborate the conception of progress which was suggested in Part I and, in particular, in **"Ulisses,"** which recalls the legend of the foundation of Lisbon to emphasize the importance of a fruitful union of myth with life.

Of the twelve poems which form Part II, the first nine present and describe Pessoa's vision of the maritime conquests of Portugal. They chronicle events as in **"O Infante"**. . . describe the voyages of discovery symbolically as a struggle between opposing forces in **"O Mostrengo"**; and reveal the paradise given to the mariners in **"Horizonte."** The tone of these first nine poems is, on occasion, sententious. . . but Pessoa is far less explanatory or prescriptive, as it were, in Part II than in Part I. Moreover, not only does a more recognizably lyric-prophetic strain appear in the last three poems of Part II but **"Prece"** anticipates the dominant prophetic tone of the final part.

If what we have called the explanatory-historic poem is less apparent in Part II, by Part III it has disappeared. Instead we find a note of urging which through incantation seeks to hasten the promised fulfillment. This part is the prophetic experience toward which the whole work has tended, and Pessoa expresses himself with very little aspiration to *despersonalização* in such poems as "**Screvo meu livro a beira-mágoa. . . .**"

Comparisons between the lyric personae of *Mensagem* often become identifications, since distinctions between them whether they are historical or contemporary, are not important. The vacuity of this world in comparison with the plenitude which is to come is as tedious for Pessoa as it was for his historical predecessors in similar circumstances. Both bewail their present existence and implore aid. When the poet probes the human core within historical events, chronological differences become unimportant. As Dr. Rickard has recently observed, "Pessoa's heroes personify the spirit of sacrifice and the sense of a spiritual mission to be fulfilled. Though dissatisfaction, not triumph, is their fate, the poet implies that their restless, questing spirit is as necessary in the twentieth century as it ever was" [*Selected Poems*, 1971]. The tentative nature of human experience will remain unchanged, except for some initiated Portuguese Mariners, until the eventuation of Pessoa's message.

The five historical characters who appear in *As Quinas* exemplify a blind, meaningless existence. Duty is but an end in itself . . . in a world in which man is not assured a just reward for his efforts. He can desire only in order to be given, at the caprice of fate, either. . . In Part II, the grief as well as the grandeur of the Portuguese maritime empire is revealed. . . While even the hopeful, visionary Part III briefly points to the frustration of the present. . . This sentiment of the tedious and tentative nature of existence diminishes as *Mensagem* progresses, while more intense lyric expression is given to appeals for relief and support. In Part I the persona adopts the tone of a suppliant appealing to an intercessor for succour. . . In Part II these demands attain a more passionate note in "**Prece,**" where the persona beseeches his Lord. . . This liturgical entreaty, so to speak, achieves its highest lyric expression in Part III. The messianic language of "**O Desejado**". . . echoes the poet's own sacerdotal voice in "**Screvo meu libro a beira-mágoa . . . .**"

The development of these two strains of lyricism in *Mensagem,* one displaying impatience and anxiety, the other imploring aid, underlines the prophetic structure of the work. As the envisioned moment approaches, tedium diminishes while imprecation increases. When the ultimate fulfillment is at hand the personae do not lament; they pray that it will come about.

In Part I and Part II Pessoa formulates the premises upon which his prophecy is based and assures us that his message has foundation in historical fact. The explanatory-historic poem predominates here. In Part III the poet foresees an event which because of its visionary, future nature is not, of course, historical. The lyric-prophetic poem predominates. A ratio or progression could therefore be formulated which would indicate that the later the poem, the more likely it is to be lyric and prophetic. . . .

There is little real drama, rather, a chorus and the sketch of an exposition, heroic, struggle, and a postponed dénouement. Pessoa offers no solution to the paradox of immanence, its tedium and absurdity, beyond that of the willed fiction of a purposeful existence revealed, after all, through heraldry, a branch of alchemy. *Mensagem* captures poignantly the agony of the poet's essential obsession with the mystery of existence.

Alex Severino (essay date 1979)

SOURCE: "Fernando Pessoa's Legacy: The *Presença* and After," in *World Literature Today,* Vol. 53, No. 1, Winter, 1979, pp. 5-9.

[*Severino examines the effect of the Presença movement in Portugal on Pessoa's enduring reputation, and his contribution to the nationalistic movement.*]

To study the extent and character of Fernando Pessoa's legacy, it is necessary to consider the circumstances surrounding the publication of his work. Practically unknown at the time of his death, Pessoa (1888-1935) possessed a reputation based solely on *Mensagem* (*Message;* 1934), a book of nationalistic verse imbedded in the occult—a little-known facet of this multifaceted poet—as well as on several dozen poems scattered throughout short-lived, inaccessible journals such as *Orpheu* (1915), *Athena* (1924-25), *Contemporânea* (1922-26) and *Presença* (1927-40).

Nor did Pessoa's known work give the true measure of his legacy. *Mensagem* was not well received, not even by some of the poet's small band of admirers. They would have preferred that Pessoa introduce himself to the public with a work of a less patriotic nature. The steady collaboration he maintained in these other journals, on the other hand, could not overcome the scandalous behavior of years past, when those "lunatics" from *Orpheu* with whom he was associated stirred sleepy Lisbon into literary awareness. For years he was known as the poet of *Orpheu,* dismissed by some for the scandal he and others had caused, hailed by others as the poet most responsible for introducing Modernism into Portugal.

Until the late forties, when the bulk of his work began to be available to the public and to the critics not directly involved with Modernism, Fernando Pessoa was admired and imitated mostly because of the boldness of the technical innovations evident from the poems in *Orpheu.* We know now that formal experimentation was only one of his many facets, the one he had assigned to "Álvaro de Campos." Among the several other selves Pessoa invented to express his many moods—the heteronyms—Campos represented the Modernist outlook and style. It was left to later generations to discover that there were other important traits in Pessoa's poetry. To the free verse and structural audacity of the Modernist Campos were added the epigrams from the Latinist "Ricardo Reis," well-wrought poems carving contemporary themes in Horatian odes. Juxtaposed to these two poets was the matter-of-fact, almost careless free verse of "Alberto Caeiro," the anti-poet, for whom only the exterior world was real. And from this symphony of poets Pessoa himself emerged as conductor, striving toward what none of the others had dared to seek—to apprehend the ineffable world beyond words, the irrational made rational through language, the intensely musical verse akin to song. It is this legacy, the attempt to express the inexpressible through the power and mystery of language, that characterizes Fernando Pessoa's influence on Portuguese poetry today.

In such a broad topic as the study of sixty-three years of Fernando Pessoa's legacy, it would be impossible, within restricted space, to present more than a summarized account of the movements and poets involved. Rather than try to be superficially comprehensive, it seems advisable to concentrate on one particular movement, the *Presença*, and to study its pioneering role in making known the novelty and excellence of Pessoa's poetry. Moving beyond esthetic affinities, I shall examine those poets from *Presença* in whose work the Pessoa legacy is most evident.

. . . . .

The first literary movement in Portugal to recognize the importance of Fernando Pessoa was *Presença*. The name was derived from a journal which in the late twenties congregated a group of young students from the University of Coimbra who wanted to transform the quality of Portuguese literature, bringing it closer to echoing European trends. The journal lasted thirteen years (1927-40). Fifty-six numbers were issued in two different series: fifty-four in the first and two in the second. During those thirteen years *Presença* defended the literary artifact with unswerving devotion, rescuing Portuguese literature from the clutches of an autocratic government bent on using folksy, easily accessible art as a means of propaganda. A steady struggle was maintained in the pages of the journal to keep literature pure, that is, to make literature an earnest and sincere spiritual activity between the writer and his craft. Furthermore, *Presença* wanted to keep literature autonomous, free from any correlative purpose, such as being used as a vehicle for exposing sociopolitical ills. In time *Presença* would be accused of promoting art for art's sake by the proponents of committed literature beginning to be heard in Portugal after 1940.

As they looked for literary vocations as genuine as their own, the *Presença* group became interested in the poets from *Orpheu*. Theirs had been an authentic and sincere poetry, and as such it needed to be revived and their authors brought back from semi-oblivion into the Modernist fold. Therefore the group that called itself "the second Modernism" set out to promote the poets from the first Modernism. In one of the journal's first issue José Régio wrote in reference to Pessoa: "For all these advan-

tages, Fernando Pessoa has the makings of a Master and is the richest in outlets of the so-called Modernists" [*Presença*, 1927]. Spurred by such acclaim, Fernando Pessoa went on to publish some of his best work in *Presença*.

Presença was founded, edited and directed at first by José Régio, a pseudonym for José Maria dos Reis Pereira (1901-1969), the most gifted writer to have emerged from the group and its principal animator; João Gaspar Simões (b. 1903), novelist and foremost critic whose weekly columns appearing in leading newspapers have helped shape Portuguese letters for the past fifty years; and Branquinho da Fonseca (1905-1974), poet and novelist, author of an excellent novel, *O barão* (*The Baron*, 1942). An important event occurred in the early stages of *Presença*'s history. Alleging that the journal's prevailing philosophy, as determined by Régio, smothered individual expression, Branquinho da Fonseca broke away from the group, taking with him Adolfo Rocha (better known as Miguel Torga, b. 1907) and Edmundo Bettancourt (1899-1973), leaving Régio and Simões to answer for the journal.

Fernando Pessoa became indirectly involved in the controversy. He was one of the "Masters" who were supposedly guiding *Presença* toward esthetic absolutism. Miguel Torga told him so in an angry letter written in reference to Pessoa's unfavorable opinion of his book *Rampa* (1930): "The era of the Masters has already passed," he wrote [*Cartas de Fernando Pessoa a João Gaspar Simões*, 1957]. As a gesture of allegiance to Régio and Simões—they were later joined by Adolfo Casais Monteiro (1908-1972)—Fernando Pessoa maintained from then on a steady presence in the journal. The *presencistas* in turn did all they could to make Pessoa's poetic genius known while he was alive and continued to do so even after his death. First they sought his active collaboration. Later, when *Presença* prospered enough to launch its own book series, the directors offered to publish his work. He declined, suggesting the publication of Mário de Sá-Carneiro's unpublished poems instead, which were in his keeping. Gaspar Simões wrote the first two critical essays on Pessoa to appear in book form—*Temas* (1929) and *O mistério da poesia* (1931).

After Fernando Pessoa died, Simões and Luis de Montalvor—the latter had been with him in *Orpheu*—went through his manuscripts and selected the poems which today make up the first four volumes of the "Complete Works," put out by Ática. Along with **Mensagem**, already published, these four volumes are the nucleus of Pessoa's poetry. Other volumes of unpublished works have since appeared. Their contents, however, have not revealed any better poems than the ones originally selected by Simões and Montalvor. Unfortunately, Simões's crowning effort on behalf of Pessoa, the monumental and controversial *Vida e obra de Fernando Pessoa* (1951), fell short of expectations. Some of the conclusions reached are based on psychological probings into the human soul, difficult to assess. Nevertheless, in spite of the impressionistic methods used, Simões's biography is still the fundamental, most complete study of Fernando Pessoa's life and work available.

Simões looked at Pessoa from the point of view of a critic. Others in the *Presença* group saw him principally as a poet whose work offered rich possibilities for their own poetic growth. Such was José Régio, at least in the early stages of his poetic career, for after the praise he bestowed on Pessoa in the first three numbers of the journal, he never again wrote a line about him. After that, Régio would always consider Sá-Carneiro the better poet. According to Simões, the reason for the sudden reversal had to do with a meeting, the first between the two poets, or rather between Régio and Campos—elusive, impersonal Campos—who had on that occasion impersonated Pessoa. Hiding behind the mask of Álvaro de Campos, Pessoa answered the young poet's questions evasively, stating during the course of the conversation that he knew little about English literature, having read only two or three English novels. Régio took Pessoa-Campos's strange behavior to be a sign of insincerity and assumed he had been wrong in identifying Pessoa's poetry with his own. The two poets' views on art had collided. For Régio, art was a means of exploring the psyche, of revealing personality, the "I," conscious and subconscious. For Pessoa, art was a means of concealing personality. Art was for him the expression of many masks, of imagined personalities differing from his own, each paradoxically interpreting truth from many points of view.

Pessoa's influence on José Régio's poetry can be traced only to his early work and is evident in "Cântico negro" (Black Canticle), a poem inserted in his first book of poetry, *Poemas de deus e do diabo* (Poems from God and the Devil, 1925). This celebrated poem, written at a time when Régio was an ardent admirer of what little portion of Pessoa's poetry had appeared in print, reveals certain affinities with **"Lisbon Revisited, 1923,"** published for the first time in *Contemporânea* in 1923. Joaquim Montezuma de Carvalho points this out in an article entitled "'Cântico negro,' um poema de José Régio," published in the literary supplement of *O Estado de São Paulo*. In spite of the similarities between the two poems, they differ in tone and style. Pessoa and Régio are, after all, quite different, as are the two movements they superiorly represented—*Orpheu* and *Presença*.

Régio's echoing of Pessoa-Campos—for it is the raving, defiant Campos who in the heteronymic family subscribes to **"Lisbon Revisited, 1923"**—may be detected in the use of free verse and irregular stanzaic form as well as, thematically speaking, in the tone of social defiance and individual affirmation, the assertion of self-reliance common to both poems. In the Campos poem, however, there is the underlying suggestion of a painful existential awareness which points to the futility of all protest. Protest is useless, according to Campos, in the face of the world's opacity. Where the poetic voice in Régio's poem is resolute, in Pessoa's it is, above all, metaphysically weary.

> "Come this way!" some tell me with gentle eyes,
> holding out their arms, so sure
> that it would be good for me to hear them
> when they say, "Come this way!"
> I eye them with weary eyes

> (fatigue and irony are in my eyes)
> and fold my arms
> and never go that way.

And in Álvaro de Campos:

> Don't take my arm!
> I don't like you to take my arm. I want to be
> alone.
> I said I am alone!
> Oh what a bore, your wanting me to be with
> people!

Régio is confident of the course to be followed. He goes forth with "songs in his lips." The madness of which he speaks is the madness of the seer, the possessed, ready to pursue a vision with obstinate idealism: "I have my own madness." Although madness is never mentioned in the Campos poem, its imminence is implicit in the widely disparate irregularity of the stanzas—some of one or two lines—and the asymmetry of the verse line, abruptly long and short. Often an exclamation mark ends the incomplete thought, as if to sustain and even repress the catapult of feeling ready to burst forth. In the Campos poem the impending madness is the madness of the despondent, the defeated—a final refuge. Moreover, the poem's overall structure contrasts sharply with Régio's relative uniformity of line and stanza in spite of the free verse. In the Régio poem the subjective voice, the "I," never loses control; it imposes itself on the extrinsic reality, while in Campos the "I" is diminished and almost smothered by the overwhelming presence of the universe.

Pessoa and Régio are similar in their devotion to the prerogatives of art, though different in their way of expressing it. Pessoa explores many aspects of truth through the several personalities he has created, far removed from the empirical self. His aim is, as he has said, relating his method to Shakespeare's, to arrive at sincerity through multiple insincerity. By disappearing as an artistic entity, a self, he introduces conflicting realities created by many selves, each an infinitesimal segment of a universal truth. Rooted in emotions Pessoa himself has felt—he too once returned to Lisbon from South Africa after a long absence—**"Lisbon Revisited, 1923,"** for example, interprets reality from the point of view of Campos. Circumscribed within the thematic and structural confines of the Campos poem, the resulting poetic reality has acquired a new dimension which is only faintly related to whatever sensations Pessoa might have felt. All the poetry written by Fernando Pessoa is characterized by this very same dramatic quality. It is the poetry of the other self; "I fly into another," Pessoa tells Simões in a letter regarding the dramatic quality of his verse (*Cartas a João Gaspar Simões*). . . .

Régio, on the other hand, is the poet of the empirical self. His poems are poetic "translations" of what he already carried inside himself when he was born, to evoke Régio's own statement in a famous essay included as a postscript to *Poemas de deus e do diabo*, beginning with the second edition. Although his declared intention is to refer his personal anguish and anxiety to that of all mankind, José Régio, like Walt Whitman, never quite succeeds in substituting the egotistical "I" for an egoism that would represent the overall human predicament. His most common theme, the myth of the "fallen angel," depicting the man who fell from grace to find the Devil, is pursued with considerable involvement of the self in spite of the intentions to relate to all mankind.

> God and the Devil guide me, no one else!
> Everyone has a father, everyone has a mother!
> But I who have no beginning nor end
> Was born of the love between God and the Devil.

Orpheu and *Presença* are two closely associated literary movements. The latter sprang from the former and identified with it in the full commitment to literature and in the innovative poetic techniques meant to bring to the surface the formerly untapped human subconscious. At the same time they are two very different movements. On one hand is *Orpheu,* never quite falling into a group pattern, led by three highly individualistic poetic personalities: the enraging, vituperative Almada Negreiros, venting his fury against the Lisbon middle class; or the intellectual, multifaceted Pessoa, hiding behind the many masks; or Sá-Carneiro, himself a sheaf of metaphors, until he becomes one grandiose metaphor, killing himself. On the other hand is *Presença,* more cohesive, led by Régio and Torga, who reaffirm the hegemony of the indivisible self as they grope torturously with Christ's presence on earth: Régio, in anguish, seeking Christ and finding the Devil; Torga immersing himself in the midst of human suffering. His is a telluric mysticism rooted in the harsh, inhospitable region of his birth, the crags and arid valleys of northern Portugal.

It is regrettable that neither Régio nor Torga perceived the religious elements in Pessoa's poetry—regrettable but not surprising. Pessoan appreciation in those days was confined mostly to the question of the simulated selves, the heteronyms. It did not allow for the serious consideration of the poems written under Pessoa's own name, more specifically, the occult poems reflecting an earnest quest for an *Ente Supremo* (Superior Being) or for the intermediate superior beings Pessoa alludes to in a famous letter to Adolfo Casais Monteiro of 13 January 1935, transcribed in Simões's *Vida e obra.* Although quite different from Régio's theocentricity, focused on Christ and on Catholicism, Pessoa's religiousness, as portrayed in his poems, is no less sincere than Régio's and its ultimate failure in offering an explanation just as poignant.

"I am basically a religious spirit," he confides to Armando Cortes-Rodrigues in a letter of 19 January 1915, included in *Cartas a Armando Cortes-Rodrigues.* The abiding quest for religious knowledge led him to the study of esoteric doctrines as expounded by such theosophical organizations as the Rosicrucians, the Knights Templars and the Theosophical Society, founded in 1888 by Madame Blavatsky, whose writings he translated into Portuguese. According to Pessoa, these writings were responsible for the reawakened spirituality he felt around 1915. Like Yeats,

another convert to Madame Blavatsky's teachings, Pessoa sought solace for an avidly religious spirit in the principles and teachings of the non-Christian theosophical societies with their promise of semi-mystical thought. . . .

Presença ceased publication in 1940. World events such as the Spanish Civil War and World War II brought about a shift in literary taste which went from the esthetic and confessional to the militant. For almost forty years Pessoa's reputation as a poet became involved in the contention between the militant poets who saw literature, and poetry in particular, as a vehicle for social reform and the craftsmen who believed that the demands of form and structure were to be met in the creation of a poem.

Challenged by the so-called "new realists," who were further alienated by nationalistic **Mensagem** and its use by the government's propaganda machine, Fernando Pessoa lost favor with the general public and the young. On the other hand, his following increased among the estheticists, who had begun to discover artistic qualities in Pessoa which had been obscured by the Modernist breakthrough he had initiated. Neglected at home by the militant poets, Pessoa's poetry traveled to other lands. Brazil adopted him as its very own, his acclaim there reaching apotheosis. The foreign recognition has helped to solidify Pessoa's reputation at home, which today knows no bounds.

For this, *Presença* was greatly responsible. The critical excellence and the artistic integrity of such writers as José Régio, João Gaspar Simões, Adolfo Casais Monteiro, Carlos Queiroz and others helped to rescue Pessoa from oblivion while contributing in no small measure to the importance of his legacy in contemporary Portuguese poetry.

Ronald W. Sousa (essay date 1982)

SOURCE: "The Structure of Pessoa's *Mensagem,*" in *Bulletin of Hispanic Studies,* Vol. LIX, No. 1, January 1982, pp. 58-66.

[*Sousa analyzes the structure of* Mensagem, *and explores its relation to the occult.*]

Over the past thirty-or-so years, criticism has raised a genre problematic about **Mensagem,** the one book of Portuguese poetry that Fernando Pessoa published in his lifetime. The basic question is: 'Is it historical, narrative, more-or-less "epic" poetry, or personal, "lyric" poetry?' The lines of the debate—recognized as such or not by the various participating critics—can be expressed in the following formulations: 'Is the book a recounting of the Portuguese past in more-or-less discrete, objectively-presented units that play a rôle akin to that of narrative episodes, or does the book's structure revolve about a subjective principle, as in "lyric"?' Allied to that question is one of readership: 'Should the reader—the general reader of poetry, not the academic critic—properly approach

Mensagem seeking to reconstruct a narratively-presented objective world or attempting the 'sympathetic', one-to-one reading of a "lyric" fabric?' It should be pointed out that the taking-up of either basic position in the controversy involves a major presupposition: that the book—comprising as it does forty-four short poems written and revised over a twenty-one-year span—constitutes a coherent poetic utterance, for practical purposes a single, though composite, poem rather than an organized collection of independent poems.

It is not my present purpose to enter the controversy. I intend instead to show first that the book (which I too take to constitute a unitary poetic movement) embodies a much more precise structure and that the individual poems within it are susceptible of much more specific readings than allowed in the concepts of reading in which the various genre arguments are grounded and, secondly, that such specificity in reading leads to comprehension of the fact that *Mensagem* is generically anomalous, a situation rendering generic categorization futile.

Since a detailed reading of the poems is easier once the structure in which they are set is clear, and since thorough-going reading will call into question further issues—such as the establishing of a completely reliable text—I shall concentrate my argument here on substantiation of the view that the book has a very precise structure, adducing passages only to support and illustrate that argument.

One additional observation constitutes a necessary preliminary to this study. My approach is grounded in a familiarity with many works that Pessoa himself had read—especially the many works dealing with occultism—and it is grounded as well in the conviction that the material contained in those works influenced in very specific ways the conception of *Mensagem*. The notion of influence from occultist sources is universally accepted—but it is viewed in general terms only; no one has dealt with what the origins of the occultist material are, what is revealed by examination of the context in which such material originally occurs, or what those revelations may have to say about overall meaning-making in *Mensagem*. And the fact that some of the language of *Mensagem* derives verbatim from occultist sources has not been pointed out.

The first utterance of the work—after the title, the implications of which will be touched on at the end of this examination—is the Latin epigraph *Benedictus Dominus Deus noster qui dedit nobis signum.* The source is a book Pessoa had read entitled *The Brotherhood of the Rosy Cross,* by Arthur Edward Waite. The significant passage from that title reads as follows:

> *Benedictus Dominus Deus noster qui dedit nobis signum.* For those who know or can discover the authorized battery of the Rite, it may happen that the door will open and that he by whom they are admitted will be Christian Rosy Cross, who after witnessing the Hermetic marriage left the Palace of the King, expecting that next day he should be Door Keeper. *Introitus*

Apertus est ad Occlusum Regis Palatium. The ways indeed are many but the Gate is one. *Valete, Fratres.* [*The Brotherhood of the Rosy Cross,* London, 1925]

Recourse to this passage makes it quite clear that Pessoa begins his book with Rosicrucian language. And he ends it in a similar manner, for in fact the last words of *Mensagem* are precisely *Valete, Fratres.* It seems, in fact, that he takes the two formulae as respectively a Rosicrucian salutation and valediction, the former pointing to an established revelatory authority and the latter indicating that an explanation of the nature of that authority has been set forth in the symbols following the salutation—in this case, in Waite's own parabolic linguistic symbolism. One should not, in my view, read the specific original implications of language such as this into Pessoa's poetry. Indeed, the incorporation of such language into *Mensagem* provides an exemplary case of the need for caution in reading. Pessoa's beginning and ending of the work with Rosicrucian formulae has the primary function of suggesting that there is a ritual aspect to the entire book, that the intervening poems comprise a series of signs that suggest revelation and/or initiation in one of many possible ways. We may not, just because of the presence of that beginning and end, read Rosicrucian tenets *en bloc* into the poem.

The poems that come between the salutation and the valediction are divided into three sections, the first entitled "Brasão", the second "Mar Portuguez", the third "O Encoberto". Each section has its own Latin epigraph. The approximate significance of the tripartite division can be deduced by recourse to analysis of a similar division in several of the systems with which Pessoa came into contact in his readings in esoterica.

The Freemasonic initiatory scale is composed of three steps, beginning with "Apprentice" and ending with "Master". The individual who reaches the third step continues upward in a personal progress through various symbolic levels. A similar structure is to be found in Theosophy, another area intowhich Pessoa delved in some depth. In Madame Blavatsky's *The Voice of the Silence,* [Peking 1927] which Pessoa translated into Portuguese, three-staged initiatory progress is a recurring theme. In one fragment of that work, each step is called a "Hall", and three "Halls" the first being terrestrial existence characterized by ignorance, the second apprenticeship or learning, and the third spiritual consciousness characterized by wisdom—lead to open-ended ascent into ever-greater degrees of self-control and awareness.

Those systems, seen in general terms, involve the following progression: first, the initiate's surrender to the master to learn his secrets, secondly, his battle for control of himself, thirdly, incipient success in that battle. The third step also includes continuous individual (sometimes called "hidden") progress in the psychic-spiritual realm.

Another tripartite scheme that appears in the readings is the cycle of life-death-rebirth. A number of Freemasonic works treat that pattern. The basic movement of this tripartite scheme involves loss of the secret of life and resulting state of spiritual benightedness, in which, according to some conceptions, glimpses of the lost truth are occasionally perceived. After a time, spiritual rebirth is achieved—through one of a number of routes. In many exegeses death is conceived as necessary to the reaching of the higher spiritual state betokened in rebirth. The entire process may represent a ritual necessarily—and sometimes (as, for example, in some conceptualizations of the process of debasement in alchemy) intentionally—embarked upon in order to achieve spiritual progress.

The three-level initiatory hierarchy and the death-rebirth cycle are conceptually dissimilar in several areas. Especially problematic is the correlation between the second level of initiatory progress and the state of spiritual death. It should be observed, however, that a hidden postulate of many practitioners of the occult in the era was the reconcilability of all such differences into one universally-true system; indeed, such unification is the precise aim of late-nineteenth- and early-twentieth-century Theosophy. For such reasons, many of the exegetes that Pessoa read saw no major inconsistencies between systems. That fact is important to an appreciation of the amalgam of disparate references that Pessoa includes in *Mensagem*.

A third similar, but not conceptually identical, pattern taken from esoterica makes a simple, unified interpretation of the implications of *Mensagem*'s structure even more difficult. It is the concept of threefold interpretation, as set forth by Franz Hartmann in *Magic, White and Black,* another title in Pessoa's collection. Briefly stated, the concept involved is that every phenomenon can be understood on three levels, the specific one at a given moment depending upon the degree of insight of the perceiver. The three levels on which reality exists are, in Hartmann's terms, the exoteric, seen by those concentrating on the material world, the esoteric, seen by those concentrating on the soul or the emotions, and the spiritual, which involves perceptual union of the types of interpretation characteristic of the first two levels. . . .

Before I apply these concepts to *Mensagem,* there is one further preliminary matter to be dealt with: the question of the status of such notions in Pessoa's work. The problem is a multifaceted one that extends well beyond just the matter of incorporation of material from occultist systems into literary texts. Limited to that sphere, however, it can be approached as follows: there is in Pessoa a tension between a wish to believe in the truth of such systems and a sense that he is drawing upon them merely as structuring elements for his work. Citations can be adduced from Pessoa to illustrate either alternative and, as well—as is usual with this complex intellect—an awareness precisely of the tension between the two. That awareness is often conceptualized in the notion that truth is by nature an aesthetically-created category, or myth, that has the merely functional value of mobilizing human action. (When such 'aesthetic' myth-making is literary, an additional postulate involving the conviction that language has, in one of several ways, great direct effects on reality must also be assumed.) Thus occultist tenets, while un-

true in themselves, can become functionally true in the myth-making action that they exert on the world through such literature as Pessoa's poetry. *Mensagem* is in many respects his most extensive and complex realization of such myth-making.

Much as does the passage reproduced from *Quinto Império, Mensagem* involves the fusion of various tripartite systems and the application of the series so produced to interpretation of Portuguese history. The Latin epigraphs indicate the nature of each section. The epigraph to "Brasão" is *Bellum Sine Bello*. The nineteen "Brasão" poems constitute an emblematic fabric that reconstructs the Portuguese coat of arms by ascribing to poetic profiles of prominent figures from the era of Portuguese glory—King John I, Nun'Álvares Pereira, Prince Henry, etc.—status as corresponding devices in that coat of arms (King John corresponds to the seventh castle of the coat of arms, Pereira to the crown atop it, etc.). Thus physical existence is focussed upon in "Brasão"—the presence of historical figures and of the visualizable emblem they figuratively incarnate. Those two "physical existences" combine to suggest the Portuguese past also made "physical". The emphasis on the physical corresponds to the first level of the various initiatory hierarchies: to life before death, to concentration on the material world in interpreting phenomena, to the first realization of a prophecy, etc. And *Bellum Sine Bello* denotes struggle on a personal-psychological level within the historical figures referred to in the poems. To be sure, there are hints of another, less tangible ethical or spiritual force at work in their lives that they do not fully comprehend. There are as well treatments in the first two poems—which, significantly, correspond to the heraldic fields upon which the other poems/devices "rest"—of the themes of national destiny (poem 1) and of the necessary relevance to the Portuguese experience of the life-death-rebirth cycle (poem 2). And there is treatment in the third poem, which corresponds to Ulysses—a mythical figure in relation to Portuguese history—, of the theme of the animating power of myth. All three of these themes will be taken up in less "tangible" ways in the second and third sections of the book.

The epigraph to "Mar Portuguez", *Possessio maris,* has with respect to both the three-step structure and the themes of the poems that it contains a relationship similar to that manifested in "Brasão". "Maris" is the key word; as is amply demonstrated in the poems of this section, the 'sea' is both an external and, simultaneously, an internal realm to be conquered, and conquest involves simultaneous overcoming of both. Further, the sea is difficult to "possess". The vicissitudes of Portugal's historical effort towards permanent maritime empire are constantly shown in reflection upon both the external and the internal realms. Finally, that effort toward empire ends in failure. The emphasis in these poems falls on mental qualities and processes and on attitudes toward the historical undertaking rather than on the biographical entities involved. "Mar Portuguez" thus corresponds to the second stage of the initiatory hierarchy, in which the initiate separates from the master and struggles toward self-control that will lead him upward (a stage, incidentally, often symbolized in occultist writings by the attempted crossing of a river or other body of water). It also corresponds to the death before, and perhaps necessary to, rebirth (indeed such is hinted thematically in the last two poems of thesection). It corresponds too to interpretive concentration on matters of the emotions, of the soul. It suggests the second realization of a prophecy.

The epigraph of "O Encoberto" is *Pax in Excelsis*. The section is divided into three subsections, which perhaps betoken continually higher levels (*excelsi?*) of initiatory progress. "O Encoberto", translatable as "The Hidden One", obviously has reference not only to King Sebastian lost but also to the third, "hidden" initiatory level. The poems of the section deal with patterns in Portuguese history, with prophecy, and with Sebastianism, making of national history a series of symbols that suggest a psychic realm and ritual framework in which Portugal can be reborn. That orientation can be glimpsed, through contrast of the Sebastian poem of "Brasão" (poem No. 15) with that of "O Encoberto" (poem No. 32). In the former the biographical Sebastian proclaims that his reckless, potentially creative daring will remain after his physical death, for it in fact is what characterizes mankind. In the later poem, he speaks of his sense that his life has a place in destiny, that it is as a symbol—of a creativity that is not merely human but, because of the degree to which he and his nation epitomize it, typically Portuguese—that he will return to his country. . . .

The section also includes a series of three poems entitled **"Avisos",** or prophets of Portuguese rebirth, each presumably, according to the notions of threefold interpretation and three realizations of a prophecy, seeing the nature of rebirth more nearly completely than his predecessor. In short, the poems of "O Encoberto" express, in several ways, the attainment of wisdom, the reaching of the totalizing symbolic level of interpretation of existence—and specifically of national history—the rebirth of a nation, the third realization of a prophecy.

That body of poetry, then, placed as it is between the Rosicrucian salutation and valediction, is presented as at the very least the appropriation of occultist elements toward the forging of a highly intricate poetic utterance and, more likely, as the serio-fanciful symbolic exposition—or perhaps inculcation—of a myth (that is, a functional truth) of some validity. There is, then, about **Mensagem** the air of a document that proposes action in the world. In fact, in the final poem of the book, after the poetic voice has gone through a process of analysing the state of the Portuguese national psyche, the last words (immediately before *"Valete, Fratres"*), "O Portugal, hoje és nevoeiro . . . / É a Hora!", constitute a final admonition emphasizing a sense that the book has shown or taught something new to be put into effect.

What, exactly? Through what agency? Not all such questions can be fully explored here. Some provisional answers can be indicated, however, through further analysis—now of the referential system embodied in the **Mensagem** poems.

That there is a foreground figure in some of the poems of **Mensagem** is undeniable. Some of the poems—Numbers 3-10, 16-20, 24, 27-28, 34, 37-38—include a foreground speaker, or *persona,* who addresses or describes the subjects of the poems, occasionally referring to the Portuguese nationality that he has in common with them. It is clearly indicated in the poems that he is looking back through the Portuguese past. The speaker is, in fact, a kind of epic voyager—one who journeys through the various ages of Portuguese history, seeking by means of his journey to learn about forces at work in his nation. These poems thus involve the present in confrontation with the past and set forth a comparison of the two eras. Most of the rest of the poems of the book—Numbers 1-2, 21, 23, 25-26,29-31, 33, 35-36, 40-44—should probably be read as the speaker's meditations on the nature of the world and of Portugal's place in it, or his mythologizing of aspects either of his world view or of Portuguese history. The key differences between this group of poems and the previous group are differences of subject-matter and of approach; the speaker's position remains the same in all thirty-six poems.

When, in those poems, the speaker refers to himself—as he often does—it is, except in the one instance of poem 30, always as *nós, Nós* in the context of these poems obviously means "we, the present-day Portuguese". Is the speaker then to be regarded as present-day Portugal in the act of introspection? The content of poem 30, however, supported by evidence from a thirty-seventh poem, refutes any theory that *nós* has only that collective antecedent. In poem 30, **"A Ultima Nau",** and in that thirty-seventh poem, the untitled eighth poem of "O Encoberto" (poem 39), the speaker is singular and clearly Fernando Pessoa. (Poem 39 is the third of the three poems dealing with prophets of Portuguese rebirth. Pessoa has, then, thematized himself as the third, and presumably definitive, recurrence in a prophetic line. And the book that, in the poem, he says he is writing is surely **Mensagem,** the very work we read.) There is, then, a specific 'I' somewhere amid the *nós*. In the light of that factor, *nós* may be seen as 'I and the other present-day Portuguese', the epic voyager would then presumably be Fernando Pessoa acting as a surrogate for all his countrymen in his examination of the national past. The nature of the framework in which the **Mensagem** poems are set, however, suggests that even that interpretation is incompletely descriptive of the full meaning of *nós,* that that interpretation commingles in *nós* with another, more exact antecedent: "you, my present-day Portuguese reader(s) and I".

We must, then, relocate our notion of the focus of perception in the book. It is not merely each historical figure profiled in "Brasão" who concentrates primarily on worldly matters but also the personified poet/reader(s) who are examining these figures. The personified poet/reader(s) then proceed, in their journey, to higher, more complex perceptual outlooks upon experience and history in the second and third sections, as though in each section the same material were being seen at a different perceptual level. Awareness of that process of step-by-step relocation of the focus of perception permits a consistent reading of the whole book, since many of the poems of "O Encoberto" are in fact highly abstract.

The nature of the relationship between the two elements within *nós* is hinted at in the title **Mensagem,** for the title too has its occultist antecedents—in Theosophy. There it refers to the concept of a divine messenger—a teacher or prophet—and his/her giving of a message to the world and thus changing of the course of civilization. The Theosophical exposition of that notion evidences the usual Theosophical tendency toward syncretism, for it sees commonality in the Master-Initiate and Guru-Neophyte relationships found in other occult systems. Such an amalgamation seems to characterize as well Pessoa's use of the concept in the structuring of **Mensagem**. In the book, he is the Master, or Guru, his reader(s) the Initiate(s), or Neophyte(s). At the same time, a large scope—in this case national rather than worldwide—is hinted at, as in Theosophy. (João Gaspar Simões's claim that Pessoa felt that **Mensagem** would exercise a formative influence on the Portuguese psyche at a time when that psyche was undergoing a crucial remodelling [*Vida e Obra,*], if true, would confirm that interpretation.)

Understanding of the nature of the initiation presumably undergone by the reader(s) involves examination of the relationship between such structural features as I analyse here and the actual themes of the poems, taken in order. Suffice it for present purposes to say that, in theory, the reader is given the material necessary to proper understanding of the mysteries of his nation and himself; he has, then, been taken by the Master Fernando Pessoa from rank neophyte to potential *frater*—through the language and structure of the book that he is reading. The final words of the last poem, "E a Hora", then, tell him that he is now made able to understand the deepest meaning of, and to act in concert with, national historical forces. In fact, those words conclude a summarizing process that draws primarily on the concept of death and rebirth found in magic, alchemy, and other esoteric systems that Pessoa knew. . . .

The lines draw on the fog imagery developed through the book as a symbol of loss and confusion—in concert with the stock image of the fog that, in traditional Sebastianism, is supposed to part to reveal the returned King. The last two lines, then, imply rebirth. This seemingly inconsistent situation is explained if one takes into account that Pessoa is drawing on the concept that when the low point of degradation or debasement is reached, rebirth is reached as well. What he is saying to his reader is in fact that the proper depths of national disarray, or 'fog'—the social confusion of late-1920s and early-1930s Portugal—have been reached, and that the reader(s) must comprehend that fact in the manner in which Pessoa explains it through **Mensagem** and see it within the dynamics of Portuguese history set forth according to the logic of the book. The reader(s), having been so initiated, will then know how to react—and Portugal will have been reborn. (The degree of reality that Pessoa ascribed to that literarily-proclaimed 'rebirth' is questionable. Like many of his other pronouncements, it treads the line between actual belief and appropriation for use in the process of making poetry.)

What, then, of the genre problematic? There is, to be sure, a sort of 'narrative' (and, in 'Brasão', loosely chronological) arrangement of 'events'. The relationship between those 'events' is, however, provided primarily by the trajectory of the Master/Initiate(s) through them rather than by relationships between the 'events' themselves. Indeed, the structuring principle of the book presupposes that trajectory. Is this narrative, 'epic' poetry? Conversely, while something akin to the stereotyped subjective, 'lyric' reception is expected of the reader—i.e., he/she is expected to penetrate into, and understand, an intensive view of experience—, that understanding is to be derived from the coordination of a series of 'events', or units, rather than from a merely thematic interpretation of poetic content.

In sum, this short book, because of the nature of its structure as outlined above, partakes in different ways of each genre, while thoroughly avoiding facile categorization into either.

Leland Guyer (essay date 1987)

SOURCE: "Fernando Pessoa and the Cubist Perspective," in *Hispania,* Vol. 70, No. 1, March 1987, pp. 73-8.

[*In this excerpt, Guyer relates Pessoa's work and poetic priorities to those of the Cubist aesthetic movement.*]

The nineteenth century in the mainstream of Western civilization was unquestionably one of those periods marked to a great degree by an enthusiastic dedication to a vision. The vision was one of order, of progress, and of the subjugation of nature to humanity's technical genius. This self-assured interpretation of one's ability to know and dominate the environment is reflected in that century's artistic interpretation of the world.

Followers of this Positivistic thought reacted with some conviction. Their reaction was a rejection of the pre-eminence of reason, order and measure. In its place, artists often allied themselves with reason's negative image. Some saw this anti-Positivistic reaction, this revaluation of the mysterious and the unknown, as an unwisely retrogressive leap to a so-called "escapism" identified with an earlier time. Perspective, form, color, sound and reason had seemed well defined and in no particular need of revision.

Others viewed the reaction not as retrogressive but as profoundly progressive. The techniques of the artist, the writer, the scientist and the social scientist were placed on trial and found lacking in their vision. They seemed to ignore what was below the surface. Among numerous responses, a renewed interest in the occult developed. Rosicrucianism flourished. Theosophy was invented. And probably most important, modern psychiatry appeared with its investigations of that slippery substance, the unconscious.

The artistic products of this anti-Positivistic reaction are well-known. Impressionism, Symbolism, Expressionism,

Dadaism, Surrealism, Cubism and any number of other revolutionary "isms" have flourished in the last hundred years or so. Of these, one of the more perplexing and vexatious tendencies in twentieth-century art history has been Cubism. Similarly perplexing and vexatious has been the unusual work of a modern Portuguese poet, Fernando Pessoa. Both Cubism and the poetry of Pessoa have been criticized as insincerely conceived creations intended primarily to shock the bourgeoisie, but these arguments have faded in the wake of decades of overwhelming acceptance. It is not my intent to offer yet another value judgment of these pivotal creations but to examine the relationship of the Cubist notion of perspective and the literary creation of Fernando Pessoa.

The term Cubism has been meticulously defined and applied. The term has also been loosely defined so that it may apply to a wide range of work that, by general consensus, has been regarded as Cubist. Gerald Kamber has provided a concise and generally applicable definition of Cubism as it may relate to art and literature. In the primary phase of Cubist technique he discerns "(1) a pulling to pieces of the object; (2) a rebuilding of the pieces into an independent composition; (3) a placing together of objects (or parts of objects) from an unrestricted range of observations; (4) a shifting of emphasis from the 'reality' of the objects to the 'reality' of the aesthetic surface".

In rejecting traditional perspective (among other sacred legacies) the Cubists found they could rearrange the object of their attention in such a way that two eyes might appear on one side of the head, or in such a way that the head might appear square-shaped, as if opened up and seen from multiple perspectives simultaneously. The image might be seen in much the same way that we see a radically deforming Mercator projection of the Earth in which the polar regions are represented far out of proportion to the equatorial regions. A viewer of any known object is aware that there is "more than meets the eye." To try to express what we know exists, free from the limited perspective and scope of the static camera eye, is to attempt to gain a fuller view of reality, deformed as it may appear to one who is accustomed to a limited perspective. In time this fundamental ideal of Cubism often either became somewhat hidden or entirely lost in much of what we now call Cubist works, but the shift of emphasis on the object to emphasis on the *idea* of the object persisted.

Where the Cubist painters rearranged the appearance of their objects and ignored traditional rules of imitative art, the Cubist poets did so also. With the literary Cubists, images became disjointed, syntax became fragmented and reorganized, perspective became radically altered, and atmosphere generally became that of a vague and uncertain mindscape, indulging itself in the apparently random trajectories of the unconscious.

Fernando Pessoa, although relegated to what often is considered the intellectual and artistic hinterland of Europe, was very much a product of the same times that spawned such better-known Cubist poets as Guillaume Apollinaire and Max Jacob. He never made the artist's nearly obligatory pilgrimage to Paris, but several of his closest friends did reside in Paris and elsewhere abroad. Through this extremely wide range of acquaintances and readings Pessoa became thoroughly familiar with all the major literary movements of ancient and modern Western tradition. His correspondence with other Portuguese writers and his literary criticism and theorizing make it abundantly clear that Pessoa was well aware of contemporary thought and literary fashion.

In his works Pessoa left us one of the major (and generally unrecognized) statements on Cubist poetics. It is so Cubist in its effect that one wonders why it has not been classified as such before. This oversight is probably due to the restricted focus we have had in the examination of Cubism and of Pessoa's work as a whole. . . .

Many modern poets from Baudelaire, Mallarmé, Rilke, Yeats, Eliot, Antonio Machado and others assume multiple poetic personae to varying degrees. . . .

It is probably Fernando Pessoa who exploited this fragmentation of the empirical self into multiple poetic personae more than anyone else. The major lyric poetry and prose of Pessoa are attributed to four names: Alberto Caeiro, Ricardo Reis, Alvaro de Campos and his own given name, Fernando Pessoa. Writing under a different name, an author is normally said to be using a pseudonym. In contrast to the rather common convention of using pseudonyms is the less common phenomenon of using what Pessoa called heteronyms. These names that he signed to his works are not just names: they represent distinct identities who created poetry and prose from differing points of view. The poetry that the author signed as Fernando Pessoa normally is referred to as his orthonymic poetry.

Although it seems that Pessoa has a neverendingly expanding universe of poetic personae, complete with detailed biographies, one may approach his poetry with an eye toward economy and relative completeness if one focuses just on the above named personae. Briefly, one may characterize these voices in the following way: the poetry of the orthonymic Fernando Pessoa normally possesses a measured, regular form and appreciation of the musicality of verse. It takes on intellectual issues, and it is marked by concern with dreams, the imagination and mystery. Campos's poetry generally reflects a freer form and places greater emphasis on the physical sensations of the surrounding world. Caeiro's poetry also reveals an emphasis on the sensations. It reflects the belief that the only reality that something may possess is that which is patently visible. His attitude of contentment contrasts with Pessoa and Campos's pervasive sense of anguish. Also contrasting in this respect, to a certain extent, is the poetry of Ricardo Reis. A persona writing with classical forms, themes and imagery, Reis finds his greatest burden to be the recognition of human mortality but finds solace applying the carpe diem principle to his life.

Some of the most complex personae one may find in poetry are of the orthonymic Pessoa himself. This persona's poetry actually represents a wide spectrum of individual personae whose multi-faceted natures can be discerned with relative ease. Principally a poet, the orthonymic persona of Fernando Pessoa was also a literary theorist who described and analyzed periods and styles of artistic activity. He even invented and wrote extensively on several styles of poetry he believed would revolutionize Portuguese, if not all of European, poetry. Among the "isms" he launched and promoted were *Paulismo, Sensacionismo* and *Interseccionismo*. And it is *Interseccionismo* that will serve to demonstrate Pessoa's most evident, but not entirely complete, link with literary Cubism.

An approach to a new vision of reality, whose inception interestingly coincided with the appearance of Pessoa's heteronyms in 1914, his *Interseccionismo* is best represented by Pessoa's poem **"Chuva Oblíqua."** Here the reader finds an accretion of shifting, intersecting, fluid planes of time and space. Here time is present and past, and mindscapes metamorphose according to the whims of the unfettered flow of apparently unconscious forces. . . . The whole poem is marked by a similar fragmentation of "traditional" linear description. The reader is transported to a dizzying world of temporal, spatial, sensorial, intellectual and oneiric sequences dovetailing into one another, providing a constantly shifting perspective and scene.

One might argue that this poem is truly representative of Pessoa's invented *Interseccionismo* and not in the Cubist mode at all, but as we know, Cubism is more of an approach to reality than a fixed set of guidelines designed to generate clones of an original. **"Chuva Oblíqua"** does conform to the general thrust of Cubism as do the works of such diverse artists as Pablo Picasso and Marcel Duchamp. This approach to poetry provided Pessoa only a temporary source of fascination. He never lost interest in the *concept* expressed by **"Chuva Oblíqua,"** but he found another approach to its further realization.

A wider vision of his multi-perspective work can be found in his orthonymic poetry alone. As just demonstrated, Pessoa conducted an experiment with a traditional approach to literary Cubism. And if we accept the assertion that a principal feature of Cubism is the reorganization of perspective, we can see that Pessoa found other ways less traditional to articulate the concerns that gave rise to the Cubist idea.

Fernando Pessoa writing in his own name reflects a complex of world views that rarely, if ever, finds a host in one author. Besides the "isms" that Pessoa invented and briefly developed, which represent the kind of experimentation one might be inclined to ascribe to any young poet's evolving tastes, Pessoa signed his own name to poems reflecting radically different and concurrent perspectives on his surroundings. Pessoa, as many others before and after him, looked to the occult for inspiration and illumination. Alchemy, astrology and magic find a persistent articulation in Pessoa's work. He also wrote from the more socially acceptable point of view of the Rosicrucians and Theosophists. There was a side of Pessoa that conceived simple, popular verse. And there was

another that wrote verse in French. The only full-length book of poetry in Portuguese that he published in his lifetime was an unabashedly and messianically nationalistic tribute to Portugal and the Portuguese—*Mensagem*. On the other hand, Pessoa was well aware of the precarious existence of Europe and the rest of the world in view of the awesome specter of a second World War and wrote some of the most profoundly felt anti-war poems ever to be written in Portuguese. But there is another, very different persona (or personae, one might argue) to whom one must pay some attention in order to learn of the complexity of the orthonymic Pessoa's amazingly faceted work. This is the poetry that Pessoa wrote in English.

Although he was born in Lisbon, he spent much of his youth in South Africa where he attended high school and excelled in a number of subjects, most notably English. The influence of this experience remained with the poet. Indeed, some believe that English remained Pessoa's first language until he died, but this is difficult, if not impossible, to prove. What is clear, however, is that he continued to read, write and speak in English until his death.

In 1918 he published a short book of English poetry entitled *35 Sonnets*. This series of poems reflects many of the concerns that can be discerned in his other verse. It was written in a style that London and Glasgow book reviewers found notable more for its faithful reproduction of Elizabethan English than for its poetic qualities. Not totally devoid of such anachronistic language is a pair of long English poems by Pessoa which give clear evidence of warring personae within the orthonymic Pessoa. I refer specifically to his tribute to human sexuality in his poems **"Epithalamium"** and **"Antinous."** Though Pessoa's biography gives no evidence that he had any practical knowledge of the subject, the urge to write of human sexuality was certainly there. What resulted are two modern classics of Portuguese soft-core pornography—**"Epithalamium,"** a celebration of heterosexual love and **"Antinous,"** a celebration of homosexual love. One poem certainly seems to be a response to the other—two views of love from radically different perspectives.

If one considers the orthonymic Pessoa as one persona, he is a very round character. In the end, though, one is likely to find more satisfaction by considering his poetry to be a collection of rather flat personae, much like the representation of structural planes in some Cubist paintings and sculptures.

Earlier I referred to the heteronymic side of Pessoa's poetry, represented by the personae Alberto Caeiro, Ricardo Reis and Alvaro de Campos. With the exception of the last heteronym, these personae are also flat articulations of ideas, although they too possess unquestionably high poetic value.

Alberto Caeiro is the seminal heteronym, the one from whom all the other major heteronyms were said to have found inspiration. He is also one of the least durable personae. (Pessoa allowed him to die of natural causes at a very early age.) He is said to have been the impetus for

Campos's *Sensacionista* poems in that for Caeiro only that which could be *sensed* had any truth. Of Caeiro, Pessoa wrote:

> He sees things with the eyes only, not with the mind. He does not let any thoughts arise when he looks at a flower. Far from seeing sermons in stone, he never even lets himself conceive a stone as beginning a sermon. The only sermon a stone contains for him is that it has nothing at all to tell him [*Páginas Intimas e de Auto-Interpretação*].

For Caeiro metaphysics is the antithesis of his approach to life. . . . Existence, in other words, precedes essence.

Another two-dimensional character is Ricardo Reis. Although possessing a rather interesting biography, his interpretation of the world is surprisingly limited. His response to his supposed seminal master, Caeiro, is deceiving. Reis is a modern pagan who urges one to seize the day and accept fate with tranquility. Where Caeiro's total disregard for the intellect stands opposed to the orthonymic Pessoa's persistent conflict between the intellect and the senses, Ricardo Reis, a "disciple" of Caeiro, reflects Caeiro's suspicion of the intellect but does so from a different perspective. . . .

This persona pleads that he and Lídia abandon the daily toil and, as the flowers whose short life should serve as an example to them, take what advantage their own short life offers. The natural backdrop suggests Caeiro, but the gardens and the sun are of Adonis and Apollo. The rigid order of his pagan cosmos is as present as the order of his poetry. His appeals are for the *future*. He has studied Caeiro, but he lacks Caeiro's sense of being present in the world. Although he suggests that he and Lídia seek another life *inscientes,* unthinkingly, the tight syllabification and extremely wrought hyperbaton do anything but suggest the natural ease and flow of Caeiro's poems. Despite what Reis would wish, his intellect, and not Caeiro, is his master.

Said to be another disciple of Alberto Caeiro, Pessoa's third major heteronym, Alvaro de Campos, presents a fuller, rounder, less static character. He is a persona subject to the oscillations of a manic-depressive evolution. His character is perhaps the most believable of the personae already described, but his work is not less a part of the pattern. Explaining these heteronyms' links to one another in the face of Campos's ideal of Sensationism, Pessoa signals a fundamental word:

> Caeiro has one discipline: things must be felt as they are. Ricardo Reis has another kind of discipline: things must be felt, not only as they are, but also so as to fall in with a certain ideal of classic measure and rule. In Alvaro de Campos things must simply be felt (*Páginas Intimas e de Auto-Interpretação*).

But, as already mentioned, Campos exhibits a clear evolution ranging between the depressive and the manic. In his earliest poem, **"Opiário"** (said to be expressive of

Campos's style before he fell under the influence of Caeiro), his opiated state accompanies him to the brink of despair and launches him on a path of intellectual speculation that would have shocked his "master" Caeiro.

After Campos found his spiritual guru he embarked wholeheartedly on the development of what he called his Sensationist phase. He made some effort to be original, but his links with Italian Futurism, often considered a derivative of Cubism in literature, painting and sculpture, are obvious. In this Futurist/Sensationist phase, with a fury of alternately passionate invective and fervent glorification, he sings exultant praise of the present age. As a representative work of this phase, **"Ode Marítima"** opens with the persona before a peaceful harbor scene. But in the scores of pages which follow, in characteristic Futurist/ Sensationist fervor, he slips in and out of the present time and space, relives other incarnations, wails alternately in English and Portuguese, and generally finds himself to be helpless before the avalanche of vision rising in his mind. As the long poem ends, a sense of order is regained, but the effect of fragmentation and disjointedness lingers in the reader's memory.

Depression sets into Campos's persona as his poetic work unfolds, however, and his major later poems reflect an existentially anguished search for meaning behind appearances, such as in his **"Tabacaria."** This kind of mystery, of course, has no place in Caeiro's universe.

Apollinaire, in his *The Cubist Painters* (1913), noted the limitations of Euclidean geometry in the twentieth century. Beyond the three dimensions that such geometry recognized, he sensed that there was a fourth, the "dimension of the infinite, . . . which endows objects with plasticity". Alvaro de Campos also recognized the pervasive influence of non-Euclidean geometry in his "Apontamentos para uma Estética Não-Aristotélica" (1924-25). Although he is at least as vague as Apollinaire on this matter, it is clear that the two Cubist poet/theoreticians were aware of similar ideas and forces in the air and of the need to find new ways to perceive reality.

Pessoa did write what we normally call Cubist poetry in the Intersectionist phase of his orthonymic poetry. Cubist poetics are also clearly to be seen in the Futurist/Sensationist phase in the poetry of the heteronymic Alvaro de Campos. But where we find the enduring commitment to the notion of the Cubist perspective is in the work of Fernando Pessoa considered as a whole.

Wylie Sypher also could have been referring to Pessoa's personae when he described the Cubist technique in which

> things exist in multiple relations to each other and change their appearance according to the point of view from which we see them—and we now realize that we can see them from innumerable points of view [*From Rococo to Cubism in Art and Literature,* 1960].

Pessoa's intersecting, fragmented, kaleidoscopic, oneiric, multi-faceted images of his early Cubist attempts were dwarfed by the scope of his montage of poetic personae. As the Cubist planes on a canvas, these personae are relatively flat, and where it seems they are not, they are actually the sum of another montage of individual flat poetic personae. The early attempts at Cubist poems merely provided a few tentative models for the macrostructure of the author's whole work.

One doesn't know which persona really speaks for Pessoa, nor does it matter. Most probably he is nowhere wholly present in any one of the personae he created. He is represented, rather, in his collection of apparent contradictions. Fernando Pessoa, the poet, is the point of intersection of many avenues which ultimately cross one another. The overall effect clearly coincides with the brand of realism that the Cubist perspective seeks to convey.

John Hollander (review date 1987)

SOURCE: "Quadrophenia," in *The New Republic,* Vol. 197, No. 3, 790, September 7, 1987, pp. 33-36.

[*Renowned American poet John Hollander reviews two editions of English translations of Pessoa's work:* The Keeper of the Sheep *and* Poems of Fernando Pessoa, *both translated and edited by Edwin Honig and Susan M. Brown. Hollander praises the translations and comments on Pessoa's significant position within the whole of modernism.*]

If Fernando Pessoa had never existed, Jorge Luis Borges might have had to invent him. This remarkable modern poet started writing in English, in which he was educated; and then, in his native Portuguese, he produced four major poetic oeuvres, one under his own name and three completely different ones by fictional poets—no mere pseudonyms—called Alberto Caeiro, Álvaro de Campos, and Ricardo Reis. This was not a matter of tragic, literal psychiatric disorder; it was a figurative revision of a multiple poetic personality that, with its complex relations among the "heteronyms" (as they are usually called to distinguish them from mere pseudonyms without full fictional identities for their bearers), betokened a strong, original, and stable poetic imagination confronting some of the major problems of modernism.

A consideration of Pessoa's poetry entails knowledge of the work of all four poets. Professional scholars will also be concerned with a number of Pessoa's other, more shadowy heteronymous figures: the authors of some of the early poems in English, Alexander Search and Charles Robert Anon; and, in Portuguese, C. Pacheco and a critic named Bernard Soares who wrote no verse, and a number of others to a projected total of 19. But it is ultimately the trilogy of poets Caeiro, Campos, and Reis—along with the orthonymic poetry, written fully in propria persona, of Pessoa himself—that is of primary importance.

Pessoa was born in Lisbon in 1888, the descendant, on his father's side, of a Jewish convert to Christianity (hence,

perhaps, the Jewish element in Campos's character). Pessoa's father was a music critic who died when the boy was five. His mother then married the Portuguese consul in Durban, and Pessoa was educated in South Africa, leaving it permanently in 1905 after having written a prize essay for admission to university there. He chose to attend the University of Lisbon, and in that city he remained, from 1908 until his death in 1935. He worked at commercial foreign correspondence for a number of firms in Lisbon, led a literary life that touched avant-garde circles, and published poems, translations, and essays. He never married, but lived both alone and with members of his family.

Until 1909 Pessoa wrote in English; there are over 100 English poems. (A responsible edition of all of Pessoa's English writings should be done.) Three years later he began to write in his native language and to read widely in French Symbolist poetry. By 1915 he was writing poems under all three heteronyms, at first publishing only some under the name of Campos.

In a letter dated ten months before his death, Pessoa told a disciple his story of the genesis of the heteronyms: suddenly, on March 8, 1914, he started writing a large number of poems under the covering title *O Guardador de Rebanhos* (*The Keeper of Sheep*)—perhaps, it has been suggested, transforming an earlier abandoned project of inventing, as a hoax, a strange sort of pastoral poet. But Alberto Caeiro is a very belated pastoralist. "I never kept sheep," begins the first of the 49 poems that make up his collected works, "But it's as if I'd done so." Here is the rest of the first strophe of his proem, in Edwin Honig and Susan M. Brown's excellent new translation:

> My soul is like a shepherd.
> It knows wind and sun
> Walking hand in hand with the Seasons
> Observing, and following along.
> All of Nature's unpeopled peacefulness
> Comes to sit alongside me.
> Still I'm sad, as a sunset is
> To the imagination,
> When it grows cold at the end of the plain
> And you feel the night come in
> Like a butterfly through the window.

The plain but quizzical style, the limpid vers libre, the systematic dramaturgy—all give Caeiro's work a power that is never simplistic.

The other heteronyms emerged around Caeiro. According to Pessoa's letter, Caeiro was born in 1889, lived with an old aunt in the country, was only minimally educated, had no profession, and died at 26; he represents, for Pessoa, what Shelley called "unpremeditated art." Ricardo Reis, a Horatian neoclassicist in whose tight, strophic odes meditation seems to crystallize, was born in 1887, says Pessoa, and was educated by the Jesuits; a doctor, he resided in Brazil because of his monarchist views. Álvaro de Campos, a naval engineer not presently employed, lives in Libson; he is well traveled, the author (like Reis and

Pessoa) of critical writings, as well as of Whitmanesque longish rhapsodic poems in a mode of free verse very different from Caeiro's.

And finally, of course, there is the orthonymic Fernando Pessoa. The rhymed lyrics of his *Cancioneiro,* and of the wonderful long sequence, published in 1934, called *Mensagem* ("message," "dispatch"—the word can also be used to mean "errand" or "summons"), seem to connect the different virtues of Campos and Reis. *Mensagem* is a sort of post-Symbolist revision of Vaz de Camões's *Os Lusiadas,* the great Portuguese Renaissance epic, a series of internalized, meditative lyrics on moments and figures in Portuguese history, perhaps in some ways analogous to Hart Crane's *The Bridge. . . .*

What is most Borgesian—or possibly Nabokovian—about this group of poets is the way in which Pessoa himself acknowledges how deep an influence Caeiro was upon his own work: "Alberto Caeiro is my master." Octavio Paz has commented that "Caeiro is the sun in whose orbit Reis, Campos, and Pessoa himself rotate. In each are particles of negation or unreality. Reis believes in form, Campos in sensation, Pessoa in symbols. Caeiro doesn't believe in anything. He exists." And Pessoa remarked of Caeiro's influential force:

> Caeiro had that force. What does it matter to me that Caeiro be of me if Caeiro is like that? So, operating on Reis, who had not as yet written anything, he made come to birth in him a form of his own and an aesthetic persona. So operating on myself, he has delivered me from shadows and letters. . . . After this, so prodigiously achieved, who will ask whether Caeiro exists or not?

There are other ways of regarding this relation among the four poets, three of whom have been invented by a fourth who nonetheless claims to derive from one of them. Pessoa invoked at various times the analogy of fully formed Shakespearean characters, and at others the context of modernist poetic impersonality. As Álvaro de Campos put it, in a manifesto called *Ultimatum,* the greatest artist will reveal himself the least (this from a true, not a trivial, Whitmanian). He will "write in the greatest number of literary genres, making use of paradoxes and dissimilarities. No artist should have only one personality."

A poet like Auden, who wrote in a variety of modes, could approximate this achievement, although his voice never changes. So can a dramatic monologuist, of which Pessoa might seem to be an extreme case. But there is another aspect to his Trilogy: it is as if the historical phases of the life of poetry itself, not merely of one artist's work, were being personified synchronically and allowed to coexist. What Renaissance scholars refer to as the Virgilian progression—from pastoral to georgic to epic—was affirmed in the canceled opening lines of the *Aeneid,* which outlined, for Renaissance poets, the model of a poetic career: "I am he who once played my song on a slender reed, then, leaving the woods, made the neighboring fields serve the farmer, however grasping—a book farmers prize; but now of Mars' bristling [arms and the man I sing . . .]."

Similarly, Caeiro's modern pastoral, the Parnassian withdrawals of Reis, Campos's great odes of imagined voyaging, are all gathered up in various ways in Pessoa's own poems. Certainly the *Mensagem* would not be possible without Caeiro's unmediated vision, or Reis's forethought, or Campos's unending quest for a hero, a subject, at once within and beyond himself. The various heteronyms can thus be heard as giving voice to drifts, strains, and impulses within one imagination, each providing a reductive version of what the revisionary New Poetry should be.

There have been several books introducing Pessoa to speakers of English, but they are all out of print. Aside from Edouard Roditi's brief essay and fine, pioneering translations of five poems in 1955, we have had a Penguin volume by Jonathan Griffin and two very useful books, both published in 1971 and both with detailed introductions and notes—one of 60 poems, translated by F. E. G. Quintanilha, and the other by Peter Rickard of Cambridge, an exemplary volume of 70 poems with excellent apparatus and free-verse translations of unusual tautness and limpidity. Both of these include the Portuguese texts, and for readers without that language but with, say, French and Spanish, the originals can be a revelation: with a dictionary, an elementary grammar, and a good knowledge of poetry, one can find out a great deal about what has been traded for what in the complex economy of verse translation.

Now Edwin Honig, who produced a smaller selection of Pessoa translations in 1971, has collaborated with Susan M. Brown on two volumes. One is a broader selection of the work of all the heteronyms, as well as of Pessoa's own English verse. The other is the complete version of Caeiro's *The Keeper of Sheep* Honig and Brown are at their best with Caeiro, and the complete oeuvre is atreasure to have. I regret strongly that there is no facing Portuguese text, particularly in the more comprehensive selection, *Poems of Ferdinand Pessoa.* Without the Portuguese, and without the kind of biographical material and annotation that Rickard gives, the poems of Reis and of Pessoa himself lose the most. Explaining some of the problems faced by the translations in Honig and Brown's larger volume involves taking a closer look at all the poets and their work. (When quoting from poems that Honig and Brown do not translate, I use my own, provisional versions.)

We might start with Pessoa's poems in English. They are worth more than a glance, not least because some of their peculiar energies and successes carry over into the later work and are immediately accessible to English readers. The series of "Inscriptions," resonant of the sepulchral epigrams of the Greek Anthology, seems related to the mode of Ricardo Reis. They are terse, elegant, graceful, and yet capable of startling:

> Me, Chloe, a maid, the mighty fates have
>   given,
> Who was nought to them, to the peopled
>   shades.
> Thus the gods will. My years were but

twice seven.
I am forgotten now in my distant glades.

Or:

There was a silence where the town was
    old.
Grass grows where not a memory lies
    below.
We that dined loud are sand. The tale is
    told.
The far hoofs hush. The inn's last light doth
    go.

Or:

I put by pleasure like an alien bowl.
Stern, separate, mine, I looked towards
    where gods seem.
From behind me the common shadow stole.
Dreaming that I slept not, I slept my dream.

"My hand/Put these inscriptions here, half knowing why;/ Last, and hence seeing all, of the passing band," concludes the fictional author in the last of these, as if Pessoa were bidding farewell, in 1920, to neoclassicism, summing up and transcending a tradition in a way analogous to that by which Alberto Caeiro would perform a final revision of pastoral.

Honig and Brown reprint ten of Pessoa's strange, somewhat crabbed English sonnets and some earlier poems, including a few by Alexander Search. One misses a bit of the long, homosexually-oriented **"Antinous"** (1915) that begins (with an echo of Verlaine, I think), "The rain outside was cold in Hadrian's soul," and whose high diction moves through fine passages like this one about Hadrian's eponymous lover:

That love they lived as a religion
Offered to gods that come themselves to
    men.
Sometimes he was adorned or made to don
Half-vestured, then in statued nudity
Did imitate some god that seems to be
By marble's accurate virtue men's again.

And the remarkable heterosexual counterpart of the Antinous poem, Pessoa's **"Epithalamium"** of the previous year (a weird version of Spenser, deriving from his diction and verse-form but without the famous refrain), concentrates on the fears and joys of the bride's sexual initiation. Thus the 12th strophe's invocation of a phallic "belfry's height" that "Does in the blue wide heaven a message prove,/Somewhat calm, of delight," and of the sun pouring light on the "ordered rout" of guests; "And all their following eyes clasp round the bride":

They feel like hands her bosom and her
    side;
Like the inside of her vestment next her
    skin,

They round her round and fold each crevice
    in;
They lift her skirts up, as to tease or woo
The cleft thing hid below. . . .

The verbal texture and formal control of the English poems operate with greater density and plangency in Pessoa's own poems, and, differently, in those of Reis. What marks Caeiro, though, is that he is always telling you what he is *not* doing: "Rhymes don't matter to me," he says. "You seldom see / Two identical trees, standing side by side." Still, he can be allusive in his negations of allusiveness and tradition, as in his rejection of the mainstream of poetic history in favor of the river flowing through his own village. (One's local stream was the emblem of one's own poetic turf throughout the Renaissance, like the Thames, the Avon, Du Bellay's Loire, and so on.) But he ends poem 20 by saying that his village river reminds one of nothing, that if one is beside it one is merely beside it. The passing wind, in another poem, talks only about the wind; the Virgilian shepherds, in yet another, played on reeds and sang in a literary way about love, "But the shepherds in Virgil poor things / are Virgil, / And nature is ancient and beautiful." He keeps protesting his conceptual innocence, and performing, like Wallace Stevens's snow man, a reduction of false imaginings.

Álvaro de Campos is a visionary wanderer, most obviously indebted for his ode forms and long rhapsodic lines to Whitman; but he is also a Shelleyan. His early **"Triumphal Ode"** (1914), tinged with Futurist rhetoric, starts out

In the aching light of the factory's large
    electric bulbs,
Fevered, I write.
I write gnashing my teeth, brutal before the
    beauty of this.
Before the beauty of this, wholly unknown
    to the ancients. . . .
Fevered and staring at the engines as if at a
    tropical Nature
Great human tropics of iron and fire and
    power—
I sing, and sing the present, and also the
    past and future.
Because the present is all of the present and
    all of the future
And Plato and Virgil within the machines
    and electric lights.

But, after much Whitmanesque incantation, this poem ends with a longing for transcendence, and a revision of Whitman's favored trope: *"Ah nõ ser en toda a gente e toda a parte!"* ("Ah not to be all people and all places!").

Campos's long, splendid **"Maritime Ode,"** with its sexual fantasies and Mallarméan withdrawals and fears of erotic shipwreck, his **"Tobacco-shop,"** his poems on **"Lisbon Revisited,"** move into realms of terror, despair, and selfquestioning of a sort Caeiro's pure assurance never explores. His diction, too, wanders from high to low. It seems to me, with my limited knowledge of Portuguese, that Honig and Brown do very well with his language and with the cadence of his lines.

Ricardo Reis is another story. He invokes Horace's Lydias, Naearas, and Chloes, without any of Caeiro's desire to avoid singing literarily of love:

> As though every kiss
> Were of departure
> O my Chloe, let us kiss now, loving.
> Perhaps this hand touching
> Our shoulders already
> Hails that barge, empty ever when it comes,
> Binding in the same sheaf
> What we were together
> With the totality of other life.

In highly crafted, syllabically counted lines, and with archaized diction and Latinate syntax, Reis promotes a guarded, intellectual, far-from-ecstatic mood of carpe diem and memento mori intertwined, asking nothing of the gods, the answer to life's questions lying beyond them: *"Os deus sõ deuses / Porque nõ se pensam"* ("The gods are gods / Because they don't think themselves up"). Literally echoing Horace, Reis proclaims that "Happy he whom gracious life / Allowed to keep the gods in mind / To see like them / These earthly things where dwells / A reflection, mortal, of immortal life." Where Caeiro rejects previous allegorizations of nature, Reis rejects moral homilies on our condition, except that he propounds the virtue of such rejections:

> To everyone, like his height justice is
> Distributed: thus fate makes
> Some tall and others happy.
> Nothing is a prize: what happens just
> happens.
> Nothing, Lydia, do we
> Owe our fate but to have it.

To preserve in English something of the tone of Reis's syntax and diction (he will use Latin words that are neologisms for modern Portuguese) and his meter (it substitutes for the classical quantitative prosody a pure syllabism) is not too difficult, and syllabic versions of Reis would give one a better sense of the almost classically modernist (in the Anglo-American, rather than the Continental mode) use of strict form as a stay against confusion. In a central, aristocratic figure, Reis rises above the storms of sensibility through which Campos perilously and ecstatically navigates: "Be whole in everything. Put all you are/Into the smallest thing you do. / The whole moon gleams in every pool, / It rides so high."

Reis has not yet had his optimum translator. Perhaps, as is frequently the case with poetic translation, a poem in Language A must pass into Language B through the enabling filter of some particular body of poetry already in B. (Recall, for example, the Tennyson that makes the blank verse of Robert Fitzgerald's wonderful English *Aeneid* so noble and powerful, as opposed to the tincture of Pound that made the same translator's *Odyssey* so strong for the modernist ear.) Perhaps the youthful Milton's unrhymed, stressed translation of Horace, "What slender youth . . . ," might provide something of such a filter. Or so might some of the diction of Landor.

The so-called orthonymic poetry of Pessoa himself requires even more in the way of adaptive resources. Pessoa has all of the control of Reis with none of his archaisms; and he has also a good deal of Campos's vigor. His negations and withdrawals are almost gnostic in their complexity, and go beyond Caeiro in wiping the slate clean. Thus in a Christmas poem of 1922 (the original rhymes, as in this version, are the words *culto* and *occulto*):

> A god is born. Others die. What never came
> Nor went was Truth. Error changed all the
>   more.
> Our new Eternity is not the same.
> The best is always what has gone before.

> Blind, Knowledge labors at the barren
>   ground.
> Crazy, Faith lives the dream of its own cult.
> A newborn god is just a new word's sound.
> Seek not then, nor believe. All is occult.

Pessoa's own verse makes rich and powerful use of rhyme, not merely for generating a melody or for pacing, but (as with all important poets) for its semantic work and play, for what it reveals of relations among words and among their referents—relations that ordinary usage keeps hidden. A poem of 1913 about a village church bell, for example, concludes:

> At each one of your strokes
> Resounding in open sky
> I feel the past more distant
> I feel longing more nigh

—except that in the original, the rhymes are on *aberto* ("open") and *mais perto* ("nearer"): the widening of possibility becomes another kind of enclosure at the incursion of *saudade* ("longing," "yearning").

In another quatrain of the same poem, Pessoa plays with the notion of repetition, saying of his village bell, sad in the evening calm, "Each stroke of your / Sounds within my soul"—bland enough in English, except that the third line about each stroke of the bell, *"Cada sua badalada,"* plays on the internal rhyme of *cada* ("every") and the word for the tolling of a bell, as if thereby to augment the number of strokes of the clapper.

One more example—they blossom everywhere in these poems—of Pessoa's verbal texture, which gets completely lost in most translations I've seen. **"The Portuguese Sea,"** poem 30 of *Mensagem,* ends:

> Quem quer passar além da Bojador
> Tem que passar além da dor
> Deus ao mar o perigo e o abismo deu
> Mas nele é que espelhou o céu.

In Honig and Brown:

> If you'd sail beyond the cape
> Sail you must past cares, past grief.
> God gave perils to the sea and sheer depth
> But mirrored heaven there.

But even without knowing any Portuguese, a reader can see the symmetry of sailing past the *Bojador* (a West African promontory, slightly south of the Canaries, once a limit of exploration) and the *dor,* the anguish now seen as its last port, in the rhymed shorter line. The pun that mirrors *Deus* and *deu,* "God" and "gave," at the end of the next line is itself brilliantly avowed in the final one, with its image of mirroring and the confirming rhyme of *céu*—"sky," "heaven." One can't ask a translator to get all of these moments, but one does keep wanting to be reminded that they, or something like them, are there, that the language of the poetry has that sort of dimension.

If English syllabics suggest a way of handling Reis's tight strophes, perhaps a way of handling Pessoa's orthonymic poetry has been pointed by Richard Howard in the superb unrhymed but accentual-syllabic verse he used for all of Baudelaire. Howard managed, in versions of poems with rhyming stanzas just like Pessoa's, to create the impression of rhyme by his end-stopping mono- and dissyllabic words; one has the feeling that the line one had just read had rhymed with an earlier one, heard but forgotten. Rhythm is more important than rhyme for holding verse together, even though it cannot often perform the magic on particular words that rhyme, assonance, and alliteration can.

Honig and Brown have done very well by Caeiro, and reasonably well by Álvaro de Campos. Ricardo Reis and Pessoa himself still may have to find their translators. But if Honig and Brown's work renews the debate about translation and leads to new versions of Pessoa, that, too, will be a measure of its success. Meanwhile this volume has brought a great poet to our attention again. Anybody who cares about poetry, about fictions of identity, about the whole of modernism, must be grateful.

Anne J. Cruz (essay date 1988)

SOURCE: "Masked Rhetoric: Contextuality in Fernando Pessoa's Poems," in *Romance Notes,* Vol. XXIX, No. 1, Fall, 1988, pp. 55-60.

[*In the following excerpt, Cruz explores the rhetorical implications of Pessoa's use of heteronyms.*]

Fernando Pessoa has made an art form of psychic fragmentation. In his poems, mask (un)covers mask in order to expound, explicate, and contradict the multifacetic poet. The creation of *heterónimos,* as he calls his poetic avatars, presupposes an interest in the ludic: unlike Antonio Machado's pseudonyms, which clearly reveal the poet's persona to the reader, Pessoa's masks contribute to his duplicity as poet. As Octavio Paz has perceptively pointed out in his introduction to Pessoa's poems, "Reis and Campos told what he [Pessoa] would never tell. In contradicting him, they expressed him, in expressing him, they made him invent himself." Pessoa's creations are motivated dramatically; by acting out his many roles, he creates himself. What Pessoa's poetry ultimately discloses, then, is not the "real poet"—whoever he may be—but the rhetorical origins of his art.

The distinction between the rhetorical and the serious has been drawn by Richard Lanham, who notes that these two modes of authorship are based on two differing types of life in western civilization, as defined by Werner Jaeger in his *Paideia:*

> There are two contrasting types of life. . . . One of them is built upon the flattering quasi-arts—really not arts at all but copies of arts. We may call it, after one of its main species of flattery, the rhetorical ideal of life. Its purpose is to create pleasure and win approval. The other, its opponent, is the philosophical life. It is based on knowledge of human nature and of what is best for it: so it is a real techné, and it really cares for man, for the body as well as the soul [Richard Lanham, *Motiues of Eloquence: Literary Rhetoric in the Renaissance,* 1976].

For Lanham, this historical as well as philosophical division has in turn produced two types of literature which need to be measured by different parameters:

> There seem to be two characteristic modes of Western literature, then, narrative and speech or serious and rhetorical, and two ranges of motive, one serious and purposive and the other dramatic and playful. The more one ponders these parallel dichotomies, the more clear it becomes that we really need two poetics to make sense of them.

The serious poet's rejection of the dramatic and playful is countered by the ludic poet's revelling precisely in his linguistic ability to play.

Pessoa's poetry places him within the category of rhetorical man who, instead of hiding his art, exults in its ostentation, since art is the only concept in which he believes. As Lanham demonstrates, the poet feels at home in his roles, knowing that to live, he must always play them, since only through his poses does he become himself: "imposture becomes sincerity. . . . Rhetorical man is an actor and insincerity is the actor's mode of being." The difference between reality and art, between truth and fiction, is exploited continuously by the rhetorical poet, as reality cannot exist without artistic formulation. The poet's language renders significance and form to the chaotic reality around him, only to lose its signifying quality and revert to pure playfulness:

> A totally serious, referential use of language never lasts long. It becomes stylized, turns playful . . . the very process of composition generates an oscillation between play and purpose. But at the same time, a

movement toward the opposite extreme, toward pure verbal play, activates our resources for making meaning, our impulse for purpose.

Investigating its own creative impulse, Pessoa's poetics develops from the tensions between play and purpose. Thus, in his often-quoted **"Autopsicografía,"** written under the name Fernando Pessoa, he creates images whose significance he then negates. . . .

To move the reader, the poet must pretend he feels nothing, divesting himself of any emotion so he may draw closer to the reader intellectually. His rational expression—the poem—is, like the poem's *calhas de roda,* the medium by which he cultivates the emotion of the reader (the *coração,* reduced to a child's toy, *comboio de corda*) in order to entertain the reader's intellect (and by entertaining the poet's reason, as the term *razão* is ambiguous here). Thus, in the poem, the difference between the rhetorical and the serious not only parallels the dichotomy between reason—the intellective faculty—and emotion, but also the function that the poet assigns to the expression of pain as the motivation of an artistic game controlled by the intellect.

The tension between emotion and reason allows the creation of the poem. The *calhas de roda* symbolize the union between the mind and the heart, a circular pathway with no beginning and no end, and one on which the heart will continuously journey, so long as it feels pain. . . .

To [Georg] Lind, Pessoa's calculated images reveal his serious intent. Yet the poem begins with an antinomy: if the poet is a *fingidor,* then it is only logical to suppose that what follows is also a fiction. Pessoa distances himself doubly from his poetry; hiding behind two masks from the reader, he narrates the poem in the third person, placing himself in the reader's role ("E os que lêem o que escreve"). By calling the poem **"Autopsicografía,"** he promises the reader at the very least a tentative self-analysis; however, he then negates any truth the poem may contain by presenting himself as his own fictive creation. Nonetheless, the poem does tell us something. It exposes the poet's belief in his ability to create an experience—however fictional—thus celebrating his own self as a creator of fiction as well as a fictional creation. . . .

If in **"Autopsicografía"** Pessoa disappears behind yet another mask to become one reader among many, in **"Isto"** he reaffirms his authorial stance through the use of the first person. Assuming the persona of the poet, he distances himself from "them" *(dizem)*—the disbelievers who take imaginative poetry to be nothing but a lie. To the author of **"Isto,"** creativity does not originate in emotion, but in the imagination, as he perceives incidents that in themselves create poetic visions. The simile of the terrace illustrates the continuity of experience, each incident opening onto the next, and offering the poet a perspective from which he draws for his creative act ("Por isso escrevo em meio / do que não está ao pé.") His attempt to engage experiences (whether real or fictive) becomes the creative force which informs as well as justifies his poem: he is free to create without emotion. Unlike in **"Autop-**

sicografía," the poet does not intend to influence the reader's reaction; by separating himself both emotionally and aesthetically, he places the responsibility of response squarely on the reader: "Sentir? Sinta quem lê!". . . .

Joanna Courteau notes [in her article "Contradiction in the Poetry of Fernando Pessoa," in *Actas do II Congresso International de Estudos Pessoanos,* 1985] that Pessoa's poetry creates and inhabits a *heteroreality,* one where "reality corresponds to the aesthetic space of art." She warns, however, that "what must not be forgotten is that this aesthetic space which we may call heteroreality is, unlike everyday reality, simply and purely a construction created by language." This in turn allows us to "set aside our logic and our senses and to participate in the poet's heteroreality" which, to Courteau, is a poetic reality constructed on the basis of contradiction.

Yet, to comprehend Pessoa's contradictions, we need to view the poems as operating not only intertextually—the "real" poet disappearing within the space created by their confrontation, as Courteau has pointed out—but also contextually: we cannot understand the one without reading the other. To read one poem without attending to its poetic response is to ignore the dialectics of Pessoa's poetry, the continual oscillations between truth and fiction, between the serious and the rhetorical, that occur not only in the poetry of his *hererónimos,* but also in the poems of Fernando Pessoa *ele-mesmo.* In the final analysis, all his poems must be read in relation to one another in order to uncover the rhetorical strategies through which Pessoa—poet and poetic creation—creates himself.

Richard Zenith   (essay date 1993)

SOURCE: "Fernando Pessoa and the Theatre of His Self," in *Performing Arts Journal,* Vol.XV, No. 2, May, 1993, pp. 47-9.

[*Below, Zenith provides a general overview of Pessoa's career and the development of his poetic persona(e).*]

Not widely known in his own country and scarcely at all outside it at the time of his death in 1935, Fernando Pessoa (born 1888) is now generally regarded as Portugal's most original poet since Luís de Camões and one of the most original poets of any land writing in the twentieth century. This phenomenal increase in stature is related more or less directly to the increasing availability of the 25,000 + manuscript sheets left by Pessoa in a large trunk and housed today at the National Library in Lisbon. Pessoa was rapidly appreciated by the Portuguese-speaking world as much of his most important poetry saw print in the 1940s, and in the last decade or so he has become a literary byword across continental Europe, with both his poetry and prose being translated on a grand scale. His work has caught on more slowly in the English-speaking world, which is ironic when we consider that Pessoa, who spent much of his childhood in South Africa, wrote all of his early poems, a number of later poems, and most of his personal notations in English. Even his final recorded words, written the day before his death, were in English: "I know not what tomorrow will bring."

A sizable portion of Pessoa's writings have yet to be published in the original, let alone in translation. Besides poetry, fiction and drama, Pessoa's legacy consists of philosophy, social and literary criticism, translations, linguistic theory, horoscopes and assorted other texts, variously typed, handwritten or illegibly scrawled in Portuguese, English and French. He wrote in notebooks, on loose sheets, on the backs of letters, advertisements and handbills, on stationery from the firms he worked at and from the cafés he frequented, on envelopes, on paper scraps, and in between the lines of his own prior texts. The Pessoa archives are a veritable labyrinth, and so it is not surprising that new and important texts are constantly turning up.

The fragmentary state of the archives is emblematic of the author's literary project of depersonalization. "Be plural like the universe!" wrote Pessoa with a flourish on a scrap of paper left in his famous trunk of manuscripts, and he set the example, multiplying himself into three major "heteronyms"—Alberto Caeiro, Ricardo Reis, and Álvaro de Campos—along with dozens of lesser "dramatis personae" who wrote poetry, stories, essays and criticism, very often about each other. Teresa Rita Lopes, one of Portugal's most knowledgeable and astute Pessoa scholars, convincingly argues that the universe of Pessoa was a vast and ongoing theatre of himself, and she cites the protean poet's own words as evidence. He wrote, for example, that the heteronyms "should be considered as distinct from their author. Each one forms a drama of sorts; and together they form another drama. . . . The works of these three poets constitute a dramatic ensemble, with careful attention having been paid to their intellectual and personal interaction. . . . It is a drama in people, instead of in acts."

The heteronyms were "born" in 1914 (they were given retroactive birth dates: 1889, 1887 and 1890, respectively) and each was endowed with an individuated biography, psychology, politics, religion, and physique. Alberto Caeiro, considered the Master by the other two, was an ingenuous, unlettered man who lived in the country and had no profession. Ricardo Reis was a doctor and classicist who wrote odes in the style of Horace. Álvaro de Campos, a naval engineer, started out as an exuberant futurist with a Whitmanesque voice, but over time he came to sound more like a brooding existentialist. The pithiest description and distinction of the heteronyms was made by Pessoa in a text he wrote in English: "Caeiro has one discipline: things must be felt as they are. Ricardo Reis has another kind of discipline: things must be felt, not only as they are, but also so as to fall in with a certain ideal of classic measure and rule. In Álvaro de Campos things must simply be felt."

Much of Pessoa's best verse was attributed to the heteronyms, but the majority of his poetry, including nearly his entire production in English, was written under his own name. Pessoa himself may be described as a neo-Symbolist poet of esoteric, patriotic, and existentialist themes. His work, the virtual opposite of Caeiro's, tends to be highly rational and analytical, rarely taking things simply as they are, at face value.

The drama of Pessoa was that there was no drama, except for the literary kind. "Real life" hardly existed for this fragmented soul, or it meant little to him. After returning from South Africa to his native Lisbon at age 17, he never again left Portugal, and almost never even left the capital city. He traveled immensely, but it was all in his writings and his imagination. The realization of a dream will always be something less than the dream, and so the secret of successful living—according to Pessoa—is to act as little as possible, taking refuge from the world in the imagination, where everything is perfect, and nothing disappoints.

Pessoa wrote his only complete play, *The Mariner,* in 1913, a year before the heteronyms burst onto the scene (though Pessoa began to invent alter egos already as a small child), and the essential drama, or non-drama, of the mature author was all contained here, in seed form. *The Mariner* is the negation of action, plot, progress, and even character. Nothing in this strange play remotely approaches reality or its semblance. All we have is a vague longing for another age, for other lands and for other seas, for whatever is *other,* and then the "story": a hazy recollection of a dream within a dream, and the dreamer suspects that she herself may be a mere figment in a dream of the mariner she dreamed about. Nothing of substance is presented in these pages—only words that "seem like people."

This anti-play or "static drama," to use Pessoa's self-contradictory epithet (*drama* deriving from a Greek verb meaning "to do, to act"), reads like a program or prophecy of the then young poet's life, for he spent the rest of his years leading a largely solitary existence but producing an astonishing quantity of words so as to *other* himself into fictitious personalities that were perhaps—he speculated—more real than he was.

Static and undramatic as it may be, *The Mariner* has been staged in a number of languages and countries. And Pessoa's *Faust,* a long and unfinished fragmentary play on which he worked throughout his adult life, has been produced in both Portuguese and French, having played last year to packed audiences in a theatre outside Paris. In this postmodern age of anti-discourse, anti-history, anti-literature and anti-art, it is surprising that some enterprising troupe in America hasn't already seen fit to give part of the stage to Pessoa's anti-theatre.

FURTHER READING

Biography

Jennings, H. D. *Os Dois Exilios: Fernando Pessoa Na Africa Do Sul.* Porto, Portugal: Centro de Estudos Pessoanos, 1984, 210 p.

This is a critical biography of Pessoa centering on his youth in South Africa.

Criticism

Anderson, Robert N. "The Static Drama of Fernando Pessoa." *Hispanofila* 104 (January 1992): 89-97.

Anderson examines questions of genre and Pessoa's conception of himself as a dramatist, and examines how readers today can theorize a dramatic genre to which Pessoa could belong.

Biderman, Sol. "Mount Abiegnos and the Masks: Occult Imagery in Yeats and Pessoa." *Luso-Brazilian Review* V, No. 1 (June 1968): 59-74.

Biderman addresses the similarities between Pessoa's and Yeats' involvements in mystical and occult movements and how these interests are manifested in their work in similar ways.

Brown, Susan Margaret. "The Whitman/Pessoa Connection." *Walt Whitman Quarterly Review* IX, No. 1 (Summer 1991): 1-14.

Brown examines the influence on Pessoa of American poet Walt Whitman.

Carreño, Antonio. "Suggested Bases for a Comparative Study of Pessoa and Antonio Machado." *Romance Notes* XX, No. 1 (Fall 1979): 24-8.

Carreño positions Pessoa and Machado as contemporaries within the Hispanic poetic tradition on the basis of their aesthetics.

Monteiro, George. "Poe/Pessoa." *Comparative Literature* XL, No. 1 (Winter 1988): 134-49.

Monteiro discusses the influence of the American tradition on Pessoa, specifically Edgar Allan Poe's.

————."The Song of the Reaper: Pessoa and Wordsworth." *Portuguese Studies* V (1989): 71-80.

Monteiro examines similarities between Pessoa's and William Wordsworth's poetry.

Roditi, Edouard. "Fernando Pessoa, Outsider Among English Poets." *The Literary Review* (Spring 1963): 372-85.

Roditi brings a biographical angle to bear upon an analysis of Pessoa's English poetry positioned within the context of the major poets writing in English at the beginning of the twentieth century.

Sousa, Ronald W. "On Pessoa's Continued Centrality in Portuguese Culture." *Ideologies & Literature* III, No. 2 (Fall 1988): 39-50.

Sousa examines the figure of "Pessoa" and its numerous appropriations in the political history of twentieth-century Portugal.

Ziomek, Henryk. "Dream and Vision in the Poetry of Fernando Pessoa." *Kentucky RomanceQuarterly* XX, No. 4 (1973): 483-93.

Ziomek examines the relationship between reality, dream and image in Pessoa's poetry.

Additional coverage of Pessoa's life and career is contained in the following sources published by Gale Research: *Twentieth-Century Literary Criticism*, Vol. 27; *Hispanic Literary Criticism*, Vol. 2; and *Contemporary Authors*, Vol. 125.

Kenneth Rexroth
1905-1982

American poet, translator, essayist, playwright.

INTRODUCTION

Kenneth Rexroth authored a large oeuvre of poetry and translations and was an instrumental figure in two different poetry movements in San Francisco. His early work is difficult, bristling with abstruse literary allusions and abstract imagery when it is not outright Cubist—the sight and sound of words dominating over sense—while his later work is almost unpoetically simple. Some of his poems contain vitriolic political screeds, while others have an extreme serenity, influenced by Buddhism. Rexroth never completed high school, yet he was enormously erudite, and translated poems from French, Spanish, Greek, Chinese and Japanese with great skill and compassion. Though he was associated with the 1940s San Francisco Renaissance and later with the Beat poets, Rexroth was never securely a part of any movement. He was unsparing in his criticism of academics and whatever seemed to him to represent the literary establishment. He always remained an outsider, and his work was not treated seriously outside a small circle during his lifetime, usually overlooked or ignored by anthologies of American poetry. His poetic styles are so disparate that it is difficult to encapsulate the totality of his work. His love poems and his nature poems, which finely render the Northern California landscape, are perhaps his most appealing and accessible, and have received the most critical attention.

Biographical Information

Rexroth had a troubled and tumultuous childhood. Born in 1905 in South Bend, Indiana, he spent his early years in Elkhart, Indiana; Battle Creek, Michigan; and Chicago, Illinois. His tubercular mother died when Rexroth was eleven, and three years later his father died of alcoholism. Rexroth spent his teen years in Chicago, nominally cared for by an aunt, attending courses at the Art Institute and at the University of Chicago. Precocious as both a painter and poet, Rexroth never graduated from high school. By the time he was seventeen he was a chronic truant, at times incarcerated in the Chicago House of Corrections, and, when he was free, was living on his own in a bohemian style, writing, painting, and acting. He traveled across the U.S. and to Europe, working odd jobs such as ship's cook and ranch hand until 1927 when he married his first wife, painter Andree Dutcher, and settled with her in San Francisco. He published his first book of poems, *In What Hour,* in 1940. Andrée, an epileptic, died after a seizure in that same year. The marriage had been all but officially over for years, and Rexroth soon married his lover, Marie

Kass. He and Marie were avid mountain climbers, camping in the Sierras for weeks at a time, and many of his finest poems were inspired by trips he took with her. His book *The Phoenix and the Tortoise* was published by New Directions in 1944, and Rexroth began a life-long friendship with New Directions publisher James Laughlin. Rexroth was a well-known figure in San Francisco both for his leftist political work and for his literary soirées, but he had no national reputation. In 1948 he received a Guggenheim fellowship which allowed him to give readings across the country, and then to travel to Europe. After the trip, he divorced Marie and had a child with Marthe Larsen, whom he had married bigamously. (Perhaps to be expected from someone noted for his amorous poems, Rexroth's personal life was complicated and full of entanglements.) Despite the prestige of the Guggenheim award, Rexroth failed to attract much critical attention, and his books continued to be published solely by New Directions. By the mid-1950s, San Francisco was the hotbed of the Beat movement, and Rexroth made himself a mentor or father-figure to many younger poets such as Allen Ginsburg and Lawrence Ferlinghetti. He published many volumes of translations, new poems, and collections of his earlier poems, including in 1958 *The*

Homestead Called Damascus, a poem he had completed when he was twenty. In 1967 he received a Rockefeller Foundation grant which allowed him to visit Japan. This visit cemented his Buddhist leanings, and heavily influenced his next book, *The Heart's Garden, The Garden's Heart.* He had published an important anthology of his earlier work, *The Collected Shorter Poems,* in 1966, and in 1968 followed it with *The Collected Longer Poems.* Now the body of his work was in print and could be read as a whole. He continued to write and publish new poems in the 1970s, and also taught at the University of California at Santa Barbara. He died of a heart attack in 1982.

Major Works

Rexroth's first major work was *The Homestead Called Damascus,* which he began writing when he was fifteen and did not publish until 1958, when he was fifty-three. A long, allusive philosophical poem, it shows the intellectual complexities Rexroth wrestled with at a very young age. His other early works are all similarly marked by intellectual force, length, and daring experimentation with language. "A Prolegomenon to a Theodicy," completed in 1927 and published in the collection *The Art of Worldly Wisdom* in 1949, is indicative even by its title of the obliqueness of Rexroth's early poems. The poems of *In What Hour,* published in 1940, are by contrast startlingly lyrical and direct. One of the best is "Toward an Organic Philosophy," which tells of several nights spent by campfires in the mountains of California. The philosophy of the poem is beautifully contained in the poet's observation of the stars, wildflowers, deer and trees.

The long poem "The Phoenix and the Tortoise" contains similar sensual descriptions of camping in the mountains, but this more complex poem mingles the speaker's nature observations with pungent political musings and quotations, some distorted, from philosophers and historical figures. This uneasy mixture of bile and lyricism may be as close as anything to the "true" Rexroth. Another long poem, "The Dragon and the Unicorn," from 1952, is a record of Rexroth's travels through Europe. It similarly combines pithily rendered descriptions of hotels and monuments: "The sandstone of the Roman / Road is marked with sun wrinkles / Of prehistoric beaches" with crotchety, dismissive musings: "Lawrence, Lawrence, what a lot / Of hogwash you have fathered. / Etruscan art is just plain bad." Some of his finest short poems are found in the 1956 volume *In Defense of the Earth.* This volume contains "Seven Poems for Marthe, My Wife," considered his most moving love poems. His later poems stand in great contrast to his early and middle works, as they are marked by Buddhist philosophy and are much simpler and more serene. "The Heart's Garden, The Garden's Heart" is the most emblematic of the later Rexroth. Toward the end of his life he was more and more interested in Asian poetry, and translated several volumes from both Japanese and Chinese. His *One Hundred Poems from the Chinese* and *One Hundred Poems from the Japanese* are perhaps his most popular books. These simple, direct, short poems influenced his style in his original English lan-

guage poems, to the point where one of his latest works, *The Love Poems of Marichiko,* only pretends to be a translation of a Japanese woman poet. These, his most erotic poems, Rexroth wrote when he was in his seventies.

Critical Reception

Rexroth's reputation while he was alive existed almost exclusively among other poets and literati in the San Francisco area. He scorned the New York literary establishment and anyone in academia, and his work was ignored by most major critics. He did little to court the scholarly community and in fact did much to make enemies of the influential figures in literary circles. Most notably, poet William Carlos Williams endorsed Rexroth's work, but reviews often tended to be dismissive in nature. Rexroth had a small following in England, and in 1972 an English publisher put out *The Rexroth Reader,* containing both poetry and prose. But Rexroth never fit neatly into any literary categories of style or historical period, and thus was excluded from many collections of American verse. Since his death, more detailed studies of his work have appeared, and, given time, critics may find much material worth examination in Rexroth's long catalog of works.

PRINCIPAL WORKS

Poetry

In What Hour 1940
The Phoenix and the Tortoise 1944
The Art of Worldly Wisdom 1949
The Signature of All Things 1950
The Dragon and the Unicorn 1952
A Bestiary for My Daughters Mary and Katharine 1955
One Hundred Poems from the Japanese [translator] 1955
Thou Shalt Not Kill: A Memorial for Dylan Thomas 1955
In Defense of the Earth 1956
One Hundred Poems from the Chinese [translator] 1956
Thirty Spanish Poems of Love and Exile [translator] 1956
Poems from the Greek Anthology [translator] 1962
The Homestead Called Damascus 1963
Natural Numbers: New and Selected Poems 1963
The Collected Shorter Poems 1966
The Heart's Garden, The Garden's Heart 1967
The Collected Longer Poems 1968
The Spark in the Tinder of Knowing 1968
Love in the Turning Year: One Hundred More Poems from the Chinese [translator] 1970
Sky Sea Birds Trees Earth House Beasts Flowers 1971
The Kenneth Rexroth Reader (poetry and prose) 1972
One Hundred More Poems from the Japanese [translator] 1974
New Poems 1974
On Flower Wreath Hill 1976
The Silver Swan 1976
The Love Poems of Marichiko 1978
The Morning Star [includes *The Silver Swan, On Flower Wreath Hill* and *The Love Poems of Marichiko*] 1979

Saucy Limericks and Christmas Cheer 1980
Selected Poems 1984

Other Major Works

Beyond the Mountains (verse plays) 1951
Birds in the Bush: Obvious Essays (essays) 1959
Assays (essays) 1961
An Autobiographical Novel (novel) 1966
American Poetry in the Twentieth Century (criticism) 1973
The Elastic Retort; Essays in Literature and Ideas (essays) 1973
World Outside the Window: The Selected Essays of Kenneth Rexroth [edited by Bradford Murrow] (essays) 1987

––––––––––––––––––

CRITICISM

William FitzGerald (review date 1940)

SOURCE: "Twenty Years At Hard Labor," in *Poetry,* Vol. LVII, No. 1, October 1940, pp. 158-60.

[*In this review, FitzGerald finds the poems of* In What Hour *largely derivative and unexciting.*]

Examples of Kenneth Rexroth's verse are by now familiar to readers of the literary and poetry journals (who may or may not confuse him with the two other Kenneths—Fearing and Patchen); this, however, is his first book. As an integrated performance it is less than notable; in many of the poems, the time-honored sources—Eliot, Pound, Stevens, Crane, Auden—fairly crackle from the page. Rexroth makes little effort to harmonize these loyalties; the result is a book hag-ridden by antecessors, of whom none contradict the critical truism: that their strength lies in their defiance of successful imitation.

Liberal citation from *In What Hour* might substantiate these remarks, but more significant is the case of Rexroth himself. He is, I believe, an "objectivist" (which is to say, a streamlined "imagist"—Pound has on occasion given his name and capacious blessing to both cliques); but the tag implies little that the verse itself cannot better demonstrate. The logomachic style, by any other name, would be as apparent; here articulation is further impeded by the ambiguity of the unarticulated idea. Rexroth's countenancing of a purgation and a correction (presumably Marxian) of modern society is obliquely expressed. The symptoms of his dissatisfaction are those common to all of his generation—all, that is, but the misanthropic few. The poet, eating, remembers the starving Spaniard; a transport plane reminds him of bombed civilians, and so on, until the swollen guilt-sense intoxicates his being with neural bewilderment. What is he to do? Like another Californian, he might forswear all communal sympathies and marry the hawk; but again, like Nicola Sacco, he might fight

and fall "for the conquest of the joy of freedom for . . . the poor workers." Of this dilemma, and its consequences to the poetic sensibility, Philip Henderson has written intuitively and at length in his book, *The Poet and Society.*

Rexroth's fulminations lack the pyrotechnics that make Auden exciting reading, but they are no less incoherent than the worst of Auden for being more cryptically conceived. Yeats's remark that "We make out of the quarrel with others rhetoric, but of the quarrel with ourselves, poetry," requires an addendum to validate the propagandizing function of rhetoric—a function, no doubt, to which Rexroth, like Auden, subscribes *ex animo.* But if Auden's career has incited a plethora of rhetoric, Eliot's has not; it remains to Rexroth to harness the pair together in such lines as:

> Before the inevitable act,
> The necessity of decision,
> The pauper broken in the ditch,
> The politician embarrassed in the council,
> Before the secret connivance,
> Before the plausible public appearance,
> What are the consequences of this adultery?

Elsewhere, Stevens is respectfully saluted:

> The avid eyes of gravid mice entice
> Each icy nostrum of the zodiac, *etc.,*

and there are "letters" to Auden and to Yvor Winters, a repudiation of Santayana, and an exercise in Whiteheadian objectivity called "Organum." Pervasive throughout the non-political items (they are few) is the predilection for "daring" metaphors and word-combinations suggestive of that disconsolate incantator, Hart Crane.

I am not unaware of the dangers of this "I've seen *you* before" indictment; Rexroth might conceivably have the stuff of a superior poet despite any number of derivations, but the hint of inadequate assimilation carried by the present book is too constant for easy dismissal. The poet has little that is new to say, and his devices for speech are fully as familiar as the polemic itself. In the poem, "August 22, 1939," he describes his literary career thus far as "twenty years at hard labor." If that is so, we could scarcely expect his poems to be greatly unlike those articles fashioned by prison inmates for a stipend. I dislike stressing the parallel, but the Rexroth of *In What Hour* sorely needs either a change of occupation or a parole.

Francis C. Golffing (review date 1945)

SOURCE: "An Uncomfortable Humanism," in *Poetry,* Vol. LXV, No. 5, February 1945, pp.260-62.

[*In this review of* The Phoenix and the Tortoise, *Golffing finds a rift between Rexroth's intelligence and his sensibility.*]

Kenneth Rexroth's new volume raises a number of interesting problems with reference to both metrics and the imaginative faculty.

Rexroth's poetic endowment is considerable and it is reinforced by a high degree of humanist culture. Yet the peculiar fusion of intelligence and sensibility, which we call, for convenience, the poetic imagination, is hardly ever completely realized in his work. His sensibility and his intelligence operate on different planes, and their respective qualities are too disparate to associate except in rare moments.

The poet's sensibility is erotic, mystical, while his reasoning tends to be trenchant and all-but-nihilistic. This division results in two contrary modes of expression, at times within the same poem. The purely rational parts are pungent, summary and uncharitable; the passages dealing with his emotional allegiances are suffused with tenderness and show the kind of patient observation which is attendant on sympathy. In other words, his imagination operates intact only on the limited territory of his personal pieties, while it disintegrates, or altogether deserts him, whenever the theme is outside his range of compassion.

A similar rift runs through most of the Graeco-Roman tradition. We find it in Catullus and Horace, in Martial and in the Alexandrine epigrammatists. At the risk of simplification, we may say that it is the pagan division of the world into pleasurable and distasteful parts, lovable and objectionable persons, with no mediation between the two groups. Such an attitude is perfectly legitimate and has redounded to the glory of both the lyric and the epigram. But it is doubtful whether it can ever reveal the whole breadth of man's destiny, for it is devoid of pity and hence of complete understanding. Though humanistic, it is not humane.

A further explanation may be found in the fact that Rexroth is not only a humanist but also a student of telluric structure and change. His knowledge of geology and mineralogy has proved a great creative asset, by extending his range of reference and imparting to his best verse a sweep and vigor very rare in contemporary poetry. Yet, by the same token, it has strengthened his geocentric bias; man is reduced to a tiny and rather ironic accident in a constant whirl of atoms:

> The earth will be going on a long time
> Before it finally freezes;
> Men will be on it; they will take names,
> Give their deeds reasons.
> We will be here only
> As chemical constituents . . .

His most ambitious poem, **"The Phoenix and the Tortoise,"** is also his best, though it too suffers occasionally from the fatal division between sensibility and intelligence. It contains passages of great delicacy, precise yet replete with warmth:

> Here, on the soft unblemished skin,
> Where ear and jaw and throat are joined,

> Where a flush begins to spread
> Under the glittering down;
> Here, where the gracious eyebrow
> Tapers over the orbit and onto the edge
> Of the blue shadowed temple . . .

or:

> One more spring, and after the bees go,
> The soft moths stagger in the firelight;
> And silent, vertiginous, sliding,
> The great owls hunt in the air;
> And the dwarf owls speak at their burrows . . .

In lines like these the fusion is complete, but quite often we get a bald congeries of abstractions, e.g.:

> And in dynamic antithesis,
> The person as priest and victim—
> The fulfillment of uniqueness
> In perfect identification,
> In ideal representation,
> As the usurping attorney,
> The real and effective surrogate . . .

which, in its context, is intelligible enough, even intelligent, but without sensual grace or form. The notions are merely juxtaposed instead of being wrought together.

Here we touch on the question of Rexroth's metrics. His point of departure is the "objectivist" movement, and a comparison with W. C. Williams may be illuminating. Both poets use speech rhythm exclusively; both are concerned with the exact rendering of sense perceptions. But while Williams is a master of rhythmic structure and counterpoint, Rexroth's cadences are casual and at times so close to prose that his line divisions seem arbitrary. Especially in some of the epigrams and paraphrases the tension is low, the rhythm indecisive. The exception is again **"The Phoenix and the Tortoise,"** where the poet employs a cumulative rhetoric and where the triple beat line is always apparent as a firm prosodic basis.

J. R. Squires (review date 1950)

SOURCE: A review of *The Art of Worldly Wisdom,* in *Poetry,* Vol. LXXVI, No. 3, June 1950, pp. 156-58.

[*In the following review of* The Art of Worldly Wisdom, *Squires claims Rexroth is held back by adherence to a finicky and zealous formal method.*]

It is a matter for wonder when a poet who is scarcely an old-timer chooses to publish a collection of earlier verse which in no way is likely to add to his reputation. And yet I suppose that the province of a review is not that of questioning the prudence of such a choice, but rather that of examining the effect for whatever interest or use it may have.

Written "in a half decade of transition and foreboding—1927-1932," *The Art of Worldly Wisdom* contains the usual defects of immaturity: the coyness of the younger poet in the presence of the poets who influence him; the tendency of short poems to damp off just when they seem to be getting a start; the tendency of longer poems to become wispy. On the other hand, considered purely as juvenilia, the poems show a wonderful exuberance of vocabulary. The impact is usually ludicrous, but one forgives it as the appetite which accompanies a growing period, quite as he forgives the exorbitant maternalism of Rexroth's learning which fosters such rare birds as medieval Latin nonsense refrains in the same nest with rather special terms from modern science. Gratifyingly enough, one catches an occasional flash of Rexroth's essential and real talent, horrendous here in its crudity, but nevertheless indicative:

> Whenever I think of England I see Wyndham
> Lewis standing in a high freezing wind on the
> plain where Mordred and Arthur fought,
> dressed only in his BVD's painfully extracting
> thorns from his chapped buttocks. It grows
> dark rapidly.

Now this *is* young! But it is also blessed with the wry, wintry alignment which points toward Rexroth's later and very brilliant adaptations of post-Augustan Latin verse—adaptations which, despite a brashness, are, in my opinion, easily the best translations in a modern idiom. But translations, however good they are, do not comprise the stature of a poet, and so, summarily, one is less likely to be astounded by the defectiveness of the greater part of the poetry or the admirableness of some of it than by the evidence of how little progress Rexroth has made in, roughly, twenty years. Nevertheless, these same poems which are the source of this bemusement also contain, I feel, the reason for it. And this is a reason which I cannot discuss without discussing the objectivist movement for which Rexroth has somewhere said he is an "unwilling spokesman."

Probably there is no other literary cult in which the members have so little congruence. However, a recognizable spirit of recusancy seems common to most of them. For example, William Carlos Williams, the most eminent of the objectivists, for a number of years has preached that American poetry must snub the traditional metrics and turn to the rhythms of American speech; that is to say, to virtually no rhythm at all. (That Williams has succeeded in producing excellent metrical effects does not mean that his theory is good, but that he has a fine ear.) Rexroth, who once sought to rejuvenate the flagging spirits of English rhythms by turning to the prosodies of the medieval *Sequentia* and primitive songs, has been considerably more reasonable than Williams. The real point is that these objectivists feel that something new *must* be done. Perhaps they are right, but the great innovations seem always to have occurred naturally, not consciously or truculently, and to have preceded the theory which explains them. And the ineluctable irony of the literary cult which insists primarily upon innovation or change is that the experiment becomes its own formula, the rebellion becomes its own convention. Thus while most poets during the last twenty years have retreated, shuddering, to the fringes of tradition, the objectivists have pioneered farther into the deserts where the imagists perished. In Rexroth's case, I feel that the alliance has been unfortunate, for it has probably confirmed him in a natural adolescent proclivity toward logomachy, an art of wordy wisdom. I say "unfortunate" because all of Rexroth's verse, whether early or recent, is evidence of a first class mind and, what is rarer, a mind that has been contoured with poetic erudition.

Frequently Rexroth has likened his technique to that of the cubist painters, a point which he reiterates in a foreword to *The Art of Worldly Wisdom*. Presumably, such a correspondence accounts for poems such as Part IV of **"A Prolegomenon to a Theodicy,"** a fifty-five line catalog of impressions: "The quivering palm / The conic of the wing / The trough of light / The rattling stones." This is an extreme example, but it is one which is relevant to most of Rexroth's work. Here, whether one is sympathetic to cubism or not, he is left at one level with the job of supplying syntactical transitions and, at a different level, of *imagining* a unity into the disparate materials. The effect is calamitous. In the first place, since equality is allowed to all these "simple forms of reality," which Rexroth deposits on the page, the surface result amounts to a dreary kind of spiritual scholarship in which one fact is as important as another. In the second place, since the poet eschews his poetical obligation to synthesize his experience into something which has, in the final analysis, only one shape, one obtains the feeling that the emotions are impure; that is to say, cluttered and impotent before the demands of their intricacy:

> Consular divides and the buttes glow.
> The sagging noon.
> We will colour the pages grey olive beige and blue
>   turning them slowly. We will break the backs of
>   letters. There the snake whirrs.
> The scoria omits nothing.
> O fugitive ostrich-porcupine.

Now I hasten to add that I do not think, or know, that Rexroth's emotions are really impure, but impurity is the impression imparted by his method which, in an odd way, is a very formal one, finicky and zealous and as self-defeating as the devotion to a "rhetoric," which ensnared, say, Simias of Rhodes or Theocritus in his late period. And the pity of it is that Kenneth Rexroth remains one of America's most interesting but nevertheless unfulfilled poets. And *The Art of Worldly Wisdom* does not so much demonstrate that he has grown up as it demonstrates that it is time he did.

Francis Golffing (review date 1950)

SOURCE: A review of *The Signature of All Things,* in *Poetry,* Vol. LXXVI, No. 3, June 1950, pp. 159-61.

[*In this review of* The Signature of All Things, *Golffing praises the poems for their combination of cosmic feeling and unclouded judgment.*]

When several years ago I reviewed Mr. Rexroth's **The Phoenix and the Tortoise** for these pages, I entertained certain doubts about the solidity of his poetic procedure. The free verse flowed a little too freely and at times could scarcely be read as verse; the lines, though crisp throughout, tended to become brittle; and there were obvious faults of style—a fondness for abstract catalogues, an unfleshing of the idea till nothing was left but the bare conceptual bone—which vitiated some of his finest productions. Many of the poems were alive with an almost uncanny insight, while others seemed to meander through channels of intellectual irrelevance or be flushed hectically with some undiscoverable excitement. A rift could be noticed in these verses between intelligence and sensibility: the intelligence usually working like a scalpel, subtle yet unpitying, in a few instances thrashing about wildly, like a flail; the sensibility reserved for the writer's personal pieties which were set forth with that microscopic precision we bestow on the things we love most. Yet the poems of the latter type, no matter how delightful, were largely outside the scope of intellect: they relied for effect on a very curious blend of sensuality and tenderness, and on the careful rendering of physical minutiae. A general misanthropy thus came to exist alongside of flights of affection almost extravagant in their intensity, with no middle ground and scarcely any recognition of the rift.

The present collection goes a long way toward closing it. Not that it has been bridged entirely: there are still instances here of that utter revulsion from the common run of humanity which disfigured the earlier volume. (Disfigured: not because the human animal does not justify such a reaction—it may or may not—but because the exploitation of that reaction makes for cheap poetry. Not even Swift succeeded at this kind of verse, except once or twice.) Yet, while still an atomist by persuasion, Mr. Rexroth now manages to populate his globe with luminous energetic matter to create a constant interplay of lively forces from which no being is any longer excluded. The "ingots of quivering phosphorescence" he celebrates in one of his poems, the "scattered chips of pale cold light that was alive" are mind and matter in one; and the poet has come to assume the role of the magus, the decipherer of hieroglyphics, interpreting "these ideograms/ Printed on the immortal/Hydrocarbons of flesh and stone." Read in these terms, each of Mr. Rexroth's poems appears as a dogged effort to reclaim living substance from decay; and, if the reading is right, we are justified in considering the erotic poems as an extreme instance of the same concern. The body of woman, so persistently extolled, is yet recognized for what it is to worm and undertaker; at the same time, this fragile frame, this lump of matter cries out for its own eternity, an eternity never settled once and for all but in need of constant renewal or better: revalidation:

> It may be
> Some distraught, imagined girl,

> Amalfi's duchess, Electra,
> Struggles like an ice bound swan,
> Out of the imagination,
> Toward a body, beside me,
> Beyond the corner of the eye;
> Or, may be, some old jealousy
> Or hate I have forgotten
> Still seeks flesh to walk in life.

Whether he reads the lineaments of a cherished face, the runes of ancient rock or the stellar enigma, Mr. Rexroth is concerned with the living mystery they disclose, with the stream rising in an anonymous past, feeding the brief present and running on into a nameless future:

> Majestic, from the most distant time,
> The sun rises and sets.
> Time passes and men cannot stop it.
> The four seasons serve them,
> But do not belong to them.
> The years flow like water.
> Everything passes away before my eyes.
>   . . . Borne headlong
> Towards the long shadows of sunset
> By the headstrong, stubborn moments,
> Life whirls past like drunken wildfire.

An essentially monistic conception, this, to which Lao-tse and Democritus have stood joint godfathers. Whether or not we endorse the poet's underlying beliefs, we must acknowledge the grandeur of the conception; nor can Mr. Rexroth be accused of wanton irrationality. There is no hint here of that studied disdain, so fashionable today, for the powers of judgment, no large statements spilling over the edges of the poem. What may strike the casual reader as the poet's private *mystique* is simply the aura within which the mind accepts, rejects, qualifies, subtilizes. Good examples of this combination of cosmic feeling and unclouded judgment may be found throughout the Chinese-inspired cycles; another instance is **"Epigram I"** where our temporal categories are made to scatter before the thunderbolt of momentary insight:

> The bleeding hearts in the garden
> Bloom early, but never fruit.
> Every year they have spread further,
> Underground, by creeping rootstocks.
> Zeno's arrow in my heart,
> I float in the plunging year.

Poems such as this are truly ideograms—dense clusters of meaning compressed into the compass of a pregnant symbol. No higher commendation is needed for any poem.

Robert Creeley (review date 1956-1957)

SOURCE: A review of *In Defense of the Earth,* in *New Mexico Quarterly,* Vol. XXVI, No. 4, Winter 1956-1957, pp. 409-11.

[In this review of In Defense of the Earth, *Creeley sees Rexroth as moving toward more readable poems.]*

In Defense of the Earth is the first more or less substantial collection of Kenneth Rexroth's poems since the publication of his **The Dragon And The Unicorn**. The latter was a long philosophical travel-poem, so that the book I am reviewing more literally goes back to **The Signature Of All Things** (1949), and is (as that book was) an accumulation of poems and translations of varying length and determination.

> Many of these poems deal with similar locations and events, seeking over and over again for the changing forms of an unchanging significance in stars, insects, mountains and daughters. They do not of course try to answer, "Why am I here?" "Why is it out there?"—but to snare the fact that is the only answer, the only meaning of present or presence . . . [Foreword by Kenneth Rexroth to **In Defense of the Earth**.]

Reading a book, or reviewing it,—one comes to ask, what does the book have, for its ideas; and, how clearly are those ideas made evident? Rexroth's title demonstrates the area of his concern, large though it surely is, and open as well to the pitfalls of an over-zealous generality. But one can, as he does, begin there.

The opening poems are for his wife, Marthe, and his daughter, Mary. Those for his wife have, among them, some of the book's best writing.

> . . . What do I know now,
> Of myself, of the others?
> Blood flows out to the fleeing
> Nebulae, and flows back, red
> With all the worn space of space,
> Old with all the time of time.
> It is my blood. I cannot
> Taste in it as it leaves me
> More of myself than on its
> Return . . .

This is the first idea. It is as well a broadening, in effect a deepening, of something, such as:

> . . . Just born to die
> Nobody will ever know anything about it
> And I have nothing more at all to say.

Which is taken from **The Art Of Worldly Wisdom** (1949), a book which marked the last large instance of Rexroth's experimentation in poems akin (as he notes) to those of Stein, Lowenfels, Arensberg, and Louis Zukofsky. After that time he made clear his intention to write in more "common" forms, and to give up at least the intensity of his concern to that point with syntactical formation, personally based. Perhaps my own statement here is unclear, but what was meant seems simply this: he became concerned with a poetry which people, in a half-hoped for generality, might be able to read, as put against that which apparently they

could not—or at least this was not to be the concern of the writer.

This is the second idea, clear in this book—that people, who are being loved, attacked, or subjected to the varying attitudes of the writer be obliged to hear that concern. The poem **"Thou Shalt Not Kill"** (for the memory of Dylan Thomas, who was himself proposed as a 'common' voice) speaks like this:

> I want to run into the street,
> Shouting, "Remember Vanzetti!"
> I want to pour gasoline down your chimneys.
> I want to blow up your galleries.
> I want to burn down your editorial offices.
> I want to slit the bellies of your frigid women.
> I want to sink your sailboats and launches.
> I want to strangle your children at their finger paintings.
> I want to poison your Afghans and poodles.
> He is dead, the drunken little cherub.
> He is dead,
> The effulgent tub thumper.
> He is Dead . . .

But—one knows what one 'speaks', or else not. Put too blandly, such address is perhaps only equalled by the equal exhortations, to buy this bread, that butter, and to eat it all. More reasonably—the addition of 'launches' to 'sailboats' belies the echoing tiredness of the man writing, it may be with the whole 'idea'.

More quietly (less 'common'):

> What can you say in a poem?
> Past forty, you've said it all.
> The dwarf black oak grows out of
> The cliff below my feet. It
> May be two hundred years old,
> Yet its trunk is no bigger
> Than my wrist, its crown does not
> Come to my shoulder . . .

I read the book making notes, so that I should not be overly embarrassed, coming to write of it. Which was my dilemma, but these poems are marked as follows: **"Seven Poems For Marthe, My Wife"** ('Positions of love—physical—loneliness. Images of possible loss—flat line. Praise.'); **"The Mirror In The Woods"** ('Good—fairy-story quality. Mirror.'); **"For Eli Jacobsen"** ('Good-old-timers, liberals, workers—the good old days—won't come again. Courage—makes taste & feelings better. Ok.'); **"Time Is The Mercy Of Eternity"** ('Philosophical—"on poetry". Up in the mts. Images of *moments:* description. Clear. *Alone*. All strips away to "knowledge".'), etc., etc.

Perception, inside or out, is 'earth', equally to be defended. In the 'Japanese Translations' at the book's end, there is this one (by Ishikawa Takuboku):

> I do not know why
> But it is as though

There were a cliff
Inside my head
From which, every day,
Clods of earth fall.

Lawrence Lipton (essay date 1957)

SOURCE: "The Poetry of Kenneth Rexroth," in *Poetry,* Vol. XC, No. 3, June 1957, pp. 168-80.

[*In the following essay, Lipton takes a hard look at Rexroth's formal and metrical experimentation.*]

In the introduction to his anthology, *New British Poets,* Kenneth Rexroth observed that "On the eve of the second war, the intellectual world generally was still dominated by the gospel of artistic impersonality, inherited from the nineteenth century 'scientific,' 'exact aesthetic,' and the opposed cult of artistic irresponsibility, 'Art for Art's Sake,' Mallarmé, Valéry, Cubism, much Marxism, the dubious 'Thomism' of M. Maritain, T. S. Eliot, Laura Riding, Robert Graves, I. A. Richards, most surrealists—it was almost universally taught and believed that the work of art was not communicative, was not 'about anything.' Instead, it should be approached empirically, from a utilitarian basis, as an object existing in its own right, a sort of machine for precipitating an 'aesthetic experience.' . . . I believe that this rigorous rationalism, this suppression of all acknowledgement of personality, feeling, intuition, the denial of communication and of the existence of emotion, is part of the general sickness of the world, the Romantic Agony, the splitting of the modern personality, the attempt to divorce the brain from the rest of the nervous system." This theory dominated European art for half a century, he went on to say, but "there is only one trouble with it, and that is that it isn't true. There is no such work of art. The paintings of Picasso, or even Mondrian, the sculpture of Brancusi, the poetry of Eliot or Valéry, the music of Stravinsky, they are all intensely personal. In fact, they are amongst the most personal works of art in the history of culture."

It is well to bear this passage in mind when one attempts to examine critically the poems of Kenneth Rexroth before 1940. Many of the poems in *The Art of Worldly Wisdom* and *In What Hour* explore the problem of form; of the former Rexroth wrote in the preface: "Technically, I suppose most of these poems represent about as an advanced position as American poetry has taken. I can think onlyof the poems of Walter Arensburg, Gertrude Stein, Walter Lowenfels, and Louis Zukofsky to compare with them. Of course, similar French poetry has long been accepted by all literate people. They are not 'difficult' poems in the sense that the Neo-Metaphysical verse of the Reactionary Generation which came after them is difficult. There are no Seven Types of Ambiguity lurking in them. Their elements are as simple as the elementary shapes of a cubist painting and the total poem is as definite and apprehensible as the finished picture." These, the poems in *The Art of Worldly Wisdom,* were pub-

lished only a few years ago, but they are, with the exception of *The Homestead Called Damascus,* his earliest, dating as they do from 1927-1932. "I have withheld them from permanent publication," he explains, "until the time which produced them was no longer an element in the judgment of their value," and he characterizes the period in which they were written as, for him, "a half decade of transition and foreboding."

Once he got over this period, he went right ahead to discover his own idiom in books like *The Phoenix and the Tortoise* and *The Dragon and the Unicorn.* He likes to think that there is an unbroken progression from first to last in his poems. "My poetry today, though it employs a more accepted idiom, does not differ fundamentally," from the poems in *The Art of Worldly Wisdom,* he says in the preface to that book. "These poems are not in quest of hallucination," he adds, as if he were clearing himself before a committee of Objectivists. "They owe nothing to the surrealism which was coming into fashion when they were being written. One poem is a sort of polemic by example against two leaders of surrealism. They are intended to be directly communicative, but communicate by means similar to those employed by the cubists in the plastic arts or by Sergei Eisenstein in his early great films—the analysis of reality into simple units and the synthesis of the work of art as a real parallel to experience." That may be the way he remembers it twenty-five years later, but it is not the way it looked and felt at the time. He tried everything, at least once, even automatic writing and hallucination. I remember it because I tried it too, along with him. We were constantly together during those years. I destroyed all but a few of my poems of that period. He preferred to publish his—twenty-five years later, in book form. They are good poems, of their sort, but they are not "built of and articulated around elements which are as simple, sensuous and passionate as I could find . . . communicative, even didactic." What is simple, sensuous and passionate about

> As A is.
> A triangular chessboard squared in two tones of
> 　gray,
> 　P to K3, KN X B.
> It's very cold under the table. A cold window.

or

> ancre ridgedge et poissoble ongpoint
> (or) KAniv ubiskysplice ubi danAe ubi diamondane
> thru oat quiv　　　　　　　　　at place
> at daybreak　　　　　　　　　shellbreak

lines which he addressed to Louis Zukofsky, to whom, presumably, they were simple and for all we know sensuous and passionate. The preceding lines were addressed to W. C. Williams. Epistolary verse is one of the favorite forms with coterie poets, and sometimes it is written in code. It's more fun that way.

Let's not be stuffy about it. Surely, after all these years it is silly to pretend that there weren't times when we were kidding ourselves and kidding each other, just for the hell of it. There is a good deal of that in *The Art of Worldly Wisdom*. I don't mean the piece addressed to Tzara and Breton, that was deliberate parody. I mean the borderline moments when we weren't sure ourselves whether we meant it, or were just playing with words to see how it felt. It was good, it was healthy, it was necessary, but there is no use pretending now that it was anything more than that. Or to pretend afterwards that it was something else which it wasn't. "In prosody, and in certain devices of syntax," says Rexroth of the poems in *The Art of Worldly Wisdom,* "they owe much to primitive songs— American Indian, Melanesian, Negro, Negrito, Bushman, etc., and to the study of languages least like the Indo-European groups—subjects which greatly interested me then and from which I hoped much new blood could be transfused into English poetry. Medieval Latin poetry, especially the great sequences—in particular of Adam of St. Victor and of Abelard—is another metrical influence." Technically as advanced a position as American poetry has taken, owing much to primitive songs, etc. No one blinks an eye, because by now we are all familiar with the radical, "advanced" position of the poet in quest of fresh beginnings in ancient sources. Much nonsense has been written about it, but in Rexroth it was no pretense, no pose. Compare, for instance,

> The word became fruitful;
> It dwelt with the feeble glimmering;
> It brought forth night:
> The great night, the long night,
> The lowest night, the loftiest night,
> The thick night to be felt,
> The night to be touched,
> The night not to be seen,
> The night ending in death.

with

> And did you dream
> The white the large
> The slow movement
> The type of dream
> The terror
> The tumbling stone

>   . . . . .

> In early dawn the plume of smoke
> The throat of night
> The plethora of wine
> The fractured hour of light
> The opaque lens
> The climbing wheel

The first is from a Maori chant, quoted by Joseph Campbell in *The Hero with a Thousand Faces,* the second from **"A Prolegomenon to a Theodicy"** in *The Art of Worldly Wisdom*. Or compare this chant for a taro feeding ceremony among the Manus of the Admiralty Islands, quoted by Margaret Mead in *Growing Up in New Guinea:*

> I give this to her mouth in order to brighten
>   the funeral fires with it,
>   the fire of gift exchange with it,
>   all that belongs to it.
> I give taro to the daughter of Paleiu,
> To the grandchild of Sanan,
> To the grandchild of Posanau.

with

>   (are you there)
> Hold my hand and keep out of the rushes
> Nothing will hurt you everybody loves you and I
>   want you to be very
>   happy
> She cried and said I've got to go I really ought to
>   go
> The master physicist
> You mustn't do that he said we don't advise it it
>   interferes with the work
>   of the committees and interrupts the sessions of
>   the congress
> Goodbye o lady goodbye

from **"When You Ask for It,"** again in *The Art of Worldly Wisdom*. And in the same piece the use of Negro folk material—"Star in the east / Star in the west / Wish that star was in my breast," a source that he was to rediscover later in the music of jazz.

But experiment in prosody was never Rexroth's primary interest nor ever held him for very long. In these, the very first of his poems there was already the foundation that he was to build into a framework of ideas. It is all, one way or another, a prolegomenon to a theodicy. "We were interested in ways of being," "The grammar of cause / The cause of grammar / The place of being" (*Art of Worldly Wisdom*). He was writing a theodicy, a justification of the divine attributes, of justice; not merely to justify a formal, technical credo, whether Zukofsky's or anybody else's, including his own.

In What Hour seems at first glance to be an interruption to the quest for a theodicy, because it has so much topical material in it. Written during the Depression years and first published, some of it, in magazines like *New Masses, Partisan Review* and *The New Republic,* it adds up for Rexroth into Lessons in Geography and History. Had We But Time, and The Place of Value in a World of Facts— the titles he gives to the parts into which he divided the book—and ends with "Ice Shall Cover Nineveh," which carries further his inquiry into the problem of good and evil, act and destiny which began with the **"Prolegomenon."** Formally, technically, it begins to approach the syllabic line of his later work, a tendency that becomes even more marked in *The Signature of All Things* and *The Phoenix and the Tortoise.* He is at pains to tell us that "sometimes after the poem is cast in syllabic lines it is broken up into cadences," and the influence, "poetic kinship," he prefers to call it, of the Chinese is making itself felt. "Against this (syllabic line) is counterpointed a rhythm primarily of quantity, secondarily of accent. In addition, close attention is paid to the melodic line of the vowels and to the evolution of consonants (p-b-k, m-r-l-y, etc.). In most cases a melody was written at the same time as the poem."

The poetry of self-exploration, which usually comes early, came late in Rexroth's writing career. It is retrospective in character, as in the title poem of *The Signature of All Things,*

>   . . . The long hours go by.
> I think of those who have loved me,
> Of all the mountains I have climbed,
> Of all the seas I have swum in.
> The evil of the world sinks.
> My own sin and trouble fall away
> Like Christian's bundle, and I watch
> My forty summers fall like falling
> Leaves and falling water held
> Eternally in summer air.

where the frequently varied eight syllable line is the metrical scheme and the metaphor is based mostly on nature—trees, skies, stars, mountains, rivers, seas, rain, snow, sun. Elegies and epistles. Memories of his first wife, Andrée, who died young. Reliving their love in memory, trying to bridge the sense of separation with unmailable letters. "These are all simple, personal poems, as close as I can make them to integral experience." Trying to relate the personal experience to the social experience. "Perhaps the integral person is more revolutionary than any program, party, or social conflict. At least I have come to think so." Trying to convince himself that in abandoning the "social" poem—**"Gentlemen, I Address You Publicly"** or the "public speech" which in the Thirties had lured even Archibald MacLeish away from a poetry that "should not mean / But be," he was still performing the function of the social poet. "And I have little doubt but that he—the irreducible man—is the great enemy of the fools and rascals who are destroying the world." And arriving at the "religious anarchism" which he would have us believe has been "the point of view . . . in all my work" from the beginning.

Iambic is the sound barrier of English verse and it is in this period that Rexroth broke the sound barrier. The vehicle he uses is the seven syllable line. Nothing breaks the habit of iambic better than the discipline of practicing to breathe, so to speak, in seven syllable intervals. Or nine syllables. Eight, if you must, but never ten. Well, hardly ever.

> Not like strident Sappho, who
> For all her grandeur, must have
> Had endemetriosis,
> But like Anyte, who says
> Just enough, softly, for all
> The thousands of years to remember.

The temptation here would have been, for a mind trained but not retrained in English verse, to start with a ten-syllable five-stress line of iambic—

> Not like strident Sappho who for all her
> Grandeur must have had. . . .

and take off from there, content to settle for a metrically more manageable word than endemetriosis. Not that the seven syllable line doesn't present the poet with Procrustean problems, any line length is bound to. Rexroth is no word-chopper with a box of hyphens in his tool chest. He prefers to let the line run on into nine syllables, or even eight, and break the rule rather than the word. I do not impute any special virtue to this practice. Others—Cummings, for one—have done wonderful things with hyphens. So has James Boyer May. But Rexroth justifies his practice in the only way any metric can be justified, by making vocally viable verse with it. Perhaps, like William Carlos Williams, he tends to think of iambic as English rather than American prosody. As late as only a few years ago Williams still thought it necessary to emphasize the distinction at a poetry conference on "Experimental and Formal Verse" held at Bard College. "We speak a language that is not English any longer. . . . It has structural elements in time and pace . . . which are not that of English. . . . It is more Mediterranean than North Sea and it is more loose-jointed than English . . . more dynamic as contrasted with the static nature of English . . . the prosody of English does not apply to American. . . . The first thing we must do as poets is to throw it out, body and soul. . . . To build, if we are men, something better . . . to invent a prosody of our own."

And no tricks, Rexroth would add. No hooks, no shock, no hypnosis. No verbal massage. Perhaps it was something like this he had in mind when he used the words "simple, sensuous and passionate."

Where a longer, more reflective line seems to be called for, he has settled for the seven- to nine-syllable line, as in *The Phoenix and the Tortoise* and *The Dragon and the Unicorn*. Speaking of the latter, in his preface, Rexroth says that since he feels "that the poet is most important socially and artistically when he speaks in his vatic role" and "the first duty of the poet is to communicate . . . there is nothing unconventional about this poem. What technical subtleties it possesses are discreetly veiled under a simple syllabic prosody." Here the line is more often one of seven or eight rather than nine syllables. The reviewers who called it "percussive" and "metronomic"—when they didn't call it "chopped up prose"—were probably giving it the old finger-counting test rather than the oral reading it requires. (How many reviewers give *any* book of poems an oral reading before sounding off in print about it? The commercial laboratory equivalent of such practice is the "sink test.") Despite the fact that Rexroth keeps repeating that his meter is based on quantity, it is not to be read like Latin or Greek verse. Lines like

> French radical youth, like
> The Wandervögel before them,
> Have a better way of marking
> Time until the monsters destroy
> Each other: Keep uncompromised;
> Stay poor; try to keep out from

Under the boot; love one another;
Reject all illusions; wait.

can be read aloud only one way: as casual speech. What distinguishes stuff like this from prose is its concentration and tension. Moreover, it is a highly flexible idiom. It can pass from the philosophical—

It is true that being is
Responsibility, beyond
The speculations of Calvin,
St. Thomas, or Augustine,
Ontology is ethical.

to the narrative—

We fill our rucksacks at a
Rôtisserie just like the ones
In Pompeii, with bread just like the
Pumice casts, and take the train
To the South. . . .

to passionate anger—

    . . . Man
Gets daily sicker and his
Ugliness knots his bowels.
On the site of several
Splendid historic brothels
Stands the production plant of
Time-Luce Incorporated.
Die Ausrottung der Besten.

without missing a beat. Could it not, then, be set up just as well like poetic prose? It could, without losing its sense or its tone, but it would lose the pace which the poet wishes to give his words. After all, that is what line-length is for: a formal notation of the poet's tempo, the pace and emphasis he prescribes for the oral rendition of the verse. There is more opportunity here for alternating legato with staccato passages than the longer, flowing line of poetic prose permits. Read the lines aloud, pausing at the line-ends no more and no less than a good actor pauses at the line-ends of Shakespeare's iambic pentameter lines, and the ear will recognize the logic of the weight and measure Rexroth has given them. Not always, of course, for all formal arrangements of sound entail some compromise with sense at times. The trick is to know when to compromise, and, when compromise is not advisable, which to favor, which is more vital to the total effect of the passage.

In the verse plays, **Beyond the Mountains,** Rexroth was faced once more with the problem of form. He calls them Noh plays on classical themes and says that he hoped to find in them "a more direct expression than philosophical elegy affords." "I have found it interesting," he says in the Introduction, "to subject my philosophical opinions to the test of dramatic speech." How well his philosophy stands the test of drama is not our concern here. The seven-syllable line stands up well in dialogue. This should not surprise anyone. I am sure it did not surprise him. It

is used flexibly, of course, as in the other books, alternating at times with shorter and longer lines, but nearly always stopping short of ten syllables, and rarely falling into iambic. Why this studied avoidance of iambic?

The answer to this question is the clue to what is central and pivotal, I think, in Rexroth's work, and I shall make it my final one. Nothing in art is natural. Art is by definition artificial. Cadenced speech, even grammar and syntax, and when it comes to that, language itself is an artifact. Every actor on the stage, even in the most naturalistic theater, is bigger than life size. When he speaks verse he is ten feet high. He is a god, and he might as well be wearing a mask, or a goat skin. One verse-dramatist writes me that he is convinced, after years of research, that the line of natural American speech today is a three-beat line. Another assures me it is the four-beat line. All are pretty well agreed—all "moderns," that is—that it is not iambic. Was it *ever* iambic? Shakespeare's clowns (countrymen and common folk) talk prose, his noblemen talk verse. Not invariably, but often enough to suggest that this was the convention of the stage. But only on the stage. In real life they talked prose, like anybody else. Iambic is no more "basic" to English speech than any other meter. The only thing that is basic to meter is a psycho-motor impulse, but all attempts to classify and correlate meters with specific emotions break down when tested by experience. Anger, for example, even towering rage, can be, and in fact is constantly being, expressed in iambics, trochees or anapests, even in glaring silence. The meter need not be "true to life." It need be true to only one rule: the rule that the poet sets up for his poem. It is justified by the inner consistency of the work of art. There is nothing in all this that Rexroth could not say Yes to, judging by what he himself has said to me personally, or in print. So his avoidance of iambic must be explained in some other way.

Iambic is tied up in the education of every English-writing poet with all the philosophical and metaphysical poets of the past. Especially iambic pentameter. It is the metrical vehicle of the Holy Sonnets, *Paradise Lost,* of Herbert and Traherne, of Wordsworth's *Prelude* as well as Pope's *Essay on Man,* of Shelley's *Prometheus Unbound* as well as Browning's *Sordello.* Hardy never quite broke through the sound barrier. "There is always something a little synthetic about Hardy's rugged verse," Rexroth remarks at one point in his Introduction to Lawrence's poems. "The smoother ones seem more natural, somehow," he says, and names Hardy's sonnet to Leslie Stephen as his best poem. The implication here is personal, and Rexroth confirms it as he goes on: "If Hardy ever had a girl in the hay, tipsy on cider, on the night of Boxing Day, he kept quiet about it . . . he never let on, except indirectly." Hardy was a pandit and iambic meter was his métier, while Lawrence was a *Wandervögel* and the freer-flying forms came naturally to him. "At the very beginning Lawrence belonged to a different order of being from the literary writers of his day."

Tinkering with the iambic in small ways was something that Rexroth passed up from the start. "Compulsion neurotics like Hopkins and querulous old gentlemen like Bridges made quite an art of metrical eccentricity. You turned an iamb into a trochee here, and an anapest into a hard spondee there, and pretty soon you got something that sounded difficult and tortured and intense." When Rexroth broke with the church-bound, creed-bound tradition of the English philosophical, religious, metaphysical poets, he went all the way and broke with their metrics too. Earlier and more completely than Lawrence did. "In 1912 he [Lawrence] said: 'I worship Christ, I worship Jehovah, I worship Pan, I worship Aphrodite. But I do not worship hands nailed and running with blood upon a cross, nor licentiousness, nor lust. I want them all, all the gods. They are all God. But I must serve in real love. If I take my whole passionate, spiritual and physical love to a woman who in turn loves me, that is how I serve God. And my hymn and my game of joy is my work. All of which I read in. . . .' Do you know what he read all that in?" asks Rexroth. "It makes you wince. He thought he found that in *Georgian Poetry, 1911-12*! In Lascelles Abercrombie, Wilfred Gibson, John Drinkwater, Rupert Brooke, John Masefield, Walter de la Mare, Gordon Bottomley!"

Lawrence thought he was a Georgian, at first, Rexroth reminds us. But he, Rexroth, with that case of mistaken self-identity before him, made no comparable mistake. Nor did he go the way of Eliot, who broke with the metric and returned to the tradition after that first brief revolt; preached the funeral oration over the grave of a dead tradition and then jumped in with the corpse. What Rexroth came to admire in Lawrence's verse was its "uncanny, 'surreal' accuracy of perception and evaluation." And what about Objectivism? "Objectivism is a hollow word beside this complete precision and purposiveness." The surrealistic, then, need not be hallucinatory. "Bad poetry always suffers from the same defect: synthetic hallucination and artifice. Invention is not poetry. . . . Poetry is vision, the pure act of sensual communion and contemplation." "Good cadenced verse is the most difficult of all to write. Any falsity, any pose, any corruption, any ineptitude, any vulgarity, show up immediately. . . . The craft is the vision and the vision is the craft." Since the vision is unteachable, the craft too becomes unteachable. And impossible to criticize? Here is a dilemma. In fact, all such reasoning leads to dilemma, and Lawrence is full of such reasoning—or, rather, such intuiting. It is attractive, and contagious. At every turn we are next door to the poet as God. And Gods do not have to learn their craft, they do not even have to think, and they are above criticism either by themselves or by others. It is a heady notion and Rexroth, for all his usual sanity of mind, fell for it while he was reading and "introducing" Lawrence.

One thing does seem fairly certain, however. That all the forms and techniques prove, on close examination, to be timelessly enduring—and forever expendable. A paradox but not a contradiction. "The sonnet or quatrain are like the national debt, devices for postponing the day of reckoning indefinitely. All artistic devices are a method of spiritual deficit-financing." We could ask whether this includes the seven syllable line? I think Rexroth would

answer Yes, if only to leave himself free to abandon it when it suits his purpose to do so. The form must change as the vision changes.

When poetry is once more a living art, performing a living social function in society, it will be easier to see, I think, that the content of a poem is the *materia poetica* of its function, and the form is the per*form*ance, in the Latin sense of *forma,* the shape or likeness of an idea or a thing, the performance of a function. In its completest form it is *sutra,* the teaching, *mantra,* the verbal and / or musical sounds of the ritual, and *mudra,* the symbolic gesture, dance; all three integrated into one. In the verse plays of *Beyond the Mountains,* Rexroth has attempted that integration. It is premature, but only as all prophecy is premature, and one of the poet's roles is the role of prophet. "Hardy was a major poet. Lawrence was a minor prophet. Like Blake and Yeats, his is the greater tradition."

William Carlos Williams (review date 1957)

SOURCE: "Two New Books by Kenneth Rexroth," in *Poetry,* Vol. XC, No. 3, June 1957, pp. 180-90.

[*In his review of* In Defense of the Earth *and* One Hundred Poems from the Chinese, *Williams defends Rexroth's unpoetic meter and diction, and lavishly praises his translations.*]

The technical problem of what to do with the modern poetic line has been solved by Kenneth Rexroth by internal combustion! Whether that can be said to be activated by atomic fission or otherwise is immaterial. The line, in Rexroth's opinion, is to be kept intact no matter if it may be true, as the painters have shown, that any part of a poem (or painting) may stand for the poem if it is well made; therefore if anything at all is done with it, keeping it intact, it must give at the seams, it must spread its confinements to make more room for the thought. We have been beaten about the ears by all the loose talk about "free verse" until Rexroth has grown tired of it.

But the problem still remains. If you are intent on getting rid of conventional verse what are you going to accept in its place? It is purely a matter of how you are going to handle the meter. Forget for a moment the meaning of the poems in this book, *In Defense of the Earth,* which is not, I think, a good title, the poet has ignored all formal line divisions save by the use of an axe.

The first ten or fifteen poems trespass perilously close upon sentimentality, they can be passed over at once as of mere personal interest to the poet himself, no matter how deeply experienced, having to do with individuals of his family. With **"A Living Pearl,"** the general interest may be said to begin, the technical and ideational interest that is inherent in the poems (there is not room enough in the pages of *Poetry* to quote the poem in full):

"A Living Pearl"

At sixteen I came West, riding
Freights on the Chicago, Milwaukee
And St. Paul, the Great Northern,
The Northern Pacific.
A job as helper to a man

. . . . .

Tonight,
Thirty years later, I walk
Out of the deserted miner's
Cabin in Mono Pass, under
The full moon and the few large stars.

And so it goes for about seventy-five lines. It is written as verse, the initial letter of every lineis capitalized as in Marlow or Lope de Vega or Edna St. Vincent Millay. But there the similarity to any verse form with which I am familiar ceases. It is a sequence we are more familiar with in prose: the words are direct, without any circumlocution, no figure of speech is permitted to intervene between the meaning of the words and the sense in which they are to be understood.

There is no inversion of the phrase. The diction is correct to the idiom in which the poet speaks, a language "which cats and dogs can read." But it is a language unfamiliar to the ordinary poetry reader. Poems are just not written in those words.

More serious is the question as to whether or not, since poems are universally thought to be musical, Rexroth has any ear for music. And if so what constitutes his music.

Can the lines be counted—forget for the moment the prosy diction? It may have been put down purposely to subvert any poetic implication in the lines that it is associated with the lies of the ordinary poem in the usual facilely lilting measures. This American author is dedicated to the truth. To hell with tuneful cadences in the manner, let us say, of Robert Burns or T. S. Eliot or Rimbaud at least while the world is being cheated and starved and befouled.

The technical problem of what to do with the modern poetic line has been solved by Kenneth Rexroth by internal combustion!

—William Carlos Williams

Rexroth is a moralist with his hand at the trigger ready to fire at the turn of a hair. But he's a poet, and a good one, for all that. So as to the music of his lines let us not be too hasty. As a translator of the Chinese lyrics of Tu Fu his ear is finer than that of anyone I have ever encountered. It has been conclusively proved to my ear, at least, that if he does

not give himself to our contemporary building of the line he doesn't want to soil himself as all others are doing.

Toward the end of this book of eighty-odd pages, after that fine poem, **"A Living Pearl,"** with its unfamiliar turns of phrase, there are some shorter pieces or longer ones broken into shorter subsections (like the one to Dylan Thomas) which are arresting by the directness of their speech: by the way, when I attempt to measure the stresses in one of his typical lines, which are short, I find that there are for the most part three. The pace is uniformly iambic, using a variable foot according to the American idiom.

The poems themselves are the importance. Their moral tone is stressed, except in the translations from the Japanese at the end. The book's seriousness, sting, and satiric punch dominate these pages. A miscellany of bitter stabs masquerading as, and meant to be, nursery rhymes, Mother Goose, a-b-c's and other accounts, scathing denunciations of our society which would have done credit to a Daumier or a Goya: **"A Bestiary For My Daughters Mary and Katharine;" "Murder Poem No. 74321;" "Portrait of the Author as a Young Anarchist"**—a grieving memorial to Vanzetti and others; and another, **"Thou Shalt Not Kill,"** a memorial to Dylan Thomas.

The latter half of the book is a diatribe of the most comprehensive virulence. It should be posted in the clubrooms of all universities so that it could never be forgotten. For the poem is the focal point for all activity among the intellectuals of the world from New York, Paris and Helsinki. Rexroth puts down many of their names here—a lunatic fringe it may be:

They are murdering all the young men.
For half a century now, every day,

. . . . .

Stephen, Lawrence ("on his gridiron"), Robinson, Masters ("who crouched in / His law office for ruinous decades"), Lola Ridge, Jim Oppenheim, Orrick Johns, Elinor Wylie, Sara Teasdale, George Sterling, Phelps Putnam, Jack Wheelright, Donald Evans, John Gould Fletcher, Edna Millay, Bodenheim ("butchered in stinking / Squalor"), Sol Funaroff, Isidor Schneider, Claude McKay, Countee Cullen, Ezra, "that noisy man," Carnevali, etc. etc.

He may sometimes be mistaken in his choice of those to remember but that is a mere choice among individuals: his sympathies are amply justified.

. . . . .

He is dead,
The bird of Rhiannon.
He is dead.

. . . . .

You killed him, General,
Through the proper channels.

You strangled him, Le Mouton,
With your *mains étendus.*

. . . . .

The gulf stream smells of blood
As it breaks on the sands of Iona
And the blue rocks of Canarvon.
And all the birds of the deep sea rise up
Over the luxury liners and scream,
"You killed him! You killed him.
In your God damned Brooks Brothers suit,
You son of a bitch."

There is another memorable passage showing the sardonic temper with which the poems have been salted down. This occurs toward the end of the "Mother Goose" (for his daughters), and note that he treats his children with the same respect as though they had been adults at whose throats their murderous weapons are addressed. Addressing his countrymen in general he tells them:

Hide the white stone
in the left fist.
Hide the white stone
In the right fist.
I am your secret brother.
Where is the white stone?
You have swallowed it.

. . . . .

It may not be welcome in a review of this kind to stress an author's pointed reference to an unlovely fact. But in this case when in the text reference has been made to Martial's satyrs whose whole mood of violent attack on the corruption of his own age has been invoked by Rexroth in his own revolt and revulsion, nothing could be more appropriate to this than the following anecdote:

There were two classes of kids, and they
Had nothing in common: the rich kids
Who worked as caddies, and the poor kids
Who snitched golf balls. I belonged to the
Saving group of exceptionalists
Who, after dark, and on rainy days,
Stole out and shit in the golf holes.

Kenneth Rexroth has been an avid reader in universal literature. He is familiar with a variety of foreign languages, ancient and modern. He is familiar with the capitals of Europe, has read extensively of philosophy and the history of the social sciences. I think, as men go, there is no better read person in America. You should see his library! all his books, and most of his collected magazine articles, filed in orderly fashion for twenty or thirty years back for ready reference.

He is an authority on his subject of modern poetry. As a lecturer he is respected (and feared) throughout the academic world.

The present book, *In Defense of the Earth,* has been dedicated *To Marthe, Mary, Katharine;* his wife and daughters whom he speaks of extensively in the first part.

. . . . .

Kenneth Rexroth has recently translated *One Hundred Poems from the Chinese,* one of the most brilliantly sensitive books of poems in the American idiom it has ever been my good fortune to read.

It must be amazing to the occidental reader, acquinted we'll say with Palgrave's *Golden Treasury,* to realize that the Chinese have a practice and art of the poem, which in subtlety of lyrical candor, far exceeds his own. I am grateful to him. Nothing comparable and as relaxed is to be found I think in the whole of English or American verse, and in French or Spanish verse, so far as I know. So that it constitutes a unique experience to read what has been set down here.

Womanhood has been engraved on our minds in unforgettable terms. Oh, I know that women can be bitches, you don't have to be a homosexual to learn that, but the exact and telling and penetrant realization of a woman's reality, of her lot, has never been better set down. It is tremendously moving, as none of our well known attempts, say, throughout the Renaissance have ever succeeded in being.

This is a feat of overwhelming importance. It is not a question of a man or woman's excess in experience or suffering, for whatever this amounted to, they have had to do; but that in their mutual love they have been made to bear their fates. What does it matter what a woman and a man in love will do for themselves? Someone will succeed and someone will die. In the poem suddenly we realize that we know that and perceive in a single burst of vision, in a flash that dazzles the reader.

The poet Tu Fu (713-770) was the first, with him it begins. Homer and Sappho with their influence on our poetry had been dead for over a thousand years. The use of the metaphor, pivotal in our own day, had not been discovered by the Chinese in these ancient masterpieces. The metaphor comes as a flash, nascent in the line, which flares when the image is suddenly shifted and we are jolted awake just as when the flint strikes the steel. The same that the Chinese poet seeks more simply when the beauty of his images bursts at one stroke directly upon us.

Dawn over the Mountains

The city is silent,
Sounds drains away
Buildings vanish in the light of dawn,
Cold sunlight comes on the highest peak,
The dust of night
Clings to the hills,
The earth opens,
The river boats are vague,
The still sky—

The sound of falling leaves.
A huge doe comes to the garden gate,
Lost from the herd,
Seeking its fellows.

                                        (*Tu Fu*)

Where is the poem? without metaphor among these pages so effortlessly put down. Occidental art seems more than a little strained compared to this simplicity. You cannot say there is no art since we are overwhelmed by it. The person of the poet, the poetess, no, the woman herself (when it is a woman), speaks to us . . . in an unknown language, to our very ears, so that we actually weep with her and what she says (while we are not aware of her secret) is that she breathes . . . that she is alive as we are.

Where is it hidden in the words? Our own clumsy poems, the best of them, following the rules of grammar . . . trip themselves up. What is a sonnet of Shakespeare beside this limpidity but a gauche, a devised pretext? and it takes fourteen lines rigidly to come to its conclusion. But with bewildering simplicity we see the night end, the dawn come in and a wild thing approach a garden. . . . But the compression without being crowded, the opposite of being squeezed into a narrow space, a few lines, a universe, from the milky way . . . vividly appears before us.

But where has it been hidden? because it is somewhere among the words to our despair, if we are poets, or pretend to be, it is really a simple miracle, like that of the loaves and the fishes. . . .

Where does the miracle lodge, to have survived so unaffectedly the years translation to a foreign language and not only a foreign language but a language of fundamentally different aspect from that in which the words were first written? The metaphor is total, it is overall, a total metaphor.

But there are two parts to every metaphor that we have known heretofore: the object and its reference—one of them is missing in these Chinese poems that have survived to us and survived through the years, to themselves also. They have been jealously, lovingly guarded . . . Where does it exist in the fabric of the poem? so tough that it can outlast copper and steel . . . a poem?

     —and really laughs and cries! it is alive.
     —It is as frightening as it is good.

And the Chinese as a race have built upon it to survive, the words of Tu Fu, a drunken poet, what I mean is DRUNK! and a bum, who did not do perhaps one constructive thing with himself in his life—or a Bodenheim.

I go to a reception and find a room crowded with people whom I cannot talk with except one, a man (or a woman perhaps) or one who wearies me with his insistencies. . . . When a few miraculous lines that keep coming into my head transport me through space a thousand years into the past. . . .

"A magic carpet" the ancients called it. It costs nothing, it's not the least EXPENSIVE!

Look at the object: an unhappy woman, no longer young, waking in her lonely bed and looking over a moonlit valley, that is all. Or a man drunk or playing with his grandchildren who detain him so that he cannot keep an appointment to visit a friend. . . . And what? A few fragile lines which have proved indestructible!

Have you ever thought that a cannon blast or that of an atomic bomb is absolutely powerless beside this?—unless you extinguish man (and woman), the whole human race. A smile would supersede it, totally.

     I raise the curtains and go out
     To watch the moon. Leaning on the
     Balcony, I breathe the evening
     Wind from the west, heavy with the
     Odors of decaying Autumn.
     The rose-jade of the river
     Blends with the green-jade of the void.
     Hidden in the grass a cricket chirps.
     Hidden in the sky storks cry out.
     I turn over and over in
     My heart the memories of
     Other days. Tonight as always
     There is no one to share my thoughts.

                                        (*Shu Chu Senn*)

or this:

     The Visitors

     I have had asthma for a
     Long time. It seems to improve
     Here in this house by the river.
     It is quiet too. No crowds
     Bother me. I am brighter here
     And more rested. I am happy here.
     When someone calls at my thatched hut
     My son brings me my straw hat
     And I go out to gather
     A handful of fresh vegetables.
     It isn't much to offer.
     But it is given in friendship.

                                        (*Tu Fu*)

These men (a woman among the best of them) were looking at direct objects when they were writing, the transition from their pens or brushes is direct to the page. It was a beautiful object (not always a beautiful object, sometimes a horrible one) that they produced. It is incredible that it survived. It must have been treasured as a rare phenomenon by the people to be cared for and reproduced at great pains.

But the original inscriptions, so vividly recording the colors and moods of the scene . . . were invariably put down graphically in the characters (not words), the visual symbols that night and day appeared to the poet. The Chinese calligraphy must have contributed vastly to this.

Our own "Imagists" were right to brush aside purely grammatical conformations. What has grammar to do with poetry save to trip up its feet in that mud? It is important to a translator but that is all. But it is important to a translator, as Kenneth Rexroth well knows. But mostly he has to know the construction of his own idiom into which he is rendering his text, when to ignore its more formal configurations.

This is where the translations that Kenneth Rexroth has made are brilliant. His knowledge of the American idiom has given him complete freedom to make a euphonious rendering of a text which has defied more cultured ears to this date. It may seem to be undisciplined but it is never out of the translator's measured control. Mr. Rexroth is a genius in his own right, inventing a modern language, or following a vocal tradition which he raises here to great distinction. Without a new language into which the poems could be rendered their meaning would have been lost.

Finally, when he comes to the end of introduction, he says, "So here are two selections of poetry, one the work of a couple of years, the other the personal distillate of a lifetime. I hope they meet the somewhat different ends I have in view. I make no claim for the book as a piece of Oriental scholarship. Just some poems."

At the very end there are data, notes, ten pages of them, annotated page for page, on the individual poems. And two and a half pages of Select Bibliography. The translations into English began in 1870 with *The Chinese Classics,* James Legge. Included is a mention of Ezra Pound's *Cathay,* 1915.

In the French there is, dating from 1862, the *Poésies Chinoises de l'Epoque Thang,* and, among others, that of Judith Gautier's, 1908, *Livre de Jade.* The German versions are still those of Klabund.

Muriel Rukeyser (review date 1957)

SOURCE: "Lyrical 'Rage,'" in *The Saturday Review,* Vol. XL, No. 45, November 9, 1957, p. 15.

[*In this review, Rukeyser praises* In Defense of the Earth.]

The fineness of Kenneth Rexroth's *In Defense of Earth* depends on several virtues. They are virtues which are rare in this year but which are apparent in almost every one of the Rexroth poems: a lyric-mindedness that has been prepared by many disciplines to summon up its music; a learning that eats the gifts of the world, knowing (like the laboratory baby before the food) how many cultures must be drawn on to make human fare; and that quality which has been talked about so much in speaking of Kenneth Rexroth and of those he has known in San Francisco: rage.

The poems included in the collection are the whole background of lyrics written by Kenneth Rexroth since 1949. Here is the exquisite **"Great Canzon"**:

> . . . She, when she goes
> Wreathed in herbs, drives every
>   other
> Woman from my mind—
>   shimmering
> Gold with green—so lovely that
>   love
> Comes to rest in her shadow, she
> Who has caught me fast between
> Two hills, faster far than fused
>   stone . . .

And here are the "web and the hidden crippled bird," landmarks of the time when Morris Graves and Rexroth first knew each other and wanted the journey to Japan; here are the moving poems for his wife, Marthe, and for the little daughter, particularly **"The Great Nebula of Andromeda," "A Maze of Sparks of Gold,"** and **"A Sword in a Cloud of Light,"** with its Christmas crowds on Fillmore Street, its Orion "spread out / On the sky like a true god," and ending:

> Believe in all those fugitive
> Compounds of nature, all doomed
> To waste away and go out.

There are here also the whiplash **"Bestiary"**; a group of epigrams and translations; and the four-part memorial for Dylan Thomas with its shattering *ubi sunt* for the poets of these years, dead of all the deaths or "stopped writing at thirty . . . How many went to work for *Time*? How many died of prefrontal / Lobotomies in the Communist Party? How many are lost in the back / Wards of provincial madhouses? How many, on the advice of their psychoanalysts, decided / A business career was best after all? How many are hopeless alcoholics?" The last part of the poem is for Dylan Thomas himself, and it carries its heaped-up accusation for murder against the specific anti-poetry, anti-religion—but you had better read this for yourself, since any description will sound like the frothing and rage with which the poem has been charged.

This would be rage, in the speaking man; and a shout and rant of frustration. But here; in the sparse, controlled poems it is something else and more: it is the sharp willingness to speak of the committed man. There is little enough control around anywhere this year, and less commitment. The sound of commitment comes through as the sound of anger. In these brief and disciplined poems of Rexroth's we have the background and tradition of "Howl" and of *On the Road.* The influence and the lyric commitment are shown naked here. They reach us, in love, jeering, bringing in other poetry from China and Japan. Read:

> Lions terrify most men
> Who buy meat at the butcher's—

and

> What happened to Robinson
> Who used to stagger down Eighth
>   Street,

Dizzy with solitary gin?
Where is Masters, who crouched in
His law office for ruinous decades?
Where is Leonard who thought he
    was
A locomotive? And Lindsay,
Wise as a dove, innocent
As a serpent, where is he?
    Timor mortis conturbat me.

It does not matter that Althea made that same last crack
in *The Way of All Flesh;* it is surely a crack as old as the
Bible. But, in context this year, the lines knock against
our lives. And now the poets come on, in their deaths and
lives: Jim Oppenheim, Orrick Johns, Elinor Wylie, Sara
Teasdale, Jack Wheelwright, Bodenheim, Edna Millay,
Genevieve, Harry, Hart, and the rest of Rexroth's line of
poets.

The title is right; this book is written "in defense," and
the parts are love, anger, willingness to act to protect. In
these poems the qualities come through with marvelous
strength, clarity, and music. This review has been held for
long enough to let readers see how many critics talk of
these poems in terms of rage, and talk of "Howl" and *On
the Road* in terms of vitality. Again, this is not rage, but
the commitment of a poet, coming through in the classic
terms of our thought, in terms of our poetry of nature, and
in terms of some attitudes identified here with Oriental
religion—quite simply, attitudes largely neglected in our
lives. Or, even more simply, in the words of a poet older
than Rexroth, Robert Frost:

Someone had better be prepared
    for rage.
There would be more than ocean
    water broken
Before God's last "Put out the
    light" was spoken.

Kenneth Rexroth is dealing with the plans of women and
men in these magnificent poems, which are harsh, full of
grace and certainty and grief: poems of the mountain nights,
of the vast crystal of knowledge encompassing the limitless
crystal of air and rock and water; of the people to be loved,
the mountain animals, the nights of stars, and, on Fillmore
Street, the night, the moon, the crowded earth.

Richard Foster   (essay date 1962)

SOURCE: "The Voice of a Poet: Kenneth Rexroth," in
The Minnesota Review, Vol. II, No. 3, Spring 1962, pp.
377-84.

[*In this essay, Foster analyses a body of Rexroth's work,
and finds him a fine lyric poet, especially in his love
poems.*]

When a couple of years ago my pleasure in reading through
Kenneth Rexroth's first collection of essays, *Bird in the*

Bush, led me to take an attentive look at his poetry, I was
struck by the anomaly that so good a poet had been so
ostentatiously ignored by the ruling literary culture of his
time. Until I looked into *Bird in the Bush* I had known
Rexroth only as a name connoting a poetry that had never
grown up to Auden, a poetry of rabid convictions and
shapeless outcries, a poetry skewered in the labor pro-
grams of the thirties and yelling ever since. I found that
the essays were not only fierce, but also funny and literate. And when I went on from there to the poems I heard
a voice all right, but it was a voice that said and sang far
more variously than I had ever guessed it could.

The only poet of major importance with a voice since
Yeats—though exceptions might be made for Robert
Graves and the later work of Wallace Stevens, and I take
it the case of Dylan Thomas is at least uncertain—is
William Carlos Williams. And though he has been universally respected and admired, he has been outside the
mainstream of twentieth-century Anglo-American poetry.
The perpetual extinction of personality has not been a
foundation principle of Williams' artistic or spiritual credo
as it has been of Eliot's, and his antipathy to Eliot's influence is well known. Rexroth, who has also been outside the mainstream, and as an early admirer of Williams
expressed much the same set of antipathies, looks rather
like the antiphon of Auden in the way that Williams is the
antiphon of Eliot. The kind of poetry Auden wrote was
"iconic"—a fancy name for what Rexroth has dubbed
"construction"—rather than expressive and personal. To
Eliot and Auden and the influential critics of the forties,
the poet is conceived of primarily as a "craftsman" of
language. But to Rexroth and Williams the poet is much
more than a craftsman. It is the difference between "Pop-
injay" and "Vates," to use two of Rexroth's own favorite
characters. The poet is conceived by Rexroth as a kind of
prophet or bard. Thus the singleness one feels in all
Rexroth's work. Not poems, but poetry—discreet local
moments in a single continuum of utterance. A voice.
And it is a voice that seems especially worth listening to
at this moment when so many new poets with voices are
beginning to be heard, and so many established voiceless
poets are trying to find their voices by exploring the very
traditions which Rexroth has been nourishing on now for
years.

Rexroth's poetry is in a much older tradition than that of
American individualist ecstasy, which he shares in to some
extent with Whitman, Hart Crane, and William Carlos
Williams. His main tradition is a less provincial one than
that, a less strident and ambitious one than that, and one
much less prone to artificial supercharging of the sort
given it recently by the so-called "Beat" poets. I don't
know quite how to name it, except to call it the *personal*
or *humane* tradition of lyric poetry—from the tragedy and
passion and humor of the late Roman and Mediaeval lyric
poets to the pathos and sweetness and dignity of the classic Japanese. Perhaps I am only saying that Rexroth is a
fine universal lyric poet whose work has affinities with
much of the best lyric poetry of the past. He is no barbaric yawper, as I had always believed. Oh sometimes, as in
his barbaric elegy for Dylan Thomas, he gets mad ("You

murdered him, you sons of bitches / In you God damn Brooks Brothers suits!"), but it is sincere anger, and it has that power. And he knows well enough, as he tells us in his fine introduction to Lawrence's poems, that sometimes when you care enough you have to become long-winded and that's that. His worst fault is his own version of official philosophical talk—the same kind of thing that blemishes some of his prose, and that many times blemished Lawrence's. In his long poems, such as *The Dragon and the Unicorn,* a one hundred and seventy-pager published in 1952, where he has lots of Occidental room to verbalize his abstract thinking, there are fistfulls of passages like "Unless we can find somewhere / In the course of rebirth the / Realization of all / Persons through transcendence / Of the self, what I have called / Extrapersonalization. . . ." Sappho and Tu Fu must have burned up thousands of infinitely better passages. And Rexroth himself ought, by every right instinct of his good human nature, to abhor such dull blather. But of course even this is part of the voice—the honest voice succumbing to its childish weakness for pedantry. It is no violation of the person, only of sanity, and it is an infrequent kind of badness to boot. Rexroth is really bad, however, *false* to the person that is his theme and to the voice that gives it being, when he falls back slackly, as he occasionally does on the ready-made rhetoric of salon wit ("History's stockholder's private disasters / Are amortized in catastrophe"), or of soapbox incendiarism ("Far / Away in distant crities / Fat-hearted men are planning / To murder you while you sleep"), or of gift book love-schmaltz (". . . I still catch fish with flies / Made from your blonde pubic hair"), which is only silly Lawrence prose.

I am cataloguing the weaknesses so I can clear the decks for the strengths and beauties of Rexroth's poetry, which are considerable and numerous. To date Rexroth has published six books of his own poetry, in addition to a volume of verse drama and several volumes of translations. His earliest work is collected in *The Art of Worldly Wisdom,* first published in 1949. Most of it is work from the late twenties and early thirties, and it is what he seems willing to call "cubist" in nature. It is arid, obscure, not much fun. Though it is stylistically one with the latter work—the language is basically the excerpting of most of the syntactical arrangements that make simple—it suffers *in extremis* from the philosophical afflatus and communication possible. Its special obscurity is roughly like a long series of grunts, mumblings, and blurtings heard muffled through a motel wall. Except for a few very oriental and very clear love poems, most of the book is dead artifact. Things pick up mightily in his first published book, *In What Hour* (1941), where there are some memorable and deeply felt articulations of the special ideological traumata of the thirties. It is refreshing to encounter, in this day of poetry's stylish inconsequence, a poem as passionately "about" something as Rexroth's **"Requiem for the Spanish Dead,"** or the chillingly prophetic **"The Motto on the Sundial,"** a kind of "Second Coming," which ends,

> It is later than you think, there is a voice
> Preparing to speak, there are whisperings now
> And murmuring and noises made with the teeth.

> This voice will grow louder and learn a language.
> They shall sit trembling while its will is made
>   known,
> In gongs struck, bonfires, and shadows on sundials.
> Once it has spoken it shall never be silenced.

Social apocalypse is the abiding context of Rexroth's poetry—the semi-farcical slaughter of bodies and souls in peace and war, out of which rises phoenix-like the living flames of persons, shaped in love, anger, visionary ecstasy, and holy dying. Self, loved ones, lovers, in moments of fulfillment or recognition, and through and over all the beauty and power of Nature, which, though it is the ultimate extinguisher of persons, is also the natural enemy of society, which is the enemy of persons. These are the themes and occasions of Rexroth's best and most characteristic poems, the best of which are in three books, *The Phoenix and the Tortoise* (1944), *The Signature of All Things* (1949), and *In Defense of the Earth* (1956).

Some of the most memorable are elegiac poems, ranging in mood from the beautiful personal elegies for the poet's mother and for his first wife, Andrée, to the superb classical assaults—some of them are adaptations or actual translations—upon the pretensions and pomposities of man in his physicality and mortality. I must quote just one of the latter, from *The Phoenix and the Tortoise,* to demonstrate their ferocious humanity:

> I know your moral sources, prig.
> Last night you plunged awake screaming.
> You dreamed you'd grown extremely old,
> Lay dying, and to your deathbed,
> All the girls you'd ever slept with
> Came, as old as you, to watch you die.
> Comatose, your blotched residues
> Shrivelled and froze between stiff sheets;
> And the faces, dim as under
> Dirty water, incurious,
> Silent, of a room full of old,
> Old women, waited, patiently.

Perhaps the truly essential Rexroth is found in the love poems. Almost all of his good poems could be said to be love poems. From the sweetly reserved translations of Chinese and Japanese poems, to Rexroth's own intense, free-flowing poems, the theme is love. Love—the recognition of mortality, the turning of the seasons and the great, silently commentative drift of the constellations overhead, and the stepping forth into full, intense, imaginative reality of mortal persons, lover, wife, child, and friend. There are so many good and true Rexroth poems of this kind that selection and discrimination is difficult. They crowd to be heard. One of the most moving of there is "' . . . About the cool water,'" from *The Phoenix and the Tortoise,* in which the words of Sappho, the effulgence of midsummer, the deep, still lateness of afternoon, and the slow, full passion of lovers lying together in the orchard of a ruined New England farm fuse, as in the momentum of a complexly counterpointed piece of music, into a love poem of astonishing immediacy. There is nothing between: the poem is intensely the act. Another

Kenneth Rexroth's *New Poems,* almost exclusively lyrics like "spindles of light," are concerned with "the ecology of infinity." "The endless dark, however, is not a terrifying interstellar hole dwarfing man. Things though in motion are in place. Rexroth's poems are composed of a flash or revelatory image and silent metamorphoses:

> Spring puddles give way
> To young grass.
> In the garden, willow catkins
> Change to singing birds.

Syntax is cleared of the clutter of subordinate clauses, that contingent grammar of a mind hesitating, debating with itself, raging against death and old age. The dynamics of his poems are marked *piano*—even storms are luminous rather than noisy. There is no harried quest for consolation: one need only step outdoors and look up at the stars and peace descends, "Orion striding / into the warm waves." This slow music exquisitely suits the feelings of the people in Rexroth's poems, who are resigned to evanescence. Heartbreak is laconically stated. The same poem can be written over and over—and is. Rexroth's own poems, his imitations of Chinese poetry, and his translations from the Chinese all share the same stylized calm, like the delicate brush strokes of a Chinese scroll. Through the formal manners of his lyrical calligraphy one moves in a serene Void and pleasant monotony that does not suppress emotion so much as it suggests the magical glidings of our dreams:

> "Composed in a Dream"
>
> On the road of Spring, rain multiplies
>   the flowers,
> And the flowers kindle the moun-
>   tains into Spring.
> I follow the brook to its hidden
>   source
> Among a thousand golden orioles.
>
> Before my eyes the flying clouds
> Change into dragons dancing in the
>   blue sky.
> Drunk, lying in the shade
> Of these rattan blinds,
> I can't tell North from South.
>   —Ch'in Kuan (1048-1100)

Thomas Parkinson (essay date 1976)

SOURCE: "Kenneth Rexroth, Poet," in *The Ohio Review,* Vol. XVII, No. 2, Winter 1976, pp. 54-67.

[*This wide-ranging essay spans Rexroth's career, but concentrates on* The Phoenix and the Tortoise *as an exemplary 20th century work.*]

Many readers have difficulty in disengaging Rexroth as poet from Rexroth as social critic, Rexroth as man of letters, Rexroth as poetic warrior carrying on a vendetta with those who do not see the world of poetry as he does. One distinguished writer remarked scornfully in my presence that he did not consider Rexroth a poet but a politician. In the interests of dinner table decorum I didn't bother to press him to a clearer definition, but the remark was so pejorative in tone that it was hardly necessary. Now the poetic community has before it the *Collected Shorter Poems* and the *Collected Longer Poems* from New Directions, and the matter is there to be explored afresh.

I say "explored" deliberately, because magisterial criticism seems to me impertinent to most current literature, and because the poetry of Rexroth is special in the contemporary canon: because it gives a world to explore, it is not predicated on convention or a break from convention, it is not tuned to the sequence of fads that absorbs so much energy better invested. In an age of fashions without style, this body of work has style. There is integrity of manner because there is integrity of vision that is not clouded by polemics or confined to the merely aesthetic. The poetry articulates, often overtly but more often by example, a devotion to the contemplative life. Insofar as it is a record of events, it records the anguish and reward of pursuing the contemplative life in a world of spiritual, religious environmental, and economic agony. When the world intrudes on the quest it is sometimes met with fury and invective, scorn, sarcasm, contempt, and hatred.

Style is a by-product. Writers of stature do not say, "I must develop a style," and then go about deliberately seeking mannerisms that will set them apart from their contemporaries and past convention. Style is a by-product of an habitual disposition toward experience. The man who devotes his life to an art or to the arts does so because he has a love for the medium of that art and what has been accomplished through that medium, and he has an intuitive and often secretly arrogant belief that he has something to do with or say through that medium, something of importance. He is persuaded (with little objective reason persuaded), with the fatality of birth, that there is something he can do that no one else can do, and that the art is his work. He has a vocation. How many people have felt that persuasion and then, after disappointment and neglect, sometimes justified, have turned to some other mode of being. Henry James said once that a man can be taught the techniques of an art but he cannot be taught the one necessity, courage. To be an artist at any time demands courage; to be an artist in California from 1927, when Rexroth first established himself in San Francisco, through the Reagan regime, when Rexroth resettled in Santa Barbara, demands heroism.

And he will have something to do with or say through that medium. The implied distinction sets Rexroth apart from, say, Ezra Pound. When Rexroth writes of the Revolution of the Word, he is saying something very complex. Certainly he has in mind the *logos,* and there is an underlying religious motive. Certainly too he is thinking of the revolution of the word that began with Baudelaire and Whitman, continued through Pound and Apollinaire, and is the heritage of the modern age, the attempt through changing the medium of verse to change sensibility and hence in effect the structuring of society. But he also means the revolution *through* the word, and his affection for the poetry of D. H. Lawrence is revealing (for Eliot was quite right in saying that in Lawrence's poetry at its most transcendent one is not aware of the poetry but of what one is seeing through the poetry). Like any poet, Rexroth is concerned with what he can do *with* the medium, but his stress is on what can be done *through* words. He uses as epigraph for his **Collected Shorter Poems** a translation from an anonymous Provencal poem:

> When the nightingale cries
> All night and all day,
> I have my sweetheart
> Under the flower
> Till the watch from the tower
> Cries, "Lovers, rise!
> The dawn comes and the bright day."

Poets growing up between 1920 and the present have used Ezra Pound's early poems as the best working out of poetic problems. Rexroth knew this, and his incidental comments in conversation on Pound's prosody set all those young associates, as I then was, wondering. Pound rendered the same poem:

> When the nightingale to his mate
> Sings day-long and night late
> My love and I keep state
> In bower
> In flower
> 'Till the watchman on the tower
> Cry:
> > "Up! Thou rascal, Rise,
> >   I see the white
> >   Light
> >   And the night
> >   Flies."

Here is a difference.

The Pound version is a pedagogue's delight, and that was one of Pound's functions. He instructed an entire generation of American poets. Seldom has the poetic game been so nakedly given away; the leading of vowel tones that Duncan talks about mysteriously is not one bit a mystery here. The diphthong *ai* becomes the long *e*, the long *e* and diphthong *ai* continue until the diphthong *au* takes control, and finally the diphthong *ai* dominates and concludes. The poem is formulated in circular design—it is all there, evident. Who can not like it, teacher, student, or poet? Rexroth knew all that, and deliberately set about determining the motive of his collected shorter poems by denying it.

The Rexroth version does not point to itself but to the experience. Anyone who thinks that this is an accident has very little sense of the recent history of poetry—the Pound version points to itself, to its fine shadings, to its subtleties, to its movement and recoil and ultimate satisfaction of expectations established in the opening line. Irresistible. I admire it gratefully—any pedagogue would—but there is something lost to the experience in the Pound version. Rexroth appeals to the common experience of the dawn song, Pound to the overt artifice of his special treatment.

The Pound poem makes a convention new: the Rexroth poem attempts to recreate a traditional experience. The difference represents in miniature Rexroth's definition of his poetic function. Conventions irritate him to the point of indifference, so that he is not even interested in destroying them. Traditions, the core experience of the race, as embodied in wisdom whether poetical or philosophical or historical or religious—these are the substance of his concern. He writes poetry to discover and render wisdom. Wisdom is useless knowledge, knowledge after the fact, and the fact never recurs in precisely that form. It is not paradoxing to say that genuine wisdom is unique in the same way that a genuine poem is. It makes a generous accurate statement about the special form that a universal recurring problem, and an insoluble one, takes. The human effort to be good, the hunger for righteousness, is its sad area for contemplation.

This is why, after the first two books, **The Art of Worldly Wisdom** and **In What Hour,** Rexroth settles into a relatively fixed mode of prosody, normally syllabic in structure. Although sympathetic to innovative writing, he publishes few experiments with language because of his basic persuasion that what poetry lets us see is more important than its texture, that verbal process is only incidentally revelatory, that knowledge, experience, understanding are the materials. His admiration for Tu Fu, Catullus, Baudelaire, Lawrence, and Stevens shows his own motivation. That is the lineage of the visionary and moral traditionalist.

But Rexroth has his special particular tone, that of the civilized man in a barbarous world, self-conscious and socially aware, speaking in an urbane ironic voice. Of art and letters, girls and wine, food and politics, children and music, nature and history, the conversation of a club that never existed on land or sea. Perhaps, thinking of the poetry, the hardest thing to comprehend is just that tone—all one can do is listen, for its modulations, its sudden surge to anger, its suave inversion of its own plausibility, its tinge of sadness, its rage against insensitivity. It goes on talking, talking, a reminder of possibility in the darkening years.

This was the ground of his appeal, especially with the poems from **The Phoenix and the Tortoise** on to the present. Nobody else was thinking of writing poetry in just those terms. Nobody else had the boldness to define his poem's subject as so large and inclusive:

> . . . And I,
> Walking by the viscid, menacing
> Water, turn with my heavy heart
> In my baffled brain, Plutarch's page—

The falling light of the Spartan
Heroes in the late Hellenic dusk—
Agis, Cleomenes—this poem
Of the phoenix and the tortoise—
Of what survives and what perishes,
And how, of the fall of history
And waste of fact—on the crumbling
Edge of a ruined polity
That washes away in an ocean
Whose shores are all washing into death.

It could have been written yesterday; it was published in 1944. Rather than talk about the two formidable collected volumes, I should prefer to look closely at the volume that for me still embodies the reasons for my admiration and indebtedness to the poetry of Rexroth.

I have several copies of **The Phoenix and the Tortoise**. One of them is worn from reading. The binding is broken. I don't know how many times I have read it. Except for books used in teaching, very few books in my library show equivalent wear.

The seasons revolve and the years change
With no assistance or supervision.
The moon, without taking thought,
Moves in its cycle, full, crescent, and full.

The white moon enters the heart of the river;
The air is drugged with azalea blossoms;
Deep in the night a pine cone falls;
Our campfire dies out in the empty mountains.

The sharp stars flicker in the tremulous branches;
The lake is black, bottomless in the crystalline
     night;
High in the sky the Northern Crown
Is cut in half by the dim summit of a snow peak.

O heart, heart, so singularly
Intransigent and corruptible,
Here we lie entranced by the starlit water,
And moments that should each last forever

Slide unconsciously by us like water.

I have been reading this poem for twenty-five years with deepening pleasure. It is not a pleasure that comes from recognizing new relations within the poem that had evaded me before but instead a joy that grows as my experience grows, makes the poem more true because I have, at least quantitatively, more opportunity for knowing what the truth is or might be. The quietness of notation, the directness of that the natural world lives on without assistance or supervision, the rightness of the perceptions. Perhaps the poem has conditioned my experience so that it has become difficult to distinguish between the two, but if so its power is dual, the power to alert the sensibility, the power to vindicate.

There are others of the short poems that show the same kind of imagination at work. The view here shown, of the break between man and nature, the adoration of a natural structure that has an integrity and beauty of design beyond human touch or apprehension, the elegiac realization of human separation from such an order, its failure to *be* in a way analogous to the biological and astronomical order—there is great poignance in it. The poem immediately following it shows knowledge, the attentiveness that lets us see in what fullness it is the same basic biological design:

Now, on this day of the first hundred flowers,
Fate pauses for us in imagination,
As it shall not ever in reality—
As these swifts that link endless parabolas
Change guard unseen in their secret crevices.
Other anniversaries that we have walked
Along this hillcrest through the black fir forest,
Past the abandoned farm, have been just the same—
Even the fog necklaces on the fencewires
Seem to have gained or lost hardly a jewel;
The annual and diurnal patterns hold.
Even the attrition of the cypress grove
Is slow and orderly, each year one more tree
Breaks ranks and lies down, decrepit in the wind.
Each year, on summer's first luminous morning,
The swallows come back, whispering and weaving
Figure eights around the sharp curves of the swifts
Plaiting together the summer air all day,
That the bats and owls unravel in the nights.
And we come back, the signs of time upon us,
In the pause of fate, the threading of the year.

James Broughton once said about the reputations of Bay Area artists, whether poets or film-makers, that they suffered in relation to those of New York artists because they were interested in, believed in, natural and aesthetic beauty, were not at all bashful in reacting to it or trying to make it. The beauty of this poem—and it is beautiful—parallels the beauty of, grows from, the natural order of the world. The poem has faith in that order, even to the weaving and unweaving of flight patterns by swift, swallow, bat, owl. The subject is old. In the Mediterranean spring and summer, whether in Italy or California, I am moved by the changing of the guard when the swallows suddenly seem to diminish and move more clumsily because the bats have taken over—there is a poem dimly in my memory on the subject. It must be one of the genuinely classical human observations.

The poem's faith in the almost military regularity of nature, the breaking of ranks by the cypress trees, the swifts' changing of guard—this is not an aesthetic but an experienced order: "The annual and diurnal patterns hold." The vocabulary of nature is limited but endless; the human entity is more varied but has a definite term, is not irreplaceable, as the fog necklaces on the fencewires are. There is pathos here without self-pity, and the curious thing is that this poet who speaks so frequently of personality as necessary to poetry, as inevitable, and does so sometimes with rancor and vigor that seem excessive to the subject, should himself become in these poems more type than person. Nobody else could have written such poems, but the style, as I have already asserted, is more the way of expressing a complex disposition toward experience than the assertion of personal uniqueness. These poems stand as refractions of general design, parts of the universe rather than expressions of a separate individualism.

The term "classic" keeps forcing itself on my attention as I contemplate this body of work. At times Rexroth exhibits that enviable gift of getting to the ground of experience that one sees in the poetry of Lawrence or Yeats when they are at their least effortful. The theme of these two poems is close to that of "The Wild Swans at Coole," but the poems are much more selfless than Yeats' moving lyric. For in one of its aspects, Rexroth's poetry strikes the same nerve as "I have a gentil cok" or "The Maidens Came," poems that are not often part of critical discussion because there is nothing much to do but admire them. His feeling toward nature has none of the egotism that afflicts Keats or Wordsworth or, to take the really egregious example, Hopkins. Perhaps this is because Rexroth has lived closer to wilderness than to what Europeans call "nature"; it is one thing to listen to a nightingale on Hampstead Heath and something very different to walk in the hills of Marin county or lie by a dwindling camp fire in the Sierra. Wilderness has a way of putting human emotions in their proper place.

At the base of many of the shorter poems, then, is the recognition of an extra-human order, non-social, transcendent. Yet there is no sentimentalizing of nature, no infusion of it with human quality. It is a measure and norm, indifferent.

Among the other shorter poems are numerous erotic poems, sometimes set in wilderness, sometimes urbanely Roman or Mediterranean. Rexroth seemed to fix on several qualities in his life in California that extended to analogies to other cultures and geographies, and his favorites were the Orient and the classic world of the Graeco-Roman tradition. His later work would result in his book of translations from Mediterranean poetry and his two books of poems from the Japanese and the Chinese—beautifully printed, lovingly rendered, these books have achieved the status of ideal Christmas presents. Their tone was already present in the translations that conclude *The Phoenix and the Tortoise,* and it infused the style of the entire book. Somehow he discovered among the dreary stretches of Ausonius the one poem surely by him and genuinely fine. From the medieval *Carmina,* he chose the brilliant "Rumor Laetalis." They are adaptations—the tone is what mattered to him.

The special quality of this poetry, however, is pleasure in the language and in the experience. The pleasure grows from the clear fact that the poet knows what he means, he says what he means and he means what he says. Sometimes the poetry appears declarative, what is sometimes disparagingly called the poetry of statement, as if cogency and fullness of statement did not in themselves have suggestion and overtone enough:

> . . . I have only the swindling
> Memory of poisoned honey.
>
> Poetry and letters
> Persist in silence and solitude.
>
> . . . In ten years
> The art of communication
> Will be more limited.
> The wheel, the lever, the incline,
> May survive, and perhaps
> The Alphabet. At the moment
> The intellectual
> Advance guard is agitated
> Between the Accumulation
> Of Capital and the
> Systematic Derangement of
> The senses, and the Right
> To Homosexuality.

These several statements, the cheated lover, the neglected poet, the saddened intellectual—all of them have the overtone of their voice, one that is widely diffused. They are characteristic, and compared to other verse of the period they have a quality of sustained judgment, of ultimate good sense, of wry factualness, that is extraordinary. The capacity for making judgments appear factual, to reify the moral imagination, is not so frequent that one can take such poetry lightly. It is not just that this was the way things were, but the way they are, their continuousness, and alas, their permanence.

The long poem. Since 1912 the quality and quantity of poetry in the United States has steadily grown. Looking at the recent output of a small press sent to me for review, I find myself murmuring Yeats' words about the Rhymers' Club, "I don't know whether any of us will become great or famous, but I know one thing—there are too many of us." The very growth of poetic technique and skill, however, had for a long time a deleterious effect. First, the exploration of new methods turned the poet's attention from what he could do through words to what he could do with them—a very salutary thing for the art. The novelist knew no such inhibitions, and from Gertrude Stein and James Joyce on, novelists incorporated the new poetic devices into their work until, finally, the novel had become so Alexandrian as to lead literary historians to declare that *Finnegans Wake* was the novel's funeral.

At the same time there was a determined effort to reclaim from the novel much of the ground lost by the modern poem's tendency toward the compact, the elliptical, the privately symbolic. These efforts are well known, and the line from the *Cantos* of Pound through Williams' *Paterson* to Olson's *Maximus* poems is clear to see. Crane's *Bridge* does not fall entirely outside that line of development, but its use of closed forms seems to shunt it toward another line of development.

The Bridge, The Four Quartets, **The Phoenix and the Tortoise.** The sequence does not seem exactly right, but it seems to me more appropriate than placing Rexroth's poem in the Pound-Williams-Olson lineage. In fact, Rexroth stands outside both lineages, but it might be helpful to see his poem in conjunction with the *Four Quartets,* which were written and published, except for the first of them, during the Second World War. For the *Quartets* are in effect war poems, poems written to celebrate the religious and historical continuity of England when that continuity seemed most menaced, poems also designed to place the poet's religious responsibility for the spiritual state of his world. **The Phoenix and the Tortoise** is also a war poem but written from outside the war, and from outside any state or national loyalty. Its loyalties are placed in another realm. At the same time, it is a religious meditative poem on history, on what abides and what perishes, on the place of man in nature and the cosmic resonance of individual responsibility.

"Meditations in a cold solitude." The cold in this line is physical, night by the sea, and the solitude of the poem comes from the contemplation of tragedy. Remote on the Pacific shore, there is nothing to sustain except what in the cultural imagination gets across the Sierra. His memory broods over, ruminates on, what makes for historical continuity as he stands

> . . . here on the edge of death,
> Seeking the continuity,
> The germ plasm of history,
> The epic's lyric absolute.

He can find that absolute in love, in the sacrament of marriage, in sexual abandon, in the imperious remoteness of geology, in courtesans and trivial survivals: the baby, the rose, the pear tree, the coin that outlives Tiberius, vulnerable mere data. Tragedy—

> . . . beyond the reach
> Of my drowsy integrity,
> The race of glory and the race
> Of shame, just or unjust, alike
> Miserable, both come to evil end.

History apart from irreducible values of biology and personality (in a sense not at all conventional) he sees from an Augustinian perspective. History, the public articulation of human energy, is evil and at best tragic, and the state is the organization on massive scale of the evil motives of men. In the midst of the Second World War, this isolated clear look has an austerity and compassion that are unique and, now, all the more accurate:

> Men drop dead in the ancient rubbish
> Of the Acropolis, scholars fall
> Into self-dug graves, Jews are smashed
> Like heroic vermin in the Polish winter.

Christianity, when its communal and metaphysical sanctions give out, places an intolerable and even paralyzing burden on the believer. Eugene O'Neill's life is one bitter monument to that fact. There are many others. Christianity cannot accommodate tragedy; all its habits and drifts are toward ultimate resolutions, and the insoluble it can-

not admit. If one maintains the ethic of Christianity without belief in its rituals and dogmas, then all that sacrifice, repentance, and prayer are self-flagellating. The Augustinian doctrine of history without a Day of Judgment leaves one caught in a world of pointless cruelty. After describing some of the horrors of the Second World War, Rexroth shifts the burden to his own shoulders:

> This is my fault, the horrible term
> Of weakness, evasion, indulgence,
> The total of my petty fault—
> No other man's.

>   And out of this
> Shall I reclaim beauty, peace of soul,
> The perfect gift of self-sacrifice
> Myself as act, as immortal person?

He walks on, through the light of nature, clouds, and sea, as the sun rises:

> My wife has been swimming in the breakers,
> She comes up the beach to meet me, nude,
> Sparkling with water, singing high and clear
> Against the surf. The sun crosses
> The hills and fills her hair, as it lights
> The moon and glorifies the sea
> And deep in the empty mountains melts
> The snow of winter and the glaciers
> Of ten thousand thousand years.

The answer is love, is sacramental marriage. In the terms of Rexroth's preface, "I have tried to embody in verse the belief that the only valid conservation of value lies in the assumption of unlimited liability, the supernatural identification of the self with the tragic unity of creative process." This is to be achieved by the movement from the self to the other, and through that other to universal commitment.

Rexroth claims no individual credit for the idea, citing Lawrence and Schweitzer as predecessors:

> The process as I see it goes something like this: from abandon to erotic mysticism, from erotic mysticism to the ethical mysticism of sacramental marriage, thence to the realization of the ethical mysticism of universal responsibility—from the Dual to the Other. These poems might well be dedicated to D. H. Lawrence, who died in the attempt to refound a spiritual family. One of thepoems is a conscious paraphrase of one of his.

> **The Phoenix and the Tortoise** is an attempt to portray the whole process in historical, personal and physical terms. I have tried to embody in verse the belief that the only valid conservation of value lies in the assumption of unlimited liability, the supernatural identification of the self with the tragic unity of creative process. I hope I have made it clear that I do not believe that the Self does this by an act of will, by sheer assertion. He who would save his life must lose it.

Unlimited liability is a product of the imagination. If a president who declared an aggressive war intervening in the lives of remote and innocent people had to conduct it by personally strangling each man, woman, and child of the "enemy," there would be no such wars. But since he has no personal responsibility, he can allow and even threaten and encourage actions that would make slow strangulation a welcome death.

One difficulty is that the people endowed with imagination are the ones most deeply hurt, in the moral sense. To live in the twentieth century with full imaginative sensibility operative at the highest level is to have a molecule painfully cut out of one's body each second of each day, as some peasant dies from fragmentation bombs, as some black chalks up another hopeless second in the concentration camps that are called corrective institutions, as some baby dwindles away from his possibilities in some disease-ridden hut or tenement. And those who are doing the cutting believe in their righteousness. "Why should we pour our money into the rat-hole of some slum? If you've seen one slum you've seen them all."

So the title poem of *The Phoenix and the Tortoise* stands in its integrity as a witness to the love of true righteousness, of mercy, of pity, of love, of knowledge and understanding. How can one be good in an evil world? the classic traditional question that never leaves us, our moral doom.

The poem seems to me the most perfect artistically of the long meditative poems of the twentieth century. It cannot be reduced to a series of barren meditations relieved by occasional bursts of lyric felicity. The texture is even in its interest and appeal. Rexroth can think in verse, and unlike so many of the large established poetic imaginations of the twentieth century, he is not a truncated man, a literary specialist with some cranky notions about economics or language or religion or history. He knows the fashions of his age, and he knows what is faddish and impertinent in them. He is not taken in by the thought of the moment that is there only to feed an empty desire for false novelties. The only comparable poems are Eliot's *Four Quartets,* and to choose them over Rexroth's poem strikes me as a foolish act. *The Phoenix and the Tortoise* is a saddening poem *not* because it doesn't shape a valid artistic form—it does—but because even the world of 1944, the agonies of that terrible war, seems more possibly habitable than the world that has come out of the post-war years. Now it would be hard to say that the annual and diurnal patterns persist, power is so heavily concentrated and so savagely misused.

I have insisted on talking of Rexroth as poet and concentrated on a single book in so doing because economy requires some selectivity. What I have said of *The Phoenix and the Tortoise* does not "cover" his poetry, which is diverse and rich beyond the limits of any single book. *The Collected Shorter Poems* and *The Collected Longer Poems* provide a massive body of work for exploration. The whole seems to me unique and overwhelmingly useful. Utility, beauty, integrity, fullness of vision, and a knowledge of the world that extends beyond the latest critical book on Mallarmé while including it. To Rexroth poetry envisions and embodies life on a scale and grandeur that none of his poetic contemporaries has attempted to reach. At the same time he has not neglected precision of observation, clarity of articulation, verbal play and prosodic invention.

In a curious way, for his fellow poets, and especially those younger ones who take him with appropriate seriousness, he doesn't tell us much about poetry. His later work, from *The Phoenix and the Tortoise* on, settles into an adaptation of Apollinaire's revivifying of the eight syllable line in French, with variations, and of modern poets in English Rexroth seems to have profited most from the study of Apollinaire. Still, if one wants the experience of Apollinaire's qualities, better to go to him directly. If one wants to learn the rich vocabulary of forms that is the heritage of the modern period, Rexroth has less to offer than Stevens, Neruda, Pound, Williams, Desnos, Eluard, Rilke, Yeats, even Auden. Rexroth offers something else, a model for emulation that one can neither imitate nor loot because it is all of a piece, a fully ordered design of a recognizable universe to which one can give imaginative assent. I don't know what the term *major* exactly means, but if the body of Rexroth's poetic work is not a major achievement, then we can forget the term.

Donald Hall (essay date 1980)

SOURCE: "Kenneth Rexroth and His Poetry," in *The New York Times Book Review,* Vol. LXXXV, No. 47, November 23, 1980, pp. 9, 43-4.

[*In this essay, Hall encapsulates Rexroth's career, sketching his poetic preoccupations, and speculating on his lack of critical acceptance.*]

In December of this year, Kenneth Rexroth will turn 75. Among his lesser accomplishments, he has appeared as a character in two famous novels: James T. Farrell put him into *Studs Lonigan,* a kid named Kenny who works in a drugstore; with more creative denomination, Jack Kerouac called him Rheinhold Cacoethes in *The Dharma Bums,* that 1958 Beat Generation testament, where he is the figure we recognize; anarchist, leader of San Francisco's literary community and poet.

For decades he has written lines like these, setting human life in a context of stone:

> Our campfire is a single light
> Amongst a hundred peaks and water-
>   falls.
> The manifold voices of falling water
> Talk all night.
> Wrapped in your down bag
> Starlight on your cheeks and eyelids
> Your breath comes and goes
> In a tiny cloud in the frosty night.

Ten thousand birds sing in the sunrise.
Ten thousand years revolve without
  change.
All this will never be again.

One thing that is without change is that everything changes. Like many of the greatest poets—Wordsworth, Keats, Frost, Eliot—Rexroth returns continually to one inescapable perception. Maybe this elegiac vision of permanent stone and vanishing flesh derives from the great private event of his middle years—the death of his first wife Andree in 1940 after 13 years of marriage. Her name and image return decades after her death.

But Rexroth is not limited to elegy; he is the most erotic of modern American poets, and one of the most political. The great public event of his young life was the execution of Sacco and Vanzetti. Years after the electrocution he wrote **"Climbing Milestone Mountain"**:

> In the morning
> We swam in the cold transparent lake, the blue
> Damsel flies on all the reeds like millions
> Of narrow metallic flowers, and I thought
> Of you behind the grille in Dedham, Vanzetti,
> Saying, "Who would ever have thought we would
>   make this history?"
> Crossing the brilliant mile-square meadow
> Illuminated with asters and cyclamen,
> The pollen of the lodgepole pines drifting
> With the shifting wind over it and the blue
> And sulphur butterflies drifting with the wind,
> I saw you in the sour prison light, saying,
> "Goodbye comrade."

In Rexroth's poems the natural world, unchanged and changing, remains background to history and love, to enormity and bliss.

When a young man, Rexroth was a Wobbly and studied Marxism as a member of a John Reed Club. Later he moved toward anarchism and pacifism, ideologies which his mature philosophic poems support with passion and argument. His politics of the individual separates him from the mass of Americans—and obviously from Stalinists of the left—and yet joins him to all human beings; it is a politics of love—and Rexroth is the poet of devoted eroticism. **"When We With Sappho"** begins by translating from a Greek fragment, then continues into a personal present:

> ". . . about the cool water
> The wind sounds through sprays
> of apple, and from the quivering leaves
> slumber pours down . . ."

> We lie here in the bee filled, ruinous
> Orchard of a decayed New England farm,
> Summer in our hair, and the smell
> Of summer in our twined bodies,
> Summer in our mouths, and summer
> In the luminous, fragmentary words

> Of this dead Greek woman.
> Stop reading. Lean back. Give me your mouth.
> Your grace is as beautiful as sleep.
> You move against me like a wave
> That moves in sleep.
> Your body spreads across my brain
> Like a bird filled summer;
> Not like a body, not like a separate thing,
> But like a nimbus that hovers
> Over every other thing in all the world.
> Lean back. You are beautiful,
> As beautiful as the folding
> Of your hands in sleep.

This passionate tenderness has not diminished as Rexroth has aged. His latest book includes the beautiful *Love Poems of Marichiko,* which he calls a translation from the Japanese; however, a recent bibliography lists the translations of Rexroth's Marichiko *into* Japanese; in the middle of his eight decade, the poet has written his most erotic poem.

His work for 40 years has moved among his passions for the flesh, for human justice and for the natural world. He integrates these loves in the long poems, and sometimes in briefer ones. *The Signature of All Things* may be the best of all. It is the strength of Rexroth's language that it proscribes nothing. Starting from his reading in a Christian mystic (Jacob Boehme, 1575-1624), he writes vividly of the natural world, he refers to "Pilgrim's Progress," he ranges out into the universe of stars and focuses back upon the world of heifers and minute phosphorescent organisms. It is a poetry of experience and observation, of knowledge—and finally a poetry of wisdom. Nothing is alien to him.

Rexroth's characteristic rhythm moves from the swift and urgent to the slow and meditative, remaining continually powerful; his line hovers around three accents most deployed over seven or eight syllables. It is remarkable how little his line has changed over 40 years, in a world of changing poetic fashion. This steadfastness or stubbornness recalls his patience over publication: He did not publish a book of poems until 1940, when he was 35 years old, although he had been writing since the early 20's. Later, in *The Art of Worldly Wisdom* (1949), he collected and published work from his cubist youth. Some had appeared in Louis Zukofsky's *An Objectivist's Anthology* (1932).

When we try to describe a poet's style, it can be useful to name starting points, but it is not easy with Kenneth Rexroth. He has said that Tu Fu was the greatest influence on him; fair enough, but there is no analogy between the Chinese line, end-stopped, with its count of characters, and Rexroth's run-on syllabics. In temperament and idea Rexroth is close to D. H. Lawrence, about whom he wrote his first major essay, in 1947; but Lawrence's best poems take off from Whitman's line—and Rexroth's prosody is as far from Whitman's as it can get. Perhaps there is a bit of William Carlos Williams in his enjambed lines; maybe Louis Zukofsky. We could say, throwing up our hands, that he is a synthesis of Tu Fu, Lawrence and Mallarmé. To an unusual extent Rexroth has made Rexroth up.

He was born in Indiana in 1905 and spent most of the 20's in Chicago's Bohemia—poet, painter and autodidact. Late in the decade he moved to San Francisco, where he has lived much of his life, moving down the Coast to Santa Barbara only in 1968. He was the poet of San Francisco even before Robert Duncan, Philip Lamantia, Kenneth Patchen and William Everson (Brother Antoninus). For decades he has advocated the poetry of the West, the elder literary figure of the city where poetry came to happen: Jack Spicer, Philip Whalen, Michael McClure, Lawrence Ferlinghetti, Lew Welch, Joanne Kyger. His influence on the young is obvious, clearest in Gary Snyder, who is worthy of his master. When young writers from the East arrived in the 50's—Allen Ginsberg, Jack Kerouac, Gregory Corso—they attended gatherings at Rexroth's house, and it was Rexroth who was catalyst for the 1955 Six Gallery reading that was the public birth of the Beat Generation.

Later, alliances altered. Talking about Kenneth Rexroth, it is easy to wander into the history of factionalism, for he has been partisan, and few polemicists have had a sharper tongue. Inventor of the parodic The Vaticide Review (apparently Partisan, but it can stand in for all the quarterlies), he wrote in 1957 of poet / professors, "Ninety-nine percent of them don't even exist but are androids manufactured from molds, cast from Randall Jarrell by the lost wax process." On the West Coast he has been a constant, grumpy presence. If the West has taken him for granted, the East has chosen to ignore him, perhaps because he has taken potshots at the provincial East forever and ever. The *Harvard Guide to Contemporary Writing* (1979), which purports to cover the scene since 1945, will do for an example; the poetry critic quotes *none* of Rexroth's poetry but sputters about his "intemperate diatribes." Nor does Rexroth make the *New York Review of Books* short-list of Approved Contemporaries.

Which is a pity, because he is better than anyone on it.

Taste is always a fool—the consensus of any moment; contemporary taste is the agreement of diffident people to quote each other's opinions. It reaffirms with complacency reputations which are perceived as immemorial but which are actually constructed of rumor, laziness and fear. As a writer ages and issues new volumes, he or she is reviewed as if the writing has remained the same, because it would require brains and effort to alter not only one's past opinion but the current professional assessment.

Perhaps the consensus of our moment, product largely of the East and the academy, is especially ignorant, especially gullible. Or perhaps it is only—in the matter of Kenneth Rexroth—that the tastemakers are offended by Rexroth's morals. In fact they *ought* to be, because the ethical ideas that Rexroth puts forward with such acerbity are old-fashioned and individual—anathema to the suburban, Volvo-driving, conformist liberalism of the academy. He stands firm against technocracy and its bureaus, of which the university is as devoted an institution as General Motors. Rexroth's morals derive in part from Indiana before the First World War, in part from centuries of Oriental thought, and in part from the radical non-Marxist thinking of late 19th-century Europe.

He has not been wholly without attention. Morgan Gibson wrote a Twayne book about him, which lists many reviews and articles about his poetry; a magazine called *The Ark* has recently devoted an issue to his work, with tributes from John Haines, W. S. Merwin, William Everson, the late James Wright and many others. His reading aloud to music, which is superb and innovative, is available on several tapes and records.

James Laughlin of New Directions has been his loyal publisher and keeps his poetry in print, including paperback editions of the *Collected Shorter Poems* (1967) and the *Collected Longer Poems* (1968). The long poems are five in number, including **"The Phoenix and the Tortoise,"** a 30-page meditative philosophic poem from the early 40's, and **"The Dragon and the Unicorn,"** from the second half of the same decade, which describes European travel and argues on a high level of abstraction. Best of the long poems is the latest, **"The Heart's Garden, the Garden's Heart"** (1967).

There are many volumes of prose: *An Autobiographical Novel* (1966), several collections of essays both literary and political, and a rapid, polemical literary history called *American Poetry in the Twentieth Century* (1971). There are volumes of translations; Rexroth has translated from Latin, Greek, French, German, Spanish, Swedish; but it is his work in Chinese and Japanese which is deservedly best known—beginning with *One Hundred Poems From the Chinese* (1956). Certainly his verse translations remain among the best in an age of translation.

However, if we look for his best work, we look to his own poems. To end with, here is the lyric **"Your Birthday in the California Mountains,"** from his *New Poems* of 1974:

> A broken moon on the cold
>   water,
> And wild geese crying high
>   overhead,
> The smoke of the campfire rises
> Toward the geometry of heaven—
> Points of light in the infinite
>   blackness.
>
> I watch across the narrow inlet
> Your dark figure comes and
>   goes before the fire.
> A loon cries out on the night
>   bound lake.
> Then all the world is silent with
>   the
> Silence of autumn waiting for
> The coming of winter. I enter

The ring of firelight, bringing to
    you
A string of trout for our dinner.
As we eat by the whispering
    lake,
I say, "Many years from now
    we will
Remember this night and talk
    of it."
Many years have gone by since
    then, and
Many years again. I remember
That night as though it was last
    night,
But you have been dead for
    thirty years.

Donald Gutierrez (essay date 1983)

SOURCE: "Natural Supernaturalism: The Nature Poetry of Kenneth Rexroth," in *The Literary Review*, Vol. 26, No. 3, Spring 1983, pp. 405-18.

[*In this excerpt, Gutierrez discusses Rexroth's nature poetry.*]

"The clarity of purposively realized objectivity is the most supernatural of all visions."
    Kenneth Rexroth, Introduction to D.H. Lawrence's *Selected Poems*

"As long as we are lost in the world of purpose we are not free."
    Kenneth Rexroth, *The Dragon and The Unicorn*

Probably there is little nature verse of any value that is simply about nature. Nature-meditation verse is perhaps a more accurate description for much of the important poetry dealing with nature as a medium for exploration of the self and the world. Yet even that phrase is too tame for the intensities and depths of meaning achieved by some poets in confronting the natural environment. Wordsworth's *The Prelude* is formidably subtle in, among other things, the reflexivities it creates in relating the individual sensibility to the "world" of nature. D.H. Lawrence in some of his best verse addresses nature with a sense of its non-human integrity so vigorous as to suggest in poems like "Fish" either an iconoclastic idea of subject and object, or the limitations of human sovereignty amid the mystery of the earth's non-human life. Nature in Kenneth Rexroth's verse is approached for various ends—as a context for love and sex, an inspiration to contemplation, a stabilizing contrast to the overwhelming corruption of twentieth century societies and experience.

But perhaps Rexroth's most memorable treatment of nature occurs when, without violating its integrity or particularity, he engages it to suggest certain philosophical ideas about the character of reality. These ideas in turn are arresting because, in the midst of the turmoil of large cities, wars, and social evil and misery, they remind us, to quote Rexroth quoting the nineteenth century English scientist John Tyndall, of "'the obliquity of the earth's axis . . . which runs through creation, and links the roll of a planet alike with the interests of marmots and men.'" (**"Fall, Sierra Nevada,"** in "Towards an Organic Philosophy," in *The Collected Shorter Poems of Kenneth Rexroth,* 1966, p. 103). Rexroth is particularly sensitive to that "roll of the planet" and its place in human sensibility and the "phenomena" of society.

His conception of nature is not Tennyson's "Nature red in tooth and claw." Nature in its malign or destructive guise figures little if at all in his verse, although his sense of the radical evil of *human* nature is sharp indeed. Thus the nature of earthquakes, volcanic eruptions, hurricanes, and animals preying on each other is seen primarily in Rexroth's social poetry, converted into a polemical verse attacking human society and institutions (as in his jeremiad on the death of Dylan Thomas, **"Thou Shalt Not Kill"**). But the natural environment itself is not allegorized into a Ted Hughes landscape of primal human ferocity and terror. As a result, there is something old fashioned yet strikingly immediate about Rexroth's nature poetry.

Rexroth's most characteristic nature poetry embodies the ancient Oriental sagacity that nature and its phenomena *are* themselves. This outlook does not mean that nature is not translated into other meanings in Rexroth's verse, but it does place more stress on the literal reality of nature than is common among 20th century poets. This philosophic literalism emerges from the clarity, particularization, and deceptive sense of artless art of his poetry, qualities to which the frequent use of declarative sentences and the virtual absence of metaphors also contribute. Rexroth's "artless" art endows the nature verse with both a smooth-surfaced, anti-allegorical "finish" and a distinctive authenticity of utterance. This poetry aspires to the difficult paradox of not meaning, but being, while implying a significant if non-discursive reality.

A Rexroth nature poem is often comprised of a movement from one crisply precise detail of knowledgeable observation to another. Frequently the result is a gradually brimming significance or an overt climactic realization. Set usually in mountain areas in central California or near the San Francisco Bay area, this verse registers an uncommon order of reality.

"Fall, Sierra Nevada," the poem that ends with the Tyndall quotation, is thick with specific details of place, flora, fauna, and weather. Located in the Sierra Nevada range in eastern California, the poem specifies landmarks, peaks like Ritter and Banner, an adjacent eastern range (the White mountains), and the salt flats of Nevada. Specific types of birds are mentioned (hermit thrush, chickadees, hummingbirds, a golden eagle, an owl—caught in two beautiful lines, "The ventriloquial billing / Of an owl mingles with the bells of the waterfall"). Also mentioned are constellations like Scorpion and the Great Bear, planets like Jupiter and Venus, time ("This morning," "At noon," "All day," "At sunset," "In the morning"), weather ("cloud shadows," "distant thunder," "far-off lightnings," "Rain is falling," "a small dense cumulus cloud"), and frost. In addition, a range of specific colors and shades is connected with all of these terrestrial and celestial details: gold, alpenglow, burnt peaks, dark sedge meadows, white salt flats, whitebark pines.

These do not comprise all the details (or even categories of details) in this 45-line poem, but they will suffice to give an idea of the texture of concreteness and specificity typical of a Rexroth nature poem. Rexroth writes with a highly accurate sense both of his specific surroundings and of the character of those surroundings over a period of time (in this poem, 24 hours, from morning to morning). There is no romantic heightening through self-indulgent emotion or a merging with nature. Rather, the descriptiveness is so precise that it creates an intense external reality, a kind of objective super-reality: "Just before moonset, a small dense cumulus cloud, / Gleaming like a grape cluster of metal, / Moves over the Sierra crest and grows down the westward slope." The poem cites a specific time of day, a literally accurate description of a cloud, followed, to intensify its reality, by a crystal-clear simile about it, and an exact description of its direction and what it passes over. The entire poem exists on this almost preternatural level of descriptive clarity, lending its climactic statement of the interrelation of all earthly life a numinosity that transcends its factual base.

Sometimes, the "purpose" of a Rexroth nature poem will become overt, as in the moving Tyndall quotation from **"Fall, Sierra Nevada"** about the common earthly interests of "marmots and men." In some poems the climax might be an elegy for a dead loved one, as in one of the three elegiac "Andree Rexroth" verses, which ends with "all the years that we were young / Are gone, and every atom / Of your learned and disordered / Flesh is utterly consumed," or an erotic vision experienced through the sheer concentration of beauty of a unique site, as in this high moment from **"Incarnation"** in which "Rexroth" has descended from a climb in the mountains and sees

> . . . far down our fire's smoke
> Rising between the canyon walls . . .
> And as I stood in the stones
> In the midst of whirling waters
> The swirling iris perfume
> Caught me in a vision of you
> More real than reality . . .

What is beautiful about the beloved is intensified by, and merged with, the beauty of the landscape:

> Forever the thought of you,
> And the splendor of the iris . . .
> And the obscure cantata
> Of the tangled water, and the
> Burning, impassive snow peaks
> Are knotted together here.

But the point in **"Incarnation"** goes deeper than an association of beauties. The clear, exact description symbol-izes a heightened state of being. This condition is partly brought on by temporarily living in mountains which causes the vivid sense of the physical environment to also intensify one's sense of the "Other." In this sort of "nature-and-love" verse, sexual intimacy takes on an unusual vividness. Depictions of natural surroundings become a revelation of relationship with the beloved and of the almost magical simplicities of existence, as in the post-coital **"Still on Water,"** "A turtle slips into the water / With a faint noise like a breaking bubble / There is no other sound . . . ," in which the description also reflects the serenity of the lovers.

In one of the other "Andree Rexroth" poems (simply called **"Andree Rexroth"**), Rexroth writes movingly about the experience of nature before and after the death of his first wife:

> Now once more gray mottled buckeye branches
> Explode their emerald stars,
> And alders smoulder in a rosy smoke
> Of innumerable buds.
> I know that spring again is splendid
> As ever, the hidden thrush
> As sweetly tongued, the sun as vital—
> But these are the forest trails we walked together,
> These paths, ten years together.
> We thought the years would last forever,
> They are all gone now, the days
> We thought would not come for us are here.
> Bright trout poised in the current—
> The racoon's track at the water's edge—
> A bittern booming in the distance—
> Your ashes scattered on this mountain—
> Moving seaward on this stream.

Although the poem has a clear-cut time structure of present-past-present, this arrangement achieves powerful emotional effects through precise descriptive and imaginative representations of nature. These effects are enhanced by an implicit contrast of the speaker alone in nature in the present and (through retrospection) together with his beloved in the same place ten years earlier. The poem opens indicating that it is spring again. If "Now once more" is the most minute of hints of a deeper sorrow to be broached, the "I-know-that" syntax of lines 5-7 enlarges the intimation of something lacking in the present, despite the continuing brilliance, beauty, and force of nature (the "emerald stars" of the buckeye branches, the "rosy smoke" of the budding alders, the melodious thrush, the vitality of the sun).

By line 8, however, it becomes increasingly clear what the veiled dissatisfaction with nature and with the present in the preceding lines means. Lines 9-12 amplify this dissatisfaction. The speaker and his wife had been so absorbed in each other and in the physical surrounding as to assume that the present would never end. The present itself was a future the lovers thought would never occur, but, like a vision of hell, it has come to pass. What this is emerges in the penultimate line of the poem: the death of Andree Rexroth.

This death—the culmination of the poem—is made heartrending by the shock of its revelation, and by the fact that what had implicitly made nature "perfect" or "complete" in that idyllic past is now mere ashes. With oblique irony, nature continues to take its course (trout ready to leap, racoons hunting for fish, the huge bittern making a mating call). By indicating that Andree Rexroth is now a part of nature, Rexroth not only evokes lines from one of the most poignant of Wordsworth's Lucy Grey poems ("Rolled round in earth's diurnal course, / With rocks, and stones, and trees"), but transcends that allusion by the pronounced context in the poem of adult love. The beloved is now a part of the nature that, at one time, had supported and beautified her relationship with the speaker, a part moving implacably towards final dissolution in the ocean.

Rexroth doesn't melodramatize his lament. Nature is—objectively—just as beautiful now as it was in the past when Andree Rexroth was alive. But of course it is no longer for him the beautiful surroundings it once was. This loss is apparent in the laconic syntax of the last five lines with its series of dependent verbal clauses, the decisive ashes line, culminating in the present participle of the last line, and the quietly mournful sense it gives that more than the beloved's ashes are "moving seaward." Through the restraints imposed by an acute fidelity to the realities of the natural environment, a fidelity reflecting his love, the loss of his beloved, and the quality of their relationship, Rexroth in **"Andree Rexroth"** embodies an exquisitely quiet sadness reminiscent of the Oriental poetry he so admired.

If in a poem like **"Falling Leaves and Early Snow,"** one beholds an almost "pure" nature poem (the opening three lines seem to allude to the opening hostilities of World War II), in **"Another Spring,"** the "deeper" meaning is poignantly tangible:

> The seasons revolve and the years change
> With no assistance or supervision.
> The moon, without taking thought,
> Moves in its cycle, full, crescent, and full.
>
> The white moon enters the heart of the river;
> The air is drugged with azalea blossoms;
> Deep in the night a pine cone falls;
> Our campfire dies out in the empty mountains.
>
> The sharp stars flicker in the tremulous branches;
> The lake is black, bottomless in the crystalline
>   night;
> High in the sky the Northern Crown
> Is cut in half by the dim summit of a snow peak.
>
> O heart, heart, so singularly
> Intransigent and corruptible,
> Here we lie entranced by the starlit water,
> And moments that should each last forever
>
> Slide unconsciously by us like water.

The poem can be seen as developing within two time frames, or, more accurately, within a framework of space within time. There is the opening broad reference to the revolving seasons and the changing years, followed by two-and-a-half stanzas dealing with one moonlit night. That these two sections of the poem are not merely descriptive is borne out by the last five lines of the poem where the simple, inevitable passing of time, taking with it the beautiful moments of love, creates an ineffable poignancy.

Indeed, some of the impact of **"Another Spring"** arises from the ostensible contrast between the careful, even "pure," descriptiveness of the first three stanzas of the poem, and the impassioned subjectivity of address in the final five lines both to the subjective self ("heart") and to the beloved. The first "objective" section of the poem contains lines that could almost stand by themselves in their clarity of presentation:

> The white moon enters the heart of the river. . . .
>
> The sharp stars flicker in the tremulous branches,

or there is

> Deep in the night a pine cone falls,

a line whose lucidity and simplicity almost make analysis seem an impertinence.

Yet from the opening lines hints of a deeper meaning are already present. Seasons and years occur without "assistance or supervision," and the moon moves through its phases "without taking thought." This is followed by the sharply etched images of stanzas two and three: the moon on the river, the azalea-drugged evening air, the dying campfire and flickering stars, and so on. This appearance of objective description is subtly complicated by the motif of clashing white and black imagery running throughout it: the moon moving through a (dark) sky and river, the campfire dying out in the (dark) mountains, the stars glittering through the (dark) branches, the stars of the Northern Crown obscured by the "dim snow peak." This build-up of imagistic contrasts contains a tension that suddenly snaps in the opening of the fourth stanza where Rexroth makes the sudden shift to an almost Yeatsian apostrophe to the principle of feeling ("O heart, heart . . .").

The implication in the final five lines that time (especially moments of love amidst nature) is like water suggests that in a way it *is* water, is one with phenomena. Something in the very movement of the seasons (a major theme in the poem) diminishes not only a gratifying contemplation of nature but also durability or steadfastness in love. The "heart," so vulnerable to change and hardness, is, like the seasons, like moving water, the "victim" of impermanence and change and thus of disaffection. The poem is all that remains to prevent beautiful moments of love in nature from vanishing, despite the revolving seasons, perhaps forever.

Time is viewed in quite a different way in the mystical **"Time Is The Mercy Of Eternity."** One of Rexroth's best poems, "Time," like much of Rexroth's nature verse, displays sharp, clear description. But one discovers several complicating factors in this more ambitious poem. There is an introductory statement about time antithetical to the mystical meanings in the title, a motif of visual recession and "mirroring," a symbolic distinction between the purity or clarity of mountain life and the confusion and corruption of city life, and a symbolic and climactic use of the image of a crystal that responds to the idea of time introducing the poem.

"Time is divided," Rexroth begins, into

> Seconds, minutes, hours, years,
> And centuries. Take any
> One of them and add up its
> Content, all the world over
> One division contains much
> The same as any other.

Time (or "times") is an indistinguishable element that cannot give experience or phenomena character or identity, and thus value. Time in this sense is *not* the mercy of eternity; rather, it is a value-neuter quantity. Yet the poem does not reach the opposite mystical apotheosis of the title through such traditional devices as "problem-solving," narrative, surprises or shocks, retrospection, or a vision of God. Instead, it develops a heightened sensitivity, through acute response and descriptive integrity and through the elements of complexity mentioned above, towards the details and events in the natural surrounding, ascending to a mystical realization.

Rexroth is encamped on a narrow ledge with a steep drop first of 500 feet, then of another 1000 feet to a river. Beyond his ledge-camp are physical elements that also become media of the transformation of reality—first, "shimmering space," then the recessiveness of "fold on / Dimmer fold of wooded hills," beyond which, in the final medium of "pulsating heat," lies the San Joaquin Valley, the flatland of "life and trouble." The world of commerce is described shortly after as the "writhing city," burning in a "fire of transcendence and commodities," a condensed, ironic allusion to St. Augustine's lustful Carthage and to Karl Marx's chapter on commodity fetishes in *Capital*. Yet even in 20th century Carthages and Babylons, realization, "the holiness of the real," is possible, love creating a mode of genuine transcendence for the "experiencer" and the lover. But this short meditation on the city, the flatland far off, suggests for "Rexroth" or the viewer a different kind of transcendence, experienced climactically through inhabiting this "higher" life of mountain, canyon, and sky over a period of several weeks.

In the latter part of the poem, two revelations occur, both suggesting an original perspective on life through a unique conception of the centers of reality. The first arises in a scene in which Rexroth is looking at a deep pool in early evening. He describes some of the water creatures—frogs, hydras, water boatmen, "a small dense cloud of hundreds / Of midges, no bigger than / My head" hovering over the pond. This leads to a deepening awareness:

> I realize that the color
> Of the water itself is
> Due to millions of active
> Green flecks of life.
>
> . . . . .
>
> The deep reverberation
> Of my identity with
> All this plenitude of life
> Leaves me shaken and giddy.

What has made this pitch of identity with nature possible is being in the midst of it ("alone/ In the midst of a hundred mountains"). But like the "cloud" of midges, it is the union of the object with the articulated experience of the object that gives both a reality more forceful for being experienced in solitude. Indeed, part of the cogency and serenity of Rexroth's nature verse stems from his skill in making his persona and its experience credible. There are no self-doubting Prufrocks here, no involuted discussions of the reality of object and subject. The object is fully "there" because of a fidelity of objective description mirroring a harmony and repose in the poem's speaker.

The second vision concludes the work, and presents a process of simplifying one's needs similar to a definition of the contemplative Rexroth makes in *The Dragon and the Unicorn* in which, by putting aside appetite and the wish for consequence from possibility, one can develop a "disinterested / Knowledge of himself, of / The simplest things, knowing them / As really perspectives into / The others" (*The Dragon and the Unicorn*). This conception is made concrete in the final 22 lines of **"Time."** Conveyed through a metaphor of the crystal, it hardens objective and subjective reality, the contemplative and the "object" of contemplation, as two crystals—"At last there is nothing left / But knowledge, itself a vast / Crystal encompassing the limitless crystal of air / and rock and water." This semi-monist condition is reached, after a transcendence of flatland mentality and divisiveness, through a residing in nature that Rexroth develops for several pages. The speaker consequently is "Suspended / In absolutely transparent / air and water and time," which in turn creates in him a "crystalline being."

Why the crystal metaphors? The stripping of the qualities of one's moral history, of "personal facts, / And sensations, and desires," that has occurred during "Rexroth's" immersion in nature, results in a purity or clarity of being that reflects "this translucent / Immense here and now" of the Object or physical surrounding. The crystalline "knowledge" attained, closely relating the natural elements to human existence in a concentration of serene and almost selfless repose, leads to the two "crystals" being "perfectly / Silent. There is nothing to / Say about them." Such is the language of a transcendence free from the pressures of the pantheistic deity one usually finds in pious nature verse. If this is a dialogue (those "others" Rexroth alludes to in the passage defining the contemplative), it is definitely a secularized "I" and "Thou." Part of the authority of **"Time"** and of Rexroth's other meditative nature poems derives from the basic implication that natural phenomena can, if sufficiently experienced, meet the deepest human needs.

Now we can consider how time is the mercy of eternity. If eternity can be regarded as a form or conception of transcendence experienced by human beings fleetingly, time *can* become the mercy or grace or "kindness" of eternity through a quintessential experience of nature by a person "suspended" in a state of contemplation (or in analogous states of integrity). The culminating image and vision of the crystalline state is granted "Rexroth" in the symbolic location halfway between the "writhing city" and "eternity." Time, seen as quantitative and valueless at the beginning of the poem, has, through the speaker's climactic experience of nature and mind as two harmonious spaces, become, at the poem's end, a "mercy" of eternity.

Even Rexroth's "pure" nature verse can surprise with the quiet force of its *literal* significance, a quality in part due to his habit, as mentioned earlier, of declarative directness, highly lucid description, and sparse figuration. In **"Clear Autumn,"** a poem from a short verse series called **"Mary And The Seasons,"** from the 1956 collection *In Defense Of The Earth,* Rexroth describes a mountain setting in which fallen leaves suggest an illumination: "New-fallen / Leaves shine like light on the floor." The light motif is not stressed; rather, it has its place amid the humming of low-flying insects, the quiet clustering nearby of Holstein cattle vistas, the floating buzzards. Yet even here a sinister image of human menace is suggested in a glimpse of "long white scrawls" in the air, the "graffiti of genocide" left by jet bombers too high to be visible.

If the fallen leaves suggest an order of naturalness separate from the captivity and menace of the human world of purpose, the final image of nature in **"Clear Autumn"** is strikingly original and delicate. Following the reference to the jets, the concluding scene opens with a description of the air as glittering with "millions of glass / Needles, falling from the zenith." We learn that this aerial miracle is

    . . . the silk of a swarm
Of ballooning spiders, flashes
Of tinsel and drifting crystal
In the vast rising autumn air.
When we get back everything
Is linked with everything else
By fine bright strands of spun glass,
The golden floor of October,
Brilliant under a gauze of light.

Rexroth has taken an unusual (and unromantic) instance of natural life, and expanded it into a symbolic image of an almost supernatural order and interconnection. The ethereal simplicity and visual uniqueness of the image also constitute its suggestive power.

Rexroth states in another poem-series, **"Aix-en-Provence"** (**"Spring,"** from his 1964 book *Natural Numbers*), that nature is primarily and ultimately itself:

       Now the buds
Are round and tight in the dim
Moonlight, in the night that
Stretches on forever, that had
No beginning, and that will
Never end, and it doesn't mean
Anything. It isn't an image of
Something. It isn't a symbol of
Something else. It is just an
Almond tree, in the night, by
The house, in the woods, by
A vineyard, under the setting
Half moon, in Provence, in the
Beginning of another Spring.

Also implied in these lines is an anti-symbolic, anti-teleological esthetic and philosophy.

A similar attitude underlines the ballooning spider webs of **"Clear Autumn."** No less effective for not being tendentious, this unique image primarily *is* its meaning. The "rightness" of the spider-web image resides not in its symbolizing of nature's innate order or "artful handiwork," but in its embodiment of the sheer autonomy of nature as seasonal unfoldings, the reign of Tyndall's "oblique axis" again. Reigning, but not obliterating. Some of the complexity of Rexroth's conception of humanity and human society in the nature verse arises from his acknowledgement of the potency of organized human murderousness and destructiveness. But within the trances and meditations of mountain life, the reality of the presences of nature is uppermost. The spiders and their magical spun glass will soon disappear, as will that particular autumn and that "golden floor." But they persist in the mind and in art as an illumination of earthly existence, "brilliant under a gauze of light.". . .

Lee Bartlett (essay date 1989)

SOURCE: "The Community of Love: Reading Kenneth Rexroth's Long Poems," in *The Centennial Review,* Vol. XXXIII, No. 1, Winter 1989, pp. 17-31.

[*In this excerpt, Bartlett traces the development of the quest theme through all of Rexroth's long poems.*]

James Wright has written that Rexroth "is a great love poet during the most loveless of times," and indeed over the past sixty years Rexroth has written some of the most moving and durable American verse of our century. Undoubtedly, Rexroth's most well-known and accessible poems are his lyrics and his translations. Additionally, however, he wrote five long "philosophical" poems; these comprise his 1968 volume, *The Collected Longer Poems*. The first of these, *The Homestead Called Damascus*, was written while he was still in his teens; the last, ***Heart's***

Garden, The Garden's Heart, was not completed until after the collection itself had gone to New Directions. In between we have **"A Prolegomenon to a Theodicy,"** *The Phoenix and the Tortoise,* and *The Dragon and the Unicorn.* Interestingly, while criticism of the last decade has found the modern long poem a fruitful area of inquiry (I'm thinking here of fine studies like M. L. Rosenthal and Sally M. Gall's *The Modern Poetic Sequence,* Barry Ahern's study of *Zukofsky's "A",* and countless books and articles on *The Cantos, Paterson, The Maximus Poems, Life Studies,* and *The Dream Songs*), Rexroth's long poems have received very little attention. Yet it seems to me that taken together these five poems form as interesting and coherent a major poetic project as any of the other of the great long poems of this century, and certainly if Rexroth's work survives it will be in large measure because of his achievement here. At the very least, his long poem offers an alternative vision and set of stylistic possibilities to what was the prevailing formalist aesthetic.

In his introduction to *The Collected Longer Poems,* Rexroth explains that he considers these poemsas sections of a larger single project, rather than as discreet entities: "All the sections of this book now seem to me almost as much one long poem as do the *The Cantos* or *Paterson.* . . . The plot remains the same—the interior and exterior adventures of two poles of personality." Further, he notes that "the political stand of the poems never changes: the only Absolute is the Community of Love with which Time ends. . . . I have tried to embody in verse the belief that the only valid conservation of value lies in the assumption of unlimited liability, the supernatural identification of the self with the tragic unity of the creative process." Though it is doubtful that Rexroth wrote *The Homestead Called Damascus,* at least, with either Pound's or Williams's notion of a grand modern epic in progress, I would like to look at the poem in some detail because it establishes the twin geometries explored by the poet in his later longer work, and is probably the least well-known of the long poems.

The publication history of *Homestead* is a little tangled. Rexroth began the poem when he was just fifteen and completed it not later than 1925. Two sections ("Adonis in Summer" and "Adonis in Winter") from Part II appeared as short poems in *The Phoenix and the Tortoise* (1944), but the poem entire was not published until 1957 in *The Quarterly Review of Literature* (where it was followed by a series of notes by Lawrence Lipton, and won a Longview Award). New Directions finally released the poem as a separate volume in its "World Poets" pamphlet series in 1963.

Homestead is juvenilia, but (like "The Lovesong of J. Alfred Prufrock," completed when Eliot was just twenty-three) it is certainly not slight. "In those days," Rexroth wrote Lawrence Lipton, "we thought *The Waste Land* a revolutionary poem," and while commentators have seen the influence of both Aiken and Jeffers in *Homestead,* it is obvious that the poem is Rexroth's youthful attempt to meet Eliot's challenge. Like *The Waste Land, Homestead* is divided into sections, its intelligibility depends upon

both a literate audience and readers willing to work through a rather discontinuous narrative structure, and throughout we sense that no less than the very core of Western Civilization is at stake. Even the language of the poem,

> And Thomas, with a narrow light,
> comes out and watches, by the gate;
> And muses in the turgid night;
> And goes into the house again.
> The library is calm and prim.
> The shepherds and the sheep have passed.
> And Botticelli ladies, slim
> And hyperthyroid, grace the walls

recalls Eliot's early work. However, while Eliot's allusiveness seems somehow fully integrated into his long poem (can we imagine a *Waste Land* without it?), Rexroth's often does not. "I was immersed in Frazier, Murray, Harrison, Jessie Weston, A. E. Waite, and was busy reading the whole corpus of the Arthuriad," the poet continued to Lipton, and many times here Rexroth seems to be wearing his learning on his sleeve, as his frequent literary, philosophical, and historical allusions are sometimes merely gratuitous. Still, I think that because of its structural complexity, the loveliness of certain passages, and the fact that the poem announces themes that will play throughout the other, more mature longer poems, *Homestead* remains an integral part of Rexroth's corpus. Andas the product of a teenage mind, it is remarkable.

The poem is divided into four numbered sections, with the fourth section divided into two parts. Lipton has noted that the "mood" of the work is that of elegiac reverie, though this reverie alternates with straight narrative passages. There are three narrative consciousnesses here—Thomas Damascan, his brother Sebastian, and a disembodied narrative voice who in his comments on the action seems (as Morgan Gibson points out in his *Kenneth Rexroth*) as dispassionate and omniscient as Eliot's Tiresias—and Rexroth has spoken of these three voice as components of a single personality, his own. Flatly stated, the plot of the poem follows the general pattern of a quest tale. It begins with a twenty-two-line meditation by, presumably, the third narrative voice which contrasts unquestioning angels ("robed / in tublar, neuter folds of pink and blue") with young minds searching for their identities ("poking in odd / Corners for unsampled vocations / Of the spirit, / While the flesh is strong"). Following, we discover that two brothers, Thomas and Sebastian (and the religious implications here are, of course, deliberate), lead rather idyllic lives on the family estate in the Catskills—hiking, reading books like *The Golden Bough,* and sitting up late "drinking wine, / Playing chess, arguing—Plato and Leibnitz, Einstein, Freud and Marx." This pastoral scene ("The sheep are passing in the snow") alternates with the thoroughly modern ("The dim lit station, the late slow train, / And the city of steel and concrete towers") as the boys contemplate the possibility of love as a stay against mortality. The section ends on a harsh note as Sebastian sets the possibility of happiness with his female neighbor Leslie against a sense of the inevitability of death, while Thomas weighs the memory of "panthers' soft cries" in their mating against "Death / Here hinges fall, a land of crusts and / Rusted keys . . . Hakeldama, the potters' field / Full of dead strangers."

In Part II, Thomas crosses the mountains for the "empty city from which / Alternate noise and utter stillness come," leaving Sebastian to make his way back home alone through the "vegetable light." Sebastian sits playing chess by himself now, drinking "bitter tea," dwelling on his loneliness. In the "deep blue winter evening" he recalls an earlier trip of his own to New York City, remembering dirty snow, pigeons, burnt fried potatoes, a streetcar, and, most vividly, a stripper who "rolls her buttocks" while "rhinestones cover her bee-stung / Pussy and perch on each nipple." But this reverie only intensifies his feeling of separation "through the level days," and his preoccupation with death. It is Good Friday, and Thomas reenters the poem involved (like Tammuz, the slain harvest god) in some sort of "involuntary" sacrifice, the martyrdom Sebastian fears. "How short a time for a life to last," the third voice muses, "So few years, so narrow a space, so / Slight a melody, a handful of / Notes."

Part III is subtitled "The Double Hellas," and here we have sexuality split into its two guises—the erotic and the domestic. We get a sense of the inexorable process of time as the section opens with a description of the earth's movement into and out of the ice age. Following, there is a description of the brothers' early pastoral life ("The yellow lights, the humming tile stove, / Father with his silver flute, / Mother singing to the harmonium") but, as Gibson suggests, this environment embodies the "bourgeois-Christian-Classical tradition" which is now, for them both, merely an "ornate, wasted fiction." The erotic is introduced as Sebastian strolls through the garden while "The floral vulvas of orange and crimson / Squirm inside his head." There are allusions to Kore (Persephone, whose yearly return to the world from Hades symbolized fecundity), Chlorus (beautiful wife to King Neleus), "Pisanello's courtesans," and Maxine (the Black stripper from part II), but these only seem to confuse Sebastian further. In the modern world there seems to be no room for passion, no room for the heroic: "the epic hero / Came, in full armour, making a huge / Clatter, and fell, struck down from behind / . . . the clock ticks measured out his death." As Maxine sleeps in her far-off "scented bed," Sebastian reads Socrates on love in solitude. "Shall personal / Loneliness give way to the enduring / Geological isolation?" he wonders. Meanwhile, Thomas comments on the nature of the family estate, "a land too well-mannered" where "the bedrooms / Mold with the sweat of bygone death beds." Unlike Sebastian, he has a distinct lack of interest in domestic sexuality: "Her thighs, her buttocks rolling like two / Struggling slugs—these things are not for me," for the "echoing in the tunneled / Sepulcher" presages death.

What follows is a meditation on presence, a comment by the third narrative voice. The beautiful world of the thing—a new brick warehouse, lovers, cattle—is for Thomas his "sacrament," an "undeniable reality": "Heraclitus said that the world was made / Of the quick red tongue between

her lips, / Or else from the honey that welled up / From the shady spring between the thighs." But again, like "the tree, moon isolate / In a moonless night, stiffens in an / Explosion of wind and rips off every / Leaf," the human world is ever-winding down, ever deteriorating, "Dun camels in the smoky desert, / The Pyramids gone crimson into time." All that is left us is "music of objects worn by careful hands."

The final section of *Homestead,* "The Stigmata of Fact," continues with images of death and deterioration: "chalk old skulls," "a crumbling kingdom," "assassins everywhere," "the thick dust / settles once more on the disordered / Bones in their endless sleep." Such is Thomas's "brilliant / Summer region, his painted landscape." For a time, Sebastian is able to make a leap of faith ("I am the Master of the / Pattern of my life") which leads him momentarily to his dying mother and Maxine; in the end, though, he finds himself a kind of Prufrock, "Dead? / No, living with a limitless sterile / Kind of life . . . naked, / Blind, salty, and relaxed on the edge / Of the blind sea alone with the blind rabbi." The great myths—Theseus, the Minotaur, the labyrinth, the Easter Island statues— have been reduced to dust by modern archaeology. Leaving Sebastian "puzzled" in the rain-soaked slums, Thomas retreats to the mountains, leaving the lights of the modern city to disappear behind the "tiny, closing doors of silence."

In *Homestead,* then, we have a number of themes which Rexroth will return to again and again. The brothers are a kind of split consciousness—the active (Sebastian) over against the reflective (Thomas); or, as Gibson prefers, "the tendency toward sacrifice and martyrdom, and the restraining tendency of skeptical withdrawal from commitment"—a split the poet will struggle with in himself throughout his life. There is the Romantic's despair over the passing of both the mythic imagination and the natural world, along with an intense sense of *carpe diem.* And perhaps most important, there is a seeking after the fact of heterosexual love, which in the contemporary world has seemingly lost not only its sacramental nature but its significance as a transformative power as well. Unlike Matthew Arnold's Dover Beach lovers, Thomas is left not with the grail but squatting in the darkness at a fire, alone.

Rexroth began **"A Prolegomenon to a Theodicy"** in 1925 and finished it two years later; this poem didn't appear until 1949, however, when it was included in *The Art of Worldly Wisdom,* and it has never been published separately. While *Homestead* is in large part meditative, **"A Prolegomenon"** is more experimental; in fact the severe dissociation and juxtaposition are reminiscent of Cubist painting, an interest of Rexroth's at the period.

Though the case might be made that here Rexroth was primarily concerned with stylistic possibilities, the poem's primary argument continues the movement of *Homestead.* A prolegomenon is a preface, an introduction; a theodicy is the concept of the vindication of the goodness of God in respect to the existence of evil. If God is supremely good and supremely powerful, goes the age-old Christian paradox, and if he cannot make an error, how is it that evil can exist in the world? The poem continues the despair of **Homestead** in its opening section: "I want something else / I want and want always wear and wear / Always / Always / But you can't have it don't you realize there / Isn't any more there isn't any more at all not / At all". The next many sections provide catalogues of objects, actions, concepts seen through the "anagogic eye," as Rexroth moves for resolution, not through logic but after "the visionary experience without which no theodicy is possible". By the poem's conclusion, its Christian imagery emerges fully developed ("The bread of light / The chalice of the abyss / The wine of flaming light"), as the poet has moved through a kind of apocalypse to the appearance of God. To my mind, this odd poem offers no satisfactory solution to its own paradox, save a kind of willed acceptance; certainly its primary question continues Rexroth's search for some kind of transcendent vision (though interestingly there is little if any reference to the power of physical love here), but finally it seems a mere exercise.

With **The Phoenix and the Tortoise** (the title poem of his second book, published in 1944), Rexroth has settled into his more mature style, and here he engages far more directly the question of "the Community of Love" he spoke about in the introduction to **The Homestead** and the Cubist experiment of **"Prolegomenon"** in favor of the far more direct, personal statement we have come to associate with Rexroth's mature work (as well as that of Western poets for whom he has been a direct influence, like Gary Snyder and William Everson). Further, the poet's political engagement becomes an important element in this poem, and it is the first of the long poems which is set, at least in part, in California.

The entire collection (the volume also contains a number of shorter lyrics, as well as translations and "imitations") attempts to develop, Rexroth tells us in his introductory note, "more or less systematically, a definite point of view . . . the discovery of a basis for the recreation of a system of values in sacramental marriage." **Phoenix** attempts "to portray the whole process" ("from abandon to erotic mysticism, from erotic mysticism to the ethical mysticism of sacramental marriage, thence to the realization of the ethical mysticism of universal responsibility") in "historical, personal, and physical terms." He dedicates the poem to Albert Schweitzer, "the man," he says, "who, in our time, pre-eminently has realized the dream of Leonardo da Vinci."

Like the first long poem, we have again a quest of sorts, as **Phoenix** opens with the poet meditating on "the geological past / Of the California Coast Ranges," figures of death along the coast:

> Of what survives and what perished,
> And how, of the fall of history
> And waste of fact—on the crumbling
> Edge of a ruined polity
> That washes away in an ocean
> Whose shores are all washing into death.

> A group of terrified children
> Has just discovered the body
> Of a Japanese sailor bumping
> In a snarl of kelp in a tidepool.

The poet is again a seeker, "seeking the continuity, / The germ plasm, of history, / The epic's lyric absolute." What, he asks, is the relationship between art and history; can anything transcend the ravages of time? History, he tells us, is composed of mere "particulars," while poetry offers "an imaginary / Order of being, where existence / And essence, as in the Diety / of Aquinas, fuse into pure act." The first section concludes with a privileging of this imaginary order, this mystic vision ("The illimitable hour glass / Of the universe eternally / turning") over such notions as will and ego.

In the next two sections of the poem, lying under the moonlight in his "folded blanket" next to his wife while "north of us lies the vindictive / Foolish city asleep under its guns," the poet expresses his anarchism: "The State is the organization / Of the evil instincts of mankind"; "War is the State"; "Man is a social animal; / That is, top dog to a slave state." The goal of history "is the achievement / Of the completely atomic / Individual and the pure / Commodity relationship . . . / The flow of interoffice / Memoranda charts the excretions / Of societal process, / The cast snakeskin, the fleeting / Quantum, Economic Man." This angry meditation on modern life and organizational man rumbles through the night until at dawn the poet wonders "would it have been better to have slept / And dreamed, than to have watched night / Pass and this slow moon sink?" Perhaps his wife's "dreams" hold more of an answer than his own "meditations in cold solitude."

A resolution to death and decay, and to man's own corporate stupidities and inhumanities, is offered in the poem's concluding section, wherein like Voltaire's Candide Rexroth turns to the garden of the personal:

> Babies are more
> Durable than monuments, the rose
> Outlives Ausonius, Ronsard,
> And Waller, and Horace's pear tree
> His immortal column. Once more
> Process is precipitated
> In the receptive womb.
> In the decay of the sufficient
> Reasonableness of sacraments
> Marriage holds by its bona fides.

Nude, he enters the water, "the prime reality," and it is the sudden appearance of his wife, also naked, which offers a transcendent, even beatific vision, a final alternative to dead men "in the ancient rubbish": "The sun crosses / The hills and fills her hair, as it lights / The moon and glorifies the sea / And deep in the empty mountains melts / The snow of Winter and the glaciers / Of ten thousand years."

The Dragon and the Unicorn (written between 1944 and 1950, and published in 1952) opens where **Phoenix** leaves off; if love is the answer to the paradox of history, just what is its nature? Written in the direct style of the earlier poem, this is by far Rexroth's longest poem (running over 6,000, primarily seven-syllable, lines), and certainly one of his most fully realized. While the setting of **Phoenix** is northern California, **Dragon** follows the poet across America, through Europe, back to San Francisco. As Rexroth notes in his preface to the volume, "The form is that of the travel poems of Samuel Rogers and Arthur Hugh Clough. The general tone is not far removed from that expressed by other American travelers abroad, notably Mark Twain." Yet again the poet is off on a quest, and yet again the quest is bodied forth, as Gibson notes, "as interior monologue of Rexroth's inquiry into the problem of love."

The first of the poem's five parts takes Rexroth (by **Phoenix,** at the very least, the question of an Eliotic persona no longer obtains, the speaker is, clearly, the poet himself) by train from San Francisco to New York, then through the British Isles. Like the previous poem, the political dimension is paramount, as Rexroth again assails the modern city as well as the corporate state. In Chicago, for example, "Man / Gets daily sicker and his / Ugliness knots his bowels. / On the site of several / Historical brothels / Stands the production plant of / Time-Luce Incorporated"; in Liverpool, he sees "bombed-out shells, / Everybody too busy / To fix them up. So Rome died." Set against the city, however, he discovers North Wales "glowing with Spring—/ Birds and wild flowers everywhere," while

> High above Yarcombe the wind
> Dies at sunset and I rest
> In a hanging meadow. The land
> Falls away for long blue miles
> Down the trough of glacial valley.
> In the deep resonant twilight
> The stars open like wet flowers.

Yet he returns to London, a place "sicker than New York," as the answer to his quest is not in the solitude of the pastoral, but again in a kind of human communion: "There is no reality / Except that of experience / And experience is the / Conversation of persons." There he searches (often humorously, as with "Nini" a sadist who "gets quite rough") for love, "the ultimate / Mode of free evaluation. / Perfect love casts out knowledge."

At the start of Part II, Rexroth receives copies of **The Art of Worldly Wisdom,** but finds in his new book's pages not the intensity of experience but "only anecdotes for company"; "I cannot find the past." The setting for this section is France, and the tone throughout is rather grim, as the poet meditates both on his own failed attempts at love and the excesses of history. Traveling along the Loire he muses that "Ultimately the fulfillment / Of reality demands that / Each person in the universe / Realize every one of the / Others in the fullness of love." Here the institution of the Church, another manifestation for him of the corporate state, "is the symbol / Of the repression of all / That I love in France." Sexual love offers an alternative, but "only for so brief a time." Rather, it is a

deeper, more lastingly transcendent love, a true communion or community, that "like all the sacraments, is a / Miniature of being itself."

In part III the scene shifts to Italy, where Rexroth travels now with his wife, Marthe. Again, he broods on the evils of collectivity—from capitalism and the Church to the State and various intellectuals; even social activism is not immune. Echoing Henry Treece's manifesto delineating the New Apocalypse aesthetic of such younger British poets as Alex Comfort and Vernon Watkins, that "the salvation of the individual man is via the individual man himself and not by way of the Commonwealth, the State, or the International Collective," Rexroth writes:

> I know of
> No association of men
> Which cannot be demonstrated
> To have been, ultimately
> Organized for purposes
> Of coercion and mutal
> Destruction. By far the worst
> Are the putative communal
> And benevolent gangsters. Lawrence pointed out
>   long ago
> That the most malignant form
> Of hate is benevolence.
> Social frightfulness had increased
> In exact proportion to
> Humanitarianism. . . .
> Every collectivity
> Is opposed to community.

And again, that community is realized through a sacramental, personal, heterosexual love that in the modern world is constantly in danger of perversion. The only absolute, the only hope of salvation, is the "full communion of lovers," and the section ends in a kind of fulfillment of his vision, with Marthe pregnant.

Section four takes the poet first to Switzerland (here he takes issue with Protestantism—"the anal ghost of Karl Barth's church / Of spiritual masochism"—and Jung) then back to Paris and Bordeaux (where he rejects Marxism—"No collectivity against / Collectivities can function / To restore community"). Finally, in section five Rexroth returns to America, and as he travels back across land to San Francisco, he is not pleased: "Calvinist and Liberal / Both strive to reduce moral / Action to the range of the / Objectively guaranteed"; "In Kansas even the horses / Look like Landon, ugly parched / Faces like religious turtles." Through capitalism, the East and heartland have become "a ruined country," their inhabitants "a ruining people," though as he moves west out of the morass of the great Eastern cities his black mood lifts. Here, out of "the world of purpose," he comes to understand that "the community of persons" transcends even the need for a god. Once again he has returned to the garden of his West to achieve in nature a transcendence of the "empiric ego."

The last of the long poems, **Heart's Garden / The Garden's Heart,** was written over twenty-five years later, in

1967 in Kyoto. The scene is Japan, and once again we have the wandering, meditative, now older poet: "A man of / Sixty years, still wandering / Through wooded hills, gathering / Mushrooms, bracken fiddle necks, / And bamboo shoots, listening / Deep in his mind to music." The mood is Taoist, feminine ("The dark woman is the gate. . . . / She is possessed without effort"), but again he is lost and confused. Pilate's question in *Dragon* appears again, "what is love," but now in his old age Rexroth seems to move beyond argument in favor of, as Gibson argues, complete presentation: "The poem *is* vision; for the sounds and silences of speech unify the poet's sensations. The unity, the harmony, of speech and perception *is* the Tao" (125). The other long poems, even *Dragon,* seem to strain for a vision, as if by enumerating the endless follies of contemporary civilization the poet will finally convince himself (and us) of the necessity of community. Here, however, Rexroth seems no longer to be struggling. The world, like the Tao, simply is, and it is lovely.

In *Homestead,* Rexroth had staked out his twin poles—the life of action (represented by Sebastian) over against the life of reflection (represented by Thomas). By the time of the publication of his collection of shorter poems, *The Signature of All Things* in 1950, however, he had already come to be drawn more closely to the latter. In that collection, which takes its title from the seventeenth-century mystic Jacob Boehme, he writes in the preface, "Perhaps the integral person is more revolutionary than any program, party, or social conduct." He is coming to accept Boehme's notion of reality, that "the whole outward visible world with all its being is a signature, or figure on the inward spiritual world . . . as the spirit of each creature sets forth and manifests the internal form of its body, so does the Eternal Being also."

I spoke earlier of *Homestead* as, at least in part, the young Rexroth's attempt to meet the challenge of Eliot's *The Waste Land;* certainly, *Heart's Garden / The Garden's Heart* in the same fashion works as a counter to Eliot's late great work, *The Four Quartets.* Where Eliot's earlier poem affects impersonal presentation, where it is discontinuous, where it is highly allusive, and where it offers at least in part a social critique, *The Four Quartets* strives for a more personal, discursive voice, is far less allusive, and eschews social critique in favor of what David Perkins calls "Romantic metaphysical exploration." All of this can be said of Rexroth's last long poem as well. However, throughout *The Four Quartets* we have the nagging sense that for all the richness of its imagery and insight Eliot's vision, tied specifically to an Anglo-Catholic theology in which the Church itself becomes the final point where "the timeless and time intersect," the final vision of the poem is rather narrowly and exclusively defined. Rexroth's final vision, on the other hand, for all its Asian imagery, is far more Emersonian, far more indigenously American, than Eliot's.

Through the first four long poems the poet's search for a perfect community of love takes him through most pathways of the world's maze, yet none offers an all-encompassing transcendent vision. Here, in his last years, as

Eliot embraces the architecture of the Church and its mythologies, for Rexroth politics, literature, sociology all give way to the "music of the waterfall," as he returns to his Penelope, "the final woman who weaves, / And unweaves, and weaves again." And it is this return to nature, quietude, and the feminine which offers the final clarity of vision:

> In the moon-drenched night the floating
> Bridge of dreams breaks off. The clouds
> Banked against the mountain peak
> Dissipate in the clear sky.

"We are unaware that we live in the light of lights," Rexroth closes in his introduction to *The Collected Longer Poems,* "Because it casts no shadow. When we become aware of it we know it as birds know air and fish know water. It is the ultimate trust."

David Barber (essay date 1993)

SOURCE: "The Threading of the Year," in *Parnassus: Poetry in Review,* Vols. 18 & 19, Nos. 2 & 1, 1993, pp. 277-88.

[*In the following excerpt, Barber contends that Rexroth's most poised and mature poetry was influenced by his direct observation of the Northern California landscape.*]

Although it's evident that Rexroth's radical disaffection from the centers of official culture made the Bay Area an appealing base of operations, it's also plain that his embrace of the California hinterlands stemmed from impulses at least as elemental as ideological. An avid and delicate alertness to his adopted region's natural history, a charged responsiveness to its open sprawl and utter scale, ground the more durable passages in *In What Hour,* revealing backcountry affinities and reflective leanings one doesn't usually associate with hardboiled anarchists:

> Autumn in California is a mild
> And anonymous season, hills and valleys
> Are colorless then, only the sooty green
> Eucalyptus, the conifers and oaks sink deep
> Into the haze; the fields are plowed, bare, waiting;
> The steep pastures are tracked deep by cattle;
> There are no flowers, the herbage is brittle.
> All night along the coast and the mountain crests
> Birds go by, murmurous, high in the warm air.
>
> (from **"Autumn in California"**)

Readers whose acquaintance with California isn't limited to glossy postcards of the Golden Gate or celluloid montages of Hollywood palms can attest to the rightness of that "sooty green" and that oak-devouring haze, but one needn't be a native to be impressed by the fine-spun attention Rexroth musters for a "mild / And anonymous season" that few writers in his day (and no great number in our own) would deem worthy of more than passing notice. A Currier and Ives calendar of stock seasonal footage is next to useless in coming to terms with the muted annual cycle of the Californian countryside, and Rexroth's precedence in paying homage to this terra incognita is a credit to both his sense of nuance and his sensible knack for "making it new." The ear must shake off the echoes of intoxicating Keatsian stanzas before it can pick up the unprepossessing stateliness of *this* ode to autumn, and that's arguably all to the good: The ruminative texture of the above passage, the chariness toward fully ripened rhyme ("Mild"—"valleys"; "green"—"deep") and verbal dazzle ("Birds go by"), seem altogether more fitting to the hazy, colorless, and anonymous character of thelandscape under scrutiny than the chiming couplets, lush pentameters, and rapturous sprung rhythms that a verdant, dramatically transitory clime wrings from its laureates.

Rexroth had been a resident of San Francisco for more than a decade when *In What Hour* came off the presses. He also had some twenty years of literary industry already behind him, much of it hyperactive philosophical college and programmatic dabblings in Objectivist serialism. These experimental proclivities apparently withered as the breadlines formed and his political activism intensified, but what really seems to have brought Rexroth back from the brink of linguistic cubism was his growing intimacy with Northern California's coastal wilds and Sierra ranges. It is surely not a trifling biographical detail that Rexroth was periodically under the employ of the Federal Writers Project during these years, contributing unsigned descriptive sketches and touring squibs to such publications as the *WPA Guide to California* and a *Field Handbook of the Sierra Nevada*. These commissions had to be a happy circumstance for an enthusiast of the trail like Rexroth, and it's safe to say that the grit and dirt he picked up along the way was a decided blessing for his poetry. Amid such abstruse set pieces as **"Dative Haruspices"** ("Film and filament, no / Donor, gift without / Reciprocity, transparent / Tactile act, an imaginary / Web of structure sweeps / The periphery of being . . .") and **"New Objectives, New Cadres"** ("By what order must the will walk impugned, / Through spangles of landscapes, / Through umbers of sea bottom, By the casein gleam of any moon / Of postulates and wishes?") that take up considerable breathing room in his first collection, one welcomes the tempered measure that marks Rexroth's epistles from the mountains:

Frost, the color and quality of the cloud,
Lies over all the marsh below my campsite.
The wiry clumps of dwarfed white bark pines
Are smoky and indistinct in the moonlight,
Only their shadows are really visible.
The lake is immobile and holds the stars
And the peaks deep in itself without a quiver.
In the shallows the geometrical tendrils of ice
Spread their wonderful mathematics in silence.
(from **"Toward an Organic Philosophy"**)

In the long day in the hour of small shadow
I walk on the continent's last western hill
And lie prone among the iris in the grass

My eyes fixed on the durable stone
That speaks and hears as though it were myself.
(from **"A Lesson in Geography"**)

Lines like these assure us that Rexroth from early on was wholly conscious of casting himself as a poet in honorable regional exile, and they also affirm the elements of style that were coalescing into trustworthy habits of composition. The "outdoors" poetry of *In What Hour*—lean and economical in its syntax and its diction, coolly observant and solemnly meditative in its essential register, its balance of trust placed in the testimony of the senses rather than the force of rhetorical address—assumes the concentrated plainspoken form that Rexroth would avail himself of increasingly in the years to come. Implicit in this streamlined prosody is a finetuned moral sensibility. Steeped in the organic rhythms and seasonal variations of the California landscape, this is verse that divines in ecology a higher ethical order that might expunge the taint of a corrupt and corrosive social ethos. More simply, the mountaintop had become for Rexroth the most reliable place to steel the conscience and clear one's head. Here is the opening of **"Hiking in the Coast Range,"** a poem commemorating the death of two dockworking unionists:

The skirl of the kingfisher was never
More clear than now, nor the scream of the jay
As the deer shifts her covert at a footfall;
Nor the butterfly tulip ever brighter
In the white spent wheat; nor the pain
Of a wasp stab ever an omen more sure;
The blood alternately dark and brilliant
On the blue and white bandanna pattern.

What bears out the intensity and urgency of these clean-hammered lines are their scrupulous attentiveness and inherent clarity: the balance of cadences and concentration of stresses ("white spent wheat," "omen more sure"), the taut quasi-scriptural deployment of successive negations and accumulating pivots, the deft interlocking of naturalistic and emblematic detail as the passage moves from "skirl" to "scream" to "wasp stab." This is not the voluble and splenetic poet who elsewhere confounds oracular power with oratorical volume; this is not the poet whose moral imperatives are largely indistinguishable from his imperious moods. It is the difference between grandiloquence and gravity; between a short fuse and a drawn bowstring.

Even so, **"Hiking the Coast Range"** is still in its own way a public poem written on the barricades. The hiker has hied to the hills to galvanize his resistance to injustice in the polis and to gird his loins for renewed class warfare. What's striking as one thumbs toward the midpoint of the *Collected Shorter* is the hush that falls over Rexroth's later backcountry poetry of the 1940's and 1950's, the hue and cry of causes and the outbursts of anathema fading out like crackling radio signals. In their place one hears a virtual liturgy of earthly delights and soulful gleanings, poems claiming sovereignty in what a later, blither generation of Californians would champion as the here and the now. A handful are examples of the forthright and singularly unaffected love poetry that is justly accorded a place of honor among Rexroth's more devoted readers. Initially most distinctive for an unblinkered erotic candor rarely encountered in mid-century American poetry . . . these amatory poems retain their boldness on the far side of the sexual revolution because they are unmuddied by either sentimentality or lubricity and unblemished by Puritan and Freudian galls alike. Up where the air is clear, Eros routs Thanatos from the field, if only for the most fleeting of interludes. As demonstrated in the exemplary **"Lyell's Hypothesis Again"** (Charles Lyell was the preeminent geologist of the early nineteenth century and one of the forefathers of modern geological time), Rexroth's sylvan settings are vivid environments, not allegorized Gardens, and his grasp of the material world vastly exceeds that of your average passionate shepherd:

Naked in the warm April air,
We lie under the redwoods,
In the sunny lee of a cliff.
As you kneel above me I see
Tiny red marks on your flanks
Like bites, where the redwood cones
Have pressed into your flesh.
You can find just the same marks
In the lignite in the cliff
Over our heads. *Sequoia*
Langsdorfii before the ice,
And *sempervirens* afterwards,
There is little difference,
Except for all these years.

Encountering other such poems (**"Floating," "Still on Water," "When We with Sappho"**) that twine in a double helix around the force of nature and power of desire, we are reminded of Rexroth's admiration for the eroticized, mystical pulse of D. H. Lawrence's poetry, which he praised in his rousing 1947 introduction to the first American edition of Lawrence's *Selected Poems,* for achieving its visionary authority in "the pure act of sensual communion and contemplation" and reaching its highest mastery in Lawrence's explicit love poems to Frieda composed during the couple's travels along the Rhine. This cluster of lyrics, declared Rexroth in his best Poundian manner, comprise "the greatest imagistic poems ever written," capturing the romantic union of a man and woman in so primal and natural a state that "everything stands out lit by a light not of this earth and at the same time completely of this earth. . . ." That line could serve as the epigraph for Rexroth's own intermittent poetry of spiritualized Eros and conjugal grace, his Lawrentian tendency—revealed nowhere more indelibly than in these closing lines of **"Floating"**—to spot the fingerprints of the divine in the couplings of humankind:

Move softly, do not move at all, but hold me,
Deep, still, deep within you, while time slides
    away,
As this river slides beyond this lily bed,
And the thieving moments fuse and disappear
In our mortal, timeless flesh.

Memorable though they are, Rexroth's present-tense lyrics celebrating a flesh-and-blood Other under an open sky are outnumbered by wilderness poems conceived in the absence of companionship or the aftermath of passion. Most of them take the form of soliloquies rather than direct addresses to the beloved, and they chronicle more hours spent in soulmaking than lovemaking. Much as Rexroth cherished having a mate by his side as he scaled peaks and forded brooks, the evidence of these poems lays bare an even deeper need to wrestle with body and spirit in perfect solitude. The impulse is ancient, and at this late date often wearily formulaic, yet the verse Rexroth mined on a "high plateau where / No one ever comes, beside / This lake filled with mirrored mountains" (**"Time Is the Mercy of Eternity"**) or "On the ground beside lonely fires / Under the summer stars, and in / Cabins where the snow drifted through / The pines and over the roof" (**"A Living Pearl"**) stands out as some of the most measured and least derivative he would ever compose. While these meditations always assume a monastic distance from the madding crowd, they seldom indulge in the presumptions of holy loneliness; while they commonly incline toward mysticism, they rarely court the thin air of worldly detachment. The rituals of purification Rexroth invokes are better described as escapes *into* the world, revolving as they do around the pleasures of the flesh and the manifestations of place, sharply specific as they are about the passage of the seasons, the changes in the weather, the fluctuation of waters and the cycles of flowerings, the comings and goings of creatures. "Nature poetry" is almost always an enfeebling appellation, but especially so for these benedictions and baptisms written at the intersection of natural history and preternatural mystery:

Forever the thought of you,
And the splendor of the iris,
The crinkled iris petal,
The gold hairs powdered with pollen,
And the obscure cantata
Of the tangled water, and the
Burning, impassive snow peaks,
Are knotted here together.
This moment of fact and vision
Seizes immortality,
Becomes the person of this place.
The responsibility
Of love realized and beauty
Seen burns in a burning angel
Real beyond flower or stone.

(from **"Incarnation"**)

"This moment of fact and vision"—here, in a phrase, is Rexroth's plumbline, the unit of measure by which he set about divining the limits of knowing and the depths of being as he lit out for the timberline. Yet the poems Rexroth consecrates to such moments have precious little in them of Romantic self-exaltation and sublimity: The visionary awakenings that grip this poet on his lonely summits or beside his rushing streams are specimen reaffirmations of recurrence, of continuity, of pattern, of the habitual and the diurnal, of responsibility. The "burning angel / Real beyond flower or stone" that appears in the closing lines of **"Incarnation"** gains all the greater purchase on reality by virtue of the fact that we are in the hands of a poet who is inordinately attentive to flowers and stones and by virtue of the fact that we have been paced through a poem that begins not in inspiration but perspiration: "Climbing alone all day long / In the blazing waste of spring snow, I came down with the sunset's edge / To the highest meadow. . . ." The elevation of the soul and the attainment of serenity pivots not on "either/ors" but hangs in the balance between infinitely renewable "ands" and "thens."

The alpine wilderness, to be sure, was where Rexroth sought a peace surpassing all understanding, and in certain poems he enshrines his waterfalls and meadows and glades as the way stations of a pilgrim. Occasionally, they verge on ecstatic experience, glimpses behind the veil. In **"The Signature of All Things"** (the title poem of Rexroth's 1949 collection, named after the seminal work of the 16th-century German mystic Jacob Boehme) he lays the text aside and "gaze[s] through shade / Folded into shade of slender / Laurel trunks and leaves filled with sun" until "My own sin and trouble fall away? Like Christian's bundle." In **"Time Is the Mercy of Eternity"** he stares into a high-country pool upon an August evening and discerns "that the color / Of the water itself is / Due to millions of active / Green flecks of life . . . / The deep reverberation / Of my identity with / All this plentitude of life / Leaves me shaken and giddy." But for the most part, in transcribing his communions with nature, Rexroth succumbs neither to grandiosity nor to giddiness. The devotional integrity of his compactly built verse paragraphs derives from their implicit insistence that looking closely, speaking directly, and feeling deeply can (and perhaps must) merge into a steadfast and continuous sacramental habit of mind.

There is a rugged humility in Rexroth's readiness to be steadied by the cyclical and his willingness to be schooled by the commonplace. Observation, these poems intimate, incubates perception; description, revelation. "Although / I expect them, I walk by the / Stream and hear them splashing and / Discover them each year with / A start," he writes of a salmon migration in **"Time Spirals."** And again, in **"Doubled Mirrors,"** tramping down a familiar road at night and descrying a "glinting / Everywhere from the dusty gravel," Rexroth hunkers down for a remedial seminar in wonder: "I suspect what it is / And kneel to see. Under each / Pebble and oak leaf is a / Spider, her eyes shining at / Me with my reflected light / Across immeasurable distance." The salmon spawn every year, it is an old story; the spiders proliferate under the leaf-fall at summer's end, there's nothing remarkable in it; and there is Rexroth, expecting and suspecting, lingering over his yoked moments of fact and vision as if they were a rosary.

Rexroth is never more firmly in possession of his tone and touch as when he seems to be simply marking time, nothing the hour, fixing the night sky, taking stock of what stirs around him. His finest poems of this ilk, with their delicacy and accuracy of perception, their owlish-

ness and gravitas, their fastidious rhythms and spare syntax literally portray a man coming to his senses. What commends them—the poems and the senses—is their exemplary composure. Time and again in this poetry of the interior Rexroth cultivates keen regard where others might have lapsed into wild rapture—dedicating himself not to leaps of faith but rather, as he articulated in one of his most lovely poems, to "pauses of fate." The poem is **"We Come Back,"** from the 1944 collection *The Phoenix and the Tortoise,* and it follows in its entirety:

> Now, on this day of the first hundred flowers,
> Fate pauses for us in imagination,
> As it shall not ever in reality—
> As these swifts that link endless parabolas
> Change guard unseen in their secret crevices.
> Other anniversaries that we have walked
> Along this hillcrest through the black fir forest,
> Past the abandoned farm, have been just the same—
> Even the fog necklaces on the fencewires
> Seem to have gained or lost hardly a jewel;
> The annual and diurnal patterns hold.
> Even the attrition of the cypress grove
> Is slow and orderly, each year one more tree
> Breaks rank and lies down, decrepit in the wind.
> Each year, on summer's first luminous morning,
> The swallows come back, whispering and weaving
> Figure eights around the sharp curves of the swifts,
> Plaiting together the summer air all day,
> That the bats and owls unravel in the nights.
> And we come back, the signs of time upon us,
> In the pause of fate, the threading of the year.

Here, I submit, is the most telling and limpid draft of "the same poem over and over" that the elder Rexroth makes reference to at the head of **"Hapax."** For all its classical elegance of bearing and the formal mastery of its syllabics, it is a supplicant's poem and a sacramental incantation. For all its worldliness, it seeks meaning in provisionality and in the shedding of metaphysical conceits and moral precepts. If any poem was ever a "sheaf of stillness" it is this one: In that pause of fate an orgy of motion becomes a tapestry of eternal forces and the vernal turns autumnal as our eye works down the page. Stated baldly in **"Hapax,"** the "ecology of infinity" is a shibboleth, a buzzline. Inscribed in the "endless parabolas" of swifts and the "fog necklaces on fencewires" that "seem to have gained or lost hardly a jewel," it's a spiritual condition made manifest and a phrase redeemed.

I don't want to give the impression that this pietistic poet of the woods and rockfaces is the "true" Rexroth or a Rexroth to be extolled at the expense of all the rest there are to go around. Nor would I venture to say that this medley of work constitutes anything so commanding as a "period" or anything as coherent as a system of thought. Notwithstanding the auspiciously titled **"Toward an Organic Philosophy,"** one of the contemplative respites among the fiery polemics of *In What Hour,* this is not a poet to whom we turn for grandly mounted summas. In the years roughly spanning Pearl Harbor and the McCarthy hearings (one instinctively reaches for political watermarks when considering a muckraker of Rexroth's caliber), Rexroth's poems cover a teeming variety of subjects in a variety of forms and registers: urbane epigrams ("**Me Again**"), erotic homages ("**A Dialogue of Watching**"), memoirs bittersweet and unrepentant ("**The Bad Old Days**," "**A Living Pearl**"), playful verse for his daughters ("**A Bestiary**," "**Mother Goose**"), outright screeds (most notoriously, "**Thou Shalt Not Kill**," an ostensible elegy for Dylan Thomas that some adherents of incendiary anaphora hail as an ur-"Howl"), and of course, the earliest of his floodtide of Chinese and Japanese translations. But I believe these intermittent Hapaxes hold up so well precisely because they occupy an honestly-arrived-at middle ground between Rexroth's more vexed compulsions and volcanic convictions, sinning neither on the side of preachiness or aloofness. For that reason they are also some of the most humane poems from Rexroth's hand, urgent without straining after effects, serious without resorting to homiletics, thoughtful without thirsting for themes. Theirs is a versification and idiom of proportion, which in turn bears out the rectitude and the scrupulousness of the speaker's self-reflection.

What they are surely not, this group of contemplative verses occasioned by travels upcountry and downriver, are California eclogues or Sierra idylls, numbers written in honor of some idealized, half-mythical territory of honeyed light and stirring vistas. Proportion presupposes equilibrium, and the landscapes that loom so large in Rexroth's field of vision are as empirical and historical as they are archetypal and sanctified. As fleshed out in poems like "**We Come Back**," "**Time Is the Mercy of Eternity**," "**Time Spirals**," or "**Lyell's Hypothesis Again**," Rexroth's California has fewer links to the legendary island that the first European mapmakers drew or the promised land that the nineteenth-century popular imagination painted than it has ancestral ties to an innately Protestant branch of debate over the conception of nature as scripture and geography as destiny. Call him Ishmael: The deeper Rexroth penetrates into the region's lonely isolation, the more inescapably he becomes entangled in uniquely American contours of imagination and realms of spirit. However much his work asks to be understood with reference to Marx or in light of Tu Fu, however boldly his personal history carries the impress of beatnik San Francisco and beatific Kyoto, his reckonings with the wilderness bear the telltale marks of Jeffersonian and Emersonian bloodlines.

Seeking expression through nature, argued Emerson in "The Poet," "is a very high sort of seeking, which does not come by study, but by the intellect being where and what it sees; by sharing the path or circuit of things through forms, and so making them translucid to others." In Rexroth's backcountry poetry, California—and the so-called American Century that he waged such a holy war against—finds a glowing ember of Transcendentalism, no longer a creed or a mission but a latent aptitude for, in Emerson's words again, "the condition of true naming . . . resigning himself to the divine aura which breathes through forms. . . ." Wherever else Rexroth's long and winding paper trail leads us, it also runs through the vicinity of

Concord, and that is where, just now, this reader would like to leave him:

> Deer are stamping in the glades,
> Under the full July moon.
> There is a smell of dry grass
> In the air, and more faintly,
> The scent of a far off skunk.
> As I stand at the wood's edge,
> Watching the darkness, listening
> To the stillness, a small owl
> Comes to the branch above me,
> On wings more still than my breath.

Donald Gutierrez (essay date 1994)

SOURCE: "The Holiness of the Real: The Short Poems of Kenneth Rexroth," in *Breaking Through to the Other Side: Essays on Realization in Modern Literature,* Whitston Publishing Company, 1994, pp. 133-36.

[*In this excerpt, Gutierrez discusses Rexroth's erotic* Love Poems of Marichiko.]

The Love Poems of Marichiko represents an order of love verse strikingly different in some ways from all Rexroth's other love verse and remarkable for a man in his late sixties. *Marichiko* is a sequential verse narrative of sixty short verses (supposedly written by a Japanese "poetess" named Marichiko) that Rexroth claims to have translated in Japan during the 1970s. Actually, Rexroth did not translate the poems; he *wrote* them. I have considered at length elsewhere why Rexroth perpetrated this curious ruse. Let it suffice to say here that the poems constitute an unforgettable union of passion and poignancy, crystallized by a context of love bliss and almost unbearable forlornness. In short, the series comprises a mini-tragedy of being loved and left. Thus the deeper thematic elements in the poem provide its searing eroticism with a process of tragic realism that is a high achievement in American love verse.

The set of poems is too long to scrutinize in its entirety here, but a quotation sketch of the work will convey its flavor and some of its force:

> I sit at my desk.
> What can I write to you?
> Sick with love,
> I long to see you in the flesh.
> I can write only,
> 'I love you. I love you. I love you.'
> Love cuts through my heart
> And scars my vitals.
> Spasms of longing suffocate me
> And will not stop.

This intensity is typical of the poem and of its dramatic desperation and anguish. Apt metaphors communicate the power of the passions running through this love. Says "Marichiko,"

Making love with you
Is like drinking sea water.
The more I drink
The thirstier I become,
Until nothing can slake my thirst
But to drink the entire sea.

With such an unquenchable appetite for love, we are subtly prepared for some strong erotic episodes, and soon get one:

You wake me,
Part my thighs, and kiss me.
I give you the dew
Of the first morning of the world. . .

in which the cunnilingual sex is partly sublimated by an apocalyptic content suggesting through poetic license the extremity of passion of this love experience. A far sharper, almost terrifying sensuality emerges some poems later:

I scream as you bite
My nipples, and orgasm
Drains my body, as if I
Had been cut in two.

This love is so obsessive and overwhelming to "Marichiko" that even daytime, the major phase of our conscious lives and strivings, is subordinated to night and dreams of love and lover:

Because I dream
Of you every night,
My lonely days
Are only dreams.

One could notice here how much effect Rexroth is getting out of concise, spare diction, short verse lines, and almost no metaphors, qualities found in some of his best love and nature poems. In the "Marichiko" poems, these traits are so condensed, so tautened as to lead through a paradoxical process of inversion to a considerable expansiveness of emotion and reference. There are just a few words and two to two-and-a-half foot verse lines, but the words are chosen with utter precision of meaning and emotion to make a powerful impact. The verse sentences of this series poem, chiseled to quintessential expression, embody a core of realized experience, evoking again Rexroth's mystical immanence of "the holiness of the real."

The poem sequence achieves a witty grammatical and semantic bliss that is as moving as it is illusionary (and it is both) in #20:

Who is there? Me.
Me who? I am me. You are you.
You take my pronoun,
And we are us.

This pronominal "jeu d'esprit" will late in the sequence imply bitter irony for the narrator, who, in merging her-self with her beloved, will lose herself disastrously, for, when "us" dissolves, "me" and "I" seem, so violently disunited, selfless and virtually dead.

Relations subtly, mysteriously change, and by #38, after a few quiet hints in two or three preceding poems, we get *this*:

I waited all night.
By midnight I was on fire.
In the dawn, hoping
To find a dream of you,
I laid my weary head
On my folded arms,
But the songs of the waking
Birds tormented me.

which is followed five poems later by

. . . Crickets sing all night in the pine tree.
At midnight the temple bell rings,
Wild geese cry overhead
Nothing else.

and

. . . My hollow eyes and gaunt cheeks
Are your fault.

Clearly, another, sinister phase of the relationship has evolved. Little reason is given for its occurrence ("Our love was dimmed by / Forces which came from without,") we are told, but that explanation is vague at best, and leads us to think that the cause of the end of love is less important than its occurrence, which (for some people) is inevitable, like the succession of the seasons, or death.

The final poems in the sequence are as fraught with grief, misery and bitterness as the earlier ones were radiant with joy and ecstasy:

. . . My heart flares with this agony.
Do you understand?
My life is going out.
Do you understand?
My life.

The final poem in the sequence implies death of life for the woman, in these concluding lines:

I hate the sight of coming day
Since that morning when
Your insensitive gaze turned me to ice
Like the pale moon in the dawn.

Thus the series does not end sensationally, on a flourish of melodrama or violence. Rather, it ends the way such matters often enough end in life, in rejection, estrangement, bitterness, one's desire to live ebbing into a darkening grayness. "Chilled through, I wake up with the first light," she says in the same poem. Life is now monotonal, dominated by the dark side of the moon of love that shone lustrously earlier in the poem sequence.

One could possibly squeeze a moral from the "Marichiko" poems, but that would falsify the pith of this verse, for the real integrity of the sequence (Rexroth's most coherent, tight-knit one) does not arise from some facile, causal explanation or moral judgment. Rather, like the Scandinavian sagas in which blood feuds erupt from either mysterious or trivial causes and move relentlessly towards doom like Fall towards Winter, the "Marichiko" poems suggest that love begins, grows, wanes and sometimes ends. One can't always explain it, love can be like that. It *does* end, and that is as much a part of the actual trajectory of life (if less palatable to our basic ideals or fantasies) as unending love or marital fidelity. Aside from such bony realism, the "Marichiko" poems are remarkable for so utterly blending romance and realism that the extremities of ecstatic love become inextricably part of the same world of experience as the acrid horror of abandonment. They are especially remarkable, though, for being so free of moral pronouncement and for the narrative they frame, which allows Rexroth's capacity for an impersonal poetics even more scope than do most of his love lyrics.

Thomas Evans (essay date 1995)

SOURCE: "Kenneth Rexroth," in *American Poetry: The Modernist Ideal,* eds. Clive Bloom and Brian Docherty, Macmillan, 1995, pp. 97-101.

[*In this excerpt, Evans explicates the influence of Buddhist philosophy on Rexroth's work, particularly in the poem "On Flower Wreath Hill."*]

In the Avatamsaka Sutra (Avatamsaka means 'flower wreath', the inspiration for Rexroth's poem **"On Flower Wreath Hill"**) occurs the image of the "Jewel Net of Indra", in which reality is likened to a net, each knot of which can be compared to a "jewel" or the perspective of an individual human being, which is reflected in all the other "jewels" or perspectives. Our separate perspectives are thus bound together by a single infinite law. By contemplation on the interdependence of all the other "jewels", rather than by selfish introspection, one becomes bound to them on an intuitive level; in Rexroth's words, everything is "in its place, the ecology / Of infinity". In the poem **"Hapax",** from which this line is taken, the Net is a feature of the organic world; the closer a community is to such an organic world, the closer it comes to perpetuating a fully integrated existence in a substantial universe—as far as this is possible in Buddhism, where all substance is impermanent.

Rexroth also uses the image of the Net in **"On Flower Wreath Hill",** to create the peace that spreads in Nature when the Net is no longer shaken or disturbed by human disharmony; even the "Spider's net of jewels has ceased / to tremble". His perception of the Net becomes a sustaining religious experience in this poem. Although it is true that he perceives this net in the architecture of nature rather than in the 'architecture' of community, the Net has a social function, as a subsidiary part of its universal purpose, since it binds together mutually supportive human beings. Significantly, Rexroth told an interviewer, "A life lived according to the Buddha law will not need much from politics". In the same interview, Rexroth maintained that "the religious experience is self-sufficient". This takes on a broader significance in the context of his desire for an organic community: the impetus provided by the experience is a compelling but intuitive force, and is the ultimate affirmation of man's link with manking. The community is bound by the experience to work for its own health and Agape becomes instinctive. . . .

I referred earlier to Rexroth's poetry as being a gateway to a perception of what lies beyond all transient matter: Sunya, the Void. This Mahayana doctrine permeates his later work; most notably in **"On Flower Wreath Hill."** It is worth concentrating on this poem; but before doing so, a fuller explanation of Sunya is necessary.

Sunyata (Voidness) is basic to the Mahayana school of Buddhism, although it has roots in the earlier school of Hinayana. It is the belief that what we know as reality is only comparatively real to us, but what exists as comparative reality is a component part of ultimate reality: "The One is all things, and is incomplete without the least of them." All things which exist in our comparative reality are impermanent and possess no real content, i.e. they are Void of content. They are manifestations of the Void, ultimate reality, which lies beyond them. For a Buddhist to fulfil the essence of this Void is enlightenment, the only absolute. This is the doctrine of Mind Only or Void Only: Sunyata.

This is the ultimate theme of **"On Flower Wreath Hill"** but the poem is also laden with references to Japanese and Buddhist mythology, and bears the powerful influence of the Late T'ang poet Tu Fu, particularly in the way Rexroth intersperses descriptive passages with personal meditations. Buddhism was at a peak in China throughout the T'ang dynasty, and the poetry of this period that is not political often contemplates the world of nature. (Ezra Pound and Arthur Waley were dissatisfied with their translations of Tu Fu, whereas Rexroth translated many of Tu Fu's poems with great sensitivity.)

Parts One and Two of the poem introduce the theme of transience by establishing links between the ancient past and the present, demonstrating the cyclical nature of time. As the narrator walks through the forest, he considers the fallen leaves and the burial mound beneath them which contains a long-dead princess; he is concerned not only with the change of tangible matter (Anicca) but with the nature even of abstract concepts such as honour and beauty: "Who was this princess under / This mound overgrown with trees / Now almost bare of leaves?" The imagery of leaves is extended when Rexroth very probably refers to an episode in the life of the Buddha, when he grasped a handful of leaves from the ground, and asked his disciples which were more numerous, the leaves in his hand or those on the trees of the forest, (the former being the truths he had told them and the latter being the ones he had not revealed).

And now, for Rexroth, on the brink of religious revelation, "There are more leaves on / The ground than grew on the trees." In the lines that follow this quotation, Rexroth considers the paradox that nostalgic memory perpetuates delusions of immortality, despite earlier intuition of impermanence. After expanding on the theme of the silence and natural glory of Autumn, in Parts Three and Four, he returns in Part Five to yet another distraction from complete knowledge of Sunyata: memories of suffering, painful memories reverberate through his consciousness like a temple bell. Each part of the poem, in sequence, depicts inner conflict or comparatively serene contemplation; for, in Part Six, he reflects with equanimity on the royal dead beneath their shattered gravestones, whom no-one remembers.

The penultimate section abandons the influence of Tu Fu upon the structure of the poem (description followed by reflection), in favour of a not entirely satisfactory combination of Buddhist mythology, and ultimately an emphatic affirmation of Annica: "Change rules the world forever. / And man buta little while". These lines bid farewell to doubt, and clear the way for the confident tone of the final section.

In the first verse of Part Eight, the narrator generates an anticipatory tension with images of the world being "alive", and of his body being penetrated with electric life. He sits in the darkness on a "Sotoba", a grave marked by symbolic stones representing earth, water, air, fire and ether. These remind him of impermanence, which for the first time leads him to contemplate directly what lies beyond, in emptiness: "The heart's mirror hangs in the void". . . . Again we return to the Avatamsaka Sutra and the Jewel Net of Indra. The imagery of the Net is handled with consummate skill; initially it is only referred to obliquely, in terms of silver and pearls that gleam on a young girl's sleeves, an image which is transposed to a mist of silver and pearls (Interestingly, Rexroth has suggested that one should approach illumination "as though an invisible mist was coming up behind you and enveloping you"). These oblique references reflect the poet's gradual progression towards full realisation of the Net.

The fifth verse of this final section reflects on Annica, change, in the organic world, in the pattern of the seasons, and acts as a precursor to the harmony of the last verse; here the Net of Indra has ceased to tremble. It prepares us for a kind of frozen tableau of a mist whose every drop is lit by moonlight—transcendental architecture in which each part is a component of a harmonious whole.

In the last fifteen lines, Rexroth experiences Absolute Reality, a revelation of Void Only. In the forest, the mist and the moon, he sees the Net of Indra, linking partial reality to Absolute Reality. The sense of perfect harmony between the temporal world and infinity is strengthened by the soundless music of Krishna's flute which summons the Gopis, or milkmaids, to dance and become Real.

"On Flower Wreath Hill" is Rexroth's most significant exposition of Buddhist philosophy. His shorter poem, **"Void Only"** is less artistically impressive, but it is an explicit statement of Sunyata which is at least effective in its concrete language, paring down his view-point to an Absolute: "Only emptiness / No limits" (there is an erotic version of this poem in **"The Silver Swan"**). What **"On Flower Wreath Hill"** and **"Void Only"** have in common is their handling of Sunyata, which is direct and explicit. But, in **"On Flower Wreath Hill",** the reader is prepared gradually for the experience, which occurs in the last verse, whereas in **"Void Only,"** the poet (and by implication, the reader) is almost surprised by it, as he wakens from a dream.

In other poems, such as **"Towards an Organic Philosophy"** and **"A Spark in the Tinder of Knowing",** Rexroth implies Voidness, rather than addressing it directly, and through this method creates the style of poetry for which he is best known. Richard Eberhart once said of Rexroth's poetry that it achieved a "calmness and grandeur, as if something eternal in the natural world has been mastered". In Buddhist terms, the Net of Indra provides that "something eternal", a successful image for the inter-relationship of all things. In **"Towards an Organic Philosophy",** he describes three landscapes which have been subjected to different kinds of change, such as glaciation in the Sierras, and finds a common factor in "The chain of dependence which runs through creation" (a quotation from Tyndall). As in **"The Dragon and the Unicorn,"** shift of scene leaves an impression of constant change, the gentle motion of Annica.

"The Spark in the Tinder of Knowing" takes a single scene in which man communes with nature and finds in himself the peace which stills the landscape, a suggestion of the Void beyond Annica. But, just as **"Towards an Organic Philosophy"** attempts to create no more than the impression of Sunyata, through an expression of nature's part in Oneness, so this poem stops short of probing the implications of Annica. In this Rexroth is putting into effect Keats's Negative Capability, thus relying on the power of transcendence.

When he came to write **"On Flower Wreath Hill,"** Rexroth did not abandon his transcendental descriptiveness, for it was a technique which had made him original and influential, but he combined it with explicit statements. Later poems such as **"Confusion of the Senses,"** **"Privacy,"** or **"Red Maple Leaves"** show that he retained his ability to sensualise his mystical organic philosophy without needing to define it. But it would be reckless to categories his poems rigidly, since there is a reflective, contemplative element in so many of them.

It is also important to realise that, despite the depth and breadth of his erudition, Rexroth was unwilling to give unconditional allegiance to any one school of Buddhism, preferring to absorb those teachings which confirmed and broadened his own intuitive and intellectual concepts. He found them in Jakob Boehme, A. N. Whitehead, Tu Fu, Whitman and many others, but it was most demonstrably in the fundamental beliefs of the Mahayana school—above all in the doctrine of Sunyata—that he encountered the consummate vision of reality that he had sought.

FURTHER READING

Biography

Hamalian, Linda. *A Life of Kenneth Rexroth.* New York: W.W. Norton, 1991, 444 p.

The only full-length biography of Rexroth.

Sagetrieb: A Journal Devoted to Poets. Vol. 2, No. 3 (Winter 1983). 159 p.

This special issue devoted to Rexroth contains several anecdotes from his life narrated by friends and forgiving enemies, as well as critical essays and portions of Rexroth's own memoirs.

Bibliography

Hartzell, James, and Richard Zumwinkle, compilers. *Kenneth Rexroth: A Checklist of His Published Writings.* Los Angeles: Friends of the UCLA Library, University of California, 1967, 67 p.

A complete bibliography of Rexroth's poetry and other writings; includes several photos, reproductions of his manuscript pages, Rexroth's drawings and magazine cover designs.

Criticism

Gibson, Morgan. *Revolutionary Rexroth: Poet of East-West Wisdom.* Hamden, CT: Archon Books, 1986, 153 p.

Covers all Rexroth's poetry, translations, and his autobiography, attempting to evaluate his worldview as a whole.

Gutierrez, Donald. "Keeping an Eye on Nature: Kenneth Rexroth's 'Falling Leaves' and 'Early Snow.'" *American Poetry* 1, No. 2 (Winter 1984): 60-4.

Close study of the two poems.

———. "Musing With Sappho: Kenneth Rexroth's Love Poem 'When We with Sappho' as Reverie." *American Poetry* 4, No. 1 (Fall 1986): 54-63.

Detailed analysis of the love poem.

Hamalian, Leo. "Scanning the Self: The Influence of Emerson on Kenneth Rexroth." *South Dakota Review* 27, No. 2 (Summer 1989): 3-14.

Partly biographical, this essay focuses on ideas of freedom and individualism Rexroth shared with Ralph Waldo Emerson.

Hamalian, Linda. "Early Versions of 'The Homestead Called Damascus.'" *North Dakota Quarterly* 56, No. 1 (Winter 1988): 131-47.

Compares early fragments—some written when the poet was as young as 15—with the published version of Rexroth's first long poem.

Hamill, Sam and Elaine Laura Kleiner. "Sacramental Acts: The Love Poetry of Kenneth Rexroth." *The American Poetry Review* 26, No. 6 (November/December 1997): 17-8.

Chronicles Rexroth's personal life as it impacted his poetry, particularly his four marriages and his often stormy relationship with poets of the Beat group.

Kazin, Alfred. "Father Rexroth and the Beats." In *Contemporaries,* pp. 480-84. Boston: Little, Brown and Company, 1962.

Rexroth is styled more of a "sorehead" than a radical in this essay dealing largely with the poet as a public figure and essayist.

Stock, Robert. "The Hazards of Art." *The Nation* 208, No. 12 (March 24, 1969): 378.

Review praises *The Collected Longer Poems,* finding their philosophy valuable for young radicals.

Additional coverage of Rexroth's life and career is contained in the following sources published by Gale Research: *Contemporary Literary Criticism,* Vols. 1, 2, 6, 11, 22, 49; *DISCovering Authors: Poets Module; Contemporary Authors,* Vols. 5-8R, 107; *Contemporary Authors New Revision Series,* Vols. 14, 34; *Concise Dictionary of American Literary Biography, 1941-1968; Dictionary of Literary Biography,* Vols. 16, 48, 165; *Dictionary of Literary Biography Yearbook,* Vol. 82; and *Major Twentieth-Century Writers.*

Georg Trakl
1877-1914

Austrian poet and dramatist.

INTRODUCTION

While the eminence and influence of Georg Trakl's poetry has been widely discussed, his work is best known for its lyric qualities. His controlled use of colors, sounds, and ciphers blending into brooding meditations, as well as the exquisite tone of his cries against man's doomed existence are two hallmarks of his work. These tendencies closely align him with German Expressionism, and both Ranier Maria Rilke and French Symbolist poet Arthur Rimbaud were inspired by his work. Conversely, Trakl's writing exhibits many of the techniques and themes employed by the Imagists, Surrealists, and Impressionists, making his work difficult to classify. Many critics believe he was a modernist before his time, citing as evidence his paratactical lines which break free from traditional poetical modes to follow musical forms and expressions to a great degree.

Biographical Information

Trakl, born in 1887 in Salzburg, was the son of affluent parents. His brief, troubled life spans years of great upheaval: the apex and decline of the Habsburg monarchy, the *Jahnhundertwende* of 1900, and the outbreak of the first World War. While this period gave rise to much artistic and cultural innovation—Freud, Mahler, Wittgenstein and Klimt were among Trakl's contemporaries—this turn-of-the-century era was in spirit marked by an awareness of the decay of all social structures and of the danger this change posed to the future of mankind. In this vein Trakl's verse proceeds: he was exceedingly aware that his world, personal as well as external, was "breaking apart," *entzweibricht,* a term he coined, causing *"Leid,"* a state of suffering. This mood prevails in his poetry.

The disparity in ages between his parents, his mother's opium habit, or the Catholic schooling he and his brothers and sisters received although growing up in a Protestant household—these may have caused deep disturbances in Trakl's personality, and contributed to the schizophrenia from which he suffered. This condition, coupled with his drug and alcohol use, led Trakl quickly to his end. By age fifteen, Trakl was experimenting with chloroform and had begun drinking heavily; by 1905 he had left school prematurely. Both he and his sister Margaret, the sibling to whom he was the closest, found the paths of middle-class life unendurable compared to the towers of their art. Their relationship, debatably incestuous, haunted him even as it

nourished him. Her figure appears often in his work as "the sister," an alter ego, a beloved, a mirror-image or *doppelganger.* Even though she married and was able to play the role of the bourgeois wife, she herself committed suicide a few years after Trakl did.

After being forced to leave school, Trakl began an apprenticeship in a pharmacy that, unfortunately and ultimately, fed his future addiction to narcotics. From this point onward, events in his life are inextricably woven into his poetry. His increasing addiction to narcotics is reflected in his use of images, synaesthesia and an inscrutable personal mythology. Likewise, his experiences during World War I also gave rise to a prolific period, but eventually proved too much for his fragile mental condition.

In August of 1914, Trakl went to Austrian-controled Poland as medic under the command of incompetent Austrian generals. After a bloody defeat at Grodek, Trakl was left to care for ninety wounded throughout two days and two nights, and without supplies or attending physicians. The battle at Grodek caused Trakl to suffer a psychotic episode upon the unit's retreat. He threatened to shoot himself in front of his fellow officers but was disarmed and restrained, and in October, ordered to the hospital at Cracow for observation. His mentor, Ludwig Ficker hurried to Cracow to secure his release because he knew that confinement would only cause Trakl's condition to deteriorate. Unable to secure the release, Ficker later received a letter from Trakl and a copy of "Grodek" and "Lament," Trakl's last two poems, the former considered to be one of his greatest lyrics. A week later, Trakl died of an overdose of cocaine.

Major Works

As early as 1904, Trakl was writing poetry. Having been influenced by Charles Baudelaire and the symbolist idea of music as the pure, non-referential art form, and having played piano himself, he joined a poet's club of young writers inspired by the spirit of the *Jahrhundertwende.* Trakl's early poetry itself was fueled by the tension between Nietzschean frenzy and Dostoevskian despair.

After being forced to leave school in 1906, Trakl wrote two one-act verse tragedies, *Totentag* and *Fata Morgana;* the former was well-received by his Salzburg audience. The other's failure temporarily blocked his creative impulses, but eventually he resumed work on a third, a three-act tragedy, *Don Juans Tod,* which was destroyed in 1912. While working toward finishing his studies, Trakl continued to write poetry and, by the time he received his master's degree in pharmacy in 1910, his work exhibited a technical mastery, and he was beginning to make his own mark on Romantic and symbolist imagery.

Trakl's patriotism led him to volunteer for a year as a medic with the Austro-Hungarian army stationed in Vienna. After that term, he was unable to adjust to working in Salzburg again and so requested to return to active duty, this time in Innsbruck. It was during 1912 that he met Ludwig von Ficker, the editor of *Der Brenner,* a literary journal of the highest caliber that was to publish a poem of Trakl's in every issue from 1912 to 1914. Ficker also provided criticism, spiritual advice, and succor to Trakl as his life deteriorated. In 1913 Trakl suffered a bout of depression in Ficker's home even as his first collection of poems, *Gedichte,* was being readied for publication. Although Trakl's mental health became increasingly unstable, he continued to be very prolific through much of 1914, the last year of his life. He revised his second collection, *Sebastian im Traum,* was published posthumously in 1915.

Critical Reception

Most critics concur that Trakl's work had a major impact on German Expressionism. Many others agree that his later works were modern in nature, exhibiting an aggregate of rhythms, grammatical structures like musical scores, and poetic logic of colors, phrasings, and figures all his own. As he developed in his craft, his poems become more impersonal, devoid of the first-person pro-

noun, employing what some critics call "mythic objectivity." As philosopher Ludwig Wittgenstein, Trakl's patron, said, "I do not understand them; but their tone pleases me. It is the tone of true genius." This objective style may be written proof of Trakl's schizophrenia; on the other hand, it may have been Trakl's superlative, horrific statement against man's corrupted condition. Indisputably his work is despairing, violent, obsessive, even perverse at times, but many argue that his Christian faith may yet serve to provide possible redemption in his work. Trakl saw himself in a hell from which he had no "absolution" to leave, his visions of heaven always too distant from earth. The nearest Trakl comes to expressing an affirmation of life comes from his pantheism, learned from Hölderlin, which imbues his work with compassion. His mature poetry makes a definitive statement or analysis of his poetry difficult, so it is that Trakl's compressed, carefully revised verse remains as a testament of this poet's life.

PRINCIPAL WORKS

Poetry

Gedichte [*Poems*] (1913)
Sebastian im Traum [*Sebastian Dreaming*] (1915)
Die dichtungen (1918)
Aus goldenem kelch (1939)
Decline: Twelve Poems by G. Trakl, 1998-1914 (1952)
Twenty Poems of Georg Trakl (1961)
Selected Poems (1968)
In the Red Forest   (1973)
Poems (1973)

Other Major Works

Fata Morgana (drama) 1906
Totentag [*All Souls Day*] (drama) 1906
Don Juans Tod [*Don Juan's Death*] (unfinished drama) 1907
Dichtungen und briefe (poetry, prose poems, and letters) 1969

*The manuscript to this three-act verse drama is believed to have been destroyed in 1912.

CRITICISM

Theodore Holmes (review date 1962)

SOURCE: A review of *Twenty Poems of Georg Trakl,* in *Poetry,* Vol. C, No. 5, August, 1962, pp. 322-24.

[*In the following excerpt, the reviewer points out the singular appeal of Trakl's abstract poetry, commenting also on Bly's and Wright's translations.*]

George Trakl died young, and his poems are the work of a young poet; they combine the social concern of Auden with the vague romanticism of unresolved emotion we find in so much of Goethe—there is a spectral quality to them that is all their own. They are the immediate violent reaction of the youthful heart to the deep numbness it feels in the face of the brutality and injustice of the world. In them there is the refuge taken in nature, the expression of our situation in terms of her changes, a violence done to her out of our own anger, that the still unclarified mind caught in the trammel of its early emotions takes for understanding. It is the way youth expresses itself while waiting for its vision to formulate itself in available terms. Trakl's moons, streams, stars, skies, trees can mean so much in their contexts that they hardly mean anything at all; just the vague alienation of nature from our interests, in all its detached coldness, is there, as the form of all the coldness of man to man. In this lies Trakl's strength: he is powerful when immediate, weak when conceptual. This is generally the weakness of romanticism—it seeks to draw its power from turning its back on the ordinary resources of understanding open to the mind. This is one of the best poems Mr. Wright and Mr. Bly give us, and their translation.

"Im Osten" ("In the East")

Den wilden Orgeln des Wintersturms
Like the wild organ-grinding of the winter storm
Gleicht des Volkes finstrer Zorn,
Is the people's dark anger,
Die purpurne Woge der Schlacht,
The purple wave of the battle,
Entlaubter Sterne.
Leafless stars.

Mit zerbrochnen Brauen, silbernen Armen
With shattered brows, silver arms
Winkt sterbenden Soldaten die Nacht.
The night waves to dying soldiers.
Im Schatten der herbslichen Esche
In the shade of the autumn ash
Seufzen die Geister der Erschlagenen.
Sigh the spirits of the slain.

Dornige Wildnis umgürtet die Stadt.
Thorny wilderness girds round the city.
Von blutenden Stufen jagt der Mond
From bleeding steps the moon chases
Die erschrockenen Frauen.
The frightened women.
Wilde Wölfe brachen durchs Tor.
Wild wolves broke through the door.

"On the Eastern Front"

The ominous anger of masses of men
Is like the wild organ of the winter storm,
The purple surge of battle,
Leafless stars.

With broken eyebrows and silver arms
The night waves to dying soldiers.

In the shade of the ash tree of autumn
The souls of the slain are sighing.

A thorny desert surrounds the city.
The moon chases the shocked women
From the bleeding stairways.
Wild wolves have broken through the door.

In italics I give the reader without German, as closely as I can, what the original says. He can compare the changes made by the translators and decide on them for himself, but I would suggest that any change, even if it *improves* the poem, is wrong. It cannot be repeated too often that the initial part of the translator is to be brave and detached enough to render simply what is there! In the light of most translating today, the authors have been amazingly accurate and faithful to the original, and as a rule their efforts in these poems at rendering Trakl are ones for which we can be grateful. Here though, I would say the inversion of the first two lines and the tenth and eleventh do not seem justified as I understand the German. True, a rearrangement of clauses is often necessary in translating German if we are to make the English sound like anything at all, but only when it is impossible to preserve the syntax in the light of English usage. The order of lines, as well as their verbal integrity, are vital units on which any important poem is built—an aspect of the artistry often not given sufficient attention by translators. To dissipate this structural texture is to dissipate to that extent the content of the poem. In each of these cases, I see no syntactical impasse or formal considerations that dictate here against giving the original in the order it was composed. Too, it would seem to me such changes as "organ" for "organ-grinding", "eyebrows" for "brows", and "have broken" for "broke" in the above, do Trakl some disservice.

D. J. Enright　(review date 1968)

SOURCE: A review of *Selected Poems,* in *The Listener,* Vol. 80, No. 2065, October 24, 1968, p. 542.

[In the following favorable review, Enright attempts to position Trakl within a particular school of poetry, at times comparing him to Holderlin.]

Georg Trakl, an Austrian, died in 1914, at the age of 27, of an overdose of drugs. This makes him, in the Germanic language of classification, an Expressionist. It only remains to find out what he expressed.

Trakl makes use of a quite constricted range of references and images (the word-counter would have an easy job here!), and many of his poems look like variations on each other. The range of meaning is much harder to assess, because Trakl's meaning is customarily difficult to establish. It is narrow, one would venture, but by no means superficial. The usual comparison is with Hölderlin, and the similarities are obvious enough and (I would say) not very significant. For one thing, Trakl is a miniaturist, whereas even Hölderlin's shortest poems convey a sense of spaciousness. Trakl is reminiscent of the older poet in the movement of his verse, in the dignity and solemnity of its tone, which modifies severely what otherwise would be a somewhat sensational subject-matter, and occasionally also in wording and in local statement. For instance, in the fine **"Caspar Hauser Song"**:

Ernsthaft war sein Wohnen im Schatten des Baums
Und rein sein Antlitz

Serious was his habitation in the tree-shade And
pure his face.

And *'Schön ist dér Mensch und erscheinend im Dunkel'* ('Beautiful is man and evident in the darkness').

The chief difference with Hölderlin, and it far outweighs the similarities, is this: in the poetry of his sanity (which *is* his poetry), Hölderlin is pursuing a line of thought, he is what can legitimately be called a "philosophical poet." The thought is there, it is of prime importance, and it can be followed with no more difficulty than is to be expected in a serious-minded author who is also a poet. What holds Trakl's poems together, in as far as they do hold together, is not a continuity of thinking. Only occasionally are these poems truly self-sufficient wholes—and I will admit that those which are, such as **"Caspar Hauser Song," "The Sun," "Summer," "Eastern Front,"** and perhaps **"Grodek,"** seem to me the most unequivocally satisfying—but more often they are a succession of images, sometimes touching, sometimes chilling, interspersed with more or less enigmatic exclamations and arbitrary assertions ("The sun desires to shine black").

For Trakl the designation that springs to mind is "Imagist." And in his book, *Reason and Energy* (1957), Michael Hamburger remarks that the term "would at least have the virtue of indicating the most distinctive characteristic of Trakl's art". It must be added, though, that Trakl is radically unlike the Anglo-American poets whom we know by this title: their imagist poems are light, and the meaning (such as it is) is not hard to find; his poems, whose meaning is very hard to find, convey an impression of weightiness. The Imagists are rather self-consciously performing literary manoeuvres, whereas Trakl is doing what he is driven to do.

Trakl's work has numerous references to "decay" and "decline", corruption and putrescence both physical and spiritual, but the verse never mimes, it maintains at such moments a cold, almost clinical air, which however is warmed by other references to the point at which the total effect is oneeven of tenderness. Perhaps it was this which led Rilke to say of Trakl's work, in his sacerdotal manner, that "falling is the pretext for the most continuous ascension". Trakl was most certainly no bard of the refuse bin or the garbage cart.

His incessant use of colours is the most obvious thing about his poetry, and the most mysterious. Blue, purple, rosy, black, silver, golden, white and brown recur with a frequency which, contemplated in cold blood, is quite staggering. In a 13-line poem we encounter 'black rooms', "rosy mirror", "white forms", "purple night-wind", "black mouths" and "blue eyelids". Blue is the most favoured among these favourite colours. In **"Childhood"** we meet "blue cave", "blue waters" and "a blue moment", besides "holy blueness" (translated here as "azure"), and the last few lines of **"Elis"** give us "blue deer", "blue fruits" and "blue doves."

Trakl's work has numerous references to 'decay' and 'decline,' corruption and putrescence both physical and spiritual, but the verse never mimes, it maintains at such moments a cold, almost clinical air, which however is warmed by other references to the point at which the total effect is one even of tenderness.

—*D. J. Enright*

The difficulty, Mr. Hamburger remarks, is in deciding to what extent Trakl's images are to be treated as symbols. The colour adjectives, he concludes, are "partly pictorial, partly emotive and partly symbolic." More often than not, it appears to me, the significance of the adjective is determined by the noun to which it is attached and on which it then reflects back. Thus "black" generally seems to indicate or emphasise corruption, melancholy, age or dread, though not of course in the repeated "black horses," nor (it would seem) when the "black flight" of birds comes together with the "holiness" of "blue flowers." "Purple" is usually found in connection with richness of taste or texture, or perfume, though "purple pestilence" and the "purple curses of hunger" are clearly exceptions. The ubiquitous "blue" commonly seems to connote youthfulness, life, spirituality, freshness (blue waters, blue springs, the blue butterfly emerging from its chrysalis), but here and there it is linked with decay. If consistency is a requirement, then clearly Trakl's colours cannot properly be called symbolic. They are pictorial, rather, and then inevitably, according to their contexts, emotive in a greater or lesser degree.

Despite the references to corruption and decay (yet contained coolly and cleanly within the sealed poem like specimens in a jar of formalin) and despite such explicit declarations as "Overwhelming is the generation's decline," to talk about "a vision of spiritual crisis in Europe" is not much more useful than ascribing these poems to hallucinatory states produced by alcohol and drugs. The images are of such an extreme clarity and sharpness, the point-blank conjunction of a few primary colours and a few simple objects, as to create a paradoxical effect of pellucid mysteriousness, as in some Surrealist paintings. Like such paintings, which seem on the point of telling a story, Trakl's poems repulse the interpretation they also appear to invite. Perhaps Wittgenstein said as much as can safely be said of this poetry: "I don't understand it; but its *tone* delights me. It is the *tone* of true genius."

Thirteen of these translations were included in the valuable anthology, *Modern German Poetry* (1962), edited by Michael Hamburger and Christopher Middleton. The versions here show a number of small changes, among them a few distinct improvements, tending to suggest that the more literal rendering is often the better one. They certainly bring Mr Hamburger's earlier assertion that Trakl's poems are "not translatable" into grave doubt.

It is unwise to offer to assess the stature of a poet of whom your understanding is uncertain. But set beside Hölderlin, Trakl has the look of a minor rather than a major poet. He could well be overestimated today, when enigmaticness is considered a sign of superiority and the fully "made" poem is looked down on. But he is a true poet and a unique voice, and it is good to have this selection of him.

Review of *Selected Poems*:

The 42 poems brilliantly translated [in *Selected Poems*] offer a tour of the nightmare landscape of Trakl's mind—a phantasmagoria of trees, weather, colors, rocks, death, and the dark. The tormented Austrian who committed suicide in 1914 at the age of 27 has been likened to Rimbaud and Hölderlin, both in the chaos of his inner life and his contorted imagery. Trakl's obsessive love for his sister produced some of his most moving lyrics such as, "Where you walk, there it is autumn and evening/A blue deer under trees and its music." Except for the present collection, only a British edition of Trakl's *Twenty Poems* is now available in English; the publishers have performed a great service in issuing this representative bilingual selection. Trakl was a major, if little-known, talent, and more than half a century after his death he seems as contemporary as Roethke, Eberhart, or Berryman.

Rosemary Neiswender, "A Review of Selected Poems,*" in* Library Journal, *Vol. 94, No. 15, September 1, 1969, p. 293.*

Michael Hamburger (essay date 1970)

SOURCE: "Georg Trakl," in *Reason and Energy: Studies in German Literature,* Weidenfeld and Nicolson, 1970, pp. 291-323.

[*In the following essay, Hamburger follows the "microcosm" of Trakl's verse vis-a-vis the poet's life.*]

Of all the early Expressionists, Trakl was the least rhetorical and the least dogmatic; and he was an Expressionist poet only insofar as he was a modernist poet who wrote in German. Expressionism happened to be the name attached to modernist poetry written in German; but Trakl

would not have written differently if there had been no movement of that name. Nor did he have any contact with the initiators of the movement, all of whom were active in Berlin; whatever he had in common with Hoddis, Lichtenstein, Heym, and Benn, he owed to the *Zeitgeist,* not to any program or theory. If Trakl had written in English—but, of course, it is inconceivable that he should have done—he would have been called an Imagist, though it is most unlikely that he ever heard or read this word. Neither label is very useful, but Imagist would at least have the virtue of indicating the most distinctive characteristic of Trakl's art; all poets express themselves, but Trakl expressed himself in images. To treat Trakl's poems as self-expression, that is to say, as fragments of an autobiography, is to misunderstand them; for Trakl's dominant aspiration was to lose himself.

Trakl has also been called an Existentialist; and I have already alluded to the intimate, though obscure, connection between an existential mode of thought and imagist practices. Just as Existentialists tend to leap straight from the bare condition of existence to the absolute—God, if they believe in Him, Nothing if they do not—so imagist poets deal with bare phenomena in the form of images, not as an ornament added to what they have to say, or as a means of illustrating a metaphysical statement, but as an end in itself. The mere existence of phenomena is their justification; and to understand their Being is to understand their significance. The poetic image, then, becomes autonomous and "autotelic," or as nearly so as the medium of words permits. It follows that the pure imagist technique is likely to break down as soon as a poet wishes to convey truths of a different order than the ontological; and that is one reason that nearly all the poets who once practiced a purely imagist technique have either modified or abandoned their practice. Poetic statements bearing on religious dogma, on ethics, history, and social institutions require such a modification, since the pure image is unrelated to all these spheres.

Every interpretation of Trakl's works hinges on the difficulty of deciding to what extent his images should be treated as symbols—to what extent they may be related to the spheres enumerated above. This, of course, raises the question of his beliefs, for belief comes into play as soon as we attempt to "interpret" an image at all; a purely existential image has no meaning other than itself. Since Trakl undoubtedly lent a symbolic significance to his images—or to some of them at least—these two basic questions are bound to be raised. Trakl's poetry is so essentially ambiguous—so "laconic," as one of his interpreters has observed—that many different interpretations of its symbolism are possible. The most one can hope to do is to avoid too heavy a personal bias toward one symbolism or another; and to allow each reader to make his own choice.

Georg Trakl was born at Salzburg on February 3, 1887. His mother, née Halik, was the second wife of Tobias Trakl, a prosperous ironmonger who belonged to a Protestant family long established in this Roman Catholic city. Both the Trakl and Halik families were of Slav descent;

the Trakls had originally come from Hungary, the Haliks—much more recently—from Bohemia. The family house at Salzburg, with its old furniture, paintings and statuary, as well as the family garden in a different part of the city contributed images to many of Trakl's poems, especially to the sequence **"Sebastian im Traum."** The whole of Salzburg—or Trakl's vision of it—is present in much of his work; it is the "beautiful city" of his earlier poems, a city in decay because its present does not live up to its past.

It is difficult to say whether Trakl's childhood was as melancholy and as lonely as his retrospective poems suggest. From accounts of him by his school friends it appears that he showed no signs of extreme introversion until his late adolescence; and the first part of **"Sebastian im Traum"** is a vision of childhood that can no more be reduced to factual narrative than any other poem of Trakl's, for all its references to identifiable objects:

> Mutter trug das Kindlein im weissen Mond,
> Im Schatten des Nussbaums, uralten Holunders,
> Trunken vom Safte des Mohns, der Klage der
>   Drossel;
> Und stille
> Neigte in Mitleid sich über jene ein bärtiges Antlitz,
>
> Leise im Dunkel des Fensters; und altes Hausgerät
> Der Väter
> Lag im Verfall; Liebe und herbstliche Träumerei.
>
> Also dunkel der Tag des Jahrs, traurige Kindheit,
> Da der Knabe leise zu kühlen Wassern, silbernen
>   Fischen hinabstieg,
>
> Ruh und Antlitz;
> Da er steinern sich vor rasende Rappen warf,
> In grauer Nacht sein Stern über ihn kam;
>
> Oder wenn er an der frierenden Hand der Mutter
> Abends über Sankt Peters herbstlichen Friedhof
>   ging,
> Ein zarter Leichnam stille im Dunkel der Kammer
>   lag
> Und jener die kalten Lider über ihn aufhob.
>
> Er aber war ein kleiner Vogel im kahlen Geäst,
> Die Glocke lang im Abendnovember,
> Des Vaters Stille, da er im Schlafe die dämmernde
>   Wendel-treppe hinabstieg.

> Mother bore this infant in the white moon,
> In the nut-tree's shade, in the ancient elder's,
> Drunk with the poppy's juice, the thrush's lament;
> And mute
> With compassion a bearded face bowed down to
>   that woman,
>
> Quiet in the window's darkness; and ancestral
>   heirlooms,
> Old household goods
> Lay rotting there; love and autumnal reverie.

> So dark was the day of the year, desolate
>   childhood,
> When softly the boy to cool waters, to silvery
>   fishes walked down,
>
> Calm and countenance;
> When stony he cast himself down where black
>   horses raced,
> In the grey of the night his star possessed him.
>
> Or holding his mother's icy hand
> He walked at nightfall across St. Peter's autumnal
>   churchyard
> While a delicate corpse lay still in the bedroom's
>   gloom
> And he raised cold eyelids towards it.
>
> But he was a little bird in leafless boughs,
> The churchbell long in dusking November,
> His father's stillness, when asleep he descended the
>   dark of the winding stair.

On the evidence of these lines it has been suggested that Trakl's mother must have been a drug addict, like her son! But narcotics and intoxicants, in Trakl's poetry, are associated with original sin. Drunkenness, traditionally, began after the Flood, when men were so far removed from their first state that life became unbearable without this means of escape. For the same reason it is with compassion that the father's bearded face looks down at the mother of this poem.

Trakl seems to have been fond of both his parents and at least one of his five brothers and sisters, Margarete, who became a concert pianist and settled in Berlin. Much has been made of Trakl's attachment to this sister, for critics of the literal persuasion insist on identifying her with the sister who appears in his poems; but neither the references to incest in Trakl's early work nor the personage of the sister in his later poems permit any biographical deductions. Incest is one of many forms of evil that occur in Trakl's work; and the personage of the sister is a kind of spiritual alter ego, an anima figure, so that in certain poems a brother-sister relationship symbolizes an integration of the self. Trakl used many other legendary or archetypal personages in his poetry; not to write his autobiography, but to compose visionary poems of an unprecedented kind.

As a boy, Trakl shared Margarete's love of music and played the piano with some skill. At school, on the other hand, he proved less than mediocre. When he failed his examinations in the seventh form, he was unwilling to sit for them again and decided that he was unfit for the professional or academic career originally planned for him. For a time he received private tuition at home. An Alsatian governess taught him French; and he took this opportunity to read the French poets, especially Baudelaire, Verlaine, and Rimbaud. Other influences on his poetry are those of Hölderlin, Mörike, and Lenau; and his thought was decisively influenced by Kierkegaard, Dostoievsky, and Nietzsche. When, toward the end of his life, he decided to do without books, it was the works of Dostoievsky with which he found it hardest to part. Already at school Trakl belonged to a literary club. Toward the end of his school years he grew taciturn, moody, and unsociable; he began to speak of suicide, drank immoderately and drugged himself with chloroform. The career he now chose, that of a dispensing chemist, gave him easy access to more effective drugs for the rest of his life.

From 1905 to 1908 Trakl was trained for this career in his native town. During this time, two of his juvenile plays were publicly performed; *Totentag,* acted in 1906, was something of a *succès de scandale; Fata Morgana,* a one-act play put on later that year, was an unqualified failure. In the same year Trakl began to contribute short dramatic sketches and book reviews to a local paper. He left Salzburg in October, 1908, to complete his training at the University of Vienna, where he took a two-year course in pharmacy. His hatred of large cities dates from this period. At this time he worked at a tragedy, *Don Juan,* of which only a fragment remains, and at an extant puppet play on the Bluebeard theme. After his second year in Vienna, during which his father died, Trakl entered on one year's military service as a dispensing chemist attached to the medical corps; he was posted to Innsbruck, then back to Vienna, but took the earliest opportunity of being transferred to the Reserve.

In 1912 he considered emigrating to Borneo; but in the same year he began to write his best work and met his patron, Ludwig von Ficker, in whose periodical *Der Brenner* most of Trakl's later poems first appeared. It was mainly owing to Ficker's friendship and support that Trakl was able to devote the remaining years of his life to the writing of poetry. In January, 1913, he accepted a clerical post in Vienna, but returned to Innsbruck after three days' work. Except for a number of other journeys—to Venice, Lake Garda, various parts of Austria, and Berlin, where he visited his sister Margarete and met the poetess Else Lasker-Schüler—and three more abortive attempts to work for his living in Vienna, Trakl moved between Innsbruck and Salzburg till the outbreak of war. In 1913 Trakl's first book, a selection of his poems made by Franz Werfel, was published by Kurt Wolff; a second collection appeared in the following year.

By 1913 Trakl had become a confirmed drug addict. In December of that year he nearly died of an overdose of veronal; but in spite of this and his alcoholic excesses, his physical strength remained prodigious, as various anecdotes testify. A prose poem, **"Winternacht,"** derives from one of Trakl's own experiences: after drinking wine near Innsbruck, he collapsed on his way home and spent the remainder of the night asleep in the snow—without suffering any ill effects. In July, 1914, Ludwig von Ficker received a considerable sum of money—100,000 Austrian crowns—with the request to distribute it as he thought fit among the contributors to *Der Brenner.* Trakl and Rilke were the first beneficiaries; but when Herr von Ficker took Trakl to the bank to draw part of the grant, Trakl's good fortune so nauseated him that he had to leave the bank before the formalities had been completed. Long after the event Ficker revealed the identity of Trakl's and

Rilke's patron; he was the philosopher Ludwig Wittgenstein, who gave away most of his inheritance at this time. Later, Wittgenstein wrote to Ficker about Trakl's poetry: "I don't understand it; but its *tone* delights me. It is the *tone* of true genius."

Late in August, 1914, Trakl left Innsbruck for Galicia as a lieutenant attached to the Medical Corps of the Austrian army. After the battle of Grodek Trakl was put in charge of ninety serious casualties whom—as a mere dispensing chemist hampered by the shortage of medical supplies— he could do almost nothing to help. One of the wounded shot himself through the head in Trakl's presence. Outside the barn where these casualties were housed a number of deserters had been hanged on trees. It was more than Trakl could bear. He either threatened or attempted suicide, with the result that he was removed to Cracow for observation as a mental case. His last poems, **"Klage"** and **"Grodek,"** were written at this time.

Trakl now feared that he, too, would be executed as a deserter. According to the medical authorities at Cracow he was under treatment for dementia praecox (schizophrenia); but his treatment consisted in being locked up in a cell together with another officer suffering from delirium tremens. During this confinement Ludwig von Ficker visited Trakl and asked Wittgenstein, who was also serving in Poland, to look after Trakl; but Wittgenstein arrived too late. After a few weeks of anguish, Trakl took an overdose of cocaine, of which he died on November 3, or 4, 1914. It has been suggested that he may have misjudged the dose in his state of acute distress; this was the opinion of his batman, the last person to whom Trakl spoke.

Apart from his juvenilia—poems, plays, and book reviews—Trakl's work consists of some hundred poems and prose poems written between 1912 and 1914, the year of his death at the age of twenty-seven. The horizontal range of these poems is not wide; it is limited by Trakl's extreme introversion and by his peculiar habit of using the same operative words and images throughout his later work. But Trakl's introversion must not be mistaken for egocentricity. "Believe me," he wrote to a friend, "it isn't always easy for me, and never will be easy for me, to subordinate myself unconditionally to that which my poems render; and I shall have to correct myself again and again, so as to give to truth those things that belong to truth." Trakl's inner experience is "objectified" in images and in the symbolic extension of those images; his concern, as he says, was with general truths and with the rendering of general truths in a purely poetic manner. For that reason, the melancholy that pervades his work was only a premise, not the substance, of what he wished to convey; it is as important, but no more important, than the key of a musical composition. It was certainly a limitation of Trakl's that he could compose only in minor keys; but the same could be said of Leopardi and of other lyrical poets whose poetry conveys a distinct mood. Nor should Trakl be assessed in terms of optimism and pessimism, categories that are largely irrelevant to his vision. As Rilke was one of the first to point out, Trakl's work is essentially affirmative; but what it affirms is a spiritual order that may not be immediately perceptible in his poems, filled as they are with images pertaining to the temporal order that he negated.

"Trakl's poetry," Rilke wrote, "is to me an object of sublime existence . . . it occurs to me that this whole work has a parallel in the aspiration of a Li-Tai-Pe: in both, falling is the pretext for the most continuous ascension. In the history of the poem Trakl's books are important contributions to the liberation of the poetic image. They seem to me to have mapped out a new dimension of the spirit and to have disproved that prejudice which judges all poetry only in terms of feeling and content, as if in the direction of lament there were only lament—but here too there is world again." This tribute is especially important for two reasons; because of Trakl's influence on Rilke's own work, and because Rilke interpreted Trakl's poetry existentially when other critics, less close to Trakl's way of thought, read it as a record of Trakl's morbid states of mind. As late as 1923, in a letter to Ludwig von Ficker, Rilke reaffirmed his admiration for Trakl's poetry. What Rilke meant by "world" in the letter cited is what professional Existentialists would call "being"; and he believed that it is the poet's business to affirm whatever aspect of being is manifested to him, whether it be bright or dark. The mood is incidental; what matters is the intensity of the poet's response to the world and his ability to render his perceptions in words and images. Rilke always insisted that praise and lament are not mutually exclusive, but complementary functions; for lament, too, is a kind of affirmation, a way of praising what is lost or unattainable, a way of accepting the limitations of human life or even—in a sense different from that intended by Blake—of "catching a joy as it flies." That is why dirges and laments are a traditional form of poetry, though poetry, by the same tradition, is always affirmative. Within the bounds of a Christian orthodoxy that has very little in common with Rilke's private existential creed—but rather more with Trakl's beliefs—the poet's dual function in an imperfect world emerges from George Herbert's lines:

> I will complain, yet praise,
> I will bewail, approve;
> And all my sowre-sweet dayes
> I will lament, and love.

It was Rilke's insight, then, which directed the attention of Trakl's readers away from the categories of optimism and pessimism and toward that "truth" which Trakl himself thought more important than his own predicament. As the work of so many of Trakl's contemporaries shows, optimism can be just as morbid a symptom as pessimism, because there is a kind of optimism that is a hysterical perversion of the truth; its premises give it the lie. Trakl, on the other hand, wrote of what he knew; he was true to his premises, and these premises were positive enough.

The temporal order that Trakl's poems negate was that of materialism in decay. That is the significance of the decaying household utensils in the first part of **"Sebastian im Traum."** To this order, Trakl opposed an existential Christian faith akin to Kierkegaard's and an unreserved

compassion akin to that of certain characters in Dostoievsky. All this is implicit in Trakl's poetry, since he rarely stated or defined his beliefs, but translated them into images. Yet all the external evidence supports this interpretation of his beliefs; and, shortly before his death, Trakl handed the following short note to Ludwig von Ficker: "(Your) feeling at moments of deathlike existence: all human beings are worthy of love. Awakening, you feel the bitterness of the world: in that you know all your unabsolved guilt; your poems an imperfect penance." Because poetry is an imperfect penance, Trakl castigated himself to the point of self-destruction.

What Trakl lamented was not the fact or the condition of death, but the difficulty of living in an age of cultural decline and spiritual corruption. The immediate background of Salzburg, an ancient and beautiful city unable to live up to its past, was one element in his melancholy, though it does not account for his own obsession with guilt and death. "No," he wrote as early as 1909, "my own affairs no longer interest me"; and in 1914—after his breakdown on active service—"already I feel very nearly beyond this world." The dead who people his poems—the mythical Elis, for instance—are more vivid, more full of life, than the living. In the poem **"An einen Frühverstorbenen" ("To One who Died Young")**, the surviving friend is haunted by the other who

> . . . ging die steinernen Stufen des Mönchbergs
>   hinab,
> Ein blaues Lächeln im Antlitz und seltsam verpuppt
> In seine stillere Kindheit und starb;
> Und im Garten blieb das silberne Antlitz des
>   Freundes zurück
> Lauschend im Laub oder im alten Gestein.
>
> Seele sang den Tod, die grüne Verwesung des
>   Fleisches . . .

> . . . walked down the stone steps of the
>   Mönchsberg,
> A blue smile on his face and strangely cocooned
> In his quieter childhood, and died;
> And the silvery face of this friend remained in the
>   garden,
> Listening in leaves or in ancient stone.
>
> Soul sang of death, the green putrefaction of flesh. . .

It is the dying friend who smiles, the survivor who becomes obsessed with death and decay. The reason, it appears from other poems, is that those who die young preserve "the image of man" intact; wherever they appear in Trakl's poems they are associated with righteousness and with images of the good life; and this, in turn, is associated with an earlier stage of civilization, opposed to modern life in the large cities. One thinks of Rilke's cult of those who died young; but Trakl's dead are symbolic of a state of innocence that cannot be identified with youth or childhood, or even with a rustic and pastoral stage of civilization. It is an innocence that precedes original sin. That is why, in his poem on the Kaspar Hauser legend,

Trakl describes the murdered boy as "unborn." Kaspar Hauser is murdered as soon as he reaches the city, after living in the woods in a wild state. The whole poem is an allegory of the relation between innocence and death, not, as one might easily think, a glorification of a "noble savage" murdered by the corrupt inhabitants of the city.

Trakl, of course, can be criticized for his inability to bear the guilt of being alive. Shortly before his death he said of himself that as yet he was "only half born"; and he did not want his birth to be completed.

Most of Trakl's later poems are written in a form of free verse that owes much to the elegies and hymns of Hölderlin. Without in fact imitating the classical hexameter, Trakl suggests its movement by the frequent use of dactyls and spondees (as in the long lines of **"Sebastian im Traum"**), but in many of his last poems he uses a short line which is also irregular, though more frequently iambic than his longer lines. These last poems are closer to Hölderlin's hymns than to his elegies; and the landscape in these poems is the grand alpine landscape of Innsbruck, as distinct from the more gentle, elegiac landscape of Salzburg and its surroundings. Trakl's long lines do not translate well into English because the language lacks the inflections that makes German so satisfactory a medium for the imitation of classical meters and cadences. Another obstacle to translation is that Trakl's adjectives carry much more weight than English usage allows; but though part of this weight might have been transferred to verbs and nouns in the English version, the result of this process would have been something altogether different from what Trakl wrote. Trakl's adjectives—and especially his color adjectives—have a function that is partly pictorial, partly emotive (often by means of synesthesia), and partly symbolic. Like all his favorite devices, the color epithets recur throughout his mature work with a persistency reminiscent of the Wagnerian leitmotiv (and Trakl is known to have gone through a youthful phase of enthusiasm for Wagner's music).

In spite of a few innocent plagiarisms, Trakl's debt to Hölderlin should not be exaggerated. Trakl also borrowed a few devices and images from Rimbaud, but very much less has been made of this debt or of his no less obvious debt to Baudelaire. It was Emil Barth, in 1937, who first treated Trakl's work as a kind of continuation of Hölderlin's, by drawing attention to the affinity between Trakl's early rhymed poems and the very last poems of Hölderlin, the rhymed poems written in his madness. The theme was developed by Eduard Lachmann; and Martin Heidegger has developed it further—to its ultralogical conclusion.

The mere fact that Heidegger has thought Trakl worthy of his particular form of exegesis, which combines what seems like close textual analysis with the most far-reaching philosophical deductions, implies one kind of affinity between Trakl and the other German poets—Hölderlin and Rilke—to whom Heidegger has devoted similar studies; this affinity, of course, is one of perception, and it undoubtedly exists. But only a poet who uses words with the utmost precision, and with the utmost consistency as

well, can be expected to bear the weight of Heidegger's exegesis; and Trakl's use of imagery, on which every interpretation of his poems must rest, was not consistent.

A comparison with Hölderlin is also implied by Heidegger's premises; for it is from Hölderlin that he derived many of his ideas about the function of poetry, and it is in the light of these ideas that he examines Trakl's work, inevitably linking it to Hölderlin's. Heidegger believes that the function of poets is "to name what is holy"; but this naming, he writes, "does not consist in merely giving a name to something already known, but only when the poet speaks the significant word is the existent nominated into what it is. Poetry is the institution in words of being." This view is not very different from Rilke's conception of poetry as affirmation and praise of the visible world, and its transformation in the poet's "inwardness" into pure significance. Heidegger goes further than Rilke only in clearly stating that poets "institute being," rather than merely affirming it in words. Hölderlin, however, had a more modest end in mind when he wrote—at the end of *Patmos*—that the function of poets is to see that "the existing be well construed." The difference, once more, is that between a religion of the *logos* and a religion of the heart. If the *logos* was at the beginning, there is no need for poets to create the world all over again by endowing it with meaning. The question, in Trakl's case, is whether his poems were intended to "institute being" or merely to construe it.

Heidegger sees Trakl as the poet of the transitional age of which Hölderlin wrote in *Brod und Wein,* an era of Night in which there is no divine revelation, but only waiting and preparation for a new epiphany. It is certainly true that, in a very different sense from the later Expressionists, Trakl wrote of a "new humanity" or at least of a humanity different from that of the present day; but he did so in the form of images and of those mythical personages who inhabit his poems, not in the form of statements that one can easily quote in support of an argument. It is also true that his images of decay, his nocturnes, autumnal landscapes, and visions of doom are often relieved by images of regeneration, which point to a reality quite distinct from his immediate circumstances. These images Heidegger interprets as intimations of a regenerate Occident.

Trakl wrote poems that refer explicitly to the Occident. These are **"Abendländisches Lied"** and **"Abendland."** The first, which is the earlier poem, begins with images of a past, feudal and pastoral, way of life; it is difficult to place these images historically, for there are allusions to shepherds, to "blood blossoming beside the sacrificial stone," to the Crusades, and "glowing martyrdom of the flesh," to the "pious disciples" now turned into warriors, to "peaceful monks who pressed the purple grape," to hunting and to castles. The general impression is that the poem moves from a remote pastoral age to New Testament times, then to the early and later Middle Ages. In the last stanza Trakl turns to the present:

> O, die bittere Stunde des Untergangs,
> Da wir ein steinernes Antlitz in schwarzen Wassern

beschaun.
Aber strahlend heben die silbernen Lider die
    Liebenden:
Ein Geschlecht. Weihrauch strömt von rosigen
    Kissen
Und der süsse Gesang der Auferstandenen.

The ambiguity of these lines is such that they are untranslatable. All one can say with certainty is that Trakl sees
the present as "the bitter hour of decline, when in black
waters we gaze at a stony face"—images that suggest a
narcissistic isolation and the guilt which, as in other poems
of Trakl's, petrifies every faculty; and that the next three
lines express a hope of regeneration. It is the nature of
that regeneration which is obscure; for "die Liebenden"
could be lovers "lifting up silvery eyelids" to look at each
other; they could be Christian worshipers raising their
eyes after prayer toward the altar. The ambiguity is maintained in the next line; for "*ein* Geschlecht" could mean
"*one* sex," "*one* kind," or "*one* generation." And the "rosy
cushions" from which incense wafts could conceivably be
hassocks, if one takes the color epithet to be symbolical.
Perhaps Trakl intended both meanings: the fusion into
one of the sexes, which symbolizes an integration of the
psyche—so that the individual is redeemed from narcissistic solitude; and the fusion of Christian worshipers into
one community by the act of worship and their redemption by Christian love. The concluding line—"and the
sweet song of the resurrected"—accords with both interpretations.

Neither interpretation, however, accords with Heidegger's
argument; for the regeneration of which he speaks is one
peculiar to his own philosophy. As for the latter of the
two poems, **"Abendland,"** it ends with a vision of unre-
lieved gloom:

> Ihr grossen Städte
> steinern aufgebaut
> in der Ebene!
> So sprachlos folgt
> der Heimatlose
> mit dunkler Stirne dem Wind,
> kahlen Bäumen am Hügel.
> Ihr weithin dämmernden Ströme!
> Gewaltig ängstet
> schaurige Abendröte
> im Sturmgewölk.
> Ihr sterbenden Völker!
> Bleiche Woge
> zerschellend am Strande der Nacht,
> fallende Sterne.

> You mighty cities
> stone on stone raised up
> in the plain!
> So quietly
> with darkened forehead
> the outcast follows the wind,
> bare trees on the hillside.
> You rivers distantly fading!
> Gruesome sunset red

> is breeding fear
> in the thunder clouds.
> You dying peoples!
> Pallid billow
> that breaks on the beach of Night,
> stars that are falling.

Heidegger argues that the second part of this poem, which
is more peaceful in mood but filled with images of decay,
cancels out the apocalyptic third part (quoted above). If
this were so, the development of Trakl's poem would be
strange indeed; it would mean that the poem proceeds
from a valid vision to one that has been invalidated by the
preceding vision. Heidegger admits the ambiguity of
Trakl's poetry—indeed, he writes that "it speaks out of an
ambiguous ambiguity!"—but his awareness of the ambiguity does not prevent him from interpreting the whole of
Trakl's work in the most general terms.

The main obstacle to such a sweeping interpretation is
that Trakl used the same images and epithets for different
purposes, sometimes descriptively, sometimes symbolically. This applies even to his favorite color epithets—
"golden coolness," "purple stars," "black pillow," "blue
animal," "rosy sighs," and even "the white night"; but
"brown tree," "yellow corn," "red flowers," "blueish
pond," "green boughs." After deciding in every instance
whether a color epithet is to be taken literally or not, one
has to go on to the much more difficult question of whether
the nonrealistic epithets are strictly symbolic or whether
they amount to nothing more than an emotive synesthesia.

Certain painters and poets of the Expressionist era were
greatly interested in the symbolism of colors; but Trakl's
color symbolism was certainly not traditional and most
probably not even conscious. His critics and interpreters,
too, disagree over this vital point. Heidegger and Emil
Barth believe that his colors are symbolic, but Barth does
not say what they symbolize and confuses symbolism with
synesthesia. Heidegger sees all Trakl's colors as symbolic—even where they conform to the conventions of realism—but believes that this symbolism is ambiguous. He
cites the instance of "golden" in Trakl's line from **"Winkel
im Wald"**: "Auch zeigt sich sanftem Wahnsinn oft das
Goldne, Wahre." ("Often to gentle madness the golden,
true, is revealed") in which "golden" is explicitly identified with "true," whereas in a different poem Trakl speaks
of "das grässliche Lachen des Golds" ("the horrible laughter of gold"). Heidegger infers that Trakl's "golden" has
two antithetical but complementary meanings, both of them
symbolic. He does not mention that in all Trakl's poems
there is only one instance where gold has unpleasant associations; and that this is one of the few poems in which
Trakl forsakes his symbolic landscapes to write about a
large city which—like his contemporary Georg Heym—
he sees as demonically possessed. The poem in question,
"An die Verstummten," is more didactic than visionary:

> O, der Wahnsinn der Grossen Stadt, da am Abend
> An schwarzer Mauer verkrüppelte Bäume starren,
> Aus silberner Maske der Geist des Bösen schaut;
> Licht mit magnetischer Geissel die steinerne Nacht

verdrängt.
O, das versunkene Läuten der Abendglocken.

Hure, die in eisigen Schauern ein totes Kindlein
gebärt.
Rasend peitscht Gottes Zorn die Stirn der
Besessenen,
Purpurne Seuche, Hunger, der grüne Augen
zerbricht.
O, das grässliche Lachen des Golds.

Aber stille blutet in dunkler Höhle stummere
Menschheit,
Fügt aus harten Metallen das erlösende Haupt.

Oh, the great city's madness when at nightfall
The crippled trees gape by the blackened wall,
The spirit of evil peers from a silver mask;
Lights with magnetic scourge drive off the stony
night.
Oh, the sunken pealing of evening bells.

Whore who in her icy spasms gives birth to a dead
child.
With raving whip God's fury punishes the brows
possessed.
Purple pestilence, hunger that breaks green eyes.
Oh, the horrible laughter of gold.

But silent in dark caves a stiller humanity bleeds,
Out of hard metals moulds the redeeming head.

The "gold" here has nothing to do with the adjective
"golden" that Trakl uses symbolically elsewhere; it stands
for nothing more esoteric than material wealth. Its function in this poem is neither antithetical nor complementary
to its function in other poems; it is simply different.

The "silver mask" of the third line could also be interpreted in terms of Heidegger's ambiguous symbolism. The
epithet "silver," he points out, "is the pallor of death and
the twinkling of stars." The inference is that Trakl's symbols and symbolic epithets are ambiguous because of his
simultaneous perception of two orders of reality, of the
present and the timeless (or future) aspect of any scene.
This Heidegger attributed to Trakl's belief in a homecoming ("Heimkunft") after the transition (Übergang") of this
life and the departure ("Abschied") of death. This homecoming Heidegger interprets as that of a new generation
or race ("Geschlecht") that will eventually succeed the
"degenerate" one of the present. "Trakl," Heidegger writes,
"is the poet of the still hidden Occident."

Very few, if any, of Trakl's poems bear out this interpretation, which simply ignores the contradictions in Trakl's
work. One of these contradictions appertains to his use of
color epithets. The "silver mask" in the above poem, for
instance, has no primary connection with either death or
the stars, but an obvious one with the artificial lights that
"drive off the night" and prevent the city dwellers from
facing their guilt and seeking redemption. In other cases,
Trakl's color epithets serve to induce that "systematic

derangement of the senses" which Rimbaud prescribed.
Nor does his color symbolism—where it is a symbolism—always agree with the traditional one preserved by
the alchemists; to them, the metal silver corresponded
not with the stars, but with the moon, and its color was
gray.

It is the last lines of the poem, with their allusion to "the
redeeming head," that may seem to support Heidegger's
thesis of a future regeneration; but these lines raise the
question of Trakl's own beliefs. From the evidence of his
poetry alone, his precise beliefs remain doubtful. Much
of his imagery derives from Roman Catholic rites, though
Trakl was a Lutheran; he went so far as to call one sequence of poems **"Rosenkranzlieder"** (**"Rosary Songs"**).
The question of his orthodoxy must remain open here;
but there can be no doubt at all that Trakl was a Christian.
According to an account by Hans Limbach of a conversation between Trakl and Carl Dallago, which took place
at Innsbruck in 1914, Trakl professed beliefs very different
from Heidegger's interpretation:

"By the way, do you know Walt Whitman's work?"
he [Dallago] asked him suddenly.

Trakl said he did, but added that he thought Whitman
pernicious.

"How so?"—D. exclaimed—"How do you mean,
pernicious. Don't you admire his work? Surely your
manner has a good deal in common with his."

F. [Ficker] observed that the two poets were really
radically opposed, since Whitman simply affirmed life
in all its manifestations, whereas Trakl was thoroughly
pessimistic. Didn't life give him any pleasure, then?—
D. continued his inquisition. Didn't his creative work,
for instance, satisfy him at all?

"Yes," Trakl admitted, "but one should be suspicious
of that satisfaction."

D. leant back in his chair in his boundless astonishment.

"Well, in that case, why don't you go into a
monastery?" he asked after a short silence.

"I am a Protestant," Trakl replied.

"Pro-te-stant?"—D. asked again. "I must say, I should
never have thought so.—Well, at least you shouldn't
live in town, but move to the country, where you'd be
far from the madding crowd and nearer to nature."

"I have no right to remove myself from Hell," Trakl
replied.

"But Christ did so," the other retorted.

"Christ is the Son of God."

D. was almost speechless.

"So you believe too that all salvation comes from Him? You take those words, 'the Son of God,' quite literally?"

"I'm a Christian," Trakl answered.

"Well, then, how would you explain such un-Christian phenomena as Buddha or the Chinese sages?"

"They too received their light from Christ."

We fell silent, pondering on the profundity of this paradox. But D. could not let the matter rest.

"And the Greeks? Don't you agree that men have sunk much lower since their time?"

"Never have men sunk so low as now, after the appearance of Christ," Trakl replied. "They *could* not sink so low," he added after a pause . . .

One can question the accuracy of this report and its relevance to Trakl's poetry; but any interpretation of his symbolism must take Trakl's Christian faith into account, allowing for the influence of Kierkegaard and the wholly undogmatic nature of Trakl's poetry. Like Rimbaud, Trakl was "an alchemist of the word"; but even alchemists could be orthodox in their acceptance of dogma, as Paracelsus protested that he was. The real issue is whether Trakl's poetry can be interpreted as a whole or whether the seeming consistency of his later work—due to his use of recurrent images and epithets—is deceptive.

Heidegger evades this issue by assuming that Trakl is a great poet and that his practice was consistent. "Every great poet creates his poetry out of a single poem," he claims; and adds that "this poem remains unspoken." I doubt that this is true of all great poets, at least on a level that permits discussion; but since the archetypal poem remains "unspoken," it is almost useless to object that some great poets may well have more than one of these archetypal poems to draw on. Even if one succeeded in showing that certain great poets derived from two or more of such archetypes, these, in turn, could be traced back to an archetype even more archetypal; but here we leave the domain of literary criticism, which is not qualified to deal in the unspeakable.

In certain of his poems, Trakl applied the epithets "silver" and "golden" in a sense that is undoubtedly symbolic. Thus in a short poem, **"Untergang" ("Decline")**, addressed to a friend:

Über den weissen Weiher
Sind die wilden Vögel fortgezogen.
Am Abend weht von unseren Sternen ein eisiger
    Wind.

Über unsere Gräber
Beugt sich die zerbrochene Stirne der Nacht.
Unter Eichen schaukeln wir auf einem silbernen
    Kahn.

Immer klingen die weissen Mauern der Stadt.
Unter Dornenbogen
O mein Bruder klimmen wir blinde Zeiger gen
    Mitternacht.

Over the white pond
The wild birds have travelled on.
In the evening an icy wind blows from our stars.

Over our graves
The broken brow of the night inclines.
Under oak-trees we sway in a silver boat.

Always the town's white walls resound.
Under arches of thorns
O my brother, blind minute-hands
We climb towards midnight.

In this poem, Trakl sees both the friend and himself as transitional figures passing though death-in-life to spiritual regeneration. The whole meaning of the poem is in the images and the symbolic epithets, the "white" and "silver," which Trakl associates with death. There are only three brief references to the two persons of the poem, at the end of each strophe. The first strophe begins with an image suggesting transience, but without direct reference to the human personages of the poem. This reference is withheld till the third line; and even this reference is indirect. The second strophe connects the malignant influence of the stars with death; but death, to Trakl, is itself a state of transition. Boats, as in Hölderlin and Nietzsche, symbolize existence; this boat is a silver one because the lives of the two friends are overshadowed by death. The concluding strophe introduces another image that symbolizes existence here and now, the temporal order; the town's white walls are white because that temporal order itself wears the color of death, because it is doomed. In an age such as the one they live in the two friends can only suffer and wait for death. The "arch of thorns" suggests both suffering in general and the Passion.

A special significance attaches to the "silver boat" of this poem, because elsewhere Trakl has a "golden boat," which is in complete contrast with this one. The golden boat occurs in one of Trakl's poems about Elis, a mythical boy who is either dead or "unborn"—in Trakl's peculiar sense of that word. We might not know that he is not of this life, but for a different poem, **"An den Knaben Elis" ("To the Boy Elis")**:

. . . Ein Dornenbusch tönt
Wo deine mondenen Augen sind.
O, wie lange bist, Elis, du verstorben.

Dein Leib ist eine Hyazinthe,
In die ein Mönch die wächsernen Finger taucht.
Ein schwarze Höhle ist unser Schweigen,

Daraus bisweilen ein sanftes Tier tritt
Und langsam die schweren Lider senkt.
Auf deine Schläfen tropft schwarzer Tau,

Das letzte Gold verfallner Sterne.

A thorn-bush sounds
Where your lunar eyes are.
O Elis, how long since you died.

Your body is a hyacinth
Into which a monk dips his waxen fingers.
Our silence is a black cavern

From which at times a gentle animal
Steps out and lowers heavy lids.
Upon your temples black dew drips.

The last gold of perished stars.

Because Elis is dead or "unborn," he is introduced by
images of an innocent mode of life in the poem called
"Elis":

. . . Am Abend zog der Fischer die schweren Netze
     ein.
Ein guter Hirt
Führt seine Herde am Waldsaum hin.
O! wie gerecht sind, Elis alle deine Tage.

Leise sinkt
An kahlen Mauern des Ölbaums blaue Stille,
Erstirbt eines Greisen dunkler Gesang.

Ein goldener Kahn
Schaukelt, Elis, dein Herz am einsamen Himmel.

. . . At nightfall the fisherman hauled in his heavy
     nets.
A good shepherd
Leads his flock along the forest's edge.
Oh, how righteous, Elis, are all your days.

Softly sinks
The olive tree's blue stillness on bare walls,
An old man's dark song subsides.

A golden boat
Sways, Elis, your heart against a lonely sky.

The significance of the "golden boat" here is indicated by
its connection with Elis' righteousness and with the images
of the good life that precede it. Both the fisherman and
the shepherd stand for an order opposed to that of modern
life, but what is important about them is their obvious
connection with Christ; they are not righteous because they
are primitive, but their primitiveness symbolizes righteousness. The golden boat, in this context, symbolizes a mode
of existence unthreatened by death or decay. "Golden,"
here, may well be symbolic of truth, for Trakl identified
truth with innocence and righteousness.

Yet the very same poem begins with a line in which
"golden" has a function that is primarily visual or emotive:
"Vollkommen ist die Stille dieses goldenen Tags . . ."
("Perfect is the stillness of this golden day . . ."). The
noun "gold" occurs again in one of Trakl's late poems of
the Innsbruck period, **"Das Herz"** (**"The Heart"**), an
angry and despairing poem closely related to the apocalyptic **"Abendland."** In this poem death, for once, is
terrible; and it is the word "gold"—used in a purely symbolic sense—that tells us why. I shall quote the whole
poem:

Das wilde Herz ward weiss am Wald;
O dunkle Angst
Des Todes, so das Gold
In grauer Wolke starb.
Novemberabend.
Am kahlen Tor am Schlachthaus stand
Der armen Frauen Schar;
In jeden Korb
Fiel faules Fleisch und Eingeweid;
Verfluchte Kost!

Des Abends blaue Taube
Brachte nicht Versöhnung.
Dunkler Trompetenruf
Durchfuhr der Ulmen
Nasses Goldlaub,
Eine zerfetzte Fahne
Vom Blute rauchend,
Dass in wilder Schwermut
Hinlauscht ein Mann.
O! ihr ehernen Zeiten
Begraben dort im Abendrot.

Aus dunklen Hausflur trat
Die goldene Gestalt
Der Jünglingin
Umgeben von bleichen Monden,
Herbstlicher Hofstaat,
Zerknickten schwarzen Tannen
Im Nachtsturm,
Die steile Festung.
O Herz
Hinüberschimmernd in schneeige Kühle.

The wild heart turned white in the wood;
O the dark fear
Of death, when the gold
Died in a grey cloud.
November evening.
By the bare gate of the slaughterhouse there stood
The crowd of poor women.
Into every basket
Rank flesh and entrails fell;
Accursed fare!

The blue dove of nightfall
Brought no atonement.
Dark trumpet call
Rang through the elm-trees'
Damp golden leaves,
A tattered banner
Steaming with blood,
So that wild in his sadness
A man gives heed.
O brazen ages
Buried there in the sunset red.

From the house's dark hall there stepped
The golden shape
Of the maiden-youth
Surrounded with pale moons
Of autumnal courtliness,
Black pine-trees snapped
In the night gale.
The steep-walled fortress.
O heart
Glistening away into snowy coolness.

Death is terrible in this poem because "the gold died in a grey cloud"; that is to say, the true, spiritual order has been momentarily obscured, so that the poet is at the mercy of that materialism to which death is simply the cessation of life—an event more fearful than any. The harsh realism of the images that follow—the poor women who are fobbed off with putrid meat and entrails—belongs to the same materialistic order; one might almost take these images as an indictment of the social order, if it weren't for their unrealistic context. The "dove of night-fall" is blue not only because certain night skies are deep blue, but because blue stands for the spiritual in Trakl's poetry: the spiritual, at present, is powerless.

The "maiden-youth" of the third strophe is "golden" because this hermaphrodite stands for a mode of being exempt from original sin; Trakl also has a personage called "die Mönchin" (female form of "monk"), who belongs to the same order. The "sister" of other late poems has the same significance; although not hermaphrodite in herself, she is the feminine complement of the poet'smasculine spirit. The absurdity of identifying this sister with Trakl's sister Margarete is evident from his last poem, in which it is the sister's shade that appears; and Trakl's sister was neither dead at the time (although she later committed suicide also) nor actually present on the battlefield. In **"Das Herz,"** it is the appearance of the "Jünglingin" that reconciles the poet to death; for "snowy" coolness denotes the whiteness both of innocence and of death.

Heidegger cites Trakl's two last poems, **"Klage"** and **"Grodek,"** as evidence that Trakl was not a Christian poet. He asks why Trakl does not invoke God or Christ in the extremity of his despair, a despair which, Heidegger claims, "is not even Christian despair." The answer is that poetry is not prayer, or a substitute for prayer; Trakl himself said that it was an "imperfect penance." Direct references to the deity are rare even in the earlier poems of Trakl, which contain unmistakable allusions to Christian sacraments—unmistakable, that is, to all but Heidegger. In the second part of *Sebastian im Traum,* for instance, Christ is quite clearly invoked, but Trakl leaves the name "unspoken":

. . . Oder wenn er an der harten Hand des Vaters
Stille den finstern Kalvarienberg hinanstieg
Und in dämmernden Felsennischen
Die blaue Gestalt des Menschen durch seine
    Legende ging,
Aus der Wunde unter dem Herzen purpurn das Blut
    rann.
O wie leise stand in dunkler Seele das Kreuz auf . . .

. . . Or holding his father's horny hand
In silence he walked up Calvary Hill
And in dusky rock recesses
The blue shape of Man would pass through his
    legend,
Blood run purple from the wound beneath his heart.
O how softly the cross rose up in the dark of his
    soul . . .

Christ is referred to as "der Mensch," which could mean either "Man" or "the man." In the same way, few would doubt that Trakl alludes to Christ in his poem **"An die Verstummten,"** since the "redeeming head" of the last line has a more explicit counterpart in **"Abendländisches Lied"**:

. . . Ruh des Abends,
Da in seiner Kammer der Mensch Gerechtes sann,
In stummem Gebet um Gottes lebendiges Haupt
    rang.

. . . Quiet of evening,
When in his room a man gave thought to
    righteousness
And for God's living head grappled in silent prayer.

It is very strange that Heidegger, who looks only for Trakl's "unspoken" poem throughout the greater part of his essay, persistently ignoring such literal evidence as the line cited above, should suddenly require literal proof of Trakl's Christian faith where it isn't provided. But Heidegger despises logic as much as he despises "values." His philosophy reduces the world to its primal chaosand then proceeds to re-create it in the shape of Heidegger's mind. Since his literary criticism is an extension of his philosophizing, one must not expect it to balk at mere facts; but it is illuminating in its own right, as pretextual rather than contextual criticism.

Of Trakl's last two poems, the earlier, **"Klage,"** does render a vision of unmitigated despair; unmitigated, that is, except for a grammatical qualification that often escapes notice. The verb in the fourth line, "verschlänge," does not render an event that has occurred but an event that is to be feared. Here is the poem **"Klage"** (**"Lament"**):

Schlaf und Tod, die düstern Adler
Umrauschen nachtlang dieses Haupt:
Des Menschen goldnes Bildnis
Verschlänge die eisige Woge
Der Ewigkeit. An schaurigen Riffen
Zerschellt der purpurne Leib.
Und es klagt die dunkle Stimme
Über dem Meer.
Schwester stürmischer Schwermut
Sieh ein ängstlicher Kahn versinkt
Unter Sternen,
Dem schweigenden Antlitz der Nacht.

Sleep and death, the dark eagles
Around this head swoop all night long:
Eternity's icy wave

Would swallow the golden image
Of man; on horrible reefs
His purple body is shattered.
And the dark voice laments
Over the sea.
Sister of stormy sadness,
Look, a timorous boat goes down
Under stars,
The silent face of the night.

What is important is that the poem deals with two different disasters. The first, which has not occurred but which the poet fears, is that "eternity's icy wave would or may swallow" the "golden image of man"; that is to say, that men will be untrue to their Creator beyond all possibility of redemption. Heidegger rightly points out that "eternity's icy wave" is not a Christian concept; but Trakl, after all, had read Nietzsche, to whom Heidegger owes so much, and his despair was bound to be colored by the current modes of unbelief. That is why he grew angry when Dallago mentioned Nietzsche to him, saying that Nietzsche was a madman suffering "from the same disease as Maupassant." In order to express his despair—a conditional despair—he had to resort to the language of unbelief; and in other late poems too, as we have seen, Trakl was overwhelmed by his foreboding of doom.

The "purple body" of man—as distinct from his "golden *image*"—*is* being shattered, for the poem alludes to the war. Since boats symbolize existence, the sinking boat of the tenth line has the effect of a final disaster: this disaster is the senseless destruction of war, a death that is mere carnage and not the expiation of guilt that Trakl welcomes in other poems. Since the sister is invoked at the end, as a witness to the sinking boat, the extinction that Trakl fears is not the physical annihilation of mankind. One would be inclined to read a reference to Trakl's own death into these lines, if the tone of the poem were not so impersonal.

Trakl's last poem, **"Grodek,"** is more hopeful; but it is no less difficult to interpret. The "unborn grandsons" of the last line have been taken too literally as a later generation who will profit by the sacrifice of war. In an earlier poem, **"Der Abend,"** Trakl writes of "the white grandsons whose dark future is being prepared by the decaying generation (or kind) which, cold and evil, inhabits the city":

Mit toten Heldengestalten
Erfüllst du Mond
Die schweigenden Wälder,
Sichelmond—
Mit der sanften Umarmung
Der Liebenden,
Den Schatten berühmter Zeiten
Die modernden Felsen rings
So bläulich erstrahlt es
Gegen die Stadt hin,
Wo kalt und böse
Ein verwesend Geschlecht wohnt,
Der weissen Enkel
Dunkle Zukunft bereitet.

Ihr mondverschlungnen Schatten
Aufseufzend im leeren Kristall
Des Bergsees.

With dead figures of heroes
The moon is filling
The silent forests,
O sickle-moon!
And the mouldering rocks all round
With the soft embraces
Of lovers,
The phantoms of famous ages;
This blue light shines
Towards the city
Where a decaying race
Lives coldly and evilly,
Preparing the dark future
Of their white descendants.
O moon-wrapped shadows
Sighing in the empty crystal
Of the mountain lake.

In another poem, **"Das Gewitter,"** Trakl has "the boy's golden war-cry and the unborn sighing from blind eyes." Both these poems are relevant to the "prophecy" that ends **"Grodek"**; and so is the despair of **"Klage,"** for the two poems are complementary. In **"Grodek,"** too, the sister appears; but she does not appear to the poet and is explicitly described as a "shadow." (In German usage "die Schwester" means both "the sister" and "*my* sister"; hence the biographical deductions. But in **"Grodek"** there is no question of any "I.")

Am Abend tönen die herbstlichen Wälder
Von tödlichen Waffen, die goldenen Ebenen
Und blauen Seen, darüber die Sonne
Düstrer hinrollt; umfängt die Nacht
Sterbende Krieger, die wilde Klage
Ihrer zerbrochenen Münder.
Doch stille sammelt im Weidengrund
Rotes Gewölk, darin ein zürnender Gott wohnt,
Das vergossne Blut sich, mondne Kühle;
Alle Strassen münden in schwarze Verwesung.
Unter goldnem Gezweig der Nacht und Sternen
Es schwankt der Schwester Schatten durch den
      schweigenden
                                                    Hain,
Zu grüssen die Geister der Helden, die blutenden
      Häupter;
Und leise tönen im Rohr die dunkeln Flöten des
      Herbstes.
O stolzere Trauer! ihr ehernen Altäre,
Die heisse Flamme des Geistes nährt heute ein
      gewaltiger Schmerz,
Die ungebornen Enkel.

At nightfall the autumn woods cry out
With deadly weapons and the golden plains,
The deep blue lakes, above which more darkly
Rolls the sun; the night embraces
Dying warriors, the wild lament
Of their broken mouths.

But quietly there in the pasture land
Red clouds in which an angry God resides,
The shed blood gathers, lunar coolness.
All the roads lead to blackest carrion.
Under golden twigs of the night and stars
The sister's shade now sways through the silent
    copse
To greet the ghosts of the heroes, the bleeding
    heads;
And softly the dark flutes of autumn sound in the
    reeds.
O prouder grief! You brazen altars,
This day a great pain feeds the hot flame of the
    spirit,
The yet unborn grandsons.

In this poem death in battle has the significance that Trakl's despair denies to it in **"Klage";** it is a sacrifice and an expiation. But "unborn grandsons" does not denote a specific generation as yet unborn; there is no conceivable reason that the third generation, rather than the second or the fourth, should be redeemed by the death of these soldiers. "Unborn," as I have pointed out, has another sense besides the literal one in Trakl's poetry; it denotes a state of innocence more complete than the innocence of childhood. It is possible that the grandsons of **"Grodek"** are not a future generation at all, but the very same generation whose "dark future" was prepared by the cold and evil city dwellers in **"Der Abend."** In that case they would be the soldiers themselves, whose expiatory death grants them a return to innocence. If we take "unborn" literally— and Trakl uses the word literally in the passage quoted from **"Das Gewitter"**—the last lines of **"Grodek"** are indeed a prophecy, but a prophecy which it is wisest to leave alone at this stage. To fix a date for its fulfillment or to specify the exact nature of the regeneration in which Trakl believed is to put too great a strain on his poetry.

Trakls' poetry is a series of microcosmic variations, poor in melodic invention, rich in harmonic correspondences.

—Michael Hamburger

If it is frustrating not to be able to end this study with a clarion call, it is also a tribute to Trakl's art. Expressionist poetry yields opportunities for any number of clarion calls, as loud and as rousing as anyone could wish. But the difficulty of summing up Trakl's work as a whole, and the much greater difficulty of interpreting it as a whole, are two reasons that his work stands out from the German poetry of his time. Trakl's plagiarisms—and especially his self-plagiarisms—lend a deceptive consistency to his work—deceptive, because his poems are essentially ambiguous. His ambiguities derive from the tension between image and symbol, the phenomenon and the Idea. Sometimes this tension remains unresolved, so that one cannot tell whether an image is to be taken descriptively or sym-

bolically, an epithet synesthetically or qualitatively. It is true that each of Trakl's poems offers some kind of clue to the next; but it is a clue that can be very misleading.

Trakl's ambiguities are not deliberate or cerebral; he was an imaginative poet, not a fanciful one. That is why his plagiarisms are never disturbing or offensive. His debt to Hölderlin alone was such that, by all the usual criteria, his work should be very nearly worthless. He appropriated Hölderlin's imagery, rhythms, and syntax; yet Trakl's originality is beyond doubt. Any group of three lines detached from one of his later poems is immediately recognizable as his own. Trakl carried plagiarism further by continually quoting himself, repeating, varying, and adding to his earlier poems. But there is no reason that a poet should not steal his own property in order to rearrange it; and this very habit points to the harmlessness of Trakl's borrowings from other poets. The laws of property do apply to literature, insofar as no writer can deliberately steal what he lacks himself and get away with the swag; but they do not apply to the imagination. The imagination can only borrow, never steal; and, by its very nature, it can only borrow those things to which it has a right.

Trakl's debt to Hölderlin is a curiosity of literature; it does not mean that his symbolism can be interpreted in terms of Hölderlin's or that his vision begins where Hölderlin's left off. Heidegger not only presupposes such a tradition of vision and prophecy, but reads his own philosophy into Hölderlin and applies this reading to Trakl. The result is a fascinating, but ruthless, gesture, which sweeps away all evidence of Trakl's own thought in order to turn him into the prophet of an Occident regenerated by the philosophy of pure being. It is true that existential creeds tend to look alike, especially if they have been expressed in poetry alone; and Trakl's Christian faith was an existential one. But this faith is essential to his poetry, as most of his critics agree. Heidegger's exegesis would not have been possible at all but for Trakl's imagist practice; because of the noncommittal character of imagism, it would also be possible to argue that Trakl was an alchemist (as his astrological metaphors confirm!) or a Marxist (because of his vision of capitalism in decay!).

In an age of conflicting creeds and sects, such openness is an advantage. Horizontally, Trakl's range is that of a minor poet, but his vertical range is out of all proportion to it. By "vertical" here I mean neither profundity nor sublimity, but a dimension related to harmony in music. Trakl's poetry is a series of microcosmic variations, poor in melodic invention, rich in harmonic correspondences. Another way of putting it is to say that his work is valid on many "levels" of meaning. It depends as little as possible on the poet's person, opinions, and circumstances. One reason is that Trakl was conscious neither of himself nor of his reader; all his poems had his undivided attention. Of T.S. Eliot's "three voices of poetry," Trakl had only the first; but because it never even occurred to him to cultivate the others, his monologue was strangely quiet and pure.

Theodore Fiedler (essay date 1972)

SOURCE: "Holderlin and Trakl's Poetry of 1914," in *Friedrich Holderlin: An Early Modern,* The University of Michigan Press, 1972, pp. 87-105.

[*In the following excerpt, Fiedler shows how specific rhetorical patterns used by Holderlin were developed in Trakl's work as it matured; he asserts that the latter poet was "modern" in his poetical achievement.*]

Trakl's interest in Hölderlin, a matter whose significance has all too readily been exaggerated by some and dismissed out of hand by others, can be traced throughout his oeuvre. As early as 1906, for example, in a rather hapless prose poem entitled **"Barrabas. Eine Phantasie,"** Trakl employed the striking title of Hölderlin's hymn "Der Einzige" to identify the figure of Christ crucified. Yet it is not until late 1912 that Trakl's interest in his predecessor, apparently focused for the first time on the odes, elegies, and hymns of Hölderlin's maturity that were available to him, contributes to some sustained changes in his poetry. Chief among these changes, as evident in the poems **"Helian"** and **"Abendlied,"** is the emergence of a historical perspective that reflects the secularized historical fiction—a past millennium, present decadence, the new millennium—informing Hölderlin's mature poetry. Even then more than a year passes before Trakl's concern with this fundamental thematic component of his predecessor's poetry merges with a dramatic interest in aspects of Hölderlin's mature style, to effect a crucial development that results in the so-called hymnic poetry of mid-1914.

The first signs that Trakl's interest in Hölderlin's major poetry was reviving after a year of dormancy occur not, as might be expected, in a verse poem but in the poet's prose masterpiece **"Traum und Umnachtung,"** written during the first weeks of 1914. One such sign is Trakl's isolated use of a kind of hyperbatic syntax that is characteristic of Hölderlin's mature poetry. I refer to the clause: *"Stille sah er und lang in die Sternenaugen der Kröte"* (Quietly he looked and long into the starry eyes of the toad), in the poem's first section. A more significant manifestation of Trakl's reviving interest in Hölderlin in his unprecedented use of the word *Geschlecht* "race, generation" in a pejorative manner in various sections of the poem. Such usage recalls not only Hölderlin's odes "Der Frieden" and "Dichterberuf," where contemporary humanity is referred to respectively as a *gärendes* and a *schlaues Geschlecht* (a seething and a sly race) but also "Der Archipelagus," in which the poet laments:

*Aber weh! es wandelt in Nacht, es wohnt, wie im
   Orkus,
Ohne Göttliches unser Geschlecht.*

(Ah, but our kind walks in darkness, it dwells as in
   Orcus,
Severed from all that's divine.)

Trakl, to be sure, narrows down the scope of the word *Geschlecht* primarily to the protagonist's family in **"Traum**

und Umnachtung"** but its frame of reference extends by implication at least to Western man. Yet, unlike Hölderlin, who continually asserted the regeneration of decadent humanity in the near future along lines known from past eras, Trakl does not hesitate, at least in the context of **"Traum und Umnachtung,"** to send contemporary humanity to its inescapable doom: in the final words of the poem, *"die Nacht das verfluchte Geschlecht verschlang"* (night swallowed up the accursed race).

Undoubtedly the most important manifestation of Hölderlin's mediation in **"Traum und Umnachtung"** is Trakl's frequent use of the conjunction *aber.* Not that Trakl had completely ignored such conjunctions as *aber, doch, denn,* and even *auch* ("but," "yet," "for," "also"; the last-named also appears once in the poem), which are an essential feature of Hölderlin's argumentative rhetoric, both in his mature poetry and in *Hyperion.* In fact, in mid-1912 after an almost principled avoidance of such conjunctions for three years, he used *aber* in **"Träumerei am Abend,"** a poem that echoes "Brod und Wein" extensively. For the next year and one-half Trakl employed *aber* and *doch* sparingly but conspicuously to indicate radical but usually obscurely motivated shifts in perspective and mood. Only in **"Traum und Umnachtung,"** however, does the use of *aber* become widespread, occurring fully ten times. Its main function, analogous to its dialectical usage in Hölderlin's poetry (compare, for example, the use of *aber* in line 7 of the opening stanza of "Brod und Wein"), is to effect and emphasize the poem's rapid transitions from idyllic to demonic states and back again. Consider, for instance, the imposing opening of the third section of **"Traum und Umnachtung"**:

> *O des verfluchten Geschlechts. Wenn in befleckten Zimmern jegliches Schicksal vollendet ist, tritt mit modernen Schritten der Tod in das Haus. O, dass draussen Frühling wäre und im blühenden Baum ein lieblicher Vogel sänge. Aber gräulich verdorrt das spärliche Grün an den Fenstern der Nächtlichen und es sinnen die blutenden Herzen noch Böses.*

(Oh, for the accursed race. When in soiled rooms each and every fate is fulfilled, then with moldering steps death walks into the house. Oh, would that it were spring outside, and that in the blossoming tree there sang a lovely bird. *But* the sparse green withers grey at the windows of the nocturnal ones, and the bleeding hearts still meditate evil.)

Here the poem moves almost breathlessly from the demonic opening apostrophe to the subjunctively stated idyll and back again, at least momentarily, to the demonic via the conjunction *aber.* Similarly, *aber* introduces a sudden reversal of imagery and mood, a shift from the malign to the benign. As in the passage immediately preceding, and hereafter throughout the essay, roman type in the German quotations—corresponding to italics in the English translations—indicates verbal parallels with Hölderlin. The following passage opens the fourth and final section of **"Traum und Umnachtung"**:

*Tief ist der Schlummer in dunklen Giften, erfüllt von
Sternen und dem weissen Antlitz der Mutter, dem
steinernen. Bitter ist der Tod, die Kost der Schuld-
beladenen; in dem braunen Geäst des Stamms zerfielen
grinsend die irdenen Gesichter. Aber leise sang jener
im grünen Schatten des Hollunders, da er aus bösen
Träumen erwachte; süsser Gespiele nahte ihm ein
rosiger Engel, dass er, ein sanftes Wild, zur Nacht
hinschlummerte; und er sah das Sternenantlitz der
Reinheit.*

(Deep is sleep in dark poisons, filled up with stars and
the white face of the mother, the one of stone. Bitter
is death, the food of those burdened by guilt; in the
trunk's brown branches, the earthen faces decomposed,
grinning. *But* softly that one sang in the green shade
of the elder bush, as we awoke from evil dreams; with
sweet playing a rose-colored angel approached him so
that he, a shy wild animal, slept into the night; and he
saw the sidereal countenance of purity.)

Some two months later Trakl continued his close imitation of Hölderlin's use of conjunctions in two poems that
mark an important juncture in Trakl's relationship to his
predecessor's poetry. Indeed, **"Gesang des Abgeschiedenen"** and **"Abendland,"** both originating in the
second half of March 1914, point in opposite directions
as far as Trakl's poetry of 1914 is concerned. Unlike
"Abendland," the first of whose several versions already
anticipates the long strophes and short dithyrambic lines
of the "hymnic" poetry of mid-1914, **"Gesang des Abgeschiedenen"** is one of the last poems Trakl wrote in the
predominantly long-line, free verse style that has its roots
in the **"Helian"** complex of late 1912/early 1913. This
fact tends to undercut the possibility that the poem, whose
rhythm is partially determined by a largely dactylic stress
pattern, represents a deliberate imitation of Hölderlin's
elegiac hexameter, though it does not rule out that possibility entirely. Not surprisingly, the lines that most clearly
recall Hölderlin's hexameter, lines 12 and 15 of **"Gesang
des Abgeschiedenen"**:

Liebend auch *umfängt das Schweigen im Zimmer
    die Schatten der Alten,*
Denn *strahlender immer erwacht aus schwarzen
    Minuten des Wahnsinns . . .*

(Lovingly *too* the silence in the room surrounds the
    shadows of the old,
For ever more radiant there awakens from the dark
    minutes of insanity . . .)

also contain the conjunctions *denn*, which occurs once
more in the poem, and *auch*. Hölderlin, like Trakl after
him, usually positioned such conjunctions at the start of
a line, as in the first and final lines of this passage from
the initial stanza of the elegy "Heimkunft":

Denn *es wächst unendlicher dort das Jahr und die
    heilgen Stunden, die Tage, sie sind kühner
    geordnet, gemischt.*
Dennoch merket die Zeit der Gewittervogel und

*zwischen Bergen, hoch in der Luft weilt er und
    rufet den Tag.*
Jetzt auch *wachet und schaut in der Tiefe drinnen
    das Dörflein . . .*

(*For* more endlessly there the year expands, and the
    holy
    Hours and the days in there more boldly are
    ordered and
        mixed.

Yet the bird of thunder marks and observes the
    time, and
    High in the air, between peaks, hangs and calls
    out a new day.
Now, deep inside, the small village *also* awakens. . .)

It is noteworthy that Trakl's use of the conjunctions *denn*
and *auch,* indicative of causality and continuity, gives
rise, in **"Gesang des Abgeschiedenen,"** to an illusion of
narrative coherence that is decidedly absent from almost
all of his poetry written after mid-1909, especially those
poems originating after mid-1912. The sharp play of
opposites—of benign and malign forces represented in
seemingly autonomous imagistic scenes—that normally
determines the structure of Trakl's mature poems is discarded in favor of an overarching harmony more appropriate to the almost hymnic celebration of the protagonist's ultimate entry into the blue realm of *Abgeschiedenheit.* Not that conflicts are absent from the poem. But we
become aware of them only as they are being absorbed
into the metaphysical blue realm that pervades the poem
and constitutes Trakl's otherworldly analogue to Hölderlin's future millennium. Clearly the conjunctions must
play a crucial role in this process of subordination and
subsumption. Thus the conjunction *denn* serves to reinforce the benign qualities of the symbolic *Abendmahl*
immediately preceding the emergence of a serious conflict in this passage from the middle of **"Gesang des
Abgeschiedenen"**:

Schon dämmert die Stirne dem sinnenden Menschen.

*Und es leuchtet ein Lämpchen, das Gute, in seinem
    Herzen*
*Und der Frieden des Mahls; denn geheiligt ist Brot
    und Wein*
*Von Gottes Händen, und es schaut aus nächtigen
    Augen*
*Stille dich der Bruder an, dass er ruhe von
    dorniger Wanderschaft.*
O das Wohnen in der beseelten Bläue der Nacht.

(Already the brow of the thinking man darkens,

And there shines a small lamp, the good one, in his
    heart
And the peace of the supper; *for* bread and wine
    are
Consecrated by God's hands, and quietly, out of
    night-filled eyes
Your brother looks at you, so that he might rest

from his thorny wanderings.
Oh, to live in the spirit-filled blue of night.)

The hymnic apostrophe to the beneficent blue realm that rounds out this passage of course also helps to contain the emerging conflict by implicitly satisfying the brother's intuitively discerned desire to be at peace. Indeed, through use of the conjunction *auch* at the beginning of the next stanza Trakl extends the conciliatory powers of this blue realm to a historical plane which, in the words *Geschlecht* and *Enkel,* recalls at least the rhetoric of Hölderlin's historical fiction if not its substance:

> *Liebend* auch *umfängt das Schweigen im Zimmer*
>   *die Schatten der Alten,*
> *Die purpurnen Martern, Klage eines grossen*
>   Geschlechts,
> *Das fromm nun hingeht im einsamen* Enkel.

> (Lovingly *too* the silence in the room surrounds the
>   shadows of the old,
> The purple martyrs, lament of a great *race,*
> That, piously, fades away in the lone *grandchild.*)

Trakl's use of such rhetoric does not end here, however. In the poem's concluding stanzas, essentially an elaboration of the all-embracing blue realm of *Abgeschiedenheit* and the benign fate of the poem's variously identified protagonist in it, Trakl goes on to characterize his fictive blue realm at least in part in terms of the Hölderlinian concepts of *Mass* and *Gesetz,* virtues that are requisite for human progress and the new millennium. In the words of the closing lines of Trakl's poem:

> *Denn strahlender immer erwacht aus schwarzen*
>   *Minuten des Wahnsinns*
> *Der Duldende an versteinerter Schwelle*
> *Und es umfängt ihn gewaltia die kühle Bläue und*
>   *die leuchtende Neige des Herbstes,*

> *Das stille Haus und die Sagen des Waldes,*
> Mass *und* Gesetz *und die mondenen Pfade der*
>   *Abgeschiedenen*

> (For everymore radiantly there awakens out of black
>   minutes of insanity
> The patient one at the petrified threshold
> And powerfully the cool blue and the radiant
>   decline of autumn surround him,

> The still house and the legends of the forest,
> *Proportion* and *law* and the moonlit paths of the
>   departed.)

It is fair to say, I think, that Trakl's use of Hölderlin's mature poetry helped him to achieve in **"Gesang des Abgeschiedenen"** a relatively unique and, in some ways, final expression of his predominantly elegiac mode of 1913 and early 1914. By the same token, it would be intriguing to discuss the first of two published versions of the much more complicated poem **"Abendland,"** which contains even more extensive signs of Hölderlin's medi-

ation, as a kind of twentieth-century analogue to the hymn "Patmos." for example. Yet my chief interest in **"Abendland"** in the present context is the poem not so much as an end in itself as in its capacity as process, not so much in several self-sufficient works as steps in the evolution of a new kind of poetry. Thus I propose to read the various stages of **"Abendland"** as a series of experiments partially on Hölderlinian forms that culminate, in however circuitous a fashion, in Trakl's darkly apocalyptic mode of mid-1914. Before proceeding, however, I would like to describe briefly the poem's somewhat complicated genesis. In retrospect the poem's first stage consists of two distinct poems, one already bearing the title **"Abendland,"** the other—which takes up such central motifs from **"Gesang des Abgeschiedenen"** as the eucharistic meal, the suffering brother, the benign otherworldly blue night, and religious patience—bearing the title **"Wanderschaft."** These poems were then integrated virtually unchanged as parts 1 and 3 into a much longer five-part poem also called **"Abendland"** that was published in the journal *Der Brenner* (this latter text is hereafter referred to as the *Brenner* version). In addition to the poem's first stage the new critical edition of Trakl's works has also brought to light a third version of the poem, which reduced the five-part *Brenner* version from 138 lines to a three-part poem consisting of only 48 lines. This version differs from the final authorized one published in Trakl's second and last book of poetry *Sebastian im Traum* only with regard to its third section, although, as we shall see, this difference is rather remarkable especially in point of Hölderlin's mediation.

At the outset it should be noted that Trakl's adaptations of his predecessor's poetry in **"Abendland"** do not fall into a consistent pattern and only a few carry over into the poetry of mid-1914. Take, for instance, Trakl's rather mechanical, primarily visual adaptation of the long strophic forms and terse lines of Hölderlin's hymns which constitute two of the three essential characteristics of his later poetry. Both the long-stanza and the short-verse form suddenly emerge full-blown in the first stage of **"Abendland,"** whose longest stanza totals fifteen lines. Yet in the *Brenner* version this same stanza is broken up, without any really noticeable difference, into two shorter stanzas. It is not until the third version of the poem, apparently written in an attempt to substitute another kind of monumentality for the one that had been lost in a deletion of ninety lines, that Trakl reinstates the long-stanza form. Another case in point is Trakl's use of Hölderlin-derived conjunctions in the poem. Though clearly not as crucial to **"Abendland,"** where they effect no more than short spurts of causality and continuity, as they were to **"Gesang des Abgeschiedenen,"** *denn* and *auch* occur conspicuously in the first and second stages of the former. One conjunction also appears in the third version and even *aber* appears once in the *Brenner* version. Yet no occurrence of either conjunction is attested in the poem's final text nor beyond that in the poetry of mid-1914.

The various stages of **"Abendland"** also reveal a variety of syntactical innovations modeled on the hyperbatic syntax of Hölderlin's mature poetry which, with one exception that I shall discuss shortly, play either a minor role or no role at all in the poetry of mid-1914. Nonetheless, as part of a process of experimentation they are clearly crucial to the evolution of Trakl's new voice. One of the more obvious examples of such syntactical innovation is Trakl's sudden use of appositions, both nominal and adjectival, as in the following example from the *Brenner* version, part 3, which also recalls a morphological aspect of Hölderlin's so-called "austere" style:

> *Gelehnt an den Hügel der Bruder*
> *Und Fremdling,*
> *Der* menschenverlassene . . .

> (Reclining on the hill the brother
> And stranger,
> The *man-forsaken one* . . .)

Other kinds of Hölderlin-inspired hyperbata in the *Brenner* version of **"Abendland"** are fewer in number but nonetheless illustrate the extent of Trakl's experimentation with his predecessor's style. Hölderlin's mediation is audible, for example, in the inverted word order of these lines from part 2 of the *Brenner* version:

> *Und es fallen der* Blüten
> Viele *über den* Felsenpfad.

> (And of *blossoms* there fall
> *Many* over the cliff path.)

These two lines recur in the final version of the poem and may well have a direct source in these lines from the opening stanza of Hölderlin's ode "Mein Eigentum":

> . . . *wenn schon der holden* Blüten
> Manche *der Erde zum Danke fielen.*

> (. . . even if, of the lovely *blossoms*
> *Many* fell to earth, for thanks.)

A somewhat more dramatic instance of hyperbatic syntax reminiscent of Hölderlin is provided by the following passage from part 5 of the *Brenner* version:

> Gross *sind die Städte aufgebaut*
> Und steinern *in der Ebene.* . . .

> (Great are the cities, built high
> And of *stone* on the plain. . . .)

The asymmetrical distribution of the attributes *gross* and *steinern* immediately brings to mind the gnomic opening of the authorized version of "Patmos":

> Nah *ist*
> Und schwer *zu fassen der Gott.*

> (Up *close,*
> That *hard* to hold fast, is God.)

While Trakl was unfamiliar with this opening, similar sentence structure occurs elsewhere in Hölderlin's mature

poetry, as, for example, in lines 92-93 of the hymn "Die Wanderung":

> Unfreundlich *ist und* schwer *zu gewinnen*
> *Die* Verschlossene . . .

> (*Unfriendly* and *hard* to win over
> Is the recluse . . .)

One final example of such syntactical asymmetry from part 3 of the *Brenner* version:

> Vieles ist ein Wachendes
> *In der sternigen Nacht*
> *Und schön die Bläue,* . . .

> (*Much is awake*
> In the starry night,
> And beautiful, the great blue, . . .)

is the more remarkable for the fact that Trakl seems to have attempted, in the phrase *"Vieles ist ein Wachendes,"* something of the enigmatic power of the well-known gnome from Hölderlin's hymn "Der Rhein"—*"Ein Rätsel ist Reinentsprungenes"* (A mystery are those of pure origin). It is doubtful whether Trakl clearly perceived Hölderlin's formulation of such gnomic truths in his hymnic poetry as a distinctive feature of the poet's high office. But it is almost certain, given the final version of **"Abendland"** and the poetry that follows it, that he fully appreciated the authoritative stance which they and related prophetic utterances in Hölderlin's mature poetry imply.

The passage just quoted is not the only instance where Trakl models the diction and imagery of **"Abendland"** after his predecessor's poetry. *"Schwerttragender Engel"* (Sword-carrying angel), for example, a line from the first stanza of the *Brenner* version of part 2, surely echoes Hölderlin's nominal epithet for Christ in "Patmos"—*"der Gewittertragende"* (the thunder-bearing one). Another passage from "Patmos." the one depicting Pentecost:

> *Darum auch sandt' er ihnen*
> *Den Geist, und freilich bebte*
> *Das Haus und die* Wetter Gottes rollten
> Ferndonnernd über
> *Die* ahnenden Häupter, *da schwersinnend*
> *Versammelt waren die Todeshelden,* . . .

> (That's why he sent them the
> Ghost, and of course, the house
> Shook and *God's thunderclouds rolled*
> *Far-rumbling over*
> Their *dawning minds,* as, heavy of heart,
> Heroes in death, they were gathered, . . .)

may well have passed through Trakl's mind as he wrote the final stanza of the *Brenner* version, part 2:

> *Anders* ahnt *die* Stirne *Vollkommenes,*
> *Die kühle, kindliche,*

Wenn über grünendem Hügel
Frühlingsgewitter ertönt.

(But the *mind,* the sober, the childlike,
Has foreknowledge of perfection differently
When *over the greening hill*
The spring thunderstorm resounds.)

It is noteworthy that Trakl's adaptation of Hölderlin's poetry tapers off sharply in his final revision of the *Brenner* version of **"Abendland"** (in the revision whose result is the shortened *"3. Fassung"*), especially if we take into account his suppression of many of the imitative innovations present in the *Brenner* version. In fact, Trakl adds only two features to the third version of the poem that recall Hölderlin. The more important of these is the compound epithet *fern verstrahlend* modeled on a kind of participial compound that is fairly widespread in Hölderlin's elegies and hymns. The Pentecostal passage from "Patmos" just quoted contains an instance of such a compound in *ferndonnernd.*

Yet, as though in counterpoint to Hölderlin's generally declining influence on the third version of **"Abendland,"** the poem's final draft contains the most dramatic instance of Hölderlin's mediation in all of **"Abendland."** It is a curiosity of literary history that the source of this mediation, the poem "Lebensalter," is not one of Hölderlin's great odes, elegies, or hymns. Along with "Hälfte des Lebens," certainly a superior work of art and the one poem most frequently cited as indicative of its author's modern sensibility, Hölderlin had salvaged "Lebensalter" from the ruins of his hymnic enterprise. Moreover, like "Hälfte des Lebens" it is easily one of Hölderlin's most pessimistic poems, though it differs from the latter thematically insofar as its rejection of the poet's usual assumptions about history is more or less explicit. For in "Lebensalter" the triadically structured historical fiction that informs Hölderlin's major poetry gives way to a dualistic one that leaves the poet stranded in the present without recourse to past or future utopias. From a secluded vantage point, the poet registers the incomprehensible but nonetheless irrevocable passing of a past civilization momentarily evoked in the poem's three opening apostrophes:

Ihr Städte des Euphrats!
Ihr Gassen am Palmyra!
Ihr Säulenwälder in der Ebne der Wüste, . . .

(You cities of Euphrates!
You streets at Palmyra!
You forests of pillars in the desert plain, . . .)

Given Trakl's fundamentally pessimistic nature, it is hardly surprising that the poem struck a responsive chord. Specifically, he adapted its three opening apostrophes, yet another type of Hölderlin's hyperbatic syntax, to fuse images and imagistic scenes from the respective conclusions of the second and third versions of **"Abendland"** and transform them, as it were, into an apocalyptic vision of the Occident, indeed of the cosmos itself. As late as the third version of **"Abendland,"** the concluding section of the poem had still dealt primarily with the fate of the individual, the outsider, the *Fremdling.* Moreover, if we briefly turn to the final lines of that version:

O Liebe, es rührt
Ein blauer Dornenbusch
Die kalte Schläfe,
Mit fallenden Sternen
Schneeige Nacht.

(O love, a blue
Bush of thorns touches
The cool temple
With falling stars,
Snowy night.)

we can discern the outlines of an enigmatic but nonetheless positive, religiously motivated resolution. But the hopeful tone, dependent on the quiet apostrophe *"O Liebe,"* which permits a positive reading of the inexplicably falling stars here, as well as the appositionally functioning "snowy night" with its benign qualities, are both decidedly absent from the conclusion of the fourth and last version of **"Abendland,"** where Trakl's three anguished and resounding, but carefully positioned apostrophes help to create the visionary terror that encompasses the outsider, civilization, nature, and the cosmos without exception:

Ihr grossen Städte
Steinern aufgebaut
In der Ebene!
So sprachlos folgt
Der Heimatlose
Mit dunkler Stirne dem Wind,
Kahlen Bäumen am Hügel
Ihr weithin dämmernden Ströme!
Gewaltig ängstet
Schaurige Abendröte
Im Sturmgewölk
Ihr sterbenden Völker!
Bleiche Woge
Zerschellend am Strande der Nacht,
Fallende Sterne.

(You great cities
Built of stone
On the plain!
So speechlessly
Does the homeless one
With dark brow follow the wind,
Bare trees on the hilltop.
You streams glimmering far-off!
Powerfully, rain-promising
Red dusk bodes fear
In a roll of stormclouds.
You dying peoples!
Pale wave
Shattering on the night beach,
Falling stars.)

One cannot help feeling at times that the most appropriate voice in which to recite this conclusion of the final version of **"Abendland"** and the related poetry of mid-1914 is a piercing scream. For what Trakl employs, and employs effectively, to integrate the three adapted structural elements that mark these poems—the monumental stanza; the terse dithyrambic line, which exposes each word to special emphasis; the bold, expansive apostrophes—is a certain shrillness of tone without parallel in the German lyric tradition. Such a tone of course is largely a reflection of the profound personal and cultural pessimism that finds expression in these poems and still informs the final war poems **"Klage"** and **"Grodek"** that Trakl wrote in the last months preceding his death in November 1914. Yet one should not underestimate the role that Hölderlin's poetry, especially the poem "Lebensalter," played in the evolution of Trakl's new-found public voice and the emergence of correlative concerns.

It is hardly surprising, then, that Trakl should attempt, in the poem **"Der Abend,"** one of the more subdued examples of his new apocalyptic mode, what seems to be an oblique but nonetheless deliberately conceived analogue to Hölderlin's poem "Lebensalter." As does his predecessor in "Lebensalter," Trakl addresses the poem's two apostrophes not to contemporary humanity, although his words are also clearly meant for its ears, but to vestiges of a past order of things and to the moon which serves the poet as a vehicle for the resurrection of this order. Indeed, Trakl takes up almost half of the one-stanza, seventeen-line poem to locate these spectral remnants of more viable pasts, and thus the potential agents of historical change in the present, in a fairly rugged natural terrain safely outside the decadent center of civilization. In terms of the poem's thematic concerns it is important to note that the generic figures that constitute these vestiges, the dead heroes and embracing lovers, play a crucial role in joining Hölderlin's past and future worlds. In the poem's middle section the regenerative forces inherent in these embodiments of past glory are represented in the form of a blue light mysteriously radiating toward a modern urban wasteland, the city, where present decadence, embodied in the *"verwesend Geschlecht,"* is perpetuating itself and thus preparing an ominous future for its innocent progeny. The rhetoric of Hölderlin's historical fiction is in part again recalled in these words of **"Der Abend"**:

So bläulich erstrahlt es
Gegen die Stadt hin,
Wo kalt und böse
Ein verwesend Geschlecht wohnt,
Der weissen Enkel
Dunkle Zukunft bereitet.

(Thus, bluish, it radiates away
In the direction of the city,
Where, cold and evil,
There dwells a decaying *race* of men,
One preparing
For white *grandchildren*
A dark future.)

The implicit upshot of this oblique interplay of opposing epochs is the absolute decline of vanished pasts as a viable force in reshaping the here and now. At least I, for one,

find little comfort or hope for change manifest in Trakl's sudden apostrophic transference of his now grieving vestiges of past glory to the pristine refuge of a remote mountain lake, as expressed in these concluding lines:

Ihr mondverschlungnen Schatten
Aufseufzend im leeren Kristall
Des Bergsees

(You shades swallowed up by moonlight
Heaving a sigh in the empty crystal
Of the mountain lake.)

Indeed, Hölderlin's own final statement in "Lebensalter":

    . . . fremd
Erscheinen und gestorben mir
Der Seligen Geister.

       (. . . strange
To me, remote and dead seem
The souls of the blessed.)

seems a good deal less wrenching by comparison.

What has emerged in the preceding discussion is, I hope, a clear sense of the selective nature of Trakl's interest in Hölderlin. Unlike a poet such as Josef Weinheber, who wrote chauvinistic odes in the Hölderlinian manner, Trakl made no attempt to assimilate all of Hölderlin to his purposes. Instead, he contented himself with experimental adaptations of Hölderlin's elevated style which were readily discarded once they had served their initial purpose lest they become unintegrated mannerisms. This is not to say, of course, that his experimentation lacked a larger aim. Especially in the case of **"Abendland"** Trakl seems to have been groping with the aid of Hölderlin's poetry toward a more monumental and expansive mode of expression that would better accommodate the increasing urgency of personal and public concerns. Nor should Trakl's experimentation imply an absence of felt existential affinities, however reductive his perception of Hölderlin may have been. Indeed the reductive nature of this perception, in so far as it can be reconstructed from the only evidence at our disposal, namely Trakl's poetry, should throw some light on the theme of this conference. Above all I would guess that Trakl saw in his predecessor a paradigm of the poet apart, the poet as outsider, which, as M. H. Abrams has observed in his recent essay "Coleridge, Baudelaire and Modernist Poetics," is one of the fundamental assumptions of literary modernism. And though Hölderlin shared with a generation of European romantics a fundamentally different view of the poet and his function, most of his life and some aspects of his oeuvre, when read out of context, corroborate Trakl's assessment.

Martin Anderle (essay date 1978)

SOURCE: "Georg Trakl: The Emergence of His Expressionist Idiom," in *Review of National Literatures: Ger-*

man *Expressionism,* Griffon House Publications, Vol. 9, 1978, pp. 70-75.

[In the following excerpt, Trakl's brief body of work is examined by way of his problematic metaphors, the absence of the poetic self, and his poetic vision.]

Georg Trakl . . . is considered by many to be the foremost poet of the German Expressionist movement, even though he was not given the time to develop into a figure of public acclaim or controversy as was the case with some other Expressionists, notably Bertolt Brecht and Gottfried Benn. The First World War put an end to the life and work of a number of young German poets, Trakl among them. The announcement of death issued by Trakl's family carries the formula "died for the fatherland," an evasive phrase which disguises a tragedy that resulted from a terrible inner necessity. Trakl, like the Expressionist movement itself, had rebelled against middleclass respectability and an existing world which for him was the Bourgeois society and its system of values. Like Nietzsche before them, the young poets of Expressionism attacked the generally accepted opinion that life and reality were rational and manageable. They did not always engage in publicly visible protest but tended rather to disregard accepted reality in their emphasis on the inner life, an attitude adopted by Rilke, Hofmannsthal, and the Neoromanticists before them.

With Trakl, we find both violence and suffering and the yearning for purity and compassion. These extemes are inextricably entwined in his poetic world. The words and images of his poetry are no longer subordinated to reality; they are not instruments used to describe what is, but are rather expressions willed by a subject. The poet claims the right to imprint a new order on the world, to present reality as it exists for him. To this end, he makes use of language which names the "true" nature of things instead of following existing opinions and descriptions. Strong expressive words—adjectives, verbs, images—are the chief instruments of this poetic art.

Trakl carried inside himself tensions which were nourished by his experiences and the course which his life took. He was born into a normal middle-class environment, and lived in places which are generally called "beautiful": Salzburg, Innsbruck, Vienna. The natural settings of these cities are known for their charm. However, if one wants, one can see ugliness. There are slaughterhouses, rats, and cripples, even in Austrian Baroque cities, with their churches, palaces, beautiful squares, and statues. The surrounding landscape, too, is not without the suffering and dying of animals and unhappy people. Even the paintings and statues in country churches and roadside shrines show martyrdom and death. To walk through this kind of landscape—Trakl was an indefatigable walker—and to see its contrasts after one's outlook has been influenced through the reading of Dostoevsky and the Naturalists—as Trakl's was—is enough to arouse in a sensitive youth the compulsion to express his perception of life, to make a truth known.

1 *Trakl's Life*

To be sure, Trakl's life—so full of deviations from the average, after a certain point—has attracted almost as much attention as his poetry. Young Trakl had to leave school after failing in major subjects; he had sought the company of local poets, used drugs and drunk heavily; he could often be found in brothels, could not pursue a career, formed a strong emotional attachment to his sister, who took her own life in 1917—three years after Trakl himself had died, of cocaine poisoning, in the first year of World War I. All of this is in sharp contrast to what could be expected from a young man born into his circumstances. Georg Trakl was one of six children of a well-to-do Salzburg merchant who saw to it that his children received a solid education. The family was Protestant in a heavily Catholic town. Young Trakl must also have noticed the deep Catholic religiousness of his mother who had only become Protestant for formal reasons. The youth was a rather somber person, who withdrew to his writing, and visibly emulated the life of some of Dostoevsky's characters as well as that of the French poètes maudits. Trakl became a pharmacist, probably because the completion of a three-year apprenticeship (1905-1908) would admit him to the University even without a high school diploma. After studying pharmacy at the University of Vienna (1908-1910), he completed one year of army service. In the three remaining years of his life, he made several attempts to work as a civil servant, but soon left the positions offered to him, in one case after only two hours. He even rejoined the army in 1912, and worked in an army hospital in Innsbruck, but left that, too, after six months. This stay in Innsbruck, however, brought him into contact with Ludwig von Ficker, the editor of the literary magazine *Der Brenner,* who was to become a close friend and ardent supporter. Many of Trakl's poems were first published in *Der Brenner* (named after the mountain pass in the Tyrol). The first book of Trakl's poetry (**Gedichte**) was published by the Kurt Wolff Verlag in Leipzig in July of 1913. The publication of the second completed book manuscript, **Sebastian im Traum,** was delayed till 1915 by the outbreak of the war. At the beginning of September, 1914, the army unit that Trakl was attached to moved into Poland. After the battle of Grodek (September 6-11), Trakl had to take care of 90 severely wounded soldiers without being able to help them. He tried to shoot himself in an attack of depression, but was disarmed by fellow officers. Some time later (October 10), he was ordered to check into the mental ward of the Cracow military hospital for observation. He died there on November 3, 1914. The cause, as already noted, was cocaine poisoning. It is not known if he intended to commit suicide; he had used drugs excessively before, sometimes with dangerous effects.

Trakl's early death seems to have been predestined. In his letters to friends, he speaks so openly about his excessive drinking and his drug mishaps that at first one suspects self-dramatization, an emulation of Verlaine, for example. One could interpret a pessimistic remark like the following as a misanthropic outburst: "I long for the day when my soul will neither wish nor be able to live in this miserable body infected with melancholy, when it will leave this monstrosity of feces and putrefaction which is only an all-too-faithful mirror image of a godless, cursed age." (Letter to L. v. Ficker, June 26, 1913.) One would wish to attribute this language to artistic exaggeration and generalization. After all, Trakl was known and appreciated as a poet by such outstanding artists as Oskar Kokoschka, Karl Kraus, Else Lasker-Schüler, Adolf Loos. In hindsight, we have to acknowledge the sincerity of his pessimistic remarks: "Yes, dear friend, in a few days my life has been unspeakably destroyed, and all that remains is silent pain that denies itself even bitterness . . . Perhaps, you could write me a few words; I don't know where to turn to any more. It's an inexpressible misfortune when the world breaks apart. O my God, what judgement has been visited upon me! Tell me that I must have the strength to live and to express the truth. Tell me that I am not insane. A stone-like darkness has fallen upon me. O my friend, how small and unhappy I have become!" (From a letter to L. v. Ficker, from the end of November 1913).

Reinhold Grimm has demonstrated that from 1908 or 1909 on, Trakl's writing was deeply influenced by the work of Arthur Rimbaud (1854-1891):

> Trakl received a decisive, indeed *the* decisive influence from Rimbaud, which was conveyed by way of [Karl] Klammer [whose translation of Rimbaud had been published in 1907]. In his work, one can find verbatim transplants of almost entire verses and sentences, far-reaching correspondence in the vocabulary, particularly in the area of the ugly and disgusting, and finally borrowing of syntactic peculiarities and of word formation; in addition, the choice of titles and names points to identical traits. . . . Above all, Rimbaud's audacious, new, and capricious metaphors and motifs, frequently cast into reiterable formulas and including the most distant analogies and allusions, have marked Trakl's poetry unmistakably. There can be no doubt that behind a directly recognizable influence of such intensity there must be an even stronger indirect one.

We must conclude that Trakl's idiom has passed through the medium of another poet's language. Consequently, Trakl's style must be the result of a conscious artistic effort. An exploration of the actual creative process documented in the preliminary versions of many poems leads us to the same conclusions. The poems, especially the images, are the result of meticulous work and reflect a poetic method. Trakl never expresses abstractly formulated thoughts or ideas. His verse, the melody of his language, and his metaphors carry the burden of expressing the world as he sees it. For him, this is The Truth.

But it is the truth of a young man who has already characterized himself as "a stranger on earth." Trakl's visions— the truth of a pure being destroyed by inner and outer torment—expressed themselves in a poetry which became, in its totality, a symbol of life itself. There are scenes of magic beauty:

> From the courtyard gently the violin sounds.
> Today they press the brown wine.

> Vom Hof tönt sanft die Geige her.
> Heut keltern sie den braunen Wein.

And still, a poem which dwells on such idyllic scenes ends with the verses:

> Wide open are the charnel houses
> And beautifully painted by sunshine.

> Weit offen die Totenkammern sind
> Und schön bemalt von Sonnenschein.

There is a resigned innocence in this juxtaposition of beauty and death. It is expanded into images of ugliness and despair that stand in contrast both to their beautiful language and to metaphysical hope:

> God's brow dreams colors,
> Feels the soft wings of madness.
> Shadows are turning on the hill
> Seamed by black decay.

> Stirne Gottes Farben träumt,
> Spürt des Wahnsinns sanfte Flügel.
> Schatten drehen sich am Hügel
> Von Verwesung schwarz umsäumt.

The ugliness of Naturalism has been joined by inner chaos, and doom accompanied by terror becomes the universal principle. However innocent he may be, man cannot escape it. The figure of **"Elis,"** one of the many that stand for man himself, is conceived as an individual beginning his life in a state of innocence:

> Perfect is the stillness of this golden day.
> Under old oak trees
> You appear, Elis, resting, with round eyes.

> Vollkommen ist die Stille dieses goldenen Tags.
> Unter alten Eichen
> Erscheinst du, Elis ein Ruhender mit runden Augen.

But at the end of the poem, Elis' demise is almost complete; there is no choice in this world of death:

> Blue doves
> At night drink the icy sweat
> That flows from Elis' crystal brow.

> On black walls
> Always God's lonely wind sounds.

> Blaue Tauben
> Trinken nachts den eisigen Schweiss,
> Der Von Elis' kristallener Stirne rinnt.

> Immer tönt
> An schwarzen Mauern Gottes einsamer Wind.

The last example in particular shows how this poetry uses images which have nothing to do with common experience. It may already be clear that Trakl's poetry, as far as its imagery is concerned, consists of an arrangement of metaphors. There is no reality beyond these metaphors, there is not even mention of a perceiving poetic self. Their commanding influence shows itself in the juxtaposition of phenomena that would not be close to each other in the world of reality, especially in the use of color. . . .

2 *The Problem of Trakl's Metaphors*

Many books and articles have been written on the metaphor in Trakl's work. Every scholar has had to face the problem of finding a definition for this peculiar imagery, in which the traditional characteristics of the metaphor as a transformation of a familiar word into a new content are no longer applicable. The duality of the metaphor, accepted even before Aristotle, presupposes, of course, a philosophical system of dualism. It is based on the assumption that a generally known reality is interpreted or even embellished through intuition, the intellect, or the rhetoric of a poet, and thus made more meaningful. Some are affected more than others by the poet's word and accept his interpretation of reality. Poetry becomes ultimately a historic metaphor as a whole, while reality is considered to be different and "normal." The poet, however, sees in reality a problem, the solution of which will be found at the end of his struggle with the disparate elements. Then thought and thing will be one, and the word will stand for everything that there is. It takes a poet of the prophetic kind, like Trakl, to cast his views in a convincing language. If poetry is truth, then the metaphor ceases to be metaphor. The transformation of outer reality has been accomplished, and the image is related only to other images with which it forms a world of their own. The context, therefore, provides the individual image with its content, uniqueness, and value, and the individual metaphor, in turn, becomes an indispensable part of the poetic system.

What we called metaphor in the introduction to this essay and what we will continue to call metaphor is therefore no longer *meta-pherein;* it is not a process of transforming one into another, neither isit a reference to a step from reality into poetry, but it is rather the end result of a transformation. The predicament in which critics of Trakl find themselves originates in the need to find a proper term for Trakl's kind of image. Heselhaus speaks of "metaphor," Killy of "chiffre," Schier of "metaphor" and "figura." The selection of a proper term becomes less important if one comes to an understanding about the function of the metaphor within Trakl's poetry. A theoretical approach laid down in a book by Cornelius Stutterheim can be of help. He discusses a definition of the metaphor as a word that aims at a reality of which man has at best only an inadequate conception, or as a word that does not mean any reality at all. The poet attempts to make this unknown known by incorporating it intuitively into his images. It is indeed the raison d'être of the metaphor to express something that is unknown or not yet known and to make it part of the poet's world. In this manner, the dualism can be abolished and the only truth, the poetic word, remains. The poet will have accomplished his task. The theoretician, however, must also deal with

the non-poetic world. He must follow the creative process, he must investigate the disturbing outside world that the poet has striven to recast in his language.

A most valuable recent contribution to the problem of Trakl's metaphor is Paul D. Schier's book on the language of George Trakl. Schier sets out to accomplish for Trakl what some philosophers of language have been trying to do in recent years: to overcome the dualism in the poetic image. Schier wants to show that the classical, dualistic approach which prevailed in German literature up to the end of the 19th century and which permeated the thinking of scholars even later is inadequate for an understanding of Trakl and of modern poetry in general. After a survey of the theories of Fritz Mauthner, Wilhelm Wundt, Emil Winkler, Hermann Pongs, and others, Schier recognizes in Erich Auerbach's theory the key to Trakl's imagery. Auerbach presents the concept of *figura,* which means that a proven spiritual value can be transferred onto a newly introduced poetic form. This creative device originates in the Biblical exegesis of the early Christian era when, for instance, prophecies of the Old Testament were interpreted as being realized in the New Testament, or when values relating to Moses were transferred to the figure of Christ. This procedure, originally used only in religious literature, was then incorporated in the technique of secular writing: for example, Dante's Virgil, as *figura,* represents also the historic Virgil, Dante himself as a poet, as well as the idealization of any leader or prophet. (A similar transformation of one established *figura* into various other poetic forms will be found in Trakl's writing.) Auerbach compares his principle of *figura* with the traditional *symbol* which for him is the immediate and direct interpretation of life and nature. Schier accepts the existence of a "symbol," although, in connection with Trakl, he prefers the term "metaphor." He sums up: "While the language of metaphor draws its significance from the object in nature, the language of *figura* derives its significance from the 'flaming word of God': the expressive power of these words is not based on the significance of natural objects but on the conviction of an eternal, divine order." This concept, applied to Trakl's poetry, seems to require two kinds of images. However, the continuous flow of images, the constant injection of spiritual insight into nature images has the effect of creating one kind of world and therefore one kind of metaphor. It is not necessary to find a name for this image or metaphor, as so many Trakl scholars have tried to do. Every phenomenon perceived supports the poet's personal philosophy. Each and every object in nature thus becomes in poetry a *figura,* the receiver of whatever eternal pain is imposed on all things in existence. If the world were one permeated by God's grace, the relationship between the spirit and the object would be the same. The important thing is that there is a spirit in the object.

3 *Trakl's Poetic Vision*

Trakl's poetry has become popular because it offers, in its entirety, a condensed philosophy, an interpretation of life as seen by a lonely, increasingly desperate man. Let us now examine two of Trakl's poems in order to understand his intentions and his technique. In early 1913, Trakl finished **"Nearness of Death,"** (**"Nähe des Todes"** [2nd Variant]), given here in the translation of Michael Hamburger.

> O the evening deep in the sombre hamlets of
>   childhood.
> The pond beneath the willows
> Fills with the tainted sighs of sadness.
>
> O the wood which softly lowers its brown eyes,
> When from the solitary's bony hands
> The purple of his enraptured days ebbs down.
>
> O the nearness of death. Let us pray.
> This night the delicate limbs of lovers
> Yellow with incense on warm pillows untwine.
>
> O der Abend, der in die finsteren Dörfer der
>   Kindheit geht.
> Der Weiher unter den Weiden
> Füllt sich mit den verpesteten Seufzern der
>   Schwermut.
>
> O der Wald, der leise die braunen Augen senkt,
> Da aus des Einsamen knöchernen Händen
> Der Purpur seiner verzückten Tage hinsinkt.
>
> O die Nähe des Todes. Lass uns beten.
> In dieser Nacht lösen auf lauen Kissen
> Vergilbt von Weihrauch sich der Liebenden
>   schmächtige Glieder.

Personification, so frequent in Trakl's poetry, furnishes an element of the spiritual and animated that is of importance, since a visible lyrical self is missing. Not only elements of nature, evening (not so evident in translation), and wood, are personified, but also the abstract word "sadness." The abstract easily blends into the image to which it is spiritually related. The very title of the poem establishes the presence of doom. It was in the evenings and in the hamlets of childhood, it is in the willow trees and ponds, it is now with the lovers whose limbs are untwining, weak and yellowed like the old ivory of the statues of saints. The optical impression of evening and darkness is accompanied by color observations. As Walther Killy has observed quite correctly, one must avoid attaching a specific meaning to a color metaphor. It is an outstanding element in Trakl's language, one which every investigation has to take into account. It would be a mistake, however, to approach it from a psychological standpoint. The "brown eyes" of this poem evoke rather the unknown mentioned by Stutterheim. One must not try to guess what could be brown in the forest. Attempting to do so means using an inappropriate theory of metaphor. This brown color is a *figura* which could represent any number of things meaningful to Trakl, something gentle and dark, a memory of a pair of eyes, and much more that can only be sensed. And these associations exist even if Trakl had chosen the word "braun" only because it forms a harmonious sound together with "Augen." Another color in the poem, purple, indicates a contrast of joy to this

indulgence in death. Purple is generally taken for a color of the sublime, beauty, satisfaction, the joyful, without having one specific meaning. Here the purple color fades away and the pale color of bone remains. It is joined by the yellow of weakness and decay. The poem **"Nearness of Death"** is the second of the three **"Rosary Songs,"** where it is preceded by **"To my Sister"** and followed by **"Amen."** The sequence speaks for itself; the celebration of the sister's delicate nature fades into decay and the final word of a prayer. At the same time, we see life as a religious process, a religion of sadness, to be sure, but not without the consolation that, in any event, all experiences point to unavoidable doom.

4 *Poetic Self and Metaphor*

Trakl's device of not relating the events in a poem to an actual poetic self but to a number of representative figures makes it easy to widen personal experience to an universal view. The human beings in the poems become humanity itself. Probably in December of 1913, Trakl completed **"Western Song"** (**"Abendländisches Lied"**), which follows here in the translation of Christopher Middleton:

> O the soul's nocturnal wingbeat:
> Shepherds we walked by dusky forests once
> And the red deer followed, the green flower and
>   babbling stream,
> Humbly. O the ancient sound of the cricket,
> Blood flowering on the sacrificial slab
> And the lonely birdcry over the pond's green calm.
>
> O you crusades and glowing tortures
> Of the flesh, descent of the crimson fruits
> In the garden at evening where long ago the pious
>   disciples walked,
> People now of war, from wounds and star-dreams
>   waking.
> O the gentle cornflower sheaf of night.
>
> O you times of quietness and golden autumns
> When peaceful monks we trod the purple grape;
> And hill and forest shone around us.
> O you hunts and castles; peace at evening,
> When in his room man meditated justice,
> Wrestled in dumb prayer for the living head of
>   God.
>
> O the bitter hour of decline,
> When we regard a stony face in black waters.
> But radiant the lovers raise their silver eyelids:
> One kin. From rosy pillows incense pours
> And the sweet canticle of the bodies resurrected.
>
> O der Seele nächtlicher Flügelschlag:
> Hirten gingen wir einst an dämmernden Wäldern
>   hin
> Und es folgte das rote Wild, die grüne Blume und
>   der
>   lallende Quell
> Demutsvoll. O, der uralte Ton des Heimchens,

Blut blühend am Opferstein
Und der Schrei des einsamen Vogels über der
   grünen
     Stille des Teichs.

O, ihr Kreuzzüge und glühenden Martern
Des Fleisches, Fallen purpurner Früchte
Im Abendgarten, wo vor Zeiten die frommen Jünger
   gegangen,
Kriegsleute nun, erwachend aus Wunden und
   Sternenträumen.
O, das sanfte Zyanenbündel der Nacht.

O, ihr Zeiten der Stille und goldener Herbste,
Da wir friedliche Mönche die purpurne Traube
   gekelxert;
Und rings erglänzten Hügel und Wald.
O, ihr Jagden und Schlösser; Ruh des Abends,
Da in seiner Kammer der Mensch Gerechtes sann,
In stummem Gebet um Gottes lebendiges Haupt
   rang.

O, die bittere Stunde des Untergangs,
Da wir ein steinernes Antlitz in schwarzen Wassern
   beschaun.
Aber strahlend heben die silbernen Lider die
   Liebenden:
Ein Geschlecht. Weihrauch strömt von rosigen
   Kissen
Und der süsse Gesang der Auferstandenen.

The poem evokes the myth of man's innocent beginnings, when humans, animals, and plants were joined together in one Orphic embrace. The shedding of blood, the loneliness, however, are almost as old, and in one of the holiest periods, the Middle Ages, the ardent belief of so many drowns in torture and blood. While other poems show clearly the influence of the Bible, Hölderlin, Rimbaud, etc., **"Western Song"** reveals Trakl's kinship with the German Romantic poet and philosopher Novalis. In his novel *Heinrich von Ofterdingen* (1802), the crusades are of some significance. Their spiritual meaning, however, exceeds their violent aspects. Towards the end of Novalis' fragmentary novel, the girl Cyane offers guidance and comfort to the poet Heinrich. Her name is alluded to in the image "Zyanenbündel der Nacht," the "cornflower sheaf of night" in Middleton's translation. The blue of the cornflower, a repeated image in Trakl's work, serves as a soothing contrast to the earlier violence. Seriousness and humility continue in the efforts of thinkers, rulers and churchmen, in the cultivation of the earth. But was not this effort in vain? Did not the "bitter hour of decline" come over us, as we see nothing but defeat in our stony faces reflected in black waters? Trakl answers with a note of transcendental hope which he again bases on Novalis, this time on his "Hymns to the Night" (1800). In part 7 of the "Hymns," Novalis writes:

Once everything will be body
One body
The blessed pair
Float in celestial blood.

Einst ist alles Leib
Ein Leib
In himmlischem Blute
Schwimmt das selige Paar.

This yearning for a union that can be achieved only in death could be accepted by Trakl. He even imitates the typographical form of Novalis' poem in one significant instance: by likewise having the word "Ein" (of the German "*Ein* Geschlecht," i.e. "One kin" in the English rendering) printed in italics. The German word "Geschlecht" may refer to mankind, also to sex, generation, kin, family. There may be, indeed, very likely is, an allusion to Trakl's sister Grete, who shared his artistic inclinations and was, like her brother, given to depressions. She was the person closest to him and, like him, unable to reconcile her art (she was a pianist) with the demands of a middle-class life. Novalis' characters do not experience much tragedy; the certainty of immortality helps them overcome life's difficulties. Life *and* death for them are spent in a state of joy. For Trakl, all mankind experiences real and visible suffering; redemption comes to us in the moment of the most ardent pain. Love means becoming one, not only with one other person, but ultimately with God. He is the suffering, the death, and the resurrection. He is always present, even in the garish burial ceremonies with pink colors and incense, and he has long ago marked the innocence and the glory of the shepherds, the warriors, the monks and the thinkers.

In his mature work, Trakl almost never uses the personal pronoun "I." One reason for this might be that modern poetry had turned away from the subjective sensual experience of Realism and Naturalism. Still, many Expressionists speak in the first person, and very emphatically so. The main reason, however, is that even the self becomes an image. The poetic self is manifest in the figures of the stranger, the lonely one, the holy brother, etc. The identification with the insane Hölderlin is very strong. Whenever Trakl says "We" or "He" or "You," the self is included. The personified abstractions contain part of the poetic self, too. The anthropomorphic forms are in turn part of the system of images. The Oneness that Trakl experiences in man's decline embraces both man and object. Thus, every object mentioned in this poetry, that is to say, every metaphor, contains something of the self's essence. It is significant that two of the greatest German poets of the middle of the 20th century, Johannes Bobrowski (1917-1965) and Paul Celan (1920-1970), whose early work was visibly influenced by Trakl, hide the self behind frequent and powerful metaphors. A language rich in images becomes an objective system. The values expressed in its images want to be preserved for eternity. This is the poet's intention. The reader attempts to fathom their meaning and may very well find in them a world suitable for himself.

5 The Critical Edition

Scores of books, articles, and dissertations, had been written on Trakl before all the materials partaining to his work and personality could be presented in the critical edition of 1969. Walther Killy and Hans Szklenar had used Friedrich Beissner's Hölderlin edition as their model. This publication, and a *Concordance* by Heinz Wetzel in 1971, made it possible for the first time to base research on authentic texts, to use all available variants of the poems, and to become acquainted with a vast amount of information regarding Trakl and his work. In its first volume the edition presents the **Gedichte (Poems)** of 1912, **Sebastian im Traum** (**Sebastian in a Dream**) of 1915, the publications in *Der Brenner* of 1914/15, other publications during the poet's lifetime, as well as Trakl's letters and his literary remains. The second volume of the two-volume edition contains in 577 pages the actual scholarly apparatus, and in addition valuable documents, the letters addressed to Georg Trakl, a chronology, and a very useful index. This edition is especially helpful in the investigation of metaphors. The comparison of the outlines and various versions of a poem makes it possible to understand the creative process. Images are noted down quite independent of a poem, then incorporated into a few verses, moved from sketch to sketch, tried in different places within a poem, transferred to another poem until they find their ultimate place. Great skill and a strong will for perfection are at work in these structures, which, to the superficial reader, seem to consist mainly of sound and color. Youthful attempts and earlier versions clearly show a lack of perfection and strike a discordant note in the reader. In a letter to an acquaintance, Trakl called it hard work "to make verses by the sweat of one's brow." More seriously, he spells out the force that drove him in a letter to his friend, Erhart Buschbeck: "You may believe that I will never find it easy to surrender to the subject to be formulated, and I will have to correct myself again and again to give Truth what she deserves." His life and his work were in the service of truth, which meant to him total penetration of what he knew as reality, and the recording of its terrifying laws.

Patrick Bridgwater   (essay date 1985)

SOURCE: "Georg Trakl," in *The German Poets of the First World War*. Croom Helm, 1985, pp. 19-37, 168-70.

[*The following excerpt analyzes Trakl's work from its perspective on war, highlighting its Kafkaesque images and techniques while citing "Kafka's verdict, that Trakl had too much imagination. . . . [and] the imagination which drove him out of his mind also made him a superb poet."*]

Georg Trakl was the most considerable Austrian poet to see active service in 1914-18. The war, when it finally came, must have seemed a mere extension of his inner world, for he lived in a haunting and at times terrifying world of Spenglerian visions, a 'proving-ground for world-destruction' (Karl Kraus) if ever there was one. He raged not against the dying of the light, but against its relentlessness, praying in vain to be able to forget his visions. In his poetry the 'infernal chaos of rhythms and images' of his life is transmuted into a series of visionary pictures of the chaos of the degenerate modern world. His poetic

world is stigmatised by a loss of essence and substantially; his deepest and most traumatic experience was that of things falling apart. What he called his 'criminal melancholy' derives from his vision of a world (of which the Habsburg monarchy was the outward sign) that lacks the spiritual strength to ensure its own survival; modern materialism filled him with as much loathing as it did Kafka; he would have approved Kafka's definition of materiality as the evil in the spiritual world. Kafka and Trakl alike sought to affirm their belief in a spiritual order of things; too many critics have seen their work as negative because they, the critics in question, have been unable to see beyond the material order which both writers negate. When Trakl wrote to Erhard Buschbeck in autumn 1911 that he aimed to give to truth what belongs to truth, he could have been speaking for Kafka as well; with both writers the poetic purity of their work stems from an obsession with truth. Trakl's definition of his poetry as an imperfect atonement shows that he shared, too, Kafka's view of the writer as the scapegoat of mankind. When Kafka told Janouch in 1921 that the terrible thing about war was that the animal in man runs riot and stifles everything spiritual, he was expressing a view which Trakl would have shared; indeed, Trakl saw the destruction of man as a spiritual being as characteristic of his time in general. Kafka saw the war as unleashing evil (to Janouch he described war as a flood of evil which had burst open the flood-gates of chaos), while Trakl saw it as a consequence of evil; in effect both saw the war as the bursting of a festering sore not just on the body politic, but on the 'crimson body of man'. Trakl's poetry no less than Kafka's prose-poetry is a form of prayer; but his war poems are prayer-like in a different sense from most front-line poetry in that he prays not that he may himself be spared, but that mankind may not be destroyed.

As poet of war Trakl stands apart from the tub-thumping *Kriegslyrik* of August 1914; the two poems that he wrote at the front are, rather, 'poems from the field of slaughter' in much the same sense as the poems of the anti-war anthology (*1914-16, Eine Anthologie*) published by *Die Aktion*. He has nothing whatsoever in common with the poeticisers of war. What sets him apart is not just the total absence of chauvinism and rhetoric, but the fact that war is a central, pre-existent part of his whole vision, the embodiment of the decline which has been his subject for some years; it is this fact which gives his poems about war an objectivity, perspective and depth that few, if any, other German-language poems of the First World War possess.

There are relatively few German-language poets of the First World War in whose work real depth of understanding is combined with real poetic quality. Georg Trakl is certainly one of them, for, despite the fact that he wrote only five poems that can be accounted war poems in one sense or another ("**Menschheit**", a prophetic vision of war comparable to Georg Heym's "Der Krieg"; a related poem, "**Trompeten**"; "**Im Osten**," a poem of foreboding written shortly before leaving for the Eastern Front; and, most important, "**Klage [II]**" and "**Grodek**", his only actual front-line poems), his originality and poetic power are such that these few poems make him one of the outstanding German-language poets of the war. It may be partly because he wrote so little that anthologists of war poetry have reacted erratically to Trakl, but it may equally well be because he wrote poems while most other poets were producing prepoetic or subpoetic statements in which the facts are left in the raw instead of being developed into another, antonomous shape. Be this as it may, he presumably owed the inclusion of **"Grodek"** in Ernst Volkmann's nationalistic anthology *Deutsche Dichtung im Weltkrieg* (1934) to the Wagnerian motif; but his omission from Rene Schickele's anthology *Menschliche Gedichte im Kriege* (1918) is inexcusable, for no poet of the war was more deeply concerned with the fate of humanity than Georg Trakl.

In a general sense all Trakl's work is relevant to his war poems, for he was obsessed by death and by a vision of disintegration, of which the war is but the summation. It is possible to separate **"Klage II"** and **"Grodek"** from **"Der Abend"** and **"Das Gewitter"** (written only weeks earlier, but before the outbreak of war) only in a very literal and arbitrary way; no interpretation of the former poems is complete if it ignores the two latter poems. But neither can any discussion of Trakl's 'war poems' ignore the two further poems whose pre-Spenglerian theme is the decline of the West: **"Abendländisches Lied"** and **"Abendland"**. Ultimately all his poems are variations on a single unwritten and unwritable poem; his imagery is not only serial, but agglomerative and indeed circular. Whereas Rilke would, I think, have done better to refuse to leave his inner world, what made Trakl into a superb war poet was the fact that he did not need to leave his inner world in order to write about war. His visionary mode has no parallel, unless it be in the work of Georg Heym.

As Trakl will have known, the most striking single poem about war by a member of his generation is Georg Heym's visionary and prophetic "Der Krieg" ("War").

Aufgestanden ist er, welcher lange schlief,
Aufgestanden unten aus Gewölben tief.
In der Dämmrung sheht er, gross und unerkannt,
Und den Mond zerdrückt er in der schwarzen Hand.

In den Abendlärm der Städte fällt es weit,
Frost und Schatten einer fremden Dunkelheit.
Und der Märkte runder Wirbel stockt zu Eis.
Es wird still. Sie sehn sich um. Und keiner weiss.

In den Gassen fasst es ihre Schulter leicht.
Eine Frage. Keine Antwort. Ein Gesicht erbleicht.
In der Ferne zittert ein Geläute dünn,
Und die Bärte zittern um ihr spitzes Kinn.

Auf den Bergen hebt er schon zu tanzen an,
Und er schreit: ihr Krieger alle, auf und an!
Und es schallet, wenn das schwarze Haupt er
        schwenkt,
Drum von tausend Schädeln laute Kette hängt.

Einem Turm gleich tritt er aus die letzte Glut,
Wo der Tag flieht, sind die Ströme schon voll Blut.

Zahllos sind die Leichen schon im Schilf gestreckt,
Von des Todes starken Vögeln weiss bedeckt.

In die Nacht er jagt das Feuer querfeldein,
Einen roten Hund mit wilder Mäuler Schrein.
Aus dem Dunkel springt der Nächte schwarze Welt,
Von Vulkanen furchtbar ist ihr Rand erhellt.

Und mit tausend hohen Zipfelmützen weit
Sind die finstren Ebnen flackend überstreut,
Und was unten auf den Strassen wimmelnd flieht,
Stösst er in die Feuerwälder, wo die Flamme
        brausend zieht.

Und die Flammen fressen brennend Wald um Wald,
Gelbe Fledermäuse, zackig in das Laub gekrallt,
Seine Stange haut er wie ein Köhlerknecht
In die Bäume, dass das Feuer brause recht.

Eine grosse Stadt versank in gelbem Rauch,
Warf sich lautlos in des Abgrunds Bauch.
Aber riesig über glühnden Trümmern steht,
Der in wilde Himmel dreimal seine Fackel dreht

Über sturmzerfetzter Wolken Widerschein,
In des toten Dunkels kalten Wüstenein,
Dass er mit dem Brande weit die Nacht verdorr,
Pech und Feuer träufet unten auf Gomorrh.

"War": He is arisen who was long asleep, arisen from vaults deep down below. He stands in the dusk, immense and unknown, and crushes the moon in his brute black hand.

Into the nightfall noises of the cities there falls far off the chill and shadow of an alien darkness. And the maelstrom of the markets solidifies into ice. Silence falls. They look around. And no one knows.

In the streets something touches their shoulder lightly. A question. No answer. A face turns pale. In the distance a peal of bells trembles thinly, and beards tremble round their pointed chins.

On the mountains he is beginning to dance, and he shouts: All you warriors, up and at them! And there is an echo when he tosses his black head, round which hangs a loudly rattling chain of a thousand skulls.

Like a tower he stamps out the last glow, where the day is fleeing the rivers are already full of blood. Numberless are the bodies already laid out in the reeds, covered white with death's strong birds.

Into the night he drives the fire across country, a red hound with the screaming of wild mouths. Out of the darkness springs the black world of nights, it edge lit up dreadfully by volcanoes.

And with a thousand tall pointed caps, flickering, the dark plains are strewn, and what is fleeing in swarms on the roads below, he casts into the forests of flame, where the flames roar.

And the flames, burning, consume forest after forest, yellow bats clawing jaggedly at the foliage, like a charcoal-burner he strikes his poker into the trees to make the fire roar properly.

A great city sank in yellow smoke, threw itself soundlessly into the belly of the abyss. But gigantic over glowing ruins he stands who brandishes his torch three times at the wild heavens

above the reflection of storm-torn clouds, into the cold wastelands of dead darkness, to dry up the night far away with the conflagration, he pours fire and brimstone down on Gomorrah.

Georg Heym, one of the major poets of his generation, was obsessed by a foreboding of war and at the same time longed for war as a forceful interruption of the monotony of his young life and of the banality of the age. Such was his longing for an heroic life—the most that man can hope for, according to his favourite philosopher, Schopenhauer—that he even dreamt, in 1911, of taking part in great battles. The disparity between his dreams of glory and his vision, in this poem, of the carnage to which the heroic leads, is striking. The form of the poem carries clear intimations of the heroic mode, but none whatsoever of the expected immortality. The pervasive enthusiasm is without any illusions; the 'heroic' line is wooden, so that the poem is more like a dance of death than anything else. When Heym wrote it in early September 1911, a year before his tragically early death, "Der Krieg" must have been at least in part a visualisation of that great battle of which he dreamt; when it was read by others, however, it appeared to be something very different. The poem was in fact to prove a potent influence on the poetry written in the early months of the war. This is why it belongs here.

What strikes the reader at once is the monumental impersonality and barbaric grandeur of the poem, which differs from most 1914-18 war poems in being not at all subjective. What Heym gives is an objective picture of war as such, war as an elemental feature of life. There is terror in this objectivity, as there is later in Ludwig Renn's novel *Krieg,* arguably the outstanding novel of the war. In poems actually written during the war such objectivity is found only in poets who are, for one reason or another, far from their subject. Heym's poem aims to shock; it consists of juxtaposed explosive images which burst like shells in the reader's mind, a technique that was to be further developed during the war, in poetry of a very different kind, by August Stramm. Since the poet sees war as an elemental feature of life, "Der Krieg" ultimately conveys a visionary and prophetic picture of reality itself. Georg Heym, like T.S. Eliot's Tiresias, 'perceived the scene, and foretold the rest'.

The heavy six-beat trochaic line in which Heym's poem is written makes the accent stalk through the poem like the incarnate demon of war through his apocalyptic landscape. The rhythm and imagery of the poem underline the extreme violence of its subject matter. Occasional deviations from the metrical pattern give the impression both of the poet's vision dominating and threatening to violate his formal resources and of violence continually erupting through the surface of life; the old world represented by the trochaic metre is continually burst open by the violence of the subject matter. The use of rhymed couplets throughout, with all the rhymes masculine ones, is highly appropriate, since the rhyme scheme thus reflects and expresses the primitive, elemental quality of Heym's subject. The poem is 'lyrical' above all in its concentration.

The opening of "Der Krieg" is majestic in its barbaric grandeur. War is immediately personified into an infernal demon who rises from below, from the collective unconscious, from the primitive depths of life, and at the end stands in all his grim majesty over the apocalyptic landscape that is both his own true element and the scene of mankind's Fall and Passion. What, if not War, is the great power which comes unprompted into men's thoughts, of which Heym wrote in his diary in October 1911. The demon War rises before our eyes on the repeated word 'aufgestanden'. One changed syllable—'auf*er*standen'— and the word would refer to a god rising from the dead, but 'aufgestanden' is appropriate here, for War is a chthonic god or demon, a great and unknown power, a figure of utter profanity. Just how terrible this power is, is suggested in the last line of the first stanza, where War is shown crushing the moon in his brute black hand; his colour is the colour of evil and death, for war is the product of evil and the product of war, the whole point and purpose of war, is death. The demon War whose name is Death brings with him the chill of life-denying darkness. In his awful presence life in the city of man is paralysed. At first (second stanza) people are nonplussed; but then (third stanza) the uncanny, threatening atmosphere overcomes them and puzzlement gives way to fear. The jerky, abrupt phrases punch home the confused reactions of men jerked out of their trivial routines who suddenly find themselves faced with primeval violence, that is to say, the violence which all the time had been lurking at the bottom of their own minds (*homo homini lupus*). The peal of bells is a *memento mori* which reduces the staid bourgeois to a figure of fun.

The scene now changes; from the city terrified by this sudden eruption of hitherto suppressed violence we see the demon War moving out into the landscape of war, a landscape that becomes increasingly a prophetic picture of what has been called 'the lunar waste of the Somme', until it finally assumes the proportions of myth: the demon War assumes the proportions of something wholly uncontrollable. Again and again personification is used to control the perspective and gain depth. Thus in the sixth stanza night, the abode of demons, is touched into independent existence by Heym's use of the plural 'nights' which implies a black world full of night demons. Similarly fire is animated into 'a red hound with the screaming of wild mouths': the mythical hell-hound itself carrying off the broken animal bodies of the dead to eternal damnation.

The volcanoes which light up the edge of the night-demons' world fill the air with the sulphurous stench of damnation, pointing forward to the final Apocalypse.

In the seventh stanza Death is again personified, as a monstrous stoker feeding the flames with the countless dead in their tall pointed caps (the 'Pickelhauben' of the German war dead in 1914-18). The whole world is turned into a ghastly crematorium. In a brilliant nightmare image deriving from Van Gogh the flames are described as 'Gelbe Fledermäuse zackig in das Laub gekrallt'; the purpose of this memorable metaphor is to be nightmarish. And still the strutting, mechanical rhythms go their incessant, senseless way.

All through the poem War is presented as the sign of evil, and at the end we see the original monster city destroyed by War, destroyed, that is, by the awakened evil within itself. Its fall is made to echo the Fall of Babylon the Great. The earth is reduced to a wasteland dominated by the gigantic figure of Death Triumphant, although at this point Christian iconography fails, for Heym's Death is strongly reminiscent of the Hindu destroyer-god Siva Bhairava with his garland of a thousand skulls and similar figures from Tibetan demonology. Within five years this wasteland was to assume concrete form on the Somme and in Galicia.

"Der Krieg" is a magnificent poem about war, even if it is not a 'war poem' as such. When Heym was writing it in 1911, Georg Trakl had just finished serving in the Austrian army medical corps as a one-year conscript; in April 1912 he re-enlisted for a six-month spell which led to his meeting with Ludwig von Ficker. Following the outbreak of war in 1914, he volunteered for active service and left Innsbruck for Austrian-occupied Poland on 24 August 1914. He wore a red carnation on his cap as he climbed into the cattle-wagon that was to take him to Galicia; his only cause for rejoicing was the hope that the chaos of his life might for a time be replaced by some kind of order short of the ordered finality of death. The unit (Field Hospital 7/14), to which he was attached as lieutenant-pharmacist, was stationed at Rudki in Galicia (the Russian poet Aleksandr Blok had, from St Petersburg, seen the Russian troops departing for Galicia), and was subsequently involved in the battle of Grodek/Rawa-Ruska of 6-11 September. During the battle of Grodek, Trakl was responsible for some 90 severely wounded men lying in a barn with no doctor available for two days and with insufficient drugs to alleviate their suffering. One of the men shot himself in Trakl's presence. Unable to bear the sight Trakl walked outside only to see a row of bodies hanging from trees (they were locals suspected of disloyalty, in other words, of the wrong kind of patriotism). An eyewitness has written of Trakl's horror and despair at what he experienced, which Trakl himself described to Ficker as involving the whole of human misery. It is this misery that is the subject of his last two poems. Trakl's mind was turned by his experiences at Grodek; he tried to shoot himself and was taken into Garrison Hospital 15 in Cracow on 7 October for observation; on 10 October he was reported writing 'various poems' (what happened to

them?); on 3 November he died as a result of taking an overdose of cocaine, thus enacting the untranslatable words he wrote in **"Helian";** 'Zur Vesper verliert sich der Fremdling in schwarzer Novemberzerstörung.'

The poems on which Trakl was reported working in the last weeks of his life will have included **"Klage [II]"** (drafted in September), **"Grodek"** (the second version dates from 25-27 October), and **"Menschliche Trauer"** (the third version of **"Menschliches Elend",** sent to Ficker on 27 October).

Two years previously Trakl may have had a premonition of the Hell of Galicia, for in 1912 he wrote a poem, **"Menschheit",** which is, except in a technical sense, almost indistinguishable from his wartime poems. By 1912 he had also written the first two versions of **"Menschliches Elend";** when he wrote the third and final version of this poem under the title **"Menschliche Trauer"** in October 1914, he changed only the title, because no other changes were needed; the whole war situation was already implicit in his work. The original title referred to the human condition as such (cf. Andreas Gryphius's poem with the same title); it is the war which is the specific cause of **"Menschliche Trauer".**

The poem **"Menschheit"** is a foreboding vision not just of war, but of world war, the last days of mankind. Like Georg Heym's "Der Krieg", written only months earlier, Trakl's poem consists of a shocking and eventually overwhelming series of images that are at once concrete and abstract:

> Menschheit vor Feuerschlünden aufgestellt,
> Ein Trommelwirbel, dunkler Krieger Stirnen,
> Schritte durch Blutnebel; schwarzes Eisen schellt,
> Verzweiflung, Nacht in traurigen Gehirnen:
> Hier Evas Schatten, Jagd und rotes Geld.
> Gewölk, das Licht durchbricht, das Abendmahl.
> Es wohnt in Brot und Wein ein sanftes Schweigen
> Und jene sind versammelt zwölf an Zahl.
> Nachts schrein im Schlaf sie unter Ölbaumzweigen;
> Sankt Thomas taucht die Hand ins Wundenmal.

"Mankind": Mankind lined up in front of fiery gorges, a roll of drums, sombre warriors' brows, footsteps through a haze of blood; black metal grinds; despair, night in sorrowing minds: here [is] Eve's shadow, hunting, and red coin. Cloud which light pierces, the Last Supper. In bread and wine a gentle silence dwells. And they are assembled, twelve in number. At night they cry out while asleep under olive-branches; Saint Thomas dips his hand into the stigmata.

War is immediately unleashed, with the rhythm beating a garish tattoo (we hear the drum-roll in the first line before it is named in the second), and within four lines leads to despair:

> Menschheit vor Feuerschlünden aufgestellt,
> Ein Trommelwirbel, dunkler Krieger Stirnen,
> Schritte durch Blutnebel; schwarzes Eisen schellt,
> Verzweiflung, Nacht in traurigen Gehirnen:

Here there is the same kind of mythical grandeur as in Heym's more famous poem. Common to **"Menschheit"** and to Trakl's four other poems is not so much a lack of particularity, as an abstract particularity; the images themselves are as concrete as may be, so that—as with Heym—we have to remind ourselves that they are mostly non-specific, that is, not 'real' (a ridiculous word; as if anything was more real for Trakl). **"Menschheit"**, like "Der Krieg", is the product of an obsession with evil, the clearest sign of which, for both poets, was the war which they foresaw. Trakl's attitude towards that war had nothing of Heym's ambivalence. The 'Verzweiflung, Nacht in traurigen Gehirnen' of Trakl's poem is caused not by the preceding vision of war, however, but by the following vision of Man dominated by Mammon. In line 4 Trakl originally wrote 'Und Fratzen gaukeln aus zerstampften Hirnen', which is both too bestial and too specific for any pre-war poem (except Heym's 'Der Krieg', in which it would not be out of place).

"Menschheit" is not only densely imagistic, but very tightly endrhymed (ababa, cdcdc) and has a clear pattern of front-rhymes and inner rhymes. The metrical pattern emphasises the way in which the poem divides into two distinct and counterbalanced halves, as well as the parallels between the halves.

The first half of the poem, beginning with **"Menschheit"** and ending with 'rotes Geld', is a picture of modern man possessed by violence, materialism and despair. The preponderant iambic pentameters and those tight, conventional end-rhymes, which look like little more than a mannerism, give the impression of a formalised, stricken civilisation that is likely to give lip-service only to its beliefs. The dominant sounds are sch and ei, which tends to confirm that we are faced with mere *Schein*, Trakl's melancholy, godless world of *Stein*. The significant rhyme is that front-rhyme to which attention is drawn by the break in the metrical pattern, Menschheit vor / Verzweiflung, for the poem is about mankind driven to despair by its own guilt. The central image in this first 'stanza' (asit really is) is that of the Fall. The first half of the poem conveys, with vivid, lurid precision, the poet's vision of impending war and the reason for it (the Fall; materialism; violence). The first half of the poem ends with the shadow of the Fall ('Hier Evas Schatten, Jagd und rotes Geld'), man's betrayal of his God ('rotes Geld' points to Judas), and his subsequent pursuit of the false god of materialism at whatever cost (the epithet 'rot' names the colour of 'Blutnebel'). This melancholy vision of evil is opposed and counterbalanced by a vision of possible salvation which forms the core of the second half of the poem.

The second half is not a mirror image of the first, but does closely follow it. The same end-rhyme scheme is there, as is the same pattern of inner rhymes within the second line (Wein ein / Schweigen, cf. Wirbel / Stirnen in line 2) and within the invisible stanza (bricht / taucht, a near-rhyme which balances and near-rhymes with the full inner rhyme of Nacht / Jagd in lines 4 and 5), and the renewed breaks in the metrical pattern that act as a kind of front-rhyme substitute (Es wohnt in / Nachts schrein im). The poem, in other words, is as tightly organised as, say, Andreas Gryphius's 'Tränen des Veterlandes, anno 1636', a classical war poem which similarly ended in a lament for lost faith. What I wish to stress, however, is that what might be thought to be the rigid formalism of the poem is in fact an *exact* expression of its subject matter: the state of modern civilisation.

The fact that the main non-structural connection between the two halves of the poem is biblical, brings us back to the matter of interpretation, for the poem can be read in different, and indeed opposite ('negative' and 'positive') ways. I think the second half of the poem, which has as its central image the Last Supper, indicates man's only hope. Trakl is here pointing to the possibility of redemption and an end to the suffering of the first half. The disciples also suffered, but were saved by their faith. As a Christian, Trakl not only believed that men had never sunk so low as in 1914, that the modern world was bereft of all spirituality; he also believed that only a renascence of primitive Christianity could save the world from destruction. The word 'Abendmahl' in the first line of the second half takes us back to the period before the godless 'Nacht' of the first half, and indeed takes us back to the central symbolical event of primitive Christianity: the Last Supper. The opening image—'Gewölk, das Licht durchbricht' (the syntax is ambiguous, but the meaning is not)—is a painterly visualisation of a famous biblical passage ('And there came a voice out of the cloud, saying: This is my beloved Son, hear him': St. Luke, IX, 35; cf. St. Matthew, XVII, 5; 2 Corinthians, IV, 6). This brings us to the first sign of meaning in the poem—the next line contains the first sentence as such—and points forward to that which Doubting Thomas was forced to recognise and which Trakl himself did recognise: the divinity of Christ. Doubting Thomas is above all an object lesson: what the world needs is faith (this was certainly Trakl's view). But it is important to stress that this *is* a matter of interpretation; the poem is fundamentally ambiguous, and rightly so, for the future can never be read with certainty. Now if Trakl's message, whether positive or negative, had been expressed in abstract moral terms, we should have been faced with a religious tract. But given that it is expressed in the most appropriate poetic terms possible, we are faced with a poem about war whose visionary content matches its visionary nature. If Heym was the first German poet to give adequate expression to the modern, tragic conception of war, Trakl was a very close second. Heym's poem shows the Fall of Mankind; Trakl points to a possible way of averting the tragedy of mankind. Having said this, Lindenberger's comment that **"Menschheit"** is a poem which 'succeeds in evoking the horrors of modern war more powerfully than any of the German poems which were to come out of the war itself is exaggerated; the fact of the matter is that, for all its quality, **"Menschheit"** is less powerful than, for instance, any of Anton Schnack's poems.

"Menschheit" was written between 26 September and 10 October 1912 and first appeared in *Der Brenner* on 1 November 1912. Closely related to it is another poem written at the same time, **"Trompeten."**

Unter verschnittenen Weiden, wo braune Kinder
 spielen
Und Blätter treiben, tönen Trompeten. Ein
 Kirchhofsschauer.
Fahnen von Scharlach stürzen durch des Ahorns
 Trauer,
Reiter entlang an Roggenfeldern, leeren Mühlen.

Oder Hirten singen nachts und Hirsche treten
In den Kreis ihrer Feuer, des Hains uralte Trauer,
Tanzende heben sich von einer schwarzen Mauer;
Fahnen von Scharlach, Lachen, Wahnsinn,
 Trompeten.

"Trumpets": Beneath pollarded willows, where brown-skinned children are playing and leaves blowing about, trumpets sound out. Blood runs cold. Scarlet pennons rush through the sadness of the acorn, cavalrymen riding past rye fields and empty mills.

Or shepherds sing at night and deer join them round their fires, the age-old sadness of the woods. Dancers get up from a black wall. Scarlet pennons, laughter [*or*: pools of blood], madness, trumpet-calls.

This poem appeared in the November 1912 issue of *Der Ruf, Ein Flugblatt an junge Menschen,* which was devoted to the theme of war. **"Trompeten"** is a much weaker poem than **"Menschheit"** (by Trakl's standards the first stanza has no memorable images); in terms of structure, however, it is no less interesting. The obvious (abba, cbbc) formal end-rhyme is complemented by a strong but apparently random pattern of internal assonantal rhymes (Wei/trei/Rei/Krei/Feu/Hai; Kind/Kirch; schauer/Schar; lach/nachts/lach/Lach; Fahnen/Ahorns/Fahnen/Wahnsinn); both the internal rhymes and the preponderance of ei, ach, sch and t sounds are 'artful' in that they are unnecessary. The metrical scheme (basically six-beat iambic) is of no particular interest; the strong caesuras are not supported by any systematic pattern of internal rhymes; indeed, they are nullified by the random pattern we have just discerned. One has the impression that the poem is a five-finger exercise. Each stanza has one long (seven-beat) line ending in the word 'Trauer', the insistent identical rhyme which puts the poem in the context of 'Menschliche Trauer', while the last line with its heavy internal rhyme of Fahnen/Wahnsinn makes Trakl's anti-war position clear. **"Trompeten"** is indeed interesting partly for the ambiguous last line, 'Fahnen von Scharlach, Lachen, Wahnsinn, Trompeten' ('Lachen' means both 'laughter' and 'pools of blood'), which Trakl described in a letter to Erhard Buschbeck as a criticism of militaristic madness, partly for the fact that Trakl specifically asked that his anti-war poem should not be followed by a sabre-rattling offering by Paul Stefan, and mainly for the fact that it contains some images (Weiden, Scharlach, des Hains uralte Trauer) which recur in **"Grodek"**, thus showing how deeply **"Grodek"** is rooted in his personal vision. Otherwise **"Trompeten"** reminds me of nothing so much as the formalism of Viennese *fin-de-siècle* poetry ('geschniegelte Wiener Kulturlyrik') which Stadler found in Hofmannsthal; in other words, theformalism which in

"Menschheit" was structurally so important, is here an unnecessary mannerism.

It took less than two years for Trakl's presentiment of war in **"Menschheit"** and **"Trompeten"** to become reality. According to Ludwig von Ficker, it was in August 1914, probably before he left Innsbruck for the Eastern Front on 24 August, that Trakl wrote **"Im Osten"**; if this really is so (and I find it hard to believe), then this, too, is a remarkably prophetic poem, for it reads like a front-line poem, differing from **"Klage"** and **"Grodek"** mainly in what seems to be its more formal, leisurely structure:

Den wilden Orgeln des Wintersturms
Gleicht des Volkes finstrer Zorn,
Die purpurne Woge der Schlacht,
Entlaubter Sterne.

Mit zerbrochnen Brauen, silbernen Armen
Winkt sterbenden Soldaten die Nacht.
Im Schatten der herbstlichen Esche
Seufzen die Geister der Erschlagenen.

Dornige Wildnis umgürtet die Stadt.
Von blutenden Stufen jagt der Mond
Die erschrockenen Frauen.
Wilde Wölfe brachen durchs Tor.

"On the Eastern Front": The people's dark wrath is like the wild organ notes of a winter storm, the crimson wave of the battle, of defoliated stars.

With shattered brows, with silver arms night beckons to dying soldiers. In the shade of the autumn ash the spirits of the slain are sighing.

Thorny wilderness engirdles the town, the moon chases terrified women from bleeding steps. Wild wolves broke through the gate.

The key line is the first, for it is the 'wilden Orgeln des Wintersturms' that the whole poem echoes; this can be seen by tracing the pattern of the dominant or/er/ur sounds and occasional variants (or er ur/ er or/ ur ur er/ er er, er er ar/ er/ er er/ er er er, or ür/ -/ er/ ur or) which persists throughout the poem and is, together with the more obvious four-line stanza pattern, the main constant feature; this pattern of sounds is equivalent to and complements the serial imagery. Otherwise the poem is far less regular than it looks. If the first half of the poem is noteworthy for a system of near-rhymes (Sturms/Zorn; Sturms/Sterne; Sturms/Armen; Zorn/Sterne), to say nothing of the full-rhyming Schlacht/Nacht, the second half as such is characterised by a strongly dactylic verse pattern which was not present in the first half (there is one dactyl in the first stanza, while there are six dactyls in each of the last two stanzas; in other words, there are three dactyls in the first half of the poem, ten in the second half); for all the ostensible difference between the poems, this dactylic pattern links **"Im Osten"** with **"Grodek"**. The near-rhymes of the first half of the poem and thedactylic, near-alcaic ('Hölderlinian') pattern of the second half show that the form of the poem is internalised as the poet moves from actual war to an interpretation first of war and then of history; both halves of the poem are held together not so much by the stanzaic structure as by the recurrent organ notes; it is these which 'order the fragments of wrath into a formal pattern', to re-use the words which Idris Parry used in another context. The successive layers of the poem ranging from obvious (stanzas) to not-so-obvious (near-rhymes) to invisible (dactyls) matches the way in which the poet's concern passes from this war to war in general and thence to human history and the destiny of man.

Sir Maurice Bowra wrote of **"Im Osten"** that Trakl 'applies to the whole shapeless panorama of battle his gift for images . . . Here the individual elements are taken from fact and give a true picture of war'; if, as we are told, the poem was written at Innsbruck, the comment is no longer valid. What is more to the point is that the 'shapeless panorama of battle' has imposed on it both a structural pattern and a pattern of images. War is seen in Hölderlinian terms—and it is Hölderlin who is revealed as the German national poet at this time—as the embodiment of 'des Volkes . . . Zorn' (cf. Hölderlin's 'das Zürnen der Welt' in 'Patmos'), the epithet 'finster' implying that this anger is damnable. By saying that the nations' wrath, war, is like the wild organ notes of a winter storm, Trakl seems to imply that war is as necessary as winter; such a cyclic view of history, possibly deriving from Hölderlin, is found elsewhere in his work. The third and fourth lines of the first stanza incorporate Trakl's characteristic symbolism: the epithet 'purpurn' in 'Die purpurne Woge der Schlacht' refers not only to violence, but to man's guilt, to the crimson body of man which can be heard breaking in **"Klage."** In the second stanza Night is likened to Christ on the cross, his brow broken by the crown of thorns, his pale arms (silver-looking in the moonlight) outstretched as though to embrace those crucified by War.

"Im Osten" and **"Klage"** are linked by the artful frameworks of violence and darkness, within which man is at the mercy, successively, of 'Die purpurne Woge der Schlacht' and 'die eisige Woge der Ewigkeit'. That the stars, signs of the spiritual, are defoliated, suggests that man is bereft of all spirituality. War is accordingly seen as a sign of man's literal beastliness or animality. The second stanza is by comparison straightforward, although there is inevitably more to it than meets the eye: the colour silver, which Trakl probably took from Hölderlin, who used it to denote the crystalline whiteness of snow, does not only refer to the silvery light of the moon, but is one of the colours of death, the otherworldly light of perdition, for already the landscape is spectral with the peaceless spirits of the slain. The last stanza opens with an allusion to the Passion: 'Dornige Wildnis' refers to Golgotha, the place of the skull (cf. Galicia), thus implying that what is to be enacted in 1914 is the passion of mankind; indeed, Trakl makes the city of man wear a crown of thorns ('Dornige Wildnis umgürtet die Stadt'). The poem ends with a reference to the unrestrained animal ('Wilde Wölfe') in man. **"Im Osten"** is basically a Christian poem of despair. The cyclic view of life implied and the reference to the Passion are the only notes of hope.

There is little sign of salvation, for the animal in man has the upper hand. Man is not only doomed, but damned by his own actions. Although **"Im Osten"**, like most of Trakl's poetry, is rooted in reality, his images constantly point beyond themselves to a greater reality. The result is that his poem has an objectivity and a depth unusual in front-line poetry. It is true, as Bowra wrote, that Trakl 'looks upon war from the anguished solitude of a prophet'; but it is certainly not true that 'he draws no conclusions and makes no forecasts', for the whole of **"Im Osten"** is a forecast, and the poet's conclusions, though implicit, could hardly be clearer.

Both his other war poems, **"Klage"** and **"Grodek"**, were the product of his personal despair. **"Klage"** is both a highly personal poem and at the same time an oracular, Hölderlinian one; for all his own spiritual agony, Trakl's greatest fear is that the war may mark the end of man as a spiritual being; he sees mankind in danger of sinking into permanent brutishness:

> Schlaf und Tod, die düstern Adler
> Umrauschen nachtlang dieses Haupt:
> Des Menschen goldnes Bildnis
> Verschlänge die eisige Woge
> Der Ewigkeit. An schaurigen Riffen
> Zerschellt der purpurne Leib
> Und es klagt die dunkle Stimme
> Über dem Meer.
> Schwester stürmischer Schwermut
> Sieh ein ängstlicher Kahn versinkt
> Unter Sternen,
> Dem schweigenden Antlitz der Nacht.

"Lament": Sleep and death, the ghastly eagles all night long whirl around this head: the golden image of man may be consumed by the icy wave of eternity. On terrible reefs the purple body shatters. And the dark voice laments above the sea. Sister of stormy sadness see how a fearful boat sinks down beneath the stars, the silent countenance of night.

Whether the opening image in **"Klage,"** the dark eagles of sleep and death, was suggested by the twin-headed eagles of the Austro-Hungarian Empire and Imperial Russia, I do not know, but it seems probable that they were, for the poem clearly has a comparatively realistic starting-point. The first two lines express a state of mind, that of collapse and despair. We assume that 'dieses Haupt' refers to the poet himself, and that it is the despair and indeed derangement to which he had been reduced following the battle of Grodek, that underlies the poem. It is possible that 'dieses Haupt' refers to the wounded soldier who shot himself in the head in Trakl's presence; the despair which the poet expresses could be this man's; but it is more likely that this man's suffering is one of the causes of Trakl's own despair. The poet fears that 'Des Menschen goldnes Bildnis', that is, man's spirituality, his spiritual being, may soon be swallowed up by 'die eisige Woge der Ewigkeit'. Heidegger pointed out that the latter is not a Christian concept, and Michael Hamburger added that Trakl's despair was bound to be coloured by current

(Nietzschean) modes of unbelief, but we can be more specific and say that 'die eisige Woge der Ewigkeit' is a variant of Nietzsche's 'Eisstrom des Daseins', which occurs in the context of Nietzsche's view that 'Socratic [modern] man has run his course'. Trakl's view of the decline of the West is strongly tinged by Nietzsche. When he wrote this poem Trakl's mind was possessed by the crimson body of man broken on the reefs of war, so that the poem is an elegy for mankind. There has been much critical discussion of the figure of the 'sister' in Trakl's poetry; in the present context I think that 'Schwester stürmischer Schwermut' refers to Trakl's own sister and that at the end of the poem he is calling upon her to witness his own demise.

In **"Grodek"**, his last poem, Trakl implies that Western civilisation has reached a turning-point:

Am Abend tönen die herbstlichen Wälder
Von tödlichen Waffen, die goldnen Ebenen
Und blauen Seen, darüber die Sonne
Düstrer hinrollt; umfängt die Nacht
Sterbende Krieger, die wilde Klage
Ihrer zerbrochenen Münder.
Doch stille sammelt im Weidengrund
Rotes Gewölk, darin ein zürnender Gott wohnt,
Das vergossne Blut sich, mondne Kühle;
Alle Strassen münden in schwarze Verwesung.
Unter goldnem Gezweig der Nacht und Sternen
Es schwankt der Schwester Schatten durch den
    schweigenden Hain,
Zu grüssen die Geister der Helden, die blutenden
    Häupter;
Und leise tönen im Rohr die dunkeln Flöten des
    Herbstes.
O stolzere Trauer! ihr ehernen Altäre,
Die heisse Flamme des Geistes nährt heute ein
    gewaltiger Schmerz,
Die ungebornen Enkel.

"Grodek": In the evening the autumn forests ring with deadly weapons, the gold plains and blue lakes, over which the sun more darkly rolls; night embraces dying warriors, the wild lament of their broken mouths. Yet in the willow-grove a red cloud gathers, in which an angry god resides, shed blood gathers, moonlike coolness; all roads end in black decay. Beneath the golden bough of night and stars the sister's shadow sways through the silent thicket to greet the ghosts of the heroes, their bleeding heads; and in the reeds the dark flutes of autumn softly sound. O prouder sorrow! You brazen altars, a mighty grief today feeds the hot flame of the spirit, the unborn grandchildren.

That **"Grodek"** 'stands at a kind of meeting point between Trakl's private poetic world . . . and the pressures of outward, public event' is clearly true. On the surface **"Grodek"** appears to be perhaps the most impersonal front-line poem ever written; beneath the surface it is desperately, painfully personal. The evening and autumn of the opening line refer neither solely nor mainly to the aftermath of the battle of Grodek; both have a historical, Spenglerian connotation and bring back the recurrent vision of the destruction of Western civilisation. There is a clear contrast between autumn 1914 and a previous age of golden plains and blue lakes (it is no chance that this ideal landscape bears the colours of Christian and indeed Catholic spirituality), on which the sun is now setting. Night—personified in the manner of George Heym and Johann Christian Günther—embraces dying warriors, the wild laments of their broken mouths; compare Charles Sorley's famous lines:

When you see millions of the mouthless dead
Across your dreams in pale battalions go,
Say not soft things as other men have said . . .

Although Trakl's scene has a bitterly personal connotation, it is presented in a totally objective, non-specific way; he could be writing about any war in history. The red cloud in which a wrathful god resides is a reflection of the bloodlust by which men's minds are hazed, a symbol of violence and indeed of the profane, finite, physical world; whether the god is Heym's demonic war-god (i.e. Mars), or the Christian god reduced to wrath by man's brutish behaviour, or Moloch, the god to whom children (the unborn grandchildren) are sacrificed, is best left open, for any poem by Trakl is the sum total of its probable interpretations. While the 'zürnender Gott' is clearly an allusion to war, it is also important to recall that the same figure occurred in a similar context in **"Das Gewitter"** (written two to three months earlier):

Magnetische Kühle
Umschwebt dies stolze Haupt,
Glühende Schwermut
Eines zürnenden Gottes

"The Storm": Magnetic coldness surrounds this proud head, glowing sorrow of an angry god.

The 'mondne Kühle' is the moonlit chill of nightfall, but has the same connotation as the 'icy wave of eternity' in the previous poem, or the 'magnetische Kühle' of **"Das Gewitter"**; in other words, the chill is the chill of death as retribution or punishment. The key line in the poem, the one certainty among so many ambiguities, is 'Alle Strassen münden in schwarze Verwesung'; 'schwarze Verwesung' refers not only to physical decay, but also to spiritual corruption (the cause of that decay) and indeed historical disintegration; black is more than one of the colours in the spectrum of putrefaction, it is the colour of damnation. The line 'Alle Strassen münden in schwarze Verwesung' may have the connotation which E.L. Marson has described as 'the coming night as a black edge of decay creeping up from the horizon to engulf Grodek'; more certainly it has the connotation of individual lives everywhere ending in death and damnation. In line 12 the ubiquitous sister is transformed into a Valkyrie figure receiving the spirits of the slain into Valhalla, an allusion to the fascination which Wagner's *Die Walküre* held for Trakl; the 'schweigenden Hain', which might appear to be an allusion to the 'schöne Menschlichkeit' of Goethe's Iphigenie and therefore of the ideal sister-figure, is most likely a Hölderlinian echo. The figures of the dead heroes first appeared some weeks earlier in a pre-war poem, **"Der Abend"**, which begins:

> Mit toten Heldengestalten
> Erfüllst du Mond
> Die schweigenden Wälder

"Evening": With the figures of dead heroes, moon, you fill the silent woods.

What is new is the context, the 'overwrought Wagnerian pathos', which is no doubt itself the result of the poet's overwrought condition. The dark flutes of autumn sound out not merely to salute the passing of the dead, but to lament a greater loss: the unborn grandsons who have been sacrificed on the brazen altars of war; 'ihr ehernen Altäre' is not only a general reference to war, it is a more specific reference to the phrase 'auf dem Alter des Vaterlandes sterben', which was almost invariably used to announce death at the front, and the pride mixed with sorrow with which such announcements were made. Trakl clearly sees an even greater loss lying behind such deaths: the hot flame of the spirit is sustained by something purer and prouder: grief at the death of the innocents and therefore of innocence. The poem ends with this ambiguous image that has been continually misinterpreted; 'unborn' has both its literal meaning and the figurative meaning of innocent. The ending of the poem, which was less concise in the lost first version, implies that Trakl sees the Fall of Man as being re-enacted on the battle-fields of 1914; future generations of innocents will not now be born because man has finally lost his innocence and is therefore doomed.

When Ludwig von Ficker visited Trakl in hospital shortly before his death, the poet asked him whether he wanted to hear what he had written at the front; he added that it was damn all ('blutwenig'), and then proceeded to read **"Klage II"** and **"Grodek"**. I imagine that it will be agreed that whatever else they are, **"Klage"** and **"Grodek"** are not 'blutwenig'. Of course, when one bears in mind the fact that between the outbreak of war and Trakl's death two million war poems were written in the German language, one can only be more than ever grateful for Trakl's poems. One of the most extraordinary things about **"Klage"** and **"Grodek"** is that they deliberately dispense with the particularity on which front-line poetry normally depends for its effect. Trakl shuns realism (cf. his use of the unrealistic words 'Krieger' and 'Haupter' in **"Grodek"**) because his visions were more real to him than the actualities of war; these were important to him only as confirming all his worst fears. It is because his conception of reality is an inward or hallucinatory one that Trakl's metaphors do not follow the normal pattern; whereas a normal metaphor starts with something familiar, Trakl's starting point is frequently something unfamiliar, so that his images tend to exist or operate at two removes from what is normally called reality; but since what is real for him are his own visions, his imagery is appropriate to express *his* reality. Besides, his images, like Kafka's, point deeper and deeper into the work itself and away from the material order which they negate. No one took the war more seriously than Trakl, but no one treated it with more contempt either; most importantly of all, no German-language poet of the war viewed war from a deeper, historic-tragic perspective than Trakl, or produced greater poems while at the front. Kafka's verdict, that Trakl had too much imagination, this being why he could not stand war, which results from an appalling lack of imagination, remains true; but the imagination which drove him out of his mind also made him into a superb poet. Albert Ehrenstein's memorial to George Trakl, which forms the preface to his *Den ermordeten Brüdern* (1919), rightly ends with the statement that no Austrian poet has ever written more beautiful poetry than Georg Trakl. . . .

Dennis Sampson (review date 1989)

SOURCE: A review of *Song of the West,* in *The Hudson Review,* Vol. 42, No. 3, Autumn 1989, pp. 508-10.

[Trakl's fevered, Christian mysticism is discussed in the following excerpt.]

Baudelaire said that Chopin's music was "like a bird of bright plumage fluttering over the horrors of the abyss," and this is an appropriate image for anyone wanting to understand the poetry of Georg Trakl. Asked why he never entered a monastery, that mysterious early twentieth-century German poet responded that he was a Protestant and had "no right to depart from hell." Does this give you an idea what to expect from this writer? *Song of the West,* translated by Robert Firmage, is marked by lyrical grace, phantasmagoric images that beg to give shape to the spiritual in which Trakl tried permanently to live. References relating particularly to the Passion and Resurrection appear and disappear: "Golden blooms the tree of grace," "In starlight the cross looms dark," ". . . his head bows down in the darkness of the olive tree." Trakl is known too for his repetitive use of the words: *countenance, blue, chamber, dark, stars, olive tree, shepherd,* among others. This serves the same purpose that it did in the work of one who recognized Trakl as a kindred spirit early on, James Wright. For both poets there was, at the center of everything, something that could never consent to description.

Obsessed with corruption, with sin, the ethereal soul of these lyrics recoils at the sight of the human city:

> Where, cold and evil,
> A rotting generation dwells
> And prepares a dark future
> For white grandchildren.
>
> "Evening"

One can also hear Blake's excoriation of industrial London in these lines:

> Whore, who bears a dead infant in icy shudders.
> God's wrath whips raging the brow off the
>   possessed,
> Crimson plague, hunger, which shatters green eyes.
> Oh the hideous laughter of gold.
>
> "To Those Grown Mute"

The thought of heaven is not heaven, although it may fill one with elation. Poor, preposterously ill-at-ease with other people, Trakl's life is not much more than one long lyrical cry, "I have been touched by the hand of God." Unlike the ecstasy of Saint Theresa, Trakl's is the grief of the visionary caught between the corporeal and spiritual: his poems seem inadvertently original—not the product of a man seeking "liberation of the poetic figure," as Rilke was quoted as saying.

What young poet of our time might have the capacity to say of prayer, "The graves of the dead / Open at your feet / When you lay your brow in your silver hands"? Would Trakl have said of God's considerable promise what Levi did of Buna-Monowitz, "it must be experienced to be understood"? Rarely do his hallucinogenic visions coalesce—the idiot savant at the piano playing a combination of Stravinsky and Scriabin. His methodology is that of the Christian mystic, harking back repeatedly to the mystery of the Crucifixion, Trakl's paradigm for everything.

Robert Firmage has captured well the foreboding tone of these apocalyptic poems without sacrificing the naiveté. While his introduction does not do much to untangle the complexities, that won't matter to those willing to give Trakl the benefit of the doubt, going into his poems with an open mind to find out what is there. . . .

Edward Foster (review date 1990)

SOURCE: A review of *Autumn Sonata: Selected Poems of Georg Trakl* and *Song of the West: Selected Poems of Georg Trakl* in *American Book Review,* Vol. 12, No. 1, March-April 1990, pp. 17-18.

[In the following excerpt, Foster compares Simko's translation with that of Firmage, noting the task is to "find the poem before it is set in language."]

Rilke thought Trakl's books important in liberating "the poetic image." Scholars and critics have expended great effort showing that what he really liberated were his sexual repressions and his religious obsessions. Was Trakl involved with his sister? Was he a suicide? Was he, in spite of all those ugly rumors, really a Christian?

Does it matter?

Trakl's life was horrible if all the speculations about his psychological torments are indeed true, yet they add nothing to the poems, which simply will not be reduced to explanation.

Jack Spicer learned from Rilke. Did he also learn from Trakl?

> The dark
> forest of words lets in some
>   light from its branches.
> Mocking them, the deep leaves

> That time leaves us
> Words, loves.

These lines conclude Spicer's "Language," but they have an affinity with Trakl. Here is the conclusion of **"Nachtlied"** in Daniel Simko's translation:

> And you, still mirrors of truth—
> Reflections of fallen angels appear
> On the ivory temples of the lonely.

Both poetries have an autonomous quality that denies interpretation. They speak with utter conviction, saying all that needs to be said. Both operate in images that are simultaneously sharp and hermetic. Both possess an Orphic inevitability that can neither compromise nor laugh. If one wants something of Trakl in English, read Spicer.

What would Spicer have said of these new translations? He was, of course, obsessed with translation; if poems were only their words, they would be as provisional as their speakers. His translations may not always be "precise," but his version of Lorca's "Ode for Walt Whitman" is itself a great poem. "The perfect poem," Spicer said, "has an infinitely small vocabulary." The translator's problem would be to find the poem as it exists before it is set in language. From **"Kaspar Hauser Lied"** in Simko's version:

> Saw that snow fell into leafless
>   branches,
> His murderer's shadow in the half-
>   lit hallway.

And in Robert Firmage's:

> Saw, that snow fell into naked
>   branches,
> And in the dusky hallway the
>   shadow of the killer.

Firmage is closer to Trakl's order ("Sah, dass Schnee fiel in kahles Gezweig / Und im dämmernden Hausflur den Schatten des Mörders."), but according to Spicer's formulation, that doesn't matter. Trakl's images have a force that transcends their words, and Simko's version works on its own terms.

These two books transform Trakl into radically different "equivalents." Firmage often tries to indicate the formal mannerisms, word order, and rhyme schemes in the original, and his English can be moody and at times archaic, as in **"Helian"**:

> . . . they open their filth-besplattered
>   garments,
> Weeping to the wind of balsam,
>   Wafting from the rosy hill.

Simko, on the other hand, is usually more direct:

> . . . they open their filthy and
>   stained robes,

Crying out to the balmy wind
   blowing from the rosy hill.

In the same poem, Firmage translates "O wie trauwig ist
dieses Wiedersehn" as "O how sorrowful is this reen-
counter," which is close to the original but awkward.
Simko gives us "How sad this reunion is." Simko's phras-
ing is more effective here than Firmage's, but Firmage
has obviously preserved something that Simko loses. Firmage translates "Umnachtung" as "derangement," while
Simko chooses "madness." Firmage gives "heaven" as an
equivalent for "Himmel;" Simko gives "sky." Simko's
diction generally makes his versions more immediate and
hence in that way powerful, but Firmage tends to be closer
to the German construction and/or sound.

To give another example, Firmage translates "mondne
Kühle" in **"Grodek,"** Trakl's last poem, as "lunar coolness," while Simko writes, "A cold moon." In Firmage:
"All roads disgorge to black decay." In Simko: "All roads
end in black decay." Simko says, "A sister's shadow staggers through the silent grove," and Firmage says, "The
sister's shadow flutters. . . ."

But the point, of course, is that even when one version is
literally wrong (Trakl says, "The sister," after all), it
doesn't matter. (Several years ago, Michael Hamburger
decided that "The sister's shade now sways through the
silent copse," and there are obviously many other ways to
construct that line.) What does matter is not Trakl's language, but what has been done with it. Neither Firmage
nor Simko offers merely a gloss, and both succeed on
their own terms.

It is interesting to read these translations side by side.
Often they both succeed, though for different reasons,
and there are passages, of course, where one version is
clearly more effective than the other. Here is the way
Firmage begins **"Kaspar Hauser Lied"**:

He truly loved the sun, which,
   crimson, descended the hill,
The paths of the forest, the singing
   blackbird
and the joy of green.

Simko's version of the first line may be stronger, but the
third is comparatively awkward:

He truly loved the sun which sank
   crimson down the hill,
The forest paths, the singing
   blackbird,
And the pleasure of the greenery.

Trakl's third line is "Und die Freude des Grüns." In this
instance, Firmage not only comes closer to the original
but also creates the more powerful line.

Firmage argues that Trakl may have had a greater influence on German poetry than Rilke, yet Trakl has been
translated much less frequently. Until now the most widely
read translations have been those collected by Christopher
Middleton and originally published in 1968 and reissued in
1984. (Hamburger's version of **"Grodek"** is printed there.)
Among other versions, there is an important set of translations by Lucia Getsi (1973), and David J. Black published
four of the prose poems as *Winter Night* in 1979. Perhaps
the best versions in English are those by James Wright in
Twenty Poems of Georg Trakl, edited by Robert Bly, and
reprinted in an appendix in Middleton's book.

None of these versions should be overlooked, and there is
room for many more. Each points, however obliquely,
toward Trakl's initial revelation—poems that are finally
outside all versions and all language. As Wright said in
"Echo for the Promise of Georg Trakl's Life":

My own body swims in a silent
   pool,
And I make silence.

Karl E. Webb   (essay date 1990)

SOURCE: "Georg Trakl and Egon Schiele: The Effects of
Rimbaud on the Themes of Their Works," in *Crossings—
Kreuzungen,* Camden House, 1990, pp. 154-63.

[*In the following excerpt, the author compares Rimbaud's
and Trakl's alienation from the city and God in their work.*]

It is unclear just when and under what circumstances
Georg Trakl first encountered Rimbaud, though it was
probably late in 1911 or in 1912. He undoubtedly learned
of Rimbaud's poetry, as critics such as Reinhold Grimm
have pointed out, through K. L. Ammer, the pseudonym
for Karl Klammer, an Austrian military officer who published the first German translations in 1907. This volume
contained a cross-section of poems and an enthusiastic
biographical sketch by Stefan Zweig. The translations of
Rimbaud were freely interpreted by Klammer not only
by his lack of precision in translating, but also by his
choice of poems to be included. For this reason, it is
important to keep in mind that it is not just Rimbaud who
enters into our comparison, but also, perhaps just as importantly, Karl Klammer's interpretation of him. . . .

In turning now to the works of [Trakl], one discovers a
number of thematic similarities to Rimbaud that emphasize
this important link in their "relationship." The first is their
distinct and common sense of separation from the various
aspects of modern life—the cities, society in general and
also the natural world. [Both] artists express their disqui-
etude toward what they perceive to be a lifeless, cold and
threatening environment, particularly the city and its inhabitants. In Rimbaud's poem: "Paris lebt auf," for example,
Paris and its inhabitants become the object of the poet's
disgust and loathing. This is a place, he tells us, of great
inhumanity, of filth, of disease, of death and despair.

Ihr Syphilitiker, ihr Gauklerpack, ihr Puppen,
   was nützen eure Gifte, eure Fetzen,

was nützt ihr selbst Paris, der grössten aller
    Metzen?

      . . . . .

du totengleiche Stadt, du Stadt von Schmerz
    geweiht . . .

As is well-known, Trakl, too, sees the city and modern "civilization" in this same light. For him clearly, the contemporary world is a place of ugliness and despair and a place in which he feels threatened and estranged. In the poem: **"Vorstadt im Föhn,"** we detect the same hideousness and the same filth and disease that we discovered in Rimbaud's poem above.

Geduckte Hütten, Pfade wirr verstreut,

      . . . . .

Am Kehricht pfeift verliebt ein Rattenchor.
In Körben tragen Frauen Eingeweide,
Ein ekelhafter Zug voll Schmutz und Räude,
Kommen sie aus der Dämmerung hervor. . . .

Closely associated with this type of separation in [the] artists' works are the figures of poor and abandoned children who, as sort of an alter-ego . . . are subjected to the inhumane surroundings of the modern world. Rimbaud wrote several poems in which such children appear, "Betterlkinder," for example:

Um das helle Kellerfenster gesteckt,
auf den Hintern gehockt und die Hälse gereckt,
    schwarz im Schnee und der Nacht,
sehn auf den Knien fünf Kleine . . .
wie das schwere blonde Brot
    der Bäcker macht;

      . . . . .

Ganz leise sagen Gebete sie her,
hingeneigt zu dem offenen Himmelsmeer,
    dem flutenden Feuerschein,

      . . . . .

und die Hemdlein flattern dünn und zerschlissen
    im Wintersturmdräun . . .

Trakl also created numerous such figures, in **"De Profundis,"** for example:

Am Weiler vorbei
Sammelt die sanfte Waise noch spärliche Ähren ein,
Ihre Augen weiden rund und golding in der
    Dämmerung

      . . . . .

Bei der Heimkehr
Fanden die Hirten den süssen Leib
Verwest im Dornenbusch. . . .

The . . . artists were not only alienated by the city, or town, and its inhabitants, they also exhibit a profound sense of separation from the modern natural world which, like the man-made cities, becomes a symbol for the dead or the dying. In an earlier epoch, epitomized by Eichendorff's Romanticism, nature symbolized a safe and protected retreat from unsatisfactory human contact, but no longer. Rimbaud describes his natural surroundings as desolate and lifeless. There is a threatening wind blowing, the river runs yellow, and the bells of the village are woefully silent. There is nothing to give encouragement or solace in this unrelentingly barren landscape.

O Herr, wenn kahl die Felder liegen,
wenn in den hingeduckten Flecken,
die sich im kahlen Land verstecken,
die langen Abendglocken schwiegen . . .

In Trakl, too, we discover similar images of a nature dying or already dead from which spiritual or physical rejuvenation is now impossible. We detect in this—one of his most common themes (particularly after his exposure to Rimbaud)—the same threatening atmosphere that we identified in the poetry above. The oft-quoted passages from **"De Profundis"** are typical:

Es ist ein Stoppelfeld, in das ein schwarzer Regen
    fällt.
Es ist ein brauner Baum, der einsam dasteht.
Es ist ein Zischelwind, der leere Hütten umkreist.
Wie traurig dieser Abend.

In a further passage from **"Drei Blicke in einen Opal,"** nature becomes even more menacing. Death has arrived and all creatures are caught in its all-encompassing devastation:

Die Purpurschnecken kriechen aus zerbrochenen
    Schalen
Und speien Blut in Dorngewinde starr und grau. . . .

A more profound and disconcerting similarity in Rimbaud and Trakl's works is their common feelings of estrangement from God and His cosmic order. This perception goes to the very essence of their existence, for they felt completely deserted and rejected by the Supreme Being. Though all three no longer professed a belief in traditional Christian precepts, they nevertheless exhibited a heightened traditional sense of "cosmic" or spiritual alienation because of their deep roots in the Christian church with its prohibition against sensuality and its primary doctrines of sin and redemption. They, themselves, chose the course of sensual, even "pagan" expression, but were then beset with an overwhelming and traditional sense of guilt. Unlike "transgressors" of the past, however, they discovered no solice in a redemptive force nor any existing way toward reunification with God.

Thematically in the works of all three artists, the above spiritual or "cosmic" alienation finds profound expression. Typically, the *persona* of the work is beset by forbidden, yet overpowering, sexual desires, the expression of which precipitates an overwhelming sense of guilt and despondency. Though at times there appears to be an attempt to escape this guilt by accepting a less complicated and more impulsive pre-Christian way of existence, escape of this sort is never fully possible in the end, and the *persona* is left with feeling rejected by God and expulsed from God's cosmic order. The repeated appearance of church-related figures such as priests, cardinals, novices, and nuns, and significantly (with Trakl and Schiele) the "sisters," either in juxtaposition to the *persona* or as alteregos, serves to heighten the sense of spiritual estrangement.

In Rimbaud's "Schlechtes Blut," the poet documents, with an undertone of sarcasm and self-derision, this sense of "cosmic" alienation:

> Das heidnische Blut kehrt wieder! Der Geist ist
> nahe; warum hilft mir
> Christus nicht and gibt meiner Seele Adel and
> Freiheit? Ach, die Zeit des
> Evangeliums ist vorbei! Das Evangelium, das
> Evangelium!
>
> . . . . .
>
> Zu wem mich wenden? Welches Tier soll ich
> anbeten? Mich auf welches
> heilige Bild stürzen? . . .
>
> Ach, ich bin so verlassen, dass ich meinen Eifer zur
> Vollendung ich weiss
> nicht welchem Götzenbilde darbringen möchte.

In Trakl's poetry, this "cosmic" alienation also assumes pivotal importance. Various religious figures, such as novices and priests, are filled with the typical sensual longing, and resultant guilt and despair. They feel estranged at the very center of their existence from God and His order.

> Die fremde Schwester erscheint wieder in jemands
> bösen
> Träumen.
> Ruhend im Haselgebüsch spielt sie mit seinen
> Sternen.
> Der Student, vielleicht ein Doppelgänger, schaut ihr
> lange vom
> Fenster nach.
>
> . . . . .
>
> Im Dunkel brauner Kastanien verblasst die Gestalt
> des jungen
> Novizen.

In **"Drei Blicke in einen Opal,"** we find a more extreme example where the monks have become crazed with sexual lust and perversion:

> Aus Schwarzen bläst der Föhn. Mit Satyrn im
> Verein

> Sind schlanke Weiblein; Mönche der Wollust
> bleiche Priester,
> Ihr Wahnsinn schmückt mit Lilien sich schön and
> düster
> Und hebt die Hände auf zu Gottes goldenem
> Schrein. . . .

In the [Rimbaud] case, the uncertainty, fear and disorientation become most evident in the prose-poem: *Ein Sommer in der Hölle,* where we discern passages of the most startling self-examination. At one point of particular despair, he cries out:

> Ich sterbe vor Müdigkeit. Das ist das Grab; ich
> gehe zu den Würmern,
> Schrecken der Schrecken!
>
> . . . . .
>
> Mein Gott, Mitleid, verbirg mich, ich halte mich zu
> schlecht!—
> Ich bin geborgen, und ich bin es nicht.

In another passage, he asks himself: "kenne ich noch die Natur? *Kenne ich mich selbst?* (italics mine).

Trakl, too, has these feelings of great uncertainty and mental anguish. His works unquestionably contribute some of the most impressive images of psychic terror to be found anywhere in modern literature. In **"De Profundis,"** we read:

> Ein Schatten bin ich ferne finsteren Dörfern.
> Gottes Schweigen
> Trank ich aus dem Brunnen des Hains.
> Auf meine Stirne tritt kaltes Metall
> Spinnen suchen mein Herz.
> Es ist ein Licht, das in meinem Mund erlöscht. . . .

One could expand this investigation to include the potential mental disintegration that possibly could have occurred as a result of the extreme alienation and resultant anguish, or to discuss Trakl's portrayal of the *Doppelgänger* or multiple personalities as an indication of this disintegration, but the confines of the present essay will not allow for it. Suffice it to say at this point that [the] artists obviously sought some solution or relief, some form of mediation, from their mental and emotional predicament. In Rimbaud's case, it was at first the escape to drugs and a completely unstructured life; later, it was his flight from Europe and from his art to a primitive existence in the remote regions of Ethiopia where he supposedly lived a "productive and harmonious life among the untouched natives." In other words, at least if we can believe Stefan Zweig, Rimbaud seems to have found a hope for the future and a lasting and harmonious solution to his estrangement. . . . The Austrian, on the other hand, was not so fortunate, living as he did at the end of an era, at the beginning of a true disintegration. For him, there was no hope for the future nor seemingly any possible flight from the realities of their existence. At most, he could rely on vague and more pleasant memories from the past and the various other artificial methods of escape. For him there was no rebirth of the lost harmony; it was dead, and only its longing remained. . . .

Eric Williams (essay date 1992)

SOURCE: "Georg Trakl's Dark Mirrors," in *Modern Austrian Literature,* Vol. 25, No. 2, 1992, pp. 15-35.

[*The following essay explores modes common to much of Trakl's verse: its reflexivity, revisionism, and its many "mirror motifs."*]

In meiner Seele dunklem Spiegel
Sind Bilder niegeseh'ner Meere,
Verlass'ner, tragisch phantastischer Länder
Zerfliessend ins Blaue, Ungefähre.

Georg Trakl

I

"I imagine," wrote Rainer Maria Rilke after reading George Trakl's first volume of poetry, published posthumously in 1915, "that even the initiated experiences these views and insights as an outsider pressed against panes of glass: for Trakl's experience occurs like mirror images and fills its entire space, which, like the space in the mirror, cannot be entered." Though Rilke's metaphor of the mirror is frequently cited as a poignant image for evoking that "alienated realm of [Trakl's] poetic experience which is fundamentally inaccessible" there is a second—and invariably overlooked—aspect of Trakl's work which is reflected in Rilke's response: the image of the mirror itself. Occurring in various forms and contexts throughout Trakl's work, the mirror (or reflexive surface) is an important, if not central, experiential metaphor in his writing. How it figures in the poet's groping exploration of the dark origins of his poetic creativity is the topic of this essay.

Unlike many modern poets, Georg Trakl wrote no critical treatises on aesthetics or poetics and, aside from two short literary reviews, a couple of cryptic literary aphorisms, and a scattering of references to poetry in letters, he left behind very little in the way of direct commentary upon poetry. As to the significance of his own poetry, he was strangely silent. About the only thing that exists in the way of commentary upon his own creativity is a number of oblique references found in letters, most of which were written fairly early in his career in 1909 and 1910. In one he mentions, for example, the delight which ensues when one "frees oneself from something which has for a long time torturously demanded release", whereas he complains in another that an acquaintance had superficially copied his "heated, hard-won," "imagistic manner," which derives from a "living fever" and "forged four image pieces in four lines of poetry into one single impression". Trakl was a compulsive poet who had little time or energy for anything but his poetic calling, and it "drove him into delirium," as he once lamented in another letter, that he

did not have enough time "to in some small measure give form to an infernal chaos of rhythms and images".

Perhaps the best source for Trakl's critical "commentary"—and certainly the most interesting—is his reflexive and often highly self-conscious work, which, as one critic recently remarked, "knows more of its method than anything the poet ever said." Though Trakl never set out to simply write poetry about poetry—he only used the words "poet" ("Dichter") and "poem" ("Gedicht") once each in all his work—his "feverish" efforts to come to terms with that "infernal chaos of rhythms and images" engendered a heightened sensitivity to the complex origins of his poetic impulse which is registered in a subtle but pervasive level of reflexivity which runs throughout his work. By focusing on the psychological implications of Trakl's interest in images denoting vision and visual reciprocity, I will show how the metaphoric function of the mirror is of central significance in his particular "poetological" exploration of the wellsprings of poetry.

The following poem, typical of his earlier work, uses the conventional form of rhymed, first person confessional verse to convey a Baroque message of death and decay that is also subtly poetological. After indulging in a series of extravagant lamentations about a horrible, dark world filled with anxiety, pestilence, and distorting shadows, the poetic persona appears to reflect upon the nature of its confessional speaking in a poem whose title is Latin for "I confess."

"Confiteor"

Die bunten Bilder, die has Leben malt
Seh' ich umdüstert nur von Dämmerungen,
Wie kraus verzerrte Schatten, trüb und kalt,
Die kaum geboren schon der Tod bezwungen.

Und da von jedem Ding die Maske fiel,
Seh' ich nur Angst, Verzweiflung, Schmach und
    Seuchen,
Der Menschheit heldenloses Trauerspiel,
Ein schlechtes Stück, gespielt auf Gräbern, Leichen.

Mich ekelt dieses wüste Traumgesicht.
Doch will ein Machtgebot, dass ich verweile,
Ein Komödiant, der seine Rolle spricht,
Gezwungen, voll Verzweiflung—Langeweile!

The first line provides the bright background against which the poem's gloomy "confiteor" is made. Taken alone, it is positive. Life paints colorful pictures, inspiring romantic images, as it were, which the remainder of the poem then dismantles. What others might see as colorful images painted by the vital force of life, the poetic persona confesses, it sees distorted by cold shadows which forever darken its visual experience and reveal life to be a heroless tragedy of pestilence and *Angst* performed badly upon corpses and graves.

Though the poem's decadent theme and expressionistic excesses are at odds with the "inspired heart" poetry of the classical-romantic tradition of the nineteenth century, its structure and thematic development are still very much under the sway of the narrative constraints of that tradition. Accordingly, the poem moves in a conventional romantic fashion from a particular situation to a more general level of abstraction. The poetic persona first recounts the particulars of what it *sees*—"colorful images painted by life"—and then states, in a more general vein, how these "colorful images" degenerate into the decadent imagery of a repulsive world in which it, ultimately, is forced by an anonymous commandment to mouth its boring role.

In lamenting about the inadequacy of its mode of speaking—by referring to itself as an actor who despairs about the boring role he is forced to speak—this early poetic persona concludes its *confession* with a subtle poetological reflection that calls into question the poetic tradition which, up to Trakl's time, had taken the confessional poetry of Goethe's era as the paradigm of authentic lyrical expression. The speaking of confessional poetry, it would seem, can no longer satisfy its expressive needs. What it speaks has become an empty compulsion, an inauthentic mouthing of a "role," a repeating of the *already written* lines of an inappropriate tradition. Unlike Goethe's early poetic personae who celebrated, in Erich Trunz' words, "the total unity of man and nature in language," this persona is trapped in an alienating world "where the mask has fallen from everything," where the bright images of life are transformed, in a heroless human tragedy, into the horrific imagery of literary decadence. Using the paradigm, this early poetic persona struggles to articulate its troublesome clash with the tradition. What results is an aesthetic dilemma in which the incommensurability of message and mode produces a poetological statement whose paradoxical nature registers the need to escape the narrative constraints of the *confiteor* mode.

Typical of Trakl's early work is his use of visual imagery to convey the transition from particular to abstract. Beginning, in this particular case, in the first two stanzas, this transition is then completed in the third stanza's general pronouncement. Here, the metaphorics of visuality give way to a more abstract, non-visual metaphor about the actor-buffoon's compulsive mode of speaking. It is interesting to note that the "colorful images"—what might be construed as a romantic idyll of unmediated pure visuality—begin to disintegrate in the second line at the point where the lyrical "I" first appears. In saying "I" in order to speak about what it sees, the persona marks a subject-object differentiation which it then articulates in the series of horrific visions in the following lines. The pure vision of line 1 thus deteriorates into a Baroque tragedy which demasks everything in the visual world ("And since the mask has fallen from everything") and transforms the poetic persona into a self-conscious speaking subject who despairs about its inauthentic speech. The poem thus begins to articulate a split between seeing and speaking which the young poet was incapable of further elaborating at this stage in his career.

II

In his mature work, Trakl effectively distances himself from the confessional mode of classical-romantic *Erlebnis-*

lyrik and achieved a kind of objective austerity and concentrated precision which broke new ground for German poetry. Here, under the sway of his "simultaneous reception" of Hölderlin and Rimbaud, Trakl put the frenzied, egocentric excesses of his earlier writing behind and began to produce controlled, almost dispassionate imagistic verse largely devoid of first person references and overt confessional content. The following, often anthologized, poem conveys the crisp efficiency and soft, muted tone of this breakthrough period. With terse elemental terms Trakl aligns an evocative constellation of images to create an unsettling landscape in which a haunting autumnal atmosphere casts its dark shadow on everything in both the natural and human sphere. Like a quiet autumn evening, this "decline" softly descends from the heavens with their foreboding departure of birds and cold wind, and ends, after passing over "our" graves in the city at the depth of night ("midnight"). The poem is entitled **"Untergang"** and was dedicated to Trakl's poet friend, Karl Borromaeus Heinrich. Though less directly reflexive and self-referential than **"Confiteor,"** the poem does nonetheless present a subtle poetological reflection upon the relationship between (obscured) vision and poetic creativity.

"Untergang"
an Karl Borromaeus Heinrich

Über den weissen Weiher
Sind die wilden Vögel fortgezogen.
Am Abend weht von unseren Sternen ein eisiger
    Wind.

Über unsere Gräber
Beugt sich die zerbrochene Stirne der Nacht.
Unter Eichen schaukeln wir auf einem silbernen
    Kahn.

Immer klingen die weissen Mauern der Stadt.
Unter Dornenbogen
O mein Bruder klimmen wir blinde Zeiger gen
    Mitternacht.

Since the poem's subtle poetological implications are more generally a product of its dense weave of imagery as a whole, it would be helpful to begin with some more general observations about the poem's particular structure and content: one is immediately struck by the poem's tight structure and repetitive vocabulary. This structural tightness is most apparent in the symmetrical repetition of "über-über" and "unter-unter" in the initial position of lines, the twice occurring "weiss" and "Nacht" as well as the punctuation pattern of the first two stanzas and its variation in the third. The sensuous quality of this poem, by contrast to Trakl's earlier work, produces a hypnotic flow of resonating sounds and somber rhythms; most notable are the hollow "o's," the eery "i's," the haunting "ei" assonances and "w" alliterations, and the various sibilants whose hissing waxes and wanes to suggest the swirling of a chilling autumn wind.

Also typical of Trakl's mature work is the dense intratextual cross-referentiality which Trakl establishes here through a play of assonance and alliteration. In the first stanza, for example, the repetition of "w" and "ei" in the "*wei*ssen *Wei*her" of the first line resonate in the "*ei*siger Wind" of the third line. More than an arbitrary play with sound, this resonance serves to associate these four elements and reinforces the sense that the white pond of the first line is frozen and lifeless. The "*wei*ssen *Wei*her," moreover, echo in the "*wei*ssen Mauern" of the third stanza, where the analogous position of "weiss" sets up a symmetry between these two stanza's first lines and, in effect, contrasts the white *pond* with the white *walls*. "Weiss" is the structural tie which contrasts the openness of the natural sphere (pond) with the closure of civilization (the white walls of the city). Trakl's choice, in this context, of the word "Weiher" is also significant. He did not use the perhaps more common term "Teich" ("pond")—which would have maintained the "ei" assonance but lost the cross-referential potential of "W"—likely because "Weiher" also conjures certain religious associations which enrich the poem's nature-civilization contrast. The German word "Weihe" ("blessing, "consecration," "solemnity"), it should be pointed out, is closely related to "Weihestätte" ("holy place") and derives from a Germanic root which means "holy," "magical," or "religious." Trakl's white pond thus suggests a holiness which is absent in the cold sterility of the "white walls of the city." If one then considers the German expression, "Er ist dem *Untergang geweiht*," the choice of "Weiher" becomes all the more meaningful in this poem of death and decline entitled **"Untergang."**

In any case, the openness of the foreboding autumnal scene in the first stanza is intensified by the distant origin of the "icy wind" in line 3. But why is this icy wind coming from "our stars"? Are they *our* stars because they bring the celestial message of our fate, our *Untergang*— "our graves" (line 4)? Such an associative reading of this typically indeterminate imagery would be strengthened by the first stanza's (southerly) flight of birds, a natural sign for the inevitable darkening decline of Fall. Parallel bird imagery also occurs in a poem entitled **"Dezember,"** which likewise progresses from a "flight of wild birds" (crossing dark) waters, in the first stanza and ends, similar to **"Untergang,"** with a nighttime image of verticality: ". . . the night follows with shattered masts." Indeed, the flight of birds, and especially birds themselves, often figure in Trakl's verse as a foreboding natural sign for Autumn and decline (literally "Untergang"). Unfortunately, tracing down such abounding parallel imagery in this verse where "each new sad-beautiful image encountered . . . is somehow already known and already read" inevitably leads to endless circuits through Trakl's "self-plagiaristic" oeuvre and yields at best vague general trends but never interpretative keys. The "zerbrochene[] Masten die Nacht" in the poem **"Dezember"** seems, for instance, to resonate in "zerbrochene Stirne der Nacht" in **"Untergang,"** which in turn resonates in the strikingly similar "zerbrochene Stirne im Munde der Nacht" in a poem entitled **"Am rand eines alten brunnens"**. A "bowing brow" likewise occurs in various poems in contexts whose similarity would invite comparative analysis. Various permutations and combinations of virtually every image in **"Untergang"**— with the exception of "we blind hands climb"—show up

in literally dozens of poems. The eery "an icy wind blows from our stars," for example, turns up almost verbatim in two other poems as "from our stars blows a snowy wind".

Another related and equally mystifying aspect of Trakl's verses was brought to light in 1969 with the publication of the definitive critical edition to his work. Presented for the first time in a lengthy critical apparatus are the numerous manuscript draft versions to a majority of his poems which had been scribbled on scraps of paper, napkins, menus, letters and envelopes. These so-called "variant" versions reveal a compulsive and, at times, seemingly illogical or somewhat random process of creation and revision in which Trakl repeatedly switched, added or deleted in line after line of composition often apparently unrelated—even contradictory—strings of individual words and, in some cases, bits and pieces of imagery which he appears to have lifted from his own poems. In an earlier version of **"Untergang,"** for example, the word "dark" in the final line "O my brother in *dark* sighs" was replaced in succession by "langen," "bleichen," "tiefen," "schwarzen" "dunklen," "schmächtigen," "schweigend" and then reworked in the final version of the poem to become "O my brother . . . we *blind* hands . . ." The strangeness of "blind hands climbing toward midnight," it should be pointed out, is partially the result of an untranslatable aspect in the German word "Zeiger," which, in addition to "hand of a clock" can also mean "indicator" or "pointer." This semantic aspect allowed Trakl to cast, in a typically expressionist manner, the human being as an inanimate thing, as an alienated being objectified, as it were, by the dehumanizing forces of the modern world. By objectifying the brothers as the "blind hands" of ticking time in a stanza beginning with "the white walls of the city sound forever," Trakl brought together a constellation of motifs in which the disintegration of pure vision (implied in "blind") interplays with images connoting the disintegrating forces of time and the alienating effects of civilization. The inescapability of these threatening forces and effects is reinforced by the temporal infinity of the city's endlessly sounding walls—sterile, blinding "white walls" which "sound forever," enclosing and entrapping the human being in the alienating and unnatural noise of civilization. Reiterating the sense of threatening entrapment is the unfriendly image of "thorn arches" beneath which the brothers are transformed into the blind hands— the indicators—of the eery darkness of "midnight."

If one then construes "my brother" of the final line as a fraternal allusion to Karl Borromaeus Heinrich to whom the poem is dedicated, one begins to see that this tersely imagistic poem is, like so much of Trakl's work, also self-referential and poetological. With the words "O my brother, *we* blind hands climb toward midnight," the distanced and restrained poetic persona quietly calls out to a kindred soul, a poetic brother who like himself blindly points to the darkness of midnight, to, perhaps, an empty transcendence in the cold, dark void of the cosmos. It is as though the very existence of these objectified indicator brothers, standing alone in their alienation, has itself become a signifying event. Exposed to the process of darkening autumnal decline they become a groping gesture which registers, like a cosmic weather vane, the darkness—blindness—of a post romantic era that can no longer *see* a reassuring bright unity in the "colorful images painted by life." This reading is indirectly confirmed, perhaps, by the final line of the poem's second version, which reads: "O mein Bruder, verwandelt sich dunkel die Landschaft der Seele." In becoming itself a darkening landscape, this (objectified) soul is, by contrast to its romantic brothers, incapable of reflecting the radiant display—the "colorful images"—of the natural world. It is a soul which reflects, as such, only the dark transformation of the romantic landscape. Iris Denneler has also commented upon the poetological potential of these final lines, musing that one may see in the words "Bruder" and "Zeiger" an allusion to the shared poetic calling of Heinrich and Trakl, who had carried on a kind of "communication . . . in the medium of literary texts.

Though critics have long been aware of Trakl's precarious emotional state—documented schizophrenia—approaches to his work were all too often shrouded in religious, existential and formalistic studies which quietly avoided the troubling question of insanity. This collective repression effectively blocked a differentiated investigation of the psychological implications of his work. It also obscured the fact that Trakl's letters demonstrate a keen capacity to observe and articulate the turmoil of his own inner states and that he was generally interested in issues of a psychological nature. In, for example, a short review essay—one of the three extant literary reviews he wrote—Trakl comments upon the psychological implications of several works by the Austrian dramatist Gustav Streicher. Here, after mentioning in passing how one of Streicher's earlier works "seeks to solve a psychological problem of the most subtle kind with the means of modern psychoanalysis ("Seelenanalyse"), Trakl goes on to praise the intense emotional effects of Streicher's most recent work, writing:

> It is strange how these verses penetrate the problem, how often the sound of the word expresses an inexpressible thought and holds fast the fleeting mood. In these lines there is something of the sweet feminine rhetoric which seduces us to listen to the melos of the word and ignore its content and meaning; the minor key of this language puts the mind into a meditative mood and fills the blood with dreamy fatigue.

Of particular interest here is the implication that the sound of the word, the "minor key" of language, has a sensuous incantatory power which is superior to the ordinary sense of words. That this sensuous power is attributed to a "feminine rhetoric" suggests that Trakl's remarks may have, at least in part, a deep psycho-sexual motivation which brings him to fantasize escaping in and through a feminine element the rational grasp of language's "content and meaning." The sense of escape is strengthened by Trakl's allusion to a state of intoxication which lulls the mind and "fills the blood with dreamy fatigue." Put in the context of Trakl's well-known alcoholism and drug addiction, this allusion to the intoxicating effects of the "minor key of language" begins to make poetic sense. The desirable in-

cantatory effects of *melo*dious poetic words, like the narcotic effect of drugs, provided him with a sensually pleasing means of escaping the torment of his (schizophrenic) self-consciousness, a torment which he sensed, vaguely perhaps, was somehow linked to the rational "content and meaning" of language—the medium of social discourse. In fantasizing a feminine rhetoric which induces a narcotic *melos,* Trakl here expresses a desire to resolve the unhappy experience of his linguistically socialized ego by re-establishing the sensuous security of a preverbal connection to a feminine—maternal—ground. Trakl's "childish ego," to borrow Erich Neumann's Jungian characterization of Georg Trakl, wishes to "escape from the hostile, alien world of normal reality," so that it can "revert to a mythical ego to which the world appears as a unitary world." This primal yearning for the sweet, intoxicating *melos* of the word, sealed off from an alienating world manifests itself in various ways from, most obviously, the rich sensuous quality of Trakl's hypnotic rhythms, resonating assonances, and alliterations to an explicit complaint about the "terrible helplessness of words". But it is also present in his synaesthetic visions of a bright, egocentric world of sound and color which, as he once confided in a letter of 1908, caused him to listen to "his inner melodies" and to "dream images which are more beautiful than all of reality". Such "dream images" figure throughout his work in the various specular motifs whose many permutations—which both idealize and problematize a brighter "unitary world" of visual integration—no doubt prompted Rilke on a second occasion to use the image of the mirror to characterize Trakl's verse, stating that his poetry presented a "mirror-image world . . . that consisted completely in falling."

Trakl's abounding mirror motifs are found almost invariably in contexts which undermine or negate the positive value of the reflecting surface. The figural result ranges from a denigration of visual experience in general to an alienating distortion of self-perception. In the first stanza of a relatively late poem entitled **"Herbstseele,"** Trakl places the dazzling, reflective surface of a pond into a typically hostile environment:

> Jägerruf und Blutgebell;
> Hinter Kreuz und braunem Hügel
> Blindet sacht der Weiherspiegel,
> Schreit der Habicht hart und hell.

A pedestrian rendition of the original German of the last line ("Blindet sacht der Weiherspiegel") might be something like, "The pond-mirror softly blinds." This translation explicitly mentions both the mirror and its (potentially) alienating effects. In itself, the pond is unproblematic; it is a natural surface whose sunny-day brilliant dazzle can blind the eye. The German, however, is not so patently positive, because Trakl did not choose a verb such as "glänzen," ("to gleam, dazzle"), but created, rather, a decidedly negative verb out of the adjective for "blind." The resulting neologism thus focuses the attention on the "not seeing" of blindness. Within the context of this stanza, the sense of blinding characterizes, in addition to the "dazzling" visual effects of the pond, an obscuring of the reflective surface itself, since Trak's neologistic verb has no specified direct object. "Blindet sacht der Weiherspiegel" can mean, in other words, that the pond-mirror itself becomes blind. The sense of "not seeing" is then subtly reiterated in the first two lines of the next stanza where "black silence" hovers ominously over "path and field." That this "black" suggests the absence of vision, is strengthened by Hans-Georg Kemper's observation that "Schweigen" is often modified in Trakl's imagery by attributes which connote "not seeing," a fact which led him to conclude that "Schweigen" corresponds to the black of not seeing. This is an important insight which would reinforce the claim that the theme of obscured vision or specularity—blindness—is associated in Trakl's work with language (and ultimately poetry), since "Schweigen" can mean "to keep silent, not to speak."

By undermining the potentially beautiful specularity of the naturally reflective pond-mirror, Trakl has also undermind the "holy," "magical" or "religious" connotations of "Weih-er." "Weiher," it might be noted, frequently occurs in images involving natural reflections—especially the reflection of stars—as is the case in the evening landscape of the first stanza of **"Untergang"** where, after the birds have flown away over the *Weiher* an icy wind blows from the stars. This obscuring of specular reflection implied in the darkening autumnal skies over the white pond emerges again in the second stanza of **"Untergang"** in the bowing darkness of the "shattered brow of the night"; in personifying the night with "brow," Trakl transforms the encroaching night into a face whose fractured darkness is incapable of reciprocating "our" gaze. The motif of a bowing brow or face occurs in other poems in images denoting or suggesting visuality and specularity, from the "brow which bends over bluish waters" to a haunting image of a Narcissus figure who "bends over silent waters to see" that his "countenance has left" him. In any case, the implied blindness of the bowing brow of the night in **"Untergang"** becomes explicit in the "blind hands" of the final stanza, a stanza in which the peaceful quiet of nature is broken by the sounding of the city's white walls. It is as though the sound of civilization and human society is somehow implicated in a darkening process which first obscured the resplendent dazzle of the magical pond and then moved on to the "brothers" in the final line, where they are transformed into the signifying event of gesturing blind hands—human indicators of the ominous black silence and blind darkness of an alienating modern world.

A similar constellation of natural scenery and civilized, darkening decline occurs in one of Trakl's best-known poems, the **"Kaspar hauser lied"** (1913). Here the poet plays off the motif of the noble and innocent savage destroyed by civilization by alluding to a legendary (and historically documented) foundling named Kaspar Hauser who, at the age of seventeen or eighteen, mysteriously appeared in Nuremberg on Whit-Monday 1828, ignorant of both language and society. Hardly able to walk and incapable of speaking, this boy had been isolated since birth, as he later recounted after acquiring the rudiments of language, in a dark dungeon-like room. As enigmatic

as his origin was his demise some five years later (he was stabbed to death in the Hofgarten at Ansbach by an assailant whose identify—like that of the perpetrators of his macabre upbringing—remains to this day a mystery). Trakl's **"Kaspar hauser lied"** belongs to a rich and varied imaginative response to the Hauser mystery that includes, more recently, Peter Handke's 1967 *Kaspar* play and Werner Herzog's 1975 film *Every Man for Himself and God against All.* Using motif and vocabulary borrowed from Verlaine's "Gaspar hauser chante" poem and (especially) Jakob Wassermann's 1908 semi-documentary novel on Kaspar Hauser, Trakl constructed a typically enigmatic and abstract poem which is only vaguely reminiscent of the Hauser story. Rather than harkening back to the foundling's dungeon-dark beginnings, Trakl's poem opens with the following measured and richly lyrical allusions to a bright, pre-social world of innocence:

> Er wahrlich liebte die Sonne, die purpurn den
>   Hügel hinabstieg,
> Die Wege des Waldes, den singenden Schwarzvogel
> Und die Freude des Grüns.
> Ernsthaft war sein Wohnen im Schatten des Baums
> Und rein sein Antlitz.
> Gott sprach eine sanfte Flamme zu seinem Herzen:
> O Mensch!
> Stille fand sein Schritt die Stadt am Abend. . .

One immediately notices the bright, warm, and colorful Arcadian imagery; here is a joyous serenity, an Eden of authentic dwelling in which Kaspar ("he") and primal nature ("sun," "hill," "forest," and "tree") coexisted harmoniously before "his footstep" entered in silence "the city in the evening." Taken by itself, the first stanza depicts—in the past tense—a bright world which, when compared with Trakl's abounding present tense scenes of autumnal decline, appears to present a pre-existing ideal state of peaceful coexistence and love. Even the setting sun, usually a foreboding sign of imminent doom, is (was) an object of love—in a stanza which itself is unified by one verb: "loved." "He truly loved" joins together all of the elements of this natural scene as the objects of Kaspar's true love. Significant, also, is the fact that the first object of this love, the sun, is a feminine noun ("die Sonne")—a primal feminine element which connotes the ultimate origin of all light and life.

Bathed in the primal warmth of the setting sun, Kaspar was at one with his world—a fanciful quiet world undisturbed by the civilized noise of society. Here, in the Edenic "joy of green," he could listen to the sweet *melos* of the blackbird's song—a kind of pure melody in an Arcadian "minor key" untainted by the loud "content and meaning" of the words forced upon him when he turned up in the city. Kaspar enjoyed, so long as he was safely isolated from the alienating world of words, a harmonious preexistence in a unitary perceptual world. He dwelled, to couch it in Lacanian psychoanalytic terms, in the resplendent but doomed imaginary world of a mirror stage—the fanciful preverbal state of a "specular I" which is conjured, or retroactively projected, by a linguistically alienated "social I."

Axiomatic to Lacan's analysis of the formation of the human ego, or self, is the belief that the psyche has a kind of inborn mirror disposition which is instrumental in the formation of the concept of self or ego. In order to overcome the fragmentary character of its experience in the early months of existence, the developmental period Lacan designates as the "mirror stage," the pre-linguistic human subject begins to form, with the help of its intra-psychic mirror, the concept of a unified self by making visual identifications with its phenomenal world. The so-called mirror stage infant thus enjoys a kind of undifferentiated visual symbiosis with its mother and environment. This visual connection, however, is broken by the acquisition of language: in learning to speak and say "I," the infant becomes increasingly aware of itself as opposed to the surrounding world rather than a (more or less) undifferentiated part of it. In trading its narcissistic visual (imaginary) identifications for the pre-formulated "already spoken" structures of language, the human psyche takes an alienating step toward fuller self-consciousness. Trakl's Kaspar Hauser is, prior to his fateful "footstep" into the "city in the evening," like a pre-verbal infant who has not yet experienced the "paranoic alienation, which dates from the deflection of the specular *I* into the social *I*. His Edenic innocence would suggest the purity of a childlike Adam who has not yet fallen from the grace of a resplendent perceptual world into the "civilized" social world of words.

It is interesting to note that a language problematic with social implications is also present in the Wassermann novel. In a chapter entitled "The Mirror Speaks," Wassermann writes about how Hauser was saddened and troubled by his confrontation with language: "It was a long way from the thing to the word. Nonetheless, the same way also led to people; indeed, it was as if people stood behind a screen of words which made their expressions strange and horrible." The words which brought Wassermann's Hauser to the society of people, also produced a frightening estrangement, for words made people's features, most importantly their faces, strange and menacing. Not surprisingly, Hauser's "favorite fantasy" was "that he someday be permitted to go home." He longed to return *home,* to a home which, significantly, would entail a kind of pre-existence prior to the menacing, socializing influence of language.

The idea of an adolescent boy who is miraculously ignorant of both language and society seems to have conjured in Trakl's imagination a sensuous—intoxicating—vision of primal innocence. It was as such a poetic vision which provided him with a kind of "vicarious access to the lost world of childhood," to, in other words, the imaginary security of a pre-verbal, specular "I." His Kaspar-Adam was thus happily "uncivilized"; he dwelled in a unitary world which contained no broken mirrors, shattered dark brow, or blinded eyes, since the purity of his perceptual world was undisturbed by the trauma associated with the endlessly ringing "white walls of the city." Unmarked by trauma, his "countenance" is "pure"—not the "mirror-image of a godless, cursed century," as Trakl once referred to himself.

Trakl, it would seem, had little trouble identifying with this homeless foundling doomed by the anonymous brutality of the city. He, in fact, once referred to himself as a "poor Kaspar Hauser" in a letter written from the city of Innsbruck—a place which he described in the same letter as "the meanest and most brutal city that exists." It is no coincidence that Trakl's late, thinly veiled autobiographical prose-poem **"Traum und Umnachtung"** carried as its original title "Der Untergang kaspar munchs." The purity of Kaspar, be he an ascetic monk or an innocent foundling, is doomed to decline—a darkening decline which transforms, within the "mirror-image world" of Trakl's later verse, a boy named Kaspar Hauser into a complex mythic figure who evokes the beautiful but impossible, unattainable state— a myth—of a nurturing perceptual world of visual integration and sensuous sound. For Trakl, the story of Kaspar Hauser was more than a literary source or convenient set of symbolic props, it was a profound existential metaphor which both reflected and elaborated his dark visions of civilization and its discontents. It was a legend which, as Frank Graziano has succinctly stated, "informs his work as much as his own biography."

The impossibility of the myth of pre-existence is evoked already by the portentous setting sun in the opening scene of Trakl's Hauser poem. This Edenic landscape contains, moreover, like Adam and Eve's garden before the Fall, a potentially dangerous tree. Hauser, we note, dwelled solemnly "in the shadow of the tree." The bright (maternal) security of his fanciful existence in the sweet feminine *melos* of the blackbird's song already stands in the shadow of a tree which conjures visions of the menacing paternal Tree of Knowledge created by God the Father. The paternal agency is and was there from the beginning—in Western culture, at least—inevitable and sure as the setting sun. This, too, makes sense from a Lacanian perspective, since the process of socialization associated with the acquisition of language is part and parcel of the Oedipal criris, whereby the child's symbiotic relationship with the mother is disrupted by the intervention of the law of the father.

The transition from the pre-verbal mirror stage to the linguistically articulated consciousness of the *social I* thus involves accepting the law of the father which underwrites and dominates, in Lacan's view, all of society and culture. Fittingly, the second stanza of Trakl's Hauser poem concludes with God's abrupt linguistic declaration— "God spoke . . . into his heart: / O man!" This marks the end of Kaspar's innocent pre-existence and sends him forth into man's noisy world of words.

Trakl's Hauser poem ends, after an allusion to the passage of seasons, "Spring and summer and beautiful the autumn / Of the righteous, his light footstep," with the following dark and violent images:

Nachts blieb er mit seinem Stern allein;

Sah, dass Schnee fiel in kahles Gezweig
Und im dämmernden Hausflur den Schatten des
    Mörders.

Silbern sank des Ungeborenen Haupt hin.

Kaspar never escaped the "shadow of the tree" whose latent menace was transformed with each quiet step he took toward the city and society into "the shadow of the killer." The silvery bright youth "exists from an alien world into which he was never really born." He leaves in an innocent unborn state, perhaps because he was never completely socialized and corrupted by the civilization of the city, but perhaps also because, to put it in Christian terms, his unborn-ness precluded his being re-born and redeemed within the Christian fellowship of man and God. Lost is the promise of re-birth and transcendental solace. The biblical myth of the Fall has become in Trakl's Kaspar Hauser world the reality of humanity's inexorable fall into the cold and brutal world of modern civilization. And yet, within the poetology of Trakl's work, the Edenic setting of the Kaspar Hauser pre-Fall world, with its bright and colorful images and pure melos of the blackbirds's song, represent the positive counter image which forever figures in Trakl's continuous lament about an autumnal world threatened by darkness and death. How an awareness of this psychic motivation reaches an aesthetic accord in the poetological reflexivity of Trakl's late work is the topic of this essay's final section.

Though essentially pessimistic, Trakl's late work is not always as patently apocalyptic as the **"Kaspar hauser lied."** Indeed, there are a number of late poems whose specular imagery hint at a creative or redemptive impulse which seems to derive from the Western world's decline—the "fall," perhaps, that Rilke saw in Trakl's work as "the precondition or pretext for ascension." Two such poems are **"Abendländisches lied"** and **"Abendlied."** These titles might indicate a weeping poetic view of the darkening "Evening-land" ("Abend-land") of the Western world.

Completed at about the same time—perhaps within a month of each other—the Kaspar Hauser poem and **"Abendländisches lied"** seem almost to form a complementary pair, so close are they in theme, development, and imagery. They contrast, however, with respect to visuality, in that the theme of vision and seeing—only implied in the deterioration of the perceptual idyll in the Kaspar Hauser poem—plays a crucial role in the final stanza of **"Abendländisches lied."** Preceded by what one critic has aptly described as "a compressed history of the Western world, progressing from prehistoric innocence" to the fallen present, this stanza contains motifs of both resplendent visual brightness andobscured self-reflection:

> O, die bittere Stunde des Untergangs,
> Da wir steinernes Antlitz in schwarzen Wassern
>   beschauen.
> Aber strahlend heben sich die silbernen Lider die
>   liebenden:
> *Ein* Geschlecht. Weihrauch strömt von rosigen
>   Kissen
> Und der süsse Gesang der Auferstandenen.

This stanza suggests that the failure of narcissictic self-reflection in the "black waters" of the present "hour of decline" need not necessarily end in the lonely demise of a Kaspar Hauser. It is as though the "silver" sinking of

Kaspar's innocent head is countered by the uplifting "silver eyelids" of lovers—over whose transfiguring unity breaks the spell of narcissistic solitude and occasions a "sweet song" of redemption. The origin of this sweet song, it may be inferred, is connected to the absence of pure visual reciprocity in a world which denies the imaginary unity of the Kaspar Hauser idyll.

A similar intertwining of obscured vision and song figure prominently in the second stanza of **"Abendland"**—a poetological stanza which explicitly relates song to the stony absence of vision:

> Leise verliess am Kreuzweg
> Der Schatten den Fremdling
> Und steinern erblinden
> Dem die schauenden Augen,
> Dass von der Lippe
> Süsser fliesse das Lied.

Note how this song benefits from the blinding of "seeing eyes," how, in other words, such "stony blindness" enables the song to flow sweeter from the lips. One cannot help but wonder whether there might also be Homeric resonances in this obvious connection of poetry and blindness. In any case, there arises, it would seem, in the absence of resplendent visual integration, a sweet song, a self-conscious *melos*—a poetic response to the absence of the blackbird's pure *melos* in a dark, post-Edenic Kaspar Hauser world. This stanza thus represents the fuller aesthetic realization of the problematic split between seeing and speaking which emerged in the frenzied lamentations of Trakl's early poem **"Confiteor,"** and was further elaborated in the "semiotic" blind hands of the poetic brothers of **"Untergang."** Rather than despairing at the frightening, dark disintegration of life's "colorful images," this composed late persona seems to recognize such disintegration as the Orphic impulse which motivates its sensuous songs of darkness, death and decline. It should come as no surprise that the mythic singer Orpheus, whose doomed backward glance and yearning for the lost feminine counterpart gave rise to beautiful melodies of lament and loss, should appear in another late poem of epic proportions **"Passion"** which, like **"Abendland,"** relates the redemptive power of poetic song to the disintegration of bright specularity.

Frustrated by the "terrible helplessness of words" and perhaps by a deep-seated aversion to the alienating (socializing) effects of language, Trakl managed—despite his schizophrenia and Kaspar Hauser paranoia—to create a profound lyrical work which recorded his Orphic descent into the darkunderworld of the human psyche. He wrote a strangely cohesive verse whose "network of tentacular roots," to borrow from T.S. Eliot's Ben Jonson essay, reach "down to the deepest terrors and desires" which most people only experience in the safe world of dreams. Gloomy but compelling, Trakl's imagistic work brought together the poet's dark visions, specular obsessions, and Orphic impulses into an aesthetic accord whose psycho-mythic reverberations find a sympathetic resonance in a postindustrial age of computers, stultifying media-barrage, and faceless urbanization. But this work also records an intense struggle with language, a poetological struggle that speaks to and from the alienations of the modern era—an era which is struggling to come to terms with the visual dis-synchronization of words and world, an era which has generated such modern and postmodern "mythologies" as the Oedipal crisis, the mirror stage, and the patro-phallocentric orders of linguistic unconscious, and an era which finds the desire of poetry lined to the impersonal menace of the Abend-land and to an unrequited need for myth in its various forms and disguises.

FURTHER READING

Biography

Sharp, Francis Michael. "Georg Trakl." In *Major Figures of Austrian Literature: The Interwar Years 1918-1938,* pp. 459-86. Riverside: Ariadne Press, 1995.

> Argues that despite his slight oeuvre and short life, Trakl sustains his appeal to readers.

Criticism

Brown, Russell E. "Attribute Pairs in the Poetry of Georg Trakl." *Modern Language Notes* Vol. 82, No. 4 (October 1974): 439-45.

> Investigates Trakl's innovations with German syntax, especially his word pairs, which fragment his world-view and creates a modernistic sense of "free-floating suspension."

Harries, Karsten. "Language and Silence: Heidegger's Dialogue with Georg Trakl." *Martin Heidegger and the Question of Literature: Toward a Postmodern Literary Hermeneutics,* pp. 155-71. Bloomington: Indiana University Press, 1979.

> Revisits Heidegger's pivotal essay on Trakl, "Language in the Poem," disputing assumptions that Heidegger held about the meaning and silences in his poetry.

Kritsch, Erna. "The Synesthetic Metaphors in the Poetry of Georg Trakl." *Monatshefte* Vol. LIV, No. 1 (January 1962): 69-77.

> Credits the presence of synesthesia in Trakl's work to its "subliminal appeal."

Lindenberger, Herbert. "The Early Poems of Georg Trakl." *The Germanic Review* Vol. XXXII, No. 1 (February 1957): 45-61.

> Presents the 1909 collection of Trakl's work.

———. "Georg Trakl and Rimbaud: A Study in Influence and Development," *Comparative Literature,* Vol. X, No. 1 (Winter 1958): 21-35.

> Traces "borrowings" and "points of contact" as well as technical innovations that Trakl and Rimbaud learned and adapted from each other's work, providing each with their mutual "success in breaking the logical juncture of conventional poetry" and helping to define a poetic "visionary experience."

Lyon, James K. "Georg Trakl's Poetry of Silence." *Monatshefte* Vol. 62, No. 4 (Winter 1970): 340-56.

> Explores four "silences" that recur in Trakl's poetry. Two states of innocence: the unborn and childhood; and two of experience: fallen man and the dead.

Marson, E.L. "Whom the Gods Love—A New Look at Trakl's Elis." *German Life & Letters* Vol. XXIX, No. 4 (July 1976): 369-81.

> Focuses on the personages in Trakl's own mythology.

Peucker, Brigitte. "The Poetry of Repetition: Trakl's Narrow Bridge." *Lyric Descent in the Romantic Tradition,* pp. 166-209. New Haven: Yale University Press, 1987.

> Examines the "language of the precursor" as the "language of exhaustion" itself in Trakl, and his struggle making this language of descent his own.

Schier, Rudolf D. "'Afra': Towards an Interpretation of Trakl." *The Germanic Review* Vol. XLI, No. 4 (November 1966): 264-78.

> An *explication de texte* pointing to Trakl's use of *figura* in the poem "Afra."

Sharp, Francis Michael. "Georg Trakl: Poetry and Psychopathology." *The Turn of the Century German Literature and Art, 1890-1915,* pp. 117-33. Bonn: Bouvier Verlag, 1981.

> Discusses Trakl's diagnosis, *dementia praecox,* in terms of the modern illness, schizophrenia.

———. *Poet's Madness: A Reading of Georg Trakl.* Ithaca: Cornell University Press, 1981, 252 p.

> Examines Trakl's poetry in light of his psychological problems.

Additional coverage of Trakl's life and career is contained in the following sources published by Gale Research: *Twentieth-Century Literature Criticism,* Vol. 5; and *Contemporary Authors,* Vol. 104.

Margaret Walker
1915-

American poet, novelist, essayist, and biographer.

INTRODUCTION

Walker's contribution to African-American literature spans six decades, from the publication of her first book of poetry, *For My People* (1942), to the most recent collection of her essays, *On Being Female, Black, and Free* (1997). Her work has shown a responsiveness to the black experience, a historical perspective and a humanism that have kept it consistently pertinent to contemporary American society. Though she has been immersed in an academic environment throughout her career as a writer, her poetry has maintained its power to reach a wide audience. Walker appropriates a broad range of styles from folk ballad to sonnet, but always remains bright and clear in meaning, and thus avoids entanglements within overly-literary characteristics that could otherwise obscure an academic poet's style.

Biographical Information

Walker was born in Birmingham, Alabama on July 7, 1915, the oldest of four children. Her father, a scholarly Methodist minister, bequeathed his love of literature to her. From her mother, a music teacher, Walker developed the rhythm intrinsic to her poetry. Her parents provided a supportive and stable home environment that emphasized the values of education, religion, and the rich heritage of black culture. Walker began writing poetry at the age of eleven. At fifteen, she attended a segregated college in New Orleans where her father and mother taught. As a college sophomore, she met the famous poet Langston Hughes who, along with her composition teacher, encouraged her to continue writing and to go North to study at a more prestigious college. She transferred to Northwestern University in Evanston, Illinois, finishing her bachelor's degree just after her twentieth birthday.

Her first professional position was as a social worker for the Works Progress Administration (WPA), and then as a writer for the WPA Writer's Project in Chicago. Through her work there, she associated with Richard Wright, Nelson Algren, Arna Bontemps, Katherine Dunham, and James Farrell. In 1940, Walker received her master's degree from the University of Iowa where she completed *For My People* as her master's thesis. She began teaching at Livingstone College in Salisbury, North Carolina in 1941. *For My People* was published by Yale University Press in 1942 and won the Yale University Younger Poet's Award. In 1943 she married Firnist James Alexander with whom

she had two sons and two daughters. Since 1949 she has been a professor of English (now Emeritus Professor) at Jackson State College in Mississippi where, in 1968, she became the director of the Institute for the Study of the History, Life and Culture of Black Peoples. She earned her doctorate, in 1965, from the University of Iowa with submission of her novel, *Jubilee,* as her dissertation. She has been the recipient of several fellowships including the Fulbright in 1971 and a National Endowment for the Arts grant in 1972. Her productive writing and teaching career has included many public readings of her poetry at literary conventions and in colleges across the country.

Major Works

Beginning with *For My People,* Walker has implored her black readers to spring forth and infuse the modern world with a sustaining faith: "We / have been believers, silent and stolid and stubborn and strong." The poems invest readers with a fresh vision of spiritual independence and a challenge to refashion a world in their own image, the image of the true egalitarian whose faith and values were forged in the crucible of oppression. This theme of *For*

My People echoes Walker's literary career in all her major works: *Jubilee, Prophets for a New Day,* and *This is My Century.* Her novel, *Jubilee,* which tells the fictional history of Walker's great-grandmother, is primarily known for its realistic depiction of the daily life and folklore of the black slave community. Walker's second volume of poetry, *Prophets for a New Day,* contains her civil rights poems, written in response to the violence of the 1960s, including the bombing of the Sixteenth Street Baptist Church in Birmingham. *This is My Century: New and Collected Poems* (1989) presents all the poems in her previous volumes: *For My People, Prophets for a New Day,* and *October Journey.* It also includes eighteen previously unpublished poems in a section entitled *This is My Century.*

Critical Reception

For My People won the Yale University Younger Poet's Award in 1942, making Walker the first American black woman to be honored in such a prestigious national literary competition. The reviews of that first volume praised her ability to awaken her readers to the plight of her race, and reviews of her subsequent publications have continued in that vein. Among her strengths as a poet, critics have noted her effective use of folk myths and Biblical allusions, her skillful use of meter, and her humanitarian themes. Her style has been called Whitmanesque in response to its rhythmic flow and its focus on common people. The occasional negative criticism that her work received has mainly focused on her sonnets, suggesting that they lack the immediacy of her other poetic forms.

PRINCIPAL WORKS

Poetry

For My People 1942
Ballad of the Free 1966
Prophets for a New Day 1970
October Journey 1973
This is My Century: New and Collected Poems 1989

Other Major Works

Come Down from Yonder Mountain (novel) 1962
Jubilee (novel) 1966
How I Wrote Jubilee (essays) 1972
A Poetic Equation: Conversations Between Margaret Walker and Nikki Giovanni [with Nikki Giovanni] (interviews) 1974
Black Women and Liberation Movements (essays) 1981
The Daemonic Genius of Richard Wright (biography) 1982; revised edition, *Richard Wright: Daemonic Genius* 1988
How I Wrote Jubilee and Other Essays on Life and Literature (essays) 1989

On Being Female, Black, and Free: Essays by Margaret Walker (essays) 1997

CRITICISM

Stephen Vincent Benét (essay date 1942)

SOURCE: "Foreword," in *For My People,* Yale University Press, 1942, pp. 5-7.

[*In this excerpt from the Foreword to* For My People, *Benét introduces Walker as a promising new poet whose sincerity and talent make her work successful.*]

Straightforwardness, directness, reality are good things to find in a young poet. It is rarer to find them combined with a controlled intensity of emotion and a language that, at times, even when it is most modern, has something of the surge of biblical poetry. And it is obvious that Miss Walker uses that language because it comes naturally to her and is part of her inheritance. A contemporary writer, living in a contemporary world, when she speaks of and for her people older voices are mixed with hers—the voices of Methodist forebears and preachers who preached the Word, the anonymous voices of many who lived and were forgotten and yet out of bondage and hope made a lasting music. Miss Walker is not merely a sounding-board for these voices—I do not mean that. Nor do I mean that this is interesting and moving poetry because it was written by a Negro. It is too late in the day for that sort of meaningless patronage—and poetry must exist in its own right. These poems keep on talking to you after the book is shut because, out of deep feeling, Miss Walker has made living and passionate speech.

"We Have Been Believers," "Delta," "Southern Song," "For My People"—they are full of the rain and the sun that fall upon the faces and shoulders of her people, full of the bitter questioning and the answers not yet found, the pride and the disillusion and the reality. It is difficult for me to read these poems unmoved—I think it will be difficult for others. Yet it is not only the larger problems of her "playmates in the clay and dust" that interest Margaret Walker—she is interested in people wherever they are. In the second section of her book you will find ballads and portraits—figures of legend, like John Henry and Stagolee and the uncanny Molly Means—figures of realism like Poppa Chicken and Teacher and Gus, the Lineman, who couldn't die—figures "of Old Man River, round New Orleans, with her gumbo, rice, and good red beans." They are set for voice and the blues, they could be sung as easily as spoken. And, first and last, they are a part of our earth.

Miss Walker can write formal verse as well; she can write her own kind of sonnet. But, in whatever medium she is working, the note is true and unforced. There is a deep sincerity in all these poems—a sincerity at times disquieting. For this is what one American has found and seen—this is the song of her people, of her part of America. You cannot deny its honesty, you cannot deny its candor. And this is not far away or long ago—this is part of our nation, speaking.

I do not know what work Miss Walker will do in the future, though I should be very much surprised if this book were all she had to give. But I do know that, in this book, she has spoken of her people so that all may listen. I think that is something for any poet to have done.

Nelson Algren   (review date 1943)

SOURCE: "A Social Poet," in *Poetry: A Magazine of Verse,* Vol. LXI, February, 1943, pp. 634-36.

[*In this review of Walker's first volume of poems, Algren compliments her on her ability to communicate as a social poet but faults her for some stylistic weaknesses.*]

In this volume the Yale Series has effected a wholesome deviation from previous presentations by giving us a poet who is not, for one, a poet's poet. Miss Walker is intense and forthright without being oratorical; she is terse and demanding without loss of rhythm. She depends upon meanings more than upon metaphysics.

> For my people thronging 47th Street in Chicago and
>   Lenox Avenue
>   in New York and Rampart Street in New
>   Orleans, lost disinherited
>   dispossessed and happy people filling the
>   cabarets and taverns and
>   other people's pockets needing bread and shoes
>   and milk and land
>   and money and something—something all our
>   own . . .
>
>   . . . We with our blood have watered these
>   fields and they belong to us.

The piece called **"Delta"** is not Miss Walker's so much as it is her people's. It is one of those songs which derive music and message from sheer weight of social pressure. It possesses the restless music that oppression makes in the human heart, and recreates the mood of the human mind under the lash. By its total mood this reader was strongly reminded of Chaim Bialik's *Night.*

Miss Walker's fondness for alliteration, however, as in **"We Have Been Believers,"** sometimes compromises her depth and originality. When she resists this tendency, as in **"Delta,"** her verse is considerably deepened. And occasionally, as in **"Dark Blood,"** she lapses into conventional romanticism:

> And when I return to Mobile I shall go by the way
>   of Panama and Bocas
>   del Toro to the littered streets and the one-room

> shacks of my
>   old poverty, and blazing suns of other lands
> may struggle then to
>   reconcile the pride and pain in me.

The point being that the American Negro doesn't go to Mobile by way of Bocas del Toro any more. That is a romanticized trek to which young Negro poets are greatly given. But it is a false journey and has led not one of them home as yet.

In the second section Miss Walker goes directly to Mobile and returns with a bagful of ballads. All of them make good stories, and some of them make good poems. Although **"Two Gun Buster and Trigger Slim"** is slight, and **"Yalluh Hammuh"** finishes feebly, **"Poppa Chicken"** and **"Teacher"** are satisfying both as stories and as poems:

> Women sent him to his doom
>   Women set the trap
> Teacher was a bad, bold man
>   Lawd, but such a sap!

When unhampered by the requirements of formal verse, Miss Walker's poetry is fuller than when, as in the final section, she commits herself to a definite form. Here she is just another poet writing sonnets. Although none are bad—since she does not write bad poetry—several do smell of the midnight oil. Fortunately, the final piece rounds out the entire volume, carrying the dignity of the title-poem's message to a well-rounded close:

> Our birth and death are easy hours, like sleep
> and food and drink. The struggle staggers us
> for bread, for pride, for simple dignity.
> And this is more than fighting to exist;
> more than revolt and war and human odds.
> There is a journey from the me to you.
> There is a journey from the you to me.
> A union of the two strange worlds must be.
>
> Ours is a struggle from a too-warm bed;
> too cluttered with a patience full of sleep.
> Out of this blackness we must struggle forth;
> from want of bread, of pride, of dignity.
> Struggle between the morning and the night.
> This marks our years; this settles, too, our plight.

R. Baxter Miller   (essay date 1981)

SOURCE: "The 'Etched Flame' of Margaret Walker: Biblical and Literary Re-Creation in Southern History," in *Tennessee Studies in Literature,* Vol. XXVI, 1981, pp. 158-72.

[*Below, Miller explores Walker's use of Biblical allusions in poems from* For my People *and* Prophets for a New Day.]

The reader [of *For My People*] experiences initially the tension and potential of the Black South; then the folk tale of both tragic possibility and comic relief involving the curiosity, trickery, and deceit of men and women alike; finally, the significance of physical and spiritual love in reclaiming the Southern land. Walker writes careful antinomies into the visionary poem, the folk secular and the Shakespearian and Petrarchan sonnets. She opposes quest to denial, historical circumstances to imaginative will, and earthly suffering to heavenly bliss. Her poetry purges the southern ground of animosity and injustice which separate Black misery from Southern song. Her themes are time, infinite human potential, racial equality, vision, blindness, love and escape, as well as worldly death, drunkenness, gambling, rottenness, and freedom. She pictures the motifs within the frames of toughness and abuse, fright and gothic terror. Wild arrogance, for her speakers, often underlies heroism, but the latter is more imagined than real.

The myth of human immortality expressed in oral tale and in literary artifact transcends death. The imagination evokes atemporal memory, asserts the humanistic self against the fatalistic past, and illustrates, through physical love, the promise of both personal and racial reunification. The achievement is syntactic. Parallelism, elevated rhetoric, simile, and figure of speech abound, but more deeply the serenity of nature creates solemnity. Walker depicts sun, splashing brook, pond, duck, frog and stream, as well as flock, seed, wood, bark, cotton field, and cane. Still, the knife and gun threaten the pastoral world as, by African conjure, the moral "we" attempts to reconcile the two. As both the participant and observer, Walker creates an ironic distance between history and eternity. The Southern experience in the first section and the reclamation in the second part frame the humanity of folk personae Stagolee, John Henry, Kissie Lee, Yallah Hammer, and Gus. The book becomes a literary artifact, a "clean house" which imaginatively restructures the southland.

But if Dudley Randall has written "The Ballad of Birmingham" and Gwendolyn Brooks "The Children of the Poor," Walker succeeds with the visionary poem. She does not portray the gray-haired old women who nod and sing out of despair and hope on Sunday morning, but she captures the depths of their suffering. She recreates their belief that someday Black Americans will triumph over fire hoses and biting dogs, once the brutal signs of White oppression in the South. The prophecy contributes to Walker's rhythmical balance and vision, but she controls the emotions. How does one change brutality into social equality? Through sitting down at a lunch counter in the sixties, Black students illustrated some divinity and confronted death, just as Christ faced His cross. Walker deepens the portraits by using biblical typology, by discovering historical antitypes, and by creating an apocalyptic fusion. Through the suffering in the Old and New Testaments, the title poem of *For My People* expresses Black American victory over deprivation and hatred. The ten stanzas celebrate the endurance of tribulations such as dark murders in Virginia and Mississippi as well as Jim Crowism, ignorance, and poverty. The free form includes the parallelism of verbs and the juxtaposition of the present with the past. Black Americans are "never gaining, never reaping, never knowing and never understanding." When religion faces reality, the contrast creates powerful reversal:

> For the boys and girls who grew in spite of these things to be man and woman, to laugh and dance and sing and play and drink their wine and religion and success, to marry their playmates and bear children and then die of consumption and anemia and lynching.

Through biblical balance, **"For My People"** sets the White oppressor against the Black narrator. Social circumstance opposes racial and imaginative will, and disillusion opposes happiness. Blacks fashion a new world that encompasses many faces and people, "all the adams and eves and their countless generations." From the opening dedication (Stanza 1) to the final evocation (Stanza 10) the prophet-narrator speaks both as Christ and God. Ages ago, the Lord put His rainbow in the clouds. To the descendants of Noah it signified His promise that the world would never again end in flood. Human violence undermines biblical calm, as the first word repeats itself: "Let a new earth rise. Let another world be born. Let a bloody-peace be written in the sky. Let a second generation full of courage issue forth. . . ."

"We Have Been Believers," a visionary poem, juxtaposes Christianity with African conjure, and the Old Testament with the New, exemplified by St. John, St. Mark, and Revelation. The narrator ("we") represents the Black builders and singers in the past, for Walker seeks to interpret cultural signs. The theme is Black faith, first in Africa and then in America. As the verse shows movement from the past to the present, the ending combines Christianity and humanism. With extensive enjambment, the controlled rhapsody has a long first sentence, followed by indented ones that complete the meaning. The form literally typifies Black American struggle. The long line is jolted because an ending is illusory, and the reader renews his perusal just as the Black American continues the search for freedom. The narrator suggests the biblical scene in which death breaks the fifth seal (Revelation 6:11). There the prophet sees all the people who, slain in the service of God, wear garments as the narrator describes them.

The authenticating "we" is more focused than either Ellison's in *Invisible Man* or Baldwin's in *Notes of a Native Son*. Their speakers are often educated and upwardly mobile people who move between White and Black American worlds. Walker's, on the contrary, are frequently the secular and religious "folk" who share a communal quest. She blends historical sense with biblical implication: "Neither the slaver's whip nor the lyncher's rope nor the / bayonet could kill our black belief. In our hunger we / beheld the welcome table and in our nakedness the / glory of a long white robe." The narrator identifies Moloch, a god of cruel sacrifice, and all people who have died for no just cause. She prepares for the myth that dominates the last three parts of the poem, the miracle that Jesus performed on the eyes of a blind man. After He instructs him to wash them in the pool of Siloam, the man sees clearly (John 9:25). Another allusion suggests the miracle that Christ worked for the afflicted people near the Sea of Galilee. Walker's narrator knows the legend, but awaits the transformation (Mark 7:37). The waiting prepares for an irony phrased in alliteration: "Surely the priests and the preachers and the powers will hear . . . / . . . now that our hands are empty and our hearts too full to pray." This narrator says that such people will send a sign—the biblical image of relief and redemption—but she implies something different. Although her humanism embraces Christianity, she adds militancy and impatience. Her rhetoric illustrates liquid sound, alliteration, and assonance: "We have been believers believing in our burdens and our / demigods too long. Now the needy no longer weep / and pray; the long-suffering arise, and our fists bleed / against the bars with a strange insistency."

The impatience pervades **"Delta,"** which has the unifying type of the Twenty-Third Psalm. Although the first part presents the blood, corruption, and depression of the narrator's naturalistic world, the second illustrates the restorative potential of nature. High mountain, river, orange, cotton, fern, grass, and onion share the promise. Dynamic fertility, the recleansed river (it flowed through swamps in the first part), can clear the Southern ground of sickness, rape, starvation, and ignorance. Water gives form to anger, yet thawing sets in. Coupled with liquidity, the loudness of thunder and cannon implies storm; the narrator compares the young girl to Spring. Lovingly the speaker envisions vineyards, pastures, orchards, cattle, cotton, tobacco, and cane, "making us men in the fields we have tended / standing defending the land we have rendered rich and abiding and heavy with plenty." Interpreting the meaning of earth can help to bridge the distance between past decay and present maturity when the narrator celebrates the promise:

> the long golden grain for bread
> and the ripe purple fruit for wine
> the hills beyond for peace
> and the grass beneath for rest
> the music in the wind for us
> and the circling lines in the sky
> for dreams.

Elsewhere a gothic undercurrent and an allusion to Abel and Cain add complexity; so does an allusion to Christ and transubstantiation. Rhetorical power emerges because the harsh tone of the Old Testament threatens the merciful tone of the New one. Loosely plotted, the verse recounts the personal histories of the people in the valley. Still, the symbolical level dominates the literal one, and the poem portrays more deeply the human condition. The narrator profits from the gothicism which has influenced Ann Radcliffe, Charles Brockden Brown, and Edgar Allan Poe. Just as Walker's pictures create beauty for the African-American, they communicate a grace to all who appreciate symmetrical landscapes. The tension in her literary world comes from the romantic legacy of possibility set against denial: "High above us and round about us stand high mountains / rise the towering snowcapped mountains /

while we are beaten and broken and bowed / here in this dark valley." Almost no rhyme scheme exists in the poem, but a predominance of three or four feet gives the impression of a very loose ballad. The fifth stanza of the second part has incremental repetition, as the undertone of Countee Cullen's poem "From the Dark Tower" heightens the deep despair, the paradox of desire and restraint: "We tend the crop and gather the harvest / but not for ourselves do we sweat and starve and spend . . . / here on this earth we dare not claim . . ." In the stanza before the final one the reader associates myth and history. While the narrator remembers the Blacks unrewarded in the Southern past, the imagery suggests Christ and transubstantiation. The speaker, however, alludes mainly to Abel slain by Cain (Genesis 4:10): "We with our blood have watered these fields / and they belong to us." Implicitly the promise of the Psalmist ("Yea though I walk through the valley of the shadow of death") has preceded.

In four quatrains, **"Since 1619"** strengthens Old Testament prefiguration. Aware of World War II, the narrator illuminates human blindness. She emphasizes the inevitability of death and the deterioration of world peace. With anaphora she repeats the Psalmist: "How many years . . . have I been singing Spirituals? / How long have I been praising God and shouting hallelujahs? / How long have I been hated and hating? / How long have I been living in hell for heaven?" She remembers the Valley of Dry Bones in which the Lord placed the prophet Ezekiel, whom He questioned if the bones could live. Whereas in the Bible salvation is external and divine, here the transformation comes fromwithin. The poem contrasts moral renewal to the spiritual death during World War II and the pseudo-cleanliness of middle-class America. Written in seven stanzas, the verse has four lines in the first section and three in the second. Initially the poem portrays the ancient muse, the inspiration of all poetry, and later it illustrates poverty, fear, and sickness. Even the portrait of lynching cannot end the narrator's quest for cleanliness. Although Americans face death, they will continue to seek solace through intoxication and sex. The beginning of the poem foreshadows the end, but the directness in the second section supplants the general description in the first. The middle-class Americans in the first part have no bombing planes or air-raids to fear, yet they have masked violence and ethnocentric myth: "viewing weekly 'Wild West Indian and Shooting Sam,' 'Mama Loves Papa,' and 'Gone By the Breeze!'" Calories, eyemaline, henna rinse, and dental cream image a materialistic nation. With a deeper cleanliness, the speaker advises the reader within an ironic context: "Pray for second sight and the inner ear. Pray for bulwark against poaching patterns of dislocated days; pray for buttressing iron against insidious termite and beetle and locust and flies and lice and moth and rust and mold."

The religious types in the second and third sections of *For My People* rival neither those in the first section nor those in *Prophets for a New Day*. When Walker ignores biblical sources, often she vainly attempts to achieve cultural saturation. Without biblical cadences her ballads frequently become average, if not monotonous. In **"Yalluh**

Hammah," a folk poem about the "Bad Man," she manages sentimentality, impractical concern, and trickery, as a Black woman outsmarts the protagonist and steals his money.

But sometimes the less figurative sonnets are still boring. **"Childhood"** lacks the condensation and focus to develop well the Petrarchan design. In the octave a young girl remembers workers who used to return home in the afternoons. Even during her maturity, the rags of poverty and the habitual grumbling color the Southern landscape still. Despite weaknesses, the poem suggests well a biblical analogue. As the apostle Paul writes "When I was a child, I spake as a child: but when I became a man, I put away childish things" (I Corinthians 13:11), Walker's sonnet coincidentally begins, "When I was a child I knew red miners . . . / I also lived in a low cotton country . . . where sentiment and hatred still held sway / and only bitter land was washed away." The mature writer seeks now to restore and renew the earth.

In *Prophets* Walker illustrates some historical antitypes to the Old Testament. Her forms are the visionary poem, free verse sonnet, monody, pastoral, and gothic ballad in which she portrays freedom, speech, death, and rebirth. Her major images are fire, water, and wind. When she opposes marching to standing, the implied quest becomes metaphorical, for she recreates the human community in the spiritual wilderness. She looks beneath any typological concern of man's covenant with God, and even the pantheistic parallel of the Southerner's covenant with the land, to illuminate man's broken covenant with himself. The human gamut runs from death ("mourning bird") to the potential of poetry ("humming bird"). Poetry recreates anthropocentric space. The speaker depicts the breadth through dramatic dialogue, sarcasm, and satire. Even the cold stone implies the potential for creative inspiration or Promethean fire. The narrator verbally paints urban corruption in the bitter cold and frozen water. Her portrait images not only the myth of fragmentation and dissolution, but the courage necessary to confront and transcend them. Her world is doubly Southern. Here the Old South still withstands Northern invasion, but the Black South endures both. One attains the mythical building beyond (sounds like Thomas Wolfe), the human house, through fire. Form is imagined silence. Poetry, both catharsis and purgation, parallels speaking, crying, and weaving. The center includes geometric space and aesthetic beauty. To portray anthropocentric depth is to clarify the significance of human cleansing.

Although the sonnets and ballads in *For My People* are weak, the typological poems in *Prophets for a New Day* envision universal freedom. But neither Walker nor her reader can remain at visionary heights, for the real world includes the white hood and fiery cross. Even the latter image fails to save the poem **"Now,"** in which the subject is civil rights. Here both images of place and taste imply filth as doors, dark alleys, balconies, and washrooms reinforce moral indignation. The Klan marks "kleagle with a klux / and a fiery burning cross." Yet awkward rhythms have preceded. In shifting from three feet to four, the speaker stumbles: "In the cleaning room and closets / with the washrooms marked 'For Colored Only.'" The ear of **"Sit-ins"** catches more sharply the translation of the Bible into history. Written in twelve lines of free verse, the lyric depicts the students at North Carolina A & T University, who in 1960 sat down at the counter of a dime store and began the Civil Rights movement. The speaker recreates Southern history. In the shining picture, the reader sees the Angel Michael who drove Adam and Eve from Paradise, but the portrait becomes more secular: "With courage and faith, convictions and intelligence / The first to blaze a flaming patch for justice / And awaken consciences / Of these stony ones." The implement that in the Bible and Milton symbolized Paradise Lost becomes a metaphor for Paradise Regained. In viewpoint the narrator gives way to the demonstrators themselves: *"Come, Lord Jesus, Bold Young Galilean / Sit Beside This Counter / Lord With Me."*

As with most of Walker's antitypical poems, **"Sit-Ins"** hardly rivals **"Ballad of the Free,"** one of her finest. The latter work portrays the heroic missions and tragic deaths of slave insurrectionists and excels through consistent rhythm as well as compression of image. At first the verse seems true to the title. Although the design of the typical ballad usually emphasizes a rhythmic contrast between two lines in succession, **"Ballad of the Free,"** stresses a contrast between whole stanzas. Of the twelve sections which comprise the poem, each of the four quatrains follows a tercet which serves as the refrain. The narrator adds a striking twist to St. Matthew (19:30; 20:16), in which Peter asks Jesus what will happen to people who have forsaken everything to follow Him. Christ replies that the social status will be reversed. Although He speaks about the beginning of the apocalypse in which all persons are judged, Walker's narrator forsees the end of the apocalypse in which all are equal: "The serpent is loosed and the hour is come. . . ."

The refrain balances social history and biblical legend. The first stanza presents Nat Turner, the leader of the slave insurrection in South Hampton, Virginia, during 1831. After the first refrain, the reader recognizes Gabriel Prosser, whom a storm once forced to suspend a slave revolt in Richmond, Virginia. With a thousand other slaves, Prosser planned an uprising that collapsed in 1800. Betrayed by fellow bondsmen, he and fifteen others were hanged on October 7 in that year. After the first echo of the refrain, Denmark Vesey, who enlisted thousands of Blacks for an elaborate slave plot in Charleston, S.C., and the vicinity, appears in the fifth stanza. Authorities arrested 131 Blacks and four Whites, and when the matter was settled, thirty-seven people were hanged. Toussaint L'Ouverture, who at the turn of the eighteenth and nineteenth centuries liberated Haitian slaves, follows the second echo of the refrain. Shortly afterwards an evocation of John Brown intensifies the balance between history and sound. With thirteen Whites and five Blacks, Brown attacked Harper's Ferry on October 16, 1859, and by December 2 of that year, he was also hanged. In the poem, as in the Southern past, the death of the rebel is foreshadowed. Gifted with humane vision, he wants to change an inegalitarian South. But the maintainers of the status quo will kill, so the hero becomes the martyr.

In order to emphasize Turner as historical paradigm, the narrator ignores the proper chronology of L'Ouverture, Prosser, Vesey, Turner, and Brown. She gives little of the historical background but calls upon the names of legend. What does she achieve, by naming her last hero, if not a symmetry of color? The ballad that began with Black Nat Turner ends with White John Brown, for if action alone determines a basis for fraternity, racial distinction is insignificant.

For a central portrait of Turner, the verse moves backward and forward in both typological and apocalyptic time. As with the narrator of Hughes's "Negro Speaks of Rivers," the speaker can comprehend different decades. Because she is outside of Time, L'Ouverture and Brown, who come from different periods, appear to her with equal clarity. Until the eleventh stanza, the biblical sureness of the refrain has balanced history. The note of prophecy sounds in the slowness and firmness of racial progress: *"Wars and Rumors of Wars have gone, / But Freedom's army marches on. / The heroes' list of dead is long, / And Freedom still is for the strong."* The narrator recalls Christ (Mark 13:7) who prophesies wars and rumors of war, but foretells salvation for endurers. The final refrain interfuses with the fable and history: "The serpent is loosed and the hour is come."

"At the Lincoln Monument in Washington, August 28, 1963," presents analogues to Isaiah, Exodus, Genesis, and Deuteronomy. Written in two stanzas, the poem has forty-four lines. The speaker dramatizes chronicle through biblical myth, racial phenomenology, and Judaeo-Christian consciousness. She advances superbly with the participant to the interpreter, but even the latter speaks from within an aesthetic mask. The poetic vision authenticates the morality of her fable and the biblical analogue. The first stanza has twenty-eight lines, and the second has sixteen. As the speaker recalls the march on Washington, in which more than 250,000 people demonstrated for civil rights, she attributes to Martin Luther King, Jr., the leader of the movement, the same rhetorical art she now remembers him by. The analogue is Isaiah: "The grass withereth, the flower fadeth: but the word of our God shall stand for ever" (40:8). Two brothers, according to the fable, led the Israelites out of Egypt. Sentences of varied length complement the juxtaposition of cadences which rise and fall. The narrator names neither King as "Moses" nor King's youthful follower as "Aaron," yet she clarifies a richness of oration and implies the heroic spirit. King, before his death, said that he had been to the mountain top, and that he had seen the Promised Land. But the speaker literarily retraces the paradigm of the life; she distills the love of the listeners who saw him and were inspired: "There they stand . . . / The old man with a dream he has lived to see come true."

Although the first eleven lines of the poem are descriptive, the twelfth combines chronicle and prefiguration. The speaker projects the social present into the mythical past. Her words come from a civil rights song, "We Woke Up One Morning With Our Minds Set On Freedom." The social activist wants the immediate and complete liberation which the rhetorician (speaker and writer) translates into literary symbol: "We woke up one morning in Egypt / And the river ran red with blood . . . / And the houses of death were afraid."

She remembers, too, the story of Jacob, who returns home with his two wives, Leah and Rachel (Genesis 30:25-43). Laban, the father-in-law, gave him speckled cattle, but now the narrator understands that Jacob's "*house* (Africa-America) has grown into a nation / The slaves break forth from bondage" (emphasis mine). In Old Testament fashion, she cautions against fatigue in the pursuit of liberty. Through heightened style, she becomes a prophet whose medium is eternal language. She has mastered alliteration, assonance, and resonance.

> Write this word upon your hearts
> And mark this message on the doors of your houses
> See that you do not forget
> How this day the Lord has set our faces toward
>   freedom
> Teach these words to your children
> And see that they do not forget them.

Walker's poetry alludes subtly to King but refers to Malcolm X directly. The verse dedicated to Malcolm portrays him as Christ. Nearly a Petrarchan sonnet, the poem is not written in the five-foot line, but has several lines of four or six feet. Neither of the last two lengths usually characterizes the form, and even a concession of off-rhyme does not make a Petrarchan scheme unfold. The comments sound repetitious because they are. As with the earlier sonnet **"Childhood,"** **"Malcolm"** appears at first to deserve oblivion because here, too, Walker fails to condense and control metrics. Still, the quiet appeal is clear. The Christ story compels rereading, and one finds it a meaningful experience. When Malcolm is associated with a dying swan in the octave, the narrator alludes to the Ovidian legend of the beautiful bird which sings just before death. Malcolm takes on Christ's stigmata: "Our blood and water pour from your flowing wounds."

Vivid and noble portraits of crucifixion, another type of martyrdom, give even more vitality to **"For Andy Goodman, Michael Schwerner, and James Chaney"** (hereafter **"For Andy"**), a poem about three civil rights workers murdered in Mississippi on June 21, 1964. The elegy complements seasonal and diurnal cycle through the reaffirmation of human growth and spiritual redemption. Despite the questionable value of martyrdom, sunrise balances sunset, and beautiful leaves partly compensate for human mutilation. In dramatic reversal, Walker's narrator uses the literary technique which distinguishes *Lycidas, Adonais,* and *When Lilacs Last in the Dooryard Bloom'd.*

The flower and the paradigmatic bird (lark, robin, mourning bird, bird of sorrow, bird of death) restore both an epic and elegiac mood. The reader half-hears the echo of the goddess Venus who mourns for Adonis; *mourning* and *morning,* excellent puns, signify the cycle and paradox of life. The short rhythm, two feet, and the longer rhythm, three or four, provide the solemn folksiness of a very loose ballad or free verse. With interior rhyme, the musical balance communicates quiet pathos: "They have killed these three / They have killed them for me." The gentle suggestion of the trinity, the tragic flight of the bird, and the slow but cyclical turning from spring to spring intensify the narrator's sadness and grief.

Just as **"For Andy"** shows Walker's grace of style, the title poem of *Prophets* illustrates that the Bible prefigures the eloquence. As with the earlier poem **"Delta,"** **"Prophets"** resists paraphrase because it abstractly portrays Black American history. The poem has three parts. The first shows thatthe Word which came to the biblical prophets endures, and the next presents the actual appearance of the ancient vision to new believers. In the third part, the reader moves to a final understanding about tragic death. While the poet marks the recurrence of sacred light, fire, gentleness, and artistic speech, she contrasts White and Black, dark and light, age and youth, life and death. Some allusions to Ezekiel and Amos now fuse with others from Ecclesiastes and Isaiah. Amos tells of a prophet-priest of sixth century B.C., a watchman over the Israelites during the exile in Babylon, by the river of Cheber (Ezek. 1:15-20). As a herdsman from the southern village of Tekoa, Judah, he went to Bethel in Samaria to preach a religion of social justice and righteousness. He attacked economic exploitation and privilege and criticized the priests who stressed ritual above justice. Because Amos is Walker's personal symbol of Martin Luther King, Jr., she provides more background about him than about others. The reader knows his name, character, and homeland.

But Walker socially and historically reinvigorates the scriptures. She is no eighteenth-century Jupiter Hammon who rewrites the Bible without any infusion of personal suffering. She feels strongly and personally that the demonstrators in the sixties antitypify the Scriptures: "So today in the pulpits and the jails, / A fearless shepherd speaks at last / To his suffering weary sheep." She implies perseverance even in the face of death, and her speaker blends the images of the New Testament with those from *Beowulf.* Her lines depict the beast:

> His mark is on the land
> His horns and his hands and his lips are gory with
>   our blood
> He is death and destruction and Trouble
> And he walks in our houses at noonday
> And devours our defenders at midnight.

The literary word images fear and sacrifice more than immediate redemption. What shadows the fate of the good? The beast

> has crushed them with a stone.
> He drinks our tears for water
> And he drinks our blood for wine;
> He eats our flesh like a ravenous lion

> And he drives us out of the city
> To be stabbed on a lonely hill.

The same scene relives the crucifixion.

Walker draws heavily upon the Bible for typological unity. Of the twenty-two poems in *Prophets,* seven of the last nine have biblical names for titles, including **"Jeremiah,"** **"Isaiah,"** **"Amos-1963,"** **"Amos (Postscript-1968),"** **"Joel,"** **"Hosea,"** and **"Micah."** A similar problem besets all, although to a different extent. The aesthetic response relies on historical sense more than on dramatized language, and passing time will weaken the emotional hold. In **"Jeremiah,"** the narrator is conscious of both the fallen world and the apocalyptic one. She suggests Benjamin Mays, who has been a preacher and educator in Atlanta for over fifty years. Seeking to lift the "curse" from the land, Mays wants to redeem the corrupted city. The mythical denotation of the place—"Atlanta"—inspires the cultural imagination. Once a girl by that name lost a race to Hippomenes, her suitor, because she digressed from her course to pursue golden apples. Yet Walker's poem does more than oppose Mays to urban materialism. Through his articulation (the spoken word), he signifies the artist and the writer. The narrator who recounts the tale is an artist, too, since Walker's speakers and heroes mirror each other. Although Jeremiah appears as a contemporary man, he exists in a half-way house between legend and reality. Despite limitations, the final six lines of the verse combine myth and anaphora, where the speaker compares the imaginative and historical worlds more closely than elsewhere. Once destroyed by fire, Atlanta suggests Babylon, capital first of Babylonia and then of Chaldea on the Euphrates river. As the scene of the biblical Exile, the city represents grandeur and wickedness. The book of Psalms portrays the despair of the Israelites who sat down and wept when they remembered Zion. With an undertone of an old folk ballad, Walker builds a literary vision. While anaphora strengthens solemnity, the voice subsumes both narrator and prophet:

> My God we are still here. We are still down here
>   Lord,
> Working for a kingdom of Thy Love,
> We weep for this city and for this land
> We weep for Judah and beloved Jerusalem
> O Georgia! "Where shall you stand in the
>   Judgment?"

Through the fire, the mark, and the word, **"Isaiah"** clarifies the typology which leads from **"Lincoln Monument,"** midway through the volume, to **"Elegy"** at the end. Jeremiah expresses himself in the public forum as well as on television. He resembles Adam Clayton Powell, Jr., a major Civil Rights activist in Harlem during the depression. Powell persuaded many Harlem businesses, including Harlem Hospital, to hire Blacks. As Chairman of the Coordinating Committee on Employment, he led a demonstration which forced the World's Fair to adopt a similar policy in 1939. He desegregated many Congressional facilities, Washington restaurants, and theatres. He proposed first the withholding of federal funds from projects which showed racial discrimination; he introduced the first legislation to desegregate the armed forces; he established the right of Black journalists to sit in the press galleries of the United States House of Representatives and in the Senate. As Chairman of the House Committee on Education and Labor in 1960, he supported forty-eight pieces of legislation on social welfare and later earned a letter of gratitude from President Johnson.

> In 1967, however, Powell's House colleagues raised charges of corruption and financial mismanagement against him. In January he was stripped of his chairmanship and barred from the House, pending an investigation. On March 1, 1967 Powell was denied a seat in the House by a vote of 307 to 116, despite the committee's recommendation that he only be censured, fined, and placed at the bottom of the seniority list. On April 11 a special election was held to fill Powell's seat. Powell, who was not campaigning and was on the island of Bimini and who could not even come to New York City because of a court judgment against him in a defamation case, received 74% of the Harlem vote cast.[Peter M. Bergman and Mort N. Bergman, *The Chronological History of the Negro in America,* 1969.]

Even more clearly, the **"Amos"** poems reconfirm Walker's greater metaphor for Martin Luther King, Jr. The first of these two verses, twenty lines in length, portrays Amos as a contemporary shepherd who preaches in the depths of Alabama and elsewhere: "standing in the Shadow of our God / Tending his flocks over the hills of Albany / And the seething streets of Selma and of bitter Birmingham." As with the first **"Amos"** poem, the second **"Postscript (1968)"** is written in free verse. With only ten lines, however, the latter is shorter. King, the prophet of justice, appears through the fluidity and the wholesomeness of the "O" sound: "From Montgomery to Memphis he marches / He stands on the threshold of tomorrow / He breaks the bars of iron and they remove the signs / He opens the gates of our prisons."

Many of the short poems that follow lack the high quality found in some of Walker's other typological lyrics. **"Joel"** uses the standard free verse, but the historical allusion is obscure. **"Hosea"** suffers from the same problem. The Bible presents the figure as having an unfaithful wife, but Walker's poem presents a Hosea who, marked for death, writes love letters to the world. Is the man Eldridge Cleaver? The letters and the theme of redemption clearly suggest him, but one can never be sure. The legend could better suit the man. The last poem in **Prophets** appropriately benefits from some of Walker's favorite books such as Ecclesiastes, Isaiah, and St. John. **"Elegy,"** a verse in two parts, honors the memory of Manford Kuhn, professor and friend. Summer and sunshine give way to winter snow and "frothy wood," since the green harvest must pass. But art forms ironically preserve themselves through fire, and engraving comes from corrosion. Eternity paradoxically depends upon decay. The first section concerns the cycle of nature which continually turns; the second, an elaborate conceit, depicts people as ephemeral artists. Reminiscent of Virgil's

Aeneid, Shelley's "The Witch of Atlas," and Danner's short lyric, "The Slave and the Iron Lace," Walker's second section begins:

> Within our house of flesh we weave a web of time
> Both warp and woof within the shuttle's clutch
> In leisure and in haste no less a tapestry
> Rich pattern of our lives.
> The gold and scarlet intertwine
> Upon our frame of dust an intricate design. . . .

Here are her ablest statement and restatement of the iamb. The "I" sound supports assonance and rhyme, even though the poem is basically free. At first the idea of human transitoriness reinforces *Ecclesiastes* which powerfully presents the theme. In a second look, however, one traces the thought to Isaiah (40:7): "The grass withereth, the flower fadeth: because the spirit of the Lord bloweth upon it. . . ." But the speaker knows the ensuing verse equally well: "The grass withereth, the flower fadeth; but the *word* [emphasis mine] of our God shall stand for ever" (40:8). Poetry, an inspired creation in words, is divine as well. To the extent that Kuhn showed Christ-like love and instruction for his students, his spirit transcends mortality. For any who demonstrate similar qualities is the vision any less true and universal? To Nicodemus, the Pharisee whom Jesus told to be reborn (John 3:8), the final allusion belongs.

> We live again
> In children's faces, and the sturdy vine
> Of daily influences: the prime
> Of teacher, neighbor, student, and friend
> All merging on the elusive wind.

Patient nobility becomes the poet who has recreated Martin Luther King, Jr. as Amos. She has kept the neatly turned phrase of Countee Cullen but replaced Tantalus and Sisyphus with Black students and sit-ins. For her literary fathers, she reaches back to the nineteenth-century prophets Blake, Byron, Shelley, and Tennyson. Her debt extends no less to Walt Whitman and to Langston Hughes, for her predecessor is any poet who forsees a new paradise and who portrays the coming. As with Hughes, Walker is a romantic. But Hughes had either to subordinate his perspective to history or to ignore history almost completely and to speak less about events than about personal and racial symbols. Walker, on the contrary, equally combines events and legends but reaffirms the faith of the spirituals. Although her plots sometimes concern murder, her narrators reveal an image of racial freedom and human peace. The best of her imagined South prefigures the future.

Eugenia Collier (essay date 1984)

SOURCE: "Fields Watered with Blood: Myth and Ritual in the Poetry of Margaret Walker," in *Black Women Writers (1950-1980),* edited by Mari Evans, Anchor Books, 1984, pp. 499-510.

[*Collier discusses Walker's use of Black myth and ritual in the poems of* For my People *and* Prophets for a New Day.]

"For my people everywhere . . . ," the reader began, and the audience of Black folk listened, a profound and waiting silence. We knew the poem. It was ours. The reader continued, his deep voice speaking not only *to* us but *for* us, ". . . singing their slave songs repeatedly: their dirges and their ditties and their blues and jubilees. . . ." And as the poem moved on, rhythmically piling on image after image of our lives, making us know again the music wrenched from our slave agony, the religious faith, the toil and confusion and hopelessness, the strength to endure in spite of it all, as the poem went on mirroring our collective selves, we cried out in deep response. We cried out as our fathers had responded to sweating Black preachers in numberless cramped little churches, and further back, as our African ancestors had responded to rituals which still, unremembered and unknown, inform our being. And when the resonant voice proclaimed the dawn of a new world, when it called for a race of *men* to "rise and take control," we went wild with ancient joy and new resolve.

Margaret Walker's **"For My People"** does that. It melts away time and place and it unifies Black listeners. Its power is as compelling now as it was forty-odd years ago when it was written, perhaps more so as we have experienced repeatedly the flood tide and the ebb tide of hope. The source of its power is the reservoir of beliefs, values, and archetypal characters yielded by our collective historical experience. It is this area of our being which defines us, which makes us a people, which finds expression *in Black art and in no other.*

Make no mistake: What we call the "universal" is grounded in particular group experience. All humans (except, perhaps, an occasional aberrant individual) share such fundamentals as the need for love, an instinct for survival, the inevitability of change, the reality of death. But these fundamentals are meaningless unless they are couched in specific human experience. And there is no person who is not a member of a race, a group, a family of humankind. Nobody exists alone. We are each a part of a specific collective past, to which we respond in a way in which no person outside the group can respond. This is right. This is good.

Margaret Walker has tapped the rich vein of Black experience and fashioned that material into art. By "Black experience" we refer to the African past, the dispersal of African people into a diaspora, and the centuries-long incubus of oppression. Included is the entire range of human emotion from despair to joy to triumph. The discussion here will be of Margaret Walker's use of this shared experience in her poetry.

Margaret Walker's signature poem is **"For My People."** Widely anthologized in Black collections and often read at dramatic presentations, it is the work most closely associated with her name. Some years ago, when I was involved in compiling an anthology of ethnic literature for high schools, the editor (white) refused to permit us to include this poem. It was too militant, he said. The man was unutterably wise: the poem thrusts to the heart of Black experience and suggests a solution that would topple him and the culture he represents from its position of power. White response to African American literature is often, and for obvious reasons, diametric to Black response; this poem is indeed a case in point.

> Margaret Walker's *For My People* . . . melts away time and place and it unifies Black listeners. Its power is as compelling now as it was forty-odd years ago when it was written, perhaps more so as we have experienced repeatedly the flood tide and ebb tide of hope. The source of its power is the reservoir of beliefs, values, and archetypal characters yielded by our collective historical experience.
>
> —*Eugenia Collier*

"For My People" exemplifies Walker's use of Black myth and ritual. [By myth is meant the wellspring of racial memories to which I have previously alluded. By ritual is meant the actions, gestures, and activities which recur in a culture and which overlap with and result from myth.] The poem first evokes the two mechanisms which have never been a source of strength to Black folk: music and religion. But even in the first stanza is implied a need to move beyond historical roles, for the "slave songs" are sung "repeatedly," the god (lower case) to whom the people pray is "unknown," and the people humble themselves to "an unseen power." Then the poem catalogues the rituals of the toil which consumes the life of the people, hopeless toil which never enables one to get ahead and never yields any answers. The stanza jams the heavy tasks together without commas to separate them, making them all into one conglomerate burden: "washing, ironing, cooking scrubbing sewing mending hoeing plowing digging planting. . . ." The poem rushes by, as indeed life rushes by when one must labor "never gaining never reaping never knowing and never understanding. . . ."

Walker now changes focus from the general to the specific—to her playmates, who are, by extension, all Black children playing the games which teach them their reality—"baptizing and preaching and doctor and jail and soldier and school and mama and cooking and playhouse and concert and store and hair and Miss Choomby and company. . . ." She shows us the children growing up to a woeful miseducation in school, which bewilders rather than teaches them, until they discover the overwhelming and bitter truth that they are "black and poor and small and different and nobody cared and nobody wondered and nobody understood. . . ." The children grow, however, to manhood and womanhood; they live out their lives until they "die of consumption and anemia and lynching. . . ."

The poem then returns to the wide angle of "my people" and continues its sweep of Black experience, cataloguing the troubled times wrought by racism.

The form of the first nine stanzas supports their message. Rather than neat little poetic lines, they consist of long, heavily weighted paragraphs inversely indented. The words and phrases cataloguing the rituals of trouble are separated by "and . . . and . . . and." There is little punctuation. Each stanza begins with a "for" phrase followed by a series of modifiers. Finally the long sentence, with its burden of actions and conditions, ends with one short, simple clause which leaves the listener gasping: "Let a new earth rise." Five words. Strong words, each one accented. Five words, bearing the burden of nine heavy stanzas, just as Black people have long borne the burden of oppression.

The final stanza is a reverberating cry for redress. It demands a new beginning. Our music then will be martial music; our peace will be hard-won, but it will be "written in the sky." And after the agony, the people whose misery spawned strength will control our world.

This poem is the hallmark of Margaret Walker's works. It echoes in her subsequent poetry and even in her monumental novel *Jubilee*. It speaks to us, in our words and rhythms, of our history, and it radiates the promise of our future. It is the quintessential example of myth and ritual shaped by artistic genius.

The volume *For My People* is the fruit of the Chicago years in the 1930s when the young poet found her voice. A lifetime's experience went into the writing of the book: the violent racism of the deep South, her gentle and intelligent parents, her bitter struggle to retain a sense of worth despite the dehumanizing forces of Alabama of the 1920s and 1930s; her disillusionment at discovering that racial prejudice was just as strong in the Midwest, where she went to college, as in the South. After her graduation from Northwestern University in the mid-thirties, she went to Chicago to work at various jobs, including the Federal Writers Project. There her developing sensitivity was nurtured by her association with young artists and intellectuals, including Richard Wright. She became interested in Marxism and, like many of her contemporaries, saw it as the key to the accomplishment of the dream. After four years she left Chicago to study in the School of Letters of the University of Iowa. The poems in *For My People,* reflecting the thoughts, emotions, and impressions of all the years, were her master's thesis. After receiving her degree, she returned to Southern soil, this time to stay.

The South is an ancestral home of Black Americans. It is true, of course, that slavery also existed in the North and that Black people have lived from the beginning in all sections of this country. But collectively it is the South that is the nucleus of Black American culture. It is here that the agony of chattel slavery created the history that

is yet to be written. It is the South that has dispersed its culture into the cities of the North. The South is, in a sense, the mythic landscape of Black America.

This landscape as portrayed vividly in this first important volume for the South is the psychic as well as the geographic home of Margaret Walker. The children in **"For My People"** play "in the clay and dust and sand of Alabama." The strong grandmothers in **"Lineage,"** who "touched earth and grain grew," toiled in the wet clay of the South. And the farm in Iowa reminds the poet of her Southern home. "My roots are deep in southern life," writes Walker in **"Sorrow Home,"** flooding the poem with sensual images of warm skies and blue water, of the smell of fresh pine and wild onion. "I want my body bathed in southern suns," she writes in **"Southern Song,"** "my soul reclaimed from southern land." This poem is rich in images of silver corn and ponds with ducks and frogs, of the scent of grass and hay and clover and fresh-turned soil.

Both poems portray what Eleanor Traylor calls the ruined world, the fragmented world of the American South, the ambivalence which ever haunts Black people. For the Southland [in **"Sorrow Home"**] is the "sorrow home, melody beating in my bone and blood!" And the speaker (for us all) demands, "How long will the Klan of hate, the hounds and the chain gangs keep me away from my own?". And the speaker, the collective "I," after portraying the peace and beauty of the Southland, pleads in graphic detail for undisturbed integration of the Self.

The poem that most completely exploits the motif of the South is the long poem **"Delta."** "I am a child of the valley," Walker asserts, and again the "I" is collective. The valley is both literal and symbolic. The images are realistic descriptions of an actual place. But the poem's essence is its symbolic meaning. The valley is, in the beginning, a place of despair, of "mud and muck and misery," hovered over by "damp draughts of mist and fog." Destruction threatens, for "muddy water flows at our shanty door / and leaves stand like a swollen bump on our backyard." Here the sounds are the dissonance of the honky-tonks, the despairing sounds of "the wailing /of a million voices strong." The speaker, in deep despair, demands that her "sorrowing sisters," "lost forgotten men," and a desperate people rise from the valley with a singing that "is ours."

This vision of hope recalls the fact that the generations-long labor of the people has made the valley theirs / ours. The snowcapped mountains tower high above the "beaten and broken and bowed" ones in "this dark valley." On the river, boats take away "cargoes of our need." Meanwhile, our brother is ill, our sister is ravished, our mother is starving. And a deepseated rebelliousness surfaces from inside our collective self. Oppression increases with the destruction of a sudden storm, and the rape and murder of all we love leaves us "dazed in wonder." From this lowest of all points, when we are threatened with total loss, we realize our love for this place, and our right to it, precisely because it is "our blood" that has "watered these fields."

"Delta" encompasses the essence of Black myth in America. The valley depicts our traditional position as the most completely oppressed people in America; the mountains, snowcapped, are our aspiration for the fulfillment of America's promise—ever before us but totally beyond our reach. Again, the rituals of toil and despair and regeneration affirm the myth. The message of the poem is that we have bought our stake in this nation with our labor, our torment, and our blood. And nothing, nothing, can separate us from what is ours.

The poems of the South portray one level of the Black American ancestral home. Walker is not unaware of the scattered places worldwide which created the Black American. "There were bizarre beginnings in old lands for the making of me," she asserts in **"Dark Blood."** The "me" is both personal and collective as she refers not only to her own immediate ancestry in Jamaica but to the eclectic background of Black people—Africa, Asia, Europe, the Caribbean. "There were sugar sands and islands of fern and pearl, palm jungles and stretches of a neverending sea." She will return "to the tropical lands of my birth, to the coasts of continents and the tiny wharves of island shores" to "stand on mountain tops and gaze on fertile homes below." This return is a psychic journey into the mythic past, a journey necessary for the Black American, for only by reuniting with the fragmented self can one become whole. On her return to the place of her physical birth, Walker writes, the "blazing suns of other lands may struggle then to reconcile the pride and pain in me." The poem thus encompasses space and time—continents and islands, antiquity and now. It thrusts deep into the Black American self.

In another section of the volume, Walker shows another aspect of our psyche: our folklore. Here the voice is that of the tale teller indigenous to Black America, especially the South, who reaches back ultimately to the people who swapped tales around the fire in ancient Africa. Using ballad forms and the language of the grass-roots people, Walker spins yarns of folk heroes and heroines: those who, faced with the terrible obstacles which haunt Black people's very existence, not only survive but prevail—with style. There are the tough ones: Kissie Lee, who learned by bitter experience that one must fight back and who "died with her boots on switching blades"; Trigger Slim, who vanquished the terror of the railroad workers' mess hall, Two-Gun Buster; and the baddest of them all, Stagolee, who killed a white policeman and eluded the lynch mob. There are the workers: Gus the lineman, who handled his live wire and survived many certain-death accidents only to drown drunk, facedown in a shallow creek; and the most famous worker, John Henry, who "could raise two bales of cotton / with one hand anchored down the steamboat," but who was killed by a ten-pound hammer. There are the lovers: Sweetie Pie, done wrong by her lover Long John Nelson; the Teacher, whose "lust included all / Women ever made;" Yalluh Hammuh, who was defeated by jealous Pick Ankle and his girl friend May; Poppa Chicken, whose very presence on the street made the girls cry, "Lawdy! Lawd!" There are the supernatural elements throughout: old Molly Means, "Chile of

the devil, the dark and sitch," whose ghost still "rides along on a winter breeze"; Stagolee's ghost, which still haunts New Orleans; Big John Henry, whom the witches taught how to conjure. These are all archetypes who recur repeatedly in Black American lore and are vital to the culture—mythic characters performing endlessly their rituals of defeat, survival, and triumph.

Contrasting with the ballads are the poems which end the volume: six sonnets. But even here the setting is the mythic landscape, the South of Walker's memory. It is peopled by "red miners" who labor incessantly and hopelessly, "painted whores," pathetic and doomed, and people who are hurt and bewildered, muttering protests against their oppression. The landscape is filled with tree stumps, rotting shacks of sharecroppers, and cold cities with tenements. The form of these poems supports their theme. For the dignified sonnet form, which emerges from a European vision of an orderly universe, substitutes here approximate rhyme rather than true rhyme, indicating that, for these people, the promise has been distorted.

The symbols in the *For My People* poems are elemental: sun, earth, and water. The sun is the primary symbol, appearing repeatedly. The sun is a beneficent force, radiating comfort; it is the source of healing. "I want my body bathed again in southern suns," she writes in **"Southern Song,"** "to lay my hand again upon the clay baked by a southern sun. . . ." In **"Dark Blood"** it is the "blazing suns of other lands" which bring together the scattered ancestry and "reconcile the pride and pain in me." Often the sun force is implied in the many agrarian images of growing grain or seeds planted with the expectation of fulfillment. In **"Sorrow Home"** the absence of the sun is symbolically significant. Declaring that "I was sired and weaned in a tropic world. . . . Warm skies and gulf blue streams are in my blood," the poet asserts her longing for the sun and the natural things it produces in contrast to the unnatural environment of the city: "I am no hot-house bulb to be reared in steam-heated flats with the music of 'L' and subway in my ears, walled in by steel and wood and brick far from the sky."

The most sustained reference to the sun is in the brief poem **"People of Unrest,"** where the speaker gazes "from the pillow" at the sun, the pillow seeming to symbolize lethargy or other conditions which prevent one from knowing one's potential and taking appropriate action. The sun is the "light in shadows"—hope when all seems hopeless. The day grows tall; it is time for action—for self-knowledge, for healing, for positiveness. We should seek joyfully the force which will make us whole and move us to positive action. For our curse of "unrest and sorrow," the sun will provide regeneration.

Earth and water are closely associated with sun. Soil, sun-warmed, is also healing. It is the womb from which springs nourishment for spirit as well as body. The sturdy, singing grandmothers "touched the earth and grain grew." The persona caught in the unnatural environment of the Northern city longs for unbroken rest in the fields of Southern earth, where corn waves "silver in the sun"

("**Southern Song**"). We need "earth beneath our feet against the storm" ("**Our Need**"). Water also is a life force, working with earth to produce nourishment and peace. The city-dwelling persona longs to "mark the splashing of a brook, a pond with ducks and frogs . . ." ("**Southern Song**").

But an imbalance between sun, earth, and water produces chaos. The valley, where there is little sun, yields "mud and muck and misery" ("**Delta**"). The soil there is "red clay from feet of beasts." The red of the clay suggests violence as "my heart bleeds for our fate." There is muddy water at our shanty door, and we are threatened by swollen levees. Rivers are the mode of transportation by which the fruits of our labor are taken from us. In the city, where there are "pavement stones" instead of warm earth and "cold and blustery nights" and rainy days instead of sun, the people shield themselves from that nature, brooding and restless, whispering oaths ("**Memory**").

The symbols of sun, earth, and water arise from racial memory of generations when nature, not Western technology, sustains life. The slave culture was an agrarian culture, and before that the African sun and earth and water in balance kept us living, in imbalance made us struggle against death. Walker uses these symbols in accordance with our history, tapping Black myth and ritual.

Something else particularly significant to Black people infuses the *For My People* poems: music. In poem after poem music is heard as a life-sustaining force. There are not only the rhythms of the long-paragraph poems and the ballads, but also the repeated references to music. It is music that reflects the emotional tone of many of the poems and often provides an essential metaphor. In "**Sorrow Home**" the music of the city is dissonant; the persona is plagued by the restless music propelling her toward home. Beneath it all is the melody of the South, the sorrow home, beating in her bone and blood. "**Today**" is itself a song, singing of the terrible images of a wartime world: "I sing these fragments of living that you may know by these presents that which we feared most has come upon us." In two poems Walker defies Black tradition. In "**For My People**," the religious songs are called "dirges" and she demands that they disappear in favor of "martial songs." In "**Since 1619**" she demands impatiently, "How many years since 1619 have I been singing Spirituals? / How long have I been praising God and shouting hallelujahs?" Music, for Walker, is a medium for communicating her message, as it has been for Black people since the beginning of time.

The poems in *For My People* thus emerge from centuries of Black American myth and ritual. Tinged with the Marxism which influenced the young poet's thinking at the time, they nevertheless reflect not only the writer's own grounding in Black Southern tradition but the generations of racial experience which were the ingredients of that tradition. The major dynamic in the book is the tension between the natural beauty of the land and the unnatural horror of racism, the poet's longing for the South but dread of its oppression and violence. The book is a demand for revolution.

The major part of this essay is concerned with these poems because this critic feels that *For My People* is Margaret Walker's most vital contribution to our culture. It is the nucleus which produced her subsequent volumes. Nearly thirty years passed before Walker published another collection of poems. Meanwhile the nation had engaged in wars, declared and undeclared, and Black people's fortunes had risen and fallen several times over.

Prophets for a New Day (1970) was the fruit of the upsurge of rebellion of the 1960s; it was published by a major Black influence of the times, Dudley Randall's Broadside Press. The poems in this small paperback volume are Walker's tribute to the people, celebrated and unsung, who contributed their agony and sometimes their lives to freedom.

Here the Souther landscape has become the battleground for the struggle for civil and human rights. As in *For My People,* the poet contrasts nature's beauty with the horror of violence and oppression. The elemental symbols of sun, earth, and water have disappeared as the scene shifts to the cities, which are the backdrop for struggle and death. Jackson, Mississippi, where lie "three centuries of my eyes and my brains and my hands," is called "City of tense and stricken faces . . . City of barbed wire stockades." The sun is destructive here, for it "beats down raw fire." The jagged rhythms and uneven rhyme underscore the tension ("**Jackson, Mississippi**"). Birmingham, Alabama, is a place where beautiful memories, tinged with fantasy, contrast with the present reality of hatred and death ("**Birmingham**").

The people on the mythic landscape are the heroes of that time. They are the "prophets." Some, like the children who were jailed, will not be remembered individually, but their collective effort is unforgettable history. Others are names whose very mention elicits floods of memories of that bitter time: Malcolm X, Martin Luther King, Medgar Evers, the three slain young civil rights workers. Walker has captured their heroism in poem after poem. She alludes often to specific events—the 1963 march on Washington, Dr. King's ringing speech there, the march on Selma, the dogs and fire hoses and cattle prods used against young and old nonviolent demonstrators, the murder of heroes. The poems are infused with rage, controlled and effective.

One difference from the *For My People* poems is immediately apparent: the biblical references in *Prophets for a New Day*. The early poems, consistent with their Marxist cast, saw religion as an opiate. "**Since 1619**" demands that "these scales fall away from my eyes" and that "I burst from my kennel an angry mongrel. . . ." In another poem from that volume, "**We Have Been Believers**" she damns all Black religion, the "black gods from an old land" and the "white gods of a new land," ridiculing the faith of the people and insisting, "We have been believers believing in our burdens and our demigods too long." She demands revolution, which she apparently sees as the antithesis of religion. *Prophets for a New Day,* however, reflects a profound religious faith. The heroes of the sixties are named for the prophets of the Bible: Martin Luther King is Amos, Medgar Evers is Micah, and so on. The people and events of the sixties are paralleled with Biblical characters and occurrences. The title poem makes the parallel clearly. It begins, seeing fire as paradigm in the burning bush of the Moses legend, the goals informing the lips of Isaiah, and as Nommo, or the Word, which inspires the prophets of today's "evil age." The religious references are important. Whether one espouses the Christianity in which they are couched is not the issue. For the fact is that Black people from ancient Africa to now have always been a spiritual people, believing in an existence beyond the flesh. African art, the music of the slave culture, and the fervor of urban storefront churches affirm the depth of this faith.

Prophets for a New Day, like its predecessor, is grounded in Black myth and ritual. It records the generation of the sixties' contribution to the history of bloody struggle against oppression and the soul-deep conviction that we— that all people—are meant by nature to be free.

Another volume, *October Journey,* a collection of poems from 1934 to 1972, was published by Broadside Press three years later. For the most part, I found these poems less impressive than the others. Some were occasional poems and some written in sonnet form, using formal diction, which this critic found artificial and lacking in spontaneity. Here I admit a personal bias: I have never found European structures such as the sonnet, nor poems written for specific occasions, to be sturdy enough vehicles to contain the weight of our centuries-long tragedy and triumph, nor of our vision which stretches from an African past to the future.

"October Journey," the title poem, is an exception. It is a fine work, rivaling the best poetry of our times in its imagery, its emotional appeal, and the way it burrows deep inside the reader. The poem is a journey into the mythic homeland. It begins with a warning fashioned out of folk beliefs, suggesting that for the traveler the "bright blaze" of autumn's rising is to be preferred to heady spring hours, or to what might be tempting summer nights; cautioning that broad expanses of water should be avoided during the full moon, and that some kind of protection should be carried. The message is that the finest journeys occur in October. Then follows a series of passionate images of the Southland in October, "when colors gush down mountainsides / and little streams are freighted with a caravan of leaves," and in all the seasons. The description is a collage of form and color and sun-earth-water. The speaker eagerly anticipates the return to the place of so many loving memories; such a return is necessary if one is to be whole. "The train wheels hum, 'I am going home, I am going home, / I am moving toward the South.'" But, as in Walker's other poems, the old ambivalence is there: ". . . my heart fills up with hungry fear. . . ." And when she arrives in homeland, the natural beauty of the place and the warmth of childhood memories are swallowed up in the dreadful reality of the ruined world, portraying brilliantly the withering of promise, the grief too deep and pervasive to be expressed, the dried blooming,

the wasted potential, sullen facets of the profound. Again Walker has portrayed brilliantly the profound historical experience of Black people, the mythic past which lies just behind our eyes.

Margaret Walker is a profoundly important poet whose works plumb the depth of our racial experience. And our racial experience is a deeply human experience no less universal than that of our oppressors and, in fact, more important. For it takes inhumanity, greed, and technology to be an oppressor; but it takes all the attributes of godly humanity to survive oppression and to emerge as victorious human beings. Margaret Walker shows us the way. The power of her emotion and poetic craftsmanship transcends ideology and bares the struggle and strength which are integral to our individual and collective selves. Despite the many images of brutality inflicted upon us, Walker's vision from the beginning has been of a people striking back at oppression and emerging triumphant. Despite her avowed abhorrence of violence Walker has ever envisioned revolution. Rapping with Nikki Giovanni, Walker admitted that her feelings about Black people and the struggle for freedom were best encompassed in an early poem published in *Prophets for a New Day,* "The Ballad of the Free." This poem unites the old urge toward revolution and the militance of Christian teachings learned from her minister father. She evokes the champions whose blood colors our history: Nat Turner, Gabriel Prosser, Denmark Vesey, Toussaint L'Ouverture, John Brown. She repeats, in a stirring refrain, words that sing our most intimate racial self. The metaphor is that of a serpent loosed, and echoing Fanon, Walker prophesied that there is more to come than merely the last being first.

Margaret Walker's poetry has mined the depths of African-American racial memory, portraying a history and envisioning a future. Like all artists, she is grounded in a particular time and thus labors under particular limits of conscious perception. Her vision of the African past is fairly dim and romantic, in spite of various individual poems on ancestry. Consciously she sees African-Americans as a minority group in the United States of America, the stepchildren, rejected, oppressed, denied, brutalized, and dehumanized by the dominant group. [See Walker's essay "Willing to Pay the Price," in *Shades of Black* by Stanton L. Wormley and Lewis Fenderson William, 1969.] But her poetry emanates from a deeper area of the psyche, one which touches the mythic area of a collective being and reenacts the rituals which define a Black collective self. When she was nineteen, Margaret Walker wrote:

I want to write
I want to write the songs of my people.
I want to hear them singing melodies in the dark.
I want to catch the last floating strains from their
    sob-torn throats.
I want to frame their dreams into words; their souls
    into notes.
I want to catch their sunshine laughter in a bowl;
fling dark hands to a darker sky
and fill them full of stars

then crush and mix such lights till they become
a mirrored pool of brilliance in the dawn.

And she has done just that.

Richard K. Barksdale (essay date 1986)

SOURCE: "Margaret Walker: Folk Orature and Historical
Prophecy," in *Black American Poets Between Worlds,
1940-1960,* edited by R. Baxter Miller, University of
Tennessee Press, 1986, pp. 104-16.

[*In the following excerpt, Barksdale examines Walker's
use of folklore in the ballads of* For My People *and the
civil rights poems of* Prophets for a New Day.]

Like Robert Hayden and Melvin Tolson, Margaret Walker
has written her poetry in the shadow of the academy.
Both of her advanced degrees from the University of
Iowa—the master's degree in 1940 and the Ph.D. in
1966—were granted because of her achievements in creative writing. Her first volume of poems, *For My People*
(1942), won the Yale Series of Younger Poets Award and
helped her to gain the master's degree; her prize-winning
novel, *Jubilee,* fulfilled the central requirement for the
doctorate. But Margaret Walker's poetry is quite different
from that written by Hayden or Tolson. Many of Hayden's
poems are full of intellectual subtleties and elusive symbols that often baffle and bewilder the reader. *Harlem
Gallery,* by Tolson, is often intellectually complex and
obscure in meaning. Margaret Walker's's poetry, on the
other hand, is clear and lucid throughout, with sharply
etched images and symbols presented in well-formed
ballads and sonnets. It is now clear in retrospect that
Hayden and Tolson were influenced by the academic poets
of the 1930s and 1940s—Ciardi, Tate, Lowell, Wilbur,
Auden, Dickey. Their poetry has an academic gloss, suggesting richly endowed libraries in the sophisticated sub-
urbs of learning. Only rarely do they seem sensitized to
problems and dilemmas confounding an unintellectual-
ized, urbanized, and racially pluralistic America, a concern which dominates Margaret Walker's poetry.

Although Walker, too, spent all of her days in academia,
she was never as a writer held captive by it. An analysis
of her poetry reveals that in subject, tone, and esthetic
texture, it is remarkably free of intellectual pretense and
stylized posturing. One finds instead the roots of the Black
experience in language simple, passionate, and direct. If
one asks how Margaret Walker as a writer remained in
the academy but not of it, the answer appears in the circumstances governing her family life and background.

Margaret Walker was the daughter of a preacher man, and
not just an ordinary one. Her father, Sigismond Walker,
was a native of Jamaica who, in 1908, four years before
Claude McKay's arrival in 1912, came to America to study
at Tuskegee. Unlike the poet McKay, however, Sigismond
Walker persevered academically, gained a degree at Atlanta's Gammon Theological Institute and then joined that

small band of educated Black methodist ministers who
ventured forth to preach the Word in the pre-World War
I South. So Margaret Walker grew up in a household
ruled by the power of the word, for undoubtedly few have
a greater gift for articulate word power than an educated
Jamaican trained to preach the doctrine of salvation in the
Black South. Indeed, personal survival in the Walker
household demanded articulateness. The poet admits that
in a home filled with song and singing inspired by her
musician mother, she struggled successfully to survive
without the gift of song; but survival without the mastery
of words and language was impossible. So by the age of
twelve, Margaret Walker was writing poetry and sharpening her communication skills; and, when, at the age of
seventeen, she transferred from New Orleans' Gilbert
Academy to Northwestern, she took her well-honed verbal
skills with her. As noted in *How I Wrote Jubilee,* she
quickly discovered at Northwestern that she did not know
how to convert the rich orature of her talking, word-filled
New Orleans household into a novel, but she was fully
convinced that she had carried the power of the word
with her to Evanston.

Not only was there a preaching father in the Walker household, but there was a talking maternal grandmother—a
grandmother full of tales of "befo' dah wah" and "duin
da time afta da wah." So there were stories to be listened
to and placed in the vault of memory. And there was also
New Orleans with its rich background of folk mythology,
its music, its red beans and rice and jambalaya, and its
assortment of racial experiences to be remembered and
recalled through the power of the word.

So Margaret Walker as a poet and as a writer was not
dependent on the academy for her subject matter, for her
style, for her authorial posture. Indeed, the rhetorical power
of the poem, **"For My People"**—the verbal arpeggios,
the cascading adjectives, the rhythmic repetitions—has its
roots in the "preacher-man" rhetoric of the Black South.
Similarly, Vyry's eloquent prayer in *Jubilee* came from
the Blacks' past and from the deep folk memories of a
trouble-driven people.

The poet would also be the first to admit that her "down-
home" grounding in the principles of the Judeo-Christian
religion, Blackstyle, protected her against the frivolous
intellectualism of the academy. She had no need to join
movements, to bow to trends, and identify with esoteric
cults. Her religion also stood her in good stead when, in
1935, she graduated from Northwestern and joined other
writers in Chicago's rather radical WPA Writer's project—
writers such as Nelson Algren, Richard Wright, Studs
Terkel, Willard Motley, James Farrell, and Jack Conroy.
In 1935, Chicago lay by the shore of Lake Michigan like
a beached whale, panting its way through the Depression, and the world and Chicago were ripe for social and
political revolution. Racism, gangsterism, corruption, and
political radicalism were everywhere. But Margaret
Walker kept her home-grown faith through it all, calling
not for violent revolution but for "a new earth" that would
"hold all the people, all the faces, all the adams and
eves."

The poet's career started out with a bang. In 1942, when, at twenty-seven, she published her first volume of poems—*For My People*—she became one of the youngest Black writers ever to have published a volume of poetry in this century. Langston Hughes had published "The Negro Speaks of Rivers" at the age of nineteen, but his first volume of poems was not published until 1926 when he was twenty-four. Moreover, when her volume won a poetry prize in 1942, Margaret Walker became the first Black woman in American literary history to be so honored in a prestigious national competition. But these achievements are not what is notable or significant about *For My People*. The title poem is itself a singular and unique literary achievement. First, it is magnificently wrought oral poetry. It must be read aloud; and, in reading it aloud, one must be able to breathe and pause, pause and breathe preacher-style. One must be able to sense the ebb and flow of the intonations. One must be able to hear the words sing, when the poet spins off parallel clusters like

> . . . the gone years and the now years and the maybe years, washing ironing cooking scrubbing sewing mending hoeing plowing digging planting pruning patching dragging along.

This is the kind of verbal music found in a well-delivered down-home folk sermon, and, as such, the poem achieves what James Weldon Johnson attempted to do in *God's Trombones:* fuse the written word with the spoken word. In this sense the reader is imaginatively set free to explore what Shelley called the beautiful "unheard melody" of a genuine poetic experience. The passage is also significant in its emphasis on repetitive "work" words describing the age-old labors of Black people. The activities are as old as slavery—slavery in the "big house" or slavery in the fields. Adding "ing" to these monosyllabic work-verbs suggests the dreary monotony of Black labor in slave times and in free times. Without the "ing," they remain command words—enforcing words, backed up by a white enforcing power structure. And behind the command has always lurked the whip or the gun or the overseer or the Captain or the boss or Mr. Charlie or Miss Ann. Indeed, Black laborers, long held captive by Western capitalism, were forced to work without zeal or zest—just "Dragging along." Somehow they remained outside the system of profit and gain; no profits accrued to them for their labor; thus, they dragged along, "never gaining never reaping never knowing and never understanding." In just these few lines, Margaret Walker performs a premier poetic function: she presents a succinct historical summary of how the Black man slipped into an economic and social quagmire when, first as a slave and then as a quasi-free man, he was forced to cope with the monster of European capitalistic enterprise. . . .

Although one cannot say that the rest of the poems in Margaret Walker's initial volume meets the same criteria for high poetic quality, they reflect the young poet's sense of "word power" and her sharp awareness of the importance of Black orature. The poems in Part II contain a series of Black folk portraits—Poppa Chicken, Kissee Lee, Yallah Hammuh. In many of these, one can trace the influence of Langston Hughes' 1927 volume of poems, *Fine Clothes to the Jew,* which contained many verses portraying Black folk and celebrating the Black urban life style. Indeed both Poppa Chicken and Teacher remind one of Hughes' "Sweet Papa Vester" in that poet's "Sylvester's Dying Bed." All three are sweet men—men who pimp for a living and generally walk on the shady side of the street. There are differences, however, between the Hughes portrait and those by Margaret Walker. Hughes' version is comically objective. Nowhere does the author obtrude an opinion in the brief story line, and everything, as in any good comic routine, is grossly exaggerated. As he lies dying, "Sweet Papa Vester" is surrounded by "all the wimmens in town"—"a hundred pretty mamas"—Blacks and "brown-skins" all moaning and crying. On the other hand, both **"Poppa Chicken"** and **"Teacher,"** written in a swinging ballad rhyme and meter, lack the broad comic touch one sees in the Hughes poem. In fact, the protagonist is a "bad dude" and not to be taken lightly:

> Poppa Chicken toted guns
> Poppa wore a knife.
> One night Poppa shot a guy
> Threat'ning Poppa's life.

Teacher similarly has no comic stature. In fact, it is the poet's opinion that

> Women sent him to his doom.
> Women set the trap.
> Teacher was a bad, bold man
> Lawd, but such a sap!

Three other poems in Part II of *For My People*, **"Kissee Lee," "Long John and Sweetie Pie,"** and **"Yallah Hammuh"** reflect a Hughesian influence. Although all three are written in a swinging ballad rhyme and meter that Hughes never used in his Black folk portraits, they all reveal a finely controlled and well-disciplined narrative technique. There is just enough compression of incident and repetitive emphasis to provoke and sustain the reader's interest. And all of the characters—Long John, Sweetie Pie, Kissee Lee, and Yalluh Hammuh—come from the "low-down" social stratum where, Hughes believed, Black men and women lived in accordance with a life style that was to be treasured simply because it was distinctively Black. Theirs is an environment filled with heroic violence, flashing knives, Saturday night liquor fights, and the magnificent turbulence of a blues-filled weekend of pleasure and joy. For instance, after Margaret Walker's Kissee Lee "learned to stab and run" and after "She got herself a little gun,"

> . . . from that time that gal was mean,
> Meanest mama you ever seen.
> She could hold her likker and hold her man
> And she went thoo life jus' ra'sin san'.

To the Kissee Lees of the world death comes soon and

> . . . she died with her boots on
>   switching blades
> On Talledega Mountain in the likker raids.

The ballad **"Long John Nelson and Sweetie Pie"** presents another story which has been repeated many times in Black folklore—the story of a very stressful romantic relationship that ends in disappointment, separation, grief, and death. There is the inevitable triangle involving Long John, who is ever a lover but never a laborer; Sweetie Pie, who cooks real good and eats far too well; and a "yellow girl," who has "coal black hair" and "took Long John clean away / From Sweetie Pie one awful day." The brief story ends when Sweetie Pie, her lover gone, wastes away and dies. To historians and literary scholars, it is a story of small, almost mean, insignificance; but to a Black folk poet interested in the rich orature of her people, this little story opened another window on the world of the Black experience.

Part II of Margaret Walker's first volume of poetry also includes poems about **"Bad Ol' Stagolee"** and **"Big John Henry,"** Black mythic folk heroes whose stories have been told and sung for generations. Since both men really lived and died, the poet in recounting their stories dips into authentic Black folk history. John Henry, the steel-driving man who would not let "a steam drill beat him down," was employed in the Big Bend Tunnel in West Virginia on the C&O Line and lost his life in a tunnel accident in 1872. Similarly, Stagolee, born in Georgia shortly after the Civil War, became a Memphis gambler who was widely known for his big stetson hat, his .44, and his everhandy deck of cards. When a fellow gambler named Billy Lyons objected to the way Stagolee shuffled the cards and, in a fit of anger, knocked off Stagolee's stetson and spit on it, Stack promptly shot him dead with his .44. In her poetic version of the John Henry and Stagolee stories, Margaret Walker does not restrict herself to the known historical facts. She shifts through the accretion of myth and incident and, in swinging couplets, tells how "Bad Man Stagolee" shot, not Billy Lyons, but "a big policeman on 'leventh street" and how John Henry was a "sho-nuff man / Whut lived one time in the delta lan'" in the Mississippi cotton country. Both men are larger than life heroes. For his murder of a white policeman, Stagolee is never caught, and no one knows how he eventually died; all that is known is

> Bad-man Stagolee ain't no more
> But his ghost still walks up
>   and down the shore
> Of Old Man River round New Orleans
> With her gumbo, rice and good
>   red beans!

On the other hand, the poet tells us how her John Henry died—"a ten-poun hammer done ki-ilt John Henry." But the manner of his dying is not nearly as important as his symbolic fame as the preeminently gifted Black laboring man. He stands for all Black men who, amid great adversity, farmed and plowed, dug and hammered, lifted and strained throughout the South to build railroads, load steamboats, and tote bricks in "the bilin' sun." But Margaret Walker embellishes her John Henry with even more heroic attributes. He consorts with witches who

> taught him how to cunjer,
> And cyo the colic and ride the
>   thunder.

He can whistle like a whippoorwill and talk to the "long lean houn'." In other words, in addition to being the symbolic Black laboring giant, he has supernatural gifts that lift him far above humankind's mortal sphere. . . .

In the 1940s and 1950s, Margaret Walker published a few occasional poems (later gathered for publication in a Broadside Press volume, **October Journey,** in 1973); but, in addition to attending to her responsibilities as wife, mother, and college professor, she devoted most of her "literary" time to researching historical and biographical data for her fictional magnum opus, *Jubilee*. When this novel was published in 1966, the South was already ablaze with the Black protest against segregation and the century-long denial of the Black people's civil rights. The events of that period—the bombings, the deaths, the marches, the big-city riots—stimulated the most exciting outburst of Black poetry since the Harlem Renaissance. These poets, with some significant exceptions, were young urban revolutionaries who were conscientiously abrasive in their racial rhetoric. Not only did they insist that wrongs be righted, but they assumed a para-military posture and demanded that the guilty be punished by fire, by bullets, or by the sheer violence of their poetic rhetoric. Inevitably, the seething racial turbulence of the times provoked a poetical response from Margaret Walker. Because of her experience, background, and training—her familial gift of word power, her intensive apprenticeship in Chicago's literary workshop in the 1930s, and her mastery of Black orature—her **Prophets For a New Day** (Broadside Press, 1970) stands out as the premier poetic statement of the death-riddled decade of the 1960s. The poems of this small volume reflect the full range of the Black protest during the time—the sit-ins, the jailings, the snarling dogs, the 1963 March on Washington, the lynching of the three Civil Rights workers in Mississippi. All of the poems in the volume touch the sensitive nerve of racial memory and bring back, in sharply etched detail, the trauma and tension and triumphs of that period. **"Birmingham"** and **"For Andy Goodman, Michael Schwerner and James Chaney"** stand out as carefully wrought poetical reactions to a city and to an event that filled the world with horror and foreboding.

Both of these poems are unusual simply because painful emotions are not recollected in tranquillity but in moods carefully textured by the delicate filigree of the poet's imagery. For instance, in **"Birmingham"** the first part of the poem is filled with the persona's nostalgic memories of the beauty of the Birmingham countryside as the twilight settles over the red hills. In this section of the poem, the reader senses the God-wrought beauty that enfolds the city—a city filled with the evil that man has wrought.

> With the last whippoorwill call of evening
> Settling over mountains
> Dusk dropping down shoulders of red hills

Cardinal flashing through thickets—
Memories of my fancy-ridden life
Come home again.

Part II of the poem is concerned with death and the images of dying. The principal persona of the poem has returned to a city engulfed by it—a city "where a whistling ghost" makes "a threnody / Out of a naked wind."

I died today.
In a new and cruel way.
I came to breakfast in my night-dying clothes
Ate and talked and nobody knew
They had buried me yesterday.

In Part III the persona longs to return to her "coffin bed of soft warm clay," far from the North's "bitter cold." For Birmingham and the South, drenched in the blood of countless Black martyrs, are good places in which to die and be buried.

The lines dedicated to the memory of Goodman, Schwerner, and Chaney, the young Civil Rights martyrs murdered by klansmen in Mississippi's Neshoba County, are also rich in imagery and symbol. There is no rhetoric of confrontation, but there is a very successful effort to filter through the nuances of memory and find the three young men again. One remembers, first, three faces—one" sensitive as the mimosa leaf," one "intense as the stalking cougar," and the third as "impassive as the face of rivers." And then one remembers that the summer of their death cannot last forever and that soon fall will come and the three young men will metamorphose into three leaves, cut adrift from life and mixing helter-skelter with nature's superb fall potpourri of wind, water, and sunlight.

Then the poet turns directly to the lives of the three young men to probe how a century of concern can be reduced to a quintessential moment in the "hourglass of destiny." Cut off prematurely, they will never know the "immortality of daisies and wheat," "the simple beauty of a humming bird," or "the dignity of a sequoia"—never know the full meaning of winter's renunciation or spring's resurrection. And who murdered the sensitive Goodman, the intense Schwerner, the impassive Chaney? The poet exercises her poetic license to castigate with a forceful alliterative phrase those who killed and entombed the three young men:

The brutish and the brazen
without brain
without blessing
without beauty. . . .

Before closing the poem, Margaret Walker once again examines the startling contradiction between the South's languorous natural beauty and the ugliness of Black lynched bodies floating in muddy rivers or buried in soggy graves shaded by fragrant magnolias and stately live oaks. The South is full of paradoxes, but the juxtaposition of floral beauty and bloody violence is the most puzzling. And nowhere is this more obvious than in Mississippi.

In the final section of *Prophets for a New Day* Margaret Walker turns to history and prophecy, linking today's Black leaders, old and young, to the biblical prophets. The volume's title poem begins with "the Word," but the final lines of the title poem throb with the poet's indignation and outrage about the unfettered power of the beast of racial hatred that roams the land.

His horns and his hands and his lips are gory with
    our blood.
He is War and Famine and Pestilence
He is Death and Destruction and Trouble
And he walks in our houses at noonday
And devours our defenders at midnight.
He is the demon who drives us with whips of fear
And in his cowardice
He cries out against liberty
He cries out against humanity.

The poems that end the volume of poetry present in brief portraits the **"Prophets for a New Day"**—Benjamin Mays (Jeremiah), Whitney Young (Isaiah), Martin Luther King, Jr. (Amos), Julian Bond (Joel), and Medgar Evers (Micah). These poems with their strong religious content prove that Margaret Walker has come full circle from the biblical source for social history back to biblical parable. She begins and closes with the Word. In the "breaking dawn of a blinding sun," she offers a promise that "the lamp of truth" will be lighted in the temple of hope and that, soon one morning, "the winds of freedom" will begin "to blow / While the Word descends on the waiting World below."

Langston Hughes, in his review of Gwendolyn Brooks' *Street in Bronzeville,* stated that all good poets are more far sighted and perceptive in discerning social problems and ills than politicians. Of Margaret Walker he would have noted her great gift for prophecy and the marvelous word power that enabled her to burrow deeply into the rich orature of her people.

Margaret Walker   (essay date 1989)

SOURCE: "Preface," in *This Is My Century, New and Collected Poems,* University of Georgia Press, 1989, pp. xiii-xvii.

[*Walker summarizes her poetic career, acknowledging sources of literary inspiration and personal assistance from family members, friends and other writers throughout her life.*]

At Northwestern I first heard of *Poetry, A Magazine of Verse,* and the Yale University Younger Poets competition. I heard Harriet Monroe read her poetry at Northwestern, and I must have seen an ad in the *Poets of America* magazine announcing the Yale competition. I vowed then to publish in *Poetry* and to enter the competition at Yale.

I graduated from Northwestern during the Depression, and after seven months looking for a job I began work on the WPA Chicago Writers' Project. Here I worked with Richard Wright, who was writing his first professional prose at the time. I was profoundly impressed with his talent, his intense driving ambition, his discipline, and his strange social theories and perspectives. The critic Robert Bone says Richard Wright led a new movement, the Chicago Renaissance, which grew out of the South Side Writers' Group organized at that time. I was a member of that group for three years.

Meanwhile, I discovered that the office of *Poetry* was on the same street, Erie, as the Project where I worked. I met Miss Geraldine Udell, who introduced me to George Dillon, the editor of *Poetry* at that time. He encouraged me to read the French Symbolist poets. I could read both French and German and had already translated poems by Goethe, Schiller, and Heine. Now I was reading Baudelaire's *Les Fleurs du mal,* Rimbaud's *Une Saison en enfer,* Mallarmé's *L'Après-midi d'un faune,* and a smattering of Verlaine and Valéry. All my life I had read English and American classics, and I especially liked the English Romantic poets and American women writers such as Edna St. Vincent Millay, Léonie Adams, Elinor Wylie, and Louise Bogan. I met Muriel Rukeyser at a cocktail party at the office of *Poetry* just after she won the Yale award for *Theory of Flight.* It goes without saying that I had also read poetry by black people all my life: Langston Hughes, Countee Cullen, Claude McKay, Sterling Brown, and James Weldon Johnson. I was privileged to meet all of them.

Shortly after my twenty-second birthday I sat down at my typewriter and in fifteen minutes wrote all but the last stanza of the poem **"For My People."** Nelson Algren read it on the Project and told me how to write the resolution and conclusion. George Dillon published it that November in *Poetry.* The next year he published **"We Have Been Believers"** and the following year in a special WPA issue celebrating twenty-five years of *Poetry* he published my sonnet **"The Struggle Staggers Us."** In connection with the celebration there was a radio program and I was on that, too, reading my sonnet.

I had been trying to write sonnets since I was sixteen and seventeen. Professor Hungerford said poets have to write sonnets because sonnets furnish the same discipline for the poet as five-finger exercises for the musician. When I was in school in Iowa in the sixties I took my qualifying oral exam on sonnets, the history of that form, and sonnet sequences.

In Iowa in the late thirties, Paul Engle, my teacher in the poetry workshop and my thesis advisor, reawakened my interest in folk ballads and I began to experiment with that form. Also at Iowa I began to correspond with one of America's greatest balladeers, Stephen Vincent Benét. In 1942, five years after **"For My People"** was published and two years after the twenty-six poems in the *For My People* collection served as my master's thesis, I won the Yale award. *For My People* was published with a foreword by Mr. Benét.

I wrote **"October Journey,"** a poem that has multiple meanings in my life, in 1943 after a few weeks at Yaddo, where I wrote the ballad **"Harriet Tubman."** I was actually making the journey South in October, and **"October Journey"** expresses my emotions at that time. I met my husband in October, and after thirty-seven years of our marriage he died in October. This poem was one of Arna Bontemps's favorites.

The decade of the sixties was a turbulent one in American society, and the civil rights confrontations made it a violent decade. The most violent year was 1963. By the time President Kennedy was assassinated in November, there had been many brutal killings in the South. Our neighbor Medgar Evers was assassinated on the street where I live. Four little girls were killed when Sixteenth Street Baptist Church in Birmingham was bombed. One of those children was the granddaughter of a neighbor from my childhood days in Birmingham. My cousins were members of Sixteenth Street Baptist Church, and they took me as a child to worship in that church. I gradually came to know many of the civil rights leaders, women and men, and so I was emotionally moved to write my civil rights poems in 1963. They are the poems in *Prophets for a New Day*.

One Sunday afternoon in 1963, ten years after my father died, I wrote ten typewritten pages of a poem called **"Epitaph for My Father."** That poem appeared in the *October Journey* collection. *Prophets for a New Day,* consisting of twenty-two poems in thirty-five pages, was published in 1970. Three years later in November 1973 the ten poems of the *October Journey* volume were published.

In 1979 I took early retirement from teaching at Jackson State University, where I had been since 1949. I immediately sat down and wrote the poems which constitute the section of this book called *This Is My Century*. Although twelve of the thirty poems in that section have seen previous publication, this is the first publication of the complete collection. In 1985 I was asked to write about Farish Street. The poems in *Farish Street,* the latest of the five sections, were printed in 1986.

All these poems have come out of my living. They express my ideas and emotions about being a woman and a black person in these United States—Land of the *Free* and Home of the Brave?

I seem to write in only three distinct forms: narratives or stories as ballads, lyrical songs as sonnets, and the long line of free verse punctuated with a short line. The characteristics of my poetry that may superficially be considered reflective of Sandburg, Masters, Jeffers, and Whitman are not derived from these poets but rather from a lifetime of reading the Bible and wisdom literature of the East— *Mahābhārata, Bhagavad-Gītā, Gilgamesh, Sundiata*—that they too had read. I have worn out four Bibles and am beginning to wear out the fifth. For twenty years I taught the Bible as literature at Jackson State University and for twenty-five years I taught the annual Bible study classes to the women in my local church. In my humanities classes

I taught the wisdom literature of the East beginning with the *Book of the Dead* from Egypt; the *Mahābhārata* and *Bhagavad-Gītā* from India; *Gilgamesh* from Babylonia; and the African epic *Sundiata*. All of these are pre-Homeric epics which my white professors denied existed.

Stephen Benét says I write my own kind of sonnet. My friends, the black male scholars and critics, speak disparagingly of my sonnets, but the editors of *The Sonnet: An Anthology,* Robert Bender and Charles Squier, say my sonnet on Malcolm X is one of the major sonnets of this century. Louis Untermeyer said my ballads were either Paul Laurence Dunbar gone modern or Langston Hughes gone sour. If I worried about what critics say I would stop trying to write, to practice the craft and the art of writing. As long as I live I shall keep trying. Why? Because I must.

I have lived most of my life in the segregated South. With the exception of one year in Meridian, Mississippi, when I was five, I lived in Birmingham, Alabama, my birthplace, until I was ten. I began writing in New Orleans, where I lived from age ten to seventeen. At seventeen I went out of the South for the first time to attend Northwestern University and, after graduation, lived and worked in Chicago for four years. I spent one year in the late thirties and three years in the sixties in Iowa, earning a master's degree in 1940 and a doctoral degree in 1965 from the University of Iowa. I began teaching at Livingstone College in North Carolina in 1941. After a year of teaching in West Virginia in 1942-43 I returned to North Carolina, where I married and resumed teaching. Since 1949 I have lived and worked in Jackson, Mississippi, going out of the South only to study, teach, or lecture. The South is my home, and my adjustment or accommodation to this South—whether real or imagined (mythic and legendary), violent or nonviolent—is the subject and source of all my poetry. It is also my life.

B. Dilla Buckner (essay date 1990)

SOURCE: "Folkloric Elements in Margaret Walker's Poetry," in *CLA Journal,* Vol. XXXIII, No. 3, March 1990, pp. 367-77.

[*In the following excerpt, Buckner defines folklore and explores the manner in which Walker uses it in her ballads.*]

Since, quite often, there are misconceptions about the definition of folklore or "fakelore" (a term coined by Richard Dorson [in *American Folklore*] in 1950, which means the falsifying of the raw data for capitalistic gain rather than totalitarian conquest), it is necessary to establish some ground rules for exploring folklore in literature. Three tests that can be used to see if an author has used folklore follow:

1. There must be biographical evidence; we should be able to establish that the author knew of and was part of the oral tradition.

2. From reading the story, we should be able to establish that the author gives an accurate description of the folk group and their customs—in other words, he has observed the group firsthand.

3. We must be able to show that the folk motifs can be found in the Motif Index and that the folk material has had oral circulation before the author included it in his story. [David Laubach, *Introduction to Folklore*]

Couple the above three-faceted test set forth by Dorson with a four-part test by Laubach—(1) Folklore is oral; (2) folklore is traditional within a certain group; (3) folklore must exist in different versions; and (4) folklore is anonymous—and one readily observes that Walker definitely utilizes the folk tradition . . . [A] close examination of any number of Walker's poems reveals just how deeply steeped she is in the folkloric traditions of black people.

"**Ballad of the Hoppy-Toad**" is an example of Walker's masterful usage of folklore elements. Surface-wise, this poem is about a protagonist's concern about an evil spell cast upon her by "the goofer man" or the "root worker." No reason is given for this act, but the spell is reversed and the caster is ultimately the victim of his own evil deed. On the surface, also, is the tall tale told in ballad form. Structurally, the poem follows most of the conventions of the traditional ballad. Each stanza consists of four lines with four beats or stresses in the first line, three in the second, four in the third, and three in the fourth. The second and fourth lines rhyme; the first and the third do not. Thus, if the word "**Ballad**" were not included in the title, one could merely scan the poem and identify its form. An example is this stanza:

The góo/pher mán/ was hól/leríng	a
"Don't kíll/ that hóp/py-tóad."	b
Sis Á/ veŕy/ she sáid/ "Hońey,	c
You boút/ to lose/ your lóad."	b

The above stanza follows the traditional ballad format, while other lines in some of the stanzas veer from this pattern; the first line of the poem is an example of such a variation (poetic license, perhaps). Yet, the rhyme scheme *abcb* pervades the poem. (It may be necessary to point out that the ballad is one of the commonest forms for relaying folk information. Note, for example, "Sir Patrick Spens" or "Barbara Allan.")

Like a number of ballads, also, the "**Ballad of the Hoppy-Toad**" has many of the properties of a full-blown short story: setting, plot, characters. This story takes place on a Saturday on Market Street, wherever, U.S.A. While the street may mean some place specific to Walker, her description leads the reader to a vivid description of the Southern Saturday marketing day, washing day, and fighting and drinking day. Thus, she gives a time, background, and place for the oncoming story. Her characters, likewise, are well established: The narrator or protagonist, the goopher man or antagonist, and Sis Avery. The rise in action begins with "the night I seen the goopher man / Throw dust around my door," and continues throughout the narrator's seeking Sis Avery's assistance in curtailing the spell. The climax of this dramatic piece is the changing of the horse to a toad with the dénouement being the toad and goopher man dying simultaneously.

In addition to the traits previously listed, the **"Ballad"** abounds in other folklore elements. There is, for example, the constant mentioning of various animals, and the animal stories are very much a part of folklore tradition. The reader is introduced to the toad, via inference, of course, in the first stanza: "When the Saturday crowd went stomping / Down the Johnny-*jumping* road." In the second stanza, the deacon's daughter is "lurching / Like a drunken alley *goat*"; the "root-worker" is a *dog* that needs to behave; and the charging *horse* is reduced to the ultimate "hoppy-toad." Paula Giddings observes that the animal imagery that Walker uses shows her indepthness. [See Giddings's excerpt, "A Shoulder Haunched Against a Sharp Concern."] . . .

Another element that authenticates this ballad as folklore is Walker's use of the conjurer or conjurers, when one considers Sis Avery. The use of magic, ju ju, mojo, voodoo, hoodoo, etc., has long been a part of the black heritage. The user of such magic (a conjurer) has a special place in black history:

> Conjurers could be pictured as exotic Old Testament type prophets or magicians: "He could turn as green as grass, most, and was just as black as a man could very well be, and his hair covered his neck and he had lizards tied on it. He carried a crooked cane. He would throw it down and pick it up and say something and throw it down and it would wriggle like a snake, and he would pick it up and it would be as stiff as any other cane!" [Lawrence Levin, "The Sacred World of Black Slaves," *Black Culture and Black Consciousness*, 1977].

Historically, while the slave conjurer, for the most part, used his powers to ward off some of his master's abuse, quite often that same power could be used against other slaves. As Lawrence Levin notes, "[t]he power of conjurers to wreak retribution upon slaves when requested to do so by other slaves was believed to be almost unlimited. . . . Other conjurers, of course, could be consulted to reverse these effects." So the conjurer with such great powers becomes highly respected, and this background information is evident in the **"Ballad of the Hoppy-Toad"** when the goopher man or root worker casts a spell on the storyteller and has it reversed by Sis Avery to his disadvantage.

One other significant aspect about the spell-casting episode is the back-and-forth play between good and evil or sacred (good) and profane (evil). The narrator tells the reader that the spell is an "evil note," and hexes usually carry a negative connotation. Yet, the other conjurer may use a counter spell to reverse the act only after the narrator has tried the Christian or "right" way via the church and prayer. Giddings notes the same dichotomy. . . .

One final observation about the **"Ballad"** is that it conforms to the Dorson test of folklore in literature: (1) it is definitely an outgrowth of the oral tradition since the story was told to Walker by someone (anonymous) from the North Carolina area; (2) the storyteller/ narrator gives a very detailed account of the characters, as noted, and their customs (any reader would recognize the description of the typical Souther-Saturday and Saturday-night episodes); and (3) the fire or prayer to ward off evil spirits, the reversal of spells or duper being duped, and the animal lore are representative folk motifs that can be found in the Motif Index.

Equally as compacted with similar folkloric elements of the **"Ballad of the Hoppy-Toad"** in content is Walker's **"Molly Means."** There is good and evil (the innocent bride and evil conjurer); there is the spell casting and its reversal; there is the animal emphasis, and the animals in **"Molly Means"** are a dog and hog. Yet Molly has all the charm of a snake. Further comparison/contrast of these two works reveals a male goopher man in the **"Ballad"** and a female witch in **"Molly Means,"** with both becoming victims of their own evil doings. Additionally, Walker, in **"Molly Means,"** tells how the witch gets her powers:

> Some say she was born with a veil on her face
> So she could look through unnatchal space
> Through the future and through the past
> And charm a body or an evil place. . . .

Yet the reader is not privy to such information in the **"Ballad's"** root worker. This particular idiom of a person's being born with a veil has been catalogued, and the belief is still widespread among the black community; however, it does not always indicate evilness. Rather, a child born with a veil (in actuality the placenta) is born for good luck and has the *gift* of being able to see into the future.

There is the lack of religious impetus to counteract the evil spirit in **"Molly Means,"** and the reader gets the implication that religion is replaced by the devout love of the husband for his young bride. As with the religion that does not work in the **"Ballad,"** the husband has to contact a conjurer, "who said he could move the spell / and cause the awful thing to dwell / On Molly Means. . . ." Details of how the conjurer accomplishes this feat are not as explicit as in the **"Ballad,"** but the resulting deaths of the evildoers are evident. While nothing remains of the **"Hoppy Toad,"** the ghost of Molly Means remains whining, crying, cackling, moaning, and, of course, barking, thus iterating that her demise, too, is somehow affiliated with an animal, more specifically, a dog. The return of a person in the form of a ghost or an animal can be found in the Motif Index, although the reasons for returning differ.

Two other folklore elements of note found in **"Molly Means"** are the use of numbers and the refrain structure. In folklore, especially modern lore, each number represents something in particular. Numbers have been catalogued, and usually the odd numbers (3, 7, 11) used by Walker indicate good luck; but these seem to mean the opposite in **"Molly Means"**: "Imp at three and wench at 'leben / she counted her husbands to the number seben."

The second point of note is that the structure of **"Molly Means"** is a variation of the traditional folk ballad; some ballads repeat the last line of each stanza, and some repeat a particular refrain. Walker thus makes use of incremented repetition in **"Molly Means"** which "involves repeating the basic structure of a line but changing it slightly (the increment) in order to move the story forward; sometimes this technique has striking dramatic effects." The first line of the refrain that follows each stanza is basically the same—"O Molly, Molly, Molly Means"—with the exception of stanzas two, three, and six, where the "O" is replaced with "Old." So the balladeer refers to Molly as "old" when describing her evilness, her "black-hand arts," and her death. The first two words of the second line of the refrain are also changed slightly to denote progression: "There goes the ghost of Molly Means"; "Dark is . . ."; "Cold is. . . ."; "Where is . . ."; "Sharp is . . ."; "This is . . ."; "Lean is. . . ." The only time Walker asks a question is before the husband goes in search of the witch, thus suggesting a change in the action of the story.

While the **"Ballad of the Hoppy-Toad"** is structurally much like the traditional ballad, **"Molly Means"** has more dissimilarities than similarities. It is, however, of the oral tradition, about a particular group of people and their customs and about a specific event. Walker is like the traditional balladeer in **"Molly Means"** because this poem is more objective; she "reports the news of the day in a very impersonal way" and "refuses to condemn." On the other hand, in the **"Ballad,"** she is author/narrator/protagonist, making judgments about the townspeople and even calling the goopher man a dog. With this subjectivity, too, comes more dialogue, particularly between the narrator and Sis Avery and between Sis Avery and the goopher man.

In further searching for folklore elements in these two works, one must take note of the language which is a part of folk tradition. According to Laubach, "[f]olk grammar often is nonstandard. . . . Particularly good examples of these usages are double negatives, such as 'I ain't got none,' and double superlatives, such as 'most kindest.'" One can readily see the differences between the more formalized English of **"Molly Means,"** which the author treats more objectively, and the non-standard English of the **"Ballad,"** in which the author/narrator seems to be one and the same. Spears [in "Black Folk Elements in Margaret Walker's *Jubilee*," *Mississippi Folklore Register*, 1980] says of Walker on this issue, though his reference is to *Jubilee*, "Walker is a dialectologist in the strictest send of the word, and her use of eye dialect for characterization is both accurate and effective. It captures the essence of black dialect in pronunciation, vocabulary items, and usage and grammar, particularly in syntax." Walker's use of dialect in both of the poems tends to lend credibility to her characters. She employs subject-verb nonagreement: "I knows just what will hex him"; auxiliary verb dropping: "And when the tale begun to spread"; double subject: "What you reckon that there mean"; folk pronunciation: "Chile of the devil, the dark, and sitch" (Chile for child and sitch for such); and folk sayings: "Honey, / You bout to lose your load." In her dialectal poems, the influence of Paul Lawrence Dunbar is quite obvious. . . .

Walker's folk heroes come in different sizes and shapes, and she celebrates the good heroes in *Prophets for a New Day* and the more diversified ones in the second section of *For My People*. Most of her prophets are fighters for civil rights, with special attention being given to Michah and Amos, Medgar Evers, and Martin Luther King. In this collection, she calls on numerous Biblical figures and images to describe her heroes; and if one considers the folklore inherent in the Bible, he need not test any of these poems for elements of lore. Of the poetry in *For My People*, Baxter Miller writes, "Without biblical cadences her ballads frequently become average, if not monotonous. In 'Yalluh Hammer,' a folk poem about the 'Bad Man,' she manages sentimentality, impractical concern, and trickery, as a Black woman outsmarts the protagonist and steals his money." Yet, in spite of Miller's observation, the weaker person's overcoming the stronger one as Lil Lad Two-Gun Buster is definitely in the folk tradition and is easily recognizable as a folk motif. In addition to the local heroes that Walker addresses—such as Poppa Chichen, the pimp, or Kissie Lee, who dies with her boots on—Walker renders more compact versions of national heroes, such as John Henry, who dies with a nine-pound hammer in his hand as opposed to a ten-pound one, and Stackerlee, who in her version does not take over hell, but rather "his ghost still walks up and down the shore / Of Old Man River round New Orleans / with her gumbo, rice, and good red beans!"

Whether Walker deals with her heroes as tragic possibilities or comic reliefs, she is always very serious about those who gave their lives to set right an inegalitarian society. When asked about her response to William Styron's *Confessions of Nat Turner,* one can almost visualize the writer's anger in her response: "The racism in that book is the damage that he does to the hero for the black child. Nat Turner represents to Black people, first of all, a preacher, and that is one of our heroes—you see, folk heroes. . . . He [Styron] attacks Nat Turner as a man; he attacks him as a preacher; and he attacks him as a folk hero." Perhaps it was out of such an attack on Nat Turner that Walker wrote **"The Ballad of the Free,"** which celebrates such insurrectionists as Turner, Vesey, L'Ouverture, and John Brown. These legendary figures, about whom there are written and oral accounts and versions, offer for Walker material to describe the heroic missions and tragic deaths of slave insurrectionists. The power of this poem may lie in the balance that Walker finds between historical fact and Biblical imagery. The facts are about the heroes, and the religious images are in the refrain:

> The serpent is loosed and the hour is come
> The last shall be first and first shall be none
> The serpent is loosed and the hour is come.

Although the above reference can be found in the Bible, it is certainly no accident that Walker uses words that are included in Nat Turner's confessions about a vision dictated to Thomas R. Gray: "And on the 12th of May, 1828, I heard a loud noise in the heavens, and the Spirit instantly appeared to me and said the Serpent was loosened, and Christ had laid down the yoke he had borne for the sins of men, and that I should take it on and fight against the Serpent, for the time was just approaching when the first should be last and the last should be first."

In conclusion, Walker's poetry is definitive proof that she is a poet of the people, her people. The folkways, customs, beliefs, or superstitions embodied in lines, even words, of her poetry reveal that she is a folklorist and, indeed, a folk poet.

Margaret Walker's century

Distinguished black poet Margaret Walker has, indeed, a claim to the century, for she has lived through most of it. She is a link to many of the most important figures in African American culture: she studied with W. E. B. Dubois, worked for the WPA Writers project with Richard Wright, talked poetry with Langston Hughes and Countee Cullen, was Medgar Evers' neighbor on the street where he was assasinated. Always immediate but classic in voice, her poetry has a timeless quality, as illustrated in her renowned sonnet to Malcolm X, which begins with an address to militants: "All you violated ones with gentle hearts; / You violent dreamers whose cries shout heartbreak." If younger poets have ranged farther in voice and content, it is because they stand high on the shoulders ofgiants such as Margaret Walker. This is a book that belongs in all public library poetry collections.

Pat Monaghan. A review of This is My Century: New and Collected Poems, *in* Booklist, *Vol. 86, No.4, October 15, 1989.*

Florence Howe   (review date 1990)

SOURCE: "Poet of history, poet of vision," in *The Women's Review of Books,* Vol. VII, Nos. 10-11, July, 1990, pp. 41-2.

[*In the following review of Walker's poetry, Howe discusses "Epitaph for My Father" from the "October Journey" section and "Fanfare, Coda, and Finale" from the "Farish Street" section of* This Is My Century.]

Last November, at the Graduate School of the City University of New York, Margaret Walker accepted The Feminist Press literary award of 1989 in honor of her "achievement as poet, novelist, critic and essayist; as teacher and fighter for human rights; and as a spirit of great empathy, compassion and understanding." The citation continued: "You came of age in a world not friendly to women or black people. You helped lead the way towards changing that world. You offer all of us, whatever our race, a vision of possibility. Without diminishing the pain of prejudice, conflict and war, you also see past the suffering and sorrow into a dif-

ferent dimension, into the moments or even the months and years of *Jubilee*." In *This is My Century: New and Collected Poems,* Walker's spirit blazes through 100 poems written during the past half-century, the early ones as powerful today as they were when *For My People* won the Yale Younger Poets Prize in 1942. . . .

I found most moving the elegy called **"Epitaph for My Father,"** a poem in which Walker recalls her father's Jamaican roots, the pain of life for him as emigrant in Jim Crow Southern cities. She brings to life not only the family's dynamic (mother's caution about money; father's wanting to be generous), but one hurtful sentence she wishes she had not spoken to him, and a vision of how it might have been, given her view of him, had she been born male, not female:

> I might have followed in his every step,
> Had preached from pulpits, found my
>   life as his
> And wandered too, as he, an alien on
>   the earth,
> But female and feline I could not stand
> Alone through love and hate and truth
> And still remain my own. He was him-
>   self;
> His own man all his life.
> And I belong to all the people I have
>   met,
> Am part of them, am molded by the
>   throng
> Caught in the tide of compromise, and
>   grown
> Chameleon for camouflage.

The image of a woman "grown / Chameleon" for survival in a white patriarchal world might suit many women of Walker's generation and mine. But it is also another way of saying that, if we search for the poet behind the poems in this volume, we need to study the people who fill its pages—from those sturdy grandmothers and their ancestral slaves to the little boy in 1963 who cried *"Hurry up Lucille or we won't get arrested with our group."* If we are searching for Margaret Walker, she is telling us, we need to find Phillis Wheatley and Harriet Tubman, Nat Turner and John Brown, Paul Lawrence Dunbar and Robert Hayden and perhaps, more surprisingly, Freud, Kierkegaard, Einstein, as well as Du Bois.

When she says she "belong[s] to all the people I have met, / Am part of them, am molded by the throng," she is describing herself as a poet of history. For those who remember the sixties' civil rights movement, Walker's poems stir memories of the fearless children who ignored threats and attended Freedom Schools, of the sit-ins, of the demonstrations and of the deaths—Medgar Evers, the children of Birmingham, Andy Goodman, Michael Schwerner and James Chaney, Malcolm X, Martin Luther King. Much of this poetry is inspirational, celebrating, often in elegies, the heroism of people who stood for human—not national or racial—dignity. It is not that Walker ignores race; the poems more often than not speak to "the color line." Rather, she speaks to it and beyond, perhaps because of that visionary quality her poetry has had from the first. Walker is the least sectarian Christian I can name. Steeped, she tells us, not only in the Bible, but in the "wisdom literature of the East," she values the lessons of the past, especially when they offer evidence of the human energy for spiritual as well as material survival.

Ultimately, then, as a poet of history, she is a poet of vision, of the flow of past not only into present, but of a reach into the future. The seven new poems called **"Farish Street"** that close the volume focus with camera-like intensity on the Southern street, its shops and people, and, at the same time, recall an ancestral African village, the "Root doctor, Hoodoo man" then and now. And in the series' final poem, **"The Labyrinth of Life,"** Walker presents herself as "traveler," looking down the road "to the glory of the morning of all life." But the poems that precede this final group remind us of the terrible world still needing mending: **"On Police Brutality," "Money, Honey, Money," "Power to the People," "They Have Put Us on Hold," "Inflation Blues"**—the titles themselves a litany of troubles for all the have-nots, all the powerless who would have space to live.

In the final poem of this section, **"Fanfare, Coda, and Finale,"** Walker returns to the form of **"For My People,"** only the rhythm is muted, slowed to a dirge:

> I buy bread of bitterness everyday in the
> markets of the world. Peace and plenty
> are never my share; every day I go
> hungry. Everyday I walk in fear, and
> no one seems to care . . .

> Out of my struggle I have sung my
> song; found hymn and flower in field
> and fort and dungeon cell. Yet now I
> have constriction in my heart where
> song is born. Such bitterness is eating
> at my vocal chords the bells within
> me, hushed, refuse to ring. Oh lift this
> weight of brick and stone against my
> neck, and let me sing.

How to conclude? Of all the poems in the collection, the one that speaks to me most personally and urgently today comes from the 1942 volume, which I first read twenty years ago. In 1990, even the title, **"The Struggle Staggers Us,"** overwhelms. For those of us who have lived through three (or more) decades of change know that we are only at the beginning (or at best in the middle) of much more to come. This 1942 poem speaks with immediacy not only to the contemporary women's movement, so interested as it is in "difference," but to a world that needs to solve the problems of poverty if it is ever to have racial and ethnic harmony inside nations and among them.

Walker tells us that being born and dying, like eating, drinking and sleeping, are "easy hours." "The struggle staggers us":

> for bread, for pride, for simple dignity.
> And this is more than fighting to exist;
> more than revolt and war and human
>   odds.

For persons are involved, individuals and their behavior that cannot be legislated:

> There is a journey from the me to you.
> There is a journey from the you to me.
> A union of the two strange worlds
>   must be.

"Struggle," Walker concludes, "marks our years" of present and future. Amen, Margaret Walker, Amen.

FURTHER READING

Biography

Giovanni, Nikki and Walker, Margaret. *A Poetic Equation: Conversations Between Nikki Giovanni and Margaret Walker*. Washington, DC: Howard University Press, 1974, 135 p.

> Giovanni questions Walker regarding her personal life and her views on history, social issues, and politics; Walker's answers include comments about how these aspects of her life have influenced her literary career.

Walker, Margaret. *How I Wrote* Jubilee *and Other Essays on Life and Literature*. New York: The Feminist Press at The City University of New York, 1990, 157 p.

> A collection of essays by Walker, some literary, but many of a personal, autobiographical nature.

Criticism

Bontemps, Arna. "Let My People Grow." *New York Herald Tribune Books* 19, No. 19 (January 3, 1943): 3.

> Recognizes Walker's poetic contribution to an understanding of the social conditions of the black race.

Hull, Gloria T. "Covering Ground." *African American Writers* 6, No. 3 (Spring 1991): 2-4.

> Points out the consistency of Walker's humanitarian themes and allegiance to her race throughout her poetic career as revealed in the poems of *This Is My Century*.

Traylor, Eleanor W. "'Bolder Measures Crashing Through': Margaret Walker's Poem of the Century." *Callaloo* 10, No. 4 (Fall 1987): 570-95.

> Thoroughly analyzes poems in *This is My Century* including scansion of specific lines, summary of themes, and explication of imagery, symbols and rhymes.

Whipple, Leon. "Songs for a Journey." *Survey Graphic.* XXXI, No. 12 (December 1942): 599-600.

> Praises Walker's "genius": her ability to speak for her race, to connect the present to the past and to fashion a better future.

Untermeyer, Louis. "New Books in Review." *The Yale Review* XXXII, No. 2 (December 1942): 370-71.

> Appreciates the emotional intensity of the poems in Part One, the free verse section, of *For My People,* but faults the sonnets and folk ballads in the rest of the book as being trite and unoriginal.

Interview

Graham, Maryemma. "The Fusion of Ideas: An Interview with Margaret Walker Alexander."*African American Review* 27, No. 2 (Summer 1993): 279-86.

> Walker discusses her political and social views and the way they influence her poetry.

Additional coverage of Walker's life and career is contained in the following sources published by Gale Research: *Contemporary Literary Criticism,* Vols. 1, 6; *Black Literature Criticism; DISCovering Authors: Multicultural Module; Black Writers,* Vol. 2; *Contemporary Authors,* Vols. 73-76; *Contemporary Authors New Revision Series,* Vols. 26, 54; *Dictionary of Literary Biography,* Vols. 76, 152; **and** *Major Twentieth-Century Writers.*

William Butler Yeats
1865-1939

Irish poet, dramatist, essayist, critic, short story writer, and autobiographer.

INTRODUCTION

Yeats is considered one of the greatest poets in the English language. He was devoted to the cause of Irish nationalism and played an important part in the Celtic Revival Movement, promoting the literary heritage of Ireland through his use of material from ancient Irish sagas. Further, Yeats employed national themes in his poetry, thereby attempting to restore the cultural unity that he felt was needed to bring an end to Ireland's internal division and suffering. Magic and occult theory were also important elements in Yeats's work. Yeats viewed the poet as kindred to the magician and the alchemist; thus he was deeply interested in spiritualism, theosophy, and occult systems. Many of the images found in his poetry are in fact derived from Rosicrucianism as well as from his own occult researches, which are described in his prose work *A Vision*.

Biographical Information

Yeats was born in Dublin to Irish-Protestant parents. His father was a painter who influenced his son's thoughts about art. Yeats's mother shared with her son her interests in folklore, fairies, and astrology as well as her love of Ireland, particularly the region surrounding Sligo in western Ireland where Yeats spent much of his childhood. Yeats's formal education began when he was eleven years old with his attendance at school first in England, then Ireland. As a youth he was erratic in his studies, shy and prone to daydreaming. In 1884 Yeats enrolled in the Metropolitan School of Art in Dublin. There he met the poet George Russell, who shared Yeats's enthusiasm for dreams and visions. Together they founded the Dublin Hermetic Society for the purposes of conducting magical experiments and "to promote the study of Oriental Religions and Theosophy." Yeats also joined the Rosicrucians, the Theosophical Society, and MacGregor Mather's Order of the Golden Dawn. He frequently consulted spiritualists and engaged in the ritual conjuring of Irish gods. In 1885, Yeats met the Irish nationalist John O'Leary, who was instrumental in arranging for the publication of Yeats's first poems in *The Dublin University Review* and in directing Yeats's attention to native Irish sources for subject matter. Under the influence of O'Leary, Yeats took up the cause of Gaelic writers at a time when much native Irish literature was in danger of being lost as the result of England's attempts to anglicize Ireland through a ban on the Gaelic language. In 1889, Yeats met the actress Maud Gonne, an agitator for the nationalist cause, whose great beauty and reckless destructiveness in pursuit of her po-

litical goals both intrigued and dismayed him. He accompanied her to political rallies, and though he often disagreed with her extremist tactics, he shared her desire to see Ireland freed from English domination. Although Gonne's repeated refusals to marry Yeats brought him great personal unhappiness, their relationship endured through many estrangements, and nearly all of Yeats's love poetry is addressed to her. In 1917 when he was fifty-two years old, Yeats married Georgiana Hyde-Lees. Through his young wife's experiments with automatic writing, Yeats gathered the materials on which he based *A Vision,* his explanation of historical cycles and his theory of human personality based on the phases of the moon. In 1922, after decades of struggle by the Irish nationalists had finally culminated in the passage of the Home Rule Bill, Yeats became a senator for the Irish Free State. He left the senate in 1928 because of failing health and devoted his remaining years to poetry. He died in France in 1939.

Major Works

Yeats's poetry evolved over five decades from the vague imagery and uncertain rhythms of *The Wanderings of*

Oisin, and Other Poems, his first important work, to the forceful, incantatory verse of the *Last Poems.* Throughout his career, Yeats found occult research a rich source of images for his poetry, and traces of his esoteric interests appear everywhere in his poems. "The Rose upon the Rood of Time," for example, takes its central symbol from Rosicrucianism, and "All Souls' Night" describes a scrying, or divination, ceremony. In his earliest poetic works, such as *Mosada,* Yeats took his symbols from Greek mythology; however, after meeting John O'Leary, he turned instead to Irish mythology as a source for his images. The long narrative poem, "The Wanderings of Oisin," was the first he based on the legend of an Irish hero. In spite of its self-consciously poetic language and immature imitations of Pre-Raphaelite poetic technique, the poem's theme— the disagreement between Oisin and St. Patrick—makes it important to an understanding of the later Yeats. The sense of conflict between vision and corporeal realities, as symbolized by the saint and the hero, is the essential dichotomy in Yeats's poetry. Additionally, Yeats recognized that only through imagination could the raw materials of life be transformed into something enduring. For Yeats, the role of the artist was the same as that of the alchemist: he must effect a transformation that obscures the distinction between form and content, between the "dancer and the dance." This theme is most effectively expressed in the later poems "Sailing to Byzantium" and "Byzantium." As Yeats grew older and more sure of his themes, his approach to the techniques of poetry changed. Recognizing that faerie songs were less suited to the tragic themes that preoccupied him than were more realistic narratives, he began, with the poems of *In the Seven Woods,* to write verses describing actual events in his personal life or in the history of Ireland, One of his most famous lyrics, "Easter 1916," about a rebel uprising that resulted in the martyrdom of all who participated, belongs to this later group. In his maturity, Yeats wrote little narrative poetry. Instead he adopted the dramatic lyric as his most characteristic form of expression. Influenced by Ezra Pound, he simplified his diction and modified his syntax to reflect more closely the constructions of common speech, and in works such as *Responsibilities, and Other Poems, The Wild Swans at Coole,* and *Michael Robartes and the Dancer,* his verses began to take on the rhetorical, occasionally haughty tone that readers today identify as characteristically Yeatsian. Critics agree that Yeats's poetic technique was impeccable. It was this mastery of technique that enabled him to perfect the subtle, forceful, and highly unusual poetic meter that he used to create the effect of a chant or an incantation in such poems as "The Tower." His remarkable creative development in his final years illustrates a lifelong determination to remake himself into his ideal image of the poet: a sacerdotal figure who assumes the role of mediator between the conflicting forces of the objective and subjective worlds.

Critical Reception

Yeats's interest in Irish politics and his visionary approach to poetry often confounded his contemporaries and set him at odds with the intellectual trends of his time. His

intent interest in subjects that others labeled archaic and perceived as an affront to their modernity delayed his recognition among his peers. Nonetheless, Yeats's poetic achievement stands at the center of modern literature. By the beginning of the twentieth century he was recognized as the best English-language, Symbolist poet while also considered to be the foremost Celtic revivalist poet. Yeats was awarded the Nobel Prize in literature in 1923, though at the time of his death in 1939, his views on poetry were regarded as eccentric by students and critics alike. This attitude held sway in spite of critical awareness of the beauty and technical proficiency of his verse. Yeats had long opposed the notion that literature should serve society. As a youthful critic he had refused to praise the poor lyrics of the "Young Ireland" poets merely because they were effective as nationalist propaganda. In maturity, he found that despite his success, his continuing conviction that poetry should express the spiritual life of the individual estranged him from those who believed that a modern poet must take as his themes social alienation and the barrenness of materialist culture. As Kathleen Raine wrote of him: "Against a rising tide of realism, political verse and University wit, Yeats upheld the innocent and the beautiful, the traditional and the noble," and, as a consequence of his disregard for the concerns of the modern world, was often misunderstood. However, as critics became disenchanted with modern poetic trends, Yeats's romantic dedication to the laws of the imagination and art for art's sake became more acceptable. Indeed, critics today are less concerned with the validity of Yeats's occult and visionary theories than with their symbolic value as expressions of timeless ideals, considering his interest in arcana as a manifestation of the truth of Wallace Stevens's statement that "poets are never of the world in which they live."

PRINCIPAL WORKS

Poetry

Mosada: A Dramatic Poem 1886
The Wanderings of Oisin, and Other Poems 1889
The Countess Cathleen, and Various Legends and Lyrics
   1892
Collected Poems 1895
The Wind among the Reeds 1899
In the Seven Woods 1903
The Green Helmet, and Other Poems 1910
Responsibilities, and Other Poems 1914
The Wild Swans at Coole 1917
Michael Robartes and the Dancer 1920
Later Poems 1922
The Cat and the Moon, and Certain Poems 1924
The Tower 1928
The Winding Stair 1929
Words for Music Perhaps, and Other Poems 1932
The Collected Poems of W. B. Yeats 1933
The King of the Great Clock Tower 1934
A Full Moon in March (poetry and dramas) 1935
New Poems 1938

Last Poems and Two Plays (poetry and dramas) 1939
On the Boiler (poetry and essays) 1939
Last Poems and Plays (poetry and dramas) 1940
The Poems: A New Edition 1983

Other Major Works

The Celtic Twilight (folklore) 1893
The Land of Heart's Desire (drama) 1894
The Secret Rose (short stories) 1897
The Shadowy Waters (drama) 1900
Cathleen ni Houlihan [with Lady Gregory] (drama) 1902
The Hour Glass [with Lady Gregory] (drama) 1903
Ideas of Good and Evil (essays) 1903
The King's Threshold [with Lady Gregory] (drama) 1903
On Baile's Strand (drama) 1904
Stories of Red Hanrahan (short stories) 1904
Deirdre [with Lady Gregory] (drama) 1906
Discoveries (essays) 1907
The Unicorn from the Stars [with Lady Gregory] (drama) 1907
The Golden Helmet (drama) 1908
Poetry and Ireland [with Lionel Johnson] (essays) 1908
At the Hawk's Well (drama) 1916
Per Amica Silentia Lunae (essay) 1918
The Player Queen (drama) 1919
Four Plays for Dancers [first publication] (dramas) 1921
Four Years: 1887-91 (memoir) 1921
A Vision (essay) 1925; also published as *A Vision* [enlarged edition] 1937
*Autobiographies (memoir) 1926; also published as *The Autobiography of William Butler Yeats* [enlarged edition] 1938
The Dreaming of the Bones (drama) 1931
The Collected Plays of W. B. Yeats (dramas) 1934; also published as *The Collected Plays of W. B. Yeats* [enlarged edition] 1952
Wheels and Butterflies (drama) 1934
The Herne's Egg (drama) 1938
Purgatory (drama) 1938
The Death of Cuchulain (drama) 1949
The Letters of W. B. Yeats (letters) 1954
W. B. Yeats: Essays and Introductions (essays) 1961

*This work includes the memoirs *Reveries over Childhood and Youth* and *The Trembling of the Veil*. The enlarged edition of 1938 also includes the memoirs *Dramatis Personae, Estrangement, The Death of Synge,* and *The Bounty of Sweden*.

CRITICISM

Lionel Johnson   (review date 1892)

SOURCE: Review of "The Countess Kathleen and Various Legends and Lyrics," in *The Academy,* Vol. 42, No. 1065, October 1, 1892, pp. 278-79.

[*Johnson, an English poet of Irish descent, was a friend of Yeats. In the following excerpt, Johnson praises Yeats for his use of Celtic themes and his ability to seize his readers emotionally.*]

Mr. Yeats has published two volumes of verse: **The Wanderings of Oisin** and **The Countess Kathleen**. Doubtless it is difficult to speak with perfect security about the first books of a living writer; but I feel little diffidence in speaking of these two volumes. In the last two or three years much charming verse has been published by many writers who may make themselves distinguished names; but nothing which seems to me, in the most critical and dispassionate state of mind, equal in value to the poems of Mr. Yeats. Irish of the Irish, in the themes and sentiments of his verse, he has also no lack of that wider sympathy with the world, without which the finest national verse must remain provincial. Yet, for all his interests of a general sort, his poetry has not lost one Irish grace, one Celtic delicacy, one native charm. . . .

The distinction of Mr. Yeats, as an Irish poet, is his ability to write Celtic poetry, with all the Celtic notes of style and imagination, in a classical manner. Like all men of the true poetical spirit, he is not overcome by the apparent antagonism of the classical and the romantic in art. Like the fine Greeks or Romans, he treats his subject according to its nature. Simple as that sounds, it is a praise not often to be bestowed. Consider the "Attis" of Catullus: how the monstrous, barbaric frenzy of the theme is realised in verse of the strictest beauty. It is not a Latin theme, congenial to a Latin nature: it is Asiatic, insane, grotesque; its passion is abnormal and harsh. Yet the poem, while terrible in its intensity of life, is a masterpiece of severe art. It is in this spirit, if I may dare so great a comparision, that Mr. Yeats has written: his poetry has plenty of imperfections, but it is not based upon a fundamental mistake; he sees very clearly where success may be found. When he takes a Celtic theme, some vast and epic legend, or some sad and lyrical fancy, he does not reflect the mere confused vastness of the one, the mere flying vagueness of the other: his art is full of reason. So he produces poems, rational and thoughtful, yet beautiful with the beauty that comes of thought about imagination. It is not the subjects alone, nor the musical skill alone, nor the dominant mood alone, but all these together that make these poems so satisfying and so haunting. They have that natural felicity which belongs to beautiful things in nature, but a felicity under the control of art.

In these poems, the immediate charm is their haunting music, which depends not upon any rich wealth of words, but upon a subtle strain of music in their whole quality of thoughts and images, some incommunicable beauty, felt in the simplest words and verses. Collins, Blake, Coleridge, had the secret of such music; Mr. Yeats sings somewhat in their various ways, but with a certain instinct of his own, definitely Irish. The verse is stately and solemn, without any elaboration; the thought falls into a lofty rhythm. Or the verse is wistful and melancholy, an aërial murmur of sad things without any affectation. . . .

In all the poems, even the most mystical in thought, there is a deep tone of sympathy with the world's fortunes, or

with the natures of living things: a curiously tender gladness at the thought of it all. . . . His ballads are full of this
natural sentiment, shown rather in their simple mention
of facts and things, as an old poet might mention them,
than in any artificial simplicity. There is humour in this
verse: a sense of the human soul in all things, a fearless
treatment of facts, a gentleness towards life, because it is
all wonderful and nothing is despicable. And through the
poems there pierces that spiritual cry, which is too rare
and fine to reach ears satisfied with the gross richness of
a material Muse. . . . There is much to distress some
readers in Mr. Yeats's poems. Cuchullin, to them, is less
familiar than King Arthur, and they know nothing about
the Irish symbolism of the Rose, and much fearless simplicity seems to them but odd and foolish. All writers of
distinction, who have a personal vision of life, and thoughts
of their own, and a music of unfamiliar beauty, must lay
their account with ridicule or misapprehension. But a very
little patience will overcome all difficulties. It is impossible to read these poems without falling under their fascination and taking them home to heart.

William Butler Yeats (essay date 1900)

SOURCE: "The Symbolism of Poetry," in *Essays and
Introductions* (reprint), Macmillan, 1961, pp. 153-64.

[*This essay, which first appeared in* The Dome *in 1900,
presents Yeats's views on symbolic poetry. In the excerpt
which follows, Yeats discusses the emotional and intellectual associations of symbolism and the power of rhythm
to evoke a state of meditation in poetry.*]

Symbolism, as seen in the writers of our day, would have
no value if it were not seen also, under one 'disguise or
another, in every great imaginative writer,' writes Mr.
Arthur Symons in *The Symbolist Movement in Literature*,
a subtle book which I cannot praise as I would, because
it has been dedicated to me; and he goes on to show how
many profound writers have in the last few years sought
for a philosophy of poetry in the doctrine of symbolism,
and how even in countries where it is almost scandalous
to seek for any philosophy of poetry, new writers are
following them in their search. We do not know what the
writers of ancient times talked of among themselves, and
one bull is all that remains of Shakespeare's talk, who
was on the edge of modern times; and the journalist is
convinced, it seems, that they talked of wine and women
and politics, but never about their art, or never quite seriously about their art. He is certain that no one who had
a philosophy of his art, or a theory of how he should
write, has ever made a work of art, that people have no
imagination who do not write without forethought and
afterthought as he writes his own articles. He says this
with enthusiasm, because he has heard it at so many comfortable dinner-tables, where some one had mentioned
through carelessness, or foolish zeal, a book whose difficulty had offended indolence, or a man who had not forgotten that beauty is an accusation. Those formulas and
generalisations, in which a hidden sergeant has drilled the

ideas of journalists and through them the ideas of all but
all the modern world, have created in their turn a forgetfulness like that of soldiers in battle, so that journalists
and their readers have forgotten, among many like events,
that Wagner spent seven years arranging and explaining
his ideas before he began his most characteristic music;
that opera, and with it modern music, arose from certain
talks at the house of one Giovanni Bardi of Florence; and
that the Pléiade laid the foundations of modern French
literature with a pamphlet. Goethe has said, 'a poet needs
all philosophy, but he must keep it out of his work,' though
that is not always necessary; and almost certainly no great
art, outside England, where journalists are more powerful
and ideas less plentiful than elsewhere, has arisen without
a great criticism, for its herald or its interpreter and protector, and it may be for this reason that great art, now
that vulgarity has armed itself and multiplied itself, is
perhaps dead in England.

All writers, all artists of any kind, in so far as they have
had any philosophical or critical power, perhaps just in so
far as they have been deliberate artists at all, have had
some philosophy, some criticism of their art; and it has
often been this philosophy, or this criticism, that has
evoked their most startling inspiration, calling into outer
life some portion of the divine life, or of the buried reality,
which could alone extinguish in the emotions what their
philosophy or their criticism would extinguish in the intellect. They have sought for no new thing, it may be, but
only to understand and to copy the pure inspiration of
early times, but because the divine life wars upon our
outer life, and must needs change its weapons and its
movements as we change ours, inspiration has come to
them in beautiful startling shapes. The scientific movement brought with it a literature which was always tending
to lose itself in externalities of all kinds, in opinion, in
declamation, in picturesque writing, in word-painting, or
in what Mr. Symons has called an attempt 'to build in
brick and mortar inside the covers of a book'; and new
writers have begun to dwell upon the element of evocation, of suggestion, upon what we call the symbolism in
great writers.

In **"Symbolism in Painting,"** I tried to describe the element of symbolism that is in pictures and sculpture, and
described a little the symbolism in poetry, but did not
describe at all the continuous indefinable symbolism which
is the substance of all style.

There are no lines with more melancholy beauty than
these by Burns:—

> The white moon is setting behind the white wave,
> And Time is setting with me, O!

and these lines are perfectly symbolical. Take from them
the whiteness of the moon and of the wave, whose relation
to the setting of Time is too subtle for the intellect, and
you take from them their beauty. But, when all are together,
moon and wave and whiteness and setting Time and the
last melancholy cry, they evoke an emotion which cannot
be evoked by any other arrangement of colours and sounds

and forms. We may call this metaphorical writing, but it is better to call it symbolical writing, because metaphors are not profound enough to be moving, when they are not symbols, and when they are symbols they are the most perfect of all, because the most subtle, outside of pure sound, and through them one can best find out what symbols are. If one begins the reverie with any beautiful lines that one can remember, one finds they are like those by Burns. Begin with this line by Blake:—

> The gay fishes on the wave when the moon sucks
> up the dew;

or these lines by Nash:—

> Brightness falls from the air,
> Queens have died young and fair,
> Dust hath closed Helen's eye;

or these lines by Shakespeare:—

> Timon hath made his everlasting mansion
> Upon the beached verge of the salt flood;
> Who once a day with his embossed froth
> The turbulent surge shall cover;

or take some line that is quite simple, that gets its beauty from its place in a story, and see how it flickers with the light of the many symbols that have given the story its beauty, as a sword-blade may flicker with the light of burning towers.

All sounds, all colours, all forms, either because of their preordained energies or because of long association, evoke indefinable and yet precise emotions, or, as I prefer to think, call down among us certain disembodied powers, whose footsteps over our hearts we call emotions; and when sound, and colour, and form are in a musical relation, a beautiful relation to one another, they become, as it were, one sound, one colour, one form, and evoke an emotion that is made out of their distinct evocations and yet is one emotion. The same relation exists between all portions of every work of art, whether it be an epic or a song, and the more perfect it is, and the more various and numerous the elements that have flowed into its perfection, the more powerful will be the emotion, the power, the god it calls among us. Because an emotion does not exist, or does not become perceptible and active among us, till it has found its expression, in colour or in sound or in form, or in all of these, and because no two modulations or arrangements of these evoke the same emotion, poets and painters and musicians, and in a less degree because their effects are momentary, day and night and cloud and shadow, are continually making and unmaking mankind. It is indeed only those things which seem useless or very feeble that have any power, and all those things that seem useful or strong, armies, moving wheels, modes of architecture, modes of government, speculations of the reason, would have been a little different if some mind long ago had not given itself to some emotion, as a woman gives herself to her lover, and shaped sounds or colours or forms, or all of these, into a musical relation,

that their emotion might live in other minds. A little lyric evokes an emotion, and this emotion gathers others about it and melts into their being in the making of some great epic; and at last, needing an always less delicate body, or symbol, as it grows more powerful, it flows out, with all it has gathered, among the blind instincts of daily life, where it moves a power within powers, as one sees ring within ring in the stem of an old tree. This is maybe what Arthur O'Shaughnessy meant when he made his poets say they had built Nineveh with their sighing; and I am certainly never sure, when I hear of some war, or of some religious excitement, or of some new manufacture, or of anything else that fills the ear of the world, that it has not all happened because of something that a boy piped in Thessaly. I remember once telling a seeress to ask one among the gods who, as she believed, were standing about her in their symbolic bodies, what would come of a charming but seeming trivial labour of a friend, and the form answering, 'the devastation of peoples and the overwhelming of cities.' I doubt indeed if the crude circumstance of the world, which seems to create all our emotions, does more than reflect, as in multiplying mirrors, the emotions that have come to solitary men in moments of poetical contemplation; or that love itself would be more than an animal hunger but for the poet and his shadow the priest, for unless we believe that outer things are the reality, we must believe that the gross is the shadow of the subtle, that things are wise before they become foolish, and secret before they cry out in the market-place. Solitary men in moments of contemplation receive, as I think, the creative impulse from the lowest of the Nine Hierarchies, and so make and unmake mankind, and even the world itself, for does not 'the eye altering alter all'?

> Our towns are copied fragments from our breast;
> And all man's Babylons strive but to impart
> The grandeurs of his Babylonian heart.

The purpose of rhythm, it has always seemed to me, is to prolong the moment of contemplation, the moment when we are both asleep and awake, which is the one moment of creation, by hushing us with an alluring monotony, while it holds us waking by variety, to keep us in that state of perhaps real trance, in which the mind liberated from the pressure of the will is unfolded in symbols. If certain sensitive persons listen persistently to the ticking of a watch, or gaze persistently on the monotonous flashing of a light, they fall into the hypnotic trance; and rhythm is but the ticking of a watch made softer, that one must needs listen, and various, that one may not be swept beyond memory or grow weary of listening; while the patterns of the artist are but the monotonous flash woven to take the eyes in a subtler enchantment. I have heard in meditation voices that were forgotten the moment they had spoken; and I have been swept, when in more profound meditation, beyond all memory but of those things that came from beyond the threshold of waking life. I was writing once at a very symbolical and abstract poem, when my pen fell on the ground; and as I stooped to pick it up, I remembered some fantastic adventure that yet did not seem fantastic, and then another like adventure, and when I asked myself when these things had happened, I found that I was remembering my dreams for many nights. I tried to remember what I had done the day before, and then what I had done that morning; but all my waking life had perished from me, and it was only after a struggle that I came to remember it again, and as I did so that more powerful and startling life perished in its turn. Had my pen not fallen on the ground and so made me turn from the images that I was weaving into verse, I would never have known that meditation had become trance, for I would have been like one who does not know that he is passing through a wood because his eyes are on the pathway. So I think that in the making and in the understanding of a work of art, and the more easily if it is full of patterns and symbols and music, we are lured to the threshold of sleep, and it may be far beyond it, without knowing that we have ever set our feet upon the steps of horn or of ivory.

Besides emotional symbols, symbols that evoke emotions alone,—and in this sense all alluring or hateful things are symbols, although their relations with one another are too subtle to delight us fully, away from rhythm and pattern,—there are intellectual symbols, symbols that evoke ideas alone, or ideas mingled with emotions; and outside the very definite traditions of mysticism and the less definite criticism of certain modern poets, these alone are called symbols. Most things belong to one or another kind, according to the way we speak of them and the companions we give them, for symbols, associated with ideas that are more than fragments of the shadows thrown upon the intellectby the emotions they evoke, are the playthings of the allegorist or the pedant, and soon pass away. If I say 'white' or 'purple' in an ordinary line of poetry, they evoke emotions so exclusively that I cannot say why they move me; but if I bring them into the same sentence with such obvious intellectual symbols as a cross or a crown of thorns, I think of purity and sovereignty. Furthermore, innumerable meanings, which are held to 'white' or to 'purple' by bonds of subtle suggestion, and alike in the emotions and in the intellect, move visibly through my mind, and move invisibly beyond the threshold of sleep, casting lights and shadows of an indefinable wisdom on what had seemed before, it may be, but sterility and noisy violence. It is the intellect that decides where the reader shall ponder over the procession of the symbols, and if the symbols are merely emotional, he gazes from amid the accidents and destinies of the world; but if the symbols are intellectual too, he becomes himself a part of pure intellect, and he is himself mingled with the procession. If I watch a rushy pool in the moonlight, my emotion at its beauty is mixed with memories of the man that I have seen ploughing by its margin, or of the lovers I saw there a night ago; but if I look at the moon herself and remember any of her ancient names and meanings, I move among divine people, and things that have shaken off our mortality, the tower of ivory, the queen of waters, the shining stag among enchanted woods, the white hare sitting upon the hilltop, the fool of Faery with his shining cup full of dreams, and it may be 'make a friend of one of these images of wonder,' and 'meet the Lord in the air.' So, too, if one is moved by Shakespeare, who is content with emotional symbols that he may come the nearer to our

sympathy, one is mixed with the whole spectacle of the world; while if one is moved by Dante, or by the myth of Demeter, one is mixed into the shadow of God or of a goddess. So, too, one is furthest from symbols when one is busy doing this or that, but the soul moves among symbols and unfolds in symbols when trance, or madness, or deep meditation has withdrawn it from every impulse but its own. 'I then saw,' wrote Gérard de Nerval of his madness, 'vaguely drifting into form, plastic images of antiquity, which outlined themselves, became definite, and seemed to represent symbols of which I only seized the idea with difficulty.' In an earlier time he would have been of that multitude whose souls austerity withdrew, even more perfectly than madness could withdraw his soul, from hope and memory, from desire and regret, that they might reveal those processions of symbols that men bow to before altars, and woo with incense and offerings. But being of our time, he has been like Maeterlinck, like Villiers de l'Isle-Adam in *Axël,* like all who are preoccupied with intellectual symbols in our time, a foreshadower of the new sacred book, of which all the arts, as somebody has said, are beginning to dream. How can the arts overcome the slow dying of men's hearts that we call the progress of the world, and lay their hands upon men's heartstrings again, without becoming the garment of religion as in old times?

If people were to accept the theory that poetry moves us because of its symbolism, what change should one look for in the manner of our poetry? A return to the way of our fathers, a casting out of descriptions of nature for the sake of nature, of the moral law for the sake of the moral law, a casting out of all anecdotes and of that brooding over scientific opinion that so often extinguished the central flame in Tennyson, and of that vehemence that would make us do or not do certain things; or, in other words, we should come to understand that the beryl stone was enchanted by our fathers that it might unfold the pictures in its heart, and not to mirror our own excited faces, or the boughs waving outside the window. With this change of substance, this return to imagination, this understanding that the laws of art, which are the hidden laws of the world, can alone bind the imagination, would come a change of style, and we would cast out of serious poetry those energetic rhythms, as of a man running, which are the invention of the will with its eyes always on something to be done or undone; and we would seek out those wavering, meditative, organic rhythms, which are the embodiment of the imagination, that neither desires nor hates, because it has done with time, and only wishes to gaze upon some reality, some beauty; nor would it be any longer possible for anybody to deny the importance of form, in all its kinds, for although you can expound an opinion, or describe a thing, when your words are not quite well chosen, you cannot give a body to something that moves beyond the senses, unless your words are as subtle, as complex, as full of mysterious life, as the body of a flower or of a woman. The form of sincere poetry, unlike the form of the 'popular poetry,' may indeed be sometimes obscure, or ungrammatical as in some of the best of the *Songs of Innocence and Experience,* but it must have the perfections that escape analysis, the subtleties that have a new meaning every day, and it must have all this whether it be but a little song made out of a moment of dreamy indolence, or some great epic made out of the dreams of one poet and of a hundred generations whose hands were never weary of the sword.

William Archer (essay date 1902)

SOURCE: "William Butler Yeats," in *Poets of the Younger Generation,* John Lane/The Bodley Head, 1902 (reprinted by Scholarly Press, 1969), pp. 531-57.

[*In the following excerpt, Archer notes that Yeats's early Celtic themes were an outgrowth of his personality and beliefs and not affectations of a current style.*]

It is with Mr. Yeats that, so far as I know, the genuine spirit of Irish antiquity and Irish folk-lore makes its first entrance into English verse. Irish poets before him have either been absorbed in love, potheen, and politics—as Mr. Yeats himself puts it, they have "sung their loudest when a company of rebels or revellers has been at hand to applaud"—or (like Goldsmith and Moore) they have become to all intents and purposes Anglicised. Even William Allingham's fairies, pleasant little people though they be, are rather Anglo-Saxon Brownies than Keltic Sheogues. In Mr. Yeats we have an astonishing union of primitive imagination and feeling with cultivated and consciously artistic expression. He does not manipulate from outside a dead and conventionalised mythological machinery. The very spirit of the myth-makers and myth-believers is in him. His imaginative life finds its spontaneous, natural utterance in the language of the "Keltic twilight." This is no literary jargon to him, but his veritable mother-tongue. When he deals with Catholicism, you see in his mental processes a living repetition of what occurred when the first missionaries evangelised Hibernia. You see the primitive pagan assimilating the Catholic mythology to his own spiritual habits and needs, and attaching purely pagan concepts to Christian names and terms. His moral ideas are enlarged, no doubt; his metaphysics are practically unaffected. Christianity, in Mr. Yeats's poems, is not a creed, but a system of folk-lore. You do not trouble about its historical basis, you neither accept nor reject its dogmas. It is part and parcel of the innumerable host of spiritual entitites and influences which beleaguers humanity from the cradle to the grave. Belief in these entities and influences is no more a matter of intellectual determination, of voluntary assent, than belief in the air we breathe. It is part of our constitution: innate, inevitable. Mr. Yeats's religion (I speak, of course, of Mr. Yeats the poet, not of the theoretical mystic and editor of Blake) is not "morality touched with emotion," but rather superstition touched with morality. It is "older than any historythat is written in any book. . . ."

[L]et us glance at Mr. Yeats's epic, *The Wanderings of Oisin*. And here it must be said that the curious crispness, delicacy, and artful simplicity of his style is the result of patient effort and slow development. His verse has now a peculiar, indefinable distinction, as of one tiptoeing exquisitely through a fairy minuet; whereas ten years ago its movement was often flat-footed and conventional enough. *The Wanderings of Oisin,* as it now stands, is very different from the poem originally published under that title.

[In its original form, the poem] is pretty, indeed, and fancifully decorative, with unmistakable foretastes of the poet's maturer quality; but it is nerveless, diffuse, and now and then commonplace. Everything of value is retained in the later version; some exquisite touches are added. . . .

[Every] change tends to heighten the racial colour of the passage (if I may call it so) and make it more characteristically Keltic. The first form might have been the work of an Englishman cleverly applying the method of *Christabel* to an Irish subject; the second form is Irish to its inmost fibre. . . . Magical and mysterious though the subject be, the design is perfectly definite, and is picked out, so to speak, in washes of brilliant, translucent, almost unharmonised colours. The picture is illuminated rather than painted, like the border of an ancient manuscript. It is characteristic of the Keltic imagination, though it may dwell by preference in the mist, to emerge at times into a scintillant blaze of light and colour.

[*The Wanderings of Oisin* is] a singularly beautiful and moving poem, in which the high-hearted bravery and the wistful beauty of the old Irish myth-cycle find the most sympathetic of interpreters. . . .

Mr. Yeats draws his true strength from his native soil. In these early experiments the conventionality of the verse was particularly noticeable. It showed scarcely a trace of individual accent, and was not to be distinguished from the blank verse of the scores of stillborn "poetic dramas" which every year brings forth. No sooner had Mr. Yeats returned to Ireland and chosen a dramatic motive from Irish folk-lore, than his individuality asserted itself not only in the idea and structure of his work but in its rhythms as well. *The Countess Cathleen* has undergone stringent revision since its first appearance; and here, as in *The Wanderings of Oisin,* the changes—and especially the rounding-off of metrically defective lines—have all been for the better. But even in its original form the poem was full of a weird impressiveness which was then new to dramatic literature.

A melancholy theme indeed is that of *The Countess Cathleen*. It can be told in a few words: The land is famine-stricken; Satan sends two demons in the guise of merchants to buy the souls of the starving peasants; the Countess Cathleen will sacrifice all her vast wealth, her "gold and green forests," to save the people; but the emissaries of hell (the heavenly powers being apparently asleep) steal her treasure, becalm her ships, delay the passage of her flocks and herds; so that at last there is nothing for her to do but to sell her own soul and feed the people with the proceeds. The absolute impotence, the practical non-existence, of the powers of good, and the perfect ease with which the powers of evil execute their plots, render the play depressing almost to the point of exasperation. It is true that at the end an Angel intervenes, and gives us to understand that Cathleen's soul is safe, because

> The Light of Lights
> Looks always on the motive, not the deed,
> The Shadow of Shadows on the deed alone.

But this is a tardy consolation to the reader, who feels, moreover, that Satan is not quite fairly dealt with, being baulked by a quibble, not openly encountered and vanquished. Oppressive melancholy, however, is the note of the folklore from which Mr. Yeats draws his inspiration; though in his delightful little book of prose, *The Celtic Twilight,* he seems inclined to contest the fact. Be this as it may, **The Countess Cathleen** (especially in its revised form) is as beautiful as it is sad. The blank verse has a monotonous, insinuating melody which is all its own, arising not only from the dainty simplicity of the diction, but from the preponderance of final monosyllables and of what the professors of Shakespearometry call "end-stopped" lines. Mr. Yeats eschews all attempt to get dramatic force and variety into his verse by aid of the well-known tricks of frequent elisions, feminine endings, periodic structure, and all the rest of it. And herein he does well. No rush and tumult of versification could suit his mournful fantasies so perfectly as this crooning rhythm, this limpid melody, which seems, as Cyrano de Bergerac would say, to have a touch of the brogue in it. . . .

In [**The Wind Among the Reeds** and **The Shadowy Waters,** Mr. Yeats's] peculiar gifts of imagination and of utterance are seen at their best. He extracts from a simple and rather limited vocabulary effects of the rarest delicacy and distinction. There is a certain appearance of mannerism, no doubt, in Mr. Yeats's individuality. One can scarcely turn a page of these books without coming upon the epithets "dim," "glimmering," "wandering," "pearl-pale," "dove-grey," "dew-dropping," and the like. His imagery is built up out of a very few simple elements, which he combines and re-combines unweariedly. The materials he employs, in short, are those of primitive folk-poetry; but he touches them to new and often marvellous beauty. What in our haste we take for mannerism may be more justly denominated style, the inevitable accent of his genius.

One other word, and I have done. It appears from the notes to **The Wind Among the Reeds,** rather than from the poems themselves, that Mr. Yeats is becoming more and more addicted to a petrified, fossilised symbolism, a system of hieroglyphs which may have had some inherent significance for their inventors, but which have now become matters of research, of speculation, of convention. I cannot but regard this tendency as ominous. His art cannot gain and may very easily lose by it. A conventional symbol may be of the greatest interest to the anthropologist or the antiquary; for the poet it can have no value. If a symbol does not spring spontaneously from his own imagination and express an analogy borne in upon his own spiritual perception, he may treasure it in his mental

museum, but he ought not to let such a piece of inert matter cumber the seed-plot of his poetry.

Times Literary Supplement (review date 1919)

SOURCE: "Tunes Old and New," a review of *The Wild Swans at Coole,* in *The Times Literary Supplement,* No. 896, March 20, 1919, p. 149.

[*In the following review, the critic praises Yeats's masterful use of sound and suggests that Yeats emphasizes both ephemeral and malignant themes in* The Wild Swans at Coole.]

Mr. Yeats is like a fiddler taking down his old dust-covered violin and lazily playing an old tune on it; or it seems an old tune at first that he is taking liberties with. How often one has heard it; and yet, suddenly, it is as new as the sunrise—or the moonlight. Go on, go on, we cry. No one can play like that; and then he ceases carelessly, and puts the fiddle away, and talks of other things. All through this book he has the effect of remembering old tunes and playing them over again and making them new. There are some players who possess you with the sense of their mastery by the way they look over the fiddle before they sound a note; and he has this power with the first words of a song. But he likes best to begin with the variation upon an old tune, the tune being implicit in the variation and fading a way out of it into a last line, that seems to stop lazily as if it were just capriciously tired of itself. So in **"The Wild Swans at Coole,"** we are tantalized; he seems to love the mere sound of his fiddle that only he can draw from it and then to grow weary as if all tunes were played and stale.

He himself is aware of this mood and even makes poetry out of it:—

> I am worn out with dreams:
> A weather-worn, marble triton
> Among the streams;
> And all day long I look
> Upon this lady's beauty
> As though I had found in book
> A pictured beauty,
> Pleased to have filled the eyes
> Or the discerning ears,
> Delighted to be but wise,
> For men improve with the years;
> And yet and yet
> Is this my dream, or the truth?
> O would that we had met
> When I had my burning youth;
> But I grow old among dreams,
> A weather-worn, marble triton
> Among the streams.

There he seems to be living on memories and to resent some malignancy in the nature of things which has made of him a work of art incompatible with artless reality. It is this sense of a malignance in things which makes Irish writers themselves so often seem malicious. It is in Synge, and even in Mr. Shaw; they whisper malice about men because to them there is malice in reality. In the second verse of another poem Mr. Yeats says:—

> I would find by the edge of that water
> The collar-bone of a hare
> Worn thin by the lapping of water,
> And pierce it through with a gimlet and stare
> At the old bitter world where they marry in
>   churches,
> And laugh over the untroubled water
> At all who marry in churches,
> Through the white thin bone of a hare.

Irish writers do seem to look at reality through the white thin bone of a hare, through some magic and isolating medium of their own, which makes reality to them far off, absurd, meaningless. And the world of meaning which they desire, for them is not. Hence their malice. They would put us out of conceit with the reality that is at least real to us, because they are out of conceit with it; and Mr. Yeats wanders lost, unable to find that universe which is yet real to him because he so much desires it.

Through all his poetry there is this beauty, a little malign, of desire that has not only failed to find its object but despairs of finding it. That is why he picks up his fiddle so lazily and plays us such short, sweet, tantalizing tunes on it. Stray things suggest to him that state of being he can never find, like the wild swans at Coole themselves:—

> The trees are in their autumn beauty,
> The woodland paths are dry,
> Under the October twilight the water
> Mirrors a still sky;
> Upon the brimming water among the stones
> Are nine and fifty swans.

And the poem ends:—

> But now they drift on the still water
> Mysterious, beautiful;
> Among what rushes will they build,
> By what lake's edge or pool
> Delight men's eyes when I awake some day
> To find they have flow away?

Because they are so beautiful they are to him visitants and have the transitoriness of his own delight in them. In his music he seems to inhabit a world that will tremble away at a touch like reflections in still water. Even in the beautiful poem in memory of Major Gregory, full of concrete things and characters, he says:—

> Always we'd have the new friend meet the old
> And we are hurt if either friend seem cold,
> And there is salt to lengthen out the smart
> In the affections of our heart,
> And quarrels are blown up upon that head;
> But not a friend that I would bring

> This night can set us quarrelling,
> For all that come into my mind are dead.

Friends too, and even friendships, are like the wild swans at Coole. But how good the poem is; both racy and passionate, like the poetry of Donne, and like that, without imitation, in its very turns of speech. While we analyse the poet's mind and seem to judge it, we are fidgeting away from the real matter, the beauty of his poetry. That justifies his mind and all its moods; and in *The Wild Swans at Coole* there are many beautiful poems, some more homely than Mr. Yeats is wont to write. Every one can enjoy the **"Two Songs of a Fool,"** or **"The Cat and the Moon,"** which is a miracle of things exactly said that seemed unsayable; and there is a truth most delicately captured in **"An Irish airmen foresees his death"**:—

> I know that I shall meet my fate
> Somewhere among the clouds above;
> Those that I fight I do not hate,
> Those that I guard I do not love;
> My country is Kiltartan Cross
> My countrymen Kiltartan's poor,
> No likely end could bring them loss
> Or leave them happier than before.

There he fiddles to an old tune, but what a new surprise of meaning he gets out of his easy, lazy, masterly fiddling. And we can only listen and be grateful.

William Butler Yeats (essay date 1937)

SOURCE: "A General Introduction for My Work" (1937), in *Essays and Introductions* (reprint), Macmillan, 1961, pp. 509-26.

[In the following excerpt, Yeats discusses the nature of his poetry and the influences of Celtic legend, his Irish heritage, and other poets on his work.]

A poet writes always of his personal life, in his finest work out of its tragedy, whatever it be, remorse, lost love, or mere loneliness; he never speaks directly as to someone at the breakfast table, there is always a phantasmagoria. Dante and Milton had mythologies, Shakespeare the characters of English history or of traditional romance; even when the poet seems most himself, when he is Raleigh and gives potentates the lie, or Shelley 'a nerve o'er which do creep the else unfelt oppressions of this earth,' or Byron when 'the soul wears out the breast' as 'the sword outwears its sheath,' he is never the bundle of accident and incoherence that sits down to breakfast; he has been re-born as an idea, something intended, complete. . . . He is part of his own phantasmagoria and we adore him because nature has grown intelligible, and by so doing a part of our creative power. 'When mind is lost in the light of the Self,' says the Prashna Upanishad, 'it dreams no more; still in the body it is lost in happiness.' 'A wise man seeks in Self,' says the Chandogya Upanishad, 'those that are alive and those that are dead and gets what the world cannot give.' The world knows nothing because it has made nothing, we know everything because we have made everything.

It was through the old Fenian leader John O'Leary I found my theme. His long imprisonment, his longer banishment, his magnificent head, his scholarship, his pride, his integrity, all that aristocratic dream nourished amid little shops and little farms, had drawn around him a group of young men; I was but eighteen or nineteen and had already, under the influence of *The Faerie Queene* and *The Sad Shepherd,* written a pastoral play, and under that of Shelley's *Prometheus Unbound* two plays, one staged somewhere in the Caucasus, the other in a crater of the moon; and I knew myself to be vague and incoherent. He gave me the poems of Thomas Davis, said they were not good poetry but had changed his life when a young man, spoke of other poets associated with Davis and *The Nation* newspaper, probably lent me their books. I saw even more clearly than O'Leary that they were not good poetry. I read nothing but romantic literature; hated that dry eighteenth-century rhetoric; but they had one quality I admired and admire: they were not separated individual men; they spoke or tried to speak out of a people to a people; behind them stretched the generations. I knew, though but now and then as young men know things, that I must turn from that modern literature Jonathan Swift compared to the web a spider draws out of its bowels; I hated and still hate with an ever growing hatred the literature of the point of view. I wanted, if my ignorance permitted, to get back to Homer, to those that fed at his table. I wanted to cry as all men cried, to laugh as all men laughed, and the Young Ireland poets when not writing mere politics had the same want, but they did not know that the common and its befitting language is the research of a lifetime and when found may lack popular recognition.

Behind all Irish history hangs a great tapestry, even Christianity had to accept it and be itself pictured there. Nobody looking at its dim folds can say where Christianity begins and Druidism ends; 'There is one perfect among the birds, one perfect among the fish, and one among men that is perfect.' I can only explain by that suggestion of recent scholars—Professor Burkitt of Cambridge commended it to my attention—that St. Patrick came to Ireland not in the fifth century but towards the end of the second. The great controversies had not begun; Easter was still the first full moon after the Equinox. Upon that day the world had been created, the Ark rested upon Ararat, Moses led the Israelites out of Egypt; the umbilical cord which united Christianity to the ancient world had not yet been cut, Christ was still the half-brother of Dionysus. A man just tonsured by the Druids could learn from the nearest Christian neighbour to sign himself with the Cross without sense of incongruity, nor would his children acquire that sense. The organised clans weakened Church organisation, they could accept the monk but not the bishop.

Into this tradition, oral and written, went in later years fragments of Neo-Platonism, cabbalistic words—I have heard the words 'tetragrammaton agla' in Doneraile—the floating debris of mediaeval thought, but nothing that did

not please the solitary mind. Even the religious equivalent for Baroque and Rococo could not come to us as thought, perhaps because Gaelic is incapable of abstraction. It came as cruelty. That tapestry filled the scene at the birth of modern Irish literature, it is there in the Synge of *The Well of the Saints,* in James Stephens, and in Lady Gregory throughout, in all of George Russell that did not come from the Upanishads, and in all but my later poetry.

Our mythology, our legends, differ from those of other European countries because down to the end of the seventeenth century they had the attention, perhaps the unquestioned belief, of peasant and noble alike; Homer belongs to sedentary men, even to-day our ancient queens, our mediaeval soldiers and lovers, can make a pedlar shudder. I can put my own thought, despair perhaps from the study of present circumstance in the light of ancient philosophy, into the mouth of rambling poets of the seventeenth century, or even of some imagined ballad singer of to-day, and the deeper my thought the more credible, the more peasant-like, are ballad singer and rambling poet. Some modern poets contend that jazz and music-hall songs are the folk art of our time, that we should mould our art upon them; we Irish poets, modern men also, reject every folk art that does not go back to Olympus. Give me time and a little youth and I will prove that even 'Johnny, I hardly knew ye' goes back.

If Irish literature goes on as my generation planned it, it may do something to keep the 'Irishry' living, nor will the work of the realists hinder, nor the figures they imagine, nor those described in memoirs of the revolution. These last especially, like certain great political predecessors, Parnell, Swift, Lord Edward, have stepped back into the tapestry. It may be indeed that certain characteristics of the 'Irishry' must grow in importance. When Lady Gregory asked me to annotate her *Visions and Beliefs* I began, that I might understand what she had taken down in Galway, an investigation of contemporary spiritualism. For several years I frequented those mediums who in various poor parts of London instruct artisans or their wives for a few pence upon their relations to their dead, to their employers, and to their children; then I compared what she had heard in Galway, or I in London, with the visions of Swedenborg, and, after my inadequate notes had been published, with Indian belief. . . . I am convinced that in two or three generations it will become generally known that the mechanical theory has no reality, that the natural and supernatural are knit together, that to escape a dangerous fanaticism we must study a new science; at that moment Europeans may find something attractive in a Christ posed against a background not of Judaism but of Druidism, not shut off in dead history, but flowing, concrete, phenomenal.

I was born into this faith, have lived in it, and shall die in it; my Christ, a legitimate deduction from the Creed of St. Patrick as I think, is that Unity of Being Dante compared to a perfectly proportioned human body, Blake's 'Imagination,' what the Upanishads have named 'Self': nor is this unity distant and therefore intellectually understandable, but imminent, differing from man to man and age to age, taking upon itself pain and ugliness, 'eye of newt, and toe of frog.'

Subconscious preoccupation with this theme brought me *A Vision,* its harsh geometry an incomplete interpretation. The 'Irishry' have preserved their ancient 'deposit' through wars which, during the sixteenth and seventeenth centuries, became wars of extermination; no people, Lecky said at the opening of his *Ireland in the Eighteenth Century,* have undergone greater persecution, nor did that persecution altogether cease up to our own day. No people hate as we do in whom that past is always alive, there are moments when hatred poisons my life and I accuse myself of effeminacy because I have not given it adequate expression. It is not enough to have put it into the mouth of a rambling peasant poet. Then I remind myself that though mine is the first English marriage I know of in the direct line, all my family names are English, and that I owe my soul to Shakespeare, to Spenser and to Blake, perhaps to William Morris, and to the English language in which I think, speak, and write, that everything I love has come to me through English; my hatred tortures me with love, my love with hate.

I am like the Tibetan monk who dreams at his initiation that he is eaten by a wild beast and learns on waking that he himself is eater and eaten. This is Irish hatred and solitude, the hatred of human life that made Swift write *Gulliver* and the epitaph upon his tomb, that can still make us wag between extremes and doubt our sanity.

Style is almost unconscious. I know what I have tried to do, little what I have done. . . . The English mind is meditative, rich, deliberate; it may remember the Thames valley. I planned to write short lyrics or poetic drama where every speech would be short and concentrated, knit by dramatic tension, and I did so with more confidence because young English poets were at that time writing out of emotion at the moment of crisis, though their old slow-moving meditation returned almost at once. Then, and in this English poetry has followed my lead, I tried to make the language of poetry coincide with that of passionate, normal speech. I wanted to write in whatever language comes most naturally when we soliloquise, as I do all day long, upon the events of our own lives or of any life where we can see ourselves for the moment. I sometimes compare myself with the mad old slum women I hear denouncing and remembering; 'How dare you,' I heard one say of some imaginary suitor, 'and you without health or a home!' If I spoke my thoughts aloud they might be as angry and as wild. It was a long time before I had made a language to my liking; I began to make it when I discovered some twenty years ago that I must seek, not as Wordsworth thought, words in common use, but a powerful and passionate syntax, and a complete coincidence between period and stanza. Because I need a passionate syntax for passionate subject-matter I compel myself to accept those traditional metres that have developed with the language. Ezra Pound, Turner, Lawrence wrote admirable free verse, I could not. I would lose myself, become joyless like those mad old women. . . . If I wrote of personal love or sorrow in free verse, or in any rhythm that left it unchanged, amid all its accidence, I

would be full of self-contempt because of my egotism and indiscretion, and foresee the boredom of my reader. I must choose a traditional stanza, even what I alter must seem traditional. I commit my emotion to shepherds, herdsmen, cameldrivers, learned men, Milton's or Shelley's Platonist, that tower Palmer drew. Talk to me of originality and I will turn on you with rage. I am a crowd, I am a lonely man, I am nothing. Ancient salt is best packing.

Louis MacNeice (review date 1940)

SOURCE: "Yeats's Epitaph," a review of *Last Poems and Plays,* in *The New Republic,* Vol. 102, No. 26 (1334), June 24, 1940, pp. 862-63.

[*In the following excerpt, MacNeice remarks on the resilience of the aging Yeats's poetic voice and observes that the poet's native Ireland features prominently in the works collected in his* Last Poems and Plays.]

During the last ten years, Yeats has had more bouquets from the critics than any other poet of our time. It was refreshing to see these critics and also many of the younger poets committing themselves to enthusiasm for an older contemporary; their praise, however, was sometimes uncritical and sometimes, on a long-term view, injurious to its subject. There were reviewers who felt Yeats was a safe bet—safe because he was an exotic; anyone can praise a bird of paradise but you have to have some knowledge before you go buying Rhode Island Reds. There is a double point that needs making—first that Yeats was not so exotic as is popularly assumed, second that on the whole his exoticism was not an asset but a liability. He was partly aware of this himself; in his middle period he fought clear of the dead hand of Walter Pater and deliberately set out to make his poetry less "poetic" and in his later years (the years when he was a devotee of Balzac) he paid at least lip-homage to the principle of "Homo sum. . . ." His failure fully to practise this principle was due to a constitutional inhumanity.

I say this in honor to his memory. If you believe a man was a genius, it is an insult to him to ignore his deficiencies and peculiarities. One of the most peculiar poets in our history, Yeats was also extraordinarily lacking in certain qualities which the greater poets usually possess; in so far as he achieved greatness it proves, not the power of inspiration or any other such woolly miracle—all that it proves is the miracle of artistic integrity. For this was a quality he possessed even though as a man he may sometimes have been a fraud. His more naïve enemies regard him as knave or fool all through—at best as a "silly old thing"; his more naïve admirers regard him as God-intoxicated and therefore impeccable. It is high time for us to abandon this sloppy method of assessment; if poetry is important it deserves more from us than irresponsible gibes on the one hand or zany gush on the other.

Take Yeats's two passions—Ireland and Art. We have to remember that, in regard to both, his attitude was conditioned by a comparatively narrow set of circumstances and that, in judging his services to Ireland and Art, we shall be very shortsighted if we reapply his own heavily blinkered concepts of either; it is a lucky thing for the artist that his work usually outruns his ideology. Yeats talked a good deal about magic and beauty and mysticism, but his readers have no right to gabble these words like parrots and call what they are doing appreciation. Beauty is *not* the mainspring of poetry and, although a few poets have been genuine mystics, Yeats, unlike his friend A.E., was certainly not one of them; he had what might be called a mystical sense of value, but that is a different thing and a thing which perhaps for *all* artists is a *sine qua non*.

Yeats's poetry reached its peak in **The Winding Stair** (1933). The **Last Poems** now published represent the Indian summer of his virile, gossipy, contumacious, arrogant, magnificently eccentric old age. Although the book as a whole certainly lacks the depth and range of **The Tower** or **The Winding Stair**, although the septuagenarian virility is sometimes too exhibitionist, although he overdoes certain old tricks and falls into needless obscurities, and although the two plays here included are flat failures, there is still enough vitality and elegance to compensate for certain disappointments. Few poets in English literature have been able to write lyrics after thirty-five; the astonishing thing about Yeats is that he remained essentially a lyric poet till the last. Even the enormous cranky pseudo-philosophy of *A Vision* only served as an occasion for further lyrics. Yeats's ingredients became odder and odder but, because they were at least dry and hard, they helped him to assert a joy of life which was comparatively lacking in his early Celtic or pre-Raphaelite twilights. The great discovery of the later Yeats was that joy need not imply softness and that boredom is something more than one gets in dreams. Axel has been refuted; "Hamlet and Lear are gay."

Ireland is very prominent in these last poems. Yeats had for a long time regarded the essential Ireland as incarnate in the country gentry and the peasantry, his ideal society being static and indeed based upon caste. The Irish "Troubles," however, evoked in him an admiration, even an envy, for the dynamic revolutionary. His thought, in assimilating this element, became to some extent dialectical; he began to conceive of life as a developing whole, a whole which depends upon the conflict of the parts. He even began to write in praise of war, a false inference from a premise which is essentially valid—

> . . . when all words are said
> And a man is fighting mad,
> Something drops from eyes long blind,
> He completes his partial mind. . . .

Physical violence being a simple thing, the Yeats who honored it took to writing in ballad forms, while the contemplative Yeats continued to use a grand rhetorical manner and a complex inlay of esoteric ideas and images; there are good examples of both in this book. There are also, as in the preceding volumes, a number of poems

about himself and his friends; once again he goes around with a highly colored spotlight; it is amusing to turn from one of these poems, **"Beautiful Lofty Things,"** which contains a reference to a public banquet in Dublin, to George Moore's account of the same banquet in "Ave." The most revealing poem in this book is **"The Circus Animals' Desertion,"** where Yeats with admirable ruthlessness looks back on his various elaborate efforts to project himself on to the world—Celtic legend, Maud Gonne, symbolic drama. In this excellent and moving poem a self-centered old man rises above his personality by pinning it down for what it is.

Donald A. Stauffer (review date 1951)

SOURCE: "A Half Century of the High Poetic Art of William Butler Yeats," in *The New York Herald Tribune Book Review*, Vol. 27, No. 38, May 6, 1951, p. 3.

[*In the following review, Stauffer praises* The Collected Poems *and briefly summarizes Yeats's poetic career, observing that in his poems, Yeats champions the integrity of the individual against society's pressure to reform.*]

For the first time in an American edition, all of the lyrics William Butler Yeats cared to own, and some of his narrative-dramatic poems, are available in one volume. In prose or poetry, probably no single volume can compete with this one if a reader seeks to understand Western literature of the last century. Or for that matter, literature today or tomorrow.

Chronologically arranged, the **Collected Poems** can be read indirectly as a history. The dates which Yeats has assigned somewhat cavalierly to pieces he tinkered with during a long lifetime range from 1889 to 1939, the year of his death. Here is half a hundred years of continuous awareness and continuous development. Here are the Nineties, when the sickness of the century took on odd pastel tones in a precious worship of art. Here are the folk and the race and the nation, the seeking in epic and saga and religion and history for greatness that will transcend time. Here are the dreams of ancient and noble ancestors and of supernatural beauty.

But in dreams begins responsibility as Yeats knew. So here, too, is action, after the "old songs or courtly shows," after the symbols that search for meanings—"those stilted boys, Lion and woman and the Lord knows what." Ireland must be given a theater, a museum, a literature of its own. Yeats himself becomes a one-man Renaissance. In the years before the First World War, this singer of roses upon the rood of time is changed, changed utterly, into a satirist, economical as Swift, immediate, cutting, who writes occasional poems to university students, or at the Abbey Theater or on the land agitation, or about the Dublin Municipal Gallery.

The period between the wars witnessed Yeats's most magnificent efforts at discovery and consolidation. He formalizes his thought in an imaginative philosophical system of his own which whether the reader understands it or not, gives death and relationships to his poems. He remains a part of his times, if one is going to demand the superficial gestures: thinking of the death of airmen, meditating on the Irish civil wars, walking among school children as a Senator of the Irish Free State, aware of the bomb that can knock the town flat. More important are his thoughts relating aristocracy and democracy, the individual and the monolithic state, tradition and immediacy, art and life, age and youth, mathematical order and murderous passion.

Such oppositions of words mean little in a review. The point is that Yeats makes them mean much in his poems. In **"The Second Coming"** he has written the best apocalyptic poem of the century, with lines that will echo in quotation at least until the second coming (the poem appeared in a 1921 volume):

> The best lack all conviction,
>   while the worst
> Are full of passionate intensity.

And for poems of as many levels as the Empire State Building, who in this or any other period has surpassed **"Byzantium"** and **"Sailing to Byzantium?"**

As is true for all great long poems, but perhaps for the first time consistently in the short lyric form, his lyrics are inexhaustible. They are "reflective" poems in a literal sense: One poem reflects facets from another, like a wilderness of mirrors. Every reading adds a new pleasure or a new thought. The shallowest piece in appearance, if the others are borne in mind, cannot be drained dry. In his last poems, Yeats achieved what so many poets have aimed at: Complete surface simplicity coupled with reverberations in depth, rhythmical control balanced perfectly with rhythmical freedom. The surface can be imitated—and is. But to achieve the genuine product one first must be Yeats and second must work fifty years.

The casual boldness and directness are breathtaking. Here is a complete poem called **"The Lover's Song"**:

> Bird sighs for the air,
> Thought for I know not where,
> For the womb the seed sighs.
> Now sinks the same rest
> On mind on nest
> On straining thighs.

The elements could not be simpler: a two-beat tall-rime stanza with slight variations; diction so stripped that one two-syllable word satisfies the whole poem; three paralel thoughts grouped to a conclusion; the idea of search or desire cast in a natural, an intellectual, and a sensual form; implicit oppositions that might be diagramed or reduced to syllogisms; and at the end the Nirvana or the blessing of fulfilment, home, consummation, death, age, sleep, night, peace rest.

Yeats's great battle, every day harder to fight, was to preserve the significance of the individual against the giant

modern conformities in thought and society. His tactics were as slippery and changing as a jiujitsu bout acted by a Proteus. To the unsympathetic. Yeats may appear a poseur, an impractical Quixote, a gullible attender at seances, a dabbler in the occult, a hierophant of a religion he has himself constructed. One hardly knows where to take him, even in the varying portraits and photographs. The publishers did well to retain as frontispiece Augustus John's portrait done in 1907 when Yeats was forty-two, just at the turning point between his two styles—with the sensuous mouth, the wild disarray, the broad platform of the upper nose, the fey quality, the bold eagle glance from the wide-set eyes, fortunately without the horn-rims which he was later to adopt and which seemed so incongruous to his particular powers of seeing.

It will become increasingly apparent, if it is not already well enough known, that Yeats saw more, and more clearly, than most of his contemporaries. Eliot's tribute is just: "He was one of those few whose history is the history of their own time, who are a part of the consciousness of an age which cannot be understood without them." His great gift—greater even than his superb and classical art—was the carving of a figure of a man, the ideal figure of Yeats as he would have liked to be, of the Irishman, of any one who cares to read. The figure is not sentimental. It is full of lust and rage; it turns into a beggarman, a fool, a Crazy Jane as well as into Cuchulain fighting the ungovernable sea, or an Irish airman foreseeing his death, or a fisherman climbing at dawn, to cast his flies. The powerful religious sense is as inverted as Blake's: "Homer is my example, and his unchristened heart." Yet there is invincible vitality in Yeats's figure: Courage, galety and "Tragedy wrought to its uttermost." Yeats cannot be read through without a sense of wonder at the transformations he achieved: he changes his own avowed timidity into images of courage, unfulfillment in his own love affair into the most galvanized amatory verse since John Donne, local history and his own daily experience into the image of man.

Yeats could well have said of his poems as he said of the odd constructs in his philosophical system: "They helped me to hold in a single thought reality and justice." And at their high points, which come with astonishing frequency, the reader may believe with Yeats that:

> It seemed, so great my happiness,
> That I was blessed and could bless.

Max Wildi (essay date 1955)

SOURCE: "The Influence and Poetic Development of W. B. Yeats," in *English Studies*, Vol. 36, Nos. 1-6, 1955, pp. 246-53.

[*In the following excerpt from an overview of Yeats's work, Wildi asserts that Yeats's poetic influence was reciprocal: even as he helped such writers as Arthur Symons, Thomas Sturge Moore, Ezra Pound, T. S. Eliot, and W. H. Auden, he was himself helped by them.*]

Any poet whose gift survives the first impulse of youth must not only learn to practise the craft of verse as a conscious discipline, he must also be capable of inward renewal. Among modern English writers both D. H. Lawrence and T. S. Eliot each in his own way show this power of transcending their earlier selves; neither of them, however, presents so astonishing an example of repeated rebirth as William Butler Yeats.

Yeats was early recognized as an original and influential poet. In the last ten years before his death younger poets looked up to him as the greatest master writing in the English language. His influence had by this time become far-reaching and unique. Like every other master, he had left his mark on the early tentative verses of many young poets, especially those of the Edwardian decade, the early verse of the Georgians and of some of the Imagists. Here, however, we are not so much concerned with this kind of influence as with a far more significant one, the influence which releases new forces, sets free and encourages contemporaries and younger writers to experiment and break loose from convention.

The most exciting thing about Yeats and this influence is, however, the fact that in many cases it is *mutual,* and is connected with crucial phases of his poetic development. In his contacts with other poets the dominating and lively personality of Yeats shows an unexpected plasticity and humility, as T. S. Eliot bore witness in his Yeats Lecture in the Abbey Theatre in 1940.

The story of the development and influence of W. B. Yeats opens with a seeming paradox: Yeats, who in his day came to influence three successive generations of poets, began by being himself deeply influenced to an extent that might at first sight appear like a total extinction of his own personality. Among these 'influences' the Pre-Raphaelites, who dominated his father's art, must be mentioned first, and of these chiefly William Morris, whom Yeats came to know personally, then all those whom the Pre-Raphaelites admired: Spenser, Shelley and Blake. There are moments when it seems as if there were nothing in the Romantic tradition from Malory and the ballads down to Swinburne and Whitman that could not influence Yeats and make him echo its tone, or colour, or emotion in his earliest verse. In this initial phase of his poetic development Yeats was mainly passive, yet even then his personality asserted itself, at least in the selection of the masters to whose influence he submitted. His gift of lyric utterance was there from the start and along with it went the power to heighten and purify the note of those he imitated. A poem like **"The Everlasting Voices"** is more hypnotic and sweet and at the same time more exciting in its nostalgic tone than anything in Morris or in the languid early verse of Blake. It is the intoxication of such chanting heady musicthat Yeats passed on to younger men like Joyce (see his poems in *Chambermusic*) and Ezra Pound, who echoes Yeats in early pieces. . . . In all this there is more of a kind of mediumistic transmission of what was in the thin air of late Romantic poetry than any dear influence. All is vague, solemn, shadowy and languorous.

The first clear case of mutual influence to be mentioned is that between Yeats and Arthur Symons. They had met in the early nineties at the Rhymers' Club, and for some time in 1895 shared rooms overlooking Fountain Court in the Temple. As a poet Symons was an impressionist, interested only in the visible scene of London's Bohemia. As an acute and penetrating critic he ranged over a far wider field. He very soon discovered that, among the members of the Rhymers' Club, Yeats was the undeniable genius. In deep admiration and friendship he joined the young Irish poet. The literary result in Symons' books of verse was echoes of his friend's richer and more powerful verse. Symons tried hard to dream. He tried to dream by taking opium or hashish and by drinking absinthe, but the dreams would not come. A few delicate impressionist miniatures, some clear and strangely cold verse and a number of very pure renderings of Verlaine and a passage or two of Mallarmé are all that survive of the poetical work of Arthur Symons. As a critic, however, he was to do incalculable service to his friend Yeats and to many other poets as well. Symons introduced the English-speaking literary world, and among it Yeats and Eliot, to the poetry of the French symbolistes, to Mallarmé and Maeterlinck, Villiers de l'Isle-Adam, Verlaine, Rimbaud and Laforgue. Symons took Yeats to the Rue de Rome, where Mallarmé held his famous 'mardis' and introduced him to the master. There is some doubt whether Yeats understood what Mallarmé said or wrote in French, but he had Arthur Symons' translations and *The Symbolist Movement in Literature,* which Symons had delicated to Yeats, to fall back on. There is no doubt whatever that Mallarmé's theory and practice made a very deep impression on Yeats. They confirmed him in his high, quasi-mystic notion of poetry as a supreme calling to which the whole man was to be dedicated as to an almost priestly function and ritual. This attitude, which he found embodied in Mallarmé's devotion to his art and expressed to the point of quixotry in Villiers de l'Isle-Adam's drama *Axel* (a book that Yeats praised and quoted again and again) implied a retirement to the *tour d'ivoire,* which appealed to one side of Yeats' nature. He came to abandon it by the turn of the century, when, in his own words "everybody got down off his stilts." What he never abandoned throughout his life was his high aspiration and unwavering belief in the mission of his art to create a higher reality to be imposed on the world of fleeting appearance and perverse, low desire by the power of words which "alone are certain good."

This lofty, idealistic conviction formed the basis of the friendship that united Yeats with the English poet, Thomas Sturge Moore, for more than 40 years. Both derived a central part of their poetic inspiration from the Pre-Raphaelites, whose visual and literary art they developed into a symbolism of their own, with the significant difference that whereas Yeats had turned to Blake and Irish folklore, Sturge Moore had started out from Matthew Arnold and retained his master's didactic note to the end. The delight both poets took in ancient myths, in speculation and imagery, and the happy balance achieved by the union between Sturge Moore's quiet, serene and independent nature and the impetuous theorizing and activity of W. B. Yeats, linked them in a lifelong friendship.

The influence Yeats exercised on his friend is best seen in Sturge Moore's lyrical dramas, some of which were suggested by Yeats. But whereas with Yeats the figures are human beings striving for purification and eternity, the dramatis personae of Sturge Moore's plays are shadowy, legendary ghosts, striving to become but never succeeding in being, human.

The correspondence between the two poets, which was published in 1953, shows, amongst many other things, how often Yeats generously gave help and as freely accepted it, in the form of precise workmanlike criticism of his verse, advice on stage decoration for his dramas and those noble book covers, all designed by Sturge Moore, that are found on the later volumes of Yeats' verse. Thanks to his frank acknowledgment we know that Yeats borrowed a short passage from Sturge Moore's "Dying Swan" and used it in **"The Tower"**; the published correspondence makes it clear that he owed Sturge Moore another debt, since one of Yeats' finest poems, **"Byzantium,"** was written as a result of Sturge Moore's criticism of the last verse of **"Sailing to Byzantium"** (Letter of April 16, 1930).

When all is said, it will, however, be found, that in the give-and-take of this long friendship, though hundreds of services were rendered on both sides, there was no such fundamental stimulus as that which Yeats owed to Mallarmé and, indirectly, to Symons, or as the decisive shock treatment that was meted out to him by a much younger man: Ezra Pound.

Pound entered Yeats' life in 1909, under a constellation radically different from that which presided over earlier friendships. A deep estrangement had come to separate Yeats from the Ireland of his youth. The patriots who had once seemed the friends of Ireland's literary Renascence had hooted *The Playboy of the Western World*. Synge, whom Yeats had worshipped and who had cured him of his dandified astheticism and helped him to create the new Irish poetic drama, was dead. Yeats was approaching middle age. He had left behind him whatever had made him popular among Victorian poetry-lovers, the nostalgic sweetness of **"The Lake Isle of Innisfree"** and the over-elaborate love-poetry of **"The Rose."** Yeats had started out on his long pilgrimage towards his own innermost self, towards unity of being and complete sincerity. One phase of his development, the phase of mainly passive reception was over. Yeats now found himself in the midst of the second phase, that of aggressive assertion, and the creation of a conscious "mask" for the active half of his being. Ezra Pound's first influence belongs to this phase. It was not till the end of the war that Yeats was to find an integral expression of his genius in the poems of *The Wild Swans at Coole* (1919) and *Michael Robartes and the Dancer* (1921).

When Yeats met Pound, some time in 1909, the latter had three slender books of verse to his name. In these the influence of Yeats (as well as that of Browning, Whitman and the poets of the Nineties) is clearly visible in many passages, showing that Pound was predisposed for the contact that followed. Both Yeats and Pound shared a proud, impatient temper with a feeling for nobility, a generous passion for the art and artifice of verse and a desire to "make it new." Yeats was beset by what Pound called "a rabble of forty-five imitators"; Pound was as yet unknown. Thus it is all the more astonishing to see the master go to school to his one-time pupil, and in consequence of this pupil's criticism remodel his style. This surprising example of humility that enabled the forty-five year old Yeats to listen to an eccentric twenty-five year old hothead and to allow Pound to bluepencil his, the acknowledged master's, verse, is unique. To understand the full significance of Pound's influence it must be remembered that those were the days that saw the birth of futurism, cubism and abstract art in general all over Europe. A revolt against passive, descriptive art had set in. The desire for more concentrated, vital and expressive art, for strict and controlled form, was felt in manyplaces. Some such desire had been at the root of the deep dissatisfaction Yeats had come to feel for his own early verse. Now he learned through Pound that poets and sculptors and painters both in England and France were trying to break away from the idyllic, the loosely romantic and rhetorical the vague and dreamy. Instantaneous vivid effects of high concentration were to be aimed at, through the creation of images in dry, clear language after the manner of the Japanese and Chinese poets. Yeats, in whom the strongly visual impulses of the English painter-poets from Blake to Morris and his own father had never died out, was keenly interested in "Imagism" and the kindred art of Wyndham Lewis. He never became one of the Imagists himself, for the programme implied in that name was too literal and narrow for him, yet verses like "A Thought from Propertius" show how far he could go in what Pound calls "that sort of poetry which seems as if sculpture or painting were just forced or forcing itself into words" (from Pound's review entitled "The Later Yeats" in *Poetry*, IV, May, 1914).

Yeats himself explained the change that had come over his art at a celebration in honour of Wilfrid Scawen Blunt, in Februari 1914, saying "If I take up to-day some of the things that interested me in the past I find that I can no longer use them. They bore me. Every year some part of my poetical machinery suddenly becomes of no use. As the tide of romance recedes I am driven back simply on myself and my thoughts in actual life" (*The Egoist*, Vol. I, 57). It is significant that Yeats, at a moment when the impersonal and objective in art was on everybody's lips, should speak of being driven back on his personal experience.

One may ask here if Yeats in his turn left any deeper mark on Pound's later verse. Juvenile imitation, as we find it in his early poems, does not count for much. The answer is: no. Pound and Yeats went different ways as poets. The important moment was, for both of them, the moment when their ways crossed in those years immediately before the first world war, when in 1913 and 1914 Yeats lived for some time with Ezra Pound and his wife in a cottage in Sussex. It was in these years and those immediately preceding that the creative and critical stimulus of their meeting enriched both. It set them free for independent development. Yeats, the richer and more complex of the two, derived from Pound's theory and practical criticism an impulse towards greater austerity on the one hand and greater human outspokenness on the other. Years were to pass before these impulses bore their full fruit in *The Wild Swans at Coole* while some of the immediate impressions went into *Responsibilities* (1914).

The last important phase in which influence and development combine is the period of the poet's old age, which saw the production of *The Tower* (1928), of *The Winding Stair and other Poems* (1923), and of the posthumous *Last Poems* of 1939.

Yeats had all his life been in search of an all-embracing unity of being. He sought it among poets and theosophists, magicians and philosophers, mystics and simple country people. In late middle age he had tried to build up a rational-irrational "Vision" of the world on the foundation of his wife's intuitions, dreams and revelations, as well as his own speculations and his reading. It served as a kind of scaffolding by the help of which some of his greatest poetry was made possible. The result of all his efforts at re-making himself, ever since the moment when he had come out of the dream of youth, had been an approach to an ever deeper and more intense reality by breaking through the screens and mists of words and illusions and through the mirrors of self-deception. When, in old age, he faced reality once more, it appeared to him full of tragic and insoluble opposites, possessing that "terrible beauty" which is both heroic and tragic, of which Yeats speaks in "Easter 1916". The effect of this lifelong search on his verse was to make it more direct than ever, achieving in places the boldness of great rhetoric, in others the magnificence of the grand style and, more surely in this last stage, the lyric note.

We have it on the testimony of T. S. Eliot that the poetry of the later Yeats caused a shock of surprise and made a very deep impression on the poets of Eliot's and W. H. Auden's generation, who had been unaffected by the dreamy, Victorian verse of the early Yeats. What did this later Yeats mean to the poets who might have been his sons or even grandsons? As T. S. Eliot in his Yeats Lecture remarks, their ideas and ideals were radically opposed to his. Nearly all the poets of the Thirties had been Marxists at one time of their career. The Yeats of *On the Boiler* and of the later poems must to them have appeared a fascist. A beggar was to Yeats a figure symbolizing human dignity and freedom, to Auden and his friends he was a plague spot of society.

Yet there was the essential Yeats, Yeats the poet, who transcended the politician, he who had helped to lead English poetry out of the house of bondage, out of naturalism, description, minor sentiment and reasoning into the large freedom of his art and taught them to use symbols and images boldly for the evocation of the passions and powers of the soul. However much they might admire Hopkins, Owen, Hardy or Eliot, it was to Yeats that they owed the example of a free use of classical mythology, of

the renewal of alexandrine and refrain, which he had delivered from tame usage, and the example of his magnificent outspokenness as a free man.

W. H. Auden recently declared in the course of a wireless talk that Yeats' poem **"The Circus Animals' Desertion"** was the best statement of the modern poet's predicament. The circus animals in this poem are his symbols, to which Yeats half-humorously alludes by pretending to be a kind of travelling circus director with a band of trained performing beasts, the lions, eagles, swans, dolphins, hawks and their companions in his verses. The predicament of which W. H. Auden spoke, which is one of the themes of the poem, lies in the fact that symbols and words may suddenly fail the poet. The glory of poetry lies in image or dream fulfilled in words, but it ultimately starts in the chaos of the restless heart, in "mire and blood," the pitiful raw-material, to which the poet is reduced.

This poem astonishes by its range, its combination of pride and humility, by the paradox of glory and mire and the insistence on the primitive and chaotic nature of reality. In some of his later verse Yeats had achieved a hardness and outspokenness that delighted the generation that was born into the bitter winds of the political Thirties. "Hardness and dryness" are words Louis Macneice used in his fine study of *The Poetry of W. B. Yeats*. They are perhaps more representative of what the younger generation looked for than of what is actually there. Hardness there certainly is, but dryness: no. Was it not rather the fanaticism, the frenzy and zest of the later Yeats that appealed to those who went to fight in Spain? Yeats had been, amongst many other things, a fierce partisan, who had shown his manhood in fighting for his friends and for the cause of symbolist art. That is probably why poets like Auden, Day Lewis and Macneice felt themselves more drawn to Yeats than to Eliot, a more bookish, more complex, withdrawn figure, whose immense influence was in the field of diction, imagery and critical doctrine, whereas Yeats influence was a personal one. "He had upheld," in the words of a young poet of our days, Christopher Middleton, "the force and wisdom of poetry in a tatterdemalion and mechanical age."

Yeats himself had begun to read the work of the youngest generation of poets shortly before he was seventy. The immediate occasion was the selection of verse for his *Oxford Book of Modern Verse,* which ranged from 1892 to 1935. As a representative selection of modern verse it proved a tantalizing book, since it freely reflected all the likes and dislikes of its compiler. Since its publication new generations and schools of poets have arisen and new anthologies have been made, which have largely superseded it. Yet it remains a precious and memorable book. With its brilliantly personal introduction it presents a mirror of its author's taste in contemporary poetry and it is a monument of his friendships. In its pages we find represented all the poets Yeats had known so well, from whom he had learned and whom he had helped: Lionel Johnson and Arthur Symons W. S. Blunt, T. Sturge Moore and Ezra Pound. Along with these goes the rich array of his Irish contemporaries, from his great friends Lady

Gregory, Æ and Synge to Joyce and the living L. A. G. Strong, F. R. Higgins and Frank O'Connor, together with Tagore and Shri Purohit Swami from India. It is an overwhelming list showing the genius for friendship which this essentially shy poet possessed. Our list gives but a faint idea of their full number and their importance in his life. We have seen how deeply some of those here mentioned influenced the development of his poetry. Finally, this poetry itself is full of the glorified images of men and women Yeats had known, loved and admired: Maud Gonne, Lady Gregory, Mabel Beardsley, O'Leary and the Irish patriots. Synge and Lionel Johnson and many others.

It is dangerous to dogmatize, but the conclusion to which all this points is that *personality* was the *forma formans* of Yeats' world. Whatever we may think of his bookish studies and abstract theories, it is heightened human personality, human nobility, as example and ideal, as medium and form that shaped the poetry and personality of W. B. Yeats. Through the mediation of friends Yeats probably learned far more than through books. His influence was in its turn the influence, not of his ideas or ideologies or his semi-mystical systems, but that of a man and a living poetical voice.

Even in his last years he made new friends among the younger poets, two of which he singled out for special praise in his anthology: W. J. Turner and Dorothy Wellesley. The latter, the present Duchess of Wellington, was his friend from 1935 to his death. His letters to her, published in 1940, show him at work on his anthology. Now, in his old age, with his style triumphantly individual, Yeats naturally turned to those among the younger writers who wrote his kind of poetry, using symbols much as he used them. Turner and Dorothy Wellesley did so, and for this very reason they were the least representative of all the younger poets. Yeats, however, tried hard to be fair to the men of the Thirties and included examples of their work.

The younger poets in their turn have amply repaid his courtesy. Louis Macneice devoted a fine and full study to his poetry and, more recently, a short assessment has appeared by a Scottish poet and critic of the youngest generation: G. S. Fraser. Sidney Keyes and Kenneth Allott have made Yeats the subject of poems of their own.

The greatest tribute, however, was paid by W. H. Auden, who wrote one of his finest poems under the impact of the news of Yeats' death in January 1939. The last three stanzas of this poem "In Memory of W. B. Yeats" express better than any other words what Yeats meant to one of the finest of the poets who came after him. In accents that echo the famous lines of Yeats' own poetical testament **"Under Ben Bulben"** W. H. Auden, while speaking to all poets, speaks magnificently of Yeats:

> Follow, poet, follow right
> To the bottom of the night,
> With your unconstraining voice
> Still persuade us to rejoice;

> With the farming of a verse
> Make a vineyard of the curse,
> Sing of human unsuccess
> In a rapture of distress;

> In the deserts of the heart
> Let the healing fountain start,
> In the prison of his days
> Teach the free man how to praise.

Charles A. Raines (essay date 1959)

SOURCE: "Yeats' Metaphors of Permanence," in *Twentieth Century Literature,* Vol. 5, No. 1, 1959, pp. 12-20.

[*In the following excerpt, Raines examines Yeats's later poems and argues that they contain metaphors which represent order amid chaos and which consequently unify Yeats's later work.*]

One of the constant themes in modern poetry, the search for permanence, grows primarily out of the idea that the twentieth century is a time of utter chaos and continual disruption, both spiritual and material, or, as Yeats describes it in a note to his poem **"The Second Coming,"** "our scientific, democratic, fact-accumulating, heterogeneous civilization." Yeats, as a modern poet, is primarily concerned with the need to synthesize chaotic and disruptive elements in our civilization with permanent elements toward the end of attaining perfection, and, therefore, order. Certain metaphors of the later poems reveal Yeats' ideas of permanence. Further, these metaphors form a unifying theme throughout a body of the later poems. A study of some representative metaphors taken from a selection of the later poems will show Yeats' idea of permanence as a theme which makes these poems interdependent.

In **"News for the Delphic Oracle," "The Delphic Oracle upon Plotinus,"** and **"The Second Coming"** similarities of idea occur in metaphors dealing with "the innocents," the sea, the dolphins, and "brute blood," and the ideas carried by these metaphors occur in varying forms in the three poems. The "innocents," considered so by Yeats because they are of an age not corrupted by heterogeneity, are discovered in **"News for the Delphic Oracle"** and in **"The Delphic Oracle upon Plotinus"** as they are about to make a journey through "the blood-dimmed tide" described in **"The Second Coming."** In this sea of vacillation the innocents presumably may be drowned or lost, or they may be carried safely to the shore. In the terminology of the first two of these poems the shore represents ultimate perfection and order. Thus, when the innocents set out on their journey they are faced with a "Golden Race," which "looks dim," and, at first, in **"The Delphic Oracle upon Plotinus,"** "salt blood" blocks Plotinus' eyes, while similarly, in **"News for the Delphic Oracle,"** Plotinus has "salt flakes" on his breast. Therefore, the symbolic sea through which the innocents must swim in order to get to the permanent shore may be thought of as the postclassical age, which, because of its unresolved heterogeneities, represents a stumbling-block to perfection. This is the point at which

> Things fall apart; the center
>   cannot hold;
> Mere anarchy is loosed upon
>   the world,
> The blood-dimmed tide is loosed,
>   and everywhere
> The ceremony of innocence is
>   drowned;
> The best lack all conviction,
>   while the worst
> Are full of passionate intensity.

The stumbling-block itself is represented in terms of blood and its attendant brutishness. There is the blood that blocks Plotinus' eyes, the "blood-dimmed tide," and the innocents' reopened wounds which give forth blood as the innocents pass through the water. Further, there are many creatures of blood which serve to contrast with the immortal innocents and the "choir of love": these are the "brute dolphins," Peleus, who stares at Thetis's naked body while

> Foul goat head, brutal arm appear,
> Belly, shoulder, bum,
> Flash fishlike;

and, in **"The Second Coming,"** a "shape with a lion body and the head of a man," and "indignant desert birds." This also reminds us of "the frog-spawn of a blind man's ditch . . ." of **"A Dialogue of Self and Soul,"** Yeats' general description of modern civilization as ". . . this pragmatical, preposterous pig of a world" (**"Blood and the Moon"**), and many other metaphors dealing with "ditch" and "blood" which might bear further investigation to show an interdependent theme in the later poems.

A more exact description of the state of permanence or perfection in Yeats' point of view, however, may be had from a closer inspection of one of these metaphors: the dolphins in **"News for the Delphic Oracle."** The spiritually perfected beings, or innocents, are borne over the sensuous and earthly mire of the water, each "steadied by a fin," the dolphins thus becoming the stable elements amid the flux of their environment. The dolphins, however, are brutes themselves, and are, therefore, a part of the flux and instability. This dependence of the philosopher-innocents upon an element of the brute-sensuous existence points up the necessity for direct association with the present life with all its heterogeneity, and, indeed, dependence upon it for final synthesis and permanence. This necessity is further emphasized by the opening of the philosophers' death wounds as they ride, so that for a time the philosophers are a part of the mire and blood and undergo a kind of transmutation or revaluation which enables them to reach a state of permanence only by virtue of a synthesis of "innocence" and "blood." The state of permanence which Yeats desires for our time, then, is not altogether divorced from the physical, heterogeneous world, but is dependent on it in some measure.

There are two major ideas of permanence, then, to be had from the treatment of the dolphins: permanence itself must be closely bound with life—both world and spirit must be represented; any worldly permanence must serve simply as a transport to final permanence, which although it is bound with the worldly, transcends the worldly because it has the added ingredient of the spiritual, for, as Yeats puts it in **"The Circus Animals' Desertion"**:

> I must lie down where all the
>   ladders start,
> In the foul rag-and-bone shop
>   of the heart.

These two ideas Yeats develops in a surprising number of poems using the stone as a central metaphor. **"Easter, 1916"** is a good example. This poem, which is concerned with transmutation of the sort undergone by the innocents in the poems previously mentioned, recounts the storming of the Dublin post office by a group of Irish rebels, who, significantly, take action against an imperament and unstable existence in an effort to re-establish the Irish national tradition. The effort toward re-establishment fails, but the rebels themselves emerge in a permanent state and a "terrible beauty is born" the poem states. That is to say, the rebels are, like Plotinus and the innocents, greeted by the "choir of love," and are "changed, changed utterly." However, this change could not have been possible without positive contact with the natural, represented by the dolphins or the stone, and it is

> Hearts with one purpose alone
> Through summer and winter
>   [that] seem
> Enchanted to a stone
> To trouble the living stream.

Later in the poem it is explained that

> Too long sacrifice
> Can make a stone of the heart.

"O when may it suffice?" then becomes the question. The answer is that the stone will suffice when it is an instrument in the change from natural to supernatural, or from the heterogenous world of the "living stream" or the "blood-dimmed tide" to a world of synthesis of the natural and supernatural. The state is described by Cleanth Brooks [in *The Well Wrought Urn*, 1947] as "the human situation itself in which the natural and supernatural are intermixed—the human situation which is inevitably caught between the claims of both natural and supernatural." We ourselves cannot know this harmony, Yeats points out in the final section of the poem, but, he says, "it is enough to know they dreamed and are dead."

This is the same sort of fusion that occurs when, in **"Easter, 1916,"** the stones lie dormant and unmoved while

> A horse-hoof slides on the brim,
> And a horse plashes with it;
> The long-legged moor-hens dive,

And the hens to moor-cocks call;
Minute by minute they live: . . .

The stone lives with this stream of life, which is not permanence itself, but an element of permanence, the stone having the advantage of being both a part of the stream of life and a permanent object itself. Thus, to paraphrase the last line of the poem, it is enough to know the stone is in the midst of life and permanent too, representing, therefore, the presence of order.

The idea of the stone in the stream of life is again presented in **"The Man and the Echo."** In this poem the protagonist goes to a pit where a "broken stone" lies and he poses questions to the ageless and permanent object with the hope of resolving in his own mind certain problems of life which have troubled him. (But note that the stone is "broken," an important variation on the stone metaphor, indicating the dispersion of worldly objects and their attendant concepts. Note, for example, **"The Spirit Medium"**:

For I would not recall
Some that being unbegotten
Are not individual,
But copy some one action,
Moulding it our of dust or sand, . . .

"dust or sand" representing a dispersed form of the stone.) The protagonist first decides that these problems of life are insoluable and thinks of suicide as a solution, but he is convinced that this action

. . . were to shirk
The spiritual intellect's great work
And shirk it in vain . . .

for this is to overlook the importance of the body, or indulgence such as that represented by the innocents and the Irish revolutionists. The conflict in the protagonist's mind, then, is between body and soul, and he seeks some permanent reconciliation between the two. Although it is a permanent object in itself, the rock can be of help, as in **"Easter, 1916,"** only when it is a part of theliving stream and, therefore, the protagonist receives answers to his questions only when he regards the stone together with the "living stream":

Up there some hawk or owl
  has struck,
Dropping out of sky or rock,
A stricken rabbit is crying out,
And its cry distracts my thought.

The rock itself, then, has not been the solution, but it has contributed to the solution. Yeats, in terms of this metaphor as well as that of the dolphins, seems to be saying that permanent institutions, or worldly concepts of permanence, in themselves cannot furnish permanence to society or to individuals, but that these institutions and ideas can contribute to permanence and that they are an indispensable part of permanence in that they act as a

transport to the final synthesis of the worldly and the spiritual and thus to ultimate transcendence. Again it is important to note that the rock is indistinguishable from the life about it, for the cry of the rabbit is distracting, much like the salt blood that distracted the innocents as they crossed the bloody mire.

The idea of the rock or stone in the stream of life is a metaphorical pattern recurring again and again in the poems from *Michael Robartes and the Dancer* (1921) to *Last Poems* (1936-1939) and points to the essential unity of almost the entire body of the later poems. It may also be noted that this theme occurs in at least one poem in an earlier book *The Wild Swans at Coole* (1919), **"Men Improve with the Years"**:

I am worn out with dreams;
A weather-worn, marble triton
Among the streams; . . .

An enumeration of some of these metaphors in the later poems is in order, since no attention has been brought to this as a pattern of imagery.

Notable examples of "rock" or "stone" are to be found in **"On a Political Prisoner," "A Meditation in Time of War," "Meditations in Time of Civil War"** (particularly sections I, III, IV, VI, and VII). The idea of permanence in civilization as a possibility is extensively discussed in **"Nineteen Hundred and Nineteen," "Spilt Milk," "The Nineteenth Century and After"** and **"His Confidence."** Of particular significance is the "desolate source" referred to in **"His Confidence"** because it throws light not only on Yeats' search for permanence and the thematic relationship of his later poetry, but reminds us of themes in Eliot, Hemingway and Faulkner, to name only three who have dealt with the idea of spiritual value out of a desolate source.

The impermanence of civilizations is dealt with notably in two poems, **"The Gyres"** and **"Lapis Lazuli,"** both of which include stone metaphors. A short view of **"Lapis Lazuli"** will show the point here. The poem begins with an announcement of the possibility of World War II (the poem appeared in 1938) and its disruption of Western Civilization. As in **"The Gyres"** there is an ironic juxtaposition of "tragic" and "gay," and Hamlet, Cordelia, Ophelia and Lear are viewed as evidence of "All men have aimed at, found and lost," showing that civilization itself, far from being permanent, is elusive and changeable, and that it may be tragically deceptive so that

All things fall and are built
  again,
And those that build them
  again are gay.

This is further evidenced, in the third stanza, by Callimachus, "Who handled marble as if it were bronze," but whose works, nevertheless, "stood but a day." This idea is finally concretized in three Chinese figures made of lapis lazuli, and, therefore, a stone image of permanence, with a "long-legged bird" flying over them, "a symbol of longevity." Imperfections in these figures, wrought by the passage of time, remind Yeats of a mountain on which these ancient persons might be sitting as they look upon "all the tragic scene" below [*The Letters of W.B. Yeats,* ed. Allan Wade, 1955], and, as one of these Chinamen, a servant, begins to play on a "musical instrument"

> Their eyes mid many wrinkles,
>   their eyes,
> Their ancient, glittering eyes,
>   are gay . . .

for they are able to look upon the passing civilizations with the wisdom of old age and to see that permanence must ultimately be a matter of transcendence. It is important to note, too, that Yeats has transformed these stone figures into living beings who transcend their earthly existence, as the innocents on the backs of dolphins, to a spiritual existence represented (in the first stanza) by the presence of the "fiddle-bow,' which has been deprecated by "hysterical women" as being of no use in the face of impending crisis.

All poems discussed thus far, then, show that it is a synthesis that Yeats desires, and this is dramatized in even fuller measure in the much-discussed poem **"Leda and the Swan."** The question posed in this poem seems to raise again the problem of how to arrive at final permanence. The question is:

> Did she put on his knowledge
>   with his power
> Before the indifferent beak
>   could let her drop?

Leda must feel the "strange heart beating" because a synthesis of Zeus' superhuman characteristics and Leda's human characteristics has taken place. Zeus, the superhuman with "knowledge" and "power," is described as in sensual contact with Leda, "her nape caught in his bill"; but he remains as supernatural and is described as "feathered glory" and "white rush" until

> A shudder in the loins engenders
>   there
> The broken wall, the burning
>   roof and tower
> And Agamemnon dead.

After this, Leda is described as having been "mastered by the brute blood of the air," recalling the "blood and mire" of earlier poems, and then there is the final question already noted. If this knowledge and power are obtained by Leda it must be because the supernatural has intermingled with the "body," and this must be so for the result of this combination is Helen, who is considered by Yeats to have provided a source of order in the sense that she began the classical age—an age which, for Yeats, represents permanence. Helen is considered a progenitor of permanence because she represents a synthesis of life (Leda) with the spiritual (Zeus), which produces permanence. Thus, "bro-

ken wall," "burning roof and tower," and "Agamemnon dead" take us forward to the end of the classical, permanent age represented by Helen, to the postclassical, impermanent age.

Further examples of persons from history who have provided sources of order are presented in **"Long-Legged Fly."** The three persons mentioned in the poem were all responsible for lasting accomplishment and are remembered for their actions: Caesar took action "that civilization may not sink," Helen began the classical age, and Michael Angelo painted for the centuries. Yeats presents these three people in insignificant actions, emphasizing the flow of life that goes on about them, and at the same time their participation in more or less ordinary life themselves. The mind of each of these persons "Like a long-legged fly upon the stream . . . moves upon silence," at the same time producing permanence and participating in the "stream of life." The long-legged fly, then, is reminiscent of the dolphins, particularly in that the fly remains above the "blood and mire" and yet is dependent on this natural element for stability. It may also be noted that while these three historical persons, like the innocents, rise above the human in their actions, they are a definite part of the stream, being human and participating in commonplace human actions—for example, Helen, whose feet "practice a tinker shuffle."

So far there has been ample evidence to show that Yeats' idea of permanence is based primarily on reconciliation of the two opposites: the life of the heterogeneous physical world and the purifying life of the spiritual; and, also, there has been ample evidence to show this as a major theme appearing in a number of Yeats' later poems. However, the metaphor of permanence is not yet complete. There are two poems, **"Two Songs From a Play"** and **"A Dialogue of Self and Soul,"** which may be said to be transitional in the sense that they stand between the poems already discussed, which introduce the idea of permanence, and other poems which represent the conclusion of this idea, as shall be seen later. Both the poems just named express the peremptory breakdown of order. This breakdown of order forces the individual to a reconciliation of opposites as the only means of obtaining absolute permanence.

In **"Two Songs From a Play"** Yeats explains this predicament of man in terms of history:

> The Babylonian starlight brought
> A fabulous, formless darkness in;
> Odour of blood when Christ was
>   slain
> Made all Platonic tolerance vain
> And vain all Doric discipline.

Given this condition of modern man, the search for permanence must be a struggle for permanence; albeit this is a "Golden Race," the salt blood of an unreconciled existence makes permanence difficult to obtain, and, in actuality, the race is no less difficult for persons of one time than of another, for the two basic elements to be reconciled, body and soul, are basic to men of all times. Realizing this predicament, the protagonist of **"A Dialogue of Self and Soul"** says:

> I am content to live it all again
> And yet again, if it be life to
> pitch
> Into the frog-spawn of a blind
> man's ditch.

As has already been seen, this is a contentment which must of necessity come if any permanence is to be gained. We must not be content with the abstract alone, but also with the "frog-spawn"—the "blood-dimmed tide" which is physical life.

Having posited the predicament of man and the difficulty of his struggle for permanence, Yeats must show how this permanence may be obtained by the individual. Yeats does this in **"Sailing to Byzantium," "Among School Children,"** and **"Byzantium."**

In **"Sailing to Byzantium"** the individual's journey to a state of imaginative perfection is begun. Byzantium, which for Yeats represents an ideal state of the mind, is possible for the mind as well as for the soul and can actually be reached in life. In this poem Yeats' basic problem of remaining in and out of life at once, of indulging in the blood and mire of life and at the same time reaching a pure state of being, or permanence, recurs. In the opening stanza we are presented with a state of youth, a sensuous life with emphasis on productivity and regeneration that is reminiscent of the "nymphs and satyrs" of **"News For the Delphic Oracle"** that "copulate in the foam." The primary opposition in the poem is that of the sensual and the intellectual, and this opposition is presented in terms of the instability of the younger generation, which is signified in the closing lines of the first stanza:

> Caught in that sensual music
> all neglect
> Monuments of unageing intellect.

The ultimate goal of the journey, then, is the fusion of "sensual music" and "monuments"; that is, the sensual with the spiritual and the temporary with the permanent. In order to effect this fusion, the protagonist must take on some of the characteristics of the innocents; therefore, he calls upon "sages standing in God's holy fire" and invokes them to "gather me into the artifice of eternity," so that

> Once out of nature I shall never
> take
> My bodily form from any
> natural thing.

Once this is realized, the body will be in the form of a Byzantine work of art, a bird which will be animate in the sense that it sings to the Emperor, but inanimate as a work of art. The permanent being, as represented in the bird, is, then, a combination of bodily form and spiritual existence, and in this sense the "starlit or . . . moonlit dome" of **"Byzantium"** also represents an artistically transcendent accomplishment which "disdains" the purely human.

The same problem of permanence is, in **"Among School Children,"** resolved by the removal of the individual from life in order for the individual to gain a proper perspective of life, and it is again a situation in which the natural and supernatural are intermixed. Plato, Pythagoras and Aristotle worship philosophy as a means of obtaining an objective view of life; in like manner "nuns and mothers worship images" as a means, they hope, of understanding the "presences" of which they are aware. The philosophers become "old clothes upon a stick to scare a bird," and the nun and mother are disappointed in their quest, both these failures coming as a result of the failure to understand the necessary reconciliation of the abstract and the body—the blood and mire. The basic metaphor in the poem becomes the chestnut tree, which represents unity of abstract "presences," or the soul, with the physical, or the body. The organic make-up of the tree points to the necessity of regarding each of the parts as equally important and to the idea that heterogeneity, and, therefore, failure result from separation of these parts. Permanence, then, cannot be a matter of objective viewpoint, for "how can we know the dancer from the dance?" But the mixture, which we cannot know objectively, constitutes permanence, and again it is enough to know there is permanence.

If **"Sailing to Byzantium"** represents the attainment of permanence in life, and **"Among School Children"** the attainment of permanence through the reconciliation of the abstract with life, then **"Byzantium"** shows how this final addition of the abstract to life is possible through co-mixture of all the subjective and objective elements of man,

> All that man is
> All mere complexities
> The fury and mire of human veins . . . ,

with his supernatural elements:

> an image, man or shade,
> Shade more than man, more
> image than shade; . . .

Which is an imaginative conception of man as existing in the afterlife. Thus the final state of permanence is conceived of as pure imagination, with man's superhuman qualities dominating his corporeal qualities but depending upon them, so that Yeats announces:

> I hail the superhuman;
> I call it death-in-life and
> life-in-death.

The final journey begun by the innocents and continued by the old man of **"Sailing to Byzantium"** and **"Among School Children"** ends

Where blood begotten spirits come
And all complexities of fury leave,
Dying into a dance,
An agony of trance,
An agony of flame that cannot
   singe a sleeve . . . ,

and the ideal situation of the after-life becomes a permanent reality when "spirit after spirit" pervades the scene "astraddle on the dolphin's mire and blood"; the heterogeneities of body and spirit are broken as "fresh images beget . . ." yet more images, forming Yeats' completed metaphor of permanence.

Yvor Winters (essay date 1960)

SOURCE: "The Poetry of W. B. Yeats," in *Twentieth Century Literature*, Vol. 6, No. 1, April 1960, pp. 3-24.

[*In the following excerpt, Winters criticizes selections from* The Collected Poems, *finding fault with many aspects of them including Yeats's philosophy, his use of symbolism, his elevated style, and the rhythm of his lines.*]

We have been told many times that we do not have to take the ideas of Yeats seriously in order to appreciate his poetry; but if this is true, Yeats is the first poet of whom it has ever been true. We need to understand the ideas of Donne and of Shakespeare in order to appreciate their works, and we have to take their ideas seriously in one sense or another, and it is possible to take their ideas seriously much of the time. A great deal of scholarly work has been done of their ideas, and some of this work has contributed to our appreciation of what they wrote. A great deal of scholarly work has been done on Yeats in recent years; unfortunately, the better one understands him, the harder it is to take him seriously.

I shall refer rather often in this essay to a recent book [*A Reader's Guide to William Butler Yeats*] by John Unterecker. The book gives a more detailed account than any other which I know of what Yeats was doing or thought he was doing. It accepts without question Yeats's ideas regarding the nature of poetry, ideas which in my opinion are unacceptable. And like almost every other publication on Yeats it accepts without question the notion that Yeats was a very great poet and it merely substitutes exegesis for criticism. For example, Mr. Unterecker explains the meaning of an early poem, **"The Two Trees,"** and I think correctly. Then, with no explanation whatever, he refers to it as "so grand a poem." The poem is obviously a bad poem: it is sentimental and stereotyped at every point. Mr. Unterecker is a split personalty: on the one hand he is a careful scholar and on the other he is a critic with neither talent nor training. In this he resembles most of the literary scholars with whose work I am acquainted, but his book is very helpful notwithstanding.

Mr. Unterecker says (*A Reader's Guide*), and I believe correctly so far as Yeats's theory goes: "Because all occult symbols linked ultimately to a universal harmony, any consistent interpretatation of one of them was 'right' since it in turn led to that harmony. The only danger, as Yeats frequently pointed out, is that the reader is likely to limit the symbol's meaning and so throw it into the area of allegory." For some readers, this passage may call for brief explanation. In terms of medieval poetry, the word *symbol* refers to an object which has a one-to-one relationship to a meaning: that is, the whale is Satan, and Dante's panther, lion and wolf are lust, pride, and avarice. When such symbols occur in the action of a narrative, we have allegory. But Yeats employs the word *symbol* as we employ it in speaking of French' symbolist poetry, and the meaning of the term is reversed. Mallarmé was the great theorist of this kind of thing: his aim was to produce a kind of poetic absolute in which rational meaning would be as far as possible suppressed and suggestion would be isolated. He was not wholly successful in his aim, for many—perhaps most—of his later poems appear to deal, as obscurely as possible, with the theory of this kind of poetry; but he tried. In so far as this kind of effort succeeds, we have, in the very words of the Master, an "aboli bibelot d'inanité sonore." This is what Frank Kermode calls the romantic image, that is, the image which is meaningless, inscrutable, the image of which the dancer with the beautiful body and the expressionless face is the perfect type. Kermode disapproves of the method and he finds it in Yeats, but he is overcome by Yeats and considers him a great poet not, withstanding. What Yeats and Mr. Unterecker mean by a "universal harmony" it would be hard to say. Mr. Unterecker says elsewhere.

> Any analogy we can construct for the symbol, any meaning we assign to it, is legitimate so long as we recognize that that meaning is *not* its meaning. Its meaning must always be more elusive than any value we can—with words—fix to it. All that the meaning we assign to a symbol can ever be is either part of its meaning or one of its possible meanings. No symbol has a meaning.

And again he tells us that the symbol does not give us meaning "but instead the feeling of meaning . . . an undefined sense or order, of rightness, of congruence at the heart of things." I discussed this theory of the feeling of meaning a good many years ago in writing of what I called pseudo-reference and a little later in my essay on Poe. And Mr. Unterecker again: "Yeats allows us to experience . . . the necessary if momentary illusions of order which give us courage to live." Foolish as these ideas may seem, they are, as nearly as I can make out, Yeats's ideas as well as Mr. Unterecker's, and they are commonly accepted in our time.

Yeats, of course, often deviated from this theory of the symbol and wrote forthright poems; and he often wrote in symbols more nearly akin to medieval symbols than to Mallarméan. But the theory provides a dark and convenient little corner into which the apologist may retreat rapidly backward whenever he is embarrassed by the meaning.

I will try to summarize the principal ideas which motivate Yeats's poetry. All good comes from the emotions, and even madness is good. *Wisdom* is a pejorative term; *ignorance* is the reverse. In Yeats's later work *lust* and *rage* become increasingly prominent and they represent virtues. Sexual union is equated with the mystical experience or at least participates in the mystical experience in a literal way. This is not the same thing as the analogy of sexual union which is sometimes used by the Christian mystics. The Christian mystics tell us that the mystical experience is absolutely different from any human experience and thus cannot be described in language, but that the experience can be suggested by analogy. This leads, I think, to a more or less fraudulent poetry, for the poet is dealing with an ineffable experience by dealing with something irrelevant to it; but the fraud is, in a sense, an honest one, for the rules of the procedure are known. But for Yeats the two experiences are of the same kind, the only difference being that the sexual experience is less nearly pure than would be the experience of disembodied spirits: we are given the pure experience in **"Ribh at the Tomb of Baile and Ailinn,"** in which Ribh reads his book by the pure light given off by the orgasm of the disembodied lovers.

Yeats's concept of what would be the ideal society is also important. Such a society would be essentially agrarian, with as few politicians and tradesmen as possible. The dominant class would be the landed gentry; the peasants would also be important, but would stay in their place; a fair sprinkling of beggars (some of them mad), of drunkards, and of priests would make the countryside more picturesque. The gentlemen sould be violent and bitter, patrons of the arts, and the maintainers of order; they should be good horseman, perferably reckless horseman (if the two kinds may exist in one); and they should be fond of fishing. The ladies should be beautiful and charming, should be gracious hostesses (although there is a place for more violent ladies—videlicet Mrs. Franch in **"The Tower"**), should if possible be musicians, should drive men mad, love, marry, and produce children should not be interested in ideas and should ride horseback, prefer ably to hounds. So far as I can recollect, the ladies are not required to go fishing. What Yeats would have liked would have been an eighteenth-century Ireland of his own imagining. He disliked the political and argumentative turmoil of revolutionary Ireland; he would scarcely have thought that the order which has emerged was sufficiently picturesque to produce poetry.

Yeats's cosmological and psychological system has been so fully discussed by others that I shall merely summarize it. He believed that history proceeds through cycles of two thousand years each. Every cycle begins in a state of objectivity (which is evil) and with violence; it proceeds through subjectivity (which is good), through pure subjectivity (which is too much of a good thing), and it then proceeds toward objectivity and ultimate dispersal and a new beginning. The life of every human goes through a similar cycle. Yeats had two diagrams for this process: the diagram of the phases of the moon and the diagram of the interpenetrating cones (gyres, pernes, or spindles). The

first of these is a circle with the twenty-eight phases of the moon marked upon it. At the top is the dark of the moon (pure objectivity, where no life is possible); at the bottom is the full moon (pure subjectivity, and at this point in the cycle of the individual man the spirit may leave the body and encounter other spirits); on the opposite sides of the circle are the two quarters. Between the dark and the first quarter we have a primitive condition of violence and elementary learning, the struggle between the spirit and brutality. Between the first quarter and the full we aproach creativity, and between the full and the second quarter we depart from creativity. The period of the greatest creativity is on both sides of the full and close to it. Between the second quarter and the dark we arein the period of wisdom, in which creativity is almost at an end, and are approaching death, in the life of a man, and the end of an era in terms of the historical cycle. The gyres are most easily represented by Richard Ellman's diagram [in *Yeats: The Man and the Masks*] of the two equilateral triangles lying on their sides: the short line of these triangles should be very short in relation to the long lines, and the tip of each triangle should reach to the middle of the short line of the other. This design gives us a cross-section of the interpenetrating cones or gyres. At the points where the long lines intersect, we have the period corresponding to the full moon on the circle. The cones rotate in opposite directions, and one of them is winding the thread of life from the other: this procedure is perning or gyring. At the end of a two-thousand year cycle there is a sudden and violent reversal and the perning starts in the other direction.

In addition to Yeats's explicit ideas, there are certain consistent attitudes which should be mentioned. In his early work of the Celtic twilight period, he relied very heavily for his subjects on the figures of Irish legend: Oisin, Cuchulain, Conchobor, Dierdre, and others, and at this time and later he created a few such characters independently: Red Hanrahan, Michael Robartes, and Owen Aherne for examples. But Yeats needed heroes for his work, and he came more and more to need contemporary heroes. The result was his attempt to transform himself and his friends into legendary heroes. The most important of the friends were Lady Gregory, Major Robert Gregory, John Synge, Shawe-Taylor, and Hugh Lane; but there were others, among them Douglas Hyde. None of these people except Lady Gregory and John Synge would be known outside of Ireland today had Yeats not written about them, and Lady Gregory would be very little known. In fact Synge's reputation in the early part of the twentieth century was due at least as much to Yeats as to Synge, and his repuation has shrunken greatly. I can remember the time when Synge was the greatest dramatist in English except Shakespeare. There is no harm in praising one's friends, but when so much hyperbole is expanded upon people of small importance, the discrepancy between the motive and the emotion becomes increasingly evident with time; there seems to be someting ridiculous about it. Maude Gonne was a special case, for Yeats was in love with her; but his equation of Maude Gonne with Dierdre, Helen of Troy, and Cathleen ni Houlihan partakes of his dramatization of himself. His concern with his uninteresting relatives and ancestors would seem to be part of the same dramatization.

I will turn to the principal poems related to the theory of the historical cycles. **"Leda and the Swan"** describes the rape of Leda by Zeus in the form of a swan, a rape which led to the birth of Helen, the destruction of Troy, and the disintegration of early Greek civilization. The rape introduced the next cycle of Greek civilization, which ended with the collapse of "Platonic tolerance," "Doric discipline," and ultimately the Roman Empire. **"Two Songs from a Play"** describe the end of the second Greek Cycle and the beginning of the Christian. **"The Second Coming"** prophesies the imminent end of the Christian cycle. Each of these works deals with violence, for every cycle begins and ends in violence. Yeats admires violence in general and has little use for Platonic tolerance, Doric discipline, or the civilization produced by Christianity. This fact is especially important when we come to read **"The Second Coming."**

The account of the rape in the first eight lines of **"Leda and the Swan"** is very impressively done, but an account of a rape in itself has very limited possibilities in poetry. The important thing here is this: that the rape is committed on a mortal girl by Zeus. In the significance of this fact will reside the power or weakness of the whole poem. In the first portion of the sestet we are told that the swan has engendered the fall of Troy and the death of Agamemnon, but there is nothing about the historical cycles: this has to be read in from what we know of Yeats's theories—which are, after all, ridiculous. The greatest difficulties reside in the remainder of the sestet. "Did she put on his knowledge with his power?" The question implies that she *did* put on his power, but in what sense? She was quite simply overpowered or raped. She did not share his power, unless we understand a mystical union in the sexual act, which I think is implied. And what about his knowledge? Was this the knowledge of the fall of Troy and the death of Agamenon? Was it the knowledge that a new cycle was about to begin (in spite of the fact that there is no reference to the cycles in the poem)? Or was it the omniscience of the god, resulting from the sexual union, a knowledge which would include the two other forms of knowledge? I suspect the last, but I would have difficulty in proving it. Next we have to consider "the brute blood of the air." The swan as such is a brute and flies through the air. Zeus may be thought of as living in the air and descending from the air. But Zeus as such was not a brute in Greek Mythology, and his animal disguises were disguises; nevertheless he often appeared in brute forms. The brute form here would appear to be connected with the identification of sexual union with the mystical experience. Satan, however, was referred to in the middle ages as the Prince of the Air, and he and his demons were said to live "in darkened air." I do not recollect that Yeats has mentioned this fact anywhere, but the fact is easily available, and it seems to me unlikely that Yeats would have overlooked it. Yeats was fascinated with the concept of demonic possession as a form of the mystical experience and with the possibility of obtaining supernatural knowledge from such possession. In **"The Gift of Harun al-Rashid,"** the young wife is possessed by a Djinn, apparently as a result of sexual awakening, and in her sleep she communicates the knowledge which her husband desires. This is a pretty fantasy, I suppose, but one can scarcely take it seriously. But we return to the question: is Zeus a god or a demon, or does it make no difference? It should make a difference if we are to adjust our emotions to the motive, for what is the motive? Then there is the difficulty that the poem ends with a question. A question, if it is really a question, is a weak way in which to end a poem, for it leaves the subject of the poem unjudged. But this question may be, as I suspect it is, a rhetorical question: in this event the answer should be either *yes* or *no*. There is nothing in the poem to help us choose, but from what I know of Yeats, I think that Yeats expected us to say *yes*. This brings us to the final difficulty: the vehicle of the poem is a Greek myth, and there is no harm in this if the tenor is serious; but the tenor is a myth of Yeats's private making, and it is foolish. That is, if we are to take the high rhetoric of the poem seriously, we must really believe that sexual union is a form of the mystical experience, that history proceeds in cycles of two thousand years each, and that the rape of Leda inaugurated a new cycle; or at least we must believe that many other people have believed these things and that such ideas have seriously affected human thinking and feeling. But no one save Yeats has ever believed these things, and we are not sure that Yeats really believed them. These constitute his private fairy tale, which he sometimes took seriously and sometimes did not. I see no way to make up one's mind about this poem except to decide that it is one of two things: an "aboli bibelot d'inanité sonore" or an "aboli bibelot de bêtise sonore." I feel sure that it is the latter, but I wish it were the former, for the former would at least be inscrutable and would call for greater skill on the part of the poet. The sonority is real, and I can appreciate it as well as the next man, but it takes more than sonority to make a great poem. Pure sonority eventually comes to seem pompous and empty.

"Two Songs from a Play" exhibit the same sonorous rhetoric and much of Yeats's private mythology: the difficulties therefore are similar to those in **"Leda,"** but there are certain passages which, as fragments, are effective. Mr. Unterecker gives a page of explanation of the poem. He equates the fierce Virgin and her Star with Virgo and Spica (of the zodiac), with Astraea and the Golden Age, with the staring Virgin (Athena) and the heart of Dionysus; and he tells us that these anticipate respectively Mary and Christ, Mary and the Star of Bethlehem, Mary and the Christian Age, and Mary and Christ's heart. This is a sufficiently complicated set of relationships for a poem of sixteen lines in the course of which the relationships are not explained, but I suspect that there is one additional complication. In the poem entitled **"A Nativity,"** a poem in which the symbolic method is medieval, we have the line: "Another star has shot an ear"; and of this and other similar figures Yeats tells us: "I had in my memory Byzantine mosaic pictures of the Annunciation, which show a line drawn from a star to the ear of the Virgin. She conceived of the Word, and therefore through the ear a star fell and was born." The fierce Virgin at the end of the first song is, of course, Mary; she must be fierce, because each new era begins in violence: we thus substitute Yeats's private myth of the Virgin for the traditional one. Similarly it was the odor of Christ's blood (in the second song) which put an end to Platonic tolerance and Doric discipline; that is to say, it was the violence of the new religion, the "Galilean turbulence" or Christ. The Babylonian starlight and the fabulous darkness indicate the same thing: we observe the starlight most clearly in the dark of the moon, which is the period of pure objectivity and of the violent reversal of the gyres. The rhetorical force in the poem is close to Yeats's best—but it is purely rhetorical. What he is saying is almost as foolish as what he says in section III of **"The Tower,"** especially the twelve lines beginning "And I declare my faith." These lines are uttered with a passion which is obviously meant to be convincing, but who can be convinced? Unless we are convinced, the passion is meaningless. The second half of the second song is an excellent elegiac stanza, but it has only a loose connection with what has preceded.

The difficulties are similar in **"The Second Coming."** In line six, the expression "the ceremony of innocence" is misleading and awkward. By reading **"A Prayer for My Daughter,"** which follows, one discovers that the phrase means the ceremonious life in which innocence flourishes; but as one comes to it in the poem, it would seem to indicate some kind of ceremony, perhaps baptismal, perhaps sacrificial, perhaps some other. Otherwise the first eight lines are very impressive if one takes them phrase by phrase: the adjective *mere* in the fourth line, for example, is a stroke of genius. But what do the lines mean? One who has lived through the last thirty years and who has not observed the date of the poem (the volume was published in 1921) may feel that Yeats was writing about the growth of fascism, naism, or communism:

> the worst
> Are full of passionate intensity.

But the first two are impossible and the third is unlikely. "The best" are the Irish aristocrats; "the worst" are the Irish engaged in politics, who were trying to establish a constitutional democracy and who eventually succeeded. The poem is an attack on civilized government made by a man who felt an intense dislike for democracy and the political activity without which democracy cannot survive—a dislike which was due in part to his native temperament but largely, I fear, to the fact that Maude Gonne was more interested in politics than in Yeats; by a man who, during much of his later life, was often tempted in the direction of fascism. The first four and a half lines of the second section are an example of Yeats's high rhetoric, but for their effect they depend upon our belief in his notion of the Spiritus Mundi. From there on we have his description of the beast, which is a fine description. But the account of the beast is not pure description. If we are to take it as seriously as Yeats's language indicates that we should, we must again accept his theory of the gyres as in some way valid. And if we do this, we must face the fact that Yeats's attitude toward the beast is different from ours: we may find the beast terrifying, but Yeats finds

him satisfying—he is Yeats's judgment upon all that we regard as civilized. Yeats approves of this kind of brutality. When we consider all of these complications, it becomes very difficult to arrive at an acceptance of the poem, an acceptance both rational and emotional. I do not deny that civilization may be coming to an end—there is no way of knowing, although I think that the chances of its surviving for a long time are fairly good. But if we are to have a poem dealing with the end of civilization, and one that we can suppose to be great, the poem must be based on something more convincing than a home-made mythology and a loose assortment of untenable social attitudes. We need to invoke the Malarméan concept of the symbol to save this poem, but we cannot invoke it because the ideas are perfectly clear. . . .

I have had something to say of Yeats's habit of excessive dramatization. I would like to be a little more explicit on this subject and then proceed to a few of his poems on his friends and on his political attitudes. I will quote two of Yeats's very minor poems and compare them briefly with two poems by John Synge on the same subjects. First is Yeats's poem **"A Coat"**: this is the last poem in **Responsibilities** and is his farewell to the style of the Celtic Twilight:

> I made my song a coat
> Covered with embroideries
> Out of old mythologies
> From heel to throat;
> But the fools caught it,
> Wore it in the world's eyes
> As though they'd wrought it.
> Song, let them take it,
> For there's more enterprise
> In walking naked.

As I have tried to show, Yeats never learned to walk naked, although he managed to shed a few of the more obvious ribbons of the eighteen-nineties. Here is Synge's poem:

> *The Passing of the Shee*
> After looking at one of A. E.'s pictures
>
> Adieu, sweet Aengus, Meave, and Fand,
> Ye plumed yet skinny Shee,
> That poets played with hand in hand
> To learn their ecstasy.
> We'll stretch in Red Dan Sally's ditch,
> And drink in Tubber Fair,
> Or poach with Red Dan Philly's bitch
> The badger and the hare.

I will now quote Yeats's poem (also from **Responsibilities**) **"On Those That Hated 'The Playboy of the Western World'"**:

> Once, when midnight smote the air,
> Eunuchs ran through Hell and met
> On every crowded street to stare
> Upon great Juan riding by:

Even like these to rail and sweat
Staring upon his sinewy thigh.

That slow, that meditative man himself wrote as follows:

The Curse
To a sister of an enemy of the author's
who disapproved of "The Playboy."

Lord, confound this surly sister,
Blight her brow with blotch and blister,
Cramp her larynx, lung and liver,
In her guts a galling give her.

Let her live to earn her dinners
In Mountjoy with seedy sinners:
Lord, this judgment quickly bring,
And I'm your servant, J. M. Synge.

Yeat's poems are inflated; they are bardic in the worst sense. Synge's poems are witty and unpretentious. Synge was not, I think, a great dramatist, but he wrote a few fine, though small, poems, of which these two are the best.

"To a Friend Whose Work Has Come to Nothing" exhibits the same inflated style and Yeats's predilection for madness. The first ten lines are plain and honest and exhibit a certain moral nobility; the last six, however, recommend madness as a cure for the problem propounded. We are told that the poem was addressed to Lady Gregory. Lady Gregory never followed the advice here given, but as she appears in this poem she is merely one in a long series of Yeatsian lunatics.

"In Memory of Major Robert Gregory" is a poem in praise of Lady Gregory's son, who was killed in the first world war. It is commonly described as one of the greatest poems in our language; I confess that I think it a very bad poem. The first two stanzas deal with Yeats's recent settling in his new house and with his thoughts about dead friends; the next three stanzas deal with three dead friends in particular: Lionel Johnson, John Synge, and Yeats's uncle, George Pollexfen; the next six stanzas deal with Robert Gregory; the final stanza is a conclusion. The first stanza is quiet and acceptable, though undistinguished. The second stanza, undistinguished in general, contains two very awkward details: the third and fourth lines employ a conversational and verbose stereotype to embody a simple matter, and the fifth line employs another. The fifth line, however, is bad in other ways: the words *up upon* make a crude combination, and the whole line, "And quarrels are blown up upon that head", gives us, like the two lines preceding, a dead metaphor but this time a mixed metaphor. Unless we are imperceptive of the possibilities of language, we visualize something being blown up on top of a head. This kind of thing is common in newspaper writing and in other vulgar writing. I remember a freshman compostion from many years ago, in which the student wrote: "This line of study is basic to my field of endeavor." It is the same kind of thing, and no apologetic reference to the virtues of colloquialism is

an adequate defense. The third stanza, which deals with Lionel Johnson, is stereotyped throughout, but it contains two especially unfortunate details. Johnson is described as "much falling", a sufficiently clumsy phrase in itself, but Pound [in "Hugh Selwya Mauberly"] tells us

how Johnson (Lionel) died
By falling from a high stool in a pub . . .

It seems likely that Pound's poem was written somewhat after that of Yeats, as far as I can judge from the dates at my disposal, and that the passage was intended as a comment on Yeats's phrase. At any rate, it is a fair enough comment. Immediately below "much falling" we get a very thin reincarnation of Roland's horn. The fourth stanza deals with John Synge. He is described as "that enquiring man," a phrase to which I do not object in itself. But every time Synge appears by name in Yeats's poems, he is described as "that . . . man", and we expect the formula as regularly as we come to expect rock, thorn trees, cold light, shaking and trembling, and scarecrows; furthermore the unnecessary use of the demonstrative adjective is one of Yeats's most obviously mechanical devices for achieving overemphasis. The remainder of this stanza is undistinguished, but one should consider these details: in line five, *certain* is used as a pronoun instead of as an adjective; in line six we have "a most desolate and stony place"; and in the last we have "Passionate and simple like his heart", a phrase which is not only one of Yeats's common clichés but one which indicates as clearly as many others the anti-intellectual bent of his work. The fifth stanza deals with Yeats's uncle, George Pollexfen, who, it seems, had been a vigorous horseman in his youth, but who had devoted himself to astrology in his later years. The diction is dull, but once again there are strange details. For example, if solid men and pure-bred horses are determined by the stars, then why not other men and horses? The limitation, I suppose, could have been clarified by such a word as *even,* but the writing is slovenly: as Pound said long ago, poetry should be at least as well written as prose. The words *outrageous, sluggish,* and *contemplative* indicate that Yeats disapproved of his uncle's later interests because they were, in some sense, intellectual; but Yeats himself was interested, throughout much of his life, in equally pseudointellectual studies. Perhaps the stanza is what Cleanth Brooks would call ironic; but it is also dull. The sixth stanza is respectably executed except for two details. In the second line "as it were" says nothing; it may have been used to fill out the line and achieve a rime, or it may have been used in the interests of colloquial style, although it is not colloquial. It seems to be lazy. The next to the last line, "Our Sidney and our perfect man," is exorbitant praise. One might accept it as a mere outburst of grief except for the fact that Yeats devotes the rest of the poem to praising Gregory in these terms: he was a great horseman, scholar, and painter; he had the knowledge to give expert advice in architecture, sculpture, and most of the handicrafts. He may well have been a great horseman, but so is many a jockey; the praise in the other departments, however, appears excessive, for if it were not we should have heard of Gregory's accomplishments from other sources. He appears to have been no Sidney, but a charming and admirable young man who dabbled in the arts. We have familiar stereotypes in the last stanzas: cold rock and thorn, stern color, delicate line, secret discipline, none of them really described or defined; we have the facile commonplaces of the final lines of stanzas eight and nine and the somewhat comical example of misplaced particularity in the final line of stanza eleven. In stanza eleven the figure of the fires is a good example of the unrealized figure of speech: that is, the two fires tell us nothing about the two temperaments except that some people live rapidly and briefly, some slowly and longer, and at the descriptive level the fires are uninteresting. In the twelfth and final stanza, Yeats tells us that he had hoped in this poem to comment on everyone whom he had ever loved or admired but that Gregory's death took all his heart for speech. He had managed to write twelve stanzas of eight lines each, however, before he stopped; but this remark serves as a kind of apology for the loose structure of the poem—a structure which remains loose in spite of the apology.

"Coole Park, 1929" is a poem in honor of Lady Gregory and her home, Coole Park, which she had been forced to sell to the Forestry Department, though she was permitted to live there until her death. The poem is a typical meditation on the virtues of old families and their patronage of the arts, but especially upon Lady Gregory as a force in bringing distinguished men together and guiding their work. The theme is therefore the intellectual force that Lady Gregory exerted upon these men: Douglas Hyde, a negligible poet who became a distinguished Celtic scholar, whose poetry Yeats apparently admired and whose scholarship he regretted; John Synge, whose plays Yeats greatly admired and vastly over-rated; Shawe-Taylor and Hugh Lane, nephews of Lady Gregory and patrons of the arts but scarcely great men; and Yeats himself. Shawe-Taylor and Lane are described as "those impetuous men". This is a Yeatsian formula to describe distinguished gentlemen, and Synge appears in the usual formula for Synge: "that slow, that meditative man." The unfortunate Hyde is buried in the worst pseudo-poeticism of all, and Yeats employs a prettily apologetic description of himself. The central figure of speech appears in the third stanza. The first two lines of the first place Lady Gregory and a swallow together in what appears to be an accidental juxtaposition, but in the third stanza the men are compared to swallows, and we are told that Lady Gregory could keep a swallow to its first intent, could control the flight of swallows. Obviously she could do nothing of the sort; we may suppose that she could control talented men in some fashion, but we are not told how. The movement of the swallows is charming; Lady Gregory's influence on the men, presumably an intellectual influence, is never given us. What he have is a fairly good vehicle with almost no tenor, or fairly good decoration of an undefined theme. In the last two lines, however, the third stanza collapses almost completely. Line seven reads: "The intellectual sweetness of those lines." At the level of the vehicle, the lines are those of the swallows' flight; at the level of the tenor, we have nothing, for "intellectual sweetness" is merely a sentimental phrase with no conceptual support. The last line of this stanza, "That cut through time or cross it withershins,"

is especially unclear. How did the line of the swallows, either as vehicle or as tenor, cut through time? As to *withershins,* the *Shorter Oxford English Dictionary* gives this account of it:

> 1. In a direction contrary to the usual; the wrong way—1721. 2. in a Direction contrary to the apparent course of the sun (considered as unlucky or causing disaster)—1545.

The last line of the first stanza is pseudo-poetic. The third and fourth lines of the last stanza are commonplace, and the sixth and seventh are baffling: why should the mourners stand with their backs to sun and shade alike, and why is the shade sensual? This is verbiage for the sake of verbiage.

The best poem of this kind, I believe, is a late one, **"The Municipal Gallery Revisited."** There are a good many characteristic defects. In his attempt to achieve a conversational tone (or perhaps out of inadvertence) Yeats wrote a fair number of lines which are awkward in movement. The poem is predominantly iambic pentameter, but if we are to read it in this meter, we encounter problems, some more serious than others. Line four can be read only as three trochees followed by two anapests. In line eight of the same stanza we get this:

> A revolútionary sóldier knéeling tó be bléssed.

That is, we have four syllables in the first foot and either three or four in the second, depending on our pronunciation of *revolutionary.* It is hard to read the first line of the second stanza as anything but an alexandrine. In line three of the second stanza, we have a trochee in the last position if we pronounce Ireland correctly, but this is the only line in the poem where this awkward variation occurs, and we are not prepared for it and are tempted to mispronounce the word for the sake of the rime. Line five in the same stanza is an alexandrine and the first lines of four, five and six are alexandrines. We have such formulae as "terrible and gay" and "John Synge . . . that rooted man". At the opening of the fourth stanza we have rhetorical exaggeration:

> Mancini's portrait of Augusta Gregory,
> 'Greatest since Rembrandt', according to
>   John Synge;

But this is followed immediately by the almost weary qualification:

> A great ebullient portrait, certainly.

At the opening of the third stanza we have the expression of emotion through physical action:

> Heart-smitten with emotion I sink down,
> My heart recovering with covered eyes.

But this is an account of an old old man looking at the portraits of his dead friends and is understandable, and it has not the empty violence of comparable passages from earlier poems. The transition from five to six is 'awkward. Yeats apparently thought that the line at the end of five needed a footnote, and I dare say it does; but he puts his footnote in parentheses at the beginning of six, and it is unimpressive as poetry, and it detracts from the unity of six. Except for this detail, six is well enough written, but its effect depends upon Yeats's view of the ideal society, "dream of the noble and the beggar-man," a view by which I find myself unmoved. The last stanza over-rates Yeats's friends, but is the moving statement of an old man who held them in high esteem and who now reviews them all in their official portraits, all of them being dead. Perhaps the best apology for this poem is to be found in a poem by Robert Bridges, written a good many years earlier, his "Elegy among the Tombs":

> Read the worn names of the forgotten dead,
> Their pompous legends will no smile awake;
> Even the vainglorious title o'er the head
> Wins its pride pardon for its sorrow's sake;
> And carven Loves scorn not their dusty prize,
> Though fallen so far from tender sympathies.

The best of the political poems, I suspect, is "**Easter 1916.**" The worst fault in this poem is the refrain, "A terrible beauty is born." One can understand the sentiment, but the diction is pure Yeatsian fustian. In the first stanza I regret the repetition of "polite meaningless words", but the defect, if it is a defect, is minor. In the line "To please a companion", however, we have an unrhythmical prose if we pronounce *companion* correctly; to save the rhythm, we have to say companee*un*. In the first seven lines of the next stanza, lines which are passably written, we have Yeats's view of what women should not do. In the next two lines,

> This man had kept a school
> And rode our winged horse.

we have a pseudo-poeticism, as bad as Hyde's sword or Roland's horn. A little farther on we have this:

> So sensitive his nature seemed.

The line is written in a very rapid tetrameter, and it occurs in a poem which otherwise is written in heavily accented trimeter, and for the moment it ruins the movement. To save the meter, we should have to read *sens'tive,* but the *Shorter Oxford English Dictionary* does not give this pronunciation. In the third stanza, the stream and the other details of momentary change are the main part of the vehicle; the unchanging stone is the rest. The vehicle, as mere description, is very well handled. The tenor, however, is this: the truly spiritual life consists of momentary change; fixity of purpose turns one to an imperceptive stone. This is familiar romantic doctrine, but I see no reason to take it seriously. In the last stanza he tells us that the Easter Martyrs turned themselves to stones and perhaps in a poor cause, but he praises them for their heroism and laments their deaths. The poem is marred by certain faults of style and by more serious faults of thinking, which we must consider virtues if we are to be greatly moved by the poem. . . .

First of all we should discard the idea that Yeats was in any real sense a Mallarméan symbolist. There is not, so far as my limited knowledge goes, any extensive translation of Mallarmé's criticism. The original prose is extremely difficult, and I do not believe that Yeats ever had a sufficient command of French to read it; he certainly had not in the years when he was forming his style. And Mallarmé's verse is more difficult than his prose The simple fact of the matter is, that Yeats (from *Responsibilities* onward at least, and often before) was usually trying to say something clearly. His obscurity results from his private symbols (mainly of the medieval variety), from the confusion of his thought, and from the frequent ineptitude of his style. From *Responsibilities* onward, in fact, he became more and more openly didactic. He quite obviously was deeply moved by his ideas and expected us to be moved by them. But unfortunately his ideas were contemptible. I do not wish to say that I believe that Yeats should be discarded, for there are a few minor poems which are successful or nearly successful, and there are many fine lines and passages in the more ambitious pieces. But in the long run it is impossible to believe that foolishness is greatness, and Yeats was not a great poet, nor was he by a wide margin the best poet of our time. There are greater poems in Bridges, Hardy, Robinson, and Stevens, to mention no others, and in half a dozen younger poets as well. His reputation is easily accounted for. In the first place there is real talent scattered through his work; in the second place our time does not recognize any relationship between thought and poetry, between motive and emotion; in the third place, Yeats's power of self-assertion, his bardic tone, overwhelmed his readers. The bardic tone is common in romantic poetry: it sometimes occurs in talented (but confused) poets such as Wordsworth, Blake and Yeats; more often it appears in poets of little or no talent, such as Shelley, Whitman, and Robinson Jeffers. For most readers the bardic tone is synonymous with greatness. If the poet asserts his own greatness long enough and in the same tone of voice the effect is hypnotic; we have seen the same thing on the political platform in such speakers as Adolf Hilter and Father Coughlin. But in time the effect wears off. While the tone is effective, however, a good deal of damage can be done and in fact is usually done. In our time Yeats has been regarded as the great poet in person, the poet of the impeccable style. He has thus become a standard of judgment for critics, with the result that the work of better poets has been obscured or minimized; and he has become a model for imitation, with the result that the work of a good many talented poets has been damaged beyond repair.

A. G. Stock (essay date 1965)

SOURCE: "From the National to the Universal," in *The Dublin Magazine,* Vol. 4, Nos. 3 & 4, Autumn/Winter 1965, pp. 28-35.

[In the following excerpt, Stock concentrates on Yeats's concern for Ireland and his involvement with magic, tracing the presence of both in his poetry throughout his career by focusing on a selection of poems that unites these interests.]

"I am persuaded," says Yeats in *Autobiographies,* "that our intellects at twenty contain all the truths we shall ever find, but as yet we do not know truths that belong to us from opinion caught up in casual irritation or momentary fantasy. As life goes on, we discover that certain truths sustain us in defeat, or give us victory, whether over ourselves or others, and it is these truths, tested by passion, that we call convictions."

Whether or not this is true of all men it is an illuminating truth about Yeats. From first to last his fundamental convictions hardly changed: his way of putting them, concentrated by the test of passion, made them look different. At first, like an untried faith, they were only expressible in intricate and visionary symbolism, but he carried them into battle with a resistant world and learnt their meaning in terms of experience. He hammered his thoughts into unity, deepening them till those that at first seemed unrelated were fused together; and for this he had to find a language that would not only convey the whole of his vision in one breath, so to speak, but would integrate it with flesh and blood experience. The continuous hammering and fusing generates the concentrated energy of his later style.

Two deeply rooted convictions seemed at first to have little enough connection: the faith in his nationality which made him aspire to be a poet of Ireland, and the equally passionate faith in the supernatural that committed him to the study of magic. In bringing them together he deepened the first into a cosmic philosophy of the rise and fall of civilizations and the second into an affirmation of the eternity of the soul, the ultimate creator and destroyer of civilizations. In a few poems widely separated in time one can trace the coming together of these two themes in a single vision.

"To Ireland in the Coming Times" was written when he was twenty-eight. Already he is troubled by the seeming contradictions between his dedication to Ireland and his preoccupation with elemental spirits, and he tries to resolve it by a meditation in three movements. In the first and longest, he brings Ireland and the elemental spirits into harmony, by seeing both as aspects of the world of time, controlled by a vision of ideal beauty existing in eternity. By the phrases and rhymes, the vision with her red-rose-bordered hem, leading all things natural and supernatural in an everlasting dance, is related to the Lady Beauty of one of Rossetti's sonnets:

> long known to thee
> By flying hair and fluttering hem, the beat
> Following her daily of thy heart and feet
> How passionately and irretrievably,
> With what fond hope, how many days and way.

Then comes the reflection that time is only time, that men and nations and spirits alike are unrealities disappearing at last in an absolute

> where may be,
> In truth's consuming ecstasy,
> No place for love and dream at all;
> For God goes by with white footfall.

And then—an afterthought colouring the whole meditation—that nevertheless the love and the dream are worth recording for generations still to be born, and to pass away. The life of time has its own reality.

The many changes in this poem, between the first version of 1892 and its final form in 1925, show that to Yeats it was a statement which mattered permanently, an imperfect statement needing to beset right. At twenty-eight he could assert confidently that Ireland possessed the vision—

> And still the thoughts of Ireland brood
> Upon her holy quietude.

But after the turbulent politics of thirty years it was discreetly tempered to

> And may the thoughts of Ireland brood
> Upon a measured quietude.

The word "measure," not in the first version at all, comes three times in seven lines ending here and several times later, so that it makes a second thread in the poem's pattern, interwoven with the recurring phrase "the red-rose-bordered hem," and makes the whole design more complex. Along with "the plummet-measured face" of **"The Statues"** and "Measurement began our might" in **"Under Ben Bulben,"** it shows how measure, or ordered proportion, grew to be a symbol of eternity embodied in time. But the relation of the three movements of thought is unaltered.

Between the two versions much had happened to Ireland and to Yeats's thoughts about Ireland. **"September 1913"** is a disillusioned contrast between heroic Ireland of the past and the men he is quarrelling with here and now—

> Romantic Ireland's dead and gone,
> It's with O'Leary in the grave.

But all the same he had to have an Ireland to write for, and a little later, in **"The Fisherman,"** he is shaping its image: an ideal image, and yet a great deal closer to his actual experience than the Cathleen Ni Houlihan of his early dreams. Though his fisherman is as far as possible from the slogan-shouting politicians who infuriate him, still, he grows from the countryside, from an Irish tradition of life that is Yeats's own—a lonely man

> Climbing up to a place
> Where stone is dark under froth

—and for that man he will write his poems.

"**The Fisherman**" comes between "**September 1913**" and "**Easter 1916.**" It looks back to the earlier exasperated mood, but the rhythm of its three-stress line, which Yeats had rarely used before, links it directly with the feeling of the later poem.

"**Easter 1916**" recants the scathing mockery of "**September 1913,**" but is by no means an impetuous wholesale recantation. The men he had dismissed so contemptuously had brought back heroism to the world, but they had not changed his distrust of the obsessive fanaticism which puts a man outside of human life. Their sacrifice might even have been needless; and yet it had changed Irish history irrevocably. He weights it all up, and without ignoring what repels him finds that admiration prevails over regret, that "A terrible beauty is born."

The heart of the poem, where he transcends his initial hostility, is the passage about the stone and the stream. It says what he feels about those dehumanising political abstractions, but the quietude of the image makes it not altogether a condemnation; and in the next stanza hostility is lost in compassion. He has found a standpoint beyond anger, where he can see the fanaticism as a part, and the greatest part, of the sacrifice Ireland needs from her sons. And to find it he went back to the haunts of his imaginary fisherman, to some place in Sligo "Where stone is dark under froth"—or perhaps to the stream by Thoor Ballylee. His understanding of Ireland grew from his love of its earth and waters.

The title of "**Nineteen Hundred and Nineteen**" makes it a third phase of his meditation on Irish history. To turn from "A terrible beauty is born" to the stark brutality of

> . . . a drunken soldiery
> Can leave the mother, murdered at her door,
> To crawl in her own blood, and go scot-free

is like falling from a high cliff on to the rocks of fact. The words recall a recent happening near Coole, one of many happenings of those days. The terrible beauty of Easter Week had let in seven years of unbeautiful violence.

But in this poem Ireland was not alone in his thoughts. All over Europe, from the revolution in Russia to the threatening labour troubles in England, he saw western civilization degenerating into anarchic violence. Two thousand years ago the sculptures of Phidias seemed imperishable; now all that modern man took most pride in—

> A law indifferent to blame or praise,
> To bribe or threat; habits that made old wrong
> Melt down, as it were wax in the sun's rays

—was following them into darkness. Ireland was close enough and mattered deeply enough to show him the catastrophe in all the horror of minute particulars, and to show it threatening everything he valued in the life of the imagination. That murdered mother focuses the picture, and Ireland epitomizes the doom of an age.

Yeats refuses to evade the reality with a reassuring formula. To save anything from the ruins of time he is thrown back on another of his truths, the solitude of the soul in eternity which gives it the power to endure all loss.

> He who can read the signs nor sink unmanned
> Into the half-deceit of some intoxicant
> From shallow wit . . .
> Has but one comfort left: all triumph would
> But break upon his ghostly solitude.

That this ultimate solitude is the soul's strength is not a new thought to him; it is to be founda quarter of a century earlier in "To his Heart, bidding it have no Fear." It stands the test of experience, but the language of experience changes it almost beyond recognition.

Though *A Vision* was not written till 1925, it was already taking shape in Yeat's mind when he wrote "**Nineteen Hundred and Nineteen.**" Its two major themes, the cyclic decay and renewal of civilizations and the passage of the soul through life after life, are both in the poem, and it is their interplay that holds it together, but they are not reduced to a formula. Yeats is contemplating his world's imminent downfall and has no direct answer to the bleak question—

> Man is in love and loves what vanishes,
> What more is there to say?

And yet by the logic of poetry, which has a different validity from Aristotelian logic, there is a kind of answer in the strangely reassuring beauty of the swan—

> The breast thrust out in pride
> Whether to play, or to ride
> Those winds that clamour of approaching night

—an image of the soul in solitude, reducing all the constructions of art and intellect to a nest from which the bird leaps into the desolate heaven. The murdered mother and the drunken soldiers are not made insignificant; nevertheless, against the world's transitory glory is set the eternity of the soul.

Pass on to 1934. The vision of doom he had lived with for fifteen years was visible now to others besides Yeats. Neither in the west nor the east was there any recovery of the ordered world he loved. Coole was a sanctuary no longer, Lady Gregory was dead. Ireland indeed was achieving a kind of stability, but there was no place in it for the old-time "big house," which stood for a way of life stretching back through feudal times right to the heroic age, focusing everything he valued in European history. That life had given place irrevocably to another with which he had no sympathy. Already the world could see the approach of war, and history seemed to have caught up with his forebodings. But Yeats had passed beyond them, and was at home in the "fabulous formless darkness" into which age after age sinks back. In a sense he had been there long ago, when he wrote of all things vanishing "Where God goes by with white footfall;" but though the thought is there, it is the language of a youth whose imagination has not grasped destruction. In the sonnet **"Meru"** he says

> . . . man's life is thought,
> And he, despite his terror, cannot cease
> Ravening through century after century,
> Ravening, raging and uprooting that he may come
> Into the desolation of reality

—and there is a lifetime of experience between the white footfall of God and "the desolation of reality."

"Meru" has all history in it; one might think Yeats had forgotten Ireland. But it would be easy to show from other poems of the period—from **"Parnell's Funeral,"** for instance—how some Irish grief or anger touches off the poem, and then, because all his thoughts converge, it becomes universalized. Even in **"Meru,"** it may be that Coole Park was Yeats's Egypt and Greece and Rome, and he could only fortify himself to bear its loss by turning himself into the soul of man contemplating the transience of history.

The last poems, posthumously published, are full of Ireland. It is not now a personified abstraction, but the men and women, the countryside and the quarrels that had moulded his creative life. The men and women were nearly all dead, but in his mind they were more alive than anything in the present, and mind is the country of eternity.

> Though grave-diggers' toil is long,
> Sharp their spades, their muscles strong,
> They but thrust their buried men
> Back in the human mind again.

Most of what he had fought for was lost, but that made it no less worth defending. Now that the world had woken up to the imminence of destruction Yeats's mind had gone beyond it to the assurance of renewal:

> Lovers of horses and of women, shall,
> From marble of a broken sepulchre,
> Or dark betwixt the polecat and the owl,
> Or any rich, dark nothing disinter
> The workman, noble and saint—

Like any Irishman who had stood up to Britain, he was unimpressed by sheer size: the greatness of tragedy was not scale but intensity:—

> Though Hamlet rambles and Lear rages,
> And all the drop-scenes drop at once
> Upon a hundred thousand stages,
> It cannot grow by an inch or an ounce.

The last poems range between the personal and the universal till you cannot say whether he is writing his own or the world's history; either is an image of the other. **"The Curse of Cromwell"** seems to me to concentrate all this. In Cromwell and his murderous crew are both modern Ireland and all the drab commercial democracy of the modern world; in the lovers and the dancers, Coole

Park and the whole world of splendid gaiety he dreamed of. With the ruined houses, ways of life have vanished that stretched back at least to Homer's day. Readers of the Odyssey will remember how the dogs in the swineherd's hut whimpered when Athena came, although except Odysseus none of the human company could see her—just as in Ireland to this day, horses and dogs are known to sense the presence of a spirit. The old wandering singer knows that the dead still live, but his knowledge increases the burden of loneliness in a world that has turned away from them. He is Yeats himself, but equally he is the spirit of a past thrust aside by the present. And all this is put with ballad-like simplicity, in a lyric that has one of the rarest of qualities in modern poetry, the easy lilt of a song.

> I came on a great house in the middle of the night,
> Its open lighted doorway and its windows all alight,
> And all my friends were there and made me
>   welcome too;
> But I woke in an old ruin that the wind howled
>   through;
> And when I pay attention I must out and walk
> Among the dogs and horses that understand my
>   talk.
>> *O what of that, O what of that,*
>> *What is there left to say?*

Marjorie G. Perloff (essay date 1969)

SOURCE: "'Heart Mysteries': The Later Love Lyrics of W. B. Yeats," in *Contemporary Literature,* Vol. 10, No. 2, pp.

[*In the following excerpt, Perloff provides explications of structure, semantics, and sound and uses biographical information about Yeats's feelings for Maud Gonne during the last two decades of his life to analyze lyrics of Yeats's second Maud Gonne cycle.*]

In the love lyrics of his last decade, Yeats, the critics would have it, finally turned from a disembodied and sterile courtly ideal to "desecration and the lover's night." The last stanza of **"Among School Children,"** for example, with its famous assertion that "Labour is blossoming or dancing where/ The body is not bruised to pleasure soul," can be viewed, as it is by Donald Davie, as the rejection of the Romantic tradition of sexual passion which comes from the courtly love of the Middle Ages through the *Vita Nuova* to the Platonism of Sidney's *Astrophel and Stella,* the tradition in which carnal consummation is delayed indefinitely or excluded altogether in the attempt to transform sexual love into something "purer"—more intellectual and spiritual. Yeats's early love poems from **The Rose** (1893) to **The Wild Swans at Coole** (1919) were clearly in this mode, but after his marriage in 1917, so the theory goes, Yeats gradually came to reject the soul in favor of the body. In an essay on the **"Words For Music Perhaps"** sequence which appeared in its final form in **The Winding Stair** of 1933, Denis Donoghue [in

"The Vigour of Its Blood: Yeats's 'Words for Music Perhaps,'" *Kenyon Review,* 1959] argues that the "biological imperative is the "principle of structure or myth of the Crazy Jane poems corresponding to the anthropological myth of *The Waste Land.* This position, downward-tending in its images, is close to that of Lawrence in *Lady Chatterley's Lover.*"

Whether or not this new "mythology of earth" is a good thing has been hotly debated, but the pervasive presence of the sexual theme in the later poetry has been accepted as axiomatic. In part Yeats himself is to blame for what I hope to show is a misconception about his love poetry. The letters of his final decade are generally addressed to the women in his life—Olivia Shakespear, Dorothy Welles-ley, Ethel Mannin—and in these Yeats frequently refers to his renewed sexual energy and to his preoccupation with sexual matters. In 1926, for example, he wrote Olivia Shakespear, "My moods fill me with surprise and some alarm. The other day I found at Coole a reproduction of a drawing of two charming young persons in the full stream of their Saphoistic [*sic*] enthusiasm, and it got into my dreams at night and made a great racket there." A year later he declared that "only two topics can be of the least interest to a serious and studious mind—sex and the dead," and in 1933, when he was correcting the proofs of *The Winding Stair,* he explained that "Sexual abstinence" prompted the new love lyrics: "I was ill and yet full of desire." Dorothy Wellesley concluded from Yeats's letters and conversations that "Sex, Philosophy and the Occult preoccupy him."

The poems themselves, however, reflect these prose statements only partially, and one remembers that Yeats was fond of striking poses even in his letters, essays, and autobiographical writings, and that the face he presents to his female correspondents is not necessarily his only one. Accordingly, the reader must be wary when Yeats tells Mrs. Shakespear that the poems in **"Words For Music Perhaps"** are "all emotion and all impersonal . . . all praise of joyous life, though in the best of them it is a dry bone on the shore that sings the praise." What is immediately striking about the later love lyrics is that those that do celebrate sexual energy, if not quite the "joyous life," are invariably dramatic monologues: the speaker is Crazy Jane, or the Woman Young and Old, or the Chambermaid, or the Irish mystic Ribh, or Solomon, or the Wild Old Wicked Man. Such extensive use of personae is the exception rather than the rule for Yeats who, in his greatest poems from **"The Wild Swans at Coole"** through **"Byzantium"** and **"A Dialogue of Self and Soul"** to **"Lapis Lazuli"** and **"The Circus Animals' Desertion,"** uses the mode of the dramatized, autobiographical "I"— the "I" of the poet himself. In a letter of 1935, Yeats told Dorothy Wellesley that he had learned to "make a woman express herself as never before. I have looked out of her eyes. I have shared her desire." This boast is made good in the "Three Bushes" sequence and in **"A Woman Young and Old,"** but, interestingly, although the Chambermaid and the Young Woman know sexual satisfaction, the "I" of the poet never does. I do not think that such "masking" is to be attributed to the poet's reticence; Yeats speaks

freely enough of his personal problems and of the private lives of his friends and relatives in his great occasional poems such as **"In Memory of Major Robert Gregory,"** **"Easter 1916,"** and **"All Souls' Night."** Rather, it would seem that Yeats's personal experience in love, which is reflected in those poems that dramatize the poet's own self, was the opposite of Donne's, whose love poetry is often linked to that of Yeats. Despite the fact that Yeats, like Donne, makes much of the fusion of body and soul in the achievement of true love, of Unity of Being, there is none of Donne's sense of joyous conquest in Yeats, for whom "one little roome" never becomes "an every where," and who can never tell his sweetheart that "reverend love" has made them "one another's hermitage."

"A Dialogue of Self and Soul," which stands as a kind of head-piece to the "little mechanical songs" of **"Words For Music Perhaps,"** contains Yeats's most famous and clear-cut statement of his commitment to life, to the re-birth that characterizes the whole *Winding Stair* volume. But what precisely is it that the speaker wants to relive? The relevant stanza is the following:

> I am content to live it all again
> And yet again, if it be life to pitch
> Into the frog-spawn of a blind man's ditch,
> A blind man battering blind men;
> Or into that most fecund ditch of all,
> The folly that man does
> Or must suffer, if he woos
> A proud woman not kindred of his soul.

The sensuous imagery ("frog-spawn," "fecund ditch") should not obscure the fact that the experience which the speaker most wants to relive is his painful and frustrating courtship of the "proud woman not kindred of his soul," the woman who does not and cannot return his love and who is, of course, Maud Gonne. Yeats's preference of Self to Soul is thus not a simple matter of preferring the active sexual life to the contemplation of "that quarter where all thought is done," earth to heaven, Swordsman to Saint. Rebirth, it turns out, can take many different forms.

The love lyrics of Yeats's later years fall into two classes, which may be called Will and Mask, or Contemplation and Action, or the Ideal and the Real. The ballads on Crazy Jane, the lyrics in **"A Woman Young and Old,"** and the "Three Bushes" sequence fall into the latter class, which might be called the Love Poetry of the Mask. It is interesting to note that in *A Vision* Yeats insists that "sexual passion" is not the *Will* but the *Mask* of the Man of Phase 17 (Yeats's own phase). The realistic love poetry of the Mask is epitomized by the all-too-often-quoted stanza in **"Crazy Jane Talks with the Bishop"**:

> 'A woman can be proud and stiff
> When on love intent;
> But Love has pitched his mansion in
> The place of excrement;
> For nothing can be sole or whole
> That has not been rent.'

Much space has been devoted to discussion of this and related passages; my own concern in this essay is with the other mode, the Love Poetry of Self. This mode encompasses a fairly large group of lyrics written between 1919 and 1939, forming what might be called Yeats's Second Maud Gonne Cycle, the first having culminated in the elegiac love poems found in *The Wild Swans at Coole* (1919), such as **"Broken Dreams"** and **"The People,"** and, more specifically, in the bitter **"Owen Aherne and his Dancers,"** in which the Heart, unable to bear the "burden" of rejected love, goes "mad." This allegorical poem, written a few days after Yeats's marriage to Georgie Hyde-Lees in 1917, marks the poet's final despair at the thought that both Maud Gonne and her daughter Iseult had rejected his offers of marriage, a despair punctuated by his wife's discovery that she could perform automatic writing. For a few years, the **"Image from a Past Life"** is absent from Yeats's poems, but by 1919 Maud Gonne reappears in **"A Prayer for My Daughter"** as the object of the speaker's love-hate: her opinionated mind and intellectual hatred are rejected in a prayer for their opposites, custom and ceremony, but the poet is obsessed by that which he rejects. The same obsession is at the heart of **"Among School Children"** (1926). Despite its affirmative last stanza with its insistence that the body should not be "bruised to pleasure soul," the speaker's meditation originates in the painful recollection of the "youthful sympathy" which once blended the natures of himself and his beloved into a "sphere," the "yolk and white of the one shell." The "heart" of the "sixty-year-old smiling public man" is driven wild by the mere thought of her Quattrocento face, of her "Ledean body."

In the first two poems of **"A Man Young and Old"** (1926-27), Maud Gonne appears in the guise of moon goddess, tempting the poet-lover ("She walked awhile and blushed awhile / And on my pathway stood"), and transfiguring him with her smile which turns out to be the same smile she bestows on all men: "Like the moon her kindness is, / If kindness I may call / What has no comprehension in't, / But is the same for all." When the lover tries to touch her, he discovers that her "heart is made of stone," an insight that nearly drives him wild and ultimately reduces him to a "bit of stone" as well. In the third poem in this sequence of mythic ballads, Maud Gonne plays the role of mermaid:

> A mermaid found a swimming lad,
> Picked him for her own,
> Pressed her body to his body,
> Laughed; and plunging down
> Forgot in cruel happiness
> That even lovers drown.

Thomas Parkinson [in "Yeats and the Love Lyric," *James Joyce Quarterly,* 1966] has argued that Yeats's love poetry composes a complete recension of the concept of La Belle Dame Sans Merci, but surely the convention behind this little poem is the Romantic one of the Belle Dame or vampire. The mermaid demands the love of the "swimming lad" but cannot return it; she feeds on his body and ultimately destroys him.

The Second Maud Gonne Cycle thus begins in bitterness and resentment. But gradually the demon is exorcised and in the 'thirties Yeats returns to the courtly mode of the *Rose* and *Green Helmet* poems, tempered by forgiveness and understanding. To the end, Maud Gonne is La Belle Dame Sans Merci, but the poet can finally renounce all claims to her mercy or even to her attention; he is satisfied with contemplation and memory. In *Dramatis Personae* (1925), his autobiography of the period 1896-1902, Yeats insisted that he hated George Moore's disclosures of "promiscuous amours" because he himself was "A Romantic, when romanticism was in its final extravagance." "I thought," he explained, "one woman, whether wife, mistress, or incitement to platonic love, enough for a life-time." Although Yeats is, of course, talking of his former self here, the remark reveals his bias. Other women might provide the joys of family life, of companionship, or of sexual pleasure; when it came to *love,* however, one woman was enough for the poet's lifetime.

During the autumn of 1931, the period in which Yeats wrote those two poems of the "biological imperative," **"Crazy Jane Talks with the Bishop"** and **"Crazy Jane and Jack the Journeyman,"** he also wrote three short personal poems: **"Quarrel in Old Age," "The Results of Thought,"** and **"Remorse for Intemperate Speech."** Both in the Cuala Press edition of *Words For Music Perhaps* (1932) and in *The Winding Stair* of 1933 these three poems, together with **"Stream and Sun at Glendalough,"** which was written in 1932, were placed by Yeats immediately preceding the twenty-five-poem sequence of **"Words For Music Perhaps."** Contrary to what is commonly held, the sequence itself is rather loosely organized. Since only the first seven of the twenty-five lyrics deal directly with Crazy Jane, it is rather inaccurate to refer to the whole series as the Crazy Jane poems. Poems VIII-XIV represent the antithesis of Crazy Jane's earthy sensuality; they celebrate the idealistic, romantic love of a young girl and a young man, and then the memory of this love that torments the same two people in old age. The rest of the lyrics in the sequence vary as to speaker, theme, and plot. **"Three Things"** (XV), one of Yeats's personal favorites, is the song of the "dry bone" in praise of the "joyous life." **"Lullaby"** (XVI), which Yeats describes in a letter of 1929 as a song a mother might sing to her child, is a paean for the great lovers Helen and Paris, Tristram and Isolde, and Zeus and Leda—a poem in the heroic tradition of the ruling passion. **"After Long Silence"** (XVII), by contrast, is a personal meditation occasioned by Yeats's perception that he and his beloved can talk about love only now that they are too old to experience it. [The poem was addressed not to Maud Gonne but to Olivia Shakespear, but it is generalized enough to be applicable to any woman who has been loved by the poet and fits tonally into the Second Maud Gonne Cycle.] The next three poems, **"Mad as the Mist and Snow," "Those Dancing Days are Gone,"** and **"I Am of Ireland,"** are experiments in blending the conventions of folk ballad and mad song. To argue, as does Walter Houghton, that the speaker of **"I Am of Ireland"** is Crazy Jane, and that she is being propositioned by Jack the Journeyman, does not seem to be warranted by the text itself. Poems XXI-XXIV introduce a new speaker, Old Tom, but again I cannot agree with Houghton and Donoghue that Tom is Jane's counterpart. His concerns, like those of his model, Poor Tom in *King Lear,* are philosophical rather than sexual; no particular woman haunts his dreams. Rather, Old Tom is Yeats's Plotinian, the "insane" oracle who knows that "All things remain in God," that "The stallion Eternity / Mounted the mare of Time, / 'Gat the foal of the world." Finally, **"The Delphic Oracle Upon Plotinus,"** the last poem in the so-called Crazy Jane sequence, is less a love poem than a generalized image of Plotinus' journey to the paradise of his more venerable predecessors, Plato and Pythagoras, an image perceived by the slightly disenchanted "I," who is none other than Yeats himself.

"Words For Music Perhaps" does not, then, have a single plot, theme, or speaking voice. If one takes the unifying theme to be what Peter Ure [in *W. B. Yeats,* 1963] calls "the heroic justification of sexuality in a naked world," one must eliminate poems VIII-XIV, the Old Tom poems, **"After Long Silence"** and **"Mad as the Mist and Snow,"** which is not a love poem at all. On the other hand, if one generalizes and takes the theme to be something like the frustrations of old age, one might just as well include **"The Tower"** or **"Sailing to Byzantium."** Nor is the unity formal: it is often assumed that what Yeats called his "mechanical songs" are all ballads with refrains, but in fact these poems have a great variety of stanza forms and many do not have refrains. At best, then, the sequence of short lyrics and ballads known as **"Words For Music Perhaps"** may be regarded as a chronological unit. If this is the case, the four short lyrics that precede the twenty-five-poem sequence can be seen as complementary poems on related themes. The first one, **"Quarrel in Old Age,"** epitomizes what I have called Yeats's love poetry of Self, of the Ideal, and is perhaps the best example of the kind of poem found in Yeats's Second Maud Gonne Cycle:

> Where had her sweetness gone?
> What fanatics invent
> In this blind bitter town,
> Fantasy or incident
> Not worth thinking of,
> Put her in a rage.
> I had forgiven enough
> That had forgiven old age.
>
> All lives that has lived;
> So much is certain;
> Old sages were not deceived:
> Somewhere beyond the curtain
> Of distorting days
> Lives that lonely thing
> That shone before these eyes
> Targeted, trod like Spring.

The occasion that prompted this autobiographical lyric must have been one of a series of quarrels that arose between Maud Gonne and Yeats after he was elected to the senatorship of the newly formed Irish Free State in

1922, thus becoming a charter member of the Establishment while Maud Gonne persevered in her revolutionary politics. She herself writes, "We had quarrelled seriously when he became a Senator of the Free State which voted Flogging Acts against young republican soldiers still seeking to free Ireland from the contamination of the British Empire, and for several years we had ceased to meet." On the surface, it is a rather slight poem: the speaker in old age wonders how his beloved has been so utterly transformed from sweet young girl to shrewish old woman. The change seems hard to forgive until the poet remembers that "All lives that has lived," that the idea of beauty remains no matter what happens to the person who embodies that beauty. As such, the poem has been labelled "Platonic" or "Plotinian" when it has been discussed at all and is generally dismissed as a marginal occasional piece. This is unfortunate, for **"Quarrel in Old Age"** represents the triumph of style of the later Yeats quite as much as do the more "daring" Crazy Jane poems.

It is easy to be misled by the diction of the poem; if one looks at isolated words and phrases, one is bound to be disappointed, for almost every line contains phraseology used in Yeats's earlier Maud Gonne poems and which therefore strikes one superficially as conventional and hackneyed. A few examples will illustrate this point:

Quarrel in Old Age	*Earlier Poems*

1. sweetness	1. 'Such a delicate high head,
	   All that sternness amid charm,
	   All that *sweetness* amid strength?'
	      —**"Peace"** (1910)

2. blind bitter town	2. 'My darling cannot understand
	   What I have done, or what would do
	   In this *blind bitter land.*'
	      —**"Words"** (1909)

3. lonely thing	3. Under the passing stars, foam of the sky
	   Lives on this *lonely face.*
	   —**"The Rose of the World"** (1892)
	
	I mourn for that most *lonely thing;*
	   and yet God's will be done:
	   I knew a phoenix in my youth, so
	   let them have their day.
	   —**"His Phoenix"** (1915)

4. trod like Spring	4. For she had fiery blood When I was young,
	   And *trod so sweetly proud* As '*twere upon a cloud.* . . .
	   —**"A Woman Homer Sung"** (1910)

A crowd
Will gather, and not know
it walks the very
street
Whereon a *thing once
walked* that seemed
a burning cloud.

—"Fallen Majesty" (1912)

| 5. Lives that lonely thing
That shone before these
eyes | 5. When the wild
thought . . .
Set all her blood astir
And *glittered in her
eyes.* |

—"To a Young Girl" (1915)

Time's bitter flood will
rise,
*Your beauty perish and
be lost*
*For all eyes but these
eyes.*

—"The Lover Pleads with his Friend" (1897)

With respect to its diction, then, **"Quarrel in Old Age"** seems to be no more than a late specimen of the pre-Raphaelite love lyric in which the young Yeats celebrates his Rose of the World, his Phoenix, his Goddess who walks on clouds, his Sun whose blaze blinds the eye and lights up the soul. Here surely is a courtly love lyric that harks back to *The Wind Among the Reeds* of 1899, the reader surmises and impatiently hurries on to Crazy Jane. But the poem repays study. Its distinguishing feature, as in the case of most of Yeats's later poems, is not its vocabulary or its overt theme but its principle of organization—the poetic structure itself.

The reader is immediately drawn into the dramatic situation of the poem by the abrupt opening question with its unexpected verb tense: "Where *had* her sweetness gone?" The use of *had* where one would expect *has* immediately pushes the quarrel into the past; it indicates that the speaker hadasked himself this question at a moment prior to the present time of the poem—he is asking it no longer. It is as if, after the event, the poet is trying to remember the steps leading up to the quarrel. The casual reference to "her" implicates the reader in the poet's drama; we feel that we must know all about *her,* the poet's intimate.

In lines 2-6, the initial question is answered with an absolute minimum of words: *whatever* (the heavily stressed indefinite pronoun "what" suggests the emptiness of the charge) the fanatic mob of Dublin can think of by way of slander or petty gossip has been brought to Maud Gonne's attention and has "Put her in a rage." But she is not, of course, only raging at the "fanatics"; as the title of the poem suggests, it is the fact that Yeats himself had evidently sided with the "blind bitter town" that precipitated the great quarrel. In this context, the last two lines of the first stanza are puzzling; there is no logical connection between them and what comes before. If it is the woman who has lost her sweetness, why must the speaker be the

one to forgive her, and what does "old age" have to do with it? The condensation of the passage is marked, but what Yeats means, I think, is that as former lover, the speaker finds it difficult enough to accept the sheer fact of Maud Gonne's old age with the concomitant loss of beauty that "distorting days" have brought, without having to "forgive" as well the bad temper and rage of an angry old woman.

The drama of the poem is that, against all better judgment, he does forgive her. The tense shifts abruptly to the present in the second stanza as the poet announces, "All lives that has lived; / So much is certain." The sharp reversal that has taken place is the result of a mental state frequently met with in the **Winding Stair** poems—the casting out of remorse—but here the act is only implicit. In a sudden moment of insight, the poet is able not only to forgive Maud Gonne but also to recover the essence of what she once was and the assurance that this essence is permanent. Somewhere behind the wrinkles, gray hair, and dimmed eyes of the old woman ("beyond the curtain / Of distorting days"), her former self survives.

The last three lines of the poem are extremely elliptical. There is nothing very unusual about the Spring image; in describing his first meeting with Maud Gonne in *The Trembling of the Veil* (1922), Yeats used the same personification: "Today, with her great height and the unchangeable lineaments of her form, she looks the Sybil I would have had played by Florence Farr, but in that day she seemed a classical impersonation of the Spring, the Virgilian commendation 'She walks like a goddess' made for her alone." The inspiration for this image was most probably Botticelli's "Primavera," a painting Yeats knew well, in which the goddess Spring has the "Hollow of cheek as though it drank the wind" which Yeats attributed to Maud Gonne in **Among School Children.**

The difficulty of the passage is caused not by its imagery or diction but by its very peculiar syntax. Since Yeats omits both connectives and punctuational clues in the last three lines, it is impossible, in the first place, to determine whether "Targeted" modifies "lonely thing" or "eyes." In 1935 when Maurice Wollman, who was editing an anthology of modern poetry, asked Yeats if "Targeted" meant "protected as with a target, a round shield," Yeats replied, "Your note on targeted is quite correct," thus suggesting that the participle must modify "lonely thing": Maud Gonne's beauty, in other words, is that of the archetypal love goddess; it is "Targeted" or protected from the frenzy of the common people, the mob. But the syntactic construction of lines 15-16 makes it equally possible to take "Targeted" as a modifier of "eyes," and in this case one can read the passage in two ways, depending on whether "before" is read as an adverb of place or one of time: (1) the poet recalls the time when the "lonely thing"—Maud Gonne's unique beauty—shone *in front* of his "Targeted" eyes, eyes which were, in other words, "hit" by the rays of her brilliant sunshine; or (2) the poet recognizes that the "lonely thing" shone even *before* Yeats's own eyes were "Targeted" by it. Both these readings, like the first one, yield conventional Petrarchan images, and they do not really contradict one another. Maud Gonne's beauty is protected from common life and cannot be contaminated; her eyes shoot arrows at those of her lover; her immortal beauty existed even before her lover was "struck." The radical condensation of the passage suggests that Yeats would have it all three ways. "Targeted" is, in any case, the key word here; it is emphasized not only by its range of meaning but also by the complex alliteration of *"Targeted, trod"* and by the heavy stress on its first syllable.

"Quarrel in Old Age" is, then, a new variant of the Neoplatonic love lyric which Yeats had supposedly renounced in his later years in favor of the poetry of the "biological imperative." "All lives that has lived": the Platonic form of Maud Gonne's beauty exists outside time and space, compensating for the "curtain of distorting days" that temporarily obscures it. This is not to say, however, that the poem points back to the mode of Yeats's earlier love lyrics; in terms of tone and structure it is, as we have seen, anything but simplistic. Thus a seemingly simple declarative statement like "Old sages were not deceived" has, in the context of the whole poem, a nice ironic edge: one suspects that Yeats is here thinking not only of Plato and Plotinus but of another old sage—the poet himself. It is, after all, he who has not been "deceived" in his instinctive love for Maud Gonne, he who has willed into existence the grand truth that "All lives that has lived." If "so much" were really "certain," there would be no need for the sweeping assertion, for the brave effort to be convincing and convinced. **"Quarrel in Old Age"** is thus a poem of the Will rather than the Mask; it celebrates feeling itself but manages to do so without the note of self-pity found in some of the earlier Maud Gonne poems. In **"Words,"** written in 1910, the poet felt sorry for himself because his "darling" could not understand "What I have done, or what would do / In this blind bitter land. . . ." In **"Quarrel in Old Age,"** on the other hand, the poet is content to contemplate Maud Gonne's essence without asking anything in return. The "sweetness" that seemed to have "gone" returns, only it is now not Maud Gonne's sweetness but the poet's own. The reversal is complete.

Sound repetition and rhythm emphasize this reversal. In the first stanza, the speaking voice almost sputters: after the initial question the lines are run on, there are numerous anapestic feet, and the combination of end rhyme, internal rhyme, and alliteration of *f*'s, *b*'s, *t*'s, *s*'s, and *n*'s creates a cacophonous sound pattern. The fourth line deviates from the three-stress norm of the poem; it contains four stresses in what might be described as two amphimac feet (/ x /) with an unstressed middle syllable: "Fántasý / or / íncide t." Since the primary stresses in this line tend to fall on unimportant prefixes or suffixes, the rhythm itself implies the futility of the mob's fantasies.

In the second stanza the rhythm slows down and becomes emphatic. Three-stress lines continue to be the norm, but there are fewer unstressed syllables, the stresses accordingly clustering together as in "Áll líves that hás líved," "Só múch is cértain," and "Líves that lónely thíng." Voiceless stops and spirants give way to voiced ones and to liquid *l*'s.

"Quarrel in Old Age" is thus a triumph of the late style quite as much as are the Crazy Jane poems, but it has received no more than passing comment from critics. **"The Results of Thought"** has been similarly slighted, although W. H. Auden cites the entire poem as an example of Yeats's metrical mastery in his famous essay on Yeats. **"The Results of Thought"** is thematically linked to **"Quarrel in Old Age"**; again, the poet is able to cast out remorse about the "bitter glory" which has wrecked the lives of Maud Gonne and of his other women friends by a sheer act of will:

> But I have straightened out
> Ruin, wreck and wrack;
> I toiled long years and at length
> Came to so deep a thought
> I can summon back
> All their wholesome strength.

Again, memory obliterates "time's filthy load" and can "Straighten aged knees." And again Yeats does astonishing things with the three-stress line. The opening couplet, for example,

> Acquaintance, companion
> One dear brilliant woman . . .

juxtaposes two six-syllable lines, one of which contains only two words and two primary stresses while the second contains four words and four primary stresses, the implication being that the "one dear brilliant woman" (Maud Gonne) is worth dozens of acquaintances and companions. A glance at the earlier drafts of this stanza, reproduced by Jon Stallworthy in his study of the manuscript revisions, indicates how thoroughly Yeats reworked the basic material for this poem.

The "summoning back" of Maud Gonne is found again within the **"Words For Music Perhaps"** sequence itself. In the first stanza of **"Young Man's Song"** (IX), the speaker is one who cannot, in the language of **"Quarrel in Old Age,"** "forgive" his sweetheart for growing old. But, as in **"The Results of Thought,"** he manages to straighten out "Ruin, wreck and wrack." His heart opposes the rational judgment that "She will change . . . into a withered crone" and asserts that all lives that has lived:

> Uplift those eyes and throw
> Those glances unafraid:
> She would as bravely show
> Did all the fabric fade;
> No withered crone I saw
> Before the world was made.

Again, Yeats is less interested in establishing Platonic truths than in insisting that, for the lover, the image of the loved one is eternal. In the third stanza, not only the poet but all men must "bend the knee" to his "offended heart," for "the heart cannot lie." As in **"Quarrel,"** the implication is that feeling, instinct, emotion—the heart—gives us a truer view of things than can any rational philosophy. We are not, after all, very far from the Romantics in this poem.

"His Confidence" (XI), for that matter, contains the Shelleyan image of the fountain. Even thoughthe poet's heart has been hit so hard that it has broken in two, he rejoices because he knows that "out of rock, / Out of a desolate source, / Love leaps upon its course." As in Shelley's poetry, the fountain, miraculously rising from "desolate rock," is a symbol of generation, rebirth. The speaker of **"His Confidence"** does not pity himself; he rejoices in his suffering. And in the third "Young Man" poem, **"His Bargain,"** the poet insists that, unlike those crass lovers Dan and Jerry Lout who "change their loves about" at random in a never-ending circuit, his own love is beyond such whirling.

Yeats, then, was never exclusively the poet of earth and of commitment to the body. The love poetry of his final volume, the *Last Poems* of 1939, ranges from the **"Three Bushes"** sequence with its rather over-insistent phallic symbolism—even Dorothy Wellesley was amused by **"The Second Chambermaid's Song,"** referring to it as "the worm poem"—to **"A Bronze Head,"** Yeats's final Maud Gonne poem, written during the last year of his life, which has nothing whatever to do with sexual possession.

"A Bronze Head" is an occasional poem inspired by Laurence Campbell's bust of Maud Gonne in the Dublin Municipal Gallery. By 1938 all of Yeats's remorse and bitterness at his former sweetheart had been "cast out"; the quarrel in old age was over. In her memorial essay on Yeats, Maud Gonne describes her last meeting with the poet which took place in June of that year:

> One of our early dreams was a Castle of the Heroes. It was to be in the middle of a lake, a shrine of Irish tradition where only those who had dedicated their lives to Ireland might penetrate; they were to be brought there in a painted boat across the lake and might only stay for short periods of rest and inspiration. . . . Our Castle of the Heroes remained a Castle in the Air, but the last time I saw Willie at Riversdale just before he left Ireland for the last time, as we said goodbye, he, sitting in his armchair from which he could rise only with great effort, said, "Maud, we should have gone on with our Castle of Heroes, we might still do it." I was so surprised that he remembered, I could not reply. . . .

A few weeks after this visit, Yeats wrote to his friend, the painter William Rothenstein, "I wish you would find some way of making a drawing of Maud Gonne. No artist has ever drawn her, and just now she looks magnificent." But nothing ever came of this project and Yeats had to be satisfied with Campbell's "bronze head."

In the poem that commemorates this work of art, Yeats finally drops the mask of Wild Old Wicked Man completely; here the body is willingly "bruised to pleasure soul" and La Belle Dame Sans Merci is forgiven. The bronze head in the gallery is less a symbol of art than of Maud Gonne's impending death. Everything in the decor of the first stanza is redolent of the tomb—"withered and mummy-dead." The speaker wonders whether, in death, anything of Maud Gonne's spirit will remain to haunt the tomb. "Which of her forms," he asks in Stanza II, "has

shown her substance right?" The "dead" bronze head with the conventional round, staring eye of Byzantine sculpture, or her bodily incarnation—"her form all full/ As though with magnanimity of light." Perhaps, the poet decides, "substance can be composite"; perhaps, as the Hegelian philosopher McTaggart thought, both forms contain her substance so that she is at once "human, superhuman," mortal and immortal.

In the third stanza, that quality of Maud Gonne which Yeats had formerly called her "intellectual hatred" or her "opinionated mind" comes to be regarded as simply her fate. Even as a young colt, "all sleek and new," she had, the poem declares, a "vision of terror" of what she would have to live through in the future. As for her lover, "Propinquity had brought / Imagination to that pitch where it casts out / All that is not itself." In memory, in other words, the poet identifies completely with the "dark tomb-haunter," and by an act of imagination he makes her fate his own. Such identification can drive a man mad: "I had grown wild / And wandered murmuring everywhere, 'My child, my child!'" But whereas **"Among School Children"** moves in the direction of the "great-rooted blossomer," the chestnut-tree whose leaf, blossom, and bole are one and indivisible, **"A Bronze Head"** moves toward dualism:

> Or else I thought her supernatural;
> As though a sterner eye looked through her eye
> On this foul world in its decline and fall. . . .

F. A. C. Wilson [in *Yeats's Iconography*, 1960] writes of these lines, "Maud Gonne is possessed by an angel, which descants through her lips and with the terrible unsentimentality of heaven, on the degradation of spirit in the modern world." But it is not necessary to read the lines quite so allegorically: Yeats says only that it is "*As though a sterner eye looked through her eye.*" Maud Gonne is "supernatural" in the same way that the lady of the Elizabethan sonneteers is supernatural—a supreme being, a goddess, a sublime spirit. In the last stanza, Yeats implies that Maud Gonne ultimately has the last word. She is beyond criticism, a heroic figure removed from "this foul world in its decline and fall." Many of Yeats's earlier Maud Gonne poems celebrated her beauty, her strength, her pride, her arrogant brilliance. But in **"A Bronze Head"** Yeats surprisingly calls her "a most *gentle* woman." The "great tomb-haunter," an image of transcendence, here replaces the "great-rooted blossomer," Yeats's symbol for Unity of Being.

"I must be satisfied with my heart," the poet announces in the most famous poem of his last years, **"The Circus Animals' Desertion."** The circus animals, the stilts and ladders of poetic language, the outward shows are stripped away, revealing the disreputable origins of poetic inspiration:

> A mound of refuse or the sweepings of a street,
> Old kettles, old bottles, and a broken can,
> Old iron, old bones, old rags, that raving slut
> Who keeps the till. Now that my ladder's gone,

I must lie down where all the ladders start,
In the foul rag-and-bone shop of the heart.

This passionate declaration of the poet's allegiance to what he calls in **"Remorse for Intemperate Speech"** "my fanatic heart," might serve as an epigraph to a volume of Yeats's love poetry, for it is the *heart* rather than the *soul* or the *body* that is at the center of the poems. The new Yeats *Concordance* bears out this generalization in quantitative terms: the word *heart* is listed as one of the ten most frequently found words in the *Variorum* text of Yeats's poems, and *heart* occurs at least twice as often as either *soul* or *body* not only in the earlier poetry but in such later volumes as *The Winding Stair* as well.

For Yeats the "joyous life"—what Richard Ellmann has called "secular blessedness"—can never be the domain of the Soul alone; such poems as **"A Dialogue of Self and Soul"** and **"Vacillation"** make this point emphatic. But the self in the former poem is by no means equivalent to the Body; its emblem, the sword, is covered with "Flowers from I know not what embroidery—/ Heart's purple," and in Part VII of "Vacillation" the debate is specifically between Soul and Heart. Again, in **"Sailing to Byzantium,"** he prays to the holy sages to "Consume my *heart* away; sick with desire," and Helen of Troy is characterized in **"The Tower"** as the woman who had "all living *hearts* betrayed." So too, in **"Words for Music Perhaps,"** the emphasis is less on what Denis Donoghue calls "the irreconcilable claims of soul and body" than on what Crazy Jane herself calls "the *heart*'s truth." The lover of **"Young Man's Song"** insists that "the *heart* cannot lie," and he is willing to kneel in the dirt "To my offended *heart* / Until it pardon me." Transformed into the old man of **"Love's Loneliness,"** he describes how in old age "Dread has followed longing, / And our *hearts* are torn."

From first to last, Yeats's love poetry centers on the "fanatic *heart*." But the milieu of the heart changes. In *The Wind Among the Reeds* of 1899, the poet is likely to refer to his "out-worn *heart* in a time out-worn," or to his "trembling *heart*," or he complains that words are "hurtling through" his *heart* like lightning. The wisdom of the later love poetry is that, even when the heart is broken in two as it is in **"His Confidence,"** the poet can rejoice in his knowledge that "out of rock, / Out of a desolate source, / Love leaps upon its course." Love, even imperfectly returned, cannot die; all lives that has lived. It is this faith that places the Yeatsian "I" in a very different world from that inhabited by Lady Chatterley or, for that matter, by Donne's enlightened lovers. The "religion of the heart" of the later Maud Gonne poems suggests that, for all Crazy Jane's insistence on "bodily lowliness," Yeats himself knew that "Love has pitched his mansion" in more than one spot.

Joyce Carol Oates (essay date 1969)

SOURCE: "Yeats: Violence, Tragedy, Mutability," in *Bucknell Review,* Vol. XVII, No. 3, December 1969, pp. 1-17.

[*In the following excerpt, Oates asserts that the violent events and "farfetched and grotesque" images of Yeats's work are a result of his view of life as a dynamic chaos that needs to be shaped and controlled through art.*]

In his last poems Yeats moves toward a contemplative and dispassionate assertion of the joy that can arise out of tragedy, and the poem that ends his career, **"Under Ben Bulben,"** leaves us with the image of a cold eye looking upon life and death equally, unmoved, like the golden bird of **"Sailing to Byzantium"** that sings equally of what is past, or passing, or to come. Yet the jagged tonalities of the last poems will not be reconciled by the theoretical claim for a dispassionate unity, just as certain poems, examined individually, will not support their apparent themes. Yeats' genius lies not in his ability to hammer his multiple thoughts into unity, but rather in his faithful accounting of the impossibility—which may lead one to the edge of madness—of bringing together aesthetic theory and emotional experience. His final work is characterized by irony, but more importantly by an incomplete blend of the "tragic" and the "mutable." What is tragic is intended to transcend or insome way justify the suffering Yeats or his legendary *personae* have experienced, and takes its most frequent immortality in the shape of a work of art; what is mutable is all that is left out, all that will not fit in—in short, life itself, the material of art itself. . . .

In **"Prometheus Unbound"** (1932) Yeats states surprisingly that it is not Blake, after all, who had most shaped his life, but Shelley: a visionary, a 'psychic' being, but an unconverted man. And he speaks of Balzac changing men's lives, saving Yeats himself from the obsessive pursuit of absolute and external beauty which, to strike a balance, would have required "hatred as absolute." His art has been carefully imagined, carefully worked and reworked; legendary, archetypal beings have been given new life in order to transform the secular age into something approaching holiness, or at any rate into an age which can, through the study of Yeats' monumental verse, appreciate the passing of holiness. Yet the effort seems out of proportion to the primary, fundamental argument of the poems. For they are continually dehumanizing their subject even to the point of thwarting the demands of a gay tragedy in **"The Gyres"** Yeats insists upon the joyousness of tragedy, he insists that those witnesses to the modern chaos look on and laugh "in tragic joy," without signs or tears:

> For painted forms or boxes of make-up
> In ancient tombs I sighed, but not again;
> What matter? Out of cavern comes a voice,
> And all it knows is that one word "Rejoice!"

The refrain "What matter?" is set against the vision of a world in which "irrational streams of blood are staining earth," where "Empedocles has thrown all things about." The soul of man has coarsened, approaching the darkness of nothing; yet the gyres will bring round all things once again, disinterring the dead. In **"Lapis Lazuli,"** which Yeats believed to be one of his most successful poems, the theme of Nietzschean gaiety is continued. We must believe that our sufferings are enacted upon a tragic stage, and that our human gaiety transfigures "all that dread." The poem ends, like the "Ode on a Grecian Urn," with a contemplation of a work of art, the Chinamen carved in lapis lazuli, whom Yeats imagines as staring down upon the tragic scene of temporal life with "ancient, glittering eyes" that are gay.

The basic difficulty with this position is its abstracting of the human, its forcing upon animate life a certain theoretic and ultimately epistemological shape. For no matter what aesthetic position we finally give to Yeats, the very fact of his various responses to formal unity and "profane perfection" will contradict it. Thus these poems, insisting upon an impersonal logic that transcends human suffering, can be read in the context of certain other poems and plays as ironic statements, partial statements, to be qualified or questioned by the poet. So long as the world is conceived dynamically one·cannot come to rest, either in a piece of lapis lazuli or in a formal, completed tragedy. Like Wallace Stevens, who inherited many of Yeats' preoccupations with the duality of man's imaginative response to the world, Yeats knows that "We keep coming back and coming back / To·the real: to the hotel instead of the hymns / That fall upon it out of the wind."

Approaching death inspires the poet to a frenzy of self-fabrication. He will "make his soul," compelling it to take on the colossal tragic shapes of Lear and Cuchulain, and the "second-best" shape of the wild old wicked man In the form of a pilgrim he journeys to the purgatorial world of the dead, only to be told in reply to his questions *Fol de rol de rolly O.* The knowledge available to man, and which becomes in turn the knowledge that the poet will give back to the world, is nonsense, verbal nonsense—*Fol de rol de rolly O.* The formal perfection of tragedy is now lost. Ironically, the poet understands in **"The Municipal Gallery Revisited,"** in the very place of formal images and "deep-rooted things," that the mathematical movement of the gyres does not promise any human salvation, any human meaning at all. It is the earth itself that is lost:

> And I am in despair that time may bring
> Approve patterns of women or of men
> But not that selfsame excellence again.

Two difficult poems, **"The Statues"** and **"News for the Delphic Oracle,"** offer us twin and warring interpretations of life. What is reality? Yeats' central question, his maddening question, deals with the extension and limitation of reality, man's power, man's will—for as he states arrogantly in **"The Tower,"** "Death and life were not / Till man made up the whole, / Made lock, stock and barrel / Out of his bitter soul"—in confrontation with the silence of nothingness, the ultimate chaos which has no meaning and is not concerned with meaning. Not human evil, but inhuman chaos, is for Yeats as it was for Shakespeare the supreme horror. Therefore, what lies beyond the human imagination, being horrible, must be constantly given a shape, "named."

In **"The Statues"** we are told of artists, men that "with a mallet or a chisel" modelled the speculative philosophers'

calculations, and "put down / All Asiatic vague immensities." It is not knowledge that redeems, for "knowledge increases unreality"; it is, rather, the power of the creative imagination, whether working in stone or with words or with certain noble men of Ireland that is important. The switch to "We Irish" is surprising, even in a poem by Yeats, since the poem has dealt with so vast a landscape, and signals the poet's ironically arrogant conclusion to the metaphysical problem he has brought up. Born into an ancient race but thrown "upon a filthy modern tide," the Irish can yet find it possible to climb to their proper level in order to "trace the lineaments of a plummet-measured face"—that is, to read with their fingers the shape of a heroic face or personality, to trace in the darkness an archetypal vision that will redeem them, since passion is equal to creation: "passion could bring character enough," and brings the living to press their lips against a work of art, as if it were indeed living. Here the living, the Irish, are to remake themselves in the image of a colossal vision. It is formlessness that is to be conquered, a climbing out of the spawning fury of the modern world. [Peter Ure sees the poem as embodying the "God" or force or "dramatist" of history, history being like the image of the dancer—its soul of meaning one with its body of accomplishment. See *Yeats*, 1963.]

"News for the Delphic Oracle," however, imagines a pastoral dimension where all the "golden codgers" lay, old men refined of the mire and fury of human blood, where the dew itself is silver. Everyone sighs, in this paradise of completed forms, of stilled gestures. Plotinus, having swum the buffeting seas of **"The Delphic Oracle Upon Plotinus"** (*Words for Music Perhaps*), now stretches and yawns. These "Innocents" relive their ancient patterns, "dreaming back through their lives," until the burden of their humanity is finally thrown off. Like the spirits of **"Byzantium,"** they have achieved "death-in-life," "life-in-death." But the third stanza focusses upon the union of Peleus and Thetis, the union of bodies and of beautiful parts of bodies. Thetis' "limbs are delicate as an eyelid" and Peleus' eyes are blinded with tears. The "intolerable" music of Pan falls upon them and suddenly the poem breaks into a confusion of jarring images, of finite, joyous, profane parts that contradict the world of golden forms:

> Foul goat-head, brutal arm appear,
> Belly, shoulder, bum,
> Flash fishlike; nymphs and satyrs
> Copulate in the foam.

The poem ends with this violent activity, an activity that hardly seems willed by human beings so much as by parts of bodies, the frenzy of the flesh one with the foaming sea. It is a stunning reversal of the poem's opening, where the "golden" people lay sighing in their completion. Their choir of love with its "sacred laurel crowns" and its Pythagorean beauty contrasts feebly with the music of Pan, felt as intolerable.

That the static resolution of human complexity cannot be sustained is examined in the famous Byzantium poems, the **"Byzantium"** of *The Winding Stair* taken as a qual-ification of **"Sailing to Byzantium"** of *The Tower*. For here purgation effects its magic only at night, when the images of the day recede. Though a golden bird can crow like the cocks of Hades (imagined as real birds?), it is curiously enough "embittered" by the moon—though why the miraculous bird should be embittered by the chang-ing, subjective moon, since it is immune to mortality, is puzzling. And the poem itself ends with images that yet "fresh images beget," the rage and wilderness of the foam-ing sea, which no amount of human artifice can transform into art. So the poem works itself out, like **"News for the Delphic Oracle,"** as a deeply ironic turning upon itself, a drama of the challenge of two opposing dimensions, whose tragic irony is visible only to the poet himself. The dialectic is grasped only by the poet: the world of artifice is immune to change, and does not exist; the world of nature is immune to abstraction, and exists only in dying generations, without control or consciousness.

For at the core of [Yeats's] mature art is the puzzled insistence upon the formlessness of all substance, and the insubstantial nature of all form—in short, a vision of human tragedy destroyed by mutability.

—*Joyce Carol Oates*

Therefore Yeats achieves, even through his intensely au-tobiographical and confessional poems, a rendering of the self's basic impersonality, at the point at which it enters art. Here he finds, to his distress, the very negation of the younger Yeats. For at the core of his mature art is the puzzled insistence upon the formlessness of all substance, and the insubstantial nature of all form—in short, a vision of human tragedy destroyed by mutability. It is no won-der that events in his work are violent, his images far-fetched and grotesque. Very little has been said about the madness of some of Yeats' images. His superhuman Cuchulain will die at the hands of a beggar, for twelve pennies, and will find himself transformed into something wildly antithetical to his soul:

> There floats out there
> The shape that I shall take when I am dead,
> My soul's first shape, a soft feathery shape,
> And is not that a strange shape for the soul
> Of a great fighting-man?

Cuchulain is answered only by the senile muttering of the Blind Man, who is trying to behead him. When Cuchulain dies he dies into song, the singing of a bird; his symbolic death "dies" us into the modern age, its music being that of some Irish Fair. A Street-Singer tells of what the harlot sang to the beggar-man, recalling "what centuries have passed" since these heroic men lived. Cuchulain himself

wakes in the poem of 1939, "Cuchulain Comforted," where the "violent and famous" man must sew his shroud in the company of convicted cowards who have died in fear. He becomes one of them, he who in life had been their op-posite; he sings with them, changing his throat into the throat of a bird, for only in such profound humiliation can his life grow sweeter. It is a conclusion like that of *The Herne's Egg*—ironic and ambiguous. "I think pro-found philosophy must come from terror," Yeats says in the essay-broadcast, "Modern Poetry," of 1936. Whatever geometrical structure he has imagined for man and histo-ry, whatever fate appears to control individuals, it is ul-timately the abyss that silences all questions:

> An abyss opens under our feet; inherited convictions, the pre-suppositions of our thoughts . . . drop into the abyss. Whether we will or no we must ask the ancient questions: Is there reality anywhere? Is there a God? Is there a Soul? We cry with the Indian Sacred Book: "They have put a golden stopper into the neck of the bottle; pull it! Let out reality!"(*Essays and Introductions*)

"The Man and the Echo" is another of Yeats' poems about death. Intensely personal, almost desperate, it shouts its secret in a place of stone:

> All that I have said and done,
> Now that I am old and ill,
> Turns into a question till
> I lie awake night after night
> And never get the questions right.

He questions his personal role in history, his effect upon certain people's lives. To what extent was he responsible for Irishmen shot by the English? (Auden's famous line in "In Memory of W. B. Yeats," "poetry makes nothing happen," is a curiously simplistic resolution of Yeats' specific doubts; one of the crucial points about Yeats' life and work is that poetry *does* make something happen.) All seems to him evil; simply to die would be to shirk "the spiritual intellect's great work." What is desired is a single, clear view that arranges an entire life. He wants to stand in judgment on his own soul, yet he ends by asking, "What do we know but that we face / One another in this place?"; and even this beautiful, helpless thought is de-stroyed by the sudden plundering of nature:

> Up there some hawk or owl has struck,
> Dropping out of sky or rock.
> A stricken rabbit is crying out,
> And its cry distracts my thought.

Understanding himself a great poet, having conceived of himself in a great tradition, Yeats is nevertheless distracted by so commonplace and brutal an event—it is reality it-self, the impersonal and gratuitous, the ever-changing, the unheroic, that cheats him of a final form. A violent ges-ture is the final gesture, simply because it silences all that has come before. Violence will disarm the tragic player, whether it rises out of his own body or out of the body of nature. It reminds us of the quiet, gentle ending of the ambitious and proud **"The Tower,"** when Yeats' death will seem no more than the clouds of the sky at twilight "Or a bird's sleepy cry / Among the deepening shades."

The most the poet can hope for is a kind of equanimity with the powerful chaos of nature. In **"High Talk"** and **"The Circus Animals' Desertion,"** Yeats dismisses his creations as "all metaphor," "those stilted boys, that burnished chariot, / Lion and woman and the Lord knows what."

> Malachi Stilt-Jack am I, whatever I learned has run wild,
> From collar to collar, from stilt to stilt, from father to child.
> All metaphor, Malachi, stilts and all. A barnacle goose
> Far up in the stretches of night; night splits and the dawn breaks loose;
> I, through the terrible novelty of light, stalk on, stalk on;
> Those great sea-horses bare their teeth and laugh at the dawn.

> **("High Talk")**

Here the poet's ego manages a difficult balance with the prodigious and unthinking forms of nature. The barnacle goose has the magical power to break loose the dawn, which will take place regardless of the poet's words; the poet's triumph is to "stalk on" through the "terrible novelty of light," keeping his own place, his own proper dark, while the sea-horses—perfect images of energy, like the nymphs and satyrs in the foam—laugh at the breaking of a new day. The poet's activity, his stalking, is a kind of animal activity; he must imitate the animals in order to partake of their power. [It is difficult to interpret the poem as a humanistic work, imagining the poet successfully imposing his will upon the cosmos itself. See B. L. Reid, *William Butler Yeats: The Lyric of Tragedy*, 1961. Reid sees the poet's passion stretching until it "dominates fate and creates its own world."]

One of Yeats' most beautiful poems is **"The Circus Animals' Desertion."** Here he confesses that his own "animals" are no more than emblematic; they have not the power of real animals, real energy. Their existence has come from the poet's own bitterness, his starvation for life, the dreams that resulted from his own deprivation. "Heart-mysteries" give rise to dreams that, in turn, enchant the poet, until he dreams several moves from reality—he himself betraying the mighty Cuchulain, for it is ultimately the symbolic Cuchulain that engrosses Yeats, his own creation: "Players and painted stage took all my love, / And not those things that they were emblems of."

The poet is able to make such images masterful and complete, simply because they are images and not reality. He creates them out of the "purity" of his mind, having refined them out of their grosser origins. Thus, the sublimative poetic process is seen to be a betrayal of nature, or an inability to deal with nature itself. Yeats' statement of 1900 (in **"The Symbolism of Poetry"**) that "Solitary men make and unmake mankind, and even the world itself, for

does not 'the eye altering alter all?'" seems the remark of a very young and ambitious artist; it is the central doctrine of Yeats' poetry, yet it cannot bear a confrontation with the dynamic world. When the world and the self collide, the marketable drama is epistemological but, more than that, it is a moral confrontation—jarring and devastating to the ego. In his essay **"Prometheus Unbound"** Yeats speaks of the incomplete art of Shelley, where "sex is sublimated to an unearthly receptivity"; the poet is compelled to imagine whatever "seemed dark, destructive, indefinite" [*Essays and Introductions*]. Shelley is like Beardsley, who was under a compulsion to include something obscene in his drawings: "Something compels me to sacrifice to Priapus." The artist, acting upon his own sense of autonomy, is nevertheless forced to "secret the obscene" in some corner of his art; sublimation is a possibility only when the artist denies his basic self. Sublimation is a "ladder" but when the ladder is gone, the poet must acknowledge the origin of all his art: "In the foul rag-and-bone shop of the heart."

Desmond Pacey (essay date 1970)

SOURCE: "Children in the Poetry of Yeats," in *The Dalhousie Review*, Vol. 50, No. 2, Summer 1970, pp. 233-48.

[*In the following excerpt, Pacey discusses the evolution of Yeats's allusions to children from those of a Romantic modified by touches of "irony" and "humour" to those of a realist who recognized that children are not ideal creatures but are in fact human beings with bad as well as good traits.*]

Yeats' multiplicity of powerful poems about sexual love, old age, and Irish society has distracted attention from his poetic treatment of children. Apart from a number of articles and essays on **"Among Schoolchildren"**, the subject remains literally unexplored. And yet four of Yeats' finest poems—**"A Prayer for My Son"**, **"A Prayer for My Daughter"**, and **"The Dolls"**, and especially **"Among Schoolchildren"** (which many readers consider his greatest single poem)—are specifically about children, and there are many references to children and childhood scattered throughout his *Collected Poems*.

The strongest single impression with which one comes away from reading Yeats' poems on children, and his references to them, is of the consistency, clearsightedness, and realism of his attitudes. Although he may have been, as he has said, a Romantic writing when Romanticism had reached its most extravagant phase, he is seldom if ever prone to Romantic exaggeration in his treatment of childhood—nor, for that matter, to any other exaggerations. Attitudes to children in literature—as they are intelligently discussed, for example in Peter Coveney's *Poor Monkey* or in Leslie Fiedler's essay "The Eye of Innocence" in his *No! in Thunder*—have generally fallen into three groups: the eighteenth-century rationalist view, which saw the child as a small adult to be regulated as quickly as possible into rational and moral perfection; the Puritan Christian view, which saw the child as a miserable sinner in desperate need of salvation; and the Romantic view, expressed most clearly by Blake and Wordsworth but given premonitory utterance by Vaughan and Traherne in the seventeenth century, which saw the child as innocent, intuitively wise, spontaneous, happy, perceptive, sensitive, or "trailing clouds of glory". Of these three attitudes, it need scarcely be said, Yeats' comes closest to the Romantic, but he is singularly free from its more extreme manifestations.

This is the more remarkable when we recall that Yeats came to maturity when the Romantic cult of the child was at its apogee of decadence, the last decades of the nineteenth century. Of those decades, Coveney writes: "Writers began to draw on the general sympathy for childhood that had been diffused; but for patently subjective reasons, their interest in childhood serves not as a means for integration of experience, but creates a barrier of nostalgia and regret between childhood and the potential responses of adult life. The child becomes a means of escape from the pressures of adult adjustment . . ." (*Poor Monkey*). Marie Corelli, J. M. Barrie, A. E. Housman, and Hugh Walpole all provide examples of this escapist tendency; in Yeats—at least in the mature Yeats—it is found not at all. Where, as in **"Among Schoolchildren"**, he is momentarily tempted into this self-pitying nostalgia, he rapidly overcomes it by self-depreciating irony, and goes on to one of the most triumphant examples in literary history of the "integration of experience", the famous final apostrophe of that poem.

As we might expect, it is in his early poems that Yeats most nearly approximates the stock Romantic attitudes towards children. Even here, however, the stress is not so much on the more doubtful of the Romantic concepts—innocence, wisdom, religious sensibility—as on the more observable, provable features of childhood: its fragility and vulnerability. The first reference is in the first poem in the first section of *Collected Poems,* and it is to "the stammering schoolboy" who awkwardly reads aloud in class some story of heroic adventure. This first reference is characteristic and indicative: Yeats was always aware of the pressures which orthodox systems of education impose upon the child. The boy's stammer is an objective correlative which sums up all his nervousness, his shyness, his sense of being entangled in some world he never made; and the emphasis is not on the boy's inherent superiority to adults but on his sense of inferiority, even if it is implied that that sense of inferiority is baseless. (In a late poem, **"A Dialogue of Self and Soul"**, Yeats was to enshrine this same perception in the memorable phrase "the ignominy of boyhood".)

The next reference to childhood, however, is not so admirable, and is one of the few examples of Yeats' falling into the trap of Romantic exaggeration. The allusion occurs in that most awkward and ugly of all Yeats' poems, **"Ephemera"**, and it reads "when the poor tired child, Passion, falls asleep". In the background of that line lie many of the clichés of Victorian poetry and fiction, those

scenes in which pitiful children die or innocent children fall asleep while maternal tears cascade upon the pillow-slip.

Another Victorian stereotype, that of the sensitive child who must escape from the harsh world of reality to some land of faery or Treasure Island of romance, occurs in **"The Stolen Child",** with its monotonous, sentimental refrain:

> *Come away, O human child!*
> *To the waters and the wild*
> *With a faery, hand in hand,*
> *For the world's more full of weeping*
> *Than you can understand.*

Even in this weak poem, however, the sentimentality is checked by irony: Yeats makes the faeries faintly ridiculous by having them whisper in the ears of "slumbering trout" to "Give them unquiet dreams", by having them lean from ferns "that drop their tears / over the young streams", and by having them foolishly congratulate themselves on the fact that "The solemn-eyed" child will

> . . . . hear no more the lowing
> Of the calves on the warm hillside
> Or the kettle on the hob
> Sing peace into his breast,
> Or see the brown mice bob
> Round and round the oatmeal-chest.

This implied endorsation of the pleasures of the real world, indeed, transposes the whole effect of the poem, and what began as a piece of sentimental escapism ends in an acceptance of familiar, domestic reality.

The Romantic concept of the spontaneous, happy child finds expression in **"The Meditation of the Old Fisherman"**, but here again it is decisively modified. The old fisherman who sees the waves "dance by my feet like children at play" and dreams nostalgically of the days "When I was a boy with never a crack in my heart", is guilty of the falsification of experience, of deliberate self-delusion. But the poem is a dramatic utterance: it is the fisherman, not Yeats, who asserts that "the waves were more gay", the Junes warmer, the herring more plentiful, and the girls more beautiful in the halcyon days of his boyhood.

Yeats himself came closer to falsification in **"The Ballad of Moll Magee"**, one of the many Romantic and Victorian poems dealing with the death of a child and the woes of its grief-stricken mother. Perhaps it was a consciousness of this fact that led Yeats to dismiss this poem, in a letter to John O'Leary, as a "mere experiment". Once again, however, romantic illusions are not allowed full play: the "little childer" to whom Moll tells her story are not romantic innocents but very real sadists—she has to begin and end her story by begging them not to throw stones at her!

In a rather similar fashion, Yeats manages to redeem **"A Cradle Song"** from the excesses of that popular nineteenth-century genre, the sentimental lullaby. Here, however, it is humour, rather than realism, which is the saving salt. The angels who stoop above the infant's bed are said to be doing so because "They weary of trooping / With the whimpering dead." Too charitably, perhaps, I take that as a bit of black humour—an attitude, however, to which Yeats himself leads some confirmation by the explicit humorous gaiety of the second stanza:

> God's laughing in Heaven
> To see you so good,
> The Sailing Seven
> Are gay with his mood.

After such comic relief, we are almost ready to swallow the unabashed sentimentality of the third and final stanza:

> I sigh that kiss you,
> For I must own
> That I shall miss you
> When you have grown.

There is a matter-of factness about that stanza, a kind of honest platitudinousness, which does something to redeem it. We know it could be so much worse in, say, Coventry Patmore.

There is at least one instance, however, where Yeats is guilty of what Coveney calls the late nineteenth-century practice of drawing on "the general sympathy for childhood", or of what I. A. Richards might have called using the child merely to elicit a stock response. It occurs in one of Yeats' most flatulent poems, **"The Lover Tells of the Rose in his Heart"**. There, declaring that "All things uncomely and broken, all things worn out and old" are "wronging your image that blossoms a rose in the deep of my heart", he suddenly, for no apparent reason except that the weeping child was a guaranteed source of facile emotion in the late Victorian period, brings in "The cry of a child by the roadway". The mature Yeats would never have allowed himself to indulge in such an unmotivated and unspecific allusion.

There are some other references to children in the early poems of Yeats, but they add nothing to what we have said of his attitudes. In these early poems we see Yeats accepting in their main outlines the Romantic and occasionally even the Victorian attitudes towards children, but always modifying them to some extent and usually to a decisive extent. Irony, realism, and humour almost always are invoked, singly or in combination, to stop the poem short of the worst excesses of idealizing or sentimentalizing of childhood. In the poems of Yeats' maturity, the poems written after 1900, the relics of the Romantic or Victorian stereotypes are very rare indeed: there is a new honesty, a new realism, in both the content and style of his allusions to children. At the same time, the main ingredient of his attitude, his tender concern for childish fragility and vulnerability, persists and is indeed strengthened.

The first hint of the mature manner comes in that poem which in so many ways marks a turning-point in Yeats'

poetic career, **"Adam's Curse"**. It comes as a mere aside, when the "beautiful mild woman" replies:

> "To be born woman is to know—
> Although they do not talk of it at school—
> That we must labour to be beautiful."

The hint is not so much in what is said—although the reference to the obliviousness of orthodox education to the real conditions of human life reflects one of Yeats' deepest convictions, and points forward to **"Among Schoolchildren"**—as in the tone and manner of expression. The tone is no longer rhetorical, nostalgic, or sentimental: rather it is sarcastic, off-hand, mordant, and dry. The words are not richly sensuous nor in any sense ornamental—they are the words of ordinary speech, in the order and rhythm of speech. There is implied a whole effort to get away from conventional attitudes and opinions, and to see things as they really are. The mood is closer to Swift than to Tennyson.

This far more thoroughgoing realism, verging now towards bitterness as in the early poems it had sometimes come dangerously close to sentimentality, is found in **"The Coming of Wisdom with Time"**. In this poem it is implied that, if childhood is indeed a time of relative happiness, its happiness is deceptive and treacherous:

> Though leaves are many, the root is one;
> Through all the lying days of my youth
> I swayed my leaves and flowers in the sun;
> Now I may wither into the truth.

We have here a strong premonition of the danger against which Yeats was to struggle—but struggle successfully—in all his late, great poems about childhood: the danger of exaggerating the tragic dimension of human experience, of indulging in easy cynicism.

The balance tips ominously towards facile cynicism in the pair of poems **"To a Child Dancing in the Wind"** and **"Two Years Later"**. Here the innocence of the child is seen rather as ignorance: the vulnerable child can dance and tumble out her hair in spontaneous joy only because she does not recognize her own vulnerability and the power of the destructive forces which surround her. To accept life, to see the world as ultimately beneficent, is to indulge in dreams; the reality is suffering and the end is tragedy:

> O you will take whatever's offered
> And dream that all the world's a friend,
> Suffer as your mother suffered,
> Be as broken in end.

Yeats, however, recognized this danger of facile cynicism in one of the best stanzas of one of his best poems, **"A Prayer for my Daughter"**:

> My mind, because the minds that I have loved,
> The sort of beauty that I have approved,
> Prosper but little, has dried up of late,

> Yet knows that to be choked with hate
> May well be of all evil chances chief.
> If there's no hatred in a mind
> Assault and battery of the wind
> Can never tear the linnet from the leaf.

This poem illustrates how Yeats did succeed in making his best poems about children a means to the integration of experience. His sense of the little girl's vulnerability, so powerfully expressed in the early references to a howling storm, the levelling wind, the screaming Atlantic gale, the flooded stream, the frenzied drum and "the murderous innocence of the sea", is complemented by his later affirmation of the values which can cushion her against the shocks of disaster: modest beauty, natural kindness, courtesy, self-reliance, custom, ceremony, and the "radical innocence" of the human soul. Here Yeats, in his emphasis upon order, discipline, and self-restraint, comes closer to the eighteenth-century conception of the child than to the Romantic conception: the child is seen as a delicate growth which needs the shelter of social and civilized values, rather than as a beautiful blossom which society will warp and wither.

If **"A Prayer for my Daughter"** illustrates the greater balance and profundity of the mature Yeats' treatment of the child, it also illustrates the advances in his mature style. The predominantly run-on lines of the first two stanzas create an effect of frightening speed; then the poem, as if by a supreme effort of will, a deliberate refusal to be stampeded into panic, slows down to a grave and dignified pace. The image of the wind, introduced in the first line, recurs several times in the first and second stanzas, in the "assault and battery of the wind" in the seventh stanza, in the "old bellows full of angry wind" in the eighth, in the "every windy quarter howl" in the ninth—and is conspicuous by its absence in the tenth and last, where the laurel tree of custom spreads its branches in a windless sky. Thus the wind, which in the first stanza was seen as all powerful and triumphantly destructive—what protection is there in a cradle-hood and coverlid against a wind that can level haystacks and roofs?—is gradually cut down, first, to the figure of an angry but impotent boxer or blustering petty criminal, next to the ridiculous form of an old bellows, then to a silly howler that can frighten no one, and finally is stilled altogether. Counterpointing the diminishing image of the wind is the steadily enlarging image of the tree: in the first stanza "Gregory's wood" is dismissed as "no obstacle" to the wind; in the second stanza the branches of the elm scream and dance in agony; in the sixth stanza the growing girl is seen as "a flourishing hidden tree" and as "some green laurel / Rooted in one dear perpetual place"; in the seventh stanza, the tree has become a safe refuge for the linnet, which the wind cannot dislodge; and in the final stanza the laurel tree, proudly spreading its branches, has defeated the wind entirely. The poem, like all Yeats' greatest poems, is a profoundly humanistic, life-affirming document. The wind, by the end of the poem, has come to symbolize all those evil forces which assault humanity, the tree to symbolize all the human values which staunchly withstand them; and there is no doubt which has triumphed.

"A Prayer for my Son" is at first glance less humanistic and more religious. Again an infant is being threatened by evil forces, but this time the forces are supernatural— "devilish things"—rather than natural, and, accordingly, supernatural powers are invoked to protect the child. "A strong ghost" is bidden to stand at the head of his bed, and Christ, the all-powerful God who has nevertheless known what it is to be a helpless infant, is asked to do the bidding. The religious figures of the poem, however, are very human persons, and the poem is at least as much a tribute to the fidelity of human love as a plea for divine intervention. Christ, "wailing upon a woman's knee", is said to have known "All that worst ignominy / Of flesh and bone", and His parents are deliberately referred to as "a woman and a man", who, when He was hunted by Herod's servants, protected Him "with human love."

This poem is a further instance of the tact and skill with which Yeats manages his material, so disposing and modulating it that it is saved from excess. The experience upon which the poem is based, detailed by Yeats on page 16 of the 1962 edition of *A Vision,* is, to say the least, bizarre, and to a sceptical mind plainly incredible:

> A little after my son's birth I came home to confront my wife with the statement "Michael is ill". A smell of burnt feathers had announced what she and the doctor had hidden. When regular communication was near its end and my work of study and arrangement begun, I was told that henceforth the Frustrators would attack my health and that of my children, and one afternoon, knowing from the smell of burnt feathers that one of my children would be ill within three hours, I felt before I could recover self-control the medieval helpless horror at witchcraft. I can discover no apparent difference between a natural and supernatural smell, except that the natural smell comes and goes gradually while the other is suddenly there and then as suddenly gone.

This does not seem a very promising basis for a tolerable twentieth-century poem, but Yeats brings it off. He does so by introducing into the strange episode so much of the familiar world. The references to the child turning in bed, to his morning meal, to the mother's very human need of sleep, to Christ's wailing upon His mother's knee, to Joseph and Mary hurrying like any anxious parents "through the smooth and rough"—these references anchor the poem in the ordinary world and give credibility and human relevance to an experience which we might otherwise reject as utterly fantastic.

Contributing to the same effect is the diction of the poem. Throughout, with one or two conspicuous exceptions to act as foils, Yeats uses the simplest, strongest, most familiar words. Think, for example, of what a subtle but fatal alteration of effect would have resulted from the use of "mighty" rather than "strong" as the adjective for the ghost, of "wail" rather than "cry", of "need of sleep" rather than "fill of sleep". Words like "fist", "devilish things", "simplest want", "knee", "flesh and bone", "servants", "a woman and a man" all humanize and domesticate the otherwise *outré* situation.

Indeed, the more closely one examines this poem the more one is impressed by its subtlety, ambiguity, and profundity. It is called a prayer, and apostrophizes Christ, but it ends by praising human love and by affirming that it was by the patient fidelity of his human parents that Christ himself was saved. It is, thus, a prayer that provides its own answer: we are felt with the clear implication that the child's strongest defence against whatever devilish things assail him is not any strong ghost nor supernatural agent but his own natural, human parents. **"A Prayer for my Son"** is only an apparent exception to Yeats' persistent humanism.

Equally humanistic in its effect is **"The Dolls"**. Here again is a poem which far transcends the occasion (the rumoured pregnancy of a mistress) which is said to have prompted it. It is a satire on those who prefer the deadly perfection of dolls to the lively imperfection of children, and it is closely related to one of the themes of **"Among School-children"**: that true meaning is to be found in organic growth rather than in static perfection. The dolls, because they do not decay with age (one of them, "being kept for show", has "lived" for many generations), and because they do not cry and defecate, think that they are superior to the human baby which their makers have suddenly produced in their midst: one of them calls the infant an insult, another calls it "a noisy and filthy thing" which will disgrace them. With a beautiful twist of irony, Yeats has the mother of the human child accept the view of the dolls, and humbly apologize to her husband for her fecundity: "My dear, my dear, O dear, / It was an accident." This, of course, suggests another of Yeats' persistent themes, that many good things come by chance, that wisdom is a butterfly and not a gloomy bird of prey.

This poem is so full of irony and ambiguity that it is odd that recent critics, so fond of these qualities in an age made tolerable only by ironic ambiguity of vision, have not paid more respectful attention to it. The proud dolls are "in the doll-maker's house": in other words, for all their pride they are only creatures of a creature, occupants of a house only on the sufferance of its rightful owners. Although they accuse the infant of being noisy, one of them bawls and the other "out-screams the whole shelf"; although the dolls accuse the child of filthiness, they are "kept for show" and thus owe any cleanliness they may claim to the efforts of those who keep them; although they feel superior to humanity, their proudest boast is that "There's not a *man* can report / Evil of this place"; and although they think they are so very knowing, they have no knowledge of the generation of children and think that the man and woman have merely *brought* the child here. The woman, instead of being proud of her capacity to generate true life, allows the dolls to convince her that her child is somehow disgraceful, and apologizes to her equally troubled husband. The relevance of all this, at a time when some people are ready to elevate the computer over the human brain, or the electronic media over the humanly imperfect book, scarcely needs pointing out. Nor do I need to describe in any detail how the poem illustrates the balanced nature of the mature Yeats' attitude to childhood: children *are* noisy and filthy, but they are also alive, and thus can grow as dolls can not.

If **"The Dolls"** has suffered undue neglect at the hands of the critics, **"Among Schoolchildren"** has suffered the opposite fate. So many essays in exegesis have been devoted to it that, if it were not so central to my theme, there would be a temptation to omit it altogether. Discussion, however, will be comparatively brief.

With all due deference to the insights of Cleanth Brooks, John Wain, Frank Kermode and Thomas Parkinson, I believe that the single most illuminating essay on this poem is "'**Among Schoolchildren**' and the Education of the Irish Spirit" by Donald T. Torchiana in the book *In Excited Reverie*. By proving that Yeats was endorsing the system of education practised and promoted by Maria Montessori, Professor Torchiana has disposed of many misinterpretations of the poem, and has permitted us to see its structure in a new light.

John Wain (in *Interpretations,* 1955) asserts that "the poem breaks into two halves", that Yeats "abandons the circular technique; after the halfway mark, there is no recurrence of the school-room, the children, the nun, the personal situation." He concludes: "Instead of circling back on itself, the poem moves forward, in the form of a bridge, then suddenly stops with no opposite shore in sight. It is not a bridge after all but a pier. It leads nowhere; its purpose is to afford us, before we turn and retrace our steps, a bleak and chastening glimpse into the deep waters." Almost every clause in the above series can be factually refuted. What has led Mr. Wain astray, perhaps, is that he has too narrowly conceived the subject of the poem, which he begins his essay by declaring to be "the relationship or interpenetration of matter and spirit." If one looks for a straightforward analysis of such an abstract problem as that the poem may seem to break into two, or to lead nowhere.

The subject of **"Among Schoolchildren"** is what its title leads us to expect it will be: a series of observations, memories, and meditations of the poet on finding himself among a class of schoolchildren. The schoolroom, the nun, the children, the classwork, the singing and the "smiling public man" are there all the time; if we are in any danger of forgetting that, Yeats jogs our memory by mentioning or alluding to one or other or several of them at intervals throughout the poem. The schoolroom, for example, is described in the first stanza, is implied in the second by the "harsh reproof", is referred to in the "there" of the third stanza, is implied by the "old scarecrow" of the fourth and "that shape with sixty or more winters on its head" in the fifth, is suggested by the reference to Aristotle birching Alexander in the sixth and to the nuns and mothers in the seventh, and is quite clearly present by contrast in the references to labour and "blear-eyed wisdom out of midnight oil" in the eighth and last. It would be possible, but impossibly tiresome to do the same kind of analysis for all the major ingredients of that first stanza. The poem is very intricately integrated.

Its structure *is* circular, but circular in a somewhat unusual way. The first stanza is the hub of the wheel; the succeeding stanzas are spokes radiating from this hub; the connections between the stanzas from the rim of the wheel; the final stanza returns to the hub. The middle six stanzas of the poem do indeed fall into two linked sequences, but the poem does not break in half. Stanzas II to IV relate to the particular case of Maud Gonne, who was once a child like these but is now an ageing woman; stanzas V to VII generalize this problem of change and decay and refer it for possible solutions to theories of reincarnation, philosophy, and religion; but there is no abrupt break between stanzas IV and V, since the "comfortable kind of old scarecrows" of IV is obviously "that shape / With sixty or more winters on its head" of V.

Yeats's attitude towards children was not rationalistic, or Puritan, or romantic, but profoundly humanistic and realistic. . . . He saw the child not as a species apart, but as one who shared the constant vulnerability and the occasional splendour of the whole human race.

—Desmond Pacey

There is not space in this essay for a detailed explication of **"Among Schoolchildren"**, but its implications for Yeats' attitude towards children may be briefly summarized. That an orthodox and repressive educational system was destructive of childish joy and spontaneity was a commonplace of Romantic discussions of childhood, perhaps the most memorable expression of it being Blake's "The School Boy":

I love to rise in a summer morn,
When the birds sing on every tree:
The distant huntsman winds his horn,
And the skylark sings with me.
O! what sweet company!

But to go to school in a summer morn,
O! it drives all joy away,
Under a cruel eye outworn
The little ones spend the day
In sighing and dismay. . . .

O! father and mother, if buds are nipp'd
And blossoms blown away . . .
How shall the summer arise in joy,
Or the summer fruits appear?

Yeats accepted this Romantic view, but instead of carrying it to the extreme of declaring, as Blake did, that "there is no use in education", he looked about for a form of education that would release and nourish the child's potentialities rather than inhibit them. His speeches to the Senate, and to the Irish Literary Society on November 30, 1925, make it clear that he saw the nearest approximation to such an ideal education in the modern Italian system as set forth by Montessori and Gentile. In Maria Montes-

sori's book, *The Montessori Method,* there are many passages which suggest the final stanza of **"Among Schoolchildren"**. Here are a few examples:

If any educational act is to be efficacious, it will be only that which tends to help toward the complete unfolding of this life. To be thus helpful it is necessary rigorously to avoid the arrest of spontaneous movements and the imposition of arbitrary tasks.

By education must be understood the active help given to the normal expansion of the life of the child. The child is a body which grows, and a soul which develops—these two forms, physiological and psychic, have one eternal font, life itself. We must neither mar nor stifle the mysterious powers which lie within these two forms of growth, but we must await from them the manifestations which we know will succeed one another.

The educational conception of this age must be solely that of aiding the psychophysical development of the individual.

The whole of the Montessori method, in fact, is based on the premise that schoolwork—"labour"—can be joyful, "blossoming or dancing", as witness this description of a child learning to write:

The child who wrote a word for the first time was full of excited joy. Indeed no one could escape from the noisy manifestations of the little one. He would call everyone to see, and if there were some who did not go, he ran to take hold of their clothes, forcing them to come and see. We all had to go and stand about the written work to admire the marvel, and to unite our exclamations of surprise with the joyous cries of the fortunate author.

Such are the ideas that underlie **"Among Schoolchildren"**, which is primarily, although by no means exclusively, a poem about the education of children. Yeats begins the poem by describing, approvingly, an ideal form of education in a model school; then, realistically, he is struck with the realization that no system of education can save us from the process of ageing; he glances at theories of reincarnation, speculations of philosophers, and the consolations of religion, only to dismiss them as inadequate attempts to find permanence amidst flux; and then in the final triumphant stanza he accepts and glories in the fact of flux, seeing the cycle of spontaneous life itself as the one permanent and self-sufficing thing. Work becomes joy when it is performed voluntarily, spontaneously, and rhythmically; life becomes joyful when body and soul function in harmony; true beauty is a spontaneous development and not something to be desperately sought after; wisdom arises from our normal, free involvement with our environment rather than by other- or self-imposed discipline; human life is not a long slow descent from childish innocence to senile despair but a cycle like the life-cycle of a tree, with each segment of the cycle having its own rightness, its own function; we cannot abstract that which performs the cycle from the cycle itself, any more than we can have a true dance without a dancer or a dancer without a dance. **"Among Schoolchildren"** is a poem of humanistic affirmation, but it is an affirmation made only after all the negative factors have been looked at squarely and long.

Another facet of Yeats' humanistic affirmation which is involved with his treatment of children is his concern with the continuity of a human tradition. We have already glanced at this concern in reference to **"A Prayer for my Daughter"**, but it is a quite frequent theme in his later poetry. In the introductory poem to *Responsibilities* he movingly regrets his own failure, up to that time, to produce offspring: "I have no child, I have nothing but a book, / Nothing but that to prove your blood and mine." But perhaps the most poignant and powerful passage on this matter occurs in the fourth section of his **"Meditations in Time of Civil War"**. There he does not suggest, as the lines just quoted from *Responsibilities* may be felt to suggest, that the mere generation of children is a guarantee of continuity. Yeats' dominant attitude, for all his occasional descents into bleak despair, is affirmative, but it is by no means a facile affirmation:

> Having inherited a vigorous mind
> From my old fathers, I must nourish dreams
> And leave a woman and a man behind
> As vigorous of mind, and yet it seems
> Life scarce can cast a fragrance on the wind,
> Scarce spread a glory to the morning beams,
> But the torn petals strew the garden plot;
> And there's but common greenness after that.
>
> And what if my descendants lose the flower
> Through natural declension of the soul,
> Through too much business with the passing hour,
> Through too much play or marriage with a fool?
> May this laborious stair and this stark tower
> Become a roofless ruin that the owl
> May build in the cracked masonry and cry
> Her desolation to the desolate sky.

A similar realism is found in Yeats' reminiscences of his own boyhood. The reminiscences in his poetry are few, and he never indulges in the facile nostalgia which was so common an ingredient in Romantic and Victorian literature. Instead of idealizing his childhood associates or himself as a child, he gives us specific memories, portraits which show the warts and all. In **"Under Saturn"**, for example, he writes:

> . . . . my horse's flanks are spurred
> By childish memories of an old cross Pollexfen,
> And of a Middleton, whose name you never heard,
> And of a red-haired Yeats whose looks, although he died
> Before my time, seem like a vivid memory.
> You heard that labouring man who had served my people. He said
> Upon the open road, near to the Sligo quay—

> No, no, not said, but cried it out—'You have come again,
> And surely after twenty years it was time to come'.
> I am thinking of a child's vow sworn in vain
> Never to leave that valley his fathers called their home.

Instead of looking back to his childhood regretfully, as did so many of the Romantics, and using nostalgia as an evasion of adult responsibilities, Yeats in his sixties declares that he has still all the faculties he had as a boy: uses his own youth, in other words, not as a saddle but as a spur. In **"The Towers"** he declares:

> Never had I more excited, passionate, fantastical
> Imagination, nor an ear and eye
> That more expected the impossible—
> No, not in boyhood when with rod and fly,
> Or the humbler worm, I climbed Ben Bulben's back
> And had the livelong summer day to spend.

Rather than as a source of boasting, he is inclined to use memories of his boyhood as a means to humility, as in the self-depreciation of the middle stanza of **"At Algeciras"**:

> Often at evening when a boy
> Would I carry to a friend—
> Hoping more substantial joy
> Did an older mind commend—
> Not such as are in Newton's metaphor,
> But actual shells of Ross's level shore.

This note of self-depreciation, balanced it is true with a certain measure of self-approbation, is also struck in **"What Then?"** the poem Yeats as an elderly man wrote for the boys of the high school he had attended. In its irony and ambiguity, the fine balance it strikes between humanistic affirmation and an awareness of the possible ultimate futility of all human effort, its realistic clear-sightedness and yet its persistent refusal to be fully daunted, this poem makes a fitting conclusion for this essay:

> His chosen comrades thought at school
> He must grow a famous man;
> He thought the same and lived by rule,
> All his twenties crammed with toil,
> *'What then?' sang Plato's ghost. 'When then?'*
>
> Everything he wrote was read,
> After certain years he won
> Sufficient money for his need,
> Friends that have been friends indeed;
> *'What then?' sang Plato's ghost. 'What then?'*
> All his happier dreams came true—
> A small old house, wife, daughter, son,
> Grounds where plum and cabbage grew,
> Poets and Wits about him drew;
> *'What then?' sang Plato's ghost. 'When then?'*
>
> 'The work is done;' grown old he thought,
> 'According to my boyish plan;
> Let the fools rage, I swerved in naught,

Something to perfection brought';
But louder sang the ghost, 'What then?'

To sum up, as is proved by this and the other poems that have been quoted or alluded to, Yeats' attitude towards children was not rationalistic, or Puritan, or romantic, but profoundly humanistic and realistic. Aware of human strength, he was also aware of human weaknesses; aware of our reach for perfection, he was also aware of the limitations of our grasp of perfection when seen *sub specie oeternitatis*. He saw the child not as a species apart, but as one who shared the constant vulnerability and the occasional splendour of the whole human race.

Thomas L. Byrd, Jr. (essay date 1978)

SOURCE: "The Environment of the Quest: The Poetic Dream," in *The Early Poetry of W. B. Yeats: The Poetic Quest,* Kennikat Press, 1978, pp. 11-38.

[*In the following excerpt, Byrd interprets animal and plant imagery as important aspects of Yeats's poetry, suggesting that such images authenticate the "poetic dream" of art's eternal power.*]

Directly connected with Yeats's use of specific landscapes are his references to the animals and plants that inhabit these areas. Yeats's poems are very heavily populated with various forms of animal and vegetable life, and in such a natural way that the reader is not so much aware of their importance as he is conscious of their presence, just as the average person is aware of the natural life around him without thinking about it. With a few obvious exceptions such as the rose, animal and plant life—mice, worms, marigolds, and the like—are presented on a level that is almost subconscious. We know they are there, but their presence is so natural in context that we think no more of it. Yet their existence is very important to the total meaning of the poems.

Concerning the poetry written before 1889, Forrest Reid [*W.B. Yeats: A Critical Study*, 1915] observes that "on nearly every page we meet with the wild, delightful creatures Mr. Yeats himself met with in the rambles of his boyhood." The rose did not overpower all the lesser flowers and animals in Yeats's poetry. Small birds, animals, and flowers appear just as frequently in the poems published between 1889 and 1900, and Yeats realizes the importance of their function. In the first poem in *The Rose,* **"To the Rose upon the Rood of Time,"** the Rose is seen as the power that relates the poet to the world of "common things that crave." The worm and the field-mouse are integral parts of the world of "heavy mortal hopes," a world Yeats knows he must not lose while seeking the "strange things said / By God to the bright hearts of those long dead." For valid poetry, the two worlds must mesh and mingle; they must be seen as one universe.

Yeats was aware of the importance of the function of animal and plant life throughout his career as a poet. From the very first, he senses the coexistence of the two worlds, and he illustrates their coterminous existence through animal and plant imagery of the same sort found in the Irish poetry. Even though his earliest poetry may seem artificial to the modern ear, Yeats counters the artificiality of Arcadia with a constant undertone of living reality. In **"The Island of Statues"** alone, the following plants and animals are mentioned at least once, and in some cases many times: daffodil, lilac, pansy, ash, willow, cypress, pine, alder, foxglove, rose, lily, sloe berries, hawthorn; heron, sheep, squirrel, crane, panther, owl, drake, woodpecker, grasshopper, bee, adder, moth, wolf, boar, steer, cuckoo, robin, lynx, kine, mouse, cankerworm, fish, kestrel, frog, otter. In addition, there are many general references to trees, flowers, and animals. The little pastoral play literally teems with life.

The poems on Indian subjects, which through mood, tone, and subject matter are the most languorous of Yeats's early poetry, do not, as one might expect, have as many references to plants and animals as Yeats's other poems. Lesser life is nevertheless present, often a more exotic life, such as the peahens and parrot in **"The Indian to His Love,"** but sometimes a life just as common to Ireland as to India. **"Anashuya and Vijaya"** contains the following: corn, flocks, panthers, poppies, flamingoes, the lion, birds, deer, antelope, the hound, lambs, kine, flies, mice.

In the Irish poetry, as Mr. Reid suggests, the animals and plants are more specifically Irish, and they do occur on virtually every page. With the exception of the rose and the lily, which more often, as in *The Shadowy Waters* and in the poems about the rose, have specifically Pre-Raphaelite and Rosicrucian overtones, the lesser life not only suggests motion; it also affirms the presence of life itself and testifies to the continuing existence of the mundane world in the presence of myth, legend, and fantasy. Taken together with the rose and the lily, the life of earth forms a background tapestry for the whole of the poetry, providing the reader with continuous reminders that the world he knows has not been abandoned or rejected.

Significantly, in **"The Man Who Dreamed of Faeryland"** the world of nature provides the visions of the land of faerie. The man standing in Dromahair and, later, by the well of Scanavin is told of the other world by extremely commonplace creatures and objects—a pile of fish, a lugworm, a small knot-grass. The fish

    . . . sang what gold morning or evening sheds
    Upon a woven world-forgotten isle
    Where a people love beside the ravelled seas;
    That Time can never mar a lover's vows
    Under that woven changeless roof of boughs.

The lugworm

    Sang that somewhere to north or west or south
    There dwelt a gay, exulting, gentle race
    Under the golden or the silver skies.

The knot-grass

Sang where—unnecessary cruel voice—
Old silence bids its chosen race rejoice.

In this poem the man is disturbed: at the end he "has found no comfort in the grave," but the world of faerie and the world of nature are seen to be directly interrelated.

By their functions as a motif of reality, as a background for the major concern, and—sometimes—as a link between man and the supernatural, the animals and plants serve to augment and amplify Yeats's use of the landscape. In all of Yeats's early poetry—on Arcadian, Indian, or Irish subjects—they reinforce the value of the natural world. The animals and plants, especially in the Arcadian and Indian poetry, provide the reader with a link of familiarity and make the setting seem less removed and foreign. In the specifically Irish poetry, these functions become more effective because the plants and animals are more tightly integrated in the totality of the poem. The landscape is already real; the animals and plants add to the existing reality. Their primary effect here is to link the legendary world to the present. We are in a world far from cities, and sometimes in a misty world of legend, but Yeats always indicates that we are in an eternal world that is always present. In **"The Madness of King Goll,"** for example, Yeats immediately plunges us into the times and places of Ireland's legendary past:

I sat on cushioned otter-skin:
My word was law from Ith to Emain,
And shook at Inver Amergin
The hearts of the world-troubling seamen.

However, instead of drifting completely into the mists of the past (as he is sometimes accused of doing), through his use of forest life Yeats relates the world of Ith and Emain to the world that is always present:

And now I wander in the woods
When summer gluts the golden bees,
Or in autumnal solitudes
Arise the leopard-coloured trees;
Or when along the wintry strands
The cormorants shiver on their rocks.

The exotic connotations of "leopard-coloured" are carefully balanced with the "ordinary" creatures, the bees and cormorants, and the four seasons of the Irish climate. Amid the natural seasons, King Goll wanders in the company of the wolf, the deer, and the hares of the forest.

Yeats often suggests motion through the use of small creatures. Animals in Yeats are not used for the sake of imagery alone. In most cases they, like the wind and the leaves in **"The Hosting of the Sidhe,"** are present in the poem because they are present in life, or occasionally, like the hound with one red ear in *The Wanderings of Oisin,* because they are present in Yeats's original source. In specific relation to the poetic dream, the function of the many fish, mice, birds, and the like, is to suggest the constant movement of these lower forms of life:

Autumn is over the long leaves that love us,
And over the mice in the barley sheaves;
Yellow the leaves of the rowan above us,
And yellow the wet wild-strawberry leaves.
("**The Falling of the Leaves**")

Amidst the yellowing decay and coming of the death of winter, Yeats does not overlook the presence of the mice.

The totality of the landscape, then, becomes more than a setting: it is a philosophical entity that, together with the other elements of Yeats's poetic vision, makes the poetry not an abstract criticism of life but the embodiment of life itself. This is not to say that Yeats subscribes to a form of pantheism, nor that he finds in nature the same type of power or inspiration that Wordsworth feels. In Yeats's poetry, the natural surroundings do more than surround: they become an integral part of existence. Man is not detached, and there is no man-nature conflict. Although Yeats does not idealize in the manner of Rousseau, he does consider man and nature to be inseparable. He does not present to us an Eden, and his views of man and environment appear primitivistic only to the modern town- or city-dweller who has lost his intimate relationship with the natural world....

In Yeats's poetry, the natural surroundings do more than surround: they become an integral part of existence. Man is not detached, and there is no man-nature conflict.

—*Thomas L. Byrd, Jr.*

In the structure of the poems related to the theme of poet-seeker, such as *The Wanderings of Oisin,* there can be discerned three levels directly informed by motion or lack of motion. *Oisin* is dominated and controlled by Oisin's wanderings, his search: in this sense it is all motion. Yet in another sense the poem is all stillness. Time is suspended for Oisin. His travels last for three hundred years; he remains on each island for one hundred years; when he again sets foot physically upon Ireland, he ages immediately. He is young throughout his travels; when he talks of them in his dialogue with Saint Patrick, he is "bent, and bald, and blind." Within the stillness of the time suspension there is the movement of lesser life—the birds, the deer, the hounds. Herein lies the tension of motion and rest. In this poem there are worlds within worlds, from the macrocosmic to the microcosmic.

The complexity of time, motion, stillness, and dream, of sound and silence, gradually becomes intensified as the poem progresses. First, in Oisin's travels outward from Ireland to the first island, and onward to the second and third islands, time becomes confused. Each time Oisin leaves the shore for the open sea, his sense of time becomes blurred; each time, until he leaves the last island

and Remembrance returns to him, the same is repeated with only slight modifications:

> I know not if days passed or hours . . .

> I do not know if days
> Or hours passed by . . .

> Were we days long or hours long in riding . . . ?

Accompanied by sound, or, on the last segment of the journey, the consciousness of lack of sound, Oisin travels farther away from the world he knows into the world of eternal mists and disillusion. In the first part of the journey, leaving Ireland, Niamh sings continuous songs of the other world; between the first island and the second, her song is "troubled" by tears; after leaving the second island, Niamh no longer sings.

Paralleling the intensifying sorrow of Niamh, the islands are progressively more removed from active, physical life and more and more involved with life as seen in a dream. In the first island, called significantly "The Island of the Living" in the 1889 version, there are many contrasts between action and stillness. After the mysterious journey over the water, we are introduced to the world of twilight and the dream. However, even though we see Aengus in his hall dreaming "a Druid dream of the end of days," when even "the stars are to wane" and a literal twilight exists throughout, there is the contrasting action of the Immortals, the movement of the dance, the sounds of the harp and the song. In eternal summer, Oisin engages in the traditional heroic sports of hunting, fishing, and wrestling. As we leave the Island of the Living, Yeats shows us a vignette of action and inaction that, in essence, summarizes the existence of the first island. In the golden light of evening, some of the Immortals move among the fountains, dance, and wander hand in hand; others sit in dreams on the water's edge, singing and gazing at the setting sun while the birds keep time to the music.

On the second island, called "The Island of Victories" in the 1889 version, Oisin finds himself in an atmosphere of greater mystery. On The Island of Fears, as it was named in the definitive edition, eternity consists of actions perpetually repeated. In the attempt to deliver a maiden chained to two ancient eagles, Oisin fights with a demon. This action begins an endless fight, for the demon perpetually renews himself: Oisin fights and defeats the demon; after the third day of the victory feast, the demon reappears. Thus, for one hundred years Oisin endures, without dreams, fears, languor, or fatigue, "an endless feast. / An endless war."

When Oisin reaches the third island, the Island of the Sleepers ("The Island of Forgetfulness" in the 1889 version), Yeats's subtlety in dealing with rest and motion reaches its height. Oisin lives only in dreaming of life:

> So lived I and lived not, so wrought I and wrought
>   not, with creatures of dreams,
> In a long iron sleep, as a fish in the water goes
>   dumb as a stone.

In describing the island, Yeats tells us that "no live creatures lived there." In context, however, much life is suggested in the description of deathly stillness:

> But the trees grew taller and closer, immense in
>   their wrinkling bark;
> Dropping; a murmurous dropping; old silence and
>   that one sound;
> For no live creatures lived there, no weasels moved
>   in the dark:
> Long sighs arose in our spirits, beneath us bubbled
>   the ground.

The trees seem to loom larger in Oisin's eyes; the trees and the ground exude noises; Oisin thinks of weasels. A few lines later the horse whinnies when he catches sight of the huge, white, sleeping bodies. The presence of owls (in spite of the statement made in line 19) provides an effective contrast of life with the slumberers:

> So long were they sleeping, the owls had built
>   their nests in their locks,
> Filling the fibrous dimness with long generations
>   of eyes.
> And over the limbs and the valley the slow owls
>   wandered and came,
> Now in a place of star-fire, and now in a shadow-
>   place wide;
> And the chief of the huge white creatures, his knees
>   in the soft star-flame,
> Lay loose in a place of shadow: we drew the reins
>   by his side.

In these lines Yeats gives us not only life but continuing life, with "generations" of owls. Perception is suggested by the use of "eyes" in line 40. The busy and ordinary activity of nest-building complements the action of Niamh and Oisin in reining their horses, while the slow wandering movement, related through inversion in line 41, effectively complements the mysterious sleepers. In addition, the movement of life is sustained in the mind of the reader throughout this island of sleep-enchantment by frequent references to life in the world of man as Oisin relates to Saint Patrick the things the island caused him to forget: "How the falconer follows the falcon in the weeds of the heron's plot"; "How the slow, blue-eyed oxen of Finn low sadly at evening tide." Yeats thus maintains an awareness of life and motion even when describing their absence. No matter how removed the dream world is from the world of men—and the islands visited by Oisin are fabled and eternal, removed from time—the dream never loses consciousness of reality. Even in the early Arcadian play *The Island of Statues,* in which one might expect from the very nature of the Arcadian subject matter a complete removal from the world, the sleepers awake from their enchantment asking about men and events from the lives they were living before the spell was cast upon them.

A clear example of Yeats's use of various types of motion and motion suggestion, of time and timelessness within the dream, can be seen in the short, nine-line **"Love Song**

from the Gaelic," which appeared in *Poems and Ballads of Young Ireland* (1888):

> My love, we will go, we will go, I and you,
> And away in the woods we will scatter the dew;
> And the salmon behold, and the ousel too,
> My love, we will hear, I and you, we will hear,
> The calling afar of the doe and the deer.
> And the bird in the branches will cry for us clear,
> And the cuckoo unseen in his festival mood;
> And death, oh my fair one, will never come near
> In the bosom afar of the fragrant wood.

This very early and immature lyric is quoted here for an important reason. Many critics, and Yeats himself, would probably refer to it as "escape poetry"; yet, even in this admittedly trivial lyric (it was never published in any edition of Yeats's works), it is clear that the so-called "escape" is not a true flight from reality, and that this escape is part of the seeker theme and an important part of the complex poetic dream. In this small poem Yeats introduces the important elements found in later, more sophisticated poetry dealing with the seeker. As in **"The Stolen Child," "The Hosting of the Sidhe,"** and *The Wanderings of Oisin,* there is the summons to go. The world into which the loved one is summoned is eternal and timeless: "death . . . will never come near"; but it is also a forest world filled with creatures. This poem does represent a yearning for the pastoral, but it is a pastoral that exists among familiar and living things. When the eternal world is gained, the best of the transitory world is not lost.

In discussing Yeats's poetry, one must be cautious in making a distinction between eternal and transitory states of existence. The question of time in Yeats's poetic dream needs further investigation, for here we reach an ambiguity that is unresolved. It is too easy to conclude that in the later verse Byzantium provides the solution when the poet is "gather[ed]" into "the artifice of eternity," for even in **"Sailing to Byzantium"** Yeats echoes the concern for old age that pervades his later verse and that is actually a manifestation of a concern found in Yeats from the beginning: Can man, through his art, conquer time? Though man dies and buildings fall into ruins, Yeats hopes that poetry is eternal. But it is a hope, not a certainty:

> I, the poet William Yeats,
> With old mill boards and sea-green slates,
> And smithy work from the Gort forge,
> Restored this tower for my wife George;
> And may these characters remain
> When all is ruin once again.
>   (**"To be Carved on a Stone at Thoor Ballylee"**)

As Yeats prophetically predicts, this very old tower—Yeats liked to think it was Norman, though no one seems to know its age—did fall into ruin (it is now being restored), and these lines, carved on a stone of the tower, do remain. Somehow, though, Yeats's hope seems wistful; the inscription of Ozymandias is the best one can hope for.

The lines carved on the tower comprise the statement of a practical man and the enunciation of a conclusion that is pessimistic and almost cynical for a poet so conscious of the importance of his art. Yeats obviously did not operate from the philosophy implied by these lines throughout his poetic career. In his use of the dream it is clear that he was searching for the true relationship existing between time and his art.

The dream state, by its very nature, involves a focus on time different from that of the waking state, and under special conditions the dream state can involve a negation of time. The true vision pierces eternity, and a state of enchantment, such as that of Oisin or the sleepers in *The Island of Statues,* can suspend time. If immortal creatures could be found, it should be in the supernatural world, but for Yeats there seems to be some doubt:

> A man has a hope for heaven,
> But soulless a fairy dies.

Is there, then, a world of eternity? If so, where does it exist?

In the poetic dream, one does not escape from reality: one escapes to reality. The true meaning of escape—the meaning indicated earlier—and the true Celtic Twilight can be seen in the short poem **"Into the Twilight."** The spiritual condition of the poet and the summons to the quest are contained in the first two lines:

> Out-worn heart, in a time out-worn,
> Come clear of the nets of wrong and right.

To find reality, the poet must escape the petty, middle-class world of the dull, smugly complacent, and spiritually ignorant shopkeeper, the "nets of wrong and right" that can ensnare a person into a world in which everything is seen in terms of black and white, good and evil; the same world discussed later in connection with Saint Patrick in *The Wanderings of Oisin*. If one can leave modern city life, the poem implies, "Eire is always young," and in Ireland the poet can find reality:

> Come, heart, where hill is heaped upon hill:
> For there the mystical brotherhood
> Of sun and moon and hollow and wood
> And willow and stream work out their will.

Eternity and the dream are found in the soil and in nature. The poet is summoned to leave the "nets of wrong and right," but he does not enter a clear, uncomplicated paradise. Yeats juxtaposes the "grey twilight" with the "dew of the morn"; the heart is summoned to laughter and sighs; the heart laughs in the greyness and sighs in the shining dew. The loneliness of God coexists with the "mystical brotherhood" of nature. This is the eternal youth of Ireland, which will remain even though "hope fall from you and love decay."

"Time and the world are ever in flight." Yeats is affirming these things that endure, the "shining dew" and the "grey twilight." Hope and love do not endure, for they are the kind of hope and love that can be destroyed "in fires of a slanderous tongue." In this context, Yeats could be implying a Neoplatonic distinction between higher and lower types of love and hope. The modern world, the world of the slanderous tongue, the world containing the type of love and hope prone to decay, is most probably the world he writes about later, in which "Romantic Ireland" has been replaced by men who

> . . . fumble in a greasy till
> And add the halfpence to the pence
> And prayer to shivering prayer, until
> You have dried the marrow from the bone.
> **("September, 1913")**

In his radio talk "Players and Painted Stage," which has been reprinted by Denis Donoghue in *The Integrity of Years,* Frank Kermode quotes Yeats's observation that art is "the struggle of the dream with the world." Kermode defines the dream as "a transcendent reality, the truth of the imagination." According to Kermode, the world is more complex than the mere opposite of the dream; it is not simply a place to be hated and shunned. He accurately defines the world as it is seen in Yeats's poetry:

> The world is something to be both hated and loved:
> the spiritless sphere of realists, shopkeepers, "thinkers,"
> and also the place of admired animal vitality—"the
> young in one another's arms"—and heroic action.

The poet is summoned not from the world but from *a* world, the world of pettiness and minor values, the "nets of wrong and right," in which the major values are obscured and lost. Yeats states his position quite clearly in **"To Ireland in the Coming Times,"** which was entitled more explicitly in the first printing in 1892 as "Apologia Addressed to Ireland in the Coming Days." This poem is the personal credo of Yeats as an Irish poet, and even though couched in the language and style of the early poetry, it is a credo he never abandoned. In the first four lines, Yeats fits himself into a tradition and shows that he is escaping *into* a world of artistic purpose:

> Know, that I would accounted be
> True brother of a company
> That sang, to sweeten Ireland's wrong,
> Ballad and story, rann and song.

In the world of the Irish poetic tradition, time operates in a special way in relation to art:

> When Time began to rant and rage
> The measure of her flying feet
> Made Ireland's heart begin to beat;
> And Time bade all his candles flare
> To light a measure here and there;
> And may the thoughts of Ireland brood
> Upon a measured quietude.

Perhaps Time's candles can, for a moment, "light a measure" even for the world of the "greasy till."

When living in a world necessarily and unavoidably governed by time, the poet is in a state of existence in which the dream is essential:

> Because, to him who ponders well,
> My rhymes more than their rhyming tell
> Of things discovered in the deep,
> Where only body's laid asleep.

This is one of Yeat's clearest statements of the function of the dream in poetry. The dreams supply the meaning of the poetry, and they become the key to the unity for which the poet is searching.

An examination of Yeats's revisions of this poem will confirm the continued and steady importance of the dream throughout his career; the revisions also reveal an earlier emphasis on the dream. The version quoted here is that of the definitive edition. Although Yeats made no revisions that directly change the meaning of this poem, he was more explicit in the versions that appeared in and before the 1924 revision of *Poems* (1895). In this and earlier editions, lines 21 and 22 read: "Of the dim wisdoms old and deep, / That God gives unto man in sleep." In all versions of this poem, both early and late, Yeats alludes, in the lines immediately following, to mysterious forces that come "about [his] table" through the dream. These forces are called "magical powers" in 1892, "elemental beings" in all versions from 1895 through 1924, and "elemental creatures" in the definitive edition. Yeats was always aware that dreams provide the poetic insight.

In **"To Ireland in the Coming Times,"** Yeats reveals that he is living in an intermediary state between the materialistic world of pounds, shillings, and pence and the eternal world for which he is searching. The dream is an essential part of the poetic search, and that search is not over: unity has not been attained and knowledge is not complete; therefore, the ambiguities, the "vagueness" and cloudiness often deplored in Yeats's early poetry are unavoidable, and indeed essential, at this stage of artistic development. The last stanza of this poem gives us the perspective we need in order to understand the dream and its importance to the poetic search:

> I cast my heart into my rhymes,
> That you, in the dim coming times,
> May know how my heart went with them
> After the red-rose-bordered hem.

In these lines the dream and the poetry itself are very closely connected. In the short life allotted to man, the poet's heart went "after the red-rose-bordered hem" that is specifically Ireland, the hem of Cathleen ni Houlihan; but by suggestion, Yeats is following all that is implied by the red rose. In his note to **"Aedh Hears the Cry of the Sedge,"** Yeats observes that "the Rose has been for many centuries a symbol of spiritual love and supreme beauty." He goes on to enumerate many uses of the rose in religion and in poetry. In the notes to *The Rose,* Yeats says that "the quality symbolised as The Rose differs from the Intellectual Beauty of Shelley and of Spenser in that

I have imagined it as suffering with man and not as something pursued and seen from afar." This last note was written in 1925, and Yeats tells us that he noticed this quality of the rose "upon reading these poems for the first time for several years." The element of pursuit is implied, however, by the use of the word *after* in the last line. Nevertheless, the retrospective statement in the note does give an added insight. A concept such as intellectual beauty is a logical goal for the poetic search, and Yeats's use of the rose in many of his early poems makes it clear that the rose is one symbol of the goal of his search. Here, though, we see the goal as something attainable, even as something present. The rose can be seen in the poetic dream.

The dreaminess, cloudiness, and ambiguity found in Yeats are usually defended or condemned primarily on artistic and philosophical grounds, following one or more of the standard methods of literary criticism. What many critics fail to see, or at least fail to mention, is the strong element of plain common sense found in Yeats. Like the peasants he admired, he could combine the affairs of daily life with glimpses and concern for the supernatural. If the trait of common sense is overlooked, there are unsurmountable difficulties in interpreting Yeats's poetry and prose. (On the other hand, it should be noted that Yeats is not a literate Margery Kempe, who was so bound to life on earth that her relation with Christ, as seen in her *Booke,* is simply another sexual affair.) Such critics as Harold Bloom [in *Yeats,* 1970], for example have difficulties with Yeats's religion and his mysticism. The confusion found in Yeats's poetry and in his comments about his symbols and his philosophy is understandable, and even sometimes erased, when they are read in the light of such statements as those found in the lines **"To be Carved on a Stone at Thoor Ballylee,"** which are quoted above. Yeats accepts the fact that man and his creations are not eternal; at the same time, ideas and thoughts can remain.

William O'Neill (essay date 1983)

SOURCE: "Yeats on Poetry and Politics," in *The Midwest Quarterly,* Vol. XXV, No. 1, Autumn 1983, pp. 64-73.

[*In the following excerpt, O'Neill suggests that Yeats's poetical interpretation of political events evolved from bitterness to acceptance as Yeats tried to impose order on chaos by applying the theories of historical cycles which he explains in his collection of poems entitled* A Vision.]

William Butler Yeats came of age during the Parnell era, a time of great political excitement in Ireland. By the mid-eighties Charles Stuart Parnell and his supporters had, by obstructionist tactics, forced the issue of home rule upon the English Parliament. Seven hundred years of English presence in Ireland seemed about to end. Then Captain O'Shea filed his famous suit for divorce, naming Parnell as corespondent. The tragi-comic debacle that brought Parnell to defeat and ended, for the time, all hope of home rule, was treated, in Yeats's early poems about it, merely as the crowning piece of evidence of the nar-

rowness of a great number of his countrymen. In the poem, **"To a Shade,"** written in 1913, he advises the spirit of the departed leader to forget about the Irish; have a look at his monument, enjoy a breath of fresh air, and return to his tomb, "For they are at their old tricks yet."

But in later years, after the cosmology of *A Vision* had been developed, Yeats claimed to understand the significance of the Parnell episode more fully. The shock of Parnell's destruction, he says in **King of the Great Clock Tower,** was the event which released the artistic energy of the literary movement which followed. Before the Kitty O'Shea episode, the Unionists and the Nationalists were separate camps, each behind its own walls. The downfall of Parnell brought a confrontation, a turmoil. The two sides clashed in the streets and in the meeting halls, and the intellectual excitement infected the writers.

In the poem, **"Parnell's Funeral,"** written forty years after the event, Parnell is likened, by implication, to Iphigenia; his sacrifice, like that of Agamemnon's daughter, makes possible an age of war, which is also an age of literary achievement. Succeeding ages create different kinds of energy, as he explains in *A Vision*:

> After an age of necessity, truth, goodness, mechanism, science, democracy, abstraction, peace, comes an age of freedom, fiction, evil, kindred, art, aristocracy, particularity, war.

The argument becomes less convincing as it becomes more elaborate. The skeptical reader may suspect that Yeats draws this generalization solely from the two examples with which he illustrates it in the poem. Yeats searches with increasing intensity for historical pattern, and, as in this example, often seems to see it where no other eye can. If his purpose is to help us understand the historical process, he fails.

The usual explanation of the value of the theory is that it helped Yeats achieve what he called "Unity of Being." A writer needs to have a position, a *persona*, a viewpoint from which to see and a platform from which to speak. The theory seems to have been particularly useful in helping Yeats to write about the political events of his time. The poems which he wrote during and soon after the writing of *A Vision*, which were published in 1928 in **The Tower,** dwell more exclusively on politics than does his work from any previous period. This could be attributed to the fact that there was a civil war going on in Ireland at this time, but there had been spectacular political events enough all during Yeats's creative life. He had dealt with them from time to time in single poems, but never until now had they formed the central theme of a book. Politics had been a subject that he had felt it necessary to look away from in his thoughts and in his writing. *A Vision* seems to have given him analytical apparatus, a means of admitting the subject in a way that would not overwhelm him and his work.

But to say this is not to explain the existence of the theory. It is, after all, a theory that no reputable historian would endorse, a theory that Yeats himself seemed to believe only part of the time—as evidenced by the fact that as he wrote succeeding drafts of such *Vision*-oriented poems as **"The Second Coming"** and **"Sailing to Byzantium,"** he eliminated all direct reference to it. As Yeats explains, *A Vision* was derived from the automatic writings of his wife, but, since the purpose of *A Vision* was to help him write poetry, I believe we will come nearer a full understanding of his idea of poetry and its relation to politics by ignoring this bit of hocus pocus and following the evolution of his thought in the poetry itself.

The first evidence of conscious thought on this subject comes at a time when he was under the influence of another Irish political figure, the Fenian leader John O'Leary. It is well known that O'Leary persuaded Yeats to write on Irish subjects, but there is also evidence that O'Leary was the source of the politics and art theme in Yeats's poetry. In the *Autobiography* Yeats tells of a conversation with O'Leary. "I was defending an Irish politician who had made a great outcry because he was treated as a common felon, by showing that he did it for the cause's sake. . . ." O'Leary responded, "There are things that a man must not do to save a nation." O'Leary, who had spent five years in an English prison for taking part in an armed insurrection in 1867, and had spent fourteen years in forced exile in Paris, had come to be concerned about the effect of the struggle with England upon the Irish personality. The bitterness engendered by years of failure threatened to destroy what it was about Ireland that made it worth fighting for.

It was during the time of his association with O'Leary, who had stayed with the Yeats family at Bedford Park, that Yeats wrote **"The Ballad of Father O'Hart."** In this simple poem, a rendering in verse of a folk tale of western Ireland, Father O'Hart places his lands in the trust of a shoneen. (The word means, roughly, "upstart"—here, a plantation Protestant whose Irish antecedents do not go back very far.) He does this because these were "penal times," times when Catholics were not allowed to own more than a small amount of property. The shoneen double-crosses John and gives the lands "as dowers to his daughters, / And they married beyond their place." John heroically refuses to become embittered. Although impoverished, he goes up and down the land preaching, freeing birds from their cages, saying with a smile, "Have peace, now," and going his way with a frown, which comes of not being quite able to forget his grievance.

Perpetual bitterness is too great a price to pay to save a nation. The prime example in the poetry of one who has paid that price is Constance Markiewicz (née Gore-Booth). Yeats had visited the Gore-Booth home in Sligo during his visits to the Pollexfens. He recalled those days in **"Easter 1916"** after she had been sentenced for her role in the rising.

> That woman's days were spent
> In ignorant good-will,
> Her nights in argument
> Until her voice grew shrill.

> What voice more sweet than hers
> When, young and beautiful,
> She rode to harriers?

The damage wrought to her by bitterness is dwelt on in the other poems about her, **"On a Political Prisoner"** and **"In Memory of Eva Gore-Booth and Con Markiewicz."**

His idea that obsession with political struggle is especially bad for women undoubtedly had to do with the fact that this had been his real rival in his long, unsuccessful wooing of Maud Gonne. Indeed, his proposal to her after the death of her husband, Captain MacBride, was made subject to her agreeing to give up politics.

Political obsession is bad for the poet, too, and not only because it creates bitterness, but also because it involves "mechanical thought." The example of his father, the rationalist who lacked the artistic confidence to finish a painting (he worked sometimes for years on a single canvas), may have given him his first hint that scientism and the intuitive arts are inimical. Yeats wore a ring which had on it a hawk and a butterfly; the hawk symbolized the straight-line flight of logical thought, that of the scientist or the politician; the butterfly symbolized the random-seeming flight of the artist's mind. The problem for the poet is to avoid mechanical thought and bitterness while keeping contact with "what is most interwoven with one's life": the life and events of his time, which in Ireland, in Yeats's time, threatened every minute to engender those things.

The predicament is a theme of the fifth poem of **"Meditations in a Time of Civil War."** First an I.R.A. man, then a Free Stater, a "brown Lieutenant," call at his door. After their visits he makes a conscious effort to turn away from their war:

> I count those feathered balls of soot
> The moor-hen guides upon the stream,
> To silence the envy in my thought.

The figure of the moor-hen is a familiar one: in **"Easter 1916"** "Hearts with one purpose alone" are likened to a stone in the moving stream, and contrasted with "The long-legged moor-hens" who dive and call to their mates. "Minute by minute they live: / The stone's in the midst of all." He must, if he is to continue to create, avoid the kind of obsession which can enchant the heart to a stone.

> . . . Homer had not sung
> Had he not found it certain beyond dreams
> That out of life's own self-delight had sprung
> The abounding glittering jet. . . .
>
> > ("Ancestral Houses")

"Life's own self-delight" is the source of femininity and also of art; the source of procreation and of creation. It is the honey of creation which, in the sixth poem, he bids the bees produce:

My wall is loosening; honey-bees,
Come build in the empty house of the stare.

There is an antithesis between the living man who feels
injustice and can hardly help but harbor bitterness, and
the creator, who must overcome it. Yeats advocates a lack
of spontaneity in this regard. It is O'Leary's thought about
Ireland: response must be measured and tempered according to the effect upon the mind of the one responding. So
Father O'Hart, in spite of the feelings which make him
frown, returns good for bad; draws away from the hopeless battle which he would have good cause for waging
and behaves according to his true nature, freeing the birds,
whose flight, like that of the butterfly or the movements
of the moor-hens, is of a kind with the movement of the
poet's intuition.

It is not an escape from reality, although this is at
times a temptation. The poem **"Nineteen Hundred and
Nineteen"** arose from the depredations of the Black
and Tans in the town of Gort and elsewhere in the
neighborhood of Thoor Ballylee. He sees in the barbarous actions of these English "special forces," following hard upon the similar barbarities of the World War,
a sign of the terminal decline of the civilization which
had reached its peak in the time of his youth when
"We pieced our thoughts into a philosophy, / And
planned to bring the world under a rule." The pieced-
together humanist philosophy has proved false; the
pieces, as of an old mosaic, are coming apart in the
storm of human events. The philosophy was naive; it
failed to take into account the evil side of the human
animal. This is a necessary oversight in the creation of
great works of art, such as the statues of Phidias, the
beauty of which derives from the ennobling of the
human subject. Now that the horrors of the twentieth
century have destroyed the vision of mankind out of
which this art was created, the temptation is to escape
into the world of pure imagination.

> He who can read the signs nor sink unmanned
> Into the half-deceit of some intoxicant
> From shallow wits. . . .

But the escape is not made in **"Nineteen Hundred and
Nineteen,"** as it is in Shelley's "Alastor," from which
comes the figure of the swan (of the third section) who
leaps into the desolate heavens tempting the poet to try to
follow.

The poet's stance will be determined, not spontaneously,
but by his artistic needs. Political obsessions, if they ensnare him, destroy the poet, and political events out of his
control threaten to destroy the civilization which embodies his poetry. Yet escape will not serve his purpose because it is the dilemma itself which provides the material
for some of Yeats's most powerful poetry. In the poem
"Words" he recognized this.

> My darling cannot understand
> What I have done, or what would do
> In this blind bitter land.

But he remembers:

> That the best I have done
> Was done to make it plain.

In the field of force between the poet and his spiritual
opposite, the world of politics, exists the energy which
creates the poetry. Yeats's theories of history allow him
to remain within the "pull" of the world of political events
without being swallowed up by it.

To make this idea clearer, let us return to the poem **"Nineteen Hundred and Nineteen"** to see it in practice. In the
first section the murder of a woman by the Black and
Tans is described:

> Now days are dragon-ridden, the nightmare
> Rides upon sleep: a drunken soldiery
> Can leave the mother, murdered at her door,
> To crawl in her own blood, and go scot-free;
> The night can sweat with terror as before
> We pieced our thoughts into philosophy,
> And planned to bring the world under a rule,
> Who are but weasels fighting in a hole.

The poem ends with the image of Lady Kyteler, a fourteenth century practicer of witchcraft, putting out charms
to attract her incubus, Robert Artisson.

In 1919 the lovely things are gone, and the amenities of
civilization have disappeared with them. The twentieth century is a time of nightmare. "But is there any comfort to be
found?" The only answer is the melancholy: "Man is in
love and loves what vanishes, / What more is there to say?"

**Yeats permits us to witness the absurd
posture of the modern man who insists
that human events have meaning.**

—William O'Neill

The idea of the patterns of history is introduced in the
second section of the poem with the image of Loie Fuller's
Chinese dancers and their shining, floating ribbon of cloth
which seems to whirl them around and hurry them off "in
its own furious path." The dance that whirls human beings along its furious path "goes to the barbarous clangor
of a gong." The historical dance and its music are unpleasant to human ears. The dance may have a purpose,
but it is evidently not a human purpose. But there is the
consolation, slight as it is, that these times are a predictable season of the Platonic year. The lovely things are
merely leaves of some deciduous tree which must be shed
so the tree can bloom again two thousand years hence.

Yeats said that the purpose of envisioning history as a
series of cycles was to help him "hold in a single thought
reality and justice." If there is any justice in the reality he

has shown us in the first section of the poem, it must be the justice of some extra-human system. The extra-human system of the Bible, which helped Milton see reality and justice whole, is no longer functional. "Avenge O Lord thy slaughtered saints" will not do for Parnell and the woman in her doorway. But his invented system, Yeats implies here, is also pathetically inadequate. It is Loie Fuller and her Chinese dancers juxtaposed against the mother murdered at her door, crawling in her own blood.

> A man in his own secret meditation
> Is lost amid the labyrinth that he has made
> In art or politics.

Art and political philosophy are like the labyrinth, which conceals, sometimes successfully and sometimes not, the destructive Minotaur. The artist and the humanist philosopher are always in some measure aware of the beast at the center, and aware of what it is that they are doing. They are creating "ingenious lovely things," those things which can make of the Robert Artisson and Lady Kyteler species, a civilization. It takes enormous ingenuity to create lovely things out of such unpromising material, and it takes a great effort of will to maintain them. They seem "sheer miracle to the multitude," who do not understand their nature, their fragility.

In **"Nineteen Hundred and Nineteen,"** as in the several poems on the demise of Parnell, he considers an event which moves him deeply, first with outrage, then he calms his rage by examining the event in the light of his pseudo-scientific theory of history. The faint discerning of a pattern, and the conclusion that it is therefore part of a dance and not mere chaos, will make it bearable.

There are three possible responses to the injustice of events: permanent bitterness and struggle, as with Con Markiewicz or Maud Gonne; cynical resignation and escape from both reality and justice, as with Alastor; or some system of reconciling reality with some larger and necessarily extra-human idea of justice. The system Yeats uses to force the raw data of history into making sense is a gimcrack one; such a one as might have been invented by one of Joyce Cary's backstreet philosophers.

> I took no trouble to convince,
> Or seem plausible to a man of sense.
> (**"The Apparitions"**)

Art is an ingenious thing; it involves self-deception. The fact that it involves self-deception is one of Yeats's themes, so it should not surprise us that he lets us in on the deception which makes his own work possible. Yeats permits us to witness the absurd posture of the modern man who insists that human events have meaning.

Elizabeth Butler Cullingford (essay date 1993)

SOURCE: "The Anxiety of Masculinity," in *Gender and History in Yeats's Love Poetry,* Cambridge University Press, 1993, pp. 11-24.

[*In the following excerpt, Cullingford examines Yeats's personality and his love poetry, suggesting that Yeats possessed feminine qualities which enabled him to write untraditional poems in praise of the women he loved.*]

Love poetry, the discourse of sexuality in verse, is inflected by the gender of the subject position adopted by its author. In this respect Yeats's work is problematic. As an Irish nationalist poet he was expected to produce "manly" verse in order to counteract the colonial sterotype of the Irish as effeminate and childish. Yet he conceived of his poetic vocation as demanding a "feminine" receptivity and passivity, and as inheritor of an organic romantic poetic he saw the production of verse as analogous to the female labor of producing a child. "Man is a woman to his work, and it begets his thought," he wrote in 1909 [*Memoirs: Autobiography—First Draft and Journal*]. Gilbert and Gubar argue that in the nineteenth century literary creativity was metaphorically defined as a male generative activity: pen as penis, author as father; but Mary Ellmann [in *Thinking*] notes an equally strong association between "childbirth and the male mind." The organic childbirth metaphor, discarded by neo-classical poets, was revivified by the Romantics. In 1911 Gonne, employing a bold gender-role reversal, deplored Yeats's absorption in theater to the detriment of love poetry:

> Our children were your poems of which I was the Father sowing the unrest & storm which made them possible & you the mother who brought them forth in suffering & in the highest beauty & our children had wings—You & Lady Gregory have a child also *the theatre company* & Lady Gregory is the Father who holds you to your duty of motherhood in true marriage style. That child requires much feeding & looking after. I am sometimes jealous for my children. [*Always Your Friend: Letters between Maud Gonne and W. B. Yeats, 1893-1938*]

"That the Night Come" shows that Yeats accepted both Gonne's masculine self-definition and her metaphors: in the "storm and strife" of her existence she resembles "a king" [*The Variorum Edition of the Poems*]. Susan Friedman argues, however, that male poets who adopt the female model of pregnancy are indulging in "a form of literary *couvade,* male appropriation of procreative labor to which women have been confined" [in "Creativity and the Childbirth Metaphor: Gender Difference in Literary Discourse." *Feminist studies* 1987]: the comparison between poetic and physical creativity, which masks women's inability to participate in cultural labor, keeps them at the work of producing babies. Nevertheless, Gonne's version of the trope, with its confident adoption of the active, stormy, and paternal role, and its comic depiction of Yeats as the submissive wife of a dominating Gregory, suggests that the use of this metaphor during the period of women's emancipation may signify a shift in power rather than an appropriative strategy. Yeats's encouragement and promotion of women artists such as Katharine Tynan, Florence Farr, Althea Gyles, Augusta Gregory, Dorothy Wellesley, and Margot Ruddock, moreover, allow us to interpret his use of the childbirth metaphor as sympathetic identification rather than usurpation. As a comrade he exhorted Wellesley: "Write verse, my dear, go on writing, that is the only thing that matters" [*The Letters*, 1954].

[Yeats] exalted emotion over reason. He loathed the Victorian myth of science and progress. . . .

—Elizabeth Butler Cullingford

Yeats was fascinated by William Sharp's attempt to reinvent himself as the Celtic poetess Fiona MacLeod; and Freudian and Jungian critics concur in describing him as female identified. [see Brenda Webster's *Yeats: A Psychoanalytic Study*] While the Freudians regard this identification as a problem, a neurosis caused by his unsatisfactory relationship with his mother [See David Lynch's *Yeats; The Poetics of the Self*], Kiberd uses the Jungian model to argue that, although in his youth Yeats was "an unconscious slave to his *anima*," he later accepted and expressed the woman within. [See Declan Kiberd's *Men and Feminism in Modern Literature*]. His insistence on the androgyny of the male artist is characteristic of the Decadence, a period during which, Jane Marcus argues [in *Art and Anger: Reading Like a Women*], the concept of androgyny "extends the range of male sexuality into the feminine, but continues to regard the extension of female sexuality into the historical masculine as perverse." Womanly men were more acceptable than mannish women. Androgyny has been condemned by feminists on the grounds that to celebrate the combination of stereotypically "masculine" and "feminine" qualities is to presume that aggression is naturally male, and passivity naturally female, and to advocate with Jung that men seek an eternal woman, women an eternal man, within themselves. Jungian formulations superimpose two essentialist stereotypes rather than revealing gender identity as a social construction. Diana Fuss [in *Essentially Speaking: Feminism, Nature and Difference*], however, claims convincingly that essentialism is neither good nor bad in itself, but as it is deployed, while Carolyn Heilbrun [in *Toward a Recognition of Androgyny*] insists that androgyny means the deconstruction of stereotypes, "a movement away from sexual polarization and the prison of gender." If we grant that for some writers the goal of androgyny was the freedom to be active or passive or a mixture of the two regardless of biology, Heilburn's contention may be acceptable Ashis Nandy claims that in India the denigration of *klibatva*, or femininity-in-masculinity, as the "final negation of a man's political identity, a pathology more dangerous than femininity itself," was part of the disastrous legacy of colonialism. Indians became convinced that to fight the aggressive, controlling, and powerful oppressor it was necessary to adopt his standards of "masculinity," and thus created an absolute sexual polarization not native to Hindu culture. Contemporary objections to Jung and to the concept of androgyny should not lead to the dismissal of an idea that challenged the dominant constructions of gender during Yeats's lifetime. Yeats once argued that, "In judging any moment of past time we should leave out what has since happened" [*Explorations*]. We cannot do that, but as historicists we should balance contemporary theoretical questions with the solutions that were intellectually possible and politically useful at a specific moment in history.

Like many Romantic poets, Yeats was unable to identify with the norms of masculinity dominant in the late nineteenth century. He exalted emotion over reason. He loathed the Victorian myth of science and progress; and his early desire to cast out of his verse "those energetic rhythms, as of a man running" and replace them by "wavering, meditative, organic rhythms" [*Essays and Introductions*] demonstrates his rejection of masculine form. He espoused an organic, Keatsian, consciously essentialist "feminine" poetics in which "words are as subtle, as complex, as full of mysterious life, as the body of a flower or of a woman." His horoscope showed him to be a man dominated by the moon, and in his later years he developed a philosophy based upon a lunar myth that privileged traditionally feminine symbolism: moon over sun, night over day. Although his father praised active men, Yeats was timid and passive, dependent upon reverie and dreams for his inspiration. While the autonomous, unified phallic self of patriarchal tradition claims sole authorship both of history and literary texts, Yeats, whose most aggressively phallic symbol, the tower, is "Half dead at the top," subverted the potency of this imperial maleness; despite his post-1903 Nietzschean posturings, it was always an ironic mask. He described himself as "one that ruffled in a manly pose / For all his timid heart." His dialogical theory of the gyres, in which opposites alternately increase and decrease in strength but contain and never obliterate each other, reveals his rejection of a unitary position.

At the beginning of his career Yeats was metaphorically ravished by a Muse who displayed the traditionally masculine qualities of aggression and initiation. Laura Armstrong, whom he described as a "wild creature" [*Autobiographies*], "woke me from the metallic sleep of science and set me writing my first play." Although Armstrong played a conventionally feminine role in rescuing Yeats from the "metallic" sterility of rational and scientific thought and turning him toward the intuitive world of poetry, Yeats's portrait of himself as a Sleeping Prince awakened by an energetic Princess reverses gender stereotypes. His account of their first meeting emphasizes his passivity:

> I was climbing up a hill at Howth when I heard wheels behind me and a pony-carriage drew up beside me. A pretty girl was driving alone and without a hat. She told me her name and said we had friends in common and asked me to ride beside her. After that I saw a great deal of her and was soon in love. I did not tell her I was in love, however, because she was engaged. She had chosen me for her confidant and I learned all about her quarrels with her lover.

Armstrong, unconventionally hatless and driving alone, literally carried off the poet, who became the passive listener to her tales of love.

The Island of Statues, written for Armstrong, explores numerous ambiguities of gender. An Enchantress lives on an island, guarding the flower of immortality within a "brazen-gated glade." Penetration of this symbolically feminine enclosure is archetypally dangerous: male questers in search of the flower must be certain to choose correctly; if they fail, the Medusan Enchantress will turn them to stone. The plucking of a flower is an ancient metaphor for the taking of virginity, and we hardly need Freud's interpretation of the Medusa as the castrating female genitals surrounded by snaky hair to see in *The Island of Statues* a thinly veiled expression of Yeats's doubts about his ability to conform to traditional standards of masculine behavior. Indeed, the impotence of all the male characters in the play is striking. The lovers of the shepherdess Naschina, Thernot and Colin, are the first of Yeats's passive poets mesmerized by inaccessible and courageous females: Aillil in early versions of *The Shadowy Waters,* Septimus in the drafts of *The Player Queen,* Aleel in *The Countess Cathleen.* (Aleel was a Yeatsian self-portrait written to be played by a woman, Farr.) Naschina favors Almintor, an ostensibly more heroic type. Yeats, however, could not yet create a successful masculine male: Almintor chooses the wrong flower and is duly turned to stone. The resourceful Naschina assumes a male disguise and confronts the Enchantress. In a Shakespearian denouement, the Enchantress falls in love with the disguised shepherdess; but her infatuation destroys her, and Naschina restores the statues to life. Like Rosalind, Portia, and Viola, the androgynous female in male clothing unites the best qualities of both sexes. Yet while Shakespeare's transvestite heroines are reincorporated into conventional patriarchal society at the close of the action, Naschina's success transforms her into a figure of the excluded Eternal Feminine: at the end of the play, unlike her lover, she casts no shadow. A resourceful woman becomes Symbolic Woman. To add to the indeterminacy of effect, Yeats presents the Enchantress's unconsciously lesbian passion for the shepherdess with sympathy: a sympathy that Gonne endorsed in favoring the Enchantress and hating Naschina [*The Collected Letters: Volume I, 1865-1895*].

"The Wanderings of Oisin" (completed before Yeats met Gonne, but substantially revised thereafter) also has a heroine who, like Armstrong, takes the sexual initiative. Niamh "a child of the mighty Shee" comes from the land of the young to claim Oisin as her lover. As Yeats climbed into Armstrong's pony cart, Oisin mounts Niamh's steed and is captured by her: "she bound me / In triumph with her arms around me." Marital status, however, changes the "amorous demon" to "a frightened bird." Once "The gentle Niamh [is] my wife," she is made timid by fear of losing Oisin. Each time an object from Ireland reminds him of the human world he has left behind, Niamh, "white with sudden cares," tries to distract him by moving on. When he finally goes back she is left lamenting like Calypso or Dido: "I would die like a small withered leaf in the autumn, for breast unto breast / We shall mingle no

more." The epic form, unlike the lyric, gave Yeats a traditional model of masculinity: the epic hero leaves his women behind. Although Yeats later mockingly represented Oisin as "led by the nose / Through three enchanted islands," he was retrospectively projecting the masterful, rejecting Gonne into the timid and devoted figure of Niamh:

> But what cared I that set him on to ride,
> I, starved for the bosom of his faery bride?

At the time of the original composition he could not have been starved for her bosom, since he had not yet encountered her. Nevertheless, the lines describing Niamh, which were minimally changed during Yeats's numerous revisions, employ many of the images later associated with Gonne:

> A pearl-pale, high-born lady, who rode
> On a horse with a bridle of findrinny;
> And like a sunset were her lips,
> A stormy sunset o'er doomed ships.

A Rossettian iconography was waiting for its incarnation.

Yeats attempted no more epics. Aware that an audience accustomed to the "manly" patriotic ballad verse of *The Spirit of the Nation* might not appreciate his lyrics, he attempted in **"To Ireland in the Coming Times"** (1892) to establish himself as a masculine writer in a political context:

> *Know, that I would accounted be*
> *True brother of a company*
> *That sang, to sweeten Ireland's wrong,*
> *Ballad and story, rann and song.*

This poem subsumes the erotic longings focused on the symbol of the Rose under a political agenda: like many Irish poets before him Yeats writes love poetry to his country under the guise of a woman. One who must insist that he is the "true brother" of Davis, Mangan, and Ferguson, however, obviously expects his audience (explicitly constructed as male, as *"him who ponders well)* to doubt his gender identification, and suspect the femininity of his subject matter:

> *Nor be I any less of them,* [the true brothers]
> *Because the red-rose-bordered hem*
> *Of her, whose history began*
> *Before God made the angelic clan,*
> *Trails all about the written page.*

Yeats knows that his pursuit of *"faeries, dancing under the moon"* situates him on the margins of acceptable discourse. The lyric writer embraces a poetics that is already culturally gendered: as Parker [in *Literary Fat Ladies: Rhetoric, Gender, Property*] suggests, "much of the history of lyric associates it with the female or the effeminate." Its characteristics of emotion, brevity, and intimacy can be negatively coded as hysteria, triviality, and embarrassing self-revelation. The lyric writer may exploit the feminine, but he is also contaminated by it.

"The Madness of King Goll" (1887), for example, depicts the renunciation of political authority and prowess in war for the metaphorically feminine domain of nature, poetry, and madness. Abandoning his defense of Ireland against the Viking invaders, Goll becomes a crazed wanderer in the woods, a celebrant of the nature goddess Orchil. Only his harp affords him relief: poetry justifies his madness and alienation from masculine pursuits. The poem ends disastrously, however, with the instrument broken and the poet still exiled from the male world of political action: "My singing fades, the strings are torn, / I must away by wood and sea." Yeats's identification with this sexual and poetic impasse is suggested by his father's portrait of him as the mad king holding the broken harp.

Goll's pattern is repeated by Fergus, who in the *Taín* is a figure of great potency, the lover of the insatiable Queen Maeve. Yeats's Fergus seeks to exchange the public responsibilities of manhood for "the dreaming wisdom" of the Druid. The Druid warns of the loss of power and diminution of masculinity inherent in the choice of wisdom, dreams, and poetry:

> Look on my thin grey hair and hollow cheeks
> And on these hands that may not lift the sword,
> This body trembling like a wind-blown reed.
> No woman's loved me, no man sought my help.

Allen Grossman [in *Poetic Knowledge in The Early Yeats: A Study of The Wind Among The Reeds*] argues that in Yeats's early poetry the wind, symbol of vague desires and hopes, also represents the shifting and unstable libido. The image of the Druid's body "trembling like a wind-blown reed" suggests that, in choosing dreams, the Druid and Fergus open themselves to the sorrow of infinite and unsatisfied desire.

Desire, in **"The Man who Dreamed of Faeryland,"** destroys what society has defined as masculinity. The dreamer is on the threshold of manhood—as lover, as money-maker, as perpetrator of violence—but he is immobilized by the image of a timeless, feminine Faeryland where "Danaan fruitage makes a shower of moons." He is ruined by his inability to adapt to the patriarchal order, and by his impossible desire for a maternal paradise. Yeats seldom wrote about his mother. When he did, he associated her with Ireland and with the oral tradition, emphasizing her fondness for exchanging stories about fairies and supernatural events with the fishermen's wives at Howth. As a collector of Irish fairy stories he associated himself with the only happiness he ever saw his mother enjoy. In 1887 the unhappily married Susan Yeats suffered a stroke, and became mentally impaired. Yeats describes people who have withdrawn from the world into total or partial insanity as "away" or absent in fairyland. His account of his mother's stroke as a liberation into "perfect happiness" suggests that he saw her too, in her twelve-year absence, as an inhabitant of fairyland. Yeats's

vision of fairyland as the place of the mother, a psychic retreat from the problems and challenges of the world, was ambivalent: the cost of feminine wisdom might be insanity. Of the fairies he wrote:

> It is natural, too, that there should be a queen to every household of them, and that one should hear little of their kings, for women come more easily than men to that wisdom which ancient peoples, and all wild peoples even now, think the only wisdom. The self, which is the foundation of our knowledge, is broken in pieces by foolishness, and is forgotten in the sudden emotions of women, and therefore fools may get, and women do get of a certainty, glimpses of much that sanctity finds at the end of its painful journey.

Women, fairies, primitives, lunatics, and saints fracture the phallic, unified Cartesian self, foundation of the Law of the Father. Yeats felt his selfhood dispersed and threatened but his poetry enabled by his identification with these marginal figures.

Male selfhood and its constitution in language are central to **"The Song of the Happy Shepherd"** and **"The Sad Shepherd."** The Happy Shepherd rejects war, philosophy, and science, but, believing that "Words alone are certain good," he clings to the masculine Logos, to the constitutive importance of language: "The wandering earth herself may be / Only a sudden flaming word." He solipsistically affirms the self and its speech as the only "truth," but male identity is sustained by an Other:

> Go gather by the humming sea
> Some twisted, echo-harbouring shell,
> And to its lips thy story tell,
> And they thy comforters will be,
> Rewording in melodious guile
> Thy fretful words a little while,
> Till they shall singing fade in ruth
> And die a pearly brotherhood.

In **"The Sad Shepherd"** the "twisted, echo-harbouring shell" is characterized as female by "her wildering whirls." As in the myth of the nymph Echo, woman is a melodious hollow chamber, a sounding-board for male complaint. The Ovidian reference, however, also ironizes the speaker by identifying him with Narcissus. The happy shepherd, a verbal narcissist, suggests that the male find a sympathetic female who will repeat his words in her own way. She will add nothing original, nor will she speak of herself: man provides the lyrics, woman the melody. This hierarchical opposition, however, is complicated by the fact that in rewording Logos the "echo-harbouring shell" also transforms it into poetry: for Yeats the supremely important act. The masculine "brotherhood" of words will take a "pearly" color from the vessel through which it has passed.

"The Song of the Happy Shepherd," moreover, is answered by its companion poem, **"The Sad Shepherd,"** in which the sea-shell retakes the initiative. When the protagonist attempts to communicate with the stars, the sea, and the dewdrops, those archetypally "feminine" natural presences are busy talking to themselves. He therefore

> Sought once again the shore, and found a shell,
> And thought, *I will my heavy story tell*
> *Till my own words, re-echoing, shall send*
> *Their sadness through a hollow, pearly heart;*
> *And my own tale again for me shall sing,*
> *And my own whispering words be comforting,*
> *And lo! my ancient burden may depart.*

The words *"I," "my,"* and *"me"* dominate this passage. The egotistical shepherd discovers, however, that the "wildering whirls" of the female sea-shell dissipate the imperial self:

> Then he sang softly nigh the pearly rim;
> But the sad dweller by the sea-ways lone
> Changed all he sang to inarticulate moan
> Among her wildering whirls, forgetting him.

The world is not a single male word, Logos, comprehensible to all, but many female voices singing "inarticulate" melodies among themselves. In Kristevan terms, one who speaks the language of the father, the language of lack and desire, confronts but cannot understand the semiotic language of the mother, the "wildering whirls" of the onomatopoeic song of self-containment: he

> Cried all his story to the dewdrops glistening.
> But naught they heard, for they are always
>   listening,
> The dewdrops, for the sound of their own dropping.

In these two poems Yeats questions the relation of gender to poetry. Femininity is figured as oceanic, the origin both of being and of verse; but Yeats complicates this familiar representation by making the female archetypes impervious to the male who seeks to use them for his own expressive ends. They sing their own song. In [Hélène] Cixous's words, Yeats is one of those poets who frequently, though not always, "let something different from tradition get through." As a man who loves women and respects their difference while he identifies with them, and as a writer aware that the anxiety of masculinity is also the anxiety of modernity, he remakes inherited forms and tropes while remaining deeply conscious of his poetic precursors.

In early poems that are explicitly addressed to a mistress, and therefore formally located in the love tradition, Yeats accepts certain conventions: the woman as goddess, as Muse, as aesthetic object. His revisions of the genre, however, are demonstrated in his handling of the *carpe diem* formula. Poems in the *carpe diem* tradition, modelled on the works of Horace, Catullus, and Ovid, urge immediate sexual enjoyment in terms that devalue the object of desire. Although he wrote several poems within the tradition, Yeats could not muster the masculine bravado required by a genre that blatantly proffers male sexuality. In assuming the existence of female sexual pleasures, the *carpe diem* poets sometimes arrive at a cheerfully lascivious mutuality: Marvell enjoins his Coy Mistress to "roll all our strength, and all / Our

sweetness, up into one ball." Behind the impatient energy lies a threat, however. In *Twelfth Night* Shakespeare's Orsino voices the master metaphor of the genre: "For women are as roses whose fair flower / Being once displayed, doth fall that very hour." Innumerable manipulators of the formula use the rosebud cliché to insist that the woman who refuses to yield her chastity will wither on the branch, her essential biological purpose unfulfilled. Edmund Waller's "Go, Lovely Rose" epitomizes a tradition in which the perennial conflation of woman with nature emphasizes the passivity of the female, whose function is to display herself for male "commendation" and consumption:

> Bid her come forth,
> Suffer herself to be desired,
> And not blush so to be admired.

Even the syntax is passive. The comparison becomes overtly coercive in the final stanza, where the rose is instructed to:

>   die! that she
> The common fate of all things rare
> May read in thee;
> How small a part of time they share
> That are so wondrous sweet and fair!

Instead of concluding that the cruel mistress feared pregnancy, objected to his character or looks, or preferred someone else, the *carpe diem* poet arrogantly insisted that the woman's virginity was like uninvested capital: unless "used" by him it was "wasted." Waller implies that he is the young woman's only chance: if she refuses him she will never find another. In "To the Virgins, to Make Much of Time" Herrick also deploys withering rosebuds to claim that a woman sexually unused is a woman dead:

> Then be not coy, but use your time;
> And while you may, goe marry:
> For having lost but once your prime,
> You may for ever tarry.

Herrick is specific about the social implications of his economic and horticultural metaphors: if a woman "spends" time without "using" it to service a man, she will become a superfluous old maid. The message is repeated in poem after poem: woman's only function is to please physically and to procreate. She needs to make the most of her brief bloom: once it has gone she is worthless. Poets admit that men die too, but their useful and natural lives more nearly coincide. Loss of manly beauty does not mean loss of manly function.

Yeats did not present Gonne with Marvell's grotesque choice: yield your virginity to me or to the worms. His rejection of this convention may be demonstrated by comparing **"When You are Old"** with Ronsard's "Quand Vous Serez Bien Vielle," from which it derives:

> *Quand vous serez bien vielle, au soir, à la*
>   *chandelle,*
> *Assise aupres du feu, devidant & filant,*

Direz chantant mes vers, en vous esmerveillant,
Ronsard me celebroit du temps que j'estois belle.

Ronsard uses the conventional theme of mutability as an "erotic threat." If his mistress fails to satisfy him, *"Vous serez au fouyer une vielle acroupie, / Regrettant mon amour et vostre fier desdain."* She will be lonely and regretful because she has missed her chance with him, and he enjoys imagining her unhappiness. Yeats does not resort to such sexual bullying. His beloved is not admonished: *"Vivez, si m'en croyez, n'attendez a demain: / Cueillez des aujourd'huy les roses de la vie."* Yeats makes no mention of those perennially transient roses, nor is his poem an attempt at seduction. The woman will age whether or not she requites his love: he offers her the poem as a source of melancholy pleasure during the sleepy twilight of old age, a reminder that

> many loved your moments of glad grace,
> And loved your beauty with love false or true,
> But one man loved the pilgrim soul in you,
> And loved the sorrows of your changing face.

Although his verses recall her lost youth they do not accuse her of cruelty towards her celebrant: love has "fled"; she has not repelled him by her "fier desdain." The deterioration caused by aging is not used as a weapon against her; instead the poet lovingly details her present charm: her "soft look" and her "moments of glad grace." Ronsard's object of desire has no specific characteristics; she is, simply and unoriginally, "belle." Yeats values particular beauties of her body, but is even more attracted by beauty of soul: unlike other suitors he loved "the pilgrim soul in you / And loved the sorrows of your changing face." In his Introduction to *The Penguin Book of Love Poetry* Stallworthy notes with pained surprise that throughout the entire amatory tradition, "We look in vain for the features, lineaments of a living woman." It is Stallworthy's surprise that is remarkable: women in this tradition are objects, not individuals. Yeats's "pilgrim soul," however, a phrase we associate with Gonne's courage and determination, provides an exception to this rule. It associates her, moreover, with the journeying quester of male mythology rather than with the passive maiden of the courtly tradition. Nor can a pilgrim soul wither like a youthful body: Yeats subverts the *carpe diem* genre even as he employs it. His refusal to imitate Ronsard's sonnet form (his poem has twelve lines instead of fourteen) may even suggest a stylistic disengagement from that most traditional vehicle of the love tradition.

Instead of using mutability as a coercive strategy, Yeats promises to love his mistress even when she has lost the bloom of youth, and whether or not she yields to him. While others may desert her, he will remain faithful:

> Time's bitter flood will rise,
> Your beauty perish and be lost
> For all eyes but these eyes.

In assuring her that what he values is a beauty that he will always see, no matter what her outward appearance, Yeats abandons the crude assumption that a woman's worth is coterminous with her beauty. **"The Folly of Being Comforted"** enacts his rejection of that assumption:

> One that is ever kind said yesterday:
> "Your well-belovèd's hair has threads of grey,
> And little shadows come about her eyes;
> Time can but make it easier to be wise
> Though now it seems impossible, and so
> All that you need is patience."
>
> Heart cries, "No,
> I have not a crumb of comfort, not a grain.
> Time can but make her beauty over again."

The beauty of Yeats's beloved, which consists in energy rather than passivity, in "nobility" rather than in freshness of the flesh, can only increase with the passage of time. Here Yeats employs a modified, couplet form of the Shakespearian sonnet, but his claim that "Time can but make herbeauty over again" challenges Shakespeare's basic premise, which is that nothing but art or procreation can withstand the depredations of "Devouring Time" (Sonnet 19). Despite his emotional use of the concluding couplet, "if she'd but turn her head, / You'd know the folly of being comforted," Yeats refuses to claim, as Shakespeare does, that "in black ink my love may still shine bright" (Sonnet 65): a claim that witnesses more to the poet's desire for personal immortality than to the qualities of the beloved. In **"The Folly of Being Comforted"** the older woman inspires a devotion unlinked to the flawless skin and auburn hair of the young beauty:

> Because of that great nobleness of hers
> The fire that stirs about her, when she stirs,
> Burns but more clearly. O she had not these ways
> When all the wild summer was in her gaze.

Yeats's insecure masculinity prevented him from employing the sexually cynical poetics of the *carpe diem* mode. His use of the woman-as-rose metaphor . . . reflected his opinion that, "The only two powers that trouble the deeps are religion and love." His Rose is not a reminder of falling petals, but a Dantesque sacred symbol and an eternally desirable image of Ireland.

FURTHER READING

Bibliography

Cross, K. G. W., and Dunlop, R. T. *A Bibliography of Yeats Criticism 1887-1965*. London: Macmillan Press, 1971, 341 p.
> Lists reviews, essays, articles, whole books, dissertations and theses about Yeats and includes a chronology of Yeats's works.

Jochum, K. P. S. *W. B. Yeats: A Classified Bibliography of Criticism,* 2d ed. Urbana: University of Illinois Press, 1990, 1176 p.

Extensive bibliography listing approximately 12,000 items. Jochum notes that his aim is to be "complete" rather than "selective."

Wade, Allan. *A Bibliography of The Writings of W. B. Yeats,* 3d edition, revised and edited by Russel K. Alspach. Suffolk, Great Britain: Richard Clay (The Chaucer Press), 1968, 514 p.

Descriptive bibliography listing Yeats's work. Includes a thorough index of individual titles and a brief list of the major works about Yeats.

Biography

Ellman, Richard. *Yeats: The Man and the Masks.* New York: Macmillan Co., 1948, 331 p.

Biographical and critical study by a prominent American critic and Yeats scholar.

———. "Yeats's Second Puberty." *The New York Review of Books* XXXII, No. 8 (9 May 1985): 10-18.

Discussion of Yeats's belief that the vasectomy he underwent in 1934 brought on a "strange second puberty" and infused much of his late poetry with wildness and passion.

Foster, R. F. *W. B. Yeats: A Life, Volume 1: The Apprentice Mage, 1865-1914.* New York: Oxford University Press, 1997, 640 p.

An extensive examination of Yeats's early life within the social and political history of his time.

Gibbon, Monk. *The Masterpiece and the Man: Yeats As I Knew Him.* London: Rupert Hart-Davis, 1959, 226 p.

Biography based largely on the reminiscences of Yeats's younger cousin, Monk Gibbon, who was also acquainted with such Irish notables as A.E., George Moore, and Maud Gonne.

Hone, Joseph. *W. B. Yeats: 1865-1939.* London: Macmillan and Co., 1943, 504 p.

Generally regarded as the finest biography of Yeats. Hone had the help of Mrs. W. B. Yeats and Maud Gonne in preparing the text, as well as access to Yeats's unpublished papers.

Lynch, David. *Yeats: The Poetics of the Self.* Chicago: The University of Chicago Press, 1979, 240 p.

Psychoanalytic study of Yeats, his poetry, and his philosophies, based on the most recent psychological theories of narcissism.

Macgloin, T. P. "Yeats's Faltering World." *Sewanee Review* XCV, No. 3 (Summer 1987): 470-84.

Discusses Yeats's role within the social context of late nineteenth- and early twentieth-century Ireland.

Moore, Virginia. *The Unicorn: William Butler Yeats's Search for Reality.* New York: The Macmillan Co., 1954, 519 p.

Examination of Yeats's religious beliefs and occult researches; Moore's volume contains many excerpts from Yeats's notebooks and records of his magical Rosicrucian experiments.

Murphy, William M. *Prodigal Father: The Life of John Butler Yeats.* Ithaca, N.Y.: Cornell University Press, 1978, 649 p.

Biography of Yeats's artist father, whose philosophy and personality markedly influenced his son's career. There are many references to W. B. Yeats throughout the text.

Webster, Brenda S. *Yeats: A Psychoanalytic Study.* Stanford: Stanford University Press, 1973, 246 p.

Argues that "the central thread of Yeats's life and work is his tireless, driven effort to'remake' himself, to bring himself as man and artist into a satisfactory relationship both with his impulses and with a threatening reality."

Criticism

Adams, Hazard. *Blake and Yeats: The Contrary Vision.* Ithaca, N.Y.: Cornell University Press, 1955, 328 p.

Extensive comparison of the symbolic systems of Blake and Yeats, maintaining that "the vortex and related images provide a main link between the poets."

Allen, James Lovic. *Yeats's Epitaph: A Key to Symbolic Unity in His Life and Work.* Washington, D.C.: University Press of America, 1982, 270 p.

Monograph on Yeats's gravestone inscription, taken from the poem "Under Ben Bulben," attempting to establish the relationship of this poem to the rest of Yeats's work.

Beum, Robert. *The Poetic Art of William Butler Yeats.* New York: Frederick Ungar Publishing, 1969, 161 p.

Examines the prosody of Yeats's major poems with detailed analyses of metrics and rhymes.

Bloom, Harold, ed. *William Butler Yeats.* New York: Chelsea House Publishers, 1986, 232 p.

Reprints essays by notable scholars including Paul de Man, Richard Ellman, and Ian Fletcher.

———. "Yeats, Gnosticism and the Sacred Void." In his *Poetry and Repression: Revisionism from Blake to Stevens,* pp. 205-34. New Haven, CT: Yale University Press, 1976.

Discusses the origins of gnosticism as well as Yeats's use of it.

Bogan, Louise. "William Butler Yeats." In her *Selected Criticism: Poetry and Prose,* pp. 86-104. New York: Noonday Press, 1955.

Reprint of a 1938 essay in which Bogan hails Yeats as the greatest living poet writing in English. She discusses his career as one of continual development and growth.

Bornstein, George. *Transformations of Romanticism in Yeats, Eliot and Stevens.* Chicago: University of Chicago Press, 1976, 263 p.

Discussion of Yeats's part in the continuance of the Romantic tradition. There are references to Yeats throughout the book.

Bradford, Curtis B. *Yeats at Work.* Carbondale, IL: Southern Illinois University Press, 1965, 407 p.

Provides excerpts and analyses of Yeats's working

manuscripts of *The Wind Among the Reeds,* "The Wild Swans at Coole," "The Tower," and others.

Brunner, Larry. *Tragic Victory: The Doctrine of Subjective Salvation in the Poetry of W. B. Yeats.* Troy, NY: Whitson Publishing Co., 1987, 184 p.

Examines the theme of redemption in Yeats's poetry and maintains that his poems express a "struggle" that "epitomizes the terrible urgency of redemption and the utter inadequacy of subjectivity to attain it."

Clark, David R. *Yeats at Songs and Choruses.* Amherst: University of Massachusetts Press, 1983, 283 p.

Interprets manuscript versions of "Crazy Jane on the Day of Judgment," "Three Things," "After Long Silence," "Her Triumph," "Colonus' Praise," "From *Oedipus at Colonus*" and "From the *Antigone.*"

Diggory, Terence. *Yeats & American Poetry: The Tradition of the Self.* Princeton, NJ: Princeton University Press, 1983, 262 p.

Compares and contrasts the confessional poetry of several twentieth-century Modernist poets with the works of Yeats.

Ellman, Richard. "Yeats and Eliot." *Encounter* XXV, No. 1 (July 1965): 53-5.

Discusses Yeats's and Eliot's criticism of each other's poetry.

Finneran, Richard J. *Editing Yeats's Poems* New York: St. Martin's Press, 1987, 144 p.

A companion to *The Poems of W. B. Yeats, A New Edition* which provides explanations of that volume and discussions of the complexity in editing Yeats's poems.

Gardner, Joann. *Yeats and the Rhymers' Club: A Nineties' Perspective.* New York: Peter Lang, 1989, 249 p.

Describes Yeats's poetic friends of the 1890's and his literary relationships to them.

Hardy, Barbara. "Passion and Contemplation in Yeats's Love Poetry." In her *Feeling in Poetry,* pp. 67-83. Bloomington: Indiana University Press, 1977.

Maintains that Yeats is primarily concerned in his love poetry with making and contemplating images of actual experience and suggests that this poetry is best typified by short, intense lyrics.

Hassett, Joseph M. *Yeats and the Poetics of Hate.* New York: St. Martin's Press, 1986, 189 p.

Claims that Yeats was preoccupied with the emotion of hate and that an understanding of his feelings sheds light on the meaning of many of his poems.

Hoffman, Daniel. *Barbarous Knowledge: Myth in the Poetry of Yeats, Graves and Muir.* New York: Oxford University Press, 1967, 266 p.

Traces Yeats's career from his beginnings in the ballad tradition to his development of a mythological framework from which to draw subjects, characters, and imagery.

Hoffpauir, Richard. "Yeats or Hardy?" *The Southern Review* 19, No. 3 (July 1983): 519-47.

Compares the critical receptions of Yeats's and Hardy's careers, suggesting that one or the other must be regarded as the preeminent poet of the twentieth century and that such a choice excludes the other poet from serious consideration.

Jeffares, A. Norman. *The Circus Animals: Essays on W. B. Yeats.* London and Basingstoke: Macmillan and Co., 1970, 183 p.

Contains essays on Yeats, his father, and his friend Oliver St. John Gogarty, including examinations of Yeats's "mask," Yeats as a critic, gyres, and women in Yeats's poetry.

————. *A Commentary on "The Collected Poems of W. B. Yeats."* Stanford: Stanford University Press, 1968, 563 p.

Line by line explications of each poem in Yeats's *Collected Poems.*

————. *A New Commentary on the Poems of W. B. Yeats.* Stanford: Stanford University Press, 1984, 543 p.

Line by line explications of each poem in *The Poems: A New Edition* cross referenced to the second edition of Yeats's *Collected Poems* (1950).

————, ed. *W. B. Yeats: The Critical Heritage.* London: Routledge & Kegan Paul, 1977, 483 p.

Reprints reviews, essays, and other critical assessments written between 1884 and 1939 by prominent commentators.

Kishel, Joseph. "Yeats's Elegies." *Yeats-Eliot Review* 7, Nos. 1 & 2 (June 1982): 78-90.

Suggests that such poetry as *The Rose* and *In the Seven Woods* can profitably be reinterpreted as "partial elegies" and critically compared with Yeats's more traditional elegiac poems such as "In Memory of Major Robert Gregory," and "Easter 1916."

Kline, Gloria C. *The Last Courtly Lover: Yeats and the Idea of Woman.* Ann Arbor, MI: UMI Research Press, 1983, 199 p.

Describes the late nineteenth- and early twentieth-century notions about Medieval courtly love and applies them to Yeats's relationships with the women in his life.

Lerner, Laurence. "W. B. Yeats: Poet and Crank." *Proceedings of the British Academy,* XLIX (1963): 49-67.

Argues that Yeats's "eccentric" and "crackpot ideas" are transformed into "universal symbols" through his poetry.

Malins, Edward, and Purkins, John. *A Preface to Yeats, Second Edition.* New York: Longman, 1994, 218 p.

Offers a concise introduction to Yeats's poetry including studies of Yeats's life, the history of Ireland as it applies to his poetry, and the literary background of the poems.

McNally, James. "Cast a Cold Eye on Yeats on Arnold." *Victorian Poetry* 25, No. 2 (Summer 1987): 173-80.

Suggests that Yeats's criticism of Matthew Arnold can

be attributed to the fact that Yeats's poetry was influenced by Arnold but Yeats "had some difficulty in acknowledging debts or obligations."

Menon, V. K. Narayana. *The Development of William Butler Yeats*. Edinburgh and London: Oliver and Boyd, 1960, 92 p.

Second edition of a study of the form and content of Yeats's poetry, first published in 1942.

Murphy, Frank Hughes. *Yeats's Early Poetry: The Quest for Reconciliation*. Baton Rouge: Louisiana State University Press, 1975, 172 p.

Traces Yeats's "efforts toward an ultimate reconciliation of the contrary forces of human experience as they are reflected in the first eight groups of his lyric poetry, as arranged in *The Collected Poems*."

Murry, J. Middleton. "Mr. Yeats's Swan Song." In his *Aspects of Literature*, pp. 39-45. London: W. Collins Sons & Co., 1920.

Negative review of Yeats's *The Wild Swans at Coole*, maintaining that in this work Yeats's creativity and imagination failed him.

O'Donnell, William. *The Poetry of William Butler Yeats: An Introduction*. New York: Ungar, 1986, 192 p.

Provides a chronological survey of Yeats's poetry emphasizing "Yeats's masterful command of language and his willingness to face squarely the full complexity of life."

O'Faoláin, Seán. Review of *Selected Poems, Lyrical and Narrative*, by W. B. Yeats. *The Criterion* IX, No. xxxvi (April 1930): 523-28.

Comments on Yeats's poetic strengths and weaknesses in a review of *Selected Poems* which contains altered versions of many of Yeats's early works. In O'Faoláin's opinion, the earlier works were better in their original forms.

O'Neil, William. "Yeats on Poetry and Politics." *Midwest Quarterly* XXV, No. 1 (Autumn 1983): 64-73.

Offers a discussion of Yeats's career in the context of Irish political and social events of the period.

Pack, Robert. "Yeats as Spectator to Death." In his *Affirming Limits: Essays on Mortality, Choice, and Poetic Form*, pp. 151-73. Amherst: University of Massachusetts Press, 1985.

Examines the presentation of death in Yeats's poetry.

Perloff, Marjorie. *Rhyme and Meaning in the Poetry of Yeats*. The Netherlands and Paris: Mouton & Co., 1970, 249 p.

Provides a close technical study of "the phonetic character of Yeats's rhymes and the relation of rhyme and meaning in his lyric poetry."

Ramazani, Jahan. *Yeats and the Poetry of Death, Elegy, Self-Elegy, and the Sublime*. New Haven: Yale University Press, 1990, 244 p.

Applies theories of death to trace the "dialogue with death" in Yeats's lyrical poetry.

Ransom, John Crowe. "Yeats and His Symbols." *The Kenyon Review* 1, No. 3 (Summer 1939): 309-22.

Contends that comprehension of Yeats's symbolism requires no special or esoteric knowledge and that in the infrequent instances when obscure symbols occur, understanding them is not necessary to the enjoyment of the poem.

Rawson, Claude. "A Question of Potency." *Times Literary Supplement*, No. 4,399 (24 July 1987): 783-85.

Considers the effects of Yeats's vasectomy on his poetry and discusses Yeats's belief that a vital connection exists between "versemaking and lovemaking."

Regueiro, Helen. "Yeats." In her *The Limits of Imagination: Wordsworth, Yeats, and Stevens*, pp. 95-145. Ithaca and London: Cornell University Press, 1976.

Dialectical criticism that sees Yeats's poetry as his quest for unity of being.

Reid, Forrest. *W. B. Yeats: A Critical Study*. London: Martin Secker, 1915, 257 p.

Early survey containing criticism of the poems written before 1899.

Rosenthal, M. L. *Running to Paradise: Yeats's Poetic Art*. New York: Oxford University Press, 1994, 362 p.

Provides thorough critical evaluations of Yeats who is assessed by Rosenthal as "the greatest poet in this century writing in English."

Scott, Clive. "A Theme and Form: 'Leda and the Swan' and the Sonnet." *The Modern Language Review*, 74, Part I (January 1979): 1-11.

Examines Yeats's experiments with the sonnet form and mythological materials.

Shaw, Priscilla Washburn. *Rilke, Valéry and Yeats: The Domain of the Self*. New Brunswick, NJ: Rutgers University Press, 1964, 278 p.

Comparative study utilizing Yeats's works as a norm "between the poetic extremes of Rilke and Valéry" because, according to Shaw, Yeats's poetry "communicates a more balanced awareness of self and world, in which the irreducible existence of each is made felt."

Stallworthy, Jon. *Between the Lines: Yeats's Poetry in the Making*. London: Oxford University Press, 1963, 261 p.

Provides excerpts from original manuscripts and comparisons of finished versions of many of Yeats's well-known poems including "Sailing to Byzantium," "Byzantium," and "The Second Coming."

———. *Visions and Revisions in Yeats's Last Poems*. London: Oxford University Press, 1969, 181 p.

Provides excerpts from original manuscripts and detailed comparisons of finished versions of Yeats's later poems including "Lapis Lazuli," and "Under Ben Bulben."

———, ed. *Yeats's Last Poems, a Casebook*. London: Macmillan and Company, 1968, 280 p.

Offers twenty-two critical essays by eminent critics including W. H. Auden, J. C. Ransom, Louis Macneice and Curtis Bradford.

Thurley, Geoffrey. *The Turbulent Dream: Passion and Politics in the Poetry of W. B. Yeats.* St. Lucia, Australia: University of Queensland Press, 1983, 235 p.

Loosely chronological survey based on a dialectical structure. Thurley treats Yeats's career in three phases: "Thesis: Fantasy," "Antithesis: Terror," and "Synthesis: Gaiety."

Ure, Peter. *Towards a Mythology: Studies in the Poetry of W. B. Yeats.* London: University Press of Liverpool, 1946, 123 p.

Assesses the role of mythology in Yeats's poems, discusses how he adapts Irish myths, and suggests that Yeats uses myth to unify the abstract and concrete.

Warren, Austin. "William Butler Yeats: The Religion of a Poet." In his *Rage for Order: Essays in Criticism,* pp. 66-83. Chicago: University of Chicago Press, 1948.

Traces prominent influences in Yeats's spiritual development, including Irish mythology and Theosophy.

Weygandt, Cornelius. *Yeats and the Irish Renaissance: English Poetry of Today Against an American Background.* New York: Russell and Russell, 1937, 460 p.

An American view of early twentieth-century English poetry, with extensive references to Yeats throughout.

Wright, George T. "Yeats: The Tradition of Myself." In his *The Poet in the Poem: The Personae of Eliot, Yeats, and Pound,* pp. 88-123. Berkeley and Los Angeles: University of California Press, 1960.

Examines the narrative voice of Yeats's poetry.

Young, David. *Troubled Mirror: A Study of Yeats's "The Tower."* Iowa City: University of Iowa Press, 1987, 153 p.

Ranks Yeats among the greatest English poets based on a close reading of the poems in *The Tower* and argues that the work functions as one long poem.

Additional coverage of Yeats's life and career is contained in the following sources published by Gale Research: *Twentieth-Century Literary Criticism,* Vols. 1, 11, 18, 31; *DISCovering Authors*; *DISCovering Authors: Dramatists Module*; *DISCovering Authors: Most-Studied Authors Module*; *DISCovering Authors: Poets Module*; *World Literature Criticism*; *Contemporary Authors,* Vols. 104, 127; *Contemporary Authors New Revision Series,* Vol. 45; *Concise Dictionary of British Literary Biography, 1890-1914*; *Dictionary of Literary Biography,* Vols. 10, 19, 98, 156; and *Major Twentieth-Century Writers.*

Poetry Criticism
INDEXES

Literary Criticism Series
Cumulative Author Index

Cumulative Nationality Index

Cumulative Title Index

How to Use This Index

The main references

Calvino, Italo
1923–1985 .... **CLC 5, 8, 11, 22, 33, 39,
73; SSC 3**

list all author entries in the following Gale Literary Criticism series:

BLC = *Black Literature Criticism*
CLC = *Contemporary Literary Criticism*
CLR = *Children's Literature Review*
CMLC = *Classical and Medieval Literature Criticism*
DA = *DISCovering Authors*
DAB = *DISCovering Authors: British*
DAC = *DISCovering Authors: Canadian*
DAM = *DISCovering Authors: Modules*
    DRAM: *Dramatists Module;* *MST*: *Most-Studied Authors Module;*
    MULT: *Multicultural Authors Module;* *NOV*: *Novelists Module;*
    POET: *Poets Module;* *POP*: *Popular Fiction and Genre Authors Module*
DC = *Drama Criticism*
HLC = *Hispanic Literature Criticism*
LC = *Literature Criticism from 1400 to 1800*
NCLC = *Nineteenth-Century Literature Criticism*
PC = *Poetry Criticism*
SSC = *Short Story Criticism*
TCLC = *Twentieth-Century Literary Criticism*
WLC = *World Literature Criticism, 1500 to the Present*

The cross-references

See also CANR 23; CA 85-88;
   obituary CA116

list all author entries in the following Gale biographical and literary sources:

AAYA = *Authors & Artists for Young Adults*
AITN = *Authors in the News*
BEST = *Bestsellers*
BW = *Black Writers*
CA = *Contemporary Authors*
CAAS = *Contemporary Authors Autobiography Series*
CABS = *Contemporary Authors Bibliographical Series*
CANR = *Contemporary Authors New Revision Series*
CAP = *Contemporary Authors Permanent Series*
CDALB = *Concise Dictionary of American Literary Biography*
CDBLB = *Concise Dictionary of British Literary Biography*
DLB = *Dictionary of Literary Biography*
DLBD = *Dictionary of Literary Biography Documentary Series*
DLBY = *Dictionary of Literary Biography Yearbook*
HW = *Hispanic Writers*
JRDA = *Junior DISCovering Authors*
MAICYA = *Major Authors and Illustrators for Children and Young Adults*
MTCW = *Major 20th-Century Writers*
NNAL = *Native North American Literature*
SAAS = *Something about the Author Autobiography Series*
SATA = *Something about the Author*
YABC = *Yesterday's Authors of Books for Children*

Literary Criticism Series
Cumulative Author Index

Ambler, Eric 1909- ...... **CLC 4, 6, 9**
See also CA 9-12R; CANR 7, 38; DLB 77;
MTCW

Amichai, Yehuda 1924- .... **CLC 9, 22, 57**
See also CA 85-88; CANR 46, 60; MTCW

Amichai, Yehudah
See Amichai, Yehuda

Amiel, Henri Frederic 1821-1881 .... **NCLC 4**

Amis, Kingsley (William)
1922-1995 ....   **CLC 1, 2, 3, 5, 8, 13, 40,
44; DA; DAB; DAC; DAM MST, NOV**
See also AITN 2; CA 9-12R; 150; CANR 8,
28, 54; CDBLB 1945-1960; DLB 15, 27,
100, 139; DLBY 96; INT CANR-8; MTCW

Amis, Martin (Louis)
1949- .... **CLC 4, 9, 38, 62, 101**
See also BEST 90:3; CA 65-68; CANR 8, 27,
54; DLB 14; INT CANR-27

Ammons, A(rchie) R(andolph)
1926- ..... **CLC 2, 3, 5, 8, 9, 25, 57; DAM
POET; PC 16**
See also AITN 1; CA 9-12R; CANR 6, 36, 51;
DLB 5, 165; MTCW

Amo, Tauraatua i
See Adams, Henry (Brooks)

Anand, Mulk Raj 1905- .. **CLC 23, 93; DAM
NOV**
See also CA 65-68; CANR 32; MTCW

Anatol
See Schnitzler, Arthur

Anaximander
c. 610B.C.-c. 546B.C. .... **CMLC 22**

Anaya, Rudolfo A(lfonso)
1937- ...... **CLC 23; DAM MULT, NOV;
HLC**
See also AAYA 20; CA 45-48; CAAS 4;
CANR 1, 32, 51; DLB 82; HW 1; MTCW

Andersen, Hans Christian
1805-1875 .... **NCLC 7; DA; DAB; DAC;
DAM MST, POP; SSC 6; WLC**
See also CLR 6; MAICYA; YABC 1

Anderson, C. Farley
See Mencken, H(enry) L(ouis); Nathan, George
Jean

Anderson, Jessica (Margaret) Queale
1916- .... **CLC 37**
See also CA 9-12R; CANR 4, 62

Anderson, Jon (Victor)
1940- .... **CLC 9; DAM POET**
See also CA 25-28R; CANR 20

Anderson, Lindsay (Gordon)
1923-1994 .... **CLC 20**
See also CA 125; 128; 146

Anderson, Maxwell
1888-1959 .... **TCLC 2; DAM DRAM**
See also CA 105; 152; DLB 7

Anderson, Poul (William) 1926- .... **CLC 15**
See also AAYA 5; CA 1-4R; CAAS 2; CANR
2, 15, 34; DLB 8; INT CANR-15; MTCW;
SATA 90; SATA-Brief 39

Anderson, Robert (Woodruff)
1917- .... **CLC 23; DAM DRAM**
See also AITN 1; CA 21-24R; CANR 32; DLB
7

Anderson, Sherwood
1876-1941 ... **TCLC 1, 10, 24; DA; DAB;
DAC; DAM MST, NOV; SSC 1; WLC**
See also CA 104; 121; CANR 61; CDALB
1917-1929; DLB 4, 9, 86; DLBD 1; MTCW

Andier, Pierre
See Desnos, Robert

Andouard
See Giraudoux, (Hippolyte) Jean

Andrade, Carlos Drummond de .... **CLC 18**
See also Drummond de Andrade, Carlos

Andrade, Mario de 1893-1945 .... **TCLC 43**

Andreae, Johann V(alentin)
1586-1654 .... **LC 32**
See also DLB 164

Andreas-Salome, Lou
1861-1937 .... **TCLC 56**
See also DLB 66

Andress, Lesley
See Sanders, Lawrence

Andrewes, Lancelot 1555-1626 .... **LC 5**
See also DLB 151, 172

Andrews, Cicily Fairfield
See West, Rebecca

Andrews, Elton V.
See Pohl, Frederik

Andreyev, Leonid (Nikolaevich)
1871-1919 .... **TCLC 3**
See also CA 104

Andric, Ivo 1892-1975 .... **CLC 8**
See also CA 81-84; 57-60; CANR 43, 60; DLB
147; MTCW

Androvar
See Prado (Calvo), Pedro

Angelique, Pierre
See Bataille, Georges

Angell, Roger 1920- .... **CLC 26**
See also CA 57-60; CANR 13, 44; DLB 171

Angelou, Maya 1928- .... **CLC 12, 35, 64, 77;
BLC; DA; DAB; DAC; DAM MST,
MULT, POET, POP; WLCS**
See also AAYA 7, 20; BW 2; CA 65-68; CANR
19, 42; DLB 38; MTCW; SATA 49

Annensky, Innokenty (Fyodorovich)
1856-1909 .... **TCLC 14**
See also CA 110; 155

Annunzio, Gabriele d'
See D'Annunzio, Gabriele

Anodos
See Coleridge, Mary E(lizabeth)

Anon, Charles Robert
See Pessoa, Fernando (Antonio Nogueira)

Anouilh, Jean (Marie Lucien Pierre)
1910-1987 **CLC 1, 3, 8, 13, 40, 50; DAM
DRAM**
See also CA 17-20R; 123; CANR 32; MTCW

Anthony, Florence
See Ai

Anthony, John
See Ciardi, John (Anthony)

Anthony, Peter
See Shaffer, Anthony (Joshua); Shaffer, Peter
(Levin)

Anthony, Piers 1934- .... **CLC 35; DAM POP**
See also AAYA 11; CA 21-24R; CANR 28, 56;
DLB 8; MTCW; SAAS 22; SATA 84

Antoine, Marc
See Proust, (Valentin-Louis-George-Eugene-)
Marcel

Antoninus, Brother
See Everson, William (Oliver)

Antonioni, Michelangelo 1912- .... **CLC 20**
See also CA 73-76; CANR 45

Antschel, Paul 1920-1970
See Celan, Paul
See also CA 85-88; CANR 33, 61; MTCW

Anwar, Chairil 1922-1949 .... **TCLC 22**
See also CA 121

Apollinaire, Guillaume
1880-1918 **TCLC 3, 8, 51; DAM POET;
PC 7**
See also Kostrowitzki, Wilhelm Apollinaris de
See also CA 152

Appelfeld, Aharon 1932- .... **CLC 23, 47**
See also CA 112; 133

Apple, Max (Isaac)
1941- .... **CLC 9, 33**
See also CA 81-84; CANR 19, 54; DLB 130

Appleman, Philip (Dean) 1926- .... **CLC 51**
See also CA 13-16R; CAAS 18; CANR 6, 29,
56

Appleton, Lawrence
See Lovecraft, H(oward) P(hillips)

Apteryx
See Eliot, T(homas) S(tearns)

Apuleius, (Lucius Madaurensis)
125(?)-175(?) .... **CMLC 1**

Aquin, Hubert 1929-1977 .... **CLC 15**
See also CA 105; DLB 53

Aragon, Louis
    1897-1982CLC 3, 22; DAM NOV, POET
    See also CA 69-72; 108; CANR 28; DLB 72;
    MTCW

Arany, Janos 1817-1882 .... NCLC 34

Arbuthnot, John 1667-1735 .... LC 1
    See also DLB 101

Archer, Herbert Winslow
    See Mencken, H(enry) L(ouis)

Archer, Jeffrey (Howard) 1940- ..... CLC 28;
    DAM POP
    See also AAYA 16; BEST 89:3; CA 77-80;
    CANR 22, 52; INT CANR-22

Archer, Jules 1915- .... CLC 12
    See also CA 9-12R; CANR 6; SAAS 5; SATA
    4, 85

Archer, Lee
    See Ellison, Harlan (Jay)

Arden, John 1930- .... CLC 6, 13, 15; DAM
    DRAM
    See also CA 13-16R; CAAS 4; CANR 31; DLB
    13; MTCW

Arenas, Reinaldo
    1943-1990 ......   CLC 41; DAM MULT;
    HLC
    See also CA 124; 128; 133; DLB 145; HW

Arendt, Hannah 1906-1975 .... CLC 66, 98
    See also CA 17-20R; 61-64; CANR 26, 60;
    MTCW

Aretino, Pietro 1492-1556 .... LC 12

Arghezi, Tudor .... CLC 80
    See also Theodorescu, Ion N.

Arguedas, Jose Maria
    1911-1969 .... CLC 10, 18
    See also CA 89-92; DLB 113; HW

Argueta, Manlio 1936- .... CLC 31
    See also CA 131; DLB 145; HW

Ariosto, Ludovico 1474-1533 .... LC 6

Aristides
    See Epstein, Joseph

Aristophanes
    450B.C.-385B.C. ... CMLC 4; DA; DAB;
    DAC; DAM DRAM, MST; DC 2; WLCS
    See also DLB 176

Arlt, Roberto (Godofredo Christophersen)
    1900-1942 .... TCLC 29; DAM MULT;
    HLC
    See also CA 123; 131; HW

Armah, Ayi Kwei 1939-..... CLC 5, 33; BLC;
    DAM MULT, POET
    See also BW 1; CA 61-64; CANR 21; DLB
    117; MTCW

Armatrading, Joan 1950- .... CLC 17
    See also CA 114

Arnette, Robert
    See Silverberg, Robert

**Arnim, Achim von (Ludwig Joachim von
    Arnim)** 1781-1831 ...... NCLC 5; SSC 29
    See also DLB 90

Arnim, Bettina von 1785-1859 .... NCLC 38
    See also DLB 90

Arnold, Matthew
    1822-1888 .... NCLC 6, 29; DA; DAB;
    DAC; DAM MST, POET; PC 5; WLC
    See also CDBLB 1832-1890; DLB 32, 57

Arnold, Thomas 1795-1842 .... NCLC 18
    See also DLB 55

Arnow, Harriette (Louisa) Simpson
    1908-1986 .... CLC 2, 7, 18
    See also CA 9-12R; 118; CANR 14; DLB 6;
    MTCW; SATA 42; SATA-Obit 47

Arp, Hans
    See Arp, Jean

Arp, Jean 1887-1966 .... CLC 5
    See also CA 81-84; 25-28R; CANR 42

Arrabal
    See Arrabal, Fernando

Arrabal, Fernando 1932-.... CLC 2, 9, 18, 58
    See also CA 9-12R; CANR 15

Arrick, Fran .... CLC 30
    See also Gaberman, Judie Angell

Artaud, Antonin (Marie Joseph)
    1896-1948 .... TCLC 3, 36; DAM DRAM
    See also CA 104; 149

Arthur, Ruth M(abel) 1905-1979 ...... CLC 12
    See also CA 9-12R; 85-88; CANR 4; SATA 7,
    26

Artsybashev, Mikhail (Petrovich)
    1878-1927 .... TCLC 31

Arundel, Honor (Morfydd)
    1919-1973 .... CLC 17
    See also CA 21-22; 41-44R; CAP 2; CLR 35;
    SATA 4; SATA-Obit 24

Arzner, Dorothy 1897-1979 .... CLC 98

Asch, Sholem 1880-1957 .... TCLC 3
    See also CA 105

Ash, Shalom
    See Asch, Sholem

Ashbery, John (Lawrence)
    1927-.... CLC 2, 3, 4, 6, 9, 13, 15, 25, 41,
    77; DAM POET
    See also CA 5-8R; CANR 9, 37; DLB 5, 165;
    DLBY 81; INT CANR-9; MTCW

Ashdown, Clifford
    See Freeman, R(ichard) Austin

Ashe, Gordon
    See Creasey, John

Ashton-Warner, Sylvia (Constance)
    1908-1984 .... CLC 19
    See also CA 69-72; 112; CANR 29;
    MTCW

Asimov, Isaac
    1920-1992 .... CLC 1, 3, 9, 19, 26, 76, 92;
    DAM POP
    See also AAYA 13; BEST 90:2; CA 1-4R;
    137; CANR 2, 19, 36, 60; CLR 12; DLB
    8; DLBY 92; INT CANR-19; JRDA;
    MAICYA; MTCW; SATA 1, 26, 74

Assis, Joaquim Maria Machado de
    See Machado de Assis, Joaquim Maria

Astley, Thea (Beatrice May)
    1925- .... CLC 41
    See also CA 65-68; CANR 11, 43

Aston, James
    See White, T(erence) H(anbury)

Asturias, Miguel Angel
    1899-1974 ... CLC 3, 8, 13; DAM MULT,
    NOV; HLC
    See also CA 25-28; 49-52; CANR 32; CAP
    2; DLB 113; HW; MTCW

Atares, Carlos Saura
    See Saura (Atares), Carlos

Atheling, William
    See Pound, Ezra (Weston Loomis)

Atheling, William, Jr.
    See Blish, James (Benjamin)

Atherton, Gertrude (Franklin Horn)
    1857-1948 .... TCLC 2
    See also CA 104; 155; DLB 9, 78

Atherton, Lucius
    See Masters, Edgar Lee

Atkins, Jack
    See Harris, Mark

Atkinson, Kate .... CLC 99

Attaway, William (Alexander)
    1911-1986 .... CLC 92; BLC; DAM
    MULT
    See also BW 2; CA 143; DLB 76

Atticus
    See Fleming, Ian (Lancaster)

Atwood, Margaret (Eleanor)
    1939- .   CLC 2, 3, 4, 8, 13, 15, 25,
    44, 84; DA; DAB; DAC; DAM
    MST, NOV, POET; PC 8; SSC 2;
    WLC
    See also AAYA 12; BEST 89:2; CA 49-
    52; CANR 3, 24, 33, 59; DLB 53; INT
    CANR-24; MTCW; SATA 50

Aubigny, Pierre d'
    See Mencken, H(enry) L(ouis)

Aubin, Penelope
    1685-1731(?) .... LC 9
    See also DLB 39

Auchincloss, Louis (Stanton)
1917- ... **CLC 4, 6, 9, 18, 45; DAM NOV; SSC 22**
See also CA 1-4R; CANR 6, 29, 55; DLB 2; DLBY 80; INT CANR-29; MTCW

Auden, W(ystan) H(ugh)
1907-1973 ... **CLC 1, 2, 3, 4, 6, 9, 11, 14, 43; DA; DAB; DAC; DAM DRAM, MST, POET; PC 1; WLC**
See also AAYA 18; CA 9-12R; 45-48; CANR 5, 61; CDBLB 1914-1945; DLB 10, 20; MTCW

Audiberti, Jacques
1900-1965 .... **CLC 38; DAM DRAM**
See also CA 25-28R

Audubon, John James 1785-1851 .. **NCLC 47**

Auel, Jean M(arie)
1936- .... **CLC 31; DAM POP**
See also AAYA 7; BEST 90:4; CA 103; CANR 21; INT CANR-21; SATA 91

Auerbach, Erich 1892-1957 .... **TCLC 43**
See also CA 118; 155

Augier, Emile 1820-1889 .... **NCLC 31**

August, John
See De Voto, Bernard (Augustine)

Augustine, St. 354-430 .... **CMLC 6; DAB**

Aurelius
See Bourne, Randolph S(illiman)

Aurobindo, Sri 1872-1950 .... **TCLC 63**

Austen, Jane
1775-1817 ..... **NCLC 1, 13, 19, 33, 51; DA; DAB; DAC; DAM MST, NOV; WLC**
See also AAYA 19; CDBLB 1789-1832; DLB 116

Auster, Paul 1947- .... **CLC 47**
See also CA 69-72; CANR 23, 52

Austin, Frank
See Faust, Frederick (Schiller)

Austin, Mary (Hunter)
1868-1934 .... **TCLC 25**
See also CA 109; DLB 9, 78

Autran Dourado, Waldomiro
See Dourado, (Waldomiro Freitas) Autran

Averroes 1126-1198 .... **CMLC 7**
See also DLB 115

Avicenna 980-1037 .... **CMLC 16**
See also DLB 115

Avison, Margaret
1918- .... **CLC 2, 4, 97; DAC; DAM POET**
See also CA 17-20R; DLB 53; MTCW

Axton, David
See Koontz, Dean R(ay)

Ayckbourn, Alan
1939- . **CLC 5, 8, 18, 33, 74; DAB; DAM DRAM**
See also CA 21-24R; CANR 31, 59; DLB 13; MTCW

Aydy, Catherine
See Tennant, Emma (Christina)

Ayme, Marcel (Andre)
1902-1967 .... **CLC 11**
See also CA 89-92; CLR 25; DLB 72; SATA 91

Ayrton, Michael 1921-1975 .... **CLC 7**
See also CA 5-8R; 61-64; CANR 9, 21

Azorin .... **CLC 11**
See also Martinez Ruiz, Jose

Azuela, Mariano
1873-1952 .... **TCLC 3; DAM MULT; HLC**
See also CA 104; 131; HW; MTCW

Baastad, Babbis Friis
See Friis-Baastad, Babbis Ellinor

Bab
See Gilbert, W(illiam) S(chwenck)

Babbis, Eleanor
See Friis-Baastad, Babbis Ellinor

Babel, Isaac
See Babel, Isaak (Emmanuilovich)

Babel, Isaak (Emmanuilovich)
1894-1941(?) .... **TCLC 2, 13; SSC 16**
See also CA 104; 155

Babits, Mihaly 1883-1941 .... **TCLC 14**
See also CA 114

Babur 1483-1530 .... **LC 18**

Bacchelli, Riccardo 1891-1985 .... **CLC 19**
See also CA 29-32R; 117

Bach, Richard (David)
1936- .... **CLC 14; DAM NOV, POP**
See also AITN 1; BEST 89:2; CA 9-12R; CANR 18; MTCW; SATA 13

Bachman, Richard
See King, Stephen (Edwin)

Bachmann, Ingeborg 1926-1973 .... **CLC 69**
See also CA 93-96; 45-48; DLB 85

Bacon, Francis 1561-1626 .... **LC 18, 32**
See also CDBLB Before 1660; DLB 151

Bacon, Roger 1214(?)-1292 .... **CMLC 14**
See also DLB 115

Bacovia, George .... **TCLC 24**
See also Vasiliu, Gheorghe

Badanes, Jerome 1937- .... **CLC 59**

Bagehot, Walter 1826-1877 .... **NCLC 10**
See also DLB 55

Bagnold, Enid 1889-1981 .... **CLC 25; DAM DRAM**
See also CA 5-8R; 103; CANR 5, 40; DLB 13, 160; MAICYA; SATA 1, 25

Bagritsky, Eduard 1895-1934 .... **TCLC 60**

Bagrjana, Elisaveta
See Belcheva, Elisaveta

Bagryana, Elisaveta .... **CLC 10**
See also Belcheva, Elisaveta
See also DLB 147

Bailey, Paul 1937- .... **CLC 45**
See also CA 21-24R; CANR 16, 62; DLB 14

Baillie, Joanna 1762-1851 .... **NCLC 2**
See also DLB 93

Bainbridge, Beryl (Margaret)
1933- ..... **CLC 4, 5, 8, 10, 14, 18, 22, 62; DAM NOV**
See also CA 21-24R; CANR 24, 55; DLB 14; MTCW

Baker, Elliott 1922- .... **CLC 8**
See also CA 45-48; CANR 2

Baker, Jean H. .... **TCLC 3, 10**
See also Russell, George William

Baker, Nicholson
1957- .... **CLC 61; DAM POP**
See also CA 135

Baker, Ray Stannard
1870-1946 .... **TCLC 47**
See also CA 118

Baker, Russell (Wayne) 1925- .... **CLC 31**
See also BEST 89:4; CA 57-60; CANR 11, 41, 59; MTCW

Bakhtin, M.
See Bakhtin, Mikhail Mikhailovich

Bakhtin, M. M.
See Bakhtin, Mikhail Mikhailovich

Bakhtin, Mikhail
See Bakhtin, Mikhail Mikhailovich

Bakhtin, Mikhail Mikhailovich
1895-1975 .... **CLC 83**
See also CA 128; 113

Bakshi, Ralph 1938(?)- .... **CLC 26**
See also CA 112; 138

Bakunin, Mikhail (Alexandrovich)
1814-1876 .... **NCLC 25, 58**

Baldwin, James (Arthur)
1924-1987 .... **CLC 1, 2, 3, 4, 5, 8, 13, 15, 17, 42, 50, 67, 90; BLC; DA; DAB; DAC; DAM MST, MULT, NOV, POP; DC 1; SSC 10; WLC**
See also AAYA 4; BW 1; CA 1-4R; 124; CABS 1; CANR 3, 24; CDALB 1941-1968; DLB 2, 7, 33; DLBY 87; MTCW; SATA 9; SATA-Obit 54

Bass, Kingsley B., Jr.
See Bullins, Ed

Bass, Rick 1958- .... **CLC 79**
See also CA 126; CANR 53

Bassani, Giorgio 1916- .... **CLC 9**
See also CA 65-68; CANR 33; DLB 128, 177;
MTCW

Bastos, Augusto (Antonio) Roa
See Roa Bastos, Augusto (Antonio)

Bataille, Georges 1897-1962 .... **CLC 29**
See also CA 101; 89-92

Bates, H(erbert) E(rnest)
1905-1974 ... **CLC 46; DAB; DAM POP;
SSC 10**
See also CA 93-96; 45-48; CANR 34; DLB
162; MTCW

Bauchart
See Camus, Albert

Baudelaire, Charles
1821-1867 ... **NCLC 6, 29, 55; DA; DAB;
DAC; DAM MST, POET; PC 1; SSC 18;
WLC**

Baudrillard, Jean 1929- .... **CLC 60**

Baum, L(yman) Frank 1856-1919 ... **TCLC 7**
See also CA 108; 133; CLR 15; DLB 22;
JRDA; MAICYA; MTCW; SATA 18

Baum, Louis F.
See Baum, L(yman) Frank

Baumbach, Jonathan
1933- .... **CLC 6, 23**
See also CA 13-16R; CAAS 5; CANR 12;
DLBY 80; INT CANR-12; MTCW

Bausch, Richard (Carl)
1945- .... **CLC 51**
See also CA 101; CAAS 14; CANR 43, 61;
DLB 130

Baxter, Charles
1947- .... **CLC 45, 78; DAM POP**
See also CA 57-60; CANR 40; DLB 130

Baxter, George Owen
See Faust, Frederick (Schiller)

Baxter, James K(eir) 1926-1972 .... **CLC 14**
See also CA 77-80

Baxter, John
See Hunt, E(verette) Howard, (Jr.)

Bayer, Sylvia
See Glassco, John

Baynton, Barbara 1857-1929 .... **TCLC 57**

Beagle, Peter S(oyer) 1939- .... **CLC 7, 104**
See also CA 9-12R; CANR 4, 51; DLBY 80;
INT CANR-4; SATA 60

Bean, Normal
See Burroughs, Edgar Rice

Beard, Charles A(ustin)
1874-1948 .... **TCLC 15**
See also CA 115; DLB 17; SATA 18

Beardsley, Aubrey 1872-1898 .... **NCLC 6**

Beattie, Ann 1947- ..... **CLC 8, 13, 18, 40, 63;
DAM NOV, POP; SSC 11**
See also BEST 90:2; CA 81-84; CANR 53;
DLBY 82; MTCW

Beattie, James 1735-1803 .... **NCLC 25**
See also DLB 109

Beauchamp, Kathleen Mansfield 1888-1923
See Mansfield, Katherine
See also CA 104; 134; DA; DAC; DAM
MST

Beaumarchais, Pierre-Augustin Caron de
1732-1799 .... **DC 4**
See also DAM DRAM

Beaumont, Francis
1584(?)-1616 .... **LC 33; DC 6**
See also CDBLB Before 1660; DLB 58, 121

**Beauvoir, Simone (Lucie Ernestine Marie
Bertrand) de**
1908-1986 ... **CLC 1, 2, 4, 8, 14, 31, 44,
50, 71; DA; DAB; DAC; DAM MST,
NOV; WLC**
See also CA 9-12R; 118; CANR 28, 61; DLB
72; DLBY 86; MTCW

Becker, Carl (Lotus) 1873-1945 ..... **TCLC 63**
See also CA 157; DLB 17

Becker, Jurek 1937-1997 .... **CLC 7, 19**
See also CA 85-88; 157; CANR 60; DLB 75

Becker, Walter 1950- .... **CLC 26**

Beckett, Samuel (Barclay)
1906-1989 ... **CLC 1, 2, 3, 4, 6, 9, 10, 11,
14, 18, 29, 57, 59, 83; DA; DAB; DAC;
DAM DRAM, MST, NOV; SSC 16;
WLC**
See also CA 5-8R; 130; CANR 33, 61;
CDBLB 1945-1960; DLB 13, 15; DLBY
90; MTCW

Beckford, William 1760-1844 .... **NCLC 16**
See also DLB 39

Beckman, Gunnel 1910- .... **CLC 26**
See also CA 33-36R; CANR 15; CLR 25;
MAICYA; SAAS 9; SATA 6

Becque, Henri 1837-1899 .... **NCLC 3**

Beddoes, Thomas Lovell 1803-1849 **NCLC 3**
See also DLB 96

Bede c. 673-735 .... **CMLC 20**
See also DLB 146

Bedford, Donald F.
See Fearing, Kenneth (Flexner)

Beecher, Catharine Esther
1800-1878 .... **NCLC 30**
See also DLB 1

Beecher, John 1904-1980 .... **CLC 6**
See also AITN 1; CA 5-8R; 105; CANR 8

Beer, Johann 1655-1700 .... **LC 5**
See also DLB 168

Beer, Patricia 1924- .... **CLC 58**
See also CA 61-64; CANR 13, 46; DLB 40

Beerbohm, Max
See Beerbohm, (Henry) Max(imilian)

Beerbohm, (Henry) Max(imilian)
1872-1956 .... **TCLC 1, 24**
See also CA 104; 154; DLB 34, 100

Beer-Hofmann, Richard
1866-1945 .... **TCLC 60**
See also CA 160; DLB 81

Begiebing, Robert J(ohn) 1946- .... **CLC 70**
See also CA 122; CANR 40

Behan, Brendan 1923-1964 **CLC 1, 8, 11, 15,
79; DAM DRAM**
See also CA 73-76; CANR 33; CDBLB 1945-
1960; DLB 13; MTCW

Behn, Aphra 1640(?)-1689 ...... **LC 1, 30; DA;
DAB; DAC; DAM DRAM, MST, NOV,
POET; DC 4; PC 13; WLC**
See also DLB 39, 80, 131

Behrman, S(amuel) N(athaniel)
1893-1973 .... **CLC 40**
See also CA 13-16; 45-48; CAP 1; DLB 7, 44

Belasco, David 1853-1931 .... **TCLC 3**
See also CA 104; DLB 7

Belcheva, Elisaveta 1893- .... **CLC 10**
See also Bagryana, Elisaveta

Beldone, Phil "Cheech"
See Ellison, Harlan (Jay)

Beleno
See Azuela, Mariano

Belinski, Vissarion Grigoryevich
1811-1848 .... **NCLC 5**

Belitt, Ben 1911- .... **CLC 22**
See also CA 13-16R; CAAS 4; CANR 7; DLB
5

Bell, Gertrude 1868-1926 .... **TCLC 67**
See also DLB 174

Bell, James Madison 1826-1902 ... **TCLC 43;
BLC; DAM MULT**
See also BW 1; CA 122; 124; DLB 50

Bell, Madison Smartt 1957- ...... **CLC 41, 102**
See also CA 111; CANR 28, 54

Bell, Marvin (Hartley) 1937- .... **CLC 8, 31;
DAM POET**
See also CA 21-24R; CAAS 14; CANR 59;
DLB 5; MTCW

Bell, W. L. D.
See Mencken, H(enry) L(ouis)

Bernhardt, Sarah (Henriette Rosine)
1844-1923 .... **TCLC 75**
See also CA 157

Berriault, Gina 1926- .... **CLC 54**
See also CA 116; 129; DLB 130

Berrigan, Daniel 1921- .... **CLC 4**
See also CA 33-36R; CAAS 1; CANR 11, 43;
DLB 5

Berrigan, Edmund Joseph Michael, Jr.
1934-1983
See Berrigan, Ted
See also CA 61-64; 110; CANR 14

Berrigan, Ted .... **CLC 37**
See also Berrigan, Edmund Joseph Michael,
Jr.
See also DLB 5, 169

Berry, Charles Edward Anderson 1931-
See Berry, Chuck
See also CA 115

Berry, Chuck .... **CLC 17**
See also Berry, Charles Edward Anderson

Berry, Jonas
See Ashbery, John (Lawrence)

Berry, Wendell (Erdman)
1934- .... **CLC 4, 6, 8, 27, 46; DAM
POET**
See also AITN 1; CA 73-76; CANR 50; DLB
5, 6

Berryman, John
1914-1972 ... **CLC 1, 2, 3, 4, 6, 8, 10, 13,
25, 62; DAM POET**
See also CA 13-16; 33-36R; CABS 2; CANR
35; CAP 1; CDALB 1941-1968; DLB 48;
MTCW

Bertolucci, Bernardo 1940- .... **CLC 16**
See also CA 106

Berton, Pierre (Francis De Marigny)
1920- .... **CLC 104**
See also CA 1-4R; CANR 2, 56; DLB 68

Bertrand, Aloysius 1807-1841 .... **NCLC 31**

Bertran de Born c. 1140-1215 .... **CMLC 5**

Besant, Annie (Wood) 1847-1933 .... **TCLC 9**
See also CA 105

Bessie, Alvah 1904-1985 .... **CLC 23**
See also CA 5-8R; 116; CANR 2; DLB 26

Bethlen, T. D.
See Silverberg, Robert

Beti, Mongo ...... **CLC 27; BLC; DAM MULT**
See also Biyidi, Alexandre

Betjeman, John
1906-1984 ... **CLC 2, 6, 10, 34, 43; DAB;
DAM MST, POET**
See also CA 9-12R; 112; CANR 33, 56;
CDBLB 1945-1960; DLB 20; DLBY 84;
MTCW

Bettelheim, Bruno 1903-1990 .... **CLC 79**
See also CA 81-84; 131; CANR 23, 61;
MTCW

Betti, Ugo 1892-1953 .... **TCLC 5**
See also CA 104; 155

Betts, Doris (Waugh) 1932- ...... **CLC 3, 6, 28**
See also CA 13-16R; CANR 9; DLBY 82; INT
CANR-9

Bevan, Alistair
See Roberts, Keith (John Kingston)

Bialik, Chaim Nachman
1873-1934 .... **TCLC 25**

Bickerstaff, Isaac
See Swift, Jonathan

Bidart, Frank 1939- .... **CLC 33**
See also CA 140

Bienek, Horst 1930- .... **CLC 7, 11**
See also CA 73-76; DLB 75

Bierce, Ambrose (Gwinett)
1842-1914(?) .. **TCLC 1, 7, 44; DA;
DAC; DAM MST; SSC 9; WLC**
See also CA 104; 139; CDALB 1865-1917;
DLB 11, 12, 23, 71, 74

Biggers, Earl Derr 1884-1933 .... **TCLC 65**
See also CA 108; 153

Billings, Josh
See Shaw, Henry Wheeler

Billington, (Lady) Rachel (Mary)
1942- .... **CLC 43**
See also AITN 2; CA 33-36R; CANR 44

Binyon, T(imothy) J(ohn) 1936- .... **CLC 34**
See also CA 111; CANR 28

Bioy Casares, Adolfo
1914- .... **CLC 4, 8, 13, 88; DAM MULT;
HLC; SSC 17**
See also CA 29-32R; CANR 19, 43; DLB 113;
HW; MTCW

Bird, Cordwainer
See Ellison, Harlan (Jay)

Bird, Robert Montgomery
1806-1854 .... **NCLC 1**

Birney, (Alfred) Earle
1904- .... **CLC 1, 4, 6, 11; DAC; DAM
MST, POET**
See also CA 1-4R; CANR 5, 20; DLB 88;
MTCW

Bishop, Elizabeth
1911-1979 ...... **CLC 1, 4, 9, 13, 15,
32; DA; DAC; DAM MST, POET;
PC 3**
See also CA 5-8R; 89-92; CABS 2; CANR
26, 61; CDALB 1968-1988; DLB 5,
169; MTCW; SATA-Obit 24

Bishop, John 1935- .... **CLC 10**
See also CA 105

Bissett, Bill 1939- .... **CLC 18; PC 14**
See also CA 69-72; CAAS 19; CANR 15; DLB
53; MTCW

Bitov, Andrei (Georgievich) 1937- ... **CLC 57**
See also CA 142

Biyidi, Alexandre 1932-
See Beti, Mongo
See also BW 1; CA 114; 124; MTCW

Bjarme, Brynjolf
See Ibsen, Henrik (Johan)

Bjornson, Bjornstjerne (Martinius)
1832-1910 .... **TCLC 7, 37**
See also CA 104

Black, Robert
See Holdstock, Robert P.

Blackburn, Paul 1926-1971 .... **CLC 9, 43**
See also CA 81-84; 33-36R; CANR 34; DLB
16; DLBY 81

Black Elk
1863-1950 .... **TCLC 33; DAM MULT**
See also CA 144; NNAL

Black Hobart
See Sanders, (James) Ed(ward)

Blacklin, Malcolm
See Chambers, Aidan

Blackmore, R(ichard) D(oddridge)
1825-1900 .... **TCLC 27**
See also CA 120; DLB 18

Blackmur, R(ichard) P(almer)
1904-1965 .... **CLC 2, 24**
See also CA 11-12; 25-28R; CAP 1; DLB 63

Black Tarantula
See Acker, Kathy

Blackwood, Algernon (Henry)
1869-1951 .... **TCLC 5**
See also CA 105; 150; DLB 153, 156, 178

Blackwood, Caroline 1931-1996 .... **CLC 6, 9,
100**
See also CA 85-88; 151; CANR 32, 61; DLB
14; MTCW

Blade, Alexander
See Hamilton, Edmond; Silverberg, Robert

Blaga, Lucian 1895-1961 .... **CLC 75**

Blair, Eric (Arthur) 1903-1950
See Orwell, George
See also CA 104; 132; DA; DAB; DAC; DAM
MST, NOV; MTCW; SATA 29

Blais, Marie-Claire
1939- **CLC 2, 4, 6, 13, 22; DAC; DAM MST**
See also CA 21-24R; CAAS 4; CANR 38; DLB
53; MTCW

Blaise, Clark 1940- .... **CLC 29**
See also AITN 2; CA 53-56; CAAS 3; CANR
5; DLB 53

Blake, Fairley
See De Voto, Bernard (Augustine)

Blake, Nicholas
See Day Lewis, C(ecil)
See also DLB 77

Blake, William
1757-1827 . **NCLC 13, 37, 57; DA; DAB;
DAC; DAM MST, POET; PC 12; WLC**
See also CDBLB 1789-1832; DLB 93, 163;
MAICYA; SATA 30

Blake, William J(ames) 1894-1969 ...... **PC 12**
See also CA 5-8R; 25-28R

Blasco Ibanez, Vicente
1867-1928 .... **TCLC 12; DAM NOV**
See also CA 110; 131; HW; MTCW

Blatty, William Peter 1928- ..... **CLC 2; DAM
POP**
See also CA 5-8R; CANR 9

Bleeck, Oliver
See Thomas, Ross (Elmore)

Blessing, Lee 1949- .... **CLC 54**

Blish, James (Benjamin)
1921-1975 .... **CLC 14**
See also CA 1-4R; 57-60; CANR 3; DLB 8;
MTCW; SATA 66

Bliss, Reginald
See Wells, H(erbert) G(eorge)

Blixen, Karen (Christentze Dinesen)
1885-1962
See Dinesen, Isak
See also CA 25-28; CANR 22, 50; CAP 2;
MTCW; SATA 44

Bloch, Robert (Albert) 1917-1994 .... **CLC 33**
See also CA 5-8R; 146; CAAS 20; CANR 5;
DLB 44; INT CANR-5; SATA 12; SATA-
Obit 82

Blok, Alexander (Alexandrovich)
1880-1921 .... **TCLC 5**
See also CA 104

Blom, Jan
See Breytenbach, Breyten

Bloom, Harold 1930- .... **CLC 24, 103**
See also CA 13-16R; CANR 39; DLB 67

Bloomfield, Aurelius
See Bourne, Randolph S(illiman)

Blount, Roy (Alton), Jr. 1941- .... **CLC 38**
See also CA 53-56; CANR 10, 28, 61; INT
CANR-28; MTCW

Bloy, Leon 1846-1917 .... **TCLC 22**
See also CA 121; DLB 123

Blume, Judy (Sussman) 1938- ... **CLC 12, 30;
DAM NOV, POP**
See also AAYA 3; CA 29-32R; CANR 13, 37;
CLR 2, 15; DLB 52; JRDA; MAICYA;
MTCW; SATA 2, 31, 79

Blunden, Edmund (Charles)
1896-1974 .... **CLC 2, 56**
See also CA 17-18; 45-48; CANR 54; CAP 2;
DLB 20, 100, 155; MTCW

Bly, Robert (Elwood)
1926- .... **CLC 1, 2, 5, 10, 15, 38; DAM
POET**
See also CA 5-8R; CANR 41; DLB 5; MTCW

Boas, Franz 1858-1942 .... **TCLC 56**
See also CA 115

Bobette
See Simenon, Georges (Jacques Christian)

Boccaccio, Giovanni
1313-1375 .... **CMLC 13; SSC 10**

Bochco, Steven 1943- .... **CLC 35**
See also AAYA 11; CA 124; 138

Bodenheim, Maxwell 1892-1954 .... **TCLC 44**
See also CA 110; DLB 9, 45

Bodker, Cecil 1927- .... **CLC 21**
See also CA 73-76; CANR 13, 44; CLR 23;
MAICYA; SATA 14

Boell, Heinrich (Theodor)
1917-1985 ... **CLC 2, 3, 6, 9, 11, 15, 27,
32, 72; DA; DAB; DAC; DAM MST,
NOV; SSC 23; WLC**
See also CA 21-24R; 116; CANR 24; DLB 69;
DLBY 85; MTCW

Boerne, Alfred
See Doeblin, Alfred

Boethius 480(?)-524(?) .... **CMLC 15**
See also DLB 115

Bogan, Louise
1897-1970 .... **CLC 4, 39, 46, 93; DAM
POET; PC 12**
See also CA 73-76; 25-28R; CANR 33; DLB
45, 169; MTCW

Bogarde, Dirk .... **CLC 19**
See also Van Den Bogarde, Derek Jules
Gaspard Ulric Niven
See also DLB 14

Bogosian, Eric 1953- .... **CLC 45**
See also CA 138

Bograd, Larry 1953- .... **CLC 35**
See also CA 93-96; CANR 57; SAAS 21; SATA
33, 89

Boiardo, Matteo Maria 1441-1494 .... **LC 6**

Boileau-Despreaux, Nicolas
1636-1711 .... **LC 3**

Bojer, Johan 1872-1959 .... **TCLC 64**

Boland, Eavan (Aisling) 1944- .. **CLC 40, 67;
DAM POET**
See also CA 143; CANR 61; DLB 40

Bolt, Lee
See Faust, Frederick (Schiller)

Bolt, Robert (Oxton) 1924-1995 ..... **CLC 14;
DAM DRAM**
See also CA 17-20R; 147; CANR 35; DLB 13;
MTCW

Bombet, Louis-Alexandre-Cesar
See Stendhal

Bomkauf
See Kaufman, Bob (Garnell)

Bonaventura .... **NCLC 35**
See also DLB 90

Bond, Edward
1934- .... **CLC 4, 6, 13, 23; DAM DRAM**
See also CA 25-28R; CANR 38; DLB 13;
MTCW

Bonham, Frank 1914-1989 .... **CLC 12**
See also AAYA 1; CA 9-12R; CANR 4, 36;
JRDA; MAICYA; SAAS 3; SATA 1, 49;
SATA-Obit 62

Bonnefoy, Yves
1923- .... **CLC 9, 15, 58; DAM MST,
POET**
See also CA 85-88; CANR 33; MTCW

Bontemps, Arna(ud Wendell)
1902-1973 .... **CLC 1, 18; BLC; DAM
MULT, NOV, POET**
See also BW 1; CA 1-4R; 41-44R; CANR 4,
35; CLR 6; DLB 48, 51; JRDA; MAICYA;
MTCW; SATA 2, 44; SATA-Obit 24

Booth, Martin 1944- .... **CLC 13**
See also CA 93-96; CAAS 2

Booth, Philip 1925- .... **CLC 23**
See also CA 5-8R; CANR 5; DLBY 82

Booth, Wayne C(layson) 1921- .... **CLC 24**
See also CA 1-4R; CAAS 5; CANR 3, 43; DLB
67

Borchert, Wolfgang 1921-1947 .... **TCLC 5**
See also CA 104; DLB 69, 124

Borel, Petrus 1809-1859 .... **NCLC 41**

Borges, Jorge Luis
1899-1986 ... **CLC 1, 2, 3, 4, 6, 8, 9, 10,
13, 19, 44, 48, 83; DA; DAB; DAC;
DAM MST, MULT; HLC; SSC 4; WLC**
See also AAYA 19; CA 21-24R; CANR 19, 33;
DLB 113; DLBY 86; HW; MTCW

Borowski, Tadeusz 1922-1951 .... **TCLC 9**
See also CA 106; 154

Borrow, George (Henry)
1803-1881 .... **NCLC 9**
See also DLB 21, 55, 166

Bosman, Herman Charles
1905-1951 .... **TCLC 49**
See also Malan, Herman
See also CA 160

Bosschere, Jean de
1878(?)-1953 .... **TCLC 19**
See also CA 115

Boswell, James
1740-1795 .... **LC 4; DA; DAB; DAC; DAM MST; WLC**
See also CDBLB 1660-1789; DLB 104, 142

Bottoms, David 1949- .... **CLC 53**
See also CA 105; CANR 22; DLB 120; DLBY 83

Boucicault, Dion 1820-1890 .... **NCLC 41**

Boucolon, Maryse 1937(?)-
See Conde, Maryse
See also CA 110; CANR 30, 53

Bourget, Paul (Charles Joseph)
1852-1935 .... **TCLC 12**
See also CA 107; DLB 123

Bourjaily, Vance (Nye) 1922- ....**CLC 8, 62**
See also CA 1-4R; CAAS 1; CANR 2; DLB 2, 143

Bourne, Randolph S(illiman)
1886-1918 .... **TCLC 16**
See also CA 117; 155; DLB 63

Bova, Ben(jamin William) 1932- ...... **CLC 45**
See also AAYA 16; CA 5-8R; CAAS 18; CANR 11, 56; CLR 3; DLBY 81; INT CANR-11; MAICYA; MTCW; SATA 6, 68

Bowen, Elizabeth (Dorothea Cole)
1899-1973 .... **CLC 1, 3, 6, 11, 15, 22; DAM NOV; SSC 3, 28**
See also CA 17-18; 41-44R; CANR 35; CAP 2; CDBLB 1945-1960; DLB 15, 162; MTCW

Bowering, George 1935- .... **CLC 15, 47**
See also CA 21-24R; CAAS 16; CANR 10; DLB 53

Bowering, Marilyn R(uthe) 1949- .... **CLC 32**
See also CA 101; CANR 49

Bowers, Edgar 1924- .... **CLC 9**
See also CA 5-8R; CANR 24; DLB 5

Bowie, David .... **CLC 17**
See also Jones, David Robert

Bowles, Jane (Sydney)
1917-1973 .... **CLC 3, 68**
See also CA 19-20; 41-44R; CAP 2

Bowles, Paul (Frederick)
1910- .... **CLC 1, 2, 19, 53; SSC 3**
See also CA 1-4R; CAAS 1; CANR 1, 19, 50; DLB 5, 6; MTCW

Box, Edgar
See Vidal, Gore

Boyd, Nancy
See Millay, Edna St. Vincent

Boyd, William 1952- .... **CLC 28, 53, 70**
See also CA 114; 120; CANR 51

Boyle, Kay
1902-1992 .... **CLC 1, 5, 19, 58; SSC 5**
See also CA 13-16R; 140; CAAS 1; CANR 29, 61; DLB 4, 9, 48, 86; DLBY 93; MTCW

Boyle, Mark
See Kienzle, William X(avier)

Boyle, Patrick 1905-1982 .... **CLC 19**
See also CA 127

Boyle, T. C. 1948-
See Boyle, T(homas) Coraghessan

Boyle, T(homas) Coraghessan
1948- . **CLC 36, 55, 90; DAM POP; SSC 16**
See also BEST 90:4; CA 120; CANR 44; DLBY 86

Boz
See Dickens, Charles (John Huffam)

Brackenridge, Hugh Henry
1748-1816 .... **NCLC 7**
See also DLB 11, 37

Bradbury, Edward P.
See Moorcock, Michael (John)

Bradbury, Malcolm (Stanley)
1932- .... **CLC 32, 61; DAM NOV**
See also CA 1-4R; CANR 1, 33; DLB 14; MTCW

Bradbury, Ray (Douglas)
1920- .... **CLC 1, 3, 10, 15, 42, 98; DA; DAB; DAC; DAM MST, NOV, POP; SSC 29; WLC**
See also AAYA 15; AITN 1, 2; CA 1-4R; CANR 2, 30; CDALB 1968-1988; DLB 2, 8; MTCW; SATA 11, 64

Bradford, Gamaliel 1863-1932 ...... **TCLC 36**
See also CA 160; DLB 17

Bradley, David (Henry, Jr.)
1950- .... **CLC 23; BLC; DAM MULT**
See also BW 1; CA 104; CANR 26; DLB 33

Bradley, John Ed(mund, Jr.)
1958- .... **CLC 55**
See also CA 139

Bradley, Marion Zimmer 1930- ...... **CLC 30; DAM POP**
See also AAYA 9; CA 57-60; CAAS 10; CANR 7, 31, 51; DLB 8; MTCW; SATA 90

Bradstreet, Anne
1612(?)-1672 .... **LC 4, 30; DA; DAC; DAM MST, POET; PC 10**
See also CDALB 1640-1865; DLB 24

Brady, Joan 1939- .... **CLC 86**
See also CA 141

Bragg, Melvyn 1939- .... **CLC 10**
See also BEST 89:3; CA 57-60; CANR 10, 48; DLB 14

Braine, John (Gerard)
1922-1986 .... **CLC 1, 3, 41**
See also CA 1-4R; 120; CANR 1, 33; CDBLB 1945-1960; DLB 15; DLBY 86; MTCW

Bramah, Ernest 1868-1942 .... **TCLC 72**
See also CA 156; DLB 70

Brammer, William 1930(?)-1978 .... **CLC 31**
See also CA 77-80

Brancati, Vitaliano 1907-1954 .... **TCLC 12**
See also CA 109

Brancato, Robin F(idler) 1936- .... **CLC 35**
See also AAYA 9; CA 69-72; CANR 11, 45; CLR 32; JRDA; SAAS 9; SATA 23

Brand, Max
See Faust, Frederick (Schiller)

Brand, Millen 1906-1980 .... **CLC 7**
See also CA 21-24R; 97-100

Branden, Barbara .... **CLC 44**
See also CA 148

Brandes, Georg (Morris Cohen)
1842-1927 .... **TCLC 10**
See also CA 105

Brandys, Kazimierz 1916- .... **CLC 62**

Branley, Franklyn M(ansfield)
1915- .... **CLC 21**
See also CA 33-36R; CANR 14, 39; CLR 13; MAICYA; SAAS 16; SATA 4, 68

Brathwaite, Edward Kamau
1930- .... **CLC 11; DAM POET**
See also BW 2; CA 25-28R; CANR 11, 26, 47; DLB 125

Brautigan, Richard (Gary)
1935-1984 ...... **CLC 1, 3, 5, 9, 12, 34, 42; DAM NOV**
See also CA 53-56; 113; CANR 34; DLB 2, 5; DLBY 80, 84; MTCW; SATA 56

Brave Bird, Mary 1953-
See Crow Dog, Mary (Ellen)
See also NNAL

Braverman, Kate 1950- .... **CLC 67**
See also CA 89-92

Brecht, (Eugen) Bertolt (Friedrich)
1898-1956 .... **TCLC 1, 6, 13, 35; DA; DAB; DAC; DAM DRAM, MST; DC 3; WLC**
See also CA 104; 133; CANR 62; DLB 56, 124; MTCW

Brecht, Eugen Berthold Friedrich
See Brecht, (Eugen) Bertolt (Friedrich)

Bremer, Fredrika 1801-1865 .... **NCLC 11**

Brennan, Christopher John
1870-1932 .... **TCLC 17**
See also CA 117

Brennan, Maeve 1917- .... **CLC 5**
See also CA 81-84

Brentano, Clemens (Maria)
1778-1842 .... **NCLC 1**
See also DLB 90

Brent of Bin Bin
See Franklin, (Stella Maraia Sarah) Miles

Brown, Sterling Allen
1901-1989 ... **CLC 1, 23, 59; BLC; DAM MULT, POET**
See also BW 1; CA 85-88; 127; CANR 26; DLB 48, 51, 63; MTCW

Brown, Will
See Ainsworth, William Harrison

Brown, William Wells
1813-1884 .... **NCLC 2; BLC; DAM MULT; DC 1**
See also DLB 3, 50

Browne, (Clyde) Jackson 1948(?)- .... **CLC 21**
See also CA 120

Browning, Elizabeth Barrett
1806-1861 ...**NCLC 1, 16, 61; DA; DAB; DAC; DAM MST, POET; PC 6; WLC**
See also CDBLB 1832-1890; DLB 32

Browning, Robert
1812-1889 .. **NCLC 19; DA; DAB; DAC; DAM MST, POET; PC 2; WLCS**
See also CDBLB 1832-1890; DLB 32, 163; YABC 1

Browning, Tod 1882-1962 .... **CLC 16**
See also CA 141; 117

Brownson, Orestes (Augustus) 1803-1876
NCLC 50

Bruccoli, Matthew J(oseph) 1931- ... **CLC 34**
See also CA 9-12R; CANR 7; DLB 103

Bruce, Lenny .... **CLC 21**
See also Schneider, Leonard Alfred

Bruin, John
See Brutus, Dennis

Brulard, Henri
See Stendhal

Brulls, Christian
See Simenon, Georges (Jacques Christian)

Brunner, John (Kilian Houston)
1934-1995 .... **CLC 8, 10; DAM POP**
See also CA 1-4R; 149; CAAS 8; CANR 2, 37; MTCW

Bruno, Giordano 1548-1600 .... **LC 27**

Brutus, Dennis 1924- ... **CLC 43; BLC; DAM MULT, POET**
See also BW 2; CA 49-52; CAAS 14; CANR 2, 27, 42; DLB 117

Bryan, C(ourtlandt) D(ixon) B(arnes)
1936- .... **CLC 29**
See also CA 73-76; CANR 13; INT CANR-13

Bryan, Michael
See Moore, Brian

Bryant, William Cullen
1794-1878**NCLC 6, 46; DA; DAB; DAC; DAM MST, POET; PC 20**
See also CDALB 1640-1865; DLB 3, 43, 59

Bryusov, Valery Yakovlevich
1873-1924 .... **TCLC 10**
See also CA 107; 155

Buchan, John 1875-1940 ..... **TCLC 41; DAB; DAM POP**
See also CA 108; 145; DLB 34, 70, 156; YABC 2

Buchanan, George 1506-1582 .... **LC 4**

Buchheim, Lothar-Guenther 1918- .... **CLC 6**
See also CA 85-88

Buchner, (Karl) Georg
1813-1837 .... **NCLC 26**

Buchwald, Art(hur) 1925- .... **CLC 33**
See also AITN 1; CA 5-8R; CANR 21; MTCW; SATA 10

Buck, Pearl S(ydenstricker)
1892-1973 ...... **CLC 7, 11, 18; DA; DAB; DAC; DAM MST, NOV**
See also AITN 1; CA 1-4R; 41-44R; CANR 1, 34; DLB 9, 102; MTCW; SATA 1, 25

Buckler, Ernest
1908-1984 .... **CLC 13; DAC; DAM MST**
See also CA 11-12; 114; CAP 1; DLB 68; SATA 47

Buckley, Vincent (Thomas)
1925-1988 .... **CLC 57**
See also CA 101

Buckley, William F(rank), Jr.
1925- .... **CLC 7, 18, 37; DAM POP**
See also AITN 1; CA 1-4R; CANR 1, 24, 53; DLB 137; DLBY 80; INT CANR-24; MTCW

Buechner, (Carl) Frederick
1926- .... **CLC 2, 4, 6, 9; DAM NOV**
See also CA 13-16R; CANR 11, 39; DLBY 80; INT CANR-11; MTCW

Buell, John (Edward) 1927- .... **CLC 10**
See also CA 1-4R; DLB 53

Buero Vallejo, Antonio 1916- ..... **CLC 15, 46**
See also CA 106; CANR 24, 49; HW; MTCW

Bufalino, Gesualdo 1920(?)- .... **CLC 74**

Bugayev, Boris Nikolayevich 1880-1934
See Bely, Andrey
See also CA 104

Bukowski, Charles
1920-1994 ...... **CLC 2, 5, 9, 41, 82; DAM NOV, POET; PC 18**
See also CA 17-20R; 144; CANR 40, 62; DLB 5, 130, 169; MTCW

Bulgakov, Mikhail (Afanas'evich)
1891-1940 ... **TCLC 2, 16; DAM DRAM, NOV; SSC 18**
See also CA 105; 152

Bulgya, Alexander Alexandrovich
1901-1956 .... **TCLC 53**
See also Fadeyev, Alexander
See also CA 117

Bullins, Ed
1935- . **CLC 1, 5, 7; BLC; DAM DRAM, MULT; DC 6**
See also BW 2; CA 49-52; CAAS 16; CANR 24, 46; DLB 7, 38; MTCW

Bulwer-Lytton, Edward (George Earle Lytton)
1803-1873 .... **NCLC 1, 45**
See also DLB 21

Bunin, Ivan Alexeyevich
1870-1953 .... **TCLC 6; SSC 5**
See also CA 104

Bunting, Basil
1900-1985 .... **CLC 10, 39, 47; DAM POET**
See also CA 53-56; 115; CANR 7; DLB 20

Bunuel, Luis
1900-1983 .... **CLC 16, 80; DAM MULT; HLC**
See also CA 101; 110; CANR 32; HW

Bunyan, John
1628-1688 .... **LC 4; DA; DAB; DAC; DAM MST; WLC**
See also CDBLB 1660-1789; DLB 39

Burckhardt, Jacob (Christoph)
1818-1897 .... **NCLC 49**

Burford, Eleanor
See Hibbert, Eleanor Alice Burford

Burgess, Anthony ... **CLC 1, 2, 4, 5, 8, 10, 13, 15, 22, 40, 62 , 81, 94; DAB**
See also Wilson, John (Anthony) Burgess
See also AITN 1; CDBLB 1960 to Present; DLB 14

Burke, Edmund
1729(?)-1797 .... **LC 7, 36; DA; DAB; DAC; DAM MST; WLC**
See also DLB 104

Burke, Kenneth (Duva)
1897-1993 .... **CLC 2, 24**
See also CA 5-8R; 143; CANR 39; DLB 45, 63; MTCW

Burke, Leda
See Garnett, David

Burke, Ralph
See Silverberg, Robert

Burke, Thomas 1886-1945 .... **TCLC 63**
See also CA 113; 155

Burney, Fanny 1752-1840 .... **NCLC 12, 54**
See also DLB 39

Burns, Robert 1759-1796 .... **PC 6**
See also CDBLB 1789-1832; DA; DAB; DAC; DAM MST, POET; DLB 109; WLC

Burns, Tex
See L'Amour, Louis (Dearborn)

Burnshaw, Stanley
1906- .... **CLC 3, 13, 44**
See also CA 9-12R; DLB 48

Burr, Anne 1937- .... CLC 6
See also CA 25-28R

Burroughs, Edgar Rice
1875-1950 .... **TCLC 2, 32; DAM NOV**
See also AAYA 11; CA 104; 132; DLB 8;
MTCW; SATA 41

Burroughs, William S(eward)
1914-1997 .... **CLC 1, 2, 5, 15, 22, 42, 75;
DA; DAB; DAC; DAM MST, NOV,
POP; WLC**
See also AITN 2; CA 9-12R; 160; CANR 20,
52; DLB 2, 8, 16, 152; DLBY 81; MTCW

Burton, Richard F. 1821-1890 .... **NCLC 42**
See also DLB 55, 184

Busch, Frederick 1941- ..... **CLC 7, 10, 18, 47**
See also CA 33-36R; CAAS 1; CANR 45; DLB
6

Bush, Ronald 1946- .... **CLC 34**
See also CA 136

Bustos, F(rancisco)
See Borges, Jorge Luis

Bustos Domecq, H(onorio)
See Bioy Casares, Adolfo; Borges, Jorge Luis

Butler, Octavia E(stelle)
1947- .... **CLC 38; DAM MULT, POP**
See also AAYA 18; BW 2; CA 73-76; CANR
12, 24, 38; DLB 33; MTCW; SATA 84

Butler, Robert Olen (Jr.)
1945- .... **CLC 81; DAM POP**
See also CA 112; DLB 173; INT 112

Butler, Samuel 1612-1680 .... **LC 16**
See also DLB 101, 126

Butler, Samuel
1835-1902 .... **TCLC 1, 33; DA; DAB;
DAC; DAM MST, NOV; WLC**
See also CA 143; CDBLB 1890-1914; DLB
18, 57, 174

Butler, Walter C.
See Faust, Frederick (Schiller)

Butor, Michel (Marie Francois)
1926- .... **CLC 1, 3, 8, 11, 15**
See also CA 9-12R; CANR 33; DLB 83;
MTCW

Buzo, Alexander (John) 1944- .... **CLC 61**
See also CA 97-100; CANR 17, 39

Buzzati, Dino 1906-1972 .... **CLC 36**
See also CA 160; 33-36R; DLB 177

Byars, Betsy (Cromer) 1928-............. **CLC 35**
See also AAYA 19; CA 33-36R; CANR 18, 36,
57; CLR 1, 16; DLB 52; INT CANR-18;
JRDA; MAICYA; MTCW; SAAS 1; SATA
4, 46, 80

Byatt, A(ntonia) S(usan Drabble)
1936- .... **CLC 19, 65; DAM NOV, POP**
See also CA 13-16R; CANR 13, 33, 50; DLB
14; MTCW

Byrne, David 1952- .... **CLC 26**
See also CA 127

Byrne, John Keyes 1926-
See Leonard, Hugh
See also CA 102; INT 102

Byron, George Gordon (Noel)
1788-1824 .... **NCLC 2, 12; DA; DAB;
DAC; DAM MST, POET; PC 16; WLC**
See also CDBLB 1789-1832; DLB 96, 110

Byron, Robert 1905-1941 .... **TCLC 67**
See also CA 160

C. 3. 3.
See Wilde, Oscar (Fingal O'Flahertie Wills)

Caballero, Fernan 1796-1877 .... **NCLC 10**

Cabell, Branch
See Cabell, James Branch

Cabell, James Branch 1879-1958 .... **TCLC 6**
See also CA 105; 152; DLB 9, 78

Cable, George Washington
1844-1925 .... **TCLC 4; SSC 4**
See also CA 104; 155; DLB 12, 74; DLBD
13

Cabral de Melo Neto, Joao
1920- .... **CLC 76; DAM MULT**
See also CA 151

Cabrera Infante, G(uillermo)
1929- ...... **CLC 5, 25, 45; DAM MULT;
HLC**
See also CA 85-88; CANR 29; DLB 113; HW;
MTCW

Cade, Toni
See Bambara, Toni Cade

Cadmus and Harmonia
See Buchan, John

Caedmon fl. 658-680 .... **CMLC 7**
See also DLB 146

Caeiro, Alberto
See Pessoa, Fernando (Antonio Nogueira)

Cage, John (Milton, Jr.) 1912- .... **CLC 41**
See also CA 13-16R; CANR 9; INT CANR-
9

Cahan, Abraham 1860-1951 .... **TCLC 71**
See also CA 108; 154; DLB 9, 25, 28

Cain, G.
See Cabrera Infante, G(uillermo)

Cain, Guillermo
See Cabrera Infante, G(uillermo)

Cain, James M(allahan)
1892-1977 .... **CLC 3, 11, 28**
See also AITN 1; CA 17-20R; 73-76; CANR
8, 34, 61; MTCW

Caine, Mark
See Raphael, Frederic (Michael)

Calasso, Roberto 1941- .... **CLC 81**
See also CA 143

Calderon de la Barca, Pedro
1600-1681 .... **LC 23; DC 3**

Caldwell, Erskine (Preston)
1903-1987 .... **CLC 1, 8, 14, 50, 60; DAM
NOV; SSC 19**
See also AITN 1; CA 1-4R; 121; CAAS 1;
CANR 2, 33; DLB 9, 86; MTCW

Caldwell, (Janet Miriam) Taylor (Holland)
1900-1985 .... **CLC 2, 28, 39; DAM NOV,
POP**
See also CA 5-8R; 116; CANR 5

Calhoun, John Caldwell
1782-1850 .... **NCLC 15**
See also DLB 3

Calisher, Hortense
1911- ..... **CLC 2, 4, 8, 38; DAM NOV;
SSC 15**
See also CA 1-4R; CANR 1, 22; DLB 2; INT
CANR-22; MTCW

Callaghan, Morley Edward
1903-1990 .... **CLC 3, 14, 41, 65; DAC;
DAM MST**
See also CA 9-12R; 132; CANR 33; DLB 68;
MTCW

Callimachus
c. 305B.C.-c. 240B.C. .... **CMLC 18**
See also DLB 176

Calvin, John 1509-1564 .... **LC 37**

Calvino, Italo
1923-1985 .. **CLC 5, 8, 11, 22, 33, 39, 73;
DAM NOV; SSC 3**
See also CA 85-88; 116; CANR 23, 61;
MTCW

Cameron, Carey 1952- .... **CLC 59**
See also CA 135

Cameron, Peter 1959- .... **CLC 44**
See also CA 125; CANR 50

Campana, Dino 1885-1932 .... **TCLC 20**
See also CA 117; DLB 114

Campanella, Tommaso 1568-1639 .... **LC 32**

Campbell, John W(ood, Jr.)
1910-1971 .... **CLC 32**
See also CA 21-22; 29-32R; CANR 34; CAP
2; DLB 8; MTCW

Campbell, Joseph
1904-1987 .... **CLC 69**
See also AAYA 3; BEST 89:2; CA 1-4R; 124;
CANR 3, 28, 61; MTCW

Campbell, Maria 1940- .... **CLC 85; DAC**
See also CA 102; CANR 54; NNAL

Campbell, (John) Ramsey
1946- .... **CLC 42; SSC 19**
See also CA 57-60; CANR 7; INT CANR-
7

Campbell, (Ignatius) Roy (Dunnachie)
1901-1957 .... **TCLC 5**
See also CA 104; 155; DLB 20

Campbell, Thomas 1777-1844 .... **NCLC 19**
See also DLB 93; 144

Campbell, Wilfred .... **TCLC 9**
See also Campbell, William

Campbell, William 1858(?)-1918
See Campbell, Wilfred
See also CA 106; DLB 92

Campion, Jane .... **CLC 95**
See also CA 138

Campos, Alvaro de
See Pessoa, Fernando (Antonio Nogueira)

Camus, Albert
1913-1960 ... **CLC 1, 2, 4, 9, 11, 14, 32,
63, 69; DA; DAB; DAC; DAM DRAM,
MST, NOV; DC 2; SSC 9; WLC**
See also CA 89-92; DLB 72; MTCW

Canby, Vincent 1924- .... **CLC 13**
See also CA 81-84

Cancale
See Desnos, Robert

Canetti, Elias
1905-1994 .... **CLC 3, 14, 25, 75, 86**
See also CA 21-24R; 146; CANR 23, 61; DLB
85, 124; MTCW

Canin, Ethan 1960- .... **CLC 55**
See also CA 131; 135

Cannon, Curt
See Hunter, Evan

Cape, Judith
See Page, P(atricia) K(athleen)

Capek, Karel
1890-1938 .... **TCLC 6, 37; DA; DAB;
DAC; DAM DRAM, MST, NOV; DC 1;
WLC**
See also CA 104; 140

Capote, Truman
1924-1984 .... **CLC 1, 3, 8, 13, 19, 34, 38,
58; DA; DAB; DAC; DAM MST, NOV,
POP; SSC 2; WLC**
See also CA 5-8R; 113; CANR 18, 62; CDALB
1941-1968; DLB 2; DLBY 80, 84; MTCW;
SATA 91

Capra, Frank 1897-1991 .... **CLC 16**
See also CA 61-64; 135

Caputo, Philip 1941- .... **CLC 32**
See also CA 73-76; CANR 40

Caragiale, Ion Luca 1852-1912 ..... **TCLC 76**
See also CA 157

Card, Orson Scott 1951- ...... **CLC 44, 47, 50;
DAM POP**
See also AAYA 11; CA 102; CANR 27, 47;
INT CANR-27; MTCW; SATA 83

Cardenal, Ernesto 1925- .... **CLC 31; DAM
MULT, POET; HLC**
See also CA 49-52; CANR 2, 32; HW; MTCW

Cardozo, Benjamin N(athan)
1870-1938 .... **TCLC 65**
See also CA 117

Carducci, Giosue 1835-1907 .... **TCLC 32**

Carew, Thomas 1595(?)-1640 .... **LC 13**
See also DLB 126

Carey, Ernestine Gilbreth 1908- .... **CLC 17**
See also CA 5-8R; SATA 2

Carey, Peter 1943- .... **CLC 40, 55, 96**
See also CA 123; 127; CANR 53; INT 127;
MTCW; SATA 94

Carleton, William 1794-1869 .... **NCLC 3**
See also DLB 159

Carlisle, Henry (Coffin) 1926- .... **CLC 33**
See also CA 13-16R; CANR 15

Carlsen, Chris
See Holdstock, Robert P.

Carlson, Ron(ald F.) 1947- .... **CLC 54**
See also CA 105; CANR 27

Carlyle, Thomas
1795-1881 .. **NCLC 22; DA; DAB; DAC;
DAM MST**
See also CDBLB 1789-1832; DLB 55;
144

Carman, (William) Bliss
1861-1929 .... **TCLC 7; DAC**
See also CA 104; 152; DLB 92

Carnegie, Dale 1888-1955 .... **TCLC 53**

Carossa, Hans 1878-1956 .... **TCLC 48**
See also DLB 66

Carpenter, Don(ald Richard)
1931-1995 .... **CLC 41**
See also CA 45-48; 149; CANR 1

Carpentier (y Valmont), Alejo
1904-1980 .... **CLC 8, 11, 38; DAM
MULT; HLC**
See also CA 65-68; 97-100; CANR 11; DLB
113; HW

Carr, Caleb 1955(?)- .... **CLC 86**
See also CA 147

Carr, Emily 1871-1945 .... **TCLC 32**
See also CA 159; DLB 68

Carr, John Dickson 1906-1977 .... **CLC 3**
See also Fairbairn, Roger
See also CA 49-52; 69-72; CANR 3, 33, 60;
MTCW

Carr, Philippa
See Hibbert, Eleanor Alice Burford

Carr, Virginia Spencer 1929- .... **CLC 34**
See also CA 61-64; DLB 111

Carrere, Emmanuel 1957- .... **CLC 89**

Carrier, Roch
1937- ..... **CLC 13, 78; DAC; DAM MST**
See also CA 130; CANR 61; DLB 53

Carroll, James P. 1943(?)- .... **CLC 38**
See also CA 81-84

Carroll, Jim 1951- .... **CLC 35**
See also AAYA 17; CA 45-48; CANR 42

Carroll, Lewis ..... **NCLC 2, 53; PC 18; WLC**
See also Dodgson, Charles Lutwidge
See also CDBLB 1832-1890; CLR 2, 18; DLB
18, 163, 178; JRDA

Carroll, Paul Vincent 1900-1968 ...... **CLC 10**
See also CA 9-12R; 25-28R; DLB 10

Carruth, Hayden
1921- .... **CLC 4, 7, 10, 18, 84; PC 10**
See also CA 9-12R; CANR 4, 38, 59;
DLB 5, 165; INT CANR-4; MTCW;
SATA 47

Carson, Rachel Louise
1907-1964 .... **CLC 71; DAM POP**
See also CA 77-80; CANR 35; MTCW; SATA
23

Carter, Angela (Olive)
1940-1992 .... **CLC 5, 41, 76; SSC 13**
See also CA 53-56; 136; CANR 12, 36, 61;
DLB 14; MTCW; SATA 66; SATA-Obit 70

Carter, Nick
See Smith, Martin Cruz

Carver, Raymond
1938-1988 ...... **CLC 22, 36, 53, 55; DAM
NOV; SSC 8**
See also CA 33-36R; 126; CANR 17,
34, 61; DLB 130; DLBY 84, 88;
MTCW

Cary, Elizabeth, Lady Falkland
1585-1639 .... **LC 30**

Cary, (Arthur) Joyce (Lunel)
1888-1957 .... **TCLC 1, 29**
See also CA 104; CDBLB 1914-1945; DLB
15, 100

Casanova de Seingalt, Giovanni Jacopo
1725-1798 .... **LC 13**

Casares, Adolfo Bioy
See Bioy Casares, Adolfo

Casely-Hayford, J(oseph) E(phraim)
1866-1930 .... **TCLC 24; BLC; DAM
MULT**
See also BW 2; CA 123; 152

Casey, John (Dudley) 1939- .... **CLC 59**
See also BEST 90:2; CA 69-72; CANR 23

Casey, Michael 1947- .... **CLC 2**
See also CA 65-68; DLB 5

Casey, Patrick
See Thurman, Wallace (Henry)

Coleridge, Mary E(lizabeth)
1861-1907 .... **TCLC 73**
See also CA 116; DLB 19, 98

Coleridge, Samuel Taylor
1772-1834 .... **NCLC 9, 54; DA; DAB;**
DAC; DAM MST, POET; PC 11; WLC
See also CDBLB 1789-1832; DLB 93, 107

Coleridge, Sara 1802-1852 .... **NCLC 31**

Coles, Don 1928- .... **CLC 46**
See also CA 115; CANR 38

Colette, (Sidonie-Gabrielle)
1873-1954 .. **TCLC 1, 5, 16; DAM NOV;**
SSC 10
See also CA 104; 131; DLB 65; MTCW

Collett, (Jacobine) Camilla (Wergeland)
1813-1895 .... **NCLC 22**

Collier, Christopher 1930- .... **CLC 30**
See also AAYA 13; CA 33-36R; CANR 13, 33;
JRDA; MAICYA; SATA 16, 70

Collier, James L(incoln)
1928- .... **CLC 30; DAM POP**
See also AAYA 13; CA 9-12R; CANR 4, 33,
60; CLR 3; JRDA; MAICYA; SAAS 21;
SATA 8, 70

Collier, Jeremy 1650-1726 .... **LC 6**

Collier, John 1901-1980 .... **SSC 19**
See also CA 65-68; 97-100; CANR 10; DLB
77

Collingwood, R(obin) G(eorge)
1889(?)-1943 .... **TCLC 67**
See also CA 117; 155

Collins, Hunt
See Hunter, Evan

Collins, Linda 1931- .... **CLC 44**
See also CA 125

Collins, (William) Wilkie
1824-1889 .... **NCLC 1, 18**
See also CDBLB 1832-1890; DLB 18, 70,
159

Collins, William
1721-1759 .... **LC 4, 40; DAM POET**
See also DLB 109

Collodi, Carlo 1826-1890 .... **NCLC 54**
See also Lorenzini, Carlo
See also CLR 5

Colman, George
See Glassco, John

Colt, Winchester Remington
See Hubbard, L(afayette) Ron(ald)

Colter, Cyrus 1910- .... **CLC 58**
See also BW 1; CA 65-68; CANR 10; DLB
33

Colton, James
See Hansen, Joseph

Colum, Padraic 1881-1972 .... **CLC 28**
See also CA 73-76; 33-36R; CANR 35; CLR
36; MAICYA; MTCW; SATA 15

Colvin, James
See Moorcock, Michael (John)

Colwin, Laurie (E.)
1944-1992 .... **CLC 5, 13, 23, 84**
See also CA 89-92; 139; CANR 20, 46; DLBY 80; MTCW

Comfort, Alex(ander)
1920- .... **CLC 7; DAM POP**
See also CA 1-4R; CANR 1, 45

Comfort, Montgomery
See Campbell, (John) Ramsey

Compton-Burnett, I(vy)
1884(?)-1969 .... **CLC 1, 3, 10, 15, 34;**
DAM NOV
See also CA 1-4R; 25-28R; CANR 4; DLB 36; MTCW

Comstock, Anthony 1844-1915 ...... **TCLC 13**
See also CA 110

Comte, Auguste 1798-1857 .... **NCLC 54**

Conan Doyle, Arthur
See Doyle, Arthur Conan

Conde, Maryse
1937- .... **CLC 52, 92; DAM MULT**
See also Boucolon, Maryse
See also BW 2

Condillac, Etienne Bonnot de
1714-1780 .... **LC 26**

Condon, Richard (Thomas) 1915-
1996 ... **CLC 4, 6, 8, 10, 45, 100; DAM NOV**
See also BEST 90:3; CA 1-4R; 151; CAAS 1;
CANR 2, 23; INT CANR-23; MTCW

Confucius
551B.C.-479B.C. . **CMLC 19; DA; DAB;**
DAC; DAM MST; WLCS

Congreve, William
1670-1729 .... **LC 5, 21; DA; DAB; DAC;**
DAM DRAM, MST, POET; DC 2; WLC
See also CDBLB 1660-1789; DLB 39, 84

Connell, Evan S(helby), Jr.
1924- .... **CLC 4, 6, 45; DAM NOV**
See also AAYA 7; CA 1-4R; CAAS 2; CANR
2, 39; DLB 2; DLBY 81; MTCW

Connelly, Marc(us Cook)
1890-1980 .... **CLC 7**
See also CA 85-88; 102; CANR 30; DLB 7;
DLBY 80; SATA-Obit 25

Connor, Ralph .... **TCLC 31**
See also Gordon, Charles William
See also DLB 92

Conrad, Joseph 1857-1924 **TCLC 1, 6, 13, 25,**
43, 57; DA; DAB; DAC; DAM MST,
NOV; SSC 9; WLC
See also CA 104; 131; CANR 60; CDBLB
1890-1914; DLB 10, 34, 98, 156; MTCW;
SATA 27

Conrad, Robert Arnold
See Hart, Moss

Conroy, Donald Pat(rick)
1945- .... **CLC 30, 74; DAM NOV, POP**
See also AAYA 8; AITN 1; CA 85-88; CANR
24, 53; DLB 6; MTCW

Constant (de Rebecque), (Henri) Benjamin
1767-1830 .... **NCLC 6**
See also DLB 119

Conybeare, Charles Augustus
See Eliot, T(homas) S(tearns)

Cook, Michael 1933- .... **CLC 58**
See also CA 93-96; DLB 53

Cook, Robin 1940- .... **CLC 14; DAM POP**
See also BEST 90:2; CA 108; 111; CANR 41;
INT 111

Cook, Roy
See Silverberg, Robert

Cooke, Elizabeth 1948- .... **CLC 55**
See also CA 129

Cooke, John Esten 1830-1886 .... **NCLC 5**
See also DLB 3

Cooke, John Estes
See Baum, L(yman) Frank

Cooke, M. E.
See Creasey, John

Cooke, Margaret
See Creasey, John

Cook-Lynn, Elizabeth
1930- .... **CLC 93; DAM MULT**
See also CA 133; DLB 175; NNAL

Cooney, Ray .... **CLC 62**

Cooper, Douglas 1960- .... **CLC 86**

Cooper, Henry St. John
See Creasey, John

Cooper, J(oan) California .... **CLC 56; DAM MULT**
See also AAYA 12; BW 1; CA 125; CANR
55

Cooper, James Fenimore
1789-1851 .... **NCLC 1, 27, 54**
See also AAYA 22; CDALB 1640-1865; DLB
3; SATA 19

Coover, Robert (Lowell)
1932- ..... **CLC 3, 7, 15, 32, 46, 87; DAM**
NOV; SSC 15
See also CA 45-48; CANR 3, 37, 58; DLB 2;
DLBY 81; MTCW

Copeland, Stewart (Armstrong)
1952- .... **CLC 26**

Coppard, A(lfred) E(dgar)
1878-1957 .... **TCLC 5; SSC 21**
See also CA 114; DLB 162; YABC 1

Coppee, Francois 1842-1908 .... **TCLC 25**

Coppola, Francis Ford 1939- .... **CLC 16**
See also CA 77-80; CANR 40; DLB 44

Corbiere, Tristan 1845-1875 .... **NCLC 43**

Corcoran, Barbara 1911- .... **CLC 17**
See also AAYA 14; CA 21-24R; CAAS 2;
CANR 11, 28, 48; DLB 52; JRDA; SAAS
20; SATA 3, 77

Cordelier, Maurice
See Giraudoux, (Hippolyte) Jean

Corelli, Marie 1855-1924 .... **TCLC 51**
See also Mackay, Mary
See also DLB 34, 156

Corman, Cid .... **CLC 9**
See also Corman, Sidney
See also CAAS 2; DLB 5

Corman, Sidney 1924-
See Corman, Cid
See also CA 85-88; CANR 44; DAM POET

Cormier, Robert (Edmund)
1925- .... **CLC 12, 30; DA; DAB; DAC;
DAM MST, NOV**
See also AAYA 3, 19; CA 1-4R; CANR 5, 23;
CDALB 1968-1988; CLR 12; DLB 52; INT
CANR-23; JRDA; MAICYA; MTCW;
SATA 10, 45, 83

Corn, Alfred (DeWitt III) 1943- .... **CLC 33**
See also CA 104; CAAS 25; CANR 44; DLB
120; DLBY 80

Corneille, Pierre
1606-1684 .... **LC 28; DAB; DAM MST**

Cornwell, David (John Moore)
1931- .... **CLC 9, 15; DAM POP**
See also le Carre, John
See also CA 5-8R; CANR 13, 33, 59; MTCW

Corso, (Nunzio) Gregory 1930- .... **CLC 1, 11**
See also CA 5-8R; CANR 41; DLB 5, 16;
MTCW

Cortazar, Julio
1914-1984 **CLC 2, 3, 5, 10, 13, 15, 33,
34, 92; DAM MULT, NOV; HLC; SSC
7**
See also CA 21-24R; CANR 12, 32; DLB 113;
HW; MTCW

CORTES, HERNAN 1484-1547 .... **LC 31**

Corwin, Cecil
See Kornbluth, C(yril) M.

Cosic, Dobrica 1921- .... **CLC 14**
See also CA 122; 138; DLB 181

Costain, Thomas B(ertram)
1885-1965 .... **CLC 30**
See also CA 5-8R; 25-28R; DLB 9

Costantini, Humberto
1924(?)-1987 .... **CLC 49**
See also CA 131; 122; HW

Costello, Elvis 1955- .... **CLC 21**

Cotes, Cecil V.
See Duncan, Sara Jeannette

Cotter, Joseph Seamon Sr.
1861-1949 .... **TCLC 28; BLC; DAM
MULT**
See also BW 1; CA 124; DLB 50

Couch, Arthur Thomas Quiller
See Quiller-Couch, Arthur Thomas

Coulton, James
See Hansen, Joseph

Couperus, Louis (Marie Anne)
1863-1923 .... **TCLC 15**
See also CA 115

Coupland, Douglas
1961- .... **CLC 85; DAC; DAM POP**
See also CA 142; CANR 57

Court, Wesli
See Turco, Lewis (Putnam)

Courtenay, Bryce 1933- .... **CLC 59**
See also CA 138

Courtney, Robert
See Ellison, Harlan (Jay)

Cousteau, Jacques-Yves
1910-1997 .... **CLC 30**
See also CA 65-68; 159; CANR 15; MTCW;
SATA 38

Cowan, Peter (Walkinshaw) 1914- .... **SSC 28**
See also CA 21-24R; CANR 9, 25, 50

Coward, Noel (Peirce)
1899-1973 .... **CLC 1, 9, 29, 51; DAM
DRAM**
See also AITN 1; CA 17-18; 41-44R; CANR
35; CAP 2; CDBLB 1914-1945; DLB 10;
MTCW

Cowley, Malcolm 1898-1989 .... **CLC 39**
See also CA 5-8R; 128; CANR 3, 55; DLB 4,
48; DLBY 81, 89; MTCW

Cowper, William
1731-1800 .... **NCLC 8; DAM POET**
See also DLB 104, 109

Cox, William Trevor 1928- .... **CLC 9, 14, 71;
DAM NOV**
See also Trevor, William
See also CA 9-12R; CANR 4, 37, 55; DLB 14;
INT CANR-37; MTCW

Coyne, P. J.
See Masters, Hilary

Cozzens, James Gould
1903-1978 .... **CLC 1, 4, 11, 92**
See also CA 9-12R; 81-84; CANR 19; CDALB
1941-1968; DLB 9; DLBD 2; DLBY 84;
MTCW

Crabbe, George 1754-1832 .... **NCLC 26**
See also DLB 93

Craddock, Charles Egbert
See Murfree, Mary Noailles

Craig, A. A.
See Anderson, Poul (William)

Craik, Dinah Maria (Mulock)
1826-1887 .... **NCLC 38**
See also DLB 35, 163; MAICYA; SATA
34

Cram, Ralph Adams 1863-1942 ..... **TCLC 45**
See also CA 160

Crane, (Harold) Hart
1899-1932 ... **TCLC 2, 5; DA; DAB;
DAC; DAM MST, POET; PC 3;
WLC**
See also CA 104; 127; CDALB 1917-1929;
DLB 4, 48; MTCW

Crane, R(onald) S(almon)
1886-1967 .... **CLC 27**
See also CA 85-88; DLB 63

Crane, Stephen (Townley)
1871-1900 .... **TCLC 11, 17, 32; DA;
DAB; DAC; DAM MST, NOV, POET;
SSC 7; WLC**
See also AAYA 21; CA 109; 140;
CDALB 1865-1917; DLB 12, 54, 78;
YABC 2

Crase, Douglas 1944- .... **CLC 58**
See also CA 106

Crashaw, Richard 1612(?)-1649 .... **LC 24**
See also DLB 126

Craven, Margaret
1901-1980 .... **CLC 17; DAC**
See also CA 103

Crawford, F(rancis) Marion
1854-1909 .... **TCLC 10**
See also CA 107; DLB 71

Crawford, Isabella Valancy
1850-1887 .... **NCLC 12**
See also DLB 92

Crayon, Geoffrey
See Irving, Washington

Creasey, John
1908-1973 .... **CLC 11**
See also CA 5-8R; 41-44R; CANR 8, 59; DLB
77; MTCW

Crebillon, Claude Prosper Jolyot de (fils)
1707-1777 .... **LC 28**

Credo
See Creasey, John

Credo, Alvaro J. de
See Prado (Calvo), Pedro

Creeley, Robert (White)
1926- .... **CLC 1, 2, 4, 8, 11, 15, 36, 78;
DAM POET**
See also CA 1-4R; CAAS 10; CANR 23,
43; DLB 5, 16, 169; MTCW

Crews, Harry (Eugene)
1935- .... CLC 6, 23, 49
See also AITN 1; CA 25-28R; CANR 20, 57;
DLB 6, 143; MTCW

Crichton, (John) Michael
1942- ...... CLC 2, 6, 54, 90; DAM NOV,
POP
See also AAYA 10; AITN 2; CA 25-28R;
CANR 13, 40, 54; DLBY 81; INT CANR-
13; JRDA; MTCW; SATA 9, 88

Crispin, Edmund .... CLC 22
See also Montgomery, (Robert) Bruce
See also DLB 87

Cristofer, Michael
1945(?)- .... CLC 28; DAM DRAM
See also CA 110; 152; DLB 7

Croce, Benedetto 1866-1952 .... TCLC 37
See also CA 120; 155

Crockett, David 1786-1836 .... NCLC 8
See also DLB 3, 11

Crockett, Davy
See Crockett, David

Crofts, Freeman Wills
1879-1957 .... TCLC 55
See also CA 115; DLB 77

Croker, John Wilson
1780-1857 .... NCLC 10
See also DLB 110

Crommelynck, Fernand
1885-1970 .... CLC 75
See also CA 89-92

Cronin, A(rchibald) J(oseph)
1896-1981 .... CLC 32
See also CA 1-4R; 102; CANR 5; SATA 47;
SATA-Obit 25

Cross, Amanda
See Heilbrun, Carolyn G(old)

Crothers, Rachel
1878(?)-1958 .... TCLC 19
See also CA 113; DLB 7

Croves, Hal
See Traven, B.

Crow Dog, Mary (Ellen) (?)- .... CLC 93
See also Brave Bird, Mary
See also CA 154

Crowfield, Christopher
See Stowe, Harriet (Elizabeth) Beecher

Crowley, Aleister .... TCLC 7
See also Crowley, Edward Alexander

Crowley, Edward Alexander 1875-1947
See Crowley, Aleister
See also CA 104

Crowley, John 1942- .... CLC 57
See also CA 61-64; CANR 43; DLBY 82;
SATA 65

Crud
See Crumb, R(obert)

Crumarums
See Crumb, R(obert)

Crumb, R(obert) 1943- .... CLC 17
See also CA 106

Crumbum
See Crumb, R(obert)

Crumski
See Crumb, R(obert)

Crum the Bum
See Crumb, R(obert)

Crunk
See Crumb, R(obert)

Crustt
See Crumb, R(obert)

Cryer, Gretchen (Kiger) 1935- .... CLC 21
See also CA 114; 123

Csath, Geza 1887-1919 .... TCLC 13
See also CA 111

Cudlip, David 1933- .... CLC 34

Cullen, Countee
1903-1946 TCLC 4, 37; BLC; DA; DAC;
DAM MST, MULT, POET; PC 20;
WLCS
See also BW 1; CA 108; 124; CDALB
1917-1929; DLB 4, 48, 51; MTCW;
SATA 18

Cum, R.
See Crumb, R(obert)

Cummings, Bruce F(rederick) 1889-1919
See Barbellion, W. N. P.
See also CA 123

Cummings, E(dward) E(stlin)
1894-1962 .. CLC 1, 3, 8, 12, 15, 68; DA;
DAB; DAC; DAM MST, POET; PC 5;
WLC 2
See also CA 73-76; CANR 31; CDALB 1929-
1941; DLB 4, 48; MTCW

Cunha, Euclides (Rodrigues Pimenta) da
1866-1909 .... TCLC 24
See also CA 123

Cunningham, E. V.
See Fast, Howard (Melvin)

Cunningham, J(ames) V(incent)
1911-1985 .... CLC 3, 31
See also CA 1-4R; 115; CANR 1; DLB 5

Cunningham, Julia (Woolfolk)
1916- .... CLC 12
See also CA 9-12R; CANR 4, 19, 36;
JRDA; MAICYA; SAAS 2; SATA 1,
26

Cunningham, Michael 1952- .... CLC 34
See also CA 136

Cunninghame Graham, R(obert) B(ontine)
1852-1936 .... TCLC 19
See also Graham, R(obert) B(ontine)
Cunninghame
See also CA 119; DLB 98

Currie, Ellen 19(?)- .... CLC 44

Curtin, Philip
See Lowndes, Marie Adelaide (Belloc)

Curtis, Price
See Ellison, Harlan (Jay)

Cutrate, Joe
See Spiegelman, Art

Cynewulf c. 770-c. 840 .... CMLC 23

Czaczkes, Shmuel Yosef
See Agnon, S(hmuel) Y(osef Halevi)

Dabrowska, Maria (Szumska)
1889-1965 .... CLC 15
See also CA 106

Dabydeen, David
1955- .... CLC 34
See also BW 1; CA 125; CANR 56

Dacey, Philip
1939- .... CLC 51
See also CA 37-40R; CAAS 17; CANR 14, 32;
DLB 105

Dagerman, Stig (Halvard)
1923-1954 .... TCLC 17
See also CA 117; 155

Dahl, Roald
1916-1990 .... CLC 1, 6, 18, 79; DAB;
DAC; DAM MST, NOV, POP
See also AAYA 15; CA 1-4R; 133; CANR 6,
32, 37, 62; CLR 1, 7, 41; DLB 139; JRDA;
MAICYA; MTCW; SATA 1, 26, 73; SATA-
Obit 65

Dahlberg, Edward
1900-1977 .... CLC 1, 7, 14
See also CA 9-12R; 69-72; CANR 31, 62; DLB
48; MTCW

Daitch, Susan 1954- .... CLC 103

Dale, Colin .... TCLC 18
See also Lawrence, T(homas) E(dward)

Dale, George E.
See Asimov, Isaac

Daly, Elizabeth
1878-1967 .... CLC 52
See also CA 23-24; 25-28R; CANR 60; CAP
2

Daly, Maureen
1921- .... CLC 17
See also AAYA 5; CANR 37; JRDA; MAICYA;
SAAS 1; SATA 2

Damas, Leon-Gontran
1912-1978 .... CLC 84
See also BW 1; CA 125; 73-76

Deighton, Leonard Cyril 1929-
See Deighton, Len
See also CA 9-12R; CANR 19, 33; DAM NOV,
POP; MTCW

Dekker, Thomas
1572(?)-1632 .... **LC 22; DAM DRAM**
See also CDBLB Before 1660; DLB 62, 172

Delafield, E. M. 1890-1943 .... **TCLC 61**
See also Dashwood, Edmee Elizabeth Monica
de la Pasture
See also DLB 34

de la Mare, Walter (John)
1873-1956 ...... **TCLC 4, 53; DAB; DAC;
DAM MST, POET; SSC 14; WLC**
See also CDBLB 1914-1945; CLR 23; DLB
162; SATA 16

Delaney, Franey
See O'Hara, John (Henry)

Delaney, Shelagh
1939- .... **CLC 29; DAM DRAM**
See also CA 17-20R; CANR 30; CDBLB 1960
to Present; DLB 13; MTCW

Delany, Mary (Granville Pendarves)
1700-1788 .... **LC 12**

Delany, Samuel R(ay, Jr.)
1942- .... **CLC 8, 14, 38; BLC; DAM
MULT**
See also BW 2; CA 81-84; CANR 27, 43; DLB
8, 33; MTCW

De La Ramee, (Marie) Louise 1839-1908
See Ouida
See also SATA 20

de la Roche, Mazo 1879-1961 .... **CLC 14**
See also CA 85-88; CANR 30; DLB 68; SATA
64

De La Salle, Innocent
See Hartmann, Sadakichi

Delbanco, Nicholas (Franklin)
1942- .... **CLC 6, 13**
See also CA 17-20R; CAAS 2; CANR 29, 55;
DLB 6

del Castillo, Michel 1933- .... **CLC 38**
See also CA 109

Deledda, Grazia (Cosima)
1875(?)-1936 .... **TCLC 23**
See also CA 123

Delibes, Miguel .... **CLC 8, 18**
See also Delibes Setien, Miguel

Delibes Setien, Miguel 1920-
See Delibes, Miguel
See also CA 45-48; CANR 1, 32; HW;
MTCW

DeLillo, Don
1936- ....**CLC 8, 10, 13, 27, 39, 54, 76;
DAM NOV, POP**
See also BEST 89:1; CA 81-84; CANR 21;
DLB 6, 173; MTCW

de Lisser, H. G.
See De Lisser, H(erbert) G(eorge)
See also DLB 117

De Lisser, H(erbert) G(eorge)
1878-1944 .... **TCLC 12**
See also de Lisser, H. G.
See also BW 2; CA 109; 152

Deloria, Vine (Victor), Jr. 1933- ..... **CLC 21;
DAM MULT**
See also CA 53-56; CANR 5, 20, 48; DLB 175;
MTCW; NNAL; SATA 21

Del Vecchio, John M(ichael)
1947- .... **CLC 29**
See also CA 110; DLBD 9

de Man, Paul (Adolph Michel)
1919-1983 .... **CLC 55**
See also CA 128; 111; CANR 61; DLB 67;
MTCW

De Marinis, Rick 1934- .... **CLC 54**
See also CA 57-60; CAAS 24; CANR 9, 25,
50

Dembry, R. Emmet
See Murfree, Mary Noailles

Demby, William
1922- .... **CLC 53; BLC; DAM MULT**
See also BW 1; CA 81-84; DLB 33

de Menton, Francisco
See Chin, Frank (Chew, Jr.)

Demijohn, Thom
See Disch, Thomas M(ichael)

de Montherlant, Henry (Milon)
See Montherlant, Henry (Milon) de

Demosthenes 384B.C.-322B.C. ...... **CMLC 13**
See also DLB 176

de Natale, Francine
See Malzberg, Barry N(athaniel)

Denby, Edwin (Orr) 1903-1983 .... **CLC 48**
See also CA 138; 110

Denis, Julio
See Cortazar, Julio

Denmark, Harrison
See Zelazny, Roger (Joseph)

Dennis, John 1658-1734 .... **LC 11**
See also DLB 101

Dennis, Nigel (Forbes) 1912-1989....... **CLC 8**
See also CA 25-28R; 129; DLB 13, 15;
MTCW

Dent, Lester 1904(?)-1959............... **TCLC 72**
See also CA 112

De Palma, Brian (Russell) 1940-....... **CLC 20**
See also CA 109

De Quincey, Thomas 1785-1859 ...... **NCLC 4**
See also CDBLB 1789-1832; DLB 110; 144

Deren, Eleanora 1908(?)-1961
See Deren, Maya
See also CA 111

Deren, Maya 1917-1961 .... **CLC 16, 102**
See also Deren, Eleanora

Derleth, August (William)
1909-1971 .... **CLC 31**
See also CA 1-4R; 29-32R; CANR 4; DLB 9;
SATA 5

Der Nister 1884-1950 .... **TCLC 56**

de Routisie, Albert
See Aragon, Louis

Derrida, Jacques 1930- .... **CLC 24, 87**
See also CA 124; 127

Derry Down Derry
See Lear, Edward

Dersonnes, Jacques
See Simenon, Georges (Jacques Christian)

Desai, Anita
1937- .... **CLC 19, 37, 97; DAB; DAM
NOV**
See also CA 81-84; CANR 33, 53; MTCW;
SATA 63

de Saint-Luc, Jean
See Glassco, John

de Saint Roman, Arnaud
See Aragon, Louis

Descartes, Rene 1596-1650 .... **LC 20, 35**

De Sica, Vittorio 1901(?)-1974 .... **CLC 20**
See also CA 117

Desnos, Robert 1900-1945 .... **TCLC 22**
See also CA 121; 151

Destouches, Louis-Ferdinand
1894-1961 ....CLC 9, 15
See also Celine, Louis-Ferdinand
See also CA 85-88; CANR 28; MTCW

de Tolignac, Gaston
See Griffith, D(avid Lewelyn) W(ark)

Deutsch, Babette 1895-1982 .... **CLC 18**
See also CA 1-4R; 108; CANR 4; DLB 45;
SATA 1; SATA-Obit 33

Devenant, William 1606-1649 .... **LC 13**

Devkota, Laxmiprasad
1909-1959 .... **TCLC 23**
See also CA 123

De Voto, Bernard (Augustine)
1897-1955 .... **TCLC 29**
See also CA 113; 160; DLB 9

De Vries, Peter
1910-1993 ...... **CLC 1, 2, 3, 7, 10, 28, 46;
DAM NOV**
See also CA 17-20R; 142; CANR 41; DLB 6;
DLBY 82; MTCW

Dorn, Edward (Merton) 1929- ... **CLC 10, 18**
See also CA 93-96; CANR 42; DLB 5; INT 93-96

Dorsan, Luc
See Simenon, Georges (Jacques Christian)

Dorsange, Jean
See Simenon, Georges (Jacques Christian)

Dos Passos, John (Roderigo)
1896-1970 ... **CLC 1, 4, 8, 11, 15, 25, 34, 82; DA; DAB; DAC; DAM MST, NOV; WLC**
See also CA 1-4R; 29-32R; CANR 3; CDALB 1929-1941; DLB 4, 9; DLBD 1, 15; DLBY 96; MTCW

Dossage, Jean
See Simenon, Georges (Jacques Christian)

Dostoevsky, Fedor Mikhailovich
1821-1881 ... **NCLC 2, 7, 21, 33, 43; DA; DAB; DAC; DAM MST, NOV; SSC 2; WLC**

Doughty, Charles M(ontagu)
1843-1926 .... **TCLC 27**
See also CA 115; DLB 19, 57, 174

Douglas, Ellen .... **CLC 73**
See also Haxton, Josephine Ayres; Williamson, Ellen Douglas

Douglas, Gavin 1475(?)-1522 .... **LC 20**

Douglas, Keith (Castellain)
1920-1944 .... **TCLC 40**
See also CA 160; DLB 27

Douglas, Leonard
See Bradbury, Ray (Douglas)

Douglas, Michael
See Crichton, (John) Michael

Douglas, Norman 1868-1952 .... **TCLC 68**

Douglass, Frederick
1817(?)-1895 .... **NCLC 7, 55; BLC; DA; DAC; DAM MST, MULT; WLC**
See also CDALB 1640-1865; DLB 1, 43, 50, 79; SATA 29

Dourado, (Waldomiro Freitas) Autran
1926- .... **CLC 23, 60**
See also CA 25-28R; CANR 34

Dourado, Waldomiro Autran
See Dourado, (Waldomiro Freitas) Autran

Dove, Rita (Frances)
1952- .... **CLC 50, 81; DAM MULT, POET; PC 6**
See also BW 2; CA 109; CAAS 19; CANR 27, 42; DLB 120

Dowell, Coleman 1925-1985 .... **CLC 60**
See also CA 25-28R; 117; CANR 10; DLB 130

Dowson, Ernest (Christopher)
1867-1900 .... **TCLC 4**
See also CA 105; 150; DLB 19, 135

Doyle, A. Conan
See Doyle, Arthur Conan

Doyle, Arthur Conan
1859-1930 **TCLC 7; DA; DAB; DAC; DAM MST, NOV; SSC 12; WLC**
See also AAYA 14; CA 104; 122; CDBLB 1890-1914; DLB 18, 70, 156, 178; MTCW; SATA 24

Doyle, Conan
See Doyle, Arthur Conan

Doyle, John
See Graves, Robert (von Ranke)

Doyle, Roddy 1958(?)- .... **CLC 81**
See also AAYA 14; CA 143

Doyle, Sir A. Conan
See Doyle, Arthur Conan

Doyle, Sir Arthur Conan
See Doyle, Arthur Conan

Dr. A
See Asimov, Isaac; Silverstein, Alvin

Drabble, Margaret
1939- ... **CLC 2, 3, 5, 8, 10, 22, 53; DAB; DAC; DAM MST, NOV, POP**
See also CA 13-16R; CANR 18, 35; CDBLB 1960 to Present; DLB 14, 155; MTCW; SATA 48

Drapier, M. B.
See Swift, Jonathan

Drayham, James
See Mencken, H(enry) L(ouis)

Drayton, Michael 1563-1631 .... **LC 8**

Dreadstone, Carl
See Campbell, (John) Ramsey

Dreiser, Theodore (Herman Albert)
1871-1945 .... **TCLC 10, 18, 35; DA; DAC; DAM MST, NOV; WLC**
See also CA 106; 132; CDALB 1865-1917; DLB 9, 12, 102, 137; DLBD 1; MTCW

Drexler, Rosalyn 1926- .... **CLC 2, 6**
See also CA 81-84

Dreyer, Carl Theodor 1889-1968 ...... **CLC 16**
See also CA 116

Drieu la Rochelle, Pierre(-Eugene)
1893-1945 .... **TCLC 21**
See also CA 117; DLB 72

Drinkwater, John
1882-1937 .... **TCLC 57**
See also CA 109; 149; DLB 10, 19, 149

Drop Shot
See Cable, George Washington

Droste-Hulshoff, Annette Freiin von
1797-1848 .... **NCLC 3**
See also DLB 133

Drummond, Walter
See Silverberg, Robert

Drummond, William Henry
1854-1907 .... **TCLC 25**
See also CA 160; DLB 92

Drummond de Andrade, Carlos
1902-1987 .... **CLC 18**
See also Andrade, Carlos Drummond de
See also CA 132; 123

Drury, Allen (Stuart) 1918- .... **CLC 37**
See also CA 57-60; CANR 18, 52; INT CANR-18

Dryden, John
1631-1700 .... **LC 3, 21; DA; DAB; DAC; DAM DRAM, MST, POET; DC 3; WLC**
See also CDBLB 1660-1789; DLB 80, 101, 131

Duberman, Martin 1930- .... **CLC 8**
See also CA 1-4R; CANR 2

Dubie, Norman (Evans) 1945- .... **CLC 36**
See also CA 69-72; CANR 12; DLB 120

Du Bois, W(illiam) E(dward) B(urghardt)
1868-1963 ... **CLC 1, 2, 13, 64, 96; BLC; DA; DAC; DAM MST, MULT, NOV; WLC**
See also BW 1; CA 85-88; CANR 34; CDALB 1865-1917; DLB 47, 50, 91; MTCW; SATA 42

Dubus, Andre
1936- .... **CLC 13, 36, 97; SSC 15**
See also CA 21-24R; CANR 17; DLB 130; INT CANR-17

Duca Minimo
See D'Annunzio, Gabriele

Ducharme, Rejean 1941- .... **CLC 74**
See also DLB 60

Duclos, Charles Pinot 1704-1772 .... **LC 1**

Dudek, Louis 1918- .... **CLC 11, 19**
See also CA 45-48; CAAS 14; CANR 1; DLB 88

Duerrenmatt, Friedrich
1921-1990 .. **CLC 1, 4, 8, 11, 15, 43, 102; DAM DRAM**
See also CA 17-20R; CANR 33; DLB 69, 124; MTCW

Duffy, Bruce (?)- .... **CLC 50**

Duffy, Maureen 1933- .... **CLC 37**
See also CA 25-28R; CANR 33; DLB 14; MTCW

Dugan, Alan 1923- .... **CLC 2, 6**
See also CA 81-84; DLB 5

du Gard, Roger Martin
See Martin du Gard, Roger

Duhamel, Georges 1884-1966 .... **CLC 8**
See also CA 81-84; 25-28R; CANR 35; DLB 65; MTCW

Edgerton, Clyde (Carlyle) 1944- ...... **CLC 39**
See also AAYA 17; CA 118; 134; INT 134

Edgeworth, Maria 1768-1849 ....**NCLC 1, 51**
See also DLB 116, 159, 163; SATA 21

Edmonds, Paul
See Kuttner, Henry

Edmonds, Walter D(umaux) 1903- ... **CLC 35**
See also CA 5-8R; CANR 2; DLB 9; MAICYA;
SAAS 4; SATA 1, 27

Edmondson, Wallace
See Ellison, Harlan (Jay)

Edson, Russell .... **CLC 13**
See also CA 33-36R

Edwards, Bronwen Elizabeth
See Rose, Wendy

Edwards, G(erald) B(asil)
1899-1976 .... **CLC 25**
See also CA 110

Edwards, Gus 1939- .... **CLC 43**
See also CA 108; INT 108

Edwards, Jonathan
1703-1758 .... **LC 7; DA; DAC; DAM
MST**
See also DLB 24

Efron, Marina Ivanovna Tsvetaeva
See Tsvetaeva (Efron), Marina (Ivanovna)

Ehle, John (Marsden, Jr.) 1925- .... **CLC 27**
See also CA 9-12R

Ehrenbourg, Ilya (Grigoryevich)
See Ehrenburg, Ilya (Grigoryevich)

Ehrenburg, Ilya (Grigoryevich)
1891-1967 .... **CLC 18, 34, 62**
See also CA 102; 25-28R

Ehrenburg, Ilyo (Grigoryevich)
See Ehrenburg, Ilya (Grigoryevich)

Eich, Guenter 1907-1972 .... **CLC 15**
See also CA 111; 93-96; DLB 69, 124

Eichendorff, Joseph Freiherr von
1788-1857 .... **NCLC 8**
See also DLB 90

Eigner, Larry .... **CLC 9**
See also Eigner, Laurence (Joel)
See also CAAS 23; DLB 5

Eigner, Laurence (Joel) 1927-1996
See Eigner, Larry
See also CA 9-12R; 151; CANR 6

Einstein, Albert 1879-1955 .... **TCLC 65**
See also CA 121; 133; MTCW

Eiseley, Loren Corey 1907-1977 .... **CLC 7**
See also AAYA 5; CA 1-4R; 73-76; CANR 6

Eisenstadt, Jill 1963- .... **CLC 50**
See also CA 140

Eisenstein, Sergei (Mikhailovich)
1898-1948 .... **TCLC 57**
See also CA 114; 149

Eisner, Simon
See Kornbluth, C(yril) M.

Ekeloef, (Bengt) Gunnar
1907-1968 .... **CLC 27; DAM POET**
See also CA 123; 25-28R

Ekelof, (Bengt) Gunnar
See Ekeloef, (Bengt) Gunnar

Ekelund, Vilhelm 1880-1949 .... **TCLC 75**

Ekwensi, C. O. D.
See Ekwensi, Cyprian (Odiatu Duaka)

Ekwensi, Cyprian (Odiatu Duaka)
1921- .... **CLC 4; BLC; DAM MULT**
See also BW 2; CA 29-32R; CANR 18, 42;
DLB 117; MTCW; SATA 66

Elaine .... **TCLC 18**
See also Leverson, Ada

El Crummo
See Crumb, R(obert)

Elia
See Lamb, Charles

Eliade, Mircea 1907-1986 .... **CLC 19**
See also CA 65-68; 119; CANR 30, 62;
MTCW

Eliot, A. D.
See Jewett, (Theodora) Sarah Orne

Eliot, Alice
See Jewett, (Theodora) Sarah Orne

Eliot, Dan
See Silverberg, Robert

Eliot, George
1819-1880 ..... **NCLC 4, 13, 23, 41, 49;
DA; DAB; DAC; DAM MST, NOV; PC
20; WLC**
See also CDBLB 1832-1890; DLB 21, 35,
55

Eliot, John 1604-1690 .... **LC 5**
See also DLB 24

Eliot, T(homas) S(tearns)
1888-1965 **CLC 1, 2, 3, 6, 9, 10, 13,
15, 24, 34, 41, 55, 57; DA; DAB; DAC;
DAM DRAM, MST, POET; PC 5;
WLC 2**
See also CA 5-8R; 25-28R; CANR 41;
CDALB 1929-1941; DLB 7, 10, 45, 63;
DLBY 88; MTCW

Elizabeth 1866-1941 .... **TCLC 41**

Elkin, Stanley L(awrence)
1930-1995..... **CLC 4, 6, 9, 14, 27, 51,
91; DAM NOV, POP; SSC 12**
See also CA 9-12R; 148; CANR 8, 46;
DLB 2, 28; DLBY 80; INT CANR-8;
MTCW

Elledge, Scott .... **CLC 34**

Elliot, Don
See Silverberg, Robert

Elliott, Don
See Silverberg, Robert

Elliott, George P(aul)
1918-1980 .... **CLC 2**
See also CA 1-4R; 97-100; CANR 2

Elliott, Janice 1931- .... **CLC 47**
See also CA 13-16R; CANR 8, 29; DLB 14

Elliott, Sumner Locke
1917-1991 .... **CLC 38**
See also CA 5-8R; 134; CANR 2, 21

Elliott, William
See Bradbury, Ray (Douglas)

Ellis, A. E. .... **CLC 7**

Ellis, Alice Thomas .... **CLC 40**
See also Haycraft, Anna

Ellis, Bret Easton
1964- .... **CLC 39, 71; DAM POP**
See also AAYA 2; CA 118; 123; CANR 51;
INT 123

Ellis, (Henry) Havelock
1859-1939 .... **TCLC 14**
See also CA 109

Ellis, Landon
See Ellison, Harlan (Jay)

Ellis, Trey 1962- .... **CLC 55**
See also CA 146

Ellison, Harlan (Jay)
1934- .. **CLC 1, 13, 42; DAM POP; SSC
14**
See also CA 5-8R; CANR 5, 46; DLB 8; INT
CANR-5; MTCW

Ellison, Ralph (Waldo)
1914-1994 .... **CLC 1, 3, 11, 54, 86; BLC;
DA; DAB; DAC; DAM MST, MULT,
NOV; SSC 26; WLC**
See also AAYA 19; BW 1; CA 9-12R; 145;
CANR 24, 53; CDALB 1941-1968; DLB 2,
76; DLBY 94; MTCW

Ellmann, Lucy (Elizabeth)
1956- .... **CLC 61**
See also CA 128

Ellmann, Richard (David)
1918-1987 .... **CLC 50**
See also BEST 89:2; CA 1-4R; 122; CANR 2,
28, 61; DLB 103; DLBY 87; MTCW

Elman, Richard 1934- .... **CLC 19**
See also CA 17-20R; CAAS 3; CANR 47

Elron
See Hubbard, L(afayette) Ron(ald)

Eluard, Paul .... **TCLC 7, 41**
See also Grindel, Eugene

Author Index

Freneau, Philip Morin
1752-1832 .... NCLC 1
See also DLB 37, 43

Freud, Sigmund 1856-1939 .... TCLC 52
See also CA 115; 133; MTCW

Friedan, Betty (Naomi) 1921- .... CLC 74
See also CA 65-68; CANR 18, 45; MTCW

Friedlander, Saul 1932-...................... CLC 90
See also CA 117; 130

Friedman, B(ernard) H(arper)
1926- .... CLC 7
See also CA 1-4R; CANR 3, 48

Friedman, Bruce Jay 1930- ...... CLC 3, 5, 56
See also CA 9-12R; CANR 25, 52; DLB 2, 28;
INT CANR-25

Friel, Brian 1929- .... CLC 5, 42, 59
See also CA 21-24R; CANR 33; DLB 13;
MTCW

Friis-Baastad, Babbis Ellinor
1921-1970 .... CLC 12
See also CA 17-20R; 134; SATA 7

Frisch, Max (Rudolf)
1911-1991 .... CLC 3, 9, 14, 18, 32, 44;
DAM DRAM, NOV
See also CA 85-88; 134; CANR 32; DLB 69,
124; MTCW

Fromentin, Eugene (Samuel Auguste)
1820-1876 .... NCLC 10
See also DLB 123

Frost, Frederick
See Faust, Frederick (Schiller)

Frost, Robert (Lee)
1874-1963 ... CLC 1, 3, 4, 9, 10, 13, 15,
26, 34, 44; DA; DAB; DAC; DAM MST,
POET; PC 1; WLC
See also AAYA 21; CA 89-92; CANR 33;
CDALB 1917-1929; DLB 54; DLBD 7;
MTCW; SATA 14

Froude, James Anthony
1818-1894 .... NCLC 43
See also DLB 18, 57, 144

Froy, Herald
See Waterhouse, Keith (Spencer)

Fry, Christopher
1907- .... CLC 2, 10, 14; DAM DRAM
See also CA 17-20R; CAAS 23; CANR 9, 30;
DLB 13; MTCW; SATA 66

Frye, (Herman) Northrop
1912-1991 .... CLC 24, 70
See also CA 5-8R; 133; CANR 8, 37; DLB 67,
68; MTCW

Fuchs, Daniel 1909-1993 .... CLC 8, 22
See also CA 81-84; 142; CAAS 5; CANR 40;
DLB 9, 26, 28; DLBY 93

Fuchs, Daniel 1934- .... CLC 34
See also CA 37-40R; CANR 14, 48

Fuentes, Carlos
1928- . CLC 3, 8, 10, 13, 22, 41, 60; DA;
DAB; DAC; DAM MST, MULT, NOV;
HLC; SSC 24; WLC
See also AAYA 4; AITN 2; CA 69-72; CANR
10, 32; DLB 113; HW; MTCW

Fuentes, Gregorio Lopez y
See Lopez y Fuentes, Gregorio

Fugard, (Harold) Athol
1932- ..... CLC 5, 9, 14, 25, 40, 80; DAM
DRAM; DC 3
See also AAYA 17; CA 85-88; CANR 32, 54;
MTCW

Fugard, Sheila 1932- .... CLC 48
See also CA 125

Fuller, Charles (H., Jr.)
1939- .... CLC 25; BLC; DAM DRAM,
MULT; DC 1
See also BW 2; CA 108; 112; DLB 38; INT
112; MTCW

Fuller, John (Leopold) 1937-............. CLC 62
See also CA 21-24R; CANR 9, 44; DLB
40

Fuller, Margaret .... NCLC 5, 50
See also Ossoli, Sarah Margaret (Fuller
marchesa d')

Fuller, Roy (Broadbent)
1912-1991 .... CLC 4, 28
See also CA 5-8R; 135; CAAS 10; CANR 53;
DLB 15, 20; SATA 87

Fulton, Alice 1952- .... CLC 52
See also CA 116; CANR 57

Furphy, Joseph 1843-1912.............. TCLC 25

Fussell, Paul 1924- .... CLC 74
See also BEST 90:1; CA 17-20R; CANR 8,
21, 35; INT CANR-21; MTCW

Futabatei, Shimei 1864-1909 .... TCLC 44
See also DLB 180

Futrelle, Jacques 1875-1912 .... TCLC 19
See also CA 113; 155

Gaboriau, Emile 1835-1873 .... NCLC 14

Gadda, Carlo Emilio 1893-1973 .... CLC 11
See also CA 89-92; DLB 177

Gaddis, William
1922- .... CLC 1, 3, 6, 8, 10, 19, 43, 86
See also CA 17-20R; CANR 21, 48; DLB 2;
MTCW

Gage, Walter
See Inge, William (Motter)

Gaines, Ernest J(ames)
1933- ..... CLC 3, 11, 18, 86; BLC; DAM
MULT
See also AAYA 18; AITN 1; BW 2; CA 9-
12R; CANR 6, 24, 42; CDALB 1968-
1988; DLB 2, 33, 152; DLBY 80; MTCW;
SATA 86

Gaitskill, Mary 1954- .... CLC 69
See also CA 128; CANR 61

Galdos, Benito Perez
See Perez Galdos, Benito

Gale, Zona
1874-1938 .... TCLC 7; DAM DRAM
See also CA 105; 153; DLB 9, 78

Galeano, Eduardo (Hughes) 1940- ... CLC 72
See also CA 29-32R; CANR 13, 32; HW

Galiano, Juan Valera y Alcala
See Valera y Alcala-Galiano, Juan

Gallagher, Tess 1943- ...... CLC 18, 63; DAM
POET; PC 9
See also CA 106; DLB 120

Gallant, Mavis
1922- .... CLC 7, 18, 38; DAC; DAM
MST; SSC 5
See also CA 69-72; CANR 29; DLB 53;
MTCW

Gallant, Roy A(rthur) 1924- .... CLC 17
See also CA 5-8R; CANR 4, 29, 54; CLR 30;
MAICYA; SATA 4, 68

Gallico, Paul (William)
1897-1976 .... CLC 2
See also AITN 1; CA 5-8R; 69-72; CANR 23;
DLB 9, 171; MAICYA; SATA 13

Gallo, Max Louis 1932- .... CLC 95
See also CA 85-88

Gallois, Lucien
See Desnos, Robert

Gallup, Ralph
See Whitemore, Hugh (John)

Galsworthy, John 1867-1933 .... TCLC 1, 45;
DA; DAB; DAC; DAM DRAM, MST,
NOV; SSC 22; WLC 2
See also CA 104; 141; CDBLB 1890-1914;
DLB 10, 34, 98, 162; DLBD 16

Galt, John 1779-1839 .... NCLC 1
See also DLB 99, 116, 159

Galvin, James 1951- .... CLC 38
See also CA 108; CANR 26

Gamboa, Federico 1864-1939 .... TCLC 36

Gandhi, M. K.
See Gandhi, Mohandas Karamchand

Gandhi, Mahatma
See Gandhi, Mohandas Karamchand

Gandhi, Mohandas Karamchand
1869-1948 .... TCLC 59; DAM MULT
See also CA 121; 132; MTCW

Gann, Ernest Kellogg 1910-1991 ...... CLC 23
See also AITN 1; CA 1-4R; 136; CANR 1

Garcia, Cristina 1958- .... CLC 76
See also CA 141

Garcia Lorca, Federico
1898-1936 ..... TCLC 1, 7, 49; DA; DAB;
DAC; DAM DRAM, MST, MULT,
POET; DC 2; HLC; PC 3; WLC
See also CA 104; 131; DLB 108; HW; MTCW

Garcia Marquez, Gabriel (Jose)
1928- .... CLC 2, 3, 8, 10, 15, 27, 47, 55,
68; DA; DAB; DAC; DAM MST, MULT,
NOV, POP; HLC; SSC 8; WLC
See also AAYA 3; BEST 89:1, 90:4; CA 33-
36R; CANR 10, 28, 50; DLB 113; HW;
MTCW

Gard, Janice
See Latham, Jean Lee

Gard, Roger Martin du
See Martin du Gard, Roger

Gardam, Jane 1928- .... CLC 43
See also CA 49-52; CANR 2, 18, 33, 54; CLR
12; DLB 14, 161; MAICYA; MTCW; SAAS
9; SATA 39, 76; SATA-Brief 28

Gardner, Herb(ert) 1934- .... CLC 44
See also CA 149

Gardner, John (Champlin), Jr.
1933-1982 .. CLC 2, 3, 5, 7, 8, 10, 18, 28,
34; DAM NOV, POP; SSC 7
See also AITN 1; CA 65-68; 107; CANR 33;
DLB 2; DLBY 82; MTCW; SATA 40;
SATA-Obit 31

Gardner, John (Edmund) 1926- ...... CLC 30;
DAM POP
See also CA 103; CANR 15; MTCW

Gardner, Miriam
See Bradley, Marion Zimmer

Gardner, Noel
See Kuttner, Henry

Gardons, S. S.
See Snodgrass, W(illiam) D(e Witt)

Garfield, Leon 1921-1996 .... CLC 12
See also AAYA 8; CA 17-20R; 152; CANR 38,
41; CLR 21; DLB 161; JRDA; MAICYA;
SATA 1, 32, 76; SATA-Obit 90

Garland, (Hannibal) Hamlin
1860-1940 .... TCLC 3; SSC 18
See also CA 104; DLB 12, 71, 78

Garneau, (Hector de) Saint-Denys
1912-1943 .... TCLC 13
See also CA 111; DLB 88

Garner, Alan
1934- .... CLC 17; DAB; DAM POP
See also AAYA 18; CA 73-76; CANR 15; CLR
20; DLB 161; MAICYA; MTCW; SATA 18,
69

Garner, Hugh 1913-1979 .... CLC 13
See also CA 69-72; CANR 31; DLB 68

Garnett, David 1892-1981 .... CLC 3
See also CA 5-8R; 103; CANR 17; DLB
34

Garos, Stephanie
See Katz, Steve

Garrett, George (Palmer)
1929- .... CLC 3, 11, 51
See also CA 1-4R; CAAS 5; CANR 1, 42; DLB
2, 5, 130, 152; DLBY 83

Garrick, David 1717-1779 .... LC 15; DAM
DRAM
See also DLB 84

Garrigue, Jean 1914-1972 .... CLC 2, 8
See also CA 5-8R; 37-40R; CANR 20

Garrison, Frederick
See Sinclair, Upton (Beall)

Garth, Will
See Hamilton, Edmond; Kuttner, Henry

Garvey, Marcus (Moziah, Jr.)
1887-1940 .... TCLC 41; BLC; DAM
MULT
See also BW 1; CA 120; 124

Gary, Romain .... CLC 25
See also Kacew, Romain
See also DLB 83

Gascar, Pierre .... CLC 11
See also Fournier, Pierre

Gascoyne, David (Emery)
1916- .... CLC 45
See also CA 65-68; CANR 10, 28, 54; DLB
20; MTCW

Gaskell, Elizabeth Cleghorn
1810-1865 .. NCLC 5; DAB; DAM MST;
SSC 25
See also CDBLB 1832-1890; DLB 21, 144,
159

Gass, William H(oward)
1924- ..... CLC 1, 2, 8, 11, 15, 39; SSC 12
See also CA 17-20R; CANR 30; DLB 2;
MTCW

Gasset, Jose Ortega y
See Ortega y Gasset, Jose

Gates, Henry Louis, Jr.
1950- .... CLC 65; DAM MULT
See also BW 2; CA 109; CANR 25, 53; DLB
67

Gautier, Theophile
1811-1872 ... NCLC 1, 59; DAM POET;
PC 18; SSC 20
See also DLB 119

Gawsworth, John
See Bates, H(erbert) E(rnest)

Gay, Oliver
See Gogarty, Oliver St. John

Gaye, Marvin (Penze) 1939-1984 ..... CLC 26
See also CA 112

Gebler, Carlo (Ernest) 1954- .... CLC 39
See also CA 119; 133

Gee, Maggie (Mary) 1948- .... CLC 57
See also CA 130

Gee, Maurice (Gough) 1931- .... CLC 29
See also CA 97-100; SATA 46

Gelbart, Larry (Simon) 1923- .... CLC 21, 61
See also CA 73-76; CANR 45

Gelber, Jack 1932- .... CLC 1, 6, 14, 79
See also CA 1-4R; CANR 2; DLB 7

Gellhorn, Martha (Ellis)
1908- .... CLC 14, 60
See also CA 77-80; CANR 44; DLBY 82

Genet, Jean
1910-1986 .... CLC 1, 2, 5, 10, 14, 44, 46;
DAM DRAM
See also CA 13-16R; CANR 18; DLB 72;
DLBY 86; MTCW

Gent, Peter 1942- .... CLC 29
See also AITN 1; CA 89-92; DLBY 82

Gentlewoman in New England, A
See Bradstreet, Anne

Gentlewoman in Those Parts, A
See Bradstreet, Anne

George, Jean Craighead
1919- .... CLC 35
See also AAYA 8; CA 5-8R; CANR 25; CLR
1; DLB 52; JRDA; MAICYA; SATA 2, 68

George, Stefan (Anton)
1868-1933 .... TCLC 2, 14
See also CA 104

Georges, Georges Martin
See Simenon, Georges (Jacques Christian)

Gerhardi, William Alexander
See Gerhardie, William Alexander

Gerhardie, William Alexander
1895-1977 .... CLC 5
See also CA 25-28R; 73-76; CANR 18; DLB
36

Gerstler, Amy 1956- .... CLC 70
See also CA 146

Gertler, T. .... CLC 34
See also CA 116; 121; INT 121

Ghalib .... NCLC 39
See also Ghalib, Hsadullah Khan

Ghalib, Hsadullah Khan 1797-1869
See Ghalib
See also DAM POET

Ghelderode, Michel de
1898-1962 .... CLC 6, 11; DAM DRAM
See also CA 85-88; CANR 40

Ghiselin, Brewster 1903- .... CLC 23
See also CA 13-16R; CAAS 10; CANR 13

Ghose, Zulfikar 1935- .... CLC 42
See also CA 65-68

Goebbels, Josef
See Goebbels, (Paul) Joseph

Goebbels, (Paul) Joseph
1897-1945 .... **TCLC 68**
See also CA 115; 148

Goebbels, Joseph Paul
See Goebbels, (Paul) Joseph

Goethe, Johann Wolfgang von
1749-1832 ... NCLC 4, 22, 34; DA; DAB;
DAC; DAM DRAM, MST, POET; PC 5;
WLC 3
See also DLB 94

Gogarty, Oliver St. John
1878-1957 .... **TCLC 15**
See also CA 109; 150; DLB 15, 19

Gogol, Nikolai (Vasilyevich)
1809-1852 ... NCLC 5, 15, 31; DA; DAB;
DAC; DAM DRAM, MST; DC 1; SSC 4,
29; WLC

Goines, Donald
1937(?)-1974 .... CLC 80; BLC; DAM
MULT, POP
See also AITN 1; BW 1; CA 124; 114; DLB
33

Gold, Herbert
1924- .... CLC 4, 7, 14, 42
See also CA 9-12R; CANR 17, 45; DLB 2;
DLBY 81

Goldbarth, Albert 1948- .... CLC 5, 38
See also CA 53-56; CANR 6, 40; DLB 120

Goldberg, Anatol
1910-1982 .... **CLC 34**
See also CA 131; 117

Goldemberg, Isaac 1945- .... CLC 52
See also CA 69-72; CAAS 12; CANR 11, 32;
HW

Golding, William (Gerald)
1911-1993 ... CLC 1, 2, 3, 8, 10, 17, 27,
58, 81; DA; DAB; DAC; DAM MST,
NOV; WLC
See also AAYA 5; CA 5-8R; 141; CANR 13,
33, 54; CDBLB 1945-1960; DLB 15, 100;
MTCW

Goldman, Emma 1869-1940 .... **TCLC 13**
See also CA 110; 150

Goldman, Francisco 1955- .... CLC 76

Goldman, William (W.)
1931- .... CLC 1, 48
See also CA 9-12R; CANR 29; DLB 44

Goldmann, Lucien
1913-1970 .... **CLC 24**
See also CA 25-28; CAP 2

Goldoni, Carlo
1707-1793 .... LC 4; DAM DRAM

Goldsberry, Steven 1949- .... CLC 34
See also CA 131

Goldsmith, Oliver
1728-1774 .... LC 2; DA; DAB; DAC;
DAM DRAM, MST, NOV, POET; WLC
See also CDBLB 1660-1789; DLB 39, 89,
104, 109, 142; SATA 26

Goldsmith, Peter
See Priestley, J(ohn) B(oynton)

Gombrowicz, Witold
1904-1969 .... CLC 4, 7, 11, 49; DAM
DRAM
See also CA 19-20; 25-28R; CAP 2

Gomez de la Serna, Ramon
1888-1963 .... CLC 9
See also CA 153; 116; HW

Goncharov, Ivan Alexandrovich
1812-1891 .... NCLC 1, 63

Goncourt, Edmond (Louis Antoine Huot) de
1822-1896 .... NCLC 7
See also DLB 123

Goncourt, Jules (Alfred Huot) de
1830-1870 .... NCLC 7
See also DLB 123

Gontier, Fernande 19(?)- .... CLC 50

Gonzalez Martinez, Enrique
1871-1952 .... **TCLC 72**
See also HW

Goodman, Paul 1911-1972 ...... CLC 1, 2, 4, 7
See also CA 19-20; 37-40R; CANR 34; CAP
2; DLB 130; MTCW

Gordimer, Nadine
1923- .... CLC 3, 5, 7, 10, 18, 33, 51, 70;
DA; DAB; DAC; DAM MST, NOV; SSC
17; WLCS
See also CA 5-8R; CANR 3, 28, 56; INT
CANR-28; MTCW

Gordon, Adam Lindsay
1833-1870 .... NCLC 21

Gordon, Caroline
1895-1981 ..... CLC 6, 13, 29, 83; SSC 15
See also CA 11-12; 103; CANR 36; CAP 1;
DLB 4, 9, 102; DLBY 81; MTCW

Gordon, Charles William 1860-1937
See Connor, Ralph
See also CA 109

Gordon, Mary (Catherine)
1949- .... CLC 13, 22
See also CA 102; CANR 44; DLB 6; DLBY
81; INT 102; MTCW

Gordon, N. J.
See Bosman, Herman Charles

Gordon, Sol 1923- .... CLC 26
See also CA 53-56; CANR 4; SATA 11

Gordone, Charles
1925-1995 .... CLC 1, 4; DAM DRAM
See also BW 1; CA 93-96; 150; CANR 55;
DLB 7; INT 93-96; MTCW

Gore, Catherine 1800-1861 .... NCLC 65
See also DLB 116

Gorenko, Anna Andreevna
See Akhmatova, Anna

**Gorky, Maxim .... TCLC 8; DAB; SSC 28;
WLC**
See also Peshkov, Alexei Maximovich

Goryan, Sirak
See Saroyan, William

Gosse, Edmund (William)
1849-1928 .... **TCLC 28**
See also CA 117; DLB 57, 144, 184

Gotlieb, Phyllis Fay (Bloom)
1926- .... CLC 18
See also CA 13-16R; CANR 7; DLB 88

Gottesman, S. D.
See Kornbluth, C(yril) M.; Pohl, Frederik

Gottfried von Strassburg
fl. c. 1210- .... **CMLC 10**
See also DLB 138

Gould, Lois ....CLC 4, 10
See also CA 77-80; CANR 29; MTCW

Gourmont, Remy (-Marie-Charles) de
1858-1915 .... **TCLC 17**
See also CA 109; 150

Govier, Katherine 1948- .... CLC 51
See also CA 101; CANR 18, 40

Goyen, (Charles) William
1915-1983 .... CLC 5, 8, 14, 40
See also AITN 2; CA 5-8R; 110; CANR 6; DLB
2; DLBY 83; INT CANR-6

Goytisolo, Juan
1931- .... CLC 5, 10, 23; DAM MULT;
HLC
See also CA 85-88; CANR 32, 61; HW;
MTCW

Gozzano, Guido 1883-1916 .... PC 10
See also CA 154; DLB 114

Gozzi, (Conte) Carlo
1720-1806 .... NCLC 23

Grabbe, Christian Dietrich
1801-1836 .... NCLC 2
See also DLB 133

Grace, Patricia 1937- .... CLC 56

Gracian y Morales, Baltasar
1601-1658 .... LC 15

Gracq, Julien .... CLC 11, 48
See also Poirier, Louis
See also DLB 83

Grade, Chaim 1910-1982 .... CLC 10
See also CA 93-96; 107

Graduate of Oxford, A
See Ruskin, John

Griffin, Peter 1942- .... CLC 39
See also CA 136

Griffith, D(avid Lewelyn) W(ark)
1875(?)-1948 .... TCLC 68
See also CA 119; 150

Griffith, Lawrence
See Griffith, D(avid Lewelyn) W(ark)

Griffiths, Trevor 1935- .... CLC 13, 52
See also CA 97-100; CANR 45; DLB 13

Grigson, Geoffrey (Edward Harvey)
1905-1985 .... CLC 7, 39
See also CA 25-28R; 118; CANR 20, 33; DLB
27; MTCW

Grillparzer, Franz 1791-1872 .... NCLC 1
See also DLB 133

Grimble, Reverend Charles James
See Eliot, T(homas) S(tearns)

Grimke, Charlotte L(ottie) Forten
1837(?)-1914
See Forten, Charlotte L.
See also BW 1; CA 117; 124; DAM MULT,
POET

Grimm, Jacob Ludwig Karl
1785-1863 .... NCLC 3
See also DLB 90; MAICYA; SATA 22

Grimm, Wilhelm Karl 1786-1859 .... NCLC 3
See also DLB 90; MAICYA; SATA 22

**Grimmelshausen, Johann Jakob Christoffel
von** 1621-1676 .... LC 6
See also DLB 168

Grindel, Eugene 1895-1952
See Eluard, Paul
See also CA 104

Grisham, John
1955- .... CLC 84; DAM POP
See also AAYA 14; CA 138; CANR 47

Grossman, David 1954- .... CLC 67
See also CA 138

Grossman, Vasily (Semenovich)
1905-1964 .... CLC 41
See also CA 124; 130; MTCW

Grove, Frederick Philip .... TCLC 4
See also Greve, Felix Paul (Berthold Friedrich)
See also DLB 92

Grubb
See Crumb, R(obert)

Grumbach, Doris (Isaac)
1918- .... CLC 13, 22, 64
See also CA 5-8R; CAAS 2; CANR 9, 42; INT
CANR-9

Grundtvig, Nicolai Frederik Severin
1783-1872 .... NCLC 1

Grunge
See Crumb, R(obert)

Grunwald, Lisa 1959- .... CLC 44
See also CA 120

Guare, John
1938- .. CLC 8, 14, 29, 67; DAM DRAM
See also CA 73-76; CANR 21; DLB 7;
MTCW

Gudjonsson, Halldor Kiljan 1902-
See Laxness, Halldor
See also CA 103

Guenter, Erich
See Eich, Guenter

Guest, Barbara 1920- .... CLC 34
See also CA 25-28R; CANR 11, 44; DLB 5

Guest, Judith (Ann)
1936- .... CLC 8, 30; DAM NOV, POP
See also AAYA 7; CA 77-80; CANR 15; INT
CANR-15; MTCW

Guevara, Che .... CLC 87; HLC
See also Guevara (Serna), Ernesto

Guevara (Serna), Ernesto 1928-1967
See Guevara, Che
See also CA 127; 111; CANR 56; DAM MULT;
HW

Guild, Nicholas M. 1944- .... CLC 33
See also CA 93-96

Guillemin, Jacques
See Sartre, Jean-Paul

Guillen, Jorge
1893-1984 CLC 11; DAM MULT, POET
See also CA 89-92; 112; DLB 108; HW

Guillen, Nicolas (Cristobal)
1902-1989 .... CLC 48, 79; BLC; DAM
MST, MULT, POET; HLC
See also BW 2; CA 116; 125; 129; HW

Guillevic, (Eugene) 1907- .... CLC 33
See also CA 93-96

Guillois
See Desnos, Robert

Guillois, Valentin
See Desnos, Robert

Guiney, Louise Imogen
1861-1920 .... TCLC 41
See also CA 160; DLB 54

Guiraldes, Ricardo (Guillermo)
1886-1927 .... TCLC 39
See also CA 131; HW; MTCW

Gumilev, Nikolai Stephanovich
1886-1921 .... TCLC 60

Gunesekera, Romesh
1954- .... CLC 91
See also CA 159

Gunn, Bill... CLC 5
See also Gunn, William Harrison
See also DLB 38

Gunn, Thom(son William)
1929- .... CLC 3, 6, 18, 32, 81; DAM
POET
See also CA 17-20R; CANR 9, 33; CDBLB
1960 to Present; DLB 27; INT CANR-33;
MTCW

Gunn, William Harrison 1934(?)-1989
See Gunn, Bill
See also AITN 1; BW 1; CA 13-16R; 128;
CANR 12, 25

Gunnars, Kristjana 1948-.................. CLC 69
See also CA 113; DLB 60

Gurdjieff, G(eorgei) I(vanovich)
1877(?)-1949 .... TCLC 71
See also CA 157

Gurganus, Allan
1947- .... CLC 70; DAM POP
See also BEST 90:1; CA 135

Gurney, A(lbert) R(amsdell), Jr.
1930- ...... CLC 32, 50, 54; DAM DRAM
See also CA 77-80; CANR 32

Gurney, Ivor (Bertie)
1890-1937 .... TCLC 33

Gurney, Peter
See Gurney, A(lbert) R(amsdell), Jr.

Guro, Elena 1877-1913 .... TCLC 56

Gustafson, James M(oody)
1925- .... CLC 100
See also CA 25-28R; CANR 37

Gustafson, Ralph (Barker) 1909- ..... CLC 36
See also CA 21-24R; CANR 8, 45; DLB 88

Gut, Gom
See Simenon, Georges (Jacques Christian)

Guterson, David 1956- .... CLC 91
See also CA 132

Guthrie, A(lfred) B(ertram), Jr.
1901(1991 .... CLC 23
See also CA 57-60; 134; CANR 24; DLB 6;
SATA 62; SATA-Obit 67

Guthrie, Isobel
See Grieve, C(hristopher) M(urray)

Guthrie, Woodrow Wilson 1912-1967
See Guthrie, Woody
See also CA 113; 93-96

Guthrie, Woody .... CLC 35
See also Guthrie, Woodrow Wilson

Guy, Rosa (Cuthbert) 1928- .... CLC 26
See also AAYA 4; BW 2; CA 17-20R; CANR
14, 34; CLR 13; DLB 33; JRDA; MAICYA;
SATA 14, 62

Gwendolyn
See Bennett, (Enoch) Arnold

H. D. .... CLC 3, 8, 14, 31, 34, 73; PC 5
See also Doolittle, Hilda

H. de V.
See Buchan, John

Haavikko, Paavo Juhani
1931- .... **CLC 18, 34**
See also CA 106

Habbema, Koos
See Heijermans, Herman

Habermas, Juergen 1929- .... **CLC 104**
See also CA 109

Habermas, Jurgen
See Habermas, Juergen

Hacker, Marilyn
1942- .... **CLC 5, 9, 23, 72, 91; DAM POET**
See also CA 77-80; DLB 120

Haggard, H(enry) Rider
1856-1925 .... **TCLC 11**
See also CA 108; 148; DLB 70, 156, 174, 178; SATA 16

Hagiosy, L.
See Larbaud, Valery (Nicolas)

Hagiwara Sakutaro
1886-1942 .... **TCLC 60; PC 18**

Haig, Fenil
See Ford, Ford Madox

Haig-Brown, Roderick (Langmere)
1908-1976 .... **CLC 21**
See also CA 5-8R; 69-72; CANR 4, 38; CLR 31; DLB 88; MAICYA; SATA 12

Hailey, Arthur
1920- .... **CLC 5; DAM NOV, POP**
See also AITN 2; BEST 90:3; CA 1-4R; CANR 2, 36; DLB 88; DLBY 82; MTCW

Hailey, Elizabeth Forsythe
1938- .... **CLC 40**
See also CA 93-96; CAAS 1; CANR 15, 48; INT CANR-15

Haines, John (Meade) 1924- .... **CLC 58**
See also CA 17-20R; CANR 13, 34; DLB 5

Hakluyt, Richard 1552-1616 .... **LC 31**

Haldeman, Joe (William) 1943- .... **CLC 61**
See also CA 53-56; CAAS 25; CANR 6; DLB 8; INT CANR-6

Haley, Alex(ander Murray Palmer)
1921-1992 ...... **CLC 8, 12, 76; BLC; DA; DAB; DAC; DAM MST, MULT, POP**
See also BW 2; CA 77-80; 136; CANR 61; DLB 38; MTCW

Haliburton, Thomas Chandler
1796-1865 .... **NCLC 15**
See also DLB 11, 99

Hall, Donald (Andrew, Jr.)
1928- .... **CLC 1, 13, 37, 59; DAM POET**
See also CA 5-8R; CAAS 7; CANR 2, 44; DLB 5; SATA 23

Hall, Frederic Sauser
See Sauser-Hall, Frederic

Hall, James
See Kuttner, Henry

Hall, James Norman 1887-1951 ..... **TCLC 23**
See also CA 123; SATA 21

Hall, (Marguerite) Radclyffe
1886-1943 .... **TCLC 12**
See also CA 110; 150

Hall, Rodney 1935- .... **CLC 51**
See also CA 109

Halleck, Fitz-Greene
1790-1867 .... **NCLC 47**
See also DLB 3

Halliday, Michael
See Creasey, John

Halpern, Daniel 1945- .... **CLC 14**
See also CA 33-36R

Hamburger, Michael (Peter Leopold)
1924- .... **CLC 5, 14**
See also CA 5-8R; CAAS 4; CANR 2, 47; DLB 27

Hamill, Pete 1935- .... **CLC 10**
See also CA 25-28R; CANR 18

Hamilton, Alexander
1755(?)-1804 .... **NCLC 49**
See also DLB 37

Hamilton, Clive
See Lewis, C(live) S(taples)

Hamilton, Edmond 1904-1977 .... **CLC 1**
See also CA 1-4R; CANR 3; DLB 8

Hamilton, Eugene (Jacob) Lee
See Lee-Hamilton, Eugene (Jacob)

Hamilton, Franklin
See Silverberg, Robert

Hamilton, Gail
See Corcoran, Barbara

Hamilton, Mollie
See Kaye, M(ary) M(argaret)

Hamilton, (Anthony Walter) Patrick
1904-1962 .... **CLC 51**
See also CA 113; DLB 10

Hamilton, Virginia
1936- .... **CLC 26; DAM MULT**
See also AAYA 2, 21; BW 2; CA 25-28R; CANR 20, 37; CLR 1, 11, 40; DLB 33, 52; INT CANR-20; JRDA; MAICYA; MTCW; SATA 4, 56, 79

Hammett, (Samuel) Dashiell
1894-1961 ... **CLC 3, 5, 10, 19, 47; SSC 17**
See also AITN 1; CA 81-84; CANR 42; CDALB 1929-1941; DLBD 6; DLBY 96; MTCW

Hammon, Jupiter
1711(?)-1800(?) .... **NCLC 5; BLC; DAM MULT, POET; PC 16**
See also DLB 31, 50

Hammond, Keith
See Kuttner, Henry

Hamner, Earl (Henry), Jr. 1923- ...... **CLC 12**
See also AITN 2; CA 73-76; DLB 6

Hampton, Christopher (James)
1946- .... **CLC 4**
See also CA 25-28R; DLB 13; MTCW

Hamsun, Knut .... **TCLC 2, 14, 49**
See also Pedersen, Knut

Handke, Peter 1942- .... **CLC 5, 8, 10, 15, 38; DAM DRAM, NOV**
See also CA 77-80; CANR 33; DLB 85, 124; MTCW

Hanley, James 1901-1985 ..... **CLC 3, 5, 8, 13**
See also CA 73-76; 117; CANR 36; MTCW

Hannah, Barry 1942- .... **CLC 23, 38, 90**
See also CA 108; 110; CANR 43; DLB 6; INT 110; MTCW

Hannon, Ezra
See Hunter, Evan

Hansberry, Lorraine (Vivian)
1930-1965 .... **CLC 17, 62; BLC; DA; DAB; DAC; DAM DRAM, MST, MULT; DC 2**
See also BW 1; CA 109; 25-28R; CABS 3; CANR 58; CDALB 1941-1968; DLB 7, 38; MTCW

Hansen, Joseph 1923- .... **CLC 38**
See also CA 29-32R; CAAS 17; CANR 16, 44; INT CANR-16

Hansen, Martin A. 1909-1955 .... **TCLC 32**

Hanson, Kenneth O(stlin)
1922- .... **CLC 13**
See also CA 53-56; CANR 7

Hardwick, Elizabeth
1916- .... **CLC 13; DAM NOV**
See also CA 5-8R; CANR 3, 32; DLB 6; MTCW

Hardy, Thomas
1840-1928 **TCLC 4, 10, 18, 32, 48, 53, 72; DA; DAB; DAC; DAM MST, NOV, POET; PC 8; SSC 2; WLC**
See also CA 104; 123; CDBLB 1890-1914; DLB 18, 19, 135; MTCW

Hare, David 1947- .... **CLC 29, 58**
See also CA 97-100; CANR 39; DLB 13; MTCW

Harford, Henry
See Hudson, W(illiam) H(enry)

Hargrave, Leonie
See Disch, Thomas M(ichael)

Harjo, Joy 1951- .... **CLC 83; DAM MULT**
See also CA 114; CANR 35; DLB 120, 175;
NNAL

Harlan, Louis R(udolph) 1922- .... **CLC 34**
See also CA 21-24R; CANR 25, 55

Harling, Robert 1951(?)- .... **CLC 53**
See also CA 147

Harmon, William (Ruth) 1938- .... **CLC 38**
See also CA 33-36R; CANR 14, 32, 35; SATA
65

Harper, F. E. W.
See Harper, Frances Ellen Watkins

Harper, Frances E. W.
See Harper, Frances Ellen Watkins

Harper, Frances E. Watkins
See Harper, Frances Ellen Watkins

Harper, Frances Ellen
See Harper, Frances Ellen Watkins

Harper, Frances Ellen Watkins
1825-1911 .... **TCLC 14; BLC; DAM
MULT, POET**
See also BW 1; CA 111; 125; DLB 50

Harper, Michael S(teven)
1938- ....**CLC 7, 22**
See also BW 1; CA 33-36R; CANR 24; DLB
41

Harper, Mrs. F. E. W.
See Harper, Frances Ellen Watkins

Harris, Christie (Lucy) Irwin
1907- .... **CLC 12**
See also CA 5-8R; CANR 6; CLR 47; DLB
88; JRDA; MAICYA; SAAS 10; SATA 6,
74

Harris, Frank 1856-1931 .... **TCLC 24**
See also CA 109; 150; DLB 156

Harris, George Washington
1814-1869 .... **NCLC 23**
See also DLB 3, 11

Harris, Joel Chandler 1848-1908 ... **TCLC 2;
SSC 19**
See also CA 104; 137; DLB 11, 23, 42, 78, 91;
MAICYA; YABC 1

**Harris, John (Wyndham Parkes Lucas)
Beynon** 1903-1969
See Wyndham, John
See also CA 102; 89-92

Harris, MacDonald .... **CLC 9**
See also Heiney, Donald (William)

Harris, Mark 1922- .... **CLC 19**
See also CA 5-8R; CAAS 3; CANR 2, 55; DLB
2; DLBY 80

Harris, (Theodore) Wilson
1921- .... **CLC 25**
See also BW 2; CA 65-68; CAAS 16; CANR
11, 27; DLB 117; MTCW

Harrison, Elizabeth Cavanna 1909-
See Cavanna, Betty
See also CA 9-12R; CANR 6, 27

Harrison, Harry (Max) 1925- .... **CLC 42**
See also CA 1-4R; CANR 5, 21; DLB 8; SATA
4

Harrison, James (Thomas)
1937- .... **CLC 6, 14, 33, 66; SSC 19**
See also CA 13-16R; CANR 8, 51; DLBY 82;
INT CANR-8

Harrison, Jim
See Harrison, James (Thomas)

Harrison, Kathryn 1961- .... **CLC 70**
See also CA 144

Harrison, Tony 1937- .... **CLC 43**
See also CA 65-68; CANR 44; DLB 40;
MTCW

Harriss, Will(ard Irvin) 1922- .... **CLC 34**
See also CA 111

Harson, Sley
See Ellison, Harlan (Jay)

Hart, Ellis
See Ellison, Harlan (Jay)

Hart, Josephine
1942(?)- .... **CLC 70; DAM POP**
See also CA 138

Hart, Moss
1904-1961 .... **CLC 66; DAM DRAM**
See also CA 109; 89-92; DLB 7

Harte, (Francis) Bret(t)
1836(?)-1902 .... **TCLC 1, 25; DA; DAC;
DAM MST; SSC 8; WLC**
See also CA 104; 140; CDALB 1865-1917;
DLB 12, 64, 74, 79; SATA 26

Hartley, L(eslie) P(oles)
1895-1972 .... **CLC 2, 22**
See also CA 45-48; 37-40R; CANR 33; DLB
15, 139; MTCW

Hartman, Geoffrey H. 1929- .... **CLC 27**
See also CA 117; 125; DLB 67

Hartmann, Sadakichi 1867-1944 ... **TCLC 73**
See also CA 157; DLB 54

Hartmann von Aue
c. 1160-c. 1205 .... **CMLC 15**
See also DLB 138

Hartmann von Aue 1170-1210 ...... **CMLC 15**

Haruf, Kent 1943- .... **CLC 34**
See also CA 149

Harwood, Ronald 1934- .... **CLC 32; DAM
DRAM, MST**
See also CA 1-4R; CANR 4, 55; DLB 13

Hasek, Jaroslav (Matej Frantisek)
1883-1923 .... **TCLC 4**
See also CA 104; 129; MTCW

Hass, Robert 1941- ... **CLC 18, 39, 99; PC 16**
See also CA 111; CANR 30, 50; DLB 105;
SATA 94

Hastings, Hudson
See Kuttner, Henry

Hastings, Selina .... **CLC 44**

Hathorne, John 1641-1717 .... **LC 38**

Hatteras, Amelia
See Mencken, H(enry) L(ouis)

Hatteras, Owen .... **TCLC 18**
See also Mencken, H(enry) L(ouis); Nathan,
George Jean

Hauptmann, Gerhart (Johann Robert)
1862-1946 .... **TCLC 4; DAM DRAM**
See also CA 104; 153; DLB 66, 118

Havel, Vaclav 1936- ... **CLC 25, 58, 65; DAM
DRAM; DC 6**
See also CA 104; CANR 36; MTCW

Haviaras, Stratis .... **CLC 33**
See also Chaviaras, Strates

Hawes, Stephen 1475(?)-1523(?) .... **LC 17**

Hawkes, John (Clendennin Burne, Jr.)
1925- **CLC 1, 2, 3, 4, 7, 9, 14, 15, 27, 49**
See also CA 1-4R; CANR 2, 47; DLB 2, 7;
DLBY 80; MTCW

Hawking, S. W.
See Hawking, Stephen W(illiam)

Hawking, Stephen W(illiam)
1942- .... **CLC 63, 105**
See also AAYA 13; BEST 89:1; CA 126; 129;
CANR 48

Hawthorne, Julian 1846-1934 .... **TCLC 25**

Hawthorne, Nathaniel
1804-1864 .. **NCLC 39; DA; DAB; DAC;
DAM MST, NOV; SSC 29; WLC**
See also AAYA 18; CDALB 1640-1865; DLB
1, 74; YABC 2

Haxton, Josephine Ayres 1921-
See Douglas, Ellen
See also CA 115; CANR 41

Hayaseca y Eizaguirre, Jorge
See Echegaray (y Eizaguirre), Jose (Maria
Waldo)

Hayashi Fumiko 1904-1951 .... **TCLC 27**
See also DLB 180

Haycraft, Anna
See Ellis, Alice Thomas
See also CA 122

Hayden, Robert E(arl)
1913-1980 ..**CLC 5, 9, 14, 37; BLC; DA;
DAC; DAM MST, MULT, POET; PC 6**
See also BW 1; CA 69-72; 97-100; CABS 2;
CANR 24; CDALB 1941-1968; DLB 5, 76;
MTCW; SATA 19; SATA-Obit 26

Hergesheimer, Joseph
1880-1954 .... **TCLC 11**
See also CA 109; DLB 102, 9

Herlihy, James Leo
1927-1993 .... **CLC 6**
See also CA 1-4R; 143; CANR 2

Hermogenes fl. c. 175- .... **CMLC 6**

Hernandez, Jose 1834-1886 .... **NCLC 17**

Herodotus
c. 484B.C.-429B.C. .... **CMLC 17**
See also DLB 176

Herrick, Robert
1591-1674 .... **LC 13; DA; DAB; DAC;**
DAM MST, POP; PC 9
See also DLB 126

Herring, Guilles
See Somerville, Edith

Herriot, James
1916-1995 .... **CLC 12; DAM POP**
See also Wight, James Alfred
See also AAYA 1; CA 148; CANR 40; SATA
86

Herrmann, Dorothy 1941- .... **CLC 44**
See also CA 107

Herrmann, Taffy
See Herrmann, Dorothy

Hersey, John (Richard)
1914-1993 ...... **CLC 1, 2, 7, 9, 40, 81, 97;**
DAM POP
See also CA 17-20R; 140; CANR 33; DLB 6;
MTCW; SATA 25; SATA-Obit 76

Herzen, Aleksandr Ivanovich
1812-1870 .... **NCLC 10, 61**

Herzl, Theodor 1860-1904 .... **TCLC 36**

Herzog, Werner 1942- .... **CLC 16**
See also CA 89-92

Hesiod c. 8th cent. B.C.- .... **CMLC 5**
See also DLB 176

Hesse, Hermann
1877-1962 ... **CLC 1, 2, 3, 6, 11, 17, 25,**
69; DA; DAB; DAC; DAM MST, NOV;
SSC 9; WLC
See also CA 17-18; CAP 2; DLB 66; MTCW;
SATA 50

Hewes, Cady
See De Voto, Bernard (Augustine)

Heyen, William 1940- .... **CLC 13, 18**
See also CA 33-36R; CAAS 9; DLB 5

Heyerdahl, Thor 1914- .... **CLC 26**
See also CA 5-8R; CANR 5, 22; MTCW; SATA
2, 52

Heym, Georg (Theodor Franz Arthur)
1887-1912 .... **TCLC 9**
See also CA 106

Heym, Stefan 1913- .... **CLC 41**
See also CA 9-12R; CANR 4; DLB 69

Heyse, Paul (Johann Ludwig von)
1830-1914 .... **TCLC 8**
See also CA 104; DLB 129

Heyward, (Edwin) DuBose
1885-1940 .... **TCLC 59**
See also CA 108; 157; DLB 7, 9, 45; SATA 21

Hibbert, Eleanor Alice Burford
1906-1993 .... **CLC 7; DAM POP**
See also BEST 90:4; CA 17-20R; 140; CANR
9, 28, 59; SATA 2; SATA-Obit 74

Hichens, Robert S. 1864-1950 .... **TCLC 64**
See also DLB 153

Higgins, George V(incent)
1939- .... **CLC 4, 7, 10, 18**
See also CA 77-80; CAAS 5; CANR 17, 51;
DLB 2; DLBY 81; INT CANR-17; MTCW

Higginson, Thomas Wentworth
1823-1911 .... **TCLC 36**
See also DLB 1, 64

Highet, Helen
See MacInnes, Helen (Clark)

Highsmith, (Mary) Patricia
1921-1995 .... **CLC 2, 4, 14, 42, 102;**
DAM NOV, POP
See also CA 1-4R; 147; CANR 1, 20, 48, 62;
MTCW

Highwater, Jamake (Mamake)
1942(?)- .... **CLC 12**
See also AAYA 7; CA 65-68; CAAS 7; CANR
10, 34; CLR 17; DLB 52; DLBY 85; JRDA;
MAICYA; SATA 32, 69; SATA-Brief 30

Highway, Tomson
1951- .... **CLC 92; DAC; DAM MULT**
See also CA 151; NNAL

Higuchi, Ichiyo 1872-1896 .... **NCLC 49**

Hijuelos, Oscar
1951- ...... **CLC 65; DAM MULT, POP;**
HLC
See also BEST 90:1; CA 123; CANR 50; DLB
145; HW

Hikmet, Nazim 1902(?)-1963 .... **CLC 40**
See also CA 141; 93-96

Hildegard von Bingen
1098-1179 .... **CMLC 20**
See also DLB 148

Hildesheimer, Wolfgang
1916-1991 .... **CLC 49**
See also CA 101; 135; DLB 69, 124

Hill, Geoffrey (William)
1932- ...... **CLC 5, 8, 18, 45; DAM POET**
See also CA 81-84; CANR 21; CDBLB 1960
to Present; DLB 40; MTCW

Hill, George Roy 1921- .... **CLC 26**
See also CA 110; 122

Hill, John
See Koontz, Dean R(ay)

Hill, Susan (Elizabeth)
1942- ... **CLC 4; DAB; DAM MST, NOV**
See also CA 33-36R; CANR 29; DLB 14, 139;
MTCW

Hillerman, Tony
1925- .... **CLC 62; DAM POP**
See also AAYA 6; BEST 89:1; CA 29-32R;
CANR 21, 42; SATA 6

Hillesum, Etty 1914-1943 .... **TCLC 49**
See also CA 137

Hilliard, Noel (Harvey) 1929- .... **CLC 15**
See also CA 9-12R; CANR 7

Hillis, Rick 1956- .... **CLC 66**
See also CA 134

Hilton, James 1900-1954 .... **TCLC 21**
See also CA 108; DLB 34, 77; SATA 34

Himes, Chester (Bomar)
1909-1984 ...... **CLC 2, 4, 7, 18, 58; BLC;**
DAM MULT
See also BW 2; CA 25-28R; 114; CANR 22;
DLB 2, 76, 143; MTCW

Hinde, Thomas .... **CLC 6, 11**
See also Chitty, Thomas Willes

Hindin, Nathan
See Bloch, Robert (Albert)

Hine, (William) Daryl 1936- .... **CLC 15**
See also CA 1-4R; CAAS 15; CANR 1, 20;
DLB 60

Hinkson, Katharine Tynan
See Tynan, Katharine

Hinton, S(usan) E(loise)
1950- .. **CLC 30; DA; DAB; DAC; DAM**
MST, NOV
See also AAYA 2; CA 81-84; CANR 32, 62;
CLR 3, 23; JRDA; MAICYA; MTCW; SATA
19, 58

Hippius, Zinaida .... **TCLC 9**
See also Gippius, Zinaida (Nikolayevna)

Hiraoka, Kimitake 1925-1970
See Mishima, Yukio
See also CA 97-100; 29-32R; DAM DRAM;
MTCW

Hirsch, E(ric) D(onald), Jr. 1928- .... **CLC 79**
See also CA 25-28R; CANR 27, 51; DLB 67;
INT CANR-27; MTCW

Hirsch, Edward 1950- .... **CLC 31, 50**
See also CA 104; CANR 20, 42; DLB 120

Hitchcock, Alfred (Joseph)
1899-1980 .... **CLC 16**
See also AAYA 22; CA 159; 97-100; SATA 27;
SATA-Obit 24

Hitler, Adolf 1889-1945 .... **TCLC 53**
See also CA 117; 147

Horney, Karen (Clementine Theodore Danielsen) 1885-1952 .... **TCLC 71**
See also CA 114

Hornung, E(rnest) W(illiam) 1866-1921 .... **TCLC 59**
See also CA 108; 160; DLB 70

Horovitz, Israel (Arthur) 1939- ...... **CLC 56; DAM DRAM**
See also CA 33-36R; CANR 46, 59; DLB 7

Horvath, Odon von
See Horvath, Oedoen von
See also DLB 85, 124

Horvath, Oedoen von 1901-1938 .... **TCLC 45**
See also Horvath, Odon von
See also CA 118

Horwitz, Julius 1920-1986 .... **CLC 14**
See also CA 9-12R; 119; CANR 12

Hospital, Janette Turner 1942- .... **CLC 42**
See also CA 108; CANR 48

Hostos, E. M. de
See Hostos (y Bonilla), Eugenio Maria de

Hostos, Eugenio M. de
See Hostos (y Bonilla), Eugenio Maria de

Hostos, Eugenio Maria
See Hostos (y Bonilla), Eugenio Maria de

Hostos (y Bonilla), Eugenio Maria de 1839-1903 .... **TCLC 24**
See also CA 123; 131; HW

Houdini
See Lovecraft, H(oward) P(hillips)

Hougan, Carolyn 1943- .... **CLC 34**
See also CA 139

Household, Geoffrey (Edward West) 1900-1988 .... **CLC 11**
See also CA 77-80; 126; CANR 58; DLB 87; SATA 14; SATA-Obit 59

Housman, A(lfred) E(dward) 1859-1936 .... **TCLC 1, 10; DA; DAB; DAC; DAM MST, POET; PC 2; WLCS**
See also CA 104; 125; DLB 19; MTCW

Housman, Laurence 1865-1959 .... **TCLC 7**
See also CA 106; 155; DLB 10; SATA 25

Howard, Elizabeth Jane 1923- ..... **CLC 7, 29**
See also CA 5-8R; CANR 8, 62

Howard, Maureen 1930- .... **CLC 5, 14, 46**
See also CA 53-56; CANR 31; DLBY 83; INT CANR-31; MTCW

Howard, Richard 1929- .... **CLC 7, 10, 47**
See also AITN 1; CA 85-88; CANR 25; DLB 5; INT CANR-25

Howard, Robert E(rvin) 1906-1936 .... **TCLC 8**
See also CA 105; 157

Howard, Warren F.
See Pohl, Frederik

Howe, Fanny 1940- .... **CLC 47**
See also CA 117; CAAS 27; SATA-Brief 52

Howe, Irving 1920-1993 .... **CLC 85**
See also CA 9-12R; 141; CANR 21, 50; DLB 67; MTCW

Howe, Julia Ward 1819-1910 .... **TCLC 21**
See also CA 117; DLB 1

Howe, Susan 1937- .... **CLC 72**
See also CA 160; DLB 120

Howe, Tina 1937- .... **CLC 48**
See also CA 109

Howell, James 1594(?)-1666 .... **LC 13**
See also DLB 151

Howells, W. D.
See Howells, William Dean

Howells, William D.
See Howells, William Dean

Howells, William Dean 1837-1920 .... **TCLC 7, 17, 41**
See also CA 104; 134; CDALB 1865-1917; DLB 12, 64, 74, 79

Howes, Barbara 1914-1996 .... **CLC 15**
See also CA 9-12R; 151; CAAS 3; CANR 53; SATA 5

Hrabal, Bohumil 1914-1997 .... **CLC 13, 67**
See also CA 106; 156; CAAS 12; CANR 57

Hsun, Lu
See Lu Hsun

Hubbard, L(afayette) Ron(ald) 1911-1986 .... **CLC 43; DAM POP**
See also CA 77-80; 118; CANR 52

Huch, Ricarda (Octavia) 1864-1947 .... **TCLC 13**
See also CA 111; DLB 66

Huddle, David 1942- .... **CLC 49**
See also CA 57-60; CAAS 20; DLB 130

Hudson, Jeffrey
See Crichton, (John) Michael

Hudson, W(illiam) H(enry) 1841-1922 .... **TCLC 29**
See also CA 115; DLB 98, 153, 174; SATA 35

Hueffer, Ford Madox
See Ford, Ford Madox

Hughart, Barry 1934- .... **CLC 39**
See also CA 137

Hughes, Colin
See Creasey, John

Hughes, David (John) 1930- .... **CLC 48**
See also CA 116; 129; DLB 14

Hughes, Edward James
See Hughes, Ted
See also DAM MST, POET

Hughes, (James) Langston 1902-1967 .... **CLC 1, 5, 10, 15, 35, 44; BLC; DA; DAB; DAC; DAM DRAM, MST, MULT, POET; DC 3; PC 1; SSC 6; WLC**
See also AAYA 12; BW 1; CA 1-4R; 25-28R; CANR 1, 34; CDALB 1929-1941; CLR 17; DLB 4, 7, 48, 51, 86; JRDA; MAICYA; MTCW; SATA 4, 33

Hughes, Richard (Arthur Warren) 1900-1976 .... **CLC 1, 11; DAM NOV**
See also CA 5-8R; 65-68; CANR 4; DLB 15, 161; MTCW; SATA 8; SATA-Obit 25

Hughes, Ted 1930- .. **CLC 2, 4, 9, 14, 37; DAB; DAC; PC 7**
See also Hughes, Edward James
See also CA 1-4R; CANR 1, 33; CLR 3; DLB 40, 161; MAICYA; MTCW; SATA 49; SATA-Brief 27

Hugo, Richard F(ranklin) 1923-1982 .. **CLC 6, 18, 32; DAM POET**
See also CA 49-52; 108; CANR 3; DLB 5

Hugo, Victor (Marie) 1802-1885 ... **NCLC 3, 10, 21; DA; DAB; DAC; DAM DRAM, MST, NOV, POET; PC 17; WLC**
See also DLB 119; SATA 47

Huidobro, Vicente
See Huidobro Fernandez, Vicente Garcia

Huidobro Fernandez, Vicente Garcia 1893-1948 .... **TCLC 31**
See also CA 131; HW

Hulme, Keri 1947- .... **CLC 39**
See also CA 125; INT 125

Hulme, T(homas) E(rnest) 1883-1917 .... **TCLC 21**
See also CA 117; DLB 19

Hume, David 1711-1776 .... **LC 7**
See also DLB 104

Humphrey, William 1924-1997 .... **CLC 45**
See also CA 77-80; 160; DLB 6

Humphreys, Emyr Owen 1919- .... **CLC 47**
See also CA 5-8R; CANR 3, 24; DLB 15

Humphreys, Josephine 1945- ..... **CLC 34, 57**
See also CA 121; 127; INT 127

Huneker, James Gibbons 1857-1921 .... **TCLC 65**
See also DLB 71

Hungerford, Pixie
See Brinsmead, H(esba) F(ay)

Hunt, E(verette) Howard, (Jr.) 1918- .... **CLC 3**
See also AITN 1; CA 45-48; CANR 2, 47

Ives, Morgan
See Bradley, Marion Zimmer

J. R. S.
See Gogarty, Oliver St. John

Jabran, Kahlil
See Gibran, Kahlil

Jabran, Khalil
See Gibran, Kahlil

Jackson, Daniel
See Wingrove, David (John)

Jackson, Jesse 1908-1983 .... **CLC 12**
See also BW 1; CA 25-28R; 109; CANR 27;
CLR 28; MAICYA; SATA 2, 29; SATA-Obit
48

Jackson, Laura (Riding) 1901-1991
See Riding, Laura
See also CA 65-68; 135; CANR 28; DLB 48

Jackson, Sam
See Trumbo, Dalton

Jackson, Sara
See Wingrove, David (John)

Jackson, Shirley
1919-1965 .... **CLC 11, 60, 87; DA; DAC;
DAM MST; SSC 9; WLC**
See also AAYA 9; CA 1-4R; 25-28R; CANR
4, 52; CDALB 1941-1968; DLB 6; SATA 2

Jacob, (Cyprien-)Max 1876-1944 .... **TCLC 6**
See also CA 104

Jacobs, Jim 1942- .... **CLC 12**
See also CA 97-100; INT 97-100

Jacobs, W(illiam) W(ymark)
1863-1943 .... **TCLC 22**
See also CA 121; DLB 135

Jacobsen, Jens Peter 1847-1885 .... **NCLC 34**

Jacobsen, Josephine 1908- .... **CLC 48, 102**
See also CA 33-36R; CAAS 18; CANR 23, 48

Jacobson, Dan 1929- .... **CLC 4, 14**
See also CA 1-4R; CANR 2, 25; DLB 14;
MTCW

Jacqueline
See Carpentier (y Valmont), Alejo

Jagger, Mick 1944- .... **CLC 17**

Jakes, John (William)
1932- .... **CLC 29; DAM NOV, POP**
See also BEST 89:4; CA 57-60; CANR 10, 43;
DLBY 83; INT CANR-10; MTCW; SATA
62

James, Andrew
See Kirkup, James

James, C(yril) L(ionel) R(obert)
1901-1989 .... **CLC 33**
See also BW 2; CA 117; 125; 128; CANR 62;
DLB 125; MTCW

James, Daniel (Lewis) 1911-1988
See Santiago, Danny
See also CA 125

James, Dynely
See Mayne, William (James Carter)

James, Henry Sr. 1811-1882 .... **NCLC 53**

James, Henry
1843-1916 ... **TCLC 2, 11, 24, 40, 47, 64;
DA; DAB; DAC; DAM MST, NOV; SSC
8; WLC**
See also CA 104; 132; CDALB 1865-
1917; DLB 12, 71, 74; DLBD 13;
MTCW

James, M. R.
See James, Montague (Rhodes)
See also DLB 156

James, Montague (Rhodes)
1862-1936 .... **TCLC 6; SSC 16**
See also CA 104

James, P. D. .... CLC 18, 46
See also White, Phyllis Dorothy James
See also BEST 90:2; CDBLB 1960 to Present;
DLB 87

James, Philip
See Moorcock, Michael (John)

James, William
1842-1910 .... **TCLC 15, 32**
See also CA 109

James I 1394-1437 .... **LC 20**

Jameson, Anna 1794-1860 .... **NCLC 43**
See also DLB 99, 166

Jami, Nur al-Din 'Abd al-Rahman
1414-1492 .... **LC 9**

Jammes, Francis 1868-1938 .... **TCLC 75**

Jandl, Ernst 1925- .... **CLC 34**

Janowitz, Tama 1957- .. **CLC 43; DAM POP**
See also CA 106; CANR 52

Japrisot, Sebastien 1931- .... **CLC 90**

Jarrell, Randall
1914-1965 .... **CLC 1, 2, 6, 9, 13, 49;
DAM POET**
See also CA 5-8R; 25-28R; CABS 2;
CANR 6, 34; CDALB 1941-1968; CLR
6; DLB 48, 52; MAICYA; MTCW;
SATA 7

Jarry, Alfred
1873-1907 ... **TCLC 2, 14; DAM DRAM;
SSC 20**
See also CA 104; 153

Jarvis, E. K.
See Bloch, Robert (Albert); Ellison, Harlan
(Jay); Silverberg, Robert

Jeake, Samuel, Jr.
See Aiken, Conrad (Potter)

Jean Paul 1763-1825 .... **NCLC 7**

Jefferies, (John) Richard
1848-1887 .... **NCLC 47**
See also DLB 98, 141; SATA 16

Jeffers, (John) Robinson
1887-1962 ...... **CLC 2, 3, 11, 15, 54; DA;
DAC; DAM MST, POET; PC 17; WLC**
See also CA 85-88; CANR 35; CDALB 1917-
1929; DLB 45; MTCW

Jefferson, Janet
See Mencken, H(enry) L(ouis)

Jefferson, Thomas 1743-1826 .... **NCLC 11**
See also CDALB 1640-1865; DLB 31

Jeffrey, Francis 1773-1850 .... **NCLC 33**
See also DLB 107

Jelakowitch, Ivan
See Heijermans, Herman

Jellicoe, (Patricia) Ann 1927- .... **CLC 27**
See also CA 85-88; DLB 13

Jen, Gish .... CLC 70
See also Jen, Lillian

Jen, Lillian 1956(?)-
See Jen, Gish
See also CA 135

Jenkins, (John) Robin 1912- .... **CLC 52**
See also CA 1-4R; CANR 1; DLB 14

Jennings, Elizabeth (Joan)
1926- .... **CLC 5, 14**
See also CA 61-64; CAAS 5; CANR 8, 39;
DLB 27; MTCW; SATA 66

Jennings, Waylon 1937- .... **CLC 21**

Jensen, Johannes V. 1873-1950 ...... **TCLC 41**

Jensen, Laura (Linnea) 1948- .... **CLC 37**
See also CA 103

Jerome, Jerome K(lapka)
1859-1927 .... **TCLC 23**
See also CA 119; DLB 10, 34, 135

Jerrold, Douglas William
1803-1857 .... **NCLC 2**
See also DLB 158, 159

Jewett, (Theodora) Sarah Orne
1849-1909 .... **TCLC 1, 22; SSC 6**
See also CA 108; 127; DLB 12, 74; SATA 15

Jewsbury, Geraldine (Endsor)
1812-1880 .... **NCLC 22**
See also DLB 21

Jhabvala, Ruth Prawer
1927- .... **CLC 4, 8, 29, 94; DAB; DAM
NOV**
See also CA 1-4R; CANR 2, 29, 51; DLB 139;
INT CANR-29; MTCW

Jibran, Kahlil
See Gibran, Kahlil

Joyce, James (Augustine Aloysius)
1882-1941 ... **TCLC 3, 8, 16, 35, 52; DA; DAB; DAC; DAM MST, NOV, POET; SSC 26; WLC**
See also CA 104; 126; CDBLB 1914-1945; DLB 10, 19, 36, 162; MTCW

Jozsef, Attila
1905-1937 .... **TCLC 22**
See also CA 116

Juana Ines de la Cruz 1651(?)-1695 ...... **LC 5**

Judd, Cyril
See Kornbluth, C(yril) M.; Pohl, Frederik

Julian of Norwich
1342(?)-1416(?) .... **LC 6**
See also DLB 146

Juniper, Alex
See Hospital, Janette Turner

Junius
See Luxemburg, Rosa

Just, Ward (Swift)
1935- ....**CLC 4, 27**
See also CA 25-28R; CANR 32; INT CANR-32

Justice, Donald (Rodney)
1925- .... **CLC 6, 19, 102; DAM POET**
See also CA 5-8R; CANR 26, 54; DLBY 83; INT CANR-26

Juvenal c. 55-c. 127 .... **CMLC 8**

Juvenis
See Bourne, Randolph S(illiman)

Kacew, Romain 1914-1980
See Gary, Romain
See also CA 108; 102

Kadare, Ismail 1936- .... **CLC 52**

Kadohata, Cynthia .... **CLC 59**
See also CA 140

Kafka, Franz
1883-1924 ..... **TCLC 2, 6, 13, 29, 47, 53; DA; DAB; DAC; DAM MST, NOV; SSC 29; WLC**
See also CA 105; 126; DLB 81; MTCW

Kahanovitsch, Pinkhes
See Der Nister

Kahn, Roger 1927- .... **CLC 30**
See also CA 25-28R; CANR 44; DLB 171; SATA 37

Kain, Saul
See Sassoon, Siegfried (Lorraine)

Kaiser, Georg
1878-1945 .... **TCLC 9**
See also CA 106; DLB 124

Kaletski, Alexander
1946- .... **CLC 39**
See also CA 118; 143

Kalidasa fl. c. 400- .... **CMLC 9**

Kallman, Chester (Simon)
1921-1975 .... **CLC 2**
See also CA 45-48; 53-56; CANR 3

Kaminsky, Melvin 1926-
See Brooks, Mel
See also CA 65-68; CANR 16

Kaminsky, Stuart M(elvin)
1934- .... **CLC 59**
See also CA 73-76; CANR 29, 53

Kane, Francis
See Robbins, Harold

Kane, Paul
See Simon, Paul (Frederick)

Kane, Wilson
See Bloch, Robert (Albert)

Kanin, Garson 1912- .... **CLC 22**
See also AITN 1; CA 5-8R; CANR 7; DLB 7

Kaniuk, Yoram 1930- .... **CLC 19**
See also CA 134

Kant, Immanuel 1724-1804 .... **NCLC 27**
See also DLB 94

Kantor, MacKinlay 1904-1977 .... **CLC 7**
See also CA 61-64; 73-76; CANR 60; DLB 9, 102

Kaplan, David Michael 1946- .... **CLC 50**

Kaplan, James 1951- .... **CLC 59**
See also CA 135

Karageorge, Michael
See Anderson, Poul (William)

Karamzin, Nikolai Mikhailovich
1766-1826 .... **NCLC 3**
See also DLB 150

Karapanou, Margarita 1946- .... **CLC 13**
See also CA 101

Karinthy, Frigyes 1887-1938 .... **TCLC 47**

Karl, Frederick R(obert)
1927- .... **CLC 34**
See also CA 5-8R; CANR 3, 44

Kastel, Warren
See Silverberg, Robert

Kataev, Evgeny Petrovich 1903-1942
See Petrov, Evgeny
See also CA 120

Kataphusin
See Ruskin, John

Katz, Steve 1935- .... **CLC 47**
See also CA 25-28R; CAAS 14; CANR 12; DLBY 83

Kauffman, Janet 1945- .... **CLC 42**
See also CA 117; CANR 43; DLBY 86

Kaufman, Bob (Garnell)
1925-1986 .... **CLC 49**
See also BW 1; CA 41-44R; 118; CANR 22; DLB 16, 41

Kaufman, George S. 1889-1961 ...... **CLC 38; DAM DRAM**
See also CA 108; 93-96; DLB 7; INT 108

Kaufman, Sue .... **CLC 3, 8**
See also Barondess, Sue K(aufman)

Kavafis, Konstantinos Petrou 1863-1933
See Cavafy, C(onstantine) P(eter)
See also CA 104

Kavan, Anna 1901-1968 .... **CLC 5, 13, 82**
See also CA 5-8R; CANR 6, 57; MTCW

Kavanagh, Dan
See Barnes, Julian (Patrick)

Kavanagh, Patrick (Joseph)
1904-1967 .... **CLC 22**
See also CA 123; 25-28R; DLB 15, 20; MTCW

Kawabata, Yasunari
1899-1972 .... **CLC 2, 5, 9, 18; DAM MULT; SSC 17**
See also CA 93-96; 33-36R; DLB 180

Kaye, M(ary) M(argaret) 1909- .... **CLC 28**
See also CA 89-92; CANR 24, 60; MTCW; SATA 62

Kaye, Mollie
See Kaye, M(ary) M(argaret)

Kaye-Smith, Sheila 1887-1956 .... **TCLC 20**
See also CA 118; DLB 36

Kaymor, Patrice Maguilene
See Senghor, Leopold Sedar

Kazan, Elia 1909- .... **CLC 6, 16, 63**
See also CA 21-24R; CANR 32

Kazantzakis, Nikos
1883(?)-1957 .... **TCLC 2, 5, 33**
See also CA 105; 132; MTCW

Kazin, Alfred 1915- .... **CLC 34, 38**
See also CA 1-4R; CAAS 7; CANR 1, 45; DLB 67

Keane, Mary Nesta (Skrine) 1904-1996
See Keane, Molly
See also CA 108; 114; 151

Keane, Molly .... **CLC 31**
See also Keane, Mary Nesta (Skrine)
See also INT 114

Keates, Jonathan 19(?)- .... **CLC 34**

Keaton, Buster 1895-1966 .... **CLC 20**

Keats, John
1795-1821 .... **NCLC 8; DA; DAB; DAC; DAM MST, POET; PC 1; WLC**
See also CDBLB 1789-1832; DLB 96, 110

Keene, Donald 1922- .... **CLC 34**
See also CA 1-4R; CANR 5

La Fayette, Marie (Madelaine Pioche de la Vergne Comtes 1634-1693 .... **LC 2**

Lafayette, Rene
See Hubbard, L(afayette) Ron(ald)

Laforgue, Jules
1860-1887 .. **NCLC 5, 53; PC 14; SSC 20**

Lagerkvist, Paer (Fabian)
1891-1974 .... **CLC 7, 10, 13, 54; DAM DRAM, NOV**
See also Lagerkvist, Par
See also CA 85-88; 49-52; MTCW

Lagerkvist, Par .... **SSC 12**
See also Lagerkvist, Paer (Fabian)

Lagerloef, Selma (Ottiliana Lovisa)
1858-1940 .... **TCLC 4, 36**
See also Lagerlof, Selma (Ottiliana Lovisa)
See also CA 108; SATA 15

Lagerlof, Selma (Ottiliana Lovisa)
See Lagerloef, Selma (Ottiliana Lovisa)
See also CLR 7; SATA 15

La Guma, (Justin) Alex(ander)
1925-1985 .... **CLC 19; DAM NOV**
See also BW 1; CA 49-52; 118; CANR 25; DLB 117; MTCW

Laidlaw, A. K.
See Grieve, C(hristopher) M(urray)

Lainez, Manuel Mujica
See Mujica Lainez, Manuel
See also HW

Laing, R(onald) D(avid)
1927-1989 .... **CLC 95**
See also CA 107; 129; CANR 34; MTCW

Lamartine, Alphonse (Marie Louis Prat) de
1790-1869 .. **NCLC 11; DAM POET; PC 16**

Lamb, Charles 1775-1834 ..... **NCLC 10; DA; DAB; DAC; DAM MST; WLC**
See also CDBLB 1789-1832; DLB 93, 107, 163; SATA 17

Lamb, Lady Caroline 1785-1828 ... **NCLC 38**
See also DLB 116

Lamming, George (William)
1927- .... **CLC 2, 4, 66; BLC; DAM MULT**
See also BW 2; CA 85-88; CANR 26; DLB 125; MTCW

L'Amour, Louis (Dearborn)
1908-1988 .... **CLC 25, 55; DAM NOV, POP**
See also AAYA 16; AITN 2; BEST 89:2; CA 1-4R; 125; CANR 3, 25, 40; DLBY 80; MTCW

Lampedusa, Giuseppe (Tomasi) di
1896-1957 .... **TCLC 13**
See also Tomasi di Lampedusa, Giuseppe
See also DLB 177

Lampman, Archibald 1861-1899 ... **NCLC 25**
See also DLB 92

Lancaster, Bruce 1896-1963 .... **CLC 36**
See also CA 9-10; CAP 1; SATA 9

Lanchester, John .... **CLC 99**

Landau, Mark Alexandrovich
See Aldanov, Mark (Alexandrovich)

Landau-Aldanov, Mark Alexandrovich
See Aldanov, Mark (Alexandrovich)

Landis, Jerry
See Simon, Paul (Frederick)

Landis, John 1950- .... **CLC 26**
See also CA 112; 122

Landolfi, Tommaso 1908-1979 .... **CLC 11, 49**
See also CA 127; 117; DLB 177

Landon, Letitia Elizabeth
1802-1838 .... **NCLC 15**
See also DLB 96

Landor, Walter Savage
1775-1864 .... **NCLC 14**
See also DLB 93, 107

Landwirth, Heinz 1927-
See Lind, Jakov
See also CA 9-12R; CANR 7

Lane, Patrick
1939- .... **CLC 25; DAM POET**
See also CA 97-100; CANR 54; DLB 53; INT 97-100

Lang, Andrew 1844-1912 .... **TCLC 16**
See also CA 114; 137; DLB 98, 141, 184; MAICYA; SATA 16

Lang, Fritz 1890-1976 .... **CLC 20, 103**
See also CA 77-80; 69-72; CANR 30

Lange, John
See Crichton, (John) Michael

Langer, Elinor 1939- .... **CLC 34**
See also CA 121

Langland, William
1330(?)-1400(?) **LC 19; DA; DAB; DAC; DAM MST, POET**
See also DLB 146

Langstaff, Launcelot
See Irving, Washington

Lanier, Sidney 1842-1881 ..... **NCLC 6; DAM POET**
See also DLB 64; DLBD 13; MAICYA; SATA 18

Lanyer, Aemilia 1569-1645 .... **LC 10, 30**
See also DLB 121

Lao Tzu .... **CMLC 7**

Lapine, James (Elliot) 1949- .... **CLC 39**
See also CA 123; 130; CANR 54; INT 130

Larbaud, Valery (Nicolas)
1881-1957 .... **TCLC 9**
See also CA 106; 152

Lardner, Ring
See Lardner, Ring(gold) W(ilmer)

Lardner, Ring W., Jr.
See Lardner, Ring(gold) W(ilmer)

Lardner, Ring(gold) W(ilmer)
1885-1933 .... **TCLC 2, 14**
See also CA 104; 131; CDALB 1917-1929; DLB 11, 25, 86; DLBD 16; MTCW

Laredo, Betty
See Codrescu, Andrei

Larkin, Maia
See Wojciechowska, Maia (Teresa)

Larkin, Philip (Arthur)
1922-1985 **CLC 3, 5, 8, 9, 13, 18, 33, 39, 64; DAB; DAM MST, POET**
See also CA 5-8R; 117; CANR 24, 62; CDBLB 1960 to Present; DLB 27; MTCW

Larra (y Sanchez de Castro), Mariano Jose de
1809-1837 .... **NCLC 17**

Larsen, Eric 1941- .... **CLC 55**
See also CA 132

Larsen, Nella
1891-1964 .... **CLC 37; BLC; DAM MULT**
See also BW 1; CA 125; DLB 51

Larson, Charles R(aymond) 1938- ... **CLC 31**
See also CA 53-56; CANR 4

Larson, Jonathan 1961(?)-1996 .... **CLC 99**

Las Casas, Bartolome de 1474-1566 ... **LC 31**

Lasch, Christopher 1932-1994 .... **CLC 102**
See also CA 73-76; 144; CANR 25; MTCW

Lasker-Schueler, Else 1869-1945 ... **TCLC 57**
See also DLB 66, 124

Latham, Jean Lee 1902- .... **CLC 12**
See also AITN 1; CA 5-8R; CANR 7; MAICYA; SATA 2, 68

Latham, Mavis
See Clark, Mavis Thorpe

Lathen, Emma .... **CLC 2**
See also Hennissart, Martha; Latsis, Mary J(ane)

Lathrop, Francis
See Leiber, Fritz (Reuter, Jr.)

Latsis, Mary J(ane)
See Lathen, Emma
See also CA 85-88

Lattimore, Richmond (Alexander)
1906-1984 .... **CLC 3**
See also CA 1-4R; 112; CANR 1

Leffland, Ella 1931- .... **CLC 19**
See also CA 29-32R; CANR 35; DLBY 84;
INT CANR-35; SATA 65

Leger, Alexis
See Leger, (Marie-Rene Auguste) Alexis Saint-
Leger

**Leger, (Marie-Rene Auguste) Alexis Saint-
Leger** 1887-1975 .... **CLC 11; DAM
POET**
See also Perse, St.-John
See also CA 13-16R; 61-64; CANR 43;
MTCW

Leger, Saintleger
See Leger, (Marie-Rene Auguste) Alexis Saint-
Leger

Le Guin, Ursula K(roeber)
1929- .... **CLC 8, 13, 22, 45, 71; DAB;
DAC; DAM MST, POP; SSC 12**
See also AAYA 9; AITN 1; CA 21-24R;
CANR 9, 32, 52; CDALB 1968-1988;
CLR 3, 28; DLB 8, 52; INT CANR-
32; JRDA; MAICYA; MTCW; SATA 4,
52

Lehmann, Rosamond (Nina)
1901-1990 .... **CLC 5**
See also CA 77-80; 131; CANR 8; DLB 15

Leiber, Fritz (Reuter, Jr.)
1910-1992 .... **CLC 25**
See also CA 45-48; 139; CANR 2, 40; DLB 8;
MTCW; SATA 45; SATA-Obit 73

Leibniz, Gottfried Wilhelm von
1646-1716 .... **LC 35**
See also DLB 168

Leimbach, Martha 1963-
See Leimbach, Marti
See also CA 130

Leimbach, Marti .... **CLC 65**
See also Leimbach, Martha

Leino, Eino .... **TCLC 24**
See also Loennbohm, Armas Eino Leopold

Leiris, Michel (Julien)
1901-1990 .... **CLC 61**
See also CA 119; 128; 132

Leithauser, Brad
1953- .... **CLC 27**
See also CA 107; CANR 27; DLB 120

Lelchuk, Alan 1938- .... **CLC 5**
See also CA 45-48; CAAS 20; CANR 1

Lem, Stanislaw
1921- .... **CLC 8, 15, 40**
See also CA 105; CAAS 1; CANR 32;
MTCW

Lemann, Nancy 1956- .... **CLC 39**
See also CA 118; 136

Lemonnier, (Antoine Louis) Camille
1844-1913 .... **TCLC 22**
See also CA 121

Lenau, Nikolaus 1802-1850 .... **NCLC 16**

L'Engle, Madeleine (Camp Franklin)
1918- .... **CLC 12; DAM POP**
See also AAYA 1; AITN 2; CA 1-4R; CANR
3, 21, 39; CLR 1, 14; DLB 52; JRDA;
MAICYA; MTCW; SAAS 15; SATA 1, 27,
75

Lengyel, Jozsef
1896-1975 .... **CLC 7**
See also CA 85-88; 57-60

Lenin 1870-1924
See Lenin, V. I.
See also CA 121

Lenin, V. I. .... **TCLC 67**
See also Lenin

Lennon, John (Ono)
1940-1980 .... **CLC 12, 35**
See also CA 102

Lennox, Charlotte Ramsay
1729(?)-1804 .... **NCLC 23**
See also DLB 39

Lentricchia, Frank (Jr.)
1940- .... **CLC 34**
See also CA 25-28R; CANR 19

Lenz, Siegfried
1926- .... **CLC 27**
See also CA 89-92; DLB 75

Leonard, Elmore (John, Jr.)
1925- .... **CLC 28, 34, 71; DAM POP**
See also AAYA 22; AITN 1; BEST
89:1, 90:4; CA 81-84; CANR 12, 28,
53; DLB 173; INT CANR-28;
MTCW

Leonard, Hugh .... **CLC 19**
See also Byrne, John Keyes
See also DLB 13

Leonov, Leonid (Maximovich)
1899-1994 .... **CLC 92; DAM NOV**
See also CA 129; MTCW

Leopardi, (Conte) Giacomo
1798-1837 .... **NCLC 22**

Le Reveler
See Artaud, Antonin (Marie Joseph)

Lerman, Eleanor
1952- .... **CLC 9**
See also CA 85-88

Lerman, Rhoda
1936- .... **CLC 56**
See also CA 49-52

Lermontov, Mikhail Yuryevich
1814-1841 .... **NCLC 47; PC 18**

Leroux, Gaston
1868-1927 .... **TCLC 25**
See also CA 108; 136; SATA 65

Lesage, Alain-Rene 1668-1747 .... **LC 28**

Leskov, Nikolai (Semyonovich)
1831-1895 .... **NCLC 25**

Lessing, Doris (May)
1919- . **CLC 1, 2, 3, 6, 10, 15, 22, 40, 94;
DA; DAB; DAC; DAM MST, NOV; SSC
6; WLCS**
See also CA 9-12R; CAAS 14; CANR 33, 54;
CDBLB 1960 to Present; DLB 15, 139;
DLBY 85; MTCW

Lessing, Gotthold Ephraim
1729-1781 .... **LC 8**
See also DLB 97

Lester, Richard 1932- .... **CLC 20**

Lever, Charles (James)
1806-1872 .... **NCLC 23**
See also DLB 21

Leverson, Ada 1865(?)-1936(?) ...... **TCLC 18**
See also Elaine
See also CA 117; DLB 153

Levertov, Denise
1923- .... **CLC 1, 2, 3, 5, 8, 15, 28, 66;
DAM POET; PC 11**
See also CA 1-4R; CAAS 19; CANR 3, 29,
50; DLB 5, 165; INT CANR-29; MTCW

Levi, Jonathan .... **CLC 76**

Levi, Peter (Chad Tigar) 1931- .... **CLC 41**
See also CA 5-8R; CANR 34; DLB 40

Levi, Primo
1919-1987 .... **CLC 37, 50; SSC 12**
See also CA 13-16R; 122; CANR 12, 33, 61;
DLB 177; MTCW

Levin, Ira 1929- .... **CLC 3, 6; DAM POP**
See also CA 21-24R; CANR 17, 44; MTCW;
SATA 66

Levin, Meyer
1905-1981 .... **CLC 7; DAM POP**
See also AITN 1; CA 9-12R; 104; CANR 15;
DLB 9, 28; DLBY 81; SATA 21; SATA-Obit
27

Levine, Norman 1924- .... **CLC 54**
See also CA 73-76; CAAS 23; CANR 14; DLB
88

Levine, Philip
1928- .... **CLC 2, 4, 5, 9, 14, 33; DAM
POET**
See also CA 9-12R; CANR 9, 37, 52; DLB 5

Levinson, Deirdre 1931- .... **CLC 49**
See also CA 73-76

Levi-Strauss, Claude 1908- .... **CLC 38**
See also CA 1-4R; CANR 6, 32, 57; MTCW

Levitin, Sonia (Wolff) 1934- .... **CLC 17**
See also AAYA 13; CA 29-32R; CANR 14,
32; JRDA; MAICYA; SAAS 2; SATA 4,
68

Levon, O. U.
See Kesey, Ken (Elton)

Locke, John 1632-1704 .... LC 7, 35
See also DLB 101

Locke-Elliott, Sumner
See Elliott, Sumner Locke

Lockhart, John Gibson
1794-1854 .... NCLC 6
See also DLB 110, 116, 144

Lodge, David (John) 1935- .... CLC 36; DAM
POP
See also BEST 90:1; CA 17-20R; CANR 19,
53; DLB 14; INT CANR-19; MTCW

Loennbohm, Armas Eino Leopold 1878-1926
See Leino, Eino
See also CA 123

Loewinsohn, Ron(ald William)
1937- .... CLC 52
See also CA 25-28R

Logan, Jake
See Smith, Martin Cruz

Logan, John (Burton) 1923-1987 .... CLC 5
See also CA 77-80; 124; CANR 45; DLB 5

Lo Kuan-chung 1330(?)-1400(?) .... LC 12

Lombard, Nap
See Johnson, Pamela Hansford

London, Jack . TCLC 9, 15, 39; SSC 4; WLC
See also London, John Griffith
See also AAYA 13; AITN 2; CDALB 1865-
1917; DLB 8, 12, 78; SATA 18

London, John Griffith 1876-1916
See London, Jack
See also CA 110; 119; DA; DAB; DAC; DAM
MST, NOV; JRDA; MAICYA; MTCW

Long, Emmett
See Leonard, Elmore (John, Jr.)

Longbaugh, Harry
See Goldman, William (W.)

Longfellow, Henry Wadsworth
1807-1882 .... NCLC 2, 45; DA; DAB;
DAC; DAM MST, POET; WLCS
See also CDALB 1640-1865; DLB 1, 59; SATA
19

Longley, Michael 1939- .... CLC 29
See also CA 102; DLB 40

Longus fl. c. 2nd cent. - .... CMLC 7

Longway, A. Hugh
See Lang, Andrew

Lonnrot, Elias 1802-1884 .... NCLC 53

Lopate, Phillip 1943- .... CLC 29
See also CA 97-100; DLBY 80; INT 97-
100

Lopez Portillo (y Pacheco), Jose
1920- .... CLC 46
See also CA 129; HW

Lopez y Fuentes, Gregorio
1897(?)-1966 .... CLC 32
See also CA 131; HW

Lorca, Federico Garcia
See Garcia Lorca, Federico

Lord, Bette Bao 1938- .... CLC 23
See also BEST 90:3; CA 107; CANR 41; INT
107; SATA 58

Lord Auch
See Bataille, Georges

Lord Byron
See Byron, George Gordon (Noel)

Lorde, Audre (Geraldine)
1934-1992 .... CLC 18, 71; BLC; DAM
MULT, POET; PC 12
See also BW 1; CA 25-28R; 142; CANR 16,
26, 46; DLB 41; MTCW

Lord Houghton
See Milnes, Richard Monckton

Lord Jeffrey
See Jeffrey, Francis

Lorenzini, Carlo 1826-1890
See Collodi, Carlo
See also MAICYA; SATA 29

Lorenzo, Heberto Padilla
See Padilla (Lorenzo), Heberto

Loris
See Hofmannsthal, Hugo von

Loti, Pierre .... TCLC 11
See also Viaud, (Louis Marie) Julien
See also DLB 123

Louie, David Wong 1954- .... CLC 70
See also CA 139

Louis, Father M.
See Merton, Thomas

Lovecraft, H(oward) P(hillips)
1890-1937 ...... TCLC 4, 22; DAM POP;
SSC 3
See also AAYA 14; CA 104; 133;
MTCW

Lovelace, Earl
1935- .... CLC 51
See also BW 2; CA 77-80; CANR 41; DLB
125; MTCW

Lovelace, Richard
1618-1657 .... LC 24
See also DLB 131

Lowell, Amy
1874-1925 ... TCLC 1, 8; DAM POET;
PC 13
See also CA 104; 151; DLB 54, 140

Lowell, James Russell
1819-1891 .... NCLC 2
See also CDALB 1640-1865; DLB 1, 11, 64,
79

Lowell, Robert (Traill Spence, Jr.)
1917-1977 ... CLC 1, 2, 3, 4, 5, 8, 9, 11,
15, 37; DA; DAB; DAC; DAM MST,
NOV; PC 3; WLC
See also CA 9-12R; 73-76; CABS 2; CANR
26, 60; DLB 5, 169; MTCW

Lowndes, Marie Adelaide (Belloc)
1868-1947 .... TCLC 12
See also CA 107; DLB 70

Lowry, (Clarence) Malcolm
1909-1957 .... TCLC 6, 40
See also CA 105; 131; CANR 62; CDBLB
1945-1960; DLB 15; MTCW

Lowry, Mina Gertrude 1882-1966
See Loy, Mina
See also CA 113

Loxsmith, John
See Brunner, John (Kilian Houston)

Loy, Mina .... CLC 28; DAM POET; PC 16
See also Lowry, Mina Gertrude
See also DLB 4, 54

Loyson-Bridet
See Schwob, (Mayer Andre) Marcel

Lucas, Craig 1951- .... CLC 64
See also CA 137

Lucas, E(dward) V(errall)
1868-1938 .... TCLC 73
See also DLB 98, 149, 153; SATA 20

Lucas, George 1944- .... CLC 16
See also AAYA 1; CA 77-80; CANR 30; SATA
56

Lucas, Hans
See Godard, Jean-Luc

Lucas, Victoria
See Plath, Sylvia

Ludlam, Charles 1943-1987 .... CLC 46, 50
See also CA 85-88; 122

Ludlum, Robert 1927- ..... CLC 22, 43; DAM
NOV, POP
See also AAYA 10; BEST 89:1, 90:3; CA
33-36R; CANR 25, 41; DLBY 82;
MTCW

Ludwig, Ken .... CLC 60

Ludwig, Otto 1813-1865 .... NCLC 4
See also DLB 129

Lugones, Leopoldo 1874-1938 .... TCLC 15
See also CA 116; 131; HW

Lu Hsun 1881-1936 .... TCLC 3; SSC 20
See also Shu-Jen, Chou

Lukacs, George .... CLC 24
See also Lukacs, Gyorgy (Szegeny von)

Lukacs, Gyorgy (Szegeny von) 1885-1971
See Lukacs, George
See also CA 101; 29-32R; CANR 62

Luke, Peter (Ambrose Cyprian)
    1919-1995 .... **CLC 38**
    See also CA 81-84; 147; DLB 13

Lunar, Dennis
    See Mungo, Raymond

Lurie, Alison 1926- .... **CLC 4, 5, 18, 39**
    See also CA 1-4R; CANR 2, 17, 50; DLB 2;
    MTCW; SATA 46

Lustig, Arnost 1926- .... **CLC 56**
    See also AAYA 3; CA 69-72; CANR 47; SATA
    56

Luther, Martin 1483-1546 .... **LC 9, 37**
    See also DLB 179

Luxemburg, Rosa 1870(?)-1919 ..... **TCLC 63**
    See also CA 118

Luzi, Mario 1914- .... **CLC 13**
    See also CA 61-64; CANR 9; DLB 128

Lyly, John 1554(?)-1606 .... **DC 7**
    See also DAM DRAM; DLB 62, 167

L'Ymagier
    See Gourmont, Remy (-Marie-Charles) de

Lynch, B. Suarez
    See Bioy Casares, Adolfo; Borges, Jorge Luis

Lynch, David (K.) 1946- .... **CLC 66**
    See also CA 124; 129

Lynch, James
    See Andreyev, Leonid (Nikolaevich)

Lynch Davis, B.
    See Bioy Casares, Adolfo; Borges, Jorge Luis

Lyndsay, Sir David 1490-1555 .... **LC 20**

Lynn, Kenneth S(chuyler)
    1923- .... **CLC 50**
    See also CA 1-4R; CANR 3, 27

Lynx
    See West, Rebecca

Lyons, Marcus
    See Blish, James (Benjamin)

Lyre, Pinchbeck
    See Sassoon, Siegfried (Lorraine)

Lytle, Andrew (Nelson)
    1902-1995 .... **CLC 22**
    See also CA 9-12R; 150; DLB 6; DLBY 95

Lyttelton, George 1709-1773 .... **LC 10**

Maas, Peter 1929- .... **CLC 29**
    See also CA 93-96; INT 93-96

Macaulay, Rose
    1881-1958 .... **TCLC 7, 44**
    See also CA 104; DLB 36

Macaulay, Thomas Babington
    1800-1859 .... **NCLC 42**
    See also CDBLB 1832-1890; DLB 32, 55

MacBeth, George (Mann)
    1932-1992 .... **CLC 2, 5, 9**
    See also CA 25-28R; 136; CANR 61; DLB 40;
    MTCW; SATA 4; SATA-Obit 70

MacCaig, Norman (Alexander)
    1910- .... **CLC 36; DAB; DAM POET**
    See also CA 9-12R; CANR 3, 34; DLB 27

MacCarthy, (Sir Charles Otto) Desmond
    1877-1952 .... **TCLC 36**

MacDiarmid, Hugh....   **CLC 2, 4, 11, 19, 63;**
    PC 9
    See also Grieve, C(hristopher) M(urray)
    See also CDBLB 1945-1960; DLB 20

MacDonald, Anson
    See Heinlein, Robert A(nson)

Macdonald, Cynthia 1928- .... **CLC 13, 19**
    See also CA 49-52; CANR 4, 44; DLB
    105

MacDonald, George 1824-1905 .... **TCLC 9**
    See also CA 106; 137; DLB 18, 163, 178;
    MAICYA; SATA 33

Macdonald, John
    See Millar, Kenneth

MacDonald, John D(ann)
    1916-1986 .... **CLC 3, 27, 44; DAM NOV,**
    POP
    See also CA 1-4R; 121; CANR 1, 19, 60; DLB
    8; DLBY 86; MTCW

Macdonald, John Ross
    See Millar, Kenneth

Macdonald, Ross .... **CLC 1, 2, 3, 14, 34, 41**
    See also Millar, Kenneth
    See also DLBD 6

MacDougal, John
    See Blish, James (Benjamin)

MacEwen, Gwendolyn (Margaret)
    1941-1987 .... **CLC 13, 55**
    See also CA 9-12R; 124; CANR 7, 22; DLB
    53; SATA 50; SATA-Obit 55

Macha, Karel Hynek 1810-1846 .... **NCLC 46**

Machado (y Ruiz), Antonio
    1875-1939 .... **TCLC 3**
    See also CA 104; DLB 108

Machado de Assis, Joaquim Maria
    1839-1908 .... **TCLC 10; BLC; SSC 24**
    See also CA 107; 153

Machen, Arthur .... **TCLC 4; SSC 20**
    See also Jones, Arthur Llewellyn
    See also DLB 36, 156, 178

Machiavelli, Niccolo
    1469-1527 .... **LC 8, 36; DA; DAB; DAC;**
    DAM MST; WLCS

MacInnes, Colin 1914-1976 .... **CLC 4, 23**
    See also CA 69-72; 65-68; CANR 21; DLB
    14; MTCW

MacInnes, Helen (Clark)
    1907-1985 .... **CLC 27, 39; DAM POP**
    See also CA 1-4R; 117; CANR 1, 28, 58; DLB
    87; MTCW; SATA 22; SATA-Obit 44

Mackay, Mary 1855-1924
    See Corelli, Marie
    See also CA 118

Mackenzie, Compton (Edward Montague)
    1883-1972 .... **CLC 18**
    See also CA 21-22; 37-40R; CAP 2; DLB 34,
    100

Mackenzie, Henry 1745-1831 .... **NCLC 41**
    See also DLB 39

Mackintosh, Elizabeth 1896(?)-1952
    See Tey, Josephine
    See also CA 110

MacLaren, James
    See Grieve, C(hristopher) M(urray)

Mac Laverty, Bernard 1942- .... **CLC 31**
    See also CA 116; 118; CANR 43; INT 118

MacLean, Alistair (Stuart)
    1922(?)-1987 ... **CLC 3, 13, 50, 63; DAM**
    POP
    See also CA 57-60; 121; CANR 28, 61;
    MTCW; SATA 23; SATA-Obit 50

Maclean, Norman (Fitzroy)
    1902-1990 ..   **CLC 78; DAM POP; SSC**
    13
    See also CA 102; 132; CANR 49

MacLeish, Archibald
    1892-1982 .... **CLC 3, 8, 14, 68; DAM**
    POET
    See also CA 9-12R; 106; CANR 33; DLB 4, 7,
    45; DLBY 82; MTCW

MacLennan, (John) Hugh
    1907-1990 ... **CLC 2, 14, 92; DAC; DAM**
    MST
    See also CA 5-8R; 142; CANR 33; DLB 68;
    MTCW

MacLeod, Alistair
    1936- .... **CLC 56; DAC; DAM MST**
    See also CA 123; DLB 60

Macleod, Fiona
    See Sharp, William

MacNeice, (Frederick) Louis
    1907-1963 .... **CLC 1, 4, 10, 53; DAB;**
    DAM POET
    See also CA 85-88; CANR 61; DLB 10, 20;
    MTCW

MacNeill, Dand
    See Fraser, George MacDonald

Macpherson, James
    1736-1796 .... **LC 29**
    See also DLB 109

Macpherson, (Jean) Jay
    1931- .... **CLC 14**
    See also CA 5-8R; DLB 53

MacShane, Frank 1927- .... CLC 39
See also CA 9-12R; CANR 3, 33; DLB 111

Macumber, Mari
See Sandoz, Mari(e Susette)

Madach, Imre 1823-1864 .... NCLC 19

Madden, (Jerry) David
1933- .... CLC 5, 15
See also CA 1-4R; CAAS 3; CANR 4, 45; DLB 6; MTCW

Maddern, Al(an)
See Ellison, Harlan (Jay)

Madhubuti, Haki R.
1942- .... CLC 6, 73; BLC; DAM MULT, POET; PC 5
See also Lee, Don L.
See also BW 2; CA 73-76; CANR 24, 51; DLB 5, 41; DLBD 8

Maepenn, Hugh
See Kuttner, Henry

Maepenn, K. H.
See Kuttner, Henry

Maeterlinck, Maurice
1862-1949 .... TCLC 3; DAM DRAM
See also CA 104; 136; SATA 66

Maginn, William 1794-1842 .... NCLC 8
See also DLB 110, 159

Mahapatra, Jayanta 1928- .... CLC 33; DAM MULT
See also CA 73-76; CAAS 9; CANR 15, 33

Mahfouz, Naguib (Abdel Aziz Al-Sabilgi)
1911(?)-
See Mahfuz, Najib
See also BEST 89:2; CA 128; CANR 55; DAM NOV; MTCW

Mahfuz, Najib .... CLC 52, 55
See also Mahfouz, Naguib (Abdel Aziz Al-Sabilgi)
See also DLBY 88

Mahon, Derek 1941- .... CLC 27
See also CA 113; 128; DLB 40

Mailer, Norman
1923- ... CLC 1, 2, 3, 4, 5, 8, 11, 14, 28, 39, 74; DA; DAB; DAC; DAM MST, NOV, POP
See also AITN 2; CA 9-12R; CABS 1; CANR 28; CDALB 1968-1988; DLB 2, 16, 28; DLBD 3; DLBY 80, 83; MTCW

Maillet, Antonine
1929- .... CLC 54; DAC
See also CA 115; 120; CANR 46; DLB 60; INT 120

Mais, Roger
1905-1955 .... TCLC 8
See also BW 1; CA 105; 124; DLB 125; MTCW

Maistre, Joseph de 1753-1821 .... NCLC 37

Maitland, Frederic 1850-1906 .... TCLC 65

Maitland, Sara (Louise)
1950- .... CLC 49
See also CA 69-72; CANR 13, 59

Major, Clarence
1936- .... CLC 3, 19, 48; BLC; DAM MULT
See also BW 2; CA 21-24R; CAAS 6; CANR 13, 25, 53; DLB 33

Major, Kevin (Gerald)
1949- .... CLC 26; DAC
See also AAYA 16; CA 97-100; CANR 21, 38; CLR 11; DLB 60; INT CANR-21; JRDA; MAICYA; SATA 32, 82

Maki, James
See Ozu, Yasujiro

Malabaila, Damiano
See Levi, Primo

Malamud, Bernard
1914-1986.... CLC 1, 2, 3, 5, 8, 9, 11, 18, 27, 44, 78, 85; DA; DAB; DAC; DAM MST, NOV, POP; SSC 15; WLC
See also AAYA 16; CA 5-8R; 118; CABS 1; CANR 28, 62; CDALB 1941-1968; DLB 2, 28, 152; DLBY 80, 86; MTCW

Malan, Herman
See Bosman, Herman Charles; Bosman, Herman Charles

Malaparte, Curzio 1898-1957 .... TCLC 52

Malcolm, Dan
See Silverberg, Robert

Malcolm X .... CLC 82; BLC; WLCS
See also Little, Malcolm

Malherbe, Francois de 1555-1628 .... LC 5

Mallarme, Stephane
1842-1898 ... NCLC 4, 41; DAM POET; PC 4

Mallet-Joris, Francoise
1930- .... CLC 11
See also CA 65-68; CANR 17; DLB 83

Malley, Ern
See McAuley, James Phillip

Mallowan, Agatha Christie
See Christie, Agatha (Mary Clarissa)

Maloff, Saul 1922- .... CLC 5
See also CA 33-36R

Malone, Louis
See MacNeice, (Frederick) Louis

Malone, Michael (Christopher)
1942- .... CLC 43
See also CA 77-80; CANR 14, 32, 57

Malory, (Sir) Thomas
1410(?)-1471(?) .... LC 11; DA; DAB; DAC; DAM MST; WLCS
See also CDBLB Before 1660; DLB 146; SATA 59; SATA-Brief 33

Malouf, (George Joseph) David
1934- .... CLC 28, 86
See also CA 124; CANR 50

Malraux, (Georges-)Andre
1901-1976 .... CLC 1, 4, 9, 13, 15, 57; DAM NOV
See also CA 21-22; 69-72; CANR 34, 58; CAP 2; DLB 72; MTCW

Malzberg, Barry N(athaniel)
1939- .... CLC 7
See also CA 61-64; CAAS 4; CANR 16; DLB 8

Mamet, David (Alan)
1947- .... CLC 9, 15, 34, 46, 91; DAM DRAM; DC 4
See also AAYA 3; CA 81-84; CABS 3; CANR 15, 41; DLB 7; MTCW

Mamoulian, Rouben (Zachary)
1897-1987 .... CLC 16
See also CA 25-28R; 124

Mandelstam, Osip (Emilievich)
1891(?)-1938(?) .... TCLC 2, 6; PC 14
See also CA 104; 150

Mander, (Mary) Jane 1877-1949 ... TCLC 31

Mandeville, John
fl. 1350- .... CMLC 19
See also DLB 146

Mandiargues, Andre Pieyre de .... CLC 41
See also Pieyre de Mandiargues, Andre
See also DLB 83

Mandrake, Ethel Belle
See Thurman, Wallace (Henry)

Mangan, James Clarence
1803-1849 .... NCLC 27

Maniere, J.-E.
See Giraudoux, (Hippolyte) Jean

Manley, (Mary) Delariviere
1672(?)-1724 .... LC 1
See also DLB 39, 80

Mann, Abel
See Creasey, John

Mann, Emily 1952- .... DC 7
See also CA 130; CANR 55

Mann, (Luiz) Heinrich
1871-1950 .... TCLC 9
See also CA 106; DLB 66

Mann, (Paul) Thomas
1875-1955 TCLC 2, 8, 14, 21, 35, 44, 60; DA; DAB; DAC; DAM MST, NOV; SSC 5; WLC
See also CA 104; 128; DLB 66; MTCW

Mannheim, Karl 1893-1947 .... **TCLC 65**

Manning, David
See Faust, Frederick (Schiller)

Manning, Frederic 1887(?)-1935 ... **TCLC 25**
See also CA 124

Manning, Olivia 1915-1980 .... **CLC 5, 19**
See also CA 5-8R; 101; CANR 29; MTCW

Mano, D. Keith 1942- .... **CLC 2, 10**
See also CA 25-28R; CAAS 6; CANR 26, 57;
DLB 6

Mansfield, Katherine .. **TCLC 2, 8, 39; DAB;
SSC 9, 23; WLC**
See also Beauchamp, Kathleen Mansfield
See also DLB 162

Manso, Peter 1940- .... **CLC 39**
See also CA 29-32R; CANR 44

Mantecon, Juan Jimenez
See Jimenez (Mantecon), Juan Ramon

Manton, Peter
See Creasey, John

Man Without a Spleen, A
See Chekhov, Anton (Pavlovich)

Manzoni, Alessandro 1785-1873 .... **NCLC 29**

Mapu, Abraham (ben Jekutiel)
1808-1867 .... **NCLC 18**

Mara, Sally
See Queneau, Raymond

Marat, Jean Paul 1743-1793 .... **LC 10**

Marcel, Gabriel Honore
1889-1973 .... **CLC 15**
See also CA 102; 45-48; MTCW

Marchbanks, Samuel
See Davies, (William) Robertson

Marchi, Giacomo
See Bassani, Giorgio

Margulies, Donald .... **CLC 76**

Marie de France c. 12th cent. - .... **CMLC 8**

Marie de l'Incarnation 1599-1672 ...... **LC 10**

Marier, Captain Victor
See Griffith, D(avid Lewelyn) W(ark)

Mariner, Scott
See Pohl, Frederik

Marinetti, Filippo Tommaso
1876-1944 .... **TCLC 10**
See also CA 107; DLB 114

Marivaux, Pierre Carlet de Chamblain de
1688-1763 .... **LC 4; DC 7**

Markandaya, Kamala .... **CLC 8, 38**
See also Taylor, Kamala (Purnaiya)

Markfield, Wallace 1926- .... **CLC 8**
See also CA 69-72; CAAS 3; DLB 2,
28

Markham, Edwin 1852-1940 .... **TCLC 47**
See also CA 160; DLB 54

Markham, Robert
See Amis, Kingsley (William)

Marks, J
See Highwater, Jamake (Mamake)

Marks-Highwater, J
See Highwater, Jamake (Mamake)

Markson, David M(errill)
1927- .... **CLC 67**
See also CA 49-52; CANR 1

Marley, Bob .... **CLC 17**
See also Marley, Robert Nesta

Marley, Robert Nesta 1945-1981
See Marley, Bob
See also CA 107; 103

Marlowe, Christopher
1564-1593 .... **LC 22; DA; DAB; DAC;
DAM DRAM, MST; DC 1; WLC**
See also CDBLB Before 1660; DLB 62

Marlowe, Stephen 1928-
See Queen, Ellery
See also CA 13-16R; CANR 6, 55

Marmontel, Jean-Francois 1723-1799 .. **LC 2**

Marquand, John P(hillips)
1893-1960 .... **CLC 2, 10**
See also CA 85-88; DLB 9, 102

Marques, Rene 1919-1979 ..... **CLC 96; DAM
MULT; HLC**
See also CA 97-100; 85-88; DLB 113;
HW

Marquez, Gabriel (Jose) Garcia
See Garcia Marquez, Gabriel (Jose)

Marquis, Don(ald Robert Perry)
1878-1937 .... **TCLC 7**
See also CA 104; DLB 11, 25

Marric, J. J.
See Creasey, John

Marrow, Bernard
See Moore, Brian

Marryat, Frederick 1792-1848 .... **NCLC 3**
See also DLB 21, 163

Marsden, James
See Creasey, John

Marsh, (Edith) Ngaio
1899-1982 .... **CLC 7, 53; DAM POP**
See also CA 9-12R; CANR 6, 58; DLB 77;
MTCW

Marshall, Garry 1934- .... **CLC 17**
See also AAYA 3; CA 111; SATA 60

Marshall, Paule
1929- .. **CLC 27, 72; BLC; DAM MULT;
SSC 3**
See also BW 2; CA 77-80; CANR 25; DLB
157; MTCW

Marsten, Richard
See Hunter, Evan

Marston, John
1576-1634 .... **LC 33; DAM DRAM**
See also DLB 58, 172

Martha, Henry
See Harris, Mark

Marti, Jose
1853-1895 .... **NCLC 63; DAM MULT;
HLC**

Martial c. 40-c. 104 .... **PC 10**

Martin, Ken
See Hubbard, L(afayette) Ron(ald)

Martin, Richard
See Creasey, John

Martin, Steve 1945- .... **CLC 30**
See also CA 97-100; CANR 30; MTCW

Martin, Valerie 1948- .... **CLC 89**
See also BEST 90:2; CA 85-88; CANR 49

Martin, Violet Florence
1862-1915 .... **TCLC 51**

Martin, Webber
See Silverberg, Robert

Martindale, Patrick Victor
See White, Patrick (Victor Martindale)

Martin du Gard, Roger
1881-1958 .... **TCLC 24**
See also CA 118; DLB 65

Martineau, Harriet 1802-1876 .... **NCLC 26**
See also DLB 21, 55, 159, 163, 166; YABC 2

Martines, Julia
See O'Faolain, Julia

Martinez, Enrique Gonzalez
See Gonzalez Martinez, Enrique

Martinez, Jacinto Benavente y
See Benavente (y Martinez), Jacinto

Martinez Ruiz, Jose 1873-1967
See Azorin; Ruiz, Jose Martinez
See also CA 93-96; HW

Martinez Sierra, Gregorio
1881-1947 .... **TCLC 6**
See also CA 115

Martinez Sierra, Maria (de la O'LeJarraga)
1874-1974 .... **TCLC 6**
See also CA 115

Martinsen, Martin
See Follett, Ken(neth Martin)

Martinson, Harry (Edmund)
1904-1978 .... **CLC 14**
See also CA 77-80; CANR 34

Marut, Ret
See Traven, B.

Marut, Robert
See Traven, B.

Marvell, Andrew
1621-1678 .... **LC 4; DA; DAB; DAC;**
DAM MST, POET; PC 10; WLC
See also CDBLB 1660-1789; DLB 131

Marx, Karl (Heinrich)
1818-1883 .... **NCLC 17**
See also DLB 129

Masaoka Shiki .... **TCLC 18**
See also Masaoka Tsunenori

Masaoka Tsunenori 1867-1902
See Masaoka Shiki
See also CA 117

Masefield, John (Edward)
1878-1967 ...... **CLC 11, 47; DAM POET**
See also CA 19-20; 25-28R; CANR 33; CAP
2; CDBLB 1890-1914; DLB 10, 19, 153,
160; MTCW; SATA 19

Maso, Carole 19(?)- .... **CLC 44**

Mason, Bobbie Ann 1940- ... **CLC 28, 43, 82;**
SSC 4
See also AAYA 5; CA 53-56; CANR 11, 31,
58; DLB 173; DLBY 87; INT CANR-31;
MTCW

Mason, Ernst
See Pohl, Frederik

Mason, Lee W.
See Malzberg, Barry N(athaniel)

Mason, Nick 1945- .... **CLC 35**

Mason, Tally
See Derleth, August (William)

Mass, William
See Gibson, William

Masters, Edgar Lee
1868-1950 .... **TCLC 2, 25; DA; DAC;**
DAM MST, POET; PC 1; WLCS
See also CA 104; 133; CDALB 1865-1917;
DLB 54; MTCW

Masters, Hilary 1928- .... **CLC 48**
See also CA 25-28R; CANR 13, 47

Mastrosimone, William 19(?)- .... **CLC 36**

Mathe, Albert
See Camus, Albert

Mather, Cotton 1663-1728 .... **LC 38**
See also CDALB 1640-1865; DLB 24, 30, 140

Mather, Increase 1639-1723 .... **LC 38**
See also DLB 24

Matheson, Richard Burton 1926- ..... **CLC 37**
See also CA 97-100; DLB 8, 44; INT 97-100

Mathews, Harry 1930- .... **CLC 6, 52**
See also CA 21-24R; CAAS 6; CANR 18, 40

Mathews, John Joseph 1894-1979 .. **CLC 84;**
DAM MULT
See also CA 19-20; 142; CANR 45; CAP 2;
DLB 175; NNAL

Mathias, Roland (Glyn) 1915- .... **CLC 45**
See also CA 97-100; CANR 19, 41; DLB 27

Matsuo Basho 1644-1694 .... **PC 3**
See also DAM POET

Mattheson, Rodney
See Creasey, John

Matthews, Greg 1949- .... **CLC 45**
See also CA 135

Matthews, William 1942- .... **CLC 40**
See also CA 29-32R; CAAS 18; CANR 12, 57;
DLB 5

Matthias, John (Edward) 1941- .... **CLC 9**
See also CA 33-36R; CANR 56

Matthiessen, Peter
1927- .. **CLC 5, 7, 11, 32, 64; DAM NOV**
See also AAYA 6; BEST 90:4; CA 9-12R;
CANR 21, 50; DLB 6, 173; MTCW; SATA
27

Maturin, Charles Robert
1780(?)-1824 .... **NCLC 6**
See also DLB 178

Matute (Ausejo), Ana Maria
1925- .... **CLC 11**
See also CA 89-92; MTCW

Maugham, W. S.
See Maugham, W(illiam) Somerset

Maugham, W(illiam) Somerset
1874-1965 .... **CLC 1, 11, 15, 67, 93; DA;**
DAB; DAC; DAM DRAM, MST, NOV;
SSC 8; WLC
See also CA 5-8R; 25-28R; CANR 40; CDBLB
1914-1945; DLB 10, 36, 77, 100, 162;
MTCW; SATA 54

Maugham, William Somerset
See Maugham, W(illiam) Somerset

Maupassant, (Henri Rene Albert) Guy de
1850-1893 .... **NCLC 1, 42; DA; DAB;**
DAC; DAM MST; SSC 1; WLC
See also DLB 123

Maupin, Armistead
1944- .... **CLC 95; DAM POP**
See also CA 125; 130; CANR 58; INT
130

Maurhut, Richard
See Traven, B.

Mauriac, Claude 1914-1996 .... **CLC 9**
See also CA 89-92; 152; DLB 83

Mauriac, Francois (Charles)
1885-1970 .... **CLC 4, 9, 56; SSC 24**
See also CA 25-28; CAP 2; DLB 65; MTCW

Mavor, Osborne Henry 1888-1951
See Bridie, James
See also CA 104

Maxwell, William (Keepers, Jr.)
1908- .... **CLC 19**
See also CA 93-96; CANR 54; DLBY 80; INT
93-96

May, Elaine 1932- .... **CLC 16**
See also CA 124; 142; DLB 44

Mayakovski, Vladimir (Vladimirovich)
1893-1930 .... **TCLC 4, 18**
See also CA 104; 158

Mayhew, Henry 1812-1887 .... **NCLC 31**
See also DLB 18, 55

Mayle, Peter 1939(?)- .... **CLC 89**
See also CA 139

Maynard, Joyce 1953- .... **CLC 23**
See also CA 111; 129

Mayne, William (James Carter)
1928- .... **CLC 12**
See also AAYA 20; CA 9-12R; CANR 37; CLR
25; JRDA; MAICYA; SAAS 11; SATA 6,
68

Mayo, Jim
See L'Amour, Louis (Dearborn)

Maysles, Albert 1926- .... **CLC 16**
See also CA 29-32R

Maysles, David 1932- .... **CLC 16**

Mazer, Norma Fox 1931- .... **CLC 26**
See also AAYA 5; CA 69-72; CANR 12, 32;
CLR 23; JRDA; MAICYA; SAAS 1; SATA
24, 67

Mazzini, Guiseppe 1805-1872 .... **NCLC 34**

McAuley, James Phillip
1917-1976 .... **CLC 45**
See also CA 97-100

McBain, Ed
See Hunter, Evan

McBrien, William Augustine
1930- .... **CLC 44**
See also CA 107

McCaffrey, Anne (Inez)
1926- .... **CLC 17; DAM NOV, POP**
See also AAYA 6; AITN 2; BEST 89:2; CA
25-28R; CANR 15, 35, 55; DLB 8;
JRDA; MAICYA; MTCW; SAAS 11;
SATA 8, 70

McCall, Nathan 1955(?)- .... **CLC 86**
See also CA 146

McCann, Arthur
See Campbell, John W(ood, Jr.)

McCann, Edson
See Pohl, Frederik

McCarthy, Charles, Jr. 1933-
See McCarthy, Cormac
See also CANR 42; DAM POP

McCarthy, Cormac
1933- .... CLC 4, 57, 59, 101
See also McCarthy, Charles, Jr.
See also DLB 6, 143

McCarthy, Mary (Therese)
1912-1989 .... CLC 1, 3, 5, 14, 24, 39, 59;
SSC 24
See also CA 5-8R; 129; CANR 16, 50; DLB 2;
DLBY 81; INT CANR-16; MTCW

McCartney, (James) Paul 1942- CLC 12, 35
See also CA 146

McCauley, Stephen (D.) 1955- .... CLC 50
See also CA 141

McClure, Michael (Thomas)
1932- .... CLC 6, 10
See also CA 21-24R; CANR 17, 46; DLB 16

McCorkle, Jill (Collins) 1958- .... CLC 51
See also CA 121; DLBY 87

McCourt, James 1941- .... CLC 5
See also CA 57-60

McCoy, Horace (Stanley)
1897-1955 .... TCLC 28
See also CA 108; 155; DLB 9

McCrae, John 1872-1918 .... TCLC 12
See also CA 109; DLB 92

McCreigh, James
See Pohl, Frederik

McCullers, (Lula) Carson (Smith)
1917-1967 ..... CLC 1, 4, 10, 12, 48, 100;
DA; DAB; DAC; DAM MST, NOV; SSC
9, 24; WLC
See also AAYA 21; CA 5-8R; 25-28R;
CABS 1, 3; CANR 18; CDALB 1941-
1968; DLB 2, 7, 173; MTCW; SATA
27

McCulloch, John Tyler
See Burroughs, Edgar Rice

McCullough, Colleen
1938(?)- .... CLC 27; DAM NOV, POP
See also CA 81-84; CANR 17, 46; MTCW

McDermott, Alice 1953- .... CLC 90
See also CA 109; CANR 40

McElroy, Joseph 1930- .... CLC 5, 47
See also CA 17-20R

McEwan, Ian (Russell)
1948- .... CLC 13, 66; DAM NOV
See also BEST 90:4; CA 61-64; CANR 14, 41;
DLB 14; MTCW

McFadden, David 1940- .... CLC 48
See also CA 104; DLB 60; INT 104

McFarland, Dennis 1950- .... CLC 65

McGahern, John
1934- .... CLC 5, 9, 48; SSC 17
See also CA 17-20R; CANR 29; DLB 14;
MTCW

McGinley, Patrick (Anthony)
1937- .... CLC 41
See also CA 120; 127; CANR 56; INT 127

McGinley, Phyllis 1905-1978 .... CLC 14
See also CA 9-12R; 77-80; CANR 19; DLB
11, 48; SATA 2, 44; SATA-Obit 24

McGinniss, Joe 1942- .... CLC 32
See also AITN 2; BEST 89:2; CA 25-28R;
CANR 26; INT CANR-26

McGivern, Maureen Daly
See Daly, Maureen

McGrath, Patrick 1950- .... CLC 55
See also CA 136

McGrath, Thomas (Matthew)
1916-1990 ...... CLC 28, 59; DAM POET
See also CA 9-12R; 132; CANR 6, 33; MTCW;
SATA 41; SATA-Obit 66

McGuane, Thomas (Francis III)
1939- .... CLC 3, 7, 18, 45
See also AITN 2; CA 49-52; CANR 5, 24, 49;
DLB 2; DLBY 80; INT CANR-24; MTCW

McGuckian, Medbh 1950- ..... CLC 48; DAM
POET
See also CA 143; DLB 40

McHale, Tom 1942(?)-1982 .... CLC 3, 5
See also AITN 1; CA 77-80; 106

McIlvanney, William 1936- .... CLC 42
See also CA 25-28R; CANR 61; DLB 14

McIlwraith, Maureen Mollie Hunter
See Hunter, Mollie
See also SATA 2

McInerney, Jay
1955- .... CLC 34; DAM POP
See also AAYA 18; CA 116; 123; CANR 45;
INT 123

McIntyre, Vonda N(eel) 1948- .... CLC 18
See also CA 81-84; CANR 17, 34; MTCW

McKay, Claude ... TCLC 7, 41; BLC; DAB;
PC 2
See also McKay, Festus Claudius
See also DLB 4, 45, 51, 117

McKay, Festus Claudius 1889-1948
See McKay, Claude
See also BW 1; CA 104; 124; DA; DAC;
DAM MST, MULT, NOV, POET; MTCW;
WLC

McKuen, Rod 1933- .... CLC 1, 3
See also AITN 1; CA 41-44R; CANR 40

McLoughlin, R. B.
See Mencken, H(enry) L(ouis)

McLuhan, (Herbert) Marshall
1911-1980 .... CLC 37, 83
See also CA 9-12R; 102; CANR 12, 34, 61;
DLB 88; INT CANR-12; MTCW

McMillan, Terry (L.)
1951- .. CLC 50, 61; DAM MULT, NOV,
POP
See also AAYA 21; BW 2; CA 140; CANR 60

McMurtry, Larry (Jeff)
1936- .... CLC 2, 3, 7, 11, 27, 44; DAM
NOV, POP
See also AAYA 15; AITN 2; BEST 89:2;
CA 5-8R; CANR 19, 43; CDALB 1968-
1988; DLB 2, 143; DLBY 80, 87;
MTCW

McNally, T. M. 1961- .... CLC 82

McNally, Terrence
1939- .... CLC 4, 7, 41, 91; DAM DRAM
See also CA 45-48; CANR 2, 56; DLB 7

McNamer, Deirdre 1950- .... CLC 70

McNeile, Herman Cyril 1888-1937
See Sapper
See also DLB 77

McNickle, (William) D'Arcy
1904-1977 .... CLC 89; DAM MULT
See also CA 9-12R; 85-88; CANR 5, 45; DLB
175; NNAL; SATA-Obit 22

McPhee, John (Angus) 1931- .... CLC 36
See also BEST 90:1; CA 65-68; CANR 20, 46;
MTCW

McPherson, James Alan 1943- ... CLC 19, 77
See also BW 1; CA 25-28R; CAAS 17; CANR
24; DLB 38; MTCW

McPherson, William (Alexander)
1933- .... CLC 34
See also CA 69-72; CANR 28; INT CANR-
28

Mead, Margaret 1901-1978 .... CLC 37
See also AITN 1; CA 1-4R; 81-84; CANR 4;
MTCW; SATA-Obit 20

Meaker, Marijane (Agnes) 1927-
See Kerr, M. E.
See also CA 107; CANR 37; INT 107; JRDA;
MAICYA; MTCW; SATA 20, 61

Medoff, Mark (Howard)
1940- .... CLC 6, 23; DAM DRAM
See also AITN 1; CA 53-56; CANR 5; DLB 7;
INT CANR-5

Medvedev, P. N.
See Bakhtin, Mikhail Mikhailovich

Meged, Aharon
See Megged, Aharon

Meged, Aron
See Megged, Aharon

Megged, Aharon 1920- .... CLC 9
See also CA 49-52; CAAS 13; CANR 1

Mehta, Ved (Parkash) 1934- .... **CLC 37**
See also CA 1-4R; CANR 2, 23; MTCW

Melanter
See Blackmore, R(ichard) D(oddridge)

Melikow, Loris
See Hofmannsthal, Hugo von

Melmoth, Sebastian
See Wilde, Oscar (Fingal O'Flahertie Wills)

Meltzer, Milton 1915- .... **CLC 26**
See also AAYA 8; CA 13-16R; CANR 38; CLR
13; DLB 61; JRDA; MAICYA; SAAS 1;
SATA 1, 50, 80

Melville, Herman
1819-1891 ..... **NCLC 3, 12, 29, 45, 49;**
DA; DAB; DAC; DAM MST, NOV; SSC
1, 17; WLC
See also CDALB 1640-1865; DLB 3, 74; SATA
59

Menander
c. 342B.C.-c. 292B.C. .... **CMLC 9; DAM**
DRAM; DC 3
See also DLB 176

Mencken, H(enry) L(ouis)
1880-1956 .... **TCLC 13**
See also CA 105; 125; CDALB 1917-1929;
DLB 11, 29, 63, 137; MTCW

Mendelsohn, Jane 1965(?)- .... **CLC 99**
See also CA 154

Mercer, David 1928-1980 .... **CLC 5; DAM**
DRAM
See also CA 9-12R; 102; CANR 23; DLB 13;
MTCW

Merchant, Paul
See Ellison, Harlan (Jay)

Meredith, George
1828-1909 ... **TCLC 17, 43; DAM POET**
See also CA 117; 153; CDBLB 1832-1890;
DLB 18, 35, 57, 159

Meredith, William (Morris)
1919- .... **CLC 4, 13, 22, 55; DAM POET**
See also CA 9-12R; CAAS 14; CANR 6, 40;
DLB 5

Merezhkovsky, Dmitry Sergeyevich
1865-1941 .... **TCLC 29**

Merimee, Prosper 1803-1870 ... **NCLC 6, 65;**
SSC 7
See also DLB 119

Merkin, Daphne 1954- .... **CLC 44**
See also CA 123

Merlin, Arthur
See Blish, James (Benjamin)

Merrill, James (Ingram)
1926-1995 **CLC 2, 3, 6, 8, 13, 18, 34, 91;**
DAM POET
See also CA 13-16R; 147; CANR 10, 49; DLB
5, 165; DLBY 85; INT CANR-10; MTCW

Merriman, Alex
See Silverberg, Robert

Merritt, E. B.
See Waddington, Miriam

Merton, Thomas
1915-1968 ... **CLC 1, 3, 11, 34, 83; PC 10**
See also CA 5-8R; 25-28R; CANR 22, 53; DLB
48; DLBY 81; MTCW

Merwin, W(illiam) S(tanley)
1927- ... **CLC 1, 2, 3, 5, 8, 13, 18, 45, 88;**
DAM POET
See also CA 13-16R; CANR 15, 51; DLB 5,
169; INT CANR-15; MTCW

Metcalf, John 1938- .... **CLC 37**
See also CA 113; DLB 60

Metcalf, Suzanne
See Baum, L(yman) Frank

Mew, Charlotte (Mary)
1870-1928 .... **TCLC 8**
See also CA 105; DLB 19, 135

Mewshaw, Michael 1943- .... **CLC 9**
See also CA 53-56; CANR 7, 47; DLBY
80

Meyer, June
See Jordan, June

Meyer, Lynn
See Slavitt, David R(ytman)

Meyer-Meyrink, Gustav 1868-1932
See Meyrink, Gustav
See also CA 117

Meyers, Jeffrey 1939- .... **CLC 39**
See also CA 73-76; CANR 54; DLB
111

Meynell, Alice (Christina Gertrude Thompson)
1847-1922 .... **TCLC 6**
See also CA 104; DLB 19, 98

Meyrink, Gustav .... **TCLC 21**
See also Meyer-Meyrink, Gustav
See also DLB 81

Michaels, Leonard
1933- .... **CLC 6, 25; SSC 16**
See also CA 61-64; CANR 21, 62; DLB 130;
MTCW

Michaux, Henri 1899-1984 .... **CLC 8, 19**
See also CA 85-88; 114

Micheaux, Oscar 1884-1951 .... **TCLC 76**
See also DLB 50

Michelangelo 1475-1564 .... **LC 12**

Michelet, Jules 1798-1874 .... **NCLC 31**

Michener, James A(lbert)
1907(?)-1997 .... **CLC 1, 5, 11, 29, 60;**
DAM NOV, POP
See also AITN 1; BEST 90:1; CA 5-8R; CANR
21, 45; DLB 6; MTCW

Mickiewicz, Adam 1798-1855 .... **NCLC 3**

Middleton, Christopher 1926- .... **CLC 13**
See also CA 13-16R; CANR 29, 54; DLB 40

Middleton, Richard (Barham)
1882-1911 .... **TCLC 56**
See also DLB 156

Middleton, Stanley 1919- .... **CLC 7, 38**
See also CA 25-28R; CAAS 23; CANR 21, 46;
DLB 14

Middleton, Thomas
1580-1627 .. **LC 33; DAM DRAM, MST;**
DC 5
See also DLB 58

Migueis, Jose Rodrigues 1901- .... **CLC 10**

Mikszath, Kalman 1847-1910 .... **TCLC 31**

Miles, Jack .... **CLC 100**

Miles, Josephine (Louise)
1911-1985 .... **CLC 1, 2, 14, 34, 39; DAM**
POET
See also CA 1-4R; 116; CANR 2, 55; DLB 48

Militant
See Sandburg, Carl (August)

Mill, John Stuart 1806-1873 .... **NCLC 11, 58**
See also CDBLB 1832-1890; DLB 55

Millar, Kenneth 1915-1983 .... **CLC 14; DAM**
POP
See also Macdonald, Ross
See also CA 9-12R; 110; CANR 16; DLB 2;
DLBD 6; DLBY 83; MTCW

Millay, E. Vincent
See Millay, Edna St. Vincent

Millay, Edna St. Vincent
1892-1950 .... **TCLC 4, 49; DA; DAB;**
DAC; DAM MST, POET; PC 6; WLCS
See also CA 104; 130; CDALB 1917-1929;
DLB 45; MTCW

Miller, Arthur
1915- ... **CLC 1, 2, 6, 10, 15, 26, 47, 78;**
DA; DAB; DAC; DAM DRAM, MST;
DC 1; WLC
See also AAYA 15; AITN 1; CA 1-4R; CABS
3; CANR 2, 30, 54; CDALB 1941-1968;
DLB 7; MTCW

Miller, Henry (Valentine)
1891-1980 ..... **CLC 1, 2, 4, 9, 14, 43, 84;**
DA; DAB; DAC; DAM MST, NOV;
WLC
See also CA 9-12R; 97-100; CANR 33;
CDALB 1929-1941; DLB 4, 9; DLBY 80;
MTCW

Miller, Jason 1939(?)- .... **CLC 2**
See also AITN 1; CA 73-76; DLB 7

Miller, Sue
1943- .... **CLC 44; DAM POP**
See also BEST 90:3; CA 139; CANR 59; DLB
143

Miller, Walter M(ichael, Jr.)
1923- .... CLC **4, 30**
See also CA 85-88; DLB 8

Millett, Kate 1934- .... CLC **67**
See also AITN 1; CA 73-76; CANR 32, 53;
MTCW

Millhauser, Steven 1943- .... CLC **21, 54**
See also CA 110; 111; DLB 2; INT 111

Millin, Sarah Gertrude 1889-1968 ... CLC **49**
See also CA 102; 93-96

Milne, A(lan) A(lexander)
1882-1956 .. TCLC **6**; DAB; DAC; DAM
MST
See also CA 104; 133; CLR 1, 26; DLB 10,
77, 100, 160; MAICYA; MTCW; YABC 1

Milner, Ron(ald)
1938- .... CLC **56**; BLC; DAM MULT
See also AITN 1; BW 1; CA 73-76; CANR 24;
DLB 38; MTCW

Milnes, Richard Monckton
1809-1885 .... NCLC **61**
See also DLB 32, 184

Milosz, Czeslaw
1911- ... CLC **5, 11, 22, 31, 56, 82**; DAM
MST, POET; PC **8**; WLCS
See also CA 81-84; CANR 23, 51; MTCW

Milton, John 1608-1674 ..... LC **9**; DA; DAB;
DAC; DAM MST, POET; PC **19**; WLC
See also CDBLB 1660-1789; DLB 131, 151

Min, Anchee 1957- .... CLC **86**
See also CA 146

Minehaha, Cornelius
See Wedekind, (Benjamin) Frank(lin)

Miner, Valerie 1947- .... CLC **40**
See also CA 97-100; CANR 59

Minimo, Duca
See D'Annunzio, Gabriele

Minot, Susan 1956- .... CLC **44**
See also CA 134

Minus, Ed 1938- .... CLC **39**

Miranda, Javier
See Bioy Casares, Adolfo

Mirbeau, Octave 1848-1917 .... TCLC **55**
See also DLB 123

Miro (Ferrer), Gabriel (Francisco Victor)
1879-1930 .... TCLC **5**
See also CA 104

Mishima, Yukio
1925-1970 CLC **2, 4, 6, 9, 27**; DC **1**; SSC
4
See also Hiraoka, Kimitake
See also DLB 182

Mistral, Frederic 1830-1914 .... TCLC **51**
See also CA 122

Mistral, Gabriela .... TCLC **2**; HLC
See also Godoy Alcayaga, Lucila

Mistry, Rohinton 1952- .... CLC **71**; DAC
See also CA 141

Mitchell, Clyde
See Ellison, Harlan (Jay); Silverberg, Robert

Mitchell, James Leslie 1901-1935
See Gibbon, Lewis Grassic
See also CA 104; DLB 15

Mitchell, Joni 1943- .... CLC **12**
See also CA 112

Mitchell, Joseph (Quincy)
1908-1996 .... CLC **98**
See also CA 77-80; 152; DLBY 96

Mitchell, Margaret (Munnerlyn)
1900-1949 .. TCLC **11**; DAM NOV, POP
See also CA 109; 125; CANR 55; DLB 9;
MTCW

Mitchell, Peggy
See Mitchell, Margaret (Munnerlyn)

Mitchell, S(ilas) Weir
1829-1914 .... TCLC **36**

Mitchell, W(illiam) O(rmond)
1914- .... CLC **25**; DAC; DAM MST
See also CA 77-80; CANR 15, 43; DLB
88

Mitford, Mary Russell 1787-1855 ... NCLC **4**
See also DLB 110, 116

Mitford, Nancy 1904-1973 .... CLC **44**
See also CA 9-12R

Miyamoto, Yuriko 1899-1951 .... TCLC **37**
See also DLB 180

Miyazawa Kenji 1896-1933 .... TCLC **76**
See also CA 157

Mizoguchi, Kenji 1898-1956 .... TCLC **72**

Mo, Timothy (Peter) 1950(?)- .... CLC **46**
See also CA 117; MTCW

Modarressi, Taghi (M.) 1931- .... CLC **44**
See also CA 121; 134; INT 134

Modiano, Patrick (Jean) 1945- .... CLC **18**
See also CA 85-88; CANR 17, 40; DLB
83

Moerck, Paal
See Roelvaag, O(le) E(dvart)

Mofolo, Thomas (Mokopu)
1875(?)-1948 ...... TCLC **22**; BLC; DAM
MULT
See also CA 121; 153

Mohr, Nicholasa
1935- .... CLC **12**; DAM MULT; HLC
See also AAYA 8; CA 49-52; CANR 1, 32;
CLR 22; DLB 145; HW; JRDA; SAAS 8;
SATA 8

Mojtabai, A(nn) G(race)
1938- .... CLC **5, 9, 15, 29**
See also CA 85-88

Moliere
1622-1673 .... LC **28**; DA; DAB; DAC;
DAM DRAM, MST; WLC

Molin, Charles
See Mayne, William (James Carter)

Molnar, Ferenc
1878-1952 .... TCLC **20**; DAM DRAM
See also CA 109; 153

Momaday, N(avarre) Scott
1934- .... CLC **2, 19, 85, 95**; DA; DAB;
DAC; DAM MST, MULT, NOV, POP;
WLCS
See also AAYA 11; CA 25-28R; CANR 14, 34;
DLB 143, 175; INT CANR-14; MTCW;
NNAL; SATA 48; SATA-Brief 30

Monette, Paul 1945-1995 .... CLC **82**
See also CA 139; 147

Monroe, Harriet 1860-1936........... TCLC **12**
See also CA 109; DLB 54, 91

Monroe, Lyle
See Heinlein, Robert A(nson)

Montagu, Elizabeth 1917- .... NCLC **7**
See also CA 9-12R

Montagu, Mary (Pierrepont) Wortley
1689-1762 .... LC **9**; PC **16**
See also DLB 95, 101

Montagu, W. H.
See Coleridge, Samuel Taylor

Montague, John (Patrick)
1929- .... CLC **13, 46**
See also CA 9-12R; CANR 9; DLB 40; MTCW

Montaigne, Michel (Eyquem) de
1533-1592 .... LC **8**; DA; DAB; DAC;
DAM MST; WLC

Montale, Eugenio
1896-1981 .... CLC **7, 9, 18**; PC **13**
See also CA 17-20R; 104; CANR 30; DLB 114;
MTCW

Montesquieu, Charles-Louis de Secondat
1689-1755 .... LC **7**

Montgomery, (Robert) Bruce 1921-1978
See Crispin, Edmund
See also CA 104

Montgomery, L(ucy) M(aud)
1874-1942 ...... TCLC **51**; DAC; DAM
MST
See also AAYA 12; CA 108; 137; CLR 8; DLB
92; DLBD 14; JRDA; MAICYA; YABC 1

Montgomery, Marion H., Jr. 1925- .... CLC **7**
See also AITN 1; CA 1-4R; CANR 3, 48; DLB 6

Montgomery, Max
See Davenport, Guy (Mattison, Jr.)

Montherlant, Henry (Milon) de
1896-1972 .... **CLC 8, 19; DAM DRAM**
See also CA 85-88; 37-40R; DLB 72; MTCW

Monty Python
See Chapman, Graham; Cleese, John (Marwood); Gilliam, Terry (Vance); Idle, Eric; Jones, Terence Graham Parry; Palin, Michael (Edward)
See also AAYA 7

Moodie, Susanna (Strickland)
1803-1885 .... **NCLC 14**
See also DLB 99

Mooney, Edward 1951-
See Mooney, Ted
See also CA 130

Mooney, Ted .... **CLC 25**
See also Mooney, Edward

Moorcock, Michael (John)
1939- .... **CLC 5, 27, 58**
See also CA 45-48; CAAS 5; CANR 2, 17, 38; DLB 14; MTCW; SATA 93

Moore, Brian
1921- .... **CLC 1, 3, 5, 7, 8, 19, 32, 90; DAB; DAC; DAM MST**
See also CA 1-4R; CANR 1, 25, 42; MTCW

Moore, Edward
See Muir, Edwin

Moore, George Augustus
1852-1933 .... **TCLC 7; SSC 19**
See also CA 104; DLB 10, 18, 57, 135

Moore, Lorrie .... **CLC 39, 45, 68**
See also Moore, Marie Lorena

Moore, Marianne (Craig)
1887-1972 .... **CLC 1, 2, 4, 8, 10, 13, 19, 47; DA; DAB; DAC; DAM MST, POET; PC 4; WLCS**
See also CA 1-4R; 33-36R; CANR 3, 61; CDALB 1929-1941; DLB 45; DLBD 7; MTCW; SATA 20

Moore, Marie Lorena 1957-
See Moore, Lorrie
See also CA 116; CANR 39

Moore, Thomas 1779-1852 .... **NCLC 6**
See also DLB 96, 144

Morand, Paul 1888-1976 .... **CLC 41; SSC 22**
See also CA 69-72; DLB 65

Morante, Elsa 1918-1985 .... **CLC 8, 47**
See also CA 85-88; 117; CANR 35; DLB 177; MTCW

Moravia, Alberto
1907-1990 ... **CLC 2, 7, 11, 27, 46; SSC 26**
See also Pincherle, Alberto
See also DLB 177

More, Hannah 1745-1833 .... **NCLC 27**
See also DLB 107, 109, 116, 158

More, Henry 1614-1687 .... **LC 9**
See also DLB 126

More, Sir Thomas 1478-1535 .... **LC 10, 32**

Moreas, Jean .... **TCLC 18**
See also Papadiamantopoulos, Johannes

Morgan, Berry 1919- .... **CLC 6**
See also CA 49-52; DLB 6

Morgan, Claire
See Highsmith, (Mary) Patricia

Morgan, Edwin (George)
1920- .... **CLC 31**
See also CA 5-8R; CANR 3, 43; DLB 27

Morgan, (George) Frederick
1922- .... **CLC 23**
See also CA 17-20R; CANR 21

Morgan, Harriet
See Mencken, H(enry) L(ouis)

Morgan, Jane
See Cooper, James Fenimore

Morgan, Janet 1945- .... **CLC 39**
See also CA 65-68

Morgan, Lady 1776(?)-1859 .... **NCLC 29**
See also DLB 116, 158

Morgan, Robin 1941- .... **CLC 2**
See also CA 69-72; CANR 29; MTCW; SATA 80

Morgan, Scott
See Kuttner, Henry

Morgan, Seth 1949(?)-1990 .... **CLC 65**
See also CA 132

Morgenstern, Christian
1871-1914 .... **TCLC 8**
See also CA 105

Morgenstern, S.
See Goldman, William (W.)

Moricz, Zsigmond 1879-1942 .... **TCLC 33**

Morike, Eduard (Friedrich)
1804-1875 .... **NCLC 10**
See also DLB 133

Mori Ogai .... **TCLC 14**
See also Mori Rintaro

Mori Rintaro 1862-1922
See Mori Ogai
See also CA 110

Moritz, Karl Philipp 1756-1793 .... **LC 2**
See also DLB 94

Morland, Peter Henry
See Faust, Frederick (Schiller)

Morren, Theophil
See Hofmannsthal, Hugo von

Morris, Bill 1952- .... **CLC 76**

Morris, Julian
See West, Morris L(anglo)

Morris, Steveland Judkins 1950(?)-
See Wonder, Stevie
See also CA 111

Morris, William 1834-1896 .... **NCLC 4**
See also CDBLB 1832-1890; DLB 18, 35, 57, 156, 178, 184

Morris, Wright 1910- ...... **CLC 1, 3, 7, 18, 37**
See also CA 9-12R; CANR 21; DLB 2; DLBY 81; MTCW

Morrison, Arthur 1863-1945 .... **TCLC 72**
See also CA 120; 157; DLB 70, 135

Morrison, Chloe Anthony Wofford
See Morrison, Toni

Morrison, James Douglas 1943-1971
See Morrison, Jim
See also CA 73-76; CANR 40

Morrison, Jim .... **CLC 17**
See also Morrison, James Douglas

Morrison, Toni
1931- ... **CLC 4, 10, 22, 55, 81, 87; BLC; DA; DAB; DAC; DAM MST, MULT, NOV, POP**
See also AAYA 1, 22; BW 2; CA 29-32R; CANR 27, 42; CDALB 1968-1988; DLB 6, 33, 143; DLBY 81; MTCW; SATA 57

Morrison, Van 1945- .... **CLC 21**
See also CA 116

Morrissy, Mary 1958- .... **CLC 99**

Mortimer, John (Clifford)
1923- .. **CLC 28, 43; DAM DRAM, POP**
See also CA 13-16R; CANR 21; CDBLB 1960 to Present; DLB 13; INT CANR-21; MTCW

Mortimer, Penelope (Ruth) 1918- .... **CLC 5**
See also CA 57-60; CANR 45

Morton, Anthony
See Creasey, John

Mosca, Gaetano 1858-1941 .... **TCLC 75**

Mosher, Howard Frank 1943- .... **CLC 62**
See also CA 139

Mosley, Nicholas 1923- .... **CLC 43, 70**
See also CA 69-72; CANR 41, 60; DLB 14

Mosley, Walter
1952- .... **CLC 97; DAM MULT, POP**
See also AAYA 17; BW 2; CA 142; CANR 57

Moss, Howard 1922-1987 **CLC 7, 14, 45, 50; DAM POET**
See also CA 1-4R; 123; CANR 1, 44; DLB 5

Mossgiel, Rab
See Burns, Robert

Motion, Andrew (Peter) 1952- .... **CLC 47**
See also CA 146; DLB 40

Motley, Willard (Francis)
1909-1965 .... **CLC 18**
See also BW 1; CA 117; 106; DLB 76, 143

Motoori, Norinaga 1730-1801 .... **NCLC 45**

Mott, Michael (Charles Alston)
1930- .... **CLC 15, 34**
See also CA 5-8R; CAAS 7; CANR 7, 29

Mountain Wolf Woman
1884-1960 .... **CLC 92**
See also CA 144; NNAL

Moure, Erin 1955- .... **CLC 88**
See also CA 113; DLB 60

Mowat, Farley (McGill)
1921- .... **CLC 26; DAC; DAM MST**
See also AAYA 1; CA 1-4R; CANR 4, 24, 42;
CLR 20; DLB 68; INT CANAR-24; JRDA;
MAICYA; MTCW; SATA 3, 55

Moyers, Bill 1934- .... **CLC 74**
See also AITN 2; CA 61-64; CANR 31, 52

Mphahlele, Es'kia
See Mphahlele, Ezekiel
See also DLB 125

Mphahlele, Ezekiel 1919-....... **CLC 25; BLC;
DAM MULT**
See also Mphahlele, Es'kia
See also BW 2; CA 81-84; CANR 26

Mqhayi, S(amuel) E(dward) K(rune Loliwe)
1875-1945 .... **TCLC 25; BLC; DAM
MULT**
See also CA 153

Mrozek, Slawomir 1930-................ **CLC 3, 13**
See also CA 13-16R; CAAS 10; CANR 29;
MTCW

Mrs. Belloc-Lowndes
See Lowndes, Marie Adelaide (Belloc)

Mtwa, Percy (?)-................................. **CLC 47**

Mueller, Lisel 1924- .... **CLC 13, 51**
See also CA 93-96; DLB 105

Muir, Edwin 1887-1959 .... **TCLC 2**
See also CA 104; DLB 20, 100

Muir, John 1838-1914 .... **TCLC 28**

Mujica Lainez, Manuel 1910-1984 ... **CLC 31**
See also Lainez, Manuel Mujica
See also CA 81-84; 112; CANR 32; HW

Mukherjee, Bharati 1940- ..... **CLC 53; DAM
NOV**
See also BEST 89:2; CA 107; CANR 45; DLB
60; MTCW

Muldoon, Paul 1951- .... **CLC 32, 72; DAM
POET**
See also CA 113; 129; CANR 52; DLB 40;
INT 129

Mulisch, Harry 1927- .... **CLC 42**
See also CA 9-12R; CANR 6, 26, 56

Mull, Martin 1943- .... **CLC 17**
See also CA 105

Mulock, Dinah Maria
See Craik, Dinah Maria (Mulock)

Munford, Robert 1737(?)-1783 .... **LC 5**
See also DLB 31

Mungo, Raymond 1946-.................... **CLC 72**
See also CA 49-52; CANR 2

Munro, Alice 1931-.... **CLC 6, 10, 19, 50, 95;
DAC; DAM MST, NOV; SSC 3;
WLCS**
See also AITN 2; CA 33-36R; CANR 33, 53;
DLB 53; MTCW; SATA 29

Munro, H(ector) H(ugh) 1870-1916
See Saki
See also CA 104; 130; CDBLB 1890-1914;
DA; DAB; DAC; DAM MST, NOV; DLB
34, 162; MTCW; WLC

Murasaki, Lady .... **CMLC 1**

Murdoch, (Jean) Iris
1919- ... **CLC 1, 2, 3, 4, 6, 8, 11, 15, 22,
31, 51; DAB; DAC; DAM MST, NOV**
See also CA 13-16R; CANR 8, 43; CDBLB
1960 to Present; DLB 14; INT CANR-8;
MTCW

Murfree, Mary Noailles
1850-1922 .... **SSC 22**
See also CA 122; DLB 12, 74

Murnau, Friedrich Wilhelm
See Plumpe, Friedrich Wilhelm

Murphy, Richard 1927- .... **CLC 41**
See also CA 29-32R; DLB 40

Murphy, Sylvia 1937- .... **CLC 34**
See also CA 121

Murphy, Thomas (Bernard) 1935- ... **CLC 51**
See also CA 101

Murray, Albert L. 1916- .... **CLC 73**
See also BW 2; CA 49-52; CANR 26, 52; DLB
38

Murray, Judith Sargent
1751-1820 .... **NCLC 63**
See also DLB 37

Murray, Les(lie) A(llan)
1938- .... **CLC 40; DAM POET**
See also CA 21-24R; CANR 11, 27, 56

Murry, J. Middleton
See Murry, John Middleton

Murry, John Middleton
1889-1957 .... **TCLC 16**
See also CA 118; DLB 149

Musgrave, Susan 1951- .... **CLC 13, 54**
See also CA 69-72; CANR 45

Musil, Robert (Edler von)
1880-1942 .... **TCLC 12, 68; SSC 18**
See also CA 109; CANR 55; DLB 81,
124

Muske, Carol 1945- .... **CLC 90**
See also Muske-Dukes, Carol (Anne)

Muske-Dukes, Carol (Anne) 1945-
See Muske, Carol
See also CA 65-68; CANR 32

Musset, (Louis Charles) Alfred de
1810-1857 .... **NCLC 7**

My Brother's Brother
See Chekhov, Anton (Pavlovich)

Myers, L(eopold) H(amilton)
1881-1944 .... **TCLC 59**
See also CA 157; DLB 15

Myers, Walter Dean 1937-..... **CLC 35; BLC;
DAM MULT, NOV**
See also AAYA 4; BW 2; CA 33-36R; CANR
20, 42; CLR 4, 16, 35; DLB 33; INT CANR-
20; JRDA; MAICYA; SAAS 2; SATA 41,
71; SATA-Brief 27

Myers, Walter M.
See Myers, Walter Dean

Myles, Symon
See Follett, Ken(neth Martin)

Nabokov, Vladimir (Vladimirovich)
1899-1977 .. **CLC 1, 2, 3, 6, 8, 11, 15, 23,
44, 46, 64; DA; DAB; DAC; DAM MST,
NOV; SSC 11; WLC**
See also CA 5-8R; 69-72; CANR 20; CDALB
1941-1968; DLB 2; DLBD 3; DLBY 80, 91;
MTCW

Nagai Kafu 1879-1959 .... **TCLC 51**
See also Nagai Sokichi
See also DLB 180

Nagai Sokichi 1879-1959
See Nagai Kafu
See also CA 117

Nagy, Laszlo 1925-1978 .... **CLC 7**
See also CA 129; 112

Naipaul, Shiva(dhar Srinivasa)
1945-1985 .... **CLC 32, 39; DAM NOV**
See also CA 110; 112; 116; CANR 33; DLB
157; DLBY 85; MTCW

Naipaul, V(idiadhar) S(urajprasad)
1932- .... **CLC 4, 7, 9, 13, 18, 37, 105;
DAB; DAC; DAM MST, NOV**
See also CA 1-4R; CANR 1, 33, 51; CDBLB
1960 to Present; DLB 125; DLBY 85;
MTCW

Nakos, Lilika 1899(?)- .... **CLC 29**

Narayan, R(asipuram) K(rishnaswami)
1906- .. **CLC 7, 28, 47; DAM NOV; SSC
25**
See also CA 81-84; CANR 33, 61; MTCW;
SATA 62

Nash, (Frediric) Ogden
1902-1971 .... **CLC 23; DAM POET**
See also CA 13-14; 29-32R; CANR 34, 61;
CAP 1; DLB 11; MAICYA; MTCW; SATA
2, 46

Nathan, Daniel
See Dannay, Frederic

Nathan, George Jean 1882-1958 .... **TCLC 18**
See also Hatteras, Owen
See also CA 114; DLB 137

Natsume, Kinnosuke 1867-1916
See Natsume, Soseki
See also CA 104

Natsume, Soseki 1867-1916 .... **TCLC 2, 10**
See also Natsume, Kinnosuke
See also DLB 180

Natti, (Mary) Lee 1919-
See Kingman, Lee
See also CA 5-8R; CANR 2

Naylor, Gloria
1950- .... **CLC 28, 52; BLC; DA; DAC;
DAM MST, MULT, NOV, POP; WLCS**
See also AAYA 6; BW 2; CA 107; CANR 27,
51; DLB 173; MTCW

Neihardt, John Gneisenau
1881-1973 .... **CLC 32**
See also CA 13-14; CAP 1; DLB 9, 54

Nekrasov, Nikolai Alekseevich
1821-1878 .... **NCLC 11**

Nelligan, Emile 1879-1941 .... **TCLC 14**
See also CA 114; DLB 92

Nelson, Willie 1933- .... **CLC 17**
See also CA 107

Nemerov, Howard (Stanley)
1920-1991 .... **CLC 2, 6, 9, 36; DAM
POET**
See also CA 1-4R; 134; CABS 2; CANR 1,
27, 53; DLB 5, 6; DLBY 83; INT CANR-
27; MTCW

Neruda, Pablo
1904-1973 ...... **CLC 1, 2, 5, 7, 9, 28, 62;
DA; DAB; DAC; DAM MST, MULT,
POET; HLC; PC 4; WLC**
See also CA 19-20; 45-48; CAP 2; HW;
MTCW

Nerval, Gerard de
1808-1855 .... **NCLC 1; PC 13; SSC 18**

Nervo, (Jose) Amado (Ruiz de)
1870-1919 .... **TCLC 11**
See also CA 109; 131; HW

Nessi, Pio Baroja y
See Baroja (y Nessi), Pio

Nestroy, Johann 1801-1862 .... **NCLC 42**
See also DLB 133

Netterville, Luke
See O'Grady, Standish (James)

Neufeld, John (Arthur) 1938- .... **CLC 17**
See also AAYA 11; CA 25-28R; CANR 11, 37,
56; MAICYA; SAAS 3; SATA 6, 81

Neville, Emily Cheney 1919- .... **CLC 12**
See also CA 5-8R; CANR 3, 37; JRDA;
MAICYA; SAAS 2; SATA 1

Newbound, Bernard Slade 1930-
See Slade, Bernard
See also CA 81-84; CANR 49; DAM DRAM

Newby, P(ercy) H(oward)
1918- .... **CLC 2, 13; DAM NOV**
See also CA 5-8R; CANR 32; DLB 15;
MTCW

Newlove, Donald 1928- .... **CLC 6**
See also CA 29-32R; CANR 25

Newlove, John (Herbert) 1938- .... **CLC 14**
See also CA 21-24R; CANR 9, 25

Newman, Charles 1938- .... **CLC 2, 8**
See also CA 21-24R

Newman, Edwin (Harold) 1919- .... **CLC 14**
See also AITN 1; CA 69-72; CANR 5

Newman, John Henry
1801-1890 .... **NCLC 38**
See also DLB 18, 32, 55

Newton, Suzanne 1936- .... **CLC 35**
See also CA 41-44R; CANR 14; JRDA; SATA
5, 77

Nexo, Martin Andersen
1869-1954 .... **TCLC 43**

Nezval, Vitezslav 1900-1958 .... **TCLC 44**
See also CA 123

Ng, Fae Myenne 1957(?)- .... **CLC 81**
See also CA 146

Ngema, Mbongeni 1955- .... **CLC 57**
See also BW 2; CA 143

Ngugi, James T(hiong'o) .... **CLC 3, 7, 13**
See also Ngugi wa Thiong'o

Ngugi wa Thiong'o 1938- ...... **CLC 36; BLC;
DAM MULT, NOV**
See also Ngugi, James T(hiong'o)
See also BW 2; CA 81-84; CANR 27, 58; DLB
125; MTCW

Nichol, B(arrie) P(hillip)
1944-1988 .... **CLC 18**
See also CA 53-56; DLB 53; SATA 66

Nichols, John (Treadwell) 1940- .... **CLC 38**
See also CA 9-12R; CAAS 2; CANR 6; DLBY
82

Nichols, Leigh
See Koontz, Dean R(ay)

Nichols, Peter (Richard)
1927- .... **CLC 5, 36, 65**
See also CA 104; CANR 33; DLB 13;
MTCW

Nicolas, F. R. E.
See Freeling, Nicolas

Niedecker, Lorine 1903-1970 .... **CLC 10, 42;
DAM POET**
See also CA 25-28; CAP 2; DLB 48

Nietzsche, Friedrich (Wilhelm)
1844-1900 .... **TCLC 10, 18, 55**
See also CA 107; 121; DLB 129

Nievo, Ippolito 1831-1861 .... **NCLC 22**

Nightingale, Anne Redmon 1943-
See Redmon, Anne
See also CA 103

Nik. T. O.
See Annensky, Innokenty (Fyodorovich)

Nin, Anais
1903-1977 .... **CLC 1, 4, 8, 11, 14, 60;
DAM NOV, POP; SSC 10**
See also AITN 2; CA 13-16R; 69-72;
CANR 22, 53; DLB 2, 4, 152;
MTCW

Nishiwaki, Junzaburo 1894-1982 .... **PC 15**
See also CA 107

Nissenson, Hugh 1933- .... **CLC 4, 9**
See also CA 17-20R; CANR 27; DLB 28

Niven, Larry .... **CLC 8**
See also Niven, Laurence Van Cott
See also DLB 8

Niven, Laurence Van Cott 1938-
See Niven, Larry
See also CA 21-24R; CAAS 12;
CANR 14, 44; DAM POP; MTCW;
SATA 95

Nixon, Agnes Eckhardt 1927- .... **CLC 21**
See also CA 110

Nizan, Paul 1905-1940 .... **TCLC 40**
See also DLB 72

Nkosi, Lewis 1936- .... **CLC 45; BLC; DAM
MULT**
See also BW 1; CA 65-68; CANR 27; DLB
157

Nodier, (Jean) Charles (Emmanuel)
1780-1844 .... **NCLC 19**
See also DLB 119

Nolan, Christopher 1965- .... **CLC 58**
See also CA 111

Noon, Jeff 1957- .... **CLC 91**
See also CA 148

Norden, Charles
See Durrell, Lawrence (George)

Nordhoff, Charles (Bernard)
1887-1947 .... **TCLC 23**
See also CA 108; DLB 9; SATA 23

Norfolk, Lawrence 1963- .... **CLC 76**
See also CA 144

Norman, Marsha 1947- .... **CLC 28; DAM DRAM**
See also CA 105; CABS 3; CANR 41; DLBY 84

Norris, Frank 1870-1902 .... **SSC 28**
See also Norris, (Benjamin) Frank(lin, Jr.)
See also CDALB 1865-1917; DLB 12, 71

Norris, (Benjamin) Frank(lin, Jr.)
1870-1902 .... **TCLC 24**
See also Norris, Frank
See also CA 110; 160

Norris, Leslie 1921- .... **CLC 14**
See also CA 11-12; CANR 14; CAP 1; DLB 27

North, Andrew
See Norton, Andre

North, Anthony
See Koontz, Dean R(ay)

North, Captain George
See Stevenson, Robert Louis (Balfour)

North, Milou
See Erdrich, Louise

Northrup, B. A.
See Hubbard, L(afayette) Ron(ald)

North Staffs
See Hulme, T(homas) E(rnest)

Norton, Alice Mary
See Norton, Andre
See also MAICYA; SATA 1, 43

Norton, Andre 1912- .... **CLC 12**
See also Norton, Alice Mary
See also AAYA 14; CA 1-4R; CANR 2, 31; DLB 8, 52; JRDA; MTCW; SATA 91

Norton, Caroline 1808-1877 .... **NCLC 47**
See also DLB 21, 159

Norway, Nevil Shute 1899-1960
See Shute, Nevil
See also CA 102; 93-96

Norwid, Cyprian Kamil
1821-1883 .... **NCLC 17**

Nosille, Nabrah
See Ellison, Harlan (Jay)

Nossack, Hans Erich 1901-1978 .... **CLC 6**
See also CA 93-96; 85-88; DLB 69

Nostradamus 1503-1566 .... **LC 27**

Nosu, Chuji
See Ozu, Yasujiro

Notenburg, Eleanora (Genrikhovna) von
See Guro, Elena

Nova, Craig 1945- .... **CLC 7, 31**
See also CA 45-48; CANR 2, 53

Novak, Joseph
See Kosinski, Jerzy (Nikodem)

Novalis 1772-1801 .... **NCLC 13**
See also DLB 90

Novis, Emile
See Weil, Simone (Adolphine)

Nowlan, Alden (Albert)
1933-1983 .... **CLC 15; DAC; DAM MST**
See also CA 9-12R; CANR 5; DLB 53

Noyes, Alfred 1880-1958 .... **TCLC 7**
See also CA 104; DLB 20

Nunn, Kem .... **CLC 34**
See also CA 159

Nye, Robert
1939- .... **CLC 13, 42; DAM NOV**
See also CA 33-36R; CANR 29; DLB 14; MTCW; SATA 6

Nyro, Laura 1947- .... **CLC 17**

Oates, Joyce Carol
1938- ... **CLC 1, 2, 3, 6, 9, 11, 15, 19, 33, 52; DA; DAB; DAC; DAM MST, NOV, POP; SSC 6; WLC**
See also AAYA 15; AITN 1; BEST 89:2; CA 5-8R; CANR 25, 45; CDALB 1968-1988; DLB 2, 5, 130; DLBY 81; INT CANR-25; MTCW

O'Brien, Darcy 1939- .... **CLC 11**
See also CA 21-24R; CANR 8, 59

O'Brien, E. G.
See Clarke, Arthur C(harles)

O'Brien, Edna
1936- .... **CLC 3, 5, 8, 13, 36, 65; DAM NOV; SSC 10**
See also CA 1-4R; CANR 6, 41; CDBLB 1960 to Present; DLB 14; MTCW

O'Brien, Fitz-James 1828-1862 ..... **NCLC 21**
See also DLB 74

O'Brien, Flann .... **CLC 1, 4, 5, 7, 10, 47**
See also O Nuallain, Brian

O'Brien, Richard 1942- .... **CLC 17**
See also CA 124

O'Brien, (William) Tim(othy)
1946- ..... **CLC 7, 19, 40, 103; DAM POP**
See also AAYA 16; CA 85-88; CANR 40, 58; DLB 152; DLBD 9; DLBY 80

Obstfelder, Sigbjoern
1866-1900 .... **TCLC 23**
See also CA 123

O'Casey, Sean
1880-1964 .... **CLC 1, 5, 9, 11, 15, 88; DAB; DAC; DAM DRAM, MST; WLCS**
See also CA 89-92; CANR 62; CDBLB 1914-1945; DLB 10; MTCW

O'Cathasaigh, Sean
See O'Casey, Sean

Ochs, Phil 1940-1976 .... **CLC 17**
See also CA 65-68

O'Connor, Edwin (Greene)
1918-1968 .... **CLC 14**
See also CA 93-96; 25-28R

O'Connor, (Mary) Flannery
1925-1964 ... **CLC 1, 2, 3, 6, 10, 13, 15, 21, 66, 104; DA; DAB; DAC; DAM MST, NOV; SSC 1, 23; WLC**
See also AAYA 7; CA 1-4R; CANR 3, 41; CDALB 1941-1968; DLB 2, 152; DLBD 12; DLBY 80; MTCW

O'Connor, Frank .... **CLC 23; SSC 5**
See also O'Donovan, Michael John
See also DLB 162

O'Dell, Scott 1898-1989 .... **CLC 30**
See also AAYA 3; CA 61-64; 129; CANR 12, 30; CLR 1, 16; DLB 52; JRDA; MAICYA; SATA 12, 60

Odets, Clifford 1906-1963 ..... **CLC 2, 28, 98; DAM DRAM; DC 6**
See also CA 85-88; CANR 62; DLB 7, 26; MTCW

O'Doherty, Brian 1934- .... **CLC 76**
See also CA 105

O'Donnell, K. M.
See Malzberg, Barry N(athaniel)

O'Donnell, Lawrence
See Kuttner, Henry

O'Donovan, Michael John
1903-1966 .... **CLC 14**
See also O'Connor, Frank
See also CA 93-96

Oe, Kenzaburo
1935- ..... **CLC 10, 36, 86; DAM NOV; SSC 20**
See also CA 97-100; CANR 36, 50; DLB 182; DLBY 94; MTCW

O'Faolain, Julia 1932- .... **CLC 6, 19, 47**
See also CA 81-84; CAAS 2; CANR 12, 61; DLB 14; MTCW

O'Faolain, Sean
1900-1991 ... **CLC 1, 7, 14, 32, 70; SSC 13**
See also CA 61-64; 134; CANR 12; DLB 15, 162; MTCW

O'Flaherty, Liam
1896-1984 .... **CLC 5, 34; SSC 6**
See also CA 101; 113; CANR 35; DLB 36, 162; DLBY 84; MTCW

Ogilvy, Gavin
See Barrie, J(ames) M(atthew)

O'Grady, Standish (James)
1846-1928 .... **TCLC 5**
See also CA 104; 157

O'Grady, Timothy 1951- .... **CLC 59**
See also CA 138

O'Hara, Frank
1926-1966 .... **CLC 2, 5, 13, 78; DAM POET**
See also CA 9-12R; 25-28R; CANR 33; DLB 5, 16; MTCW

O'Hara, John (Henry)
1905-1970 .... **CLC 1, 2, 3, 6, 11, 42; DAM NOV; SSC 15**
See also CA 5-8R; 25-28R; CANR 31, 60; CDALB 1929-1941; DLB 9, 86; DLBD 2; MTCW

O Hehir, Diana 1922- .... **CLC 41**
See also CA 93-96

Okigbo, Christopher (Ifenayichukwu)
1932-1967 .... **CLC 25, 84; BLC; DAM MULT, POET; PC 7**
See also BW 1; CA 77-80; DLB 125; MTCW

Okri, Ben 1959- .... **CLC 87**
See also BW 2; CA 130; 138; DLB 157; INT 138

Olds, Sharon 1942- .... **CLC 32, 39, 85; DAM POET**
See also CA 101; CANR 18, 41; DLB 120

Oldstyle, Jonathan
See Irving, Washington

Olesha, Yuri (Karlovich)
1899-1960 .... **CLC 8**
See also CA 85-88

Oliphant, Laurence
1829(?)-1888 .... **NCLC 47**
See also DLB 18, 166

Oliphant, Margaret (Oliphant Wilson)
1828-1897 .... **NCLC 11, 61; SSC 25**
See also DLB 18, 159

Oliver, Mary 1935- .... **CLC 19, 34, 98**
See also CA 21-24R; CANR 9, 43; DLB 5

Olivier, Laurence (Kerr)
1907-1989 .... **CLC 20**
See also CA 111; 150; 129

Olsen, Tillie 1913- ...... **CLC 4, 13; DA; DAB; DAC; DAM MST; SSC 11**
See also CA 1-4R; CANR 1, 43; DLB 28; DLBY 80; MTCW

Olson, Charles (John)
1910-1970 .... **CLC 1, 2, 5, 6, 9, 11, 29; DAM POET; PC 19**
See also CA 13-16; 25-28R; CABS 2; CANR 35, 61; CAP 1; DLB 5, 16; MTCW

Olson, Toby 1937- .... **CLC 28**
See also CA 65-68; CANR 9, 31

Olyesha, Yuri
See Olesha, Yuri (Karlovich)

Ondaatje, (Philip) Michael
1943- .. **CLC 14, 29, 51, 76; DAB; DAC; DAM MST**
See also CA 77-80; CANR 42; DLB 60

Oneal, Elizabeth 1934-
See Oneal, Zibby
See also CA 106; CANR 28; MAICYA; SATA 30, 82

Oneal, Zibby .... **CLC 30**
See also Oneal, Elizabeth
See also AAYA 5; CLR 13; JRDA

O'Neill, Eugene (Gladstone)
1888-1953 .... **TCLC 1, 6, 27, 49; DA; DAB; DAC; DAM DRAM, MST; WLC**
See also AITN 1; CA 110; 132; CDALB 1929-1941; DLB 7; MTCW

Onetti, Juan Carlos 1909-1994 ... **CLC 7, 10; DAM MULT, NOV; SSC 23**
See also CA 85-88; 145; CANR 32; DLB 113; HW; MTCW

O Nuallain, Brian 1911-1966
See O'Brien, Flann
See also CA 21-22; 25-28R; CAP 2

Opie, Amelia 1769-1853 .... **NCLC 65**
See also DLB 116, 159

Oppen, George 1908-1984 ...... **CLC 7, 13, 34**
See also CA 13-16R; 113; CANR 8; DLB 5, 165

Oppenheim, E(dward) Phillips
1866-1946 .... **TCLC 45**
See also CA 111; DLB 70

Origen c. 185-c. 254 .... **CMLC 19**

Orlovitz, Gil 1918-1973 .... **CLC 22**
See also CA 77-80; 45-48; DLB 2, 5

Orris
See Ingelow, Jean

Ortega y Gasset, Jose 1883-1955 .... **TCLC 9; DAM MULT; HLC**
See also CA 106; 130; HW; MTCW

Ortese, Anna Maria 1914- .... **CLC 89**
See also DLB 177

Ortiz, Simon J(oseph)
1941- .... **CLC 45; DAM MULT, POET; PC 17**
See also CA 134; DLB 120, 175; NNAL

Orton, Joe .... **CLC 4, 13, 43; DC 3**
See also Orton, John Kingsley
See also CDBLB 1960 to Present; DLB 13

Orton, John Kingsley 1933-1967
See Orton, Joe
See also CA 85-88; CANR 35; DAM DRAM; MTCW

Orwell, George . **TCLC 2, 6, 15, 31, 51; DAB; WLC**
See also Blair, Eric (Arthur)
See also CDBLB 1945-1960; DLB 15, 98

Osborne, David
See Silverberg, Robert

Osborne, George
See Silverberg, Robert

Osborne, John (James)
1929-1994 .... **CLC 1, 2, 5, 11, 45; DA; DAB; DAC; DAM DRAM, MST; WLC**
See also CA 13-16R; 147; CANR 21, 56; CDBLB 1945-1960; DLB 13; MTCW

Osborne, Lawrence 1958- .... **CLC 50**

Oshima, Nagisa 1932- .... **CLC 20**
See also CA 116; 121

Oskison, John Milton
1874-1947 .... **TCLC 35; DAM MULT**
See also CA 144; DLB 175; NNAL

Ossoli, Sarah Margaret (Fuller marchesa d')
1810-1850
See Fuller, Margaret
See also SATA 25

Ostrovsky, Alexander 1823-1886 .. **NCLC 30, 57**

Otero, Blas de 1916-1979 .... **CLC 11**
See also CA 89-92; DLB 134

Otto, Whitney 1955- .... **CLC 70**
See also CA 140

Ouida .... **TCLC 43**
See also De La Ramee, (Marie) Louise
See also DLB 18, 156

Ousmane, Sembene 1923- .... **CLC 66; BLC**
See also BW 1; CA 117; 125; MTCW

Ovid
43B.C.-18(?) .... **CMLC 7; DAM POET; PC 2**

Owen, Hugh
See Faust, Frederick (Schiller)

Owen, Wilfred (Edward Salter)
1893-1918... **TCLC 5, 27; DA; DAB; DAC; DAM MST, POET; PC 19; WLC**
See also CA 104; 141; CDBLB 1914-1945; DLB 20

Owens, Rochelle 1936- .... **CLC 8**
See also CA 17-20R; CAAS 2; CANR 39

Oz, Amos
1939- ...... **CLC 5, 8, 11, 27, 33, 54; DAM NOV**
See also CA 53-56; CANR 27, 47; MTCW

Ozick, Cynthia
1928- .... **CLC 3, 7, 28, 62; DAM NOV, POP; SSC 15**
See also BEST 90:1; CA 17-20R; CANR 23, 58; DLB 28, 152; DLBY 82; INT CANR-23; MTCW

Ozu, Yasujiro 1903-1963 .... **CLC 16**
See also CA 112

Pacheco, C.
See Pessoa, Fernando (Antonio Nogueira)

Pa Chin .... CLC 18
See also Li Fei-kan

Pack, Robert 1929- .... CLC 13
See also CA 1-4R; CANR 3, 44; DLB 5

Padgett, Lewis
See Kuttner, Henry

Padilla (Lorenzo), Heberto 1932- ..... CLC 38
See also AITN 1; CA 123; 131; HW

Page, Jimmy 1944- .... CLC 12

Page, Louise 1955- .... CLC 40
See also CA 140

Page, P(atricia) K(athleen)
    1916- ...   CLC 7, 18; DAC; DAM MST;
    PC 12
See also CA 53-56; CANR 4, 22; DLB 68;
    MTCW

Page, Thomas Nelson 1853-1922 .... SSC 23
See also CA 118; DLB 12, 78; DLBD 13

Pagels, Elaine Hiesey 1943- .... CLC 104
See also CA 45-48; CANR 2, 24, 51

Paget, Violet 1856-1935
See Lee, Vernon
See also CA 104

Paget-Lowe, Henry
See Lovecraft, H(oward) P(hillips)

Paglia, Camille (Anna) 1947- .... CLC 68
See also CA 140

Paige, Richard
See Koontz, Dean R(ay)

Paine, Thomas 1737-1809 .... NCLC 62
See also CDALB 1640-1865; DLB 31, 43, 73,
    158

Pakenham, Antonia
See Fraser, (Lady) Antonia (Pakenham)

Palamas, Kostes 1859-1943 .... TCLC 5
See also CA 105

Palazzeschi, Aldo 1885-1974 .... CLC 11
See also CA 89-92; 53-56; DLB 114

Paley, Grace
    1922-.CLC 4, 6, 37; DAM POP; SSC
    8
See also CA 25-28R; CANR 13, 46; DLB 28;
    INT CANR-13; MTCW

Palin, Michael (Edward) 1943- .... CLC 21
See also Monty Python
See also CA 107; CANR 35; SATA 67

Palliser, Charles 1947- .... CLC 65
See also CA 136

Palma, Ricardo 1833-1919 .... TCLC 29

Pancake, Breece Dexter 1952-1979
See Pancake, Breece D'J
See also CA 123; 109

Pancake, Breece D'J .... CLC 29
See also Pancake, Breece Dexter
See also DLB 130

Panko, Rudy
See Gogol, Nikolai (Vasilyevich)

Papadiamantis, Alexandros
    1851-1911 .... TCLC 29

Papadiamantopoulos, Johannes 1856-1910
See Moreas, Jean
See also CA 117

Papini, Giovanni 1881-1956 .... TCLC 22
See also CA 121

Paracelsus 1493-1541 .... LC 14
See also DLB 179

Parasol, Peter
See Stevens, Wallace

Pareto, Vilfredo 1848-1923 .... TCLC 69

Parfenie, Maria
See Codrescu, Andrei

Parini, Jay (Lee) 1948- .... CLC 54
See also CA 97-100; CAAS 16; CANR 32

Park, Jordan
See Kornbluth, C(yril) M.; Pohl, Frederik

Park, Robert E(zra) 1864-1944 ...... TCLC 73
See also CA 122

Parker, Bert
See Ellison, Harlan (Jay)

Parker, Dorothy (Rothschild)
    1893-1967 ..... CLC 15, 68; DAM POET;
    SSC 2
See also CA 19-20; 25-28R; CAP 2; DLB 11,
    45, 86; MTCW

Parker, Robert B(rown)
    1932- .... CLC 27; DAM NOV, POP
See also BEST 89:4; CA 49-52; CANR 1, 26,
    52; INT CANR-26; MTCW

Parkin, Frank 1940- .... CLC 43
See also CA 147

Parkman, Francis, Jr. 1823-1893 .. NCLC 12
See also DLB 1, 30

Parks, Gordon (Alexander Buchanan)
    1912- ..... CLC 1, 16; BLC; DAM MULT
See also AITN 2; BW 2; CA 41-44R; CANR
    26; DLB 33; SATA 8

Parmenides
    c. 515B.C.-c. 450B.C. .... CMLC 22
See also DLB 176

Parnell, Thomas 1679-1718 .... LC 3
See also DLB 94

Parra, Nicanor
    1914- ...CLC 2, 102; DAM MULT; HLC
See also CA 85-88; CANR 32; HW;
    MTCW

Parrish, Mary Frances
See Fisher, M(ary) F(rances) K(ennedy)

Parson
See Coleridge, Samuel Taylor

Parson Lot
See Kingsley, Charles

Partridge, Anthony
See Oppenheim, E(dward) Phillips

Pascal, Blaise 1623-1662 .... LC 35

Pascoli, Giovanni 1855-1912 .... TCLC 45

Pasolini, Pier Paolo
    1922-1975 .... CLC 20, 37; PC 17
See also CA 93-96; 61-64; DLB 128, 177;
    MTCW

Pasquini
See Silone, Ignazio

Pastan, Linda (Olenik)
    1932- .... CLC 27; DAM POET
See also CA 61-64; CANR 18, 40, 61; DLB 5

Pasternak, Boris (Leonidovich)
    1890-1960 .... CLC 7, 10, 18, 63; DA;
    DAB; DAC; DAM MST, NOV, POET;
    PC 6; WLC
See also CA 127; 116; MTCW

Patchen, Kenneth 1911-1972 ... CLC 1, 2, 18;
    DAM POET
See also CA 1-4R; 33-36R; CANR 3, 35; DLB
    16, 48; MTCW

Pater, Walter (Horatio) 1839-1894 .. NCLC 7
See also CDBLB 1832-1890; DLB 57, 156

Paterson, A(ndrew) B(arton) 1864-1941
    TCLC 32
See also CA 155

Paterson, Katherine (Womeldorf)
    1932- .... CLC 12, 30
See also AAYA 1; CA 21-24R; CANR 28, 59;
    CLR 7; DLB 52; JRDA; MAICYA; MTCW;
    SATA 13, 53, 92

Patmore, Coventry Kersey Dighton
    1823-1896 .... NCLC 9
See also DLB 35, 98

Paton, Alan (Stewart)
    1903-1988 .... CLC 4, 10, 25, 55; DA;
    DAB; DAC; DAM MST, NOV; WLC
See also CA 13-16; 125; CANR 22; CAP 1;
    MTCW; SATA 11; SATA-Obit 56

Paton Walsh, Gillian 1937-
See Walsh, Jill Paton
See also CANR 38; JRDA; MAICYA; SAAS
    3; SATA 4, 72

Paulding, James Kirke 1778-1860 ... NCLC 2
See also DLB 3, 59, 74

Paulin, Thomas Neilson 1949-
See Paulin, Tom
See also CA 123; 128

Paulin, Tom .... CLC 37
See also Paulin, Thomas Neilson
See also DLB 40

Paustovsky, Konstantin (Georgievich)
1892-1968 .... CLC 40
See also CA 93-96; 25-28R

Pavese, Cesare
1908-1950 .... TCLC 3; PC 13; SSC 19
See also CA 104; DLB 128, 177

Pavic, Milorad 1929- .... CLC 60
See also CA 136; DLB 181

Payne, Alan
See Jakes, John (William)

Paz, Gil
See Lugones, Leopoldo

Paz, Octavio
1914- .... CLC 3, 4, 6, 10, 19, 51, 65; DA;
DAB; DAC; DAM MST, MULT, POET;
HLC; PC 1; WLC
See also CA 73-76; CANR 32; DLBY 90; HW;
MTCW

p'Bitek, Okot
1931-1982 .... CLC 96; BLC; DAM
MULT
See also BW 2; CA 124; 107; DLB 125;
MTCW

Peacock, Molly 1947- .... CLC 60
See also CA 103; CAAS 21; CANR 52; DLB
120

Peacock, Thomas Love
1785-1866 .... NCLC 22
See also DLB 96, 116

Peake, Mervyn 1911-1968 .... CLC 7, 54
See also CA 5-8R; 25-28R; CANR 3; DLB 15,
160; MTCW; SATA 23

Pearce, Philippa .... CLC 21
See also Christie, (Ann) Philippa
See also CLR 9; DLB 161; MAICYA; SATA 1,
67

Pearl, Eric
See Elman, Richard

Pearson, T(homas) R(eid) 1956- .... CLC 39
See also CA 120; 130; INT 130

Peck, Dale 1967- .... CLC 81
See also CA 146

Peck, John 1941- .... CLC 3
See also CA 49-52; CANR 3

Peck, Richard (Wayne) 1934- .... CLC 21
See also AAYA 1; CA 85-88; CANR 19, 38;
CLR 15; INT CANR-19; JRDA; MAICYA;
SAAS 2; SATA 18, 55

Peck, Robert Newton
1928- ... CLC 17; DA; DAC; DAM MST
See also AAYA 3; CA 81-84; CANR 31; CLR
45; JRDA; MAICYA; SAAS 1; SATA 21,
62

Peckinpah, (David) Sam(uel)
1925-1984 .... CLC 20
See also CA 109; 114

Pedersen, Knut 1859-1952
See Hamsun, Knut
See also CA 104; 119; MTCW

Peeslake, Gaffer
See Durrell, Lawrence (George)

Peguy, Charles Pierre 1873-1914 .. TCLC 10
See also CA 107

Pena, Ramon del Valle y
See Valle-Inclan, Ramon (Maria) del

Pendennis, Arthur Esquir
See Thackeray, William Makepeace

Penn, William 1644-1718 .... LC 25
See also DLB 24

PEPECE
See Prado (Calvo), Pedro

Pepys, Samuel
1633-1703 .... LC 11; DA; DAB; DAC;
DAM MST; WLC
See also CDBLB 1660-1789; DLB 101

Percy, Walker
1916-1990 ... CLC 2, 3, 6, 8, 14, 18, 47,
65; DAM NOV, POP
See also CA 1-4R; 131; CANR 1, 23; DLB 2;
DLBY 80, 90; MTCW

Perec, Georges 1936-1982 .... CLC 56
See also CA 141; DLB 83

Pereda (y Sanchez de Porrua), Jose Maria de
1833-1906 .... TCLC 16
See also CA 117

Pereda y Porrua, Jose Maria de
See Pereda (y Sanchez de Porrua), Jose Maria
de

Peregoy, George Weems
See Mencken, H(enry) L(ouis)

Perelman, S(idney) J(oseph)
1904-1979 .... CLC 3, 5, 9, 15, 23, 44, 49;
DAM DRAM
See also AITN 1, 2; CA 73-76; 89-92; CANR
18; DLB 11, 44; MTCW

Peret, Benjamin 1899-1959 .... TCLC 20
See also CA 117

Peretz, Isaac Loeb
1851(?)-1915 .... TCLC 16; SSC 26
See also CA 109

Peretz, Yitzkhok Leibush
See Peretz, Isaac Loeb

Perez Galdos, Benito
1843-1920 .... TCLC 27
See also CA 125; 153; HW

Perrault, Charles 1628-1703 .... LC 2
See also MAICYA; SATA 25

Perry, Brighton
See Sherwood, Robert E(mmet)

Perse, St.-John .... CLC 4, 11, 46
See also Leger, (Marie-Rene Auguste) Alexis
Saint-Leger

Perutz, Leo 1882-1957 .... TCLC 60
See also DLB 81

Peseenz, Tulio F.
See Lopez y Fuentes, Gregorio

Pesetsky, Bette 1932- .... CLC 28
See also CA 133; DLB 130

Peshkov, Alexei Maximovich 1868-1936
See Gorky, Maxim
See also CA 105; 141; DA; DAC; DAM
DRAM, MST, NOV

Pessoa, Fernando (Antonio Nogueira)
1888-1935 .... TCLC 27; HLC; PC 20
See also CA 125

Peterkin, Julia Mood 1880-1961 .... CLC 31
See also CA 102; DLB 9

Peters, Joan K(aren) 1945- .... CLC 39
See also CA 158

Peters, Robert L(ouis) 1924- .... CLC 7
See also CA 13-16R; CAAS 8; DLB 105

Petofi, Sandor 1823-1849 .... NCLC 21

Petrakis, Harry Mark 1923- .... CLC 3
See also CA 9-12R; CANR 4, 30

Petrarch
1304-1374 ... CMLC 20; DAM POET;
PC 8

Petrov, Evgeny .... TCLC 21
See also Kataev, Evgeny Petrovich

Petry, Ann (Lane)
1908-1997 .... CLC 1, 7, 18
See also BW 1; CA 5-8R; 157; CAAS 6;
CANR 4, 46; CLR 12; DLB 76; JRDA;
MAICYA; MTCW; SATA 5; SATA-Obit
94

Petursson, Halligrimur 1614-1674 .... LC 8

Phaedrus 18(?)B.C.-55(?) .... CMLC 24

Philips, Katherine 1632-1664 .... LC 30
See also DLB 131

Philipson, Morris H. 1926- .... CLC 53
See also CA 1-4R; CANR 4

Phillips, Caryl
1958- .... CLC 96; DAM MULT
See also BW 2; CA 141; DLB 157

Phillips, David Graham
1867-1911 .... TCLC 44
See also CA 108; DLB 9, 12

Phillips, Jack
See Sandburg, Carl (August)

Phillips, Jayne Anne
1952- .... **CLC 15, 33; SSC 16**
See also CA 101; CANR 24, 50; DLBY 80;
INT CANR-24; MTCW

Phillips, Richard
See Dick, Philip K(indred)

Phillips, Robert (Schaeffer)
1938- .... **CLC 28**
See also CA 17-20R; CAAS 13; CANR 8; DLB
105

Phillips, Ward
See Lovecraft, H(oward) P(hillips)

Piccolo, Lucio 1901-1969 .... **CLC 13**
See also CA 97-100; DLB 114

Pickthall, Marjorie L(owry) C(hristie)
1883-1922 .... **TCLC 21**
See also CA 107; DLB 92

Pico della Mirandola, Giovanni
1463-1494 .... **LC 15**

Piercy, Marge
1936- .... **CLC 3, 6, 14, 18, 27, 62**
See also CA 21-24R; CAAS 1; CANR 13, 43;
DLB 120; MTCW

Piers, Robert
See Anthony, Piers

Pieyre de Mandiargues, Andre 1909-1991
See Mandiargues, Andre Pieyre de
See also CA 103; 136; CANR 22

Pilnyak, Boris .... **TCLC 23**
See also Vogau, Boris Andreyevich

Pincherle, Alberto
1907-1990 .... **CLC 11, 18; DAM NOV**
See also Moravia, Alberto
See also CA 25-28R; 132; CANR 33;
MTCW

Pinckney, Darryl 1953- .... **CLC 76**
See also BW 2; CA 143

Pindar
518B.C.-446B.C. .... **CMLC 12; PC 19**
See also DLB 176

Pineda, Cecile 1942- .... **CLC 39**
See also CA 118

Pinero, Arthur Wing
1855-1934 .... **TCLC 32; DAM DRAM**
See also CA 110; 153; DLB 10

Pinero, Miguel (Antonio Gomez)
1946-1988 .... **CLC 4, 55**
See also CA 61-64; 125; CANR 29; HW

Pinget, Robert
1919-1997 .... **CLC 7, 13, 37**
See also CA 85-88; 160; DLB 83

Pink Floyd
See Barrett, (Roger) Syd; Gilmour, David;
Mason, Nick; Waters, Roger; Wright,
Rick

Pinkney, Edward 1802-1828 .... **NCLC 31**

Pinkwater, Daniel Manus
1941- .... **CLC 35**
See also Pinkwater, Manus
See also AAYA 1; CA 29-32R; CANR 12, 38; CLR
4; JRDA; MAICYA; SAAS 3; SATA 46, 76

Pinkwater, Manus
See Pinkwater, Daniel Manus
See also SATA 8

Pinsky, Robert
1940- .... **CLC 9, 19, 38, 94; DAM
POET**
See also CA 29-32R; CAAS 4; CANR 58;
DLBY 82

Pinta, Harold
See Pinter, Harold

Pinter, Harold
1930- **CLC 1, 3, 6, 9, 11, 15, 27, 58, 73; DA;
DAB; DAC; DAM DRAM, MST; WLC**
See also CA 5-8R; CANR 33; CDBLB
1960 to Present; DLB 13; MTCW

Piozzi, Hester Lynch (Thrale)
1741-1821 .... **NCLC 57**
See also DLB 104, 142

Pirandello, Luigi
1867-1936 **TCLC 4, 29; DA; DAB; DAC;
DAM DRAM, MST; DC 5; SSC 22; WLC**
See also CA 104; 153

Pirsig, Robert M(aynard)
1928- .... **CLC 4, 6, 73; DAM POP**
See also CA 53-56; CANR 42; MTCW; SATA 39

Pisarev, Dmitry Ivanovich
1840-1868 .... **NCLC 25**

Pix, Mary (Griffith)
1666-1709 .... **LC 8**
See also DLB 80

Pixerecourt, Guilbert de
1773-1844 .... **NCLC 39**

Plaatje, Sol(omon) T(shekisho)
1876-1932 .... **TCLC 73**
See also BW 2; CA 141

Plaidy, Jean
See Hibbert, Eleanor Alice Burford

Planche, James Robinson
1796-1880 .... **NCLC 42**

Plant, Robert 1948- .... **CLC 12**

Plante, David (Robert)
1940- .... **CLC 7, 23, 38; DAM NOV**
See also CA 37-40R; CANR 12, 36, 58;
DLBY 83; INT CANR-12; MTCW

Plath, Sylvia
1932-1963 .. **CLC 1, 2, 3, 5, 9, 11, 14, 17,
50, 51, 62; DA; DAB; DAC; DAM MST,
POET; PC 1; WLC**
See also AAYA 13; CA 19-20; CANR 34; CAP 2;
CDALB 1941-1968; DLB 5, 6, 152; MTCW

Plato 428(?)B.C.-348(?)B.C. ... **CMLC 8; DA;
DAB; DAC; DAM MST; WLCS**
See also DLB 176

Platonov, Andrei .... **TCLC 14**
See also Klimentov, Andrei Platonovich

Platt, Kin 1911- .... **CLC 26**
See also AAYA 11; CA 17-20R; CANR 11;
JRDA; SAAS 17; SATA 21, 86

Plautus c. 251B.C.-184B.C. .... **DC 6**

Plick et Plock
See Simenon, Georges (Jacques Christian)

Plimpton, George (Ames) 1927- .... **CLC 36**
See also AITN 1; CA 21-24R; CANR 32;
MTCW; SATA 10

Pliny the Elder c. 23-79 .... **CMLC 23**

Plomer, William Charles Franklin
1903-1973 .... **CLC 4, 8**
See also CA 21-22; CANR 34; CAP 2; DLB
20, 162; MTCW; SATA 24

Plowman, Piers
See Kavanagh, Patrick (Joseph)

Plum, J.
See Wodehouse, P(elham) G(renville)

Plumly, Stanley (Ross) 1939- .... **CLC 33**
See also CA 108; 110; DLB 5; INT 110

Plumpe, Friedrich Wilhelm
1888-1931 .... **TCLC 53**
See also CA 112

Po Chu-i 772-846 .... **CMLC 24**

Poe, Edgar Allan
1809-1849 ... **NCLC 1, 16, 55; DA; DAB;
DAC; DAM MST, POET; PC 1; SSC 1,
22; WLC**
See also AAYA 14; CDALB 1640-1865; DLB
3, 59, 73, 74; SATA 23

Poet of Titchfield Street, The
See Pound, Ezra (Weston Loomis)

Pohl, Frederik 1919- .... **CLC 18; SSC 25**
See also CA 61-64; CAAS 1; CANR 11, 37;
DLB 8; INT CANR-11; MTCW; SATA 24

Poirier, Louis 1910-
See Gracq, Julien
See also CA 122; 126

Poitier, Sidney 1927- .... **CLC 26**
See also BW 1; CA 117

Polanski, Roman 1933- .... **CLC 16**
See also CA 77-80

Poliakoff, Stephen 1952- .... **CLC 38**
See also CA 106; DLB 13

Police, The
See Copeland, Stewart (Armstrong); Sum-
mers, Andrew James; Sumner, Gordon
Matthew

Polidori, John William
1795-1821 .... **NCLC 51**
See also DLB 116

Pollitt, Katha 1949- .... **CLC 28**
See also CA 120; 122; MTCW

Pollock, (Mary) Sharon
1936- .... **CLC 50; DAC; DAM DRAM, MST**
See also CA 141; DLB 60

Polo, Marco 1254-1324 .... **CMLC 15**

Polonsky, Abraham (Lincoln)
1910- .... **CLC 92**
See also CA 104; DLB 26; INT 104

Polybius c. 200B.C.-c. 118B.C. ...... **CMLC 17**
See also DLB 176

Pomerance, Bernard 1940- .... **CLC 13; DAM DRAM**
See also CA 101; CANR 49

Ponge, Francis (Jean Gaston Alfred)
1899-1988 .... **CLC 6, 18; DAM POET**
See also CA 85-88; 126; CANR 40

Pontoppidan, Henrik 1857-1943 .... **TCLC 29**

Poole, Josephine .... **CLC 17**
See also Helyar, Jane Penelope Josephine
See also SAAS 2; SATA 5

Popa, Vasko 1922-1991 .... **CLC 19**
See also CA 112; 148; DLB 181

Pope, Alexander
1688-1744 .... **LC 3; DA; DAB; DAC; DAM MST, POET; WLC**
See also CDBLB 1660-1789; DLB 95, 101

Porter, Connie (Rose) 1959(?)- .... **CLC 70**
See also BW 2; CA 142; SATA 81

Porter, Gene(va Grace) Stratton
1863(?)-1924 .... **TCLC 21**
See also CA 112

Porter, Katherine Anne
1890-1980 .... **CLC 1, 3, 7, 10, 13, 15, 27, 101; DA; DAB; DAC; DAM MST, NOV; SSC 4**
See also AITN 2; CA 1-4R; 101; CANR 1; DLB 4, 9, 102; DLBD 12; DLBY 80; MTCW; SATA 39; SATA-Obit 23

Porter, Peter (Neville Frederick)
1929- .... **CLC 5, 13, 33**
See also CA 85-88; DLB 40

Porter, William Sydney 1862-1910
See Henry, O.
See also CA 104; 131; CDALB 1865-1917; DA; DAB; DAC; DAM MST; DLB 12, 78, 79; MTCW; YABC 2

Portillo (y Pacheco), Jose Lopez
See Lopez Portillo (y Pacheco), Jose

Post, Melville Davisson 1869-1930 **TCLC 39**
See also CA 110

Potok, Chaim
1929- .... **CLC 2, 7, 14, 26; DAM NOV**
See also AAYA 15; AITN 1, 2; CA 17-20R; CANR 19, 35; DLB 28, 152; INT CANR-19; MTCW; SATA 33

Potter, (Helen) Beatrix 1866-1943
See Webb, (Martha) Beatrice (Potter)
See also MAICYA

Potter, Dennis (Christopher George)
1935-1994 .... **CLC 58, 86**
See also CA 107; 145; CANR 33, 61; MTCW

Pound, Ezra (Weston Loomis)
1885-1972 ... **CLC 1, 2, 3, 4, 5, 7, 10, 13, 18, 34, 48, 50; DA; DAB; DAC; DAM MST, POET; PC 4; WLC**
See also CA 5-8R; 37-40R; CANR 40; CDALB 1917-1929; DLB 4, 45, 63; DLBD 15; MTCW

Povod, Reinaldo 1959-1994 .... **CLC 44**
See also CA 136; 146

Powell, Adam Clayton, Jr.
1908-1972 .... **CLC 89; BLC; DAM MULT**
See also BW 1; CA 102; 33-36R

Powell, Anthony (Dymoke)
1905- .... **CLC 1, 3, 7, 9, 10, 31**
See also CA 1-4R; CANR 1, 32, 62; CDBLB 1945-1960; DLB 15; MTCW

Powell, Dawn 1897-1965 .... **CLC 66**
See also CA 5-8R

Powell, Padgett 1952- .... **CLC 34**
See also CA 126

Power, Susan 1961- .... **CLC 91**

Powers, J(ames) F(arl)
1917- .... **CLC 1, 4, 8, 57; SSC 4**
See also CA 1-4R; CANR 2, 61; DLB 130; MTCW

Powers, John J(ames) 1945-
See Powers, John R.
See also CA 69-72

Powers, John R. .... **CLC 66**
See also Powers, John J(ames)

Powers, Richard (S.) 1957- .... **CLC 93**
See also CA 148

Pownall, David 1938- .... **CLC 10**
See also CA 89-92; CAAS 18; CANR 49; DLB 14

Powys, John Cowper
1872-1963 .... **CLC 7, 9, 15, 46**
See also CA 85-88; DLB 15; MTCW

Powys, T(heodore) F(rancis)
1875-1953 .... **TCLC 9**
See also CA 106; DLB 36, 162

Prado (Calvo), Pedro 1886-1952 ... **TCLC 75**
See also CA 131; HW

Prager, Emily 1952- .... **CLC 56**

Pratt, E(dwin) J(ohn)
1883(?)-1964 .... **CLC 19; DAC; DAM POET**
See also CA 141; 93-96; DLB 92

Premchand .... **TCLC 21**
See also Srivastava, Dhanpat Rai

Preussler, Otfried
1923- .... **CLC 17**
See also CA 77-80; SATA 24

Prevert, Jacques (Henri Marie)
1900-1977 .... **CLC 15**
See also CA 77-80; 69-72; CANR 29, 61; MTCW; SATA-Obit 30

Prevost, Abbe (Antoine Francois)
1697-1763 .... **LC 1**

Price, (Edward) Reynolds
1933- ..... **CLC 3, 6, 13, 43, 50, 63; DAM NOV; SSC 22**
See also CA 1-4R; CANR 1, 37, 57; DLB 2; INT CANR-37

Price, Richard
1949- .... **CLC 6, 12**
See also CA 49-52; CANR 3; DLBY 81

Prichard, Katharine Susannah
1883-1969 .... **CLC 46**
See also CA 11-12; CANR 33; CAP 1; MTCW; SATA 66

Priestley, J(ohn) B(oynton)
1894-1984 .... **CLC 2, 5, 9, 34; DAM DRAM, NOV**
See also CA 9-12R; 113; CANR 33; CDBLB 1914-1945; DLB 10, 34, 77, 100, 139; DLBY 84; MTCW

Prince 1958(?)- .... **CLC 35**

Prince, F(rank) T(empleton)
1912- .... **CLC 22**
See also CA 101; CANR 43; DLB 20

Prince Kropotkin
See Kropotkin, Peter (Aleksieevich)

Prior, Matthew 1664-1721 .... **LC 4**
See also DLB 95

Prishvin, Mikhail 1873-1954 .... **TCLC 75**

Pritchard, William H(arrison)
1932- .... **CLC 34**
See also CA 65-68; CANR 23; DLB 111

Pritchett, V(ictor) S(awdon)
1900-1997 .... **CLC 5, 13, 15, 41; DAM NOV; SSC 14**
See also CA 61-64; 157; CANR 31; DLB 15, 139; MTCW

Private 19022
See Manning, Frederic

Probst, Mark 1925- .... **CLC 59**
See also CA 130

Raine, Kathleen (Jessie) 1908- ...... **CLC 7, 45**
See also CA 85-88; CANR 46; DLB 20;
MTCW

Rainis, Janis 1865-1929 .... **TCLC 29**

Rakosi, Carl .... **CLC 47**
See also Rawley, Callman
See also CAAS 5

Raleigh, Richard
See Lovecraft, H(oward) P(hillips)

Raleigh, Sir Walter
1554(?)-1618 .... **LC 31, 39**
See also CDBLB Before 1660; DLB 172

Rallentando, H. P.
See Sayers, Dorothy L(eigh)

Ramal, Walter
See de la Mare, Walter (John)

Ramon, Juan
See Jimenez (Mantecon), Juan Ramon

Ramos, Graciliano 1892-1953 .... **TCLC 32**

Rampersad, Arnold 1941- .... **CLC 44**
See also BW 2; CA 127; 133; DLB 111; INT
133

Rampling, Anne
See Rice, Anne

Ramsay, Allan 1684(?)-1758 .... **LC 29**
See also DLB 95

Ramuz, Charles-Ferdinand
1878-1947 .... **TCLC 33**

Rand, Ayn
1905-1982 .... **CLC 3, 30, 44, 79; DA;
DAC; DAM MST, NOV, POP; WLC**
See also AAYA 10; CA 13-16R; 105; CANR
27; MTCW

Randall, Dudley (Felker)
1914- .... **CLC 1; BLC; DAM MULT**
See also BW 1; CA 25-28R; CANR 23; DLB
41

Randall, Robert
See Silverberg, Robert

Ranger, Ken
See Creasey, John

Ransom, John Crowe
1888-1974 ...... **CLC 2, 4, 5, 11, 24; DAM
POET**
See also CA 5-8R; 49-52; CANR 6, 34; DLB
45, 63; MTCW

Rao, Raja 1909- ...... **CLC 25, 56; DAM NOV**
See also CA 73-76; CANR 51; MTCW

Raphael, Frederic (Michael)
1931- .... **CLC 2, 14**
See also CA 1-4R; CANR 1; DLB 14

Ratcliffe, James P.
See Mencken, H(enry) L(ouis)

Rathbone, Julian 1935- .... **CLC 41**
See also CA 101; CANR 34

Rattigan, Terence (Mervyn)
1911-1977 .... **CLC 7; DAM DRAM**
See also CA 85-88; 73-76; CDBLB 1945-1960;
DLB 13; MTCW

Ratushinskaya, Irina 1954- .... **CLC 54**
See also CA 129

Raven, Simon (Arthur Noel)
1927- .... **CLC 14**
See also CA 81-84

Rawley, Callman 1903-
See Rakosi, Carl
See also CA 21-24R; CANR 12, 32

Rawlings, Marjorie Kinnan
1896-1953 .... **TCLC 4**
See also AAYA 20; CA 104; 137; DLB 9, 22,
102; JRDA; MAICYA; YABC 1

Ray, Satyajit
1921-1992 ..... **CLC 16, 76; DAM MULT**
See also CA 114; 137

Read, Herbert Edward 1893-1968 ..... **CLC 4**
See also CA 85-88; 25-28R; DLB 20,
149

Read, Piers Paul 1941- .... **CLC 4, 10, 25**
See also CA 21-24R; CANR 38; DLB 14;
SATA 21

Reade, Charles 1814-1884 .... **NCLC 2**
See also DLB 21

Reade, Hamish
See Gray, Simon (James Holliday)

Reading, Peter 1946- .... **CLC 47**
See also CA 103; CANR 46; DLB 40

Reaney, James
1926- .... **CLC 13; DAC; DAM MST**
See also CA 41-44R; CAAS 15; CANR 42;
DLB 68; SATA 43

Rebreanu, Liviu 1885-1944 .... **TCLC 28**

Rechy, John (Francisco)
1934- .... **CLC 1, 7, 14, 18; DAM MULT;
HLC**
See also CA 5-8R; CAAS 4; CANR 6, 32; DLB
122; DLBY 82; HW; INT CANR-6

Redcam, Tom 1870-1933 .... **TCLC 25**

Reddin, Keith .... **CLC 67**

Redgrove, Peter (William)
1932- .... **CLC 6, 41**
See also CA 1-4R; CANR 3, 39; DLB
40

Redmon, Anne .... **CLC 22**
See also Nightingale, Anne Redmon
See also DLBY 86

Reed, Eliot
See Ambler, Eric

Reed, Ishmael
1938- ... **CLC 2, 3, 5, 6, 13, 32, 60; BLC;
DAM MULT**
See also BW 2; CA 21-24R; CANR 25,
48; DLB 2, 5, 33, 169; DLBD 8;
MTCW

Reed, John (Silas) 1887-1920 .... **TCLC 9**
See also CA 106

Reed, Lou .... **CLC 21**
See also Firbank, Louis

Reeve, Clara 1729-1807 .... **NCLC 19**
See also DLB 39

Reich, Wilhelm 1897-1957 .... **TCLC 57**

Reid, Christopher (John)
1949- .... **CLC 33**
See also CA 140; DLB 40

Reid, Desmond
See Moorcock, Michael (John)

Reid Banks, Lynne 1929-
See Banks, Lynne Reid
See also CA 1-4R; CANR 6, 22, 38; CLR 24;
JRDA; MAICYA; SATA 22, 75

Reilly, William K.
See Creasey, John

Reiner, Max
See Caldwell, (Janet Miriam) Taylor (Holland)

Reis, Ricardo
See Pessoa, Fernando (Antonio Nogueira)

Remarque, Erich Maria
1898-1970 ..... **CLC 21; DA; DAB; DAC;
DAM MST, NOV**
See also CA 77-80; 29-32R; DLB 56;
MTCW

Remizov, A.
See Remizov, Aleksei (Mikhailovich)

Remizov, A. M.
See Remizov, Aleksei (Mikhailovich)

Remizov, Aleksei (Mikhailovich)
1877-1957 .... **TCLC 27**
See also CA 125; 133

Renan, Joseph Ernest
1823-1892 .... **NCLC 26**

Renard, Jules 1864-1910 .... **TCLC 17**
See also CA 117

Renault, Mary .... **CLC 3, 11, 17**
See also Challans, Mary
See also DLBY 83

Rendell, Ruth (Barbara)
1930- .... **CLC 28, 48; DAM POP**
See also Vine, Barbara
See also CA 109; CANR 32, 52; DLB 87; INT
CANR-32; MTCW

Renoir, Jean 1894-1979 .... **CLC 20**
See also CA 129; 85-88

Rizal, Jose 1861-1896 .... **NCLC 27**

Roa Bastos, Augusto (Antonio)
1917- .... **CLC 45; DAM MULT; HLC**
See also CA 131; DLB 113; HW

Robbe-Grillet, Alain
1922- .... **CLC 1, 2, 4, 6, 8, 10, 14, 43**
See also CA 9-12R; CANR 33; DLB 83;
MTCW

Robbins, Harold
1916- .... **CLC 5; DAM NOV**
See also CA 73-76; CANR 26, 54; MTCW

Robbins, Thomas Eugene 1936-
See Robbins, Tom
See also CA 81-84; CANR 29, 59; DAM NOV,
POP; MTCW

Robbins, Tom .... **CLC 9, 32, 64**
See also Robbins, Thomas Eugene
See also BEST 90:3; DLBY 80

Robbins, Trina 1938- .... **CLC 21**
See also CA 128

Roberts, Charles G(eorge) D(ouglas)
1860-1943 .... **TCLC 8**
See also CA 105; CLR 33; DLB 92; SATA 88;
SATA-Brief 29

Roberts, Elizabeth Madox
1886-1941 .... **TCLC 68**
See also CA 111; DLB 9, 54, 102; SATA 33;
SATA-Brief 27

Roberts, Kate 1891-1985 .... **CLC 15**
See also CA 107; 116

Roberts, Keith (John Kingston)
1935- .... **CLC 14**
See also CA 25-28R; CANR 46

Roberts, Kenneth (Lewis)
1885-1957 .... **TCLC 23**
See also CA 109; DLB 9

Roberts, Michele (B.) 1949- .... **CLC 48**
See also CA 115; CANR 58

Robertson, Ellis
See Ellison, Harlan (Jay); Silverberg, Robert

Robertson, Thomas William
1829-1871 .... **NCLC 35; DAM DRAM**

Robeson, Kenneth
See Dent, Lester

Robinson, Edwin Arlington
1869-1935 ..... **TCLC 5; DA; DAC; DAM
MST, POET; PC 1**
See also CA 104; 133; CDALB 1865-1917;
DLB 54; MTCW

Robinson, Henry Crabb
1775-1867 .... **NCLC 15**
See also DLB 107

Robinson, Jill 1936- .... **CLC 10**
See also CA 102; INT 102

Robinson, Kim Stanley 1952- .... **CLC 34**
See also CA 126

Robinson, Lloyd
See Silverberg, Robert

Robinson, Marilynne 1944- .... **CLC 25**
See also CA 116

Robinson, Smokey .... **CLC 21**
See also Robinson, William, Jr.

Robinson, William, Jr. 1940-
See Robinson, Smokey
See also CA 116

Robison, Mary 1949- .... **CLC 42, 98**
See also CA 113; 116; DLB 130; INT 116

Rod, Edouard 1857-1910 .... **TCLC 52**

Roddenberry, Eugene Wesley 1921-1991
See Roddenberry, Gene
See also CA 110; 135; CANR 37; SATA 45;
SATA-Obit 69

Roddenberry, Gene .... **CLC 17**
See also Roddenberry, Eugene Wesley
See also AAYA 5; SATA-Obit 69

Rodgers, Mary 1931- .... **CLC 12**
See also CA 49-52; CANR 8, 55; CLR 20;
INT CANR-8; JRDA; MAICYA; SATA
8

Rodgers, W(illiam) R(obert)
1909-1969 .... **CLC 7**
See also CA 85-88; DLB 20

Rodman, Eric
See Silverberg, Robert

Rodman, Howard 1920(?)-1985 .... **CLC 65**
See also CA 118

Rodman, Maia
See Wojciechowska, Maia (Teresa)

Rodriguez, Claudio 1934- .... **CLC 10**
See also DLB 134

Roelvaag, O(le) E(dvart)
1876-1931 .... **TCLC 17**
See also CA 117; DLB 9

Roethke, Theodore (Huebner)
1908-1963 .. **CLC 1, 3, 8, 11, 19, 46, 101;
DAM POET; PC 15**
See also CA 81-84; CABS 2; CDALB 1941-
1968; DLB 5; MTCW

Rogers, Thomas Hunton 1927- .... **CLC 57**
See also CA 89-92; INT 89-92

Rogers, Will(iam Penn Adair)
1879-1935 ..... **TCLC 8, 71; DAM MULT**
See also CA 105; 144; DLB 11; NNAL

Rogin, Gilbert 1929- .... **CLC 18**
See also CA 65-68; CANR 15

Rohan, Koda .... **TCLC 22**
See also Koda Shigeyuki

Rohlfs, Anna Katharine Green
See Green, Anna Katharine

Rohmer, Eric .... **CLC 16**
See also Scherer, Jean-Marie Maurice

Rohmer, Sax .... **TCLC 28**
See also Ward, Arthur Henry Sarsfield
See also DLB 70

Roiphe, Anne (Richardson)
1935- .... **CLC 3, 9**
See also CA 89-92; CANR 45; DLBY 80; INT
89-92

Rojas, Fernando de 1465-1541 .... **LC 23**

**Rolfe, Frederick (William Serafino Austin
Lewis Mary)** 1860-1913 .... **TCLC 12**
See also CA 107; DLB 34, 156

Rolland, Romain 1866-1944 .... **TCLC 23**
See also CA 118; DLB 65

Rolle, Richard c. 1300-c. 1349 ...... **CMLC 21**
See also DLB 146

Rolvaag, O(le) E(dvart)
See Roelvaag, O(le) E(dvart)

Romain Arnaud, Saint
See Aragon, Louis

Romains, Jules 1885-1972 .... **CLC 7**
See also CA 85-88; CANR 34; DLB 65;
MTCW

Romero, Jose Ruben 1890-1952 .... **TCLC 14**
See also CA 114; 131; HW

Ronsard, Pierre de 1524-1585... **LC 6; PC 11**

Rooke, Leon 1934- .. **CLC 25, 34; DAM POP**
See also CA 25-28R; CANR 23, 53

Roosevelt, Theodore 1858-1919 ..... **TCLC 69**
See also CA 115; DLB 47

Roper, William 1498-1578 .... **LC 10**

Roquelaure, A. N.
See Rice, Anne

Rosa, Joao Guimaraes 1908-1967 .... **CLC 23**
See also CA 89-92; DLB 113

Rose, Wendy
1948- .... **CLC 85; DAM MULT; PC 13**
See also CA 53-56; CANR 5, 51; DLB 175;
NNAL; SATA 12

Rosen, R. D.
See Rosen, Richard (Dean)

Rosen, Richard (Dean) 1949- .... **CLC 39**
See also CA 77-80; CANR 62; INT CANR-
30

Rosenberg, Isaac 1890-1918 .... **TCLC 12**
See also CA 107; DLB 20

Rosenblatt, Joe .... **CLC 15**
See also Rosenblatt, Joseph

S. S.
See Sassoon, Siegfried (Lorraine)

Saba, Umberto 1883-1957 .... **TCLC 33**
See also CA 144; DLB 114

Sabatini, Rafael 1875-1950 .... **TCLC 47**

Sabato, Ernesto (R.)
1911- .... **CLC 10, 23; DAM MULT; HLC**
See also CA 97-100; CANR 32; DLB 145; HW; MTCW

Sacastru, Martin
See Bioy Casares, Adolfo

Sacher-Masoch, Leopold von
1836(?)-1895 .... **NCLC 31**

Sachs, Marilyn (Stickle)
1927- .... **CLC 35**
See also AAYA 2; CA 17-20R; CANR 13, 47; CLR 2; JRDA; MAICYA; SAAS 2; SATA 3, 68

Sachs, Nelly 1891-1970 .... **CLC 14, 98**
See also CA 17-18; 25-28R; CAP 2

Sackler, Howard (Oliver)
1929-1982 .... **CLC 14**
See also CA 61-64; 108; CANR 30; DLB 7

Sacks, Oliver (Wolf) 1933- .... **CLC 67**
See also CA 53-56; CANR 28, 50; INT CANR-28; MTCW

Sadakichi
See Hartmann, Sadakichi

Sade, Donatien Alphonse Francois, Comte de
1740-1814 .... **NCLC 47**

Sadoff, Ira 1945- .... **CLC 9**
See also CA 53-56; CANR 5, 21; DLB 120

Saetone
See Camus, Albert

Safire, William 1929- .... **CLC 10**
See also CA 17-20R; CANR 31, 54

Sagan, Carl (Edward)
1934-1996 .... **CLC 30**
See also AAYA 2; CA 25-28R; 155; CANR 11, 36; MTCW; SATA 58; SATA-Obit 94

Sagan, Francoise .... **CLC 3, 6, 9, 17, 36**
See also Quoirez, Francoise
See also DLB 83

Sahgal, Nayantara (Pandit)
1927- .... **CLC 41**
See also CA 9-12R; CANR 11

Saint, H(arry) F. 1941- .... **CLC 50**
See also CA 127

St. Aubin de Teran, Lisa 1953-
See Teran, Lisa St. Aubin de
See also CA 118; 126; INT 126

Saint Birgitta of Sweden
c. 1303-1373 .... **CMLC 24**

Sainte-Beuve, Charles Augustin
1804-1869 .... **NCLC 5**

Saint-Exupery, Antoine (Jean Baptiste Marie Roger) de
1900-1944 .... **TCLC 2, 56; DAM NOV; WLC**
See also CA 108; 132; CLR 10; DLB 72; MAICYA; MTCW; SATA 20

St. John, David
See Hunt, E(verette) Howard, (Jr.)

Saint-John Perse
See Leger, (Marie-Rene Auguste) Alexis Saint-Leger

Saintsbury, George (Edward Bateman)
1845-1933 .... **TCLC 31**
See also CA 160; DLB 57, 149

Sait Faik .... **TCLC 23**
See also Abasiyanik, Sait Faik

Saki .... **TCLC 3; SSC 12**
See also Munro, H(ector) H(ugh)

Sala, George Augustus .... **NCLC 46**

Salama, Hannu 1936- .... **CLC 18**

Salamanca, J(ack) R(ichard)
1922- .... **CLC 4, 15**
See also CA 25-28R

Sale, J. Kirkpatrick
See Sale, Kirkpatrick

Sale, Kirkpatrick
1937- .... **CLC 68**
See also CA 13-16R; CANR 10

Salinas, Luis Omar
1937- .... **CLC 90; DAM MULT; HLC**
See also CA 131; DLB 82; HW

Salinas (y Serrano), Pedro
1891(?)-1951 .... **TCLC 17**
See also CA 117; DLB 134

Salinger, J(erome) D(avid)
1919- .... **CLC 1, 3, 8, 12, 55, 56; DA; DAB; DAC; DAM MST, NOV, POP; SSC 2, 28; WLC**
See also AAYA 2; CA 5-8R; CANR 39; CDALB 1941-1968; CLR 18; DLB 2, 102, 173; MAICYA; MTCW; SATA 67

Salisbury, John
See Caute, David

Salter, James
1925- .... **CLC 7, 52, 59**
See also CA 73-76; DLB 130

Saltus, Edgar (Everton)
1855-1921 .... **TCLC 8**
See also CA 105

Saltykov, Mikhail Evgrafovich
1826-1889 .... **NCLC 16**

Samarakis, Antonis 1919- .... **CLC 5**
See also CA 25-28R; CAAS 16; CANR 36

Sanchez, Florencio 1875-1910 .... **TCLC 37**
See also CA 153; HW

Sanchez, Luis Rafael 1936- .... **CLC 23**
See also CA 128; DLB 145; HW

Sanchez, Sonia 1934- ..... **CLC 5; BLC; DAM MULT; PC 9**
See also BW 2; CA 33-36R; CANR 24, 49; CLR 18; DLB 41; DLBD 8; MAICYA; MTCW; SATA 22

Sand, George
1804-1876 ... **NCLC 2, 42, 57; DA; DAB; DAC; DAM MST, NOV; WLC**
See also DLB 119

Sandburg, Carl (August)
1878-1967 ...... **CLC 1, 4, 10, 15, 35; DA; DAB; DAC; DAM MST, POET; PC 2; WLC**
See also CA 5-8R; 25-28R; CANR 35; CDALB 1865-1917; DLB 17, 54; MAICYA; MTCW; SATA 8

Sandburg, Charles
See Sandburg, Carl (August)

Sandburg, Charles A.
See Sandburg, Carl (August)

Sanders, (James) Ed(ward) 1939- .... **CLC 53**
See also CA 13-16R; CAAS 21; CANR 13, 44; DLB 16

Sanders, Lawrence
1920- .... **CLC 41; DAM POP**
See also BEST 89:4; CA 81-84; CANR 33, 62; MTCW

Sanders, Noah
See Blount, Roy (Alton), Jr.

Sanders, Winston P.
See Anderson, Poul (William)

Sandoz, Mari(e Susette) 1896-1966 .. **CLC 28**
See also CA 1-4R; 25-28R; CANR 17; DLB 9; MTCW; SATA 5

Saner, Reg(inald Anthony) 1931- .... **CLC 9**
See also CA 65-68

Sannazaro, Jacopo 1456(?)-1530 .... **LC 8**

Sansom, William
1912-1976 .. **CLC 2, 6; DAM NOV; SSC 21**
See also CA 5-8R; 65-68; CANR 42; DLB 139; MTCW

Santayana, George 1863-1952 .... **TCLC 40**
See also CA 115; DLB 54, 71; DLBD 13

Santiago, Danny .... **CLC 33**
See also James, Daniel (Lewis)
See also DLB 122

Schulz, Charles M(onroe)
1922- .... **CLC 12**
See also CA 9-12R; CANR 6; INT CANR-6;
SATA 10

Schumacher, E(rnst) F(riedrich)
1911-1977 .... **CLC 80**
See also CA 81-84; 73-76; CANR 34

Schuyler, James Marcus
1923-1991 .... **CLC 5, 23; DAM POET**
See also CA 101; 134; DLB 5, 169; INT
101

Schwartz, Delmore (David)
1913-1966 ..... **CLC 2, 4, 10, 45, 87; PC 8**
See also CA 17-18; 25-28R; CANR 35; CAP
2; DLB 28, 48; MTCW

Schwartz, Ernst
See Ozu, Yasujiro

Schwartz, John Burnham 1965- .... **CLC 59**
See also CA 132

Schwartz, Lynne Sharon 1939- .... **CLC 31**
See also CA 103; CANR 44

Schwartz, Muriel A.
See Eliot, T(homas) S(tearns)

Schwarz-Bart, Andre 1928- .... **CLC 2, 4**
See also CA 89-92

Schwarz-Bart, Simone 1938- .... **CLC 7**
See also BW 2; CA 97-100

Schwob, (Mayer Andre) Marcel
1867-1905 .... **TCLC 20**
See also CA 117; DLB 123

Sciascia, Leonardo
1921-1989 .... **CLC 8, 9, 41**
See also CA 85-88; 130; CANR 35; DLB 177;
MTCW

Scoppettone, Sandra 1936- .... **CLC 26**
See also AAYA 11; CA 5-8R; CANR 41; SATA
9, 92

Scorsese, Martin 1942- .... **CLC 20, 89**
See also CA 110; 114; CANR 46

Scotland, Jay
See Jakes, John (William)

Scott, Duncan Campbell
1862-1947 .... **TCLC 6; DAC**
See also CA 104; 153; DLB 92

Scott, Evelyn 1893-1963 .... **CLC 43**
See also CA 104; 112; DLB 9, 48

Scott, F(rancis) R(eginald)
1899-1985 .... **CLC 22**
See also CA 101; 114; DLB 88; INT
101

Scott, Frank
See Scott, F(rancis) R(eginald)

Scott, Joanna 1960- .... **CLC 50**
See also CA 126; CANR 53

Scott, Paul (Mark) 1920-1978 .... **CLC 9, 60**
See also CA 81-84; 77-80; CANR 33; DLB
14; MTCW

Scott, Walter
1771-1832 .. **NCLC 15; DA; DAB; DAC;
DAM MST, NOV, POET; PC 13; WLC**
See also AAYA 22; CDBLB 1789-1832; DLB
93, 107, 116, 144, 159; YABC 2

Scribe, (Augustin) Eugene
1791-1861 .... **NCLC 16; DAM DRAM;
DC 5**

Scrum, R.
See Crumb, R(obert)

Scudery, Madeleine de 1607-1701 .... **LC 2**

Scum
See Crumb, R(obert)

Scumbag, Little Bobby
See Crumb, R(obert)

Seabrook, John
See Hubbard, L(afayette) Ron(ald)

Sealy, I. Allan 1951- .... **CLC 55**

Search, Alexander
See Pessoa, Fernando (Antonio Nogueira)

Sebastian, Lee
See Silverberg, Robert

Sebastian Owl
See Thompson, Hunter S(tockton)

Sebestyen, Ouida 1924- .... **CLC 30**
See also AAYA 8; CA 107; CANR 40; CLR
17; JRDA; MAICYA; SAAS 10; SATA 39

Secundus, H. Scriblerus
See Fielding, Henry

Sedges, John
See Buck, Pearl S(ydenstricker)

Sedgwick, Catharine Maria
1789-1867 .... **NCLC 19**
See also DLB 1, 74

Seelye, John 1931- .... **CLC 7**

Seferiades, Giorgos Stylianou 1900-1971
See Seferis, George
See also CA 5-8R; 33-36R; CANR 5, 36;
MTCW

Seferis, George .... **CLC 5, 11**
See also Seferiades, Giorgos Stylianou

Segal, Erich (Wolf)
1937- .... **CLC 3, 10; DAM POP**
See also BEST 89:1; CA 25-28R; CANR 20,
36; DLBY 86; INT CANR-20; MTCW

Seger, Bob 1945- .... **CLC 35**

Seghers, Anna .... **CLC 7**
See also Radvanyi, Netty
See also DLB 69

Seidel, Frederick (Lewis) 1936- .... **CLC 18**
See also CA 13-16R; CANR 8; DLBY 84

Seifert, Jaroslav 1901-1986 .. **CLC 34, 44, 93**
See also CA 127; MTCW

Sei Shonagon c. 966-1017(?) .... **CMLC 6**

Selby, Hubert, Jr.
1928- .... **CLC 1, 2, 4, 8; SSC 20**
See also CA 13-16R; CANR 33; DLB 2

Selzer, Richard 1928- .... **CLC 74**
See also CA 65-68; CANR 14

Sembene, Ousmane
See Ousmane, Sembene

Senancour, Etienne Pivert de
1770-1846 .... **NCLC 16**
See also DLB 119

Sender, Ramon (Jose)
1902-1982 ... **CLC 8; DAM MULT; HLC**
See also CA 5-8R; 105; CANR 8; HW; MTCW

Seneca, Lucius Annaeus
4B.C.-65 ..... **CMLC 6; DAM DRAM;
DC 5**

Senghor, Leopold Sedar
1906- .... **CLC 54; BLC; DAM MULT,
POET**
See also BW 2; CA 116; 125; CANR 47;
MTCW

Serling, (Edward) Rod(man)
1924-1975 .... **CLC 30**
See also AAYA 14; AITN 1; CA 65-68; 57-60;
DLB 26

Serna, Ramon Gomez de la
See Gomez de la Serna, Ramon

Serpieres
See Guillevic, (Eugene)

Service, Robert
See Service, Robert W(illiam)
See also DAB; DLB 92

Service, Robert W(illiam)
1874(?)-1958 .... **TCLC 15; DA; DAC;
DAM MST, POET; WLC**
See also Service, Robert
See also CA 115; 140; SATA 20

Seth, Vikram
1952- .... **CLC 43, 90; DAM MULT**
See also CA 121; 127; CANR 50; DLB 120;
INT 127

Seton, Cynthia Propper
1926-1982 .... **CLC 27**
See also CA 5-8R; 108; CANR 7

Seton, Ernest (Evan) Thompson
1860-1946 .... **TCLC 31**
See also CA 109; DLB 92; DLBD 13; JRDA;
SATA 18

Seton-Thompson, Ernest
See Seton, Ernest (Evan) Thompson

Shimazaki Toson 1872-1943 .... **TCLC 5**
See also Shimazaki, Haruki
See also DLB 180

Sholokhov, Mikhail (Aleksandrovich)
1905-1984 .... **CLC 7, 15**
See also CA 101; 112; MTCW; SATA-Obit
36

Shone, Patric
See Hanley, James

Shreve, Susan Richards 1939- .... **CLC 23**
See also CA 49-52; CAAS 5; CANR 5, 38;
MAICYA; SATA 46, 95; SATA-Brief 41

Shue, Larry
1946-1985 .... **CLC 52; DAM DRAM**
See also CA 145; 117

Shu-Jen, Chou 1881-1936
See Lu Hsun
See also CA 104

Shulman, Alix Kates 1932- .... **CLC 2, 10**
See also CA 29-32R; CANR 43; SATA 7

Shuster, Joe 1914- .... **CLC 21**

Shute, Nevil .... **CLC 30**
See also Norway, Nevil Shute

Shuttle, Penelope (Diane) 1947- .... **CLC 7**
See also CA 93-96; CANR 39; DLB 14, 40

Sidney, Mary 1561-1621 .... **LC 19, 39**

Sidney, Sir Philip
1554-1586 .... **LC 19, 39; DA; DAB;
DAC; DAM MST, POET**
See also CDBLB Before 1660; DLB 167

Siegel, Jerome 1914-1996 .... **CLC 21**
See also CA 116; 151

Siegel, Jerry
See Siegel, Jerome

Sienkiewicz, Henryk (Adam Alexander Pius)
1846-1916 .... **TCLC 3**
See also CA 104; 134

Sierra, Gregorio Martinez
See Martinez Sierra, Gregorio

Sierra, Maria (de la O'LeJarraga) Martinez
See Martinez Sierra, Maria (de la
O'LeJarraga)

Sigal, Clancy 1926- .... **CLC 7**
See also CA 1-4R

Sigourney, Lydia Howard (Huntley)
1791-1865 .... **NCLC 21**
See also DLB 1, 42, 73

Siguenza y Gongora, Carlos de
1645-1700 .... **LC 8**

Sigurjonsson, Johann
1880-1919 .... **TCLC 27**

Sikelianos, Angelos 1884-1951 .... **TCLC 39**

Silkin, Jon 1930- .... **CLC 2, 6, 43**
See also CA 5-8R; CAAS 5; DLB 27

Silko, Leslie (Marmon)
1948- .... **CLC 23, 74; DA; DAC; DAM
MST, MULT, POP; WLCS**
See also AAYA 14; CA 115; 122; CANR 45;
DLB 143, 175; NNAL

Sillanpaa, Frans Eemil
1888-1964 .... **CLC 19**
See also CA 129; 93-96; MTCW

Sillitoe, Alan
1928- .... **CLC 1, 3, 6, 10, 19, 57**
See also AITN 1; CA 9-12R; CAAS 2; CANR
8, 26, 55; CDBLB 1960 to Present; DLB
14, 139; MTCW; SATA 61

Silone, Ignazio 1900-1978 .... **CLC 4**
See also CA 25-28; 81-84; CANR 34; CAP 2;
MTCW

Silver, Joan Micklin 1935- .... **CLC 20**
See also CA 114; 121; INT 121

Silver, Nicholas
See Faust, Frederick (Schiller)

Silverberg, Robert
1935- .... **CLC 7; DAM POP**
See also CA 1-4R; CAAS 3; CANR 1, 20, 36;
DLB 8; INT CANR-20; MAICYA; MTCW;
SATA 13, 91

Silverstein, Alvin 1933- .... **CLC 17**
See also CA 49-52; CANR 2; CLR 25; JRDA;
MAICYA; SATA 8, 69

Silverstein, Virginia B(arbara Opshelor)
1937- .... **CLC 17**
See also CA 49-52; CANR 2; CLR 25; JRDA;
MAICYA; SATA 8, 69

Sim, Georges
See Simenon, Georges (Jacques Christian)

Simak, Clifford D(onald)
1904-1988 .... **CLC 1, 55**
See also CA 1-4R; 125; CANR 1, 35; DLB 8;
MTCW; SATA-Obit 56

Simenon, Georges (Jacques Christian)
1903-1989 .... **CLC 1, 2, 3, 8, 18, 47;
DAM POP**
See also CA 85-88; 129; CANR 35; DLB 72;
DLBY 89; MTCW

Simic, Charles
1938- .... **CLC 6, 9, 22, 49, 68; DAM
POET**
See also CA 29-32R; CAAS 4; CANR 12, 33,
52, 61; DLB 105

Simmel, Georg 1858-1918 .... **TCLC 64**
See also CA 157

Simmons, Charles (Paul) 1924- .... **CLC 57**
See also CA 89-92; INT 89-92

Simmons, Dan
1948- .... **CLC 44; DAM POP**
See also AAYA 16; CA 138; CANR 53

Simmons, James (Stewart Alexander)
1933- .... **CLC 43**
See also CA 105; CAAS 21; DLB 40

Simms, William Gilmore
1806-1870 .... **NCLC 3**
See also DLB 3, 30, 59, 73

Simon, Carly 1945- .... **CLC 26**
See also CA 105

Simon, Claude
1913- .... **CLC 4, 9, 15, 39; DAM
NOV**
See also CA 89-92; CANR 33; DLB 83;
MTCW

Simon, (Marvin) Neil
1927- .... **CLC 6, 11, 31, 39, 70; DAM
DRAM**
See also AITN 1; CA 21-24R; CANR 26, 54;
DLB 7; MTCW

Simon, Paul (Frederick)
1941(?)- .... **CLC 17**
See also CA 116; 153

Simonon, Paul 1956(?)- .... **CLC 30**

Simpson, Harriette
See Arnow, Harriette (Louisa) Simpson

Simpson, Louis (Aston Marantz)
1923- .... **CLC 4, 7, 9, 32; DAM
POET**
See also CA 1-4R; CAAS 4; CANR 1, 61; DLB
5; MTCW

Simpson, Mona (Elizabeth)
1957- .... **CLC 44**
See also CA 122; 135

Simpson, N(orman) F(rederick)
1919- .... **CLC 29**
See also CA 13-16R; DLB 13

Sinclair, Andrew (Annandale)
1935- .... **CLC 2, 14**
See also CA 9-12R; CAAS 5; CANR 14, 38;
DLB 14; MTCW

Sinclair, Emil
See Hesse, Hermann

Sinclair, Iain 1943- .... **CLC 76**
See also CA 132

Sinclair, Iain MacGregor
See Sinclair, Iain

Sinclair, Irene
See Griffith, D(avid Lewelyn) W(ark)

Sinclair, Mary Amelia St. Clair 1865(?)-1946
See Sinclair, May
See also CA 104

Sinclair, May .... **TCLC 3, 11**
See also Sinclair, Mary Amelia St. Clair
See also DLB 36, 135

Sinclair, Roy
See Griffith, D(avid Lewelyn) W(ark)

Spurling, Hilary 1940- .... CLC 34
See also CA 104; CANR 25, 52

Spyker, John Howland
See Elman, Richard

Squires, (James) Radcliffe
1917-1993 .... CLC 51
See also CA 1-4R; 140; CANR 6, 21

Srivastava, Dhanpat Rai 1880(?)-1936
See Premchand
See also CA 118

Stacy, Donald
See Pohl, Frederik

Stael, Germaine de
See Stael-Holstein, Anne Louise Germaine
Necker Baronn
See also DLB 119

Stael-Holstein, Anne Louise Germaine Necker
Baronn 1766-1817 .... NCLC 3
See also Stael, Germaine de

Stafford, Jean
1915-1979 .... CLC 4, 7, 19, 68; SSC 26
See also CA 1-4R; 85-88; CANR 3; DLB 2,
173; MTCW; SATA-Obit 22

Stafford, William (Edgar)
1914-1993 .... CLC 4, 7, 29; DAM
POET
See also CA 5-8R; 142; CAAS 3; CANR 5,
22; DLB 5; INT CANR-22

Stagnelius, Eric Johan
1793-1823 .... NCLC 61

Staines, Trevor
See Brunner, John (Kilian Houston)

Stairs, Gordon
See Austin, Mary (Hunter)

Stannard, Martin
1947- .... CLC 44
See also CA 142; DLB 155

Stanton, Elizabeth Cady
1815-1902 .... TCLC 73
See also DLB 79

Stanton, Maura 1946- .... CLC 9
See also CA 89-92; CANR 15; DLB 120

Stanton, Schuyler
See Baum, L(yman) Frank

Stapledon, (William) Olaf
1886-1950 .... TCLC 22
See also CA 111; DLB 15

Starbuck, George (Edwin)
1931-1996 .... CLC 53; DAM POET
See also CA 21-24R; 153; CANR 23

Stark, Richard
See Westlake, Donald E(dwin)

Staunton, Schuyler
See Baum, L(yman) Frank

Stead, Christina (Ellen)
1902-1983 .... CLC 2, 5, 8, 32, 80
See also CA 13-16R; 109; CANR 33, 40;
MTCW

Stead, William Thomas
1849-1912 .... TCLC 48

Steele, Richard 1672-1729 .... LC 18
See also CDBLB 1660-1789; DLB 84, 101

Steele, Timothy (Reid) 1948- .... CLC 45
See also CA 93-96; CANR 16, 50; DLB 120

Steffens, (Joseph) Lincoln
1866-1936 .... TCLC 20
See also CA 117

Stegner, Wallace (Earle)
1909-1993 ... CLC 9, 49, 81; DAM NOV;
SSC 27
See also AITN 1; BEST 90:3; CA 1-4R; 141;
CAAS 9; CANR 1, 21, 46; DLB 9; DLBY
93; MTCW

Stein, Gertrude
1874-1946 .... TCLC 1, 6, 28, 48; DA;
DAB; DAC; DAM MST, NOV, POET;
PC 18; WLC
See also CA 104; 132; CDALB 1917-1929;
DLB 4, 54, 86; DLBD 15; MTCW

Steinbeck, John (Ernst)
1902-1968 .... CLC 1, 5, 9, 13, 21, 34, 45,
75; DA; DAB; DAC; DAM DRAM,
MST, NOV; SSC 11; WLC
See also AAYA 12; CA 1-4R; 25-28R; CANR
1, 35; CDALB 1929-1941; DLB 7, 9; DLBD
2; MTCW; SATA 9

Steinem, Gloria 1934- .... CLC 63
See also CA 53-56; CANR 28, 51; MTCW

Steiner, George 1929- ... CLC 24; DAM NOV
See also CA 73-76; CANR 31; DLB 67;
MTCW; SATA 62

Steiner, K. Leslie
See Delany, Samuel R(ay, Jr.)

Steiner, Rudolf 1861-1925 .... TCLC 13
See also CA 107

Stendhal
1783-1842 ... NCLC 23, 46; DA; DAB;
DAC; DAM MST, NOV; SSC 27;
WLC
See also DLB 119

Stephen, Leslie 1832-1904 .... TCLC 23
See also CA 123; DLB 57, 144

Stephen, Sir Leslie
See Stephen, Leslie

Stephen, Virginia
See Woolf, (Adeline) Virginia

Stephens, James 1882(?)-1950 .... TCLC 4
See also CA 104; DLB 19, 153, 162

Stephens, Reed
See Donaldson, Stephen R.

Steptoe, Lydia
See Barnes, Djuna

Sterchi, Beat 1949- .... CLC 65

Sterling, Brett
See Bradbury, Ray (Douglas); Hamilton,
Edmond

Sterling, Bruce 1954- .... CLC 72
See also CA 119; CANR 44

Sterling, George 1869-1926 .... TCLC 20
See also CA 117; DLB 54

Stern, Gerald 1925- .... CLC 40, 100
See also CA 81-84; CANR 28; DLB 105

Stern, Richard (Gustave) 1928- .... CLC 4, 39
See also CA 1-4R; CANR 1, 25, 52; DLBY
87; INT CANR-25

Sternberg, Josef von 1894-1969 .... CLC 20
See also CA 81-84

Sterne, Laurence
1713-1768 .... LC 2; DA; DAB; DAC;
DAM MST, NOV; WLC
See also CDBLB 1660-1789; DLB 39

Sternheim, (William Adolf) Carl
1878-1942 .... TCLC 8
See also CA 105; DLB 56, 118

Stevens, Mark 1951- .... CLC 34
See also CA 122

Stevens, Wallace
1879-1955 ... TCLC 3, 12, 45; DA; DAB;
DAC; DAM MST, POET; PC 6; WLC
See also CA 104; 124; CDALB 1929-1941;
DLB 54; MTCW

Stevenson, Anne (Katharine)
1933- .... CLC 7, 33
See also CA 17-20R; CAAS 9; CANR 9, 33;
DLB 40; MTCW

Stevenson, Robert Louis (Balfour)
1850-1894 ... NCLC 5, 14, 63; DA; DAB;
DAC; DAM MST, NOV; YABC 2
See also CDBLB 1890-1914; CLR 10, 11; DLB
18, 57, 141, 156, 174; DLBD 13; JRDA;
MAICYA; YABC 2

Stewart, J(ohn) I(nnes) M(ackintosh)
1906-1994 .... CLC 7, 14, 32
See also CA 85-88; 147; CAAS 3; CANR 47;
MTCW

Stewart, Mary (Florence Elinor)
1916- .... CLC 7, 35; DAB
See also CA 1-4R; CANR 1, 59; SATA 12

Stewart, Mary Rainbow
See Stewart, Mary (Florence Elinor)

Stifle, June
See Campbell, Maria

Stifter, Adalbert
1805-1868 .... NCLC 41; SSC 28
See also DLB 133

Still, James 1906- .... **CLC 49**
See also CA 65-68; CAAS 17; CANR 10, 26;
DLB 9; SATA 29

Sting
See Sumner, Gordon Matthew

Stirling, Arthur
See Sinclair, Upton (Beall)

Stitt, Milan 1941- .... **CLC 29**
See also CA 69-72

Stockton, Francis Richard 1834-1902
See Stockton, Frank R.
See also CA 108; 137; MAICYA; SATA 44

Stockton, Frank R. .... **TCLC 47**
See also Stockton, Francis Richard
See also DLB 42, 74; DLBD 13; SATA-Brief
32

Stoddard, Charles
See Kuttner, Henry

Stoker, Abraham 1847-1912
See Stoker, Bram
See also CA 105; DA; DAC; DAM MST, NOV;
SATA 29

Stoker, Bram
1847-1912 .... **TCLC 8; DAB; WLC**
See also Stoker, Abraham
See also CA 150; CDBLB 1890-1914; DLB
36, 70, 178

Stolz, Mary (Slattery) 1920- .... **CLC 12**
See also AAYA 8; AITN 1; CA 5-8R; CANR
13, 41; JRDA; MAICYA; SAAS 3; SATA
10, 71

Stone, Irving
1903-1989 .... **CLC 7; DAM POP**
See also AITN 1; CA 1-4R; 129; CAAS 3;
CANR 1, 23; INT CANR-23; MTCW; SATA
3; SATA-Obit 64

Stone, Oliver (William) 1946- .... **CLC 73**
See also AAYA 15; CA 110; CANR 55

Stone, Robert (Anthony)
1937- .... **CLC 5, 23, 42**
See also CA 85-88; CANR 23; DLB 152; INT
CANR-23; MTCW

Stone, Zachary
See Follett, Ken(neth Martin)

Stoppard, Tom 1937-**CLC 1, 3, 4, 5, 8, 15, 29,
34, 63, 91; DA; DAB; DAC; DAM DRAM,
MST; DC 6; WLC**
See also CA 81-84; CANR 39; CDBLB
1960 to Present; DLB 13; DLBY 85;
MTCW

Storey, David (Malcolm)
1933- .... **CLC 2, 4, 5, 8; DAM DRAM**
See also CA 81-84; CANR 36; DLB 13, 14;
MTCW

Storm, Hyemeyohsts
1935- .... **CLC 3; DAM MULT**
See also CA 81-84; CANR 45; NNAL

Storm, (Hans) Theodor (Woldsen)
1817-1888 .... **NCLC 1; SSC 27**

Storni, Alfonsina
1892-1938 .... **TCLC 5; DAM MULT;
HLC**
See also CA 104; 131; HW

Stoughton, William 1631-1701 .... **LC 38**
See also DLB 24

Stout, Rex (Todhunter)
1886-1975 .... **CLC 3**
See also AITN 2; CA 61-64

Stow, (Julian) Randolph
1935- .... **CLC 23, 48**
See also CA 13-16R; CANR 33; MTCW

Stowe, Harriet (Elizabeth) Beecher
1811-1896 .... **NCLC 3, 50; DA; DAB;
DAC; DAM MST, NOV; WLC**
See also CDALB 1865-1917; DLB 1, 12, 42,
74; JRDA; MAICYA; YABC 1

Strachey, (Giles) Lytton
1880-1932 .... **TCLC 12**
See also CA 110; DLB 149; DLBD 10

Strand, Mark
1934- .... **CLC 6, 18, 41, 71; DAM
POET**
See also CA 21-24R; CANR 40; DLB 5; SATA
41

Straub, Peter (Francis)
1943- .... **CLC 28; DAM POP**
See also BEST 89:1; CA 85-88; CANR 28;
DLBY 84; MTCW

Strauss, Botho 1944- .... **CLC 22**
See also CA 157; DLB 124

Streatfeild, (Mary) Noel
1895(?)-1986 .... **CLC 21**
See also CA 81-84; 120; CANR 31; CLR 17;
DLB 160; MAICYA; SATA 20; SATA-Obit
48

Stribling, T(homas) S(igismund)
1881-1965 .... **CLC 23**
See also CA 107; DLB 9

Strindberg, (Johan) August
1849-1912 .... **TCLC 1, 8, 21, 47; DA;
DAB; DAC; DAM DRAM, MST; WLC**
See also CA 104; 135

Stringer, Arthur 1874-1950 .... **TCLC 37**
See also DLB 92

Stringer, David
See Roberts, Keith (John Kingston)

Stroheim, Erich von 1885-1957 ..... **TCLC 71**

Strugatskii, Arkadii (Natanovich)
1925-1991 .... **CLC 27**
See also CA 106; 135

Strugatskii, Boris (Natanovich)
1933- .... **CLC 27**
See also CA 106

Strummer, Joe 1953(?)- .... **CLC 30**

Stuart, Don A.
See Campbell, John W(ood, Jr.)

Stuart, Ian
See MacLean, Alistair (Stuart)

Stuart, Jesse (Hilton)
1906-1984 .... **CLC 1, 8, 11, 14, 34**
See also CA 5-8R; 112; CANR 31; DLB
9, 48, 102; DLBY 84; SATA 2; SATA-
Obit 36

Sturgeon, Theodore (Hamilton)
1918-1985 .... **CLC 22, 39**
See also Queen, Ellery
See also CA 81-84; 116; CANR 32; DLB 8;
DLBY 85; MTCW

Sturges, Preston 1898-1959 .... **TCLC 48**
See also CA 114; 149; DLB 26

Styron, William
1925- .... **CLC 1, 3, 5, 11, 15, 60; DAM
NOV, POP; SSC 25**
See also BEST 90:4; CA 5-8R; CANR 6, 33;
CDALB 1968-1988; DLB 2, 143; DLBY 80;
INT CANR-6; MTCW

Suarez Lynch, B.
See Bioy Casares, Adolfo; Borges, Jorge Luis

Su Chien 1884-1918
See Su Man-shu
See also CA 123

Suckow, Ruth 1892-1960 .... **SSC 18**
See also CA 113; DLB 9, 102

Sudermann, Hermann
1857-1928 .... **TCLC 15**
See also CA 107; DLB 118

Sue, Eugene 1804-1857 .... **NCLC 1**
See also DLB 119

Sueskind, Patrick 1949- .... **CLC 44**
See also Suskind, Patrick

Sukenick, Ronald
1932- .... **CLC 3, 4, 6, 48**
See also CA 25-28R; CAAS 8; CANR 32; DLB
173; DLBY 81

Suknaski, Andrew 1942- .... **CLC 19**
See also CA 101; DLB 53

Sullivan, Vernon
See Vian, Boris

Sully Prudhomme 1839-1907 .... **TCLC 31**

Su Man-shu .... **TCLC 24**
See also Su Chien

Summerforest, Ivy B.
See Kirkup, James

Summers, Andrew James 1942- .... **CLC 26**

Summers, Andy
See Summers, Andrew James

Summers, Hollis (Spurgeon, Jr.)
1916- .... CLC 10
See also CA 5-8R; CANR 3; DLB 6

**Summers, (Alphonsus Joseph-Mary Augustus)
Montague** 1880-1948 .... TCLC 16
See also CA 118

Sumner, Gordon Matthew 1951- ...... CLC 26

Surtees, Robert Smith
1803-1864 .... NCLC 14
See also DLB 21

Susann, Jacqueline 1921-1974 .... CLC 3
See also AITN 1; CA 65-68; 53-56;
MTCW

Su Shih 1036-1101 .... CMLC 15

Suskind, Patrick
See Sueskind, Patrick
See also CA 145

Sutcliff, Rosemary
1920-1992 .... **CLC 26; DAB; DAC;
DAM MST, POP**
See also AAYA 10; CA 5-8R; 139; CANR 37;
CLR 1, 37; JRDA; MAICYA; SATA 6, 44,
78; SATA-Obit 73

Sutro, Alfred 1863-1933 .... TCLC 6
See also CA 105; DLB 10

Sutton, Henry
See Slavitt, David R(ytman)

Svevo, Italo
1861-1928 .... TCLC 2, 35; SSC 25
See also Schmitz, Aron Hector

Swados, Elizabeth (A.)
1951- .... CLC 12
See also CA 97-100; CANR 49; INT 97-
100

Swados, Harvey 1920-1972 .... CLC 5
See also CA 5-8R; 37-40R; CANR 6; DLB
2

Swan, Gladys 1934- .... CLC 69
See also CA 101; CANR 17, 39

Swarthout, Glendon (Fred)
1918-1992 .... CLC 35
See also CA 1-4R; 139; CANR 1, 47; SATA
26

Sweet, Sarah C.
See Jewett, (Theodora) Sarah Orne

Swenson, May
1919-1989 ...... **CLC 4, 14, 61; DA; DAB;
DAC; DAM MST, POET; PC 14**
See also CA 5-8R; 130; CANR 36, 61; DLB 5;
MTCW; SATA 15

Swift, Augustus
See Lovecraft, H(oward) P(hillips)

Swift, Graham (Colin)
1949- .... CLC 41, 88
See also CA 117; 122; CANR 46

Swift, Jonathan
1667-1745 . **LC 1; DA; DAB; DAC;
DAM MST, NOV, POET; PC 9;
WLC**
See also CDBLB 1660-1789; DLB 39, 95, 101;
SATA 19

Swinburne, Algernon Charles
1837-1909 .... **TCLC 8, 36; DA; DAB;
DAC; DAM MST, POET; WLC**
See also CA 105; 140; CDBLB 1832-1890;
DLB 35, 57

Swinfen, Ann .... CLC 34

Swinnerton, Frank Arthur
1884-1982 .... CLC 31
See also CA 108; DLB 34

Swithen, John
See King, Stephen (Edwin)

Sylvia
See Ashton-Warner, Sylvia (Constance)

Symmes, Robert Edward
See Duncan, Robert (Edward)

Symonds, John Addington
1840-1893 .... NCLC 34
See also DLB 57, 144

Symons, Arthur 1865-1945 .... TCLC 11
See also CA 107; DLB 19, 57, 149

Symons, Julian (Gustave)
1912-1994 .... **CLC 2, 14, 32**
See also CA 49-52; 147; CAAS 3; CANR
3, 33, 59; DLB 87, 155; DLBY 92;
MTCW

Synge, (Edmund) J(ohn) M(illington)
1871-1909 ... **TCLC 6, 37; DAM DRAM;
DC 2**
See also CA 104; 141; CDBLB 1890-1914;
DLB 10, 19

Syruc, J.
See Milosz, Czeslaw

Szirtes, George 1948- .... CLC 46
See also CA 109; CANR 27, 61

Szymborska, Wislawa 1923- .... CLC 99
See also CA 154; DLBY 96

T. O., Nik
See Annensky, Innokenty (Fyodorovich)

Tabori, George 1914- .... CLC 19
See also CA 49-52; CANR 4

Tagore, Rabindranath
1861-1941 ... **TCLC 3, 53; DAM DRAM,
POET; PC 8**
See also CA 104; 120; MTCW

Taine, Hippolyte Adolphe
1828-1893 .... NCLC 15

Talese, Gay 1932- .... CLC 37
See also AITN 1; CA 1-4R; CANR 9, 58; INT
CANR-9; MTCW

Tallent, Elizabeth (Ann) 1954- .... CLC 45
See also CA 117; DLB 130

Tally, Ted 1952- .... CLC 42
See also CA 120; 124; INT 124

Tamayo y Baus, Manuel
1829-1898 .... NCLC 1

Tammsaare, A(nton) H(ansen)
1878-1940 .... TCLC 27

Tam'si, Tchicaya U
See Tchicaya, Gerald Felix

Tan, Amy (Ruth)
1952- ...... **CLC 59; DAM MULT, NOV,
POP**
See also AAYA 9; BEST 89:3; CA 136; CANR
54; DLB 173; SATA 75

Tandem, Felix
See Spitteler, Carl (Friedrich Georg)

Tanizaki, Jun'ichiro
1886-1965 .... **CLC 8, 14, 28; SSC 21**
See also CA 93-96; 25-28R; DLB 180

Tanner, William
See Amis, Kingsley (William)

Tao Lao
See Storni, Alfonsina

Tarassoff, Lev
See Troyat, Henri

Tarbell, Ida M(inerva)
1857-1944 .... TCLC 40
See also CA 122; DLB 47

Tarkington, (Newton) Booth
1869-1946 .... TCLC 9
See also CA 110; 143; DLB 9, 102; SATA 17

Tarkovsky, Andrei (Arsenyevich)
1932-1986 .... CLC 75
See also CA 127

Tartt, Donna 1964(?)- .... CLC 76
See also CA 142

Tasso, Torquato 1544-1595 .... LC 5

Tate, (John Orley) Allen
1899-1979 .... **CLC 2, 4, 6, 9, 11, 14, 24**
See also CA 5-8R; 85-88; CANR 32; DLB 4,
45, 63; MTCW

Tate, Ellalice
See Hibbert, Eleanor Alice Burford

Tate, James (Vincent)
1943- .... **CLC 2, 6, 25**
See also CA 21-24R; CANR 29, 57; DLB 5,
169

Tavel, Ronald 1940- .... CLC 6
See also CA 21-24R; CANR 33

Taylor, C(ecil) P(hilip)
1929-1981 .... CLC 27
See also CA 25-28R; 105; CANR 47

Taylor, Edward
1642(?)-1729 ... **LC 11; DA; DAB; DAC; DAM MST, POET**
See also DLB 24

Taylor, Eleanor Ross 1920- .... **CLC 5**
See also CA 81-84

Taylor, Elizabeth
1912-1975 .... **CLC 2, 4, 29**
See also CA 13-16R; CANR 9; DLB 139;
MTCW; SATA 13

Taylor, Frederick Winslow
1856-1915 .... **TCLC 76**

Taylor, Henry (Splawn) 1942- .... **CLC 44**
See also CA 33-36R; CAAS 7; CANR 31; DLB
5

Taylor, Kamala (Purnaiya) 1924-
See Markandaya, Kamala
See also CA 77-80

Taylor, Mildred D. .... **CLC 21**
See also AAYA 10; BW 1; CA 85-88; CANR
25; CLR 9; DLB 52; JRDA; MAICYA;
SAAS 5; SATA 15, 70

Taylor, Peter (Hillsman)
1917-1994 .... **CLC 1, 4, 18, 37, 44, 50,
71; SSC 10**
See also CA 13-16R; 147; CANR 9, 50; DLBY
81, 94; INT CANR-9; MTCW

Taylor, Robert Lewis 1912- .... **CLC 14**
See also CA 1-4R; CANR 3; SATA 10

Tchekhov, Anton
See Chekhov, Anton (Pavlovich)

Tchicaya, Gerald Felix
1931-1988 .... **CLC 101**
See also CA 129; 125

Tchicaya U Tam'si
See Tchicaya, Gerald Felix

Teasdale, Sara 1884-1933 .... **TCLC 4**
See also CA 104; DLB 45; SATA 32

Tegner, Esaias 1782-1846 .... **NCLC 2**

Teilhard de Chardin, (Marie Joseph) Pierre
1881-1955 .... **TCLC 9**
See also CA 105

Temple, Ann
See Mortimer, Penelope (Ruth)

Tennant, Emma (Christina)
1937- .... **CLC 13, 52**
See also CA 65-68; CAAS 9; CANR 10, 38,
59; DLB 14

Tenneshaw, S. M.
See Silverberg, Robert

Tennyson, Alfred
1809-1892 .. **NCLC 30, 65; DA; DAB;
DAC; DAM MST, POET; PC 6;
WLC**
See also CDBLB 1832-1890; DLB 32

Teran, Lisa St. Aubin de .... **CLC 36**
See also St. Aubin de Teran, Lisa

Terence
195(?)B.C.-159B.C. ...... **CMLC 14; DC 7**

Teresa de Jesus, St. 1515-1582 .... **LC 18**

Terkel, Louis 1912-
See Terkel, Studs
See also CA 57-60; CANR 18, 45;
MTCW

Terkel, Studs .... **CLC 38**
See also Terkel, Louis
See also AITN 1

Terry, C. V.
See Slaughter, Frank G(ill)

Terry, Megan 1932- .... **CLC 19**
See also CA 77-80; CABS 3; CANR 43; DLB
7

Tertz, Abram
See Sinyavsky, Andrei (Donatevich)

Tesich, Steve
1943(?)-1996 .... **CLC 40, 69**
See also CA 105; 152; DLBY 83

Teternikov, Fyodor Kuzmich 1863-1927
See Sologub, Fyodor
See also CA 104

Tevis, Walter 1928-1984 .... **CLC 42**
See also CA 113

Tey, Josephine .... **TCLC 14**
See also Mackintosh, Elizabeth
See also DLB 77

Thackeray, William Makepeace
1811-1863 **NCLC 5, 14, 22, 43; DA;
DAB; DAC; DAM MST, NOV;
WLC**
See also CDBLB 1832-1890; DLB 21, 55, 159,
163; SATA 23

Thakura, Ravindranatha
See Tagore, Rabindranath

Tharoor, Shashi 1956- .... **CLC 70**
See also CA 141

Thelwell, Michael Miles
1939- .... **CLC 22**
See also BW 2; CA 101

Theobald, Lewis, Jr.
See Lovecraft, H(oward) P(hillips)

Theodorescu, Ion N. 1880-1967
See Arghezi, Tudor
See also CA 116

Theriault, Yves
1915-1983 .... **CLC 79; DAC; DAM MST**
See also CA 102; DLB 88

Theroux, Alexander (Louis)
1939- .... **CLC 2, 25**
See also CA 85-88; CANR 20

Theroux, Paul (Edward)
1941- ...... **CLC 5, 8, 11, 15, 28, 46; DAM
POP**
See also BEST 89:4; CA 33-36R; CANR 20,
45; DLB 2; MTCW; SATA 44

Thesen, Sharon 1946- .... **CLC 56**

Thevenin, Denis
See Duhamel, Georges

Thibault, Jacques Anatole Francois 1844-1924
See France, Anatole
See also CA 106; 127; DAM NOV; MTCW

Thiele, Colin (Milton) 1920- .... **CLC 17**
See also CA 29-32R; CANR 12, 28, 53; CLR
27; MAICYA; SAAS 2; SATA 14, 72

Thomas, Audrey (Callahan)
1935- .... **CLC 7, 13, 37; SSC 20**
See also AITN 2; CA 21-24R; CAAS 19;
CANR 36, 58; DLB 60; MTCW

Thomas, D(onald) M(ichael)
1935- .... **CLC 13, 22, 31**
See also CA 61-64; CAAS 11; CANR 17, 45;
CDBLB 1960 to Present; DLB 40; INT
CANR-17; MTCW

Thomas, Dylan (Marlais)
1914-1953 ..... **TCLC 1, 8, 45; DA; DAB;
DAC; DAM DRAM, MST, POET; PC 2;
SSC 3; WLC**
See also CA 104; 120; CDBLB 1945-1960;
DLB 13, 20, 139; MTCW; SATA 60

Thomas, (Philip) Edward
1878-1917 .... **TCLC 10; DAM POET**
See also CA 106; 153; DLB 19

Thomas, Joyce Carol 1938- .... **CLC 35**
See also AAYA 12; BW 2; CA 113; 116;
CANR 48; CLR 19; DLB 33; INT 116;
JRDA; MAICYA; MTCW; SAAS 7; SATA
40, 78

Thomas, Lewis 1913-1993 .... **CLC 35**
See also CA 85-88; 143; CANR 38, 60; MTCW

Thomas, Paul
See Mann, (Paul) Thomas

Thomas, Piri 1928- .... **CLC 17**
See also CA 73-76; HW

Thomas, R(onald) S(tuart)
1913- .... **CLC 6, 13, 48; DAB; DAM
POET**
See also CA 89-92; CAAS 4; CANR 30;
CDBLB 1960 to Present; DLB 27;
MTCW

Thomas, Ross (Elmore) 1926-1995 ... **CLC 39**
See also CA 33-36R; 150; CANR 22

Thompson, Francis Clegg
See Mencken, H(enry) L(ouis)

Thompson, Francis Joseph
1859-1907 .... **TCLC 4**
See also CA 104; CDBLB 1890-1914; DLB
19

Thompson, Hunter S(tockton)
1939- ..... **CLC 9, 17, 40, 104; DAM POP**
See also BEST 89:1; CA 17-20R; CANR 23,
46; MTCW

Thompson, James Myers
See Thompson, Jim (Myers)

Thompson, Jim (Myers)
1906-1977(?) .... **CLC 69**
See also CA 140

Thompson, Judith .... **CLC 39**

Thomson, James
1700-1748 ... **LC 16, 29, 40; DAM POET**
See also DLB 95

Thomson, James
1834-1882 .... **NCLC 18; DAM POET**
See also DLB 35

Thoreau, Henry David
1817-1862 ... **NCLC 7, 21, 61; DA; DAB;**
DAC; DAM MST; WLC
See also CDALB 1640-1865; DLB 1

Thornton, Hall
See Silverberg, Robert

Thucydides c. 455B.C.-399B.C. .... **CMLC 17**
See also DLB 176

Thurber, James (Grover)
1894-1961 ... **CLC 5, 11, 25; DA; DAB;**
DAC; DAM DRAM, MST, NOV; SSC
1
See also CA 73-76; CANR 17, 39; CDALB
1929-1941; DLB 4, 11, 22, 102; MAICYA;
MTCW; SATA 13

Thurman, Wallace (Henry)
1902-1934 .... **TCLC 6; BLC; DAM**
MULT
See also BW 1; CA 104; 124; DLB 51

Ticheburn, Cheviot
See Ainsworth, William Harrison

Tieck, (Johann) Ludwig
1773-1853 .... **NCLC 5, 46**
See also DLB 90

Tiger, Derry
See Ellison, Harlan (Jay)

Tilghman, Christopher 1948(?)- .... **CLC 65**
See also CA 159

Tillinghast, Richard (Williford)
1940- .... **CLC 29**
See also CA 29-32R; CAAS 23; CANR 26,
51

Timrod, Henry 1828-1867 .... **NCLC 25**
See also DLB 3

Tindall, Gillian 1938- .... **CLC 7**
See also CA 21-24R; CANR 11

Tiptree, James, Jr. .... **CLC 48, 50**
See also Sheldon, Alice Hastings Bradley
See also DLB 8

Titmarsh, Michael Angelo
See Thackeray, William Makepeace

Tocqueville, Alexis (Charles Henri Maurice
Clerel Comte) 1805-1859 ... **NCLC 7, 63**

Tolkien, J(ohn) R(onald) R(euel)
1892-1973 .... **CLC 1, 2, 3, 8, 12, 38; DA;**
DAB; DAC; DAM MST, NOV, POP;
WLC
See also AAYA 10; AITN 1; CA 17-18; 45-48;
CANR 36; CAP 2; CDBLB 1914-1945;
DLB 15, 160; JRDA; MAICYA; MTCW;
SATA 2, 32; SATA-Obit 24

Toller, Ernst 1893-1939 .... **TCLC 10**
See also CA 107; DLB 124

Tolson, M. B.
See Tolson, Melvin B(eaunorus)

Tolson, Melvin B(eaunorus)
1898(?)-1966 .... **CLC 36, 105; BLC;**
DAM MULT, POET
See also BW 1; CA 124; 89-92; DLB 48, 76

Tolstoi, Aleksei Nikolaevich
See Tolstoy, Alexey Nikolaevich

Tolstoy, Alexey Nikolaevich
1882-1945 .... **TCLC 18**
See also CA 107; 158

Tolstoy, Count Leo
See Tolstoy, Leo (Nikolaevich)

Tolstoy, Leo (Nikolaevich)
1828-1910 ..... **TCLC 4, 11, 17, 28, 44;**
DA; DAB; DAC; DAM MST, NOV; SSC
9; WLC
See also CA 104; 123; SATA 26

Tomasi di Lampedusa, Giuseppe 1896-1957
See Lampedusa, Giuseppe (Tomasi) di
See also CA 111

Tomlin, Lily .... **CLC 17**
See also Tomlin, Mary Jean

Tomlin, Mary Jean 1939(?)-
See Tomlin, Lily
See also CA 117

Tomlinson, (Alfred) Charles
1927- .... **CLC 2, 4, 6, 13, 45; DAM**
POET; PC 17
See also CA 5-8R; CANR 33; DLB 40

Tomlinson, H(enry) M(ajor)
1873-1958 .... **TCLC 71**
See also CA 118; DLB 36, 100

Tonson, Jacob
See Bennett, (Enoch) Arnold

Toole, John Kennedy
1937-1969 .... **CLC 19, 64**
See also CA 104; DLBY 81

Toomer, Jean 1894-1967 .... **CLC 1, 4, 13, 22;**
BLC; DAM MULT; PC 7; SSC 1; WLCS
See also BW 1; CA 85-88; CDALB 1917-1929;
DLB 45, 51; MTCW

Torley, Luke
See Blish, James (Benjamin)

Tornimparte, Alessandra
See Ginzburg, Natalia

Torre, Raoul della
See Mencken, H(enry) L(ouis)

Torrey, E(dwin) Fuller 1937- .... **CLC 34**
See also CA 119

Torsvan, Ben Traven
See Traven, B.

Torsvan, Benno Traven
See Traven, B.

Torsvan, Berick Traven
See Traven, B.

Torsvan, Berwick Traven
See Traven, B.

Torsvan, Bruno Traven
See Traven, B.

Torsvan, Traven
See Traven, B.

Tournier, Michel (Edouard)
1924- .... **CLC 6, 23, 36, 95**
See also CA 49-52; CANR 3, 36; DLB 83;
MTCW; SATA 23

Tournimparte, Alessandra
See Ginzburg, Natalia

Towers, Ivar
See Kornbluth, C(yril) M.

Towne, Robert (Burton) 1936(?)- ..... **CLC 87**
See also CA 108; DLB 44

Townsend, Sue 1946- .... **CLC 61; DAB; DAC**
See also CA 119; 127; INT 127; MTCW; SATA
55, 93; SATA-Brief 48

Townshend, Peter (Dennis Blandford)
1945- .... **CLC 17, 42**
See also CA 107

Tozzi, Federigo 1883-1920 .... **TCLC 31**
See also CA 160

Traill, Catharine Parr
1802-1899 .... **NCLC 31**
See also DLB 99

Trakl, Georg
1887-1914 .... **TCLC 5; PC 20**
See also CA 104

Transtroemer, Tomas (Goesta)
1931- .... **CLC 52, 65; DAM POET**
See also CA 117; 129; CAAS 17

Transtromer, Tomas Gosta
See Transtroemer, Tomas (Goesta)

Traven, B. (?)-1969 .... **CLC 8, 11**
See also CA 19-20; 25-28R; CAP 2; DLB 9,
56; MTCW

Treitel, Jonathan 1959- .... CLC 70

Tremain, Rose 1943- .... CLC 42
See also CA 97-100; CANR 44; DLB 14

Tremblay, Michel
1942- ... CLC 29, 102; DAC; DAM MST
See also CA 116; 128; DLB 60; MTCW

Trevanian .... CLC 29
See also Whitaker, Rod(ney)

Trevor, Glen
See Hilton, James

Trevor, William
1928- .... CLC 7, 9, 14, 25, 71; SSC 21
See also Cox, William Trevor
See also DLB 14, 139

Trifonov, Yuri (Valentinovich)
1925-1981 .... CLC 45
See also CA 126; 103; MTCW

Trilling, Lionel 1905-1975 ...... CLC 9, 11, 24
See also CA 9-12R; 61-64; CANR 10; DLB
28, 63; INT CANR-10; MTCW

Trimball, W. H.
See Mencken, H(enry) L(ouis)

Tristan
See Gomez de la Serna, Ramon

Tristram
See Housman, A(lfred) E(dward)

Trogdon, William (Lewis) 1939-
See Heat-Moon, William Least
See also CA 115; 119; CANR 47; INT 119

Trollope, Anthony
1815-1882 .... NCLC 6, 33; DA; DAB;
DAC; DAM MST, NOV; SSC 28; WLC
See also CDBLB 1832-1890; DLB 21, 57, 159;
SATA 22

Trollope, Frances 1779-1863 .... NCLC 30
See also DLB 21, 166

Trotsky, Leon 1879-1940 .... TCLC 22
See also CA 118

Trotter (Cockburn), Catharine
1679-1749 .... LC 8
See also DLB 84

Trout, Kilgore
See Farmer, Philip Jose

Trow, George W. S. 1943- .... CLC 52
See also CA 126

Troyat, Henri 1911- .... CLC 23
See also CA 45-48; CANR 2, 33; MTCW

Trudeau, G(arretson) B(eekman) 1948-
See Trudeau, Garry B.
See also CA 81-84; CANR 31; SATA 35

Trudeau, Garry B. .... CLC 12
See also Trudeau, G(arretson) B(eekman)
See also AAYA 10; AITN 2

Truffaut, Francois
1932-1984 .... CLC 20, 101
See also CA 81-84; 113; CANR 34

Trumbo, Dalton 1905-1976 .... CLC 19
See also CA 21-24R; 69-72; CANR 10; DLB
26

Trumbull, John 1750-1831 .... NCLC 30
See also DLB 31

Trundlett, Helen B.
See Eliot, T(homas) S(tearns)

Tryon, Thomas
1926-1991 .... CLC 3, 11; DAM POP
See also AITN 1; CA 29-32R; 135; CANR 32;
MTCW

Tryon, Tom
See Tryon, Thomas

Ts'ao Hsueh-ch'in 1715(?)-1763 .... LC 1

Tsushima, Shuji 1909-1948
See Dazai, Osamu
See also CA 107

Tsvetaeva (Efron), Marina (Ivanovna)
1892-1941 .... TCLC 7, 35; PC 14
See also CA 104; 128; MTCW

Tuck, Lily 1938- .... CLC 70
See also CA 139

Tu Fu 712-770 .... PC 9
See also DAM MULT

Tunis, John R(oberts) 1889-1975 ...... CLC 12
See also CA 61-64; CANR 62; DLB 22, 171;
JRDA; MAICYA; SATA 37; SATA-Brief 30

Tuohy, Frank .... CLC 37
See also Tuohy, John Francis
See also DLB 14, 139

Tuohy, John Francis 1925-
See Tuohy, Frank
See also CA 5-8R; CANR 3, 47

Turco, Lewis (Putnam) 1934- ...... CLC 11, 63
See also CA 13-16R; CAAS 22; CANR 24, 51;
DLBY 84

Turgenev, Ivan 1818-1883 .... NCLC 21; DA;
DAB; DAC; DAM MST, NOV; DC 7; SSC
7; WLC

Turgot, Anne-Robert-Jacques
1727-1781 .... LC 26

Turner, Frederick 1943- .... CLC 48
See also CA 73-76; CAAS 10; CANR 12, 30,
56; DLB 40

Tutu, Desmond M(pilo)
1931- .... CLC 80; BLC; DAM MULT
See also BW 1; CA 125

Tutuola, Amos 1920-1997 ...... CLC 5, 14, 29;
BLC; DAM MULT
See also BW 2; CA 9-12R; 159; CANR 27;
DLB 125; MTCW

Twain, Mark ... TCLC 6, 12, 19, 36, 48, 59;
SSC 26; WLC
See also Clemens, Samuel Langhorne
See also AAYA 20; DLB 11, 12, 23, 64, 74

Tyler, Anne
1941- ...... CLC 7, 11, 18, 28, 44, 59, 103;
DAM NOV, POP
See also AAYA 18; BEST 89:1; CA 9-12R;
CANR 11, 33, 53; DLB 6, 143; DLBY 82;
MTCW; SATA 7, 90

Tyler, Royall 1757-1826 .... NCLC 3
See also DLB 37

Tynan, Katharine 1861-1931 .... TCLC 3
See also CA 104; DLB 153

Tyutchev, Fyodor 1803-1873 .... NCLC 34

Tzara, Tristan 1896-1963 ...... CLC 47; DAM
POET
See also Rosenfeld, Samuel; Rosenstock, Sami;
Rosenstock, Samuel
See also CA 153

Uhry, Alfred 1936- ... CLC 55; DAM DRAM,
POP
See also CA 127; 133; INT 133

Ulf, Haerved
See Strindberg, (Johan) August

Ulf, Harved
See Strindberg, (Johan) August

Ulibarri, Sabine R(eyes)
1919- .... CLC 83; DAM MULT
See also CA 131; DLB 82; HW

Unamuno (y Jugo), Miguel de
1864-1936 ...... TCLC 2, 9; DAM MULT,
NOV; HLC; SSC 11
See also CA 104; 131; DLB 108; HW; MTCW

Undercliffe, Errol
See Campbell, (John) Ramsey

Underwood, Miles
See Glassco, John

Undset, Sigrid
1882-1949 .... TCLC 3; DA; DAB; DAC;
DAM MST, NOV; WLC
See also CA 104; 129; MTCW

Ungaretti, Giuseppe
1888-1970 .... CLC 7, 11, 15
See also CA 19-20; 25-28R; CAP 2; DLB 114

Unger, Douglas 1952- .... CLC 34
See also CA 130

Unsworth, Barry (Forster) 1930- ..... CLC 76
See also CA 25-28R; CANR 30, 54

Updike, John (Hoyer)
1932- ... CLC 1, 2, 3, 5, 7, 9, 13, 15, 23,
34, 43, 70; DA; DAB; DAC; DAM MST,
NOV, POET, POP; SSC 13, 27; WLC
See also CA 1-4R; CABS 1; CANR 4, 33, 51;
CDALB 1968-1988; DLB 2, 5, 143; DLBD
3; DLBY 80, 82; MTCW

Very, Jones 1813-1880 .... NCLC 9
See also DLB 1

Vesaas, Tarjei 1897-1970 .... CLC 48
See also CA 29-32R

Vialis, Gaston
See Simenon, Georges (Jacques Christian)

Vian, Boris 1920-1959 .... TCLC 9
See also CA 106; DLB 72

Viaud, (Louis Marie) Julien 1850-1923
See Loti, Pierre
See also CA 107

Vicar, Henry
See Felsen, Henry Gregor

Vicker, Angus
See Felsen, Henry Gregor

Vidal, Gore
1925- .... CLC 2, 4, 6, 8, 10, 22, 33, 72;
DAM NOV, POP
See also AITN 1; BEST 90:2; CA 5-8R;
CANR 13, 45; DLB 6, 152; INT CANR-
13; MTCW

Viereck, Peter (Robert Edwin)
1916- .... CLC 4
See also CA 1-4R; CANR 1, 47; DLB 5

Vigny, Alfred (Victor) de
1797-1863 .... NCLC 7; DAM POET
See also DLB 119

Vilakazi, Benedict Wallet
1906-1947 .... TCLC 37

**Villiers de l'Isle Adam, Jean Marie Mathias
Philippe Auguste Comte**
1838-1889 .... NCLC 3; SSC 14
See also DLB 123

Villon, Francois 1431-1463(?) .... PC 13

Vinci, Leonardo da 1452-1519 .... LC 12

Vine, Barbara .... CLC 50
See also Rendell, Ruth (Barbara)
See also BEST 90:4

Vinge, Joan D(ennison)
1948- .... CLC 30; SSC 24
See also CA 93-96; SATA 36

Violis, G.
See Simenon, Georges (Jacques Christian)

Visconti, Luchino 1906-1976 .... CLC 16
See also CA 81-84; 65-68; CANR 39

Vittorini, Elio 1908-1966 .... CLC 6, 9, 14
See also CA 133; 25-28R

Vizenor, Gerald Robert 1934- .... CLC 103;
DAM MULT
See also CA 13-16R; CAAS 22; CANR 5, 21,
44; DLB 175; NNAL

Vizinczey, Stephen 1933- .... CLC 40
See also CA 128; INT 128

Vliet, R(ussell) G(ordon)
1929-1984 .... CLC 22
See also CA 37-40R; 112; CANR 18

Vogau, Boris Andreyevich 1894-1937(?)
See Pilnyak, Boris
See also CA 123

Vogel, Paula A(nne) 1951- .... CLC 76
See also CA 108

Voight, Ellen Bryant 1943- .... CLC 54
See also CA 69-72; CANR 11, 29, 55; DLB
120

Voigt, Cynthia 1942- .... CLC 30
See also AAYA 3; CA 106; CANR 18, 37, 40;
CLR 13; INT CANR-18; JRDA; MAICYA;
SATA 48, 79; SATA-Brief 33

Voinovich, Vladimir (Nikolaevich)
1932- .... CLC 10, 49
See also CA 81-84; CAAS 12; CANR 33;
MTCW

Vollmann, William T.
1959- .... CLC 89; DAM NOV, POP
See also CA 134

Voloshinov, V. N.
See Bakhtin, Mikhail Mikhailovich

Voltaire
1694-1778 .... LC 14; DA; DAB; DAC;
DAM DRAM, MST; SSC 12; WLC

von Daeniken, Erich 1935- .... CLC 30
See also AITN 1; CA 37-40R; CANR 17,
44

von Daniken, Erich
See von Daeniken, Erich

von Heidenstam, (Carl Gustaf) Verner
See Heidenstam, (Carl Gustaf) Verner von

von Heyse, Paul (Johann Ludwig)
See Heyse, Paul (Johann Ludwig von)

von Hofmannsthal, Hugo
See Hofmannsthal, Hugo von

von Horvath, Odon
See Horvath, Oedoen von

von Horvath, Oedoen
See Horvath, Oedoen von

von Liliencron, (Friedrich Adolf Axel) Detlev
See Liliencron, (Friedrich Adolf Axel) Detlev
von

Vonnegut, Kurt, Jr.
1922- .... CLC 1, 2, 3, 4, 5, 8, 12, 22, 40,
60; DA; DAB; DAC; DAM MST, NOV,
POP; SSC 8; WLC
See also AAYA 6; AITN 1; BEST 90:4; CA
1-4R; CANR 1, 25, 49; CDALB 1968-
1988; DLB 2, 8, 152; DLBD 3; DLBY 80;
MTCW

Von Rachen, Kurt
See Hubbard, L(afayette) Ron(ald)

von Rezzori (d'Arezzo), Gregor
See Rezzori (d'Arezzo), Gregor von

von Sternberg, Josef
See Sternberg, Josef von

Vorster, Gordon 1924- .... CLC 34
See also CA 133

Vosce, Trudie
See Ozick, Cynthia

Voznesensky, Andrei (Andreievich)
1933- .... CLC 1, 15, 57; DAM POET
See also CA 89-92; CANR 37; MTCW

Waddington, Miriam 1917- .... CLC 28
See also CA 21-24R; CANR 12, 30; DLB
68

Wagman, Fredrica 1937- .... CLC 7
See also CA 97-100; INT 97-100

Wagner, Linda W.
See Wagner-Martin, Linda (C.)

Wagner, Linda Welshimer
See Wagner-Martin, Linda (C.)

Wagner, Richard
1813-1883 .... NCLC 9
See also DLB 129

Wagner-Martin, Linda (C.)
1936- .... CLC 50
See also CA 159

Wagoner, David (Russell)
1926- .... CLC 3, 5, 15
See also CA 1-4R; CAAS 3; CANR 2; DLB 5;
SATA 14

Wah, Fred(erick James)
1939- .... CLC 44
See also CA 107; 141; DLB 60

Wahloo, Per
1926-1975 .... CLC 7
See also CA 61-64

Wahloo, Peter
See Wahloo, Per

Wain, John (Barrington)
1925-1994 .... CLC 2, 11, 15, 46
See also CA 5-8R; 145; CAAS 4; CANR 23,
54; CDBLB 1960 to Present; DLB 15, 27,
139, 155; MTCW

Wajda, Andrzej 1926- .... CLC 16
See also CA 102

Wakefield, Dan 1932- .... CLC 7
See also CA 21-24R; CAAS 7

Wakoski, Diane
1937- .... CLC 2, 4, 7, 9, 11, 40; DAM
POET; PC 15
See also CA 13-16R; CAAS 1; CANR 9, 60;
DLB 5; INT CANR-9

Wakoski-Sherbell, Diane
See Wakoski, Diane

Watkins, Paul 1964- .... **CLC 55**
See also CA 132; CANR 62

Watkins, Vernon Phillips
1906-1967 .... **CLC 43**
See also CA 9-10; 25-28R; CAP 1; DLB
20

Watson, Irving S.
See Mencken, H(enry) L(ouis)

Watson, John H.
See Farmer, Philip Jose

Watson, Richard F.
See Silverberg, Robert

Waugh, Auberon (Alexander)
1939- .... **CLC 7**
See also CA 45-48; CANR 6, 22; DLB 14

Waugh, Evelyn (Arthur St. John)
1903-1966 .... **CLC 1, 3, 8, 13, 19, 27, 44;
DA; DAB; DAC; DAM MST, NOV,
POP; WLC**
See also CA 85-88; 25-28R; CANR 22;
CDBLB 1914-1945; DLB 15, 162;
MTCW

Waugh, Harriet 1944- .... **CLC 6**
See also CA 85-88; CANR 22

Ways, C. R.
See Blount, Roy (Alton), Jr.

Waystaff, Simon
See Swift, Jonathan

Webb, (Martha) Beatrice (Potter)
1858-1943 .... **TCLC 22**
See also Potter, (Helen) Beatrix
See also CA 117

Webb, Charles (Richard) 1939- .... **CLC 7**
See also CA 25-28R

Webb, James H(enry), Jr. 1946- .... **CLC 22**
See also CA 81-84

Webb, Mary (Gladys Meredith)
1881-1927 .... **TCLC 24**
See also CA 123; DLB 34

Webb, Mrs. Sidney
See Webb, (Martha) Beatrice (Potter)

Webb, Phyllis 1927- .... **CLC 18**
See also CA 104; CANR 23; DLB 53

Webb, Sidney (James)
1859-1947 .... **TCLC 22**
See also CA 117

Webber, Andrew Lloyd .... **CLC 21**
See also Lloyd Webber, Andrew

Weber, Lenora Mattingly
1895-1971 .... **CLC 12**
See also CA 19-20; 29-32R; CAP 1; SATA 2;
SATA-Obit 26

Weber, Max 1864-1920 .... **TCLC 69**
See also CA 109

Webster, John
1579(?)-1634(?) .... **LC 33; DA; DAB;
DAC; DAM DRAM, MST; DC 2; WLC**
See also CDBLB Before 1660; DLB 58

Webster, Noah 1758-1843 .... **NCLC 30**

Wedekind, (Benjamin) Frank(lin)
1864-1918 .... **TCLC 7; DAM DRAM**
See also CA 104; 153; DLB 118

Weidman, Jerome 1913- .... **CLC 7**
See also AITN 2; CA 1-4R; CANR 1; DLB 28

Weil, Simone (Adolphine)
1909-1943 .... **TCLC 23**
See also CA 117; 159

Weinstein, Nathan
See West, Nathanael

Weinstein, Nathan von Wallenstein
See West, Nathanael

Weir, Peter (Lindsay) 1944- .... **CLC 20**
See also CA 113; 123

Weiss, Peter (Ulrich)
1916-1982 .... **CLC 3, 15, 51; DAM
DRAM**
See also CA 45-48; 106; CANR 3; DLB 69,
124

Weiss, Theodore (Russell)
1916- .... **CLC 3, 8, 14**
See also CA 9-12R; CAAS 2; CANR 46; DLB
5

Welch, (Maurice) Denton
1915-1948 .... **TCLC 22**
See also CA 121; 148

Welch, James
1940- ...... **CLC 6, 14, 52; DAM MULT,
POP**
See also CA 85-88; CANR 42; DLB 175;
NNAL

Weldon, Fay
1933- ...... **CLC 6, 9, 11, 19, 36, 59; DAM
POP**
See also CA 21-24R; CANR 16, 46; CDBLB
1960 to Present; DLB 14; INT CANR-16;
MTCW

Wellek, Rene
1903-1995 .... **CLC 28**
See also CA 5-8R; 150; CAAS 7; CANR 8;
DLB 63; INT CANR-8

Weller, Michael 1942- .... **CLC 10, 53**
See also CA 85-88

Weller, Paul 1958- .... **CLC 26**

Wellershoff, Dieter 1925- .... **CLC 46**
See also CA 89-92; CANR 16, 37

Welles, (George) Orson
1915-1985 .... **CLC 20, 80**
See also CA 93-96; 117

Wellman, Mac 1945- .... **CLC 65**

Wellman, Manly Wade 1903-1986 .... **CLC 49**
See also CA 1-4R; 118; CANR 6, 16, 44; SATA
6; SATA-Obit 47

Wells, Carolyn 1869(?)-1942 .... **TCLC 35**
See also CA 113; DLB 11

Wells, H(erbert) G(eorge)
1866-1946 ... **TCLC 6, 12, 19; DA; DAB;
DAC; DAM MST, NOV; SSC 6; WLC**
See also AAYA 18; CA 110; 121; CDBLB
1914-1945; DLB 34, 70, 156, 178; MTCW;
SATA 20

Wells, Rosemary 1943- .... **CLC 12**
See also AAYA 13; CA 85-88; CANR 48; CLR
16; MAICYA; SAAS 1; SATA 18, 69

Welty, Eudora
1909- ..... **CLC 1, 2, 5, 14, 22, 33, 105;
DA; DAB; DAC; DAM MST, NOV; SSC
1, 27; WLC**
See also CA 9-12R; CABS 1; CANR 32;
CDALB 1941-1968; DLB 2, 102, 143;
DLBD 12; DLBY 87; MTCW

Wen I-to 1899-1946 .... **TCLC 28**

Wentworth, Robert
See Hamilton, Edmond

Werfel, Franz (V.) 1890-1945 .... **TCLC 8**
See also CA 104; DLB 81, 124

Wergeland, Henrik Arnold
1808-1845 .... **NCLC 5**

Wersba, Barbara 1932- .... **CLC 30**
See also AAYA 2; CA 29-32R; CANR 16, 38;
CLR 3; DLB 52; JRDA; MAICYA; SAAS
2; SATA 1, 58

Wertmueller, Lina 1928- .... **CLC 16**
See also CA 97-100; CANR 39

Wescott, Glenway 1901-1987 .... **CLC 13**
See also CA 13-16R; 121; CANR 23; DLB 4,
9, 102

Wesker, Arnold
1932- .... **CLC 3, 5, 42; DAB; DAM
DRAM**
See also CA 1-4R; CAAS 7; CANR 1, 33;
CDBLB 1960 to Present; DLB 13; MTCW

Wesley, Richard (Errol) 1945- .... **CLC 7**
See also BW 1; CA 57-60; CANR 27; DLB
38

Wessel, Johan Herman 1742-1785 .... **LC 7**

West, Anthony (Panther)
1914-1987 .... **CLC 50**
See also CA 45-48; 124; CANR 3, 19; DLB
15

West, C. P.
See Wodehouse, P(elham) G(renville)

West, (Mary) Jessamyn
1902-1984 .... **CLC 7, 17**
See also CA 9-12R; 112; CANR 27; DLB 6;
DLBY 84; MTCW; SATA-Obit 37

Wilding, Michael 1942- .... CLC 73
  See also CA 104; CANR 24, 49

Wiley, Richard 1944- .... CLC 44
  See also CA 121; 129

Wilhelm, Kate .... CLC 7
  See also Wilhelm, Katie Gertrude
  See also AAYA 20; CAAS 5; DLB 8; INT
  CANR-17

Wilhelm, Katie Gertrude 1928-
  See Wilhelm, Kate
  See also CA 37-40R; CANR 17, 36, 60;
  MTCW

Wilkins, Mary
  See Freeman, Mary Eleanor Wilkins

Willard, Nancy
  1936- .... CLC 7, 37
  See also CA 89-92; CANR 10, 39; CLR 5; DLB
  5, 52; MAICYA; MTCW; SATA 37, 71;
  SATA-Brief 30

Williams, C(harles) K(enneth)
  1936- .... CLC 33, 56; DAM POET
  See also CA 37-40R; CAAS 26; CANR 57;
  DLB 5

Williams, Charles
  See Collier, James L(incoln)

Williams, Charles (Walter Stansby) 1
  886-1945 .... TCLC 1, 11
  See also CA 104; DLB 100, 153

Williams, (George) Emlyn
  1905-1987 .... CLC 15; DAM DRAM
  See also CA 104; 123; CANR 36; DLB 10,
  77; MTCW

Williams, Hugo 1942- .... CLC 42
  See also CA 17-20R; CANR 45; DLB
  40

Williams, J. Walker
  See Wodehouse, P(elham) G(renville)

Williams, John A(lfred)
  1925- ..... CLC 5, 13; BLC; DAM MULT
  See also BW 2; CA 53-56; CAAS 3; CANR
  6, 26, 51; DLB 2, 33; INT CANR-6

Williams, Jonathan (Chamberlain)
  1929- .... CLC 13
  See also CA 9-12R; CAAS 12; CANR 8; DLB
  5

Williams, Joy 1944- .... CLC 31
  See also CA 41-44R; CANR 22, 48

Williams, Norman 1952- .... CLC 39
  See also CA 118

Williams, Sherley Anne
  1944- .... CLC 89; BLC; DAM MULT,
  POET
  See also BW 2; CA 73-76; CANR 25; DLB
  41; INT CANR-25; SATA 78

Williams, Shirley
  See Williams, Sherley Anne

Williams, Tennessee
  1911-1983 .. CLC 1, 2, 5, 7, 8, 11, 15, 19,
  30, 39, 45, 71; DA; DAB; DAC; DAM
  DRAM, MST; DC 4; WLC
  See also AITN 1, 2; CA 5-8R; 108; CABS 3;
  CANR 31; CDALB 1941-1968; DLB 7;
  DLBD 4; DLBY 83; MTCW

Williams, Thomas (Alonzo)
  1926-1990 .... CLC 14
  See also CA 1-4R; 132; CANR 2

Williams, William C.
  See Williams, William Carlos

Williams, William Carlos
  1883-1963 .... CLC 1, 2, 5, 9, 13, 22, 42,
  67; DA; DAB; DAC; DAM MST, POET;
  PC 7
  See also CA 89-92; CANR 34; CDALB
  1917-1929; DLB 4, 16, 54, 86;
  MTCW

Williamson, David (Keith) 1942- ...... CLC 56
  See also CA 103; CANR 41

Williamson, Ellen Douglas 1905-1984
  See Douglas, Ellen
  See also CA 17-20R; 114; CANR 39

Williamson, Jack .... CLC 29
  See also Williamson, John Stewart
  See also CAAS 8; DLB 8

Williamson, John Stewart 1908-
  See Williamson, Jack
  See also CA 17-20R; CANR 23

Willie, Frederick
  See Lovecraft, H(oward) P(hillips)

Willingham, Calder (Baynard, Jr.)
  1922-1995 .... CLC 5, 51
  See also CA 5-8R; 147; CANR 3; DLB 2, 44;
  MTCW

Willis, Charles
  See Clarke, Arthur C(harles)

Willy
  See Colette, (Sidonie-Gabrielle)

Willy, Colette
  See Colette, (Sidonie-Gabrielle)

Wilson, A(ndrew) N(orman)
  1950- .... CLC 33
  See also CA 112; 122; DLB 14, 155

Wilson, Angus (Frank Johnstone)
  1913-1991... CLC 2, 3, 5, 25, 34; SSC
  21
  See also CA 5-8R; 134; CANR 21; DLB 15,
  139, 155; MTCW

Wilson, August
  1945- . CLC 39, 50, 63; BLC; DA; DAB;
  DAC; DAM DRAM, MST, MULT; DC
  2; WLCS
  See also AAYA 16; BW 2; CA 115; 122; CANR
  42, 54; MTCW

Wilson, Brian 1942- .... CLC 12

Wilson, Colin 1931- .... CLC 3, 14
  See also CA 1-4R; CAAS 5; CANR 1, 22, 33;
  DLB 14; MTCW

Wilson, Dirk
  See Pohl, Frederik

Wilson, Edmund
  1895-1972 .... CLC 1, 2, 3, 8, 24
  See also CA 1-4R; 37-40R; CANR 1, 46; DLB
  63; MTCW

Wilson, Ethel Davis (Bryant)
  1888(?)-1980 .... CLC 13; DAC; DAM
  POET
  See also CA 102; DLB 68; MTCW

Wilson, John 1785-1854 .... NCLC 5

Wilson, John (Anthony) Burgess 1917-1993
  See Burgess, Anthony
  See also CA 1-4R; 143; CANR 2, 46; DAC;
  DAM NOV; MTCW

Wilson, Lanford
  1937- .... CLC 7, 14, 36; DAM DRAM
  See also CA 17-20R; CABS 3; CANR 45; DLB 7

Wilson, Robert M. 1944- .... CLC 7, 9
  See also CA 49-52; CANR 2, 41; MTCW

Wilson, Robert McLiam 1964- .... CLC 59
  See also CA 132

Wilson, Sloan 1920- .... CLC 32
  See also CA 1-4R; CANR 1, 44

Wilson, Snoo 1948- .... CLC 33
  See also CA 69-72

Wilson, William S(mith) 1932- .... CLC 49
  See also CA 81-84

Wilson, Woodrow 1856-1924 .... TCLC 73
  See also DLB 47

**Winchilsea, Anne (Kingsmill) Finch, Countess
of** 1661-1720 .... LC 3

Windham, Basil
  See Wodehouse, P(elham) G(renville)

Wingrove, David (John) 1954- .... CLC 68
  See also CA 133

Wintergreen, Jane
  See Duncan, Sara Jeannette

Winters, Janet Lewis .... CLC 41
  See also Lewis, Janet
  See also DLBY 87

Winters, (Arthur) Yvor
  1900-1968 .... CLC 4, 8, 32
  See also CA 11-12; 25-28R; CAP 1; DLB 48;
  MTCW

Winterson, Jeanette
  1959- .... CLC 64; DAM POP
  See also CA 136; CANR 58

Winthrop, John 1588-1649 .... LC 31
  See also DLB 24, 30

Xenophon c. 430B.C.-c. 354B.C. ... **CMLC 17**
See also DLB 176

Yakumo Koizumi
See Hearn, (Patricio) Lafcadio (Tessima Carlos)

Yanez, Jose Donoso
See Donoso (Yanez), Jose

Yanovsky, Basile S.
See Yanovsky, V(assily) S(emenovich)

Yanovsky, V(assily) S(emenovich)
1906-1989 .... **CLC 2, 18**
See also CA 97-100; 129

Yates, Richard 1926-1992 .... **CLC 7, 8, 23**
See also CA 5-8R; 139; CANR 10, 43; DLB 2; DLBY 81, 92; INT CANR-10

Yeats, W. B.
See Yeats, William Butler

Yeats, William Butler
1865-1939 .... **TCLC 1, 11, 18, 31; DA; DAB; DAC; DAM DRAM, MST, POET; PC 20; WLC**
See also CA 104; 127; CANR 45; CDBLB 1890-1914; DLB 10, 19, 98, 156; MTCW

Yehoshua, A(braham) B.
1936- .... **CLC 13, 31**
See also CA 33-36R; CANR 43

Yep, Laurence Michael 1948-............ **CLC 35**
See also AAYA 5; CA 49-52; CANR 1, 46; CLR 3, 17; DLB 52; JRDA; MAICYA; SATA 7, 69

Yerby, Frank G(arvin)
1916-1991 ..... **CLC 1, 7, 22; BLC; DAM MULT**
See also BW 1; CA 9-12R; 136; CANR 16, 52; DLB 76; INT CANR-16; MTCW

Yesenin, Sergei Alexandrovich
See Esenin, Sergei (Alexandrovich)

Yevtushenko, Yevgeny (Alexandrovich)
1933- .... **CLC 1, 3, 13, 26, 51; DAM POET**
See also CA 81-84; CANR 33, 54; MTCW

Yezierska, Anzia 1885(?)-1970 .... **CLC 46**
See also CA 126; 89-92; DLB 28; MTCW

Yglesias, Helen 1915- .... **CLC 7, 22**
See also CA 37-40R; CAAS 20; CANR 15; INT CANR-15; MTCW

Yokomitsu Riichi 1898-1947 .... **TCLC 47**

Yonge, Charlotte (Mary)
1823-1901 .... **TCLC 48**
See also CA 109; DLB 18, 163; SATA 17

York, Jeremy
See Creasey, John

York, Simon
See Heinlein, Robert A(nson)

Yorke, Henry Vincent 1905-1974 ...... **CLC 13**
See also Green, Henry
See also CA 85-88; 49-52

Yosano Akiko 1878-1942 .... **TCLC 59; PC 11**

Yoshimoto, Banana .... **CLC 84**
See also Yoshimoto, Mahoko

Yoshimoto, Mahoko 1964-
See Yoshimoto, Banana
See also CA 144

Young, Al(bert James)
1939- .... **CLC 19; BLC; DAM MULT**
See also BW 2; CA 29-32R; CANR 26; DLB 33

Young, Andrew (John) 1885-1971 ...... **CLC 5**
See also CA 5-8R; CANR 7, 29

Young, Collier
See Bloch, Robert (Albert)

Young, Edward 1683-1765 .... **LC 3, 40**
See also DLB 95

Young, Marguerite (Vivian)
1909-1995 .... **CLC 82**
See also CA 13-16; 150; CAP 1

Young, Neil 1945- .... **CLC 17**
See also CA 110

Young Bear, Ray A. 1950- ...... **CLC 94; DAM MULT**
See also CA 146; DLB 175; NNAL

Yourcenar, Marguerite
1903-1987 ...... **CLC 19, 38, 50, 87; DAM NOV**
See also CA 69-72; CANR 23, 60; DLB 72; DLBY 88; MTCW

Yurick, Sol 1925- .... **CLC 6**
See also CA 13-16R; CANR 25

Zabolotskii, Nikolai Alekseevich
1903-1958 .... **TCLC 52**
See also CA 116

Zamiatin, Yevgenii
See Zamyatin, Evgeny Ivanovich

Zamora, Bernice (B. Ortiz)
1938- .... **CLC 89; DAM MULT; HLC**
See also CA 151; DLB 82; HW

Zamyatin, Evgeny Ivanovich
1884-1937 .... **TCLC 8, 37**
See also CA 105

Zangwill, Israel 1864-1926 .... **TCLC 16**
See also CA 109; DLB 10, 135

Zappa, Francis Vincent, Jr. 1940-1993
See Zappa, Frank
See also CA 108; 143; CANR 57

Zappa, Frank .... **CLC 17**
See also Zappa, Francis Vincent, Jr.

Zaturenska, Marya 1902-1982 ...... **CLC 6, 11**
See also CA 13-16R; 105; CANR 22

Zeami 1363-1443 .... **DC 7**

Zelazny, Roger (Joseph)
1937-1995 .... **CLC 21**
See also AAYA 7; CA 21-24R; 148; CANR 26, 60; DLB 8; MTCW; SATA 57; SATA-Brief 39

Zhdanov, Andrei A(lexandrovich)
1896-1948 .... **TCLC 18**
See also CA 117

Zhukovsky, Vasily 1783-1852 .... **NCLC 35**

Ziegenhagen, Eric .... **CLC 55**

Zimmer, Jill Schary
See Robinson, Jill

Zimmerman, Robert
See Dylan, Bob

Zindel, Paul
1936- .... **CLC 6, 26; DA; DAB; DAC; DAM DRAM, MST, NOV; DC 5**
See also AAYA 2; CA 73-76; CANR 31; CLR 3, 45; DLB 7, 52; JRDA; MAICYA; MTCW; SATA 16, 58

Zinov'Ev, A. A.
See Zinoviev, Alexander (Aleksandrovich)

Zinoviev, Alexander (Aleksandrovich)
1922- .... **CLC 19**
See also CA 116; 133; CAAS 10

Zoilus
See Lovecraft, H(oward) P(hillips)

Zola, Emile (Edouard Charles Antoine)
1840-1902 **TCLC 1, 6, 21, 41; DA; DAB; DAC; DAM MST, NOV; WLC**
See also CA 104; 138; DLB 123

Zoline, Pamela 1941- .... **CLC 62**

Zorrilla y Moral, Jose 1817-1893 .... **NCLC 6**

Zoshchenko, Mikhail (Mikhailovich)
1895-1958 .... **TCLC 15; SSC 15**
See also CA 115; 160

Zuckmayer, Carl 1896-1977 .... **CLC 18**
See also CA 69-72; DLB 56, 124

Zuk, Georges
See Skelton, Robin

Zukofsky, Louis
1904-1978 .... **CLC 1, 2, 4, 7, 11, 18; DAM POET; PC 11**
See also CA 9-12R; 77-80; CANR 39; DLB 5, 165; MTCW

Zweig, Paul 1935-1984 .... **CLC 34, 42**
See also CA 85-88; 113

Zweig, Stefan 1881-1942 .... **TCLC 17**
See also CA 112; DLB 81, 118

Zwingli, Huldreich 1484-1531 .... **LC 37**
See also DLB 179

Cumulative Nationality Index

Cumulative Title Index

463

Title Index

Title Index

Title Index

Title Index

Title Index

Title Index

ISBN 0-7876-1591-9

90000

9 780787 615918